THE SLAVE'S CAUSE

THE SLAVE'S CAUSE

A History of Abolition

Manisha Sinha

Yale

UNIVERSITY

PRESS

New Haven & London

Published with assistance from the Annie Burr Lewis Fund.

Published with assistance from the foundation established in memory
of James Wesley Cooper of the Class of 1865, Yale College.

Yale University Press books may be purchased in quantity for educational,
business, or promotional use. For information, please e-mail sales.press@yale.edu
(U.S. office) or sales@yaleup.co.uk (U.K. office).

Set in Electra and Trajan Pro types by Newgen North America.
Printed in the United States of America.

Library of Congress Control Number: 2015948091
ISBN 978-0-300-18137-1 (cloth : alk. paper)

A catalogue record for this book is available from the British Library.

This paper meets the requirements of ANSI/NISO Z39.48–1992 (Permanence of Paper).
10 9 8 7 6 5 4 3 2 1

For Karsten,
My German Philosopher

But while endowing her imaginary heroes with every perfection under the sun, Jo was discovering a live hero, who interested her in spite of many human imperfections. . . . There were lines upon his forehead, but Time seemed to have touched him gently, remembering how kind he was to others.

—Louisa May Alcott, *Little Women* (1868)

CONTENTS

vii

Illustrations follow page 192

ACKNOWLEDGMENTS

This book has taken me ten years to write, and my debts are numerous. Perhaps the largest is the one I owe to my research home away from home, the American Antiquarian Society, where this project began during a yearlong National Endowment for the Humanities fellowship. I have done the bulk of the research for this book there, enjoying the luxury of reading abolitionist newspapers in print and the excitement of coming across pamphlets personally signed and donated to the society by the black abolitionist Martin Delany. I thank the AAS community, for whom I became a fixture: Joanne Chaison, Ellen Dunlap, Paul Erickson, Babette Gehnrich, John Keenum, Marie Lamoureux, Elizabeth Pope, Caroline Sloat, and the numerous staff members who assisted me. Jaclyn Penny generously reproduced many of the illustrations that grace this book. I am thrilled that President Barack Obama has recognized this national treasure with a National Humanities Medal. I also thank the librarians and staff at the Boston Public Library, the Library Company of Philadelphia, the Library of Congress, the Historical Society of Pennsylvania, the New-York Historical Society, the Schomburg Center for Research in Black Culture of the New York Public Library, the Massachusetts Historical Society, the Rare Book and Manuscript division of Butler Library at Columbia University, the Houghton and Widener Libraries at Harvard University, and the W. E. B. Du Bois Library at the University of Massachusetts, Amherst, for their assistance. Nicole Joneic and Krystal Appiah of the Library Company of Philadelphia also provided invaluable assistance gathering images. Chris Densmore of the Friends Historical Library at Swarthmore College shared his expertise on Quaker history with me.

The Gilder Lehrman Institute of American History and its director, James Basker, who shares my passion for all things antislavery, Deborah Schwartz of the Brooklyn Historical Society, and Pamela Green of the Weeksville Heritage Center, who hired me as the lead consultant for the exhibition *In Pursuit of Freedom* on Brooklyn's abolitionists, facilitated my research trips to New York City. Above all, I would like to thank the benefactor of many of the institutions mentioned above, Sid Lapidus. A delightful visit to his personal library of early antislavery literature was the highlight of my research.

Much of the writing of this book was done at the AAS, during a faculty fellowship year at the Charles Warren Center for Studies in American History, Harvard University, and a sabbatical supported by the Howard Foundation at Brown University and the University of Massachusetts. I thank all the fellows: Daniel Carpenter, Dorothy Sue Cobble, Cornelia Dayton, Francoise Hamlin, Maartje Janse, Albrecht Koschnick, Daniel Kryder, Cindy Lobel, Christopher Lukasik, Lisa Materson, Timothy McCarthy, Lisa McGirr, Lisa Tetrault, and Susan Ware. Dan Carpenter's tremendous project of digitizing all known abolitionist petitions will long prove a boon to scholars of antislavery. I thank Nicole Topich for sending the entire database to me and Jennifer Fauxsmith of the Massachusetts Archives for permission to reprint a petition gratis.

I want to acknowledge my professional home of nearly twenty years, the University of Massachusetts, Amherst, where this book was conceived and written. I cannot possibly name them all, but my colleagues in the Afro-American; American; Women, Gender, and Sexuality Studies; and History Departments deserve special mention. I thank all those who attended my presentations at the Five Colleges History Seminars, one at the start and the other at the end of this book project: Chris Appy, Joyce Berkman, Joye Bowman, David Glassberg, Jennifer Heuer, John Higginson, Margaret Hunt, Bruce Laurie, Laura Lovett, Lynda Morgan, Kym Morrison, Brian Ogilvie, Mary Renda, Leonard Richards, James Smethurst, Susan Tracy, Robert Weir, and all the graduate students. Neal Salisbury's comments at the first presentation and Frank Couvares's at the last were much appreciated. The Massachusetts Society of Professors and the College of Humanities and Fine Arts provided me with a generous budget for acquiring images.

I am particularly grateful to those who took the time to read my manuscript when it was well over a thousand pages, truly a labor of friendship: Eric Foner, who has always been there for me and who invited me to contribute to his anthology *Our Lincoln,* and Graham Russell Hodges and James Sidbury, both of whose work on early African American history I greatly admire. All three gave me excellent advice on how to trim the manuscript and asked good questions. John Stauffer has been a superb coadjutor, as the abolitionists would say. I value his unstinting support.

I thank other scholars who supported me, sent me their work, solicited my input, commented on parts of the book at conferences, and invited me for talks: A. J. (Amy) Aiseirithe, Erica Ball, Edward Baptist, Ira Berlin, Robin Blackburn, David Blight, Evelyn Brooks Higginbotham, Steve Bullock, Chris Cameron, the late Stephanie Camp, Erik Chaput, Robert Churchill, Mathew Clavin, A. Glenn Crothers, David Brion Davis, Andrew Delbanco, Allison Efford, Daniel Feller, Sharla Fett, Barbara Fields, François Furstenberg, Sarah Gronningsater, Leslie Harris, Stanley Harrold, Mischa Honeck, Martha Jones, Prithi Kanakamedala, Jeffrey Kerr-Ritchie, Ethan Kytle, Drew McCoy, Richard Newman, James Oakes, John Quinn, Patrick Rael, Stacey Robertson, the late Christopher Schmidt-Nowara, David Smith, Mitchell Snay, Elizabeth Strodeur-Pryor, Kristin Waters, and Michael West. Sam Haselby and Adam Rothman made me shorten the title. I thank my current and former graduate students: Sean Alexander, Kabria Baumgartner, Julia Bernier, Emahunn Campbell, Alex Carter, Nneka Dennie, Crystal Donkor, Vanessa Fabien, David Goldberg, Erin Judge, Michael Landis, Christopher Lehman, David Lucander, Zebulon Miletsky, Johanna Ortner, Ousmane Power-Greene, Rita Reynolds, David Swiderski, Crystal Webster, Robert Williams, and Peter Wirzbicki.

I owe a lot to my agent extraordinaire, Sandra Dijkstra, and to John Donatich, the director of Yale University Press, for acquiring this book. The advice of my wonderful editor, Christopher Rogers, was always stellar and consistently encouraging. It has been a genuine pleasure to work with him. Erica Hanson, Susan Laity, and Lawrence Kenney expertly shepherded the manuscript into production.

My personal debts are also many. My ninety-year-old father and eighty-nine-year-old mother, Srinivas and Premini Sinha, are still looking out for me. I value the good cheer and support of my extended family, friends, and neighbors, especially Abha "Bunty" Sawhney, Jean DiPanfilo Hahn, Malini Sood, Al and Suzanne Thomas. I dedicate this book to my partner of over thirty years, Karsten Stueber. There really is no other. Our sons Sheel and Shiv have lived with this book. It has nearly spanned Sheel's school years and Shiv's entire life. Sheel worked with the illustrations and read the proofs on the eve of his departure to college. Shiv learned well from the abolitionists. He added a whipping post and auction block to his school project on slavery. I could have finished this book a bit earlier if I had not watched all their soccer, basketball, and baseball games. But I wouldn't have it any other way.

Abbreviations

AASS	American Anti-Slavery Society
ACS	American Colonization Society
AFASS	American and Foreign Anti Slavery Society
AMA	American Missionary Association
AMHL	Anti-Man Hunting League
AMRS	American Moral Reform Society
BFASS	Boston Female Anti Slavery Society
British & Foreign ASS	British and Foreign Anti Slavery Society
BVC	Boston Vigilance Committee
CA	*Colored American*
CFASS	Concord Female Anti Slavery Society
DAS	Delaware Abolition Society
ENYASS	Eastern New York Anti Slavery Society
GCA	General Colored Association
KAS	Kentucky Abolition Society
LNYCASS	Ladies New York City Anti Slavery Society
MAS	Maryland Abolition Society
MASS	Massachusetts Anti Slavery Society
NASS	*National Anti Slavery Standard*
NCMS	North Carolina Manumission Society
NEASS	New England Anti Slavery Society
NHASS	New Hampshire Anti Slavery Society
NYASS	New York Anti Slavery Society
NYMS	New York Manumission Society
OASS	Ohio Anti Slavery Society

PAS	Pennsylvania Society for the Abolition of Slavery
PASS	Pennsylvania Anti Slavery Society
PFASS	Philadelphia Female Anti Slavery Society
PVC	Philadelphia Vigilance Committee
RIASS	Rhode Island Anti Slavery Society
SEAST	Society for Effecting the Abolition of the Slave Trade
TMS	Tennessee Manumission Society
UGRR	Underground Railroad
VC	Vigilance Committee (various)
WASS	Western Anti Slavery Society
WNYASS	Western New York Anti Slavery Society

THE SLAVE'S CAUSE

Introduction: The Radical
Tradition of Abolition

The conflict over the contours and nature of American democracy has often centered on debates over black freedom and rights. The origins of that momentous and ongoing political struggle lie in the movement to abolish slavery. This book tells the story of abolition. It is a comprehensive new history of the abolition movement that extends its chronological parameters from the classical pre–Civil War period back to the American Revolution and rejects conventional divisions between slave resistance and antislavery activism. A history of abolition in the longue durée, it centers African Americans in it. Abolition was a radical, interracial movement, one which addressed the entrenched problems of exploitation and disfranchisement in a liberal democracy and anticipated debates over race, labor, and empire.

Caricatured as unthinking, single-minded fanatics who caused a "needless war," abolitionists are often compared unfavorably to political moderates and compromise-minded statesmen. Their resurrection as freedom fighters during the modern civil rights era has been relatively brief. It is often dismissed as neoabolitionist history. While a bland celebration of the abolitionist movement with its radical edges shorn off inhabits popular culture, the dominant picture of abolitionists in American history is that of bourgeois reformers burdened by racial paternalism and economic conservatism.[1] Neither the scholarly nor the lay consensus on abolition does justice to the movement's rich, diverse, and contentious history.

Slave resistance, not bourgeois liberalism, lay at the heart of the abolition movement.[2] Slave rebellions paralleled isolated criticisms of slavery in colonial America. The enslaved inspired the formation of the first Quaker-dominated abolition and manumission societies as well as the first landmark cases that inaugurated emancipation in the Western world. The actions of slave rebels and runaways, black writers and community leaders, did not lie outside of but shaped abolition and its goals. As most abolitionists understood, the story of abolition must begin with the struggles of the enslaved. The connection between slave resistance and abolition in the United States was proximate and continuous. Prominent slave revolts marked the turn toward immediate abolition. Fugitive slaves united all factions of the movement and led abolitionists to justify revolutionary resistance to slavery. Recent historians have declared black resistance to enslavement passé, but it was central to abolition. Not restricted to wartime emancipation, the American abolitionist moment unfolded in a hundred-year drama in law, politics, literature, and on-the-ground activism. To reduce emancipation to an event precipitated by military crisis is to miss that long history.

The history of abolition is an integrated story even though it is usually not told in that manner. Black abolitionists were integral to the broader, interracial milieu of the movement. To read them out of the abolition movement is to profoundly miss the part they played in defining traditions of American democratic radicalism. The insidious divide between white thought and black activism that pervades some books on abolition is both racialist and inaccurate. There was no such racial division of political labor in the abolition movement. Early African American literature, black abolitionists' intellectual response to the pseudoscience of race, and debates over citizenship and emigration performed the work of political protest. The theoretical sophistication of black abolitionist thought should finally put to rest the influential yet glib view of it as imitative, mired in the strictures of middle-class reform and elitism, and divorced from the plight of southern slaves and northern masses. Black and white abolitionists also went beyond a simple appeal to the American republican tradition that sought to include African Americans in its promise. They generated a powerful critique of the slaveholding Republic and constructed a counternarrative that highlighted its origins in the slave trade and slavery.[3]

The alternative nature of abolitionism is showcased by its diverse membership, which gave rise to cooperation as well as to creative conflict across rigid lines of race, class, and gender that characterized early American society. The abolition movement, in which the disfranchised, including women, played a seminal role, was driven by passionate outsiders. Women were abolition's foot soldiers and, more controversially, its leaders and orators. In birthing the first women's rights movement, abolition again revealed its radical face. The abolition movement married the black struggle against slavery to progressive white evangelicalism and to the iconoclasm of more secular reformers. Its steady radicalization on women's rights, organized religion, politics, and direct action made it quickly outgrow the empire of religious benevolence and moral reform.[4]

Abolition was a radical, democratic movement that questioned the enslavement of labor. The best works on abolition have tried to understand it by overturning simplistic social control models that emphasized social and ideological conformity to legitimize an emerging capitalist economy. Scholars have long known that modern racial slavery fostered the growth of early capitalism. If slavery is capitalism, as the currently fashionable historical interpretation has it, the movement to abolish it is, at the very least, its obverse. The history of capitalism illustrates that it has rarely marched in lockstep with democracy. The fraught relationship between capitalism and democracy is characterized more by contestation. Modern racial slavery was a monstrous hybrid that combined the horrors of an archaic labor system with the rapacious efficiencies of capitalism.[5] Like the slave system they opposed, abolitionists were hybrids, old-fashioned moralizers as well as modern exponents of human rights. It is no coincidence that the brief, incomplete triumph of the abolitionist vision resulted in the greatest expansion of American democracy, and that the demise of abolition went hand in hand with the greatest contraction of democracy. At the heart of that movement lay the slave's struggle for freedom and human dignity.

Never the so-called monomaniacs they were lampooned as, abolitionists recognized that the oppression of slaves was linked to other wrongs in their world. More than a few abolitionists joined such international radical movements as utopian socialism, feminism, and pacifism and championed Native American, immigrant, and workingmen's rights. Some even anticipated contemporary American scourges, criticizing the criminalization of blackness and the use of capital punishment and force by the state. Abolitionists were the intellectual and political precursors of twentieth-century anticolonial and civil rights activists, debating the nature of society and politics, the relationship between racial inequality and democracy, nation and empire, labor and capital, gender and citizenship. They used the vehicle of antislavery to criticize the democratic pretensions of Western societies and expose their seamier side. Abolitionists were opponents of rather than stalking horses of new forms of servitude and imperialism. As radical agitators, they were not so much theorists of liberal democracy as critics of it. In prioritizing the abolition of slavery, they did not ignore and certainly did not legitimize other forms of oppression in the modern world. Only by conflating the state with the social movement can historians view abolition as the progenitor of European imperialism.[6]

Abolitionists were original and critical thinkers on democracy, not simply romantic reformers who confined themselves to appeals to the heart. The movement against slavery made a signal contribution to the discourse of both human rights and humanitarianism. The depiction of abused black bodies in abolitionist print culture, from slave narratives dripping with blood to abolitionist newspapers and pamphlets, has appeared to many scholars as bourgeois sentimentality, voyeuristic pornography, and racist objectification of the enslaved. This scholarly gaze, the vast condescension bestowed on the very real history of black suffering under the political economy of a harsh slave regimen, leads people astray. It is based on a whitewashed understanding of abolition that reads out the black presence in it completely. Its roots lie in slaveholders' defensive response to abolitionist criticism, and it fundamentally misreads abolitionist agitation, the attempt to evoke radical empathy from an audience whose very comforts were dependent on the exploitation of those deemed inferior and expendable.[7] Those lessons remain useful today.

Confronted by a reactionary, expansionist slaveholding class that dreamed of a global empire based on slavery, the real Slave Power rather than a figment of paranoid imagination, abolitionists developed an uncompromising response to its imperialist aggressions at home and abroad. As the movement matured in the teeth of strong slaveholding opposition and state power in the United States, the cause of the American slave became intertwined with that of democracy, civil liberties, and the emancipation of women and labor. Far from being an extremist formulation with no relevance to national politics and the important events of the day, abolitionists' political project, the overthrow of the slavery-based polity of the nineteenth-century American Republic, was at the vanguard of antislavery. Some abolitionists became disenchanted with their country and government, while others sought to harness the power of the state against slavery. The history of abolition is an ideal test case of how radical social movements generate engines of political change. As they do in all social movements, questions of principle versus expediency permeated abolition, giving rise to divisions over tactics. Abolitionists debated the culpability of the church, state, and society as well as their amenability to change: whether society could be transformed through political action and whether the state was an arena of conflict or a tool of the Slave Power. It is a mistake, however, to equate slaveholders' political power with modern state formation. For good reason the conservative political tradition of American slaveholders, who dominated the federal and their state governments from inception and used all the repressive powers of the state to further the interests of slavery, was strongly antistatist.[8]

During the Civil War and Reconstruction the enslaved and their radical allies pushed the nation to realize their ideal of an interracial democracy. And for a brief period, as W. E. B. Du Bois wrote, the slave stood in the sun before being shoved back into the shadows. The overthrow of Reconstruction had little to do with the alleged poverty of the abolitionist vision and a lot to do with the enduring power of abolition's opponents. When the horror of racial injustice settled in again, not just the formerly enslaved but democracy as a whole suffered. The fate of American democracy lay not in the hands of the powerful, with their dreams of wealth and empire, but in the postwar movements for racial, gender, and economic autonomy.[9] The abolitionist project of perfecting American, indeed global, democracy remains to be fulfilled. In that sense, its legacy is an enduring one.

A new historical narrative of abolition, this book challenges long-standing interpretive binaries. For too long historians of abolition have told its story in a fragmented fashion and continue to do so along the lines of race and gender. Older historical debates over the relative importance of Garrisonians versus the evangelicals and political abolitionists, that is, eastern versus western abolitionists, revisit and rehash abolitionist divisions, at times uncritically adopting the positions of their subjects. I have found them to be far less important than the attention lavished on them suggests and highly conducive to the perpetuation of stereotypes that defy the historical record.

Recent syntheses on abolition provide global histories of slavery and emancipation in the modern West.[10] By contrast, my book narrates a movement history of abolition in the United States in a transnational context. It stresses continuity rather than rupture in the abolitionist tradition, which from its inception was an interracial one and tied to the development of democracy. From the early Quaker and black protests against slavery to the rise of the Anglo-American movement against the slave trade in the late eighteenth century to the golden age of abolitionism in the years before the Civil War, abolitionists were united by their devotion to the slave's cause. Even after bitter divisions sundered the movement, nothing brought all abolitionists together more readily than the fugitive slave's desperate bid for freedom. The title of the book comes from the words of abolitionists, who commonly used the phrase to describe their movement, signing their letters, "Yours for the slave."

It has taken me many years of archival research and reading of the enormous historical scholarship on abolition to do justice to this topic. Abolitionists were not just quintessential agitators but also wordsmiths. Whatever they lacked in power, they made up for by outproducing their mighty opponents in newspapers, books, pamphlets, letters, diaries, memoirs, material, and artwork, creating a huge, complicated historical archive. Any history of abolition must begin with that archive, as it opens a window into their worldview. In narrating a history of abolition, I engage the ideas and actions of men and women, black and white, who proved to be a match for the New World's slaveholding ancien régime. They were the disfranchised themselves and the allies of the disfranchised. They understood that the slave's cause never dies.

Part I.

THE FIRST WAVE

PROPHETS WITHOUT HONOR

The history of abolition begins with those who resisted slavery at its inception. In 1721 an unnamed African woman informed her enslaved compatriots aboard the English slaver *Robert* anchored off the coast of Sierra Leone that an unusually small number of sailors were standing guard on deck that night. She brought them weapons that she took from sailors onboard the ship and instigated the start of a rebellion. The rebels, led by a Captain Tomba, who was whipped unmercifully for refusing to submit to inspection, killed three of the five sailors on watch before being subdued by the rest of the crew. The woman was hanged by her thumbs, whipped, and slashed with knives until she was dead. Two of the rebels were forced to eat the heart and liver of a dead sailor before being executed. African resistance to enslavement was epitomized in shipboard insurrections that dot the four centuries of the slave trade and in the formation of *quilombos*, the Afro-Portuguese term for communities of runaway slaves, on the West African coast. African opposition to the slave trade and slavery, spurred by specific ethnic and national identities, is often forgotten in the literature on African participation in it. The first antislavery propaganda, which was born in West Africa, viewed European slave traders as cannibals and as brutal, treacherous tricksters. How else explain the ever-increasing numbers of Africans who disappeared in the transatlantic trade?[1]

The story of the rise of abolition is an interracial one. The devastation wrought by the Atlantic slave trade on West African nations and communities and the horrific nature of that trade inspired such early abolitionists as Anthony Benezet, the Quaker schoolteacher in Philadelphia credited with originating the movement. Writers of African descent were among the first to wrestle with the problems of race and slavery in the modern West. Slave rebellions complemented pioneering antislavery protests by Quakers and other Protestant dissenters in British North America. In Britain, runaway slaves, building on colonial precedent, led Granville Sharp to apply English notions of law and liberty to Africans. Black resistance to slavery was the essential precondition to the rise of abolitionism.

PIONEERS

Early modern Europe lacked a systematic antislavery tradition. With a few exceptions, Western thinkers had justified rather than challenged slavery. But popular prejudice against slavery had long been prevalent, at least since the collapse of serfdom in western Europe. Notions of inherent racial inferiority served to counter this sentiment. Starting in the medieval period, some European countries defined their territories as free soil, a nationalist conceit that predated the rise of modern racial slavery. Serfs who ran away to cities, *Stadtluft Macht Frei* (the German saying that city air makes free), began a fugitive tradition of creating free spaces that extended to the enslaved of all nationalities in Europe and colonial America. It is not widely known that a slave who claimed his freedom on the grounds that any slave who entered the city of Toulouse was free helped inspire the French political theorist Jean Bodin to write against slavery. Even Spain and Portugal, who followed the ancient law of Roman slavery, at times enforced the "freedom principle" within their national boundaries. State formation and servile resistance interacted in the creation of freedom in Europe's metropolises.[2]

Before their encounter with Europeans, Africans and Native Americans had their own traditions of slavery and captivity. The institution of colonial slavery in the New World led to incipient criticism of it. The Spanish Jesuit Bartolomé de las Casas, in his widely translated and reprinted *Brief Account of the Destruction of the Indies by the Spanish* (1552), recommended the enslavement of Africans to protest the treatment of Native Americans, though he came to regret his solution to the problem of labor in the Americas. In its detailed exposé of Spanish atrocities, Las Casas's book anticipated abolitionist writing even though he was complicit in the conquest and subjugation of native populations. The debates in Valladolid, Spain, between him and the proslavery natural law philosopher Juan Ginés de Sepúlveda, who dismissed antislavery as German-inspired Lutheran heresy, were the first public discussions on racial slavery in colonial America. Las Casas's early efforts and a petition to the pope resulted in a papal bull in 1537 against the enslavement of Indians, although this was mainly a symbolic gesture.

Some Dominican priests went further. Antonio de Montesinos preached against the ill-treatment of Indians in Santo Domingo and for an end to the Spanish forced labor systems of *encomienda* and *repartimiento*. Bartolomé de Albornoz of Mexico, whose antislavery book was censored by the Inquisition, condemned the enslavement of Africans as illegal. Tomás de Mercado and the Jesuit Luis de Molina criticized the African slave trade. In 1555 Fernando Oliveira denounced not just the slave trade but also the perpetual nature of racial slavery. In his *On Restoring Ethiopian Salvation* (1627), the Jesuit priest Alonso de Sandoval of Cartagena de Indias, criticized the conduct of the slave trade and slavery while arguing for the Christianization of Africans. But Sandoval, who subscribed to the biblical story of the curse of Ham popularized by Islamic, Jewish, and Christian theologians to justify the enslavement of Africans, did not publicly avow abolition. Most Catholic clerics made their peace with racial slavery, advocating only the Christianization of slaves and amelioration of slavery.

The church and state in the Spanish and Portuguese American colonies squelched individual reservations about slavery. Brazilian authorities summarily expelled Jesuit priests who argued that the enslaved should be treated more humanely. Among the petitions against the slave trade submitted to the Vatican in the seventeenth century were two by an Afro-Brazilian, Lourenço da Silva de Mendouça. In 1684 Mendouça, who claimed to be of royal Kongolese descent, questioned the slave trade and the permanent enslavement of Christian descendants of Africans, describing graphically and at length the "diabolic abuse of such slavery." Appointed procurator of a black Catholic confraternity in Madrid, similar to those in the Kongo, he journeyed to Rome to personally present his petitions on behalf of enslaved Africans. In his second petition representing Christian African slaves in Brazil and Lisbon, Mendouça appealed to the bigotry of the church, citing instances of Christian slaves enslaved by Jewish masters. Combined with the petition decrying the abuses of the slave trade that Capuchin missionaries in Kongo tendered in 1685, Mendouça's petitions in 1686 resulted in a papal denunciation of the slave trade. Early Catholic antislavery sentiment did not engender an abolition movement or prevent the expansion of American slavery with the full collusion of the church. While Spanish slave law, the Siete Partidas, and the church offered some protections to slaves, a concerted abolition movement first arose in the British Atlantic world.[3]

In the British colonies white indentured servants and Irish, Scottish, and Native American prisoners of war condemned to lifetimes of servitude initially suffered and labored in conditions similar to those of African slaves and servants. The use of various kinds of unfree labor, Indian slavery, and black and white servitude gradually gave way to African slavery. In the seventeenth century, when slavery, unknown to English common law but prevalent in the Spanish and Portuguese colonies, emerged in British America, pioneering antislavery protests appeared in the colonies. As early as 1652, Rhode Island, inspired by Roger Williams's objections to Indian slavery, had tried unsuccessfully to abolish slavery by limiting the term of servitude for Indians and Africans. Thirty years later William Penn similarly failed in his effort to prohibit lifetime servitude in Pennsylvania, and he came to view the slave trade as essential to the infant colony's prosperity. By 1663 antislavery Mennonites led by Peter Cornelius Plockhoy had banned slavery in their settlement on the Delaware Bay. When the English took over the colony, the Mennonites moved to Germantown, Pennsylvania. Even as black and white servants plotted on how to gain their freedom in the tobacco plantations of Virginia and Maryland, a petition of 1688 signed by four German and Dutch Mennonite converts to Quakerism from Germantown argued, "We shall doe to all men like as we will be done ourselves; making no difference of what generation, descent or colour they are." The petition censured Quaker slaveholders for treating human beings like cattle. Early Quaker abolitionists were not just individual voices having no impact; at their meetings they inaugurated an ongoing discussion of the propriety of slaveholding: the Chester Quarterly Meeting took the lead in recommending action against slavery and the slave trade. Even earlier, Quaker slaveholders in Barbados insisted on taking their slaves with them to their meetings.

Quaker abolitionism was a reaction to emergent capitalism and the commercialization of the faith rather than an expression of it. In 1693 Quakers disowned George Keith, the main author of an antislavery pamphlet castigating the Friends for their involvement in the slave trade and slavery. Keithians condemned the New World practice of buying the "Bodies of men for money." The riches of the "Merchants of the Earth" were based on the "cruel Oppression" of blacks and "Taunies," who he contended were as much a part of humankind as "*White* Men." Three years later Cadwalader Morgan called for the abolition of slaveholding among Quakers. William Southeby, whose antislavery writings earned him several reprimands from the Philadelphia meeting, petitioned the Pennsylvania legislature to abolish slavery in 1712. Quaker meetings in New York and New England silenced William Burling, who wrote a tract against slavery, and John Farmer. If the slaves rose in rebellion, wrote another Quaker abolitionist, Robert Piles, in 1698, "and if they should bee permitted to doe us harm," it was not clear "whether our blood will cry innocent [or] whether it will not bee said you might have left them well alone."[4]

Not all Quakers were antislavery, but most abolitionists in the British colonies were Quakers. George Fox, the founder of Quakerism, had called for the

Christianization of Africans and Native Americans and expressed qualms over the permanent uncompensated nature of racial slavery. In a letter of 1657 to his followers in the colonies, Fox laid down the Christian foundation for abolition, evoking the Golden Rule and arguing that God was no "*Respecter of Persons*" and that "he hath made all *Nations of One Blood.*" After visiting Barbados in 1671, he recommended the freeing of slaves after a term of faithful service and asked that they be compensated for their labor and not be freed "*empty handed.*" While Fox did not urge outright abolition, Quaker abolitionists used his testimony to great effect. The Irish Quaker William Edmundson, who was Fox's traveling companion and who returned to the colonies four years later, condemned the enslavement of Africans, asking "many of you count it unlawfull to make Slaves of Indians, and if so, then why the Negroes?" Alice Curwen became the first Quaker woman to call for the Christianization of slaves and for abolition.[5]

Early Quaker abolitionists in colonial America emerged from that class of colonial society which could identify with the miseries of slaves. For example, John Hepburn, a tailor from New Jersey who had immigrated to America as an indentured servant in 1684, and Elihu Coleman, a carpenter from Nantucket, were men of modest means. Hepburn, in his written dialogue between a Christian and a "negro master," condemned "this *Inriching Sin,* in making Slaves of Men." A Quaker minister, Coleman developed a scriptural argument against slavery, writing that for "all the riches and glory of this world," he would "not be guilty of so great a sin." The hunchbacked, vegetarian, Quaker dwarf Benjamin Lay begged forgiveness at the end of his abolitionist book because "it was written by one that was a poor common Sailor, and an Illiterate Man." Like the white servants and Indians who slept, worked, and ran away with Africans in the colonial period as well as the sailors, pirates, outlaws, and lower classes who conspired and socialized with slaves, these men, though more sober and religiously inclined, felt a sense of kinship with enslaved black people.[6]

Quaker abolitionists subsumed their opposition to slavery under a broader critique of warfare, wealth making, and commerce. Hepburn ridiculed slave owners and merchants as "fine powdered Perriwigs, and great bunched Coats" with wives who "paint their Faces, and Puff, and powder their Hair," growing fat on the cruelties inflicted on slaves. The Gospel according to Ralph Sandiford "excepts not nor despises any for their complexions." Sandiford was a shopkeeper, but he too excoriated ill-gotten wealth. Lay was convinced that Quaker elites had hurried Sandiford to an early grave because of their ostracism of him. Lay, who republished Burling's tract, renounced all worldly materials, especially those made by slave labor, and thought no good ever came from the pursuit of "Riches." Hepburn argued, "Riches, gotten by wronging the Labourer, is cursed." Quaker abolitionists urged boycotts of goods made through the exploitation of slaves. Lay smashed his wife's teacups to condemn the consumption of sugar, the first cash crop produced by large numbers of slaves. Far from justifying free trade and the advent of a capitalism based on free labor, they asserted that putting money before men contradicted their religious beliefs. Their opposition to slavery was part of a larger criticism they unleashed on the wealthy and powerful. If Quakerism perfected values well suited to the growth of a capitalist mentalité, it also engendered its most effective opponents.[7]

Other radical dissenting Protestant and antimonarchical sects who were part of Oliver Cromwell's army during the English Civil War also gave birth to antislavery ideas. The Levellers, a radical political group, explicitly condemned all forms of servitude, including personal slavery. In 1673 the English Puritan Richard Baxter wrote against the practice of slavery for equating men with brutes and treating them as such. While he acknowledged that a limited servitude as a penalty for crimes committed may be permissible, he called the African slave trade the worst sort of thievery and held that purchasing such slaves constituted a sin against Christianity and humankind. Eleven years later the vegetarian poet Thomas Tryon, who had worked as a hatter in Barbados and whose writings were published by Quakers, decried the violence inherent in the enslavement of Africans in the colonies. Tryon wrote of their "complaints against the Hard Usages and Barbarous Cruelties Inflicted upon them." He re-created a dialogue between a "Negro-slave" and his American master. After getting the master to enunciate the principles of Christianity, the supposedly heathen Ethiopian describes the behavior of Christian slaveholders and concludes that the "*Hypocrite Christians*" had shed more blood than all the heathens of the world. When the master objects to white Christians being compared with "*black Heathenish Negroes*," the slave gives him a lesson on the natural equality of all human beings: God made both blacks and whites, "'tis the Livery of our Creator" suited to particular climates and soil and to despise blackness was to despise him. Tryon, whose dietary prescriptions Benjamin Franklin observed, also criticized excess in the food, luxury, and lifestyle of the wealthy, "the feasting of the Rich" at the expense of their "Vassals."[8]

The Christianization of Africans—Portuguese priests, for instance, perfunctorily baptized slaves just before they began their terrible transatlantic passage to the Americas—had long been used as a justification for the African slave trade and slavery. Enslaving the heathen other was seen as a legitimate practice in early modern Europe, and slaveholders initially resisted the Christianization of their slaves, fearing it might lead to emancipation. Slaves themselves presumed that Christianity meant emancipation, and some brought freedom lawsuits against their masters once they had converted. In his *The Negros and Indians Advocate* (1680), the Anglican minister Morgan Godwyn, who was influenced by Fox's call to Christianize Africans and Native Americans and who had ministered to slaves in Virginia and Barbados, argued that *"The* Negros *(both Slaves and others) have naturally an* equal Right *with other Men to the* Exercise and Privileges of Religion." He rebuked the "hellish principles" of slaveholders that denied the humanity of black people and mercilessly abused slaves. The real heathens, he maintained, were slave owners who kept Africans in a *"Soul-murthering and Brutifying-state of Bondage."* An Ethiopian, could become a disciple of Christ, *"no longer a Slave but a Son, even* Abraham's *seed."* Godwyn's Christian universalism was not respectful of African religions, but it contained a plea for black spiritual equality and vehemently rejected arguments condoning racial inferiority drawn from the Bible. The title of his last work, *Trade Preferr'd before Religion and Christ Made to Give Place to Mammon* (1685), said it all when it came to the treatment of slaves in the British Empire. Godwyn was murdered for his antislavery views.[9]

As the numbers of enslaved Africans in North America grew, fueled by the British domination of the African slave trade in the early eighteenth century, most divines and denominations confined Christianity's role to that of concern for the spiritual well-being of slaves. The Anglican missionary Thomas Bacon and groups like the Society for the Propagation of the Gospel in Foreign Parts made systematic attempts to convert Africans, although they were largely unsuccessful. George Whitefield, the preacher who set the colonies on fire during the First Great Awakening, assured slaveholders that the conversion of their slaves did not threaten their mastery over them or the institution of slavery itself. Some figures were active in securing colonial laws that explicitly denied that slaves' conversion to Christianity would emancipate them. The efforts of the Anglican bishop George Berkeley led to the proslavery Yorke–Talbot decision of 1729, which clarified that Christianization does not lead to emancipation and that the rights of colonial slaveholders were respected in England.

Yet Christian missionaries, critical of some of the most horrific features of colonial slavery, promoted slave education. Whitefield excoriated the treatment of slaves in the southern colonies and preached sermons specifically geared toward slaves and African Americans, though he eventually purchased a plantation to support his orphanage in Georgia. The Anglican missionary Francis Le Jau documented the intense abuse of slave labor in South Carolina. The English Quaker John Bell recommended good treatment of slaves and servants, asking slaveholders to show mercy to their slaves, attend to their material needs, and avoid *"extream Labour"* and *"severe Chastisement."* The French Huguenot priest Elias Neau opened a school for African Americans and Native Americans in New York in 1704. The Virginian Presbyterian Samuel Davies was known for both the conversion of slaves and his advocacy of slave literacy. The Associates of Dr. Bray, named for Rev. Thomas Bray, who was sent to the colonies by the Anglican Church, operated the first black schools in Philadelphia, New York, and Williamsburg, Virginia. The radical printer Samuel Keimer, his protégé Franklin, and John Stephen (Jean-Etienne) Benezet, the father of the great Quaker abolitionist, supported these schools.[10]

Eighteenth-century Christian paternalism inspired antislavery attitudes and was not yet yoked to proslavery dogma. New England Puritan ministers such as Samuel Willard evinced a special interest in the state of the souls of Africans and Indians. John Eliot was known for his mission to the Indians and opposed their enslavement. His short-lived "praying towns" would fall victim to Puritan–Indian warfare. The Massachusetts Bay Colony's *Body of Liberties* (1641), which legalized the enslavement of Native American prisoners of war and so-called strangers sold to the colonists, also included an injunction that slaves should have some of the "liberties and Christian usages" of biblical and English law. Cotton Mather, an admirer of Eliot and Willard, proselytized among Africans and learned the West African technique of smallpox inoculation from his biblically named slave Onesimus. In his long pamphlet on the Christianization of the slaves, Mather dismissed arguments for racial inferiority based on skin color, the Bible, and the claim that Africans lacked a soul and the power to reason. Christian slaves become "amiable spectacles," and though they remain servants they become "the Children of God." Since Mather was known for his advocacy of the Christianizing of blacks, a "company of poor Negroes" approached him in 1693 about "a design which they had, of erecting a meeting for the welfare of their miserable nation that were servants among us." Mather oversaw this first attempt to set up an organized society by people of African descent in British North America. The rules he devised for the Society of Negroes and had his slave Spaniard deliver to the antislavery judge Samuel Sewall epitomized Christian paternalism. The rules emphasized orderly and pious behavior in meetings overseen by "some Wise and Good Man of the *English*." An expression of cultural imperialism even in its most benevolent mode, evangelical Christianity abandoned its commitment to native and black education, especially in the southern colonies. Some of these divines were slaveholders themselves and collected Indian body parts, anticipating the insidious brew of racialist science and religious parochialism that would characterize proslavery Christianity.[11]

Sewall, who came to regret his role in the Salem witchcraft trials and was appalled at the growth of slavery, warfare, and captivity in Massachusetts, emerged as the voice of Puritan antislavery. In his pamphlet *The Selling of Joseph* (1700), he wrote, "How horrible is the Uncleanness, Mortality, if not Murder, that the Ships are guilty of that bring great Crouds of these miserable Men and Women." The pamphlet evoked the biblical injunction against man stealing and refuted the commonly held assumption that all Africans were descendants of Ham and therefore cursed to slavery. He emphatically rejected the Christianization of Africans as justification of slavery, noting, "Evil must not be done, that good may come of it." Even though Sewall saw African slaves "in our Body Politick as a kind of extravasat [foreign] Blood," he employed scriptural arguments against racial distinctions. Sewall confessed six years later that he was met with "*Frowns and hard Words . . . for this Undertaking*," and in 1716 he published a more conventional essay advocating the Christianizing of Indians and Africans. Sewall's pamphlet inspired Quaker abolitionists such as Hepburn, Sandiford, and Lay, who quoted extensively from it. Slaves, in turn, had inspired Sewall. He was moved to write on reading an African couple's petition for freedom.[12]

Antislavery sentiment among a handful of American colonists grew in tandem with black resistance to slavery. Sewall's pamphlet elicited a proslavery response from the Boston merchant John Saffin, who had denied his slave Adam freedom despite a prior agreement to release him from bondage after seven years. Sewall filed Adam's successful freedom suit against Saffin and presided over the case that freed him in 1703. Adam's actions were indicative of the various antislavery strategies employed by enslaved African Americans. With the help of sympathetic whites, they brought freedom suits against their masters on various grounds: Christianization, verbal or written agreements granting freedom, self-purchase, ill-usage and brutality, or evidence of white ancestry. The same year a "mulatto" slave in Connecticut named Abda successfully sued to gain his freedom. Outside the realm of law, slave resistance in the form of runaways, conspiracies, and rebellions was ubiquitous throughout the colonial era. Starting with the Germantown protest of 1688, antislavery writers regularly alluded to slave resistance as evidence of the injustice of slavery. According to Hepburn, "We disgrace ourselves [when] we condemn and punish our Negroes for seeking by Running away to get their freedom." Sandiford called slaveholders "man stealers," who "whipped naked to common view" and "racked and burned to death" recalcitrant and rebellious slaves.[13]

The early eighteenth century witnessed the hardening of plantation slavery and an epidemic of slave resistance in the Americas from the Caribbean to the mainland colonies. Runaway slave advertisements were a mainstay of colonial newspapers. In 1739 an antislavery petition signed by eighteen Scotsmen from Darien, Georgia, gave slave rebellion or "daily invasion" as a prime reason for restricting the establishment of slavery in that colony, which was founded as an experiment in free labor and philanthropy by James Oglethorpe. Oglethorpe, a member of the governing board of the slave-trading Royal African Company, was fearful of the growing fugitive slave population in the Spanish-controlled settlement of St. Augustine in present-day Florida. The petitioners wrote, "It is shocking to human Nature, that any Race of Mankind and their posterity should be sentenc'd to perpetual Slavery; nor in Justice can we otherwise think of it, that they are all thrown amongst us to be our Scourge one day or other for our Sins: And as Freedom must be as dear to them as to us, what a Scene of Horror it must bring about!"

Colonial slave revolts led by Africans, including slave conspiracies in New York in 1712 and 1741, fomented mainly by Akans in collusion with Indians and lower-class whites, a slave conspiracy in New Jersey in 1734, and the Stono rebellion by West Central Africans in South Carolina in 1739, bolstered their argument. Some blamed the New York conspiracy of 1741 on Whitefield's religious revivals. The Stono rebels hoped to follow the steady stream of runaway slaves to Spanish Florida, where a large free black community at Gracia Real de Santa Teresa de Mosé, or Fort Mose, flourished under Francisco Menéndez, a Mandinga runaway. The South Carolinian planter Hugh Bryan, a follower of Whitefield, wrote in his journal that the "repeated Insurrections of our Slaves" were proof that "God's just judgments are upon us." Bryan was forced to retract his public statements against slavery by state authorities.[14]

Two years before the slave Jemmy led a revolt replete with Kongolese Catholic rituals and military tactics on the banks of the river Stono, Benjamin Lay published his 271-page philippic *All Slave-Keepers that keep the Innocent in Bondage, Apostates.* Sickened by the brutalities of the African slave trade and slavery he had witnessed in Barbados, Lay kidnapped the son of a Quaker slaveholder to acquaint him with the grief of Africans who were torn apart from their families. He disrupted a Quaker meeting by splattering the Bible with pokeberry juice, representing the blood of slaves. Calling slavery a vile and hellish practice and slaveholders, especially slave-owning ministers, a "Parcel of Hypocrites, and Deceivers . . . under the greatest appearance and Pretensions to Religion and Sanctity that ever was in the World," he charged that those who consumed sugar, molasses, and rum literally consumed the blood and flesh of slaves. Images of slaves mangled by punishment, bent from work, starving and naked dotted his book. Once he stood barefoot in the snow to draw attention to the frostbitten toes and fingers of ill-clad slaves. He wore a sackcloth and lived in exile in a cave after the death of his wife. Lay rejected plans to free slaves only after they had reached adulthood. That, he said, "[will not] salve the Sore, it is too deep and rotten." Quoting the scriptures as if to justify slave rebellion, he wrote, *"Its better to die by the Sword than by Famine."* As a God-fearing Quaker, Lay stated that he would say no more. But the "notorious lies" that slaves are content "will never go down well." If that were true, he asked simply, "why should they be against it?" He predicted that the "Satanical Practice of SLAVE-KEEPING" would certainly bring "sudden Destruction among us."[15]

If Lay's dramatic and uncompromising testimony against slavery alienated many Quakers, John Woolman made abolitionism respectable. Using the system of visiting Friends' meetings, Woolman roamed throughout the colonies trying to convince his coreligionists of the sin of slaveholding. A self-supporting tailor and later a successful retailer, Woolman used moderate language and deferred to Quaker practice. According to his journal, published by the Quaker Committee on the Press after his death, Woolman came to his antislavery convictions on being asked by his master to write a bill of sale for a slave woman. Subsequently he refused to write wills for slaveholders who sought to bequeath their slaves to their heirs, convincing many of them on their deathbeds to free their slaves, and he acted on behalf of at least two slaves who were attempting to secure their freedom. In his travels to the plantation colonies, Woolman noted how slaves were sold separately from their families, whipped to work, and deprived of an education as well as how bondage had a corrupting effect on society. A visit to Newport, Rhode Island, likewise opened his eyes to the horrors of the slave trade.

Self-love, or "self-interest," rather than devotion to the common good, Woolman reasoned, was the cause of slavery, and he gave a host of reasons for opposing slaveholding. Like earlier Quaker abolitionists, he chastised people for their pursuit of luxuries and wealth, developing an incipient critique of market society and, with Lay, pioneering the antislavery tactic of encouraging the nonconsumption of goods produced by slave labor. Opposition to imperialist warfare as part of their peace testimony during the Seven Years' War of 1756–63 between England and France, which spanned North America, Europe, and Asia, pushed Quaker reformers, who had long debated the rectitude of slavery, in the direction of organized abolition. The same war inspired a massive slave revolt in Jamaica in 1760–61. In 1758 Woolman had played an important role in the Philadelphia Yearly Meeting's condemnation of the importing, buying, selling, and keeping of slaves. As a member of the meeting's antislavery committee of visiting ministers and "Committee of Negroes," he convinced other meetings of the iniquity of slavery, spurring a coherent approach to abolitionism through his quietist tactics and writings. That same year the London Yearly Meeting issued an epistle against the slave trade, enlarging on some early reservations about it, as well as, in 1761, a "Strong Minute," or directive opposing it.[16]

Woolman's antislavery built a bridge between the separatist Quaker attempt to rid their community of slavery and the revolutionary abolition movement in the Anglo-American world. In 1754 he published the first half of his antislavery pamphlet *Some Considerations on the Keeping of Negroes*, which he first composed in 1746 after visiting the southern colonies. Woolman recognized that "customs generally approved, opinions received by youth from their superiors, become like the natural produce of a soil, especially when they are suited to favorite inclinations." He questioned what Nathaniel Hawthorne would call custom so old that it seems like nature. In 1762 he published the second half of his pamphlet, in which he again likened slavery to "Unrighteousness . . . justified from one Age to the other." He elaborated on his previous reasoning but added quintessential Enlightenment ideas that would become stock arguments of organized abolition in the 1770s, including an appeal to the natural rights of man, humanitarianism, and the attributing of physical differences to environmental causes. The "Idea of Slavery being connected with the Black Colour, and Liberty with the White" were "false ideas . . . twisted into our Minds," ideas which "with Difficulty we get fairly Disentangled." "The Colour of Man," he wrote, "avails nothing, in Matters of Right and Equity." He ended with an indictment of the slave trade and, at his most passionate, warned of divine vengeance against "the most haughty People" that would give "Deliverance to the Oppressed."

In his "A Plea for the Poor," published long after his death in 1793, Woolman married his antislavery to concerns about the deteriorating condition of the working classes and the destruction of the environment by early industrialization. Wealth, as he put it in his opening sentence, was the destroyer of virtue. He drew attention to the plight of the working poor and the exploitative nature of British imperialism and early capitalism. Another version of this text, "A Word of Remembrance and Caution to the Rich &c," has been dated to 1763. Like his contemporary Quaker abolitionist Joshua Evans, Woolman was a thoroughgoing reformer who combined antislavery testimony with concern for Native Americans, animal abuse, violence and war, excessive drinking, and conspicuous consumption. He died in 1772 in England before the revolutionary abolition movement came of age, but his successor in the role of the preeminent Quaker abolitionist became its founding father.[17]

ABOLITIONISTS BEFORE ABOLITION

If there was an eighteenth-century abolitionist who matched the pivotal role of William Lloyd Garrison in the nineteenth century, it was Anthony Benezet. Of Huguenot descent, the cosmopolitan Benezet was born in France, was educated in Belgium, and moved to Philadelphia in 1731. A schoolmaster who began teaching African Americans in his home and an indefatigable writer, Benezet orchestrated the antislavery campaign of the revolutionary era besides protesting the treatment of Native Americans and refugee French Acadians from Canada. He wrote countless letters to like-minded influential men and women in Europe and America and compiled several antislavery pamphlets. Benezet began his abolitionist career supporting Woolman's attempts to restrict slaveholding and the buying of slaves among Quakers, building on his predecessor's use of Quaker institutions and methods, printing, visiting, and correspondence to propagate antislavery. In 1754 he wrote the Philadelphia Yearly Meeting's *Epistle of Caution and Advice*, which drew attention to the inhumanity of the slave trade. In his first antislavery pamphlet, published five years later, Benezet, declaring that no practice was "stained with a deeper Dye of Injustice, Cruelty and Oppression" than the slave trade, compiled evidence from European slave traders on its brutalities.[18]

Benezet occupies a pride of place in early abolitionist thought, as his ideas transcended the boundaries of Quakerism. In his pamphlet *A Short Account of that part of Africa Inhabited by the Negroes* (1762) he combined the Quaker abolitionist critique of "the Love of Gain" and "Pleasures and Profits" that blind men to the "Sufferings of their Fellow Creatures" with an exhaustive account of West African societies culled from the writings of European traders and factors. The investigative nature of his pamphlet, a hallmark of modern antislavery, effectively allowed Benezet not only to rebut racialist myths surrounding Africa and its inhabitants but also to highlight the "Calamities" the Atlantic slave trade visited on their countries. Benezet read the popular geography of North Africa written by the traveler and writer Leo Africanus and strove to write from an African perspective. Even though he did not characterize African societies in all their complexity, Benezet, in an adept reversal of imagery, made Africans appear as the civilized victims of European barbarism. The romanticization of Africa was an antidote to the poisonous caricatures that later abounded in Western literature.

Did Benezet's interactions with people of African descent and their oral testimony influence his writings, as his most recent biographer speculates? Certainly his long descriptions of African societies reveal that his sources of antislavery inspiration lay as much in Africa as in the ideas of Quaker Christianity and the Enlightenment. Benezet's close connections to Philadelphia's black community and his lifelong commitment to black education undoubtedly gave birth to his strong antiracialism. Africans in the slave societies of the Americas had little opportunity to develop their natural talents, he wrote, forced as they were to be "constantly employed in servile Labor." "The Negroes," he concluded, "are equally intitled to the common Priviledges of Mankind with the Whites, that they have the same Rational Powers; the same natural Affections, and areas susceptible to Pain and Grief as they, that therefore the bringing and keeping them in Bondage, is an Instance of Oppression and Injustice of the most grie[v]ous Nature, such as is scarcely to be paralleled by any Example in the present or former Ages." Benezet's writings, circulated through the Quaker "Antislavery International" headquartered in London and Philadelphia, laid the foundation of the first Anglo-American abolition movement.[19]

If Benezet was the preeminent American abolitionist of his age, then Granville Sharp surely was his British counterpart. By 1765 the English legal theorist William Blackstone had affirmed in his influential *Commentaries on the Laws of England* that English law did not recognize slavery but clarified in later editions of his work that a master's "right to service" continued. That year a slave named Jonathan Strong solicited Sharp's help to protect him from being returned to his abusive master, David Lisle of Barbados, who had left him bloodied and bruised in the streets of London. Sharp's brother, a doctor, nursed him back to health. When Lisle reclaimed his slave and sold him, Sharp argued Strong's case, and he was set free. Sharp published his conviction that slavery or human property was incompatible with English law in his *A Representation of the Injustice and Dangerous Tendency of Tolerating Slavery; Or, Of Admitting the Least Claim of Private Property in the Persons of Men, in England* (1769). Other fugitive slaves such as Thomas Lewis, John and Mary Hylas, and James Somerset, who had run away from his master Charles Steuart, formerly of Virginia, recruited Sharp in their quest for freedom. Somerset was recaptured and imprisoned aboard a brig awaiting transportation to Jamaica. He and Lewis both were rescued through a writ of habeas corpus. Steuart had resided in Boston, and the colonial precedent of freedom suits may well have influenced Somerset, who sued him for freedom. In his decision in the *Somerset v. Steuart* case, Lord Chief Justice William Murray, Earl of Mansfield (who had adopted his nephew's mixed-race daughter Dido), denied colonial slaveholders the right to forcibly transport their slaves from England. The decision represented a happy marriage between black resistance and English law.

Somerset was widely interpreted as having abolished slavery in Britain. It damaged slaveholders' prerogatives and rendered the enslavement of Africans insecure there. A runaway slave instigated a historic antislavery ruling, and it is only fitting that his name graces the landmark Anglo-American decision. Black people throughout the British Atlantic breathed life into the decision, celebrating it as the end of slavery in England and using it as a reason to abscond from their masters. While colonial slavery continued to flourish and benefit European nations, slaves and their abolitionist allies worked to achieve hard-won concessions to their liberty. During this time slaves in France also petitioned and sued their masters for freedom. The Francisque case of 1758 freed a slave from Pondicherry, India, and in 1770 the case of a Louisiana slave named Roc against his master, Poupet, the French equivalent of the *Somerset* decision, further vindicated the freedom principle in France. Henrion de Pansey, the French Granville Sharp, argued the case and went on to write Roc's antislavery memoir.[20]

Like Benezet, Sharp wrote some of the age's most compelling abolitionist arguments. Besides his pamphlet of 1769, Sharp edited Benezet's pamphlet of 1762 for publication in Britain, and Benezet reprinted Sharp's pamphlet. The two men began a correspondence in 1772 when Benezet sent Sharp his antislavery treatises. Sharp published four important antislavery tracts in 1776, one containing a reprint of his essay from 1773 against slavery in an appendix. Emulating Benezet, Sharp issued "a Serious Warning to Great Britain and her Colonies" over the "national crime" of the African slave trade that would engender "*National Retribution*" and divine vengeance, illustrated with copious details from the Old Testament. In his second pamphlet, Sharp, who was sympathetic to the American cause, argued that British and American slave traders and slaveholders were equally responsible for colonial slavery. He recommended that the British, like the Spanish, allow their slaves one day to work for wages and purchase their freedom. In a clear reference to Bishop Berkeley, Sharp asserted in his third pamphlet that Christian obedience of servants to masters or the "law of passive obedience" did not justify slavery. In the fourth, Sharp wrote that the "royal law of liberty" was based on the Gospel's injunction to love thy neighbor and therefore slavery was illegal. Withholding the fruits of the slave's labor was the worst kind of domination, and the British, he reiterated, were guilty of violations of "*Brotherly Love and Charity*" and "the most detestable and oppressive *Slavery*."[21]

But no pamphlet inspired eighteenth-century abolitionists more than Benezet's *Some Historical Account of Guinea*, published in 1771 and reprinted many times. In 1774 the founder of Methodism, John Wesley, in his *Thoughts on Slavery*, lifted entire passages from it, as did many others, and the British abolitionist Thomas Clarkson attributed his conversion to it. A compilation and extension of Benezet's earlier writings, the work was a comprehensive indictment of the slave trade and slavery. Benezet described the cruelties of the Middle Passage and the brutal nature of slavery in the Americas, especially in the West Indies, where, he noted, the slave population "*is under necessity of being entirely renewed every sixteen years.*" Evoking Lay's rhetoric, he wrote that the colonies have "enriched themselves at the expense of the blood and bondage of the Negroes." Benezet disputed claims of slaves' racial inferiority by using environmental reasoning and comparing black slaves favorably with white servants. He rejected the contemporary equation of climate and race, holding that European laborers could just as easily cultivate the plantations in the Americas. Benezet, who opened a school for black children in 1770, "found amongst them a variety of Talents, equally capable of improvement, as amongst a like number of Whites" and dismissed notions of black inferiority as "a vulgar prejudice, founded on the Pride or Ignorance of their lordly Masters." He advocated emancipation and proposed that "every Negroe family" be granted a small tract of land in the southern or western part of the country. In its plea for black equality and autonomy, Benezet's pamphlet was a truly abolitionist tract.[22]

Besides his published works, Benezet's numerous letters to abolitionists on both sides of the Atlantic created an antislavery network. He corresponded with such prominent Quakers as David Barclay and Samuel and John Fothergill in London, Israel, John, and James Pemberton in Philadelphia, Robert Pleasants in Virginia, and Moses Brown in Providence, Rhode Island, to enlist their services in his cause. His correspondents included Selena Hastings, the Countess of Huntingdon, Queen Charlotte in England, Empress Catherine of Russia, and the Abbé Raynal in France. He urged the countess, a patron of black writers and of Methodism, to release the slaves who worked for her Orphan House in Georgia founded by Whitefield. In his last pamphlet he wrote an introduction to extracts from Raynal's multivolume *Histoire philosophique et politique des établissements et du commerce des Européens dans les deux Indes* (1780), which indicted European colonialism for its treatment of Native Americans and enslavement of Africans. Benezet eschewed simple racialism and condemned equally the African and English villains who conducted the trade with the buyers of slaves in the colonies. He died in 1784 bequeathing to the abolition movement an abundance of antislavery tracts and most of his estate to his school for African Americans. Little wonder that one of his admirers, the American patriot Benjamin Rush, dreamed of him presiding over freed slaves in heaven. As Rush pointed out in a letter to Sharp, Benezet was the foremost advocate of abolition before the American Revolution. Hundreds of black Philadelphians marched in his funeral procession.[23]

ORIGINS OF BLACK ANTISLAVERY

The origins of black antislavery can be traced to African writers and thinkers in the early modern West. As Henry Louis Gates Jr. has observed, people of African descent had to read and write their way to humanity in the post-Enlightenment Western world. Enlightenment thought proved to be a double-edged sword for them. At the very least, black men and women of letters challenged racist myths justifying the enslavement of Africans. In its politically most sophisticated forms black literature rendered a pointed critique of slavery and racism, contributing significantly to the abolitionist project. Black writers created, in Paul Gilroy's words, "the counter-culture of modernity." Africans were "conscripts of modernity," who exposed the fact that "freedom is a race myth."[24]

The first African writers in Europe were isolated figures who wrote in the style and form of dominant Western literary discourses. From the start, the "double consciousness" elaborated by Du Bois characterized black identity in the West. Juan Latino, an African slave who rose to be a professor of classics at the University of Granada in sixteenth-century Spain, was referred to mockingly by Miguel de Cervantes, a champion of the Spanish vernacular, in *Don Quixote* for his classical learning and erudition. Latino was best known for his Latin elegies celebrating the Spanish victory at the Battle of Lepanto and King Phillip II. He married a Spanish noblewoman and, unlike most enslaved Africans brought to the Iberian Peninsula, achieved fame and wealth. Latino asserted his African identity, referring to himself as such, but also claimed to be a worthy subject of the Catholic monarch of Spain. Leo Africanus, or Hassan ibn Muhammad al-Wazzan al-Fasi, was a Moor from Granada. During the Reconquista, when the Moors were driven out of Spain, he returned to Morocco but was captured by the Spanish and presented to Pope Leo X. He was baptized and became a teacher of Arabic in Rome. Leo Africanus published his celebrated *Description of Africa* (1550), which was translated into English as *A Geographical Historie of Africa*. He ultimately returned to North Africa and reconverted to Islam. Whereas Latino assumed an Afro-Iberian identity, Leo Africanus rejected the Western Christian world.[25]

African scholars in Europe in the eighteenth century, when racial slavery had become the norm in the Americas, dealt directly with the issue of human bondage. Anton Wilhelm Amo, whose brother was sold into slavery in Surinam, was a favored slave of Duke Anton Ulrich of Braunschweig-Wolfenbüttel, who freed him. He studied philosophy at the University of Halle in Germany. The rector of the University of Wittenberg touted him as an exemplar of "the natural genius of Africa." In 1729 he wrote a Latin disputation titled "On the Rights of Moors in Europe" in which he argued that since African nations were recognized under Roman law, Africans could not be enslaved. Unfortunately, this treatise is lost to history, and only his works of philosophy have survived. Amo taught at Wittenberg and Jena, but in 1747, disillusioned with European racism after being accused of falling in love with a woman "above his station," Amo returned to the Gold Coast. A statue of him survives in Wittenberg, and his grave is in modern Ghana.

Unlike Amo, Jacobus Elisa Johannes Capitein, brought to Holland by a Dutch slave trader, in his Latin dissertation of 1742 justified the enslavement of Africans on evangelical grounds. Capitein's question, "Is slavery compatible with Christian freedom or not?," which he answered in the affirmative, was a plea for the Christianization of Africans and a claim for their spiritual equality. On the face of it proslavery, his dissertation was a refutation of the racist idea that Africans could not make good Christians. Capitein spent his last years in Africa as a missionary, where he was increasingly at odds with the authorities of the Dutch West India Company. The French abolitionist Abbé Henri-Baptiste Grégoire used the examples of both Amo and Capitein to argue for black equality in his antiracist work *An Enquiry Concerning the Intellectual and Moral Faculties, and Literature of Negroes* (1808).[26]

Most early narratives of African captivity in the West were written not by black authors but by British ones. For the English at this time, the injustice of these individuals' slavery outweighed the racial justification of their enslavement. In 1734 Thomas Bluett wrote the story of the captivity of Ayuba Suleiman Diallo (Job Ben Solomon), a literate Muslim who was kidnapped into slavery from the kingdom of Bondu and enslaved in Maryland. Rescued and brought to England by Oglethorpe, Diallo managed to return to his family in Gambia. Diallo himself had traded and owned slaves. In 1749 William Dodd published romantic poems describing the real-life separation of William Ansah Sessarakoo, Prince of Annamaboe, from his lover, Zara. In the 1770s two so-called princes of Calabar, Little Ephraim Robin John and Ancona Robin Robin John, managed to win their freedom in the wake of the *Somerset* decision and secured their passage back to Africa. They found antislavery patrons in Charles and John Wesley but continued to trade in slaves on their return to Africa.[27] The inexhaustible European demand for slaves had transformed West Africa into a slave-producing region that put all people of African descent, regardless of their status, in danger of being enslaved. These works by British authors criticized not racial slavery per se but the enslavement of exceptional Africans.

Black writers in English, who first emerged in colonial America, cast doubt on the racist logic that dehumanized Africans as slave property. Educated by her mistress, Lucy Terry Prince, in her unpublished poem "Bars Fight" (1746), described an Indian raid on Deerfield, Massachusetts, from the perspective of the colonists. The poem is usually viewed as adopting a white mindset and attitudes, but one might speculate about the relish with which Prince describes in detail the killing of the colonists, including the grisly tomahawking of the unfortunate young Eunice Allen. Satire was a common mode of expressing resistance in the larger oral culture of African slaves in eighteenth-century New England. A resourceful, articulate woman, Prince did not hesitate to petition the governor for protection on behalf of her husband, Abijah Prince, and family against her considerably more wealthy neighbors, the Noyes family. Two of her sons, Ceasar and Festus, fought in the Revolution. She argued on behalf of the two boys' land claims before the Vermont Supreme Court and fought unsuccessfully to get one of them admitted to Williams College. The black abolitionist Congregational minister Lemuel Haynes eulogized Prince on her death in 1821:

> And shall proud tyrants boast with brazen face,
> Of birth—of genius, over Africa's race:
> Go to the tomb where lies their matron's dust . . .
> How long must Ethaopia's murder'd race
> Be doom'd by men to bondage & disgrace?[28]

Like Prince's satirical poem, the narrative of Briton Hammon published in 1760 appears to adopt the views of European colonists toward Native Americans. It refers to Indians as devils and savages and celebrates English liberty. Hammon's narrative reads like any other adventure-filled Indian captivity narrative, a popular colonial genre with Iberian roots. Hammon describes his escape attempts from the Spanish, prefiguring aspects of fugitive slave narratives. Hammon's astonishing reunion with his master at the end after suffering through Indian captivity in Florida, Spanish dungeons in Havana, Cuba, and poverty on the streets of London was not a simple endorsement of American slavery. If anything, it illustrated the highly precarious existence of the Atlantic Creole, people of African descent, slave and free, who navigated the confusing world of European imperialism in the Americas.[29]

Twelve years after Hammon, James Albert Ukawsaw Gronniosaw chronicled his narrative of enslavement from the African country of Bournou by the Dutch, his life as a domestic slave in New York, his education and emancipation by his last master, and, finally, his life of extreme poverty in England, a fate he shared with a majority of the black British population in the eighteenth century. He was befriended by Whitefield and traveled to Holland before marrying a poor English widow. Gronniosaw's story reads like a conversion narrative, as he discovers the "talking book," the Bible. Its religious imprimatur was reinforced by Gronniosaw's amanuensis, a "young lady," and by Rev. Walter Shirley, who wrote the foreword. Dedicated to the Countess of Huntingdon, who sponsored its publication, the work sought to raise money for its author, and in fact, having been published in the immediate aftermath of the *Somerset* case, it became a best seller. Though assisted by Quakers, who refused to baptize his dead child, Gronniosaw describes a life of trials. A veritable black book of Job, Gronniosaw's narrative emphasizes his Christian piety and forbearance, poignantly revealing the un-Christian character of the society he inhabits.[30]

The ideological underpinnings of black antislavery lay in an antiracist construction of Christianity. The rise of religious egalitarianism and evangelical Christianity, based on the spiritual equality of slaves, initially posed a challenge to the institution of slavery, one that Africans, who started to convert in large numbers with the First Great Awakening, were quick to recognize. Slaves adapted evangelical Christianity to their own largely African-inspired styles of worship. Despite their early commitment to abolitionism, Quakers' spare liturgy attracted few African Americans. Like most Quaker abolitionists, evangelicals were suspicious of the acquisitive, self-interested nature of early capitalism, which propelled the expansion of racial slavery in the Americas. The Methodists John Wesley, Francis Asbury, and Thomas Coke were antislavery, and separatist Baptists preached a message of humility and spiritual equality that appealed to African slaves, Native Americans, and women. The Moravians allowed black women such as Rebecca from the Danish colony of St. Thomas to assume positions of authority in their church. After the death of her German husband, Rebecca married an Afro-Dane Moravian, Christian Protten, a contemporary of Amo and Capitein. Like them, the Prottens spent their last days in Africa as missionaries in an uneasy relationship with their European sponsors.[31]

For black writers of the eighteenth century, a Christian identity became a way to challenge slavery. The "democratization of American Christianity" in its forms and style of worship resulted in the growth of a distinct African American Christianity. Blacks began the long process of making Christianity their own, developing a liberation theology that identified with the enslaved Israelites as the chosen people of God and the story of Exodus. In 1669 the biblically named Hagar Blackmore, an enslaved woman impregnated by her master's son, was brought up on charges of fornication in Massachusetts. She pointed out that she had been stolen from Africa from her husband and baby. Her charge of "man stealing," sure to resonate in the Puritan court, became a staple of early black Christian antislavery. In 1754 a slave named Greenwich in Canterbury, Connecticut, issued a Christian indictment of the enslavement of Africans. Racial slavery transgressed the biblical injunctions against imprisoning a man "if he hath done the[m] no harm" and against man stealing, which was punishable by death. In 1759 South Carolinians executed a black preacher named

Philip Johns for preaching earthly deliverance to the slaves. Two decades later David Margrett (also known as Margate), the first ordained black preacher with the Huntingdon Connexion, the Countess of Huntingdon's Methodist church, said, "God would send Deliverance to the Negroes, from the power of their Masters, as He freed the Children of Israel from Egyptian Bondage." He narrowly escaped being lynched in South Carolina before returning to England.[32]

The Christian origins of early African American literature gave it an antislavery cast. Starting with Phillis Wheatley, black writers and poets confronted the colonial social and intellectual order that ranked them at the bottom by representing themselves as especially worthy and pious Christians. In terms of the history of abolition, Wheatley is particularly important. In her own time, Wheatley was a subject of debate among antislavery proponents and slaveholders, and she met such prominent abolitionists and American revolutionaries as Sharp and Franklin. Wesley and Thomas Paine reprinted her poems. Rush alluded to her talents in his debate on race and slavery with the West Indian planter Richard Nisbet, who dismissed her "silly poems." Thomas Jefferson singled out the poetry of this young slave girl from Massachusetts for heavy-handed criticism. That Wheatley could evoke the ire of Jefferson and the praise of the French philosophe Voltaire and Clarkson probably secures her place in history. John Paul Jones, the daring patriot naval commander, also a Wheatley admirer, sent his verses to her. So remarkable were her poems that a bevy of Boston worthies, including John Hancock, examined her poems and testified on their authenticity.[33] Wheatley's work is the earliest literary expression of an African American consciousness and reveals an antislavery purpose. Wheatley secured her manumission on the basis of her literary talents, which became an argument for the emancipation of the entire race.

A majority of Wheatley's poems are elegies on the dead. Death was a motif that haunted the lives of African slaves. Incarceration in the holds of a slave ship was a "living death" and enslavement itself, as the sociologist Orlando Patterson has put it, "social death." While death portended Christian salvation, suicide as a form of resistance and the belief that one's soul would transmigrate to Africa were common among enslaved Africans. Named after the slaver in which she was brought in 1761, the seven-year-old Phillis became a privileged slave of John and Susannah Wheatley, who had lost their daughter, who was Phillis's age. Educated by her owners, Wheatley mastered English as well as Latin and composed her first poem in 1765. She was a genius by any standard. Literary scholars have debated the meaning of her mastery and use of contemporary and classical styles of poetry. More interestingly, Wheatley, like her predecessors, repeatedly asserted her identity as an "Ethiop" and African, anticipating the naming practices of northern free blacks. Africa in her writings is a pagan continent but also a "blissful plain," the land of her childhood from which she was snatched. Her poem "On Recollection," asks "MNEME" to inspire "Your vent'rous Afric in her great design" to remember "the acts of long departed years." There is no doubt that Wheatley was referring to her own history in writing,

> By her unveil'd each horrid crime appears,
> Her awful hand a cup of wormwood bears.
> Days, years misspent, O what a hell of woe!
> Hers the worst tortures that our souls can know.[34]

Although the British writer Aphra Behn wrote a fictional account of a slave rebellion in *Oroonoko* (1688) that preceded her work, Wheatley originated a distinct genre of antislavery literature, poems written by women. Throughout the Anglo-American world, female antislavery poets would refer to her well after her death. As early as 1771 Jane Dunlap called the "young Afric damsel" an inspiration in her book of religious poems on Whitefield published in Boston. Wheatley dedicated her anthology *Poems on Various Subjects Religious and Moral* (London, 1773) to her patron, the Countess of Huntingdon, and one of her most famous poems was on the death of Whitefield. Christianity, not the crimes perpetrated against Africans, is the dominant motif in Wheatley's most well known poem, "On being brought from Africa to America." In the poem Wheatley thanks "mercy" for saving her "benighted soul," but she makes it clear that "once I redemption neither sought nor knew." It ends with a Christian condemnation of racism. "Some view our sable race with a scornful eye, 'Their colour is a diabolic dye,'" but she reminds her readers that "*Christians, Negros,* black as *Cain,* / May be refin'd and join th' angelic strain." Similarly, Francis Williams, a free black Jamaican whose antiracist Latin poem was ironically translated by the proslavery writer Edward Long in his *History of Jamaica* (1774), wrote:

> This rule was 'stablish'd by th'Eternal Mind;
> Nor virtue's self, nor prudence are confin'd
> To *colour*; none imbues the honest heart;
> To science none belongs, none to art.

Christian universalism, for black writers, was an antidote to the new science of man that classified humankind in a Great Chain of Being in which Europeans were on top and Africans at the bottom.[35]

Christian motifs pervade the poetry of another of Wheatley's contemporaries, the slave poet from Long Island, New York, Jupiter Hammon. The self-taught Hammon was a preacher and held a position of trust in his master's family, the Lloyds, as an accountant in their community store. His patriot master had escaped the British occupation and relocated his slaves, including Hammon, to Hartford, Connecticut. Wheatley's poetry evoked a response from Hammon. He had published his first poem, a prayer titled "An Evening Thought: Salvation by Christ, with Penitential Cries," in a broadside of 1760 and was far more steeped in the Bible than Wheatley. In his "An Address to Miss Phillis Wheatley" (1778) Hammon emphasized the regenerating power Christianity held for enslaved Africans like the young poet who had been "Tost o'er the raging main" and saved "From the dangers that come down." Hammon's poetry was not a simple capitulation to Christian servitude. In his dialogue between a "kind master" and "dutiful servant," the latter asserts, "The only safety that I see, Is Jesus' holy word." His master's suicide, which resulted from his mistaken belief that the Americans had lost the war, only underscored his slave's claim to spiritual superiority.[36]

Wheatley, who is often portrayed as a lone genius, was in fact representative of an emerging African American antislavery critique of revolutionary republicanism. She saw herself as a member of an oppressed people rather than as just the pet slave of the Wheatley family or the exotic black poetess of the Atlantic world. As her letter to the British evangelical John Thornton, with whom she stayed while in London, attests, God is "no respecter of Persons," and he should "Therfor disdain not to be called the Father of Humble Africans and Indians; though despised on earth on account of our colour, we have this Consolation, if he enables us to deserve it." Wheatley's letters to a fellow slave named Obour Tanner and her moving poem to Scipio Moorhead, the African painter most likely responsible for producing the woodcut that graced her book of poems, testify to her attempts to seek out a community of African Americans. Most of her extant letters are to Tanner, to whom she wrote, "It gives me very great pleasure to hear of so many of my Nation." A similar impulse no doubt led Hammon to address his poem to her. In searching for literary predecessors in the West, Wheatley evoked not the European poets she emulated but the African poet Terence from antiquity, though Jefferson insisted he was "of the race of whites."[37]

Wheatley openly questioned the enslavement of Africans. In championing the cause of the colonists in a poem dedicated to the Earl of Dartmouth, principal secretary of state for North America, she explains that her "love of *Freedom*" springs from her personal experience:

> I, young in life, by seeming cruel fate
> Was snatch'd from *Afric's* fancy'd happy seat:
> What pangs excruciating must molest,

> What sorrows labour in my parent's breast?
> Steel'd was that soul and by no misery mov'd
> That from a father seiz'd his babe belov'd:
> Such, such my case. And can I then but pray
> Others may never feel tyrannic sway?

In her unpublished poem on the death of Gen. David Wooster she recited her opinion of slaveholding patriots freely:

> But how, presumptuous shall we hope to find
> Divine acceptance with th' Almighty mind —
> While yet (O deed ungenerous!) they disgrace
> And hold in bondage Afric's blameless race?

In a letter of 1774 to the Native American minister Samson Occom, published in several newspapers throughout New England, she caustically writes, "By the leave of our Modern Egyptians I will assert, the same Principle [love of freedom] lives in us." She remarks on "the strange Absurdity of their Conduct whose Words and Actions are so diametrically opposite. How well the Cry for Liberty, and the reverse Disposition for the exercise of oppressive Power over others agree, — I humbly think it does not require the Penetration of a Philosopher to determine."[38]

During the American Revolution, Wheatley became actively engaged in the politics of freedom and slavery. Her poem to George Washington, written in 1775 and read usually as pure flattery, gently chides him for his order excluding African Americans, including those who had fought in the initial revolutionary battles of Bunker Hill, Lexington, and Concord, from the Continental Army:

> Shall I to Washington their praise recite?
> Enough thou knows't them in the fields of fight.
> Thee, first in place and honours, — we demand
> The grace and glory of thy martial band.

A recent biographer of Washington attributes the growth in his views on race — as he evolved from a provincial Virginia planter to the more cosmopolitan revolutionary military commander — to his encounter with Wheatley (Washington invited her to his headquarters on receiving her poem, although they may have never met). Wheatley chose to fight her battles in America. She rejected acclaim in Britain and when asked to return to Africa as a missionary wrote that there she would appear to be a barbarian (a telling usage that belies the notion that she viewed Africa as an inferior, uncivilized continent), having forgotten the language of her childhood. Through Rev. Samuel Hopkins, the abolitionist

Congregational minister in Newport, Rhode Island, she became aware of the missionary work of Philip Quaque, the African minister in the Society for the Propagation of the Gospel who condemned the patriots for their hypocrisy: "I behold with Sorrowful sighing my poor abject Countryman over whom You, without the Bowels of Christian Love and Pity, hold in cruel Bondage."

Wheatley claimed an African American identity that, while evoking Western Christianity and the colonists' struggle for liberty, remained critical of both. As a Christian, she wrote that Africa was suffering from a "Spiritual Famine" but "Europe and America have long been fed with the heavenly provision, and I fear they loathe it." She later married John Peters, a free black storekeeper, doctor, and lawyer of sorts who was known to plead cases for people of color. Though unable to publish a second edition of her poems dedicated to Franklin, whom she met in London and whose antislavery reputation she was undoubtedly aware of, stories of her later poverty and her husband's alleged shiftlessness are exaggerated. Peters, who was charged with barratry for his litigious nature, was imprisoned for debt but recovered much of his fortune after Wheatley's death. All three of the children she had with Peters died, and she herself died shortly before the youngest, in 1784. Her "An Elegy on Leaving," published by Wesley that year, was prescient. Despite Wheatley's cosmopolitan background and international life—she was born in Africa, experienced slavery in America, and traveled to Britain—she chose to live as a free woman identifying with the emerging African American community in the United States. She became the black female icon of the Anglo-American abolition movement, her poems reprinted by the abolitionist Quaker printer Joseph Crukshank of Philadelphia in 1786. In the 1830s Garrison published a memoir of her by a Wheatley family descendant, Margaretta Matilda Odell. Despite Odell's attempt to reduce Wheatley to a faithful and exceptional servant favored by her owners, the introduction averred that Wheatley's poetry was proof of "African genius."[39]

Forgotten antislavery voices and actions of Quaker and African pioneers, slave rebels and runaways, radical, dissenting Christianity, English antislavery lawyers and judges, and early black writers all played a part in laying the foundation of revolutionary abolitionism. During the American War of Independence their ideas gained currency.

REVOLUTIONARY ANTISLAVERY
IN BLACK AND WHITE

It is an irony of history that one of the first martyrs of the American Revolution was an Afro-Indian sailor and runaway slave from Framingham, Massachusetts, Crispus Attucks. In 1770 nervous British soldiers shot on a crowd of belligerent patriots, killing three of them, including Attucks, instantly and wounding eight others, two of whom later died, in what came to be known as the Boston Massacre. Attucks thought he had a stake in the fight. He had had the temerity to write to Gov. Thomas Hutchinson charging him with crimes against the "people in general." John Adams defended the Redcoats and blamed the episode on the unruly "saucy boys, negroes and mulattoes, Irish teagues and outlandish jack-tarrs." A few years later Adams adopted Attucks's name to use as a pseudonym for an essay he wrote on liberty. His cousin Sam Adams, the mastermind behind the Sons of Liberty, organized the funeral procession of the five patriots who fell in Boston. Abolitionists used the symbolism of Attucks's martyrdom well into the nineteenth century.[1]

The story of revolutionary antislavery is an interracial one, flowing in distinct streams and converging in particular moments of challenges to slavery. The Age of Revolution, starting with the American, French, and Haitian Revolutions in the late eighteenth century and ending with the Latin American Wars of Independence in the 1810s and 1820s and the failed European revolutions of the 1830s and 1848, gave birth to the first wave of abolition.[2] Abolitionists subjected the revolutionary pretensions of American slaveholders to rigorous critique. Black resistance acquired new potency during the War of Independence and destabilized slavery.[3]

The Haitian rather than the American Revolution, in which slave resistance, revolutionary republicanism, and abolitionism came together in a heady mix, marks the high point in the history of revolutionary antislavery. The only instance of a successful slave rebellion in world history, it created the first independent modern black nation.[4] Despite its subsequent tragic history, Haiti answered the cry of millions of enslaved Africans: we have no country. It became the source of an alternative revolutionary tradition for abolitionists throughout the Atlantic world.

REVOLUTIONARY ABOLITIONISTS

The heritage of the Enlightenment was a mixed blessing for Africans, giving a powerful impetus to antislavery but also containing elements that justified their enslavement. The French philosophes and Scottish thinkers condemned slavery, but more than a few made exceptions to their general theories on the basis of climate, race, and region. As Benjamin Rush asked, how had Europe, "civilized as it is, and thoroughly versed in the laws of nature, and the rights of mankind" authorized "the daily outrages against human nature, permitting them to debase man almost below the level of the beasts of the field?" In his answer to the proslavery and racist response of the West Indian planter Richard Nisbet to his antislavery pamphlet, Rush asserted the intellectual and moral equality of Africans to Europeans. To the English thinker John Locke slavery was abominable and outside the social contract but the enslavement of Africans was legitimate, a condition of prisoners taken in a "just war." Locke's notion of property as a natural right also bolstered slaveholders' claims. The liberal political philosopher helped write the feudal constitution of South Carolina in 1665 and was a shareholder in the slave-trading Royal African Company. Racial slavery was the material basis for the growth of white republicanism in Virginia. But belief in republican principles also posed a threat to slavery, which in turn weakened commitment to revolutionary ideals.[5]

No "contagion of liberty" flowed inexorably according to its own logic to slaves. They and their antislavery allies transformed revolutionary currents into a call for African liberty. James Otis, in a pamphlet of 1764 vindicating the colonists' rights in the aftermath of the Sugar Act, argued that "all men . . . white or black" are "by the law of nature freeborn." The abolitionist pamphleteers Nathaniel Appleton of Boston and David Cooper, a Quaker from New Jersey, pointed to the hypocrisy of the patriots. Benezet asked in his *A Caution and a Warning to Great Britain and her Colonies* (1766) how, "at a time when the general Rights and Liberties of Mankind" had become the "Subjects of Universal Consideration," the "Advocates of Liberty, [can] remain insensible and inattentive" to the condition of those kept in "the most deplorable State of

Slavery." John Trumbull of Connecticut mocked the colonists' "natural, moral, and divine right of enslaving the Africans" in his satirical article. In 1775 the inhabitants of Darien, Georgia, evoking the vestigial antislavery premise on which their state had been founded, expressed their "disapprobation and abhorrence of the unnatural practice of Slavery in America." The New Jersey patriot and Presbyterian minister Jacob Green pointed out "what a shocking consideration [it was], that people who are so strenuously contending for liberty, should at the same time encourage and promote slavery! And being thus guilty, expose themselves to the judgment of Heaven!" After independence, Green did not allow slaveholders into his congregation.[6]

The most radical revolutionary of the Atlantic world, Thomas Paine, not only wrote a compelling plea for American independence, *Common Sense*, but also published indictments of African slavery. In an essay from 1775 often attributed to Paine, the author advised all European governments to emancipate their slaves. Slavery, he wrote, was "contrary to the light of nature, to every principle of Justice and Humanity, and even good policy." The son of a Quaker stay maker and a spokesman for revolutionary republicanism, Paine published another essay contending that Africans had a natural right to their bodies, their freedom, and their labor. Some claim he wrote the preamble of the first abolition law, Pennsylvania's gradual emancipation act of 1780. Paine joined the Pennsylvania Abolition Society in 1787, but his energies were mostly consumed in promoting the cause of revolution across the Atlantic. Nonetheless, he stood far above most American revolutionaries in his objections to slavery. He unsuccessfully advised Jefferson to remain neutral during the Haitian Revolution and to oppose the introduction of slavery into the Louisiana territory. In the antebellum period, while northern free soilers, who opposed the expansion of slavery, repeatedly invoked Jefferson's few antislavery pronouncements, abolitionists such as Garrison and Moncure D. Conway looked to Paine for ideological inspiration.[7]

Revolutionary abolitionists mocked the colonists' plight when compared to the oppression suffered by black slaves. William Dillwyn, a follower of Benezet who became influential in the British movement against the slave trade, questioned how the colonies could base their claims on "a disinterested generous love to liberty, founded on principle—on publick virtue, and a conviction that it is the unalienable right of man," when they subject "the Africans . . . to the most abject state of perpetual personal slavery." The Baptist minister and patriot John Allen put it more strongly: "Blush, ye pretended votaries of freedom! Ye trifling patriots! Who are making a vain parade of being the advocates of the liberties of mankind . . . by trampling on the sacred natural rights and privileges of the Africans." While "fasting, praying, non-importing, . . . remonstrating, resolving," they continued the "cruel, inhuman, and abominable practice of enslaving your fellow creatures."[8]

Religious revival spurred revolutionary abolition. In New England, some ministers, like Allen and the Calvinists Elhanan Winchester and Benjamin Colman, constructed a Christian antislavery argument. The Connecticut New Divinity adherents of Jonathan Edwards, the theologian of the First Great Awakening, began writing and preaching that slavery was an obstacle to religious virtue. Edwards himself was a slave owner who defended slaveholding clergy from criticism and argued only for the Christianization of blacks and Indians. But he criticized the slave trade, and his followers referred to his ideas in preaching against slavery. In their essays Ebenezer Baldwin and Jonathan Edwards Jr., who went further than his father, refuted Christian and biblical arguments for slavery. Nathaniel Niles and Levi Hart, students of Edwards's disciple Joseph Bellamy, meditated on the relationship between civil and religious liberty and condemned as sinful spiritual slavery as well as actual slavery and the enslavement of Africans.[9]

The most noted abolitionist New Divinity theologian was Rev. Samuel Hopkins. Hopkins was appalled by the Atlantic slave trade and widespread slaveholding in Newport, Rhode Island. He included African Americans in his relatively poor congregation and worked with them on antislavery and racial uplift. The devout and indigent Sarah Osborn, who led a religious revival in Newport in the 1760s and held prayers in her home for the poor, free, and enslaved blacks and for women, had been instrumental in procuring his ministry. Besides Osborn, a handful of religious women such as her friend Susanna Anthony and the Quaker revivalist Rebecca Jones, a follower of Benezet and Dillwyn, became associated with the first wave of abolition in the eighteenth century. Like Osborn, Hopkins stressed the spiritual education of his black flock, but he also made their earthly freedom a priority. Hopkins, who had once held and sold a slave, came to regret his actions and started preaching against the slave trade and slavery. To Hopkins, as to the early Quaker abolitionists, they were symptoms of the corrupt, acquisitive nature of commercial society. His doctrine of disinterested benevolence, an early version of the social gospel, steered New Divinity ideas in an abolitionist direction.

Hopkins was influenced by his contact with both enslaved and free Africans. He persuaded the more conservative Ezra Stiles, who had undergone a similar conversion when confronted with the plight of his slave, to join with him in a plan to educate and send two black missionaries, Bristol Yamma and John Quamine, to Africa. Both had attended Osborn's meetings. They won a lottery ticket and with some help from Hopkins bought their freedom. Yamma and Quamine were educated at Princeton under the personal supervision of its president, John Witherspoon, a proslavery man. Yamma frequently acted as a go-between for Hopkins and Moses Brown, the prominent Quaker abolitionist in Providence. Hopkins and Brown, who intervened in many cases of wrongful enslavement, led the early abolition movement in Rhode Island. Before Hopkins could implement his plans, Quamine died in 1779 aboard a privateer, and Yamma died in North Carolina fifteen years later. Hopkins was also an admirer of Wheatley's. He purchased a copy of her book of poems and started corresponding with her about his plans for a mission to Africa. Hopkins, however, did not argue for the wholesale colonization of African Americans. The duty of the abolitionist, according to him, was to improve the condition of free blacks and work for their education so that they might attain "an acknowledged equality with the white people."[10]

If Benezet's works were highly effectual utterances of revolutionary abolitionist thought, the writings of Hopkins and Cooper were equally compelling. The two addressed their pamphlets to the newly formed American government, hoping to capitalize on the moment of state formation to make a case for abolition. A patriot who came to view the British occupation of Newport as divine punishment for the sins of slavery and the slave trade, Hopkins dedicated his dialogue of 1776 on slavery to the Continental Congress. In their introductory letter the editors wrote that they presented the dialogue on "behalf of more than half a million persons in these colonies, who are under such a degree of oppression and tyranny as to be wholly deprived of all civil and personal liberty" to those who had gained "the respect and veneration of nations" for acting "in the important, noble struggle for LIBERTY."

Trying to expand the revolutionary antislavery consensus that condemned the slave trade but not slavery, interlocutor B in Hopkins's dialogue tries to convince A that slavery is just as reprehensible. As a clergyman, Hopkins was particularly determined to demolish the religious justification for African slavery, refuting the idea that slavery had resulted in the Christianization of Africans (he argued that it had instead brought Christianity into disrepute in Africa), the biblical justification of slavery (he evoked the story of Israelites escaping Egyptian slavery), and the curse of Ham (if true, he argued, then Africans could make slaves of Europeans since there was no correlation between the posterity of Canaan and Africans). Speaking against the popular stance that exhorted slaveholders to merely become good Christian masters, Hopkins contended that the true Christian duty of slaveholders was to free those who were wrongfully denied their freedom. Responding to A's objection that abolitionists incited slaves to rebellion by making them conscious of their situation, B replies with some authority (Hopkins ministered to Africans Americans) that when they "behold the sons of liberty oppressing and tyrannizing over many thousands of poor blacks," they are "shocked with the glaring inconsistencies and wonder" why the colonists themselves do not see it. Responding to A's claims of black inferiority and of masters who bore the expense of caring for their slaves, B argues that all whites not capable of taking care of themselves should then also be enslaved and that all "lordly, selfish" employers complain of giving too much to laborers. In a separate address Hopkins asked "the owners of negro slaves in the American colonies" to relieve themselves of the sin of slaveholding, though he saw it as the provenance of legislatures, magistrates, and "the body of the people" to do away with slavery.[11]

If Hopkins's dialogue was a high point in abolitionist protest at the start of the war, David Cooper's *A Serious Address to the Rulers of America* (1783) revealed abolitionist disappointment at its end. Cooper had published an abolitionist dialogue in 1772 and may very well have inspired Hopkins. Benezet had copies of Cooper's address distributed to all members of Congress in Philadelphia, and Washington's private library in the Boston Athenaeum contains a copy with Cooper's signature. Cooper assailed the patriots, comparing their oppression by Britain to that of "ours to negroes" as "a barley of corn to the globe we inhabit." The men who make "pompous declarations" of natural liberty are slaveholders, and when it comes to making laws they say they meant the *"rights of white men, and not all men."* The work of abolition, Cooper acknowledged, had begun but not in a manner that would produce "the desired *end,* the entire *abolition* of slavery." He pinpointed the problem with revolutionary antislavery sentiment: "Few among us are now hardy enough to justify slavery, and yet will not release their slaves; like hardened sinners, acknowledge their guilt, but discover no inclination to reform." He recounted specific instances when slaves of Tory masters had been sold to finance the battle for American independence, and "a great declaimer" of freedom had attempted to reenslave those who had been freed by his debtor. Ten years had passed since foreign restraints on American lawmaking had been removed, and it was a matter, he concluded, of "anxious sorrow" to the "true friends" of the Republic that no measure had been taken to achieve the complete abolition of slavery. Similarly, the radical British clergyman Richard Price, a supporter of the revolution and an abolitionist, praised Americans for "discountenancing" the slave trade, but urged them to get rid of "the odious slavery which it has introduced." He recommended the British metropolitan example by which a *"Negro* becomes a *freeman* the moment he sets his foot" there. For it to have true global meaning, Price argued, the American Revolution must become abolitionist.[12]

Some historians have posited that by focusing on the metaphor of political slavery, or the enslavement of the American colonists by the British Crown, patriots at best ignored and at worst justified chattel slavery and fought to protect their property rights in slaves. Even those with antislavery views became defensive when it came to slavery. Arthur Lee's diatribe of 1764 against "negroes in Africa" and vindication of the southern colonies in response to Adam Smith's criticism of slavery preceded his antislavery address of 1767 drawn from Montesquieu. In the latter, Lee called slavery a "Violation both of Justice and Religion," one that gave rise to a "fatal train of Vices" in the master and the slave. He still referred to Africans as an "unfortunate and detestable people." Franklin argued that American slaves were better off than British miners, who, he pointedly noted, were white under the smut, and impressed sailors and soldiers.[13]

Jefferson's most famous revolutionary writings, *A Summary View of the Rights of British America* (1774) and the Declaration of Independence (1776), contained condemnations of slavery and the slave trade. In the first he decried the British veto of colonial laws seeking to prohibit the slave trade, an "infamous practice" that "deeply wounded" the "rights of human nature." He called "the abolition of domestic slavery the great object desire" of the colonies but indicated that an end to the slave trade must precede "the enfranchisment of the slaves we have." In his draft of the Declaration of Independence, Jefferson elaborated on that indictment of the British monarch for waging a "cruel war against human nature itself," against the "life and liberty of a distant people who never offended him," carrying them into slavery and a "miserable death." He called the slave trade an "execrable commerce." His "vehement phillipic against negro slavery," according to Adams, was removed at the behest of lower south slaveholders from South Carolina and Georgia. But Jefferson's censure of the British monarch for inciting the "domestic" enemies of the colonists, presumably slaves and Indians, remained.[14]

Revolutionary rhetoric marked the apex of antislavery expression by the founders. Patrick Henry frankly admitted to the abolitionist Virginian Quaker Robert Pleasants that he could not do without the labor of his slaves. The prosperous trader and owner of slaves Henry Laurens of South Carolina, goaded by his idealistic son John, made a few antislavery pronouncements but took no action against the institution. Richard Henry Lee, the brother of Arthur, bemoaned the slave trade and slavery but did little for emancipation. James Madison acknowledged that his runaway slave Billy coveted the same liberty as he but did not free his slaves. Some upper south slaveholders manumitted their slaves, the most famous being the wealthy "King" Robert Carter of Virginia. But none of the prominent southern founders, except for Washington, who stipulated in his will that his slaves should be freed after the death of his wife, did so. John Dickinson of Delaware, who was originally from Pennsylvania and was influenced by his Quaker wife, manumitted all his slaves during his lifetime. Nor did any of the southern founders join abolition societies except Luther Martin, a founding member of the Maryland Society for Promoting the Abolition of Slavery.[15]

Most of the northern founders did both. Adams, who never owned slaves, was for gradual emancipation but feared a race war in the South. Sam Adams and John Hancock pushed for a law to abolish the slave trade to Massachusetts and condemned slavery. Franklin, like some other antislavery founding fathers, for example, John Jay of New York, was a slaveholder. He came late to abolition even though he had published abolitionists like Lay and Sandiford and was an admirer of Tryon, Sharp, and Benezet. He and Jay eventually freed their slaves and, along with Alexander Hamilton, lent the prestige of their names to the abolition movement after the war. Franklin's views on race were contradictory. While he voiced his personal preference for white people, referring to the English "Saxons" rather than the "swarthy" Germans and southern Europeans, Franklin, influenced by his antislavery wife and as a member of the Associates of Dr. Bray, vouched for the intellectual aptitude of black students, whom he found to be just as adept as whites. The sectional division over slavery belies generalizations of either an antislavery revolutionary generation or the equally flattening notion of a proslavery consensus among the founders. Antislavery sentiment among the founding fathers may have been widespread, but committed abolitionists were few and far between.[16]

BLACK ABOLITIONISM

African Americans of the revolutionary era, unlike most Euro-Americans, accepted abolitionism in word and deed as an article of faith. Revolutionary leaders were not the only ones to grapple with the contradiction of slavery in a republic, and their British critics, including Samuel Johnson, were not alone in noting that the loudest "yelps for liberty" came from holders of slaves. The petitions for black freedom reveal that from the start African Americans did not hesitate to voice the severity of their situation and question the revolutionary professions of American patriots. A petition from January 1773 of slaves in Boston and other towns in Massachusetts to the colony's governor and General Court signed simply "Felix" pointed out dramatically that they "had [lived] every Day of their Lives imbittered with the most intolerable Reflection, That, let their Behaviour be what it will, nor their Children to all generations, shall ever be able to do, or possess or enjoy any Thing, no not even Life itself, but in a Manner as the Beasts that perish. We have no property! We have no Wives! No Children! We have no City! No Country!" Couched in deferential language, the petitioners claimed not to want to inflict "the least Wrong and Injury to our Masters" but asked for an abolition law that "to us will be as Life from the dead."[17]

Black petitioners supported the antislavery efforts of contemporary whites, who borrowed their ideas and words. In April 1773 they asked James Swan to reprint his pamphlet *A Disuasion to Great Britain and the Colonies from the Slave Trade to Africa* (1772) and presented their freedom petition together with the pamphlet to the General Court. In 1774 Allen reprinted his *An Oration on the Beauties of Liberty, or the Essential Rights of Americans*, to which he added "Remarks on the Rights and Liberties of the Africans." He maintained that even if slaves were "used in the kindest manner," their "minds must be imbittered with the melancholly reflection, that let their behavior be what it may, they and their children are to be held in *Bondage* so long as they live!" Allen not only lifted the words of the Felix petition but also reprinted the freedom petition of Peter Bestes, Sambo Freeman, Felix Holbrook, and Chester Joie submitted in April 1773. The four had formed an antislavery committee that spoke "in behalf of our fellow slaves in this province." Yet another abolitionist pamphlet, by "A lover of constitutional liberty," urged the Massachusetts legislature to act against *"man stealing"* and *"slave keeping"* by heeding the slaves' petition. It reprinted the original Felix petition, a small essay titled "Thoughts on Slavery" signed by "The Sons of Africa," and an essay from the *Massachusetts Spy* demanding emancipation. The writer stated that he had been inspired by the slaves' petition and asked the General Court to "think candidly of their dejected state." In 1775 the Worcester county convention, in response to a freedom petition from "Negroes in the counties of Bristol and Worcester" to the local Committee of Correspondence, resolved "That we abhor the enslaving of any of the human race, particularly the NEGROES in this country."[18] The antislavery committee of slaves and the Sons of Africa, modeled most likely after the Sons of Liberty, predated the formation of the first abolition society in Philadelphia by two years.

By using revolutionary language, the black freedom petitions written by organized groups of slaves in the New England colonies during the 1770s imbued their demand for freedom with immediacy. In June 1773 yet another petition by slaves in Massachusetts read, "Your Petitioners apprehend they have in comon with other men a naturel right to be free." A petition of May 1774 by some Massachusetts blacks asked for "an act of the Legislative to be pessed that we may obtain our Natural right our freedoms and our children be set at lebety." In 1779 twenty "natives of Africa" from Portsmouth, New Hampshire, petitioned for freedom "for the sake of justice, humanity, and the rights of mankind" and pointed out that "the God of nature gave . . . [us] . . . life and freedom, upon the terms of the most perfect equality with other men; That freedom is an inherent right of the human species." The same year a petition from the slaves of a Loyalist slaveholder to the Connecticut General Assembly questioned the legitimacy of their enslavement on racial grounds: "Though they have flat noses, crooked shins, and other queerness of make, peculiar to Africans, are yet of the human race, free-born in our own country, taken from thence by man-stealers, and sold in this country as cattle in the market, without the least act of our own to forfeit liberty." As good "Whigs," they should be set free to contribute to the patriot cause, and their Tory master should be enslaved! Pomp, a slave in Norwalk, also petitioned the assembly for his freedom based on the fact that his master had deserted to the British. He could "well-provide for Himself" and his wife, a free woman, and their child. The Connecticut legislature freed Pomp.[19]

The freedom petitioners implied that compared to the sufferings of black people the American cause was trivial. As they sarcastically noted, "The efforts made by the legislative of this province in their last sessions to free themselves from slavery, gave us, who are in that deplorable state, a high degree of satisfaction. We expect great things from men who have made such a noble stand against the designs of their *fellow-men* to enslave them." A petition from 1777 submitted by eight black Bostonians, including Prince Hall, the founder of black Masonry, while repeating the language of earlier petitions, expressed "Astonishment that It have Never Bin Considered that Every Principle from which America has Acted in the Cours of their Unhappy Dificulties with Great Briton Pleads Stronger than A thousand arguments . . . that they may be Restored to the Enjoyments of that which is the Naturel Right of all men." A group of Connecticut blacks declared in their petition of 1779 that it was a "flagrant Injustice" that those "contending, in the Cause of Liberty" deny what "Reason and Revelation join to declare, that we are the Creatures of that God, who made of one Blood, and Kindred, all the Nations of the Earth."[20] The petitioners condemned racism that prevented colonists from including Africans in conceptions of American liberty.

African American petitioners also raised the question of compensation and redress, proposing concrete plans for securing black freedom. Like Sharp, Bestes et al. proposed adopting the Spanish system, which allowed slaves to work for themselves one day a week to earn money to purchase their freedom and "from our joint labours procure money to transport ourselves to some part of the coast of *Africa*, where we propose a settlement." In June 1774 blacks in Massachusetts resubmitted their May petition, asking the General Court to "give and grant to us some part of unimproved land, belonging to the province, for a settlement" so that they may enjoy the fruits of their labor. The slave committee's petition from 1773 had led to the passage of a bill that abolished the slave trade to Massachusetts, but Governor Hutchinson did not sign it and dissolved the General Court. Prince Hall's petition of 1777, which asked that all slaves be freed at the age of twenty-one, generated an abolition bill in the General Court, but it too was allowed to die.[21] The black freedom petitions were not just cries in the wilderness but, along with early Quaker petitions, helped put emancipation on the agenda of the revolution. Their demand for some sort of reparation or "freedom dues," a colonial custom that had marked the end of servitude, though, fell on deaf ears.

If the revolution engendered black antislavery protest, it also made African Americans subject its premises to criticism. The New England freedom petitions laid the foundations of black abolitionism and its preoccupation with exposing American republicanism. They did not simply appropriate revolutionary ideology but critically engaged it to highlight their plight. In 1774 two black essayists trained their sights on the colonists. Caesar Sarter of Newburyport, a former slave, asked, "If you are sensible, that slavery is in itself, and in its consequents a great evil, why will you not pity and relieve the poor, distressed, enslaved Africans?" Even though black people bore the most shocking bondage, it was thought of too little by those who "enjoy the profits of their labour." Sarter advised the patriots to consider the liberation of "oppressed Africans" as "the first step," and only then may they "with confidence and consistency of conduct" strike off their own shackles. Similarly, the anonymous "A Son of Africa" asked, "Are not your hearts also hard, when you hold them in slavery who are intitled to liberty, by the law of nature, equal as yourselves?" He asked the colonists to "pull the beam out of thine own eyes" first. Africans "are a free people" and "were never conquered by any nation." The Christianization of Africans was merely a "cloak to fill their [masters'] coffers and to screen their villainy." Slavery was contrary to the laws of God and Britain, he wrote, referring to *Somerset*. Both essayists warned the colonists of divine vengeance.[22]

The most erudite black abolitionist was Rev. Lemuel Haynes, a Congregational clergyman who spent much of his life ministering to a white church in Vermont. In the nineteenth century, abolitionists viewed Haynes as an heir to a long line of pious, gifted Africans, including Cyprian and Augustine, and his works were seen as a means to "mitigate the unreasonable prejudices against the Africans in our land." Abandoned by his white mother and an unknown black father, Haynes was a self-taught indentured servant and preached his first sermon to his master's devout family. He volunteered as a minuteman in 1774 and served in the Continental Army in 1776 until he was discharged for ill health. After that he worked for clergymen, acquiring instruction in Latin, Greek, and theology. In 1783 he married a white teacher, Elizabeth Babbit, with whom he had nine children. He was ordained in 1785. Haynes's first biographer, who had heard a few of his sermons, remembered his "impassioned eloquence" and "simplicity and striking effect." He acquired the approval of President Timothy Dwight of Yale University for challenging the liberal theology of Hosea Ballou, who rejected the doctrine of original sin in his widely reprinted *Universal Salvation*. Haynes's theological opponents never failed to draw attention to his color in their rejoinders.[23]

Haynes's ballad celebrating the Battle of Lexington, published in 1775, reveals that like other African Americans in New England he experienced the revolution as an "enfranchising experience." Signed by "Lemuel a young Mollato," the poem evokes the legacy of Puritan forefathers who tamed a wilderness and fought a "savage Brood" for freedom and life. The battle, he wrote, recalled the "awfull Scenes" of King Philip's War. But he inserted a critique of slavery in an otherwise conventional narrative of New England history. "For Liberty," he tells his readers, "each Freeman Strives As it's a Gift of God" and would rather pay for it with blood than live the life of a "Surviving Slave."[24]

Haynes gave vent to his abolitionist views in an essay from 1776 titled "Liberty Further Extended: Or Free Thoughts on the Illegality of Slave Keeping." Unlike Haynes's later sermons, it was never published. The essay is clearly influenced by Benezet, whom Haynes quoted extensively. Like the freedom petitioners, he asked every "son of Freedom," as they engaged in an "important struggle," to "turn one Eye into our own Breast, for a little moment, and See, whether thro' some inadvertency, or a self-contracted Spirit, we do not find the monster [tyranny] Lurking in our own Bosom." Haynes's signal contribution was his extended meditation on race, nation, and freedom. Everyone acknowledged, he wrote, that "an Englishman has a right to his Liberty," but an African also has *an undeniable right to his Liberty: Consequently, the practice of Slave-keeping, which so much abounds in this Land is illicit.* He quoted the biblical injunction against racism: God has made *of one Blood all nations of men, for to dwell upon the face of the Earth.* Color, he further averred, should not be the "Decisive Criterion" to deprive one of a natural right, as "whence is it that an Englishman is so far Distinguished from an Affrican in point of Natural privilege?" Some men forfeited their liberty for crimes, but if anyone was guilty of a crime, Haynes points out, it is their enslavers. The condition of blacks in the New World he concluded is "hell upon Earth; and all this for filthy Lucres sake."[25] Slavery put mammon before humans and God.

Haynes was known to follow the "same principles as Edwards and White-field" and to scorn the heresy of Arminianism; he was a "labourer" in the religious revivals of his region and an advocate of an educated ministry. He had read Edwards, Bellamy, and Hopkins, but he applied the tenets of Calvinism to criticize both slavery and racialism in a manner that went beyond the ideas of white, New Divinity ministers. Like Hopkins, Haynes ends his pamphlet with an address to slaveholders but in much stronger language condemns their hypocrisy by evoking the authority of the Bible: "Therefore is it not high time to undo these heavy Burdens, and Let the Oppressed go free?" He warned, "While you thus Sway your tyrant Scepter over others, you have nothing to Expect But to Share in the Bitter pill," and if they did not "Break these intollerable yoaks," they would find it around their own necks.[26] The notion of slaves as instruments of revolution and divine vengeance reflected both his orthodox Calvinism and alternative republican views.

To African Americans, abolition was an important component of the revolutionary agenda. In 1782, "A Black Whig" published a pamphlet, *A Sermon on the Present Situation of the Affairs of America and Great-Britain,* in Philadelphia that called for nationwide abolition. It was dedicated to the "Americans in General But to the Citizens of South-Carolina in Particular." This anonymous black patriot claimed he had "taken the liberty of a citizen" to make his case. Firmly identifying himself with the American cause and viewing Britain as "the low abyss of tyranny and despotism," he even decried British attempts to arm slaves. But in confidently predicting American success, he requested, "And now my virtuous fellow citizens, let me intreat you, that, after you have rid yourselves of the British yoke, that you will also emancipate those who have been all their life subject to bondage." "Though a descendant of Africa," he hoped in the end "may we be a free people for ever!" A truly free American republic, he avowed, would come about only with the demise of slavery.[27]

Revolutionary black abolitionists also developed the Christian critique of slavery. In his published religious sermons, Haynes did not address slavery specifically. Yet starting with his first published piece, "A Sermon on John, 1776" until his valedictory to his Rutland congregation, "The Sufferings, Support, and Reward of Faithful Ministers, Illustrated, 1820," he stressed the theme of spiritual regeneration. Christian redemption and his own life as a model clergyman were a standing rebuke to slavery and racism.

Unlike Haynes, who wrote most of his explicitly antislavery remarks in his political essays, Jupiter Hammon published two pamphlets in Hartford during the war that dealt with the problem of slavery and freedom from an Afro-Christian perspective, or what one scholar has called "biblical hermeneutics." In the first, "A Winter Piece," published in 1782, Hammon addressed those "who have had the advantage of studying" and objected to his writings. Here he made clear that only education, not inherent racial difference, separates him from his white critics. He refers to Africans as a "poor despised nation" brought by God to a "Christian land." But rather than warrant that Christianization was a justification of their enslavement, Hammon wrote that thousands of slaves "have been born in what are called Christian families," questioning the Christianity of their enslavers. He criticizes his "objectors" for failing to baptize and educate their slaves. Hammon subtly casts aspersions on the Christian nature of masters and encourages slaves to become exemplary Christians. While concerned with the spiritual well-being of slaves, Hammon approved of their longing for freedom from slavery: "Many of us are seeking a temporal freedom and I wish you may obtain it." Denying the rumor that he had petitioned a court "against freedom," he explicitly denied that blacks should restrict their quest to spiritual freedom. In his second pamphlet, "An Evening's Improvement," Hammon reiterated that "we are many of us seeking for a temporal freedom, and I pray that God would grant your desire." At the "advanced age of seventy-nine years," he did not "desire temporal freedom" for himself. Hammon rejected racial hierarchy by insisting that Christ died for the sin of all humankind. God was "no respecter of persons" and embraced black slaves even as he did enslaved Jews.[28]

Antislavery pervaded black writing during the revolutionary era. While steeped in the idioms and ideas of their times, black abolitionists developed alternative and oppositional understandings of Christianity and revolutionary republicanism to criticize both slavery and racism. African American actions on the ground complemented these views.

THE BLACK REVOLUTION

A black revolution, if not the white one, confronted racial slavery. Taking advantage of the chaos engendered by the Revolutionary War, African Americans sought freedom in various ways: by running away, taking up arms, and abandoning the land of their enslavement. The revolution facilitated slave rebelliousness and black military action. African Americans, slave and free, participated in the crowd action against British rule as early as the Stamp Act crisis. They were a part of the revolutionary mob led by the Sons of Liberty that took down King George III's statue in New York. Even in the heart of slavery in the Deep South, Charleston, South Carolina, African Americans marched to the revolutionary slogan "Liberty." A rash of slave revolts and conspiracies spread through the Caribbean and the southern colonies in the 1770s. In 1775 authorities uncovered two slave conspiracies led by black water pilots in the Carolinas. The leaders were whipped and their ears cropped; a free black pilot by the name of Thomas Jeremiah, who was probably innocent, was executed.[29]

With the outbreak of the War of Independence, African Americans waged their own battle for emancipation. Despite the voluminous rhetoric on liberty produced by the patriots, the British were the first to recruit slaves as a matter of military policy. Historically, most slave societies have been reluctant to arm slaves, but European powers, especially the Spanish, recruited free blacks, even slaves during moments of crisis, whether they were fighting each other or Native American nations or both. Slaves were an essential source of manpower in colonial America, and even slaveholders could not afford to ignore that fact during times of war. But military service did not automatically translate into freedom or even into more privileges for slave soldiers, though the Spanish did grant rights to their free black militias. The American Revolution changed that, thanks to the British governor of Virginia, John Murray, Earl of Dunmore. His Proclamation of November 7, 1775, offered freedom to slaves and any others who would fight for the British, raising the stakes considerably for blacks who wished to remain loyal. The idea originated with runaway slaves who offered their services to Dunmore. In Massachusetts a handful of black men had done the same to the British governor, Thomas Gage. After Lord Dunmore's Proclamation was issued, over a thousand slaves as well as some white servants and convicts escaped to the British in Virginia. Dunmore's Royal Ethiopian Regiment fought in the tattered clothing of slaves but no doubt subscribed to the sentiment of the legendary white sashes proclaiming "Liberty to Slaves" that they supposedly donned. Many succumbed to smallpox, and only around three hundred, including women and children, left Virginia with Dunmore in 1776.[30]

African Americans fought on both sides to gain their freedom. Abolitionists, arguing for black military service and citizenship during the Civil War, recovered the history of black patriots who had helped secure the liberties of the white Republic. A handful of black men, including Haynes and one Prince Esterbrook, a slave belonging to a local farmer, fought with the ragtag colonial militia in the battles of Lexington and Concord in 1775. At a decisive moment in the Battle of Bunker Hill a black soldier, either Peter Salem, a slave promised his freedom by his patriot master, or Salem Poor, a particularly honorable black soldier, purportedly distinguished himself by killing the officer leading the British charge, Maj. John Pitcairn. One hundred and fifty African Americans fought at Bunker Hill. When Washington took charge of the Continental Army, he and the Continental Congress, in October 1775, banned African Americans from serving on the American side. In the aftermath of Dunmore's Proclamation, Washington allowed free blacks, but not slaves, to enlist in the army, a decision supported by Congress.[31]

Some states allowed masters to use their slaves as substitutes and received compensation for them. Patriot forces used slaves confiscated from Tories for military labor and in some southern states offered slaves themselves as bounties for military service. Desperation at Valley Forge forced Washington to lift his ban, as he and the Continental Congress accepted a proposal to allow Rhode Island to recruit slaves. A 1778 law in Rhode Island enlisted and freed slaves, though it was later rescinded. The 1st Rhode Island Regiment, which initially contained all-black companies, was chosen by Washington as part of a combined Rhode Island Regiment to lead the Continental Army in the final Battle of Yorktown. Two other all-black companies fought on the patriot side, the Massachusetts Bucks of America, led by an African American, Col. George Middleton, and the 6th Company from a Connecticut battalion. A French contingent of five hundred Haitians probably included André Rigaud and Henri Christophe, leaders of the Haitian Revolution.[32]

All the northern states followed Rhode Island in allowing slaves to enlist and granting them freedom for their military service. Virginia and Maryland allowed only free blacks to serve, though many slaves in the Chesapeake, pretending to be free or in lieu of their masters, joined the Continental Army. While some masters freed slaves they owned for their wartime service, others remanded them back to slavery. Virginia freed slaves who had served in the patriot forces, but the government there also sold state-owned slaves who had served in the navy. The Continental Congress, responding to British general Henry Clinton's Phillipsburg proclamation of 1779, which offered freedom and even gave confiscated patriot land to slaves who declared loyalty to the Crown, and to British military success in the lower south, approved of slave enlistment in Georgia and South Carolina. This plan was the brainchild of John Laurens, Washington's aide-de-camp, whose distaste for slavery matched his patriotic zeal. Educated in Geneva and influenced by the egalitarian ideas of the French political philosopher Jean-Jacques Rousseau, Laurens recommended recruiting slaves and freeing them after their military service. Washington's other aide-de-camp, Hamilton, who proposed a similar plan to Governor Jay in New York, supported him, and Laurens procured a commission to lead such a regiment. Long derided for his alleged rashness, Laurens has only recently been recognized for his abolitionist beliefs. Despite his efforts, both states refused the proposition.

Instead, patriot militias in these states hunted down slaves fleeing to the British. Laurens, the lone voice of antislavery to emerge from the lower south political establishment, tragically died in a skirmish during the war.[33]

At least five thousand, if not more, African Americans fought in the Continental Army and Navy, most of them in integrated units. In the latest edition of their *Forgotten Patriots* project, the Daughters of the American Revolution have raised that count to sixty-six hundred black and Native American patriots. Black Revolutionary War veterans included Haynes, Prince and Primus Hall, rumored to have shared a blanket with Washington, and Peter Williams Sr. in New York. James Forten of Pennsylvania enlisted as a powder boy in a ship in Stephen Decatur's fleet and was held prisoner in a British man-of-war for refusing to renounce the American cause. Prince Whipple, who served with his master, William Whipple, signed the New Hampshire freedom petition of 1779.[34] All of these men became pioneering black abolitionists.

Black Loyalists, including thousands of escaped slaves, far outnumbered blacks who fought with the patriots. Responding first to Dunmore and later to Clinton's Phillipsburg proclamation, slaves defected to British lines in all thirteen colonies, some belonging to revolutionary luminaries such as Washington, Jefferson, Henry, and Madison. During the British occupation of Charleston in 1781–82, seven hundred slaves were recruited into the Black Dragoons, armed, and used as patrols around the city. In New Jersey a slave named Titus fled his Quaker master and, as Colonel Tye, led the Black Pioneers formed by Clinton against the patriots until his death in 1780. Black Loyalist guerillas accumulated supplies for the British, and the British army used African Americans as military laborers, foragers, spies, and soldiers, but they did not make the revolution into a war about black liberation.

Unlike the American Civil War, the Revolutionary War was not fought by either side in the cause of slavery or its abolition. A desperate Lord Cornwallis, in a display of imperial indifference, abandoned many slaves to disease, starvation, and the tender mercies of their former masters at Yorktown. One of the largest slave-trading and slave-owning powers in the world, the British did not fight an abolition war. They were solicitous of Loyalist masters' right of slave ownership, and some slaves of Loyalists found themselves transported from American to West Indian slavery. An exception was George Liele, whose Loyalist master freed him but who was wrongfully imprisoned until a British officer came to his rescue and helped him purchase his family's freedom. He founded the first black Baptist churches in Savannah, Georgia, and Kingston, Jamaica. Andrew Bryan, who bought his freedom after the death of his evangelical master Jonathan Bryan, took over the Savannah church. The latter was the brother of none other than Hugh Bryan, who had written against slavery earlier in the century. Both Liele and Andrew Bryan were persecuted by slaveholding authorities in Jamaica and Georgia for their preaching: Liele was imprisoned and Bryan whipped.[35]

It was the slaves who attempted to make the Revolutionary War into an abolition war, especially in the southern colonies. Most, including entire families and communities, women, children, and the elderly, used the disruption of wartime to simply flee. David George, after seeing his family cruelly abused and himself being "whipped many a time on my naked skin," explained that his "master's rough and cruel usage" was the reason for him to abscond. Boston King ran away to escape his master's cruelty and found the "happiness of liberty" as well as smallpox in British lines. Runaways like Prince Whitten fled from the lower south states to Spanish Florida, as they had done during the colonial era. The numbers are staggering: around thirty thousand in Virginia, twenty to twenty-five thousand in South Carolina, and ten to fifteen thousand in Georgia. A recent estimate has scaled down these figures, originally proposed by Jefferson, showing that at most twenty thousand slaves ran away to the British, twelve thousand from the South. Even so, Gary Nash has called this the largest unknown slave rebellion in American history. The anti–slave trade movement would fail in the short run because of the determination of some lower south slaveholders to make good their revolutionary losses, which were also caused by the suspension of the African slave trade during the war. Slaveholders and the new American Republic made compensation for lost slave property a sticking point in their negotiations with the British in the aftermath of the war. Despite the massive scale of slave defection, there were more slaves in the infant Republic at the end of the revolutionary era than at its beginning owing to the natural increase in the slave population.[36]

The British for the most part honored their commitment to black Loyalists. Nearly seven thousand slaves and black Loyalists left from Charleston and another four thousand from Savannah. Many left with their Loyalist masters from these ports and from St. Augustine in Spanish Florida, increasing dramatically the black and slave population of the British West Indies. In defiance of Article 7 of the Treaty of Paris, which promised the return of "negroes" and other property to the victorious Americans, Sir Guy Carleton evacuated another three thousand African Americans, listed in a "Book of Negroes" compiled by the British, from New York in 1783. Carleton's secretary was none other than Maurice Morgann, who had first proposed emancipation in the British Empire. Despite Washington's personal intervention and attempts by masters to recover their slaves, Carleton refused to break faith with the runaway slaves, and the

British government backed his position. Boston King reported that when the slaves heard a rumor that they would be returned to their "old masters from Virginia, North Carolina and other parts," whom they saw seizing their slaves in the streets of New York, they were filled with "inexpressible anguish and terror." Nearly ten thousand black Loyalists departed as free men and women. Some were literally "fleeing the Founding Fathers." A remnant who were not evacuated continued to fight as the King of England soldiers in the swamps near Savannah until being subdued by state authorities.[37]

The saga of black Loyalists' quest for freedom did not come to an end with the American War of Independence. They found themselves dispersed all over the British Empire, from the streets of London to the penal colony of New South Wales, Australia. In 1787 over four hundred blacks, assisted by the philanthropic Committee for the Relief of Black Poor, sailed from Plymouth, England, to found the colony of Sierra Leone on the west coast of Africa as a haven for London's blacks. For many British advocates of colonization, Sierra Leone was simply a way to get rid of the black population. First proposed by the naturalist Henry Smeathman, the project was initially supported by Sharp and the black abolitionist Olaudah Equiano as an experiment in black self-government. Equiano, appointed a commissary to the expedition, left the project after falling out with a corrupt official. Sharp modeled the colony after a romanticized notion of ancient Anglo-Saxon governance and solicited the consent and participation of native Africans. But Sharp's utopian plans foundered on the political dictates and rapacity of local officials of the Sierra Leone Company, founded in 1791, and raids by the local Temne. Some colonists joined the slave traders at Bunce Island, the site of an important British slave trading post that sent thousands of enslaved Africans to the Americas, even though one of the founding aims of the colony was to put an end to "the abominable slave trade."

Black Loyalists in Canada, who faced white hostility, an unforgiving soil and climate, and long indentures, were also attracted to Sierra Leone. According to King, who became a Methodist preacher, "poverty and distress prevailed on every side." Denied and cheated of land grants promised by the British government, they sent a representative, Thomas Peters, to London to plead their case in 1790. A runaway slave millwright from North Carolina who had joined the Black Pioneers, Peters made common cause with British abolitionists like Sharp and Thomas Clarkson. Clarkson's younger brother, John, a naval officer who became governor of the colony, led an exodus of over a thousand black Nova Scotians to Sierra Leone in 1792. David George, a Baptist preacher and protégé of Liele, reported that "the White people in Nova Scotia were very unwilling that we should go, though they had been very cruel to us, and treated many of us as bad as though we had been slaves." Inspired by black preachers like George, King, Moses Wilkinson, and John Marrant, Loyalist émigrés viewed Sierra Leone as the Promised Land.

Black settlers in Sierra Leone were left to wage yet more battles for their political rights and economic independence against company officials, some losing their lives to fulfill their dreams of acquiring land and liberty. John Clarkson and Peters, who died shortly thereafter, quarreled, and, accompanied by George, Clarkson returned to England at the end of the year. Another abolitionist governor, Zachary Macaulay, who came into conflict with the colonists for enforcing the company's demand for quit rents, left Sierra Leone. His son Thomas Babington Macaulay became a thoroughgoing imperialist. In 1800 the Nova Scotians, including Harry Washington, a former slave of George Washington, led an uprising against the company. The rebellion was put down, and authorities unleashed the newly arrived Jamaican Maroons against the rebellious former American slaves. Nearly forty black settlers were executed or banished from the colony. In 1808 Sierra Leone became a British colony, no longer an abolitionist experiment in black autonomy. Despite this outcome, the black migrations to Sierra Leone represented "a black antithesis," a reversal of the Atlantic slave trade and enslavement in the New World.[38]

THE HAITIAN REVOLUTION

More than the American Revolution and its aftermath, the Haitian Revolution constituted a landmark in the history of abolition. The Black Jacobins of the French Revolution, which began in 1789, helped abolish slavery. In Saint-Domingue slave rebellion was the face of French revolutionary republicanism. While some scholars still debate the contradictory effects of the Haitian Revolution, Haiti "saved the honor of the New World Revolutions" as far as slavery was concerned. Revolutionary black abolitionism was exemplified in the words and deeds of Haiti's free and enslaved rebels.[39] The Haitian Revolution not only instigated slave rebelliousness throughout the Americas but also, long after the fact, continued to inspire the abolitionist imagination.

Thanks to the rebels of Saint-Domingue, revolutionary resistance to slavery became a part of the abolitionist lexicon. Appropriating French republican ideas on the rights of man, free men of color like the martyr Vincent Ogé, who suffered a torturous death at the hands of colonial authorities for his troubles, led the fight for black citizenship. In their petition of 1789 to the French National Assembly, "citizens of color" asked for "those inalienable rights based on nature and the social contract, those rights you have so solemnly recognized and faithfully established." Even earlier the enslaved had established a tradition of *petit marronage*, or forming of communities of runaway slaves, and resistance under slave rebels such as Macandal. Starting in 1791 slaves of African descent inspired by Vodou and led by Boukman waged a relentless war against their enslavers. Slave rebellion in the French Caribbean and the efforts of free colored people to secure citizenship pushed the French Republic to grant the franchise to children of free blacks and to all free blacks a year later. It was the slave rebels and their revolutionary allies who married abolition to radical republicanism. In 1793 the Jacobin commissioner Léger Félicité Sonthonax, an admirer of the French abolitionist Jacques-Pierre Brissot de Warville, issued an edict abolishing slavery in Saint-Domingue. Revolutionary deputies from Saint-Domingue at the National Convention in Paris the next year pushed for the abolition of slavery by the French Republic.

United under the brilliant military leadership of Toussaint Louverture, who warded off challenges to his authority by slaveholders, free colored leaders, French emissaries, and the armies of the slave-owning empires of England and Spain, black Saint-Dominguans laid the foundation for Haitian independence during thirteen years of warfare. Louverture articulated the aims of the Haitian revolutionaries: "Let the sacred flame of liberty that we have won lead all our acts. . . . Let us go forth to plant the tree of liberty, breaking the chains of those of your brothers still held captive under the shameful yoke of slavery. Let us bring them under the compass of our rights, the imprescriptible and inalienable rights of free men." Even slaveholders were impressed with the Haitian leader, especially with his unpopular decrees binding freed slaves to plantations to revive the island's coffee- and sugar-based plantation economy. Though Louverture was imprisoned and died in France in 1802, his successors, Jean-Jacques Dessalines and Henri Christophe, defeated the world-conquering army of Napoleon, which was undone by yellow fever and the refusal of former slaves to return to slavery.

Over three hundred years after Columbus landed in Hispaniola, destroyed its native population, and introduced African slavery, the island witnessed the birth of the independent Republic of Haiti, its native name, on January 1, 1804. Warning the French to leave the island, the Haitian declaration of independence simply stated, "We have dared to be free, let us be thus by ourselves and for ourselves." The Haitian Constitution denied citizenship to whites, except for a handful of white women, children, Germans, and Poles who had defected to the Haitian cause, and it defined all Haitians as blacks. However, it ended with a universal appeal to all "friends of liberty" and "those who love mankind in every country" from a "free people, civilized and independent." Whites who rejected slavery and French rule were welcome to join the black nation.[40] This bloody, decisive challenge to slavery and white supremacy, notwithstanding Haiti's political instability and poverty, aggravated by the colonial policies of its erstwhile rulers and enemies, became sanctified in abolitionist memory.

While much has been written about the proslavery response to the Haitian Revolution and the efforts of Europeans and the United States to form a cordon sanitaire around the black republic, abolitionist reaction to it is understudied. The radical antislavery views of the French philosophe Denis Diderot, who predicted the rise of a black Spartacus, and the socialist Jean de Pechmeja had appeared in Raynal's compilation, *Histoire des deux Indes*. From the start, French abolitionists in the Société des Amis des Noirs, or society of friends of blacks, founded in 1788 by Brissot and Etienne Clavière, supported the free colored fight for citizenship led by Ogé, M. Joly, and Julien Raimond and linked it to the abolition of the slave trade. The society counted the Marquis de Condorcet, comte de Mirabeau, and the Marquis de Lafayette, a hero of the American Revolution, among its members. Mirabeau, a member of the Constituent Assembly, worked closely with Clarkson in the attempt to abolish the slave trade and published the journal of the society, in which he printed the writings of British abolitionists. Condorcet was known for his abolitionism and support of women's rights. In his pamphlet of 1781 *Reflections on Negro Slavery*, republished in 1788, he referred to black men as his brothers and to slavery as a crime. He also wrote the constitution of the Amis des Noirs. Raimond, who had been a slaveholder, became a member of the Amis des Noirs and, later, of a Jacobin Club. He wrote one of the first systematic refutations of racism, *Observations on the Origin and Progress of the Prejudice of White Colonials against the Men of Color* (1791). His writings served as a riposte to the white planters of Saint-Domingue, who lobbied the National Assembly against abolition and black rights. Raimond, like Condorcet, advocated gradual emancipation through self-purchase as a way to elicit the slaves' loyalties for the republic. Appointed as republican commissioner to Haiti by the French Directory, he became a supporter of Toussaint. Condorcet and Brissot were imprisoned and killed during the Reign of Terror, and Raimond, who was briefly imprisoned at the start of the Haitian Revolution, died on the eve of Napoleon's ill-fated attempt to reconquer Haiti.[41]

The French abolitionist most associated with the vindication of the Haitian Revolution was the liberal Catholic priest Abbé Henri Grégoire. He was converted by Raimond and enlisted into the Amis des Noirs as a champion of free colored rights. Until his death in 1831, Grégoire was the most prominent French opponent of both slavery and racism. In a letter he assured the free colored citizens of the French West Indies that their country would no longer "be a land of exile, where you meet none but tyrants on one hand, and companions in misfortune on the other; the former distributing, and the latter receiving contempt and outrage." By leading slaves "progressively to liberty," he asked them to "fulfill a duty" and "do honor to humanity." Grégoire, despite his stated preference for the gradual abolition of slavery, remained a staunch defender of Haiti as the custodian of revolutionary republicanism. Haiti, not America, he said, would be a beacon to the world. Grégoire forged a relationship with the southern republic of Alexandre Petion and the united Haitian republic in 1820. He predicted that Haiti would exercise "great influence on the destiny of Africans in the New World."[42]

Clarkson, an admirer of the French Revolution, had met Ogé in London on his way back to Saint-Domingue and supported his fight for free black rights. Clarkson wrote one of the first briefs in defense of the Haitian rebels in 1792. According to him, the revolution was a result of the efforts of slaves to win the "Rights of Man." Taking advantage of the white planters' "vanity and guilty obstinacy," slaves had struck against slavery. Reversing the popular claim of the Jamaican historian Bryan Edwards that abolitionists had instigated rebellion, Clarkson felt that abolitionists should be inspired by the rebels to double their efforts against the African slave trade. The Haitian Revolution contributed to the resurgence of abolition in Britain led by men like Henry Brougham, who wrote influential pamphlets against the African slave trade. Later, both Clarkson and William Wilberforce corresponded with Christophe of Haiti's northern kingdom to discuss ways in which to assist the new black nation, what Wilberforce called "the African cause." Clarkson became Christophe's adviser and unofficial ambassador of Haiti, lobbying the French government to recognize the black nation. The Haitian government named one of its man-of-wars *Wilberforce*. The abolitionist lawyer and Wilberforce's brother-in-law James Stephen recommended an alliance with the "sable heroes and patriots" of Haiti and wrote a hagiographic biography of Louverture, the first of many such biographies written by abolitionists.[43] Rather than championing European colonialism, abolitionists were ardent defenders of the new black nation.

The abolitionists' understanding of the Haitian Revolution was strongly influenced by one of the few sympathetic eyewitness accounts of it. In 1805 Marcus Rainsford, a soldier in the West India Regiment, wrote a massive book on the rise of Haiti and bore witness to the fact that "negroes were capable of repelling their enemies, with vigour." Richly illustrated with portraits of Louverture, images of cruelties practiced by the French and of bloodhounds being loosed against the black population, and a letter in Louverture's handwriting, the work disavowed having any antislavery intentions, but it blamed the "opulence and dissipation" of the planters for the rebellion. Rainsford's laudatory description of Louverture and condemnation of Napoleon's treachery were widely adopted in abolitionist writings. He also defended the actions of Dessalines as a reaction to French atrocities. Rainsford concluded that he was "untinctured with prejudice of any kind, unless the spirit can be so called, which inclines towards truth and humanity," and added an appendix of several important documents from the revolution. Rainsford's book, dismissed by historians as having no effect on the perception of the Haitian Revolution compared to the gory stories that dotted Edwards's account, was widely accepted in abolitionist circles. In later years, Haitian writers like Louis Félix Boisrond-Tonnerre, the author of the Haitian declaration of independence, and Pompée Valentin, Baron de Vastey, who served under Christophe, fully vindicated the revolution and spelled out its significance to antislavery.[44]

The Haitian Revolution stimulated black assertiveness throughout the Western hemisphere. In the 1790s black Jacobinism spread to Río de la Plata in Uruguay and to Maracaibo, Cartagena, Demerara, and Coro in Venezuela, and the Second Maroon War broke out in Jamaica. In 1812 the Aponte uprising of slaves and free people of color in Cuba came on the heels of the institution of a liberal constitution and the debate over abolition in the Spanish Cortes at Cádiz. Colonial authorities confiscated an illustrated book from the home of the militia veteran José Antonio Aponte containing portraits of African kings, the Spanish king, Aponte's ancestors, black soldiers defeating whites as well as Washington, Louverture, Dessalines, and Christophe. Slave rebels often invoked Haiti to justify their plans for rebellion. Christophe of the northern kingdom of Haiti helped rebels in neighboring Santo Domingo against Spanish rule. In 1821 Haiti conquered Santo Domingo and enacted abolition there. Latin American revolutionaries like José San Martín and Simón Bolívar turned to Haiti for assistance in their anticolonial struggle against Spain. Petion sent aid to them on the condition that abolition and black rights be part of their revolutionary agenda. He also instituted a policy of declaring free any runaway slaves who made their way to the black republic, making Haiti free soil. The Haitian Revolution was an important precedent for slave runaways and free black soldiers who demanded emancipation during the Latin American Wars of Independence. Like the free coloreds in Haiti, free blacks insisted on political equality with whites. By the 1820s nearly all the former Spanish colonies in Latin America where abolition was expedited by warfare had decreed a gradual end to slavery.[45]

Slave resistance inspired by the Haitian Revolution fueled fears of rebellion in the United States. In 1793 a shadowy Secret Keeper plot led by a black preacher named Gowan Pamphlet involved slaves in Norfolk and Richmond,

Virginia, and Charleston, South Carolina. Black Baptists led by the brothers Moses and Gowan Pamphlet had been meeting secretly outside Williamsburg since the Revolutionary War. By the 1790s Gowan Pamphlet's congregation numbered five hundred. In Charleston the revolutionary French counsel and soldiers were suspected of fomenting slave rebellion. Four years later some so-called French negroes in the city, slaves of émigrés from Saint-Domingue, were accused of arson and of planning to start a rebellion. In 1795 the Pointe Coupee slave conspiracy in Louisiana, inspired in part by the events of the French and Haitian Revolutions, led to the execution of twenty-three slaves and the whipping and deportation of thirty-one others. In 1800 Gabriel, an enslaved black-smith from Henrico County, Virginia, led a large, well-organized conspiracy that included slaves and free blacks, including literate artisans well versed in revolutionary ideology and partisan dissension in the early American Republic. Gabriel, "the American Toussaint," planned to march under the revolutionary slogan "Death or Liberty." He was determined to spare those with an antislavery reputation—poor whites, mechanics and artisans, Quakers and Methodists, Frenchmen—and attack only planters and merchants. Two Frenchmen were also implicated, and the plot involved nearly a thousand slaves and free blacks. The aptly named Pharaoh and Tom revealed Gabriel's plans on the eve of rebellion, which led to the quick trials and execution of Gabriel and twenty-six other rebels.

One slave conspirator taunted his republican oppressors by reporting that he could say only what Washington would have said had he been caught by the British, namely, that he was a "willing sacrifice" for the liberty of his people. A New England poet, possibly Timothy Dwight, warned,

> Remember ere too late,
> The tale of St. Domingo's fate.
> Tho Gabriel dies, a host remains
> Oppress'd with slavery's galling chain.

Two years after Gabriel's attempt was discovered, an Easter conspiracy led by a slave named Sancho spread from southern Virginia to Halifax County, North Carolina. Slave ferrymen like Sancho who plied the inland waterways of this region were implicated in the scheme, which was put down summarily in both states. Black seamen had been instrumental in disseminating news of the Haitian Revolution along the informal communication network between slave communities on the Atlantic seaboard. Southern states, starting with South Carolina in the aftermath of the Denmark Vesey conspiracy of 1822, felt threatened enough by their presence to pass the Negro Seamen laws, which confined them to jail during their stay in slave ports. As Edwin C. Holland of South Carolina bemoaned, the slaves of his state were the "true Jacobins" and anarchists. Other Carolinian slaveholders continued to blame the abolitionists, particularly the Amis des Noir, "who set on foot the Insurrection at St. Domingo."[46]

In 1811 Haiti finally came to America. Charles Deslondes, a mixed-race slave driver, led a group of slaves in rebellion at Manuel Andry's plantation in Louisiana, killing his son Gilbert and wounding Manuel. Donning European military garb like the Haitian rebels, these men started the largest slave rebellion in U.S. history, the German Coast rebellion. For days Deslondes had plotted the rebellion with two African-born slaves bearing the Akan day names Kook and Quamana and a Virginian slave carpenter, Harry Kenner. Eventually two hundred to five hundred mostly young male slaves "armed with plantation tools and primed by revolutionary ideals" escaped from their plantations on the Mississippi River, joined forces with Maroons, and marched east toward New Orleans. They burned plantations along the way, killing at least one sadistic planter. Fleeing planters spread news of the rebellion, and in New Orleans Gov. William Clairborne called on the U.S. Army and militia volunteers to secure the city and put down the rebellion. As the slave army strategically retreated, enraged armed planters alerted by the wounded Andry cornered it from behind. Venting their rage on the rebels, the planters killed and beheaded their victims in a pitched battle. Slave-hunting bloodhounds brought down a fleeing Deslondes. Kook, Quamana, and Kenner were tried and went to their deaths without betraying their compatriots. In a display of state-sanctioned terror, planters posted the rotting heads of a hundred rebels on pikes dotting the road from Andry's plantation to New Orleans.

Unlike the Haitian rebels, who were able to best the might of the Napoleonic empire, American slaves were no match for the slaveholding republic's empire of liberty. Around the same time, nervous slaveholders detected slave conspiracies in Virginia, North Carolina, and Georgia. Haiti continued to pop up as a source of inspiration in slave rebellions throughout the antebellum period. Vesey had not only visited Haiti but also planned to gain assistance and shelter there. In the wake of Nat Turner's rebellion, a former slave named Nero warned of a rebellion led by a Virginian slave trained in Haiti with about thirty-five others who "were taking lessons from the venerable survivors of the Haytian Revolution." If the uprising proved to be unsuccessful, Haiti would offer "asylum for those who survive the approaching carnage."[47]

American abolitionists praised the Haitian Revolution from the start. In 1791 Abraham Bishop of Connecticut wrote a three-part series called "The Rights of Black Men," the first systematic antislavery response to the rebellion in

Saint-Domingue in the United States. Bishop linked the black fight for freedom
with the American Revolution, asking, "Is not their cause as just as ours?" He
asked Americans to be consistent and not to "sacrifice principle to a paltry partiality for colour." He castigated the new American Republic, where "blacks are
still enslaved. . . . The Indians are driven into the society of savage beasts, and we
glory in the equal rights of men, provided that *we white men can enjoy the whole
of them.*" Slaves had no choice but to take up arms to fight for their freedom,
Bishop argued, mocking those who would ask Africans in a slave ship to petition
their enslavers. Bishop's article was also a call to arms for antislavery societies
to assist the Saint-Domingue revolutionaries with "pen, the tongue, the counsel, the sword, and . . . money." He deplored the proslavery and racist cast of
American public opinion, which "evinced a great zeal in favor of the whites. . . .
One can hardly wish the blacks to be victorious without exposing himself to
censure, calumny and opprobrious names." Bishop was part of the abolitionist milieu in Connecticut at this time, a Federalist convert to Jeffersonian Republicanism. In his pamphlet *Negro Slavery Unjustified* (1802) Rev. Alexander
McLeod, an abolitionist Presbyterian minister from New York, also reasoned
that "the courage and skill of the negroes in war will no longer be disputed, after
their transactions in St. Domingo," and "great must be his prejudice who can
deny to the black Toussaint the qualifications of a Warrior and a statesman."[48]

The anti-French Federalist administration of John Adams briefly fulfilled
abolitionist expectations. Earlier, Jefferson, as Washington's secretary of state,
had, over Hamilton's objections, authorized aid to the beleaguered French
colonists, and the governor of South Carolina, Charles Pinckney, had offered
his state's assistance to them, as had slaveholding colonial governments from
Spanish Venezuela to the Caribbean. Adams's secretary of state, Timothy Pickering, a man of antislavery sympathies, bolstered Louverture's position against
his internal rivals with an American naval presence, and the U.S. government
entered into favorable trade agreements with him. The counterrevolutionary
policies of Jefferson's Republican administration after "the Revolution of 1800"
inaugurated a long period of political and economic embargo against the black
nation. Jefferson's initial hope that free blacks could be colonized in Haiti was
quickly overtaken by his support for Napoleon's proslavery policies. Ironically,
Haitians facilitated Jefferson's acquisition of Louisiana by destroying Napoleon's
hope of building a French empire in the New World. Jefferson, who called the
Haitian revolutionaries "cannibals of the terrible republic," set into motion a
policy of isolating the black nation. The abolitionists' call for the recognition of
Haiti throughout the antebellum period was in vain. Not until the administra-

tion of Abraham Lincoln would the American government extend diplomatic recognition to Haiti.[49]

The most direct consequence of the Haitian Revolution in the United States was the influx of refugees into cities like New York, Philadelphia, Baltimore, Charleston, and New Orleans. Fleeing planters, many of whom arrived with their slaves, elicited the sympathy of whites and relief efforts by local, state, and federal governments, alarming slaveholders with their horror stories. Memoirs and works written by white slaveholding expatriates reinforced and encouraged racist depictions of the Haitian rebels. Médéric-Louis-Élie Moreau de Saint Méry, a former planter and staunch opponent of black rights and freedom, published an influential two-volume book on Saint-Domingue. Born in Martinique, he had worked and married into a slaveholding family in Saint-Domingue, studied and lived in France, and fled to Philadelphia during the French Revolution. But the story of Saint-Dominguan exiles is not primarily a white one.

Enslaved Saint-Domiguans solicited the help of abolitionists in their legal quest for freedom. The Pennsylvania Abolition Society assisted in 456 manumissions of so-called French slaves even though their owners tried to get around the state's emancipation laws. The standing committee of the New York Manumission Society recorded several instances of intervening on behalf of slaves from "St. Domingo." In 1807 it recorded the case of a Frenchman who illegally transported three black boys to New Orleans. Many French slaves ran away, and one committed suicide, thereby inspiring an abolitionist address. The author, Edward Darlington, used the occasion to point to the culpability of the entire nation in upholding slavery. The largest contingent from the second influx of Saint-Dominguan refugees in 1809 went to New Orleans, which had long-standing connections with Saint-Domingue under French rule. Colored Saint-Dominguans reinforced the creole culture of free blacks in New Orleans. They fought against the British under Andrew Jackson in the Battle of New Orleans in the War of 1812, and during Reconstruction their community emerged as a powerful voice for black rights. Some, like Rosalie of the Poulard nation, persistently sought to have her own freedom and that of her family legally established in their new home and bestowed a legacy of self-determination and activism to her descendants. In Baltimore free colored women of Haitian descent founded the first black order of nuns, the Oblate Sisters of Providence.[50]

The most well known black Haitian immigrant was Pierre Toussaint, who had accompanied his master's family to New York as a teenager. He enjoyed considerable success as a hairdresser, supported his mistress, and managed to buy his sister's and his wife's freedom. In a peculiar reversal of the master–slave relationship, one which he no doubt relished, Toussaint supported his master's family, even sending expensive gifts to his poverty-stricken white godmother in France. These women who accepted his generosity not only made him pay for his sister's freedom but also advised him not to support black women, who they felt should be gainfully employed. Toussaint's mistress freed him only on her deathbed in 1807. A devout Catholic whose canonization is being championed today, Toussaint was once refused entrance to the church he frequently attended and where he had a pew. Religion and language—in his memoir, written by a close friend, he is represented as speaking only broken English—isolated him from New York's activist black community even as his business gained him access to the highest social and political circles. Unlike Toussaint, the Haitian emigrant John Appo in Philadelphia converted to Episcopalianism and became allied with the leading black abolitionist there, James Forten. Yet another emigrant, Joseph Cassey, married the daughter of the black abolitionist Peter Williams. He joined Forten in supporting Garrison and was an agent for the *Liberator*.[51]

The Haitian Revolution had an impact on black activism in the United States. The year Haiti became independent, an anonymous writer reported that black Philadelphians had formed themselves into military companies, robbing and assaulting whites, and that they damned "any white person who came near them . . . declaring 'they would shew them St. Domingo.'" This manufactured tale, repeated uncritically by historians, contrasted sharply with the politically sophisticated way in which African Americans did note the significance of Haiti. Black Philadelphians commended the French National Assembly for abolishing slavery in the colonies. Prince Hall, in his charge to the African Masonic Lodge in 1797, asked African Americans not to be "cast down under these and many other abuses" but to look for inspiration to the slave rebellion in Saint-Domingue. Only six years earlier he reminded them, "Our African brethren . . . in the French West Indies" were tortured, whipped, and killed to gratify "their masters pride, wantonness and cruelty." But now "doth Ethiopia begin to stretch forth her hand, from a sink of slavery to freedom and equality." The fact that the Haitian republic was established on January 1, 1804, probably contributed to the rise of January First celebrations in black communities that commemorated the end of the slave trade. Black Bostonians drank toasts to the "liberty of our African brothers in *St. Domingo*, and elsewhere" and to Haiti, "the only country on earth where a man of color walks in all the plenitude of his rights" at their celebrations. In 1818 Prince Saunders, an advocate of emigration to Haiti, recapitulated the proud history of the slave revolution and praised the "traits of bravery and heroism that belong to the Haitian people."[52]

Black abolitionists began composing justifications of the Haitian Revolution after the country's unification in 1820 under President Jean Pierre Boyer. Dessalines's assassination in 1806 had plunged Haiti into civil war and resulted in its division into two countries, a northern monarchy ruled by Christophe and a southern republic under Petion. In 1823 Rev. Jeremiah Gloucester of Philadelphia, the son of the founder of black Presbyterianism John Gloucester, quoted Louverture in his slave trade oration of 1823. He praised the "sons and daughters" of Africa who "effectually broke their chain in the Island of St. Domingo, and have proclaimed the imprescribable rights of man, sealing the covenant made with liberty, by their blood." He predicted that "ages to come will read with astonishment, the history of their brilliant exploits! Yes, liberty, which they have been invincible defenders of, has found an asylum in the bosom of a regularly organized independent government." For Gloucester, January 1 was to be celebrated not only for the closing of the African slave trade but also for the establishment of the first black nation.

Black New Yorkers named their lodge the Boyer Masonic Lodge in honor of the Haitian president, and the black abolitionist John B. Vashon named his son George Boyer Vashon. Forten argued that Haiti proved Africans "could not always be detained in their present bondage" and that they "would become a great nation." African American gatherings in Boston and Baltimore led by Rev. Thomas Paul, an advocate of black emigration to Haiti, and William Watkins marked the recognition of Haiti as an independent nation by France in 1825. Watkins noted that Haiti was "an irrefutable argument to prove . . . that the descendants of Africa were never designed by their Creator to sustain an inferiority, or even a mediocrity, in the chain of being." Black Americans drank toasts to Haiti's independence, to Washington, Bolivar, and Toussaint, and to abolition societies.[53] They saw the Haitians as part of the revolutionary abolition movement.

In 1826 John Brown Russwurm gave a rousing vindication of the Haitian Revolution in his commencement address at Bowdoin College in Maine. Born in Jamaica to a Virginian merchant and slave woman and educated in Canada and New England, Russwurm became one of the first black college graduates in the country. Black advocates of Haitian emigration, Saunders and Paul mentored Russwurm, who, like Saunders, taught at the African school in Boston. Of all recent interesting events, the Haitian Revolution held, Russwurm said, a "conspicuous place." Haitians had declared themselves independent on the "auspicious day" of January 1 and courted death over slavery. The excesses of its revolution were only "retaliatory measures." The Haitian Revolution, Russwurm concluded, had shown the world that "slavery may benumb, it cannot entirely destroy our faculties" and that all men, even those of a "darker complexion," were "sensible to all the miseries of slavery and to all the blessings of freedom." Upon graduating, Russwurm briefly considered emigration to Haiti. His graduating class consisted of the prominent northern doughfaces the future president Franklin Pierce and his friend Hawthorne. He, rather then they, was chosen to deliver the commencement address. Russwurm also wrote a twenty-two-page essay that was marked by the "hagiographical treatment of Louverture prevalent in abolitionist writings."[54]

By the antebellum era, abolitionists, black and white, regularly evoked Louverture and the Haitian Revolution. Revolution in the Americas, which began with a white settler rebellion, ended with a powerful statement on behalf of black freedom. The best exponents of revolutionary abolition were the slaves themselves, whose world historical actions forever changed the dynamic in the battle between slavery and freedom in the Americas.

3

THE LONG NORTHERN EMANCIPATION

Enslaved African Americans helped initiate the first emancipation in the Atlantic world. In 1781, Bett, also known as Mumbet, and a fellow slave named Brom sued their master, Col. John Ashley, a prominent revolutionary soldier from Berkshire County in western Massachusetts, for their freedom. His wife, Annetje Ashley, had struck Mumbet with a shovel when she tried to shield her sister from her mistress's wrath. In court Mumbet insisted on giving an abolitionist interpretation to the new state constitution. She had heard that it had set all slaves free. Her lawyer and later her employer, Theodore Sedgwick, said of this remarkable woman that she "had nothing of the submissive or subdued character, which succumbs to superior force."[1] Mumbet's freedom suit, along with that of another slave, Quok Walker, led to the judicial abolition of slavery in Massachusetts.

The long northern emancipation started during the Revolution in Vermont and ended well after the revolutionary impulse was spent in New Jersey. Most northern states enacted emancipation laws that were gradual, but abolitionist activism instigated and completed that process. Blacks struggling for freedom complemented the early white antislavery societies. Together they made the courts and statehouses of the new Republic an arena for contesting black freedom claims. If African Americans and abolitionists put emancipation on the political agenda, state implementation of post nati, or what the Spanish called free womb, emancipation laws, which freed children of slaves when they reached majority, regulated that process. Economic considerations hindered northern emancipation, with laws balancing slaveholders' rights to property and labor with slaves' rights to liberty and education. Gradual northern emancipation was an experiment in state-mandated self-purchase and apprenticeship meant to regulate the transition to freedom.[2] Slaves and their abolitionist allies hastened and implemented the process of emancipation, preventing abuse and backsliding. In the South lack of state support and proscription of abolitionist activism nipped emancipation plans in the bud, despite a spurt in manumissions in the upper south.

REVOLUTIONARY EMANCIPATION

During the American War of Independence, small antislavery steps toward abolition had been taken. The much-excoriated Atlantic slave trade to the colonies came to a halt. Financial considerations, colonial indebtedness, and fears of slave rebellion due to the growing numbers of enslaved Africans in the population had led some colonies to restrict the trade, attempts that failed because of the opposition of the British government. Slave resistance thus underlay this initial anti–slave trade movement. In 1774 many colonies banned the trade, and others instituted high duties on the import of slaves. The Continental Congress extended this prohibition when it included the slave trade in its nonimportation agreement against the British. The only successful move against slavery itself came from the Quakers, who managed to prohibit slaveholding among their members. In 1774 the Philadelphia Yearly Meeting disowned slave traders. Two years later, following meetings in New England, it expelled slaveholders from membership. Meetings in New York and New Jersey followed suit. By 1783 virtually all Quakers had forsaken slaveholding, and some meetings gave slaves compensation for their years in servitude. The same year, the Society of Friends presented its first anti–slave trade petition to the Continental Congress with over five hundred signatures. Benezet, one of the signatories, led a delegation that read the petition before Congress. In 1785 a Quaker address demanded the complete abolition of slavery.[3]

Abolitionist mobilization and the desire of blacks for freedom rather than the North's waning economic interest in slavery were the dominant forces behind revolutionary emancipation, even though slavery did not occupy the same place in northern economies that it did in the plantation states of the South. Slave labor was central to cities like New York, which contained the largest urban slave population outside of Charleston, South Carolina, in colonial America, certain farming areas in the middle colonies, and rural Connecticut and Rhode Island. Even in New England, the area with the fewest slaves, one of every twenty persons was enslaved in 1750. The New England states, especially Rhode Island, were also centers of slave trading.[4] Northern slaveholders and commercial interests resisted emancipation. The economic motives of northerners weakened the process of emancipation by making lawmakers solicitous of slaveholders' property interests.

In New England, where slaves possessed certain judicial and civil rights, including the right to sue their masters for freedom, African Americans initiated and enforced emancipation. From the start Puritan courts were known to free those who could prove they had been unjustly enslaved. In 1645 two Africans were released from bondage in Boston because they had been kidnapped, an act condemned as man stealing in the Bible, by a slave trader reputed to have killed over a hundred people in a slave raid in Africa. The next year Massachusetts specifically provided foreigners and the enslaved the right to bring suit and petition the court for unlawful enslavement. Like the number of slave runaways, that of slaves petitioning and suing their masters for freedom on various grounds increased dramatically during the revolutionary era. In 1762 Jenny Slew of Ipswich, Massachusetts, sued her master, John Whipple, for having "kept her in servitude as a slave in his service and restrained her of her liberty." Even though Slew was able to sue because she had a white mother, one of the judges in the Essex Superior Court who ruled in her favor four years later argued that "this is a Contest between Liberty and Property—both of great Consequence, but Liberty of most importance of the two." She received her freedom and four pounds in court costs and damages. After the Slew case, a number of freedom suits came up in Massachusetts courts. Nearly all the plaintiffs in the twenty-eight recorded freedom suits in colonial and revolutionary Massachusetts were successful. Only one, Amos Newport of Hatfield, an African who had been kidnapped, failed. His case, begun in 1766, went all the way to the Superior Court in 1768. Amos lost his suit, but his descendants gained their freedom.[5]

Even in cases of outright constitutional abolition, black activism was necessary to make freedom a reality. In 1777 the newly created state of Vermont, with its minuscule black population, became the first state to abolish slavery. Its liberal state constitution not only instituted universal manhood suffrage but also outlawed slavery as a violation of "natural, inherent and unalienable rights." The constitution's antislavery clause stated that no man could be bound to servitude after the age of twenty-one years and no woman after the age of eighteen. This clause allowed for the apprenticeship of children and was indifferently implemented. African Americans constituted less than 2 percent, around a thousand persons, of the state's population, but they helped enforce its constitutional ban on slavery. In 1779 a female slave of a Congregational minister successfully sued her master for freedom, as did an enslaved man, Pompey Brakee, who received four hundred pounds in compensation. In 1784 a runaway slave was able to win his freedom despite the fact that his master produced a bill of sale in court. By 1802 Vermont judges ruled that a bill of sale for a slave was not admissible as evidence in a case involving an enslaved woman, Dinah. Evidence of continued enslavement even after constitutional abolition suggests that the end of slavery in Vermont was contested rather than immediate. In 1786 and again in 1806 the state was forced to pass laws prohibiting out-of-state slave sales and kidnapping.[6]

Nowhere was black initiative in the process of emancipation illustrated better than in Massachusetts. In 1776 the state's General Court passed a law to prevent the sale of two Africans seized on the high seas, but attempts to abolish slavery by law were stillborn. The first draft of the state's constitution in 1778 recognized slavery and denied blacks the right to vote, to the chagrin of some residents in Sutton, who argued that it added "to the already accumulated Load of guilt lying upon the Land." They called for emancipation, warning of divine vengeance. Although the Massachusetts constitution of 1780 removed the color bar for voting and included a bill of rights, it did not abolish slavery. But the slaves gave antislavery meaning to it. Soon after its adoption, an observer reported, "One negro after another deserted the service of those who had been their owners." Those who were remanded back to service "brought actions against those who had been their masters, and the success of the negroes in these suits operated to the liberation of all."[7] Puritan legal tradition granted the enslaved some legal and civil rights, and antislavery public opinion helped, as juries and judges decided in favor of enslaved plaintiffs.

Two historic freedom suits brought by Quok Walker and Mumbet against their owners inaugurated emancipation in Massachusetts. In 1754 James Caldwell purchased nine-month-old Quaco (an Akan day name for a boy born on Wednesday) and his parents, Mingo and Dinah. Before his death Caldwell promised Quok his freedom at the age of twenty-five. Caldwell's widow acquired Quok, but her second husband, Nathaniel Jennison of Barre, was determined to keep him enslaved. Quok deserted Jennison and began working for John and Seth Caldwell, either siblings or children of James. Jennison assaulted Quock and tried to forcibly seize him. Quok Walker sued Jennison for damages in 1781. The jury in the Worcester Inferior Court of Common Pleas ruled against Jennison and declared Walker a free man. Jennison appealed the decision and sued the Caldwells for enticing his slave away. This time the court decided in favor of Jennison, and the Caldwells appealed this decision. Later in the year the Supreme Judicial Court overturned the decision in *Jennison v. Caldwell.* In this case, Levi Lincoln, the antislavery lawyer who represented Walker and the Caldwells, made the broader argument that slavery violated "the law of nature," "the law of God," and the Declaration of Independence. The court decided against Jennison on the grounds that the state constitution declared that "all men are born free and equal" and thus had abolished slavery. Jennison then petitioned the General Court, seeking clarification on the legal status of slavery in Massachusetts.

The legislature did not respond to his petition, but in the criminal case against Jennison for assault, *Commonwealth v. Jennison* in 1783, Judge William Cushing charged the jury that "the doctrine of slavery and the right of Christians to hold Africans in perpetual servitude, and sell and treat them as we do our horses and cattle" was simply a "usage" bequeathed by European nations in pursuit "of trade and wealth." In America, "a different idea has taken place . . . more favorable to the natural rights of mankind, and to that natural, innate desire of Liberty, with which Heaven (without regard to color, complexion, or shape of noses, features) has inspired all the human race." Slavery, he declared, was inconsistent with "our own conduct and Constitution." There can "be no such thing as perpetual servitude of a rational creature, unless his liberty is forfeited by some criminal conduct or given up by personal consent or contract." Having failed not only in his attempt to enslave Quok Walker but also ironically contributing to the demise of slavery in the commonwealth, the unrepentant Jennison took the rest of his slaves, one of whom was Quok's brother, to Connecticut and sold them there. That very year Cushing also justified the freeing of fugitive slaves from South Carolina who had been captured by Massachusetts ships from privateers during the Revolutionary War on a writ of habeas corpus, leading the governor of South Carolina to threaten disunion. Twenty had chosen to return to their masters, but about fourteen found freedom and new lives in the Bay State. Massachusetts's laws took precedence over the slave code of South Carolina; it would take the fugitive slave clause in the Constitution to subvert that equation.[8]

African American women played an active role in bringing freedom suits against their masters. Starting with one of the first freedom suits in the colonies, that of Elizabeth Key in seventeenth-century Virginia, and continuing with Jenny Slew in Massachusetts and the anonymous slave woman in Vermont who sued her master, black women's readiness to use the courts as an instrument of liberation is noteworthy. In 1777 an enslaved woman named Cuba, who had been captured from a British ship, petitioned the Massachusetts Council for her freedom and won it against her captors, who sought to sell her in Jamaica. Between 1716 and 1783 fourteen black women sued for their freedom in New England.[9] The freedom suit of Mumbet, also credited with giving an antislavery interpretation to the state's constitution, bolsters this conclusion. Mumbet renamed herself Elizabeth Freeman after gaining her freedom. Colonel Ashley of Sheffield had acquired Mumbet at the age of six months when he married into the slaveholding family that owned her. Earlier, another slave, Zach Mullen, had sued the Ashleys for assault. Theodore Sedgwick, a slaveholding lawyer with antislavery leanings, and Tapping Reeve, the Federalist jurist who would found the Litchfield Law School in Connecticut, represented Mumbet and Brom in their case in 1781. In *Brom and Bett v. Ashley*, the jury in the Court of Common Pleas ruled for giving the slaves their freedom and awarded them damages. Sedgwick built on Mumbet's testimony and argued ingeniously that Massachusetts had never instituted slavery by law and that the constitution nullified the practice. Sedgwick also represented a Connecticut master trying to reclaim a female slave, and he went on to vote for the Fugitive Slave Law of 1793.

Only the enslaved showed a consistent devotion to antislavery principle. Even Cushing's slave had challenged the antislavery judge. Elizabeth Freeman became a legend in her time, and another famous black from western Massachusetts, W. E. Burghardt Du Bois, claimed kinship with her. She married Jack Burghardt, a Revolutionary War veteran eighteen years her junior. Even though Freeman refused an offer from Colonel Ashley to work for him for wages, her husband rode with him to put down Shays's Rebellion. According to family lore, Freeman saved some property of the Sedgwick family from the rebels. Burghardt also fought in the War of 1812, which was wildly unpopular among New England Federalists, revealing a political independence that belies simple notions of patron–client relationships among antislavery whites and African Americans. Freeman became a widely respected nurse and retained her adopted name after marriage. When she died in 1829, she said to the daughter of her benefactor, Catherine Sedgwick, "Any time while I was a slave, if one minute's freedom had been offered to me, and I had been told I must die at the end of that minute, I would have taken it—just to stand one minute on God's airth a free woman—I would." In an abolitionist lecture he delivered in 1831, Theodore Sedgwick II specifically attributed his views to Freeman and her quest for freedom: "But for the care of one of this calumniated race, I should not now, probably, be living to give this testimony." He refuted racist ideas, noting, "Having known this woman as familiarly as I knew either of my parents, I *cannot* believe in the moral or physical inferiority of the race to which she belonged." His son Theodore Sedgwick III defended the *Amistad* rebels in 1839. Freeman had converted the influential Sedgwick family to abolition.[10]

Another enslaved woman from Massachusetts, Belinda, made the first formal demand for compensation or reparations for her years in slavery. In 1782

Belinda petitioned for an allowance from her Tory master's abandoned estate. Recounting her abduction as a young girl from Africa, the horrors of the Middle Passage, and her enslavement in America, Belinda argued that she "by the laws of the land, is denied the enjoyment of one morsel of that immense wealth, a part whereof had been accumulated by her own industry, and the whole augmented by her servitude." The General Court granted Belinda's petition, partly because her master, Isaac Royall Jr., was a Loyalist, and allotted her an allowance for a year. In 1787 Belinda petitioned again for an allowance and was granted a pension from her former master's estate for another year. Belinda's petition evoked the old colonial practice of giving freedom dues to those released from servitude. Despite the parsimony of the legislature, her petition raised the issue of compensated freedom, not for the slaveholder but for the freed slave. In 1777 an abolitionist Presbyterian minister from Salem, Timothy Pickering, had petitioned the General Court against the slave trade and slavery and demanded reparations for slaves: "Our Slavers are advised to pay their Africans for their Past Services and to Let Them Goe Free."[11]

African Americans in Massachusetts argued that citizenship was a necessary corollary to freedom. The Quaker sea captain Paul Cuffe and six other "poor negroes and mulattoes" from the town of Dartmouth, including his brother John, put black rights on the antislavery agenda in their petition of 1780 asking for relief from taxation. The Cuffes were jailed for failing to pay their taxes for three years. The petition pointed out that "being chiefly of the African extract and by reason of long bondage and hard slavery, we have been deprived of enjoying the profit of our labour or the advantage of inheriting estates from our parents." Yet after gaining their freedom they were made to pay poll taxes on "that small pittance of estate" accumulated by much "hard labour and industry . . . to sustain ourselves and families withal." They were "aggrieved, in that, *while we are not allowed the privilege of freemen of the State, having no vote or influence in the election of those that tax us*, yet many of our color (as is well known) have cheerfully entered the field of battle in the defense of the common cause, and that (as we conceive) against a similar exertion of power (in regard to taxation), too well known to need a recital in this place." While demanding these specific political rights, the petition highlighted the plight of "we poor destresed miserable Black people" who did not have "an equal chance with white people," had "no larning, no land and also no work." The Cuffes were forced to pay their taxes despite pleading for exemption on the basis of their Indian lineage. A year later they petitioned the town of Dartmouth, asking for equal political rights and privileges for "all Free Negroes and Mullatoes" or relief from taxation "under our present depressed circumstances." Their petitions perhaps contributed to the dropping of the color bar to voting in the state's constitution of 1780.[12]

Even in Pennsylvania, the heartland of Quaker abolition, African Americans played a role in the coming of emancipation. The Anglo-American abolition movement got its organizational expression here with the formation of the Society for the Relief of Free Negroes Unlawfully Held in Bondage on April 14, 1775, at the initiative of a group of ten Quaker artisans and shopkeepers in Philadelphia. These men were young and poor, not part of the wealthy elite of the city. Most of them were associates of the English-born Quaker tailor Thomas Harrison and were not particularly religious, some being "lapsed" and "disowned" Quakers. Harrison, like his wife, Sarah, was a committed abolitionist. The society met to help a woman of mixed Indian and African heritage from New Jersey who was interned in the Philadelphia workhouse, Dinah Nevil. She was about to be sold into slavery with her four children even though she claimed to be free. The very title of the society suggests how blacks' striving to gain freedom inspired the white abolitionist organization. The society met only four times that year but brought to court six cases of wrongful enslavement. Its preamble echoed Benezet, who some claim was its first president: to aid the efforts of "poor unhappy sufferers" in loosening the bonds of slavery, an endeavor which should appeal to "all professors of Christianity, but more especially when justice, liberty and the laws of the land are the general topics among most ranks and stations of men." It did not meet regularly owing to the disruptions of war and general suspicion of Quaker pacifism. Harrison bought Nevil and her two surviving children. In his will Benezet named Harrison one of his heirs. Harrison helped reorganize the society at the end of the revolution.[13]

During the revolution, Pennsylvania, like Vermont, adopted a liberal state constitution, reflecting the rise of a radical group of patriots. George Bryan, one of the radicals, presented a gradual emancipation bill that became law on March 1, 1780. Benezet personally lobbied each member of the unicameral legislature on behalf of the bill. The law not only linked racial slavery with the fight against "political slavery" but also challenged the racial justification of slavery. It is not "for us to enquire why" men are distinguished by "feature or complexion," the first section stated. All human beings are the work of God, subject "equally to his care and protection." The times that tried men's souls had "weaned . . . those narrow prejudices and partialities we had imbibed." The law freed only the children of slaves who were born after March 1 and who had served their masters until the age of twenty-eight. The assembly rejected proslavery amendments such as a ban on interracial marriage and the binding of free blacks into servitude. It also required slaveholders to register their slaves by November 1, and noncompliance would result in the emancipation of the slaves. In response, twenty-three members of the assembly entered a protest, calling the measure imprudent and premature and warning that "free negroes" were liable to commit atrocities against the state at the behest of its enemies. Not only did slaveholders oppose the law, they shirked its provisions by failing to register slaves, selling them to other states, and demanding a law for the reenslavement of those who had been freed by their masters' failure to register them.[14] Post nati emancipation laws created a terrain of contestation between proslavery and antislavery forces in the north.

African Americans were not silent spectators to these controversies. Slaves in Pennsylvania ran away in record numbers during the 1780s, hastening and at times extending the process of emancipation to those (born before March 1) left out by the law. Blacks contributed to the "storm of protest" that prevented proslavery endeavors to pass laws that would reenslave unregistered slaves by extending the date of registration to January 1782 and exempting southern slave-holding refugees from the emancipation law. In two petitions to the legislature, free blacks in Philadelphia protested against the proposed law. The petition of "divers Negroes" argued that "the question of slavery or liberty, is too important for us to be silent. . . . If we are silent this day, we may be silent forever; returned to slavery, we are deprived of even the right of petitioning." A "poor negro" called Cato wrote in the *Freeman's Journal* that "to make a law to hang us all, would be *merciful*, when compared with this law; for many of our masters would treat with us with unheard barbarity, for daring to take advantage (as we have done) of the law made in our favor." Reenslaving free men, he argued, was a crime worse than the original one of slavery. "I have read the act that made me free," and, alluding to the preamble of the act of 1780, he asked, "What must we think of the meaning of all those words in the beginning of the said law, which seem to be a kind of creed respecting slavery?" The attempt to reenslave the nonregistered failed. In 1781 the legislature exempted southern refugees from the emancipation law but required them to register their slaves within six months of entering the state and to hold them for no longer than six months.[15]

Dramatic instances of black protest reenergized the abolition movement in Pennsylvania after emancipation. In 1784 two tragic cases of suicide, in which a black man hanged himself after his writ of habeas corpus was denied and another drowned himself in the Delaware River after he was forcefully separated from his family and sold to the South, revived the moribund Society for the Relief of Free Negros. It was reorganized as the Pennsylvania Society for the Abolition of Slavery (PAS), again, by Quakers but including antislavery patriots like

Rush. Between 1784 and 1787 its new secretary, Tench Coxe, reported that the society represented over a hundred African Americans who had sought it out for legal assistance. In 1787 it was reorganized yet again, this time as the Pennsylvania Society for Promoting the Abolition of Slavery, and the Relief of Free Negroes Unlawfully Held in Bondage. It now included many of the city's leading men, such as the banker Robert Morris, Benjamin Franklin, and numerous lawyers, who were crucial in representing African Americans in the state's courts and in implementing its emancipation laws. The group also promoted black education and, although all its members were white, explicitly prohibited only slaveholders from membership. A petition campaign led by the society and supported by the Society of Friends resulted in the passage of another law in 1788 that prevented slaveholders from circumventing the emancipation law by sending pregnant slave women out of the state, selling slaves who were about to be freed to the South, and separating slave families. It also fought to restrict the slave trade, strictly implement the six-month transit rule for slaves, and prevent the kidnapping of free blacks.[16]

Rhode Island and Connecticut, two New England states with substantial investment in slavery, emulated Pennsylvania's road to abolition in 1784. Both states passed gradual emancipation laws that freed children of slaves born after March 1 of that year. In Connecticut they would serve their masters until the age of twenty-five and in Rhode Island until the age of twenty-one for males and eighteen for females. Both states had earlier freed African Americans who had fought in the Continental Army, many times as substitutes for their masters. State courts and laws also facilitated individual manumissions. In 1774 Connecticut banned the slave trade to the state, and in 1779 Rhode Island prohibited the sale of slaves outside the state. The latter law was inspired by the actions of a slave woman from South Kingston named Abigail. Bought by a North Carolinian slaveholder, she refused to let her new master carry her and her three young children to the South. The General Assembly ordered that Abigail and her children be kept within the limits of the state and passed the law prohibiting such sales. Connecticut had to pass similar laws in 1788 and 1792 to prevent the sale of term as well as lifetime slaves to the South. In 1797 it reduced the age of freedom for term slaves from twenty-five to twenty-one. Slavery steadily decayed rather than disappeared in the two states.[17]

African Americans hastened the process of gradual emancipation by running away, striking deals with their masters, and launching legal challenges. In Connecticut slaves petitioning for freedom during the revolution helped initiate the movement toward emancipation. James Mars, a term slave born in 1790, repeatedly ran away, once with his family to prevent being taken to Virginia by their master. The white citizens of Norfolk hid the Mars family, who eluded capture.

Mars published his narrative during the Civil War for "many of the people" who do not "know that slavery ever lived in Connecticut." Even though a term slave, he was sold away from his family. He eventually became a free man, a deacon in his church, and a prominent black abolitionist.

Antislavery sentiment also contributed to the emancipation process in the state. In 1775 the New Divinity clergyman Levi Hart proposed a plan for gradual emancipation that compensated masters for their lost property as a matter of "public faith" by the government, which made it legal for them to own slaves in the first place. Hart thought it was the state's responsibility to enact abolition and argued that it was a matter of justice because of the "injury done to the Negroes." He suggested that slaves serve their masters until the age of twenty-four or -five to compensate them for their education and that masters receive compensation in exact proportion to the amount of labor lost to them by developing a mathematical table that tied compensation to the age of the slave freed. Slaveholders would get nothing for superannuated slaves but would be responsible for their upkeep as money due to them for years of service. A conservative minister, Hart contended that freed blacks should be prohibited from intermarrying with whites but should enjoy the same benefits and treatment under the law as whites. He put forward the idea of appointing an overseer to supervise them but vindicated their ability "to conduct their own affairs & provide for themselves." Finally, he proposed repatriation back to Africa. The Connecticut legislature adopted Hart's plan except that it freed only the children of slaves and offered no compensation to masters.[18]

Rhode Island, like Connecticut, was a center of New Divinity Hopkinsianism and home to a crusading abolitionist, Moses Brown. Brown, who freed his own slaves and converted to Quakerism, campaigned vigorously for the abolition of the slave trade and slavery in the 1770s. The disastrous voyage of the Brown family's slaver *Sally* in 1765, during which most of the enslaved Africans committed suicide by drowning and starving themselves after a failed uprising, had turned him against the slave trade. He proposed a plan for the gradual emancipation of slavery similar to the one eventually adopted by his state. Unlike Hart, Brown was not interested in colonization. A Quaker "Petition and Remonstrance" against the slave trade and slavery in December 1783 had led the state assembly to pass the gradual emancipation law in 1784. Hopkins commended the act but called for the education of slave children and a complete end to the slave trade. By this time he had also started barring slaveholders from attending his church. He died in 1803, having taken several futile steps to implement his African missionary project. With the revival of the African slave trade after the revolution, abolitionists like Brown and Hopkins renewed their work. Opposition from commercial and slave-trading interests, ironically headed by

Brown's slave-trading brother John Brown, managed to remove fines for violation of the act prohibiting the slave trade and allowed the state's slave traders to
ply their business elsewhere.

Brown emerged as the strongest voice of abolition in the state and continued
his antislavery work after emancipation, becoming active in the anti–slave trade
movement. In 1789 he helped form the Providence Society for the Abolition
of the Slave Trade, which, like the PAS, assisted slaves and helped free blacks
escape enslavement and kidnapping. Brown developed ties with local blacks,
many of whom sought out his aid and advocacy. As John Quamine wrote to
him, "Having some late understandings of your noble and distinguished character, and boundless benevolent engagements, with regard to the unforfeited
rights, of the poor unhappy Africans in this province; and of your sundry petitions to the General Assemblies in their favours, [there] has existed [in] one of
that nation, though an utter stranger, [a desire] to present thee with gratitude
and thanks." In 1819 Brown purchased and then donated land for the construction of a meetinghouse and school for the African Union Society. He lived long
enough to witness the emergence of Garrisonian abolition, which he heartily
approved of, in the 1830s.[19]

By 1784 all the New England states and Pennsylvania had abolished slavery.
As elsewhere, slaves in New Hampshire had resisted slavery by running away,
petitioning, and filing freedom suits. As early as 1748 one Peter Johnson had
successfully sued his master for freedom. In 1778 Peter Hanson, a free black
man, requested a divorce from his enslaved wife, Venus, using the occasion to
criticize slavery: "Making slaves of any of the human race is unrighteous in the
sight of God." The court could either grant his divorce petition or free Venus so
that he would not father slave children. New Hampshire's state constitution of
1783, which like that of Massachusetts contained a bill of rights, was construed
to have abolished slavery. In 1789 a revenue act deliberately excluded slaves as
taxable property. However, over one hundred slaves remained in the state at the
time of the first federal census in 1790. The Granite State still recorded three
slaves in the census of 1830 and one in that of 1840. Not until 1857 would a law
clarify that the state had abolished slavery and give African Americans full citizenship rights.[20] That northern abolition could be a long, drawn-out affair was
further exemplified by emancipation in New York and New Jersey.

EMANCIPATION IN THE NEW REPUBLIC

In the early American Republic slaveholders managed to win valuable concessions that helped contain abolition. The U.S. Constitution (1787) safeguarded

the institution of slavery even though it did not specifically protect slave property. Southern, especially lower south, opposition to a slave trade prohibition and to antislavery led to compromises over slavery. However historians have interpreted the nature of the Constitution, the end product became subject to contestation between slaveholders and men of antislavery faith. Revolutionary scruples prevented the Constitutional Convention from using the words *slaves* and *slavery*, but the three-fifths clause, which counted slave property for representation and taxation, the clauses postponing the African slave trade ban to 1808 and requiring the federal government to suppress domestic insurrections, and most important, the fugitive slave clause, which enforced southern laws of slavery in the free states and territories, gave slavery ironclad guarantees. The principles of federalism, which assumed the garb of states' rights, and property rights protected slaveholders' interests. Even the Northwest Ordinance of 1787 contained a fugitive slave provision while prohibiting slavery in territories north and west of the Ohio River. Slavery was eliminated in the old northwest, but the prohibition was contested vigorously. While the ordinance at least represented antislavery goals, the Constitution reflected a proslavery reality. Many northern anti-Federalists based their objections to the Constitution on the compromises over slavery. Eventually, northern Federalists emerged as the staunchest critics of "Slavery's Constitution."[21]

Whether the Constitution was a conservative counterrevolution or not, it privileged the creation of a strong federal government and Union over anti-slavery. Rush and Franklin decided not to present an anti–slave trade petition from the PAS to the convention and neither did Alexander Hamilton for the newly formed New York Manumission Society (NYMS) for fear of endangering intersectional unity. One of the few antislavery voices at the convention, Gouverneur Morris, who had earlier tried, unsuccessfully, to add an abolition clause to New York's constitution, condemned it unequivocally for its slavery clauses. Of all the framers, only Morris argued that not only the continuation of the slave trade but also the existence of slavery in the Republic called forth the "curse of heaven." And only he resisted threats by South Carolinians and Georgians to leave the Union if the Constitutional Convention did not give in to proslavery demands. It was better, he said, that the free and slave states "at once take friendly leave of each other." Elbridge Gerry of Massachusetts identified the three-fifths clause as the fatal flaw of the Constitution that would lead to southern domination of the national government. John Dickinson also criticized the three-fifths clause as a "new principle of founding the right to govern Freemen on a power derived from Slaves." James Pemberton of the PAS, Brown, and Hopkins lamented the Constitution's failure to end the slave trade immediately and to enact a plan of general emancipation. Referring to the fugitive slave clause, Brown averred that instead of "Extending Humanity and good Will" to black people, the convention had "very Unhappily Wounded the Cause of Liberty and the rights of Men."

Luther Martin of Maryland excoriated the Constitution's provision allowing the African slave trade to continue. He pointed out how the three-fifths clause made it in the interest of the lower south to continue "that infamous traffic." He would base his opposition to the Constitution on the grounds that slavery was "inconsistent with the genius of republicanism" and that the slave trade had received the sanction of the general government. The father of the Constitution, James Madison also called the twenty-year reprieve for the slave trade dishonorable. The upper south presumably had slaves enough and would soon get rid of its surplus human property in a profitable domestic slave trade to precisely the regions these men criticized. In his speech against the trade, George Mason, who, like Jefferson, criticized slavery and the slave trade in the abstract but did not free his slaves, noted that the fugitive slave clause was not strong enough for southern security. The two Virginian anti-Federalists Patrick Henry and Mason, like Rawlins Lowndes of South Carolina, opposed the creation of a strong federal government that could abolish slavery.[22]

Delayed abolition inspired proslavery opposition in the two northern states of New York and New Jersey. Slavery had more widespread roots in these two states, and neither boasted a history of antislavery like Pennsylvania's. The process of emancipation was concomitantly slower there. Nearly 12 percent of New York's population, including twenty thousand slaves, was African American, and slave labor was widespread in the rural counties of the Hudson River Valley and Long Island as well as in the city of New York. At the end of the revolution at least four hundred black New Yorkers left with the contingent of three thousand African American Loyalists for Canada. A New York law of 1781 had compensated patriot masters and given freedom to slaves serving in the Continental Army. At the end of the war the state confiscated Loyalists' property, including slaves. In 1785, however, New York failed to follow Pennsylvania, Rhode Island, and Connecticut along the path of gradual emancipation. Gov. George Clinton, a lawyer for the NYMS, and his council vetoed a bill that abolished slavery but severely restricted black citizenship by withholding the franchise and office holding. Legislators, although agreeing to rescind an anti-interracial marriage clause in the bill, refused to remove political and civil disabilities on black freedom. Instead, the state banned the importation of slaves and eased restrictions on manumission.[23]

The failure of abolition in the state in 1785 gave birth to the second abolition society after the PAS, the NYMS, which had a large contingent of Quakers but also included New York's prominent founders, Hamilton, John Jay, and Aaron Burr, who proposed immediate abolition in the legislature. All three men were slaveholders but had long been on record as favoring emancipation and ended up freeing their slaves. Burr was the grandson of the Calvinist theologian Jonathan Edwards and was probably influenced by the antislavery views of his grandfather's New Divinity followers. Unlike the PAS, the NYMS did not exclude slaveholders and represented the elite of the state. The society gave "the Violent Attempts lately made to seize, and export for Sale, several free Negroes who were peaceably following their respective Occupations in the City" as a reason for its formation. The NYMS campaigned for statewide emancipation, regularly petitioning the legislature against the slave trade, domestic and foreign, as well as for emancipation. Members visited slaveholders after the Quaker fashion to encourage individual manumissions. The society republished Hopkins's *Dialogue* of 1776 and address to slaveholders. In 1788 a successful petition campaign by the society resulted in the passage of a law prohibiting the sale of slaves outside the state. The NYMS was adept in gaining the freedom of slaves who belonged to Loyalists and whose property was confiscated. At times members of the society acted as arbitrators between masters and slaves, changing lifetime slavery to term servitude and intervening in numerous cases of wrongful enslavement, as in the case of a young black girl from Nova Scotia who was sold into slavery in New York. Between 1792 and 1814 the NYMS assisted over four hundred slaves in their quest for freedom. African Americans who bought relatives out of slavery or negotiated terms of freedom with their owners were responsible for more manumissions.[24]

The debate over emancipation in New York was dominated by the discourse of race and citizenship. Even before the society launched its antislavery campaign, a handful of black writers challenged the proslavery articles that appeared in the New York press in the 1780s, some of which mocked African American speech and abolitionist ideas about racial equality. The black voice was clearly important to the antislavery project, as both critics and defenders of slavery tried to mimic or represent the African American perspective. But blacks needed no surrogates. The most well known black New Yorker at this time was Jupiter Hammon. In 1787 Hammon published his third pamphlet, "An Address to the Negroes in the State of New York," which was reprinted in Philadelphia at that time and again in 1806 at the behest of Quaker abolitionists. In his last pamphlet Hammon once again addressed his "dear brethren" who were in "the poor, despised, and miserable state" of slavery. Evoking authority on the basis of his color, age, and previous publications, he advised the slaves of New York to behave in a manner that would not jeopardize the course of emancipation and provide fodder to proslavery opponents. Hammon returned to one of his favorite themes, that African Americans should exhibit by their exemplary behavior that they are better Christians than "a great many white people . . . some who are rich and great gentlemen." In one of his most forthright criticisms of American hypocrisy he wrote, "Liberty is a great thing we know from our own feelings, and we may likewise judge so from the conduct of white people in the late war. How much money has been spent and how many lives have been lost to defend their liberty! I must say that I have hoped that God would open their eyes, when they were so much engaged for liberty, to think of the state of the poor blacks and pity us. He has done it in some measure and has raised us up many friends, for which we have reason to be thankful and to hope in his mercy." Hammon acknowledged the rise of the abolition movement and asked slaves by their "good conduct [to] prevail on our masters to set us free."[25]

The same year Cyrus Bustill of Philadelphia issued a similar address to the slaves. Born a slave in New Jersey, Bustill refused to marry until he became free, which he did in 1769. He owned a bakery and supplied the Continental Army with bread during the revolution, earning a commendation from George Washington. A leading member of Philadelphia's black community, Bustill was the patriarch of a family that continued to be active in abolitionist circles well into the nineteenth century. His daughter Grace Bustill Douglass and granddaughter Sarah Mapps Douglass were founding members of the Philadelphia Female Anti Slavery Society. Adopting the Quaker garb and religion of his third master, who freed him and taught him the skills of a baker, Bustill urged temperance, obedience, and faithfulness. He reminded slaves that God was "no respecter of persons," and his chosen people were "all ye that Labour and are havy Laden." In fact, God himself was engaged in delivering African Americans "from the bond of Slavery, in [this] world and that which is to Come." To Bustill, Christianity, especially the Quaker tradition of antislavery, was the religion of black liberation. One of the founding members of the Free African Society in Philadelphia, he died in 1806.[26]

While Hammon's and Bustill's views were in keeping with the moral strictures of Quaker abolitionism, others staked out bolder ground. Slaves in New York, as elsewhere, ran away in record numbers in the 1780s and 1790s, hastening the collapse of the institution. Even in writing, some black abolitionists went further. In an essay published in the *American Museum* in 1788, Othello criticized Americans' "frigid silence" and "torpid indifference" to black slavery.

He warned that America will be considered an "abandoned and deceitful country" in the eyes of the world because after having won its own freedom it "basely commences oppression in her turn." The "luster" of the Constitutional Convention was forever diminished by its failure to end the slave trade, "this cruel species of reprobated villainy." He urged New York to follow the abolitionist example of Pennsylvania rather than the conduct of South Carolina, which "can never be too strongly execrated." Instead of abolition, South Carolinians had enacted a law prohibiting slaves from acquiring literacy in an "attempt to enslave" even "their minds."[27]

The next year the *American Museum* published an exposition on racism written by A Free Negro. The letter was apparently first published in Britain. The author argued that the first order of the day was to remove racial prejudices, "which are so unjustly entertained against us." He wrote that physical characteristics "of very little moment in themselves" had become "a source of the greatest misery" for Africans. Trying to highlight the absurdity of racism, he set out "to prove that we are men—a truth which is difficult to proof only because it is difficult to imagine by what argument it can be combated." Paraphrasing Shylock's famous speech in *The Merchant of Venice*, he asked if a "Negro" had eyes, "hands, organs, dimensions, senses, affections, passions." Are they not fed with the same food, subject to the same diseases, "If you prick us do we not bleed? If you poison us, do we not die?" Racism, he pointed out, was the lie that "our inhuman masters" have "so industriously and too successfully propagated in order to palliate their own guilt by blackening the helpless victims of it and to disguise their own cruelty under the semblance of justice." Ideas about race were not the result of objective scholarship but the invention of self-interested parties: "We are examined, not by philosophers, but by interested traders; not as nature formed us, but as man depraved us." A Free Negro also illustrated how racism vitiated revolutionary republicanism. The rights of man cease to operate when it comes to black people, and "patriotism in the heart of the African" becomes treason.[28]

White pamphleteers from the NYMS joined blacks in calling for emancipation. In 1796 the NYMS revised its constitution and reinvigorated its campaign for emancipation. It printed annual discourses delivered to its meetings representing the voice of organized antislavery in the state. In an oration of 1797 Samuel Miller, a Presbyterian minister, invoked the nation's founding principles and called slavery a crime against humanity, justice, and religion. Trying to answer racist objections to emancipation, Miller vouched for the scholarly abilities of black children in the Free African schools founded by the society. He responded to the argument that abolition resulted in the infringement of slaveholders' property rights: "The right which every man has to his personal liberty is paramount to all the laws of property. The right which everyone has to *himself* infinitely transcends all other human tenures." Scripture revealed that "*God has made of one blood all nations of men that dwell on the face of the earth.*" Miller even quoted Jefferson, who, he noted, cannot be "suspected of undue partiality for the depressed Africans," that God's justice cannot sleep for long, and in a conflict between slaves and their enslavers God has no "attribute that can take side with us in such a conflict." He recommended gradual emancipation but hailed the example of Massachusetts, where slaves "were all emancipated in a single day."[29]

The following year E. H. Smith, the secretary of the NYMS and a physician who died of yellow fever, delivered an impassioned address for emancipation. Identifying slavery with the "reign of oppression" in human history, he said that "negro slavery . . . was wrought into a system of enterprising cruelty, and maintained by all the force of watchful and suspicious tyranny." Smith argued that emancipation must be accomplished gradually only "if its [slavery's] sudden removal be dangerous." Calling slaveholders who contended that they had simply inherited the institution "miserable sophisters," he warned them about the kind of compensation they could expect: "Would the tyrants demand triple recompense for their injustice? Recompence they shall have, and thrice threefold,— but let them tremble in expectation!" He did not shy away from referring to the Haitian Revolution to goad slaveholders. Looking beyond New York, he adverted to "the Legislators of America, you are the real upholders of slavery! You, yes you, Legislators of this Commonwealth, you foster and protect it here! Is it not recognized by your laws? And in the very face of your Constitution?"[30]

If not the legislators of America, those of New York at least did finally succumb to abolitionist pressure. In a public letter to Gov. John Jay in 1796 urging emancipation, the black abolitionist William Hamilton, alleged to be Alexander Hamilton's illegitimate son, wrote, "How falsely & contradictory do the Americans speak when this land a land of Liberty & equality a christian country when almost every part of it abounds with slavery and oppression." Africans had never harmed or injured Americans and had an "indisputable right" to freedom, as they were enslaved against their will. As elsewhere in the North, freedom came to black New Yorkers in halting steps. While slaveholding interests held fast against abolition, the New York city delegation and new northern and western counties of the state comprised an antislavery majority in the legislature. In 1799, with Federalists like NYMS's Governor Jay and Republicans like Burr uniting behind emancipation, New York finally passed a gradual emancipation law freeing children of slaves born after July 4, 1799, once they had served their masters until the age of twenty-eight for men and twenty-five for women. The NYMS now lobbied for complete abolition, and in 1817 New York passed a law freeing all slaves in the state on July 4, 1827. Gov. Daniel D. Tompkins, a member of the NYMS, recommended passage of the law. Slaves born between 1817 and 1827 would have to serve their masters until the age of twenty-one, and those born earlier were still subject to the provisions of the act of 1799. But the law also contained protections for bound children, and the NYMS continued to assist them, hastening the process of emancipation.

The Connecticut abolition society, founded in 1790, had lobbied for a similar general emancipation law and nearly succeeded in 1794. Three years later the state legislature reduced the length of servitude of slave children and repealed the state's colonial slave code. Connecticut did not pass a complete abolition law until 1848, and Rhode Island's state constitution of 1843 freed all remaining slaves. When slaveholding refugees from Haiti petitioned the Pennsylvania legislature to keep their slaves, the PAS and Quakers lobbied for a new law providing for total abolition. Revealing the depth of African Americans' commitment to emancipation, two groups of free blacks even volunteered to be subject to a special tax in order to purchase the freedom of those still held as slaves. Abolitionists in Pennsylvania failed to procure a general emancipation law or judicial decision despite making several tries. They did, however, succeed in preventing their state from passing laws restricting black migration and freedom. New York was the only northern state to pass a law freeing those not covered by gradual emancipation before the antebellum era, a testimony to the antislavery commitment of some state leaders and to the abolitionist activism of blacks and their allies in the NYMS.[31]

New Jersey, the last northern state to abolish slavery, underwent a more protracted process of emancipation, and a few slaves resided in the state until the Civil War. Slave labor in New Jersey, as in New York, was widespread in its small-farming eastern counties, leading at least one historian to call it a slave society despite the lack of a plantation system. During the revolution most of the state's African Americans had allied themselves with the British, earning the ire of New Jersey's patriots. The legislature freed those who had fought with the patriots, and after the revolution individual manumissions increased. The revolutionary governor of the state, William Livingston, a man of antislavery convictions, proposed abolition as early as 1778. Two years later the Quaker abolitionist John Cooper made a strong argument for immediate abolition and rejected gradualism: "If we keep our present slaves in bondage, and only enact laws that their posterity might be free . . . we save that part of our tyranny . . . which to us . . . is of the most value."

In 1785 David Cooper and other Quakers such as Samuel Allinson petitioned the legislature for emancipation. As in New York, a gradual abolition bill
failed despite the support of Livingston. The legislature instead passed a law
in 1786 that facilitated manumissions, required masters to educate their slaves,
increased penalties for slave abuse, and banned the slave trade. Restrictions on
black freedom of movement and rights tacked on to the law gave it a proslavery
cast. In 1788 Livingston managed to get the legislature to pass a stronger law
against the slave trade to the state and the kidnapping of free blacks. Slaves also
could not be sold out of the state without their consent, a stipulation violated by
unscrupulous masters. African Americans, for their part, sued Loyalist masters
for freedom, and many ran away to the anonymity of New York City.[32]

Organized antislavery in New Jersey was a late bloomer, though the pioneering Quaker abolitionist John Woolman hailed from the state, and its revolutionary governor William Livingston was antislavery. In 1793 the New Jersey Society
for Promoting the Abolition of Slavery was founded at the prompting of the PAS
by Joseph Bloomfield, a patriot and future abolitionist governor of the state, and
Elias Boudinot, New Jersey's representative to Congress and a future Supreme
Court justice, a prime example of the Quaker strategy of involving prominent
non-Quakers in the abolitionist enterprise. It was a mostly Quaker organization
in west New Jersey. Overall, the Quaker-dominated western counties near Pennsylvania were more favorable to abolition than the slavery-dominated east New
Jersey. Abolitionists' repeated efforts to get the state to pass a gradual emancipation law in the 1790s failed, though their attempts at increasing manumissions
helped many slaves negotiate with their masters for freedom. Allinson's son,
William, toured the state trying to convince individual slaveholders to manumit
their slaves, and abolitionist lawyers helped to prosecute freedom suits and antikidnapping cases. Nevertheless, the slave population in New Jersey grew, and
in 1798 a revised slave code recognized the enslavement of blacks and Indians.
Although the state's revolutionary constitution of 1776 contained no bar against
black voting, which was explicitly prohibited in 1807, a host of laws against free
blacks restricted their rights.

In 1804, under Bloomfield's leadership, New Jersey finally enacted a gradual
emancipation law supported by Federalists and Republicans that freed all slave
children born after July 4 once they had served their masters until the age of
twenty-five for males and twenty-one for females. The large vote for abolition
despite strong proslavery opposition arose from the support of Jeffersonian Republicans and an abandonment clause, modeled after a similar provision in the
New York emancipation law. This clause provided backhanded compensation
for slaveholders who claimed state funds after abandoning and then reemploy-

ing their slaves as servants. Such duplicity was a drain on the state treasury until it was done away with in 1811. In 1846 New Jersey finally declared all remaining slaves apprentices for life and freed the children of apprentices born after 1846 instantly. In the last federal census before the Civil War, the state was still home to eighteen "lifetime" apprentices. Despite the passage of laws in 1788 and 1812 that required the consent of the enslaved and term slaves for sale or transport outside the state, instances of an illegal trade to the South compromised abolition. A law in 1818 strengthened the earlier laws prohibiting out-of-state sales but, unlike those of other northern states, New Jersey's abolition law did not apply to slaves visiting from the South. The quick demise of the state's abolition society further aggravated the plight of New Jersey slaves, who now had few allies except for the far-off PAS and NYMS to plead their cause in unsympathetic state courts.[33] Emancipation in New Jersey proved to be painfully gradual.

In the North it was the enslaved—most of whom were required by law to serve their masters until they were adults—rather than slaveholders or the state that bore the burden of emancipation. Gradual emancipation, like many revolutionary-era manumissions, was self-purchase by enslaved African Americans writ large. In return, they received an uneven education and some apprenticeship training on abolitionist insistence, rather than freedom dues, or compensation for generations of unpaid labor.

THE FAILURE OF SOUTHERN EMANCIPATION

If the process of emancipation ground out slowly in the lower north, it came to a complete halt in the South. Slave resistance, revolutionary ideology, and the decline of the tobacco economy spurred individual manumission rather than emancipation in the upper south states. Virginia, the new nation's oldest and largest slave society, led the way with a law in 1782 that allowed individual masters to free their slaves, overturning its legal restriction on manumissions. Black initiative played a role, as a freedom petition from a slave named George to the state assembly preceded the law. Antislavery pressure from southern Quakers like Robert Pleasants, who founded the state's abolition society, Warner Mifflin, and John Parrish also expedited the passage of the manumission law. In 1780 Virginia's Yearly Meeting had petitioned the legislature for the repeal of a law from 1723 against manumissions. Two years later they renewed their petition. Even earlier, Virginian Quakers had made slaveholding a disownable offense and, after passage of the manumission law, most freed their slaves. Mifflin attributed his antislavery beliefs not just to his Quakerism but also to a young male slave who had asked him whether it was right for slaves to work in order to send him to school; the young man reminded Mifflin that his children would also be forced to do the same for Mifflin's children.

While slaveholders used manumission as a way to reward slave loyalty and service, African Americans seized the opportunity to buy themselves and their relatives out of slavery. Many also brought freedom suits against their masters, but, although slaveholders could serve on the juries for such suits, members of antislavery societies were discouraged both from representing blacks in 1795 by being fined in unsuccessful suits and, three years later, from sitting on juries of freedom suits. In the 1790s the state assembly passed a number of laws that narrowed the grounds for freedom suits, and abolition societies in Winchester and Alexandria were forced to curtail their activities. In most cases, only white or Indian ancestry resulted in the freedom of the enslaved plaintiffs. In 1793 the legislature also barred the entry of free blacks into the state. Between 1782 and 1806, when Virginia passed an antimanumission law requiring all freed slaves to leave the state, around ten thousand slaves acquired their freedom through manumissions. Purchase of self and family members by African Americans and negotiated agreements with masters rather than slaveholder benevolence caused a surge in manumissions. It did not lead to emancipation and was quickly halted when it threatened the stability of slavery in the state.[34]

Proslavery sentiment and fear of a large free black population doomed emancipation in the upper south. Nearly half of Virginia's white population owned slaves at this time, and the weak antislavery of the state's leading men was no match for its strong slavery interests. Pleasants, who founded the Virginia Abolition Society in 1790, and Warner's father, Daniel Mifflin, Virginian Quakers who had freed their slaves, failed to persuade Henry, Madison, or Washington to endorse the abolition movement. The revolutionary hero the Marquis de Lafayette, who freed and settled his slaves on land given to him by a grateful American government, also failed to convert Washington and Jefferson to the cause of emancipation. As president, Washington sought to recover his runaway slave Ona Judge from New Hampshire. Remarkably, local officials rebuffed him. Instead, religious radicals carried the torch of abolition in revolutionary Virginia. Evangelical preachers such as the Baptists John Leland and David Barrow, who freed his slaves, the Presbyterian David Rice, and the Methodists Francis Asbury, Thomas Coke, James O'Kelly, and the itinerant Freeborn Garrettson of Maryland preached against slavery, thereby courting personal persecution. In 1785 Asbury and Coke unsuccessfully tried to solicit Washington's signature for an antislavery petition to the Virginia assembly asking for "the immediate or Gradual Exterpation of Slavery." The Methodist petition argued that "Negroes in this State have been robbed of" their right to liberty and that the proslavery "Argument drawn from the difference of Hair, Features, and Colour, are so beneath a Man of Sense, much more the Christian." Several proslavery petitions countered this petition, which was voted down handily. When Virginian Quakers formed an abolition society, none of the state's leading men joined it. Methodists and Baptists mostly failed to implement antislavery rules for their denominations. Asbury soon called only for Christianization and better treatment of slaves.[35]

No one reflected the situation in Virginia better than Jefferson, whose antislavery was severely compromised by his racism. Jefferson had written a gradual emancipation and colonization amendment to the laws of Virginia that would have freed and deported children of slaves after they had served their master to a certain age. He never submitted the plan to the General Assembly for consideration. This proposal was coupled with antiblack provisions that would have outlawed or forced all freed slaves and white women who bore children of black or mulatto men to leave Virginia and prohibited free blacks from entering the state.

In his *Notes on the State of Virginia*, first published in Paris in 1785, Jefferson touted his emancipation cum deportation proposal. He argued that blacks could not be incorporated into the state because white prejudices and black recollections of "injuries they have sustained" would permanently divide them. Slavery transformed whites into despots and blacks into enemies who lacked "amor patriae." Blacks could never become citizens of the Republic because they would not love their country after suffering enslavement, and a slave may legitimately take "a little from one, who has taken all from him, as he may slay one who may slay him." In answer to Query XVIII in the *Notes* and with an eye on French antislavery sentiment, Jefferson famously condemned slavery as unrepublican, "the perpetual exercise of the most boisterous passions, the most unremitting despotism on the one part, and degrading submissions on the other." Jefferson trembled for his country when he remembered that "God is just; that his justice cannot sleep forever" and that God had no "attribute that can take side with us in such a contest." Writing before the outbreak of the Haitian Revolution, he concluded that the revolution already portended "total emancipation" and hoped it would come "with the consent of the masters" rather than their "extirpation." Jefferson did not doubt the capacity of black slaves to rebel, though he belittled it as foolhardy bravery devoid of forethought.

Racism vitiated Jefferson's rhetoric on the injustice of slavery. His *Notes* was also a disquisition on race that questioned black equality and citizenship in the United States. According to him, natural and physical and moral distinctions, which he enumerated in a racist catalog about color, smell, beauty, sexuality, and even capacities for sleep, imagination, reason, and art, made black removal necessary. He flirted with the most crude speculations of the racial pseudoscience of his day, including the fantastic idea touted by the Jamaican planter and historian Edward Long that orangutans copulated with Africans. Jefferson claimed that male orangutans revealed a uniform preference for African women, just as African men supposedly coveted white women. His racism allowed him to blame the victims of enslavement rather than the enslavers for the degraded conditions of slaves. Jefferson differentiated between white slaves from antiquity and black slaves and offered the opinion, albeit with "great diffidence," that blacks "are inferior in the faculties of reason and imagination." Jefferson's suspicion that black people were "inferior to the whites in the endowments both of body and mind," he admitted, acted as a "powerful obstacle to the emancipation of these people." If blacks were to be freed, they must "be removed beyond the reach of mixture." He entered into a long-term relationship with one of his female slaves, Sally Hemings, the half sister of his deceased wife, and probably fathered all six of her children, contributing to the "mixture" he deplored in theory.[36]

The most deliberate refutations of Jefferson's views on race came from his admirers. The cosmopolitan Gilbert Imlay, born in New Jersey and a veteran of the Continental Army with Jacobin sympathies, was Mary Wollstonecraft's lover and the father of her child. He published A *Topographical Description of the Western Territory of North America* in London in 1792. It was republished the next year in New York and in an enlarged edition in 1797. He was ashamed, Imlay wrote, to learn that the most "enlightened and benevolent" of his countrymen entertained "disgraceful prejudices" against the "unfortunate Negro." He attributed each one of Jefferson's arguments on race to prejudice and recommended gradual emancipation, which would allow African Americans to accumulate property and acquire an education and white racism to abate. While complimenting Jefferson on his antislavery views, Imlay expressed disbelief and disgust at his speculations on black women and orangutans. In supporting intermarriage and voicing his admiration of black bodies and intellect Imlay directly contradicted Jefferson. Why would Jefferson propose banishing people of color when they could be made useful citizens, he wondered. Imlay quoted Wheatley's poem "On Imagination" and vigorously defended her and the Afro-British writer Ignatius Sancho from Jefferson's criticisms. He hoped that philanthropy would destroy domestic tyranny and that odium would stick not to black people but to "leachers of human blood, as flagrant as they are contemptible." Like Imlay, William Short, who freed his slaves and, as the American chargé d'affaires in Paris, joined the Société Amis des Noirs, disputed his mentor's racism and advocated intermarriage and black citizenship. Short's express hope that Jefferson would lead a movement for abolition was met with silence.

Racism suited proslavery aims and crippled antislavery efforts. It compelled others to engage Jefferson on the slippery terrain of race theory. The Presbyterian clergyman Samuel Stanhope Smith, the president of the College of New Jersey, later Princeton University, used arguments drawn from climate, civilization, class, and condition to explain racial differences. But he defended monogenesis, criticizing Lord Kames, a polygenist who believed that the races constituted distinct species, and Jefferson's speculations on innate racial differences. Jefferson influenced the antislavery geographer Jedidiah Morse, who quoted him to deplore racial intermixture and proposed plans for emancipation and colonization. In 1797 even Rush contended that the color, features, and smell of Africans were due to a curable leprosy. Once blacks ceased being black, there would be no rationale to oppress them.[37]

Acute contradictions marred Jefferson's ideas, and his political career followed a downward trajectory from passively antislavery to explicitly proslavery. His best antislavery actions came when he was a young man and lacked the political power to implement them. Jefferson proposed a resolution to allow manumissions as early as 1769 and unsuccessfully represented a mixed-race, nearly white indentured servant in his quest for freedom. During the revolution Jefferson withheld his plan for emancipation and deportation from the Virginia House of Delegates, noting that the "public mind" was not ready for the proposition. When a state convention met to write Virginia's constitution in 1783, he again proposed gradual emancipation and colonization, which, unlike the manumission law of 1782, required freed blacks to leave the state. In 1784 Jefferson proposed the original federal ordinance to prevent the spread of slavery into western territories that met with virtually unanimous southern opposition. Jefferson's ban would have allowed for the continuation of slavery in the west until 1800, but it would also have included territories in the old southwest, which would have profoundly altered the course of American history if enforced. The history of the United States reveals, however, that all territories open to slavery became slave states. Three years later Federalists such as Rufus King, Timothy Pickering, and Nathan Dane wrote an immediate ban on slavery in territories north of the Ohio River in the Northwest Ordinance. The law exempted the southwest from the slavery prohibition and contained a fugitive slave clause.

Jefferson supported plans to convert slaves to tenants and wage laborers in plantations, notions that were popular among French abolitionists such as Condorcet and Lafayette, but he did nothing to implement them. He refused to act on the Polish patriot Tadeusz Kościuszko's bequest, which would have compensated him for freeing, educating, and settling his own slaves. Despite attempts to use the money to found a black school under the auspices of the American Colonization Society nothing came of Kościuszko's plan. Well into the nineteenth century black abolitionists like Samuel Cornish, William Cooper Nell, and Frederick Douglass demanded that Kościuszko's dying wishes be fulfilled. Jefferson's proslavery actions came when he had attained fame and the office of president. They shaped the course of the new Republic. With the Louisiana Purchase of 1803, he was responsible for the greatest territorial expansion of slavery in the nation's history. His "empire of liberty" became one of slavery. However, Jefferson did take the initiative in December 1806, calling for the constitutionally permissible ban on the Atlantic slave trade in his message to Congress. Like most slaveholders from the upper south suspected of fostering the domestic slave trade, he opposed the foreign slave trade. As a slave owner, Jefferson was an active participant in the interstate slave trade. A recent exposé of Jefferson as a slaveholder portrays him as a calculating master who put profits and his personal comforts before the liberty of his slaves and national wealth before national ideals as well as engaged in the casual cruelty of slaveholding on a daily basis. Jefferson owned around six hundred slaves through the course of his life, many of whom he sold. He never freed his slaves except for Hemings's children and two other favored slaves. During the political crisis over the admission of Missouri as a slave state, Jefferson endorsed slavery expansion in the guise of the ostensibly antislavery diffusion theory. Diffusing the slave population into the west, he argued implausibly, given the expansion and growing strength of southern slavery, would lead to the demise of slavery and the disappearance of Africans.[38]

All gradual emancipation plans in Virginia like Jefferson's remained just plans, coupled with proposals for deportation. In 1789 Madison, considering the consequences of emancipation, proposed that freed slaves be colonized in the "wilderness of America" or the "Coast of Africa," offering that the latter might be most suitable. The next year Ferdinando Fairfax, a substantial planter and Washington's protégé and neighbor, also proposed emancipation and colonization in Africa. In 1796 the Virginian jurist St. George Tucker's scheme, though it rejected colonization, included provisions to deport freed slaves out of the state and denied all political and civil rights to free blacks. In a list of queries he sent to Jeremy Belknap, the pastor of a Boston church and a known advocate of emancipation, Tucker wanted to know how Massachusetts had abolished slavery and what was the condition of free blacks, their rights, conduct, and rates of intermarriage with whites. Belknap circulated his queries and compiled a response to them. Tucker was interested in getting rid of both slavery and black people in Virginia.

After a lengthy discussion of the history and laws of slavery in Virginia, Tucker concluded in his *Dissertation on Slavery* that the institution could not be defended. But quoting Jefferson on race, he also maintained that free blacks could not be incorporated into Virginia society even though Belknap had assured him that "it is neither birth nor colour, but education and habit, which form the human character." Tucker's plan stipulated the freeing only of female slaves at the age of twenty-eight and their progeny, with the children serving the master until they were twenty-eight. The freed people would live in a state of semiservitude with severely curtailed rights, a stipulation aimed at forcing them to emigrate out of the state. Tucker's plan was so gradual that had it been put into effect, slavery in Virginia would have lasted for another hundred years, longer than the abolition of slavery during the Civil War. While abolitionists like Pleasants objected to both its gradualism and its assault on black rights, the Virginia House of Delegates rejected it outright. In freedom suits that came before him, Judge Tucker came down firmly on the side of slaveholders' property interests. He did not free his own slaves and sold many in the domestic slave trade. It is overly generous to call Tucker an emancipationist. By the time of his death, he, like Jefferson, had cast his lot with the Virginian slaveholding planter class, whose veneer of paternalism barely hid the crass commercialism of American slavery.

A few years later, in 1801, in the aftermath of Gabriel's rebellion, St. George's namesake and cousin George Tucker published a pamphlet against slavery, calling it an "eating sore" and "growing evil" that would lead to greater unrest. This Tucker called for emancipating the slaves and removing them to the west. After the Virginia slave conspiracies of 1800 and 1802, the legislature and Gov. James Monroe proposed colonizing free blacks and freed slaves, not just the indicted slave rebels, outside the country. But the failure to find a suitable place, despite repeated requests to President Jefferson, caused this incipient plan for gradual emancipation and colonization to be dead on arrival. Given a chance to implement his favored scheme, Jefferson remained passive.[39]

Unlike Virginia, Maryland and Delaware proceeded unchecked with manumissions through the nineteenth century, but they too failed to pass emancipation laws. Quaker- and Methodist-dominated antislavery societies in these states, as in Virginia, fought unsuccessfully for emancipation. In 1787 Delaware passed a promanumission law that allowed masters to free slaves without posting a bond for them. The state's active Quaker abolitionists, such as David Ferris and the Virginia transplant Warner Mifflin, did much to promote manumission.

Mifflin was often a party to freedom suits brought by Delaware slaves. Maryland, with its much larger black population, passed a manumission law in 1790 and another in 1796 that recognized so-called delayed manumissions. Many of Maryland's manumitters were not slaveholders but free black people who had saved enough money to buy relatives out of slavery. In both Maryland and Delaware masters and slaves entered into delayed manumission agreements that created a population of term slaves resembling those in the North who had to reach majority before attaining their freedom. But in slave states like Maryland, terms of servitude could be extended as punishment, the children of female term slaves were born into slavery, and, except in Delaware, those who proved recalcitrant could always be sold south. In Delaware, John Dickinson, known for his antislavery beliefs, supported an end to the African trade as well as to the interstate slave trade. Slaves had recourse as well to freedom suits or running away to Pennsylvania, but most bore the price of delayed manumissions.

Again unlike Virginia, Maryland and Delaware had established abolition societies earlier, and they lasted longer. In 1789 Luther Martin helped found the Maryland Society for the Promotion of the Abolition of Slavery and the Relief of Free Negroes Unlawfully Held in Bondage (MAS), but it was promptly censured by the state legislature. In the same year the eminent lawyer William Pinckney, who had represented slaves in freedom suits, made an eloquent plea for repealing the state law that prohibited emancipation. In an address before the MAS dedicated to Jefferson, George Buchanan argued that variations in human type and color were "flimsy pretexts" to enslave others. After dwelling on the horrors of the slave trade, he cited the examples of Sancho and Wheatley to illustrate the injustice of racial slavery. Three years later another abolition society was founded in Chestertown. In the 1790s the state abolition society had over two hundred members. Even though repeated attempts to pass an emancipation law failed, abolitionists assisted the enslaved in presenting freedom petitions. In Maryland free black people came to constitute nearly half of the black population, and in Delaware just over 90 percent of the black population was free on the eve of the Civil War, but slavery remained legal in both states. Individual manumissions came closest to a general emancipation in Delaware, where Quakers established two abolition societies in 1788, one in Dover and the other in Wilmington. Richard Bassett, a devout Methodist who cofounded the Dover society with Mifflin, got the state to pass a law prohibiting the sale of slaves to the lower south a year earlier. By 1810 New York and New Jersey had more slaves in their population than Delaware. The state's abolitionists worked hard to prevent kidnappings and illegal sale of slaves out of the state. In Maryland and Virginia the prolific interstate slave trade to the expanding Cotton Kingdom gave a new lease on life to slavery despite the decline in tobacco cultivation. As they did elsewhere, African Americans bargained for their freedom and ran away. Delaware's large free black population was known to assist fugitive slaves and abolition. In 1825 Abraham Dorcas left one hundred dollars to the Wilmington abolition society.[40]

In the face of evangelical Christianity's retreat on the slavery question in the South, antislavery there lost ground rapidly. The institution was legal in the new states of Kentucky and Tennessee, which were composed of lands ceded by Virginia and North Carolina. Virginian evangelicals such as the Baptist David Barrow, the Methodist William McKendree, and the Presbyterian David Rice carried their antislavery preaching to Kentucky. In his address of 1792 to the Kentucky constitutional convention, *Slavery Inconsistent with Justice and Good Policy*, Rice called slaveholders "licensed robbers" who did not have any property rights in their slaves. Slavery, he asserted, was a "national vice of Virginia," and Kentucky, as a separate state, now had the choice either to adopt it as our "national crime" or to bear "testimony against it." He admiringly referred to the slave rebels of Saint-Domingue as "fired with a generous resentment of the greatest injuries, and bravely sacrificing their lives on the altar of liberty." Despite Rice's appeal, in the end Kentucky's constitution contained an article that prevented the legislature from passing a gradual emancipation law without the consent of slaveholders and compensation to them. In 1799, when antislavery advocates joined the constitutional reform movement, the young Henry Clay came out in favor of eliminating the constitutional clause on slavery and of instituting gradual emancipation. "All America acknowledges the existence of slavery as an evil," he stated. But the new states of Kentucky and Tennessee made their commitment to slavery clear. In 1797 a Quaker migrant from Pennsylvania, Thomas Embree, managed to organize antislavery societies in two eastern Tennessee counties, which petitioned for manumission and gradual emancipation laws. The state's slaveholders, however, still needed the approval of the state legislature and, in 1801, the county courts in order to manumit their slaves. State laws discouraged rather than encouraged manumission in the two new slave states.[41]

In the Carolinas and Georgia neither manumission nor emancipation was ever on the agenda. Bucking the revolutionary trend, these states increased rather than liberalized restrictions on manumission. In 1784 the North Carolina legislature freed a slave named Ned Griffin, who had petitioned for his freedom because his master, in whose place he had served during the Revolutionary War, had reneged on his promise to free him. That year North Carolina ceded its western territories but repealed the act when the "state of Franklin" seceded from the state. Throughout this dispute the continued enslavement of Africans was never an issue, as western leaders were just as eager to acquire land and slaves as those in the East. In 1790 North Carolina asked the federal government explicitly not to prohibit slavery in lands ceded to it, lands which became the state of Tennessee. The state legislature also protected slavery at home, denouncing its Quaker citizens' practice of manumitting slaves as "evil and pernicious." Instead of passing a manumission law, the legislature authorized county sheriffs to seize and sell any freed slave manumitted in violation of state law. The state required all free blacks entering the state to post bond with the local sheriff.[42]

The lower south came down even harder on challenges to racial slavery. South Carolina and Georgia were the only states that did not have an antislavery society in the revolutionary era, and representatives from both became vocal proslavery proponents in the national political arena. In the Constitutional Convention the two states threatened disunion at the hint of opposition to slavery, delayed the ban on the African slave trade, and in the early Republic they emerged as staunch proslavery opponents of Quaker, African American, and abolition societies' petitions to restrict the slave trade and end slavery. In 1800 South Carolina passed an antimanumission law requiring masters to seek permission from a magistrate and a jury before freeing slaves. Three years later the Palmetto state proclaimed its unequivocal commitment to racial slavery by reopening the African slave trade until its federal prohibition in 1808, drawing abolitionist condemnations from across the Atlantic world. South Carolina imported well over fifty thousand Africans during this period.

Antislavery made a belated and brief appearance in South Carolina in 1810, when Lewis Dupré published a pamphlet in Charleston. Contradictory antislavery and racialist assumptions suffused the work. In his warning to southerners, the author compared "intellectually . . . degraded and brutified" slaveholders with "industrious starving slaves" and "degraded Africa" with "rapacious sons of refined Europe." And while divine retribution awaited slaveholders, in South Carolina, Dupré affirmed, African color and features had been "improved" at the cost of European Christians. In a subsequent pamphlet Dupré proposed a "rational and benevolent plan" for emancipation under the auspices of a "Virginia and Carolina Emancipation Society" open in membership to blacks and whites. The society would buy slaves, who could then compensate it by hiring themselves out. But slaves were required to be vegetarians, and those who proved to be "unworthy of freedom" could be "exchanged." Dupré's was a lone, eccentric antislavery voice, and his plans for a southern abolition society came to naught.[43]

Besides the failure of abolition in the South, the new federal government enacted laws that seemed to write black people out of the Republic. In 1790 and 1792 Congress passed naturalization and militia laws that explicitly excluded people of African descent. In 1793 it passed a stringent Fugitive Slave Law implementing the fugitive slave clause of the Constitution. The law was passed to address a dispute between Virginia and Pennsylvania stemming from the kidnapping and enslavement of a free black man, John Davis, by three Virginian bounty hunters. Davis's Virginian master had not complied with Pennsylvania's registration law, and the PAS had tracked Davis back to Virginia and freed him until his master had him brought back forcibly. The fact that the first federal Fugitive Slave Law was passed in response to a case that fudged the line between kidnapping and fugitive slave rendition made the freedom of all African Americans tenuous. Davis died in slavery. For the federal government, slaveholding claims trumped black freedom, until some northern states rose in revolt. Free blacks were prohibited even from carrying the U.S. mail. Not only would southern slavery persist and expand after the cotton revolution of the 1790s, but the slaveholding Republic rejected the idea of black freedom and citizenship in large and petty ways alike.[44]

Abolitionists drew attention to the manner in which the persistence of southern slavery cast a pall over freedom in the country. In an early antislavery article, Hopkins called slavery a "national sin" of the "first magnitude." He argued that in denying Africans liberty the American Republic was guilty of "wicked contradiction and inconsistence." He wrote, "Instead of rising to honor, dignity and respect among the nations, we have suddenly sunk into disgrace and contempt." While Americans were horrified when Barbary pirates carried a few seamen into Algerian captivity, most ignored the thousands of Africans enslaved at home. Mifflin complained that many free blacks had been kidnapped from Maryland and his adopted state of Delaware into slavery. A new domestic slave trade that linked states in the upper south to lower south states like Georgia tore "Familes . . . asunder" and violated the "Marriage Tie." Though "salutary Laws have been enacted in some States . . . yet still the evil [slavery] is continued in other parts of America in a most glaring degree." Similarly, the Irish Methodist preacher James O'Kelly, in his *Essay on Negro Slavery* (1789), wrote, "Arbitrary power over the unalienable rights of thousands prevails" in the new Republic. According to Buchanan, the history of slavery "to the eternal infamy of our country . . . will be handed down to posterity, written with the blood of African innocence." Americans had become "apostates to their principles, and riveted the fetters of slavery upon unfortunate Africans." The Republic could rise to "eminence among mankind" and a "new theatre of glory" by abolishing slavery or be "stigmatized with the infamous reproach of oppression, and her citizens be called Tyrants."[45]

First-wave abolitionists did not acquiesce to the limits of emancipation in the new Republic but renewed their organizational efforts. Besides the failure of general emancipation and an immediate ban on the African slave trade, the implementation of gradual emancipation in the North and the fight for black rights consumed the energies of early abolition societies. Northern emancipation and upper south manumissions had been achieved not through the unfolding of some inexorable revolutionary logic but through ongoing contestations between slaveholders' power and legal prerogatives and enslaved black people and their abolitionist allies. They were about the meaning and parameters of black freedom and American democracy.

4

THE ANGLO-AMERICAN ABOLITION MOVEMENT

In 1875 abolitionists gathered to celebrate the centennial of the PAS. In his speech Frederick Douglass noted that he had "no sympathy with those who despise and neglect the origin of the anti-slavery movement." Men like Isaac T. Hopper, Thomas Earle, and Thomas Shipley of the PAS, he recalled, assisted thousands of slaves.[1] The largely forgotten first wave of abolition that Douglass spoke of faced an uphill task after the failure of general emancipation and the dramatic rise in racial proscription in the American Republic. Not only did abolition fail in the South, but with the rise of the Cotton Kingdom slavery began its antebellum career of economic expansion and political consolidation. Slavery died hard in Brazil, Cuba, Puerto Rico, and the United States. If eastern Europe had a second serfdom, these areas, also fueled by the growth of early capitalism, experienced a "second slavery."[2]

In the face of these obstacles, American abolition did not, as is commonly assumed, wane. State societies regrouped nationally and initiated transnational connections, especially with the British movement for the abolition of the slave trade. In making general emancipation rather than colonization their goal, abolitionists distinguished themselves from those who mouthed antislavery sentiment yet proposed plans to deport African Americans. Early abolitionist societies viewed blacks, slave and free, not only as objects of their benevolence but also as future fellow citizens. Abolitionist paternalism could be grating for a newly free people, but it could also offer invaluable assistance in securing freedom, in education, and in confronting the abuses of northern emancipation laws.[3] Some even subscribed to an unapologetic brand of revolutionary abolitionism, justifying slave rebellions and advocating black equality. It is perhaps best to judge the early abolition movement through the eyes of the enslaved and the newly free. In the context of a revolutionary backlash, abolitionists were a singular minority in the slaveholding Republic.

THE ABOLITION OF THE AFRICAN SLAVE TRADE

The British movement to end the slave trade inspired abolitionist organization and tactics. In an anonymous pamphlet from 1760, *Two Dialogues on the Man-Trade*, a Mr. Philmore rejoices at the news of a slave revolt even though it comes at the cost of English lives. Europeans compounded their crime of man stealing and murder of Africans in the trade with their "barbarous treatment" in the colonies. Philmore converts a slave trader, Mr. Allcraft, who confesses that his "love of money" had led him astray. Benezet included parts of this dialogue in his pamphlets against the slave trade. Twelve years later, inspired by *Somerset*, Maurice Morgann, a British administrator, proposed a plan for the abolition of slavery in the colonies. Morgann suggested founding a colony of free blacks in Florida and giving them land grants. The colony would act as a buffer between the British and Spanish empires and outcompete the slave colonies, as free blacks acquired skills, intermarried with whites, and created a gradation of color from the South to the North so that color would no longer be a "mark of distinction" or the "object of hatred and hostility." Steeped in Enlightenment views of race and climate, Morgann's imperial yet racially flexible vision sought to banish slavery and racial distinctions. It was not until the mid-1780s that the movement to abolish the slave trade took off. By then the British were more receptive to abolitionist appeals, eager to accrue "moral capital" in the face of defeat in North America.[4]

The loss of the American colonies, however, also facilitated the abolitionist critique of an imperial economy based on the enslavement of Africans. In 1783 British Quakers, who were wealthier and lagged behind their American counterparts on the slavery question, submitted a petition to Parliament on behalf of "our Fellow Creatures, the Oppressed Africans." William Dillwyn, a coauthor, played a crucial role in the organization of British abolition. Quakers founded the Committee of the Society for Effecting the Abolition of the Slave Trade (SEAST) in London in 1787 and placed Granville Sharp at its head. Both Sharp and Thomas Clarkson sympathized with revolutionaries in America and France and were critics of British imperialism. The German philosopher Johann Gottfried Herder referred to the Quakers' commitment to abolition as a noteworthy example of his notion of *Humanitat* in his critique of slavery and colonialism, *Ideas for the Philosophy of History of Mankind* (1784–85).

Nine of the original twelve SEAST members were Quakers and adept propagandists. The potter Josiah Wedgwood proposed the seal for the society, a kneeling slave with the motto "Am I Not a Man and a Brother?," and the printer James Phillips published most of its anti–slave trade literature. Abolitionist pamphlets and images transformed the African slave trade from a cog in the imperial machine to an exemplary instance of cruelty and inhumanity. They sought to render the enslaved African visible to the widest possible audience. The plan of the "regulated" slave ship *Brooks* with its decks of packed human-ity, first composed by William Elford and the Plymouth abolition committee and elaborated by the London Committee, became the most widely circulated broadside of British abolitionism. Mirabeau called it a living coffin. This single image evoked the Middle Passage as experienced by Africans and centered it in abolitionist discourse. In portraying the victimization of Africans by the slave trade and slavery, abolitionists did not render them passive. The iteration of it in 1794 included a shipboard rebellion. Abolitionist art blossomed in the nine-teenth century from anonymous depictions to carefully delineated humanistic portraits. In the 1820s the British Quaker abolitionist Elizabeth Heyrick trans-formed the image of the kneeling slave to that of an upright black man with the emphatic statement, "I am a man and a brother." The *Brooks* diagram lives on in the modern black artistic imagination.[5]

Clarkson's anti–slave trade pamphlets, most significantly his award-winning paper at Cambridge University, *Essay on the Slavery and Commerce of the Hu-man Species, Particularly the African* (1785), edited and published by Phillips in 1786, built on the Quaker abolitionist tradition. (He went on to write the history of the movement to abolish the slave trade in 1808 as well as admiring books on Quakerism and William Penn.) Clarkson insisted that Africans deserved liberty and the rights of man, holding that the slave trade butchered thousands annually and contradicted the very spirit of Christianity. Citing Wheatley, he denied the myth of racial inferiority and summarized the climatic theory of race popularized by eighteenth-century environmentalists. The SEAST published a concise version of it, *A Summary View of the Slave Trade and Probable Conse-quences of its Abolition*, in 1787. In *An Essay on the Impolicy of the African Slave Trade, in Two Parts* (1788), Clarkson broke new ground, avowing that the slave trade was not just immoral but impolitic. He performed yeoman's work, travel-ing to the British seaports of Bristol and Liverpool to investigate the conditions of the trade and interview sailors; he published much of this research in his *The Substance of the Evidence of Sundry Persons on the Slave Trade*. A consummate abolitionist essayist, Clarkson wrote two more pamphlets. In *An Essay on the Comparative Efficiency of Regulation or Abolition, as applied to the slave trade* (1789), dedicated to Sir William Dolben, he argued that only abolition would get rid of the evils that Dolben's bill sought to regulate. The following year his *Letters on the Slave Trade*, written from Paris, restated the case for abolition.

Not surprisingly, Samuel Taylor Coleridge called him the movement's "moral steam engine." Clarkson campaigned for a ban on the slave trade in revolutionary France and spent his last days advocating the abolition of slavery in the West Indies and the United States.[6]

British abolitionists opposed not just the slave trade but also slavery. As early as 1778 Rev. James Ramsay proposed emancipation. He published his views in *An Essay on the Treatment and Conversion of African Slaves in the British Sugar Colonies* (1784), an eyewitness account of the brutality of West Indian slavery. The essay posited that better treatment, state protection, conversion, and access to freedom would make slavery more humane until "liberty shall claim every exiled African for her own child." He refuted the racism of David Hume and the polygenism of Lord Kames, prefacing his pamphlet with abolitionist clergymen's favorite biblical injunction, "God Hath Made of One Blood all Nations of the Earth." The same year he published his *An Enquiry into the Effects of Putting a Stop to the African Slave Trade, and of Granting Liberty to the Slaves in the British Sugar Colonies.* To ministers who would stop at Christianization, Ramsay argued that while a Christian slave was more valuable than a heathen slave, a Christian freeman was more valuable than a Christian slave. Ramsay spent the rest of his life in debilitating debate with the West India slave interests who sought to discredit him and died in 1789. Rev. John Newton, a former slave trader who composed the famous hymn "Amazing Grace," wrote his belated condemnation of the slave trade from the perspective of a repentant participant. The SEAST also distributed the slave trader Alexander Falconbridge's *Account of the Slave Trade on the Coast of Africa* (1788), a report on its brutalities. William Cowper, Newton's congregant, wrote antislavery poems, including his famous "The Negro's Complaint."[7]

British women contributed to anti–slave trade poetry. The influential evangelical Hannah More's poem "Slavery" (1788) was written to coincide with the parliamentary debate over the slave trade and reprinted on both sides of the Atlantic. Before her death in 1833, More was elected to the committee of the Bristol Female Anti-Slavery Society. Wheatley inspired female poets like Mary Scott, who wrote admiringly that she had "fair nature's charms display'd!" The pioneer feminist Mary Wollstonecraft established the long-lasting antislavery trope that compared the slavery of sex with the enslavement of Africans in *A Vindication of the Rights of Woman* (1792). Literary antislavery was not a sentimental preoccupation removed from the horrors of the slave trade. James Field Stanfield, a former seaman on a slaver, wrote one of the best poetic condemnations of it. Despite their racial romanticism, antislavery British writers and poets were critics of the sordid business of empire.[8]

Even as antislavery spread in popular culture, the uphill political battle for abolition was waged in Parliament. British abolitionists perfected the tactics of lobbying, petitioning, publication of antislavery tracts, and boycott of slave-produced goods, particularly sugar. Abolitionist mass mobilization in Britain was unprecedented and took the form of a broad-based social movement that cut across class lines and used the public sphere and democratic modes of communication to influence policy. During the mass petition campaigns of 1788 and 1792, over one hundred and over five hundred petitions, respectively, were sent to Parliament. In 1792 some four hundred thousand people signed abolitionist petitions, many from the booming industrial city of Manchester, revealing the working-class roots of popular abolitionism. If not the printed word, abolitionist illustrations reached the masses. Issac Cruikshank's sensational print from 1792 of a slave girl suspended by her ankle on a ship's deck was based on the actual murder of two enslaved African women. An indefatigable abolitionist agent, Clarkson spread the abolition message into provincial English towns and to France, where he was a liaison between SEAST and the Amis des Noir.[9]

Abolitionist activism at the grassroots was indispensable in the face of the profitability of the slavery-based British Empire and entrenched racism. While antislavery sentiment was confined to the aristocratic patrons of black Christian writers, abolitionism found favor among the masses. Rather than provide ideological cover for capitalism and the status quo, popular abolitionism was based on a critique of market relations and social hierarchy. The African slave trade and colonial slavery were profitable businesses that sustained the imperial economy. The logic of British imperialism and political economy was embedded not in abolition but in the proslavery response to the abolitionists that touted the economic growth, political power, naval superiority, and national ascendance generated by slavery and the slave trade. It would take a long-fought and hard campaign to detach British national identity from slavery to antislavery. And even after the triumph of abolition, the logic of empire remained closely tied to the ideological and economic rationale not of abolition but of the institution that birthed it, racial slavery: the exploitation rather than the liberation of those deemed irrevocably inferior and uncivilized.[10]

Not surprisingly, abolition was repeatedly defeated, as the government proved to be unresponsive to popular pressure and protective of West India interests. After years of intense mobilization, British abolition suffered a setback with the defeat of slave trade abolition bills in 1791 in the House of Commons and in the House of Lords the subsequent year. The massive evidence on its brutality, largely collected by the tireless Clarkson during the hearings on the slave trade, is still an invaluable historical source. The parliamentary effort to abolish the slave trade was led by William Wilberforce, a convert to evangelical Christianity and abolition, and succeeded only in 1807. Wilberforce, who belonged to the Clapham Sect, emerged as the political leader of the movement. He joined the SEAST and initiated the petition campaign of 1792. From then on he would assiduously introduce bills calling for the abolition of the slave trade nearly every year. Wilberforce's eloquent speeches against the slave trade, "so much misery condensed in so little room," initially bore little fruit. For conservatives of all stripes, despite Wilberforce's support of sedition laws and criticism of the Sierra Leone uprising, abolition was closely associated with democracy at home and revolutionary Jacobinism abroad. Most abolitionists like Clarkson endorsed the extension of franchise and sympathized with the French Revolution and black colonists in Sierra Leone. The imprisoned working-class radical Thomas Hardy of the London Corresponding Committee was an abolitionist. The English Jacobin John Thelwall connected the suffering of labor with that of colonial slaves. The MP Charles James Fox, who introduced the successful abolition bill, was known for his sympathy for the French Revolution and opposed sedition laws. In France, ironically, the Amis des Noir was viewed as a stalking horse for British interests.

In the 1790s fears of French revolutionary radicalism prevented the British government from acting against the slave trade. During this time Bryan Edwards published his influential proslavery volumes on the history of the West Indies and Saint-Domingue, blaming French and British abolitionists for inciting slave rebellion. During the abolitionist doldrums, when Clarkson went into semiretirement and the SEAST virtually stopped meeting, antislavery sentiment grew steadily in popular and print culture. Thomas Paine responded to Edmund Burke's conservative criticism of the French Revolution, and the Anglo-Irish abolitionist poet and playwright William Preston published a scathing response to Edwards. In his *National Sins Considered* (1796), the radical newspaper editor Benjamin Flower condemned British inaction even after the slave trade's "atrocities have been repeatedly exposed to view" by abolitionists. The next year Sharp weighed in, calling the slave trade and colonial slavery inconsistent with the *"foundations of English Law and Constitution!"* His duty, Sharp insisted, despite SEAST's decision to strategically restrict abolition to the slave trade, was to illustrate the "monstrous impiety and cruelty" of both.[11]

The politically cautious Wilberforce continued to raise abolition in Parliament throughout this period. His steady efforts at building support for abolition eventually bore fruit. In 1804 the SEAST was revived at his instigation. Converts to the antislavery cause included his brother-in-law James Stephen and Henry Brougham as well as powerful political allies such as the prime ministers

William Pitt and Lord Grenville, who linked abolition to national interest and reputation. Wilberforce used news of the impending abolition by the United States to urge British action. His major work against the slave trade, *A Letter on the Abolition of the Slave Trade*, written to his constituents, was published on the eve of abolition. Wilberforce drew on the testimony of European travelers and slave traders to protest that the slave trade engendered wars and a perverted legal system in Africa designed to secure a continuous supply of slaves. He challenged the notion that Africa lacked civilization and refuted Edward Long, who held that colonial slavery was better than African servitude. Wilberforce described the racial degradation of West Indian slavery because "the feelings of sympathy towards Blacks, as fellow-creatures, or of decency respecting them as of our own species" was "largely extinct." He advocated a series of reforms, including an end to whipping and corporal punishment. If Clarkson helped launch the anti–slave trade movement, Wilberforce's censure of racism and slavery presented the finished abolitionist argument. The enslaved soon deployed his name and strategies in their struggles against slavery.

Parliamentary defeat and the constitutionally mandated delay in America ensured that Britain and the United States abolished the African slave trade virtually simultaneously in 1807, passing laws that took effect on January 1, 1808. But only in Britain did abolition come about as a result of mass agitation. In the United States it was more of a constitutional postscript enacting the clause prohibiting the federal government from abolishing the African slave trade before 1808. Despite a virtually unanimous vote on abolition in Congress, a sectional divide in debates over petitions demanding the ending of the slave trade was evident. Northerners such as James Sloan, a Republican, doomed to political oblivion by his southern-leaning party, recommended the freeing of all Africans illegally enslaved, and Theodore Dwight, a Federalist, advocated the death penalty for violation of the slave trade prohibition. Southerners who opposed them got their way, though subsequent legislation in 1819 and 1820 allowed for the repatriation of recaptives to Africa and defined the foreign slave trade as piracy punishable by death.[12]

The long British campaign against the slave trade gave birth to transnational abolitionism, which was marked by cosmopolitan cooperation rather than competition for national glory. The PAS corresponded with the London Committee and the Abbé Raynal. Sharp was made an honorary member of the PAS and NYMS. Lafayette asked Hamilton to have his name included in the membership of the NYMS. American magazines and the Quaker-dominated antislavery press reprinted the *Brooks* illustration and Clarkson's essays against the slave trade. In 1793 the Maryland abolition society published a letter from Sharp warning that southerners would be subject to divine vengeance if they did not abolish slavery. The SEAST inspired the formation of the Amis des Noir and elected Brissot as an honorary member. The French society published translations of Benezet, Wesley, and Clarkson. Quakers inspired its very name, Friends of the Blacks. The PAS published its addresses and Brissot's oration on its founding, and Brissot urged Frenchmen to follow the example of SEAST and the Quakers in America.[13]

Brissot visited Britain frequently and the United States in 1788. Like Clarkson, he was an ardent admirer of the Quakers. Montesquieu and Voltaire also contributed to the "Quaker legend" of tolerance and antislavery in their writings. The PAS elected Brissot as a member, and he reported that it "appointed committees to assist me in my work and opened their archives to me" during his visit. In 1785 St. John de Crèvecoeur, who dedicated his *Letters from an American Farmer,* in which he too praised the Quakers, to Raynal and Lafayette, became a founding member of the NYMS. In 1791 Brissot published Crèvecoeur's American travelogue. Influenced by the French racial caste system, Brissot argued for racial equality for northern free blacks and emigration to Africa for freed slaves. He noted the southern states' opposition to abolition: "Here there is no talk of freeing the Negroes, no praise of the antislavery societies in London and America. Nobody reads Clarkson's works." Bearing a letter of introduction from Lafayette, he met Washington, whose personal library contained abolitionist tracts. Washington and Hamilton, close friends of Lafayette, as well as Jefferson and Franklin, both of whom had spent time in Paris, were aware of the transnational abolitionist network. Jefferson had started to translate Condorcet's abolitionist pamphlet during his stay in Paris. But Brissot, like many before, failed to recruit them. Jefferson's speculations on black inferiority served as fodder for an opponent of Brissot's, the Marquis de Chastellux, when he wrote his proslavery, antiblack, anti-Quaker diatribe. Jefferson had more in common with men of the slaveholding planter class such as Edwards and Moreau de Saint-Méry than with the abolitionists.[14]

The Anglo-American abolition movement assiduously cultivated transnational ties. The PAS opened correspondence not just with the Amis des Noir but also with the revolutionary envoys of the French Republic to Saint-Domingue, Sonthonax and Raimond, in the late 1790s. French abolitionists recommended to the PAS's care the colored and black refugees leaving the island for Philadelphia and reported on the victories of Louverture. In 1806 Wilberforce and Zachary Macaulay renewed the SEAST's correspondence with the American abolition societies, and James Pemberton, the president of the PAS, corresponded with the Abbé Henri Grégoire. After slave trade abolition,

British abolitionists launched yet another campaign on the eve of the Congress of Vienna, the meeting of European nations called by Metternich to stem the tide of French revolutionary republicanism. They collected three-quarters of a million signatures on petitions to pressure the British government to work for the international prohibition of the African slave trade. They also urged continental abolitionists such as the Prussian naturalist and geographer Alexander von Humboldt and Madame de Staël and her abolitionist family in France to secure an international ban on the slave trade. British abolitionists played an important role in making slave trade prohibition a part of foreign policy in the nineteenth century, but they cannot be held responsible for the manner in which the British government used it to further its national and imperial interests. Within the British colonies they demanded a registry of slaves and amelioration of harsh slave laws, seeding their final campaign for the abolition of slavery.[15] They also bequeathed a legacy of mass mobilization to American abolitionists.

ABOLITION IN THE EARLY AMERICAN REPUBLIC

Contrary to conventional wisdom, the abolition movement persisted and broadened its reach in the early Republic. Quaker and abolition societies pressured the new federal government to act against the slave trade and slavery. In 1789 the Yearly Meeting of Quakers from the middle states sent an anti–slave trade petition to the recently organized federal Congress, precipitating a debate over slavery along sectional lines. While the South Carolina and Georgia representatives opposed the petition and ridiculed the Quakers, Elias Boudinot of New Jersey, the former president of the Continental Congress, came to their defense. The petition was tabled. In 1790 a PAS memorial to Congress signed by Benjamin Franklin as its president went further to argue for "*securing the blessings of liberty to the people of the United States . . . without distinction of Colour.*" Southerners questioned the constitutionality of antislavery petitions, and Madison intervened to commit the memorial. The Select Committee of the House of Representatives stated that Congress had no authority to end the slave trade before 1808 or interfere with slavery in the states. But it could exercise its power to regulate the conditions of the slave trade and tax slave imports. Lower south slaveholders attacked Quakers as traitors to the nation and demanded an informal gag on the subject of slavery as the price of union, threatening secession. Boudinot again came to the defense of abolitionists, vouching for Franklin's sanity, which had been questioned by southern congressmen. On the eve of his death, Franklin skewered their proslavery speeches in satirical

letters defending Algerian piracy and the enslavement of Christians. An abolitionist pamphlet, *The American in Algiers* (1797), revived that comparison in an
imaginary conversation between an American captive from Boston in Algiers
and an enslaved African in the United States.[16]

Antislavery petitions gave rise to more exchanges between southern slaveholders and abolitionists. In 1792 the abolition societies of states from Rhode
Island to Virginia submitted memorials to Congress calling for the abolition of
slavery and restriction of the slave trade. While some were careful to ask only for
the exercise of constitutional powers, others evoked revolutionary principles to
declare that "the whole system of African slavery is unjust in its nature." Southern congressmen claimed that since the memorials were unconstitutional and
incited slave rebellions, they should be expunged from the house journals. This
attempted gag measure elicited a lengthy protest from Warner Mifflin. Warning that the blood of oppressed Africans would cling to the garments of every
member of Congress, he protested its failure to act on the slave trade and its acceptance of southern preconditions not to act against slavery in territories ceded
to the federal government. Mifflin proclaimed that a "natural black skin" was
never the occasion of degradation before God and that Congress should show
as much concern over enslaved Africans in America as they do over captured
Americans in Algiers. The South Carolinian William Loughton Smith, known
for his vociferous proslavery speeches, dismissed Mifflin's remonstrance as the
"mere rant and rhapsody of a meddling fanatic," and the House decided to
return his memorial to him. Mifflin led a virtually one-man antislavery lobby
in Washington at this time, cornering southern congressmen on the subject
of slavery. An object of both Brissot's and Crèvecoeur's admiration, he died
in 1798.[17]

During the first two decades of the Republic, abolition societies published
pamphlets by influential religious, political, and intellectual figures in the
north. They made a case for the complete eradication of slavery and, sometimes, of racial distinctions. This was especially true in Connecticut, a center of
New Divinity antislavery. In 1788 Simeon Baldwin, the future secretary of the
state abolition society, in his Fourth of July address warranted that the revolution was not complete until the slave trade and slavery were abolished. Antislavery Calvinist clergymen such as the Yale presidents Ezra Stiles and Timothy
Dwight and Federalist lawyer politicians founded the Connecticut Society for
the Promotion of Freedom and Relief of Persons Unlawfully held in Bondage in
1790. Stiles, influenced by Hopkins, came to regret his purchase of a slave boy,
whom he manumitted and educated. He wrote the constitution of the society,
became its first president, and ministered to African Americans in Newport and

New Haven. The Connecticut society published several influential pamphlets initially delivered as addresses to the society, in which it urged the immediate ending of the slave trade and the abolition of slavery. The society's Committee of Correspondence, like the PAS and NYMS, intervened in cases in which slaveholders tried to elude the state's emancipation law or when attempts were made to kidnap free blacks.

Painting a benign picture of New England's history of slavery, Congregational ministers like Jedidiah Morse and Dwight contrasted southern and West Indian slavery with Connecticut's republican and Christian culture. Rev. James Dana of New Haven, known for his religious liberalism, spoke of Christian liberty as opposed to the history of the slave trade for the better part of an address he gave in 1790. Dana admitted that all slavery was obnoxious and condemned ideas of Africans being a different and inferior "species" as going against the "Mosaic history of the creation." He called for the spiritual and political regeneration of the Republic. In 1792 Stiles's protégé Rev. William Patten of Newport delivered a similar anti–slave trade address.[18]

Connecticut abolitionists' religious and political jeremiads dissented radically from the spread-eagle nationalism of the early Republic. The anticlerical Republican Zephaniah Swift reached the same conclusions as these ministers in his address of 1791 to the state society in Hartford. He decried America as "the theatre of most extensive slavery" and railed that "the black native of the burning climes of Africa, and the copper-coloured savages of the wilds of America, have long mourned the day Columbus sailed from Europe." In his address Jonathan Edwards Jr. called racial slavery a worse crime than the political enslavement of Americans by Britain. Ridiculing race as a reason to enslave and the idea that God condemned any part of humankind to perpetual slavery, he predicted the intermingling of races in an appendix. Edwards argued quixotically that slaveholders should compensate "Negroes for the injury which they had done them" by either intermarrying with them and "raising their colour to partial whiteness" or leaving "to them all their real estates." That year the Connecticut society sent a petition and address to Congress criticizing "the unhappy policy of this country, to impose slavery and want on those who are brought from Africa; while we hold forth the prospects of liberty and plenty to emigrants from all other countries." The Yale graduate and poet Joel Barlow in his *The Columbiad* warned of God's vengeance for "the nation's crime" that held "inthrall'd the millions of my race," speaking as Atlas, the guardian of Africa.[19]

Two of the early Republic's foremost educators made clear their distaste for slavery. Noah Webster, the lexicographer known for his dictionary, published *Effects of Slavery on Morals and Industry* (1793), an expanded version of his oration before the Connecticut society. Webster chose to construct his anti-slavery argument pragmatically, not evoking natural rights, law, and humanity, which, he pointed out, others had done, but policy, interest, and necessity, meeting proslavery opponents "upon their own ground." Slavery, he said, produced laziness and criminality that led some, like Jefferson, to speculate on the alleged inferiority of blacks. Webster contended that "*oppression is the mother of all crimes*" and that slavery had similar effects on slaves of all nations. The etymologist pointed out that serfs had long been referred to as villains and knaves, and Anglo-Saxons called their servants *lazzi*, the root of the English word *lazy*. While Webster opposed immediate abolition of slavery in the South, he rejected colonization. It was not only impractical but also unfair to black people, most of whom "are born in this country and are total strangers to Africa" and "a flagrant act of injustice, inferior only to the first act of enslaving them." Instead, slaves should be converted into free tenants and eventually propertied republican citizens. Webster insisted that emancipation was beneficial because slavery, like serfdom, was detrimental to national industry and wealth, an incipient free labor critique of slavery. By the 1830s Webster called abolitionists "absolutely deranged" and, departing from his earlier analysis of slavery as a national evil, said slavery was "a great sin and calamity, but it is not our [i.e., a northern] sin."[20]

Besides Webster, the Connecticut-born bookseller and publisher Caleb Bingham wrote well-reasoned denunciations of slavery and racial superiority. Bingham ran a private school for girls in Boston, and his first book of grammar for young women outsold Webster's dictionary. A prolific author, he published *The American Preceptor* in 1794 and the more famous *The Columbian Orator* in 1797. The latter contained an exchange between a master and a runaway slave, which inspired Douglass's oratory, who took its lessons to heart. Bingham also reprinted the speeches of Pitt, Fox, and Rev. Samuel Miller of the NYMS in his book. Like other abolitionists, Bingham inverted the categories of savagery and civilization when writing about Europeans and Africans and Native Americans.[21]

Though Bingham, like Barlow, was a Jeffersonian, Federalist New England proved to be a breeding ground for an antislavery culture. In the 1790s Federalists emerged as critics of the Jacobin reign of terror in France and their American Republican allies. The administration of John Adams passed the Alien and Sedition Acts to root out foreign radicalism. Federalist criticism of Jacobinism complemented their indictment of slavery and the slaveholding Virginia dynasty. In his address of 1794 before the Connecticut society, Theodore Dwight objected to the three-fifths clause. He noted, "Enjoying no rank in the community, and possessing no voice, either in elections, or legislation, the slaves are bro't into existence, in the Constitution of the United States, merely to afford opportunity for a few more of their masters, to tyrannize over their liberties." The southern states especially, where "domestic despotism rides triumphantly over the liberties and happiness of thousands of our fellow-creatures," were "pretended republics." A republic, according to him, had no right to make any law on slavery except as compensation to slaves. He cited the rebellion in Saint-Domingue, where slaves attacked their "tyrannical masters" and "established themselves on the firm pillars of freedom and independence" and warned that the slave South might suffer the same fate.

Drolly calling societies formed to promote freedom in a republic a solecism, Dwight asked for immediate abolition. His brother Timothy Dwight published his epic poem "Greenfield Hill" as part of the society's campaign to pass a law for general emancipation in Connecticut. In it he portrayed slavery as being contrary to republicanism. Later, he wrote a poem hailing Gabriel's abortive rebellion in Virginia. In 1795 the Massachusetts Federalist congressman Samuel Dexter proposed an amendment to the Naturalization Act of 1790 that excluded all nonwhites. Aimed at the fleeing planters from Saint-Domingue, it required all immigrants to the United States to renounce slaveholding. Federalist clergymen were incensed with Jefferson's suggestion that blacks belonged to a different species, pointing out that it was "the strongest argument for their state of slavery." They believed that slaveholders, not slaves, constituted the gravest threat to the Republic. Small wonder that black men who enjoyed the right to vote in the early Republic tended to vote Federalist.[22]

The emergence of New England as a center of antislavery belies the notion of the region as a conservative backwater until the emergence of Garrisonian abolition. In Rhode Island the Providence Society for Abolishing the Slave Trade, founded in 1789, led the abolitionist charge. One of its stalwart members, George Benson, became Garrison's father-in-law. Hopkins, who had complained to Moses Brown about forming an abolition society that restricted its purpose to the slave trade only, made sure that he included the elimination of both the slave trade and slavery as worthy abolitionist goals in his discourse of 1793 before the society. Reiterating that slavery violated the precepts of Christianity, Hopkins regretted that the Constitution allowed for the continuance of the slave trade and that Congress had neglected to pass any law against it or to promote the emancipation and education of American slaves. The Providence society also assisted those held illegally in slavery to gain their freedom. Northern slaveholders repeatedly accused abolitionists of encouraging slaves to run away and hastening their emancipation.[23]

Instead of letting the issue of slavery subside, abolitionists consolidated and stepped up their activities. In 1793, in order to coordinate antislavery efforts at the national level, the NYMS called for all the abolition societies to meet in a convention in Philadelphia. Nine societies gathered at the American Convention of Abolition Societies in 1794. It planned to replicate at a national level the work of the state societies: sending memorials and petitions to federal and state governments, publishing antislavery pamphlets, assisting free black people, and expediting emancipation. In an address to the people of the United States written by a committee led by Rush, the convention announced the abolition of "domestic slavery in our country" as its goal. Slavery, the address stated, was a species of despotism that imperiled the revolutionary effort to overthrow the "tyranny of kings" and threatened the safety and liberties of the new nation. It ought to be opposed also as a matter of "sound policy." The convention called for an immediate end to the slave trade and proposed founding more abolition societies to work for the improvement of the condition of Africans and their descendants. In its memorial to Congress the convention asked that American citizens be prohibited from participating in the slave trade and the outfitting of slavers in American ports, a request which soon became law.

In 1795 the convention concentrated on antislavery action at the state rather than federal level. Through much of its existence it regularly issued addresses to all state societies to coordinate abolitionist activity. The convention also composed memorials asking South Carolina and Georgia, which lacked abolition societies, to end the slave trade and pass manumission and gradual emancipation laws. It called upon all societies to take steps toward "the absolute repeal" of all laws on slavery in their states. The 1790s were the high point of abolitionist activism in the early Republic. By 1798 the convention was complaining of a lack of representatives from state societies. It continued to meet until 1838, although it stopped meeting annually after 1806, and abolition societies gradually became defunct in New England and most of the southern states. In the end only Pennsylvania and New York maintained a substantial presence in the convention. The PAS served as a center of organized abolitionist activism not just in Pennsylvania but also in the bordering slave states of Virginia, Maryland, and Delaware.[24]

The American Convention of Abolition Societies anticipated the controversies over slavery in the nineteenth century. In an address to the people of the United States in 1804, the convention pointed to the revival of the African slave trade in South Carolina in 1803, antimanumission laws in the South, the kidnapping of free blacks, and the expansion of slavery in the west as urgent reasons to continue the abolition crusade. Citing the precedent of the Northwest Ordinance, it submitted a memorial to Congress asking for a law to restrict the spread of slavery into the newly acquired Louisiana territory. While assuring its critics that it did not mean to violate state or property laws, the convention called for general emancipation. Despite discouraging news from abolitionists in the South, the convention of 1805 appended a model act for the gradual abolition of slavery to its minutes to be submitted to the states where slavery was still legal. In 1806 the convention urged the state societies to submit petitions to Congress to exercise its constitutional powers and end a resurgent domestic slave trade that would carry around a million slaves from the upper south states to the expanding Cotton Kingdom.[25]

After the abolition of the African slave trade in 1808, the convention concentrated on working for abolition in the South. It argued that "nearly a million human beings remain in a state of abject bondage in the United States" and that "those who have been liberated . . . require the fostering care of the advocates of freedom." The convention reiterated its goals of preventing the "inhuman practice of kidnapping," attending to the "religious, moral and literary improvement" of free blacks, and *the gradual and final extinction of slavery in the United States.* It also revived international antislavery connections, printing a letter from Wilberforce and recommending Clarkson's history of the abolition of the slave trade and officially thanking him for his labors. By 1812 the convention added a new society in Kentucky to its ranks and promptly issued an encouraging address to it. Founded in 1808, the Kentucky Abolition Society had only fifty members, but its contact with the PAS and the convention helped alleviate the hostility shown toward its activities.[26]

Abolitionists remained a dedicated minority in the early Republic even as antislavery sentiment made considerable headway in popular culture. Philip Freneau, the so-called bard of the revolution, had written a poetic condemnation of West Indian rather than southern slavery. Wheatley inspired the anonymous "Matilda," who wrote that Phillis proved "her Country's claim To Freedom, and her own to deathless Fame." The well-known poet Sarah Wentworth Apthorp Morton of Boston published, under the pseudonym Philenia, "Tears of Humanity" (1791) and the popular "The African Chief" (1792), which was reprinted several times. Her "Beacon Hill" called attention to American slavery: "If mid their bloom the cultivating captive bleed!" Antislavery sentiment entered the American stage with the performance of popular British plays such as Thomas Southerne's *Oroonoko,* based on Aphra Behn's novel, and George Coleman's *Inkle and Yarico.* The Philadelphia hairdresser John Murdock wrote two antislavery plays, *The Triumphs of Love, or Happy Reconciliations* (1795), sponsored by Rush and Tench Coxe of the PAS, and *The Politicians, or A State of Things* (1798).[27]

Abolitionists used print culture to make their case against slavery in the early American public sphere. In his widely distributed *Remarks on Slavery* (1806), John Parrish, a Quaker abolitionist from Maryland, addressed American citizens, especially those who held office and were slaveholders. "Enslaving our fellow-men . . . [was] a national evil" which "will . . . most assuredly draw down national judgments," he exclaimed, and "the axe should be laid to the root of this corrupt tree." He pointed to the growing domestic slave trade and to slaves sold "into unconditional bondage" in the "Southern Governments." This trade, Parrish contended, equaled the African slave trade in its cruelty: black people were driven like a "herd of cattle," jailed, kidnapped, and stowed in garrets and ships. The fugitive slave law operated to apprehend fleeing blacks and return them to southern slavery while the "fugitives for murder or theft" went free. The "immediate liberation of all slaves," he admitted, "may be attended with some difficulty," and he asked southerners to consider Jefferson's plan for gradual emancipation and colonization. Instead of repatriation to Africa, Parrish, who helped several slaves gain their freedom, recommended that each black family be given two hundred acres of land in the "western wilderness." A Quaker missionary, Parrish did not propose land for blacks at the cost of Native American nations. He had long promoted a lasting peace between Native Americans and the U.S. government. He died in 1809.[28]

Thomas Branagan, a former Irish slave trader, also published a plan for emancipation at this time. He counseled that steps be taken to mitigate slavery. Slaves should be educated and Christianized, hold property, be guaranteed a minimum allowance in food and clothing, have weekends off, and have their families protected; excessive punishments should be outlawed and slaveholders prosecuted for the murder of slaves. Branagan wrote an epic poem against slavery, "Avenia." The juvenile version, "The Penitential Tyrant," condemns British imperialism: "Their complicated villany explore / From Afric's golden coast to India's shore; / Their pride, rage, lust, and tyranny extend." In "Serious Remonstrances" Branagan abandoned abolition and proposed the colonization of free blacks. Quoting Jefferson and turning on African American leaders who had supported him, he called blacks "the inveterate enemies of America" and ended with a racist diatribe against intermixture. The North should welcome hardy and laborious immigrants from Ireland and Germany rather than free blacks. He knew that such words would anger abolitionists who planned on "liberating the Africans of the South, and manufacturing them into citizens of

the North." By the 1830s he was a staunch advocate of black removal.[29] Branagan proved to be an apostate to abolition.

AFRICAN AMERICANS AND EARLY ABOLITION

The first abolition movement bucked the trend that defined the American
Republic as a white man's country. One of the main aims of early abolition
societies was to seek "relief of free negroes" and to "improve the condition of
the free black population." Rush, whose involvement in organized abolition
began in the 1790s after he freed his slave, asserted in his presidential address to
the PAS that "when we have broken his chains and restored to the African his
rights, the work of justice and benevolence is not done, newborn citizens must
receive instruction, educate him in the highest branches of sciences and learning, prove to enemies of truth that despite the degrading influence of slavery
they are in no wise inferior to the more fortunate inhabitants of Europe and
America." Abolitionist notions of racial uplift were tied to a commitment to
civic equality. As Hopkins put it, "Let us consult and determine what we may
do in favor of the blacks among us, especially those who are free, in protecting
them from oppression and injuries, . . . and promote morality, virtue, and religion among them, and providing for the education of their children in useful
learning, that they may be raised to an acknowledged equality with the white
people."[30]

Abolitionists' plans for the protection and improvement of blacks included
securing citizenship for them. In an address in 1789 the PAS announced that
"attention to emancipated black people, it is . . . to be hoped, will become a
branch of our national policy." Its "committee for the improvement of the condition of the free negroes" consisted of twenty-four members divided into four
subcommittees on inspection, guardians, education, and employment. The
Committees of Inspection and Guardians intervened regularly in instances of
abuse, as in the case of John Trusty, who was "cruelly beaten" by his foreman.
The PAS had a warrant issued for the foreman's arrest. It assisted black people
in looking for employment and required two PAS attorneys to be present when
indentures were contracted. In 1788 the NYMS had established a Committee for Preventing Irregular Conduct in Free Negroes to regulate free blacks'
behavior. But in 1796 the preamble of its revised constitution stated that "struggling with poverty against obstinate and hostile prejudices, and habituated to
submission, the unhappy Africans are least able to assert their rights."[31]

Abolitionists' assistance and advice, while paternalistic, was nonetheless invaluable to a newly freed people. In 1795 the American Convention of Abolition

Societies recommended that state societies work for the amelioration of restrictive laws against blacks, the education of black children, and improving the
condition of free blacks. A year later, an address to "Free Africans" dispensed
a few "articles of Advice . . . dictated by the purest regard for your welfare": to
attend a place of public worship, to acquire education "as early as possible,"
to tend to the "instruction of your children" and teach them "useful trades," to
solicit help from friends before signing contracts, to be diligent and frugal, avoid
alcohol, "dissipation, and vice," to save their earnings, and to display "good
conduct." In 1797, adding gaming to its list of vices, it went on to voice a compliment: "We can with peculiar satisfaction inform you, that schools and places
of worship have been established, and that they are well attended by people of
your color."[32]

Early abolitionists visualized a better position for free blacks in society than
as menial laborers not fit for political equality. In its address to black Philadelphians in 1800, the PAS not only repeated the convention's homilies but added
that besides educating their children, free blacks should teach their children
useful trades or make them "farmers, rather than house servants." The reality
was far different. The PAS reported that a majority of free blacks in Philadelphia
were day laborers, waiters, mechanics, and seamen. The convention warned
that "in vain do you liberate the African, while you neglect to furnish him with
the means of properly providing for himself, and of becoming a useful member
of the community." By 1804 it changed its name to the American Convention
for Promoting the Abolition of Slavery and Improving the Condition of the African Race. It looked forward to "converting" slaves into upstanding republican
citizens.

Racial paternalism was not the only rationale for abolitionists' concern with
black improvement. The Delaware society's address invoked compensation:
"Let it be deeply impressed in our minds that we owe the descendants of Africa
a debt of immense magnitude. We are bound by the laws of equity, by the solemn requisitions of justice to pay that debt. Can we discharge our obligations in
any way so effectually as by communicating to the children of those (from the
sweat of whose brow we have derived many of our external comforts) a portion
of that knowledge which has been the source of our enjoyments and power?"
The NYMS noted, "Nor does it become us to stigmatise or reproach the blacks,
for vices which are chiefly produced by the state to which our injustice has
reduced them. We ought rather to double our exertions to repair the wrongs we
have inflicted on them, and remove as far as possible the evil consequences of
Slavery." Like the PAS, the NYMS encouraged the education of black children
and apprenticeship of black boys under skilled master craftsmen.[33]

Abolitionists claimed that making free black people model citizens of the Republic would hasten the demise of racial slavery. The convention's address to free blacks in 1804 argued, "As you are free men, we wish you to place a proper estimate on your privileges, and to act in a manner becoming your character; that, by your worthy conduct, you may destroy the prejudices which some persons entertain against you." The convention thought abolition societies should meet with free blacks regularly to instruct them on their religious and moral duties. It stressed independence, temperance, and education and reminded them that they affected the future of those still enslaved. The New Jersey society insisted that the behavior of free blacks contrasted well "with that of the poorer class of whites" and that many exhibited "sobriety, industry, oeconomy, and uprightness, well worthy of imitation." In 1816 the Delaware society reported its pleasure at the "state of the free black population," especially given the hardships that the enslaved and they endured. The PAS, while exhorting African Americans to become virtuous citizens, complained that racial prejudices had not been abolished after emancipation, as whites restricted blacks to the most "menial offices."[34]

Model black behavior and institutions like the black churches and schools that abolitionists admired as evidence of the success of emancipation and black achievement provoked rather than deflected racism. Many whites took umbrage at African Americans who supposedly stepped out of their place by displaying economic independence, political assertiveness, and social skills. In the context of the disfranchisement and economic plight of most free blacks, early abolitionists held progressive ideas about race and class. The fear of a large class of vagrant poor who would become public charges or the source of social disorder haunted colonial society, and poor laws had influenced emancipation policy. In New England so-called strangers were regularly warned out of colonial towns. Part of abolition societies' concern over free black employment and education stemmed from this history and from debates in northern states during emancipation over the upkeep of freed slaves. At the same time, abolitionists imagined a racially inclusive republic composed of worthy black citizens.

The convention also sought to protect itself from charges of sedition in a post–Haitian Revolution era rife with fear of slave rebellions. The Virginia abolition societies reported to the convention that Gabriel's conspiracy had a chilling effect on antislavery efforts and led to repressive measures against free blacks and Sunday schools operated by them. In 1801 the convention sent five thousand copies of an address to the state societies deploring the attempted rebellion but advising gradual emancipation in the South as a solution. The convention warned free blacks to be careful "in all your communications with those of your brethren who remain in slavery." Clearly, abolitionists were worried when slaveholders and southern state governments used the pretext of rebellion to clamp down on their efforts and on free blacks. The convention asked abolition societies to consider themselves "the paternal protectors and friends of the people of colour" and acknowledged the strength of racial prejudice, calling for more antislavery publications to convert white Americans.[35]

Abolitionist uplift, particularly in black education, bore fruit. In 1789 a group of young Quaker men in Philadelphia formed a society for the education of black people. A "free school for the instruction of children of color of both sexes" operated since 1793 by a black woman, Eleanor Harris, received aid from the PAS. The PAS funded schools run by the local black leaders Rev. Absalom Jones and Cyrus Bustill and ran an evening school for black men as well as a Sunday school. The black abolitionist Quomony Clarkson, who probably chose his African abolitionist name, taught in the PAS schools. In 1813 the PAS's Committee of Education formed itself into a board of education and built a school, Clarkson Hall (also named after the British abolitionist) for black boys, and it aided a school for black girls run by Elizabeth Clendinen. It also founded Sandiford Hall, named for the Quaker abolitionist, as a library and meeting place for African Americans. The PAS board of education successfully lobbied to have black public schools established by the Philadelphia Board of Education, and its Clarkson Hall became a popular venue for Clarkson associations dedicated to black education. The PAS's educational activism continued after the war. It established the Laing school in Mt. Pleasant, South Carolina, for freed people, the school where the civil rights activist Septima Clark obtained her education. The Maryland Abolition Society took out a subscription for a school in 1792 and erected the African Academy in 1797. Five years later African Americans purchased the academy and established a Methodist church in the building. The black abolitionists Daniel Coker and William Watkins served as longtime teachers there.[36]

The NYMS's African schools were among the most successful examples of cooperation between organized abolition and the independent free black communities. Since founding the African Free School in 1787, the NYMS made the "moral and intellectual improvement" of free blacks a central goal. Funded by the abolitionist John Murray, it was modeled on the Quaker Free Schools, and although initially restricted to free blacks it opened its doors to enslaved children. The NYMS established a female institute, and its schools were incorporated in 1794. Between 1799 and 1805 the black educator and activist John Teasman was appointed teacher of the African school. He successfully introduced the Lancasterian system of education, which relied on one teacher and senior students to educate others. The NYMS reported that Teasman "executes commendably the trust reposed in him" and commented favorably on the school's progress throughout his tenure. In 1804 it reported that the school had over a hundred students. Teasman, a Republican, left the school partly because of political differences with the Federalist-dominated NYMS. Early black abolitionists, including Peter Williams Jr., William Hamilton, Henry Sipkins, and Adam Carman, were students of his. Prominent black abolitionists in antebellum New York were graduates of these schools, among them James McCune Smith, Henry Highland Garnet, Samuel Ringgold Ward, George Downing, and Alexander Crummell.[37]

In 1808 the NYMS itself was incorporated in order to better assist its African schools and sewing schools for female students. In 1812 it reported that the African Free School was flourishing under the administration of the British educator Charles C. Andrews, with 130 students of both sexes. The black community also employed teachers for three other schools and formed a society to start a school for black orphans. A new public school sponsored by them also drew some black children. The convention commended the black orphans' school run by African Americans. "The best fruits of education" had begun to appear among free blacks, who revealed a "just conception of the value of education, and a provident and active concern for those who may be destitute of obtaining it." In 1828 students of the African Free School sent several tokens of their appreciation, including antislavery poems and letters, to the convention. The twelve-year-old George Allen wrote that he and his schoolmates wished that they may "prosper in your arduous and glorious undertakings; and that all your labours may be crowned with success." Fifteen-year-old George Moore thanked them for the "great things" they had done, and Eliver Reason prayed that the "Supreme Being" reward them "ten fold for the good you do for us." The young Isaiah De Grasse wrote that "advocates of abolition . . . deserve the gratitude and thanks of our whole race." A young McCune Smith was chosen to commend the visiting Marquis de Lafayette "as a friend to African Emancipation."

Community leaders worked with the NYMS to encourage and increase enrollment in the schools despite ongoing conflicts over their administration. The schools' curriculum in the liberal arts and vocational training was broad ranging and included the history and geography of Africa; the girls' education was confined to basic literacy and domestic arts. Black women such as Isaiah De Grasse's mother, Maria, and Peter Williams's sister Mary formed the African Dorcas Association to sew clothes for needy students. In 1832, when Andrews adopted views on colonization that were unpopular with the black community, enrollment in his school dropped. A strict disciplinarian, he was taken to task for his caning of students, and ultimately the trustees replaced him with a black teacher, John Adams. By 1834, the last year they were controlled by the NYMS before being incorporated into the public school system, the seven African schools reported between fourteen and sixteen hundred students. Lacking the NYMS's relationship to the black community, the schools saw a drop in enrollment, and under the public school system they never regained their former glory.[38]

Perhaps the most important work done by early abolitionists was their representation of enslaved black people in their quest for freedom and their vigorous prosecution of cases involving wrongful enslavement and kidnapping. The records of the two largest, longest-standing abolition societies, the PAS and NYMS, are replete with hundreds of instances in which abolitionists intervened on behalf of enslaved Africans in the courts and against abusive masters. Grassroots black activism sought abolitionist intervention, and black leaders acted as conduits between the enslaved and the abolition societies. Many northern slaves gained their own and their family's freedom through purchase and running away. The NYMS and particularly the PAS also helped slaves raise funds to purchase their freedom and that of family members. The abolitionists' assistance, too quickly dismissed by historians as merely paternalistic and insignificant, constitutes an important part of the story of the first emancipation. Committed members of the NYMS standing committee like the Quaker Jacob Mott, in whose home the committee met in the 1790s, and its lawyers, including Melancton Smith and Daniel Tompkins, intervened in cases of abuse. The committee showed remarkable humility about the limitations of its efforts, noting in 1791 that its purview extended to the city and not to the rest of the state or even the neighboring state of New Jersey, which lacked an abolition society at this time and where the PAS intervened occasionally in cases of wrongful enslavement. The committee saw African Americans as friendless and unprotected while their oppressors were powerful and strong, and the NYMS saw itself as being misunderstood and misrepresented. It nevertheless resolved to "render property in slaves precarious" and "traffic in them disreputable," to do away with "objections raised against their manumission," and to combat the racial prejudices of the "misinformed" as well as the "malevolent."

The reports of the committee teem with hundreds of instances in which it intervened on behalf of slaves in cases of wrongful enslavement in the 1790s, including cases of Indian slavery. Before emancipation the NYMS successfully prevented slaveholders from incarcerating their recalcitrant slaves in city prisons like Bridewell. Alexander Rhodes won his freedom on the claim that his master intended to free him. Rosanna Cook sought the help of the NYMS against her master. Her husband, William Cook, had paid for her freedom, but as he was at sea she was kept enslaved. The NYMS also took up several cases of brutality, indicting one Amos Broad and his wife for "inhuman and barbarous treatment of their slaves" and intervening in the case of a fourteen-year-old girl confined to the hospital for "severe laceration." The committee kept meticulous records of cases it adjudicated, noting where they had been successful or unsuccessful in gaining the freedom of the claimants in "discharged" cases. It took several cases of "unlawful slavery" per month. In 1808 it reported that the situation of enslaved children called for intervention because unprincipled masters did not register their birth dates and retained them in servitude long after they had reached the legal age of freedom.

While the number of local cases of wrongful enslavement dwindled, the committee continued to prosecute cases of slaves from far-off places like Jamaica, Saint-Domingue, Nova Scotia, Madeira, and even Calcutta. Complicated jurisdictional issues allowed some, like the Haitian refugee and widow Volunbrun, to move from New York to Baltimore with her slaves despite the efforts of the NYMS and free blacks. In Maryland the abolitionist Daniel Raymond prosecuted the case, but the widow sold the slaves to New Orleans. Cases of the kidnapping of free blacks into southern slavery, especially after the passage of the Fugitive Slave Act of 1793, were also prosecuted by the NYMS. By 1815 the committee noted that while acts of kidnapping had become rare and its caseload was dropping dramatically, the "spirit of oppression" still prevailed. In its heyday the NYMS helped to attain the freedom of hundreds and to enforce state laws against slavery and the slave trade. Teasman, who had a falling out with the society, had only praise for "the ingenious and heroic exploits of the standing Committee of the Manumission Society in the diminution of slavery and oppression" and in maintaining the African schools.[39]

Even more impressive than the activities of the NYMS in securing black freedom were those of the PAS. The PAS, which had over two thousand members in the early nineteenth century, intervened and represented thousands of enslaved black people not just in Pennsylvania but also in bordering slave states where folks sought its assistance. The PAS Acting Committee, like the NYMS Standing Committee, dedicated itself to fighting cases of wrongful enslavement and the kidnapping of free black people. The most active were a "lawyerly" cadre consisting of such famous legal minds as William Rawle and also the activist lawyers Thomas Shipley, Thomas Earle, and David Paul Brown, who prosecuted cases of wrongful enslavement, and activists like the Quaker abolitionist Isaac T. Hopper, whose annals of fighting for black freedom became a staple of the Garrisonian *National Anti-Slavery Standard*. Shipley, Earle, Brown, and

Hopper lived long enough to join the second wave of abolitionism. Black activism undergirded the PAS's legal strategies. Fugitive slaves as well as free blacks and term slaves secured the services of PAS lawyers through the city's activist black clergy. Hundreds of slaves from surrounding slave states sought Shipley's and Hopper's assistance to buy their freedom and have their freedom recognized in the eyes of the law.[40]

The abolition societies, except for the PAS in its later years, did not have black members, although their constitutions did not contain any specific prohibition. This de facto exclusion distinguishes them from antebellum interracial abolitionism, but African Americans bridged the gap between the two waves of abolition. A graduate of the African School and one of the first ordained black priests of St. Philips's Episcopalian church, Peter Williams Jr. became a member of the Garrisonian American Anti-Slavery Society (AASS) and a mentor to McCune Smith. In 1806 Williams wrote an unsolicited letter to the convention acknowledging its "indefatigable zeal" on behalf of "the African race." He commended the "humane men, of different denominations" who "saw, and sympathized in our sorrows, and rising above the mean prejudices imbibed against us, united their efforts in order to rescue from slavery and misery the unfortunate sons of Africa." Abolitionists "fly to our assistance" when blacks were threatened by kidnappers and make sure that "equal justice is distributed to the black and white." He lauded their efforts to "elevate us to a state of respectability" and erect "schools to enlighten our minds." He thanked "ye philanthropic men for espousing the cause of an injured, an oppressed, and a despised race."[41]

Contemporary black leaders bore testimony to how important early abolitionism had been in securing black freedom and education. Jones wrote to Sharp thanking him not only for his donation to his church but also for his long "labours of love to our afflicted nation. You were our advocate when we had but few friends on the other side of the water." Olaudah Equiano thanked the Quakers after visiting their "free-school" for blacks in Philadelphia, "with our inmost love and warmest acknowledgements; and with the deepest sense of your benevolence, unwearied labour, and kind interposition, towards breaking the yoke of slavery, and to administer a little comfort and ease to thousands and tens of thousands of very grievously afflicted and too heavy burthened negroes." Richard Allen, the founder of the African Methodist Episcopal Church, wrote a paean to abolitionists, "A Short Address to the Friends of Him Who Hath no Helper." In his view, abolitionists had not only worked for black freedom and uplift but also were "not ashamed to call the most abject of our race brethren." Allen compared abolitionists and slaveholders in his sermon on charity, a life devoted to the poor and needy over against one that was devoted "to the pomps and vanities of this wicked world, or the gratification of the sinful lusts of the flesh." William Hamilton praised the NYMS for "planning the means of the emancipation of large numbers of the enslaved" and for establishing a "seminary of learning." For that, free blacks owed it their "highest tribute of gratitude."

Orations on the end of the slave trade by black abolitionists celebrated the Anglo-American abolition movement. According to Jones, "Abolition societies and individuals" as well as God "came down to deliver our suffering country-men from the hands of their oppressors." Williams dedicated his oration to "the different societies for the abolition of slavery" for "their assiduous, energetic, and benevolent exertions, in the cause of injured humanity." African Americans painstakingly mentioned and honored a long list of abolitionists starting with early Quaker abolitionists such as Lay, Sandiford, Woolman, Benezet, Dillwyn, and Rush and including British and French abolitionists like Sharp, Clarkson, Wilberforce, and the Abbé Grégoire.[42]

In heaping praise on abolitionists, these accomplished black men were hardly belittling their own efforts. Nor did they view themselves only as ob-jects of white benevolence. They purposefully bestowed recognition on those who had fought for black liberty as worthy allies. In New York several black societies and organizations were named in honor of abolitionists, among them the African Clarkson Society, the Wilberforce Philanthropic Society, and the Brooklyn African Woolman Benevolent Society, a testament to the antislavery consciousness of the free black community. Similarly, many of Philadelphia's black societies were named after Benezet and Rush. African Americans recog-nized pioneering black antislavery voices as well, naming their literary and fra-ternal organizations after Benjamin Banneker, Allen, and Wheatley. Jeremiah Gloucester reflected this comingling of abolitionist and black identities when he referred to his audience as members "of the Angolian society, and not only as members of the Angolian, but as the sons of Africa, and not only the sons of Africa . . . but as the Rush Beneficial, and not only as the Rush Beneficial, but as the Granville Harmony, Benezet Philanthropic, Wilberforce, Farmers, Mechanics, Warner Mifflin, and as the Union Sons of Africa, and not only as members of the different societies, but as fathers, as men."[43]

The activities of abolitionist societies in turn were shaped by their connec-tions to the black community. The Quaker abolitionist Elisha Tyson, a found-ing member of the MAS and an advocate of Indian rights, not only helped erect black schools and churches but also continued to fight for black freedom in Baltimore's streets and courts well into the nineteenth century. His death was mourned by the black community and in his native Philadelphia at Al-len's church, where he was lauded as "a very influential and efficient friend of the people of color, known for his many acts of humanity and hospitality for upwards of forty years." The Baltimore cabinetmaker John Needles, the brother of the Philadelphia abolitionist Edward Needles, sent furniture wrapped in antislavery literature to the South and ran a black school taught by an African American woman, Prudence Gardiner. American abolitionists also publicized voices of black protest. Parrish's pamphlet contained an appendix with African American petitions to Congress and James Forten's letter to Congressman George Thatcher of Massachusetts commending his defense of black petitioners. He also reprinted notices of runaway slaves, revealing how slave resistance inspired abolitionists.

Black abolitionists commemorated those who had formed enduring legal and political alliances with free black communities. On Shipley's death, a "numerous and respectable meeting of the people of colour" asked Robert Purvis, the only black member of the PAS, to deliver a eulogy of him, "whose unwearied exertions have contributed much to the melioration of the long neglected condition of our people." Shipley, they noted, had "devoted his talents, a great amount of time, and no small share of his pecuniary means" to the freedom of black people. Thousands of blacks attended his funeral in Philadelphia, and Purvis in his tribute praised Shipley for standing as a "vigilant watchman" over the emancipation laws of the state. In 1841 Purvis paid similar tribute to Brown, who went on to head the Pennsylvania Anti Slavery Society, presenting him with an engraved silver pitcher on behalf of the black community for "advocating . . . the liberties of the oppressed in this country." On Rush's death, "Africans . . . solicited leave to walk to the grave before his body, hung their pulpits in mourning, and delivered their unlettered and affectionate eulogiums to his memory." This racist and condescending observer remarked on the esteem in which Philadelphia's free black community held him. In his tribute to Mifflin, Allen pointed out that his "labors and anxiety were great for the freedom of our race; who for many years devoted his time to that service, and who has been instrumental in the hands of God, in liberating hundreds, if not thousands of the African race." Allen also praised "the most worthy and benevolent character of Dr. Benjamin Rush," who had assisted the independent black churches.[44] Despite its exclusive nature, first-wave abolitionism forged strong connections with free black communities.

AFRO-BRITISH ABOLITIONISTS

Black abolitionism in Britain came of age in the 1780s with the rise of the movement to abolish the slave trade. Afro-British writers followed in the footsteps of early black thinkers in adopting the "trope of the talking book." They gave birth to a radical tradition of black abolitionism that not only appealed to Western political and religious values but also subjected them to criticism. Their "mastery of form" attempted the "deformation of mastery," to use an argument applied to a later generation of African American writers.[45]

The preacher John Marrant exposed white Christian practice in his narrative of conversion and Indian captivity published in London in 1785. Marrant was converted by Whitefield and, before returning to his family in Charleston, South Carolina, spent three years with the Cherokees and Creeks, who he says "recollect that the white people drove them from the American shores." He describes his narrow escape from execution and his success at converting his captors to Christianity. On his return Marrant faces Christian slaveholders who torture their slaves for praying with him: "Men, women, and children were strip'd naked and tied, their feet to a stake, their hands to the arm of a tree, and so severely flogg'd that the blood ran from their backs and sides to the floor, to make them promise they would leave off praying, &c. though several of them fainted away with the pain and loss of blood, and lay upon the ground as dead for a considerable time after they were untied." In an adept role reversal, Marrant shows how Christianity redeems Indians' supposed savagery, and slavery converts nominal Christians into savages. Christian universalism was Marrant's response to modern racism designed to justify the enslavement and conquest of non-Europeans. Patronized by the Countess Huntingdon and ordained in her chapel, Marrant became a Methodist preacher to black loyalists in Nova Scotia and traveled between Canada, England, and the United States, where he developed close ties with the black Masonic leader Prince Hall. An advocate of the black exodus from Nova Scotia to Sierra Leone, he died in England in 1791.[46]

Unlike the little-known Marrant, the Afro-British writer Ignatius Sancho was touted on both sides of the Atlantic as proof of blacks' ability. Clarkson referred to his letters in his prize-winning essay. Jefferson dismissed the letters as "wild and extravagant," escaping "every restraint of reason and taste," and as "incoherent and eccentric." In case others judged his letters favorably, Jefferson concluded that it could not be proven whether Sancho was their sole author or had "received amendment" from others. Born during the Middle Passage, Sancho lived a life that personified that of an Atlantic Creole. His owner took him from Spanish New Granada, where he was baptized Ignatius by a Catholic priest, to England and gave him to three spinster sisters who added Sancho, after Miguel de Cervantes's Sancho Panza, to his name. Sancho attracted the attention of their powerful neighbor, the Duke of Montagu, known, like the Countess of Huntingdon, to be a patron of blacks. Sancho acquired an education under Montagu and after his patron's death was employed as a butler by his widow and son-in-law. The latter set Sancho up as a grocer when he was unable to continue as his valet owing to ill health. Sancho composed music and published two plays and a book, *Theory of Music*, lost to history. He died in 1780, and the letters he wrote in the 1760s and 1770s were published in 1782. His widow received over five hundred pounds from the approximately one thousand subscribers of his letters, which were so successful that they were republished in subsequent editions by his son.[47]

The abolitionist tone of Sancho's letters is significant. He admonishes Julius Soubise, a West Indian slave and a notorious rake, "Look around upon the miserable fate of almost all of our unfortunate colour—superadded to ignorance,—see slavery, and the contempt of those very wretches who rol in affluence from our labours superadded to this woeful catalogue—hear the ill-bred and heart-wracking abuse of the foolish vulgar." Sancho urges Laurence Sterne, the author of *Tristram Shandy*, to write on slavery, as "the subject, handled in your striking manner, would ease the yoke (perhaps) of many." In his letter to the abolitionist Jabez Fisher of Philadelphia, Sancho praises the Quakers and Benezet, "the friendly Author—as a being far superior to any great name upon your continent," whose writings on the "unchristian and most diabolical usage of my brother Negroes" and "the illegality—the horrid wickedness of the traffic—the cruel carnage and depopulation of the human species" Fisher had sent him. Referring to Wheatley as "genius in bondage," he judged that her poetry does "credit to nature" and does not reflect "the generosity of her master," who "glories in the *low vanity* of having in his wanton power a mind animated by Heaven."

Sancho writes that while he is grateful for the freedom and blessings he enjoys in Britain, its "conduct has been uniformly wicked in the East—West-Indies—and even on the cost of Guinea.—The grand object of English navigators—indeed of all Christian navigators—is money—money—money." He condemns "the Christians' abominable traffic for slaves" that "sours my blood." Sancho calls himself Africanus and states tersely, "I am not sorry I was born in Afric." His satirical references to himself as "a poor Blacky grocer," "a coal-black, jolly African," and "a poor, thick-lipped son of Afric!" expose British racism. Despite his criticism of Christian practice, Sancho expressed faith in the capacity of Christianity to overcome racism. Christ, he writes, "died for the sins of all—all—Jew, Turk, Infidel, and Heretic;—fair—sallow—brown—tawney—black—and you—and I—and every son and daughter of Adam."[48]

More than Sancho, Ottobah Cugoano deserves pride of place for publishing the first black abolitionist pamphlet, its title reminiscent of Clarkson's essay: *Thoughts and Sentiments on the Evil and Wicked Traffic of the Slavery and*

Commerce of the Human Species in 1787. A French translation of Cugoano's pamphlet was published the next year and an abridged version of it in 1791. In a short autobiographical note Cugoano explained that he was kidnapped and sold into slavery in Africa at the age of thirteen, enslaved in Grenada, and then was slave to one Alexander Campbell in the West Indies, who brought him to Britain in 1772. Cugoano was baptized John Stuart. On becoming free, he reverted to his African name and expressed a desire to emigrate to Sierra Leone and found a school. He died shortly after publishing his pamphlet. Cugoano, who may have published his pamphlet under the auspices of SEAST, quoted Sharp, Ramsay, Clarkson, and Benezet. In the second edition he mentioned Wilberforce as well as Lord Mansfield and Counsellor Hargrave (the lawyer for James Somerset).

Cugoano, though, did not simply replicate the premises of Anglo-American abolitionism but created a peculiar vantage, that of a black abolitionist. His collaboration with Equiano and other like-minded blacks in London led to the formation of a self-styled black abolitionist group of around seven to nine men, Sons of Africa, the name first used by Massachusetts slaves during the revolution. These men wrote letters to British abolitionists, and they must have met occasionally. Like their counterparts in America, free blacks in Britain named their societies and called themselves African as a mark of racial solidarity and of a new composite African identity. No longer claiming specific nationalities and ethnicities, they had become African in the Atlantic world. The Sons of Africa was a common moniker for early black abolitionists. The second edition of Cugoano's pamphlet was addressed to the Sons of Africa from "a Native."[49]

Not since Lay had any abolitionist excoriated slaveholders in the manner that Cugoano does. He called "the great and opulent banditti of slaveholders in the western part of the world" robbers and kidnappers. Cugoano acknowledged that he was using "harsh words and comparisons" to describe their "enormous wickedness and brutal avarice" and "atrocious crimes." Slaveholders were a "bramble of ruffians, barbarians . . . grown up to a powerful luxuriance in wickedness," and they were "at the head" of all "oppression and crimes." After describing the details of his own capture and incarceration during the Middle Passage, he refuted the proslavery argument of James Tobin, a West India planter. The condition of the African slave, he argued, was much worse than that of a poor Englishman, who, he observed, would not exchange his position with that of the slave. Cugoano admitted that Africans were involved in the slave trade and that slavery existed in Africa for criminals, debtors, and prisoners of war. But Africans had been further corrupted and vitiated "by their intercourse with Europeans" and could ill conceive the horrors of racial slavery in the Americas.

He scorned the racism of Hume and reversed the racial argument for slavery, referring to the "inhuman, barbarous European" and the "poor, unfortunate Black Africans." Cugoano drew a parallel between Africans and the enslaved children of Israel, as the chosen people of God, and warned that Europeans would be subject to judgment.[50]

If Cugoano's is the most uncompromising voice of eighteenth-century black abolitionism, Equiano's narrative of capture, enslavement, and freedom is the first abolitionist slave narrative, a prototype for the well-known nineteenth-century slave narratives. Equiano, too, uses his African name even though he was known by his given name in slavery, Gustavus Vassa. The literary scholar Vincent Carretta has raised the possibility that Equiano was not born in Africa, as he claimed. The evidence he has uncovered, a baptism record and the records of the Royal Navy, state that Equiano was born in South Carolina, but the places of birth of enslaved Africans were often misreported or assumed from their last known destination by persons doing the recording. The identity of displaced Africans was highly malleable and subject to arbitrary categorization by European authorities. Carretta's evidence, in short, is not definitive.[51]

Though it resembles travel and conversion narratives, Equiano's autobiography is primarily an abolitionist text sprinkled with observations on the injustice and absurdity of slavery and racism. The only substantial account of the trade from the perspective of enslaved Africans, it occupies a central place in the abolitionist literary canon. Published in 1789, it was reviewed widely (and favorably by Mary Wollstonecraft), published in nine editions, and translated into Dutch, German, French, and Russian. It gave Equiano a measure of financial security and some international renown. Its subscribers included Sharp, Ramsay, Clarkson, the Countess of Huntingdon, the Duke of Montagu, Cugoano, and Sancho's son. Wesley apparently read it on his deathbed. After the publication of his narrative, Equiano undertook a book tour of the British Isles. In 1791 antislavery Quakers and some New York City artisans active in revolutionary republican politics sponsored its publication in the United States. In 1827 the first black abolitionist newspaper, *Freedom's Journal*, cited Equiano's narrative as an early refutation of black intellectual inferiority, and ten years later Garrison and Isaac Knapp republished it in Boston. If early print culture represented "technologies of power" to non-Europeans, writers like Equiano used it as an instrument of black liberation.[52]

Equiano joined the abolition movement. He had approached Sharp for help in preventing John Annis from being shipped back to West Indian slavery and had alerted him to the infamous *Zong* case, in which the crew of a slaver threw more than 130 Africans overboard and drowned them to claim insurance. As the presiding judge, Lord Mansfield overturned the insurance claim, but the captain and crew were not tried for mass murder, as Sharp and Equiano wanted them to be. In 1785 Equiano presented an address of thanks to the Society of Friends on behalf of "those captivated, oppressed and afflicted people." A similar address in 1787 by the Sons of Africa to Sharp, signed also by Cugoano and four other Africans, thanked him for his "long, valuable and indefatigable labours and benevolence towards using every means to rescue our suffering brethren in slavery." Equiano published appeals to Parliament and letters in London newspapers commending abolitionists. He led a black delegation to the House of Commons and was received by Pitt and Dolben among others. Equiano defended Ramsay from his critics and entered into debate with such proslavery authors as Tobin, Gordon Trumbull, and Rev. Raymond Harris, who argued that the Bible sanctioned the slave trade. To kidnap Africans and keep them in "perpetual servitude" simply because they "differ in complexion" was, he warranted, unchristian and "a crime as unjustifiable as cruel." In a letter to William Dickson, a former private secretary to the governor of Barbados, Equiano and eight other Sons of Africa, including Cugoano, praised his "Letters on Slavery" as convincing to everyone "except the Oran Otang philosophers," indicting racists with their own fantastic theories.[53]

Equiano's narrative was central to his abolitionist activism. After describing his idyllic childhood in the kingdom of Benin among the Ibo and his kidnapping and separation from his sister, Equiano wrote about his terror in viewing a slave ship on the coast in which "a multitude of black people of every description" were "chained together." Describing his first reaction to Europeans, Equiano writes that he was in a world of "bad spirits" and fears being eaten by "white men with horrible looks, red faces, and long hair." Equiano presents an alternative to European stories of cannibalism and instead calls attention to the cannibalistic nature of the slave trade that figuratively consumed thousands of Africans. His classic description of the Middle Passage, the suffocating, disease-ridden holds of a slaver packed with Africans, is a literary equivalent of the *Brooks* illustration. As a slave aboard a British naval ship, Equiano recounts his sense of displacement when he wishes that his skin was the same color as that of a white playmate. On being taught the Bible, whose stories reminded him of the "laws and rules of my country" and "tended to impress our manners and customs more deeply in my memory," he adopts a new identity as a "black Christian."

Equiano's impressions of plantation slavery stress the barbarity of slaveholders. He describes a "black woman slave" whose mouth was fitted with an "iron muzzle" so that she "could scarcely speak." He drew attention to the sexual abuse of slave women and dwelt on slaves who had pieces of their flesh cut off and were tortured with lighted wax, iron hooks, and thumbscrews, locked in coffin-like wooden boxes, beaten till their bones were broken, and sold apart from their families. He ends this catalogue of horrors with an appeal for better treatment of slaves. Slavery, he concludes, is unchristian because it gave "one man a dominion over his fellows which God could never intend!" Equiano expresses a strong sense of kinship with cargoes of "poor oppressed natives of Africa" taken on board the ship he was serving and in a plantation on the Mosquito coast where he was an overseer. He notes as well the pious nature of the "unenlightened Indians" in contrast to the savagery of Christian slaveholders. His assessment of places is determined by the geography of plantation slavery. He is abused and mistreated in Georgia and South Carolina and writes fondly of Philadelphia. But even here, Equiano commented, free blacks "live in constant alarm for their liberty, which is but nominal." Despite his strong Christianity, Equiano writes approvingly of the continuance of African practices, rituals, and funeral traditions in places with large slave populations like Jamaica.

The turning point in Equiano's narrative is his purchase of his freedom. He writes, "Heavens! Who could do justice to my feelings at this moment? . . . My feet scarcely touched the ground for they were winged with joy." His happiness, he wrote, exceeded that of conquering heroes, the recovery of an infant by its mother, the sight of a port for a "weary hungry mariner," and the reunion of lovers. Even though Equiano uses biblical analogies, he celebrates his transformation upon emancipation from a "slave in the morning, trembling at the will of another, now . . . my own master, and completely free." He reproduced his instrument of manumission to illustrate the dominion one man has over another in slavery. In a reversal of the conversion narrative, Equiano wrote that he had now reverted to his "original free African state."[54]

Equiano also put the demise of slavery and black rights on the abolitionist agenda. In a petition that he presented to the queen "on behalf of my African brethren" in 1788, he wrote, "I supplicate your Majesty's compassion for millions of my African countrymen, who groan under the lash of West Indian tyranny." He implored the queen's "interposition with your royal consort, in favor of the wretched Africans; that, by your Majesty's benevolent influence, a period now be put to their misery; and that they may be raised from the condition of brutes, to which they are at present degraded, to the rights and situation of men, and be admitted to partake of the blessings of your Majesty's happy government." He signed the petition, "The oppressed Ethiopian." His deferential tone notwithstanding, Equiano was no monarchist. He joined the London Corresponding Committee when it was decidedly dangerous to do so and was befriended by Hardy, in whose home he revised his narrative. He died in 1797, three years after his English wife, Susanna. Equiano's narratives made enough money for him to leave a substantial bequest to his daughter. His will stipulated that if she did not survive him his estate should be divided among missionaries and a school in Sierra Leone.[55]

The first wave of Anglo-American abolition was not, as is commonly thought, an all-white movement. Black testimony was foundational to its cause. Abolitionists of African descent gave the British anti–slave trade movement authenticity, that is, its ability to speak for millions of enslaved Africans in the Western world. Black abolitionism would flourish in the American Republic, where free black communities and a large enslaved population provided it with a broad social base and institutional autonomy.

5

BLACK ABOLITIONISTS IN THE SLAVEHOLDING REPUBLIC

The founders of the first black churches, Absalom Jones and Richard Allen, led a walkout at St. George's Methodist Church in Philadelphia in 1792. They had dared to pray in the front pews reserved for whites rather than in the segregated gallery constructed for black worshippers. Zealous church authorities had interrupted their prayers and forced them to rise to their feet. As the story goes, this unseemly incident was the impetus for the founding of the African Episcopal Church by Jones and the Methodist Mother Bethel Church by Allen. Jones and Allen had long contemplated establishing a separate black church, and the unchristian behavior of white Methodists bolstered their case for religious independence. In 1805 Rev. Thomas Paul, an ordained Baptist minister from New Hampshire, staged a similar walkout in Boston, leading to the formation of the African Baptist Church.[1]

The institution-building efforts of newly free northern communities laid the social foundation of black abolitionism. African Americans were quick to ally with antislavery organizations but also developed an independent, community-based abolitionism. They gave birth to an autonomous tradition of activism and an alternative discourse of abolition. The early black public sphere, or "counter-public," fostered a skeptical view of the slaveholding Republic.[2]

Black abolitionists laid the foundations of a two-pronged antislavery strategy that emphasized racial solidarity and used a highly critical public voice against the persistence of enslavement and discrimination. The free as well as the enslaved voiced their denunciation of slavery in letters, pamphlets, poems, hymns, slave narratives, eulogies, sermons, and orations. They emerged as the most uncompromising voice for abolition and black rights. As quintessential outsiders, they questioned the very foundations of the early American Republic. Black abolitionists were not so much black founders as the founding critics of the country.[3]

BLACK FOUNDERS, BLACK ABOLITIONISTS

The organizational impulse for black abolitionism emerged among free communities, which gave birth to independent religious and social institutions. The founding generation of black abolitionists, most of whom had experienced slavery and were just a generation or two removed from Africa, forged a distinct identity, acquiring new names and naming many of their societies, churches, and schools African. While their enslaved predecessors had refashioned African rituals in the Negro Election Day in New England and the Pinkster festivals in New York, parading and carnivals in most black communities gradually gave way to institutional organization. This was not just black leaders' aspiring to middle-class respectability but the growing political sophistication of newly free communities. Black civil society was an autonomous social space that grew for the most part outside of and without state sanction. Prominent exceptions were the African Methodist Episcopal Church and the New York African Society for Mutual Relief, which received charters of incorporation.[4] For the most part, black institutions bred community autonomy and independent abolitionism.

The first such institution, the Free African Union Society, was founded in the home of Abraham Casey in Newport in 1780. Composed mostly of free black men, it was led by Anthony Taylor, Ceasar Lyndon, Newport Gardner, and Salmar Nubia. The society suffered from a serious shortage of funds when even officeholders like Nubia were unable to pay their membership dues. It frequently bought lottery tickets in hopes of raising money. Hardly expressions of bourgeois respectability, these societies struggled hard just to survive. The society's surviving records from 1787 disclose that its members advocated a Back to Africa program and functioned as a prayer meeting. They regularly invited Hopkins to preach and expressed an "earnest desire of returning to Affrica and settling there." The society proposed to send "a number of Men from among Ourselves," who would return with information for others to migrate with their families. Gaining a "proper and good title" to African lands rather than missionary work was its goal and only "want of Money" prevented implementation. Gardner, who led the society, was born in Africa and was self-educated and an accomplished musician. His African name was Occramar Marycoo. He bought his freedom and was involved in a number of community uplift efforts. In 1826, at the age of eighty, Gardner along with Nubia migrated to Liberia, where both died of yellow fever.[5]

A Pan-African vision undergirded the society. It was organized to "consider what good can be done for our good and the good of all Affricans." To remedy the "wretched state of many hundreds of thousands of our brethren who are in abject slavery" and "the Nations of Affrica, from whom we spring . . . many of them so foolish and wicked as to sell one another into slavery," it ambitiously proposed redeeming both Africans in America and Africa. In 1791, true to its abolitionist calling, the society excluded from membership those Africans who had in any way been involved in enslaving other Africans. It was also staunchly independent. William Thornton, the Quaker planter from the Virgin Islands who proposed to emancipate and settle his slaves in Sierra Leone and got seventy members of the society to sign on, reported, "The Blacks in this Country cannot be expected to form a colony for any European power." Black Bostonians led by Prince Hall also tried to solicit the legislature to finance Back to Africa voyages. Thornton met with African Americans in Boston, Newport, and Philadelphia, but most were wary of letting him control any emigration project. Later, Thornton suggested purchasing Puerto Rico and settling freed slaves there, and, unlike most free blacks, he supported the formation of the American Colonization Society.[6]

The African societies created a network of activism among northern black communities. In 1789 Bristol Yamma, one of Hopkins's protégés, helped found the Providence African Society to implement the Newport society's "Grand Proposals" and gave a well-received address before it. The two societies corresponded with Hall and William Allen in New York and sent the Newport society's constitution to the Free African Society of Philadelphia via the latter's emissary, Henry Stewart. In 1794 the Providence society proposed sending a representative ("a man of our own complexion, one whome we may depend upon") along with one from Boston and another from Philadelphia to explore migration to Sierra Leone. The Newport society backed the plan but also planned to send its own representative, Gardner. This plan fell through because of a lack of funds, even though the society petitioned the Rhode Island legislature and appealed to the abolition societies for help. The Providence society managed to send James McKenzie to Sierra Leone in 1795, but its plan for mass migration never got off the ground. The Newport society praised abolitionists like Hopkins, who supported Back to Africa efforts, calling them "sincere friends." The Philadelphia society concurred and looked forward to the day when "captivity shall cease, and buying and selling mankind have an end."[7]

In the late 1790s the Newport society renamed itself the African Humane Society and began taking on community functions, ensuring proper funerals for its members (an important rite of passage in West African cultures), registering births, deaths, and marriages, building independent places of worship, and founding black schools. In 1807 it became the African Benevolent Society (ABS), whose main purpose was to establish and run a black school. In his oration before the society on the closing of the slave trade, Rev. William Patten called for donations and hoped that the society's efforts would be "crowned with great success." Appended to his speech was a constitution of the society that restricted its membership to people of color who paid fifty cents to subscribe to its constitution. The society met annually. Initially, membership in the ABS was open to men and women, but by 1809 a separate African Female Benevolent Society assisted its efforts. At least three African free schools—one run by Mary Davis and the female benevolent society, one by Gardner in his home, and the other by Arthur Flagg, the president of the ABS—were founded at this time. Black education and racial uplift rather than emigration occupied the energies of these two descendants of the original Newport society. The directors of the ABS complimented their members for raising "the next generation out of that state of ignorance and depression." Similarly, the African Union Meeting and School House, the successor of the Providence society, made education its priority, rejecting "the stale imputation of inferiority in mental capacities." Housed on land donated by Moses Brown, the society rendered him "the sincere thanks of all coloured people, for this, and every other instance of his generosity toward them." Black teachers and preachers such as Rev. John Ormsbee and Asa Cruger Goldsbury ran the school.[8]

Black Bostonians shared the emigrationism and uplift strategies of the Rhode Island societies. The first independent black organization in Boston was a brotherhood of fifteen black Masons initiated by an Irish Military Lodge in 1775. Two years later it received permission to meet and parade with St. John's Provincial Grand Lodge. Led by Hall, African Lodge No. 459 received its charter from London in 1787. Uncertainty surrounds Hall's place and date of birth. A former enslaved leatherworker, Prince and his son, Primus Hall, served during the Revolutionary War and offered the services of the African Lodge to put down Shays's Rebellion in 1786. Though Hall owned property, he died in poverty in 1807. By that time black Masonry, or Prince Hall lodges, had spread to Newport, Philadelphia, Providence, and New York. As early as the 1730s African Americans in New York had attempted to found a black Masonic lodge, and black Freemasonry in the Caribbean predated the Prince Hall lodge. The fraternal rituals of Masonry resembled those of West African secret societies. In the hands of people of African descent they became "rituals of race." In 1782, when a Boston newspaper poked fun at them, calling them "St. Blacks Lodge of Free and Accepted Masons," Hall responded that their name was African. They did not "aspire after high titles" and advocated only "love to God and universal love to all mankind."[9]

Under Hall's leadership, black Masonry became a venue for antislavery uplift and emigrationist sentiment. Slaves in Massachusetts had requested repatriation to Africa in their very first petition to the General Court in 1773. Hall, who had signed the freedom petition of 1777, wrote another emigration petition in 1787 that was signed by seventy-three black men. It posited Africa as a land of freedom and the United States as the country of slavery, where even free blacks had to deal with "very disagreeable disadvantageous circumstances." It proposed forming a "civil society, united by a political constitution" to implement its plan. In another petition sent the same year, Hall asked the state to provide "for the education of colored people." Though they were taxed for the support of schools, Hall pointed out, African Americans received no benefit from "the free schools of Boston." In 1788 he submitted yet another petition to the assembly signed by twenty others. It drew attention to the kidnapping of three seamen from Boston and a number of others from Salem into slavery. It also protested the conduct of the African slave trade from Boston and asked the legislature to rectify "our weighty grievances." An earlier Quaker petition against slave trading and another against kidnapping by the Boston clergy, combined with Hall's petition, moved the General Court to pass a law banning the African slave trade before the national prohibition and to punish the kidnapping of free blacks.[10]

Hall elicited John Marrant, a Back to Africa proponent like himself, to become the chaplain of his African Lodge in 1789. That year Marrant delivered a sermon to black Masons, reminding them of the biblical history of "Africans who were truly good, wise, and learned men, as eloquent as any nation whatever, though at present many of them [are] in slavery, which is not a just cause of our being despised." Marrant and Hall shared a Christian "Ethiopianism" that recalled the ancient Christianity of Ethiopia and refuted the view of Africa as the land of heathen darkness. Marrant held up Masonic lodges of "different nations and different colors" as an example of universal Christian brotherhood that challenged racism. Black Masons were under a double obligation to "relieve the needy, support the weak, mourn with your fellow man in distress." Their primary duty, according to him, was to the slaves.[11]

Despite Hall's activism, this pioneering black abolitionist has been historically neglected. Jeremy Belknap referred to him as the "*Primus Interpares* of the blacks in this town." His two charges to the African Lodge best illustrate the nature of early black abolitionism. The charge of 1792 was a Christian indictment of racism and a rallying cry for human brotherhood. Hall argued that God demanded that all assist their "fellow men in distress let them be of what color or nation." The "great Architect" had said that "*Aethiopia shall stretch forth her hands unto me*" and "he that despises a black man for the sake of his colour, reproacheth his Maker." Hall's charge of 1797 was an indictment of the slaveholding Republic. Hall recalled how Africans had been "dragg'd from their native country by the iron hand of tyranny and oppression . . . to a strange land . . . and there to bear the iron yoke of slavery & cruelty till death as a friend shall relieve them." He alluded to the "bloody wars" that had destroyed Native Americans and asked his listeners to "sympathize with them in their troubles, and mingle a tear of sorrow with them." Africans and Indians must weep together. Free blacks had to bear "daily insults" and were "shamefully abus'd" in America. The "great gun" or "glittering . . . swords" had led "African kings and princes . . . into bloody wars" that plunged "millions of their fellow countrymen into slavery and cruel bondage." Hall called instead for African unity and invoked the example of the Haitian Revolution.[12]

Besides Masonic lodges, black Bostonians organized African societies, schools, and churches. In 1796 they founded a mutual benefit African society to visit the sick and care for members' widows and children. The society published an essay on freedom entitled "The Sons of Africans," evoking the title of black abolitionist organizations in Massachusetts and Britain. Written by an anonymous member, the essay countered the racialist idea that Africans were descendants of Ham by reasoning that Cain's envy and pride were actually the malicious spirit of slavery, which "hath ever a tendency to spread ignorance, darkness, poverty and distress in the world." In 1805 Reverend Paul and Scipio Dalton, a Mason, founded the African Baptist Church in Boston. It allowed white Baptists to become members. From 1806 until his resignation in 1829 Paul was the pastor of the African church and a mentor to abolitionists. In the antebellum period the African Baptist Church was wracked with dissension, but its successors, such as the Twelfth Baptist Church, remained important sites of antislavery activism.

The African school was housed in the Baptist church. Primus Hall ran a school at his home until 1803, when it moved to a carpenter's shop on Belknap Street. The Revolutionary War veteran "Colonel" George Middleton of the Bucks of America and a member of the African society were employed as teachers. Sixty-seven members of the African society had signed Hall's petition of 1800 for a school. In 1808 the school moved to the basement of the Baptist church, also known as the African Meeting House, on the same street. Primus Hall, Abel Barbadoes, probably the father of the black abolitionist James Barbadoes, and Cyrus Vassell plastered its classroom. Black abolitionists like Prince Saunders and John Russwurm taught in the school.[13]

African American societies and churches in Philadelphia and New York also gave birth to abolitionist activism. Philadelphia, with its large free black population and as the center of Quaker abolitionism, produced a vigorous tradition of black abolitionism. In 1787 Jones and Allen, ministers and former slaves from Delaware, founded the city's Free African Society. It met at the home of Allen and then at Sarah Dougherdy's, indicating that it had female members. The leadership, though, remained firmly in male hands. Its leading members were Allen, Jones, the former Virginia slave Moses Johnson, the black Quaker Cyrus Bustill, and the Revolutionary War hero and black abolitionist James Forten, and from 1791 it met at the Friends' Free African School. Its constitution stipulated that only a Quaker should hold the post of treasurer, and it adopted Quaker rituals and a system of visitations. Blacks in Philadelphia combined a desire for autonomy with eliciting the support of sympathetic, antislavery whites. Like the Newport society, it secured a proper burial ground as one of its first actions. As early as 1782 Philadelphia's blacks had petitioned the city to fence off the field known as Strangers Burial Ground. The society excluded drunkards and disorderly persons and expelled a member for abandoning his wife and child and taking up with a "common woman." In one of its letters to the Newport society, it advised all free blacks to give up "gaming and feasting." Such frivolous activities "while . . . many of our complexion are starving under cruel bondage" took scarce resources and energies away from political activism.[14] Black leaders, many of them a step removed from slavery and poverty themselves, viewed racial uplift as essential to self-determination.

The Philadelphia society evolved into independent black churches, centers of community activism, black leadership, and abolitionism. In 1789 Allen seceded from the organization because of religious differences, but he and Jones continued to cooperate in the building of an African church. In 1791 the African society held several "religious meetings" that would become the basis of the African Episcopal Church of St. Thomas, led by Jones. The next year Jones and Allen led their famous walkout from St. George's Methodist Church. Allen had preached at the church since he arrived in Philadelphia in 1786, and black contributions had helped build it. In 1794, with the help of Rush of the PAS and contributions from the Newport society, George Washington, and Granville Sharp, among others, the African church opened its doors, eventually boasting over four hundred members. Rev. Samuel Magaw's discourse at the inauguration carried a religious antislavery message. After walking in the darkness of slavery, he preached, Africans partook of the light of religion, education, and an abolitionist spirit extending back to Lay, Woolman, and Benezet. The church allowed only "descendants of the African race" the power to elect or be elected officials of the church. White ministers and assistant ministers would not have the right to "vote at our elections." Jones, who came to head the church at the age of forty-nine, was a self-taught slave. Brought by his master to Philadelphia in 1762 after his entire family had been sold, he married and managed to buy a lot for a house while still a slave. After repeated applications, his master manumitted him in 1784. Jones was known for his visitations to the needy and sick and commended for his "active cooperation with every effort put forth for the advancement of his race." He died in 1818.[15]

Along with Jones, Allen laid the foundations of black abolitionism in Philadelphia. As a slave, Allen was convinced that "I should one day enjoy my freedom; for slavery is a bitter pill." He bought his freedom after the antislavery Methodist preacher Freeborn Garrettson converted his master. Allen became an itinerant preacher, earning his keep through hard physical labor. In his memoir he proudly asserted that he had never been a charge to the "Methodist connexion." Allen turned down an offer to tour with Bishop Francis Asbury in "slave countries" because he was forbidden to "intermix with the slaves." His devotion to Methodism, however, was strong enough that he rejected a ministry in Jones's African church. But it was a black Methodism that he prized, recalling that in Delaware slaves had been at the heart of the Methodist revival. His mission was "seeking and instructing my African brethren, who had been a long forgotten people and few of them attended religious worship."[16]

Allen's Bethel church became the kernel of the largest independent black denomination. Allen founded, as it was later called, Mother Bethel in 1794 in a blacksmith's shop, and it was incorporated in 1796. According to its Articles of Association, only "Africans and descendants of the African race" were permitted to be trustees and vote in the church, but it ceded considerable governing authority to the Methodist Episcopal Conference. In 1807 Allen composed an "African Supplement" to proclaim his church's rejection of white control. Not just the incident in St. George's, but white Methodists' repeated attempts to take over the property of Bethel and impose their own preaching led Allen to proclaim the church's independence. In 1815 he was forced to repurchase his church after white Methodists tried to sell it out from under him. Allen won an important court victory when the Pennsylvania Supreme Court ruled that his church as an incorporated entity had the right to self-determination. The next year the court reaffirmed that decision. Allen then issued a call to black Methodists in Baltimore, Philadelphia, and surrounding areas. They all shared similar experiences of ill treatment of black members and white preachers who "became such tyrants, and more especially to the coloured people." Delegates from Pennsylvania, New Jersey, Delaware, and Maryland met and founded the

African Methodist Episcopal Church, and Allen, who cowrote the denomination's *Doctrines and Discipline* in 1817, became its first bishop.[17]

The independent African churches of Philadelphia propelled community organization. The men in the African Methodist Episcopal Church formed the African Friendly Society in 1795, and the following year the women formed the Female Benevolent Society. In 1797 Prince Hall received a request from eleven men in Philadelphia to organize a Masonic lodge. Jones was inducted as master of the African Lodge, and Forten was elected treasurer. Members of the Philadelphia lodge were sailors, church members, and nonnatives. White Masons visited the African Lodge and at times marched with black Masons, practices that distinguished it from the Boston lodge. In 1804 the African church founded a black school, and in 1809 a "Society for Suppressing Vice and Immorality." By the early 1800s black societies proliferated in Philadelphia: the Angolian Society and the Angola Beneficial Society were founded in 1808, the Sons of Africa in 1810, the African Female Benevolent Society and the Male African Benevolent Society in 1819. Between 1802 and 1812, in the space of ten years, black Philadelphians founded ten societies. In 1809 Henry Simmons, a former slave from Virginia, formed the African Baptist Church, and in 1811 John Gloucester, a former slave from Tennessee educated by his master, founded the First African Presbyterian Church after preaching to an all-black congregation for nearly four years. Rush, a fellow Presbyterian, was instrumental in helping Gloucester purchase the freedom of his family. By 1813 over two thousand African Americans attended seven black churches in the city. Black women formed the backbone of the congregations, though they were absent in the church leadership. The most well known was Black Alice, an African slave who was brought to Pennsylvania and died at the venerable age of 116 in 1802. Allen's first and second wives, Flora Allen and Sarah Bass Allen, were also active in the church and community. As Rush toasted at the raising of the first African church in Philadelphia, African churches had replaced "African bondage."[18]

Allen and Jones laid the institutional foundation of black abolitionism in Philadelphia. Members of black churches and societies led in antislavery petitioning. The first black petition to Congress signed by members of Philadelphia's African Society has been dated to around 1792. The petition called for gradual emancipation by the federal government and proposed emigration to Sierra Leone. It was never presented and was written in a less polished fashion than most of Jones's and Allen's works. Its author was perhaps James (Oronoko) Dexter, a member of the African church who worked for James Pemberton of the PAS. The language of the petition, which evokes "an Unalinauble Right to life Liberty & the pursiut of happiness," is reminiscent of the early New England slave petitions.[19]

A petition to Congress in 1797 protested the fugitive slave law of 1793. It highlighted the plight of four former slaves from North Carolina and others threatened by kidnapping and reenslavement. Jones wrote the petition on their behalf. The law, they held, was "a flagrant proof how far human beings, merely on account of color and complexion, are, through prevailing prejudice, outlawed and excluded from common justice and common humanity." The petition stressed the "unconstitutional bondage in which multitudes of our fellows in complexion are held" and the reenslavement of those who were free by kidnappers and man stealers. It chided, "Is not some remedy for an evil of such magnitude highly worthy of the deep inquiry and unfeigned zeal of the supreme Legislative body of a free and enlightened people?" Its lofty tone was a hallmark of black abolitionism in the early Republic.[20]

While Federalist and Republican congressmen from Massachusetts supported the petition, extreme and moderate southerners alike, including William L. Smith of South Carolina and James Madison of Virginia, argued against its reception. A sectional divide was evident as Nathaniel Macon of North Carolina supported Madison's argument that state courts should decide such cases, while Aaron Kitchell of New Jersey questioned the rationale of sending free black men back to a slave state. In the end the House of Representatives voted 50 to 33 against considering it. The same year a Quaker memorial called Congress's attention to "the oppressed state of our brethren the African race" and to the plight of North Carolina's free blacks, who were subject to reenslavement. In the long debate that followed, Macon accused the Quakers of being "war mongers" for waging a war against slavery. George Thatcher of Massachusetts, who had voted against the fugitive slave law of 1793, defended them. This time the house issued a report stating that the state judiciary alone had the authority to mediate in such cases. In 1798 Thatcher, supported by Joseph Varnum of Massachusetts and Albert Gallatin of Pennsylvania, led an unsuccessful minority effort to bar slavery from the Mississippi territory and the entrance of slave states into the Union.[21]

Jones can be credited with pioneering the argument that slavery was unconstitutional long before the rise of political abolitionism. Signed by him and seventy-three others, his petition of 1799 claimed to speak on behalf of the slaves, who were "objects of your representation in your public councils," a pointed reference to the three-fifths clause. But the petition made clear that it was not slaveholders but free blacks who best represented the slaves. It stressed that free blacks "humbly conceive ourselves authorized to address and petition you on their behalf." It claimed that the slave trade and kidnapping violated the preamble of the Constitution. The petition concluded, "In the Constitution and Fugitive Bill, no mention is made of black people, or slaves; therefore, if the Bill of Rights, or the Declaration of Congress are of any validity, we beseech, that as we are men, we may be admitted to partake of the liberties and unalienable rights therein held forth." Many of his signatories were illiterate and signed with an X next to their names, belying the oft-repeated claim that black abolitionism was a narrow, elitist concern. Early black abolitionism was a community-wide affair that cut across class. Only Thatcher, one of seven congressmen who had voted against the Fugitive Slave Act, defended the illiterate petitioners ridiculed by southern congressmen. John Rutledge of South Carolina likened receiving the petition to the French convention receiving "emissaries from St. Domingo [sic]" demanding freedom for their "species." Most members of the House expressed their "pointed disapprobation" at receiving petitions from free blacks. Thatcher's was the only vote cast in favor of hearing the petition.[22]

To recognize Thatcher's lone effort in Congress to gain black Americans a hearing, Forten wrote a public letter to him in 1800. Forten was the third party of the triumvirate that included Jones and Allen that led black antislavery efforts in Philadelphia. Schooled at the Friends' Free African School, Forten rose from apprenticeship to acquire his master's sailmaking business. A wealthy sailmaker who had white and black apprentices working for him, he became a preeminent advocate for black rights and bankrolled Garrison's the *Liberator*. Forten's letter is notable not only because he recognized Thatcher's vote but also because he laid out the black abolitionist program of emancipation and black rights: "Seven hundred thousand [approximately the number of African Americans in the United States according to the Census of 1790] of the human race were concerned in our Petition; their thanks, their gratitude to you they now express . . . we derive some comfort from the thought that . . . there is one who shall use all his endeavours to free the slave from captivity . . . and preserve the free black in the full enjoyment of his rights." Challenging racist aspersions, he reasoned, "Though our faces are black, yet we are men; and though many of us cannot write, yet we all have the feelings and passions of men, and are as anxious to enjoy the birth-right of the human race."[23]

Blacks in New York matched the organizational and antislavery activism of those in Philadelphia. As early as the seventeenth century black New Yorkers sought to ensure the proper burial of their deceased, who were excluded from white church cemeteries. They formed a religious society that became the African Society in 1784. By 1795 the original Negro Burial Ground was destroyed. That year the African Society petitioned the New York Council for land to build a church and cemetery, and a year later black Methodists, including such prominent leaders as Peter Williams Sr., James Varick, and William Hamilton, began holding independent prayer meetings. In 1799 they seceded from the John Street Methodist Church and the next year built the African Methodist Episcopal (AME) Zion Church. Williams and the itinerant Methodist preacher George White, among others, signed its charter and articles of agreement. Despite an attempt led by White and Abraham Thompson to join Allen's denomination, Varick decided to form a new denomination, the AME Zion. It seceded from the Methodist Conference, was incorporated in 1820, established its own doctrine and discipline, and elected Thompson and Varick as elders. In 1828 Christopher Rush was elected superintendent and wrote a history of the church. The AME Zion's address explained, "When the Methodist society in the United States was small, the Africans enjoyed comfortable privileges among their white brethren in the same meeting-house, but as the whites increased very fast, the Africans were pressed back; therefore, it was thought essentially necessary for them to have meeting-houses of their own." While AME Zion cooperated with New York's black Asbury Church, which was still under the control of the Methodist Episcopal Conference, it established a history of rivalry with Allen's AME.[24]

The independent black church movement grew in New York after the establishment of the AME Zion. In 1808 New York's black Baptists formed the Abyssinian Baptist Church with help from Paul. Since 1792 black Episcopalians had repeatedly petitioned the Trinity Episcopal Church for land on which to build a church and school. By 1819 they had their own congregation, St. Phillip's Episcopal Church, pastored by Peter Williams Jr. Williams was ordained a priest in 1826 and became a leading black abolitionist until his death in 1840. His father was Peter Williams Sr., the founding member of the AME Zion. In 1821 the black abolitionist minister Samuel Cornish founded the city's First Colored Presbyterian Church. By 1826 African Americans in New York had founded ten black churches. As in Philadelphia, black women formed the backbone of these churches despite a male-dominated leadership. Women composed two-thirds of the Zion congregation and 75 percent of the Abyssinian Baptist Church's. As early as 1802 they formed a separate Female African Benevolent Association.[25]

Black New Yorkers also produced the longest-lived African American mutual aid society in the country, the New York African Society for Mutual Relief (NYASMR) (1808–1945). Founded by the city's black abolitionists William Hamilton, its first president, Henry Sipkins, Adam Carman, James Latham,

and John Teasman, it was incorporated by the legislature in 1810. Its charter
was extended in 1825 and 1840, and it adopted a new charter in 1869. The black
abolitionists Charles B. Ray and Philip Bell were presidents of the society in
the antebellum period. In a speech in 1809 Hamilton saw its aim as addressing
indigency and "deep poverty and distress" in the black community through its
motto, "MUTUAL INTEREST, MUTUAL BENEFIT, AND MUTUAL RELIEF." He argued
that "mere socialities" were not its object but the "noble employment" of helping the sick, poor, widowed, and orphaned. He noted that the society had more
members than "any civil institution yet attempted among us." The NYASMR's
constitution stipulated specific amounts to be given to members' families to allay the expenses of death, sickness, old age, infirmity, and permanent disability.
The African Marine Fund, founded in 1810, granted similar benefits to New
York's large population of black seamen. Most of these societies established
schools and, together with the NYMS, led the effort to secure education for
blacks.[26] Community self-help and autonomy as well as antislavery were the
legacy of the early black societies.

The proliferation of independent black organizing in New York created a
large cadre of secular black leaders and abolitionists. Hamilton, a carpenter
who had helped found the Zion church and the NYASMR, developed the uncompromising language of black abolitionism. Even more than Hall, Allen,
and Jones, he wrote some of the most stinging rebukes of American republicanism. Like that of Peter Williams Jr., his antislavery career spanned the first
and second waves of abolitionism, and he became one of the leading organizers of the antebellum national black convention movement. When he died
in 1836, nearly all of the city's numerous black societies and churches held
funeral services in his memory. The so-called elite of the black community
were united by their common schooling in the African Free Schools and commitment to education, black rights, independent organizations, and antislavery.
Only a few seemed to have acquired some measure of economic security, such
as the Downing family, which owned a popular oyster bar. Most, like Sipkins,
who was a porter, led economically precarious existences, but their political
activism, cosmopolitanism, and leadership of black institutions bolstered their
position as spokesmen of the black community.[27] They were the first generation
of "race men."

New York's African American fraternal organizations, benevolent societies,
and churches, like those elsewhere in the North, were preeminent sites not
only of black leadership but also of mass participation. Parades and celebrations
organized by these groups became venues for abolitionist oratory and addresses.
Discouraged by city authorities and even by their antislavery allies, black lead-

ers like Teasman and Hamilton insisted on celebrating their community, societies, and the abolition of slavery and the slave trade, staking their claim to manhood and citizenship in military displays and antislavery banners. These parades formed a link between colonial-era slave festivals and the institutional life of the newly free black community. As popular celebrations they revealed the depth of antislavery consciousness in black communities that transcended status. In the antebellum period, violent reactions by whites and some black leaders' curtailing of popular demonstrations dealt a deathblow to this tradition. But in the early nineteenth century, black New Yorkers paraded to celebrate their freedom and the end of slavery. While analogous to parades by white artisans and other groups claiming republican citizenship, they represented a vibrant, distinct black popular culture of music, dance, and performance represented by the short-lived African Theatre and in the city's oyster houses and dance cellars.[28]

Black organizations and churches arose in other cities, especially in the upper south states, where nearly half of the free black population resided. In Baltimore the Colored Methodist Society tried to form an independent church as early as 1795. In 1801 they established a meetinghouse under the stewardship of the Methodist Episcopal Church. In 1815 Daniel Coker, a deacon, led a secession from the church and formed the independent African Methodist Bethel Society. The next year Coker's church joined Allen's AME denomination. Coker was the son of an English servant and an enslaved father. He converted to Methodism after escaping to New York and returned to Baltimore in 1807. He worked as a teacher at the Sharp Street Church school, the African Academy. Elected with Allen to be a bishop in the AME, he withdrew when Allen objected. After that, Coker's fortunes waned, and, wracked by personal, professional, and financial troubles, he migrated to Liberia in 1820.

In the early nineteenth century the independent black church movement spread to smaller northern and southern cities. Black Methodist, Baptist and a few Episcopalian and Presbyterian churches were founded in Albany, Pittsburgh, Cincinnati, Wilmington, Washington, and Richmond. The AME acquired a large membership even in Charleston, South Carolina, until the church was destroyed in the wake of the Denmark Vesey conspiracy in 1822. In Savannah, Georgia, Andrew Bryan led the oldest black Baptist church in the country. After suffering much persecution, he died in 1812. The original church eventually split into three. Independent black religious activity was frowned on in the slave South, especially after Nat Turner's rebellion. For the most part, southern blacks, above all, the enslaved, were forced to worship in white churches or under white supervision until Reconstruction.[29]

The organizational impulse also manifested itself among southern free blacks. Membership in benevolent societies like the Brown Fellowship Society, founded in Charleston in 1790, was exclusive to its so-called free mulatto class. Although it sponsored black education, the society survived because it did not dabble overtly in antislavery politics. In 1791, however, a few men, on behalf of "Free-Men of Colour," petitioned the assembly for the right to give testimony and trial by jury, forbidden by the state slave code of 1740. They reasoned that they contributed to the "support of the Government by chearfully paying their Taxes," while prudently disclaiming a desire to be put on an "equal footing" with whites. Their petition was summarily rejected. Two years later free blacks in Camden and Charleston protested in vain against the poll taxes levied on them. Most of the southern free black societies, such as the Resolute Beneficial Society of Washington, founded in 1818, and the Burying Ground and Beneficial Society of Richmond, founded in 1815, stuck to mutual self-help and relief. Under Spanish and French rule, free black militias flourished in New Orleans, and free blacks regularly attended the Catholic church. The introduction of a more rigid racial order with the American takeover encouraged "gentlemen of color" to develop separate organizations and social lives. With the exception of Baltimore, organized black abolitionism in southern cities, where free blacks were forced to live a more restricted life subject to slave codes, was stillborn.[30] Antislavery in the South went underground and became the province of slave rebels and fugitives with allies among free blacks and a few whites.

BLACK ABOLITIONIST DISCOURSE

Militant rhetoric belied the staid institutional face of black abolition. Early black abolitionists were apt to recall a history of oppression and suffering under slavery and demand freedom not simply as an act of mercy or benevolence but as acts of justice and retribution. They were far more likely to expose the hollowness of American republican pretensions than to simply evoke its principles. They created a distinct discursive style, a radical antislavery rhetoric that would flower in the antebellum interracial abolition movement. If republicanism and the early American public sphere were mutually constitutive, an oppositional black counterpublic rendered a profound critique of it. Black abolitionists were not so much the best exponents as the best critics of American republicanism.

One of the most noted black men in the early Republic, the astronomer and mathematician Benjamin Banneker, publicly challenged Jefferson on slavery and race. Descended from an English indentured servant and an African chieftain named Bannka, Banneker was the son of their oldest daughter, Mary, and her free black husband, Robert. Born free in Maryland in 1731, Banneker was educated by his grandmother and a Quaker schoolmaster. He is known for the six almanacs he published in twenty-eight editions between 1792 and 1797 containing his annual weather calculations. Banneker's public letter to Jefferson in 1791, republished in his almanac, catapulted him onto the national stage. He took Jefferson to task: "But Sir how pitiable it is to reflect, that . . . in detaining by fraud and violence so numerous a part of my brethren under groaning captivity and cruel oppression, that you should at the Same time be found guilty of that most criminal act, which you professedly detested in others, with respect to yourselves." No doubt aware of Jefferson's disparaging racial remarks in his *Notes*, Banneker assured him that he was "of the African race, and in that colour which is natural to them of the deepest dye."[31]

Banneker's exchange with the most representative figure of American republicanism symbolized the role of public critics that African Americans assumed. Banneker's unpublished poem also gave voice to his abolitionist criticism of the country:

> Those Afric sons which Nature formed free . . .
> Behold them herefrom torn by cruel force,
> And doomed to slavery without remorse
> This act, America, thy sons have known;
> This cruel act, relentless they have done.

Jefferson responded courteously, but his private remarks, like his published ones on Wheatley and Sancho, cast doubt on Banneker's achievements. Jefferson wrote, "We know he had spherical trigonometry enough to make almanacs, but not without the suspicion of aid from Ellicott, who was his neighbor and friend, and never missed an opportunity of puffing him. I have a long letter from Banneker, which shows him to have had a mind of very common stature indeed." "Ellicott," Banneker's neighbor, was George Ellicott, a cousin of Maj. Andrew Ellicott, who helped him publish his first almanac. Banneker's letter and Jefferson's public reply were widely printed in newspapers, published in pamphlet form in 1792, and in Banneker's almanac of 1793. Even in responding, Jefferson earned the ire of proslavery South Carolinian Federalists like Henry W. DeSaussure and William Loughton Smith, who smirkingly asked, "What shall we think of a *secretary of state* thus fraternizing with negroes?"[32]

Banneker's work became an argument for racial equality. In his letter to Andrew Ellicott, who was asked to confirm the calculations, Banneker wrote that he had worked to gratify "the curiosity of the public, than for any view of profit, as I suppose it to be the first attempt of the kind that ever was made in America by a person of my complexion." Ellicott was so impressed that he asked Banneker to assist him in surveying land for the new capital in the District of Columbia. Banneker's almanac was published first in Baltimore and later in Philadelphia under abolitionist auspices. All his publishers were known to print abolitionist pamphlets or were abolitionists themselves. His Quaker neighbors, the Ellicotts, made sure that it reached Pemberton, and abolitionists touted it as evidence of African genius. As in the cases of the enslaved mathematician Thomas Fuller of Virginia and the black doctor James Derham of New Orleans, abolitionists saw Banneker as living proof of black intellectual achievement. His almanac of 1792 contained an endorsement from the physician James McHenry, a Revolutionary War veteran and senator from Maryland who saw the work as a "striking contradiction to Mr. Hume's doctrine, that 'Negroes are naturally inferior to the whites and unsusceptible of attainments in arts and sciences.'" McHenry had freed his slaves. The preface to the 1797 almanac proclaimed, "The labours of the justly celebrated *Banneker* will likewise furnish you with a very important lesson, courteous reader, which you will not find in any other Almanac, namely that the maker of the Universe is no respecter of colours; that the colour of the skin is in no ways connected with the strength of mind or intellectual powers."[33]

Nearly all of Banneker's almanacs contained abolitionist ephemera, probably reflecting both the author's and his sponsors' wishes. They included an excerpt from David Rittenhouse, the president of the American Philosophical Society and an eminent astronomer who had also verified Banneker's calculations, against slavery and the slave trade. The 1793 almanac, published by the Quaker printer Joseph Crukshank, himself the author of a well-known antislavery poem, republished numerous antislavery commentaries. That almanac contained a plan for world peace attributed to Rush and uncovered the influence of Quaker ideas. Included in this version were speeches by British parliamentarians against the slave trade, antislavery poetry by William Cowper and Thomas Wilkinson, and even Jefferson's asides against slavery from the *Notes*. The 1795 almanac contained an account of the yellow fever in Philadelphia, controversy over which would inspire Allen and Jones to publish their first abolitionist pamphlet. Banneker's later almanacs had poems by Wheatley and those written in honor of him. His popular almanacs, in short, became a medium to disseminate abolitionist arguments. Banneker died in 1806, continuing to make his calculations every year until his death. The PAS, the MAS, and admirers publicized his works, and later generations of black abolitionists memorialized him.[34]

The first black autobiography published in the early Republic, written by Venture Smith (Briton Hammon's narrative was published before independence, Gronniosaw and Marrant were published in England, and Equiano's was a republication), was also a criticism of slavery and racism. Smith notes his African American identity in the title of his narrative, describing himself as "A Native of Africa: But Resident Above Sixty Years in the United States of America." A former Connecticut slave, Smith, calling himself Broteer of Dukandarra in Africa, was enslaved at the age of eight. Published in 1798, his narrative is rarely read as an abolitionist tract. The preface, written by his scribe Elisha Niles, a Connecticut schoolteacher, laid out its antislavery purpose. Smith, Niles observed, was a black founder comparable to Franklin and Washington, but his story of the American founding was a counternarrative of slavery and racial oppression.

Smith's spare narrative of the commodification of Africans as property is an indictment of the worldwide system of commerce that included the Atlantic slave trade and the market society he came to inhabit. Unlike Equiano, who dwelt on the horrors of the Middle Passage, Smith recounted in detail the broad swath of destruction and indiscriminate enslavement of entire villages by a band of fierce African warriors and kidnappers. Cognizant of the broader forces that motivated them, he writes, "They were instigated by some white nation who equipped and sent them to subdue and possess the country." Like his contemporary abolitionists, Smith eschewed a simplistic racial analysis and instead pointed out how his African enslavers' lust for wealth led them to participate in the enslavement process and in the torture and murder of his father. The very name he is given by his first master, Venture (he was bought for four gallons of rum and some calico), illustrates his transformation into human capital. Smith related how many times he was "pawned," hired, and sold and told of his superhuman efforts to escape slavery and poverty. His is a story not of a "Venture Capitalist," as some scholars claim, or of assimilation of bourgeois values but of a laboring man, one who carefully kept track of the amount and type of work he did in order to buy his and his family's freedom. It is the value of his labor that Smith cherished, revealing how employers constantly cheated their workers. Thus Smith's grief at his son's death is compounded by the fact that he lost the money paid for his freedom. The labor theory of value informs his entire narrative. Smith mentions the amount he paid the doctor for his dying daughter, thereby underscoring that only the rich have the luxury and good taste to indulge in sentiment over hard emotional and material losses.

Smith unveils the underside of market society, where dishonesty and finagling ruled. His master charges him an enormous sum for his freedom, an Irish servant steals from him and two other runaways, foiling their plot to escape. Smith buys fellow slaves out of slavery either to liberate them or have them work with him, but they cheat him. Courts, contracts, and market rules did not dispense justice but sided with the powerful and wealthy. When he was made to pay a client for damages, Smith remarks, "but Captain Hart was a *white gentleman*, and I a *poor African*; therefore it was *all right, and good enough for the black dog.*" Forced to play by rules stacked against him, Smith, despite his achievements, determines that workingmen and black men like him in particular will always be the losers. His is no uplifting tale of liberation but a revelation of the hypocrisy and unfairness of a world governed by the cash nexus or, in his words, where Africans and their freedom could be converted "into cash." Smith died in 1805, and his tombstone captures his sense of the injustice of his enslavement and his pride in the labor that bought his freedom: "Sacred to the Memory of Venture Smith an African tho the son of a King he was kidnapped & sold as a slave but by his industry he acquired Money to purchase his Freedom."[35] His tale of loss and betrayal in isolated, rural New England stands in sharp contrast to the institutions of communal solidarity built by free black urban populations.

The first black abolitionist pamphlet came from that milieu. Jones and Allen published a vindication of the race in their pamphlet of 1794 defending the actions of the black community during the yellow fever epidemic in Philadelphia against the aspersions of Mathew Carey, who claimed that blacks had stolen and profited from the victims of the fever. In reply, they asserted that while Carey had fled the city and now profited from his pamphlet on the yellow fever, African Americans had ministered to the sick, and they were no more and in most cases less guilty than whites, who had charged patients enormous amounts or pilfered from them. They told the stories of black men and women who had assisted the sick and helped bury the dead "at the peril of our lives." Allen himself was laid up during the epidemic. Jones and Allen estimated that they had bled over eight hundred patients at Rush's direction, who said they were indefatigable. Rush also came to their defense, remarking, "The merit of the blacks in their attendance to the sick is enhanced by their not being exempted from the disorder," as was initially assumed. Allen and Jones became the first black authors to obtain a copyright when they registered their yellow fever pamphlet.[36]

They appended a radical abolitionist appeal, "An Address to Those Who Keep Slaves and Uphold the Practice," to their pamphlet, which bluntly declared, "You have been and are our great oppressors." The two black ministers reminded whites that slavery is "hateful . . . in the sight of God" and that "God himself was the first pleader of the cause of the slaves." They countered pro-slavery justifications in writing, "Will you, because you have reduced us to the unhappy condition our colour is in, plead our incapacity for freedom, and our contented condition under oppression, as a sufficient cause for keeping us under the grievous yoke?" Slaves were not content because, they argued, referring in all likelihood to the rebellion in Saint-Domingue, the "dreadful insurrections they have made, when opportunity has offered, is enough to convince a reasonable man, that great uneasiness and not contentment, is the inhabitant of their hearts."[37]

Allen's eulogy on Washington's death, which was published in the *Philadelphia Gazette* on December 31, 1799, also sought to deliver an abolitionist message to the country on behalf of the overwhelming majority of African Americans who remained in slavery. He contended that Washington was not just the father of the nation but also a "sympathizing friend" to black people. Allen knew that he had contributed to the building of the African Church and that he had drawn attention to a Quaker petition against slavery in his last address to the Senate. Washington's courteous reply to Wheatley and the Federalist Party's more liberal stance on black rights compared to the Jeffersonian Republicans were well known. But it was Washington's dying legacy of freeing his slaves in his will, to be implemented after his wife's death, that endeared him to African Americans. As Allen wrote, "He whose wisdom the nations revered thought we had a right to liberty. Unbiased by the popular opinion of the state (Virginia) in which is the memorable Mount Vernon—he dared do his duty, and wipe off the only stain with which man could ever reproach him. . . . Deeds like these are not common." To Allen, Washington's emancipation of his slaves, to whom he also granted land, was an exemplary act for the nation and a surprising gift of justice to African Americans. Rather than dwell on the paternalistic slaveholder of popular imagination, Allen sought to appropriate Washington's legacy for abolition.[38]

Allen was a proponent of a black liberation theology. Not many of his sermons are extant, but he compiled a book of "Hymns and Spiritual Songs from Various Authors." If Allen's selection of these hymns for the AME church is any indication of his religious beliefs, then, in his view, racial liberation and an end to slavery were an essential part of the black Christian project. The African American criticism of the land of slavery was embodied in the hymn "Lord, What a wretched land is this." The message Allen intended for his enslaved and newly freed congregants reflected black Israelite Christianity. The hymns spoke of the "great and awful" yet glorious days of judgment when God would punish slaveholders and redeem enslaved people, who were his chosen children. In his short writings on acts of faith, acts of hope, and acts of love, Allen revealed the highly religious inspiration for his abolitionism. It was not interracial harmony that he advocated so much as African American unity and autonomy based on a shared history of oppression: "Blessed are the sufferings which are endured." In an address "To the People of Color," he wrote of how "the love of God" had sustained him in slavery when "the prospect of liberty vanished away, and I was in darkness and perplexity." If faith did not result in earthly liberty, then it led to everlasting life when the "power of the most cruel master ends." Allen did not advocate religious quietism. He was convinced that God was on the side of the slaves.[39]

Black abolitionists did not ignore racialist discourses of social disorder and black criminality inaugurated by the legal codification of racial slavery, nor did they remain indifferent to the hardships of poverty, crime, and injustice. Execution narratives, or the dying testimonies of accused criminals, were a popular literary genre. The narratives of enslaved men like Pomp and Thomas Powers not only contained their confessions but also criticized their enslavement. In 1808 Allen compiled the execution narratives of John Joyce and Peter Mathias, two black men accused of murdering one Sarah Cross. Allen wrote that both men had repented, but he questioned the criminalization of blackness. John was aiming to recover wages due to him, and Peter had merely accompanied him. Writing in two pamphlets about the unjust imprisonment of the Boorn brothers, both white, for the murder of Russel Colvin, the black abolitionist minister Lemuel Haynes averred that their case was "particularly interesting to those among us who have lately been remarkably emancipated from bondage, slavery and death."[40] Allen's and Haynes's works were prescient in drawing parallels between imprisonment, punishment, and slavery.

Orations on the abolition of the African slave trade in 1808 reveal African American abolitionists' concerted endeavor to construct a counternarrative of slavery and freedom to the dominant national story of freedom inaugurated by the American Revolution. Most of them were delivered in black churches and societies in northern cities. Black institutional independence encouraged antislavery radicalism. The celebrations on January 1 were a pointed rejoinder to those on the Fourth of July in the new Republic. The slave trade, rather than the revolution, is the starting point of these counternarratives, and their main motif is slavery rather than liberty. The United States was a land of captivity, of slavery, and the discovery of the New World represented not the founding of the shining city on a hill but the start of the crime against Africans.[41]

In his thanksgiving sermon on the abolition of the slave trade, Jones insisted that America was the new Egypt. With the abolition of the slave trade at least the "dear land of our ancestors" would not be stained by the blood "shed by British and American hands." Recapitulating the history of the Americas in his speech, Rev. Peter Williams Jr. charged that the first European colonists, motivated by "the desire for gain," had enslaved "the harmless aborigines, compelled them to drudge in the mines" and carried Africans "into cruel captivity." Similarly, Russell Parrott of Philadelphia in his oration in 1814 noted, "It is from this period, that we may date the commencement of the sufferings of the Africans, and the discovery of the new world; which, to one portion of the human family, has afforded such advantages, to the unfortunate African, has been the source of the greatest misery." In a speech in 1815 Hamilton "[wished] to God that Columbus with his exploring schemes had perished in Europe ere he touched the American Isles." Africa then would have "been spared the terrible calamity she has suffered."[42]

By dwelling on the horrors of the slave trade, early black abolitionists exposed the unseemly side of Western civilization. Williams urged the "descendants of African forefathers" not to forget the "horrid inhumanities" perpetrated on Africa and the scenes of "unfathomable distress" of the slave ship. Hamilton felt he should forbear describing the cruelties of the slave trade, as it would make his listeners "mad for revenge on the murderers of your brethren"; but he went on to describe in graphic detail the story of a ten-year-old boy whipped to death on board a slaver. The history of the slave trade and slavery in the United States, according to Sipkins, was one of "relentless tyranny" and torture. Henry Johnson argued that he drew attention to the cruelties of the slave trade not to inflame the minds of his people but to "cast just obloquy" against oppressors. In an oration in 1823 Jeremiah Gloucester continued this tradition, commenting that the "cruelties that were practiced, ties that were broken, by those traffickers in blood, and panders of avarice, no tongue can paint."[43]

Rather than sing paeans to American republicanism and "legitimate" commerce, black abolitionists fashioned a radical critique of slavery and early capitalism. In his remarkable oration of 1811 on behalf of "our injured race," Adam Carman attacked the economic basis of slavery and the system of European commerce that reduced a black person to a "vendible article." Under the institution of slavery in the New World, Africans came to be "viewed and considered as commercial commodities; thus we became interwoven into the system of commerce, and the revenue of nations; hence the merchant, the planter, the mortgagee, the manufacturer, the politician, the legislators, and the cabinet minister, all strenuously advocated the continuance of the Slave Trade."[44] Carman posited that Western commerce and civilization, far from containing the keys to Africa's redemption, sounded its death knell.

Black abolitionists denounced as well the growth of racism in the slaveholding Republic. If all men were created equal, then the persistence of slavery and
racial inequality implied that black people were less than human or inferior. To
Williams, the slave trade and slavery were "flagrant violations of human rights."
In his oration in 1813 on the abolition of the slave trade, George Lawrence
stressed the problem of American racism and disputed it on intellectual and
moral grounds. As he put it, "Vacuous must the reason of that man have been,
who dared to assert that genius is confined to complexion, or that nature knows
difference in the immortal soul of man." Hamilton argued, "The European
with his bloated pride, conceives himself an order of being above any other order of men" and boasts "of their superior understanding, their superior genius,
their superior souls." Recounting the "cruel, barbarous treatment" of slaves,
including whippings and instruments of torture, he ended by saying, "If these
are some of the marks of superiority may heaven in mercy always keep us inferior." In a similar vein, Carman asserted, "These very savage-like manstealers,
brand us with inferiority of sensibility. My brethren, Africans and descendants
of Africans, it would be condescending from the dignity of Africans, to notice
what these invidious pedantic nizies [do-gooders] have asserted." In his eyes,
American racists displayed a "depravity of mind or proflicacy [*sic*] of morals
inferior to that imputed to us." To those who would argue that Africans "are not
of the same flesh and blood" as whites, Gloucester responded with the biblical
injunction that "God had made of one blood all the nations of men to dwell on
the face of the earth." Teasman's address to the NYASMR on the first anniversary of its incorporation in 1811 also rendered a religious indictment of racism.
Despite all that blacks and their abolitionist allies had achieved, "it is asserted
that your genius is inferior." He held up God's "revelation" against the pseudoscience of race and God's works in black achievement and "acquired abilities"
as constituting a double refutation of racism.[45]

The slave trade orations mark a distinct black tradition of protest, praising
abolitionist allies but being oppositional in content. By contrast, white sermons
on the closing of the slave trade, delivered mostly in Boston, were far more optimistic and conciliatory. In a sermon of 1808 Rev. Jedidiah Morse, for example,
commended the antislavery activism of free blacks but adopted a congratula-
tory tone. The sermons praised both the United States and Britain for their
philanthropy and spent considerable time comparing slavery to sin, urging free
black people to exemplary behavior and advocating gradual emancipation. By
1822 Rev. Thaddeus Mason Harris was recommending colonization. In one important respect, however, these orations resembled the speeches made by black
orators. God hath made of one blood all the nations of the world, they insisted,

and any attempt to ascribe to African Americans the status of a separate species or race was blasphemous. These antislavery Federalist clergymen criticized southern slavery and Jeffersonian Republicans, for whom race was a prominent exception to their creed of equality.[46]

Though as president Jefferson signed the law prohibiting the international slave trade, black orations on abolition were highly critical of him. Clearly referring to Jefferson, Hamilton claimed that the "proposition . . . advanced by men who claim a preeminence in the learned world, that Africans are inferior to white men in the structure both of body and mind" was spurious. Most black abolitionists were Federalists like Joseph Sidney, who developed an extensive criticism of Jeffersonian republicanism, "the Slavery-hole of democracy," in his speech. Even more radical in tone was an anonymous letter written by a slave to Jefferson in 1808 that lay unpublished in his papers until recently. Jefferson acknowledged that it was written by "a negro slave" but dismissed it as a "rhapsody of inconsistencies." Rather than congratulate the Republic on the closing of the African slave trade, "A Slave" wrote that "America can vie any nation in the world" when it came to "oppress & enslave mankind." He lay before Jefferson "our exquisite torment" and the "inhuman conduct" of slaveholders. Quoting the Declaration of Independence back to him, A Slave asked, "What think you now sir; are we men, or are we beasts?" The abolitionist tone of the letter is clear, and, like Banneker's almanacs, it quotes liberally from a work by the British Quaker abolitionist Thomas Wilkinson titled *An Appeal to England, on Behalf of the Abused Africans, a Poem* (1789). In a personal rebuke composed in vivid language, A Slave wrote, "O! Thomas, you have had a long nap, and spent a great number of years in ease & plenty, upon our hard earned property, while we have been in the mean time, smarting under the cow hide and sweating in the fields to raise provision to nurse tyrants[,] to cut your throat[,] and perpetuate our own bonds." It ends with the hope that Jefferson would free his own slaves, offer "reparation for the insult offered them," and start a "general immancipation."[47]

Black abolitionists like Sidney were especially censorious of slaveholding Republicans: "No people in the world make louder pretensions to 'liberty, equality, and the rights of man.' . . . And yet, strange as it may appear, there is no spot in the United States where oppression reigns with such unlimited sway!" According to Lawrence, the slave South was "so biased by interest" that it had "become callous to the voice of reason and justice." African Americans, like their Afro-British counterparts, portrayed slaveholders as the hated enemies of black people. Taking on the proslavery argument that the southern slave "is better fed and clad, than the poor of civilized Europe," Lawrence asked those "sophists whom avarice had armed in her cause" to pay attention to the real condition of slaves, who were deprived of any semblance of justice, protection, or citizenship. Nearly all the orations on the slave trade ended with a call for an end to southern slavery. While Sidney specifically asked for gradual emancipation in the South, most simply called for "African emancipation."[48] The abolitionist project, they all indicated, had not been achieved by ending the slave trade.

In his pamphlet of 1810, *A Dialogue between a Virginian and an African Minister*, Coker made emancipation in the slaveholding Republic a priority by juxtaposing black abolitionism with the slaveholding Virginia dynasty that dominated the nation. The fictitious Virginian, who is impressed by the black minister's civility, tries to convince him that his advocacy of abolition is wrong, as it would dispossess slaveholders of their property. The minister replies that abolition was a matter of humanity, not property, and that the slave's right to liberty outweighed the slaveholders' right to property. "Shall we hesitate a moment," the minister asks, "to determine who is the greatest sufferer, who is treated with the greatest injustice?" He goes on to recommend the Spanish system championed by Sharp, namely, allowing slaves to work one day a week for themselves in order to purchase their freedom, and asks the Virginian to Christianize and educate his slaves. Coker, who dedicated his pamphlet to the "people of colour," closed by saying he would not stop speaking about "the suffering of my people." In an appendix, he added a long list of black ministers and churches and excerpts from the slave trade orations, living "proofs" or exemplars of black abolitionism.[49]

The second act in establishing American independence and nationhood, the War of 1812 against the British, reinforced the alternative nature of black abolitionism. Proscribed from serving in the federal militia by the federal militia law of 1792, only a few African Americans served in integrated units of state militias. By the end of the war, the New York state legislature and congressional laws opened up recruitment to black men, who were defined as natives of the country rather than citizens. African Americans from the northern states, including the black abolitionist John B. Vashon of Pittsburgh, fought for the United States. The free colored militias in New Orleans played a crucial role in the American victory at the Battle of New Orleans, earning them a commendation from Andrew Jackson, who had solicited their assistance. Black abolitionists would repeatedly reprint it right up until the Civil War as an argument for black citizenship. Black sailors made up 15 to 20 percent of the integrated U.S. Navy and saw action throughout the war, from the battles in the Great Lakes bordering Canada to the Gulf coast. The British captured so many of them, over a thousand, that they occupied racially separate living quarters in Dartmoor prison. Slaves supplied much of the labor used to fortify and defend New Orleans, and around twenty-five hundred free black volunteers organized by Forten and Parrott helped dig trenches around Philadelphia after the bombardment of Washington. In New York and Baltimore the black community did the same. Despite free blacks' contributions, the nationalism that was given a fillip by the war was exclusively white, and the "era of good feelings" that followed it was marked by the growing virulence of popular racism and legal discrimination against black people.

African Americans, particularly the enslaved, were perceived as an internal enemy. Runaways flocked to British lines and played a role in shaping military strategy. Thousands of fugitive slaves supplied information, labor, and military service to the British, and multiple slave conspiracies were unearthed in Maryland, North Carolina, and Virginia. In the Chesapeake, Adm. Alexander Cochrane deliberately planned to encourage slaves to flee and thereby demoralize their owners. His proclamation of 1814 reprised Lord Dunmore's offer of freedom to slaves and included their families. Over three thousand slaves defected to the British, and some fought as uniformed Colonial Marines. All-black West India regiments also fought alongside English soldiers in New Orleans. For many enslaved blacks, impressment by the Royal Navy, one of the causes of the conflict, was preferable to American slavery. In Florida hundreds of slaves escaped to the so-called Negro Fort at Prospect Bluff, joining the British and their Indian allies. Some British officers such as Edward Nicolls of the Royal Marines harbored strong antislavery beliefs and became a conduit for Anglo-American abolitionism to this Maroon community of runaway slaves. When Jackson had the fort destroyed in 1816, the survivors joined up with the Seminoles on the frontier. Other fugitives from American slavery ended up in the British West Indies, particularly Trinidad, where they were called Mericans. Nearly two thousand runaway slaves were settled in Nova Scotia, following the path of black Loyalists after the revolution. These "black refugees" made their permanent home there. For a majority of the enslaved, fighting on the side of the British was a better path to freedom than laboring for their republican masters. They and their Indian allies continued to wage war on the United States in Spanish Florida, with encouragement from antislavery British officers like George Woodbine and Richard Ambrister, who had served with Nicolls. The First Seminole War was a direct result of Jackson's territorial ambitions and his determination to root out this node of black and Indian resistance, a beacon to runaway slaves from the Carolinas, Georgia, and Alabama.[50]

When Mr. Madison's War was over, the United States was more than ever a white man's country. In 1813 Forten's *Letters from a Man of Colour* put black rights on the abolitionist agenda. He challenged a proposed Pennsylvania law that would restrict black entry to the state, directed against fugitive slaves from neighboring slave states. It required state authorities to advertise unregistered blacks as fugitives so that their owners could reclaim them, and if not, they could be sold, put to hard labor, or fined heavily for not registering. The bill jeopardized the freedom of all black people in the state. Forten acknowledged the late Rush, who protested the bill just before his death that year and questioned the notion that American citizenship was racially exclusive. The Declaration and the Constitution, he wrote, embraced "the Indian and the European, the Savage and the Saint, the Peruvian and the Laplander, the white man and the African." Referring to the attacks on free blacks during the Fourth of July festivities, Forten opined that such laws encouraged racism. As he put it, "Are not men of colour sufficiently degraded? Why then increase their degradation." Forten issued a telling indictment of American racism: "Search the legends of tyranny and find no precedent." God had left no "record declaring us a different species" and "the same power which protects the white man, should protect the black." There was no point, he concluded, in black people forming organizations for their improvement or aspiring to become "honest and useful members of society" because "all our efforts by this bill, are despised and we are doomed to feel the lash of oppression:—As well may we be outlawed." Forten alerted the people of Pennsylvania to "the unhappy fate of thousands of our countrymen in the Southern States and the West Indies."[51]

Unlike Forten's letters, Jacob Oson's pamphlet against American racism has been forgotten. First delivered as a speech to African Americans in New Haven and then in New York, *A Search for Truth Or, An Inquiry for the Origin of the African Nation* (1817), written by this Connecticut minister and teacher, is not so much a history of African Americans as a biblically inspired impeachment of racism. In resorting to the Bible story of creation—Adam and Noah had a "common father," he wrote—Oson sought to answer racists who believed in the multiple origins of man. He pointed to the heathen nature of European Christians, who had committed "rapine and carnage" and violated "laws human and divine" by enslaving thousands of Africans and holding them "in bondage and subjection." The Western world, he avowed, owed most of its science and learning to Egypt. He noted the progress of early modern commerce, arguing that trade should not be the gauge of a nation's success. It had brought ruin to some, he said, referring to the slave trade: "Commerce produces luxury, and that brings down the wrath of God." Oson pointed to the light of emancipation that had spread from New England to New York and New Jersey and hoped it would glow all over the Americas as far as the Strait of Magellan, wherever Africans were "trodden under foot" and held in "cruel slavery."[52]

The publication of black spiritual narratives during this time was part of the emerging tradition of black abolitionism. George White and John Jea detailed not just their conversion experiences but also their strong condemnation of racial slavery. White, who was born a slave in Virginia and became a Methodist preacher in New York and New Jersey, wrote an account of his life in "this land of human oppression and barbarity." After gaining his freedom, he determined to devote his life to preaching the Gospel to his "African brethren." One of his sermons was titled "Loose him and let him go." Like Allen's, White's Christianity was a theology of black liberation. White, who recounted his long struggle to gain a preaching license from the Methodist Episcopal Conference, helped found a branch of Allen's AME church in New York in 1806.[53]

The life story of the "African preacher" Jea also offered a telling indictment of slavery. Born in Africa, Jea recalled the hard labor of his years as a slave belonging to a Dutch New York family. "We dared not murmur," he wrote, for fear of being "flogged . . . in a manner too dreadful to behold." Slaveholders "used us in a most cruel manner," murdering their slaves "in order to appease their wrath and thought no more of it than if they had been brutes." Much of Jea's narrative is an account of cruel masters who called their slaves black devils and deprived them of the word of God. Like many black converts, Jea portrayed his masters as the real heathens: "Though they professed Christianity, they knew nothing of what it meant." He was sold to three separate masters, all of whom suspected him of corrupting their slaves by his "talking and preaching." Describing his religious and personal trials (his first wife murdered their child), Jea's miraculous acquisition of literacy and abolitionist friends who helped purchase land to build a meetinghouse "for us poor black Africans to worship in" marked the start of a new chapter in his life as a free man. He became a sailor and traveled all over the world, preaching in England and Ireland. Only in the West Indies and the slave states of Virginia and Maryland did he encounter severe treatment, being imprisoned by persons attempting "to make me a slave."

Jea published his narrative and a hymnbook in Britain in 1815 and 1816, respectively, and was disparaging of the American Republic. As a slave, he witnessed colonists celebrating their victory over Native Americans and marveled that "*these* people made a great mourning when *God* killed one man, but they rejoice when *they* kill so many." Later in his narrative, when he refuses to fight against the British, he insists that "I was not an American, but I was a poor black African, *a preacher of the gospel.*" Africans as a persecuted people could identify with the suffering Christ: "For the world hated him and the world knew him not . . . neither do they know us, because he has chosen us out of the world." In his book of hymns Jea wrote of his family, "We all were stole away" from Africa. God, he wrote, would deliver Africans from bondage the way he did the Israelites from Egypt: "When we were carried across the 'main, / To great America, / There we were sold, and we were told, / That we had not a soul! / . . . But God who did poor Joseph save, / Who was in Egypt sold, / So did he unto us poor slaves, / And he'll redeem the whole."[54]

Like those of Jea, White, and Allen, Haynes's sermons conveyed an abolitionist message. Haynes was resolute in believing in the importance of religion to civil government and that the duty of all governments was to act virtuously and philanthropically. In making this argument, he was not only criticizing what New England Federalists viewed as the atheism of the Jeffersonian Republicans but also laying the philosophical ground for abolitionist appeals to the higher law of God. He opposed the War of 1812 from a Federalist standpoint as an unjust war and going against the biblical injunction "Thou Shall Not Kill." In "The Influence of Civil Government on Religion," Haynes reproved those who invade "our liberties" and challenge "the rights of man . . . under the soothing titles of *Republicanism, Democracy*." In a sermon in 1814, "Dissimulation Illustrated," Haynes critiqued all kinds of dissembling and hypocrisy that mar love for one's neighbor and a republican devotion to the common good: "It is a species of dissimulation, when we justify that in ourselves, which we condemn in others." Repeating the Federalist accusation that Virginian presidents like Madison and Jefferson raised the issue of impressment of American sailors while enslaving over three hundred human beings for life, he argued that "partial affection, or distress for some of our fellow-creatures, while others even under our notice, are wholly disregarded, betrays dissimulation." Haynes represented Washington as a true republican: "He was an enemy to slaveholding, and gave his dying testimony against it, by emancipating, and providing for those under his care." In "The Nature and Importance of True Republicanism" (1801) Haynes had written that slavery was a species of monarchism, not of republicanism. The state of the "poor Africans among us" show the effects of despotism.[55]

By the time Abbé Henri Grégoire published his *De la littérature des Nègres* in 1808 in Paris, black abolitionism had emerged in the United States as a coherent movement. Designed to refute Jefferson's racist views in the *Notes*, Grégoire, a member of the Société des Amis des Noirs, dedicated his book to abolitionists and antislavery writers from different countries and called for an end to slavery. Compiling a long list of slave rebels and African thinkers and writers, Grégoire sought to disprove notions of racial inferiority. Notwithstanding his measured response to the abbé, Jefferson dismissed it as diatribe and "rubbish massed together." Grégoire was unaware of a rising cadre of black abolitionists across the Atlantic. His slim volume, published in the United States in 1810, could have been expanded exponentially. His hope—"May Africans, raising their humiliated fronts, give spring to all their faculties, and rival whites in talents and virtues only; avenging themselves by benefits and effusions of fraternal kindness"—was a prescient description of the discourse and organizations of black abolitionism in the slaveholding Republic.[56]

6

THE NEGLECTED PERIOD OF ANTISLAVERY

Antislavery protest did not disappear with the waning of the first wave of abolition. In 1817 Jesse Torrey of the PAS interviewed an enslaved mother who had jumped from the window of a tavern in Washington, D.C., after slave traders "carried my children off with 'em to Carolina." Torrey's recounting of the plight of the bedridden, paralyzed woman, Anna, with an accompanying illustration of her jumping from the building became a classic indictment of the domestic slave trade and was reprinted in abolition journals for years to come.[1] Abolitionists confronted the explosive expansion of slavery into the trans-Mississippi West and an interstate slave trade whose dimensions—nearly two million sold to the Cotton Kingdom and in local sales—far exceeded the African slave trade to mainland North America.

During the "neglected period of anti-slavery," when slavery, far from disappearing, became the cornerstone of the national economy, abolitionists experimented with tactics that paved the way for second-wave abolition. The roots of antebellum abolition lay in the virtually unanimous rejection by blacks of the program of the American Colonization Society (ACS), founded in 1816 to colonize black Americans in Africa. Controversy over the colonization movement reinforced abolitionists' demands for black citizenship. By positioning themselves against colonization, African Americans rejected any solution to slavery that did not encompass black rights. Their misgivings about colonization, though, must be distinguished from independent, black-led emigration efforts.[2]

Northern unease over the growth of southern slavery also set the stage for the rise of immediate abolition. The debate over the admission of Missouri as a slave state in 1819–20 reenergized abolitionists. Besides national politics, transnational developments influenced American abolitionists. A revived British abolition movement became a powerful model of antislavery activism, inspiring comparable ideas in the United States.[3]

EMIGRATION VERSUS COLONIZATION

The African American road to immediate abolition took a detour through movements for emigration thanks to Paul Cuffe. A black Quaker sea captain from Massachusetts, Cuffe was the son of an Akan father, Kofi, and a Wampanoag mother. By the early 1800s the enterprising Cuffe, building on his Quaker connections, had established himself as a successful trader, sailing along America's slavery-riddled coastline and to faraway Scandinavian countries. From his early antitaxation petitions to his later career as an emigrationist, Cuffe revealed an abiding concern for black economic autonomy. He wrote to abolitionists in Britain and America, alerting them to his plans for trade with Africa. With an all-black crew he set sail for Sierra Leone in 1811, noting in his logbook that he read Clarkson's history on the abolition of the slave trade during the voyage, which "Ba[p]tized my mind." Cuffe organized a "Friendly Society" in Sierra Leone. Its president was John Kizell, a former slave from South Carolina and black Loyalist from Nova Scotia. Kizell, who had been enslaved from this very region as a young boy and was miraculously reunited with his African family, shared Cuffe's Pan-African vision. Kizell's former owners were German immigrants who had established a Friendly Society in South Carolina. In one of its first acts, Cuffe's society petitioned for more emigrants and permission to conduct independent trade. There was no reason, Cuffe wrote, why Sierra Leone should "not become a Nation to be Numbered among the historians nations of the World."

James Pemberton alerted Cuffe to the African Institution, a society founded in London in 1807 to end the the slave trade in Africa and remedy the conditions of slaves in the British colonies. Its members included the radical Quaker pharmacist William Allen, Dillwyn, Sharp, Clarkson, Macaulay, and the antislavery parliamentarians James Stephens and Lord Henry Brougham. From Sierra Leone, Cuffe sailed to England and was cordially received by them and by Wilberforce, who assisted him in recovering two members of his ship impressed by the British navy. Cuffe received a six-month trading license through the intervention of Allen, a longtime supporter of black settlers and critic of colonial authorities in Sierra Leone. Kizell had corresponded with Allen, apprising him of the abuse of settlers by company officials. He also presented Clarkson with an African gold ring "as a token of [his] love and respect" and sent his eight-year-old son with Macaulay to be educated in England. Allen and Clarkson formed a separate society to encourage black emigration at Cuffe's and his behest. Cuffe presented the Duke of Gloucester, the honorary president of the African Institution, with African artifacts "to Shew that the Affricans Was Capebell of mantel Endowments."[4]

Cuffe kept abolitionists apprized of his travels and established African Institutions in Philadelphia and New York. He corresponded with John Murray of the NYMS and his partners Samuel Fisher and John James in Pennsylvania. Moses Brown assisted him in gaining an audience with President Madison, when the American government impounded his ship laden with British goods for violating the Embargo. He became the first black leader to meet with an American president. The next such meeting would not take place until the Civil War. Cuffe was often subject to racial harassment but reported that Madison and Secretary of State Albert G. Gallatin, known for his antislavery sympathies, received him courteously. Madison evinced some interest in his plans, as did other colonizationists, including Jedidiah Morse, Samuel J. Mills, a Congregational clergyman from the Andover Theological Seminary, and the Presbyterian Robert Finley, who wanted to mine his knowledge of the West African coast.[5]

Cuffe's Pan-African vision was distinct from the movement to colonize African Americans, which took off after his death. He hoped that an "open Communication between America-Africa and England" would connect the black diaspora in three continents. Africans, he wrote, should "become their own Carryer and imploy their Citizens as meriners." In a short pamphlet that he published after his return, Cuffe argued that only as a "national body" could Africans escape laboring "under the narrow predict that had ben so Long hanging our heads." Racial uplift was part of his message. In an address to "my African Breatheren and fellow Countreymen" in Sierra Leone, he urged piety, temperance, duty, and faithfulness. He attached a similar exhortation from the American Convention to the free people of color. Cuffe thought an economically prosperous black nation would redeem all Africans. In a memorial of 1813 he requested the American government to allow him to trade with Sierra Leone. He hoped it could be prevailed upon "at Some future day when the liberation of Slavery become more General" to support his expeditions.

For his second voyage to Sierra Leone in 1816, Cuffe, with the help of local black leaders, rounded up thirty-eight emigrants and got the African Institutions in Philadelphia and New York to address Sierra Leone's Friendly Society. In a letter to the directors of the African Institution in London, Forten and Parrott, on behalf of the African Institution in Philadelphia, inquired what "privilege your Government would be disposed to grant" future black emigrants. On the eve of his death in 1817, Cuffe recommended the founding of two black nations, one in Africa and one in the western territories that would include Native Americans. His wife, Alice Pequit, who was a Wampanoag like his mother, had refused to relocate to Africa. To black abolitionists, Cuffe was a model leader. In his eulogy, Peter Williams said, "It was in his active commiseration in behalf of his African brethren, that he shone forth most conspicuously." He argued that blacks, however, ought to "suspend [their] judgments" on the ACS, sounding a warning against the new colonization movement claiming Cuffe's mantle.[6]

By the end of the decade a large bisectional coalition of religious and political leaders from the North and upper south, including Sen. Henry Clay and President James Monroe, sought to solve the problem of slavery and race by promoting the colonization of African Americans. The ACS, modeled after societies like the American Bible Society, the American Sunday School Union, and the American Tract Society and as yet another exercise in religious benevolence, was founded by clergymen, including Finley, Morse, Mills, Nathan Lord, and Leonard Bacon. They supported colonization as a plan for gradually ending slavery and for Christianizing Africa. In his *Thoughts on the Colonization of Free Blacks,* Finley, posing the question, "What shall we do with the free people of color?" proposed *"the gradual separation of the black from the white population."* He rejected Cuffe's idea of a black state in the west, fearing it would become a haven for fugitive slaves and an ally of Indians, Europeans, and other enemies of the American nation. Finley, who had worked as a tutor in South Carolina, knew that this is exactly what had happened on the Florida frontier. He contended that the black presence was harmful to "our industry and morals" and resulted in racial intermarriage. Emancipation could be enacted only on the condition of colonization, and it would be so imperceptible and slow as to prepare whites for the end of slavery. Finley sought the backing of the federal government for colonization and circulated his pamphlet widely among congressmen.[7]

Support for colonization crossed party and sectional lines. The ACS was launched at a meeting in Washington on December 21, 1816, that, besides clergymen like Finley and Mills, included the prominent lawyers Francis Scott Key, famous for composing the national anthem, and Elias B. Caldwell, Finley's brother-in-law and a clerk in the Supreme Court, and the politicians John Randolph of Roanoke, Daniel Webster, and Clay, who presided. In his speech, Clay, a Kentucky slaveholder whose distaste for slavery led him to colonization, recommended getting "rid . . . of a useless and pernicious, if not dangerous portion of" the American population and bringing "redemption from ignorance and barbarism of a benighted quarter of the globe!" A week later, when the American Society for Colonizing the Free People of Color in the United States met, the future president Andrew Jackson, Secretary of the Treasury William

Crawford of Georgia, and the states' rights champion John Taylor of Caroline attended. In January 1817 the Supreme Court justice Bushrod Washington, the nephew of George Washington, was elected president, and the ACS submitted its first memorial to Congress asking for an African colony. To "National Republicans," colonization complemented the promotion of domestic manufactures and internal improvements. The American System, Clay's blueprint for national economic development, stipulated the elimination of slavery and black people.

A mixture of men and motives, from southern slaveholders to northern ministers, characterized colonization, but its center of gravity emanated from the South. Even before the founding of the ACS, the Federalist Charles Fenton Mercer, godfather to Bushrod Washington, persuaded the Virginia House of Delegates to adopt resolutions requesting the federal government to sponsor colonization, a proposition the state had been pushing since Gabriel's rebellion. A conservative nationalist, Mercer deplored lower classes of all colors, especially free blacks, who he claimed lived mainly by pilfering. Robert Goodloe Harper of Maryland, in a letter to the ACS secretary Elias Caldwell, called free blacks a "nuisance and a burden" who increased pauperism and crime and corrupted the slave population. After Finley's premature death, Mercer assumed leadership of the movement. In 1819 he sponsored the law that allowed the ACS to receive federal money to resettle African "recaptives" apprehended from the illegal Atlantic slave trade. This initial funding allowed the ACS to conduct its first voyages to West Africa and acquire land for the colony of Liberia, whose capital was named Monrovia in honor of the president. Within a decade the ACS had auxiliaries in nearly all the states, and independent state colonization societies were formed. Despite its critics in the proslavery lower south, the ACS had more auxiliaries in the South than in the North. Distinguishing itself from the American Convention, the ACS proclaimed that colonization of degraded free blacks, not abolition, was its goal. As the Powhatan auxiliary stated in its memorial, colonization would not undermine slaveholders' "rights of property" and would remove the "baneful and contaminating" influence of free blacks on the enslaved. Despite avowing that free blacks would be colonized "with their own consent," colonizationists continued to denigrate them. The creation of a lily-white, slaveholding republic was predicated on the removal of free blacks and the disappearance of Native Americans.[8]

African Americans registered their opposition to colonization and refuted aspersions on their character. A large meeting of free black people at Philadelphia's Bethel Church in January 1817 chaired by Forten, with Parrott as secretary, resolved that they would never be banished from a country whose soil had been "manured" by the "blood and sweat" of their ancestors and that they abhorred "the unmerited stigma attempted to be cast upon the reputation of the free people of color." It further resolved that "we will never separate ourselves voluntarily from the slave population of this country; they are our brethren by the ties of consanguinity, of suffering and of wrong." Forten reported that at least three thousand people were present, and not one was in favor of colonization. They "think that slaveholders want to get rid of them so as to make their property more secure." Forten, who had written to Cuffe that "they will never become a people until they come out from amongst the white people," remained silent. Other black leaders also followed rather than led the meeting. A few months later another meeting issued an address signed by Forten and Parrott that emphatically stated, "We . . . renounce and disclaim every connexion with it; and respectfully and firmly declare our determination not to participate in any of it." The "heart-rending agonies" endured by their African forefathers would be repeated by sending free blacks to Africa. The address concluded, "Let not a purpose be assisted which will stay the cause of the entire abolition of slavery in the United States, and which may defeat it altogether . . . and which must insure to the multitudes whose prayers can only reach you through us, MISERY, *sufferings, and perpetual slavery.*" Finley's visit to Philadelphia was in vain, as blacks firmly rejected colonization.[9]

In the slave states, where the condition of free blacks was legally akin to masterless slaves, opposition to colonization was more muted yet clear. Richmond blacks asked to be settled in the west rather than in Africa. A meeting in Georgetown asked for territory within the United States and sought to galvanize free blacks all over the country against colonization. A majority of free blacks who left for Liberia came from the border slave states. Colonization followed the failure of even the most gradual kind of abolition in the postrevolutionary South. In the antebellum period it afforded one avenue for the manumission of slaves in southern states that had anti-emancipation laws that required former slaves to leave on obtaining their freedom. Slaves used any opportunity, including colonization, to negotiate the terms of their freedom. The ACS and the Pennsylvania Colonization Society helped transport hundreds of emancipated slaves, but this hardly made a dent in the South's flourishing peculiar institution. Colonization, pace its proslavery critics, was not a stalking horse for abolition. It was an alternative to general emancipation for a few conscientious slaveholders, many of whose heirs tried to undo their wishes through protracted legal battles in southern courts. Slaves who secured their freedom found that removal to Liberia was the price they paid for liberty.[10]

The founding of Liberia was a result of the missionary zeal of colonizationist clergymen. In an initial fact-finding mission in 1818, Mills, on behalf of the American Bible Society, and Ebenezer Burgess of Burlington College, set out for West Africa. On Clarkson's suggestion, they decided on an American settlement at Sherbro island and elicited the help of Kizell. Despite the reluctance of the native population to part with their land, Mills and Burgess composed a glowing report of the feasibility of colonization, but Mills died en route home. He became the first of many colonizationist martyrs, a group that included Rev. Samuel Bacon of Sturbridge, who led the ill-fated expedition of 1820 to Sherbro and died in Africa. After the failure to colonize Sherbro, Lt. Richard Stockton of the U.S. Navy procured land at gunpoint in Cape Mesurado to establish the American colony of Liberia in 1821. Rev. Leonard Bacon best articulated the sensibility behind the founding of Liberia in his "Plea for Africa." Africa, in Bacon's eyes, was synonymous with barbarism, imbecility, depravity, savage warfare, and the slave trade. Only its "exiled sons" could rescue the dark continent through Christianity and civilization, as white men could not flourish there. Rev. Jehudi Ashmun, the ACS agent who resisted what he called native attacks and fractious black settlers, put the colony on a firm footing the next year. He fell ill and came home to die in New Haven in 1828. In his eulogy Bacon called Ashmun a "victim to his labors and privations and afflictions under the burning sun of Africa." Even a fierce critic of colonization like the black abolitionist David Walker had kind words for Ashmun.[11]

Colonizationists were interested in redeeming "poor benighted Africa." While their writings praised the past glories of Africa, their views of contemporary African societies were decidedly unfavorable. According to Ashmun, native Africans "enjoy animal existence in perfection" and their miseries, slavery and polygamy, were of a moral nature. Colonization would "build up among barbarians the Church of God and a republican empire." As another colonizationist grandiosely put it, "The germ of an Americo-African empire has been planted; and though our society should be dissolved tomorrow, it will flourish and expand until it overshadows a continent." The Ladies Colonization Society of Fredericksburg and Falmouth argued that if India was "the appropriate sphere of action" for the British, Africa was for the United States. This protoimperialist discourse complemented colonizationists' derogatory view of free black people. The energetic secretary of the ACS, Rev. Ralph Randolph Gurley, asked free blacks suffering from degradation and debasement to save Africa from barbarism and heathenism.[12]

The colonial structure and ideology of the ACS constrained blacks' efforts to achieve autonomy. African Americans who migrated to Liberia were confronted by white control and native resentment. The only prominent black abolitionist to participate in early colonization was Daniel Coker. He joined the expedition of 1820 along with ninety other black emigrants. It was Coker who led the retreat to Sierra Leone after the failure at Sherbro. He viewed his voyage to Africa as a homecoming: "Will not Africa open her bosom, and receive her weeping and bleeding children that may be taken from slave ships or come from America?" In an address to his "African brethren in America," Coker, calling for missionaries and emigrants to Christianize Africa and end the slave trade, wrote that his "soul cleaves to Africa." He described the natives as generally hospitable and praised Kizell for his support. Unfortunately, this state of affairs did not last long; the bitter rivalry between the two doomed any chance of a united black leadership and left the colony firmly in the hands of the ACS's white agents. Both men preferred to cast their lot in Sierra Leone, where they lived and worked, rather than in Liberia.[13]

The experience of African American settlers revealed the nature of white-directed colonization. Ashmun, who preferred white agents, felt that the settlers lacked moral and religious fiber and were further corrupted by the "vitiating example of natives of this country." But a few left their mark in Liberia. Rev. Lott Cary and Colin Teague, from Richmond, established a Baptist church in Monrovia, and Forten's apprentice, Francis Devany, originally a slave of Langdon Cheves in South Carolina, was one of a handful who prospered in the colony. He died in 1834 from consumption. Cary, who led a minirevolt against white authorities, became Ashmun's right-hand man. Model emigrants like Cary, colonizationists claimed, underwent an "absolute reversal" of character and cast off their former "profane and vicious habits." Cary, a preacher who had bought himself and his children from slavery and who was as responsible for the survival of the colony as Ashmun, was in no need of moral instruction. Ashmun remarked that he was still given to "fits of turbulence." Cary gained his trust for defending the colony against a native invasion and was appointed vice agent when Ashmun returned to the United States. He died shortly thereafter, in 1828, in a gunpowder accident.

A large number of colonists found disease and an early death. High mortality rates plagued Liberia throughout its existence and increased black opposition to colonization. Settlers did not realize Cuffe's Pan-African unity but were placed in an untenable position of conflict with the surrounding African nations whose land was appropriated. They were also dependent on the ACS and their former masters for supplies, and the native populations remained enmeshed in the slave trade. Colonial notions of superiority soon infiltrated the settler population, giving rise to divisions that mark the history of Liberia until today. The *Liberian Herald* wrote, "The Liberian is certainly a great man, and what is more, by the natives he is considered a white man." The colonist George C. Brown went so far as to relate that "the natives bow at our feet as if we are giants; and they are no more than grasshoppers." In their address of 1827 to the people of color, the colonists contended, "We know nothing of that debasing inferiority with which our color stamped us with in America" and asked free blacks to join them in "founding a new Christian empire." In a trenchant critique of their views of native Africans, Jeremiah Gloucester asked, "Is it not obvious that the inhabitants of Africa notwithstanding they are heathens, can teach the greater part of those that have gone to Africa in a great many respects?"[14]

A majority of African Americans who were interested in emigrating chose Haiti rather than Liberia as their destination. While a trickle of emigrants went to Liberia, around eight thousand emigrated to Haiti in the 1820s. The man most responsible for the Haitian emigration movement was Prince Saunders, a Boston abolitionist, teacher, and Masonic leader, and the son-in-law of Cuffe. Born in Connecticut, Saunders was a schoolteacher at an African school in Colchester and a landowner in Vermont by the age of twenty-one. He was briefly educated at Dartmouth, where he attracted the attention of President John Wheelock. Wheelock recommended him to William Ellery Channing in Boston, and Saunders became a teacher in the city's African school. He also became secretary of the African Masonic Lodge and persuaded Abiel Smith to bequeath a large amount to the African school, henceforth named after its benefactor. Through much of his life Saunders championed black education and emigration. He visited England in 1815 with Rev. Thomas Paul, representing the Prince Hall Masons, and both he and Paul were converted to the cause of Haitian emigration by Wilberforce and Clarkson. Saunders helped found schools in Haiti and wrote the *Haytian Papers*, a compilation of the history and conditions of Haiti containing several official proclamations of King Henri Christophe aimed at attracting black emigrants to the island. On his return to the United States in 1818, Saunders extolled the virtues of education and Haiti in an address to the Pennsylvania Augustine Society for the Education of the People of Colour. He also presented a memoir to the American Convention recommending Haiti as an asylum for free blacks and slaves. He migrated to Haiti, became its attorney general, and wrote the country's criminal code. Saunders died there in 1839.[15]

Haitian emigration rather than colonization appealed to African Americans and abolitionists for whom the republic symbolized antislavery and black self-government. The movement took off in the 1820s with the unification of Haiti and the Haitian government's plans to lure black emigrants to revive the island's economy. In 1820 President Jean Pierre Boyer issued an appeal to African Americans, promising land and citizenship. Black wounds, he said, would be "healed by the balm of equality and their tears wiped away by the protecting hand of liberty." A Haitian emigrant to South Carolina, Silvain Simonisse, returned to his country to bolster free black settlement and joined its Emigration Bureau. Rev. Loring Dewey, a Presbyterian minister and agent for the ACS, observed abolitionists' opposition to colonization: "Among the Colored People themselves, a preference of Hayti over Africa was frequently expressed, and among the whites there was not only an opposition to colonization in Africa manifested by many, but an assurance given of their ready aid to promote emigration to Hayti." Dewey entered into correspondence with Boyer as an "ardent friend to the injured sons of Africa," and as a result the New York colonization society disowned him. He visited Haiti on a fact-finding mission in 1824 and published a plan for gradual emancipation, encouraging black women especially to emigrate so that their children might be born free.

Black abolitionists headed Haitian emigration societies as they had the African Institutions. Paul visited Haiti as a Baptist missionary, as did Williams. Rev. Samuel Cornish, who opposed colonization, was a proponent of Haitian emigration. Richard Allen's son John traveled to Haiti and reported favorably on conditions there. Allen, who led the Haitian Emigration Society in Philadelphia, wrote to Boyer that while the United States was a land of oppression for people of African descent, Haiti represented black freedom and equality. In his letter of 1824 from Haiti, Paul said the island was "the best and most suitable place of residence which Providence has hitherto offered to emancipated people of colour, for the enjoyment of liberty and equality with their attendant blessings." Composed of "active and brave men, who are determined to live free or die gloriously in the defense of freedom," Haiti "must possess advantages highly inviting to men who are sighing for the enjoyment of the common rights and liberties of mankind."

Boyer sent an agent, Jonathan Granville, to the United States to meet with black leaders and promised to defray the costs of transportation and grant land to all emigrants. The Haitian secretary of state, Gen. Balthazar Inginac, wrote to Allen that Haiti was "grateful to you for the trouble you give yourself to reunite the great family, those of your compatriot descendants of African blood." Hezekiah Grice of Baltimore, the founder of the black convention movement, migrated to Haiti in 1832 and became director of public works in Port-au-Prince. Cuffe's namesake and son, a seafarer like his father, visited Haiti, "peopled by free blacks" and "having a republican form of government." He described the "commanding aspect" of Boyer and his "superbly dressed and equipped" bodyguard.[16]

Abolitionists, as noted, preferred Haitian emigration to colonization. In Massachusetts the abolitionist John Kenrick corresponded with Inginac. When

George Flowers, an English farmer and confidante of the abolitionist feminist Frances Wright, faced his neighbors' ire for leading a black communitarian society in Illinois, he transported twenty black men to Haiti in 1823. Led by Aaron Coffin, the manumission society of North Carolina transported over a hundred freed slaves to Haiti in 1826, and the Society of Friends in North Carolina transported seven hundred more to get around the state's antimanumission laws. The Quaker abolitionist Benjamin Lundy was a champion of Haitian emigration and twice escorted black emigrants from North Carolina and Maryland to Haiti. Lundy founded the Baltimore Emigration Society in 1825 with his fellow abolitionist Daniel Raymond. He published his numbers on emigration to Haiti and debated colonizationists in his newspaper, the *Genius of Universal Emancipation.* Raymond, a political economist, argued that Haiti would grow economically once it became politically stable. Lundy also corresponded with Inginac, suggesting ways to promote emigration to Haiti. The black abolitionist William Watkins, who strongly opposed colonization, upheld the notion of a "movement emanating from a branch of our own people who cannot but have the welfare of the whole race at heart." Even after the Haitian emigration movement faltered, Lundy published articles on the Haitian republic and "Sketches" of its historic revolution in 1826 and 1827. In 1829 he and his new coeditor William Lloyd Garrison were still publishing advertisements for Haitian emigrants.[17]

The American Convention enthusiastically endorsed Haitian emigration. In its report of 1823, the convention reasoned that "it appears that the Haytians, have made a progress in Civilization and intellectual improvement, nearly if not altogether unparalleled in the history of nations." Haiti should interest all "friends of African rights," as it refuted "prejudices against the Blacks" and acted as a "refuge for those Coloured persons who may be unwilling to endure the degradation they are doomed to suffer in other countries." The PAS resolved to take no action on Haitian emigration, and while it did not take a stance against colonization, it did not endorse the ACS. The NYMS actively encouraged Haitian emigration, opening up a correspondence first with Christophe and then with Boyer and Inginac. It rejected colonization and helped found the Society for Promoting the Emigration of Free Persons of Colour to Hayti. Its standing committee, which had assisted slaves in their quest for freedom, became involved in Haitian emigration in the 1820s. It requested information from the Haitian government on what it would do for the black emigrants and kept a list of emigrants and their families. People of color in New York, the committee observed, deeply felt their oppression and were willing to migrate to Haiti to avail themselves of the privileges of citizenship.[18]

African Americans' ideological identification with the black republic could not withstand differences in language, culture, and religion, the hardships emigrants encountered, and the withdrawal of funding by the Haitian government. Most emigrants returned to the United States. Unlike colonization, however, abolitionists' promotion of Haitian emigration was based on a vindication of black equality.

ABOLITIONISTS OF THE MIDDLE PERIOD

Abolitionists in the middle period paved the way for the second wave. One of the most important was the Quaker reformer Elias Hicks, many of whose followers joined the abolition movement. Echoing earlier abolitionist Quakers, Hicks condemned not just slavery but all wealth making and market society. Like Woolman, he traveled extensively and left a journal of his ministry. In 1811 Hicks published his *Observations on the Slavery of Africans and their Descendants*, in which he noted that "custom and education" made many believe that African slavery was consistent with "justice and social order." But simply because slavery was sanctioned by manmade laws, it could not "alter the nature of justice." In a series of queries Hicks established that Africans were unjustly deprived of their natural rights and that racism was special pleading, a cloak based on selfish motives to cover unrighteous conduct. Slavery was an act of war upheld by violence and "an avaricious thirst of gain." Enslaving a person and then taking away all the products of his or her labor was robbery. Calling for the immediate abolition of slavery by law, Hicks felt that gradual emancipation, which was "the best step" yet taken, was not fully consistent with "justice and equity." He pointed out that while whites attained adulthood early, black people in the North were forced to labor for their masters for a longer time before they were freed. At the very least, slaveholders ought to educate slave children.

Hicks held consumers and purchasers of slave goods just as culpable in upholding slavery. Like Lay, he called on people to abstain from using products produced by slave labor in order to curb the "luxury and excess . . . the gain of oppression" of slaveholders. Hicks's ideas and the British Quaker example of a boycott of goods made by slave labor became the basis of the free produce movement led by Quakers and African Americans in Philadelphia, an abolitionist precursor to modern consumer activism. Hicks called on free blacks, "fellow citizens," who knew from experience how "hateful the oppressor is," to lead the movement on behalf of their "oppressed countrymen." He was also a founder of the Underground Railroad (UGRR) on Long Island, where his abolitionist daughter, among others, continued assisting fugitives. Radical

Hicksites sympathized with communitarian movements, workingmen's rights, and Wright's feminism. Hicks's preaching led to a split among Quakers in 1827–28, when orthodox Quakers tried to read him out of the Society of Friends. Later, even Hicksite followers of George F. White came to oppose abolitionists in favor of quietism.[19]

Early voices of abolition deserve a larger space in the history of antislavery than they currently occupy. At a time of relative quiescence, Jarvis Brewster of New Jersey, the English-born Presbyterian minister George Bourne in Virginia, Kenrick, and Torrey published notable abolitionist books. In *Exposition of the Treatment of Slaves in the Southern States* (1815), Brewster explained that he was compelled to write when comparing the growing prosperity of white Americans with "the most painful and miserable slavery" of blacks. He argued that laws protecting slaves passed at this time, what historians have called the domestication of southern slavery, were "disregarded and trampled under foot with impunity," and the South not only recognized slavery in principle but enforced it with a "cruel and unrelenting hand." While justice demanded "total emancipation," Jarvis called for protecting the rights of slaves. He communicated that slaves continued to be ill clad, underfed, and "driven like beasts to the field of labor." He wrote about cruel overseers and inhuman masters, of slave women and children, the aged and the young being treated in a brutal manner, of whippings, and the domestic slave trade. Jarvis appended a petition to the legislatures of the southern states to establish a "SLAVES' COURT OF APPEAL" to prevent abuses.[20]

The abolitionist Theodore Weld republished Jarvis and Bourne in his *American Slavery As It Is*. Hounded out of Virginia for his abolitionism, Bourne published *The Book and Slavery Irreconcilable* in 1816. He discarded all talk of moderation, condemning not just the slave trade but slavery itself as man stealing. Slavery was an abomination in the sight of God, and slaves were justified in fleeing from it and resisting their kidnappers. He asked all good Christians to assist them, as the Gospel could not be reconciled with slavery. A human being could not be reduced to "an article of traffic." The motto of all slaves and their allies must be, *"peaceably if we can, forcibly if we must."* Bourne reserved his special ire for the hypocrisy of religious leaders, especially the elders and ministers of his church, whose abuse of slaves he had witnessed, and the villainy of politicians, who held "declarations of Independence" in one hand and whips in the other. He pithily concluded, *"Slavery is the climax of cruelty."* In its unsparing condemnation and appeal to a higher law, Bourne's book anticipated antebellum abolition. He became a founding member of the New York Anti Slavery Society, and the black abolitionist David Ruggles published his works. He died in 1845.[21] A Baptist clergyman, Kenrick, who converted to Quakerism, also lived long enough to join the Garrisonians. He published the speeches of Wilberforce and Fox, among others, and excerpts from Clarkson's history of the abolition of the slave trade in his *Horrors of Slavery* (1817). Kenrick also reprinted Cowper's poems, the writings of Brissot and Abbé Raynal, and American abolitionists such as David Rice, David Barrow, and Jarvis. Kenrick's pamphlet was mainly a compilation of abolitionist opinion from across the world directed at shaming American slaveholders into action. The long title of his pamphlet encapsulated immediatist rhetoric: "Demonstrating that slavery is *impolitic, antirepublican, unchristian and highly criminal*: and proposing measures for its complete abolition through the United States." He became the president of the New England Anti Slavery Society (NEASS) and died at the age of seventy.[22]

Torrey's *A Portraiture of Domestic Slavery in the United States*, also published in 1817, was conciliatory in tone, asking slaveholders in the interest of self-preservation to abolish slavery. Disavowing that he was for "*unconditional emancipation*," Torrey asked masters to become patrons and guardians to their slaves, to educate them, and convert them into tenants and indentured servants. He appended the proceedings of the initial meetings of the ACS to his book. Torrey's gradualism and advocacy of colonization belied the content of his book. He enumerated desperate instances of black resistance to the domestic slave trade and his own attempts to free kidnapped African Americans, for which Thomas Shipley, the president of the PAS, commended him. Garrison also recommended his book as an effective indictment of southern slavery.[23]

During these years the American Convention met biennially, at times adjourning for a year to meet again so that it met nearly every year. These meetings were hardly desultory, ineffective gatherings. Tactics debated by abolitionists of the middle era anticipated second-wave abolition. The most important of these was the convention's rejection of colonization as impracticable and injurious to the people of color and not a path to general emancipation. This was noteworthy because in 1816 the convention itself had proposed emancipation and settlement of African Americans in the western territories in a memorial to Congress. It had also corresponded with the African Institution in London to discuss black emigration. With the founding of the ACS, it resolved that "the gradual and total emancipation of all persons of colour, and their literary and moral education, should precede colonization." A year later, after inviting Forten to speak on colonization, it issued a report criticizing it and appended the anticolonization resolutions of black Philadelphians.

In 1821 the convention proposed a plan for the "general emancipation of the slaves" of the United States, arguing, "We owe to the injured race an immense debt, which the liberation of their bodies alone would not liquidate." Slaves should be attached to the soil like the serfs of Russia, educated, not be liable to sale or arbitrary punishment, given land for which they would pay rent, and receive wages for work performed for their masters. It also issued passionate condemnations of the domestic slave trade and the kidnapping of free blacks, and it continued to make black education and uplift a priority, issuing addresses to state societies urging the establishment of schools and apprenticeship of African Americans into skilled trades. By 1829 the American Convention halfheartedly endorsed colonization, but only if it expedited emancipation in the South. On behalf of the committee considering gradual abolition, Thomas Earle of the PAS said they "do not look to the transportation of the whole colored population, at any period. Emancipation will be effected without it. But partial emigration may aid the cause; particularly in its early stages, by preparing the way for the repeal of the laws against education and against voluntary emancipation."[24]

While the NYMS, now led by Cadwallader D. Colden, Theodore Dwight, and Peter Jay, the son of John Jay, and the PAS, led by William Rawle, Earle, Robert Vaux, and Shipley, continued to dominate the American Convention, new abolition societies emerged in the upper south. At this time only the Kentucky Abolition Society (KAS), founded by David Barrow in 1808, was active in the South. Antislavery evangelicals such as Barrow and Carter Tarrant had founded the Baptists Friends of Humanity in 1805, a loose association of antislavery congregations which, according to "Tarrant's Rules," barred all slaveholders from fellowship. Barrow, who attended the convention, condemned the idea of perpetual slavery as an *unnatural* and *devilish usurpation*." The KAS languished after his death because of slaveholder opposition and the migration of abolitionist clergymen to the North. Kentucky abolitionists such as David Rice and Barrow visualized an end not just to slavery but also to racial differences, predicting that a mixed race was destined to inhabit America. Besides the KAS, the Delaware Abolition Society (DAS) continued to send representatives to the convention.

In 1815 Charles Osborne, a North Carolina Quaker who migrated to Tennessee, helped found the Tennessee Society for Promoting the Manumission of Slaves (TMS). In its inaugural address to the "free men" of the state, it called attention to "the iron hand of oppression" and the "various kinds of misery, hardship and distress" that slaves "daily groan under." Its most active member was another Quaker, Elihu Embree. His father, Thomas, was a Pennsylvania Quaker who had issued a public letter to the new state of Tennessee in 1797 calling for the gradual abolition of slavery. Embree, a clerk of the TMS, was responsible for two memorials, signed by him and the president of the society, James Jones, to the state legislature in 1817 asking for an end to the separation of slave families and the slave trade. He published an abolitionist newspaper, the *Manumission Intelligencer* in 1819, and its successor, the *Emancipator*, in 1820. Embree made clear that his newspaper was devoted to the cause of "equal rights to the now neglected sons of Africa" and the "love of African liberty." The paper published excerpts from Clarkson's history and the constitution, memorials, and various addresses of the manumission society. Embree sent his newspaper to the governors of Georgia and Alabama, who returned their package unopened. He was forced to pay return postage for the opened package sent to the governor of North Carolina and for a letter from Gov. George Poindexter of Mississippi accusing him of being a meddling northern abolitionist. After his death, the paper ceased publication. By 1823 the TMS reported to the convention that it had twenty branches with over six hundred members.[25]

The American Convention encouraged the formation of new state abolition societies, and southern Quakers responded to its call. The Coffin, Swaim, and Mendenhall families of Guilford and Randolph counties in North Carolina founded the North Carolina Manumission and Colonization Society (NCMS) in 1816. The NCMS had a strong colonizationist contingent, but abolitionists managed to prevent the society from becoming an auxiliary of the ACS and dropped the word *colonization* from its title in 1824. In its address of 1826 to the convention, the NCMS laid out its principles of gradual emancipation and recounted that after nearly falling apart in 1823 it had shown signs of growth and vigor in the past two years. Antislavery Quakers like Samuel Janney and Benjamin Hallowell, among others, most of them identified with Hicksites, founded the Benevolent Society of Alexandria for Ameliorating and Improving the Condition of the People of Color in 1827. Janney wrote a number of antislavery essays recommending gradual emancipation and colonization and corresponded regularly with the convention. The society picked up on the work of defunct local abolition societies in Virginia despite state laws "abolishing the Abolition societies," restricting freedom suits, and manumissions. It built on the work of its predecessor, the Quaker-dominated Alexandria Society for the Relief and Protection of Persons Illegally Held in Bondage, founded in 1795. This society had represented slaves in the courts and opened a school for black children. It had sixty-two members in 1797, received twenty-six complaints of illegal enslavement, pursued freedom suits in Virginia and North Carolina, and secured the support of the PAS. After Gabriel's rebellion, the society, unable to withstand persecution, held its last meeting in 1801. By 1827, however, there were 106 antislavery societies in the upper south, and 9 in Virginia and the District of Columbia had over three hundred members each.

Yet antislavery was overtaken by colonization sentiment and proved to be relatively short-lived in the upper south states. The Benevolent Society of Alexandria ceased all activity owing to a conservative backlash after Nat Turner's rebellion in 1831. The NCMS also ceased to meet after 1834, as did the TMS. Upper south antislavery was stillborn, but it produced a cadre of committed abolitionists such as Bourne, James Duncan, who moved from Kentucky to Indiana, Levi Coffin, who moved from North Carolina to Indiana, and John Rankin, who moved from Tennessee and Kentucky to Ohio. Coffin and Rankin became famous for their daring activism in the UGRR. Most abolitionists and Quakers emigrated out of the slave states to the old northwest. Janney remained in Alexandria and resumed his antislavery advocacy in the 1840s on hearing the abolitionist feminist Hicksite minister Lucretia Mott. Besides developing a free labor critique of slavery, he responded to southern clergymen's biblical defense of slavery. He was indicted for inciting a slave insurrection in 1849 and, though not convicted, gave up public advocacy.[26]

Antislavery organization in the border states received a boost with the emergence of societies—most with the words *humane, benevolent,* and *protection* in their names—to prevent the kidnapping of free blacks and the sale of northern term slaves to circumvent gradual emancipation laws. By 1819 at least eight local Union Humane Societies from Ohio sent two delegates, President Thomas Genin and Henry Crew, to the convention. These societies reported that they had "done something towards liberating those improperly held in bondage; some are engaged in considerable lawsuits in relation thereto." One of the first female antislavery societies, the Female Association of Cincinnati for the Benefit of Africans, was also founded in 1817. The next year Elisha Tyson, one of the founders of the defunct MAS, called for the formation of the Protection Society of Maryland. His nephew and biographer John S. Tyson led the new society. State governments also acted, New York passing its law of 1817 freeing all slaves by July 4, 1827, thanks to the work of the NYMS's Jay, Colden, and Governor Tompkins. Between 1813 and 1820 nearly all free states bordering the slave South passed antikidnapping laws calling for severe punishment of convicted kidnappers. African Americans who brought freedom suits against illegal enslavement generally received a sympathetic hearing in northern courts at this time. Even so, the explosive growth of slavery led to hundreds, if not thousands, of free blacks being kidnapped and sold into Deep South slavery, a development that galvanized border state abolitionism. It breathed new life into the activities of the PAS and NYMS.[27]

In his address of 1818 to the Union Humane Society of Mt. Pleasant, Genin said that only when "the fire of avarice" and the "gloom of prejudice" lessened would blacks be emancipated. Though a gradualist, he repudiated colonization as a scheme to "perpetuate and extend" rather than "contract the empire of slavery." Tracing the history of the "iniquitous thralldom of the Africans" in the New World, he devoted his entire speech to dismantling racist ideas designed to justify slavery. In Haiti, he pointed out, "emancipated slaves pursue a better course of moral instruction and civil legislation" and "were abundantly diligent in defending their acquirements, and preventing new aggressions." Genin argued that freed slaves should be "formed for good citizens" of the American Republic. Long before Lincoln did, he predicted, quoting the Bible, "A kingdom divided in itself shall fall."[28]

The man most responsible for the emergence of border state abolition was Lundy, a John the Baptist to Garrison's Christ in the eyes of devout abolitionists. Like most Quaker abolitionists, Lundy was of humble origins, a saddle maker by profession. Born in New Jersey, he was converted to abolition when he witnessed the sale of slaves in Wheeling, Virginia, an important depot in the domestic slave trade. Inspired by Osborne, who now published an antislavery reform newspaper, the *Philanthropist*, in the Quaker stronghold of Mt. Pleasant, he founded a Union Humane Society in neighboring St. Clairsville in 1816 and became an agent, writer, and assistant editor for Osborne's newspaper. While Quaker reformers such as Elisha Bates, who took over the *Philanthropist*, made antislavery one among many concerns, Lundy made it his primary one. He began publishing the *Genius* in Mt. Pleasant and moved the newspaper to Greenville in eastern Tennessee after Embree's death in 1821. Lundy represented the TMS at the American Convention of abolition societies, which recommended his newspaper to the various abolition societies. The PAS supported it financially by taking out a number of subscriptions.

The *Genius* quickly became the preeminent abolitionist newspaper in the United States in the 1820s. In the first issue published in Tennessee, Lundy wrote that his paper would rise like a phoenix from the ashes of Embree's *Emancipator*. He declared that "domestic slavery is the hot bed of tyranny, and those districts in which it is tolerated are the nurseries of aristocracy and despotism." In 1824 Lundy moved again with his newspaper to Baltimore, Maryland. He assiduously published the addresses of the NCMS, TMS, KAS, and the Benevolent Society of Alexandria, the speeches and proclamations of Haitian leaders and British abolitionists, Sancho's letters; he made his newspaper a clearinghouse for antislavery information and communication. Sharply critical of ACS leaders like Bushrod Washington, who sold fifty-four of his slaves, and Clay, who, he wrote, wanted black people to remain "hewers of wood and drawers of water," Lundy felt that southerners would accept emancipation only if coupled with emigration.[29]

Despite the failure of emancipation in the South, Lundy took heart at the progress of global antislavery: black "self government in St. Domingo, under so many disadvantages, the abolition of slavery in several of the South American provinces, and recently in Mexico, and the efforts of the British," as the American Convention put it. In 1823 a national society devoted to the mitigation and gradual abolition of slavery was formed in London. An aged Wilberforce retired and Thomas Fowell Buxton and Lord Brougham now led the parliamentary fight for abolition. A new generation of British abolitionists, some of them, like James and George Stephen, children of those involved in the slave trade crusade, reinvigorated the movement. A slew of pamphlets, among them Wilberforce's appeal on behalf of West Indian slaves, Clarkson's on emancipation, and investigations of colonial slavery by James Stephen and Macaulay, were published between 1823 and 1826. In 1825 the *Anti-Slavery Monthly Reporter* began publication. By the 1830s a successful lecturing agency system and well over a thousand local antislavery societies were formed. Massive petition campaigns once again pushed abolition to the forefront of politics. Most abolitionists adopted the cause of parliamentary reform in 1832, and even the English radical William Cobbett, a critic of Wilberforce, voted for emancipation a year later.[30]

The American Convention published extensive material from the London Antislavery Society, parliamentary proceedings, and the petition campaign. In its address of 1828 to the convention, the National Anti Slavery Tract Society, founded by Lundy to reprint British antislavery literature, hailed the power of the press and predicted that the "doom of British West Indian Slavery is sealed." Lundy tried to bring British tactics to the United States, launching a mass petition campaign for the abolition of slavery and slave trade in the District of Columbia. Colonizationists distanced themselves from Lundy's campaign, but the convention endorsed it. Lundy also supported the free produce movement led by Quakers. Inspired by Hicks and British women's boycott of slave-grown produce, abolitionists in Philadelphia founded a Free Produce Society, and the convention, starting in 1827, admitted delegates from free produce societies at its meetings. Hicksite women such as Mott and Lydia White and African American women in Philadelphia formed female free produce associations. White ran a store that sold only goods produced by free labor.

In 1835 Isaac Hopper published all of Charles Marriott's free produce writings and letters from the 1820s in a pamphlet addressed to the Society of Friends. To Marriott, the consuming of products of slave labor was participating in its robbery, and he compared it to the unjust trade embargo against Haiti. (Hopper, Marriott, and Hopper's son-in-law James Gibbons would be disowned for their radical abolitionism by the New York monthly meeting at George White's behest.) The following year the Philadelphia Female Anti Slavery Society (PFASS) published Elizabeth Heyrick's call for a boycott of goods produced by slave labor. Two years later abolitionists such as Garrison and Gerrit Smith participated in the founding of the American Free Produce Association by the Requited Labor Convention in Philadelphia to search for alternatives to slave-grown products. Its address to abolitionists pinpointed the love of money as the root of the evil of slavery and products of slave labor as stolen goods. In 1846 Philadelphia abolitionists published the *Non-Slaveholder* devoted to free produce. In the decades before the Civil War, the Quaker abolitionist George Taylor, Quaker free produce associations in the northwest, and Elihu Burritt's newspaper kept the movement alive even as most abolitionists gave up on its efficacy.[31]

Women played a crucial role in the Anglo-American turn to immediatism. Laura Townsend formed the first female antislavery society in Birmingham, England, and by 1833 there were seventy-three antislavery ladies' associations in Britain initiating petition campaigns and the boycott of slave-produced goods. In 1824 Elizabeth Heyrick anonymously published three pamphlets: her defense of the slave rebels in the British colony Demerara, her landmark *Immediate not Gradual Abolition*, and the lesser-known *No British Slavery*, all of which pushed gradualist antislavery leaders to adopt immediatism. In 1826 she published yet another pamphlet advocating the "prompt extinction" of British slavery. A prolific writer, Heyrick published two pamphlets in 1828 pressing British women to boycott slave-produced goods and defending their antislavery activism. Heyrick's abolitionism, like Clarkson's, was of a Jacobin stripe and included the advance of workingmen's rights. In her most famous pamphlet on immediate abolition, which was republished in New York in 1825, Heyrick charged that British attempts to stop the slave trade were hypocritical as long as the nation "rivets the chains upon her own slaves." Rejecting the post nati American model of gradual emancipation, Heyrick wrote, "There is something unnatural, something revolting to the common sense of justice, in reserving all the sweets of freedom for those who never tasted the bitter cup of bondage . . . when public sympathy is diverted . . . from the *living* victims of colonial bondage to their unborn progeny." With much greater reason, a workingman, "whose only property is his labour," may demand protection more than the "West Indian capitalist." She pointed out that it was the slaves rather than the slaveholders who were owed compensation for their years of unpaid labor. Most women's antislavery organizations endorsed immediatism before the male-dominated societies did. In 1830 a revamped national Anti-Slavery Society in Britain committed to immediatism.[32]

The American Convention praised the growing presence of women in abolition: "We cannot withhold the tribute of our respect and admiration from those patriotic females who have associated for this purpose in England and America, and heartily, recommend their example, as one worthy of universal imitation." Lundy serialized *Immediate and not Gradual Abolition* in his newspaper and raised a subscription to republish Heyrick's pamphlet of 1826. He also published the Quaker abolitionist Elizabeth Margaret Chandler of Philadelphia. Chandler became known for her antislavery poems "The Slave Mother" and "The Kneeling Slave." Sarah Mapps Douglass, a teacher and founding member of the PFASS, thanked Chandler for "her beautiful writings on behalf of my enslaved brethren and sisters." In 1829 Chandler started managing the ladies' department of Lundy's paper and published Wheatley's poems. In "An Appeal to the Ladies of the United States" on behalf of "our African slave population," Chandler insisted that abolition was the responsibility of American women. Responding to censures of women's antislavery advocacy, she averred that antislavery did not violate "feminine propriety" but made women act in a manner true to religion and on behalf of female slaves. Slavery, she wrote in one of her numerous antislavery essays, corrupted the female character and made women prone to fashion, vanity, and materialism. An advocate of female education and the free produce movement, she asked women not to use slave produce in their households. In her "Letters on Slavery," she again maintained that the "female sex [have] a duty to perform for the advancement of abolition." In 1830 Chandler migrated to Michigan and founded the state's first antislavery society with the Quaker abolitionist and teacher Laura Haviland. She died there in 1834. According to Lundy, who wrote Chandler's memoir, "*She was the first American female author that ever made this subject [abolition] the principal theme of her exertions.*"[33]

Lundy combined a gradualist temper with immediatist tactics and goals. In this sense, he was truly a transitional figure in the history of American abolition. He attacked the expanding domestic slave trade, especially its premier practitioners in Baltimore, the slave-trading Woolfolk family. In 1826 he wrote of a failed slave mutiny aboard a Woolfolk slaver, the *Decatur*. The slaves had planned to escape to Haiti, but as they sailed toward the island the *Decatur* was overtaken by another ship and brought to New York. Most of the rebels escaped, but William Hill (alias Bowser) was caught and hanged. Angered by the article, which praised Bowser's demeanor and criticized him, Austin Woolfolk assaulted Lundy. In the resulting case for battery, the proslavery judge castigated Lundy and fined Woolfolk one dollar. Embarking on a lecture tour of the North in 1828, Lundy inspired future leaders of immediatism, including James and Lucretia Mott in Philadelphia, Arthur Tappan, an evangelical merchant in New York who bankrolled the abolition movement, William Goodell, a reform-minded editor in Providence, Rev. Simeon Jocelyn of New Haven, who ministered to a black congregation, the Quaker poet John Greenleaf Whittier, and the young journalist Garrison in Boston. In Garrison, Lundy "discovered a disciple" and "the antislavery movement would never be quite the same again."[34]

Lundy experimented with radical reform, aiding the freethinking Wright in her goal of marrying abolition with feminism, communitarian, and working-men's movements. Wright, one of the first women in abolition to speak publicly, was influenced by Robert Owen, who was known for his model textile factory in New Lanark, Scotland, and the communitarian settlement New Harmony in Indiana. Her compatriot Robert Dale Owen, Robert's son, attributed his socialist beliefs to his father, who stood up to British "cotton lords" who were exploiting child labor, and his abolitionism to a memorable meeting with Clarkson. He recalled that Lord Brougham had come to his father's defense when mill owners attacked him. Dale Owen and Wright founded an inter-racial commune modeled after New Harmony in Nashoba, Tennessee, in 1825 to prepare slaves for freedom. Flowers joined this experiment in interracialism, cooperative labor, and abolition, but it failed amid charges of sexual impropriety and foundered as well on a lack of resources. Dale Owen pronounced it a "pecuniary failure," and Wright came under fire for her unconventional views on marriage, sex, labor, and property. Most incendiary was her advocacy of interracial unions based on mutual respect and affection, which would create a new race to "undermine the slavery of color existing in the North American republic." Eventually Wright emancipated the thirty-odd slaves in Nashoba and accompanied them to Haiti. Wright and Dale Owen also edited the radical, freethinking newspapers the *New Harmony Gazette* and, later, the *Free Enquirer* in New York, where they became proponents of educational reform, birth control, and workingmen's rights along with the land reformer George Henry Evans and Thomas Skidmore. Skidmore not only advocated the equal distribution of property but also women's rights and abolition.

Abolitionists like Lundy were swayed by the communitarian movement and flirted with radical critics of an emerging bourgeois order. He corresponded with Owen and Wright, published her accounts of Nashoba, and defended her against conservative critics. He complained of the "want of gallantry" displayed by American editors toward Wright, who coined the term *Fanny Wright-ism* to lampoon her unconventional and Jacobinic views of workingmen's and women's rights. Lundy praised Nashoba's *"more especial object, the protection and regeneration of the race of color, universally oppressed and despised in a country self-denominated free,"* although he did not agree with Wright's views on religion and marriage. He also proposed founding a cooperative community of freed slaves in the South. One of Lundy's former editors, a Hicksite named Amos Gilbert, helped Dale Owen and Wright edit their paper. The NYMS's Colden was among the trustees of Nashoba to whom Wright entrusted her property when she left the country. Dale Owen returned to New Harmony and was elected a Democratic congressman from Indiana. In his public letters to Lincoln during the Civil War, he urged emancipation. He became a Radical Republican and an advocate of black citizenship.[35] Transnational radicalism intersected with abolitionism, a pattern reinforced with the rise of Garrisonian abolition.

NATIONAL POLITICS AND ANTISLAVERY

Partisan political controversies also gave a fillip to northern antislavery. After Jefferson's election and the Louisiana Purchase, New England Federalists attempted to introduce a constitutional amendment to repeal the three-fifths clause. Federalist opposition to the Embargo and the War of 1812 centered on the national political dominance of Republican slaveholders, particularly what was called the Virginia dynasty. While Republicans tarred the antiwar Hartford Convention of 1814 with the brush of treason for contemplating disunion, New England Federalists criticized Republican War Hawks for launching an unprovoked war against the British as well as for their treatment of Native Americans and enslaved Africans. Federalist criticism of the war gave birth to the American peace movement and denunciations of slavery. Quakers also linked their peace testimony to antislavery. Antiwar sentiment birthed state peace societies. William Ladd, who founded the American Peace Society in 1828, was a staunch critic of the War of 1812.

Federalist politicians such as the Massachusetts congressman Josiah Quincy and the abolitionist clergymen Elijah Parish and Nathan Perkins connected the tyranny of racial slavery with the political domination of the North by southern slaveholders, the Slave Power. Perkins saw the war as divine punishment for sundry sins, especially the "national crime" of slaveholding. Parish asked New

Englanders to resist southern tyrants. Let them, he argued, "be satisfied by inflicting the bloody lash on more than ten hundred thousand *African* slaves." Elijah P. Lovejoy, the abolitionist editor murdered while defending his press, was named after this fiery Federalist cleric. Theodore Dwight Weld also bore the name of his Federalist abolitionist ancestor Theodore Dwight. Quincy, who retired from politics to become president of Harvard University, wrote against the extension of slavery during the Missouri Crisis and on the Slave Power well into the 1850s. His son Edmund Quincy joined Garrison, as did the Federalist John Phillips's son, Wendell Phillips. Abolitionists who later identified with the Democratic Party, Joshua Leavitt, and the editor William Cullen Bryant had Federalist antecedents. As a printer's apprentice at the Federalist *Newburyport Herald* in 1818, Garrison absorbed their views.[36]

By the end of the decade the Federalist critique of slavery resonated even with northern Republicans. Despite abolitionist protest, southern slave states entered the Union without much opposition—Louisiana in 1812, Mississippi in 1817, and Alabama in 1819. The conflict over the expansion of slavery took place in the northwest, in areas where Article VI of the Northwest Ordinance specifically prohibited slavery. In local struggles over the recognition of slavery, Republicans in Ohio, Indiana, and Illinois condemned slavery as an aristocratic, unrepublican institution that devalued democracy and competed with free labor. In Ohio the initiative to gain short-term recognition of slavery in the Virginia Military District set aside for revolutionary soldiers from that state failed miserably, and it entered the Union as a free state in 1803. In Indiana the battle was more drawn out, mainly because of Gov. William Henry Harrison's efforts to overturn Article VI and the strength of proslavery forces in the neighboring territory of Illinois. An antislavery majority in Indiana repealed indentured servitude laws that allowed slaveholders to retain their human property, and in 1816 it entered the Union as a free state with Article VI as part of its state constitution. Two important state supreme court decisions in 1820 and 1821 in freedom suits brought by black women outlawed slavery and indentured servitude in Indiana. Illinois joined the Union as a free state in 1818, but proslavery residents retained servitude laws and tried to legalize slavery. Its antislavery governor, Edward Coles of Virginia, who had freed and settled his slaves in Illinois, thwarted such attempts, as did Congress's determination to implement the slavery restriction clause of the Northwest Ordinance. In 1824 the state constitutional convention voted down the attempt to make Illinois a slave state, but servitude laws remained in force.

Northern migrants and southern "migrants against slavery" managed to officially defeat proslavery forces in the old northwest, but all three states passed "black laws" restricting the entry and rights of African Americans. Political antislavery could subsume abolitionism with racist attempts to keep the west free of a black presence. The northwest, however, also attracted genuine abolitionists, Quakers, southern antislavery evangelicals, fugitive slaves, free blacks, and antislavery politicians like Coles. These were the men and women who fought to keep the area free of slavery in the face of the relentless national expansion of slavery and a remote federal government. Southerners who migrated with their slaves, who used unfree labor in mines, and who welcomed vacationing slaveholders and their "servants" in hotels kept slavery alive even as it was in retreat. In the old northwest, a succession of federal proslavery appointees and the use of enslaved labor by the government and army bolstered the persistence of slavery in an area designated free.[37]

The sectional conflict over the admission of Missouri as a slave state in 1819, then, was not, in Jefferson's words, a sudden "firebell in the night" but the high point of a broader struggle over the status of slavery in the west. A year earlier Arthur Livermore, a New Hampshire Republican, had proposed a constitutional amendment to bar the entry of slave states into the Union. The eventual admission of Missouri as a slave state energized proslavery forces in Illinois. The first major political controversy over slavery expansion, the Missouri Crisis, revealed that free soilism, or efforts to restrict the expansion of slavery, was far more popular in the North than abolition and that slaveholders would not accept any restriction on slavery. The Republican representative James Tallmadge, who had introduced New York's immediate emancipation law and opposed the admission of Illinois into the Union because its constitution was not sufficiently antislavery, put forward the amendment to prohibit the entry of slaves to Missouri and provide for the gradual emancipation of slaves already there. Tallmadge's amendment set off a sectional debate in Congress, with most northerners speaking for the restriction of slavery and southerners adamantly opposed. His colleague from New York, John Taylor, attempted to introduce a similar slavery restriction clause to the Arkansas territory bill but failed when Clay broke a tie to open it to slavery.

The Missouri controversy boosted northern antislavery. Speeches by such northern Republicans as Tallmadge and Taylor and by Federalists like Rep. John Sergeant of Philadelphia and Sen. Rufus King of New York gave voice to abolitionist ideas as well as to arguments for the superiority of free soil and free labor. The northern demand for slavery restriction was not just a Federalist plot, as Jefferson argued, but he was probably right to blame his old enemies for first raising the slavery issue in national politics. In defending his amendment, Tallmadge clarified that he was not an abolitionist but interested in a *"great* and *glorious cause,* setting the bounds to a *slavery,* the most cruel and debasing the world has ever witnessed." Others highlighted the constitutional and political authority for slavery restriction. Taylor, who reintroduced the amendment after Tallmadge left Congress, emphasized that Missouri was in the "same latitude" as Indiana and Illinois. Sergeant evoked the precedent of the Northwest Ordinance and the constitutional power of Congress to stipulate conditions while admitting new states. The power to establish slavery, he pointedly concluded, was not "essential to the character of a free republican state." King best articulated the constitutional position of northern restrictionists. He alluded to the long-standing Federalist criticism of the three-fifths clause, a "concession" to the "slaveholding states," which, he argued, should not apply beyond the original thirteen states. He noted that "the existence of slavery impairs the industry and power of the nation" and was therefore against the general welfare, security, and interest of the Union. Barring slavery from the trans-Mississippi west would extend and strengthen "the principles of freedom," not an empire for slavery. King also voted against discriminatory property-holding qualifications for black voters at New York's constitutional convention in 1821. Secretary of State John Quincy Adams expressed his disgust at the "flagrant . . . inconsistency" of "Southern slave-holding Republicans." While slaveholders professed to be antislavery, the Missouri Crisis, he wrote, had "betrayed the secret of their souls." In the last years of his life, John Adams, who admired King's speeches, supported nonextension.[38]

On the other hand, William Smith of South Carolina, who was incensed by the writings of Kenrick and Torrey, articulated the increasingly popular "positive good" theory of slavery. Led by the Old Republicans, including John Randolph of Virginia, southerners used states' rights theory to defend slavery. Whether they argued for the superiority of slave labor like some lower south planter politicians or for the diffusion of slavery like upper south slaveholders, the result was the same, an ironclad commitment to the spread of slavery. Randolph, who had enough qualms about slavery to free his slaves on his death, was furiously opposed to the alleged intervention of the federal government into slavery. Even southern nationalists such as William Lowndes of South Carolina began spouting states' rights theory. The Missouri Crisis, thanks to men like Randolph, Nathaniel Macon of North Carolina, and the Virginian John Taylor of Caroline, who predicted civil war in his pamphlets against federal "consolidation," forever linked states' rights with the defense of slavery. Southerners resorted to threats of disunion if Missouri was not admitted as a slave state. Abolitionists in Delaware, the only slave state legislature to vote for slavery restriction, and in pockets of Maryland, Tennessee, Kentucky, and Virginia

represented antislavery sentiment in the upper south rather than the function-
ally proslavery states' rights diffusionists, whose ranks included men like Jefferson, Randolph, Monroe, and the influential Thomas Ritchie, the editor of the
Richmond Enquirer. They touted diffusion as an antislavery plan to spread and
thin out slavery and championed colonization of free blacks.[39]

Restrictionists lost Missouri to slavery, but the crisis revealed the potential
of sectional controversy to rally northern public opinion. The compromise of
1820, introduced by Sen. Jesse Thomas of Illinois, passed in an antirestrictionist
Senate and in two separate acts in the mostly restrictionist House of Representatives, thanks to the political skills of Clay. It allowed the entrance of Missouri
as a slave state but prohibited slavery north of its southern boundary at latitude
36°30′ in the rest of the Louisiana Purchase. The compromise, as southerners
realized to their chagrin, recognized the authority of the federal government to
legislate on slavery in the territories. In a separate bill, Maine entered the Union
as a free state, retaining the balance between free and slave states. Missouri's
constitution, which barred the legislature from passing an emancipation law
and required it to prohibit the entry of free blacks, thereby violating the equal
protection clause of the Constitution, rekindled the crisis. But after another
round of debates it was resolved in 1821 by another compromise proposed by
Clay, which required Missouri to declare that it would pass no law that violated
the Constitution. The Missouri legislature did so but in such defiant terms as to
undermine its acquiescence.

The privileges of citizenship for African Americans continued to be whittled
away. Most northwestern states already required them to post bond on entering,
and the harsher Missouri clause, which emulated other slave states' prohibition of the entry of free blacks, was allowed to stand. In Randolph's phrase, a
few doughfaces, northern men with southern principles, combined with a solid
South to pass the compromise. Missouri had squeaked into statehood by only
three votes in the House in 1820, with a handful of northerners abstaining or
voting with the South. By 1821 many more northern Republicans, including
restrictionists like Taylor, who was now Speaker of the House, stood behind
compromise and the Union. But sectional polarization on slavery did not completely disappear. In 1824 Ohio's legislature passed resolutions recommending
gradual emancipation and colonization in the South, resolutions that were endorsed by eight northern states. The reaction in the lower south, especially in
South Carolina, was vociferous.[40]

Abolitionists, who had promoted slavery restriction in the territories long before the controversy, viewed it as a godsend. In 1818 the American Convention
sent a memorial to Congress asking for the prohibition of slavery in all the

territories and new states entering the Union. Lundy, who named one of his sons after Tallmadge, traveled to Missouri, unsuccessfully attempting to rally antislavery sentiment there. Elias Boudinot organized an antislavery meeting in Burlington, New Jersey, to urge northern legislatures to take a firm stance against slavery extension. In Baltimore, Elisha Tyson helped organize an anti-Missouri meeting, which sent a memorial to Congress with thousands of signatures. In Massachusetts, Josiah Quincy and Daniel Webster, among others, led a free soil meeting that asked Congress to prohibit slavery in all new states admitted into the Union. The PAS rallied against slavery in Missouri and pro-slavery forces in Illinois. It noted with pleasure the "decided opposition made by a majority of the representative branch of Congress, to the admission of new States into the Union, whose constitution of government shall not prohibit slavery among them." The DAS deemed it "of the highest national importance to . . . prescribe limits to the future extension of slavery" and issued a lengthy report vindicating the constitutionality of the power of Congress to restrict slavery in the territories. The NYMS published Tallmadge's speech and praised him and Taylor for their "manly and persevering efforts . . . to prevent the further extension of the evils of slavery." Both men responded, hoping for the "full accomplishment" of its "humane and benevolent objects."

The American Convention presented yet another remonstrance to Congress against the admission of slave states and published a thousand copies of the speeches of Taylor, Tallmadge, King, the DAS report, and a letter from John Jay to Boudinot asserting the constitutionality of congressional restriction of territorial slavery. It prepared an anti-Missouri memorial "to prevent the introduction of Slaves, and to guard the rights of the free people of colour" and coordinated antislavery strategy with Sergeant, who led the opposition to Missouri's constitution in the House. The TMS's Embree wrote that "hell is about to enlarge her borders and tyranny her domain" on Missouri's admission as a slave state. Despite their failure, Lundy praised restrictionists for having "stepped forth so boldly and plead the cause of liberty so manfully." By the end of the decade, he had written a lengthy report on the superiority of free to slave labor for the convention, drawing examples from areas where slavery had been abolished, Mexico, Latin America, and Haiti. The report absorbed the northern Republican critique of slave labor and represented an abolitionist response to proslavery writers who maintained that the abolition of slavery would lead to economic collapse.[41]

Historians of the Missouri Crisis have failed to explore abolitionists' influence on restrictionists and their critique of southern diffusionists. In *The Missouri Question* (1819) Raymond called slavery "an enormous, and an alarming evil" and effectively demolished the diffusion theory, exposing its proslavery results. Slaveholders admitted for the most part that slavery was a curse but "*at the same time* adopt measures *calculated* to increase and perpetuate it to the latest generations." He said they had done nothing but magnify, perpetuate, and extend all its horrors. Raymond predicted that the spread of slavery would not end the institution but have the contrary effect of preventing the South from ever getting rid of it. He asked rhetorically, "Who ever heard that increasing the demand for an article, was the means of diminishing its quantity or preventing its increase?" The mischief would be "heightened ten fold. . . . This would be establishing the slave trade in our country with a vengeance." Raymond also criticized their advocacy of colonization. The idea that the ACS "under any circumstances, [can] have any perceptible effect in eradicating slaves from our soil, is chimerical." A year later, in his book-length pro-labor pamphlet on political economy, Raymond concluded, "Diffusion is about as effectual a remedy for slavery as it would be for the small pox, or the plague." Going beyond restriction, he suggested that southern states emulate Maryland in liberalizing their manumission laws. In his speeches Sergeant used Raymond's ideas that diffusion was a disguise for the perpetuation of slavery and the expansion of the domestic slave trade. Raymond argued that the introduction of slavery was an infringement of a republican form of government, the only constitutional stipulation for the admission of new states. Northern congressmen repeated his argument on the constitutional guarantee of republican government during the Missouri debates.[42]

Restrictionists like Tallmadge and Robert Walsh of Philadelphia also reacted to foreign antislavery criticisms of America. In the aftermath of the conservative triumph at the Congress of Vienna of 1815, they wished to hold up their experiment in republicanism against Europe's absolute monarchies, but slavery, they asserted, robbed the American example of its potency. Theodore Dwight's *New York Daily Advertiser* and Walsh's *National Gazette and Literary Register* played an important role in molding northern public opinion. In 1819 Walsh published a book defending the American Republic from criticism by British abolitionists and a pamphlet advocating the restriction of slavery in Missouri. He avowed that in America slaves were treated better than they were in the West Indies. But in his pamphlet Walsh quoted Wilberforce and acknowledged that the presence of "*negro-slavery*" gave the nation's "revolutionary creed . . . an air of imposture or infatuated selfishness." He insisted that the founders had deemed slavery "*a great political and moral evil*" and that "*slavery could find no shelter under the constitution.*"

Similarly, Joseph Blunt, in his *An Examination of the Expediency and Constitutionality of Prohibiting Slavery in the State of Missouri*, held that the "enlightened Europeans, who are well inclined towards our republic, are continually shocked at the glaring inconsistency of our conduct and principles." He decried "local prejudices" and "local interests" that sacrificed national welfare and called slavery "repugnant to the fundamental principles of the republic." Blunt put forth the Republican case against slavery. He argued that colonization, though well intended, would not solve the problem, and the only solution lay in the "emancipation and instruction" of the slaves. Only when slavery was destroyed could the United States truly boast of its "free institutions." Hezekiah Niles of Baltimore also expressed skepticism about colonization and published plans for gradual emancipation in a series of articles titled the "Mitigation of Slavery" in his influential *Register*. William Duane of the Jeffersonian newspaper *Aurora* in Philadelphia, who had been educated in Ireland and had been an editor in India, criticized slavery and advocated its restriction in Missouri. Like other northern Republicans beholden to a southern-dominated party, Duane saw his views on slavery swing like a pendulum from proslavery to antislavery and back again. Earlier, James Sloan, a Republican congressman from New Jersey, had been consigned to political oblivion for his antislavery views.[43]

The Missouri controversy revived northern Federalist criticisms of southern slavery. In his *Crisis* essays on Missouri, James Hillhouse, who had opposed the Louisiana Purchase and joined the Hartford Convention, called slavery a "disgrace to the American name" and a "blot on the human character." Slavery was not only "pernicious as it is immoral and unjust but it is totally inconsistent with the principles and security of a republican government," and a "blush of shame" should "tinge the countenance of every citizen of the United States." Hillhouse wrote that "those who justify African slavery deny the truth of God" and the unity of humankind. He warned that a new interracial population "will never suffer the degradation of their mothers" and would lead a Haitian-style slave rebellion. Hillhouse's satirical pamphlet *Pocahontas* was a mock proclamation by Virginian slaveholders "to the people of the nonslaveholding states" issued in the "imperial City of Richmond." It denounced what it called the treason of the state of New York to Virginia in asking for slavery restriction. Finally, it proclaimed that in the west, "slave dealers, kidnappers, and negro drivers shall run to and fro through the land, and greatly multiply." Bucking the trend, Tench Coxe underwent a transformation from antislavery Federalist stalwart of the PAS to a racist Republican defending slavery. Coxe recognized the centrality of slave-grown cotton to national economic development and married the

Federalist promotion of manufactures with the Republican drive for western expansion. During the Missouri Crisis, he referred to all people of color as the helots of America and declared them ineligible for citizenship. Coxe, who had once championed black citizenship, now recommended colonization for free blacks and repudiated abolition. The northern free labor argument against slavery ran up against the economic reality of the enormous profitability of slave-grown cotton and its centrality in the nation's economy.[44] Before the Civil War, cotton was the largest item of export from the United States, and its value exceeded the value of all other items of export from the country.

In the aftermath of the crisis, the nationalism of antislavery constitutional theory fed off the southern states' rights position. Long before the birth of free soilism and the Republican Party, abolitionists had demanded that the federal government separate itself from slavery and stand for freedom. The American Convention began sending memorials to Congress in the 1820s asking it to act against slavery where it constitutionally could—restricting slavery in Florida and other federal territories, abolishing slavery in Washington, and regulating and prohibiting the interstate slave trade. The convention even charged representatives from the nonslaveholding states with ignoring the wishes of their constituents and being recreant to their duty to act against slavery. It investigated economic or free labor arguments against slavery and welcomed the Delaware Free Labor Society to its ranks. Dwight also became a proponent of free labor. The abolitionist championing of free labor grew out of a republican producer ideology that lauded the dignity and independence of labor rather than out of a bourgeois justification of wage labor.

Men who had taken the lead in the Missouri debates became prominent in abolition. Sergeant was a PAS delegate and was elected president of the American Convention in 1825. Raymond joined Lundy in founding the Maryland Antislavery Society in Baltimore that year. They backed both the efforts of Rep. Charles Miner of Pennsylvania, a member of the PAS, to end slavery in the District of Columbia and a plan proposed by King to use a portion of the revenues from the sale of public lands to finance emancipation. As early as 1826 Miner offered resolutions for the abolition of slavery in the district. Like Quincy, Miner published pamphlets against slavery extension well into the 1850s. Raymond ran unsuccessfully for the Maryland legislature as an antislavery candidate. He and Lundy helped make Baltimore, for a few years, the center of the abolition movement. The American Convention met there in 1826 and in an adjourned session in 1828, and Lundy published its proceedings. Lundy later moved to Washington, where he helped form a "respectable anti-slavery society." At his prompting, the convention met in the nation's capital in order to pursue the strategy of pressuring the federal government to act against slavery. Under its auspices Lundy orchestrated the first mass petition campaign against slavery and the slave trade in the District of Columbia in 1827–29. Thousands of abolitionists in Pennsylvania and other northern states signed these petitions. Buoyed by the campaign, Miner asked for an investigation into the slave trade in the district. In his speech Miner documented the kidnapping of free blacks and the rendition of fugitive slaves, which had torn apart black families. Recounting the story of a slave woman who was separated from her free husband and three children, he said she was "more heart-broken than any creature" he had ever seen. There were, he said, many such cases "of equal cruelty." His was a lone voice for abolition in Congress.[45]

Not only would immediatists continue the strategy of criticizing slavery and the slave trade in the nation's capital with the petition campaigns of the 1830s, but political antislavery reemerged with a vengeance in the free soil campaigns of the 1840s and 1850s. Hardly just a footnote in the history of antislavery, abolitionists in the middle, supposedly neglected period inaugurated many of the tactics and ideas used by their successors in the antebellum period. The history of abolition is marked as much by continuity as by disjuncture.

Early Quaker Abolitionists

Benjamin Lay

John Woolman

Anthony Benezet

Early Black Antislavery Figures

Phillis Wheatley

Olaudah Equiano

Absalom Jones

Lemuel Haynes

British Abolition

Granville Sharp

Thomas Clarkson

William Wilberforce

Cross-Section of the slave ship Brooks

Interracial Immediatism

James Forten

Samuel Cornish

William Lloyd Garrison, painted by the black
abolitionist artist Robert Douglass Jr., c. 1835

Theodore Dwight Weld

The Abolitionist Petition Campaign

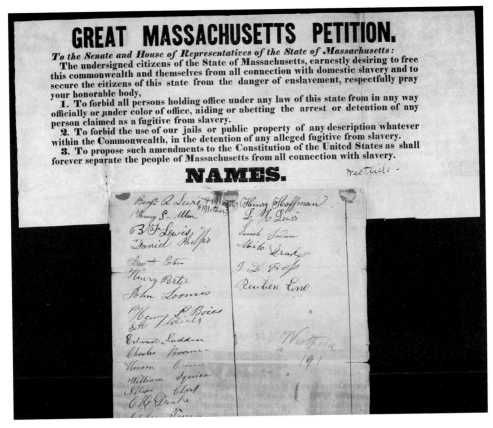

Abolitionists sent thousands of petitions to Congress and northern state legislatures. This is one of more than three thousand antislavery and anti-segregation petitions sent to the Massachusetts General Court: the Great Massachusetts Petition of 1843 demanding the severing of all connections between the Commonwealth and laws upholding slavery after the Latimer case. (Courtesy of the Massachusetts Archives; digitized by Harvard University)

Black Abolitionists

William Whipper

James W. C. Pennington

Charles Lenox Remond

Robert Purvis

James McCune Smith

Martin R. Delany

William Cooper Nell

Alexander Crummell

Women Abolitionists

Lucretia Mott

Angelina Grimké

Abby Kelley Foster

Sojourner Truth

Lucy Stone

Frances Ellen Watkins Harper

Garrisonians

Wendell Phillips

Samuel J. May

Henry C. Wright

Lydia Maria Child

Maria Weston Chapman

Evangelical and Political Abolitionists

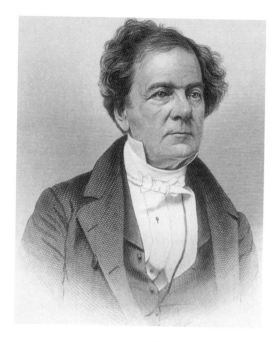

Lewis Tappan

William Jay

Gerrit Smith

William Goodell

Joshua Leavitt

Alvan Stewart

James G. Birney

Slave Resistance and the Making of American Abolition

Toussaint Louverture, leader of
the Haitian Revolution

Sengbe Pieh, painted by Nathaniel
Jocelyn, brother of Simeon Jocelyn

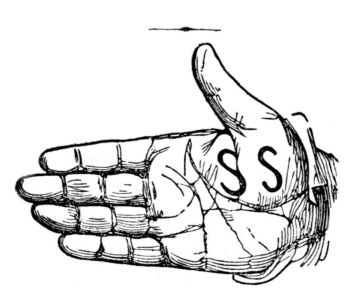

Jonathan Walker's branded hand, SS for "Slave Stealer"

Cartoon depicting abolitionists Isaac Hopper and David Ruggles of the
New York Committee of Vigilance, and Barney Corse of the New York
Manumission Society confronting John Darg, a Virginian slaveholder

The Christiana Uprising in Pennsylvania

The Abolitionist Underground

Levi Coffin   Thomas Garrett

John Rankin

Henry Bibb

Jermaine W. Loguen

Harriet Tubman

Laura Haviland

Theodore Parker

William Still

John Brown

This popular rendition of John Brown encountering a slave mother
and her child on the way to his execution reflected his wish that a slave
mother rather than a proslavery minister preside over his funeral.

Antislavery Politicians

John Quincy Adams

Joshua R. Giddings

Salmon P. Chase

Charles Sumner

William H. Seward

Thaddeus Stevens

Owen Lovejoy

This lithograph depicts abolitionists with antislavery politicians and other popular antislavery figures. *Clockwise from the top*: John Quincy Adams, William Lloyd Garrison, Joshua R. Giddings, Cassius M. Clay, Benjamin Lundy, Owen Lovejoy, Gerrit Smith, William Cullen Bryant, Henry Ward Beecher. *Center*: John Greenleaf Whittier (*top*), Wendell Phillips (*left*), Charles Sumner (*right*)

Black Reconstruction Leaders

This lithograph traces the black protest tradition from early leaders to prominent black abolitionists to black officeholders. *Top:* Robert B. Elliot (*left*), Blanche K. Bruce; *center:* Frederick Douglass; *clockwise from top:* William Wells Brown, Richard T. Greener, Richard Allen, Joseph H. Rainey, Ebenezer D. Bassett, John Mercer Langston, P. B. S. Pinchback, Henry Highland Garnet

THE SECOND WAVE

7

INTERRACIAL IMMEDIATISM

In 1827 the Baptist minister Rev. Nathaniel Paul of Albany, New York, exhorted African Americans to "enter the field with a fixed determination to live and die in the holy cause" of abolition. David Walker, the author of *Appeal . . . to the Colored Citizens of the World* (1829), also called the fight against slavery and for black rights a "holy cause."[1] While historians have written extensively about the origins of immediate abolition in the religious revivals and reform movements of this time, they have until recently ignored its black roots. The story of black abolitionist radicalism has still not been fully told. Not just black protest but instances of slave rebellion ignored in histories of abolition shaped immediate abolition.

Initially, immediatism represented a mindset rather than a fully articulated program for emancipation. Outstanding abolitionists from the revolutionary era could be called immediatists for their strong condemnation of slavery as an unmitigated evil and belief in racial equality. Practical implementation of abolition could vary from the legislative plans of the American Convention to a more fiery call to arms. By the 1820s a perfect storm of social and moral reform movements, the British example, and southern intransigence had laid the foundation for the rise of immediate abolition.[2] A growing band of abolitionists, predominantly black, formed an insistent voice of protest in a nation committed to racial slavery.

Interracial immediatism brought together the moral and religious sensibility of white reform efforts and the antislavery tactics of early abolitionists in Britain and the United States with the black tradition of protest. Just as the First Great Awakening and the rise of evangelical Christianity contributed to the growth of antislavery in the eighteenth century, the Second Great Awakening fostered the moral argument against slavery as an eradicable sin and facilitated its spread.[3] Abolition's distinct roots in the black protest tradition, however, made it a uniquely radical, interracial social movement that challenged the parameters of religious benevolence.

BLACK ROOTS OF IMMEDIATISM

African Americans had long fashioned a radical critique of the slaveholding Republic. There is an existing literature on black abolitionists who preceded Garrison in opposing colonization and calling for racial equality, but slave resistance has yet to be incorporated in the rise of immediate abolition.[4] The only example of immediatism before the 1830s was the Haitian Revolution. The black roots of immediatism can be traced to the slave rebellions of this era as well as to free black militancy. Free and enslaved resistance formed two sides of the same coin.[5]

Slave rebels inspired abolitionists. Despite recent claims that authorities and witnesses under duress concocted a slave conspiracy, it is highly likely that in 1822 a literate free black carpenter, Denmark Vesey, tried to orchestrate a slave uprising in Charleston, South Carolina. Vesey, who had bought his freedom on winning a lottery, planned a black exodus to Haiti. Two domestic servants revealed the conspiracy. Vesey and his principal lieutenants, Rolla Bennett, Peter Poyas, the African conjurer Gullah Jack Pritchard, and Monday Gell, were executed. Thirty-five slaves were hanged, while others were transported out of the state, whipped, or acquitted. That Vesey or any of the enslaved artisans and servants arrested should imagine President Boyer of Haiti as their liberator and that they were aware of the antislavery speeches of Sen. Rufus King during the Missouri Crisis and of South Carolina's law of 1820 that made manumission harder by requiring the sanction of the legislature indicated their political sophistication. Vesey was a class leader in the AME Church, which had been visited by members of Allen's Philadelphia church in 1817. State authorities harassed church members and used the conspiracy as an excuse to destroy it and banish Rev. Morris Brown and Rev. Henry Drayton. Brown succeeded Allen as head of the AME.[6]

Vesey and his followers may have failed in the short run, but they helped sow the seeds of slavery's destruction. The conspiracy generated a host of proslavery pamphlets in South Carolina. The state passed new restrictive laws on slavery, including the notorious Negro Seamen's Act, which imprisoned all visiting black sailors in violation of federal law and treaties, and Carolinian planter politicians began their antebellum career as leading spokesmen of disunion and slavery. Abolitionists drew the opposite lesson. Commenting on the conspiracy, Theodore Dwight, who had praised the Haitian Revolution, wrote that African slaves "kidnapped by white men and dragged into endless slavery, cannot be expected to be contented with their situation." Walker, the son of a free black woman and an enslaved father, born around 1796 in North Carolina and also a member of the AME, visited Charleston during the conspiracy. In the 1850s the fugitive slave abolitionist Henry Bibb published an account of Vesey's conspiracy, while Henry Highland Garnet and Douglass evoked Vesey's example. In a fitting coda, Robert Vesey, his son, helped rebuild the Charleston church in 1865, after emancipation. Four years later Garnet described the murder of one of Vesey's hapless betrayers in the streets of New York.[7]

Slave rebellion gave birth to radical abolitionism. Even before the Vesey conspiracy, the Camden slave plot in South Carolina and Bussa's rebellion in Barbados in 1816 gave notice of slaves' restiveness. Following on the heels of Vesey, the Demerara rebellion of 1823 in present-day Guyana, involving over ten thousand slaves, played an important role in British abolitionists' turn to immediatism. The enslaved themselves were inspired by rumors of freedom, Wilberforce's reputation as a powerful friend, abolitionists' attempts to ameliorate the conditions of slavery, and evangelical Christianity in the person of the missionary John Smith. Like the men who assumed leadership in Vesey's conspiracy, the leaders of the Demerara revolt, Quamina, the African deacon, and his son Jack Gladstone, were skilled slaves with positions of authority in their plantations and in Smith's Bethel church. They had called for withholding of labor. As was the case in most slave rebellions, much of the violence was visited on slaves rather than perpetrated by them.

Not noticed by historians, in 1824 Elizabeth Heyrick coupled her call for immediatism with a defense of the Demerara slave rebels. According to Heyrick, Haiti was living proof of its success, and she blamed the massacres of the revolution on the excesses of planters. In an addendum to her pamphlet on immediate abolition, she reported that the slave insurgents in Demerara had been hanged, some receiving the "protracted torture" of a thousand lashes and being forced to work in chains for the rest of their lives. Are slave rebellions "not in the cause of self-defense from the most degrading and intolerable degradation?" she asked rhetorically. The British extolled Greek resistance to tyranny but handed the slave rebels "a gibbet."[8] Heyrick coupled her call for immediate abolition with a passionate defense of slave resistance.

Besides the large slave rebellions that marked the rise of immediatism, free blacks adopted a militant stance. Robert Wedderburn from Jamaica became a well-known advocate not just of black freedom but also of English radicalism.

The son of a Scottish slaveholder and a slave mother who was sold while she was pregnant on the condition that her unborn child would be free, Wedderburn served in the Royal Navy and migrated to England in 1778. His first publication, in 1795, recounted his conversion to Wesleyan Methodism, but he went on to become a freethinker. A follower of the English radical Thomas Spence, who advocated the common ownership of land, Wedderburn published his short-lived antislavery periodical, *The Axe Laid to the Root, or A Fatal Blow to Oppressors* (1817), in the form of addresses to slaves and planters. In his first number he demanded "in the name of God, in the name of natural justice, and in the name of humanity, that all slaves be set free." He asked the slaves "not to follow the example" of Haiti but praised the Haitian rebels and the Jamaican Maroons. Anticipating the Demerara rebellion, he called on slaves to withhold their labor from their masters for an hour by organizing what can only be called a sleep-in. As a Spencean, he counseled them to never forfeit their rights to the land they toiled because then their "oppressors would have the power to starve you to death." Wedderburn connected the sufferings of the landless English poor with the oppression of slaves and signed himself as a "West-Indian, a lover of liberty." In his second address, he recommended a plan of government that was as much a blueprint for a postemancipation utopian black polity as a critique of British and slave society. Ironically, officials who spied on him recorded many of his incendiary speeches for history.

Wedderburn's other significant work, his autobiography titled *The Horrors of Slavery*, was published the same year as Heyrick's immediatist pamphlet in 1824 but has been ignored by historians of abolition. It was dedicated to the pious Wilberforce, who visited him in prison when he was jailed for blasphemy. (His satirical *Cast-Iron Parsons* on the invention of robotic parsons in much the way machines were replacing starving "labourers and artizans" is suspected of having been ghostwritten by a fellow Spencean.) Employing a familiar trope in slave narratives, Wedderburn emphasized his personal testimony against slavery, against "the injustice and inhumanity of my father" and the cruelty visited on the rebellious and resourceful enslaved women who raised him, his mother and his grandmother. Like the West Indians William Davidson, a fellow Spencean, and William Cuffay, who was active in Chartism, Wedderburn saw no conflict between abolition and social radicalism. He was buried in 1835 in a pauper's unmarked grave with the scores of poverty-stricken blacks and whites to whom he had preached.[9]

The 1820s witnessed a turn toward radicalism among black abolitionists in the United States too. By the early nineteenth century Baltimore had the largest free black population in the country, the free outnumbering enslaved blacks there by a ratio of three to two. It emerged as a center of abolitionism, rivaling Philadelphia, New York, and Boston. The line between slavery and freedom in Baltimore was blurred by runaway slaves, kidnapped free blacks, a vigorous domestic slave trade, and African American churches and schools feeding antislavery activism. In his farewell address to the people of color in 1824, Elisha Tyson conventionally exhorted free blacks to model conduct, but he also asked them to render "assistance . . . to those of your color." To an overflow audience in the city's largest black church he proposed forming an antislavery society, and a subscription was collected for the "cause of emancipation." Tyson visualized an independent black abolitionist organization, and in 1826 African Americans formed the Baltimore Society for the Protection of Free People of Color, replacing the defunct white society.[10]

Black abolitionism in Baltimore was spurred by the debate over colonization. John H. Latrobe and Charles G. Harper, the son of Robert Goodloe Harper, revived the local colonization movement, attracting Quakers like Moses Sheppard, a cousin of Tyson's. Even Tyson, who had worked with Coker, solicited the help of the ACS in the repatriation of Africans rescued from the illegal Atlantic slave trade. Harper ran on a colonizationist platform against the abolitionist Daniel Raymond for the state legislature in 1826, forcing Raymond to include colonization in his plan for emancipation. The same year Latrobe and Harper ghostwrote a procolonization memorial on behalf of African Americans to the citizens of Baltimore after convening meetings at the city's black Methodist churches. Harper complained that African Americans forced him to edit the memorial so that aspersions against them would be removed, and most seemed to have opposed it. But the ACS published it as a reflection of black support for colonization. It read in part, "But if you have every reason to wish for our removal, how much greater are our inducements to remove!" and it promised to carry "your language, your customs, your opinions and Christianity" to the "desolate shore" of Africa. Colonizationists' attempt to represent them provoked black Baltimoreans to speak out against colonization. By the end of the decade William Watkins, Coker's successor in the Sharp Street Methodist Church and a teacher, emerged as the leading critic of colonization.[11]

For abolitionists, the issue of black rights at home became intertwined with the abolition of slavery. As early as 1807 New Jersey clarified that its constitution did not allow women or blacks to vote. In 1811 New York passed a law requiring African Americans to prove their freedom before being granted the franchise, and in 1818 Connecticut disfranchised blacks while providing for adult manhood suffrage for whites. In 1821 the New York constitutional convention followed suit by raising the property-holding qualification for voting for black men while eliminating it for white men. Though some northern Republicans had endorsed slavery restriction, most seemed intent on whittling away black rights. Legal discrimination went hand in hand with popular racism. "Bobalition" broadsides caricaturing African Americans, their institutions, parades, manners, speech, and politics became ubiquitous in northern cities like Boston, New York, and Philadelphia. Republican newspapers like Mordecai Noah's *National Advocate and Enquirer* whipped up antiblack sentiment. A white mob in 1822 destroyed New York's African Grove Theatre, which was founded by William Brown and had hosted the famous black actors Ira Aldridge and James Hewlett.[12]

The final abolition of slavery in New York in 1827 came on the heels of increasing restrictions on black citizenship. Despite debates over how best to commemorate the event, African Americans marked the occasion in halls festooned with the names of Jay, Wilberforce, Clarkson, Tompkins, and a bust of Boyer. In his oration at the African Zion Church, William Hamilton attacked the new blasphemy of racism that "the Negroes have no souls, they are not men, they are a species of ourang outang. . . . They are a species inferior to white men." If there was a difference between the races, he pointedly added, then "the difference is in favor of the people of colour." American slavery, he observed sarcastically, bespoke "superior legislation and . . . superior minds." He boldly took on Jefferson on race: "I know I ought to speak with caution; but an ambidexter philosopher, who can reason contrarywise, first tells you 'that all men are created equal . . . ,' next proves that one class of men are not equal to another, which by the bye, does not agree with axioms in geometry, that deny that things can be equal, and at the same time unequal to one another."

Black abolitionists used the occasion to launch an assault on slavery and racism. Austin Steward, a former slave from Virginia, in his speech commemorating emancipation in Rochester, asked, "Why should we remember, in joy and exultation, the thousands of our countrymen who are to-day, in this land of gospel light, this boasted land of civil and religious liberty, writhing under the lash and groaning beneath the grinding weight of Slavery's chain?" Free blacks in the South celebrated the end of slavery in New York. In Fredericksburg they raised toasts to New York, hoping that Virginia would follow suit, and to the memory of Rufus King. In Baltimore they drank toasts to Jay, Tyson, and Lundy's *Genius*. Making their sentiments on colonization clear, one toast pronounced, "Emancipation without emigration, but equal rights on the spot; this is republicanism."[13]

Black abolitionists in New York issued indictments of the slaveholding Republic rather than simply evoke its ideals. Instead, they praised Anglo-American abolitionists. In a speech on July 5, Paul demanded universal rather than partial emancipation. Whether Paul chose July 5 to avoid white attacks or as a black protest against the Fourth of July, his tactic was widely adopted. In New York City a parade with representatives from various black societies celebrated the demise of slavery that day. Frederick Douglass also delivered his famous Fourth of July oration on the fifth. Paul highlighted American hypocrisy:

> It is a fact that can neither be denied or controverted, that in the United States of America, at the extirpation of fifty years after its becoming a free and independent nation, there are no less than fifteen hundred thousand human beings still in a state of unconditional vassalage. . . . Yet America is the first in the profession of the love of liberty, and loudest in proclaiming liberal sentiments towards all other nations, and feels herself insulted, to be branded with anything bearing the appearance of tyranny or oppression. Such are the palpable inconsistencies that abound amongst us and such is the medley of contradictions which stain the national character, and renders the American republic a by-word, even among despotic nations.

At the same time, Paul linked abolition with anticolonization and citizenship rights. In a speech in Troy on the second anniversary of abolition in New York, he denounced colonization as "utterly chimerical and absurd" and declared, "We claim this as *our country*, as the land of our nativity."[14]

With the publication in 1827 of *Freedom's Journal*, the first African American newspaper, black abolitionism took off. Founded by Samuel Cornish and coedited by a young John Russwurm, it became the voice of black protest. In their prospectus for the newspaper, the two editors argued that the press was the most economical way to achieve the "moral, religious, civil and literary improvement of our injured race." Moreover, "daily slandered, we think that there ought to be some channel of communication between us and the public: through which a single voice may be heard, in defence of *five hundred thousand free people of colour.*" Its opening editorial, written by Cornish, proclaimed, "We wish to plead our own cause. Too long have others spoken for us." Cornish was a pioneer in many ways. Born free in Delaware and trained in the Philadelphia Presbytery, he had founded the First Colored Presbyterian Church in New York in 1824. By the time Cornish left its active editorship, *Freedom's Journal* had over a thousand subscribers, an overwhelming majority of them African American.[15]

Freedom's Journal articulated the concerns of and connected communities across the North, building on networks established by earlier black organizations and churches. The newspaper, in the words of its editors, was "a medium of intercourse between our brethren in different states." It acquired agents even in Canada, Britain, and Haiti. Its list of agents was a veritable who's who of black abolitionism: Walker in Boston, the brothers Thomas and Nathaniel Paul and Steward in Rochester, Hezekiah Grice in Baltimore, John B. Vashon in Pennsylvania, and John Remond in Salem. It also published black abolitionists, including Forten, Watkins, Walker, Hamilton, and Peter Williams Jr. Lundy reprinted pieces from it in the *Genius,* and the American Convention recommended it. The editors advocated abolition by federal law or constitutional amendment, even though they published articles in favor of gradual abolition. They made their position clear: "Give as much importance as we may to other subjects, to us SLAVERY is an all absorbing one."

Black abolitionists used the newspaper to advertise their uncompromising rhetoric. In a long article, the writer, Aristides, adopting the name of an ancient Athenian statesman, called slavery "a record of crime" and "perpetual warfare." To those defenders of slavery who argued that it had existed since antiquity, he replied that so had robbery and murder. Proslavery had its origins in a "depraved heart." American liberty had been purchased with the slaves' blood. The Sage of Monticello held in "perpetual bondage his fellow-men!!! No man's patriotism appears better upon paper, but how is it developed upon his plantation?" Aristides concluded that colonization was a "barbarous and cunning" trick cloaked in religion to get rid of free blacks and perpetuate slavery. Since Walker used the same term, "the colonizing trick," in his *Appeal,* and Hamilton had voiced a similar critique, either could have been Aristides.[16]

Freedom's Journal did not hesitate to take on the "insolent remarks of a Southern Editor" in defense of abolitionists and manumission societies. The latter were "the man of colour's 'best friends,'" not, as the offending editor had claimed, the slaveholders. An article on the domestic slave trade warned that unless the evils of slavery were ended, "the day will come, when all we have read about Spartacus and his servile band—of the horrors of the revolutionary scenes of St. Domingo, will be re[en]acted before our eyes." Another on a southern Baptist minister pursuing his escaped slave referred to the perversions and misinterpretations of the Bible by proslavery clergymen. The paper also refuted the racist opinions of other newspapers. A correspondent accused Noah of scurrility and assured him that he had no desire, nor did he consider it an "honour," to marry his daughter, sleep in his bed, or walk arm in arm with him. In a long rebuttal entitled "Major Noah's Negroes," the editors accused him of making an "unmanly and slanderous attack on the coloured population" and of being "the cat's paw" of slaveholders. The next year a committee of black Philadelphians led by William Whipper, F. C. Webb, and James Cornish, among others, published their riposte to the editor of a Philadelphia newspaper who had referred to free blacks as eyesores fit only for colonization. Russwurm published a series of numbers "On the Varieties of the Human Race," disputing the "racial science" of the day and attributing all human variation to climate.[17]

Freedom's Journal visualized its stated goals of African American emancipation, enlightenment (education), and citizenship (exercising the right to vote) within a broader transnational context, for example, "the establishment of the Republic of Hayti" and "liberal ideas in South America," where abolition had resulted at times in black citizenship and office holding. The editors published materials from the British *Antislavery Reporter* and the proceedings of the London Antislavery Society. Despite the failure of Haitian emigration, the newspaper revealed that Haiti, or "the firm establishment of a free government by those who lately were in the bonds of slavery," exercised a powerful influence on the black abolitionist imagination. They noted that "no one wished" the Haitian Revolution well, as they had the American and French ones. The fact that "in their glorious career, alone and unaided . . . the Haitians withstood the power of the greatest monarch," Napoleon, "struck [them] with astonishment and admiration." In its first year of publication, *Freedom's Journal* devoted many pages to the history of Haiti and to a glowing biography of Toussaint Louverture. The next year the editors published a melodramatic historical fiction, "Theresa—A Haytien Tale," set during the revolution.[18] The newspaper's full-throated defense of the Haitian Revolution underscores that it was more than just a vehicle of uplift for the literate black middle class. Its advocacy of education and self-improvement was intrinsically connected to its politics of radical abolition.

Freedom's Journal emerged as a staunch critic of the ACS. Influential colonizationists ended their subscription to the newspaper. In 1829 the New York State Colonization Society was formed with the backing of the wealthy philanthropist Gerrit Smith. The editors differentiated black-led emigration movements like Cuffe's, whose memoir they published, and Haitian emigration from colonization. Writing as "A Man of Color," Forten pointed out that the procolonization memorial of Baltimore blacks was opposed by two-thirds of those present and that the main aim of the ACS was to force the emigration of southern free blacks by making their condition intolerable. Watkins, writing as "A Colored Baltimorean," wrote, "It appears very strange to me that those benevolent men should feel so much for the condition of free coloured people, and, at the same time . . . feel so little concern for those who are held in bondage by themselves." In a critique of colonization, Investigator remarked, "The measures of the Colonization Society, have not only been contrary to the wishes of our brethren, but against their repeated remonstrances." The editors published long procolonization letters from John H. Kennedy of Philadelphia and from a subscriber disgruntled with their anticolonization position. In reply, Investigator reasoned, "Colonizing the free people of colour in Africa is never going to facilitate emancipation, but rather to retard its progress." Another anticolonizationist, Clarkson, observed that the same antiblack spirit that made South Carolina imprison free black sailors motivated colonizationists.[19]

By 1828 *Freedom's Journal* had lost much of its original vitality, reprinting more articles and making frequent appeals for payment of past dues. Russwurm, who took over the editorial duties from Cornish in September 1827, became increasingly ambivalent about colonization. Earlier he had contemplated migrating to Haiti. On February 14, 1829, Russwurm announced that his views on colonization had "materially altered" and acknowledged that he was advancing "doctrines in opposition to the majority of the readers." It was, he felt, "a waste of words to talk of ever enjoying citizenship in this country." He published a defense of the ACS and of the "flourishing colony" of Liberia and started publishing more procolonization articles. Once Russwurm decided to support colonization, the newspaper collapsed within a month. Boston Crummell, in whose house the paper was founded, asked him to cease printing it. Black abolitionists disavowed Russwurm after he migrated to Liberia in September. Russwurm asked the "young men . . . wasting the best days of their lives in the United States" to flock to "this land as the last asylum of the unfortunate." He took over as editor of the *Liberian Herald*, which colonizationists pronounced "free of those tinges of barbarism . . . rarely found entirely blanched from the African intellect." To Russwurm, Liberia was "a republic in miniature" and presented a "great field of usefulness" for African Americans, who would be like "pilgrims in search of Liberty." He was one of only a handful of black abolitionists to embrace colonization.[20]

If the honor of publishing the first black abolitionist newspaper goes to New York, the founding of the first black abolitionist organization took place in Boston. In 1826 black Bostonians founded the General Colored Association (GCA), devoted to "racial betterment and slave abolition." The organization lasted as a separate entity until 1832, when it became a part of Garrison's NEASS. Rev. Thomas Paul, John Telemachus Hilton, James Barbadoes, Joshua Easton, William G. Nell, and Walker were prominent GCA members. It met to pass resolutions in favor of *Freedom's Journal* and raised funds for the safe return of Abduhl Rahhaman (Abd al Rahman Ibrahima), a Muslim prince enslaved in Mississippi. He was manumitted and traveled around the country to raise money for his family's freedom and his transportation back to Africa. Free black communities throughout the North contributed money to their "fellow countryman," the one instance in which they were willing to cooperate with the ACS, which eventually arranged for Ibrahima's transportation to Liberia. But Ibrahima, who was forced to leave his enslaved children and grandchildren behind, sent back decidedly unfavorable accounts of the colony and died shortly after his arrival. In their public dinner for him, black Bostonians drank toasts not to the ACS but to Lundy and Wilberforce. Thomas Dalton, the president of the GCA, raised a glass to "Liberty and Equality. . . . May the time be not far distant when the sons and daughters of Africa who are now in bondage, shall be enabled to exclaim 'We are free.'"

A majority of the GCA, like most African Americans, worked in menial or black-dominated service professions. Dalton was a bootblack, Hilton and Barbadoes barbers. Its most dynamic member was Walker, who had settled in Boston as a used clothes dealer by 1825. He became a pillar of the community, joining the African Masonic Lodge and the black Methodist May Street Church pastored by Rev. Samuel Snowden, a former slave and ardent abolitionist. In his address of 1828 before the GCA's semiannual meeting, Walker issued a call for abolitionist organization among blacks. As he put it, "Do not two hundred and eight years of intolerable sufferings teach us the actual necessity of a general union among us?" Five hundred thousand free blacks united, he exhorted, could perform "mighty deeds" in the cause of abolition. The same year Hosea Easton delivered a ringing address against racial prejudice to the free black community in Providence and called for cultivating "the principles of concord and unanimity among us." Easton, who began his address by comparing America's reputation for liberty with its avarice as illustrated by the slave trade and the "hellish scourge" of slave whippings, condemned the "*Colonizing Craft*" as a "diabolical pursuit."[21]

Walker's *Appeal*, the first abolitionist pamphlet of the second wave, was not a lone voice of black radicalism, as is commonly depicted, but its most effective statement. Abolitionists like Garrison, Maria Stewart, and Garnet invoked it long after the author's premature death. Published in three editions, it urged black resistance to slavery, criticized the American Republic and the colonization movement, and contained a rebuttal of racist and, in Walker's opinion, anti-Christian views of African Americans. His object, Walker stated in the preamble, was "a spirit of enquiry and investigation respecting our miseries and wretchedness in this *Republican Land of Liberty!!!!!*" He cataloged the long list of political and civil rights denied to most free black people: the right to vote, hold office, and sit on juries, among others. Whites not only reduced black people to the "wretched state of slavery" but also inflicted on them "*insupportable insult*" by claiming that they were not part of the "*human family*" and descended from "*Monkeys or Orang-Outangs.*" Walker felt that the "charges of Mr. Jefferson [must] be refuted by blacks *themselves.*" Jefferson's speculations on racial inferiority had "in truth injured us more, and . . . been as great a barrier to our emancipation as any thing that has ever been advanced against us," as they had "sunk deep into the hearts of millions of the whites and never will be removed this side of eternity." Walker retorted that whites were an "unjust, jealous, unmerciful, avaricious and blood thirsty set of beings," the "*natural enemies,*" murderers, tyrants, and oppressors of African Americans. As in "Hayti, the glory of the blacks and the terror of tyrants," Walker predicted, "my colour will root some of them out of the face of the earth."

Education, or knowledge of their oppression, religion, or African American Christianity, and political unity held the key to black liberation for Walker. He used instances of betrayal of slave resistance to assert that blacks should stamp out ignorance, submission, and treachery to their race. It was the task of free men of color in particular, he wrote, to "*go to work and enlighten your brethren*" and not be satisfied with servile positions. Walker's call for self-improvement and resistance complemented each other. His aim was the "*entire emancipation of your enslaved brethren all over the world.*" Walker targeted slaveholding Christianity, which taught blacks to submit to slavery, and warned instead of divine vengeance: "I tell you Americans! That unless you speedily alter your course, *you* and your *Country are gone!!!!!!* . . . your destruction *is at hand*, and will be speedily consummated unless you REPENT." He mocked whites' empire of religious benevolence, especially efforts to colonize free blacks. Reformers and ministers formed societies against intemperance, Sabbath breaking, and infidelity, while ignoring the "fountainhead" of evil, slavery.

In the last of his four articles Walker concentrated on a systematic refutation of colonization. Recognizing the earlier efforts of Watkins, "that very judicious colored Baltimorean," and quoting extensively from colonization speeches, he charged that the real purpose of the ACS was to rid the country of free black people and keep slaves "secure in wretchedness and ignorance" and render them more obedient. Walker wrote, quoting "the truly Reverend Divine" Allen, "this land which we have watered with our *tears* and *our blood*, is now *our mother country.*" He recommended Cornish's short-lived anticolonization newspaper *Rights of All*, which had succeeded *Freedom's Journal*, to all his brethren. Americans had "grown fat on our blood and groans" and the "colonizing trick" was merely a way to perpetuate racial slavery. Walker quoted the Declaration not just to evoke its ideals but also, like the freedom petitioners of the eighteenth century, to compare its relatively trivial complaints with the cruelties and murders inflicted on blacks and their fathers by whites and their fathers without any provocation. His appeal was a powerful indictment of American slaveholding republicanism and a revolutionary call for abolition.[22]

The year that Walker issued his *Appeal*, Robert Alexander Young published *The Ethiopian Manifesto*. Unlike Walker, Young was not part of the black abolitionist milieu. He was a "working class preacher" of mixed race from Baltimore, "who plied his trade in the streets of New York City." Young, like Walker, stated that blacks enjoyed few "rights of government" as "our race" was reduced to an enslaved state, and "to raise it from its degenerate sphere, and instill into it the rights of men, are the ends intended of these our words." Again like Walker, he castigated slaveholders as "cruel fellow-men" and a "fiendish cast of men" for their barbarities and warns them that "intuitive justice" and "an outraged and goading conscience" required them to free their slaves. He counseled slaves to submit "to your present state of suffering" because God himself would break their "vile shackles of slavery." Young's ideas were somewhat eclectic, perhaps the reason his work was neglected by his contemporaries. He ended with a mystical prediction of a messiah, a white man born of a black woman in Granada, who would become their "liberator from the infernal state of bondage."[23]

The publication of these two pamphlets coincided with one of the era's worst race riots, which took place in Cincinnati. Bordering slavery, the city had an economy with a southern orientation. It seemed "little better" than Virginia to emigrants like John Malvin. During the 1820s the city's black population had grown, established a branch of the AME, and founded black schools. Led by Malvin, black Cincinnatians demanded the repeal of Ohio's Black Law of 1807, which required blacks to post a bond of five hundred dollars when entering the state. Despite Malvin's success in negotiating a six-month stay in enforcing the law, white opposition to the black presence came to a head in August 1829, when mobs burned black homes, businesses, churches, and schools in a weeklong spree of racially motivated violence. The Ohio Colonization Society fanned the flames by calling for the removal of "this class of people as a serious evil among us," and the ACS upheld state laws regulating the settlement of black people. Even though free blacks here as elsewhere rejected colonization, emigrationists led by James C. Brown made plans to buy land in Upper Canada and form an all-black colony named Wilberforce. In 1824 African Americans had organized the Cincinnati Haytien Union to explore the possibility of emigrating to Haiti. The riot accelerated the exodus of nearly two thousand African Americans from the city, a substantial number of whom moved to Wilberforce on land purchased by Israel Lewis and Thomas Crissup. Their plight became a national cause célèbre among African Americans. Wilberforce, portrayed by abolitionists as a model black community, attracted emigrants like Steward and Paul but was torn by dissension and lack of funds. Malvin moved to Cleveland and remained active in the struggle to repeal the state's black laws.[24]

During its short publication history Cornish's *Rights of All* documented black outrage over the Cincinnati riot and the brazen attempt, legal and extralegal, to drive black Americans from their homes. As he wrote, "The conduct of the authorities to the colored people of Ohio, forms a blot in the history of our country, that would have stamped with everlasting infamy and disgrace the most barbarous nation of the dark ages." Cornish protested the silence of the white press at the "cruel illegality" of the black laws and contended that they were unconstitutional, as they prevented blacks from New York from migrating freely to Ohio. In an editorial entitled "Barbarism in America," Cornish called upon African Americans not to leave their "native land." He linked the tendency to view blacks as a "separate people," an "extraneous mass," and a "dangerous evil" with efforts to colonize them. Cornish, nevertheless, recommended black emigration to Canada, illustrating that black opposition to colonization never implied accommodation to racism.[25]

New York's black abolitionists took the lead in advocating emigration. Williams gave an anticolonization speech for the benefit of the "Colored Community of Wilberforce" in Upper Canada on the Fourth of July, 1830. Anticipating the themes and indeed the words of Douglass's famous Fourth of July speech, he stated, "The festivities of this day serve to impress upon the minds of reflecting men of colour a deeper sense of cruelty, the injustice, and oppression of which they have been victims." While "others rejoice," he said, "they mourn." Williams maintained that black freedom in the North was defective, as it had been separated from equality. He used words that black abolitionists would often repeat: "We are natives of this country, we ask only to be treated as well as foreigners." Williams criticized settler colonialism in general, noting the ruin of Native Americans, and appealed for support of their "brethren exiled from Cincinnati." A year later black New Yorkers met to pass resolutions against the formation of a colonization society in the state. Its address dissected colonizationist discourse, "which acknowledging our wrongs commits a greater by vilifying us." The ACS were "less friendly to our welfare as citizens of the United States." Writing from Liberia, Russwurm opposed Canadian emigration.[26]

In response to the Cincinnati riot and to foster Canadian emigration, African Americans convened a national convention in 1830. The idea came initially from Grice, was seconded by black New Yorkers, and ultimately called by the seventy-year-old Allen in Philadelphia. Delegates included Whipper from Pennsylvania, Steward from New York, and Abraham Shadd, the son of Jeremiah

Shadd, from Delaware. The national conventions met annually until 1835 and were revived in 1843; during this hiatus state conventions met regularly. Until the Civil War and even beyond they were powerful symbols of black political organization, articulating the demands of and debates within black communities and encouraging activism at the state and local levels. As the American Convention became virtually defunct after 1829 and before the organization of the American Anti Slavery Society (AASS) in 1833, black conventions were the only national antislavery gatherings. The first national black convention established the "American Society of Free persons of Colour, for improving their condition in the United States; for purchasing lands; and for the establishment of a settlement in the Province in Upper Canada" and elected Allen president. Its address to the free people of color called attention to "our forlorn and deplorable situation" and "laws [that] have been enacted in some of the states of this great republic, to compel an unprotected and harmless portion of our brethren, to leave their homes and seek an asylum in foreign climes." It rejected colonization but promoted emigration to Canada. Abolitionists, including Garrison, would support Canadian emigration throughout the antebellum period. Finally, it recommended the formation of local auxiliaries. Grice founded the Legal Rights Association in Baltimore.[27]

The abolitionist nature of the national black convention and the spur it gave to interracial immediatism became more evident at its second meeting in 1831. Its ranks now included Sipkins, Hamilton, Thomas L. Jennings, Williams, Peter Vogelsang, Crummell, Thomas Downing, Philip Bell, and James W. C. Pennington from New York, Forten, Robert Purvis, Whipper, and Robert Douglass Sr. from Philadelphia, and Hosea Easton, Robert Roberts, Barbadoes, and Snowden from Boston. With the death of Allen, these men constituted its leadership. Abolitionists such as Lundy, Garrison, Arthur Tappan, Simeon Jocelyn, and Thomas Shipley of the PAS attended its proceedings and received a special vote of thanks. Instead of Canadian emigration, a black manual labor school in New Haven proposed by Garrison and Jocelyn emerged as its main concern.

The convention adopted the role of the American Convention, recommending abolitionist newspapers like Lundy's *Genius*, Garrison's *Liberator*, and the *African Sentinel and Journal of Liberty*, a black newspaper edited by a John Stewart in Albany. Stewart's proposal called the "descendants of Africa" to "destroy that hydra-headed, canker worm of prejudice, encourage education, Temperance and morality, and urge the distribution of equal justice and equality." The convention set aside July 4 as a day of "humiliation, fasting and prayer" to break the "shackles of slavery" and obtain "our sacred rights." It disdained "public processions" in favor of political organization, not just as a nod to white racism or middle-class respectability but as a more sustained, permanent, and modern form of black protest. According to its address, "the spirit of persecution" in "this boasted land of freedom" was the cause of its meeting. Commending the progress of general emancipation in Britain and Denmark, it added, "Would to God we could say thus of our own native soil." Garrison remarked, "The colored people begin to feel their strength, and begin to use it." According to Joseph Willson, who published a book on Philadelphia's blacks, "To the 'first annual Convention' certainly belongs the credit of having blown the first great blast, by which the people were awakened to the importance of their own united and energetic action, in removing their disabilities and securing equal rights with other men."[28]

Except in 1834 the early national conventions met in Philadelphia, the antislavery capital of the country and home to an activist free black community. By 1831 the city boasted of numerous benevolent, literary, and fraternal organizations, women's organizations outnumbering male societies twenty-nine to sixteen. These local black associations in northern cities were important stepping-stones to a national organization. Leadership of the conventions, like that of black churches and societies, remained firmly in male hands. Along with Allen, Forten, and his son-in-law Purvis, Whipper emerged as a leading voice of black abolitionism. He was born in Lancaster in 1804 and began his career as a laborer, a "steam scourer" of clothes. In 1835 he moved to Columbia, where he developed a successful partnership with Stephen Smith, a businessman dealing in lumber and coal. Whipper was active in black civic life and one of the main figures in the convention movement of the 1830s. In an address in 1828 to the Colored Reading Society for Mental Improvement, Whipper delineated the benefits of a liberal education and castigated slaveholders for their antislave literacy laws. These "avowed advocates of slavery" claimed to be religious and moral, but, he exclaimed, "I deny them the privilege, for there is not a slaveholder under the canopy of heaven possesses one of these titles, or else I am mistaken in the articles of justice." He was sorry to note that the national government contained a "majority of these misanthropists." Whipper hoped that the reading society would produce a Wilberforce, Jay, Clarkson, Franklin, or Rush, his pantheon of abolitionist heroes. A race riot in Philadelphia in 1829 and the popularity of Edward Clay's racist illustrations lampooning black Philadelphians led Forten to call a meeting to subscribe to *Rights of All* and promote a national abolitionist organization.[29]

The decade that incubated black abolitionism began and ended with dramatic instances of slave resistance. In 1831 two major slave revolts shook the foundations of Anglo-American slavery. On August 22 Nat Turner led a slave uprising in Southampton County, Virginia. The transcriber of Turner's "Confessions," the Virginian attorney and planter Thomas Gray, recognized the import of an "open rebellion of the slaves . . . attended with such atrocious circumstances of cruelty and destruction." Coming on the heels of Walker's pamphlet and the publication of Garrison's *Liberator*, the revolt became irrevocably linked to the birth of radical abolitionism. Walker had sent copies of his *Appeal* to the Baptist minister Rev. Henry Cunningham in Savannah and the New England–born editor Elijah Burritt in Milledgeville, Georgia, who fled north shortly afterward. The pamphlet also surfaced among free blacks and slaves in Virginia and North Carolina and was carried by sailors to the lower south ports of Charleston and New Orleans. The Virginian governor John Floyd was convinced that Turner's rebellion was the product of "Yankee peddlers," reform societies, and the "incendiary publications of Walker, Garrison and Knapp." A wave of slave resistance in North Carolina and Louisiana, of which Turner's revolt was a culmination, alarmed authorities, who passed repressive laws against slaves, free blacks, and suspected abolitionists.[30]

Born in 1800, the year Gabriel was hanged and Vesey bought his freedom, Turner and the people around him believed he was destined for greatness. Communicating with the "Spirit," which sent him many signs to start a rebellion, Turner, a slave preacher, chose July 4 as the day to start the rebellion, but bad weather delayed his plan. He wanted to march to the town of Jerusalem, seize an arsenal, and escape to the Dismal Swamp, a hideout for "outlyers" and Maroons. Nearly sixty slaves followed him, and fifty-seven white men, women, and children were killed. Turner was captured after eluding authorities for a few days. When asked by Gray, "Do you not find yourself mistaken now?" Turner uttered his most famous words: "Was not Christ crucified?" Gray, who accused him of "gloomy fanaticism" and murder, evinced reluctant admiration of Turner for his "natural intelligence and quickness of apprehension" and his "calm, deliberate composure." In its memorable description of Turner in prison, bloodied and in rags "yet daring to raise his manacled hands to heaven, with a spirit soaring above the attributes of man," Gray's *Confessions* contributed to his legend. Thirty rebels were sentenced to death, nineteen were hanged, and many were transported out of the state. In a final act of desecration, physicians dissected Turner's body, keeping gruesome mementos. Hundreds of slaves and free blacks fell victim to white vigilantism, far exceeding the number of whites who had died in the rebellion. Three fugitive slaves from the area, Harriet Jacobs, Charity Bowers, and Henry "Box" Brown, left vivid accounts of the reign of terror in the aftermath of the revolt.

Turner inspired a great many abolitionists in the antebellum period. Garnet evoked the legacy of slave rebellion embodied by Turner, Vesey, Toussaint, and the later shipboard rebellions led by Cinque and Madison Washington.

William Wells Brown said Turner was a "martyr to the freedom of his race," and J. Sella Martin included Turner "among the bravest and best in history." Thomas Wentworth Higginson wrote a sympathetic account of Turner's rebellion, as he did of Vesey's conspiracy. Harriet Beecher Stowe made her slave character in *Dred* the son of Vesey and modeled him after Turner. In Martin Delany's novel, the slave rebel Blake traveled in the South and Cuba, where he heard slaves talk about Vesey and Turner. John Brown, who in 1859 would himself lead an aborted revolt, was an admirer of Turner. The *Anglo African* in 1859 invoked both Brown and Turner to demand action against slavery. In a speech on black military recruitment during the war, Douglass referred to Turner's rebellion, an instance of black men taking up arms against slaveholders, as worthy of emulation.[31]

Turner's rebellion put emancipation on the agenda of Virginia's legislature in 1831–32. William Henry Roane, the grandson of Patrick Henry, presented, among other measures, a Quaker petition for gradual abolition, and Thomas Jefferson Randolph, Jefferson's grandson, introduced a plan for gradual emancipation and the deportation of free blacks. While representatives from the western, predominantly nonslaveholding part of the state favored its "whitening" through emancipation and colonization, slaveholders rallied behind racial slavery and against even the most gradualist, antiblack plans for abolition. The legislature passed a law further proscribing free black rights and recommending colonization as a way to get rid of its free rather than its slave population. Over a hundred free blacks from Southampton County left for Liberia in the wake of the rebellion. Thomas R. Dew's famous review of the Virginia debates articulated the upper south's proslavery position that masqueraded as antislavery. While vociferously opposing all plans for emancipation as impractical and defending slavery, he hoped for an eventual end to slavery. Maryland restricted free black rights, and a similar debate proved to be a boon to the new Maryland State Colonization Society, which was incorporated and received government funding. In 1833 it declared emancipation to be one of its goals and founded a new colony in Cape Palmas, located to the south of Liberia.[32]

Turner's revolt bred fears of slave rebelliousness. Samuel Warner, a northern antislavery writer, believed it was the start of a more widespread rebellion in adjoining North Carolina and Maryland and that the slave rebels, like the Haitians, had one object in mind, "the extermination of whites." He concluded that they should not be doomed to "cruel bondage" in a "Land of liberty" and that the ideas of the Declaration and the Constitution's Bill of Rights be extended to African Americans. The anonymous Nero letter in Governor Floyd's possession, which posited that oppression bred revenge, seemed to confirm suspicions that abolitionists were instigating rebellions. Nero, a Bostonian and runaway slave from Virginia, advised that his race would "not shrink from our holy and laudable purpose of vengeance." Besides a rebellion led by a Haitian-trained "Chief," the letter warned of abolitionist agents. The proslavery Virginian aristocrat Benjamin Watkins Leigh, ironically adopting the pseudonym Appomattox, conjectured that "the seditious practices of negro preachers, . . . the machinations of the organized convention of free blacks in Philadelphia, . . . the dissemination of the incendiary writings of *The Liberator,* or *The African Sentinel,* or *The Genius of Universal Emancipation,*" and the slavery debates would destroy slavery.[33]

While slave resistance prompted debates over emancipation in America, it precipitated British abolition. In December 1831 the charismatic Samuel "Daddy" Sharpe led the so-called Baptist War or Christmas Rebellion in Jamaica, which involved nearly sixty thousand slaves. It was preceded by a wave of slave resistance and free black activism in the West Indies. Free "coloreds" in Jamaica had won equal rights in 1830, and earlier in the year British abolitionists launched a huge petition campaign for the immediate abolition of slavery. With its long history of Maroon wars and slave rebellions it was perhaps inevitable that Jamaica was the site of the largest slave revolt in the history of the British colonies. Slaveholders blamed Baptist missionaries, in whose church Sharpe was a deacon, and abolitionists for the rebellion. Fourteen whites died, and colonial authorities ruthlessly killed over five hundred slaves in reprisal and imprisoned Baptist missionaries. The slave rebels, who planned a strike in the beginning, had mainly burned down the symbols of their oppression, factories and plantations. Like Turner, Sharpe evoked crucifixion, confessing that he would rather "die upon yonder gallows than live in slavery." The abolitionist minister Henry Bleby, who published his firsthand account decades later, wrote that Sharpe was "immolated at the polluted shrine of slavery." Initially alarmed at the uprising, British public opinion veered toward antislavery when news of its brutal suppression and mistreatment of missionaries made its way home. As Bleby noted, the revolt dealt a wound to colonial slavery and "accelerated its destruction." One week after Sharpe's execution in 1832, Parliament appointed a select committee to explore the expediency of "effecting the Extinction of Slavery throughout the British Dominions." The Reform Act, which democratized parliamentary elections, and abolitionist petitions ensured the passage of emancipation in 1833.[34]

The year of Sharpe's rebellion witnessed the publication of the first female slave narrative. Written by Mary Prince, a slave who was brought to England, it detailed the brutalities of West Indian slavery. It ran through three editions in the first year of its publication. Prince left her abusive owners and eventually sought assistance from the Anti-Slavery Society. She was determined to make the slaves' case: "I have been a slave—I have felt what a slave feels and I know what a slave knows; and I would have all the good people in England know it too, that they may break our chains, and set us free." Her abolitionist employer, Thomas Pringle, made it clear that the narrative, though written by her amanuensis Susannah Strickland, was her idea. Prince's story was marked by family separation and slave sales, where "strange men" examined her like a butcher examined animals for slaughter. She referred to her owners' treatment of her as being transferred from "one butcher to another." In her descriptions of frequent whippings, which Pringle's wife vouched left her back "distinctly scarred, as if it were *chequered*," of her ceaseless and painful labor making salt, and her hints that her second, "indecent master" abused her, Prince directly responded to those who were convinced that slaves were better off than the English working poor.

Prince was forced to choose between slavery and staying with her husband in Antigua and freedom in England. In at least two other cases, including the well-known one of the slave Grace in 1827, enslaved women who "voluntarily" returned to colonial slavery did not benefit from the protections of the *Somerset* decision. Prince's narrative led to two lawsuits for libel, one brought by Pringle against *Blackwood's Magazine* for challenging its authenticity, and the other by her last owners, Mr. and Mrs. Woods, against Prince and the antislavery society. Described even by her benefactors as being self-important and proud, Prince testified that she had chosen to live with a white man, a Captain Abbot, for seven years. Like another female slave author, Harriet Jacobs, Prince defied gender conventions and made unconventional choices in order to elude her enslavers. Her testimony performed abolitionist work that was just as important as that of the petitions and writings of Englishwomen that marked the turn to immediatism in Britain.[35] Even more than the first wave of abolition, the second was an interracial radical movement shaped by black protest.

GARRISONIANISM

Historians have traditionally dated the second wave of abolition to the publication of Garrison's *Liberator*. But Garrison himself was keenly aware of its antecedents in the Quaker-dominated first wave, the British abolition movement, and the black tradition of protest. At the paper's inception, immediatism was defined by its largest constituency, the activist black communities in the urban North, Canada, and even Haiti. What distinguished Garrisonians from previous generations of abolitionists was how firmly Garrisonianism's roots lay in black abolitionism.

Descended from indentured servants and born on December 12, 1805, in Newburyport, Massachusetts, Garrison in his early years led a life that contributed to his empathy for the enslaved and working poor. Abandoned by his father, he suffered long separations from his devout mother, experienced extreme poverty and hunger, ran away from his guardians, and was put to hard labor as a child before he settled down as a printer's apprentice. At the *Newburyport Herald*, Garrison learned how to set type. Yet in journalism he discovered not a calling but a means to an end. After writing for a succession of newspapers associated with reform, he was invited to edit the *Journal of the Times*, a newspaper in Bennington, Vermont, that was a proponent of John Quincy Adams. The paper under Garrison contained so many antislavery pieces that it earned the commendation of Lundy and the American Convention.[36]

Garrison commenced his abolitionist career with an unusually radical Fourth of July address at Boston's Park Street Church in 1829. His words mirrored those of black abolitionists comparing the "pitiful detail of grievances" in the Declaration with the much greater "wrongs which our slaves must endure!" He was "sick of our unmeaning declamation in praise of liberty and equality; of our hypocritical cant about the unalienable rights of man"; and his cheeks blushed with shame at his "country's barbarity and despotism." He too warned of God's vengeance, "the catastrophe of republican America" on a day meant to celebrate it. The Haitian Revolution would pale in comparison, he predicted. This was not a conventional Fourth of July address but an abolitionist jeremiad. Garrison called for making slaves "useful, intelligent and peaceable citizens" and argued that if the enslaved were white no constitutional scruples would prevent their emancipation. The ACS had sponsored Garrison's speech, but he was not, as is commonly assumed, a member. Ten days later Garrison attended a celebration on the abolition of the slave trade organized by the African Freehold Society, a black benevolent organization. Garrison took note of the audience's audible disapproval of the two speakers, a clergyman and temperance advocate who orated that the slaves should not be freed without a long period of preparation and an ACS spokesman who also recommended gradualism and colonization.[37] Garrison's doubts on colonization became convictions.

Garrison came into sustained contact with Baltimore's black abolitionists later that year, when he accepted Lundy's invitation to coedit the *Genius*. He virtually took over the editing of the paper from Lundy, who devoted most of his time to Haitian emigration, and started publishing black abolitionists' denunciations of colonization. Watkins and Jacob Greener played a crucial role in pushing Garrison toward an anticolonization stance. Greener, a teacher, printer, and agent for the *Genius*, like Watkins, was a champion of black education. Earlier, Lundy had published Watkins's toasts on Haitian independence and advertised Greener's school for indigent children. Lundy and Garrison lived in a Quaker boardinghouse with them, practicing and preaching interracialism. Garrison soon announced his conversion to immediatism.

In a way, Garrison served an apprenticeship not only with Lundy but also with Watkins and Greener. Watkins debated black advocates of colonization like John Hepburn. He excoriated the "Americo-African empire" of Liberia and Rev. George McGill's claim that black Americans were "received and treated as white men" there. Colonizationists should be fighting the "demon of slavery" and a domestic slave trade that even Hepburn acknowledged annually shipped "one thousand or more, before all the virtue and wisdom of our Republic, without shame." Greener was known to disrupt colonization meetings and ask that the money raised be invested in black education instead. When a Reverend Hewitt drew attention to black degradation in the cause of temperance, "A Colored Observer" noted that "moral degradation can never justify oppression." Garrison in his editorial comment seconded that it was a "flimsy excuse" for slavery. Watkins eventually migrated to Canada, and his son, William J. Watkins, and adopted niece, Frances Ellen Watkins, became prominent abolitionists. Greener's sons became agents for the *Liberator*, and his grandson, Richard T. Greener, a professor in South Carolina during Reconstruction.[38]

Not just the anticolonizationist stance of black Baltimoreans but also Garrison's exposure to the prolific border state slave trade influenced him. He was imprisoned for libel after revealing in the *Genius*'s Black List that a prominent merchant, Francis Todd from his hometown in Massachusetts, participated in the slave trade. In prison Garrison witnessed slave traders and slaveholders apprehend and sell recalcitrant slaves. Rather than focus on his alleged martyrdom, he wrote that he felt ashamed that he done so little for the plight of the enslaved. Arthur Tappan bailed him out, and he left Baltimore in 1830 as an advocate of immediate abolition and black rights and a critic of colonization. He made a series of anticolonization speeches in Philadelphia and New York to mixed audiences of African Americans and white abolitionists and in Jocelyn's black church in New Haven. Tried in absentia, he was fined one thousand dollars. Garrison regarded his case as a matter of the freedom of the press and refused to pay it.[39]

Lundy did not wholly approve of the "sweeping denunciations" of colonization by this "intrepid advocate of African emancipation." But Lundy also disapproved of the ACS because, as he commented, it was interested not in

the "*abolition of slavery*" but in the "removal of the *free people of color.*" After
Garrison's departure, he reverted to a monthly edition of the *Genius* and, on
leaving Baltimore, wrote, "The spirit of tyranny in Maryland became too strong
and malignant for me." Baltimore soon ceased to be a center of abolition. In
the next two years Lundy traveled in the North and Canada, printing the *Genius* wherever he could. In 1831 the *Liberator* quickly overtook it as the premier
abolitionist newspaper. Lundy also traveled to Texas and Mexico to establish
a black colony. He promoted an emancipation scheme by which the federal
government would buy slaves and settle them in the southwest. Yet Texas became a bastion of slavery, not of black freedom. In one of his last antislavery
contributions, Lundy denounced the introduction of slavery to Texas. He published an abolitionist newspaper devoted to free produce and opposed to Texas
annexation, the *National Enquirer*, in Philadelphia and died in 1839 in Illinois,
printing the last copies of the *Genius* there.[40]

Garrison took abolition in a new direction organizationally and ideologically.
He had published the prospectus for his abolitionist newspaper in August 1830
and managed to solicit one hundred dollars from Tappan for it. After failing
to acquire a press in Washington, Garrison, together with the printer and his
longtime collaborator Isaac Knapp, published the *Liberator* in Boston. The first
issue appeared on January 1, 1831, a day fraught with meaning for black Americans, as it marked the abolition of the African slave trade and the founding of
Haiti in 1804. Forten also subsidized the printing of the newspaper with a check
for fifty-four dollars for twenty-seven subscriptions. A month later he sent Garrison another twenty dollars with new subscribers. Four hundred and fifty of the
five hundred subscribers to the *Liberator* in its first year were African Americans, sustaining the young editor with their financial, moral, and political support. In turn, Garrison published their speeches and letters, proceedings of local meetings and the national conventions, and the obituaries of Thomas Paul
and Richard Allen. Even after the subscription list of the newspaper expanded
to over two thousand, African Americans remained a quarter of its readers.

The paper, Garrison explained, did not belong to whites—"they do not sustain
it"—but "emphatically to the people of color—it is their organ." The *Liberator*,
Forten wrote, revived "our drooping hopes." Tappan, a successful merchant,
asked Garrison not to include his name in the list of agents for fear of angering
his clientele, but black abolitionists willingly became the *Liberator's* first agents:
Watkins and Greener in Baltimore, Cornish and Bell in New York, Vashon
in Pittsburgh, and Joseph Cassey in Philadelphia. Stewart, the editor of the
defunct *African Sentinel* of Albany, was an agent. The agents Abraham Shadd
in Delaware, John Remond in Salem, Massachusetts, and Jehiel C. Beman

in Middletown, Connecticut, headed distinguished abolitionist families. Local black leaders such as Henry Ogden in New Jersey and James E. Ellis, George Wyllis, and Alfred Niger in Providence were also agents. Black emigrants, including William Bowler in Port-au-Prince, Haiti, and Steward in Wilberforce, Canada, spread the word about the paper among blacks in emancipated spaces. Cassey, who had been recommended by Forten, was an especially effective agent, gaining for the *Liberator* a foothold in Philadelphia's activist black community. Charles Lenox Remond, the son of John Remond, became a successful agent and the first black lecturer for immediatism. Garrison's first apprentice was an African American, the son and namesake of Thomas Paul; his practice of hiring black apprentices would continue for much of his lifetime.[41]

When his white "coadjutors" asked Garrison to temper his language, black people sustained him in his judgment to be "as harsh as truth and as uncompromising as justice." Garrison adopted not just the black abolitionist program of anticolonization and citizenship but also its style and rhetoric. He told African Americans that "your rights, and the defence of your character, will be the leading object of the paper," observing that they had been "struggling against wind and tide." In his letters to blacks he signed off as their unflinching and untiring advocate. Garrison published a series of what he called truisms mocking American racism: all men are equal except Africans; whites who kill tyrants are heroes, and a slave who killed his master is called a murderer and burned; slaves have no intellect and southern laws against literacy "are owing simply to an itch for superfluous legislation"; and so on. He followed *Freedom's Journal* in publishing anticolonization articles by African Americans. As A Colored Baltimorean, Watkins wrote that he would rather live under the cruel laws of Maryland than be "driven like cattle to the pestilential clime of Liberia." Garrison was initially mistaken for a black man. When he met an astonished Thomas Fowell Buxton a year later in England, he received this misconception as the best compliment.[42]

The impact of black abolitionism on Garrison can be gauged by his reaction to Walker and Turner. While he wrote that he deprecated violence, he defended both men. Even Lundy criticized Walker's *Appeal* as a "bold, daring, inflammatory pamphlet" and as the "wildest strain of reckless fanaticism," but Garrison could barely conceal his admiration for Walker's rhetoric, choosing the *Appeal* as the first abolitionist work to be reviewed at length and respectfully in his newspaper. An anonymous reviewer, V, published large extracts from Walker verbatim and praised it for its correct facts and "just inferences." V liked Walker's spirit and closed by saying, "Well done David Walker." To those who would question its authorship and its intentions, Garrison replied that no white

man was capable of writing such a tract and that "if any people were ever justified in throwing off the yoke of their tyrants, the slaves are that people." Walker's
widow gave their son the middle name Garrison.

Although denying charges of inciting rebellions, Garrison clearly aligned
himself with slave resistance. Garrison was a pacifist but, remarking on Turner's
rebellion and its brutal aftermath, he wrote, "A dastardly triumph, well becoming a nation of oppressors." Slave rebels, Garrison judged, deserved no more
censure than the revolutionary generation or contemporary European freedom
fighters most Americans admired. In any other circumstance, he claimed, another Virginian slave rebel, Gabriel, would be revered as a revolutionary hero.
Garrison refused as well to repudiate the Haitian Revolution. He published an
imaginary dialogue between Washington and Toussaint, to the former's disadvantage, and a sympathetic history of Haiti, which he claimed "has been so
misunderstood and misrepresented, affords unanswerable evidence" for immediatism. Southerners, who demanded Garrison's arrest and the shutting down
of the *Liberator,* and northern newspapers, conservatives, and colonizationists
viewed his words as provoking slave rebellion. The state of Georgia put a price
of five thousand dollars on his head. Garrison became used to receiving death
threats and even published some. Boston's mayor, Harrison Gray Otis, sent a
sheriff to intimidate him and dismissed the newspaper as one read mainly by
black people. Garrison provoked outrage as a madman, a fanatic, or, in Reverend Bacon's assessment, a man who prided himself in winning the support of
blacks.

African Americans rallied around Garrison. During this time he lectured
mainly to black audiences, his speech published as *An Address to the Free
People of Color* (1831). In Philadelphia he stayed at the home of Purvis and
formed a lifelong bond with the Forten–Purvis family. Addressing the national
convention, Garrison said he never addressed black audiences without feeling
ashamed of his skin color. To him, blacks' support "outweighs in consolation all
the abuse heaped on me."[43]

If Watkins, Forten, and Walker converted Garrison on colonization, the rise
of Garrisonian abolition reinvigorated black opposition to it. African Americans
throughout the North held meetings, passed resolutions, and made speeches endorsing the *Liberator* and condemning colonization. In Boston, Robert Roberts,
the author of a popular manual on domestic work, chaired an anticolonization
meeting. In Philadelphia, Forten, Whipper, and Purvis pronounced Garrison
"the efficient and unwavering advocate of human rights." In New York, Peter
Vogelsang and Thomas Jennings led a meeting recommending the *Liberator.*
In Baltimore, Watkins and William Douglass denounced colonization as selfish

policy and not in accordance with black wishes. In Brooklyn, Pennington, and in Pittsburgh, Vashon led anticolonization meetings. In smaller, northern towns, including Hartford and Middletown, Connecticut, Providence, Rhode Island, Nantucket and Salem, Massachusetts, Columbia and Lewistown, Pennsylvania, Trenton, New Jersey, and Rochester, New York, black gatherings criticized the ACS and praised Garrison. In Cincinnati they drank toasts to Allen, Williams, Boyer, and Garrison. In a meeting at the Boyer Lodge in New York, a younger generation of black abolitionists, among them William P. Johnson, David Ruggles, and Thomas Van Rensselaer, congratulated Garrison for the "bold and fearless stance" he had taken on behalf of the "colored race." From Boston's black abolitionists came word that "the descendants of Africa had their eyes fixed" on him. They resolved, "Go then friend and patron of our cause; and whatsoever aid we can render you shall be promptly rendered."[44]

The upsurge of anticolonization, pro-*Liberator* meetings among African Americans led Garrison to publish *Thoughts on African Colonization* in 1832. A year earlier the Massachusetts Colonization Society had been organized by reputed antislavery men such as Theodore Sedgwick, Benjamin F. Varnum, and Charles Tappan, the brother of Arthur and Lewis. In response Garrison called for the organization of a National Anti-Slavery Society and promised to expose the false philanthropy, emancipation "on condition of banishment," of the ACS. The book, which contained extensive materials from the speeches and pamphlets of colonizationists and the *African Repository*, summarized and expanded on the black abolitionist argument against it. Garrison presciently critiqued colonization's imperialist consequences: "If the gospel cannot be propagated but by the aid of the sword . . . it is better to leave the pagan world in darkness." He also differentiated between black-led emigration efforts to Haiti, Mexico, and Canada and African colonization, contending that the former areas were too close for slaveholders' comfort. He published Steward's and Paola Brown's glowing reports on Wilberforce and a letter signed by a "colored female" from Philadelphia who recommended emigration to Mexico in the *Liberator*. Garrison deplored the fact that colonization incited the persecution of African Americans, rattling off a series of recent laws, beginning with Ohio's, which restricted black rights. He recapitulated black denunciations of colonization, including what he called the "conciliatory and generous language" of Walker, who was "denounced as a blood-hound and monster," and Easton's, Watkins's, and Forten's words. His most effective indictment of colonizationists lay in their accommodation to and incitement of an unchristian and unrepublican racial prejudice. The ACS, he charged, derived "malignant satisfaction" from the oppression of free blacks, and he mounted a spirited defense, pointing to their rich institutional life. To those who accused him of fostering anticolonization sentiment among blacks, he set the record straight. He had followed African Americans on this issue rather than vice versa. The second part of his book was entirely devoted to reproducing the proceedings of anticolonization black meetings.[45]

In yet another respect Garrison followed in black footsteps. From John Marrant to Paul Cuffe, black abolitionists traveled to Britain to build an international "antislavery wall" against American slavery. Immediately preceding Garrison was Nathaniel Paul, who was sent to Britain to raise money for Wilberforce. Once there Paul delivered anticolonization speeches at the cost of his original mission. In letters to Garrison he warned of the ACS agent Elliot Cresson's efforts to win British support for colonization. By 1833 Garrison decided to travel to Britain to oppose colonization and to raise funds for a black manual labor school. Black Bostonians led by Primus Hall, Hilton, and Barbadoes, and Forten, Purvis, Robert Douglass, and James McCrummell in Philadelphia approved of his mission. A meeting in New York led by Jennings, Vogelsang, Sipkins, and Johnson asked Garrison to stop Cresson from spreading "detestable misrepresentations of our known wishes." In his farewell address to the people of color, Garrison promised to plead their cause and argue against colonization. African Americans plied him with donations, gifts, and even food. In England, Paul and the British abolitionists Charles Stuart, who had written pamphlets against colonization, Joseph Phillips, and James Cropper were indispensable allies. Stuart forwarded five hundred dollars to Garrison for his proposed manual labor school. Paul lectured with Garrison and lent him money to return home. When Garrison returned, Vashon presented him with another sixty dollars. Garrison formed connections with British abolitionists, especially the radical George Thompson, a lecturing star of the antislavery society's agency system, and the Irish nationalist Daniel O'Connell.[46]

Paul's and Garrison's British lecture tour was the first triumph of interracial immediatism. While Cresson avoided debating Paul, whom he dismissed as a "mulatto" preacher, and Garrison, his cause was effectively dead. The newly formed British colonization society was minuscule and excoriated by abolitionists. Garrison capped his stay with a large meeting at Exeter Hall, where he accused the slaveholding Republic "of disfranchising and proscribing nearly half a million free people of color . . . of suffering a large portion of her population to be lacerated, starved and plundered . . . of trafficking in the bodies and souls of men . . . of stealing the liberties of two millions . . . of being callously indifferent to the accumulated wrongs and sufferings of her black population." Paul defended Garrison from Cresson's allusion to his imprisonment. Garrison was imprisoned for opposing the slave laws of the United States that gave men the liberty to buy and sell human beings, a standard by which, Paul warranted, the entire antislavery society of Britain could be jailed. The Exeter meeting resulted in the abolitionist "Protest against colonization," signed by Wilberforce, Buxton, Allen, George Stephen, and Macaulay. Paul's appeals were effective enough to prevent the aging Clarkson from lending his name to colonization, but he remained neutral. In 1841 Clarkson, in a public letter to Garrison, would finally repudiate colonization. Paul married an Englishwoman and returned to his church in Albany, where he died in 1839.[47]

While abolitionists were a despised American minority, British abolitionists represented a powerful example to them. As Garrison wrote, it cheered his spirits to be in a country where so much was being done for African emancipation. In 1833, just before his return, he witnessed the passage of the abolition bill in the reformed House of Commons and received news of Wilberforce's death. Besides the PAS, Rev. Benjamin F. Hughes of the African Presbyterian Church in New York and Whipper were the first to eulogize him. Recalling Wilberforce's "eloquent and forcible appeals," Whipper detailed his long antislavery career with great precision. In contrast to the victorious history of abolition in Britain, he noted that "the oppressed of all nations and castes" could gain shelter in the United States "EXCEPT THOSE OF AFRICAN ORIGIN." Abolitionists hailed the British precedent not because they were naïve but to hold the slaveholding Republic in contempt. And they reserved their admiration not for the government but for abolitionists. Garrisonians were critical of the British government's implementation of emancipation, which compensated slaveholders and decreed a long period of apprenticeship for former slaves. They acknowledged that "though the proposed measure is far from doing complete justice to the slave, it is yet immeasurably in advance of the present system."[48]

In calling for the immediate, uncompensated (to slaveholders) abolition of slavery and black rights Garrison gave the movement its programmatic clarity. He personally "converted" white immediatists, including the Unitarian minister Samuel J. May, the attorneys Samuel E. Sewall, a descendant of his antislavery Puritan namesake, and Ellis Gray Loring, the editors Oliver Johnson and David Lee Child, the German Charles (Karl) Follen, a professor at Harvard, and Robert B. Hall of Connecticut. Knapp and his future in-laws, the Benson family, soon joined him. The Bensons had been active in the revolutionary era abolition movement, as were the Quaker Garrisonians, the hatter Arnold Buffum and Joshua Coffin. Whittier, taught by Coffin and befriended by Garrison, was a natural convert. Garrison published May's discourse on slavery and early champions of black equality like Jocelyn. From Ohio, he published not just the black abolitionists Rev. Owen and Rev. David Nickens but also the lectures of Professors Beriah Green and Elizur Wright of Western Reserve College. He announced the conversion from colonization to immediatism of Arthur Tappan, a financier of religious and moral reform, including temperance and antiprostitution. Through Tappan he recruited Theodore Dwight Weld, the most outstanding itinerant lecturer for reform.

After scrambling to find twelve men, the "apostolic" number, who would endorse his brand of immediate abolition, Garrison in 1832 again chose January 1 on which to convene the inaugural meeting of the NEASS in the basement of the historic black Baptist church on Belknap Street. Boston's black abolitionists, already organized in the GCA, signed their names alongside the twelve, which included its first president, Buffum, Knapp, Hall, Coffin, and Johnson. Sewall, Loring, and Child, who balked, came around. The GCA worked with the NEASS on a petition campaign against slavery in the District of Columbia. The NEASS encouraged black employment and passed resolutions defending free blacks against colonizationist strictures. In his inaugural address, Hall held up Haiti as an exemplar of immediatism. Within two years, the NEASS acquired nearly two thousand members, and Buffum's and Garrison's lecture tours laid the foundations of immediatism in New England.[49]

Garrison unveiled the tactic of "moral suasion" or persuasion, which was geared to awakening public opinion on slavery and racism. For him, the most important abolitionist work was the conversion of white Americans, convincing them to recognize African Americans as their "fellow countrymen." In his sermon *On Prejudice*, May preached that "it behooves every one, if he would not be made the blind instrument of injustice, oppression, cruelty, to bear in mind that he is *individually* responsible for his conduct and his feelings." In advocating moral suasion, Garrison was strongly influenced by John Rankin's *Letters on Slavery*. Garrison reprinted them in the *Liberator* and in a book as a successful example of moral suasion, the method employed by early Quaker abolitionists. Originally published in 1824 in the newspaper *Castigator* and two years later as a book, Rankin's letters were meant to convert his brother in Virginia, who he learned had purchased slaves. Rankin felt it was his duty to liberate his mistaken brother of his racial prejudices and his "love of gain," which made him enslave black people. His stance against the "twin born" evils of slavery and racism and his opinion that slaves should be given all the "privileges of freemen" aligned well with Garrisonianism. He referred to his fellow Presbyterian John Gloucester as proof of black equality. Having lived in the South, Rankin testified to slavery's "scenes of blood and cruelty" and the disruption of families through the interstate slave trade. Rankin's brother freed his slaves and, like Rankin, moved to Ohio.

Another minister, Rev. James Duncan of Indiana, championed immediatism as early as 1824 in his *A Treatise on Slavery*. Duncan's writings reprehended slavery as a "heinous sin" and criticized northern gradual emancipation laws for robbing the slaves of their labor and liberty until they reached adulthood. Slavery, Duncan wrote, was the "double robbery" of a slave's person and labor. He predicted a Haitian Revolution in America and praised the Vesey rebels as the "fifty martyrs suffering death in Charleston . . . for attempting that which their cruel prosecutors and murderers would have considered heroic virtue in their own persons, if their condition had been the same as the slaves." Duncan avowed that it was the duty of slaves to escape slavery, and if they rose "in rebellion against their tyrants," citizens of the free states and the federal government were forbidden by "moral law" to assist in their suppression. Duncan claimed that slavery violated the Constitution, making him popular with political abolitionists, and argued that African Americans had a "natural right" to American citizenship. Evangelical abolitionists, searching for non-Garrisonian origins of immediatism, resurrected his book in the 1840s.[50]

With the addition of the Tappan brothers, Weld, Wright, Green, Joshua Leavitt, the editor of the New York *Evangelist*, and William Goodell, the editor of the *Genius of Temperance*, immediatism acquired an influential evangelical wing. Weld, a follower of Stuart, who had traveled to Canada and America, and the popular preacher Charles Grandison Finney, proved to be the most effective proselytizer for abolition, and Lewis Tappan its most effective manager. Abolition soon treaded the path of Finney's religious revivals from the "burned over" districts of upstate New York to the Western Reserve district of Ohio. New England emigrants to upstate New York, western Ohio, and the upper tier of the states of the old northwest were particularly susceptible to abolition. Nearly fifty antislavery societies modeled after the NEASS sprang up in places like Bath and Portland, Maine, where around five hundred African Americans heard Garrison lecture, Providence, Plainfield in Connecticut, Rochester, Paint Valley, Ohio, Farmington in Michigan territory, and in Quaker-settled Lancaster and Chester counties, Pennsylvania. Owen Brown, the father of John Brown, was the secretary of the Western Reserve Anti Slavery Society in Ohio, founded by Professors Wright and Green and the college president, Charles B. Storrs. In New Haven, Jocelyn and Timothy Dwight, the namesake and son of the Yale president, started an antislavery society. By October 1833 the New York Anti Slavery Society (NYASS) was founded by the Tappans, Goodell, Wright,

Leavitt, and Williams. Cornish and his protégé Theodore S. Wright, also a Presbyterian minister, joined the society.[51] Most evangelicals remained colonizationists and decried abolition. Eventually Garrison's religious and philosophical radicalism led him to part ways with the evangelical wing of abolition, but its accession added to the strength, prestige, and resources of immediatism.

Garrison proposed the formation of a national society devoted to abolition and black rights. In 1831 Arthur Tappan had convened a meeting attended by Bourne, Jocelyn, Weld, Leavitt, and Goodell to form an antislavery organization, but nothing came of it. On his return from England, Garrison persuaded the Tappans and their followers to issue a call for a meeting in Philadelphia, home to the still-active PAS. Garrison no doubt chose Philadelphia because of its history as the capital of Quaker-inspired abolition and its activist black community. While some, like Robert Vaux, who were sympathetic to Cresson and colonization, shunned the meeting, others, including Evan Lewis, Shipley, and Edwin Atlee, joined the AASS. On December 3, 1833, sixty-three delegates assembled at Adelphi Hall, which belonged to a black benevolent society. Garrison stayed at the home of the black dentist James McCrummell, where he wrote the society's declaration. Six black abolitionists were named managers of the new society, McCrummell, Purvis, Barbadoes, who accompanied Garrison from Boston, Williams, Vashon, and Shadd, who had moved from Delaware to Chester County. The first three also attended the founding convention. Blacks in Carlisle selected J. Miller McKim, a young abolitionist minister whose daughter Lucy, a pioneering collector of slave songs, would marry Garrison's son, as their delegate.

A large New York delegation led by Tappan and Goodell and a western contingent led by Green and Wright attended the founding convention. Besides some members of the PAS, Bourne, Moses Brown, and George Benson were present. New England immediatists, including Sewall, May, Jocelyn, Hall, and a young Congregationalist clergyman named Amos Phelps, who became an effective agent for the society, also were there. Quakers, especially Hicksites such as James Mott and, on Garrison's urging, Whittier, formed the largest group present. When none of the venerable Philadelphia Quakers agreed to preside, Green was chosen president on the suggestion of Lucretia Mott, the wife of James and one of four Quaker women observing the meeting from the gallery. She proffered editorial changes to the declaration and mentored McKim. While Garrison was the ideologue of the movement, its managers emerged from the New York wing. Arthur Tappan was named president, Wright, secretary of domestic correspondence, and, after his successful British tour, Garrison, secretary of foreign correspondence. Weld, who could not attend because of ill health, wrote, "I am deliberately, earnestly, solemnly, with my whole heart and soul and mind and strength, for the immediate, universal, and total abolition of slavery."[52]

All agreed on the central role of Garrison in the organization of the AASS. The convention singled out two men for special praise, Lundy and Garrison. In his speech Lewis Tappan averred that Garrison had pushed the antislavery movement forward single-handedly by nearly a quarter of a century. Purvis spoke of the high esteem "colored Americans" had for him. Garrison composed the pivotal document of the convention, the Declaration of Sentiments. It claimed to represent the two million enslaved and announced that American "oppression is unequalled by any other on the face of the earth." Arguing for "immediate and general" emancipation and equal rights for "all persons of color," it rejected as "delusive, cruel, and dangerous any scheme of expatriation." Distinguishing the program of American abolition from its British counterpart, Garrison emphasized that no compensation should be given to slaveholders: "If compensation is to be given at all, it should be given to the outraged and guiltless slaves." The declaration laid out the AASS's goals: to organize societies, employ agents, print and circulate antislavery literature, purify proslavery churches, and boycott slave-produced goods. Of all the literature he had written, Whittier reminisced, he was proudest of having his name associated with the declaration.

The AASS constitution balanced the radical aims of the declaration with circumspect means. It specified using moral suasion or "arguments addressed" to the "understanding and consciences" of slaveholders to abandon slavery and to persuade Congress to act in constitutionally permissible ways to end slavery in the District of Columbia, to outlaw the slave trade, and to not admit any new slave states. It followed Whittier's pamphlet *Justice and Expediency*, which called for immediate abolition but stressed the constitutional power of the federal government to abolish slavery in areas under its jurisdiction. It also made the elevation of the "character and condition of the people of color" a central concern, while it explicitly discountenanced physical force. The AASS appointed Garrison, May, Phelps, and Weld agents of the society. Wright pressured Weld to accept the commission. Green closed the convention with a rousing call for abolition to be "entwined around the very fibers of our hearts."[53]

The founding of the AASS broke the national consensus over slavery and race. It would be wrong, however, to blame abolitionists for the disappearance of the supposed southern moderation on slavery. Proslavery extremism predated radical abolitionism. Even before the rise of immediatism, South Carolinian planter politicians, during the nullification crisis of 1828–33 over federal tariff laws, had served notice that they would defend the permanence of slavery at any cost, including secession. Coming soon after British emancipation, the specter of an interracial abolition movement alarmed slaveholders.[54] Interracial immediatism, even in its infancy, posed a latent threat to slaveholders' political and economic power, and they recognized it as such.

8

ABOLITION EMERGENT

In 1836 Theodore Dwight Weld met his match in anti-abolition mobs that refused to let him speak at a local church in Troy, New York. Goaded by the mayor and at least one police officer, they dragged him from the pulpit and stoned him all the way to his lodging. Weld suffered a concussion that ended his speaking career. The mayor warned him to get out of town.[1]

The emergence of radical abolitionism unveiled the relationship between a social movement, society, class, and the state as reflected in mob violence, law, partisan politics, and civil disobedience. State repression and popular persecution tied the cause of the slave to that of civil liberties and to American democracy itself. Anti-abolitionist riots were also racial pogroms, targeting northern black communities and their institutions. The movement's interracial nature and programmatic radicalism posed a latent challenge to the slaveholding Republic.

Though abolitionists remained a significant minority, they acted as the ideological vanguard of a growing antislavery sentiment. Political outsiders, abolitionists nonetheless took advantage of the print, transportation, and communication revolutions. Organizationally, they developed a lecturing agency system, a network of newspapers, and modes of political action that were a blueprint for subsequent radical movements. Ideologically, Christian notions of universal brotherhood gave birth to abolitionists' systematic articulation of human rights. The complicity and conservatism of northern elites engendered critiques of political institutions, market society, cultural conformity, and social hierarchies that fractured the movement. Abolition's very growth exposed fissures within it. It was a "movement emergent" in the 1830s.[2]

CIVIL LIBERTIES

Perhaps no phenomenon illustrated the radical nature of abolition more vividly than the virulence of the racist response to it. Commentators from the French statesman and author Alexis de Tocqueville to contemporary historians have remarked on the prevalence of racism in the North. In the South abolitionists were treated like slave rebels, felons subject to the highest penalties of law and vigilante violence. Anti-abolitionist violence exposed the profoundly limited nature of American democracy and citizenship when it came to slavery and race. In this atmosphere of a major attack on their civil liberties and persons, abolitionists gained their first adherents.[3]

Controversies over black education gave an inkling of the depth of white opposition to racial equality. Abolitionists proposed the building of a black manual labor college in 1831. Supported by Garrison and Jocelyn, it received the enthusiastic backing of the black convention, which appointed Cornish as an agent to raise funds and a committee to manage it. Arthur Tappan donated one thousand dollars. Known for its public school system, female academies, Yale College, and an African Improvement Society devoted to black education, New Haven seemed like an ideal place to build the college. The manual labor movement called for a unified program of mental and physical education that emphasized the dignity and value of labor. It made education accessible to the working poor and familiarized the privileged with physical work. Weld was educated in manual labor at the Oneida Institute in New York.

The united opposition of the city's elite, the mayor, colonizationists, Yale, and working-class immigrants, who competed for jobs and residential space with the black population, doomed the college. At a raucous town meeting only Roger Sherman Baldwin, the future lawyer for the *Amistad* rebels, and James Donaghe, a Virginian abolitionist, voted with Jocelyn for the college. In resolutions, the town leaders voiced their opposition to abolition: "that the propagation of sentiments favorable to the immediate emancipation of slaves . . . is unwarrantable and dangerous interference with the internal concerns of other States, and ought to be discouraged." The incident stripped the mask of racial benevolence from the colonization movement, which promoted the education of missionaries to Africa. The state colonization society was headquartered in New Haven, home to the influential Leonard Bacon. Garrison condemned Yale and New Haven of behavior "worthy of the dark ages."[4]

Connecticut's colonizationists did not hesitate to use more heavy-handed tactics. In 1833 Prudence Crandall, educated in Moses Brown's school, admitted

Sarah Harris, a young black girl, to her female academy in Canterbury. Crandall was asked to admit Sarah by Ann Marcia Davis, who worked for Crandall and sat in her classes. Ann was engaged to Sarah's brother Charles Harris. Their father, William Harris, was an agent for the *Liberator*. Sarah had pleaded her case eloquently before Crandall. When parents and townspeople protested, Crandall dismissed her white students and opened her academy to black girls. She met Garrison, who became an ardent ally and advertised her school in his newspaper. Connecticut, acting on a petition from Canterbury, passed a law banning the instruction of African Americans from out of state, and Crandall was arrested. Andrew T. Judson, a local Democratic politician, led the opposition to Crandall. Her case went all the way to the state supreme court, where it was dismissed because of insufficient evidence, but the so-called black law was allowed to stand. After Crandall was freed, townspeople launched a campaign of intimidation, fouled the school's well water with manure, hurled stones through its windows, pelted students with garbage, and attempted to burn it down, falsely accusing a black man of the crime. They arrested her black student Ann Eliza Hammond of Providence for vagrancy.

The persecution of Crandall and her black students aroused abolitionists. Garrison published letters from Crandall's "colored scholars," one of whom struggled, she said, to find Christian forgiveness toward her enemies. He commented, "To colonize these shameless enemies of their species [rather than blacks] to some desert country would be a relief and blessing to society." In his *The Right of Colored People to Education Vindicated*, May denounced the "inveterate . . . prejudices of whites against those of African descent" and the "aristocracy of color" in the United States. With monetary assistance from Tappan, he hired lawyers for Crandall and published the *Unionist* in her defense. Charles C. Burleigh, whose brother William taught at Crandall's academy, edited it. Garrison published a pamphlet with the arguments of Crandall's lawyers because they raised the question of black citizenship. Forty-three men and women from Canterbury and neighboring towns formed an antislavery society. The NEASS's *Abolitionist* published "A Canterbury Tale" detailing the harassment of Crandall and her students. John Bowers, a black abolitionist from Philadelphia, commissioned her portrait, collecting twenty-five dollars to pay for it, so that posterity may know the "great heroines whose names but seldom adorn the history of Modern America." Crandall, who could not guarantee her students' safety, closed the academy and married a Baptist minister, Rev. Calvin Philleo. During the Civil War a black Union regiment raised money for her upkeep. Owing to a petition initiated by Mark Twain, the state of Connecticut paid her an annuity of four hundred dollars as reparation. Sarah and her sister Mary Harris became teachers and active abolitionists. Sarah named one of her daughters after Crandall, and Mary, together with her husband, worked in freedmen's schools in Louisiana during Reconstruction. In October 1995 the Connecticut General Assembly declared Prudence Crandall a State Heroine.[5]

In 1835 a mob in Canaan emulated the people of Canterbury, destroying the Noyes Academy. That year abolitionists in New Hampshire started publishing the *Herald of Freedom* in Concord with the immediatist motto, "No compromise with slavery." They appealed to the citizens of the state to disavow "an unhallowed prejudice" and asked that the "abused Negro" be enfranchised. When they built a school on land deeded by Samuel Noyes, townspeople voted for it despite some opposition. Its trustees included Sewall and David Lee Child. Unlike Yale, Dartmouth College supported the effort, visualizing Noyes as a feeder school to the college and building on its checkered history of benevolence toward Native Americans. On Hosea Easton's suggestion, fourteen black students were admitted to Noyes, among them Henry Highland Garnet, Alexander Crummell, the son of Boston Crummell, and Thomas Sidney, all three graduates of the African school, and Thomas Paul, Garrison's apprentice. The three New Yorkers were forced to make the journey to Canaan on top of a stagecoach, which took a toll on the sickly Garnet. Not deterred, they gave impressive speeches before the New Hampshire Anti Slavery Society (NHASS), much to the delight of their teachers but to the annoyance of townspeople.

Paul wrote in the *Liberator* of mounting opposition to the interracial academy. On July 4, administrators led by Timothy Tilton turned away a mob bent on asserting the racially exclusive nature of American republicanism. A month later, with the sheriff leading them, the mob returned to bulldoze the building by tying it to a cart pulled by teams of oxen. They surrounded the black students, who boarded with the faculty, and shot at them with guns. Garnet fired back and was credited with having saved the students. Both Garnet and Crummell became famous abolitionists, the latter naming one of his sons Sidney Garnet to honor the two classmates who had undergone the ordeal with him. The three eventually graduated from Oneida, which was remade into an abolitionist school by Beriah Green. Crummell recalled "3 years of perfect equality" with the white students there. The black abolitionists Jermaine Loguen, Amos Beman, William G. Allen, and Forten's son, William D. Forten, also graduated from Oneida. Their teacher at Noyes, Nathaniel Peabody Rogers, became the editor of the *Herald of Freedom*.[6]

Cutting across class lines, with "gentlemen of property and standing" taking the lead, anti-abolition mobs in the mid-1830s reacted to the rise of immediatism in an orgy of violence. They frequently targeted blacks who appeared to be stepping out of their place and were symbols of black achievement as well as churches and schools. A race riot started by drunken white sailors in Providence in 1831 alarmed Garrison, but it was an example of a regular pattern. Some of the most spectacular incidents of violence occurred at the very places where organized abolition was born. Of the seventy-plus instances of anti-abolition violence, over half, forty-six, occurred between 1834 and 1837, just as the movement was gaining ground. Threats from "southrons" accompanied the call in 1833 for the founding of the NYASS, and anti-abolitionists forced a last-minute change of venue. Garrison, who had returned from England, was excoriated in the press for his anti-Americanism. He barely escaped from New York, whose business elites had close ties to slavery. Contemporary critics blamed abolitionists' "martyr complex" for inciting violence.[7]

Colonizationist opposition, a jingoistic and racist press, the lackadaisical response by and complicity of law enforcement authorities, and conservative elites' dread of disrupting economic and political ties with the slave South stoked violence to stamp out the infant movement. The New York City riot of 1834 destroyed black homes and churches sympathetic to abolition and led to the ransacking of Lewis Tappan's home. James Watson Webb, the editor of the *New York Courier and Enquirer,* whose racist ranting and colonizationist views became a regular in the *Liberator*'s "Refuge of Oppression" section, accused abolitionists of promoting racial amalgamation. Garrison's call for the repeal of the Massachusetts law against interracial marriage infuriated Webb. The riot forced the resignation of Peter Williams, whose church was nearly destroyed, from the AASS board of managers under pressure from his superior in the Episcopal church, Bishop Onderdonk, a colonizationist. But Williams refused to renounce his membership and participated in antislavery meetings until his death in 1840. In a public letter to Mayor Cornelius Lawrence signed by the Tappans, Goodell, Leavitt, and Cornish, among others, the AASS disavowed promoting interracial marriage and raised the issue of freedom of speech. Garrison was more critical of the magistrates of New York, who he opined had been delinquent.

A month later a race riot in Philadelphia, which began as a fight between black and white firefighters at a carnival, wreaked havoc on black homes, businesses, and churches. Irish immigrants, victims of discrimination themselves, vented their anger on blacks, and a PAS report pointed to colonizationist complicity in fostering racist sentiment. One black man was killed and several more were injured. Whites were told to light candles in their windows to escape the mobs. A "citizens' committee" blamed competition over jobs as well as abolitionist activism in preventing the rendition of fugitive slaves for provoking violence. At least four anti-abolition riots in New Jersey, New Hampshire, and Connecticut occurred that year alone. In 1835 a mob again attacked black homes in Philadelphia.[8]

Contemporaries noted the respectable nature of anti-abolition mobs made up of merchants, politicians, and local law enforcement officials. In 1833 a public debate between Green and Rev. Joshua Danforth over colonization in Utica had resulted in the burning in effigy of Green and Alvan Stewart, a local abolitionist. City authorities in Utica issued grand jury presentments against a convention called by Stewart to form the NYASS in 1835. The Common Council, however, voted to let them hold the convention at the courthouse. Led by Samuel Beardsley, a local Democratic politician, an anti-abolitionist meeting that included the mayor and local bankers forced the council to reverse its decision. An opposing meeting of "respectable mechanics" backed the abolitionists' right to gather. Abolitionists moved their convention to the Bleecker Street Presbyterian Church. A committee of twenty-five led by the ubiquitous Beardsley and a local judge shouted down the speakers, destroyed church property and antislavery literature, and threatened to cane the minister. Beardsley became the attorney general of New York and a state supreme court justice. Stewart argued that northern mobs were doing the work of slaveholders. He and Goodell launched an abolitionist newspaper they called *Friend of Man* in 1836, and Utica soon became a stronghold of abolition.[9] Aversion to anti-abolitionist violence made many join the movement.

Mob violence made its way to Garrison's doorstep as well. He received threatening notes and found an elaborate gallows with two nooses constructed in front of his house, for him and the British abolitionist George Thompson. Thompson's lecture tour in the United States was disrupted by mobs pelting him with rotten eggs and garbage in Maine, New Hampshire, and Massachusetts. He and, earlier, Charles Stuart were commonly portrayed as foreign agents sent to destabilize the Union. Invited by Garrison, Thompson was refused accommodations in a New York hotel because of a southern guest's complaints. Other NEASS lecturers, mistaken for Thompson, received the same treatment. But black audiences received him cordially. One of his staple lectures was a true history of Haiti, in which he justified the use of violence in self-defense by slaves.[10]

Black Bostonians started watching Garrison's home and following him to work and back. Garrison insisted he would not allow America to disown abolitionists, and he issued an appeal on behalf of the slaves modeled after the Declaration of Independence. In August the colonizationist lawyer Peleg Sprague and the former mayor Harrison Gray Otis made inflammatory speeches at an anti-abolition meeting at Faneuil Hall. Garrison excoriated Sprague's suggestion that abolitionists plead their cause in the South, where they could be lynched. He rebuked Otis for tainting his family's revolutionary heritage by becoming an *"apologist for slavery"* and excluding black countrymen from his patriotism. On October 21, after having dinner with Vashon at his home, Garrison attended a Boston Female Anti Slavery Society (BFASS) meeting, where he was finally mobbed. A howling crowd of thousands had gathered to rough up Thompson and got Garrison instead. Disheveled, his clothes ripped and spectacles lost, with a noose around his body, Garrison owed his life to a carpenter who hid him in his shop, two burly truckmen who protected him, and an intrepid black carriage driver who whisked him to the city jail while keeping the mob at bay with his whip. Mayor Theodore Lyman, who disbanded the BFASS meeting, jailed Garrison for his protection but only after formally charging him and the thirty-odd abolitionist women for provoking disorder. Garrison and his wife, Helen (a BFASS member), who was pregnant and witnessed his mobbing, named their firstborn after Thompson. According to Garrison, the "American nation in 1835" was a "picture of infamy," "mobocracy" had triumphed in Boston, and freedom of speech and press were a "mockery."[11]

The mobbing of abolitionists converted those appalled at the open violation of civil liberties. The most important of these were Wendell Phillips, the scion of a Boston Brahmin family, the physician Henry I. Bowditch, and Francis Jackson, who had offered his home as a venue to the BFASS after the Boston mobbing. Phillips's conversion was hurried along by his fiancée, Ann Greene, who had been trapped by the mob. William Jay, the accomplished jurist and son of the founder John Jay, joined the movement after the New York City riot, and Gerrit Smith announced his conversion from colonization to abolition because "the right to free discussion" was threatened. Smith offered his estate in Peterboro to the antislavery convention driven out of Utica. He argued that abolitionists should modify their language and work for gradual emancipation. Garrison noted that Smith blew "hot and cold," but his repudiation of colonization was an important victory. Immediatism bothered some, like the antislavery Unitarian theologian William Ellery Channing. In his influential *Slavery*, Channing endorsed abolitionist ideas, committing, Garrison observed, *"moral plagiarisms."* He chided abolitionists for their extremism but condemned their persecution. May and Lydia Maria Child criticized Channing for accepting abolitionist logic but criticizing abolitionist activism. Channing deplored the fact that antislavery societies included blacks instead of appealing to the respectable elements of society.[12] Attacks on the civil liberties of whites led many to abolition.

Slaveholders knew no restraint when suspected abolitionists and slave rebels were apprehended. Just as the publication of the *Liberator* coincided with Turner's insurrection, the AASS's moral suasion campaign to mail antislavery literature to the South coincided with the slave insurrection hysteria of 1835 in Mississippi. Rumors of a rebellion and sensational accounts of the shady activities of John Murrell, who was suspected of starting a revolt, resulted in the torture, lynching, and hanging of at least nineteen slaves and a number of whites, including gamblers in Vicksburg deemed suspicious by vigilante committees. The execution of suspected rebels, abolitionists, and criminals exposed the unsavory reality of the new empire of cotton built on slaveholders' visions of wealth and power. Abolitionists, who viewed the lynching as the fruit of slavery, found themselves classed with "slave stealers" and "horse thieves."[13]

That year northerners and blacks came under suspicion all over the South. In August Amos Dresser, a student at Lane Seminary in Ohio, was arrested in Nashville for being an abolitionist planning to start a rebellion. Dresser sold Bibles wrapped in the newspaper of the AASS, the *Emancipator,* to raise money for his education. He also sold a copy of Rankin's *Letters on Slavery* and had in his possession abolitionist pamphlets. Dresser confessed that he thought slaveholding violated divine law but disavowed any intention to incite slaves. A committee of slaveholders debated whether to subject him to the customary thirty-nine lashes doled out to recalcitrant slaves and settled for twenty. Shocked that his rights were so flagrantly violated, Dresser refused to disavow abolition. He became one of the most effective lecturing agents for the AASS. In 1837 John Hopper, the son of the Quaker abolitionist Isaac Hopper, narrowly escaped being lynched in Savannah, Georgia.[14]

During the long summer of 1835 two police constables arrested Reuben Crandall, a physician and the brother of Prudence, in Washington, a southern city that doubled as the national capital, on the charge of circulating abolitionist literature. Earlier, an eighteen-year-old slave named Arthur Bowen had been arrested for demanding freedom and threatening his mistress with an axe. A predominantly Irish mob tried to lynch Bowen and Crandall, but, frustrated by the heavily guarded jail, they went on a rampage against black churches and homes. They targeted the popular restaurant of a mixed-race former slave named Beverly Snow and the Presbyterian church and the school of Rev. John F. Cook. The colonizationist district attorney Francis Scott Key brought an indictment of sedition against Crandall. Eager to demonstrate a link between slave rebelliousness and abolition, Key was also behind the arrest and conviction of Bowen. Snow migrated to Canada, where he reopened his restaurant, and Cook fled to Pennsylvania, where he rebuilt his church. Crandall admitted to being an abolitionist and led authorities to his collection of antislavery litera-ture. In his trial a year later, Judson, now a representative from Connecticut, testified, surprisingly, on his behalf, recalling his attempts to dissuade his sister from running a colored school. The defense counsel, quoting colonizationists, including Key, on the evils of slavery, raised the issue of freedom of speech. The grand jury returned a verdict of not guilty, but Crandall, who languished in jail for over eight months because of a prohibitive bail set by a proslavery judge, contracted tuberculosis in the "unwholesome dungeon" and died in 1838.[15]

In the latter half of the decade, abolition became interwoven with freedom of the press, as abolitionist editors came under sustained attack. Mobs disrupted the annual meeting of the Ohio Anti Slavery Society (OASS) and the founding of the *Philanthropist* by James G. Birney, a slaveholding convert to abolition. Birney's father supported David Rice's attempt to make Kentucky a free state, and he grew up hearing David Barrow of the KAS preach. A successful lawyer, Birney started representing slaves and Native Americans. Initially a coloniza-tionist, he was converted to immediatism by Weld. Birney established the Ken-tucky Anti-Slavery Society in 1835 and tried to start a newspaper before being warned out of the state. When a public meeting in Alabama classed abolition-ists with "*blacklegs, gamblers,* or other idle *suspicious persons*" who deserved death, Birney published his vindication of abolition. Abolitionists were, he ex-plained, nearly forty thousand men and "unoffending and respectable females." The real criminals were slaveholders, who scourged slaves so that they could lead lives of splendor.

In 1836 a mob led by Cincinnati's mayor destroyed Birney's press and de-scended on his home, where his son William kept them at bay. Birney and the OASS, which adopted the *Philanthropist* as its official organ, charged merchants and bankers with southern business connections and native Kentuckians for the violence. The mob also preyed on black homes and churches as well as broth-els and saloons that encouraged interracial fraternization. African Americans responded in self-defense. When Dennis Hill, the president of the Cincinnati Union Society of Colored Persons, distanced the society from abolition in or-der to protect the community, twenty-eight of its members repudiated his state-ment. Weld advised African Americans to stay away from the OASS's annual meeting because of threats of violence. A black man who attended was badly assaulted. When a law-and-order group of artisans, including Charles Ham-mond, the editor of the *Cincinnati Gazette* and a member of an early protection society, called a meeting to protest the violence, the meeting was hijacked by the very forces that led the mobs, who had the gall to blame abolitionists for the violence. In a letter of sympathy the executive committee of the NYASS argued that slavery could last only "on the ruins of a free press." Slaveholders and their northern "aristocratic brethren" wanted "to crucify the freedom of the free, in order to secure the continued slavery of the slave." Channing wrote to Birney that they were "sufferers for the liberty of thought, speech, and the press." The *Philanthropist* resumed publication and increased its subscriptions. Abolitionist literature thrown out by the mob apparently made converts of passersby.[16]

Despite a concerted campaign to blame the victims, anti-abolition violence generated support for the movement in the North. The most notorious incident in this period was the murder of Elijah Lovejoy, an abolitionist editor in Alton, Illinois, in 1837. Lovejoy was born in Maine, his mother was a Garrisonian, and his brother Joseph an agent for the *Liberator*. In 1834 Lovejoy began publishing an evangelical antislavery newspaper, the *Observer*, in St. Louis. He condemned the lynching of a black man, Floyd McIntosh, who was burned alive over a slow fire. Lovejoy came across his dismembered body. The appropriately named Judge Luke Lawless did not indict his murderers. Lovejoy criticized the judge, leading a mob to destroy his printing materials. The lynching and the hounding out of the AASS agent Rev. David Nelson from Missouri convinced Lovejoy to relocate. In Alton a mob led by some Missourians destroyed Lovejoy's press as soon as it arrived on the docks. City leaders condemned the action, but once Lovejoy founded an antislavery society they turned against him. His articles criticizing speculation by the wealthy during the Panic of 1837 and threats by Missourians to cut off business ties did not help. The local colonization society and the Kentucky-born attorney general of the state, Usher Linder, demanded that Lovejoy cease publishing the *Observer*. The controversy led to the formation of the Illinois Anti Slavery Society, but mobs repeatedly destroyed his press. Edward Beecher, the president of Illinois College and the son of the famous minister Lyman Beecher, asserted that it was a matter of freedom of the press. Lovejoy and his supporters resisted when a mob attacked his press a fourth time. An exchange of fire led to the death of Lovejoy, who was riddled with five bullets, as well as that of one person in the crowd. Linder made sure no one was prosecuted for his murder.

Abolitionists would not commemorate the death of one of their own in a similar manner until the execution of John Brown twenty-two years later. At the AASS meeting in the Broadway Tabernacle, Green drew attention to the "legalized man-murder" of slaves and asked, "Will not thousands and millions of our countrymen who have hitherto been indifferent, be thereby *roused to the claims of the enslaved?*" Garrison too compared Lovejoy's murder with two million enslaved martyrs and the plight of his young widow to that of slave women. Garrison, who lined his columns in thick black lines of mourning, chided the hypocrisy of those who criticized Lovejoy and endorsed anti-abolition violence. Channing, who moved closer to abolition with each new outrage, called for a meeting to condemn the murder. City officials attempted to deny abolitionists the use of Faneuil Hall. Held nearly two months later because of the controversy, the meeting was interrupted by Attorney General James Austin, who portrayed the mob as revolutionary heroes. Phillips rose to school him in New England's revolutionary tradition, thereby embarking on his career as the orator of the movement. Many years later Phillips recalled the agony he felt on hearing about Lovejoy's death. Edmund Quincy announced that resistance to tyranny was obedience to God and sent his donation to the Massachusetts Anti Slavery Society (MASS). Charles Lenox Remond also delivered a rebuttal to Austin's "lawless speech," skewering his racist logic that compared slaves to a pack of dangerous animals in a menagerie. At a black protest meeting Thomas Jinnings noted that Lovejoy's "horrid murder" was a fruit of the "foul system" of slavery.[17]

State repression complemented mob violence. Describing the disruption of a meeting in Mansfield by a mob beating drums and by the town clerk, who rang the church bell continuously, Isaac Stearns, a farmer, felt that men of "high standing" and "aristocratic feeling" should cease to dictate "what we shall hear and what we shall not hear." George Storrs, an NEASS agent, was arrested in New Hampshire, May had several meetings disrupted, once by a stone thrown into a church that injured a woman in the audience, and Rev. George B. Cheever was imprisoned for libel. In Baltimore the black minister Charles W. Gardner was arrested. In Harrisburg a mob stoned the AASS agent Jonathan Blanchard. Marius Robinson was tarred and feathered and severely injured with a scythe in Ohio. To add insult to injury, he was tried for inciting violence.

Abolitionists found it difficult to secure venues for their meetings either because most town leaders were anti-abolitionist or because of fears that the buildings would be destroyed. In 1838 a mob in Philadelphia burned down Pennsylvania Hall, built by abolitionists with mostly small donations from blacks, women, and working people. The Pennsylvania Anti Slavery Society (PASS) had been founded a year earlier, and a colonization convention had started publishing the *Anti-Abolitionist*. In 1835 city merchants, mindful of their southern trading connections, had dumped abolitionist literature into the Delaware. As abolitionists addressed the second women's antislavery convention in the hall, a loud mob heckled and broke the windows. Abolitionists appealed for protection, but the next day the hall was burned down. Whittier, now the editor of the *Pennsylvania Freeman*, called it a sacrifice to the "Demon of Slavery." The mob also attempted to torch the Colored Orphan Asylum and Bethel church. While the rioters escaped punishment, a grand jury led by Cresson blamed abolitionists. Lundy, who lost most of his papers in the fire, and the PASS received minor damages for their loss. Nearly ten years later, after much legal wrangling, the managers of Pennsylvania Hall received more compensation. The British antislavery political economist Harriet Martineau described "the short life of American abolitionism . . . so crowded with events and achievements." Violence, May reported, prevented the timid from joining antislavery societies. The black minister Theodore S. Wright, speaking on behalf of slaves, assured abolitionists that in being stoned, imprisoned, and mobbed they would "seed" the movement.

Abolitionists pioneered civil disobedience tactics in response to repression. The AASS issued an elaborate set of directives composed by Weld that instructed its agents on how to face down mobs, anticipating strategies used by civil rights workers against violent retaliation in the twentieth century. In its report of 1836 the MASS commented, "The violence and recklessness of our opposers have given a notoriety to the project of the Abolitionists, which, otherwise, it would not have so soon attained."[18] The movement was baptized by fire.

ABOLITION VERSUS COLONIZATION

The 1830s were consumed in a war of words between abolitionists and colonizationists. The Irish political economist Mathew Carey of Philadelphia wrote a series of pamphlets advocating colonization. Carey influenced Henry Clay's American System, which cited colonization as a way of ridding the country of what modernizers viewed as the economically backward institution of slavery and a "degenerate" race. Carey evoked culture, biology, the environment, and Humean moral sense to argue for racial separation. He criticized abolitionists for opposing "the fundamental laws of human nature" and "inequalities arising from unequal intellectual cultivation, a dissimilarity of moral sense." A black writer adopting the pseudonym Paul Cuffe responded that Carey, who had libeled blacks during the yellow fever epidemic, was "woefully ignorant of the dispositions of our people." In their address to the people of the United States, the managers of the ACS remarked on the "transformation, from imbecility and hopelessness, to activity, and confidence, and manliness and high expectations" of black colonists in Liberia. A meeting of blacks in New Bedford retorted that the ACS represented "terror, prejudice, and oppression" rather than "the warm and beneficent hand of philanthropy." It "teaches the public to believe that it is patriotic and benevolent to withhold from us knowledge and the means of acquiring subsistence, and to look upon us as unnatural and illegal residents in the country, and thus by force of prejudice, if not by law, endeavor to compel us to embark for Africa."[19]

Colonizationists' racism and anti-abolitionism fed off each other. Wilbur D. Fisk, the colonizationist president of Wesleyan University who refused admission to the abolitionist Charles B. Ray, argued that abolitionists had raised the expectations of blacks and had rendered "the offensive object still more unwelcome and revolting." Colonizationists accused Garrison of sowing hostility between the races and justified opposition to the college in New Haven and Crandall's school by citing local prejudices. J. K. Converse, a colonizationist pastor from Vermont, resorted to invective, saying that free blacks were debased, sunk in wickedness and vice, had deceitful hearts, and were "citizens in nothing." Even if granted political equality, they would remain inferior to whites. Similarly, the New Jersey Colonization Society pronounced that "nature has drawn a line of distinction, in color, which can never be obliterated" and that free blacks tended to become "unhappy, indolent, vicious, and revengeful." William Fowler of the Vermont Colonization Society cast further aspersions, calling for the removal of blacks, who were "comparatively ignorant, as everyone knows; addicted to vice, as proved by the records of the prison; poor and improvident, as proved by the annals of the alms-house."

In his address to the Massachusetts Colonization Society, the conservative Whig politician Caleb Cushing accused the AASS of arousing "the jealousies of the free blacks." Rev. Joseph Tracy deplored the misapplication of the "Jacobinical doctrine of the Rights of Man" and natural equality that resulted in a demand for black equality. One colonizationist called immediatism the "principle of agrarianism" since it "leveled all distinctions in society, of rank, color, caste, and sex." Some even argued that American slavery was better than African barbarism. They criticized abolitionists for not understanding that masters as well as slaves had rights.[20]

A few tried to assert an antislavery mission for the ACS. Robert J. Breckinridge, a Presbyterian pastor in Kentucky, called slavery a national crime but adhered to colonization as the best way to avoid slave rebellion and racial amalgamation. Bacon, in his review of Garrison's, Stuart's, and Cropper's anticolonization pamphlets, judged that colonization would lead to abolition and that Liberia had done more "to make the negro character respectable by mankind" than Haiti. He predicted that slavery would not survive "free and open discussion." Ironically, Bacon wrote this amidst the campaign of terror against abolition. He, Lyman Beecher, and Fisk founded the short-lived American Union for the Relief and Improvement of the Colored Race, which attracted the support of Arthur Tappan. Bacon edited the *Journal of Freedom* to represent anti-slavery colonizationists. The opposition of Garrison, Lewis Tappan, and the frigid reception accorded the union by African Americans sealed its fate. Breck-inridge and Bacon eventually threw their weight behind another antislavery colonizationist, Abraham Lincoln. The colonizationist Ebenezer Baldwin in a pamphlet of 1834 set out to prove the fallacy of the idea that blacks were naturally inferior to whites. With the death of Baldwin and the defection of Gerrit Smith, who bemoaned the lack of love for blacks in the ACS, the society ceased to contain an effective antislavery wing.

Some colonizationists waxed lyrical on the ancient glories of Egypt and Africa. In 1836 Rev. Frederick Freeman, an Episcopal minister from Pennsylvania, published an updated version of Bacon's plea for Africa in his book *Yaradee*. Despite the best efforts of the ACS secretary, Ralph Randolph Gurley, and Calvin Colton, who held that abolition was a schism from colonization, to promote missionary efforts in Africa, colonization became literally and figuratively bankrupt by the end of the decade.[21]

Abolitionists challenged colonizationists' antislavery bona fides in the North. In *The Sin of Slavery and Its Remedy* (1833), Elizur Wright argued that the ACS was a predominantly slaveholding organization which sought to secure slave property. A bad cause—colonizationists were in favor of racially discriminatory laws, he noted—could not be made good by a few antislavery adherents. He debated the ACS agent Robert S. Finley, and Jocelyn and May took on Gurley. On the request of John Remond, Buffum debated the elitist Danforth, who disparaged his opponent's lowly origins as a hatter. At Western Reserve College, Green, Wright, and Storrs initiated one of the earliest considerations of the merits of abolition versus colonization. Birney refuted Fisk and lectured in Converse's church. Thompson debated the colonizationist president of Centre College in Danville, Kentucky, and Breckinridge during the latter's visit to England. Goodell challenged Bacon, Henry B. Stanton debated Tracy and Freeman, and Robinson refuted Elisha Whittlesey.[22]

The most extended debate took place at Lane Seminary in Cincinnati. Founded in 1829, Lane was bankrolled by Arthur Tappan and headed by Beecher. In 1831 a Rev. Samuel Crothers published letters against slavery in a local paper, and a year later Stanton, a student at Lane, held that the North should not help the South put down a slave rebellion. In 1834 Weld and his followers from Oneida became students at Lane. With the charismatic Weld leading off, students armed with literature from the ACS and the AASS explored immediatism for eighteen days in two-hour-plus sessions. The most dramatic testimony came from James Bradley. Enslaved in Africa, he "cut up . . . *white objections*" to abolition. Bradley, who had bought his freedom, inverted slave-holding logic, reasoning that slaves were used to taking caring of their masters and would take care of themselves better *"when disencumbered from this load."* They wanted *"liberty and education,"* not expatriation. Even the southern students James A. Thome of Kentucky and William Allan of Alabama converted, engendering optimism about moral suasion. Slaveholders' violent repression of abolition ensured that debates like the ones at Lane would not occur in the South.

To the dismay of the administration, the students not only formed an antislavery society but also started teaching in Cincinnati's black community. Beecher and his daughter Catharine tried unsuccessfully to effect a reconciliation. Contact with African Americans made the Lane rebels even more committed to immediatism and against colonization. Their activities caused an uproar, and school authorities sought to ban discussion of slavery. Two of the students, Augustus Wattles and Marius Robinson, began to teach full-time in black schools. Weld never forgot his experience with black Cincinnatians, many of whom had bought themselves out of slavery and continued to scrape money together to buy friends and families. Recounting their stories, he "was forced to stop from sheer heart-ache and agony." Led by Weld, seventy-five students left the seminary, and fifty-one signed the "Statement of Reasons" defending freedom of discussion. Financed again by Tappan, most moved to the fledgling Oberlin Collegiate Institute, cofounded by a Finneyite, Rev. John Jay Shipherd. Professor John Morgan and the former Lane trustee Asa Mahan, who became president of Oberlin, joined them. Finney enlisted as professor of theology.

As Oberlin became a pioneer in interracial and women's higher education and a "movement center" of abolition, Weld embarked on a lecture tour of Ohio, western Pennsylvania, and New York. Stanton did the same in New England. Weld helped found the OASS, with many of the Lane rebels signing on, and Stanton, drawing on local abolitionist networks, helped form the Rhode Island Anti Slavery Society (RIASS). Lane students formed the backbone of the AASS's agency system, the biblically named Seventy, actually just over sixty agents trained by Weld. They apprised Weld of their labors, complaining when Finney tried to get them to ride the religious circuit instead of preaching abolition. At the first anniversary of the AASS, Thome testified that colonization had served to "lessen my conviction of the evil of slavery, and to deepen and sanctify my prejudice against the colored race." In contrast to colonization, Stanton declared, defeating racial prejudice was an important abolitionist aim. Weld also kept in touch with the abolitionist teachers Phebe Mathews, Emmeline Bishop, and Susan Lowe, recruited by Wattles. Weld became the premier theoretician of what he called a "living abolitionism."[23]

Colonization was on the defensive among its original constituency, northern clergymen. When Rev. Samuel H. Cox visited England he was confronted with the question of whether the ACS had the support of the free people of color. Cox undertook an independent investigation and determined that because of "the non-consent and unanimous opposition of the colored people . . . the Society is morally annihilated." His interviews with New York's black clergymen settled the question. In his pamphlet against colonization, he printed Cornish's letter that denounced it as a "system of proscription and cruelty." The Andover-educated Amos Phelps persuaded 124 ministers to sign a declaration condemning colonization and endorsing immediatism. Phelps told them it was their duty to change public sentiment and public conscience. His four lectures on slavery established that slaveholding was "in all cases a sin," as it was based on the principle of man stealing. Phelps caustically observed that if the Bible justified slavery, it also justified polygamy. The abolition movement composed of "Mr. Working-man" and "Mr. Philosopher" should unite on immediate abolition. To those who claimed that immediatism was dangerous, Phelps answered that only when the Haitians were threatened with reenslavement did they retaliate. When freed, American slaves, like their counterparts in Haiti, would "under the new order of things . . . march . . . towards their ancient splendor." In the appendix, a letter from Joshua Coffin listed all the slave rebellions in North America as a sign of divine vengeance and criticized colonizationists for fostering unchristian prejudice.[24]

Abolitionists discredited the independent Maryland Colonization Society, which made emancipation one of its goals. Watkins accused the "Maryland scheme" of "pseudo philanthropy" in denying enslaved blacks a "liberty of choice," forcing them to leave the country to obtain their freedom. Our "true friends," he wrote, were the "persecuted abolitionists." After receiving a letter from an emigrant detailing the hardships encountered in Cape Palmas, Watkins said that colonization rewarded slaves for their "years of grievous privation and unrequited toil with exile, disease, starvation and death." Following Watkins, Garrison denounced the Maryland plan as a "new scheme of villainy." In his second, lesser-known pamphlet against colonization, Garrison reviewed Maryland's colonization design and the increasingly oppressive laws against free blacks in that state. Instead of "righting the wrongs" of slavery, he criticized the state's policy of "making the condition of the free so uncomfortable, that they will be glad to escape, and by riveting the chain of the slave forever, except he consent, when emancipated, to be exiled." Colonization was a scheme to abolish the "whole colored population." In 1840 black Marylanders protested what they saw as an atrocious law that barred free blacks from entering the state and fined them for doing so, the money raised designated to the state colonization society. Black abolitionists in New York convened an anticolonization meeting led by Wright, Ray, Cornish, Thomas Downing, the Reason brothers, James McCune Smith, and John J. Zuille against Maryland colonization. Black meetings in Worcester, Buffalo, and Albany also condemned it.[25]

The colonizationists in Maryland made a direct appeal to the black community, touting emigrant success stories under the motto, "Where Freedom is, there is my country." The society appointed John Russwurm, who became disenchanted with the bigotry of ACS agents and married McGill's daughter, governor of Cape Palmas in 1836. Colonizationists published letters from black emigrants, highlighting the accomplishments of McGill's son Samuel Ford McGill and Russwurm. The *African Repository* published reports of a procolonization meeting among free persons of color in Charleston. An anonymous black Charlestonian argued that "popular prejudice" stood as an unconquerable barrier to "our advancement in knowledge" and recommended removal to Liberia, where "you will enjoy moral and political liberty." But disillusioned black colonists like Louis Sheridan, a prosperous free black man from North Carolina, and Thomas Brown, a carpenter who possessed substantial property in his native South Carolina, provided fodder for abolitionists' position. Describing the dismal conditions in Liberia, Sheridan, in a letter to Lewis Tappan, complained that he had not left "the US to be freed from the tyranny of the white man" to find himself at the mercy of another. The ACS extorted money from emigrants for the cost of their transportation to Liberia, a majority of whom, he said, would leave if they could. He also wrote that the slave trade from the area proceeded unchecked. Brown, who had migrated at his own expense, noted that while the ACS and Cresson pressured him to report favorably on Liberia, the AASS treated him fairly. He testified to the high mortality rates suffered by colonists, refuting the racialist logic of placing black people in their so-called natural environment. Brown confessed that he was forced to deal in alcohol, guns, tobacco, and powder to survive.[26]

Besides black testimony, Birney and Jay put the finishing touches to the abolitionist argument against colonization. In his *Letter on Colonization* (1834) to Rev. Thornton J. Mills of the Kentucky Colonization Society, Birney observed that colonization was a strange mixture of true with utterly false principles. In trying to address the evil of slavery, it fostered a "persecuting and malignant spirit against free people of color." A year later Jay published his *Inquiry into the Character and Tendency of the American Colonization and American Anti-Slavery Societies.* Jay's sharpest critique of colonizationists rested on their opposition to black education and improvement and their desire to get rid of black people. He pointed out that Haiti had proven the "ability of the African race to value, defend, and enjoy the blessings of freedom," and he welcomed signs that the British were doing away with gradualism and apprenticeship in the West Indies. He opposed compensation to slaveholders as "morally impossible."[27]

The black abolitionist David Ruggles was also a premier ideologue of anti-colonization immediatism. Born in Lyme, Connecticut, in 1810, educated in Sabbath schools and by the colonizationist author Lydia Sigourney, Ruggles moved to New York City in 1828. He was at various points a sailor and a grocer, but his true vocation was abolition. Ruggles founded a Garrisonian society and an antislavery reading room and library, attended the black conventions, and became an agent for the *Emancipator*. He published a formidable body of pamphlets in response to the physician David M. Reese, a vehement colonizationist. Reese charged abolitionists with foisting "the project of a forced and unnatural elevation of the African race." He dismissed their speeches as the "ravings of a mad man" and their conventions as a "motley assemblage of blacks and whites." Ruggles characterized Reese's racism as "hyperbole and cant." He treated the colonizationist Heman Howlett, who was devoid of Reese's racism, more respectfully, adding that he was a "better writer." Ruggles predicted that "my little book, pregnant with truth, shall survive the revolution of ages, and even give Dr. Reese himself a reluctant immortality!" His second reply, written under the pseudonym Martin Mar Quack MD LLD etc., spoofed Reese's medical degrees. Reese did not deign to answer Ruggles and instead replied to Jay. He contended that most blacks had been treated kindly by whites until "the spirit of Garrisonism was infused among these depressed people and . . . from being quiet and unassuming . . . they now began to assume an attitude of pride and independence. They were taught to regard themselves as perfectly equal to the whites in every aspect, and to attribute their separation, which long custom had rendered tolerable, as the fruits of robbery and oppression." In *Humbugs of New York* (1838), Reese blamed the "black and white fanatics who constituted the Executive Committee of the American Anti Slavery Society" for inciting violence against themselves. He even defended the "quiet and orderly people of Alton" for murdering Lovejoy. Ruggles fired back with *An Antidote for a Poisonous Combination*. Reese's remarks, he wrote, were a mixture of "scurrility, abuse and falsehood" and put upon him "the indelible mark of infamy."[28]

Black abolitionists remained the standard-bearers in opposing colonization. They convened giant anticolonization meetings on December 20, 1838, and January 8, 1839, in New York. Marveling at the fact that black people had opposed colonization for over twenty years, the meeting passed a resolution written by McCune Smith that called *"the whole scheme . . . anti-republican, anti-christian, and anti-humane."* McCune Smith considered the ACS an aristocratic organization that preached the "natural inequality" of American citizens. Cornish followed, deprecating the "criminal hatred of color" encouraged by colonizationists. Bell mocked colonizationist efforts to variously flatter, cajole, bribe, and intimidate blacks. Thomas Van Rensselaer admitted that he was wrong to think that the colonizationists were harmless, as they continued to poison the public mind. The *Colored American* opined that it was a "cruel, utopian system" that had lost much of its vitality under the abolitionist onslaught. Black meetings in Cleveland and Cincinnati passed resolutions against the society. Stephen Gloucester reported that colonizationists approved of the burning of Pennsylvania Hall and abused blacks and abolitionists alike. Contested in the North and virtually nonexistent in the militant proslavery lower south, colonization societies persisted mainly in the border states. By the end of the decade abolition had displaced colonization as the dominant force for antislavery in much of the upper north.[29]

ANATOMY OF A MOVEMENT

Abolitionist ideology illustrated the radical nature of the movement. It exposed northern complicity in upholding slavery, connected the sufferings of slaves to national wealth, and developed a discourse of human rights. The NEASS characterized immediatism as a principle that recognized "equal natural rights" of black people and defined slavery as a crime akin to robbery, kidnapping, or piracy. C. P. Grosvenor, the abolitionist Baptist minister, argued that since slavery was based on "the love of money, the root of all evil," no reformation of the system was possible. It was better to reduce the oppressor to pauperism than to keep two million oppressed slaves in poverty. For "so long as national wealth is bottomed, in part, on the labor of the oppressed . . . pouring all their earnings to the national Treasury, the Free States are partakers of this ill gotten wealth." Amos Savage believed that all Americans were implicated in the "national sin of slavery," and Rankin opined that the "oppression of the poor is one of the greatest sins."[30]

Notwithstanding their formal commitment to nonviolence, abolitionists continued to evoke the revolutionary example of Haiti. Grosvenor and James Dickinson defended the Haitian rebels: "Who does not applaud the colored people of St. Domingo for their refusal to submit to the cruel yoke of slavery?" William

Dexter Wilson lauded "Hayti, the first spot to receive African slaves, . . . the first spot of successful resistance to the whites; and the first spot to establish a government of free blacks in the western world." David Lee Child extolled the day "Hayti triumphed; single handed and against the world." The people of Haiti, according to one abolitionist, were "on a level, in point of cultivation and intelligence, with any people in the world; whatever prejudice and malice may object to the fact." According to Garrison, Haiti should be the object of "universal admiration" and the "acclamations of the world." In 1837 the *Liberator* published Whittier's hagiographic poem on Louverture and reported on the formation of a Haitian Abolition Society against American slavery. Two years later the *Philanthropist* combined its protest against the annexation of Texas with a demand for the recognition of Haiti by the American government. In its first issue the *Anti-Slavery Record* published a rejoinder to proslavery apologists who regularly evoked the "horrors of St. Domingo." Weld persuaded Birney to publish parts of W. W. Harvey's *Sketches of Hayti* (1827) to challenge unsympathetic depictions of the revolution. New York City's ASS argued that the safety of immediate abolition had been proven in Haiti, South America, and Mexico and called for cultivating it as a "moral sentiment."[31]

The West Indies, after the end of the apprenticeship system, also served as a successful example of immediatism. Birney pointed out that while all the nations in South America and the British West Indies had moved toward emancipation, the United States and Brazil upheld the "most contemptible of all despotisms." Henry Peterson averred that West Indian emancipation had proven the failure of gradualism. In 1838 the AASS published Thome and J. Horace Kimball's book based on their six-month investigative tour of the West Indies. Their report stressed the superiority of immediate emancipation in Antigua, where freed people enjoyed civil and political rights, including education and suffrage. In comparison, apprenticeship in Jamaica and Barbados illustrated that halfway measures between slavery and complete freedom gave rise to abuses by former masters and government. They compiled the testimony of officials, magistrates, missionaries, free blacks, and former slaves and indicated that there was "*unjustifiable inequality*" in the apprenticeship laws that worked as "additional compensation" for masters and a "modified form of slavery." Weld prepared the book for publication because Kimball, the former editor of *Herald of Freedom*, had died. The British abolitionists Joseph Sturge and Thomas Harvey went on a similar mission. They all viewed the West Indian experiment as proof of the advisability of immediate emancipation.[32]

Abolitionists sustained the doctrine of immediatism against any sign of backsliding. In his letter to the NEASS convention, Jocelyn warned that immediate emancipation should remain the watchword of abolitionists. When David Paul Brown, the president of the PASS, vacillated between immediatism and gradualism in his speech of 1838, the PASS and the MASS republished Heyrick's pamphlet to show how it had converted Wilberforce from gradualism to immediatism. The experience of gradual emancipation and racism in the North was another argument for immediatism. An NHASS report argued against "a lingering emancipation." Immediatism would convert *"our negro-hating and negro-scorning countrymen."* Oliver Johnson judged that no slaveholder would ever do anything to prepare his slaves for freedom. Abolitionists rejected the notion of compensating slaveholders. May pointed out to those who maintained that abolitionists disregarded slaveholders' property rights, that the slaves were the ones whose "dearest rights" had been violated. The Indiana Anti-Slavery Society, one of the last state societies organized, encapsulated the abolitionist principle in its constitution, immediate emancipation and the inalienable rights of humans "without respect to color." Green juxtaposed arguments against the practicability of abolition with God-given directives against slavery, an early version of the higher law argument.[33]

While fundamentalist proslavery ministers appealed to the written word of the Bible or to biblical literalism, abolitionist theology was interpretive, scholarly, and humanistic. Like that practiced by early Quakers and Unitarians, abolitionist Christianity was tempered by rationalism and humanitarianism. Abolitionists viewed slavery as a crime against humanity rather than merely a religious sin. In his four sermons on abolition, Green reasoned that slavery violated the ethical principle of disinterestedness and that selfishness, its opposite, was the source of oppression. He stressed the Gospel's notion of brotherhood, especially the divine injunction of whatsoever you "did to the least of me ye did to me." Anticipating the Social Gospel movement, the Christian socialists, and liberation theologians of the twentieth century, abolitionists condemned the oppression of the laboring poor. Even the more freethinking Garrison regarded the poor and the oppressed as God's chosen people. The Anti Slavery Society of Worcester County stressed the criminality of slavery and believed that the arm of a just God would be stretched out toward the oppressed rather than the oppressor.

Weld's highly influential *The Bible Against Slavery*, which was reprinted in four editions in 1837–38, invoked the Gospel's "LAW OF LOVE" as an abolitionist principle. Like Green, he insisted that the chattel principle or the converting of men into property, not just deprivation of rights and privileges, defined slavery. Slaveholders were man stealers, and they violated both moral law and biblical commandments. Weld derived the very essence of human rights, "MAN IS INVIO-

LABLE" from the Bible. Human beings could not be reduced to articles of commerce, he wrote, not just countenancing "self ownership" but also questioning the very idea of human beings as property. He demolished the racial grounds of proslavery divines that attempted to link blackness with "Cain's mark" or the curse on Ham. He later rejected biblical creed and became a Unitarian. Even when they were appealing to the Bible, abolitionists appealed not just to the word of scripture but to historical facts and common sense. In his letters to Rev. John L. Wilson, the South Carolinian colonizationist, Rankin claimed that Christianity had abolished slavery in the Roman Empire. Responding to Rev. John Smylie of Mississippi, Gerrit Smith warranted that most primitive Christians were slaves rather than slaveholders. He emphasized Paul's homily, "Remember them that are in bonds as bound with them." The subtitle of Weld's book announced that it concerned the "subject of Human Rights."[34]

Abolitionists were pioneers in developing the modern concept of human rights. From 1835 to 1839 the AASS published a monthly journal entitled *Human Rights,* the first time the term was used extensively. Slavery, it announced in its opening issue, is "the greatest possible violation of human rights." Garrison printed an occasional column under the new moniker. According to the RIAS convention, there could be no compromise over the principle of "human rights," and David Root, the president of the NHASS, called slavery an "outrageous infraction" of it. In a secular counterpart to Weld's arguments, Goodell defended human rights as timeless and changeless over slaveholding politicians' invocation of states' rights to defend slavery. Channing made human rights the lodestar of his critique of slavery.[35]

The abolitionist vindication of human rights challenged the ideology of paternalism that slaveholders assiduously propagated in the face of criticism. With the assistance of Sarah and Angelina Grimké, the South Carolina sisters who converted to Quakerism and abolition, Weld produced the most effective counterargument, *American Slavery As It Is,* published by the AASS in 1839. Until the publication of the slave narratives of the 1840s and 1850s and *Uncle Tom's Cabin,* its place was untouched. It sold more than a hundred thousand copies in a year and was reprinted and circulated in Britain. The book was culled mainly from advertisements in southern newspapers for runaway slaves and the sale of slaves and eyewitness descriptions of slavery. It damned slaveholders with their own words and with descriptions of maimed, scarred slaves. In his introduction Weld demolished the logic of slaveholding paternalism in pithy sentences: "Protesting their kind regard for those whom they hourly plunder of all they have and all they get . . . Plunderers of their liberty, yet careful suppliers of their wants." Paternalist pretensions of taking care of slaves' physical well-being were also not accurate, Weld wrote, citing case after case of ill-fed slaves and physical cruelty. Southern interest, law, custom, and practice treated slaves as disposable property. So effective was his indictment that modern historians of slaveholder paternalism have spent considerable time refuting it.[36]

Abolitionists not only developed an ideological response to slaveholders but also challenged their national political power. In the summer of 1835 Postmaster Alfred Huger in Charleston impounded abolitionist literature sent out by the AASS. The man behind the society's postal campaign was Lewis Tappan. A Carolinian mob called Lynch Men burned the allegedly incendiary material as well as effigies of Arthur Tappan and Garrison. Southerners elsewhere followed suit, likening the campaign to an abolitionist invasion. Postmaster General Amos Kendall agreed that the "higher law" of slaveholders' self-preservation trumped the crime of interfering with the federal mail. Postmaster Samuel L. Gouverneur of New York State, the son-in-law of the former president James Monroe, decided to withhold the delivery of all AASS mail addressed to the South. President Andrew Jackson suggested printing the names of those receiving abolitionist literature, prompting the AASS to ask those who wished to take their names off their mailing list to contact the society.

The federal postal system, which excluded black carriers, hardly functioned as an abolitionist network and was highly susceptible to censorship. Garrison criticized the United States in comparison to the "truly enlightened" Haitian government, which made all mail deliveries free of charge. When Jackson called for a federal law authorizing censorship of abolitionist mail in his annual message to Congress, the AASS responded with a letter composed by Jay and signed by its executive committee, including Cornish and Wright, which stated, "We never intend to surrender the liberty of speech, or press, or of conscience." The Democratic editor William Leggett, who criticized Kendall and Gouverneur, predicted that southern demands "would make abolitionists of our whole two millions of inhabitants" in New York. The abolitionist argument gained enough traction that the postal law of 1836 prohibited interference with the federal mail. It was a dead letter in the South, where state laws allowed for censorship and harsh punishment for the distribution of abolitionist literature. Sen. John C. Calhoun's prescription of "state sovereignty" on all questions relating to slavery became a reality even though the "great nullifier's" demand for censorship of the national postal system was narrowly defeated in the Senate.

The "freedom of thought struggle" led to the effective suppression of any discussion or activity that threatened slavery in the South. Anti-abolition meetings led by slaveholding politicians called for the arrest of abolitionists. Southern legislatures passed resolutions demanding that northern states exact legal punishments for the publication and distribution of abolitionist material. Most southern states already had such laws on the books. After 1835 they became more draconian, stipulating death for those guilty of circulating antislavery literature or even publicly challenging the legitimacy of slaveholding. While northern states did not pass similar laws, abolitionists had to put up a strong fight against censorship proposals. In the Massachusetts General Court, May, Sewall, Loring, Goodell, Follen, and Channing successfully linked abolition to the question of representative government. Garrison argued that the "nation itself will be in bondage." Where, he demanded, "are our STATE RIGHTS?"[37]

Besides the mail controversy, the long struggle over the right to petition exposed the reality of the Slave Power, which was hardly a symptom of paranoia. In December 1835 abolitionists revived the petition campaign for the abolition of the interstate slave trade and slavery in the District of Columbia, both under the constitutional jurisdiction of the federal government. Calhoun, whose resolutions of 1837 declared any interference with slavery by abolitionists or the federal government unconstitutional, demanded outright rejection of the petitions. The Gag Rule compromise, proposed by Henry Pinckney of South Carolina and supported by most Democrats, stipulated their automatic tabling. The House gag of 1836, renewed every year, was strengthened in 1840 to Calhoun's prescription of a standing rule that did not allow abolition petitions to be even received, until it was rescinded in 1844. A lesser-known Senate gag based on a procedural motion to table the reception of abolition petitions lasted well into the 1850s. The one-term senator Thomas Morris of Ohio led the fight for the right to petition, excoriating "the putrid mass of prejudice" designed "to keep the colored race in bondage." He was read out of the Democratic Party and became the vice presidential candidate of the abolitionist Liberty Party.

The former president John Quincy Adams, now a congressional representative from Massachusetts, defended the right to petition, emerging as the abolitionists' first political hero. As early as 1831 Adams presented antislavery petitions, though he distanced himself from their demands. He became the dean of northern "conscience Whigs," an antislavery bloc composed of the congressmen William Slade of Vermont, Seth M. Gates of New York, and Sherlock J. Andrews and Joshua R. Giddings of Ohio. Using ingenious parliamentary tactics, Adams embarrassed his opponents on more than one occasion. In 1837 he presented a petition from the women of Fredericksburg against the slave trade. A Virginia representative expostulated that they were not ladies but free black women, one of whom was of an infamous character, and then spent the rest of the time explaining that he had no personal knowledge of her. When Adams asked to present a petition from slaves, sent to him as a prank, to the horror of southerners he revealed that the slaves had petitioned against abolition. He took on the abolitionists' battle at considerable risk, receiving death threats. His speeches became increasingly antislavery, reflecting his long-standing private aversion to the institution.

Southern politicians and their northern doughface Democratic allies halted congressional debate on slavery, but abolitionists responded energetically to the political silencing of their movement. The executive committee of the AASS issued a declaration "to the people of the United States or such Americans who value their rights and dare to maintain them." It informed that "a crisis has arrived" when "hundreds of citizens peaceably assembled [can be] forcibly dispersed" and when the right to petition is threatened by congressional gags. In his public letter to Clay, Smith called the right to petition a "natural right." The Gag Rule inspired a deluge of abolition petitions printed in standard format by the AASS and its auxiliaries. Thousands of petitions against the annexation of Texas and the Gag Rule and for the recognition of Haiti joined earlier petitions on the District of Columbia in a mass petition campaign. Antislavery societies sent over six hundred thousand petitions with nearly two million signatures to Congress and state legislatures. The average number of signatures per petition increased dramatically, from tens in the early thirties to hundreds in the latter part of the decade. While many were members of antislavery societies, others were fellow travelers who signed particular petitions. Unlike voting, commonly confined to adult white men, the act of petitioning politicized women, who took the lead and outsigned men. The mass petition campaigns were highly effective tools for abolitionist mobilization. To southerners, the petitions were an invitation to rebellion, as they claimed had happened in Haiti and the Caribbean.[38] They were also responding to the growth of the abolition movement.

It is possible to develop an anatomy of the movement. Historians, like abolitionists themselves, have counted antislavery societies, their membership, subscription lists for abolitionist newspapers, and signatures in abolitionist petitions. In 1836 Garrison reported the formation of 7 state antislavery societies with over 500 auxiliaries. The AASS reported a total of 527, the largest numbers in Ohio (133), New York (103), and Massachusetts (87). The AASS also shared members with the old PAS and NYMS, although those societies did not formally belong to it, and it was in touch with British abolition societies, black emigrants to Canada, the French and Haitian Abolition Societies. Abolition grew rapidly in the last years of the decade. By 1838 the AASS had over 1,000 auxiliaries with around 100,000 members, according to its secretary, Birney, in his answer to Rep. Franklin Harper Elmore, who, at Calhoun's behest, posed a series of questions on the nature and aims of antislavery societies. Historians follow Rep. James Henry Hammond's estimate of 250,000. Birney, who wrote that he had given the lowest possible membership figures, claimed that one in ten persons in the northernmost states was an abolitionist and one in twenty in the middle states. Second-wave abolition, as South Carolinian planter-politicians realized, was a mass movement. New modes of communication, the penny press, the mail, and democratic fund-raising proved crucial in the formation of the movement. The AASS raised over forty thousand dollars in 1838 from members as diverse as a revolutionary soldier from Maine, a four-year-old boy, and a "colored woman" who sold apples in the streets of Boston. For a penny a week, the most humble could sustain the antislavery society. The MASS developed weekly contribution boxes decorated with abolitionist ephemera and a journal, the *Monthly Offering*, to coordinate its fund-raising. Antislavery societies also disseminated antislavery cards, poems, broadsides, and wafers with popular abolitionist sayings. Few of their opponents could match the sheer volume of abolitionist handicrafts, art, and literature.

Contrary to conventional wisdom, abolition was hardly a middle-class affair. Though African Americans formed its core constituency, abolitionism spread among white men and women in the North. Opponents made much of the lowly origins of radical abolitionists like Buffum, Thompson, and Garrison, many of whom lacked formal education. Henry C. Wright and Orange Scott emerged from the ranks of the working poor. Most delegates barely had enough money to travel to Philadelphia to found the AASS in 1833. Garrison's travel expenses, along with those of Whittier and Barbadoes, were underwritten by benefactors, but some abolitionists were unable to attend because of financial difficulties. With the prominent exception of the Tappans, a handful of New York merchants in their coterie, and the land magnate Gerrit Smith, most full-time activists, including Garrison, Weld, and the Childs, barely managed to make ends meet. Well-to-do abolitionists like the Tappan brothers, Henry G. Chapman, Francis Jackson, and Wendell Phillips risked their businesses and faced ostracism on joining the movement. Follen lost his Harvard professorship. Birney, the Grimké sisters, and the South Carolinian Baptist minister W. H. Brisbane forsook their slaveholding patrimony. Abolitionists did not belong to a cultural and intellectual elite either. While they attracted the support of a few prominent figures, abolitionists' uncompromising activism differentiated them from the northern political and cultural establishment. As Louis Filler put it, "It would misconstrue the abolitionist crusade not to appreciate its roots in ordinary people." Farmers, mechanics, and artisans formed its base. Most of the signatures in urban abolition petitions were those of workingmen, a fact that challenges the portrayal of abolition as a predominantly bourgeois endeavor. A majority of petitioners owned less property than their fellow citizens and were skilled workers—shoemakers, carpenters, painters, blacksmiths—or laborers. Not a few were propertyless, wage-earning journeymen. As one abolitionist vindicating the right to petition proclaimed, "Our Government is a democracy. We, the farmers and mechanics, are the rulers. We are the governors—you, our servants."[39] The northern haute bourgeoisie, whose fortunes were closely tied to slavery, were arrayed in opposition. The growth of capitalism proved to be a bulwark of slavery rather than its bête noir.

Furthermore, abolition was a young people's movement. Most of its leaders, including Garrison, were in their twenties and represented a new generation. In 1831 a meeting of "colored young men" at the Boyer Lodge led by Ruggles, William P. Johnson, and Van Rensselaer endorsed immediatism. Not a few of the antislavery societies in Western Reserve, Amherst, Union, Andover, Middlebury, and Marietta Colleges and Phillips Academy were founded by students who, like the Lane rebels, defied colonizationist college authorities. Others, such as Oberlin and Knox Colleges, owed their success to abolition. Like the female antislavery societies, young men's antislavery societies proliferated in the 1830s. The Boston Young Men's Anti-Slavery Society published David Lee Child's *The Despotism of Freedom*, denouncing the "inveterate, cruel and . . . ferocious prejudice" against blacks. On Stanton's prompting, the New York Young Men's Anti-Slavery Society announced, "Our duty to the colored people of this land is urgent." By 1838 there were enough young men's antislavery societies to hold a national convention.[40]

The young men and women who joined the abolition ranks became parents, and abolitionists developed a juvenile wing. A fond father, Garrison and his wife, Helen, raised their children schooled in activism and named them after prominent abolitionists. In a poem written to commemorate the birth of his first son, a poem admired by blacks in particular, Garrison dwelt on the grief of slave mothers and fathers. The *Liberator* had a juvenile department, in which Garrison published Isaiah De Grasse's elegant essay to the American Convention. Black Bostonians took the lead in establishing the first antislavery juvenile society, which they named after Garrison, and Susan Paul, the daughter of Thomas Paul, conducted the society's juvenile colored choir. Garrison was especially taken with Paul, writing, "In all that constitutes female excellence" no one was her superior. The choir performed regularly for the NEAS conventions and antislavery meetings in Boston and Salem. Garrison protested vehemently when they were barred from riding stagecoaches to perform. He also published an exchange between Susan's students and some white Sabbath school students from

Amesbury and Salisbury, who donated their pocket money to Paul's school. Paul wished that all white children felt and acted in the same way.

Susan Paul wrote one of the first antislavery juvenile didactic books, a biography of one of her students, James Jackson, who died at an early age in 1835. The memoir recounted James's habits of piety, obedience, and industry. But it also imparted important lessons in abolition and antiracism. Paul exhorted her young readers to have the courage to "love anybody who is good" regardless of skin color, and she deplored the early racism imbibed by white children who were taught to fear black people. If everyone followed the Golden Rule, she argued, "no person would be despised or abused because they are poor, or because they had a dark skin." Paul recounted the time when she told her pupils about enslaved children. In response, James prayed regularly, she wrote tellingly, for the liberty of the slaves.[41]

Like Susan Paul, Henry C. Wright, the young minister, was involved in the Sunday school movement. Paul or Sarah Mapps Douglass was probably the "negro school teacher" Wright was accused of escorting on his arm after an antislavery meeting. An advocate of children's education and nonresistance who questioned parental authority to physically discipline their children, Wright was the AASS agent for juveniles. The Mansfield and Foxboro Juvenile ASS consisted of boys and girls between the ages of five and ten. The juvenile antislavery society of Pawtucket, Rhode Island, held its own fair to raise money for abolition. In 1837 Wright reported that children had collected fifty-two dollars by contributing a penny each. Wright was the author of *A Kiss for a Blow* (1842), a popular children's tract advocating abstention from conflict. The AASS published a monthly journal directed at children, the *Slave's Friend*, from 1836 to 1839. It taught them to refer to blacks as "colored Americans" and reported on the AME bishop Daniel Payne's speech to children. Containing stories like that of a "small colored girl" who shared her plums with a racist white girl, hoping her kindness would change her views, it achieved notoriety when Hammond waved it in Congress during his anti-abolition speech. Scholars have focused on the occasional children's antislavery catechisms, hymns, and prayers in the journal. But most of the fairly substantial articles were on the history of the slave trade and African Americans, letters from black children, and the proceedings of juvenile antislavery societies as well as on prejudice, petitions, Haiti, Lovejoy, anti-abolition mobs, extracts from slave narratives, and Thome and Kimball's book on West Indian emancipation. The journal afforded children a serious education in abolition. Rather than social control, abolitionists' educational activism displayed a healthy respect for minors as rational, ethical agents.[42] The movement's diverse membership, innovative tactics, radical ideology, and political impact set it apart from other antebellum reform endeavors.

SCHISM

The politicization of abolition inevitably led to differences over strategy and ideology. Growth fueled divisions. The cause of the friction lay not only in what Garrison's contemporary and later detractors called Garrisonianism, a compound in their view of religious, political, and social heresies, but also in differences over the future direction of abolition. Nor was it simply a matter of reformists versus radicals. All abolitionists were radicals when it came to slavery and race. While it is perhaps unfair to tar all of Garrison's opponents with the same conservative brush, Aileen Kraditor correctly drew attention to Garrison's belief in a big tent philosophy for the movement. It was Garrison's critics who wanted to read him, his newspaper, and the AASS itself out of abolition.[43] The stakes were high, each side viewing the other as harming the slave's cause. To Garrison, opposition to him and his followers translated into opposition to abolition. To his opponents, Garrisonianism threatened to subvert abolition itself.

The division was strategic but articulated in ideological disputes over Garrison's religious infidelity, belief in nonresistance, and support for women's rights. Abolitionists shared similar positions on the church before the schism. At the first meeting of the AASS, Jocelyn, who represented the evangelical wing, argued that the "American Church" was stained with the blood of innocent souls in sustaining slavery, sounding like a radical Garrisonian. At its next meeting the AASS passed Bourne's resolutions asking all Christians to petition their churches on the question of slavery. Even Lewis Tappan was forced out of his Presbyterian church for his abolitionism. Birney and Weld made strenuous efforts to get the Presbyterians to accept abolitionism and reported on their division between the orthodox Old Lights and the New Lights in 1837. Abolitionist ministers such as Scott, Le Roy Sunderland, Grosvenor, and Nathaniel Colver waged a battle against slaveholding within the Methodist and Baptist denominations, forming the abolitionist Wesleyan Methodist Connection of America and the American Baptist Anti-Slavery Convention. Eventually both denominations split into northern and southern wings in 1844–45 under the pressure of the slavery controversy, a precursor to political disunion. Garrisonian as well as evangelical abolitionists pressured the churches to act against slavery.[44]

But the evangelicals found Garrison's religious iconoclasm hard to stomach. Their differences could be encapsulated in the competing mottoes of the *Liberator* and the official organ of the AASS, the *Emancipator*, edited by Joshua

Leavitt. The former's was inspired by Thomas Paine, "Our Country is the World, Our Countrymen are Mankind," to which Garrison added "Universal Emancipation," and the latter's was the biblical "Proclaim Liberty to the Captive." In 1838 Garrison embraced Paine, viewed by many as a radical atheist rather than as a revolutionary hero. He echoed Paine's skepticism of the Bible as the revealed word of God, going a step further than most abolitionists' rejection of proslavery fundamentalism. Garrison also antagonized those involved in religious benevolence by questioning the Sabbath. Like Quakers, he believed that every day, not just Sunday, should be observed as a holy day, and he excoriated racial segregation, the "negro pew," in the churches. Even the Quakers segregated blacks in their meetings, and Garrison asked them to renew their "ancient zeal."[45]

Clerical abolitionists criticized the inflammatory controversies between Garrison and evangelical editors. In 1837 they began a sustained campaign to read him out of the movement. The Congregationalist pastoral letter against the Grimké sisters' public speaking tour in Massachusetts was followed by a clerical appeal in which Rev. Charles Fitch and Rev. Joseph Towne of Boston complained of criticisms in the *Liberator* of the church and slaveholding ministers. According to them, such denunciations deterred abolition from gaining more followers within the church. Rev. Amos Phelps, the general agent of the MASS and, later, a leader of the anti-Garrisonian faction, came to Garrison's defense. The abolitionist common front against orthodoxy soon collapsed. Abolitionists in the Andover Theological Seminary issued their own appeal against Garrison's critique of the church and missionary societies and his support of women's rights. The Andover Appeal also accused him of fomenting *"disorganization and anarchy"* by advancing the idea of nonresistance, or the rejection of all human governments based on force.

Garrisonian nonresistance antagonized both religious and political abolitionists. This radical pacifism, which went beyond the American Peace Society's antiwar stance, translated into a rejection of the use of force by the state. He opposed capital punishment, perceiving early on its differential racial application, and called his opponents "hanging clergymen." Garrison was influenced by John Humphrey Noyes, the founder of the Oneida community, who described the American government as "a bloated, swaggering libertine, trampling on the Bible—its own Constitution—its treaties with Indians—the petition of its citizens: with one hand whipping a negro tied to a liberty-pole, and on the other dashing an emaciated Indian to the ground." No doubt this characterization appealed to Garrison after the violent campaign to stamp out abolition, in which the state often colluded. As he put it, "Non resistance versus brickbats and bowie-knives! . . . Divine law against lynch law!" Garrison was swayed not only by the religious perfectionism of Noyes, who believed that humans could perfect themselves and free themselves from all sin, but also by Adin Ballou, a nonresistant and the founder of the Hopedale community. He began publishing articles on "peace principles" and nonresistance, articles written mostly by Henry C. Wright. In 1838 he and Wright formed the New England Non-Resistance Society with its own paper, the *Non Resistant*. Garrison believed all governments involved tyranny, violence, and inequality and were contrary to equality, peace, and freedom. He rejected "all human politics, worldly honors and stations of authority," especially military office, armaments, and war.

Garrison's embrace of nonresistance, combined with his support for women's rights, provoked opposition from clerical abolitionists. Rev. James Woodbury of Acton issued a wide-ranging condemnation of Garrison's views of the Sabbath and the ministry, his partiality to nonresistance, Wright's rejection of "family government," that is, parental violence, and his "Fanny Wrightism." In a personal attack, Woodbury declaimed that to most abolitionists "Garrison is the god of their idolatory. He embodies abolition. He is abolition personified and incarnate." The only way for religious abolitionists to distance themselves from Garrison's views was to disown him. In reply, Garrison was forced to defend his abolition credentials, recalling that he "was a poor, self educated mechanic" with "no family connexions, without influence, without wealth, without station. . . . The clergy was against me—the rulers of the people were against me—the nation was against me," when he began his crusade. Two more clerical appeals followed Woodbury's letter, leading Garrison to sever all connections between the *Liberator* and the MASS, to the newspaper's financial disadvantage. A committee led by Jackson took charge of its finances. The clerical offensive only strengthened Garrison's suspicions of organized religion.

Garrison was upset by the failure of the AASS executive committee and the *Emancipator* to defend him against the attack. In a long letter Lewis Tappan explained to him that the committee, even though it did not approve of the clerical appeals and recognized his "early, unremitting and invaluable devotion to the cause," could not enter into a controversy between him and abolitionist clergymen in Massachusetts.

Women and African Americans, however, rallied to Garrison's defense, and he in turn defended their right to speak for abolition. In her forceful, book-length defense of Garrison, Maria Weston Chapman alluded to his pioneering efforts and to the history of the growing religious opposition to him. The black population of Boston was unanimously behind Garrison, since the ministers had remarked adversely on their religiosity. Purvis sent a letter in which he hailed the *Liberator* as a beacon to the abolition cause. The Abington Female ASS called the clerical appeals an attack on abolition itself, and the BFASS accused them of misrepresenting the scriptures. When the NEAS convention, in May 1838, decided to seat women on an equal footing, Phelps, Rev. Charles Torrey of Salem, and Fitch resigned. Tappan regretted associating with "ungodly men" in the antislavery enterprise and tried to persuade Phelps to start a new organization. Like Elizur Wright, they believed that issues like women's rights, religious perfectionism, and nonresistance impaired the abolitionist cause. Garrison reiterated, "As an abolitionist, we examine no man's political or religious creed, and care not who it is that is willing to assist us in breaking the yoke of slavery. But our liberal feelings are not met by others. We are willing to walk with them, but they are not willing to walk with us."[46]

Before his conversion to nonresistance, Garrison favored political action, and his opponents were as critical of the state and church. At its third annual meeting the AASS passed Garrison's resolution denouncing the American Republic as a *"land of religious despotism"* and *"home of republican injustice."* As late as 1836 Birney held that abolition was above "political predilections" and was not a political movement. Nor were Garrison and his followers strictly nonpolitical before the schism, as their opponents never failed to point out. Garrison supported the mass petition campaign and published verbatim the speeches of antislavery politicians. He supported the candidacy of the abolitionist Amasa Walker to Congress, asking African Americans to vote for him, inveighed against the annexation of Texas, and wrote paeans to Adams. David Lee Child, along with Lundy, led the abolitionist charge against Texas, and Henry C. Wright proposed a resolution against the admission of Arkansas into the Union at the AASS annual meeting. At the NEAS convention in 1837, Garrison devoted his speech to Texas, and it unanimously passed an anti-annexation resolution. The next year Stanton and Phelps led a large anti-Texas meeting in Faneuil Hall. Stanton, Weld, and Stewart as well as Garrison and Phillips addressed the legislatures of Massachusetts, Ohio, and New York on the Gag Rule and fugitive slaves. By 1838 the AASS was encouraging interrogation of candidates on slavery and voting only for those who supported abolition. On Stewart's prompting, the NEAS convention did the same. Garrison himself stirred his readers to vote against proslavery politicians.[47]

But while Garrison embraced nonresistance, Christian perfectionism, and women's rights, Elizur Wright, Birney, Leavitt, and Stanton moved toward political abolitionism. Like Garrison, they were moved by the events of the 1830s in their contemplation of the future direction of the movement, which they believed lay in entering politics. Stanton had enjoyed considerable success in politics. His widely reported two-day speech before the Massachusetts assembly not only defended the right to petition and Congress's constitutional power over slavery and the slave trade in the District of Columbia but also mounted a defense of political abolitionism. It led to the passage of resolutions supporting the abolition of slavery in the district. Stanton recalled that he had addressed ten legislative committees in seven states and traveled to Washington to defend the right to petition. He claimed to have predicted the passage of a constitutional amendment to end slavery as early as 1838. The *Philanthropist* editorialized that politics would not result in gradualism or a falling away from abolitionist principles, as many feared, but allowed abolitionists to "operate with increased vigor" and "enlarged hope of success." Birney felt that abolitionists needed to combat the political power of slaveholders through the ballot box. He was appalled by Wright's nonresistance articles in the *Liberator* and suggested that those who championed extraneous, unpopular concerns should resign from the AASS. If Garrisonians advocated the reformation of a corrupt state and society, political abolitionists wanted to take over the reins of government. They wanted to read out the Garrisonians by moving the AASS in a purely political direction.[48]

The showdown between them came at the annual meeting of the MASS in January 1839, at which Stanton attacked Garrison for "lowering the standard of abolition." Black abolitionists defended Garrison by acclamation, and John T. Hilton called him a "simon pure, sincere abolitionist," leading one of Garrison's detractors to remark that if he went to hell, black people would follow him there. Hoping to challenge Garrison's views on voting, Stanton asked him whether he thought voting was a sin, to which Garrison replied, "Sin for me." Not wanting to abide by Garrison's live-and-let-live philosophy, political abolitionists wanted to make voting the duty of all abolitionists. Their resolutions were handily defeated, and Phelps, Alanson St. Clair, and Torrey, who ironically were also presenting resolutions denying women the right to vote in antislavery meetings, began their own newspaper, *Massachusetts Abolitionist*. In an effort to allay divisions, the MASS annual report was generous to Phelps and Stanton but defended women's rights to participate equally in antislavery societies.

Already suspicious of the maneuverings of the executive committee represented by Tappan, Elizur Wright, and Birney, Garrison correctly suspected it of aiding his opponents. The committee made the move toward politics official policy. In "A Letter on the Political Obligations of Abolitionists," Birney tried to purge the "no government" men, as he called them, from the AASS. He pointed out that its constitution specifically enjoined abolitionists to take political action against slavery and influence Congress. Outraged that Birney's call for expulsion was printed in the *Emancipator,* the official organ of the AASS, Garrison replied as a "framer, member and manager" of the AASS. He protested Birney's "bold attack" on the "pacific views" of some abolitionists and his attempt to convert the AASS into a political organization. Garrison claimed that the AASS constitution did not exclude nonresistance. No person could be a nonresistant and not an abolitionist, though an abolitionist need not be a nonresistant. The Garrisonian-dominated MASS also got into a financial dispute with the executive committee. Arthur Tappan suffered near bankruptcy after the Panic of 1837, and the AASS was in dire straits, aggravating matters.

The financial panic, brought on by rampant speculation, including in the slave-based cotton economy, fed the crisis in the abolition movement. The boom and bust nature of early American capitalism led abolitionists like Henry C. Wright to condemn the unholy partnership between southern slavery and northern capital. The AASS pointed to the fact that the entire nation, including northern consumers and businesses, profited from the exploitation of slave labor. A parasitic and idle slaveholding class living off the enslaved was the cause of hard times, according to Stewart. Leavitt diagnosed the problem as the chokehold of the Slave Power on the nation's political economy. To Leavitt, inspired by British corn law opponents and pro-labor political economists' opposition to the tariff, the answer lay in free trade. In adopting the Democratic opposition to protection, he left Whiggish abolitionists unimpressed. Garrison viewed free trade as the watchword of slaveholding nullifiers. It never became economic orthodoxy among abolitionists, and even in Leavitt's Liberty Party economic radicalism trumped laissez-faire.[49]

The schism was a tripartite one between Garrisonians, evangelicals, and political abolitionists but with considerable crossover. The *Liberator* teemed with the correspondence of Garrisonians versus political and evangelical abolitionists. Anti-Garrisonians pushed to have their positions endorsed at the annual AASS meeting presided over by Smith but did not gain the upper hand. Birney, Stanton, and Goodell made the case for independent political action, leading to a debate with Cornish, who liked the idea of acting politically but disagreed with a requirement to vote only for abolitionists, as African Americans were behind all who were for black suffrage. The AASS passed Whittier's resolution in favor of voting to promote abolition but also gave women the right to vote. Phelps and other clerical abolitionists left the MASS after failing to exclude women at the NEAS convention. They formed the rival Massachusetts Abolition Society in May 1839, which was recognized as an auxiliary by the AASS. Its formation led, according to Garrison, to the "strange spectacle" of having two abolition societies in one state, and he denounced it as schismatical, intolerant, and exclusive. Elizur Wright, who became the editor of the *Abolitionist*, came into conflict with the clerical abolitionists, who had founded the "new organization" MAS. In a letter to Stanton that Garrison published, Wright disparaged the MAS and urged the formation of a political party.

A group of abolitionists based mostly in upstate New York, Stewart, Green, Leavitt, Stanton, Birney, Smith, and Goodell, became convinced of the necessity of a third party. Led by Stewart and Myron Holley, a veteran of the Anti-Mason party, they tried to jump-start an abolitionist party. In 1839 Stewart, a founder of the NYASS, recommended a third party to its executive committee. Political abolitionists held conventions in Albany and Cleveland but were opposed by many abolitionists, who remained suspicious of entering politics. Birney was offered their presidential nomination but felt the move was premature, as the two major parties had not yet held their nominating conventions. The physician Francis J. LeMoyne of Pennsylvania, who was nominated for the vice presidency, wrote to Birney that in his view abolition was a "religious enterprise" rather than a political movement. Tappan thought that forming a political party was contrary to the principles of the AASS constitution. (He would later change his mind.) He gave a brilliant speech at the AASS meeting on the complicity of the church and ministers in slavery and was more interested in starting an evangelical antislavery society to replace the AASS. Smith initially held aloof from both sides, writing to Weld that he was "heart sick" of the divisions.[50]

Whereas political abolitionists seriously underestimated the strength of the Garrisonians, which included most of the female membership of the society, the evangelicals underestimated abolitionists' loyalty to the original society. This became apparent at the seventh anniversary meeting of the AASS in 1840. The executive committee refused to accede to Garrison's request to delay the crucial gathering. Garrison had undertaken a lecturing tour of Massachusetts the previous year to rally the faithful. The MASS's new agent John A. Collins made sure that a large New England contingent dominated the meeting. Blacks and a majority of female antislavery societies rushed to Garrison's defense against the new organization men. A meeting in Boston led by Hilton and William Cooper Nell, the son of the GCA's William G. Nell, called Garrison "the colored people's best friend." Grace and Sarah Douglass wrote from Philadelphia that no one could ever convince them that Garrison was "recreant to the cause of the slave." A meeting in New Bedford led by Nathaniel Borden and William Powell called him "our true and faithful friend." Steamboats chartered for the meeting suspended their segregated seating, ensuring the attendance of a large number of African American delegates. Garrison called them "our unflinching friends, our most powerful allies." Forgotten in the histories of the schism, the speech of the convention was delivered by Henry Highland Garnet, who argued that black people, as American citizens, "demand redress for the wrongs we have suffered, and ask for the restoration of our birth right privileges." According to Garrison, "Patrick Henry never spoke better, on any occasion."

Some political abolitionists endorsed women's rights, and some Garrisonians supported political action, but the schism forced them to choose sides. In April Holley et al. had already met in convention at Albany and nominated Birney and Thomas Earle of Pennsylvania on an independent Abolitionist ticket, and the Liberty Party, as it was named a year later, was born. Of the 121 delegates, 104 were from New York. Those sympathetic to political action but wary of third parties and independent nominations, including Gamaliel Bailey, the editor of the *Philanthropist*, and Whittier, were soon won over. By this time Garrison was fighting for the very survival of the AASS. Lewis Tappan handed over control of the *Emancipator* to the New York City ASS just before the AASS meeting. Arthur Tappan refused to preside, and Jackson took his place. After the election of Abby Kelley to the business committee, the entire evangelical wing walked out of the meeting. The AASS passed resolutions on voting according to one's personal conscience, criticized the church for its criminal silence on slavery, and commenced the publication of the *National Anti-Slavery Standard* (NASS) to replace the *Emancipator*.[51]

The seceders, led by the Tappans, formed the American and Foreign Anti Slavery Society (AFASS), emulating the British and Foreign ASS, with whom it forged good connections. In his presiding speech, Arthur Tappan spoke out against the idea that all human governments are sinful and argued ingenuously that the substitution of *men* by *persons* in the AASS rules for voting and officeholding could include not just women but also children, probably a swipe at Wright. Despite the presence of Birney and Stanton, the AFASS would not officially endorse the Liberty Party until 1843. The AFASS briefly published the *American and Foreign Anti Slavery Reporter* and tracts written mostly by Lewis Tappan. During its short history (1840–55), the AFASS and the clerical abolitionists continued to pressure the churches to move against slavery and assisted fugitive slaves. In 1846 Lewis Tappan formed the American Missionary Association (AMA), which played a crucial role in freedmen's education after the Civil War. Evangelical abolitionists, most trained at Oberlin, devoted their energies to missionary work at home and abroad, in Canada, the West Indies, and Africa. Unlike their eastern counterparts, the western evangelicals based at Oberlin steered clear of the schism but became supporters of the Liberty Party. All factions of the movement signed off on an appeal for Oberlin written by Weld.[52]

Black abolitionists deplored the schism as distracting and unnecessary. A meeting of the Marine Benevolent Society fulsomely praised Garrison but in addition cited the Tappans, Jay, Birney, Stewart, and Smith in its accolades. Ruggles defended Garrison, saying that if he was convicted of religious apostasy, black people would stand by him. At a meeting in New York chaired by Theodore S. Wright, Van Rensselaer, in whose house Garrison was staying, tried to have resolutions passed in favor of him. Garrison and Tappan addressed the meeting. Ray and Cornish led the opposition to Van Rensselaer's attempt to endorse only the Garrisonian delegation to the world antislavery convention in London, as it would appear that they had cast censure on the rival AFASS delegation. As Ray explained, "If the colored people of this City, or any section of this country, do manifest less warmth of feeling than formerly towards *Mr. Garrison*, it is in part owing, to our *Friends* having multiplied who are equally active, & equally efficient with Mr. *Garrison*, & as a necessary consequence our good feeling is scattered upon all, instead of being concentrated upon one, as when Mr. Garrison stood alone." Some, like John Lewis, wanted to "assume a strict neutral ground" and resigned as an agent of the NHASS. Ray's newspaper, the *Colored American*, feared that divisions in the movement led to "forgetting the slave and the outraged colored community" and recommended "independence of thought and principle" among black abolitionists. He decided to remain with the AASS for the present but published the annual call for meetings of both the AASS and AFASS.

Eventually most of New York City's black abolitionists, including Ray, aligned with the political evangelical wing of the movement. That alignment was natural given their geographical and ideological proximity to the Tappanites. Many of them were clergymen who were conservatives when it came to the woman question. Cornish had criticized Garrison's nonvoting stance, noting that it would be unwise for abolitionists to disfranchise themselves when black men were fighting for the right to vote. A meeting of Albany's colored citizens endorsed the Liberty Party. Van Rensselaer, a member of the AASS's executive committee, was one of the few black New Yorkers who remained allied with the Garrisonians. Posing the question, "When doctors disagree, who shall decide?" William P. Powell, a founding member of the AASS, doled out a strong dose of Garrisonian medicine with its respect for women's rights and rejection of slaveholding governments. In Boston and Philadelphia most blacks remained allied with the Garrisonians.[53]

The schism permeated the movement even though some antislavery societies refused to identify with either side. What had been a source of strength, the movement's diversity, became the cause of division. An ideal solution was retaining the AASS as an organization for agitation and the formation of the Liberty Party as the political arm of the movement. That is what happened, but it did so in the midst of recriminations and one-upmanship. Differences between Garrison and his critics sharpened as the incentive to accommodate disagreements ceased to exist. Despite the bitter personal animosity, abolitionists cooperated with each other on distinct issues. In Ohio the line between Garrisonians and Libertyites was blurred despite the founding of the Garrisonian Ohio American Anti Slavery Society in 1842, which became the Western Anti Slavery Society (WASS). Weld, close to the evangelical and political abolitionists but a supporter of women's rights, also stayed above the fray. In 1843 he refused to join the AFASS because of its "*denial* of the equal membership of women."[54] The woman question was an essential facet of the schism.

9

THE WOMAN QUESTION

Women were abolition's most effective foot soldiers. The best answer to anti-abolitionist violence came from black and white women who marched arm in arm to shield each other from the howling mobs during the Boston riot and at Pennsylvania Hall. As Angelina Grimké put it in a letter that caught Weld's attention, if abolitionists had to pay with their blood for the oppression of a guilty nation, they were prepared to do it. So seminal were women's contributions, effect, and influence on abolition that Hammond singled them out as women who "unsex themselves to carry on this horrid warfare against Slaveholders."[1] Female antislavery societies were some of the first founded, and women abolitionists emerged as leading orators, writers, and organizers of abolition.

Historians have searched for the roots of nineteenth-century women's activism in the cult of true womanhood, which viewed women as religious creatures and custodians of moral virtue. In this reading, middle-class women often parlayed alleged moral superiority into political activism, transcending the confining domestic, private roles prescribed for them by the separate spheres theory. Women's participation in the growth of evangelical Christianity and in religious benevolence is often portrayed as the foundation of their activism in antislavery and women's rights. But most women abolitionists, like their male counterparts, hailed from humbler backgrounds. Female moral reform societies, temperance, and abolition, which required regulating male behavior and challenging social mores and political institutions, revealed class and ideological tensions among those who stuck to conventional gender roles and others who were radicalized by their activism.[2]

If not all female abolitionists became women's rights activists, pioneering feminists owed their public careers to abolition. They questioned racial as well as gender hierarchies, posing a challenge to bourgeois gender conventions, religious authority, and the white man's democracy.

WOMEN ABOLITIONISTS

African American women played a crucial part in the rise of militant black abolitionism. Despite its use of the language of manhood and conventional gender roles, *Freedom's Journal* published anonymous letters and poems by black women, a certain Matilda pleading for female education, and notices of the African Dorcas Association. Black women established a tradition of activism in the church and in social and literary organizations. Associational activities were not confined to literate, churchgoing, middle-class black women. Nearly two hundred working-class black women formed the Daughters of Africa in Philadelphia, which supported its members with a weekly allowance of $1.50 when they were sick.[3] Black women's independent associations were staging grounds for political activism. Their claims to respectability and a public antislavery persona challenged the devaluation of black womanhood and the dehumanization of African Americans in the slaveholding Republic.

Black women's abolitionism came of age in the writings and speeches of remarkable women like Maria Stewart, Sarah Mapps Douglass, Sarah Louise Forten, and Jarena Lee. Garrison published Stewart's innocuously titled *Religion and the Pure Principles of Morality* in 1831. Many years later he recounted meeting her in the "flush and promise of a ripening womanhood." The beautiful, brilliant Stewart was one of the first American women to speak publicly (Frances Wright was British). She included an introductory sketch of herself in her book: her birth in Hartford, Connecticut, in 1803, an orphan at the age of five bound to a clergyman's family, how her "soul thirsted for knowledge," her education in Sabbath schools, her marriage at the age of twenty-three to the War of 1812 veteran James W. Stewart, and her widowhood three years later. Mentored by David Walker and befriended by the "noble-hearted" Garrison, she issued an early call to arms against "slavery and ignorance." She asked "ye daughters of Africa," to "Awake! Arise!" and "distinguish yourselves." Stewart's message was not restricted to a plea for female education. She asked blacks to "promote and respect ourselves," to "patronize each other," "improve our own talents," and be silent no longer. The "great and mighty men of America," the "rich and powerful ones" may "kill, tyrannize, and oppress," but they could not crush the "fearless and undaunted spirits of the Africans forever." To Americans who had "acknowledged all the nations of the earth, except Hayti," she emphasized, "WE CLAIM OUR RIGHTS."

Stewart was soon lecturing before the NEASS and the African Masonic Lodge, the preeminent organization of black men in Boston, to mixed audiences of blacks and whites, men and women. She was hoodwinked out of her inheritance and criticized "prejudice, ignorance and poverty" for the plight of free blacks. She argued, "Continual and hard labor irritates our tempers and sours our dispositions, the whole system becomes worn out with toil and fatigue." While Stewart clarified that she did not think it "derogatory . . . for persons to live out to service," she resented the fact that "most of our color have dragged out a miserable existence of servitude from cradle to the grave." She exhorted black men to speak out "in the defence of African rights and liberty" and to work for abolition: "Let every man of color throughout the United States, who possesses the spirit and principles of a man, sign a petition to Congress to abolish slavery in the District of Columbia, and grant you the rights and privileges of common free citizens." Her frequent admonitions against men's vices like dancing, drinking, and gambling at the cost of antislavery activism may have bothered some. On the eve of her departure from Boston she justified her right to speak out. "What if I am a woman?" she asked, asserting that women were "by turns, martyrs, apostles, warriors" and "divines and scholars." Well before the Grimké sisters, Stewart contended that neither sex nor race marked a person but the "principle formed in the soul." She published her collected works in 1835.[4]

A letter Alexander Crummell wrote on her behalf reveals that Stewart became a teacher at Williamsburg and a member of the Colored Ladies Literary Society (CLLS) upon moving to New York, where she probably lectured too. She attended the first Women's Antislavery Convention in 1837. Crummell recalled meeting her, "a young woman of my own people full of literary aspiration and ambitious authorship." She moved to Baltimore in 1853 and then to Washington, where she ran Sabbath schools for black children. She did not stop lecturing and publishing, as is commonly believed. She delivered a suitably religious lecture on the proper training of children before the St. James' Protestant Episcopal Church in 1860 and wrote a semiautobiographical story on an orphaned black girl. Stewart heard the reading of the Emancipation Proclamation and, like many abolitionists, became involved in freedmen's relief during the war. When she finally received her husband's pension, she invested it in a new edition of her speeches in 1879, including a letter from Garrison reminiscing on their early collaboration. They both died that year. Black abolitionists also bracketed her life: Thomas Paul presided at her wedding and Crummell at her funeral.[5]

Black women took the lead in female antislavery organizing too. Stewart was the moving force behind the organization of the Afric-American Female Intelligence Society (AAFIS) of Boston in 1832. Its constitution, written perhaps by her, was devoted to the "diffusion of knowledge" and "suppression of vice and immorality." In her address to the AAFIS, Stewart declared, "It is useless for us any longer to sit with our hands folded." Inspired by the Quaker free produce movement, black women in Philadelphia's Bethel church formed the Colored Female Free Produce Society in 1831. That year Jocelyn proposed the organization of the all-black Female Literary Association (FLA) of Philadelphia, whose members critiqued one another's work. The CLLS in New York and the Minerva Literary Society in Philadelphia were founded in 1834. At least five black women's associations met in New York's AME Zion church. Their membership cut across class lines. Garrison published the constitutions of the AAFIS, FLA, and the Colored Female Religious and Moral Society of Salem, formed as early as 1818, and the works of members of the "Society of colored ladies in Providence" and of the FLA. The *Liberator* had a "Ladies Department," and Garrison published women in the main body of his paper too.

Abolition nurtured women's activism. Susan Paul and Prudence Crandall were the only two lifelong female members of the NEASS and the first to join antislavery societies. Paul struggled to support her family on the death of her father, and Garrison bemoaned her early death in 1841, the result of her exposure to the elements while aboard a Jim Crow steamer. A black women's Garrison Society, which may have included Paul and Stewart, met in Boston in 1832 to converse about the sufferings of "our enslaved sisters." In February Garrison reported the formation of the first antislavery society in Salem (SFASS) made up entirely of "females of color." He commended the black female antislavery societies in Middletown, Connecticut, led by women of the abolitionist Beman family, and in Rochester, New York, urging "colored and white ladies" to follow their example. In 1835 Ruggles published a pamphlet (previously attributed to George Bourne) on the sexual abuse of female slaves. He asked American women to join antislavery societies in order to protest the "debasing bondage colored women are held, by which they are defiled and destroyed."[6]

Black women were at the forefront of female abolitionism. Sarah Mapps Douglass of Philadelphia was the granddaughter of Cyrus Bustill, whose biography she wrote in 1854, and the daughter of the abolitionists Grace Bustill Douglass and Robert Douglass, a prosperous barber and leading black Presbyterian. Her brother Robert Douglass Jr., an artist of some repute, was known for his early portrait of Garrison. Garrison published his exuberant description of

Haiti's Independence Day celebrations and Sarah's essays signed Sophonisba, which reminded free women to make "our captive sisters . . . the subject of our daily conversation, our daily prayers." In letters she signed Zillah, Douglass reiterated that African Americans wanted to stay in the land of their nativity. She condemned colonizationists as "our enemies," who feared that education would "elevate us to an equality with themselves." Douglass began her teaching career in New York's African schools and was secretary of the FLA. An address to the FLA, probably given by her, exhorted its members to "elevate yourselves to the station of rational, intelligent beings accountable for the use made of the talents committed to your care." Similarly, Elizabeth Jennings, the daughter of Thomas Jennings, in her speech to the CLLS, asked black women to "stand forth in the field of improvement." Douglass encouraged black women to patronize the *Genius* and the *Liberator,* as they were "devoted to your cause." She importuned Garrison to publish the FLA's constitution and purchased a copy of his colonization pamphlet for the society. Douglass married Rev. William Douglass, the pastor and historian of the city's historic African church, St. Thomas's. The first woman to attend the Female Medical College of Pennsylvania, she became known for her pioneering lectures on female anatomy and physiology.[7]

Like Douglass, the Forten sisters of Philadelphia, Margaretta, Harriet, and Sarah, belonged to a distinguished black abolitionist family and with their mother, Charlotte, were active members of the interracial PFASS. Whittier was so impressed by them that he wrote a poem titled "To the Daughters of James Forten." Margaretta and Sarah taught school, and Harriet married Robert Purvis and was active in his Vigilant Committee, which assisted fugitive slaves. Sarah published poems and essays in the *Liberator* under the pseudonyms Ada and the Indian Magawisca. In "The Abuse of Liberty" she decried northern racism. In a poem published by the first women's antislavery convention, she wrote, "Our skins may differ, but from thee we claim, / A sister's privilege, and a sister's name." Sarah noted that her family frequented only familiar places out of fear of encountering racial proscription. Douglass complained of racism even in Quaker meetinghouses. Their efforts and those of people sympathetic to them, like the Grimkés, bore fruit in the resolution passed by the convention condemning "prejudice against color" as the "spirit of slavery." Sarah's career was cut short by her marriage to Joseph Purvis. Unlike his brother, Joseph was not an activist, and she settled for domesticity.[8]

Black women preachers championed abolition and breached the barriers of female decorum. Jarena Lee was the first in a list that included Zilpha Elaw, Rebecca Cox Jackson, Julia Foote, and Sojourner Truth. Lee, who published her spiritual narrative in 1836, traced her conversion to a sermon by Richard Allen. She approached Allen for permission to preach, and he suggested that she hold prayer meetings since the Methodist Discipline did not "call for women preachers." Lee abided by his decision but queried, "And why should it be thought impossible, heterodox, or improper for a woman to preach, seeing the Saviour died for the woman as well as the man?" She commenced itinerant preaching but resigned herself to married life with a black clergyman. After his death, Lee felt the call to preach again. Witnessing her sermonize spontaneously, as the pastor "seemed to have lost the spirit," Allen finally agreed to let her preach. Lee took the greatest delight in converting "a great slave holder" who "had been very cruel" to his slaves. In 1840 she joined the AASS and subsequently published two more editions of her narrative. Lee mentored Elaw and contested the AME's ban on women ministers. Like the more famous Truth, who donned Quaker garb to evoke respectability and the Friends' tradition of female preaching, she used religious testimony to condemn slavery and female inequality.[9]

Quaker women were an early mainstay of antebellum abolition. Laura Haviland called on "American women" to shed their "indifference manifested to the cause of the female slave." "We wish," she concluded, "that every woman should feel her accountability on this subject." Originally from Canada, Haviland migrated to Michigan via New York with her husband. She and Elizabeth Margaret Chandler founded the first western antislavery society in October 1832. The most notable was Lucretia Coffin Mott, who was born in Nantucket and settled with her husband, James Mott, in Philadelphia. She was active in the free produce movement and an early supporter of Lundy and Garrison. Used to speaking in Quaker meetings as a minister, Mott became a formidable proponent of abolition. She was the only active female participant in the founding convention of the AASS, which called for the formation of female antislavery societies.

Quakers such as Mott, Esther Moore, and Lydia White and black women abolitionists founded the interracial PFASS in December 1833. James McCrummell presided over their meeting, May addressed them, and Mott became corresponding secretary. Margaretta Forten and Sarah McCrummell, the wife of James, helped draft its constitution, and Sarah became its recording secretary. The wife of Joseph Cassey, Amy, was also a member. Not all the black women in the PFASS were related to black abolitionists. Its managing board included Hetty Reckless, who was active in the underground railroad and moral reform, and Hetty Burr, a founding member. Sarah Pugh was its president for much of its existence, and Mary Grew, its longtime corresponding secretary, wrote most of the annual reports. Writing to Elizabeth Whittier, the sister of the poet, Sarah Forten, also a member, commended Thompson's lecture on Haiti before the PFASS. The society grew dramatically in the 1830s to over two hundred members and retained an activist core of around ninety women in later decades. Roughly 12 percent of its membership was black. It supported Douglass's school, meddling with its management to her ire, until 1840.[10]

Even before the PFASS, a group of twelve women founded the BFASS in October 1833. It would not formalize its constitution until a year later and its rationale for female abolitionism was a combination of traditional and radical ideas on gender. Its first annual report claimed that the women became abolitionists "for our CHILDREN" but also called on those who were ready to "cast away pride, prejudice, self-interest, coldness, timidity and aristocracy" to join it. The BFASS was prodded by Garrison to include black women, and twenty-five, including Paul, became members. In 1836 the BFASS protested the treatment meted out to "*free* women of color, of high moral and intellectual character and cultivation, and of those strong powers which no prejudice can entirely crush, have been refused the accommodation of public conveyances, out of deference to the prejudice of the south against freedom." The BFASS was larger than its Philadelphia counterpart, drawing nearly six hundred members from Boston and the surrounding areas. While historians know a lot about a coterie of prominent women, we know little about a larger group of women married to artisans. The society also contained a substantial number of single women, most of whom, like Paul and Julia Williams, were teachers, and some working-class women, seamstresses, and domestic servants. Williams, who had enrolled in Crandall's school and Noyes Academy, taught a school for black children run by the BFASS members Martha and Lucy Ball. Phillis Salem and her Quaker employers, Sarah and Thankful Southwick, were members. The BFASS supported the Samaritan Asylum for Colored Orphans. Its first president was Charlotte Phelps, the wife of Amos Phelps.

Much like the Forten sisters, the Weston sisters, especially the formidable Maria Weston Chapman, who stood up to anti-abolition mobs, were active in the BFASS. Chapman was known for her annual reports, *Right and Wrong in Boston*, her expert editorship of the BFASS gift book *Liberty Bell*, published as a fund-raiser, and her management of its extremely successful antislavery fairs, which inspired similar efforts by other female antislavery societies. As the foreign corresponding secretary, she initiated correspondence with British and French abolitionist women, including Madame de Staël and Duchess De Broglie. The lucrative *Liberty Bell* showcased the feminist and internationalist nature of Garrisonian abolition, containing articles by Martineau and Lady Byron's plea for black education and equality. Chapman wrote a history of Haiti, complaining that whereas the history of the American Revolution fills volumes few knew the history of the black republic. Quincy wrote "Two Nights in St. Domingo," detailing the start of the slave rebellion in 1791. Chapman published articles by the Irish abolitionists Richard D. Webb, James Haughton, and Richard Allen and an article on the Hibernian Anti-Slavery Society by the MASS agent John A. Collins. It also published leading abolitionists as well as BFASS members like Eliza Follen, the wife of Charles Follen, who died in 1841, Maria's sister, Ann Warren Weston, and Lydia Maria Child.[11]

Child, a writer and the wife of David Lee Child, a founding member of the NEASS, was the most famous abolitionist woman in Boston. Known for her iconoclastic novels, her popular advice book for housewives, and her expert editorship of the first children's magazine, the *Juvenile Miscellany*, Child used her considerable talents to write an influential abolitionist text, *An Appeal in Favor of that Class of Americans called Africans* (1833). It led George Ticknor, a professor at Harvard, to boot her out of his literary salon, and the Boston Athenaeum revoked her membership. Child's book was an exposé of slavery on the decidedly unfeminine grounds of history, philosophy, political economy, and ethics. She took on proslavery apologetics: the master's property interest was the slave's only security, but rationality could be upended by human passion and avarice. Child argued that the slave South ruled the Republic through the three-fifths clause, and the North, "grown opulent," supported them. She deconstructed American racism—"We made slavery, and slavery makes the prejudice"—and the false idea that Africans did not resist their enslavement, which ignored the fact that thousands had "stabbed themselves for freedom—jumped into the waves for freedom—starved for freedom—fought like very tigers for freedom! But they have been hung, burned, and shot—and their tyrants have been their historians!" As for the alleged black tendency to crime, she retorted, "We hear a great deal of the negroes' crimes, we hear very little of their provocations." Northerners with their discriminatory laws, Child charged, were culpable for the real crime of racism.[12]

If Whittier was the poet laureate of the movement, Child was its muse. In 1834 she published *The Oasis*, an annual gift book containing abolitionist writings. Chapman modeled the *Liberty Bell* after it. A year later Child published *Authentic Anecdotes of American Slavery*. Culled from stories recounted by fugitive slaves whom she met in Philadelphia, abolitionists, and others, it was a precursor of Weld's *American Slavery As It Is*. In 1836 she published the *Anti-Slavery Catechism*, which answered each objection to immediatism in a series of questions and answers. The same year she published *The Evils of Slavery and the Cure of Slavery,* in which she quoted eminent southerners from Washington to Clay arguing that slavery was evil. She illustrated the efficacy of abolition in Haiti, in the newly independent Latin American nations, and in the British West Indies and concluded, "America has no excuse to screen her from the strong disapprobation of the world." In 1835 she wrote a two-volume global history of women. It described women's lives and gender conventions in Asia, Africa, Europe, and the Americas without making an explicit argument for equality. Her sympathetic discussion of African women kept antiracism at the forefront of her writing. Child became the first female editor of an abolitionist newspaper, the NASS, and she edited Harriet Jacobs's slave narrative, *Incidents in the Life of a Slave Girl.* Child championed Native American rights, prison reform, an end to capital punishment, the rights of the poor and working classes, and women's rights. She preferred integrated antislavery societies but acted as a liaison between the BFASS and the PFASS, encouraging the BFASS to emulate the free produce tactics of the PFASS and asking the latter to open correspondence with English abolitionists, as the BFASS had done.[13]

While the BFASS and PFASS were the most prominent female antislavery societies, two others were founded in New York, the Female Anti-Slavery Society of Chatham Street Chapel in 1834 and the Ladies New York City Anti-Slavery Society (LNYCASS) in 1835. The Chatham Street society was composed mainly of women active in the New York Moral Reform Society and Female Benevolent Society. The LNYCASS's membership was dominated by women related to the evangelical wing, among them the eldest daughter of Lewis Tappan, Juliana, who was also the corresponding secretary of the Anti-Slavery Sewing Society. The LNYCASS was formed after a rousing lecture by Thompson, and the society thanked him in its first report. The Glasgow Ladies Auxiliary Emancipation Society financed Thompson's tour, illustrating the transatlantic network of female abolitionism. The LNYCASS report noted that womanhood offered no protection to abolitionist or slave women. It was critical of the church, the "handmaid of oppression," and it opened up a correspondence with the BFASS. Unlike the BFASS and PFASS, the two New York female antislavery societies did not have any black members. Angelina Grimké pronounced the LNYCASS "utterly inefficient" because of its exclusivity. The only formal restriction in the Chatham Street society's constitution was against slaveholders, but its annual dues of a dollar excluded poor women. African American women in New York organized separately. The CLLS and the Rising Daughters of Abyssinia attended the antislavery women's convention and provided funds to publish its proceedings. In 1840 black women formed the Manhattan Abolition Society.

Conservative on the questions of race and gender, the two New York societies disintegrated after the woman question tore the movement apart.[14]

By 1835 the AASS reported that it had acquired 24 female auxiliaries in towns such as Portland, Maine, Plymouth and Concord, New Hampshire, and Providence, Rhode Island, and it predicted a tenfold growth of women's antislavery societies. The pioneering SFASS was reconstituted as an interracial society in 1834. A Providence Female Anti-Slavery Society founded in 1832 lasted barely a year. In 1834 Providence boasted of a new society with 106 members as well as a juvenile female antislavery society. Most of the officers of the Providence FASS were related to male abolitionists. As in New York, the Concord FASS in New Hampshire was formed at Thompson's urging. Its first annual report, written by its erudite corresponding secretary Mary Clark, recorded the progress of female abolitionism in New England, which had bloomed into 65 female antislavery societies by 1836. The CFASS report invoked the names of historic forbears such as Anne Hutchinson and Anne Bradstreet and the history of women's associations to justify their activism. An astute historian, Clark is a forgotten figure. She died in 1841.

The women's antislavery movement spread west with the founding of numerous societies in Ohio. By 1837 Massachusetts had over 40, and by 1838 Ohio had 30 female antislavery societies. Women abolitionists formed a statewide Ohio FASS to coordinate their activities. The number of female antislavery societies that year jumped to 139, fueled by the petition campaign, and by 1855 over 200 had been formed all over the North. A majority of the women were wives and daughters of farmers and mechanics. The societies in Lynn, a center of the shoemaking industry that supplied the slave South, and in the mill town of Lowell were predominantly working class. The Lowell girls connected their oppression to that of the slaves, an imagined solidarity opposing the alliance of the "lords of the loom and lords of the lash" built on the slave-grown cotton that fed the textile factories of New England.

The female antislavery societies corresponded with each other, as did the individual members, encouraging themselves in a hostile environment. Frances Harriet Whipple of the Providence FASS appealed to American women to lead on the question of abolition, and Maria Sturges published a letter to the women of Ohio to circulate and sign antislavery petitions. Lucy Wright, the sister of the abolitionist Elizur Wright, writing on behalf of the Portage County Ladies Society of Ohio, reported that it had grown from a founding membership of 37 to nearly 400 and asked for exchange of "kindred sentiments" with other female antislavery societies, as their hopes, fears, and aims were similar. Some, like the

BFASS, PFASS, SFASS, and the FASS of Ashtabula County, Ohio, coordinated mass petition drives and antislavery fairs and developed new female auxiliaries. The Providence FASS encouraged the formation of local auxiliaries throughout Rhode Island. The CFASS developed its own auxiliaries in Dunbarton and Durham and a Young Ladies juvenile antislavery society in Concord. The LNYCASS, which obtained 800 signatures on an anti–slave trade petition the year it was formed, issued an address to the Christian women of America to act against slavery. The PFASS republished Heyrick's pamphlets, including her defense of female antislavery societies. In their address to the women of Massachusetts, the BFASS exhorted them as "wives, mothers, daughters and sisters . . . responsible for the influence we exercise on the human race" to sign a petition against the slave trade in the District of Columbia. The Reading FASS, one of the first to be formed, declared that their enemies may rage but could not suppress women's demand for justice.[15]

Abolitionists justified women's activism and challenged bourgeois gender conventions. In his address to the CFASS, John Putnam noted that it was women who tipped the scales for abolition in Britain and charged his audience, as "members of the great human family" and as "rational, immortal and social beings," to do their duty for abolition. James A. Thome's *Address to the Females of Ohio* was a thoughtful defense of female abolitionism and challenged the idea of separate spheres. He condemned the fact that a *"sphere* is arrogantly assigned to woman, narrowed down to the circuit of the parlor, or measured by the circumference of her spinning wheel" and that the moment she steps out of it, "she is branded with every ungenerous and abusive epithet, and bid back to her *proper sphere.*" He asked them not to shrink from a *"political* subject" and to empathize with the abuse of slave women. Thome listed specific tasks for abolitionist women to petition Congress, circulate abolitionist material, write on behalf of the slave, support black schools, and convert other women and their own families to abolition.[16]

Women abolitionists did yeomen's work that was critical to sustaining the movement. The female antislavery societies were efficient fund raisers, selling subscriptions to abolitionist newspapers, purchasing pamphlets and tracts, financing the underground railroad, and paying the salaries of antislavery agents. The unpaid voluntary labor of countless unknown women kept abolition afloat. Goods with antislavery logos, mottoes, and illustrations were effective propaganda devices and a tribute to the creativity and productivity of abolitionist women. Female antislavery writing, the essays of Child and the poems of Sophia Little of Rhode Island, figured prominently in the *Liberty Bell*, sold annually at the BFASS fair. Antislavery sewing circles created articles, spreading abolitionist homilies like "May the use of our needles prick the consciences of slave-holders," sold at antislavery fairs and bazaars. Besides a fair sampling of abolitionist women's handiwork, items sold in the fairs could range from fashionable imports to homegrown goods donated by local abolitionist farmers. Most female antislavery societies emulated Chapman's elaborate fairs for the MASS, which succeeded the BFASS fairs. The *Liberator* published maps of the huge MASS fairs with specific tables displaying items from female antislavery societies all over the state. In Ohio Sarah Otis Ernst founded the Cincinnati Anti Slavery Sewing Circle and held a successful antislavery fair. These fairs usually coincided with the state antislavery conventions and meetings of local societies. While Ernst's fair funded an annual abolition convention in Cincinnati uniting all factions of the movement, the Salem Garrisonians held their own annual Western Anti-Slavery fair. Black women in Cincinnati and Philadelphia held fairs to fund black newspapers. The largest was held in New York by wives of the city's black clergymen on the eve of the war to raise funds for the Colored Orphan Asylum. The Providence FASS held its fair during commencement at Brown University to attract the largest number of buyers, while others held their gatherings during the holidays.[17]

Abolitionist women sewing, baking, and holding bazaars did not explicitly challenge gender norms, but their participation in the massive petition campaigns catapulted them into the political realm. Northern women involved in religious benevolence had petitioned against Indian removal earlier, but the female antislavery societies formed the backbone of the abolitionist petition campaign, Garrison noted. Women outnumbered male signatories, sometimes by a margin of two to one, and coordinated the campaign to gather signatures. They soon graduated from handwritten petitions to the standard printed versions handed out by the AASS and state antislavery societies. The BFASS asked the women of New England to cast aside selfishness and indolence and receive four rolls of paper each to affix their names to first and then canvass door to door for signatures. The petition campaign not only allowed women to participate in the national political debate over slavery in the District of Columbia, the interstate slave trade, the annexation of Texas, and the Gag Rule but also proved to be a stepping-stone to demands for female citizenship. Sturges remarked that the nation's capital was a "citadel of slavery," and they would not be "bantered from the field" just because they were women. Couched initially in deferential terms to the "fathers and rulers" of the country, female petitioners came to identify themselves as citizens. Gathering signatures was hard, daunting work but also a political education, introducing a whole generation of women, even those who were relatively conservative, to grassroots campaigning. Juliana

Tappan remarked, "I met with more intelligence in the families of some colored persons in my district, than in the splendidly furnished drawing rooms of wealthy citizens in Hudson Square."

In Congress, southern slaveholding politicians caricatured the women as unsexed spinsters, "grannies and misses," and the abolition movement as consisting supposedly of hoydenish women, effeminate men, and uppity blacks overturning natural gender and racial hierarchies. They disdained receiving petitions from women, noncitizens in their view. But the BFASS reminded the women of New England that representation was based on numbers, not on sex. Long after the national campaign was over, abolitionist women in Massachusetts coordinated a successful petition drive to overturn the state law against interracial marriage, and the women of Rhode Island, along with the black community, petitioned against Jim Crow. The petition campaigns were a foundational experience for many women's rights activists, who received their first political education in networking, canvassing, mobilizing, and movement formation in abolition.[18]

FEMALE ABOLITIONISM AND ITS DISCONTENTS

As women came to define abolition, their presence became controversial. Sarah and Angelina Grimké of South Carolina were instrumental to that debate. Sarah, who nursed her dying father in Philadelphia, converted to Quakerism. Her sister and goddaughter Angelina, thirteen years her junior, soon followed. Sarah's antislavery was shaped by an abolitionist of another generation, John Woolman, whose journal she read. Angelina rejected her slaveholding destiny, noting in her diary in 1829 on the eve of her departure to Philadelphia that "a Carolina mistress was literally a Slave Driver & I tho't it degrading to the female character." In 1835 she wrote her eloquent letter to Garrison and joined the PFASS. The next year Angelina published *Appeal to the Christian Women of the South*, asking them to penetrate the wall that southerners had built around their states against abolitionist reasoning. Slavery, she wrote, violated God's laws, the Declaration of Independence, and human rights. Angelina exhorted southern women to read, pray, speak, and act for abolition, even if it entailed persecution. She claimed that abolition was women's work. Like most incendiary religious women in world history, she asked women to obey God rather than man. Her pamphlet was published in three editions, one with an introduction by Thompson for an English audience. In 1836 Sarah also published *An Epistle to the Clergy of the Southern States*, a more religious and less successful document than Angelina's pamphlet. She admonished that they were stoning and killing the prophets sent to deliver them and ignoring God's "awful denunciations against those 'who rob the poor because he is poor.'" Ministers bore a "tenfold weight of guilt" for preaching that God approved of slavery with its "infinity of horrors." By converting humans into property, a "chattel personal," southern laws of slavery violated divine decrees. In their letter of 1837 to "Clarkson," the Grimké sisters delineated the actions northerners could take against slavery.[19]

The Grimkés earned notoriety not for their writings but for speaking publicly before what were called promiscuous audiences of men and women. Elizur Wright invited Angelina to attend the convention of antislavery agents in 1836. The sisters were the only women to have attended the training sessions conducted by Weld. They launched their famous speaking tour the following year and were deluged with invitations from female antislavery societies. In New York and New Jersey they had spoken before mostly female audiences, except in one black gathering that included men. In Massachusetts, men curious to hear or debate them attended their meetings. The Grimkés addressed over forty thousand people during their tour. Alarmed at their success, the General Association of Massachusetts Congregational ministers issued a pastoral letter in June 1837 written by Rev. Nehemiah Adams, who would compose the proslavery tract *A South-Side View of Slavery* (1854). The "clerical bull," as Garrison called it, was an attempt by conservative ministers to bar abolitionists from New England's churches. The ire of anti-abolitionist ministers was concentrated on the Grimkés and the Garrisonians who supported them. They were accused of threatening "the female character with widespread and permanent injury." It condemned abolitionists for encouraging "any of that sex who so far forget themselves as to itinerate in the character of public lecturers and teachers." As Angelina observed, "We have given great offense on account of our womanhood, which seems to be as objectionable as our abolitionism."

Female antislavery societies rallied to the Grimkés' defense. The BFASS and PFASS issued directives asking women to support them. The BFASS denounced the pastoral letter and praised the sisters as "women of genius and eloquence"; its members left Adams's church. The PFASS predicted that Angelina, like any abolitionist, would not only have to endure the "sneers of the heartless multitude" but also be subject to "grave charges of infractions of the laws of female delicacy and propriety." Garrisonians also came to their defense. In his address to the CFASS, Rogers maintained that it was not women who had lost sight of their sphere but gentlemen. If men would not perform the "rougher work" of abolition, then women had to step in. In the religious press Angelina was called Devilina, and the devout sisters, loose women. Clerical abolitionists like Phelps deplored their speaking to mixed audiences, but Henry C. Wright cheered them on. Angelina was exhausted after numerous lectures and depressed when Weld, with whom she had fallen in love, and Whittier warned the sisters to avoid the woman question. She protested that she lectured for the slave rather than for women's rights. Weld had early encouraged the sisters and designated them agents. He now asked them to assert their rights through their actions rather than engage their critics extensively. Sarah was determined not to "surrender my right to discuss any great moral subject" and heartened by the bolstering of "dear brother Garrison," who "united fully with us on the subject of the rights of woman." Similarly, Angelina felt that a "woman could do hundred times more for the slave if she were not fettered."[20]

The Grimké sisters could ill afford to ignore the woman question. In *Essay on Slavery and Abolitionism with Reference to the Duty of American Females*, Catharine Beecher, an advocate of female education and colonization, criticized Angelina. Unlike Mary Lyons and Emma Willard, Beecher is less known for founding schools than for her writings on domestic management, women's health, religion, and education. Ironically, Angelina had wanted to attend her Hartford Female Seminary but was refused permission by her Philadelphia Quaker meeting. The debate between Beecher and Angelina can be cast as one between difference and equality feminism, but abolitionist women employed a range of arguments from a conservative domestic rationale to a more activist, public one for their work. The more meaningful divide was one between reformers involved in religious benevolence and colonization and abolitionists. Beecher had participated in the movement against Cherokee removal coordinated by her father and other ministers in New England, which included calling public meetings, a petition campaign to Congress, and the publication of a circular. For her, acting against Indian removal was an exercise in female virtue but not abolition.

Beecher noted that Angelina mistook the opinion of northerners, who were averse to both slavery and abolition. Instead of attacking racism, she said, abolitionists should make the disagreeable object, African Americans, more agreeable. Abolitionists irritated whites and apparently made blacks envious and revengeful. She deplored Garrison's harsh language for inciting slave rebellion, sectional hatred, and lack of respect for Christian institutions. Beecher delineated the "just bounds of female influence" and objected to organizing women into antislavery societies. Abolition threw women out of their "appropriate sphere" of "piety, charity, maternal and domestic duty" and exposed them to the ridicule of the public sphere. She opposed women's lecturing, "if the female advocate chooses to come upon a stage, and expose her person, dress, and elocution to public criticism, it is right to express disgust." She likened the Grimkés' lecturing to that of the much-reviled Frances Wright. Beecher eventually signed an antislavery petition in 1854 but opposed woman suffrage.[21]

Beecher's critique and ministerial censure provoked the Grimké sisters. Angelina replied to her in a series of thirteen letters, and Sarah vindicated the equality of the sexes in her fourteen letters. They were published in the *Liberator* and reprinted as pamphlets in 1838. Angelina reasserted the abolitionist argument: slaveholders were man stealers, and the North was complicit. She rejected gradualism and held up Heyrick as a model for immediatists. Angelina vouched "as a southerner" that slavery was the mother of all abominations. In a rebuke of Beecher's colonizationist views, she professed that Haiti was ample proof of black men's capabilities. The colored man was not an *"unfortunate inferior"* but *"an outraged* and *insulted equal."* She even argued that *"it is now the duty of the slaves of the South to rebuke their masters* for their robbery, oppression and crime."[22]

The Grimkés broadened the abolitionist conception of human rights to include gender. In one of her last letters, entitled "Human Rights not Founded on Sex," Angelina famously averred, "The investigation of the rights of the slave has led me to a better understanding of my own." This was no simplistic equation of women's oppression with that of the slave but a philosophical argument that linked abolition to the cause of human rights in general. She wrote that women were just as guilty of the crime of slavery as men, and it was incumbent on them to fight against it. In republican America the right to petition was one of the few political rights available to them. The doctrine of human rights equated the slave to Lyman Beecher, she argued, and made woman equal to man. Had she ever thought of enslaved black women, she asked Beecher, in writing her "cold and heartless pages." Turning the tables on her, Angelina seemed to be asking who the true woman was here.

In her letters on the equality of the sexes addressed to Mary Parker, the president of the BFASS, Sarah sought to correct a "corrupt public opinion" and a "perverted interpretation" of the scriptures on the province of woman. Holding that woman was subject only to God, she indicted male domination: "All history attests that man has subjected woman to his will, used her as a means to promote his selfish gratification, to minister to his sensual pleasures, to be instrumental in promoting his comfort." Relying heavily on Child's book, she argued further that "the page of history teems with woman's wrongs, and it is wet with woman's tears." Ranging widely on the intellect, dress, and legal disabilities of women as well as on marriage, she constructed a full-throated feminist argument on their contemporary oppression and moral equality. Sarah concluded her letters with a plea for women's ministry, a subject close to her heart. Exemplifying the abolitionist turn against Christian fundamentalism, she reasoned that if Paul's injunction on female silence was taken literally, then women could not sing in churches or conduct Sabbath schools.[23]

The high point of female abolitionism was the annual meetings of the Anti-Slavery Convention of American Women. The BFASS issued the call for the first convention to form a national executive committee to better coordinate the petition campaign. The Boston, Philadelphia, and New York women, with seventy-one delegates, dominated the first convention, held in May 1837 in New York City. Parker was elected president and Sarah, Mott, Child, Martha Storrs, Gerrit Smith's wife, Ann, and Abby Cox of the LNYCASS were elected vice presidents. Angelina, Grew, Pugh, and Ann Weston were secretaries. Black women played an important role as well, Grace Douglass serving as vice president and the Forten sisters as delegates. The wives and daughters of New York's black abolitionists, such as Mrs. Rebecca Downing, Mrs. Maria Vogelsang, Misses Matilda and Sarah Jennings, and Julia Williams of the BFASS, attended. The delegates voiced their preference as to whether or not they should be addressed as Mrs. or Miss.

The Grimkés, Child, and Mott took a prominent part in the proceedings, proposing resolutions on the rights of fugitive slaves and against prejudice, segregation in the churches, the complicity of northern merchants and manufacturers in upholding southern slavery as well as on the right to petition and women's rights. The compromise resolution, passed by the convention, defended women's activism as the legitimate work of mothers. Angelina composed its pivotal document, *An Appeal to the Women of the Nominally Free States*. A call to abolitionist action, the appeal eschewed simple notions of gendered solidarity. Slave women were victims of slavery, and slaveholding women were "female tyrants." Abolitionists must conquer prejudice before they "storm the citadel of slavery" and defeat the "ministerial advocates of slavery." Northern women should avoid using slave grown products, fight against the prejudice visited on their "colored sisters," join antislavery societies, sign and circulate petitions against slavery. She asked, "Are we aliens?" because they are women or "bereft of citizenship" because they are mothers, wives, and daughters.[24]

The next year Angelina made history by becoming the first woman to address the Massachusetts House of Representatives, defending women's activism and the right to petition. The notion that women ruled the world by influencing men, she argued, appealed to the "baser passions of man" rather than to women's moral and intellectual power. Women should be regarded as citizens, as "moral being[s], endowed with precious and inalienable rights." Weld and Angelina married on May 14, 1838, just prior to the meeting of the second antislavery women's convention in Philadelphia, marred by the burning of Pennsylvania Hall. Angelina made the most riveting speech of the convention, which was also addressed by Mott and Chapman, with a loud mob heckling outside. She said that even if they were attacked, it would not compare with what slaves had to endure. While men may use the ballot box, women must petition. Evoking the example of British women, she concluded that Congress would be forced to legislate when "all the maids and matrons of the land" come knocking at its doors. It would be her last speech. Waiting in the wings was a Quaker schoolteacher from Lynn, Massachusetts, Abby Kelley, whose speech so impressed Weld that he anointed her Angelina's successor.

With Parker presiding again, the convention's vice presidents included Paul and Chapman of the BFASS; Juliana Tappan was one of its secretaries, Sarah M. Douglass treasurer, Angelina and Hetty Burr served on its business committee. It passed resolutions upholding the right to petition and decrying the effort to deprive black men of the vote in Pennsylvania, an issue that would haunt the abolitionist–feminist coalition after the Civil War. Two hundred and eight delegates attended, and it had seventy-five corresponding members. It received letters from local female antislavery societies, for instance, Harriet Kimball reported that the Fitchburg FASS had grown from a membership of thirty to over a hundred. In its address to antislavery societies, the convention justified women's activism as a matter of justice, humanity, religion, and patriotism. Women were encouraged to devote themselves to the education of black children and use free produce. Its address to the free people of color buttressed their efforts against disfranchisement in Pennsylvania. Filled with didactic advice on good conduct and racial unity and tightly braiding notions of uplift with resistance, it asked them to patronize Haitian goods so that Haiti might be accorded respect as an independent nation and to take part in vigilance committees assisting fugitive slaves. An overtly political address to Congress proclaimed that the quarter million members of the antislavery societies were "wielding a power stronger than political parties." It criticized northern representatives for being overawed by the "dark spirit of slavery" and thanked William Slade and Thomas Morris for their manly defense of their insulted petitions.[25]

The third convention of antislavery women met again in Philadelphia the following year. Presided over by Sarah Lewis, it was a smaller affair with half the number of delegates, as abolitionists became divided over women's proper role in the movement. But black women made their concerns central to it. Grace Douglass was once again vice president and her daughter Sarah, treasurer. Julia Williams and Harriet Forten Purvis attended both Philadelphia conventions.

Clarissa Williams of the SFASS spoke of the "monster" prejudice that black women confronted daily: "We are blamed for not filling useful positions in society; but give us light, give us learning and see what places we occupy." An address to the Society of Friends demanded more abolitionist activism. The convention's most interesting document was an appeal to American women on "prejudice against color." It chided them for doing nothing about their own "violent prejudices" or the fight against the racism that was grinding African Americans into the dust. It criticized the delicacy of white women, compromised by "social intercourse with a colored sister" but "her worldly dignity increased in a wonderful ratio by every additional colored *servant* whom she can display in her train," exposing racial and class fissures. Its circular asked women to work on canvassing petitions as "our only means of direct political action."[26]

Women also redefined the personal politics of abolition. Angelina's marriage to Weld was made by the movement. The wedding, presided over by a black and a white minister and attended by Garrison, who read the certificate of marriage, and by black friends and former Grimké slaves, was an abolitionist ceremony. It was, both Lewis Tappan and Ann Weston observed, a first for a women's rights advocate, an experiment in whether a marriage of equals was possible. The passionate letters Weld and Angelina wrote to each other reveal that they elevated the idea of companionate marriage into a shared commitment to human rights. Weld formally renounced his authority over his wife and spelled out his vision of an equal marriage. Angelina's lecturing was cut short by the births of her children, which resulted in a painful prolapsed uterus and a hernia, and by Weld's and Sarah's preference to avoid the limelight.[27]

To marry an abolitionist was to marry the movement. Contrary to the claim that while Garrison was committed to women's rights in theory he consigned his wife to a domestic position, Garrison urged Helen to form a female antislavery society. Helen demurred, though she became a member of the BFASS. Their courtship in letters is comparable to the Weld–Grimké correspondence, and theirs was a happy, long marriage. Ann Phillips was an abolitionist, although her debilitating illness prevented her from gaining the recognition Wendell enjoyed. In the case of the Childs and Motts, it was the women who were the more gifted. On James's sixty-first birthday Lucretia wrote to him about the "forty years that we have loved each other with perfect love." Abolitionist friends and family celebrated the Motts' fiftieth anniversary before James's death in 1868. Gerrit and Nancy Smith shared a passion for reform, and all the -isms of their day, including abolitionism and spiritualism. Henry B. Stanton, who married the young Elizabeth Cady, and David Lee Child were supportive of their wives' activism, though their marriages were not idyllic. Henry G. Chapman bankrolled his wife Maria's abolitionism until he died in Haiti. Marius Robinson and Augustus Wattles married the "Cincinnati sisters" Emily Rakestraw and Susan Lowe, who taught in black schools. The Philadelphia Quaker Benjamin Jones and his wife, Elizabeth Hitchcock Jones, lectured with Kelley and jointly edited the *Anti-Slavery Bugle*.

Some abolitionist couples personified what the women's rights activist Lucy Stone called "true marriages," or an equal partnership in the cause. Charles and Gertrude Burleigh, Oliver and Mary Ann Johnson, James and Charlotte Forten, Robert and Harriet Forten Purvis, Robert and Grace Douglass, Henry Highland and Julia Williams Garnet, Charles and Henrietta, and his second wife, Charlotte, Ray were activist couples. Garnet, who met Williams at Noyes Academy and courted her at the first antislavery women's convention, wrote, "She seems to have everything that beautifies a female, a good Christian and a scholar." Kelley and Stone married men who lived out their commitment to abolition and women's rights. Stephen Foster raised their daughter while Abby lectured, and Henry Blackwell joined Lucy in the struggle for women's rights. Stone was probably the first woman in America who did not take her husband's name after marriage inspiring latter-day "Lucy Stoners" to do the same.

Some feminist abolitionists, such as Grew, Parker, Betsey Mix Cowles of Ohio, and Susan B. Anthony, chose to remain single. A few abolitionist couples like Sherman and Mary Booth of Wisconsin parted company after Sherman stood accused of molesting their young babysitter. Charles and Josephine Griffing of Ohio got divorced. Charles was convinced that his wife had come under the influence of the free love doctrines of the abolitionist Parker Pillsbury. Black women like Mary Ann Shadd Cary, who lived apart from her considerably older husband, Frances Ellen Watkins Harper, and Forten's granddaughter Charlotte, who married the much younger Francis Grimké, the nephew of the Grimké sisters, had unconventional marriages. Fugitive slave abolitionists such as Frederick Douglass and William Wells Brown failed to find marital happiness, being married with women not particularly involved in or positively hostile to abolition. But William and Ellen Craft embarked on an abolitionist career together after their remarkable escape from slavery. The lives of ex-slaves seem to bear out the abolitionist indictment of slavery as destructive of marital bonds. Truth, Harriet Tubman, and Jacobs had partners who left them or whom they left.[28]

If Garrisonians supported women in the movement, evangelical abolitionists were troubled by their presence. Though a proslavery minister wrote the pastoral letter against the Grimkés, it was the opening blow of a wide-ranging clerical offensive against Garrisonian notions of female equality. The last straw for many of them was Garrison's support of women's rights, which, they argued, violated Christian doctrine and brought infamy to abolition. Most female abolitionists tended to side with Garrison, grateful for his support and his critique of the church, as clergymen were opponents of women's rights. In 1838 the NEAS convention became the first abolitionist organization to formally grant women equal voting rights, much to the dismay of the clerical abolitionists led by the Reverends Charles Torrey, Alanson St. Claire, and Phelps. Torrey and Phelps complained that the MASS had become a "woman's rights, non-government Anti-Slavery" society. From then on, Garrisonians fought to include women in their definition of *persons* participating in an antislavery organization, and their critics sought to restrict the word as applying only to men. At the AASS's annual meeting in 1839 Garrison and Smith successfully pushed for the equal participation of women in the society over the objections of the anti-Garrisonian faction led by Rev. Nathaniel Colver, Lewis Tappan, and James Birney. The meeting passed an amendment allowing women to be included in the roll call by 184 to 141 votes. Phelps tried to confine women's participation by excluding them from speaking or holding office, but his resolution was defeated. Tappan argued that while he valued "female cooperation," women should act separately. Birney presented the protest, signed by 123 delegates, against women voting or holding office in antislavery societies. When it came to female voting, Garrisonians rather than their opponents became advocates of the suffrage. Lydia Maria Child expressed surprise at some abolitionists' newfound opposition to women's equal role in antislavery societies. Despite his opposition to introducing the woman question into abolition, Birney defended Angelina against Rev. Leonard Bacon's strictures that likened her to Quaker women who allegedly ran around naked disrupting church worship in early New England. Birney's daughter-in-law wrote the first biography of the Grimké sisters.[29]

The formal division in the abolition movement came over the election of Abby Kelley to the business committee of the AASS in 1840. Garrisonians balanced nominations to the committee between the two factions, putting forward the names of Phelps, Tappan along with that of Garrison, and Kelley, the sole female nomination. Speaking in her own defense, Kelley noted, "I rise because I am not a slave." Born in a modest farming family, Kelley, a schoolteacher, was educated, like Crandall, at the Moses Brown Academy. She represented the Lynn FASS at the women's antislavery conventions. Predictably, the anti-Garrisonians led a walkout when the convention voted 557 to 451 to elect Kelley. Mott, Child, and Chapman replaced them in the business committee, sealing the women's victory. Garrison's vindication of women's voting rights had set the stage for this outcome, as female delegates voted overwhelmingly for Kelley. As Whittier put it, the AASS had "*blown up*," and Abby was the "bomb-shell that *exploded* the society." Ray nominated Hester Lane, a black woman known to purchase and free slaves. Her nomination was withdrawn: "The 'principle' could not carry her color," he wrote. But Van Rensselaer contended that Lane was opposed to female equality in antislavery societies and had allied with the AFASS. The AFASS allowed women to form separate auxiliaries but with no right to vote, hold office, or speak publicly. Some women's organizations, like the LNYCASS led by Juliana Tappan, affiliated with the new organization. Most remained Garrisonian, though many, such as the Holliston FASS in Massachusetts, favored political action.[30]

The abolitionist schism was replicated in the BFASS, where Chapman, Thankful Southwick, and Henrietta Sergeant led the Garrisonian women in passing resolutions commending the election of Kelley and vindicating their rights against the "spiritual mob." In 1839 Parker attempted to dissolve the society and instigated the formation of the Massachusetts Female Emancipation Society (MFES), allied with the new Massachusetts Abolition Society. The MFES's first address harked back to the conservative rhetoric of female benevolence. In the BFASS, religious liberals like the Unitarians and Quakers sided with the Garrisonians, and the more religiously orthodox with the new organization. The rivalry between the Weston, Southwick, and Sergeant sisters versus the evangelical Parker and Ball sisters, who controlled the BFASS offices on the eve of schism, extended back to 1837, when conservative clergymen started criticizing Garrison and the Grimké sisters. The Garrisonian women were also members of the New England Non Resistance Society. Most black women sided with the Garrisonians. An exception was the wife of Rev. Jehiel Beman of the AME Zion church, who opposed Julia Foote's preaching and was allied with the "new organization" evangelical abolitionists. The evangelical women retired from active abolitionist work, and the MFES, like the LNYCASS, withered quickly. The Garrisonian women became agents and leaders in the integrated MASS.[31]

By contrast, the PFASS remained united and staunchly Garrisonian, a model of female abolitionism. Unlike Child and Kelley, Mott felt that women's antislavery societies were necessary if integrated organizations were to be formed. As she wrote to Kelley, she was happy to see men and women "lose sight of distinctions of sex as to act in public meetings, on the enlightened and true ground of Christian equality," but there was no "better or speedier mode of preparing them for this equality" than to act in separate organizations. Though she deplored the BFASS division in her letters to Chapman, Mott identified with the Garrisonian wing and attended the first anniversary meeting of the Non-Resistance Society in 1839. The next year she got the better of an anti-abolitionist mob in Delaware, which many viewed as the practical application of nonresistance. Mott was a prominent spokeswoman of women's rights, non-resistance, and abolition. Members of the PFASS like Mott, Grew, Pugh, and Elizabeth Neall became PASS officers without any controversy, four, including Mott, were members of its executive committee, and they became leading voices in the women's rights movement. In 1853 Grew strongly opposed a proposal to dissolve the PFASS and admit men into the society. The female antislavery societies were important breeding grounds for the fight for women's equality within abolition. The PFASS disbanded in 1870 after the passage of the Fifteenth Amendment.[32]

The heyday of female antislavery societies was over after the schism. Some signaled their allegiances to the opposing abolitionist groups via their names, Garrisonian societies now using *women* rather than *female*, and those affiliated with the AFASS using *ladies* and *emancipation* in their titles, after the LNYCASS and the MFES. The strongly Garrisonian SFASS, the first female antislavery society, like the PFASS, persisted until the Civil War and was marked by the concerns of its original black members. But the dramatic growth of female antislavery societies and national antislavery women's conventions came to an abrupt end. The untimely deaths of some early pioneers such as Susan Paul, Grace Douglass, Mary Clark, and Mary Parker and the withdrawal of others like Maria Stewart and the Grimké sisters facilitated the process. The west bucked the trend: sixteen new female antislavery societies were formed there in the 1840s. Relying on a pragmatic version of abolition, western women for the most part shied clear of the ideological divisions roiling the eastern societies. Some abolitionist women retreated to more gender-appropriate organizations like antislavery sewing circles, though they raised money to finance women's rights activists such as Stone. Kelley was also a member of the Worcester Anti-Slavery Sewing Circle, and Ernst's antislavery sewing circle in Cincinnati included Garrisonians like herself as well as more moderate abolitionists. Similarly, the AFASS-affiliated Ladies Anti-Slavery Society of Dover, New Hampshire, reconstituted as the Dover Anti-Slavery Sewing Circle, circulated petitions, tracts, and calls for meetings to protest the expansion of slavery into Kansas in the 1850s. Women's abolitionism did not die out and was reignited by the fugitive slave issue, partisan politics, and eventually the fight for emancipation during the Civil War.[33]

WOMAN RIGHTS

The nineteenth-century woman rights movement, as it was called, grew out of abolition. Those abolitionist women who fought for equality, abolitionist feminists, inaugurated it. Their staging ground was the World's Antislavery Convention in London. Historians of the women's movement, who highlight the role of Elizabeth Cady Stanton, have downplayed its longer lineage among abolitionist women. In 1839 the newly formed British and Foreign ASS invited delegates to the first international convention of abolition societies the following year. Sturge sent out the call on behalf of the executive committee, better known as the London Committee, but the idea originated with the *Emancipator*. Garrisonians called it the World's Convention, popularized by Whittier in a poem bearing that title. After the formal organizational split of 1840, both factions of American abolitionists sent competing delegations to it. The AASS selected Garrison, Rogers, Charles Remond, and Mott as its delegates, vindicating its belief in "EQUAL BROTHERHOOD of the entire HUMAN FAMILY, without distinction of color, sex, or clime." The MASS sent female delegates such as Emily Winslow and Abby Southwick, and it nominated Chapman, Child, and Kelley, none of whom could make the journey, and Martineau, who did not attend because of ill health. The PASS sent its PFASS officers, Grew, Pugh, Neall, and Abby Kimber. The AFASS sent political abolitionists, including Birney and Stanton, and ministers like Colver and Rev. Elon Galusha. Birney was elected as one of the vice presidents, and Phillips, who was touring England with his wife, Ann, and Stanton were made secretaries. Garrison, Rogers, and Remond arrived when the convention was well under way.[34]

Accompanying Stanton was his wife, Elizabeth, who became the leading thinker on women's rights. Born in 1815 to a distinguished upstate New York family, she was exposed to abolition from an early age. While her Federalist father, Judge Daniel Cady, was no reformer, her mother, Margaret, was an abolitionist and signed a woman suffrage petition after the war. Educated in Willard's Troy Female Seminary, she recalled growing up at a time when "the antislavery question was up for hot discussion," and famous abolitionists lived in her neighborhood. Her cousin was Gerrit Smith, whom she visited frequently. In his Peterboro estate, where abolitionists, former slaves, and assorted reformers were recipients of Smith's largesse, she met her future husband. The newly wed Stantons visited the Grimké–Weld household. Weld recommended that she adopt the dual surname Cady Stanton. They spent their honeymoon at the world convention.

In the massive history of the woman suffrage movement, Stanton and her coauthors emphatically believed that "above all other causes of the 'Woman Suffrage Movement,' was the Anti-Slavery struggle in this country" and dated the start of their movement to the convention. This origins story should be stretched back to the black abolitionist women and female antislavery societies of the 1830s. Stanton was taken with Mott, who introduced her to the work of Wollstonecraft. Mott, she wrote, was "an entirely new revelation of womanhood" to her. In her eulogy for Mott, Stanton again recalled the importance of a "life . . . dedicated to the rights of humanity." Whether Stanton planned the first women's rights convention with Mott in London, as she recalled, or later, as historians contend, her encounter with some of the leading abolitionist feminists crystallized her commitment to women's rights. When it came to the woman question, Stanton found herself in agreement with the Garrisonians rather than the wing of the movement represented by her husband. Garrison remarked, "Mrs. Stanton is a fearless woman, and goes for woman's rights with all her soul."[35]

The World's Convention was the site of another conflict over the woman question. The London Committee, many of whose members were wary of Garrison's radicalism, was far more in sympathy with their American namesake the AFASS. Most British abolitionists, including women, wanted to avoid controversy. Sturge tried to persuade Mott and the American women not to insist on being seated, as it would hamper the convention's business. The evangelical Charles Stuart was even more hostile to female equality. Thompson, who had done so much to inspire female abolitionism, was lukewarm on the question. O'Connell was absent when the vote to seat female delegates was taken and later had to clarify to Mott that he was for women's equality. Clergymen, who composed one-fifth of the convention and included the anti-Garrisonian Rev. John Scoble, opposed seating women and invoked the theory of separate spheres. The other powerful group, orthodox, so-called aristocratic Quakers, who formed one-fourth to one-third of the convention, deplored the Hicksite Motts and joined in opposition. When the convention was over they issued a public letter disowning the Motts, which elicited a strong response from James. The London Committee refused to seat women delegates, and Lucretia's idea to hold a separate women's convention came to naught. Despite divisions, Phillips worked with Birney and Stanton to elicit British help, resolutions for dissemination of abolitionist literature, against Texas annexation, and for the right to petition, among others. After the convention, Garrison and Mott gave speeches on subjects dear to their hearts, the former on universal reform and the latter on free produce.

Garrisonians noted their debt to women. Phillips introduced the motion to seat them. He drew attention to the self-devotion of female abolitionists, who had traveled thousands of miles, leaving their families and occupations to attend and whose aid in abolition could not possibly be enlisted if their male colleagues deserted them. Col. Jonathan Miller pointed out that women in

Vermont had preceded men in the movement. In silent protest, Garrison, Rogers, Remond, William Adam, and George Bradburn joined the rejected female delegates in the galleries. Remond stated that he would not dishonor the female antislavery societies, which had paid for his trip to England. On behalf of the "American women delegates from Pennsylvania," Pugh wrote a letter protesting the decision to "exclude women from a seat in the convention as coequals in the advocacy of Universal Liberty." Some of those in opposition, like Sturge, acknowledged women's contributions but still viewed it as an extraneous issue. Phillips entered a protest, written by Adam, against the discrimination. It was tabled and not recorded in the convention minutes. Garrisonians found new British allies, the radical lawyer William Ashurst, the Quaker abolitionist Elizabeth Pease, and feminists like the physician John Bowring, who predicted, "AMERICA . . . WILL INSTRUCT ENGLAND" on women's rights. Lady Byron also sympathized with them. Pease, of the Darlington Ladies' Antislavery Society, had corresponded with Angelina. After the convention, British women breathed life into the "transatlantic sisterhood of abolitionists," raising funds for the Americans and supporting fugitive slaves. The emergence of British feminism remained behind that of its American counterpart, but a female public sphere allied with abolition helped birth the women's rights movement there too.[36]

The woman question dominated abolitionist debates. Before leaving for the convention Garrison had pointed to the fact that a woman ruled Britain and asked in what assembly "is that almost peerless woman, LUCRETIA MOTT, not qualified to take an equal part?" In a superb speech on his return, Garrison argued that women's rights was not an extraneous issue for abolitionists. "I wrong the slave," he said, "in dishonoring or casting one obstacle in the way of his female advocate." Exposing the class-based hypocrisy of Victorian gender conventions in Britain, Garrison remarked that he had seen women breaking stone in the highway, carting dung from the streets, laboring in the fields, and yet they were not allowed to participate in an antislavery convention. Rev. Charles Denison, in a long letter to Garrison in which he fondly recalled his past associations with him, regretted the division. Denison conceded that women should be allowed to vote but, he demurred, not hold office. At the tenth anniversary meeting of the AASS in 1844, he was still debating Garrison and Kelley on the propriety of women's public speaking. Phelps tried to explain away his initial support of the Grimkés, holding that women's "physical constitutions" unfit them for public life. In his reply to Colver, Garrison retorted that to claim women's rights overthrew the institution of marriage was similar to charges that abolitionists incited insurrection and murder when they argued for black rights.

Garrison and Henry C. Wright planned a world's convention of human rights to prove their point.

Abolitionists' differences over women's participation were at times a family quarrel. Stanton clarified that he had not voted to admit women into the London convention, even though Cady Stanton later claimed he had made a speech asking them to be seated. Rev. Henry Grew voted against seating women delegates at London and withdrew his subscription from the *Liberator* by the end of the year. His daughter Mary was a PFASS stalwart and suffragist. At the women's rights convention in 1854, when he objected to women speaking in public, Mott silenced him by referring to his accomplished daughter.[37]

The most important theoretical defense of women's equality at this time came from the pen of Margaret Fuller. Born in 1810, Fuller was educated by her father in the Western classics and read widely in Italian, German, and French literature after graduating from Miss Prescott's seminary. On her father's death, she taught young girls in Boston and at the transcendentalist Bronson Alcott's Temple School. By 1840 Fuller had become the editor of the transcendentalist *Dial*, an "avant garde intellectual journal." Besides Sarah Josepha Hale, the longtime editor of *Ladies' Magazine* and then *Godey's Lady's Book*, who was a colonizationist and conservative on women's rights, Fuller and abolitionists such as Chapman and Child of the NASS and Grew of the *Pennsylvania Freeman* were the first female editors. Antislavery women's rights advocates like Clarina Nichols and Jane Swisshelm soon joined them. Though not an abolitionist, Fuller admired Child and the *Liberator*, which she said was the only American newspaper with fresh insights.[38]

In the *Dial* Fuller published fellow transcendentalists and her own pieces, one of which, "The Great Lawsuit. Man *versus* Men. Woman *versus* Women.," advocating gender equality, led to her pathbreaking feminist text *Woman in the Nineteenth Century* (1845). Fuller's ideas on gender, marriage, sexuality, and women's equality were revolutionary. She was well aware of the abolitionist origins of feminism, writing, "Of all its banners, none has been more steadily upheld, and under none have more valor and willingness for real sacrifices been shown, than that of the champions of the enslaved African. And this band it is, which, partly from a natural following out of principles, partly because many women have been prominent in that cause, makes, just now, the warmest appeal in behalf of Woman." She singled out Angelina and Kelley, "women who speak in public" and who have the ability to "subdue the prejudices of their hearers." She facetiously suggested the founding of an antislavery party for women. In a letter to Chapman she also expressed dissatisfaction with the abolitionist argument for women's rights: "There is a reason why the foes of African slavery seek more freedom for women; but put it not upon that ground, but on the ground of right."

Fuller reasoned that women's equality must be raised independently on the basis of women's self-dependence, self-reliance, self-respect, and self-help. Her demand for complete equality—"We would have every path laid open to Woman as freely as to Man"—was accompanied by innovative ideas about gender and marriage. Heroic and intellectual qualities, she wrote, were just as womanly as they were manly. Rather than an androgynous notion of gender, Fuller sought to uncouple conventions of femininity and masculinity from man and woman. She argued that "there is no wholly masculine man, no purely feminine woman" and that man "partakes of the feminine" and "woman of the masculine." Her notion of marriage rejected shallow romantic "idolatory," quoting John Quincy Adams to "love and revere the female sex" and "*not to flatter them.*" Commending Child's defense of a woman who had killed her lover, Fuller rejected sexual double standards and the notion of female and male sexuality as inherently distinct. It is a "vulgar error" to think "a love" is a woman's "whole existence," she wrote, even though her own life was marked by passionate love affairs. Fuller is often critiqued for only highlighting women's inequality, but she called for a gendered solidarity: "Women are the best helpers of one another. Let them think; let them act; till they know what they need." She was known for her famous "Conversations" for women on various subjects. The abolitionists Child, Louisa Gilman Loring, the wife of Ellis Loring, and Ann Phillips as well as Cady Stanton attended sessions that "nurtured" women's "autonomous intellectual tradition." They set an early precedent for women's conventions and clubs. The author of three books, a memoir, and several articles, Fuller thought of *Woman in the Nineteenth Century* as her life's "foot-print" on earth. The authors of the history of woman suffrage, in search of foremothers, anointed Fuller a harbinger of the women's rights movement.[39]

As a critic for the *New York Tribune*, Fuller moved closer to abolitionist and labor concerns. Her many reviews praising abolitionist writings, particularly Frederick Douglass's narrative, popularized them for larger audiences. Repeatedly, she asserted that black works proved "their *claims* need no argument." In her most forthrightly antiracist piece in support of black suffrage, "What fits a man to be Voter? Is it to be White within, or White without?" she did for race what she had done for gender. Beginning with an allegorical story of a woman and a black man, Mary and Jesus, sent to enlighten their dimwitted countrymen, it ends with a critique of racism as learned but unjust behavior. In her review of Charles Burdett's *The Wrongs of American Woman*, Fuller took issue with the notion of a "hallowed domestic sphere" that ignored the sufferings and difficulties of laboring women. Her articles addressed the plight of the working poor, prostitutes, and criminals. Like Child at the *NASS*, she drew attention to class inequality and urban poverty.[40]

Fuller's cosmopolitan life illustrated the intertwining of international and domestic radicalism. Utopian socialists such as Robert Owen, Charles Fourier, and Henri de Saint-Simon were early champions of women's equality and influenced not only Fuller but also European feminists, Jeanne Deroin in France, Catherine Barmby in England, and Louise Otto in Germany. With the prominent exception of the anarchist journalist Pierre-Joseph Proudhon, European radicals championed women's rights. Fuller's departure for Europe in 1846 and her marriage to Giovanni Ossoli put her in the thick of the Italian Risorgimento and the revolutions of 1848. Confessing her conversion to socialism and "red republicanism," Fuller wrote partisan dispatches on the revolutions. Representatives of the "first international women's movement" created by the revolutions, including the Jewish feminist Ernestine Rose and the German abolitionist feminist Mathilde Anneke, joined the American women's movement. Anneke formed a close partnership with the wife of the abolitionist Sherman Booth, Mary Booth. The polyglot Rose, who had lived in Germany and France, corresponded with Deroin and translated Anneke. After the fall of the Roman republic, Fuller sailed back with her husband and young son in 1850, only to drown in a shipwreck within sight of the American shore.[41] Viewed from a transnational perspective, women's rights was part of a wave of international radicalism.

In 1848, the year Karl Marx and Friedrich Engels published *The Communist Manifesto*, a group of abolitionist women and men issued the first declaration of women's rights at Seneca Falls, New York. Rather than a singular event, a synergy of international, national, and local activism led to that founding moment. Local campaigns for women's legal and marital rights jump-started the women's movement. In New York the struggle over women's property rights, begun in 1836, had involved activists like Rose, who addressed the legislature five times, and Stanton, who briefly lobbied for it. Assemblyman Thomas Hertell's speech vindicating married women's property rights as a matter of equal rights was widely disseminated in 1839. Petitions supporting women's property rights, and one by six women from Jefferson County demanding political and civil rights, including the right to vote, to the state constitutional convention preceded Seneca Falls. Hertell sponsored New York's Married Women's Property Rights Act of 1848, which became a model for other northern states and some southern states that passed similar laws to protect property from creditors.

Grew circulated petitions for women's property rights, and Pennsylvania passed a married women's property law the same year.

Not just women's legal rights but advocacy of their marital and sexual rights came to the fore. Marriage reformers built on the work of the Female Moral Reform societies that challenged the sexual double standard and illicit male behavior. In 1843 the Maine Quaker reformer John Neal published his stinging critique of the supposed privileges of women, which anticipated demands for women's equality in all spheres of life, public and private. According to the women's rights activist Paulina Wright Davis, it was "extensively copied" and reviewed. Mary Gove, who escaped her abusive husband, lectured on female physiology and sexuality. Together with her second husband, Thomas Nichols, she became an advocate for sexual reform. Similarly, Clarina Howard Nichols, whose eloquent editorials helped secure the passage of the married women's property act in Vermont in 1847, struggled to secure a divorce and recover her children from her first husband. The Garrisonian Francis Jackson became a benefactor of women's rights after his daughter was involved in a lengthy custody case with her estranged husband. Henry C. Wright was a leading spokesman not just for children's rights but also for marriage reform. The fight for women's marital rights allowed opponents to tar abolitionist feminists with accusations of free love.[42]

Abolition laid the groundwork for the women's rights movement in upstate New York. It was long the site of Quaker and abolitionist activism, represented by the Hunt, McClintock, Wright, Post, and Hallowell families. Members of the Liberty Party, whose stronghold was in central and western New York, presented petitions for equal property rights. May recalled how the Grimké sisters had "dispelled my Pauline prejudice" against women speaking in public. He delivered a sermon, "The Rights and Condition of Woman," that, when published in 1846, became a staple of tracts distributed by the women's rights convention. May rejected the separate spheres theory and asked that women's rights be "recognized as equal [in] every way." He aided struggling needlewomen in Syracuse in forming a Sewing Protection Society, combining his advocacy of the rights of labor and of women, and opened his pulpit to former slaves as well as to women's rights advocates. During her lecture tour that led to the formation of the Western New York Anti Slavery Society (WNYAS) in 1842, Kelley braved vicious misogynistic crowds and slander. After bruising meetings in Connecticut and Rhode Island, she took upstate New York by storm during the MASS's "one hundred conventions" campaign. Garrison, Douglass, and Stephen Foster lectured with her. On her appointment as the general agent of the AASS, one abolitionist grumbled at the "gynecrocy" of Chapman and Kelley. The indefatigable Kelley inspired Wright Davis and those who had to brave the wrath of their ministers to hear her. One of them, Rhoda Bement, ended up in Seneca Falls. The notion that black women were absent in the early stirrings on women's rights is false. M. E. Mills of Albany wrote to Smith in 1846, "The colored woman who would elevate herself must contend not only with prejudice against poverty [and] prejudice against color but prejudice against her sex. Which of these is most cruel I am not prepared to say. But that all three combined are enough to crush a Lion I am prepared to testify."[43]

When Stanton moved to Seneca Falls in 1847 she tapped into these strains of activism to articulate a distinct vision for women's equality. A fellow traveler rather than an abolitionist, she became the leading spokeswoman for women's rights by deploying abolitionist networks. Fortuitously, at this time Douglass relocated to Rochester and began publishing the *North Star* with its feminist abolitionist motto, "Right is of no Sex—Truth is of no Color—God is the father of us all, and we are all brethren." Stanton had met Douglass in Boston, where she attended meetings of abolitionists and socialized with them. She, Mott, who was visiting her sister Marcia Coffin Wright, and Mary Ann McClintock issued the call for the first women's rights convention at the home of Jane Hunt. All were Quaker women active in abolition. Douglass attended the historic meeting of nearly three hundred in July 1848 and backed Stanton's controversial call for women's right to vote, which even Mott thought would make the convention seem ridiculous. Douglass praised the "brilliant talents and excellent dispositions" of the women and gave a full-throated endorsement of female equality. As Stanton recalled, even though they were subject to widespread censure, the abolitionist press stood "manfully" behind them. James Mott, the longtime president of the PASS, presided. Other abolitionists and sympathizers, Thomas McClintock, Samuel Tillman, Ansel Bascom, Isaac and Amy Post, a founder of the WNYASS, attended. Mott gave the opening address, followed by Stanton, Wright, Elizabeth and Mary Ann McClintock, who also recorded the minutes.

Stanton, assisted by Elizabeth McClintock, formulated its founding document, the Declaration of Sentiments, modeled after the Declaration of Independence. Despite her contention that she rejected the antislavery model, Stanton used the title of Garrison's AASS declaration, evoked abolitionist tactics in calling for agents, tracts, petitions, conventions, and words: the "immediate admission" of women to all the rights and privileges denied to them and enlisting "the pulpit and the press" on behalf of women's rights. In their history of woman suffrage, Stanton, Anthony, and Matilda Gage not only pointed to abolition as a source of their activism but also dedicated their volumes to the outstanding women who had fought for gender equality, including Wollstone-craft, Wright, Mott, Martineau, the Grimké sisters, Child, Fuller, and Wright Davis, among others. The dedication was not just a construction of a tradition but also an accurate genealogy of early feminist thought. Nothing illustrated Stanton's polemical powers better than her declaration. While paraphrasing Jefferson, she drew on the long history of women's protest writing: "The history of mankind is a history of repeated injuries and usurpations on the part of man toward woman, having in direct object the establishment of an absolute tyranny over her." Her rejection of separate spheres and demand for education, politi-cal and civil rights, and social and economic equality conjured earlier feminist protest. Sixty-eight women and thirty-two men signed it. The use of a revolu-tionary framework in Stanton's declaration was a stroke of political genius, but feminism rather than republicanism gave it its theoretical heft and met the ideological needs of the new women's rights movement.[44]

A month later Stanton and Elizabeth McClintock attended a smaller con-vention at Rochester, where the Posts presided over an interracial reform com-munity committed to peace, the rights of women, Native Americans, working men and women, and the abolition of slavery and capital punishment. Roch-ester was also home to the Anthony family, and Susan B. Anthony's parents and sister attended the convention and signed the Seneca Falls Declaration, preceding her in the cause she came to personify. Garrison's former apprentice William C. Nell, the son of William G. Nell, a founding member of the GCA, who was helping Douglass edit his newspaper, earned a rebuke from Mott for flattering women as superior beings. Unapologetic in its demand for political rights, the convention elected a woman, Abigail Bush, to preside over its pro-ceedings and included Stanton's demand for just wages for domestic servants. While relying on the natural rights theory of Jean-Jacques Rousseau for its Dec-laration of Rights, Sarah Owen criticized him for excluding women from its purview. Like abolitionists, these women did not simply invoke revolutionary ideas, they reformulated them. The convention reprinted Chapman's poem composed in response to the Grimké ministerial critics, "The Times that Try Men's Souls."[45]

Women's rights activists responded to their critics after the conventions. Stanton and McClintock wrote a letter to those clergymen who based female subordination on the Bible, pointing out that it had also been used to defend slavery and war. In her first recorded speech on women's rights, Stanton gave a spirited defense of the new movement. Though laced with a sliver of elitism that grew after the war (she resented "ignorant foreigners," idiots, rowdies, and "silly boys" being given the vote before women), like Child and Fuller, she reached back in history and across nations for examples of heroic women, from Joan of Arc to Zenobia. A new era was dawning, she predicted, when woman "will stand redeemed regenerated and disenthralled." In 1849 Mott's answer to Richard Henry Dana's address, which criticized the women's movement for going against women's alleged nature, was widely distributed as her "Discourse on Woman." Adulation of women made them a "plaything or toy of society" and cultivated a "kind of effeminacy." Nature had made women physically different, she said, but "neglect and mismanagement increased this difference." She called for developing women's physical, moral, and intellectual capacities by "suitable exercise" and "by reason of use." Mott repeated the feminist demands, equality in education, marriage, political and civil rights, work, and wages.[46]

Abolition was the midwife of women's activism and helped it grow organizationally in the 1850s. In conventions, women's rights activists charted their own course but often in close collaboration with abolitionist and temperance movements, as many of them lent their energies to both causes. Anthony was a temperance activist before she became an abolitionist. Another temperance advocate, Amelia Bloomer, who started publishing the women's rights magazine the *Lily* in 1849, popularized the pantaloons invented by Gerrit Smith's daughter, Elizabeth Smith Miller. On the eve of the Civil War, some of the leading champions of women's rights, like Lucy Stone, were abolitionists. An Oberlin graduate and popular agent for the MASS, Stone resolved to lecture for abolition during the week and for women's rights during the weekends. With good reason slaveholders linked the dreaded *-isms* of their day, socialism, feminism, and abolitionism. Controversy after the war over the Reconstruction amendments that introduced the word *male* into the Constitution and restricted voting to men tested that alliance. A divided women's movement took a longer time to achieve its goals in a conservative political environment not fertilized by abolitionist radicalism and antislavery politics. In losing its moorings in abolition, the American women's movement lost its antebellum commitment to racial equality. Some things were gained, but much was lost.[47]

THE BLACK MAN'S BURDEN

In its inaugural editorial in 1837 the black abolitionist newspaper *Weekly Advocate* promoted "Universal Suffrages and Universal Education," and promised that "we shall oppose all Monopolies, which oppress the Poor and laboring classes of society." Black abolitionism was not imitative, elitist, or a failure hobbled by racism. It was broad in conception. Moral reform and racial uplift were constitutive of rather than an alternative to the politics of resistance. Black abolitionists did not simply deploy bourgeois values, prove black worthiness in white eyes, and stigmatize the working poor; they also developed complementary strategies to challenge slavery and community-wide problems of racism and poverty that cut across class lines. Nor did their efforts lie outside the abolition movement, as a recent historian has proposed; in fact, they came to define its agenda.[1]

Despite the rise of interracial immediatism, the fight against racial proscription gave black abolitionism a distinctive character. African Americans pioneered a theoretical critique of the pseudoscience of race and confronted the growth of legal and popular racial discrimination. Their struggle against disfranchisement, segregation, and racial violence is often forgotten in the history of abolition. The black fight for equal rights, however, did not mean acquiescence to racist conditions at home. Emigration remained an integral part of black abolitionism. Critiquing and perfecting American democracy was the black man's burden.

INSTITUTIONS

Black abolitionists transcended modern ideological boxes of integration and separation, uplift and activism, and laid the foundation of a distinct protest tradition that encompassed all of these strategies. The convention movement marked the independent organization of black abolitionism. Black abolitionists dominated their proceedings. Calls for the national conventions put out by Junius Morel, a former slave and abolitionist, regularly appeared in the *Liberator*.[2] The successors to the conventions of 1830 and 1831 established the contours of antebellum black abolitionism.

The national conventions were not staid gatherings of self-appointed leaders but sites of protest. The convention of 1832, held in Philadelphia, was attended by twenty-nine delegates from eight states and included for the first time delegates from New England. Presided over by veteran black abolitionists like Henry Sipkins and John Vashon, it hosted a debate between Rev. R. R. Gurley and Rev. Robert Breckinridge of the ACS and abolitionists like Garrison, Shipley, Evan Lewis, Vashon, and Morel. The business committee expressed qualified approval for Canadian emigration but strong disapproval of colonization, which had "raised the tide of our calamity." It suggested concentrating resources to improve conditions at home and condemned racist opposition to black education. Its address to the free people of color censured slavery, colonization, and intemperance, tying their struggle as an "*oppressed people*" to gain citizenship to "personal and mental elevation."

Whatever rivalries separated the large Pennsylvania and New York contingents to the conventions, there was no dispute over the simultaneous promotion of moral reform and political rights. Despite William Hamilton's attempt to move the convention to New York, it met again in Benezet Hall in Philadelphia in 1833. Nearly sixty delegates from all the northern states and border slave states attended. Resolutions presented by Ruggles and Purvis voiced support for abolition. The same year, a local convention in New York City led by Thomas Jennings demanded immediate emancipation and black rights. The committee on temperance, headed by Pennington, created the Colored American Conventional Temperance Society (CACTS), which developed twenty-three branches in eighteen cities, though the first black temperance societies were formed as early as 1829. Pennington was also the secretary of the Brooklyn Temperance Society, founded in 1830. Whipper headed the committee that wrote the CACTS's constitution. It promoted temperance as part of the struggle against those "who are forever prating about . . . *African inferiority.*" The convention's reports again condemned colonization but praised Canadian emigration as a way to escape laws that "would have been a disgrace to the most barbarous nations of antiquity." Its address, by Shadd as the president, seamlessly linked the black struggles against "slavery, ignorance, and misery."[3]

The next year the convention finally met in New York. In his presidential address Hamilton drew attention to the "demon of prejudice and persecution" that "beset the path" of black people. He connected the fight against "tyranny, cruelty, prejudice and slavery" with improvement and reformation. It was important for black people to "closely attend to their own particular interest," he said, even as he recommended cooperating with the new antislavery societies. Elizur Wright and Arthur Tappan addressed the convention. Resolutions decried the systematic economic discrimination faced by "colored workmen" from both journeymen mechanics, who refused to work alongside them or include them in their guilds, and master craftsmen, who refused to hire them. The convention stepped up its organization, forming a new constitution and regularizing the election of delegates from state and local organizations. Its Declaration of Sentiment, addressed to all citizens, issued a telling indictment: "That we find ourselves, after the lapse of three centuries, on the American continent, the remnants of a nation amounting to three millions of people, whose country has been pillaged, parents stolen, nine generations of which have been wasted by the oppressive cruelty of this nation." Theirs was a revolution against "*American slavery* and *American prejudice.*" The Colored Anti-Slavery Society of Newark proclaimed, "It is our opinion, that if all the blood of our colored brethren, shed by the people of the United States, since the Declaration of Independence, was kept in a reservoir, the framers of that instrument, and their successors might swim in it."[4]

The last national convention of the decade met in Philadelphia in 1835 and gave birth to a new organization, the American Moral Reform Society (AMRS). Often portrayed as having hijacked the convention movement, it did not abandon activism for moral reform. The AMRS evoked a higher allegiance to human rights and called for a struggle against racial discrimination. It also called for the training and hiring of black mechanics and supported an independent black press. Buffum, Shipley, and Edwin Atlee addressed this convention. Though the convention called for a meeting in New York the next year, the AMRS supplanted it. While Forten, Purvis, and Whipper were associated with the formation of the AMRS, others like Shadd, Cornish, Watkins, and Lewis Woodson of Pittsburgh were its delegates, agents, and officers. The convention's address to the American people and the AMRS identified racism as an acute moral failing of the nation. It put forward education, temperance, economy, and universal liberty "as principles of moral reform" and the "destruction of all vice universally." As its constitution put it ambitiously, they sought "the successful resuscitation of our country from moral degeneracy." The problem lay not with blacks but with white racism. The convention also called for political action and endorsed the abolitionist petition campaign against slavery in the District of Columbia and federal territories.[5]

The creation of the AMRS coincided with the antebellum flowering of black civic culture. In his sketch of the black community in Philadelphia, Joseph Willson used statistics compiled by the AMRS to showcase the city's black literary and fraternal societies. The black abolitionist adoption of moral reform was neither a naïve blame-the-victim strategy nor simply imitative of the dominant culture of benevolent reform. It had deep roots in the community-building efforts of northern free blacks and their abolitionist allies. Access to schools, trades, professions, and public facilities represented community-wide concerns. At the convention in 1833 Hamilton had recommended the formation of Phoenix societies after New York's Phoenix Society, known for its educational activism. Literary societies, such as Philadelphia's Library Company of Colored Persons and New York's Philomathean Society, and, later, the Adelphic Union in Boston and the Banneker Literary Institute in Philadelphia, became springboards of racial activism. Black autonomy symbolized in churches, societies, and fraternal associations like black Masonry did not abate but provoked severe racism, which periodically degenerated from lampooning in broadsides and the penny press to violence. The civic activism of black Philadelphia's "higher classes," which included former slaves, master chimney sweeps, "hog drivers," and porters, benefited the entire community. Willson, himself a former slave from Georgia, spent considerable time demonstrating their worthiness because, with a handful of exceptions, they barely qualified as middle class. Class, as a category, takes on a whole new meaning in the context of a largely impoverished, severely proscribed northern black population. Leading abolitionists such as Pennington and Ruggles suffered debilitating poverty. Nor did cultural elitism characterize these men, whose aspirations found an outlet in racial activism.[6]

Black abolitionists made compelling analogies between slavery, ignorance, and vice on the one hand, and freedom, literacy, and virtue on the other. In his speech of 1834 to the Colored Temperance Society, Whipper condemned the "national cruelties" of slaveholding countries that oppress the enslaved physically, morally, and intellectually. He noted that only blacks suffered the ravages of slavery, yet they were "not more intemperate than the whites." Quoting Clarkson, he alluded to the "murderous effects" of alcohol on their "mother country" and "its excruciating effects on upwards of two millions of our brethren in this our native land." His speech was no bland, bourgeois reformism but used abolitionist appeals to enlist support for temperance. Whipper did not attend the Pennsylvania temperance convention, being well aware of its racial exclusivity and conservative politics. At the first meeting of the AMRS in Philadelphia in 1836, Watkins, one of the vice presidents, also cast ignorance with racism. Learning should not be characterized by mere "scientific and literary" attainment, he said, it should eschew all bigotry. He coauthored an AMRS address to the colored churches urging greater activism and the boycott of goods produced by slave labor.[7]

The AMRS acted as a national black abolitionist organization and met annually until 1841. At the meeting in 1837 the society's endorsement of education was coupled with resolutions thanking Adams for his championing of abolitionist petitions, abolitionist women laboring in the cause of "Universal Freedom," Thompson, and Lundy; in addition, there was a resolution against the admission of Texas. A competing Association for Moral and Mental Improvement in Philadelphia, founded in 1839, also devoted itself to promoting education and abolition. Unlike its white counterpart, which included a few evangelical abolitionists, the AMRS admitted women. The white AMRS stressed religious infidelity, but the black AMRS deployed moral reform in the fight against slavery and racial discrimination. John F. Cook dwelled on the four principles of the latter organization, changing the last from "universal liberty" to "universal love" in order to include the struggle against racism. The black abolitionist rhetoric of reform claimed moral superiority over blacks' oppressors. In his address to the society, James Forten Jr., the namesake and son of the black abolitionist, stated that its foremost aims were "to palsy the Herculean arm of prejudice" and advance education. As the secretary of the AMRS, a regular contributor to the *Liberator*, and a member of the Young Men's Antislavery Association, the younger Forten was an abolitionist in his own right. In a speech before the PFASS, he defended abolitionist women from attacks by southern congressmen.[8]

The AMRS's Whipper soon came under severe criticism from Cornish, Watkins, Woodson, and the former slave and abolitionist Frederick Hinton. They opposed Whipper not because of his advocacy of moral reform, an idea they too endorsed, but because of his theoretical and, in their opinion, impractical critique of the idea of race. On Whipper's suggestion, the national convention in 1835 rejected the use of *colored* and *African* to designate themselves and their institutions after an "animated and interesting discussion." The so-called naming controversy symbolized a debate over larger issues. Whipper's attempt to abolish the myth of race, or "racecraft," broke on the shoals of the black tradition of protest. Unable to chart a middle course between rejection of all forms of racism and an identity based on racial oppression, Whipper demanded the rejection of racial monikers and the theoretical rejection of racially exclusive organizations. Practically, he knew that the AMRS was an all-black body whose sole white delegate was Leavitt. Unlike Purvis and Forten, Whipper ironically was not active in interracial antislavery societies. He remained in black abolitionist organizations, a participant in the UGRR and the revived national conventions, and became an advocate of Canadian emigration.[9]

The debate between Whipper and his critics received full exposure with the reemergence of a black newspaper after a hiatus of ten years. Devoted to the "moral and political interests of our people," the independent black press was another site for the maturation of black abolitionism. In a message to prospective subscribers, the *Weekly Advocate*, renamed the *Colored American* (CA) in March 1837, made "IMMEDIATE EMANCIPATION" its guiding principle. Founded by Philip Bell, the paper offered abolitionist content that included antislavery poems and articles on the slave trade and on the "galling chains of prejudice." By the end of 1837 it had over a thousand subscribers, and by 1838 the number had doubled. Black antislavery societies such as the Pittsburgh Juvenile Anti-Slavery Society, led by George Boyer Vashon, the son of John Vashon, and David Peck, sent donations to sustain it. Though dependent almost entirely on black subscribers, it called for "whole souled abolitionists" to contribute to it financially. Cornish took over the editorship of the paper, Bell became its proprietor and agent, and for much of its life a committee of New York abolitionists, including Bell, Cornish, Wright, and Ray, published it. Justifying the name change, Cornish claimed the name "American" from "those who would rob us of our nationality and reproach us as exoticks," and, in a reproach to Whipper, "But why colored? some have said; why draw this cord of cast[e]?—because the peculiarity of our circumstances require[s] special instrumentalities and action." Sending a five-dollar donation from Rochester, Steward wrote that the newspaper would "pull down the strong holds of tyranny and oppression."

The CA became the national voice of black abolitionism. In an appeal for backing, Ray noted, "This is the only weekly paper published in this country, entirely under the management and control of colored men; and we know of but one other in the world," referring to a newspaper in Jamaica. Seeing itself as part of a larger, transnational movement, the paper warned, "Let slaveholders think of St Domingo and tremble." It also urged African Americans to continue supporting the *Liberator*, "the GREAT ENGINE of the colored man's liberty, and of the colored man's rights." In its fifth annual report, the AAAS recommended the CA as "efficient and useful . . . in the cause of human rights" and called for abolitionists to patronize it. The AASS and the *Liberator* solicited subscriptions for it. Ray collected forty dollars for the newspaper at a single meeting of the NYASS. Born in Massachusetts and educated in the Wesleyan Academy at Wilbraham, Ray was a reporter and agent who took over as editor in 1839.[10]

The failure of the AMRS to endorse the CA as its official organ, even though it commended the paper as a "valuable acquisition to our cause," irked Cornish. That honor went to the local abolitionist paper, Lundy's *National Enquirer*, founded in 1836 in Philadelphia. Cornish dismissed the AMRS for being "visionary in the extreme." He criticized its refusal to devote itself exclusively to black people and its "BOMBASTIC, HUMBUG EFFORTS" to redeem the whole country. For Hinton, too, the AMRS's refusal to adopt racial identification crippled its effectiveness. Whipper defended the AMRS on principle: "Now, what is it that deprives us of the benefit of institutions of learning—churches—the social circles—schools—the mechanic arts—elective franchise—the privileges and protection of government—the favor of just and equitable laws—trial by jury—mercantile employments—riding in stages and steamboats on a footing with 'white people,' but that odious distinction in language, principle, and practice, that confers the boon of favor on those that are known by the distinctive appellation of 'white people.'"

Whipper's theoretical objections to racial identification made no sense to most black abolitionists. Morel was in favor of "retaining the term 'Colored Man,'" as, he wrote, it carried no "inherent degradation." He argued that, like Quakers, black people should appropriate designations meant to denigrate them and make them a source of pride. Cornish protested that the "good sense of our brethren in Philadelphia has forsaken them" when they suggested *Oppressed American* as a substitute for *Colored American*. Or as Philos put it, no organization or newspaper working for the uplift of black people should be "VAGUELY" styled. In his Augustine letters Woodson wrote that since black people had been enslaved as a "distinct class" they should organize as such. Born a slave in Virginia, Woodson first moved to Ohio and then to Pittsburgh, where he became a minister, schoolteacher, and mentor to Martin Delany. Often seen as the original "father of black nationalism," Woodson differed with Whipper on black organizations and with Cornish on emigration. But Woodson shared their commitment to "moral elevation" and called for the support of Sabbath schools. The Cranberry auxiliary of the AMRS fully concurred with Augustine. Woodson's letters were published under the heading "Moral Work for Colored Men." When Peter Paul Simons, a black porter, in a speech to the African Clarkson Association in 1839, repudiated "MORAL ELEVATION" in favor of physical and political activism, Cornish refused to publish his speech except as a paid advertisement.[11]

Cornish aired his and other black abolitionists' differences with Whipper in a respectful manner, loath to make it a source of ongoing conflict. While he felt that the venerable Forten should step down as president of the AMRS, Cornish could not help but praise Whipper's and Forten Jr.'s speeches as evidence of the "talents of colored men." He reprinted in full Whipper's speech on nonresistance. Perhaps Cornish appreciated Whipper's classic antiracist argument that those responsible for brutish treatment of other human beings were closer to an animal state than their victims. Responding to the racist discourse on black criminality, Whipper argued that crime and violent punishment of it by the state fed off each other. The CA gave brief but favorable reports on the proceedings of the AMRS, praising its conduct, inclusion of women, and a few of its resolutions but characterizing others as unsound. It welcomed Whipper's decision to start publishing a new paper for the society. Morel expressed fears that starting a newspaper might endanger the CA and stressed the importance of racial unity. Whipper dissented, calling for the necessity of debate, "free discussion," and even controversy among African Americans.[12]

Whipper's theoretically logical yet practically ineffective effort to get rid of all racial categories and champion universal reform received a full airing in his short-lived newspaper the *National Reformer*, published from 1838 to 1839. He reiterated that "in our reciprocal duties to each other, we should never be guided by national or complexional preferences" and that "the highest impulse of human duty ought to be exerted in aid of the oppressed." He observed that his philosophy was consistent with the African American fight against invidious racial distinctions, as in the attempt to introduce the word *white* into Pennsylvania's state constitution and disfranchise all black voters. He professed even that his nonracialism challenged colorism within the black community, in which too often fair skin and European features were admired and whites were seen as the human norm. Racism, he wrote, had *"dethroned the dignity of our human nature. The evil is so deeply buried . . . that our anti-slavery societies cannot penetrate it. Legislation cannot reach it."* He published the new prospectus of the CA for 1839 but still objected to calling it a colored paper. Whipper also published Watkins's critique of his ideas. Watkins's parable of a drowning white man and black man, the former gaining the sympathy of many and the latter of none, forcefully made the case for racially conscious activism. In the last issue of his paper, Whipper renounced all "COMPLEXIONAL ALLEGIANCE" but was apologetic: "We take no pleasure in giving offence." The fight for racial equality was dependent on "the improvement of the white man's heart, not the colored man's mind." Black people should simply present their "certificates of our BIRTH and NATIVITY" to obtain their rights.

Whipper appealed to the New York abolitionists to attend the annual AMRS meetings. Its board of managers admitted that "little has been done to advance the great principles of our Society." The most active auxiliaries to the AMRS were based in Philadelphia and within Pennsylvania. By 1841 it had ceased to exist. Its nonracial philosophy simply did not appeal to the racially proud traditions of black protest. Moral reform and temperance, however, continued to be popular among all black abolitionists. In Cincinnati, members of the Colored Education Society formed a local moral reform society devoted to the "entire extinction of slavery, oppression, and ignorance in every quarter of the land." In Connecticut, Pennington, James Mars, and Rev. Amos Beman led a statewide temperance and moral reform convention in 1840, which Wright and Ray attended. The black state temperance societies coalesced into the States Delavan Union Temperance Society of Colored People in 1842. Like moral reform groups, black temperance societies linked their cause to that of abolition.[13]

Calls for revival of the convention movement eclipsed Whipper's crusade against racial essentialism. In 1837 Hamilton proposed a national convention addressing those involved in the early conventions. Woodson also recommended the revival of the national conventions. Pennington wrote a series of proconvention letters as the Long Island Scribe. Cornish too favored the renewal of black conventions. In 1841, writing as Sidney (this was probably Garnet since Sidney had died in 1840), Garnet challenged Whipper's color-blind abolitionism in a series of letters and defended a black state convention that met in Albany. In his second letter Sydney (same as Sidney) replied that the "combined efforts of the oppressed" were the only answer to racism. Arguing for the natural connection between free blacks and slaves, he contended, *"They* [white abolitionists] are our allies—OURS is the battle." In his last letter Sidney gave an unapologetic defense of the word *colored*, arguing once again, "We sustain relations to our own people, so peculiar that white men cannot assume them." Garnet led the revival of the convention movement in the 1840s.[14] Most black abolitionists endorsed the idea of a racially conscious activism. Independent institutions had proven to be the breeding ground of black abolitionism.

INTELLECT

In developing an intellectual response to racism, black print culture constituted a genuine counterpublic. A CA editorial pointed out that "we are the first people ever oppressed by a christian nation, for their PHYSICAL CONFORMATION." It published a multi-issue exposé, "Prejudice in the Church," decrying the segregated "negro pews." Racist conduct, Cornish agreed, "in the cruel and

ungodly manner in which it is done in this Republic, would disgrace the barbarous ages and the savage tribes." The "American aristocracy of skin" was just
as cruel, irrational, and arbitrary as European aristocracies. In an appeal for the
newspaper, Ray admonished that as far as racism was concerned, "Here, at least,
our white friends will allow they may learn from us." The newspaper argued that
"the real battle ground between liberty and slavery is prejudice against color.
. . . The friends of humanity have as yet but possessed a few out-posts upon its
frontiers. They have not yet undisputed possession of the field, even in their
own hearts." At the same time, it approvingly quoted an abolitionist newspaper
that castigated "colorphobia" as the "national insanity." Woodson delineated
the kinds of prejudice, from partiality to one's family and ethnocentrism or "*national prejudice*" to "*prejudice of caste*," which he condemned as springing from
"that proud and sinful desire in our nature, for exaltation and dominion over
our fellows." Henry Scott of Worcester complained that "notwithstanding your
boast of your free institutions, you at the same time grind the colored people
in the dust, by destroying their spirit of self respect and independence—and by
degrading them by your haughty and unjust regulations."[15]

Black abolitionists produced the first full-blown analyses of American racism.
In 1834 the national convention, to combat racial prejudice, sponsored the writing of a true history of black people by the abolitionist Charles Denison. In 1837
Rev. Hosea Easton, whose father, James Easton, had participated in the conventions, published a treatise on racism, signing off as A Colored Man. Ranging
over biblical, ancient, and medieval history, Easton contended that Egypt and
Africa were the birthplace of civilization and Europeans were the historical and
cultural descendants of barbarians. It is remarkable, he wrote, that these "barbarous people," "staining their route with blood" across the Atlantic, professed
intellectual and religious superiority. Disputing modern philosophers of the
"negro character" who compared African Americans to "ourang outangs," he
argued that slavery, not any "original hereditary cause," was the determinant of
racism. The malignant nature of popular racism had secreted into the "very vi-
tals of the colored population." It was "slavery in disguise . . . the very essence of
hell." Easton exposed the perniciousness of racism by repeating grotesque racist
language in describing black bodies. He disputed the emerging pseudoscience
of race, writing, "Analyze a black man, or anatomize him, and the result of the
research is the same as analyzing or anatomizing a white man." Easton was the
pastor of the Talcott Street Congregational Church in Hartford. Mobs attacked
his congregants and burned his church down in 1836, and he spent the last year
of his life collecting money to rebuild it. Garrison and Knapp published his
book and a long eulogy on him.[16]

Robert Benjamin Lewis's history of the "colored and Indian race" was printed a year earlier than Easton's book and republished in 1844 by a Boston committee of "colored gentlemen" led by Thomas Dalton, the former president of the GCA. The printer was Benjamin F. Roberts, the son of Robert Roberts. In the introduction Lewis was identified as the "descendant of the two races he so ably vindicates." His seemingly chauvinistic history claimed not just Egypt but also, by association, nearly all the important figures and discoveries of antiquity for Africa. Treating the Bible as a historical text, he invoked historical truth as a refutation of modern racism. Lewis posited an etymological explanation for racism. The word *negro* he traced to the Moors, who used *niger* to "designate any inferior object or animal." Europeans had adopted it "in order to oppress and degrade us as a people." Especially drawn to linguistic explanations, he pointed to African and Indian languages as evidence that both groups were "descendants of Israel." Lewis ended his book with the speech of an Indian chief, who recounts European rapacity in the New World. In the second edition of his book, perhaps at the prompting of his sponsors, he added a chapter called "Modern Eminent Colored Men," which included the founding of an "independent government, administered by a *colored* people" in Haiti. A peculiar postscript on color gradations among African Americans and Indians called for racial unity: "We are all one, and oppressed in this land of boasted Liberty and Freedom."[17]

So-called racial science, with its notions of biological racial inferiority and polygenesis, or the multiple origins of alleged human races, was a handmaiden of the proslavery argument. The American faux science of race gained popular and scholarly currency in the works of scientific racists such as the craniologist Samuel Morton of Philadelphia and, later, his followers the English Egyptologist George Gliddon, the physicians Josiah Nott of Alabama and Samuel Cartwright of Louisiana, and the Swiss naturalist Louis Agassiz, the president of Harvard University. Pennington published an extended response to the new racial pseudoscience in 1841. An escaped slave from Maryland, he settled in Brooklyn and taught in a black school in Long Island. He was an early participant in the convention movement and regularly advocated black education in the CA. Pennington audited theology classes at Yale—he was not allowed to enroll—became an ordained Presbyterian clergyman, and took over the Talcott Street church on Easton's death. He sought to write a history of black people that would cultivate a "right state of feeling on the total subject of HUMAN RIGHTS."

Using the Bible as his touchstone, he refuted the purported scientific theories of race on the premise that the *"notion of [racial] inferiority is not only false but absurd and therefore ought to be abandoned."* He challenged the idea that "there is an *inferior order of intellect, and that those of this order are radically and constitutionally inferior, so that no means can change that constitution or raise them from that order.*" He argued that "*intellect is identical in all human beings*" and is "the great distinguishing point between man and brute creation." It was a God-given gift to human beings, and it was both inconceivable and blasphemous to contend that there were diverse, inferior orders of intellect in humans. Pennington gave Jefferson the benefit of the doubt that he had denied to black slaves, writing that the Virginian had "plainly discovered to the world the adverse influence of slavery on his great mind." In a small chapter on race, Pennington reasoned that difference of color was mainly attributable to climate and environment, using both the Comte de Buffon and Johann Friedrich Blumenbach. But he challenged Rush, who held that blackness was the result of leprosy or a skin disease.

More significantly, Pennington developed a sustained moral and philosophical argument against racism. He categorized racism as sacrilegious, "*supreme selfishness,*" "emphatically *ill will,*" and illuminated its tendency toward violence, as illustrated in mob attacks against abolitionists in the 1830s, "*blindness of mind,*" or ignorance, and its resulting vices among whites of injustice, dishonesty, hypocrisy, and "*brutish and uncivil manners.*" Racism, according to him, was "*carrying the total nation to a state of refined heathenism.*" Pennington portrayed black Americans as superior Christians who must educate, "*love and pity*" these "*men hating Christians.*" His widely advertised book echoed Whipper's aim to reform racist whites.[18]

That year Pennington assisted the daughter of one of his congregants, Ann Plato, an Afro–Native American schoolteacher, to publish her book of poems and essays, writing in the introduction that it showed the "fallacy of the stupid theory" that "*nature has done nothing but fit us for slaves, and that art cannot unfit us for slavery.*" Plato's essays ranged from universal subjects like education, religion, and benevolence, where she borrowed heavily from the colonizationist Lydia Sigourney's work, to the particular, airing her views on gender and race. Writing about two of her female students, one given to hard work, the other to frivolity, she remarked, "Time was, when the temple of science was barred against the foot of woman." In another essay Plato wrote that her views on race came from the wisdom of an "aged sire" who said that "God hath made of one blood all who dwell upon the face of the earth." Two of her poems, "The Natives of America" and "To the First of August," which celebrated British emancipation, were overtly antiracist and antislavery. She also published poems in the CA. An abolitionist essay of 1839 by A Colored Woman that appeared in a Hartford reform journal may well have been written by her. It called on women to sign petitions against the slave trade even though "our GREAT and WISE men in the nation's BLACK LAW FACTORY have decided that *you have no right to ask for mercy* in their behalf." The essay was reprinted in many abolitionist newspapers. According to her latest biographer, Plato left Connecticut to settle in Iowa.[19]

Another free black woman in Boston, Harriet E. Wilson, published the recently rediscovered semiautobiographical novel *Our Nig* in 1859. It was a searing critique of northern racism. Wilson nevertheless wrote, "I would not from these motives even palliate slavery at the South, by disclosures of its appurtenances North. My mistress was wholly imbued with *southern* principles." Her purpose was to show, as the subtitle announces, that "slavery's shadows fall even there." The novel begins with the story of a fallen white woman who marries a black man. On his death she "was expelled from the companionship of white people; this last step—her union with a black—was the climax of repulsion." She abandons her seven-year-old daughter, Frado, Wilson's alter ego, to the Bellmonts. Frado's servitude closely resembles slavery, as she is subject to hard labor, whippings, and blows at the hands of her cruel mistress. Her master, however, insists on sending her to school, where a kind teacher prevents her from being bullied. The last chapter, rather than being an exposure of northern racism, a staple of abolitionist discourse, instead explains the book's lack of reception among abolitionists. Frado, having married and then been abandoned by a man claiming to be a fugitive slave who would occasionally lecture, bitterly criticizes the heart of the movement. Her husband discloses that "his illiterate harangues were humbugs for hungry abolitionists!" She is alone, poor, and abandoned in the end, her only child, for whose benefit she published her story, dead at the age of seven. Wilson eventually became a successful entrepreneur, selling hair products, and was involved with the spiritualist movement before she died in 1900.[20]

More than the obscure Plato and Wilson, black abolitionists developed a concerted intellectual response to American racism. The abolitionist physician James McCune Smith was trained in Glasgow because he was denied admission in American medical schools. The son of a slave woman from South Carolina, Smith was freed by New York's gradual emancipation law and had excelled in Andrew's Free African School. His early essays, such as "The Destiny of the Colored Race" (1843), challenged the notion that blacks were an alien race. Smith predicted that they would be absorbed into a composite American nationality. He rejected the false science that challenged the "unity of the human race" and recommended an impartial study of cultural and ethnic variations. Smith counterposed racial denigration—"We are compelled to endure the stings of insult and calumny, frequently without opportunity of reply, or the hope of redress by law"—to black artistic accomplishment. Black people, he wrote, were destined to produce the music, literature, and oratory of the nation. In *Frederick Douglass' Paper* Smith published realistic portraits of black men and women in his series "Heads of the Colored People," which was influenced by the popular but sham science of phrenology. Douglass balked at these accurate descriptions, which were at odds with abolitionist paeans to black achievers, yet Smith revealed a strong empathy with the mostly working-class people he wrote about. He took on the popular craniologists of his day, systematically deconstructing racist conjectures based on facial angles, size and shapes of skulls and brains, texture of hair, and the color of skin. Douglass probably approved of the elaborate "Afric-American Gallery" published in the *Anglo-African Magazine* in 1859 by the Brooklyn abolitionist and schoolteacher William J. Wilson. Writing as Ethiop, Wilson, who had published a letter in *Frederick Douglass' Paper* about the complete erasure of blacks from a gallery he had visited, created an artistic panorama of black history, starting with the slave ship through a genealogy of resistance, Louverture, the black conventions, the UGRR, and visions of black vengeance. Wilson's Afric-American gallery anticipated Du Bois's elaborate historical pageant, the Star of Ethiopia.

Smith also brought his scholarly expertise to bear on the sectional debate over race and slavery. In one of his last essays on race he refuted Jefferson's notion of "physical and mental distinctions between the negro and the white man." Instead of asking how to get rid of blacks, Smith declared, Jefferson, had he possessed the "insight or sagacity for which he is so celebrated, would have welcomed their presence as one of the positive elements of natural progress." In 1844 Smith produced a statistical refutation of the flawed data of the U.S. Census of 1840 on free blacks, which Calhoun had used to prove that African Americans fared better under slavery than under freedom. Slavery, Smith affirmed, murdered black people, and the proslavery opinion that "emancipation has made the free blacks deaf, dumb, blind, idiot, insane, &c &c" was a concoction of lies. A table he compiled revealed that the numbers of insane blacks listed in towns of the state of Maine in the census exceeded the total number of black inhabitants. He concluded pithily, "Freedom has not made us mad." Smith's work played a large role in discrediting the census data on free blacks, in the eyes of Edward Jarvis, the founder of the American Statistical Society.[21]

Delany, Douglass, and Garnet furthered the denunciation by blacks of scientific racism. Garnet's speech on race before the all-black Female Benevolent Society of Troy showcased how black men, women, and community institutions were involved in a common endeavor to challenge the new racial science. It was published as a pamphlet, *The Past and Present Condition and Destiny of the*

Colored Race (1848). Garnet refused to even engage the idea of different races: "In order to pursue my subject I must, for the sake of distinction, use some of the improper terms of our times. I shall therefore speak of *races*, when in fact there is but one race, as there was one Adam." He avowed that it was the condition of the colored race rather than physical attributes or nature that shaped racism. Like Pennington, he invoked the biblical as well as secular history of Africans to refute racist ideas, and, like Smith, he forecast that "this western world is destined to be filled with a mixed race."[22]

Douglass and Delany also battled the growing popularity of American ethnology. In his speech "The Claims of the Negro Ethnologically Considered" (1854), Douglass, prefiguring Du Bois's opinion that the problem of the twentieth century is the problem of the color line, stated, "The relation subsisting between the white and black people of the country is the vital question of the age." No amount of "scientific moonshine" or the "southern pretenders to science" could place black people on a "sliding scale of humanity." He complained that racists compared the most "degraded" blacks with "those of the highest cultivation," so that the "very crimes of slavery become slavery's best defense." He developed an abolitionist critique of the new racial science: "I say it is remarkable—nay it is strange that there should arise a phalanx of learned men—speaking in the name of *science*—to forbid the magnificent reunion of mankind in one brotherhood. A mortifying proof is here given, that the moral growth of a nation, or an age, does not always keep pace with the increase of knowledge, and suggests the necessity to increase human love and human learning." Years later Delany, who advocated the separation of the races after the fall of Reconstruction, published his *Principia of Ethnology*. But he too continued to discard the pseudoscientific theory of polygenesis and anticipated the findings of modern science in insisting that Africans were the original humans.[23] Black abolitionists had better politics and better science than their opponents. In developing a theoretically sophisticated response to the spurious science of race and racism, they made an original intellectual contribution to abolition.

The antebellum abolition movement, founded on an ideological commitment to racial equality, was receptive to their ideas. In 1831 Garrison drew attention to the "unjust and grievous disabilities" of free black people and their treatment in the North as an "inferior caste." Throughout its history the *Liberator* documented numerous instances of the ill-treatment of African Americans and leading black abolitionists. In 1833 David Lee Child, in his *The Despotism of Freedom*, an exposé of racism, argued that free people of color were subjected to "inveterate, cruel, and, I will add ferocious prejudice against their skins" and that in no country of the world did racism exist as strongly as it did in the

American Republic. The next year Garrison proclaimed that abolition would not be successful until "all unequal laws, having respect to the color of the skin, shall have been universally expunged from the statute-books, and prejudice scouted as a fiend, and the cord of caste burnt to ashes."[24]

Abolitionists criticized the pervasiveness of racial discrimination in the North. African Americans were excluded from all institutions, leading Garrison to quip, "Hardly any doors but those of our State Prisons, were open to our colored brethren." Elizur Wright reported that Williams College admitted a black man who looked nearly white on the condition that he leave for Liberia on graduating. Child asked abolitionists to use only those public conveyances that did not discriminate against African Americans, and Ellis Gray Loring demanded the repeal of all racially discriminatory laws. At the NEAS convention in 1837, John Levi, a former slave from the West Indies, said he did not know what racial prejudice was until he came to the United States.

African Americans testified to the depth of racist treatment and ill-usage. In 1834 Rev. William C. Munroe of Portland, Maine, reported that when he applied for admission to Amherst, Dartmouth, and Bowdoin colleges, which had graduated the first African Americans, he "met with immediate rejection" or admission upon "such degrading terms" that he could not accept. Two years later a man named Caples from Boston testified how his "heart had bled" at the discrimination he had encountered in churches and schools. Abolitionists, he decided, have done much, but they needed to do more to ensure that blacks could enter the trades. Roberts, frustrated in his efforts to print a black newspaper, the *Antislavery Herald*, in Boston, complained, "[It is] altogether useless to pretend to affect the welfare of colored people, unless the chains of prejudice are broken." In 1839 Rev. Andrew Harris reminded abolitionists that the poison of slavery does not stop at the South but "presses down upon the free people of color" in the North as well.[25]

African Americans led the way when it came to resisting racial discrimination. They demanded that abolitionists compile statistics on the free black communities in the North, initiate practical measures in finding gainful employment, and combat racism more vigorously. In 1835 Easton called on the AASS to compile information on free black people. An OASS convention report mentioned the growth of churches and schools among the state's black population and the persistent discrimination encountered by them in law, popular prejudice, and exclusion from mechanical associations and public institutions; it recommended education as a way to combat legal disabilities and "unyielding prejudice on the part of whites." At the third annual convention of the AASS, Wright asked that the society compile statistics on the free black population in the country and undertake "strenuous efforts" to improve their conditions.[26]

The black abolitionist Rev. Theodore S. Wright was most responsible for raising the issue of racism. The son of the black abolitionist R. P. G. Wright, he was named after the Federalist antislavery lawyer Theodore Sedgwick. Wright attended Princeton Theological Seminary and, mentored by Cornish, he took over Shiloh Presbyterian in New York, the largest black Presbyterian church in the country. As a student Wright had defied the colonizationist views of his professors, selling subscriptions to *Freedom's Journal.* A founding member of the Phoenix Society as well as of the board of managers of the NYASS and a member of the AASS executive committee, Wright was a prominent abolitionist. In a dramatic speech delivered in 1836 he drew attention to the "spirit of slavery" which surrounded black people like an atmosphere. That year Wright was assaulted for sitting on a bench in a Princeton chapel, and his sick wife died after exposure while riding in a Jim Crow boat. Wright argued that racism "scourges us from the table, it scourges us from the cabin, from the stage-coach, from the bed, wherever we go." A year later, in another speech commending the progress of abolition, Wright talked of eliminating racism. "It is an easy thing to ask," he said, "about the vileness of slavery in the South, but to call the dark man a brother, heartily to embrace the doctrine advanced in the second article of the constitution [of the AASS] . . . that is the test." Abolitionists must first "annihilate in their own bosom the cord of caste," and they must "burn out this prejudice, live it down, talk it down." In 1842 the black abolitionist Stephen Myers of Albany, in his short-lived *Northern Star and Freeman's Advocate*, also wrote that abolitionists must help blacks practically by hiring them and by eradicating *"prejudice from their own hearts."*[27]

Antislavery societies like the ASS of Meriden, Connecticut, responded to black admonitions. It made the fight against racism part of its constitution. At the RIASS convention Jocelyn exhorted abolitionists to prove their love for the slave by working to improve the condition of free people of color. In Indiana a convention to organize a state ASS in 1838 deemed racial prejudice "rebellion against God." The NEAS resolved in 1837 "not only to educate and elevate the free people of color, but also to eradicate from our white population, and especially from abolitionists themselves, the remains of the irrational, unnatural and unchristian prejudice, which, while it operates most injuriously upon our colored brethren, at the same time degrades, pollutes and disgraces those who in any degree cherish and retain it." The next year at the annual anniversary meeting of the AASS, Gerrit Smith importuned abolitionists to purge their hearts of the wickedness of racism, saying that, as a movement, abolition should aim to revolutionize the world on matters of race. An abolitionist pamphlet condemning segregated "negro pews" in churches asked those who called themselves "friends of the colored man" to examine their hearts. It reprinted Wright's speech.[28] Black abolitionists had made the struggle against racism central to the abolitionist program.

CITIZENSHIP

Attempts to restrict black rights in "the white man's democracy" led black abolitionists to inaugurate the fight against disfranchisement. In their memorial of 1832 to the Pennsylvania legislature, Forten, Purvis, and Whipper criticized attempts to prevent black migration to the state and to overturn the personal liberty law of 1826 that afforded runaway slaves some legal protections. In a separate statement of evidence, they showed that free blacks were a tiny fraction of the population of the city's almshouses and that, despite racial proscription, they had churches, schools, beneficent societies, and employment in mechanical arts. Arguing for disfranchisement, the colonizationist lawyer John F. Denny judged that Pennsylvania's laws were too mild when it came to the treatment of black aliens who were polluting the state's body politic. Black abolitionists condemned proposals to disfranchise them in the state constitutional convention in 1837. Rev. Charles Gardner, a member of the AMRS and a founding member of the PASS, quoted Garrison: "Let it be remembered, that the man of color has to labor against wind and tide." The next year he led protest meetings and at a large gathering in his church proposed a day of humiliation, fasting, and protest. A memorial to the convention composed by him and Hinton pointed out that distinction of color was unknown to God and violated the immutable principle that all men are created free and equal. People of color in Pittsburgh expressed their "holy indignation" at such "contracted, narrow-minded doings." The convention, dominated by Democrats, refused to consider the memorials and expelled black observers.[29]

The best-known protest against the convention's decision to disfranchise black men came from a committee headed by Purvis that composed *Appeal of Forty Thousand Citizens Threatened with Disfranchisement to the People of Pennsylvania*. Purvis asked his fellow citizens if they intended to make "political rights depend upon the skin in which a man is born." Disfranchisement bolstered schemes to colonize free blacks, but Purvis countered, "We are Pennsylvanians." Bowers lambasted the colonizationist aims of the convention, which was trying to force them "to look to Africa for a home." It had sacrificed the rights of black Pennsylvanians upon "the altar of slavery." The constitution of 1838 disfranchising black men was ratified in a referendum. Combined with the burning of Pennsylvania Hall, this act revealed the anti-abolitionist mood of northerners, who, together with slaveholders, viewed black rights as a threat to the Union. Black Pennsylvanians did not give up, sending fifty-one petitions to the legislature for enfranchisement and some even to Congress. In a public letter in 1841 Purvis protested in vain that he was denied the vote yet had to pay taxes.

Racial violence accompanied black disfranchisement. That year a race war, which began as a confrontation between black and Irish workers, resulted in the destruction of the *Philanthropist* press in Cincinnati. The race-baiting Democratic *Cincinnati Enquirer* incited mob fury. African Americans armed themselves against the rioters until officials persuaded them to disarm. The rioters then proceeded to go on a rampage and raped some black women. The authorities arrested a number of black men and enforced the state's black laws. Only the intervention of Gov. Thomas Corwin prevented further violence. The flagrant miscarriage of justice revived the sagging fortunes of the *Philanthropist*. After the Philadelphia race riot of 1842, Purvis despaired, lamenting, "[The] Press, Church, Magistrates, Clergymen and Devils—are against us. The measure of our suffering is full. . . . I am convinced of our utter and complete nothingness in public estimation." Purvis, Gardner, and Daniel Payne wrote another protest detailing the indiscriminate attacks on black men, women, and churches. [30]

Abolitionists rallied against black disfranchisement. In 1837 Stanton, in a speech to the Massachusetts legislature, said that there should be no tests for citizenship "on account of *color*." The PAS commissioned a study of the condition of the people of color in Philadelphia and vicinity to highlight their achievements. The committee included the veteran abolitionists Edward Needles, Joseph and Isaac Parrish, and Edward Hopper as well as James Mott and William Harned. The two reports, published in 1838, used a census of the city's black population and information gathered by Gardner. An appended address to the people of color sympathized with them in their "dark and gloomy" hour and warned that their disfranchisement would "render your condition more insecure and dangerous." Blacks had been met with insult and injury and lawless violence, the reports observed, while praising their admirable associations of mutual aid and schools. In his pamphlet William Jackson of Chester County, posed "a general amalgamation of the two races" as a way to end racial prejudice. [31]

That year the Baptist abolitionist William Yates of Troy published his *Rights of Colored Men to Suffrage, Citizenship and Trial by Jury*. Pointing to the disfranchisement of African Americans in Connecticut, New Jersey, New York, and, most recently, Pennsylvania, Yates reminded whites that black people had been citizens of the Republic from its inception and fought in its War of

Independence. While a lot had been written pleading the slave's cause, Yates pointed out that in the North "prejudice against color, let it be understood, is the battle ground between the friends and foes of human rights in a contest for equal laws." He acidly suggested a "*chronometer* by which we may in all cases measure the hue of a man's skin, and ascertain whether it reaches a shade which robs a native American of his property and rights, and renders him an alien in the land of his birth." The CA recommended his book as an important publication that should be "in the hand of every colored man and colored man's friend." A black juvenile antislavery society promptly named themselves after him.[32]

In 1839 William Jay published his pamphlet against racial discrimination. In mapping the "geography of prejudice," he listed the legal and popular disabilities confronted by free blacks, noting that their number exceeded the total number of inhabitants in such states as New Jersey and Connecticut. They were denied the franchise, as prejudice had grown with the country, and could not serve in the nation's army or militias. Their "right of locomotion" was impaired by the black laws of slave and free states like Ohio, which also denied free blacks the right to testify against whites. They faced "impediments to education," religion, and industry. Most egregiously, they could be kidnapped into slavery and subjected to insult and outrage. A supporter and donor to the CA, Jay was aware of the black fight for citizenship.[33]

The movement for black suffrage gained its greatest momentum in New York, buoyed by the growing strength of political abolitionism. The CA led the charge, publishing extracts from the New York constitutional convention of 1821, which had limited black voting by a property-holding qualification of $250, under such headings as "On the Rights of the Colored people to Vote" and "On the Injustice of Disfranchising them." The editors wrote, "The tens of thousands of foreigners that annually come into our state, soon climb to all the rights and immunities of citizens," while Africans Americans were denied the vote. In 1837 black New Yorkers formed ward committees to gather signatures and forwarded three petitions to the legislature demanding the right of trial by jury for fugitive slaves and the removal of the property-holding voting qualification. The CA and its many correspondents called for a black convention to combat colonization and black disfranchisement. In Pittsburgh, Vashon, John Peck, Woodson, and Delany also called for a state black convention. From Harrisburg, Morel recommended a convention of colored people that would utter its "deep condemnation" of the proceedings in Pennsylvania. In June that year New York's leading black abolitionists along with Remond formed the New York Political Association to fight for equal suffrage and called for a convention in Albany. The AASS endorsed its efforts.[34]

The abolitionist schism and the fight for equal voting rights spurred autonomous black activism in New York. Those who had led black conventions and fraternal societies, Hamilton, Sipkins, and Peter Williams Jr., all died between 1837 and 1840. A younger generation, including Ray, the Reason brothers, Patrick, an accomplished artist and engraver, and Charles, a schoolteacher, whose parents had emigrated from Haiti and Guadeloupe, and Alexander Crummell spearheaded the move to hold a state black convention. Samuel Ringgold Ward, a former slave and clergyman, remarked that since whites "have yet to learn to crucify prejudice against color," independent black action was crucial. Making an exception for his Liberty Party allies, Ward alleged that although abolitionists had fought for their own civil liberties, they had not done enough for black rights. Willis Hodges, who with his brother William fled Virginia and settled in Brooklyn, said that black men must act for themselves, as abolitionists were "men of words [more] than [of] deeds."

Nathaniel P. Rogers, the editor of the NASS, scorned exclusive conventions, and even McCune Smith had reservations about all-black conventions. Like Whipper, Rogers felt that if African Americans drew a color line it would simply reinforce rather than challenge racial separation. Van Rensselaer initially opposed Rogers but was eventually convinced by Smith. Ray justified black state conventions as a way to redress local political disabilities faced by blacks, but he did not deem a national convention necessary. Woodson and Vashon in Pittsburgh and a meeting led by Scott in Worcester supported Ruggles's call for a national convention. A "national reform convention" convened by Ruggles at Hartford in 1840, attended mainly by black abolitionists from Philadelphia and New England but opposed by Amos Beman of New Haven, proved to be a failure. Ruggles, Pennington, Mars, Vashon, and William C. Nell of Boston formed the short-lived American Board of Disfranchised Commissioners, which met the following year in New York. Black abolitionists in New York signed on to the call for a state convention in Albany. The Albany convention criticized the national reform convention.[35]

The state conventions of the early 1840s, however, led to the revival of the national black convention and made the fight for citizenship central to black abolitionism. The first state convention met in Albany in August 1840, chaired by Ray with Austin Steward as president. Disagreement arose between those such as Ray and Wright, who urged black men to acquire property to become eligible to vote, and radicals like Garnet and Crummell, who simply wanted to do away with the requirement. Differences also arose between those who wished to endorse the Liberty Party and those who wanted the convention to fight only for voting rights. A committee of six, including Wright, Ray, the Reason brothers, and Crummell, composed an address to the people of the state. "We can find no system of moral or political ethics in which rights are based on the conformation of the body, or the color of the skin," they wrote. The address linked the oppression of blacks with that of Native Americans and the Irish and with the "degradation of the Greeks" and of the lower castes in India, revealing the cosmopolitan nature of black abolitionism. Despite being a target of mob violence by immigrants, African Americans did not endorse nativism.

A petition to the legislature asked for equal political rights. The convention formed a committee to coordinate a petition campaign and county committees to acquire signatures. An address to colored fellow citizens written by Garnet, Ray, and Wright called for protests against disfranchisement in every corner and hamlet of the state. Meetings in Troy, Schenectady, Buffalo, Albany, all in the upstate heartland of the Liberty Party, and in Brooklyn demanded equal franchise. The Albany convention inspired a meeting in Newark led by Cornish, Amos Freeman, and W. F. Gardner against disfranchisement in New Jersey. Ray, reporting that a meeting in Michigan led by Robert Banks and William Munroe also protested disfranchisement, exulted, "It is really inspiring to see the effect of the Albany Convention upon our brethren of other States, and how easily they take *fire*, from the action of that body."

The attempt to extend "impartial suffrage" to African Americans came to naught, despite Garnet's eloquent address before the Judiciary Committee on the presentation of black suffrage petitions. Not deterred by this setback, the CA sent out a call for another state convention. Local meetings sent delegations to the state convention in Troy in 1841. The Troy convention issued an address "To the Electors of the State of New York," again trying to convince whites that to take away the political rights of some was to destroy the entire edifice of republican government. One by one it answered objections to black voting—that black people would vote en masse, that they demanded social equality when the object was political equality, and that they were too ignorant and degraded—holding that if immigrants who came from monarchical European countries were given the franchise then African Americas reared in the American Republic should be accorded the same privilege. Large county conventions in Albany and New York following the Troy convention revived the suffrage movement at the local level and the petition campaign.

In 1844 the state convention in Schenectady, led by Garnet and Myers, was still calling for another petition campaign for black suffrage. Its highlight was a debate over a protest by Ray and Wright against resolutions passed by the Rochester convention a year earlier denouncing both Whigs and Democrats as being proslavery at the behest of the Liberty men. They objected to partisan politics being introduced into the conventions, which they felt should maintain a united front. Garnet opposed the protest, and the Garrisonian William P. Powell approved of it. In the end, the convention voted it down resoundingly 38 to 11, revealing growing support for political abolitionism among black New Yorkers. McCune Smith and Powell, representing, they said, twenty thousand people in New York City, resigned in protest. The last of the New York suffrage conventions was held in Geneva in 1845. The convention received a letter from the antislavery Whig governor, William H. Seward, who supported black suffrage, conveying his regrets in not attending the convention. Seward noted that "a dark skin never covered a doughface."[36]

Black agitation for suffrage gained enough momentum to be debated at New York's constitutional convention in 1846 and received the backing of the Whig Party. Though the Democratic-dominated convention refused to do away with the property requirement, it authorized a referendum on the question, which was decisively defeated 224,336 to 85,406. Not until the eve of the Civil War would the issue of black suffrage emerge again in state politics. Gerrit Smith sought to circumvent the property-holding requirement in a spectacular gesture the same year. In a public letter to Wright, Ray, and McCune Smith, he announced his plans to deed 120,000 acres of his land to three thousand black men. It was, the three men responded, a "great experiment" for the race. For McCune Smith, his "generous deeds" shone through the "sad memories of crushed hope" excited by the "terrible majority" against black suffrage. Though the land turned out to be rocky and infertile, black abolitionists advocated landownership as a way to gain the right to vote and the advantages of a rural farming life.[37]

The state conventions in Pennsylvania were likewise devoted to repealing black disfranchisement. Woodson, Delany, Peck, and Vashon presided over a convention in Pittsburgh in 1841. A resolution asking the convention to attend to the accommodation of ladies and gentlemen disclosed that, unlike the New York conventions, women were in attendance here. Ray had shot down the idea of women delegates, though they were spectators. The convention petitioned the legislature to amend the state constitution and "remove all restrictions on account of color." It counseled education and temperance, adopted the CA as its organ, and called for holding county conventions to promote its aims. Its address to the "colored freemen" of the state, composed by Vashon and Woodson, among others, endorsed suffrage, farming, and an independent press but disavowed the strategy of withholding taxes to protest disfranchisement. Nearly ten years earlier, when the Rhode Island legislature had refused to receive a petition from African Americans demanding exemption from taxation because

they did not have the vote, Garrison advised that they decline to pay taxes and
sue the government. New York abolitionists voiced reservations about this strategy adopted by black Rhode Islanders, complaining that it could be used as an
excuse to deny black men the vote.

In a familiar pattern, Rhode Island had disfranchised black men in 1822, and
two years later whites had attacked black homes in the Hard Scrabble area of
Providence. In the 1830s a committee that included laborers such as George
Willis and the barber Alfred Niger in Providence demanded the right to vote.
By 1841 a suffrage movement geared to removing property-holding qualifications and led by Thomas Dorr, a former member of the RIASS, held out some
hope to blacks. But the suffrage associations excluded African Americans and
restricted their demand to democratize the vote to whites only. The people's
convention rejected a petition prepared by Ichabod Northrup and Crummell,
who was now a pastor of the Christ Church in Providence, to remove the word
white from its constitution despite Dorr's support for black voting. Dorr managed to ensure jury trial for fugitive slaves and insert a mandatory provision to
put the whites-only clause to a referendum. But African Americans rejected the
people's constitution, and Kelley, Douglass, Foster, and Pillsbury campaigned
against it. The racial animosity of Dorrites allied blacks with conservative state
authorities. The Law and Order Party put black suffrage on the ballot in 1842,
and it was approved by voters. The state constitution of 1843 gave black men
the right to vote. After his imprisonment for leading the rebellion against state
authorities, Dorr became a proslavery Democrat. Rhode Island was the only
northern state to reverse black disfranchisement.

The fight for suffrage continued in Pennsylvania, where the easterners Purvis,
Stephen Smith, Whipper, Shadd, McCrummell, and Bowers dominated the
second state convention, which met in Harrisburg in 1848. Vashon, Peck, and
Remond also attended. The convention's address to voters as "arbiters of our
political destiny" again asked for the removal of the word *white* from the state
constitution, invoking the names of Franklin, Rush, Benezet, and Woolman
as well as the European revolutions of 1848. Its appeal to colored citizens read,
"Our fathers sought personal freedom—we now contend for political freedom."
Even if their object was not realized, "we will gain in the consolidation of our
people on the subject of our rights." It hoped to plant the "seeds of revolution."
The convention constituted itself into the "Citizens' Union of the Commonwealth of Pennsylvania" in order to carry on the struggle for voting rights. In
1855 the state's disfranchised black citizens submitted a memorial to Congress
detailing that seventeen years of disfranchisement had led to the burning of
black churches and institutions and mob violence and calling the attempt to list
all the outrages they were subject to a "Herculean task."[38]

The revival of the national conventions also spurred the fight for black citizenship. In his speech of 1843 to the national convention in Buffalo, meeting after a hiatus of eight years, President Samuel Davis noted that while abolitionists had made "noble efforts in behalf of the poor slave . . . We, ourselves, must be willing to contend for the rich boon of freedom and equal rights." The meeting became famous for Garnet's "Address to the Slaves," but much of its business was geared to reviving a national network of independent black activism, the establishment of a black press, and the economic growth of northern black communities. Two years later the national convention in Troy, on Garnet's behest, called on folks to *"agitate!* AGITATE!! AGITATE!!!" The national convention of 1848, held in Cleveland and presided over by Douglass, took up the topics of gender and class. A Mrs. Sanford asked for the "Elective Franchise" and the right to property. She encouraged the convention to fight for *"unqualified citizenship of the United States."* The convention's address to the colored people pointed out that whereas they were held as slaves in the South, in the North they were "the slaves of the community." Debate over Delany's resolution that black people avoid servile jobs resulted in a compromise mediated by Douglass. The address urged moving out of menial positions but refuted the notion that they were a mark of degradation.[39]

The conventions did not stem the tide of black disfranchisement but acted as sites of resistance, especially in the more racially intolerant northwest with its large southern-born populations and black laws that penalized African Americans for entering the region's states. The black laws were sporadically enforced, and the rise of abolition posed a challenge to them. Black conventions held in Indiana in 1842, 1847, and 1851 took up many issues, but the right to vote was their foremost demand. The last convention met on the eve of the passage of a law that, implementing an article in the new state constitution, prevented blacks from entering the state. The meeting's president, John G. Britton, insisted that "[as] Americans we are entitled to all the rights, privileges, and immunities of citizenship." Abolitionists protested the exclusionary law and rejected state-sponsored colonization schemes. Given the dismal conditions faced by black Indianans, colonization found favor among antislavery men like Robert Dale Owen and the Methodist minister Rev. James Mitchell, who would be recruited by the Lincoln administration as emigration commissioner to promote colonization. Illinois and Oregon too had antiblack immigration clauses in their constitutions.

In the antislavery upper northwest, black abolitionists and their political allies managed to initiate state referendums on black suffrage. Detroit's activist black community called for a state convention in 1843, identifying African Americans "as an oppressed people wishing to be free" who will gain their liberties only by their "own exertions in their own cause." Despite repeated disturbances over the issue of rightful delegates, the Michigan convention was one of the most successful. Its resolutions made the gaining of the right to vote its primary aim, protesting that blacks were "passive instruments of the law." On the initiative of the fugitive slave Henry Bibb it passed resolutions demanding the immediate abolition of slavery and praising abolitionists, starting with Wilberforce, Clarkson, and Lovejoy and adding local abolitionists. Its address to the citizens of Michigan referred to the ancient history of Africa to refute the charges of inherent racial inferiority deployed as an excuse to deny equal political rights. A new state constitution in 1850 extended voting to immigrants and Indians, but black suffrage went down to defeat by a vote of 32,000 to 12,000. In neighboring Wisconsin, which entered the Union in 1848, a black suffrage proposal was rejected despite winning a majority because most voters abstained. In 1857 black suffrage was defeated in Iowa.[40]

The states in the northwest modeled their "black laws" after Ohio's. In the 1830s the legislature turned down abolitionist petitions against the black laws and in 1839 denied African Americans the right to petition against them. Black abolitionists such as Peter Clark and William O'Hara had long agitated for civil rights. In 1834 the light-skinned Williams family from Xenia sued to gain admittance to the public schools, and black Ohioans held "education conventions." Ohio held the greatest number of state conventions. The address of the Columbus convention held in 1843 to the citizens of Ohio, written by George Boyer Vashon and others, insisted, "WE ARE AMERICANS" and condemned the "pseudo-philanthropy" of colonizationists. The broad-based nature of the conventions was evident in its call for farmers to leave their land, mechanics to put down their tools, laborers to abandon their work, and domestic servants to "leave their lords." It invited white abolitionists to attend "without the privilege of voting" or without compromising its character as sites of independent black activism. It targeted the removal of legal disabilities, which barred blacks from giving testimony. They were "oppressed, disfranchised and otherwise degraded on account of complexion by certain infamous and most tyrannical laws."[41]

The Ohio convention of 1849 made the repeal of the state's black laws its primary concern. The political emergence of the Free Soil Party and Salmon P. Chase, who was elected to the Senate, made it an auspicious time for repeal. The delegates invited "ladies to share in the doings of the Convention" after they had protested their exclusion. The Oberlin-educated black abolitionists William Howard Day, born in New York, and Charles and John Mercer Langston dominated the proceedings. The Langston brothers, sons of a Virginian planter and his enslaved common-law wife, migrated to Chillicothe, Ohio, home to the pioneering Colored Antislavery Society, founded in 1834. The convention's address demanded the desegregation of the state's schools and ended with the slogan, "Repeal, Repeal, Repeal" the black laws. Black protest and electoral victory of a Free Soil Democratic coalition orchestrated by Chase resulted in the overthrow of the black laws. The convention in 1850 capitalized on this success. It formed the Ohio Colored American League, demanded the right of suffrage, and asked that all discriminatory laws be done away with. It also recommended that Day be appointed superintendent of the colored schools. The next year the convention appointed a commission to the governor and sent an address to the Ohio Constitutional Convention demanding suffrage. Day and James Watson spoke before the legislature on black suffrage. The constitutional convention, however, voted it down by 75 to 15. Undeterred, the Ohio conventions in the 1850s made suffrage their central demand.[42]

The struggle for the franchise also dominated the New Jersey and Connecticut black conventions of 1849. The New Jersey convention at Trenton, which was addressed by Van Rensselaer and led by the physician John Swett Rock, who became a prominent abolitionist in Massachusetts, launched a petition campaign for black suffrage. It also recommended obtaining signatures of white citizens and issued an address to them appealing for their support to make the state "the first consistent reformer of human rights in the Western World." The Connecticut convention's call noted, "We are dead to citizenship — struck down by an unrighteous State Constitution, and our life spark quenched by a cruel and unreasonable prejudice." Amos G. Beman led the convention, which was attended by his father, Jehiel Beman, and Bibb. Despite the presence of black women, the demand for black citizenship remained male centered, especially when citing black military service in the revolution and the War of 1812 as a reason for enfranchisement. The address to the colored men of Connecticut held that disfranchisement assailed their "manhood and Citizenship." The appeal to the voters of the state, written by Amos Beman and others, listed southern proslavery actions as akin to opposition to black citizenship, rebuked racism as an unchristian "corrupt public sentiment," and listed black achievements as arguments for free suffrage. In the 1850s the state convention movement spread to Illinois, California, Kansas, and even Maryland. Nearly all focused on demanding the right to vote, civil rights, and equality before the law.[43]

Black abolitionists also made the desegregation of public facilities integral to abolition. The question of segregation became entangled with factionalism when Charles Reason, responding to Van Rensselaer's criticism of the city's black abolitionists affiliated with the AFASS, accused Van Rensselaer of not serving him and Crummell in his restaurant. Van Rensselaer replied that as a matter of principle he served blacks in his establishment, even though that had cost him business among whites. In 1839 Crummell publicized Bishop On-derdonk's efforts to exclude him from the Episcopalian General Theological Seminary. Earlier, Isaiah De Grasse had been admitted and then was forced to leave the seminary. A few years later Onderdonk's brother obstructed Crum-mell's attempt to found an Episcopalian church in Philadelphia, demanding that neither Crummell nor his church be seated at his convention. In his intro-ductory remarks to the history of the Episcopalian church, Jay used the Crum-mell case to indict it for racism, as did his son John Jay II in his pamphlet *Caste and Slavery in the American Church* (1843), based on material Crummell forwarded to him. Smith sent Crummell twenty dollars, the latter writing that the "kindnesses of friends" had helped soften the blow. Black abolitionists led by George T. Downing, John J. Zuille, Wilson, and Bell held a meeting protest-ing Crummell's treatment. Onderdonk also refused to ordain Charles Reason. The Onderdonk brothers soon fell from grace, accused of womanizing and alcoholism.

The *Liberator* and CA regularly reported the experiences of blacks encoun-tering Jim Crow. Cornish protested the exclusion of his children from the pub-lic school system in New Jersey, and Van Rensselaer for being thrown off a steamboat. Ruggles recounted being defrauded by a Rhode Island steamboat and "lynched" in the Stonington railroad. In 1841 Downing was unsuccessful in his suit against the Harlem Railroad Track Company for a "barbarous out-rage upon him." Black abolitionists circulated a petition for the removal of the company as a nuisance to black citizens. It also denied black women access to the ladies' cars, repudiating their claims to respectability. In 1854 the eviction of Elizabeth Jennings, a schoolteacher and the daughter of Thomas Jennings, and her female companion from a streetcar by an Irish conductor instigated community protest and a successful lawsuit argued by the future Republican president Chester Arthur. Jennings, McCune Smith, and Pennington founded a Legal Rights Association to contest segregation in the streetcars. The next year Pennington was evicted from a streetcar but lost his suit. The association pros-ecuted a number of cases of discrimination, and it developed a female branch. Pennington and Garnet reported that they had successfully desegregated certain streetcar lines in the city. When Day and his wife were denied cabin accommo-dations on a steamboat, he pursued his case against the owner all the way to the Michigan Supreme Court only to lose. In 1864 Ellen Anderson, thrown out of a whites-only car in New York by the conductor and a policeman, sued the police commission. She won her case and effectively desegregated public transit when the city police stopped enforcing segregation. The battle against streetcar segregation was not won completely. Well after the war Sojourner Truth asserted that she had been sent so often to the smoking car that she smoked in self-defense, swallowing "her own smoke [rather] than another's."[44]

Desegregation was most successful in Massachusetts, where "the story of civil rights [was] born in the age of abolitionism." Garrison had called for the repeal of the law against interracial marriage. Female antislavery societies in the state led by Kelley conducted annual petition campaigns against the law since 1839. With positive committee reports in successive years, the legislature came close to passing the repeal in 1842. The next year Nell submitted a black petition against the discriminatory law. In March, despite the strong opposition of some members, the legislature passed a law proposed by the abolitionist George Bradburn of Nantucket that repealed the marriage prohibition. The Liberty Party played a crucial role in negotiating the final passage of the repeal. Garrison hailed it as "a signal victory over prejudice and the spirit of caste."

Black abolitionists spearheaded the campaign to desegregate public transportation and schools in Massachusetts. In 1840 the *Liberator* reported on the mistreatment of Thomas Jinnings by the Eastern Railroad Company and of Ruggles in the Nantucket steamboat and at the railroad depot in New Bedford. Ruggles, who was evicted from his seat, lost his glasses and his bag and tore his clothing in the scuffle, unsuccessfully sued the railroad company for damages. The next year the AASS agents Douglass and Collins were assaulted while attempting to travel together on the notorious Eastern Railroad. Collins sustained a bad cut on his lip from blows to his head and face, and Douglass tore up a good number of seats resisting removal. They were targeted precisely because they were "damned abolitionists" and traveled in interracial groups. In protest, Garrison and Phillips chose to travel in the dirty Jim Crow cars with black abolitionists like Nell. Shadrach Howard and Jeremiah Sanderson had to face charges in court for their confrontation with the conductor of the New Bedford Railroad. Mary Newhall Green of the Lynn ASS was assaulted by a conductor for traveling in a whites-only car, an attack that injured her, the baby in her arms, and her husband. White bystanders who came to the aid of African Americans were also mistreated, one Daniel Mann, represented by Sewell, losing his suit for assault. Garrison published a travel directory for black readers with information on the policies of local railroads and steamboats and a lengthy essay against racism by the Haitian writer S. Linstat.

Abolitionists began a petition campaign against Jim Crow railroads after failing to obtain redress in the courts. The petitions and mass meetings condemning the Eastern Railroad created a wave of public sympathy, as editorials in newspapers across the state sided with them. Garrison was hard on the Quaker superintendent of the Eastern Railroad, saying, "Quaker garb ill becomes him," as he was "lost to shame" and gloried in his brutality. But the Quaker abolitionist Nathaniel Barney, a stockholder in the New Bedford line, donated all his dividends to the abolitionist fight against segregation. Most Massachusetts railroads voluntarily desegregated their cars because of abolitionists' protests. A hearing over Jim Crow transportation in the legislature in 1842, in which Phillips, Loring, and Remond testified, revealed that only the Eastern and New Bedford–Taunton railroads persisted in their policy of segregation. The committee reported that Jim Crow violated the rights of black citizens and counseled a law prohibiting it. The law failed to pass the legislature, but Gov. Marcus Morton assured abolitionists that African Americans would receive redress. The Eastern Railroad desegregated on the prompting of its stockholders. As Garrison put it, "The corporation has proved, beyond dispute or cavil, that neither convenience, accommodation nor improvement is the ruling principle with them, but monopoly and profit."[45]

Remond was prominent in the fight against segregated transportation. During his first lecture tour in Maine, he had faced "mobocrats, eggs and brickbats" and even debated the Democratic representative Hannibal Hamlin, Lincoln's future vice president. An effective agent, he had organized antislavery societies in Maine, Massachusetts, and Rhode Island and became a member of the AASS business committee. Known for his polished speeches, Remond acquired considerable fame as a delegate to the Antislavery Convention in London. On his return, he was ejected from the Eastern Railroad along with several whites who were eager to hear about his tour. At a large meeting in Faneuil Hall, Remond pointed out that while he had been treated as an honored guest in England and Ireland, he could not safely travel in his own country. Similarly, Nancy Prince, who had been received in the Russian court, wrote to Garrison that she was thrown off a steamboat for which she had purchased a ticket and dislocated her shoulder. Remond reasoned that "complexion can in no sense be construed a crime, much less be rightfully made the criterion of rights," thereby linking desegregation with the quest for equal citizenship. Maria Chapman observed that in a few words black abolitionists could convey an argument against racial prejudice that might take a white man all day.

Black abolitionists tested the boundaries of segregation by initiating boycotts and lawsuits. In 1845 the New Bedford Lyceum's refusal to admit Nathaniel Borden and David W. Ruggles (not to be confused with David Ruggles of New York) resulted in an abolitionist boycott during which popular lecturers like Ralph Waldo Emerson, Charles Sumner, and Theodore Parker canceled their engagements. The issue of segregation in theaters emerged in 1853, when Nell,

Sarah Parker Remond, and Caroline Remond, sisters of Remond, challenged segregated seating at the Howard Athenaeum in Boston. Sarah, who was pushed down the stairs and hurt herself, was awarded five hundred dollars as compensation after bringing a criminal complaint against the guard who assaulted her. Three years later Julian McCrea and John Stephenson sued the same theater for refusing to seat them but lost their suit. Not until 1865 did Massachusetts outlaw segregation in all public spaces.[46]

Black abolitionists led by old stalwarts such as John Hilton and by the young Nell and Robert Morris became involved in a protracted struggle to desegregate Boston's public school system. Nell, who led a decade-long fight for "equal school rights," was Garrison's printing apprentice, running an employment registry for blacks in the *Liberator* and becoming a writer of some repute. As a student, Nell was recognized for scholarly distinction but, unlike white students, was denied the Franklin medal and given a voucher for purchasing Franklin's biography. Excluded from the ceremony, he attended as a waiter. Nell developed a lifelong commitment to ending educational discrimination. He initiated numerous petition drives for the desegregation of Boston's school system, one of the last holdouts in the state. Blacks had successfully desegregated public schools in Nantucket, Lowell, and Salem. The petitions asked for the dismantling of the all-black Smith school, where deplorable conditions and an abusive white schoolteacher had resulted in a boycott by a majority of parents. The school committee denied their requests despite the dissent of the abolitionist member Henry I. Bowditch. By bringing in the Dartmouth-educated Thomas Paul Jr. as head of the Smith school, the committee bolstered a small faction led by his cousin Thomas Paul Smith that defended the school as a community institution.

In 1849 Roberts sued the committee on behalf of his daughter Sarah Roberts, who, rather than attend the school, which was near her home, was forced to walk a mile to an all-black school. Morris, who had learned law under Loring and became the first black lawyer to be admitted to the Massachusetts bar, argued the Roberts case. His cocounsel was the antislavery politician Charles Sumner. In his brief, used a hundred years later by plaintiff's counsel in *Brown v. Board of Education*, which mandated school desegregation, Sumner contended that *"all men without distinction of race or color are equal before the law,"* that separate was inherently unequal, and that segregation harmed black as well as white children. Chief Justice of the Supreme Judicial Court of Massachusetts Lemuel Shaw upheld segregation and thereby established the only legal precedent for *Plessey v. Ferguson*, in which the U.S. Supreme Court declared racial segregation constitutional in 1896. Despite this setback, Nell did not give up. A resurgent boycott of the Smith school, in which activists surrounded the school and even beat up Thomas Paul Smith, led to its collapse. Nell noted the cooperation of black mothers, who made the action successful. In 1853 Morris sued the city schools again on behalf of Edward Pindall. The fight against Jim Crow schools resulted in the passage of a law by the Know-Nothing legislature and governor in 1855 that desegregated the states' schools. The nativist party contained enough free soilers such as Henry Wilson and the state legislator Charles Slack to ensure this abolitionist triumph. Armed with a stack of petitions, Nell had enlisted Slack for his cause. Slack presented a report for desegregation, liberally borrowing Sumner's words, which led to the passage of the law. The black community duly honored Nell at a meeting addressed by Garrison, Hilton, Phillips, Remond, and Slack after this long, hard-fought victory. While Phillips jokingly noted that he was tired of Nell's petitions, Garrison remarked that desegregation had been achieved mainly because of his "indefatigable efforts."[47]

The state's success with school desegregation was not replicated elsewhere. A similar movement in Rhode Island begun by Downing, the son of Thomas Downing and a wealthy caterer who moved to the state in 1846, failed. Educated at Hamilton College, New York, Downing was unable to enroll his children in the public schools. In 1857 he coauthored a petition with Northrup, *Will the General Assembly Put Down Caste Schools?* They compiled evidence from Boston, New Bedford, Nantucket, and Cambridge to tout the benefits of integration. The assembly failed to pass a desegregation bill the next year. In 1859 black abolitionists issued a statement for integration, *To the Friends of Equal Rights in Rhode Island*, but the Providence school committee refused to desegregate the schools. The assembly considered desegregation again that year, but a counterpetition from forty-five black men against disbanding the all-black schools doomed it. Garrison noted that the entire press was arrayed against Downing's persistent efforts. The battle for school integration was won only after the war, in 1866. If the antebellum North birthed Jim Crow, it also gave rise to the abolitionist struggle for black citizenship and desegregation, a forgotten nineteenth-century antecedent to the long civil rights movement.[48]

THE RISE OF EMIGRATION

Black abolitionists' rejection of colonization and fight for citizenship were coupled with approval of emigration. "Black cosmopolitanism" posited an identity of interest among all people of African descent in the Western world.[49] Emigration was a declaration of black independence that transcended national borders. It was not just a nationalist but a Pan-African project. Emigration to free spaces like Canada, Haiti, the West Indies, and Africa found acceptance among a growing minority.

Starting with the colony at Wilberforce, emigration to Canada received the support of abolitionists in the United States and Britain. Wilberforce virtually ceased to exist in 1836, consumed by the rivalry between Israel Lewis, one of the settlement's original founders, and Steward, who headed it from 1831 until its demise. Lewis, accused of misappropriating funds he had raised for the colony, was declared persona non grata by the abolitionist press, the Wilberforce board of managers headed by Steward, and the AASS. Steward's vision of black economic and political independence, plans of buying an entire township, and even sending "one of our own race" to represent the colony as a member of Parliament never came to pass. Following Wilberforce, Rev. Hiram Wilson, one of the Lane rebels; the fugitive slave Josiah Henson, who previously headed a small black settlement in Colchester, Canada West; and James Fuller from Skaneateles, New York, founded Dawn in 1841. A year later they opened a manual labor school, the British–American Institute. This colony also fell victim to financial woes and internal disputes between Henson and Wilson on one side and Rev. Isaac Rice, a poor Presbyterian minister from Ohio, and William P. Newman, a black Baptist minister, on the other. Henson, accused of mismanagement of funds, traveled to England in 1849 to raise money for the heavily indebted settlement. Wilson left Dawn and became an AMA missionary at St. Catherine's in 1850. The British and Foreign ASS sent John Scoble, cordially despised by Garrisonians for his conservatism, to investigate. He proved to be a self-aggrandizing administrator who alienated the black residents. Within two decades Dawn was sold to found the Wilberforce Education Institute at Chatham.

Canadian emigration was an alternative to colonization. A new settlement founded north of Amherstburg in 1846 by the Windsor black convention and its "Sandwich mission" became the Refugee Home Society (RHS) in the 1850s, attracting fugitives and black emigrants from Michigan. Aided by Tappan's AMA, the society counted Henry Bibb and his wife, Mary, among its founders. On Bibb's death in 1854, the society collapsed. The most successful black settlement, in Elgin, was founded by William King, an abolitionist Presbyterian minister who inherited and freed his wife's slaves, and rejected the Wilberforce–Dawn system of fund-raising. Despite the hostility of neighboring whites, it was largely self-sufficient and, like the RHS, geared toward the settlement of former slaves. It housed King's Buxton Mission, named after Sir Thomas Fowell Buxton, black schools, churches, and libraries.

Black emigrants to Canada faced discrimination and whites' hostility, but they enjoyed formal political rights. In the east a largely unknown wave of black refugees, many of them slaves from the Chesapeake region after the War of 1812, created a large black community in Halifax, Nova Scotia, with its own African churches and an African Abolition Society in 1846. It too was a haven for fugitive slaves. For black migrants like Jehu Jones, the first ordained black Lutheran minister, civil liberties enjoyed by black Canadians compared favorably with racial proscription in the United States. Around forty thousand fugitive slaves and free blacks immigrated to Canada before the Civil War.[50]

The most passionate proponent of Canadian emigration was Mary Ann Shadd, the daughter of the black abolitionist Abraham Shadd, the only black man elected to public office in Canada before the Civil War. Educated in a Quaker school, Shadd, a schoolteacher, published *Hints to the Colored People in the North* in 1849. She regarded public celebrations as a waste of scarce resources, as they did not address the needs of the masses of poor black people. The pamphlet is lost to history, but it was excerpted in Douglass's paper. A year later, in a letter to Douglass, she called for practical action rather than speeches and conventions. Shadd migrated to Canada. In 1851, together with her father, she attended the Great North American Anti-Slavery Convention in Toronto called by Bibb. Prominent emigrationists such as James Theodore Holly, Ward, and Delany participated. That year Bibb started publishing *Voice of the Fugitive*, with prominent black abolitionists serving as his agents. Shadd ran a school in Windsor, supported by the AMA. In 1852 she published *A Plea for Emigration, Notes of Canada West*. Bristling with information on Canadian climate, soil, crops, society, and government, Shadd's book, like Bibb's editorials, advocated emigration to Canada and the British West Indies as opposed to African colonization, which "invites moral and physical death" under the "escort" of the most "bitter enemies" of black people. Comparing other sites for emigration like Haiti, Mexico, and Central America, she averred that only the British government was powerful enough to withstand the expansion of slavery.

Canadian emigration became the focus of a bitter dispute between the Bibbs and Shadd. The Bibbs recommended separate communities and institutions, Shadd integration into Canadian society. The feud started over the school issue, Mary Bibb lobbying for an all-black government school and Shadd rejecting the idea of racially segregated schools. She targeted separate churches, schools, and Bibb's proposed all-black agricultural leagues as fostering prejudice. Despite her praise of Bibb's newspaper, Shadd criticized the RHS for welcoming fugitive slaves but not impoverished free blacks. Their falling out, fueled by rival accounts to the AMA, which sponsored the missionary and educational activities of both, did not end until Bibb's death. Both had partisans among missionaries and black emigrationists, Holly supporting the Bibbs and Ward, Shadd. Shadd lost AMA backing of her school, and her rivalry with Bibb was sharpened by gender, free versus freed, and ideological differences. In 1853 Bibb's printing office was destroyed by fire. Shadd's *Provincial Freeman*, named after the one abolitionist newspaper that had noticed the publication of her emigrationist tract, the *Pennsylvania Freeman*, soon overtook his newspaper. Shadd's stinging editorials excoriating Canadian prejudice as well as the financial malfeasance of the leaders of Wilberforce, Dawn, and the RHS, Bibb, Henson, and Wilson, and the "begging" system of fund-raising, ruffled many feathers. In 1856 she married the much older Thomas Cary, who invested in her paper, which she published until 1859. After the Civil War and his death, she returned to the United States. A pioneering abolitionist, Shadd Cary was not only the first black woman editor but also, after studying at Howard University, the first black woman lawyer.[51]

Shadd's coeditor in Canada, Ward, had edited the Liberty Party newspaper the *Impartial Citizen*. His name appeared as the editor of the *Provincial Freeman* in its first years of publication mainly for the sake of propriety. Ward's family had escaped slavery. Born in Maryland, he became a teacher in New York. By 1839 he was an AASS agent and a licensed preacher for the Congregational church, known for his dynamic lecturing style. Like a majority of black ministers, Ward, who called himself a Christian abolitionist, followed the Tappanite wing out of the AASS. Moving to upstate New York, he became a successful journalist and an admirer of political abolitionists like Smith, Goodell, and Green. Ward fled for Canada after being indicted in the "Jerry Rescue" fugitive slave case in Syracuse. Like Bibb, who condemned "Color-Phobia in Canada," Ward argued that "Canadian Negro Hate" was "MEANER," as it was gratuitous. But he felt that Canadian emigration acted as a "powerful influence upon our cause in the United States." Holly, a shoemaker from Vermont, also remarked that Canadian emigrants would "hang like an ominous *black cloud* over this guilty nation." Ward applied for a commission as an AMA missionary, and he belonged to the AMA's board of managers. By 1853 he left for Britain on a fund-raising tour as an agent of the Canadian ASS but became embroiled in a financial dispute and sent back very little money for the *Freeman*, earning Shadd's ire.[52]

African Americans proved to be receptive to the idea of emigration to Trinidad and the West Indies after the British abolished slavery. Woodson advocated voluntary and free emigration to "colonies of our own choice" in Canada and the British West Indies and urged African Americans to form independent communities. In 1839 the legislative council of Trinidad offered passage money for colored laborers from Canada and the United States. Replying to Hinton, who helped a shipload of black emigrants from Philadelphia move to Trinidad, Whittier noted that abolitionists, although opposed to colonization, had never opposed voluntary emigration to Canada or Haiti and were willing to consider emigration to Trinidad. The CA rejected emigration as policy and warned that the islands and British Guiana needed cheap labor. When offered a chance to migrate to Trinidad, Canadian blacks refused to jeopardize their dearly won freedom, especially given fears of reenslavement.

Abolitionists were critical of West Indian emigration schemes sponsored by colonial authorities. The antislavery Baptist missionary William Knibb perceived that emigration for cheap labor was another name for slavery. Prince, who published an account of her stay in Jamaica in 1841, wrote that most migrants ended up unacclimated, poor, duped into paying for their passage, and "ruing the day they left their country." Reverend Renshaw reported that Jamaican authorities simply wanted the *"the lowest caste of laborers."* By 1840 the AASS, Garrison, black abolitionists in Philadelphia led by Purvis, Bowers, and Robert Douglass, the AFASS, and the British and Foreign ASS announced their combined opposition to West Indian emigration. Lewis Tappan wrote to James G. Barbadoes, whose family was from the West Indies and who died there, that he would not recommend emigration to Trinidad to his colored friends. The Albany convention also passed an anti-emigration resolution over the objections of Charles Reason and Crummell. The next year African Americans, noting the involvement of Maryland colonizationists in the Trinidad scheme, held anti-emigration meetings in New York and New Jersey. They welcomed Rev. T. P. Hunt, who had gone on a fact-finding mission, and thirty-eight emigrants returning from Trinidad. If African Americans were possessed of the "migrating spirit," the CA recommended the new territories of Iowa and Wisconsin. Only Maryland free blacks entered a counterstatement willing to explore emigration to British Guiana after the failure of Trinidad. Despite abolitionists' reservations, a few hundred blacks from Boston to Baltimore migrated to Jamaica, Trinidad, and British Guiana in the 1830s and early 1840s.[53]

The biggest booster of Haitian emigration in the 1830s was not an abolitionist but the slave trader and planter Zephaniah Kingsley. Kingsley had written a proslavery treatise in 1828, married an African slave, and had children with her and other enslaved women. Unable to protect his family once Florida was acquired by the United States, Kingsley proposed Haitian emigration. Like abolitionists, he sang the praises of the black republic, denigrated Liberia, and in

1839 relocated his son George and "liberated African slaves" to Haiti. After his death in 1843, his son and wife, Anna, successfully fought Kingsley's white relatives for his property. Lydia Maria Child met him before he died, puzzled by the contradictions of his life, and abolitionist newspapers like the *Philanthropist* approved of his Haitian scheme. The *African Repository and Colonial Journal* criticized the Kingsley emigration. It touted the "government of freemen" in Liberia and Cape Palmas as opposed to Haiti, where blacks would be "slaves of the government," and the West Indies and Canada, where they would never be treated as equals.[54]

Confronted with failure at home and abroad, the ACS devolved into an emigration society relying on the private philanthropy of slaveholders. John McDonogh of Louisiana struck a bargain with his slaves, training them and making them work to pay for their passage to Liberia. McDonogh noted that he had to sell two of his slaves for bad behavior but that the promise of freedom made his slaves industrious and moral, so that they earned him enough money to buy a fresh batch from Virginia. The first of his slaves left in 1842 and the last in 1859, nine years after his death, according to the provisions of his will. In a letter from Liberia one of his former slaves wrote, "Here we enjoy the same rights & privileges that our white brethren does in America. It is our only home." Another slaveholder, Capt. Isaac Ross of Mississippi, gave his slaves the choice between freedom in Liberia and being sold on his death. Northern auxiliaries like the Pennsylvania Colonization Society (PCS) helped raise money to manumit and transport freed slaves to Liberia, many of whom negotiated the terms of their freedom. In the two decades before the Civil War, manumitted slaves outnumbered free black emigrants to Liberia. Appropriations by upper south state governments and smaller contributions from northern states allowed the ACS and state societies to send nearly four thousand emigrants to Liberia between 1848 and 1854.[55]

Black abolitionists, however, continued to critique colonization. In 1840 Cornish and Wright, identifying themselves as pastors of the Colored Presbyterian churches in Newark and New York, published *The Colonization Scheme Considered* in response to Sen. Theodore Frelinghuysen and Benjamin F. Butler. Frelinghuysen, the so-called Christian statesman, presided over the American Tract and Bible Societies, opposed Indian removal, and promoted the Christianization of Africa. He was Clay's running mate on the Whig ticket in 1844 and the vice president of the ACS. The religiosity of the Pilgrims and of William Penn's followers, Cornish and Wright argued, did not lead to the survival of Native Americans. Most Christian colonies led to resentment by the natives and to their oppression. This reaction had occurred "irrespective of the color" of the colonists in Liberia, where colonists waged incessant wars with the surrounding native populations.[56]

The rhetoric of the ACS became emigrationist after Liberia's independence in 1847. Joseph J. Roberts, a wealthy Monrovia merchant from Virginia whose enslaved mother bought his freedom, was elected president. The motto of the new nation read, "The love of liberty brought us here." The ACS and the NYCS reported a spike of interest in emigration to Liberia among blacks. The "black nationality of Liberia is a fact not to be gain-sayed or resisted," the thirty-second annual report of the ACS proclaimed. According to Ephraim Peabody, Liberia had proven that black men were capable of supporting civilized government. In 1849 Archibald Alexander, in his mammoth history of colonization, included an appendix containing the Liberian Declaration of Independence and its new Constitution. The British abolitionist Wilson Armistead used the independence of Liberia to argue for black equality. He was particularly impressed by the inaugural address of Roberts and an "eloquent speech" by the Liberian senator Hilary Teague.[57]

Colonizationists deployed increasingly nationalistic appeals to free blacks. Breckinridge noted the ACS's "sublime design" to "organize a real and enduring nationality" for black people "in its original seats." Acquiring state funds and money from the federal government to relocate recaptives taken from the illegal African slave trade, the ACS and the state societies published a barrage of information on emigration to Liberia in the 1850s. Jacob Dewees of the PCS argued that American Africans, by redeeming the continent, repaid America's debt to it. Alluding to Buxton's African Civilization Society's exploration of the Niger River valley in 1841–42, he recommended that it become the site of a free black state. He concluded that without a black nation, Africa would be brought under "colonial vassalage to the white race." Rev. C. Van Rensselaer rebuked both abolitionists for failing to promote black nationality and proslavery ministers like George Armstrong of Virginia for fostering the permanence of slavery.[58]

Prominent Liberians promoted black emigration. As the governor of Liberia, Roberts was a proponent of independence and toured the United States in 1844 to encourage emigration. Russwurm admonished that if the ACS was *"actuated by a right spirit"* it could have acted as a vehicle for black emigration instead of being forced to "seek Emigrants." As the governor of Cape Palmas, Russwurm praised the Maryland Colonization Society for its experiment in elevating men of color to offices of great trust and responsibility. He died in 1851. The Maryland colony declared its independence in 1854 and joined Liberia three years later. In the 1850s a number of other blacks made the case for Liberian emigration. In their report of 1852 Thomas Fuller and Benjamin Janifer wrote, "There is not a single office filled by a white man" in Liberia. For Rev. William B. Hoyt, Liberia was a land of hope. Rev. Daniel H. Petersen extolled his missionary calling in Africa and contended that black people must employ a national point of view. H. W. Ellis, sent by the Presbyterian Synod of Alabama and Mississippi, hoped to "live, labor and die in Africa."[59]

The project of a modern black nation represented an amalgam of romantic nationalism and black autonomy. Before he left for Liberia, Crummell in his writings fell in line with abolitionist criticisms of colonization. In 1847, attracted to missionary work in the newly independent nation, he met President Roberts in London. Like most emigrationists, Crummell was a product of Western education, and his nationalist project was primarily a political one. Christianity and civilization would redeem Africa, in his view, as it had Europe. At the same time, Crummell confronted the racism of white missionaries and colonizationist authorities. He criticized the treatment of native Africans by American settlers but regarded it as the duty of the African diaspora to save Africa through Christianization, commercial development, and education. The West Indian–born intellectual Edward Wilmot Blyden saw Liberia as "destined . . . to revolutionize for good the whole of that portion of Africa." Blyden, who migrated to Liberia in 1851 and taught at Liberia College, was Liberia's first ambassador to England and died in Sierra Leone.[60]

Other black abolitionists announced their conversion to Liberian emigration. Lewis Putnam in New York founded the Liberian Agriculture and Emigration Society. When the wrath of the entire black leadership descended on him for his "Judas-like" turn to traitor, he disavowed any connection with the ACS. The Committee of Thirteen led by Pennington, Cornish, Bell, and Downing convened to oppose both Putnam and the colonizationist Gov. Washington Hunt. A black delegation waited on Hunt to oppose state funding of the ACS. In 1860 Putnam would issue another appeal for emigration. Augustus Washington, a teacher from New Jersey who, financed by Lewis Tappan and Samuel Cox, studied at Dartmouth and then worked as a daguerreotypist in Hartford, published *Thoughts on the American Colonization Society* in 1851. Containing a judicious overview of abolition and colonization, it detailed Washington's interest in forming a "separate state" for black people. African Americans must be the "architects of our own fortunes." He advocated a coming together of abolition and colonization so that abolitionists might acknowledge the disabilities free blacks labored under and colonizationists support black education and uplift rather than simply removal. Washington asked the American government to recognize Liberia and endorsed the ACS plan to supply a line of steamers for mass black emigration. In 1853 he migrated to Liberia. A year later Washington, in a letter that was widely reprinted, detailed the less-than-ideal conditions in Liberia. It was "no Paradise, no Elysium, no Eldorado," but if Pennington and Douglass could plead for black rights in America, which consistently denied African Americans full citizenship, Washington asked black migrants to correct abuses and oppression in Liberia. In 1863 he planned to visit New York but was "afraid to venture" in the aftermath of the Draft Riots, which became a racial pogrom against the city's black community, a reminder of why he had left in the first place.[61]

Black abolitionism existed as a distinct phenomenon in the years before the Civil War, with its own institutions and concerns. African Americans made antiracism, at a programmatic as well as intellectual level, an essential part of the abolitionist project. They remained instrumental in developing movement strategy and ideology, taking on the burden of redefining the white man's democracy.

THE ABOLITIONIST INTERNATIONAL

"Our Country is the World—Our Countrymen are Mankind" was the motto that adorned the *Liberator*'s masthead from 1831 to 1865. As Garrison's adoption of Thomas Paine's slogan indicated, abolitionists, especially Garrisonians, developed a transnational appeal seeking to harness progressive international forces against slavery. Abolitionists did not just articulate a civic nationalism of liberal democratic values or a naïve celebration of Anglo-American virtue. While they supported other radical movements of the mid-nineteenth century, abolitionists insisted that they rid themselves of racial parochialism. They posited an alternative notion of universal human rights, one that had its origins in Enlightenment thought but went beyond its typical articulation in the West, which excluded or rested on the oppression of disfranchised groups.[1]

Emancipation, in this understanding, included not only the abolition of slavery but also the liberation of all oppressed people. Abolitionists were never single-issue agitators. They linked the abolition of slavery with the plight of Native Americans, labor, and immigrants, holding no truck with nativism or racism. Contrary to conventional historical wisdom, they developed an incipient critique of capitalism that linked the emancipation of the slaves with that of all laboring people. Rather than acting as stalking horses for imperialism, American abolitionists, informed by their long struggle for racial equality and against the civilizationist discourse of colonization, developed an early response to it. As the movement matured, it remained ideologically consistent, sympathizing with labor and communitarian movements, the radical side of the revolutions in Europe, and the emergence of anti-imperialism in Ireland and India. Far from reinforcing the sanctity of bourgeois society, the nation-state, and empire, abolition bolstered radical internationalism.[2]

THE BLACK INTERNATIONAL

Black abolitionists insisted that their struggle receive an international hearing. They acted as abolition's ambassadors, creating a cordon sanitaire around southern slavery. Touring Britain and Europe became a rite of passage for many, who experienced their trips abroad as "liberating sojourns" away from the all-encompassing pall of American racism. At the same time, their criticism of Western racism played out on a global stage.[3]

African Americans invented a popular transnational antislavery tradition, the annual celebration of British emancipation, the first of August, though they were hardly naïve or uncritical celebrants of Britain. In 1834 David Lee Child's speech on the historical origins of British emancipation first marked the occasion. But African Americans regularly observed West India Day, reviving black emancipation commemorations of the abolition of the slave trade and northern slavery. In 1836 a committee of New York's black abolitionists, Cornish, Wright, Van Rensselaer, Sipkins, and Thomas Downing, arranged the first mass celebration of August First. In his address Cornish criticized the "weak and foolish" aspects of British abolition, namely, slaveholder compensation and the apprenticeship system, but noted that while eight hundred thousand slaves in the West Indies were free, over two million remained enslaved in the United States. He laid out an international agenda for black abolitionism, saying, "We will fill every continent and island with the story of the WRONGS done to our brethren." That year black Philadelphians celebrated the anniversary with the active participation of women. After the abolition of apprenticeship, Garrison addressed a record all-black meeting of nearly four thousand at the Broadway Tabernacle in New York. In Philadelphia, William Douglass delivered a First of August address to a black audience. Pennington in his West India address in Newark in 1839 argued that the month of August would henceforth be associated with black freedom rather than with Augustus Caesar. Black abolitionists in Boston, Rochester, Pittsburgh, Detroit, Poughkeepsie, Lynn, Albany, Buffalo, Troy, Dayton, and Cincinnati, as well as Wilmington, where Abraham Shadd delivered an "appropriate and excellent address," celebrated West India Day.[4]

In 1842 John Collins suggested antislavery picnics to mark August First as a recruiting tool for the movement. Rev. Jehiel Beman, who had parted company with Garrisonians, insisted that the day belonged to colored men. Samuel J. May promoted annual interracial mass celebrations on August First, and by the 1850s the MASS hosted a yearly event in Abington, as did other abolition societies in New England. Remond, Nell, Rock, and the fugitive slave abolitionist William Wells Brown, besides Garrison and Phillips, were the star speakers at these gatherings. Abolitionists did not use this opportunity to advocate the peaceful, orderly, legal abolition of slavery or praise Britain uncritically. Phillips pointed out that the British government had to be bullied by abolitionists into legislating emancipation. As a former slave himself, Wells Brown warranted he would not advocate nonresistance to the slaves. The First of August addresses invoked Haiti in the same breadth as West Indian emancipation. As Rock put it, he was more proud of Haiti since England was generous to the planters but left the slaves to "test the charities of an unfriendly world." In 1858 the guest of honor at the annual MASS antislavery picnic was the West Indian Baptist minister Rev. Henry Bleby. His speech eulogized the slave rebel Sam Sharpe as a "perfect model man" executed in "cold blood" by colonial authorities. Emancipation had not ruined the slaves, he remarked, but compensation had ruined the planters.[5]

West India Day remained a predominantly black celebration, thousands gathering to observe it even in small towns like Urbana, Brooklyn, Harrisburg, and Canandaigua, Medina, Geneva, Lockport, among others in upstate New York. Accompanied by antislavery fairs and bazaars, dance, music, and food, the First of August celebrations became more and more popular and plebeian. The mass celebrations demonstrated the depth of abolitionism in black communities across class lines. In his address of 1854 in Columbus, Ohio, William J. Watkins said that African Americans shall not esteem the Fourth of July orators of slaveholding America. And while they could not "sing the Funeral Requiem of Slavery in this Land of Liberty," they could rejoice over abolition in the world. Two years later Pennington, in his First of August address in Hartford, advocated "the reasonableness of the abolition of slavery at the South, a legitimate inference from the success of British Emancipation." All-black gatherings continued in Boston and Providence. First of August celebrations spread to émigré and fugitive slave communities in Canada, changing from loyalist demonstrations to more radical affairs. Bibb excoriated discrimination in the new homeland as "second hand imitations" of the slaveholding Republic rather than simply sing paeans to the British. In 1859 black Baltimoreans and expatriates in Liberia celebrated the First of August. So engrained was this tradition that when slavery was abolished in the District of Columbia in 1862, the black community chose to celebrate on August 1. During the war, abolitionists used the occasion of West India Day to demand emancipation.[6]

Throughout the antebellum period black abolitionists traveled to Europe to make their case against American slavery as ambassadors of the movement. Nathaniel Paul and Robert Purvis, who went armed with Garrison's letters of introduction, conducted lecture tours in Britain in the 1830s. McCune Smith,

studying medicine at Glasgow, made a name for himself delivering abolitionist speeches before the Glasgow Emancipation Society (GES). Remond's successful one-year tour of the British Isles after the London World Antislavery
Convention of 1840 made black speakers a mainstay of the British abolitionist
lecture circuit. News of Remond's speeches denouncing American racism and
asking the Irish not to emigrate to such a despotic country filled the abolitionist
press. Like Paul, Remond, whose visit coincided with that of R. R. Gurley of the
ACS, was an effective lecturer against colonization. So were Birney and Stanton, lecturing under the auspices of the British and Foreign ASS, which was
allied with the AFASS and opposed Collins's fund-raising trip for the AASS.[7]

Black abolitionists abroad usually steered clear of factional divisions. Pennington undertook two successful lecture tours of England, his first coincid-
ing with that of Tappan, Leavitt, and Phelps, all of whom were attending the
second World Antislavery Convention in London in 1843. Pennington attended
as a delegate of both the Connecticut ASS and his Union Missionary Society
and church. He drew attention to Jim Crow and introduced the British to the
unique concerns of African Americans. He read out loud the address of the
national black convention and provided a comprehensive history of the growth
of black churches and institutions. Despite incurring criticism for starting a
new society in Glasgow, Pennington read from the *Liberator* to highlight racial
discrimination and referred to Garrison's *Thoughts* against colonization. He argued that American slavery was not a domestic question but one that affected
all humankind. In a rousing speech on a resolution condemning the British
government's shipping of indentured labor from Africa and India at the annual
meeting of the British and Foreign ASS, he affirmed, "What I gain anywhere
and everywhere, I gain for every manacled slave in America, and for every benighted African in the world."

Pennington's triumph set the stage for his tour of Europe in 1849. As a mark
of his growing international celebrity, Pennington published his narrative in
London. His erudite lectures condemned slavery as robbery, murder, and rapine and racism as a gross violation of Christian precepts. Pennington met the
pacifist and abolitionist Friedrich Wilhelm Carove of the University of Heidelberg at the Paris peace congress, from whom he deliberately sought an honorary
doctorate of divinity "as a recognition not for himself, as for his color, which
represented by him, and which is so deeply disdained in America." Carove appended Pennington's considerable body of published work to his petition, and
he became the first African American to receive the honor. "Germany," Pennington responded, "stands high in our affections, not only on account of her
literary fame, but because of the fidelity her sons in America have shown to the

cause of human liberty," complimenting German immigrants for their free soil sentiments. When Carove died two years later, the AFASS, of whose executive committee Pennington was a member, held a memorial service.[8]

Despite receiving international acclaim, black abolitionists described the racial indignities they were subjected to during their travels abroad. In 1837 an American ship captain had refused cabin accommodations to McCune Smith on his return to New York from Glasgow. Purvis got the better of a slaveholder who had objected to traveling with a black man on the way to England. The same man unknowingly invited the light-skinned Purvis to share his table on the return journey. Remond was unable to purchase a ticket for his transatlantic voyage without the intervention of his traveling companion, William Adam. He and Adam were forced to give up their berths in a shared cabin, confined to steerage, and constantly harassed by the crew. Remond's sister Caroline Remond Putnam was forced to give up her first-class cabin in a British Cunard steamer, a line that was known to discriminate against blacks. Ward recounted his journey to Canada: American ships had given him a cabin passage, but a British liner compelled him to travel on the deck, leading him to say, "The boast of Englishmen of their freedom from social negrophobia, is about as empty as the Yankee boast of democracy." When America's most famous fugitive, Frederick Douglass, traveled to Britain, he and James Buffum were forced to travel steerage in the *Cambria*, illustrating, he said, American customs on a "British steamer, under the British flag." Douglass delivered a fiery indictment of slavery accompanied by the abolitionist Hutchinson family singers, arousing the ire of slaveholders, who threatened him. A few, like Nancy Prince and David Dorr, who wrote travel memoirs, noted the lack of a rigid color line in Europe.

African Americans were denied passports and declared noncitizens by the U.S. government in the wake of the *Dred Scott* decision of 1857. They were forced to travel at their own peril unless, like Dorr, they accompanied their masters as slaves. The antislavery secretary of state of Massachusetts John Gorham Palfrey issued certificates for blacks, and at times the federal government issued them on a case-by-case basis. Purvis was one of the few who obtained a passport through the intervention of Robert Vaux of the PAS. In 1859 Sarah Parker Remond managed to secure a passport, but the American legation in London refused to stamp a visa for her visit to Paris.[9]

Black abolitionists sought to undo the legacy of the Middle Passage, the object of their travels being distinct from that of the American elite on European Grand Tours. As Ward put it, "God helping me wherever I shall be, at home, abroad, on land or sea, in public or private walks, as a man, a Christian, especially as a black man, my labours must be anti-slavery labours, because mine must be an anti-slavery life." His narrative, published in Britain, contained a systematic condemnation of racism in the Anglo-American world. He alluded to the scores of fugitive slaves and black abolitionists who had won international renown and argued for the continued need to battle proslavery racists and British "colonists." In Ireland he commented on the deplorable condition of the Irish and lamented that immigrants became "negro haters" even though they shared a history of extreme oppression with African Americans. Ward, however, fashioned himself as an imperial subject, dedicating his narrative to the Duchess of Sutherland and inadvertently commending a proslavery missionary society patronized by Lord Shaftesbury.[10]

Black abolitionists found England to be far from a racial paradise. Raising funds for his congregation at home, Crummell, in his correspondence with John Jay II, agonized over his decision to study in Cambridge. Eventually Crummell identified the cause of his own education with that of the race. In Cambridge one of Crummell's professors referred to his children as black pickaninnies, and an Irish maid called his wife a black devil. In a careful exegesis of Genesis, Crummell argued that "the negro race" was not biblically cursed to slavery. Only with the rise of modern racial slavery, "anti-negro" and proslavery ideas dominated European literature. The reality of racism in supposedly enlightened Britain helped Crummell decide to migrate to Liberia.[11]

Black abolitionists made antiracism a part of their mission abroad, especially as black face minstrelsy and the pseudoscience of race made racism popular and intellectually respectable in Britain. In 1848 Wilson Armistead of the Leeds ASS dedicated his mammoth *A Tribute to the Negro* to "JAMES W. C. PENNINGTON, FREDERICK DOUGLASS, ALEXANDER CRUMMELL, AND MANY OTHER NOBLE EXAMPLES OF ELEVATED HUMANITY IN THE NEGRO." Part one of the book deconstructed scientific racism, and part two contained short biographies of eminent blacks from Wheatley to Garnet as well as abolitionist indictments of slavery. Douglass, who was critical of the superimposed smile on his face in the book, nonetheless praised its contents. The same year Armistead published a book on Liberia in which he reprinted Garnet's Troy speech on the condition and destiny of the colored race. Armistead presented this book to the Boston Anti-Slavery Bazaar, revealing the transatlantic circulation of abolitionist antiracist ideology and the seminal role of African Americans in its construction.[12]

While in England, the fugitive slave abolitionist William Wells Brown criticized the famous essayist Thomas Carlyle, who was much admired on both sides of the Atlantic, for his crude racism and opposition to West Indian emancipation. Carlyle's satirical "Occasional Discourse on the Negro Question" (1849) was republished as a popular pamphlet, "Occasional Discourse on the Nigger

Question," supporting Governor Eyre for his brutal suppression of the Morant Bay rebellion in Jamaica in 1865. Wells Brown critiqued Carlyle's "laborious article in favor of the reestablishment of the lash of slavery," saying that he existed "not by sympathy but by antipathy." He highlighted Carlyle's contradictions: his concern for Irish farmers and the British working poor, but Jamaicans should be whipped into working. Wells Brown, who initially was for emigration to the West Indies, now opposed it as a second servitude. Notwithstanding his own success as an author, he discouraged African Americans from coming to England to lead lives of poverty and obscurity. His *The Black Man* (1863) a prosopography of black abolitionists, rebels, and writers was a "full-scale retort" to the race science of his times.[13]

As John Brown, a Georgia runaway, found out, riding the abolitionist lecture circuit and living as a black person in England, where most joined the swelling ranks of the urban working poor, were two entirely different propositions. After being unable to find work and noting, "There is prejudice against colour in England," Brown started lecturing under the auspices of the British and Foreign ASS and published his narrative with the help of its energetic new secretary, Louis Alexis Chamerovzow, in 1855. Hitting just the right notes for a British audience, Brown recounted the story of a black British sailor arrested in Georgia under the state's Negro Seamen's Act and the murder of a Scotsman by his master because he angered local slaveholders by offering wages to slaves. When the price of cotton rises in England, Brown observed, the slaves feel its effects immediately, being driven harder. Besides numerous tortures inflicted on him and his fellow slaves, Brown told of how his body had been used by his master, a doctor, in gruesome medical experiments testing the endurance of darker skinned people to heat to find a cure for sunburns.[14] He exposed the horrific reality that undergirded the discourse of racial science.

In 1853 William G. Allen published his exposé of racism, *The American Prejudice Against Colour*, in London, calling himself a refugee from this form of "American despotism." A frequent contributor to the *Liberator*, Allen edited Garnet's short-lived *National Watchman* in Troy and worked at the law offices of Loring before becoming a professor of Greek and rhetoric at New York Central College. Allen's marriage to a white student, Mary King, caused an uproar. Both fled to Britain, narrowly escaping a lynch mob led by town leaders. Allen's book challenged "American caste and skin-deep democracy" and contained an account of the episode in which he paid tribute to King's "moral heroism." King's family was deeply divided, her father initially and her sister supporting her while her brothers and stepmother were opposed. Allen resigned his position, and the college, an abolitionist experiment in interracial education, closed down amidst charges of racial amalgamation. He appended his narrative, his birth as a free man in Norfolk, Virginia, the shutting down of his school after Turner's revolt, and his upbringing at the federal Fort Monroe to his book. Allen pointed out that even some abolitionists opposed his marriage, yet he complimented Samuel Porter and his wife, who helped him escape the mob, Gerrit Smith, on whose recommendation he studied at Oneida, and his teacher there, Beriah Green. Porter was fired from his teaching job for his troubles. Allen's interracial romance became the subject of one of Louisa May Alcott's stories.

In England, Allen gave a lecture called "American Slavery and the Prejudice Against Color" and a lecture entitled "History, Literature and Destiny of the African Race," which was popular on both sides of the Atlantic. The genius of the American nation, he claimed, like Garnet earlier, lay in the intermingling of the races. On the other hand, he pointed out that Banneker was of pure African blood, as was the successful opera singer Elizabeth Greenfield. Refuting Samuel Morton, Allen maintained that the greatness of Egypt belonged to the African race. When McCune Smith, writing as Communipaw, took Allen to task for speaking about different races when there was but one race of man, Allen replied that he was forced to adopt the language of ethnology, the contemporary science of humankind, even when refuting it. After living as an impoverished schoolteacher in England, he blamed his failure on "a spirit not supposed to usually exist among Englishmen" and contemplated migrating to Liberia.[15]

On the eve of the Civil War, the most effective black abolitionist in Britain was Sarah Parker Remond, who launched her career in 1856 as an agent for the AASS, accompanying her brother on a lecture tour. Denied admission to Salem high school, she, like her sisters, studied in a black school in Newport. In 1858 Remond left for Britain accompanied by May. Thousands attended her speeches, which condemned slavery, racism, the exploitation of slave women, and the partiality of the conservative British press for southern secessionists. As she put it, "The negroes and their descendants, whether enslaved or free, desire and need the moral support of Great Britain." In 1861 Garnet, Day, and the Boston clergyman John Sella Martin joined her to make the abolitionist case against recognizing the Confederacy. Remond was active in the London Emancipation Society and the Freedmen's Aid Society during the war. British women abolitionists presented her with an inscribed watch as a token of their regard and in recognition of her work. She attended college in Britain and medical school in Florence, marrying at the age of fifty-two. Remond practiced medicine in Italy, joined there by her sisters, until she died in 1894.[16] By that time, many black abolitionists had helped internationalize the fight against slavery and racism.

THE ABOLITIONIST CRITIQUE OF CAPITALISM

In its early years the abolition movement had garnered more sympathy from the working classes than from the better sort. In New York City the only editor to condemn anti-abolition violence was William Leggett of the *New York Evening Post,* known for his championing of workingmen's rights. Labor leaders and land reformers like Thomas Skidmore and George Henry Evans were antislavery. Evans was the only editor besides Garrison to defend Nat Turner's rebellion and the Haitian Revolution. He vindicated abolitionists' right to be heard, though he had little in common with the city's evangelical abolitionists, led by the Tappans. The labor and abolition movements shared a discourse of oppression: working-class reformers adopted the term *wage slavery* to describe the abysmal conditions of workers, as slavery remained the benchmark of oppression. In 1835 the AASS reported that the "honest, hard working, clear headed free laborers of the North" had yet to fully support abolition, but it was optimistic about a future alliance. Working-class activists involved in the ten-hour-a-day movement in New England adopted the language of reform. The enslavement of labor represented its degradation in the eyes of most working-class leaders, even those not sympathetic to abolition.

Less known is the fact that abolitionists sympathized with the plight of labor. As the president of the NYASS, William Jay contrasted the voluntary nature of free labor to that of slave labor. But he denounced the criminal prosecution of labor unions, comparing it to the widespread toleration of anti-abolition violence. He noted, "Journeymen mechanics are indicted and punished for violations of law utterly insignificant in their character and tendency compared to the outrages committed last year." Nathaniel P. Rogers wrote about the oppressions of the factory system and argued that abolition asserted *"the dignity and freedom of Labor."* Rev. Moses Thacher asked, "Is there a manufactory in New England, whose walls are not built up on the sighs, tears, and groans of bondage?" Henry C. Wright assailed northern "great merchants" for their anti-abolitionist, proslavery stance and said that the Panic of 1837 was a just punishment for their economic ties with southern slaveholders. Burleigh contended that the slaveholding aristocracy could not enslave the northern laborer even though the northern mercantile aristocracy may kowtow to them. William Dexter Wilson averred that both slaves and free labor were "subject to the will of the monied few."[17]

In critiquing slavery, abolitionists did not legitimize wage labor, however much historians have speculated on the theoretical implications of their arguments. Rather, they drew a connection between the oppression of slaves and that of the wageworker. The RIASS argued for the enfranchisement of colored as well as white laborers. It pointed out that the proslavery position could be just as "easily applied to white laborers as to colored ones," exposing its undemocratic essence: "'Bleached or unbleached'—white or colored—the *laboring man* is pronounced a 'dangerous element of the body politic. . . .' The *laboring classes of mankind* are incapable of self government, and ought to be under the control of their superiors!" As David Root of the NHASS put it, "Let our laboring men, our mechanics, the operatives in our factories, the free yeomanry of New England think of that, and ponder it in their hearts." Isaac Stearns, who apologized for his lack of education, explained that abolitionists "do not believe in giving to the rich who have defrauded the poor, and then sending the poor, empty away, who have earned all these riches." In the view of Rogers, abolition was a movement on behalf of human labor since labor everywhere was disrespected and degraded. One Philadelphia abolitionist contended that "the abolition of slavery, in our country, is indispensably necessary to make labor respectable, and the working man respected—as well as insure to those who toil and sweat their just reward." The second annual report of the NHASS claimed that slaveholders despised the "white menial" as much as they did the slave. According to Green, the manual laborer was always subject to "varying degrees of oppression" until he is reduced to slavery. "Hence the multiplied injuries which have fallen so heavy on him. Hence the reduce of his wages from one degree to another, till at length, in the case of millions, fraud and violence strip him of his all, blot his name from the record of *mankind*, and, putting a yoke upon his neck drive him away to toil with the cattle. *Here you find the slave.*"[18]

Garrison, whose anticapitalism is vastly underestimated, acknowledged that labor had many legitimate grievances but sanguinely noted that in a republican society an "industrious artisan" would always be "held in better estimation than a wealthy idler." He soon realized that this was an overly optimistic assessment of workingmen's position in the slaveholding Republic. In announcing his approval of the ten-hour-a-day movement, he cited "the exorbitant exaction of labor and time," the neglect of children's education, the "severe regulations" of the factory system and how "rich capitalists . . . grind the face of the poor." In a hint to workingmen, Garrison published an extract reflecting that both the labor and antislavery movements represented the fight between aristocracy and democracy. On his departure to England, he wrote a heartfelt critique of financial capitalism: "I am writing in Wall Street, where the money-changers congregate, and where affluence and beggary are seen side by side, but acknowledging no relationship by creation, and at mutual enmity with each other. It is rightly named—*Wall* Street—for those who habitually occupy it in quest of riches at the expense of mankind, are *walled* in from the sympathies of human nature, and their hearts are as fleshless and hard as the paving-stones on which they tread, or the granite and marble buildings which they have erected and dedicated to their idol Gain." While attending the World Anti-Slavery Convention, Garrison argued that the British working class was "grievously oppressed" and abolitionists "are sympathetic with the oppressed as well as the enslaved throughout the world." Although he wrote that poverty was not slavery, Garrison highlighted the abuse of women and children in British industries, "a Manchester factory girl" who was a "rich man's slave" and the landless English peasant. He even reprinted "The Workingman's Appeal" from the Jacksonian anti-abolitionist newspaper the *Washington Globe*.

Ideological affinity but political separation marked the abolition and early labor movements. Some working-class leaders such as Seth Luther and John Pickering held implausibly that their condition was worse than that of slaves, while others, like Theophilus Fisk and Ely Moore, issued racist denunciations of abolition. In his review essay of Carlyle's *Chartism*, "The Laboring Classes," Orestes Brownson, the Transcendentalist labor activist, pronounced slavery less oppressive than free labor, though he claimed to be "heartily opposed to it as any modern abolitionist can be." In 1838 Brownson wrote to Garrison that he advocated the abolitionists' right to freedom of speech and press but that he was against slavery of all kinds, including that of the poor. The two men debated amicably over which cause should be given priority. Brownson decided that both promoted "universal emancipation," and Garrison lauded his refutation of Calhoun's notion that slavery was the best solution to the conflict between labor and capital. In the 1840s Evans's the *Workingmen's Advocate* compared the oppression of northern labor to that of slaves, calling for the abolition of "wage slavery" before "chattel slavery." In response, Garrison reversed the order, and Edmund Quincy asserted that anyone who saw wage slavery as worse than chattel slavery was an enemy of abolition.

Garrison was respectful of labor critics, such as William West, publishing their letters and articles in his paper. He debated Charles M'ewan, a Scottish Chartist who identified himself as a white slave and took Garrison to task for distinguishing between slavery and wage labor. Garrison praised the letter's manly spirit and reiterated his opposition to slavery as well as to workers' oppression. The Chartists represented a just cause, but he disagreed with M'ewan's censure of abolitionists. A few years later Garrison debated the labor leader James

Mitchell, who accused Irish abolitionists such as James Haughton of feeling "extra sympathy" for Africans and ignoring the misery of the working poor. Garrison defended Haughton, whom he quoted as saying that those who sympathized with slaves but not with the poor are hypocrites and that "we should be diligent in laboring for the abatement of the evils that afflict our own poor." He added that the greater hypocrite was one who pretends sympathy for the English poor and ignores African slaves. Men such as Carlyle, Garrison wrote, did not care for either the slave or the working poor. William J. Willicott, too, responded that Mitchell was mistaken, as abolitionists were for the abolition of all oppression.

During his visit to England the socialist-minded Collins cemented the alliance between abolitionists and Chartists, who presented an address to him signed by M'ewan himself. The address challenged the notion that British workers were indifferent to the plight of "our colored and enslaved brethren" and condemned slavery as the "climax of human wretchedness." It also scolded American workers for their coolness to abolition and called on them to join the abolitionists. The British, Collins noted, exercised "that same prejudice against poverty" as the Americans did in the matter of color. He called it a "dangerous species of slavery," as it was "subtle and intangible." Other abolitionists reprehended the condition of workers. William I. Bowditch condemned the "heartless, soul-destroying competition" that gave rise to wage slavery. Even the Tappanite wing of the movement held that God's wrath was visited on nations that "oppress the poor and the hireling in his wages," though the AFASS steered clear of linking abolition to other causes and was particularly critical of Collins's radicalism.[19]

Garrison and his allies tried to build an internationalist vision for abolition. While they sympathized with protests against the protectionist Corn Laws in Britain that led to high food prices, aggravated famine in Ireland, and benefited the landed elite, Garrisonians espoused a transnational abolitionism through an alliance with labor and radical reform. Just as labor leaders in Britain were skeptical of the free trade doctrines of the anti–Corn Law leaders, Garrison was suspicious of the laissez-faire proclivities of slaveholding politicians like George McDuffie and Calhoun. He published letters by Chartists like the anonymous Sophia as well as Wendell Phillips's favorable assessment of British Chartism. Harriet Martineau opposed government regulation but supported the Chartist movement and believed in workers' cooperatives, leading Robert Owen to attempt to convert her to socialism. Joseph Sturge forged an alliance with the Chartists and backed their fight for suffrage. Even militant Chartists like Feargus O'Connor, who was critical of Sturge, worked for his failed candidacy for

Parliament. Though allied with the British and Foreign ASS, Sturge's activism resembled the Garrisonian approach to abolition.

During his third visit to England Garrison gave organizational form to the abolitionist alliance with the Chartists. He, Wright, Douglass, Thompson, and William Lovett and Henry Vincent of the London Workingmen's Association founded the Anti-Slavery League in Britain in 1846, modeled after Richard Cobden's and John Bright's Anti–Corn Law League. Vincent identified the cause of labor with that of abolition, and Garrison declared himself to be a workingman who was one with the Chartists. Commending Lovett and Vincent "for pleading the cause of starving operatives," Garrison wrote, "such men I honor and revere." The league was a radical alliance unlike the conservative reformism of the World Temperance Convention and the Evangelical Alliance, which rescinded its antislavery report at Americans' insistence. Garrison realized that his association with "unpopular reformatory movements" alienated the "good society folks" from abolition, but, he concluded, "the cause of my enslaved countrymen cannot possibly be injured by my advocacy of the rights of all men, or by my opposition to all tyranny." The genteel John Estlin deplored his attempts to appeal to the lower classes. But the British Garrisonians William Henry Ashurst, Elizabeth Pease, William Smeal of the GES, and Richard Webb, Haughton, and Richard Allen in Ireland bolstered Garrison's endeavor to establish transnational networks of radical protest. (Webb had written to Garrison about Vincent early on.) They became regular contributors to the *Liberator*, drawing telling parallels between oppressed workers, starving Irish peasants, and slaves. Ashurst and Pease, a "superior woman" as Garrison described her (he named his second daughter after her), were ardent supporters of the Chartist movement. Most American abolitionists were supportive of the Chartists and their goal, universal suffrage for workingmen. The political abolitionist Gamaliel Bailey, though, thought abolition was more important than Chartism, as the former fought for natural rights, the latter for conventional ones.[20]

Black abolitionists deconstructed one of the mainstays of proslavery ideology, the idea that the condition of American slaves was better than that of the European working classes. As Pennington pointed out, it was not material conditions but the commodification of human beings that defined slavery. To African Americans comparing the condition of slaves and the working classes was like comparing apples and oranges. They deeply resented those who used the labor question to shore up the proslavery argument. An infuriated Powell responded that workers were neither "chattels personal" nor subject to "corporeal punishment." Allen, informing Sumner of his involvement in educational and penal reform, wrote, "The blows which Englishmen strike at American Slavery are really best parried by the references which Americans make to the poverty and uneducated state of what are termed the lower classes in this country." Black abolitionists, however, were not unsympathetic to the laboring poor. Remond, Douglass, and Wells Brown remarked on the utter wretchedness of starving Irish peasants, and the British working classes flocked to hear African Americans in far greater numbers than white abolitionists. Sarah Parker Remond saw an identity of interest: the slaves constituted the working class of the South. She wrote, "The free operatives of Britain are, in reality, brought into almost personal relations with slaves in their daily toil. They manufacture the material which the slaves have produced." During the Civil War, according to the American apostle of "pure and simple unionism" Samuel Gompers, English Tories and cotton manufacturers openly sympathized with the Confederacy, but British workers influenced by the spirit of Chartism and revolution identified with the Union and abolitionists, despite the fact that they faced "hunger and want" owing to the cotton famine brought on by the blockade.[21]

Long before contemporary historians did, abolitionists drew attention to the connection between the growth of capitalism and slavery and the central place of slave-labor-grown cotton in the national and global political economy. Sen. Thomas Morris of Ohio condemned the unholy alliance between the Slave Power and the money power, while Sumner upbraided the textile mill owners of New England, the "lords of the loom," and southern slaveholders, the "lords of the lash." Radical political abolitionists such as William Goodell and Gerrit Smith were critical of the rise of capitalism and connected it to their battle against racial slavery. Goodell was a staunch critic of market society and the aristocracy of wealth, reasoning that white workers were threatened with enslavement if slavery was not abolished. He indicted the system of paying the hireling inadequate wages and condemned slavery as "LABOR WITHOUT WAGES." Rogers, refuting the proslavery ideologues William Harper and Thomas R. Dew, made a similar argument. In his *Democracy of Christianity*, Goodell contrasted the egalitarianism of primitive Christians with the economic inequalities of capitalism, anticipating the social gospel movement of the twentieth century. Perhaps the greatest irony is that the proslavery theorist George Fitzhugh used Goodell's criticisms of labor exploitation in the North to defend slavery.

Goodell and Smith supported land reform as a way to address the systemic inequalities of capitalism. In 1844 Evans's National Reform Association (NRA) brought together utopian socialists, former Chartists, and labor activists with the slogan "Vote yourself a farm." Evans sanctioned abolition, women's rights, and Indians' rights, whose land, he noted, had been robbed by monopolists. His ideas built on a radical tradition going back to Paine's *Agrarian Justice* (1796) and his early rival Skidmore's *The Rights of Man to Property* (1829). Smith, a land magnate, was a convert to Evans's crusade against land monopoly and pronounced himself an agrarian. Smith refused to concede Evans's argument that wage slavery was a worse species of oppression than chattel slavery, though he responded sympathetically to Evans's call for uniting abolition with the cause of labor and land reform. In 1846 Smith deeded thousands of acres not just to blacks but also to the landless and poor, men and women. Most of the Smith grantees sold their lands for payment of taxes, but his experiment in land redistribution was unique. In 1848 Evans's Industrial Congress nominated Smith, a Liberty Party man, for the presidency even though he declined the honor. Evans's NRA also opposed the annexation of Texas and the extension of slavery. Elected to Congress in 1850 on the Liberty ticket, Smith championed the distributing of public lands to the landless. After the war the abolitionist journalist James Redpath and Garrison's son, William Lloyd Garrison Jr., became leading advocates of Henry George's single-tax plan for land redistribution. George, whose radicalism was inspired by the abolitionist crusade, wrote to Sarah Mifflin Gay in 1880 suggesting that, as the daughter of Sydney Howard Gay, she could put the abolitionist imprimatur on his program.[22]

Political abolitionists such as Elizur Wright backed land reform and the demands of labor, paving the way for the rise of free soilism. Wright's encounter with the British working poor and his own economic straits made him sympathetic to the condition of labor. As the editor of the *Chronotype* and later the *Commonwealth* in Boston, Wright supported abolition, labor, and women's rights. Smith, Goodell, and Wright formed the Liberty League in 1847, which combined abolition with economic and labor reform. In Massachusetts, Wright, with other Libertyites and Free Soilers, formed viable alliances with labor at the local and state levels, and the NRA endorsed Liberty Party candidates. Even Lewis Tappan admonished George Alexander of the British and Foreign ASS that the "rich would be better off if half or two-thirds of their wealth were distributed among their poor fellow men." He recommended "sub-divisions of landed property" and cultivation of small farms to achieve more "equality in property."

In New York Horace Greeley, the editor of the *New York Tribune*, combined antislavery with labor reform, becoming a leading proponent of land redistribution and utopian socialism. Early on, Greeley had called for the abolition of slavery in all its forms and, to the ire of abolitionists, advocated the settling of blacks in separate townships. Having the largest circulation in the nation, the *Tribune* became a mainstream outlet for northern reformism, forging connections with labor and partisan politics. Greeley was an advocate of what one might call today social democracy. He criticized untrammeled competition and individualism, which reduced workers to "abject want." The anti-rent rebellion in New York along with the NRA brought together land reformers like Evans and Greeley, an undertaking that culminated in the Republican Party's homestead platform. Land reformers and abolitionists also supported the homestead exemption for debtors. During Reconstruction, Greeley renounced his pro-labor, antislavery politics, becoming the presidential candidate of Liberal Republicans and Democrats, that is, of laissez-faire principles and white supremacy. Before the war, though, he popularized antislavery and labor reform. By the end of the 1840s workingmen's conventions and labor reform associations made opposition to the Mexican War and the extension of slavery one of labor's goals.[23]

Rejecting electoral politics, Garrisonians were more interested in utopian communities, most founded in the wake of the Panic of 1837 and inspired by early socialist thinkers such as Owen, Fourier, and Saint-Simon. The connection between abolition and communitarianism went back to the days of Frances Wright and Robert Dale Owen, freethinkers who supported abolition, workingmen's rights, and women's equality. The antebellum communitarian movement inspired by Fourierism complemented abolitionists' "come outer" philosophy of rejecting corrupt institutions, the state and church, as well as those built on precedents set by separatist religious communities such as the Shakers and Rappites. Garrison's conservative critics accused him of harboring radical "no government" as well as "no property" theories. In England, Collins reported that Garrison was "considered of the Owen school." In an editorial on "social reorganization" sympathetically evoking Owen and Fourier, Garrison commended the idea of cooperative associations personified in the abolitionist Northampton Association for Education and Industry led by his brother-in-law George Benson, William Adam, David Mack, and E. D. Hudson. He also lauded his fellow nonresistant Adin Ballou's Hopedale community, which, like Northampton, was founded in 1842, the transcendentalist community at George Ripley's Brook Farm, and Collins's journal the *Communitist*, which advocated communal ownership of property.

Remond, Douglass, and Kelley butted heads with Collins for airing "no-property" views and deflecting attention from slavery at abolition meetings, but Garrison was rather fond of him. In 1843 Collins left abolition for the utopian socialist community in Skaneateles. Two years later his Laboring Man's Reform Association joined Evans's NRA. Quincy was disappointed when Collins did not return to abolition after the failure of his communitarian project but instead joined the Whig Party and moved to California. Garrison expressed reservations at Collins's conversion to Owen's morally "absurd and dangerous" doctrine that absolved men of individual responsibility by making them mere creatures of their circumstances, an argument based on necessity that slaveholders often deployed. But he did not renounce the principle of social cooperation. He published a series of letters by Albert Brisbane, the leading American advocate and translator of Fourierism and Saint-Simonianism. Brisbane's most prominent convert was Greeley, for whose newspaper he wrote. Brisbane also influenced Ripley, and Brook Farm became Fourierist in 1843. His American Union of Associationists, like nearly all nineteenth-century radical movements, modeled its organization and lecturing system after abolition and invited abolitionists to attend their national convention. Some Fourierists accused abolitionists of prioritizing abolition over reforming capitalism. But as Karl Marx's criticism of utopian socialism makes clear, Fourierism was not necessarily more radical than abolitionism.[24]

Garrison was also critical of the otherworldly aspects of communitarians even though he was influenced by Ballou's nonresistance and John Humphrey Noyes's "Bible communism." He predicted that their success or failure hinged on the conduct of their members rather than on the larger society, as some of them experimented with social and sexual arrangements and fell victim to their leaders' misdoings. Many of these communities combined aspects of capitalism with cooperative principles like Owen's new model factory in Lanark, Scotland. Ballou's Hopedale community was based on principles of "Practical Christian Socialism" that he claimed were superior to all others, as they sought to strike a balance between "the Scylla of threatening Communism" and the "Charybdis of selfish, unscrupulous Individualism." Ironically, Ballou's experiment in Christian Socialism was eventually replaced by a ubiquitous symbol of Gilded Age rapacious capitalism, a company town led by the Draper family. Similarly, the Oneida community, which was founded on the perfectionist doctrines of Noyes in 1848 and its many offshoots, ended up as a joint-stock company. Noyes's ideas on "male continence" and "complex marriage" proved to be controversial, and after the war he fled to Canada to escape prosecution for statutory rape. Noyes wrote a history of American Socialisms, but Oneida came to be known for its manufacturing success, particularly its silverware, rather than for its communitarian principles.

Other utopian communities were associated with abolition. The Transcendentalist Amos Bronson Alcott's short-lived vegetarian community Fruitlands, founded in 1843, barely survived a year with its peculiar dietary and work restrictions. The founders of Brook Farm modified their commitment to Transcendentalism and radical individualism with the communal values of Fourierism. "Social transcendentalists" such as William Henry Channing, Alcott, and

Ripley were abolitionists. Unlike his famous uncle, Channing led an activist life as an advocate of Christian socialism, abolition, and women's rights. The Northampton Association combined Garrisonian nonresistance and abolitionism with Fourierism and ideas of cooperative labor. Many abolitionists saw communities based on principles of cooperation as a way to criticize slavery and inequality and were attracted to their experiments with health, social arrangements, the role of women, property, and labor. Weld and the Grimkés joined Marcus Spring's utopian society at Raritan Bay Union, New Jersey, where they ran a school at Eagleswood based on Fourier's educational principles. Elizur Wright also promoted Fourierist urban cooperatives as a solution to the woes of labor.

The abolitionist Northampton Association alone had prominent black members, and its radicalism on challenging race, gender, and class hierarchies made it the butt of conservative evangelical criticism. After the collapse of the Kingdom of Mathias, Sojourner Truth joined it. Ruggles spent his last years there as a "hydropathic" doctor and treated many, including Garrison, with his water cure. The fugitive slaves Basil Dorsey and Stephen C. Rush were also longtime members. The association experimented in communal living and developed an incipient critique of capitalism and the wage system. Though the association struggled, Garrison noted that the success of the experiment would cheer friends of universal reform. With its demise in 1846, the attempt to marry abolitionism with communitarianism came to an end. Unlike Oneida, Northampton was not economically successful and, as happened at Hopedale, a factory village replaced it.[25]

African Americans also created independent landowning communities, a counterpart to white communitarianism. One of the oldest black communities in New York was Seneca Village, founded in 1825 and razed in 1857 to make room for Central Park. This predominantly black community, which came to include German and Irish immigrants, boasted of churches, including the AME Zion, and colored schools. Composed mainly of working-class property holders, it was home to the black abolitionists James Gloucester and Charles Ray. Weeksville, founded in 1835 by the black Brooklynites James Weeks, Sylvanus Smith, Henry C. Thompson, and George Hogarth, was also a site of independent black activism, home to black newspapers, churches, schools, and abolitionism. In 1847 Morel moved to Weeksville, becoming a teacher and principal in its colored schools and continuing his work in the black conventions and antislavery societies. In Ohio free blacks and fugitive slaves founded the "freedom town" of Brooklyn in 1830, later known as Lovejoy after the dead abolitionist. It survived as a black majority, multiracial town well into the twentieth century.

Abolitionists helped found independent black communities. The Lane rebel Augustus Wattles started an agricultural community in Carthagena, Ohio, in 1835, where he built a manual labor school called Emlen Institute after a Quaker benefactor. In 1846 mobs dispersed John Randolph's emancipated slaves, who were deeded land and attracted to Wattles's school, illustrating the threats to such experiments. In 1836 Robert Rose founded a black community in Silver Lakes, Pennsylvania, but it was short-lived. A year earlier Free Frank, who purchased his own and his family's freedom, established the town of New Philadelphia in Illinois. Black communities such as Timbucto, consisting of black settlers on Smith's land grants, Weeksville, Seneca Village, Carthagena, and New Philadelphia made landownership, education, and economic and social independence a pathway to citizenship. These black settlements, predecessors of all black towns at the turn of the century, challenge simplistic dualisms of separation and integration. They sought political rights as well as economic autonomy.[26]

The sectional crisis over slavery did not divert either the communitarian or labor movements from their goals since there was considerable cross-fertilization of ideas and organizing between abolition and them. Garrisonian support for communitarian principles and Chartism and political abolitionists' and free soilers' championing of the cause of labor and land reform should lead to a reevaluation of the perception that abolitionists were moralistic, bourgeois individualists. With good reason, conservative critics of Garrison and Dale Owen lumped them together as "degraded infidels." Anarchistic communes, Modern Times in Long Island, founded by the former Owenite Josiah Warren, and the "free love" advocate and abolitionist feminist Stephen Pearl Andrews supplanted older communitarian experiments. By then most labor leaders agreed with abolitionists that slaveholders' supposed solution to the plight of labor, its enslavement, was an insult. Proslavery ideologues like James Henry Hammond, known for the letters he wrote to Clarkson in 1844, in which he compared the condition of the English working class unfavorably with that of slaves, best articulated this argument in his famous "Cotton is King" speech of 1858. The northern working classes, like southern slaves, Hammond maintained, constituted the dangerous "mudsill," or lowest class, of society, and only an intersectional alliance of the propertied ruling classes could keep both in check. Garrison gave the speech pride of place in his "Refuge of Oppression" column. The platform of the antislavery Republican Party rested on evoking the dignity of free labor against an idle, corrupt slaveholding aristocracy and keeping slavery out of the west. It should come as no surprise that during the Civil War, most workers cast their lot against slavery.

In the 1850s abolitionists began raising the cause of labor in antislavery meetings with increasing frequency. At the NEAS convention, Channing, a socialist-abolitionist, argued, "Logically, I have never been able to separate the Anti Slavery movement from all those directed to raise *Labor* universally." Though he still disagreed with those labor leaders who felt that the elevation of free labor must precede abolition, he felt that abolitionists must make a greater effort to convince workers of this doctrine. Garrison added that labor should also remove the "foul spirit of caste," or racism, from its midst. Stephen Foster and Parker Pillsbury, the New Hampshire abolitionists who were Roger's protégés and heirs to his ideological radicalism, supported Channing's call for "interlinking" the two movements. Pillsbury, who had worked as a teamster, strongly upheld the labor movement and referred to the working classes as the "bone and sinew of the nation." Garrison approvingly published resolutions from a workingmen's meeting that condemned the "despotic attitude of the slave power of the South and the domineering ascendancy of a Monied Oligarchy in the North as equally hostile" to labor and to "the preservation of popular rights." He was one of the friendly editors who supported a journeymen printers' strike against wage reductions in Boston. The antislavery Republican political economist from North Carolina Daniel R. Goodloe voiced his support of a shoemakers' strike in 1860 in the *National Era*. But like another antislavery North Carolinian, Hinton R. Helper, Goodloe opposed Radical Reconstruction.

Congruity rather than conflict characterized the relationship between abolition and the early labor movement in the age of the Civil War. Henry C. Wright characterized the war as the "Rebellion of Capital against labor" and as "an effort of slave-driving capitalists to enslave the labor of the entire nation . . . *white as well as black*." After the war both Phillips and Garrison backed the machinist Ira Steward's eight-hour-a-day movement. Phillips joined the labor movement, and Steward came from an abolitionist family. Smith recommended that they should fight for a six-hour day, and Garrison, who sent a contribution to the Eight Hour League, admonished that it should not give any "countenance to the spirit of complexional caste in regard to any of the working classes." The NASS, the official organ of the AASS, joined the National Labor Union and the International Workingmen's Association (IWA) in supporting the eight-hour-a-day movement.[27] Labor movements after the war saw themselves as heirs of the abolition movement.

THE IRISH QUESTION

Mass immigration and refugees from the revolutions of 1848 shaped the labor question in the abolition movement. Garrison tried to replicate his alliance with the Chartists and Irish nationalists at home. He publicized a call by D. S. Grandin to form a Workingmen's Protective Union, a cooperative, and Lovett's speech calling slavery a link in the chain of labor oppression. He gave working-class voices access to his paper, publishing letters from a mechanic who condemned the "love of gain" and another from Grandin advocating land reform. In 1845 he, Phillips, and Channing attended a meeting of the revived New England Workingmen's Association and reported on it sympathetically, noting its support of abolition. These efforts were eclipsed by Michael Walsh, the Irish labor leader, who sought an alliance with the Calhounite wing of the Democratic Party. Walsh launched an unprovoked attack on Douglass in his newspaper, calling him a "semi-baboon" and "impertinent black vagabond" and criticizing his relationship with English women as an illustration of "practical amalgamation." Garrison bemoaned the fact that a man like Walsh was at the head of New York's working classes, denouncing his over-the-top racism as "malevolent conduct" and loathsome dabbling in "Subterranean [a pun on the title of his newspaper] pollution." Walsh's "vitriolic anticapitalism" was matched by his equally vitriolic racism.

The incorporation of most of the urban immigrant working class into the southern-leaning Democratic Party, which was staunchly anti-abolitionist, alienated them from abolition and instigated mob violence. The local party boss Capt. Isaiah Rynders and Walsh had led a meeting in opposition to the Wilmot Proviso of 1846, the attempt by northern Democrats to restrict the expansion of slavery, upholding the idea of noninterference in slavery and threatening opponents with violence. In 1850 John Gordon Bennett of the *New York Herald* wrote a series of race-baiting articles condemning abolitionists as disunionists, Douglass as a black man, Garrison as a mulatto man, and Phillips as white "merely from blood." That year Rynders, who had lived in South Carolina, led a mob to disrupt the annual meeting of the AASS in New York. Garrison, Douglass, and Ward were more than a match for Rynders and a Professor Grant, a scientific racist. Grant described black people as belonging to a "monkey tribe." Greeley wryly reported that the audience was convinced that if anyone was a "dull orangutan" it was Grant and that if anybody was "the first cousin of a very vicious monkey" it was Rynders. But Rynders's mob forced the AASS to abandon New York for abolitionist-friendly Syracuse to hold its annual meeting. Rynders contended that the condition of northern labor was worse than that of southern slaves, who, he testified from personal experience, were treated with greater humanity. As a U.S. marshal in the 1850s he was zealous in implementing the Fugitive Slave Law and lax with the laws against the African slave trade.[28]

While immigrants' hostility to abolition was the result of a process of Americanization through which they sought to accrue the benefits of "whiteness" and hypernationalism or demonstrate loyalty to their adopted country, abolitionists deplored nativism in principle and appealed to immigrants to join their cause. The evangelical abolitionists George Bourne and Elijah Lovejoy were critics of the Catholic Church, but Garrison, whose mother was of Irish descent, early on condemned the burning of the Catholic convent in Charlestown in 1834, published a series of numbers on the "starving" Irish, and the anti-abolitionist William Cobbett's impressions of Ireland. Abolitionist efforts to woo the Irish failed, but not because of a lack of effort or a failure to address the conditions faced by impoverished Irish immigrants. John Rankin reported an incident in which Irish workers were whipped like slaves in the South, and the abolitionist state legislator George Bradburn of Massachusetts repeatedly drew attention to the dismal conditions faced by Irish immigrants. Amasa Walker complained that while abolitionists sympathized with "the oppressed and half paid operatives of England" and the "half starved peasantry of Ireland," they had no sympathy for America's two million black slaves. Evincing a Garrisonian horror at the misdeeds of the U.S. government, including its treatment of Native Americans, Jonathan Walker issued a special appeal to them. He wrote, "The chain that you have been helping to secure upon the limbs of the southern chattel slaves, has its other end fastened upon your own."[29]

Abolitionists sought to recruit working-class immigrants. Garrison criticized British rule in Ireland as the root of all its sufferings. In the 1840s he made a concerted effort to court the Irish by favoring the repeal of the British union with Ireland. Whether Garrison got his ideas on disunion from the Irish Repeal movement or not, he clearly sought to link the oppression of the Irish with that of black Americans. He elicited the services of Irish abolitionists and the great Irish nationalist Daniel O'Connell, who had befriended him in 1833. On his return to the United States in 1841, Remond brought with him an "Address from the People of Ireland, to their Countrymen and Countrywomen in America," composed by Irish abolitionists and signed by O'Connell, Father Theobald Mathew, a temperance advocate, and sixty thousand others, urging Irish immigrants to "UNITE WITH THE ABOLITIONISTS." Garrison thought it a "noble effusion of Irish love and sympathy."

Abolitionists publicized the Irish Appeal in mass meetings in Boston and Philadelphia, but Irish American leaders, especially those associated with the Democratic Party and the Catholic Church, such as Bishop John Hughes, challenged its veracity and condemned it, ironically, as "foreign interference." The Appeal did little to ease competitive tensions between immigrants and blacks in northern cities over jobs and housing. Unlike most blacks, though, Irish immigrants had the right to vote, which most did for the increasingly proslavery Democratic Party as the Whigs were closely associated with evangelical Protestantism. In an open letter James Canning Fuller urged the Irish to live up to their heritage of hating slavery and loving liberty. Garrison, after the Cincinnati and Philadelphia riots of 1841–42, censured those who had incited immigrants in a "murderous assault" and taught them to hate "a more unfortunate class than themselves without a cause." Irish American Repealers tried to distance O'Connell from abolitionists because as a devout Catholic he deplored Garrison's unorthodox religious views. Garrison responded that his beliefs on the Sabbath were no different from those of Quaker abolitionists like Webb and Sturge, whom O'Connell admired.

But O'Connell refused to renounce abolition. When O'Connell expressed reservations about Gerrit Smith's call for a slave rebellion, Smith defended his views as well as Garrison's anti-Sabbath views. In reply, O'Connell reiterated his firm support of peaceful abolition, leading to the dissolution of a repeal association in South Carolina. Garrison commended his "masterly reply," censuring the Cincinnati Repeal Association for its proslavery views and the actions of the Philadelphia mob. Refuting Reverend McGarahan of Mobile, Alabama, O'Connell declared that he hated slavery in all forms, and while he welcomed American support he would not countenance any justification of slavery. Smith immediately dispatched a donation of a hundred dollars to the Irish Repeal Association, and he donated generously to Irish famine relief. Garrison praised O'Connell's "scorching rebuke" of proslavery repealers. A race-baiting, anti-abolition speech by Robert Tyler, a slaveholder and the son of President John Tyler, before the Irish Repeal Association of Philadelphia, over which he presided, angered abolitionists. The Philadelphia repeal association, according to McKim, was anti-abolitionist and proslavery. Eventually, a new organization split off from it. The Cincinnati Repeal Association included prominent Democratic politicians, such as the former vice president from Kentucky, Richard M. Johnson (known for his common-law marriages to enslaved women). Salmon Chase, the antislavery lawyer and politician, led a meeting of the friends of liberty, O'Connell, and repeal to counteract the proslavery association. The Irish abolitionists Haughton and Allen lauded O'Connell and Garrison for linking Irish Repeal with abolition, unlike their "unfortunate countrymen" in the United States who chose the slaveholding Tyler to lead their national repeal convention. As O'Connell famously wrote to them, "It was not in Ireland you learned this cruelty." After his release from prison by the British government and on the eve of his death, O'Connell condemned the annexation of Texas, further alienating Irish Americans in an expansionist Democratic Party. Even he could not counteract the conservative influence of the Catholic Church and the Democratic Party on the slavery question. Garrison's eulogy on O'Connell was also a eulogy on his unsuccessful efforts to recruit Irish immigrants for the abolition movement.

Rather than being mired in the nineteenth-century discourse of romantic nationalism and despite most immigrants' coolness to abolition, an internationalist perspective made abolitionists strong critics of nativism as another species of prejudice. In a blistering editorial of 1844 on the rise of the Native American Party, Garrison scathed nativism as an antirepublican and tyrannical strain that must be "discountenanced by every friend of human brotherhood." Nativism, he believed, was akin to the spirit of slavery and racial caste, and in turning their backs on antislavery Irish immigrants were reaping the "whirlwind." But Garrison's connection to Ireland did not falter. He distinguished the Irish in Ireland from the "recreant Irish" in America, who had adopted the oppressive ways of their new country. He published reports on the Irish famine by Allen and Webb and pressed every town in the United States to vote for giving assistance to its victims. Webb disdained the narrow love of nation but eventually supported repeal, alluding to his countrymen as the "white niggers" of the British Isles. The final nail in the coffin of Garrison's dream of converting the Irish to abolition was Father Mathew's visit to the United States in 1849. Mathew refused to endorse abolition despite repeated appeals from Garrison. His reluctance was a backsliding on the slavery question since he had signed the Irish Appeal. Garrison was reduced to reprinting O'Connell's views to counteract his silence. Mathew's prime allegiance to the church and temperance and his desire not to alienate Irish Americans squelched whatever antislavery sentiments he had.[30]

On the Irish question, domestic failure crowned international success for abolitionists. In the 1850s John Mitchel, the exiled Irish leader, became an ardent defender of slavery, contending that blacks were inferior by nature. Abolitionists marveled at the fact that a man banished by the British government and forced to work like a slave in a penal colony in Tasmania should become a champion of American slavery. To Henry C. Wright, Mitchel only proved the narrowness of all nationalisms that sought liberty for themselves and slavery for others. Unlike O'Connell's and Haughton's love of all humankind, Mitchel's patriotism was shallow, Wright said, and Ireland was well rid of him. Purvis pointedly contrasted a black association formed by him to promote Irish Repeal to the racist Mitchel, "the braggart traitor to liberty." Abolitionists like Purvis and James Redpath remained strong supporters of Irish independence until their death. Mitchel, who published the *Citizen* with Thomas Francis Meagher in New York, responded to Haughton's plea for abolition with a proslavery diatribe. Owning, breeding, and selling slaves was not a crime, and he wished he had a plantation in Alabama "stocked with healthy negroes." Mitchel's brand of proslavery apologetics was too much for even some of his countrymen, who wrote him a public letter expressing their "mortification and disgust" at his conduct. Mitchel moved to Knoxville, Tennessee, where he published the *Southern Citizen*, which recommended the reopening of the African slave trade. The *Tribune* reported that the advocate of Irish emancipation had become a slaveholder and secessionist. Mitchel's sons fought for the Confederacy, and he returned to Ireland after the war.

Immigrants' hostility to abolition and black equality set the stage for the deadly New York City Draft Riots during the Civil War, when predominantly Irish mobs mercilessly attacked African Americans and burned the Colored Orphan Asylum, venting their anger against not just conscription but also emancipation. Legitimate grievances of the urban immigrant working class paled before this ugly demonstration of visceral racism. Over a hundred blacks were murdered, eleven men lynched, homes destroyed, and the black population was dealt a blow from which it would not recover for a long time. In the postwar era, radical Irish nationalists like the Fenians, labor leaders, and land leagues found common cause with abolitionists and land reformers like Henry George, finally realizing the abolitionist dream of a progressive alliance with Irish working-class immigrants at home. One of George's chief allies was the Irish nationalist and labor reformer Patrick Ford, who had worked for Garrison and fought in the Union army. He renamed his newspaper in 1878, the *Irish World and American Industrial Liberator*.[31]

THE SPIRIT OF 1848

The European revolutions of 1848 for representative government and national liberation helped internationalize social movements like abolition. In the 1830s, when Americans bolstered the Greeks and Poles in their quest for freedom from the Ottoman and Russian empires, abolitionists pointed to their hypocrisy in shedding tears for freedom struggles all over the world but being blind to the sufferings of slaves at home. Nonetheless, abolitionists sympathized with international movements for freedom, black abolitionists adopting the Byronic slogan "Hereditary bondsmen, know ye not who would be free, themselves must strike a blow," from *Childe Harold,* as their own. George Gordon, Lord Byron, had fought for Greek independence and written his poem for that cause. Whittier referred to slaves as the "Greeks of America," noting that Colonel Miller of Vermont, who had fought against the Turks, was also an abolitionist. The most famous abolitionist graduate of the Greek and Polish wars of independence was the physician Samuel Gridley Howe, whose reformism included the treatment of the blind, deaf, insane, and disabled and whose revolutionary sympathies translated into support for John Brown. David Lee Child, who had fought for the liberation of Spain from France, became an abolitionist. Garrison connected slavery to the oppression of British India, Greeks, Poles, and the Irish Catholics, viewing all these causes as embodying the fight for freedom. European "friends of liberty" looked up to the American Republic, Henry C. Wright wrote in 1846 from England, but that example was tainted by the existence of slavery.[32]

Abolitionist appeals to a revolutionary tradition were rarely confined to the American Revolution. They viewed the revolutions of 1848, which produced radical democratic, socialist, and feminist ideas, as kindred movements. The antislavery actions and words of European revolutionaries won high praise from abolitionists. In 1847 the Italian nationalist Giuseppe Mazzini wrote for the *Liberty Bell,* as did the French abolitionist Victor Schoelcher. Maria Chapman, who was living in France at this time, reported on the activities of the feminist Jeanne Deroin. She also corresponded with the Russian exile and opponent of serfdom Nicholas Tourgueneff, to whom she sent abolitionist newspapers and literature. When the Second Republic in France abolished slavery in 1848, mainly at Schoelcher's instigation, Garrison convened a special meeting of the AASS at Faneuil Hall to congratulate the French Republic, which was attended by Garrisonians, Libertyites such as Elizur Wright and Henry I. Bowditch, and free soilers like Sumner. Besides Margaret Fuller, others, including the antislavery poet and writer James Russell Lowell, a correspondent for the NASS, wrote in praise of the revolutions in prose and poetry.[33]

Abolitionists and free soilers identified the despotic Slave Power of the United States with European forces of reaction and their own battle against slavery with European revolutionary struggles. Most American conservatives typically balked at the "red republicanism" of the revolutions in 1848. Slaveholders like Calhoun, who rejoiced at the failure of the Chartists, moved unsuccessfully to table resolutions in the Senate congratulating the French on the formation of their republic, especially after the Free Soil senator from Maine John P.

Hale added abolition as one reason to congratulate the French. Brownson, who had metamorphosed from a radical labor reformer to a conservative Catholic, denounced the revolutionaries in his *Quarterly Review*. Sumner noted the opposition of the northern propertied classes to the revolutions, and the proslavery *New York Herald* commended the brutal suppression of the Paris workers. Schoelcher fled France after Louis Napoleon's coup and, refusing amnesty, returned only with the establishment of the Third Republic.

Southern proslavery writers saw abolition as akin to the dangerous -*isms* of the revolutions, Fourierism, socialism, communism, "free lovism," feminism, "bloomerism," agrarianism, and "Proudhonism." Fitzhugh said, "We treat the Abolitionists and Socialists as identical, because they are notoriously the same people, employing the same arguments and bent on the same schemes. Abolition is the first step in Socialism; the former proposes to abolish negro slavery, the latter all kinds of slavery—religion, government, marriage, families, property—nay, human nature itself." Jefferson Davis argued that socialists were correspondents of American abolitionists, the latter wanting to abolish slave property, the former all property. While historians have detected similarities between the proslavery argument and the socialist criticism of capitalism, contemporaries saw them as opposites. According to the Carolinian senator James Chesnut, red republicanism in America had merely "blacked its face."[34]

The overthrow of the French Republic, documented by Marx in *The Eighteenth Brumaire of Louis Napoleon*, and Mazzini's Roman Republic and the dispersal of the Frankfurt Parliament and Viennese radicals may have reenforced a sense of American exceptionalism. But for abolitionists, socialists, feminists, and other assorted radicals it threw into sharp contrast the nineteenth-century vogue of narrow nationalism versus universal human values and rights they advocated for disfranchised sections of the nation. When the Hungarian patriot Louis [Lajos] Kossuth toured the United States in 1851–52 in search of arms and financial support, abolitionists fully expected him to tie the cause of Hungarian liberty to that of abolition. But Kossuth, not wanting to alienate slaveholders who occupied a prominent place in government, was, Garrison said, "deaf and dumb" on slavery. To Phillips, he was a "mere Hungarian exile" who had "sacrificed the cause of liberty itself." According to Henry C. Wright, Kossuth had sacrificed humanity on the altar of nationalism. Smith observed that Kossuth, absorbed in the wrongs of his country, had forgotten the deeper wrongs of others and was just a nationalist, not a philanthropist. The antislavery Mazzini was a better representative of the spirit of 1848, he opined.

In the 1850s Mazzini cemented his reputation among abolitionists by writing public letters against slavery. Garrison published a pamphlet on Mazzini, whom he met in 1846 in England and with whom he formed a lasting friendship, and on the German naturalist and geographer Alexander von Humboldt. Humboldt's rebuke of a proslavery southerner for editing out his antislavery opinions from his work and his chiding of Americans for going backward on the slavery question earned him high praise from abolitionists. At his behest, Prussia declared slaves who landed in its territory free in 1857. The NASS dedicated two issues to Humboldt on his death. Garrison compared Mazzini's cosmopolitan love of humanity with Kossuth's narrow patriotism. In his *Letter to Louis Kossuth* (1852), Garrison wrote that it was easy to reprehend European despotism in America and American slavery in Europe, but the true test was to uphold "principles of justice and humanity" on both sides of the Atlantic. He held up for Kossuth Europeans who had been true to the cause of humanity. American revolutionaries such as Washington, Jefferson, and Henry, whom Kossuth admired, Garrison argued, had sacrificed much for the liberty of their country, but they were slaveholders who drew "their sustenance, in part, from the unrequited toil, the tears and blood of their plundered vassals." The real revolutionaries, he said, were slaves, "and where has there appeared a more heroic spirit than that of NATHANIEL TURNER, the unfortunate but indomitable slave leader in the Southampton insurrection?"[35]

Other abolitionists tried to appropriate Kossuth's revolutionary credentials for their cause. The AFASS sent a flattering letter to Kossuth, forcing Tappan to defend himself from Garrison's barbs. The MASS denounced the free soiler Horace Mann's defense of Kossuth. In a speech on slavery in Congress, Mann likened Kossuth's plight to that of fugitive slaves and avowed that only proslavery northerners and southerners had been critical of the Hungarian. Bailey's the *National Era* praised Kossuth and defended him from southern and conservative attacks, but when he refused to commit himself on slavery, the paper was disappointed in his display of "a little too much reserve." William Jay defended Kossuth for not wanting to denounce a country in which he was a guest. But, echoing the peace committee in London led by Sturge, he was alarmed at the military demonstrations at Kossuth's reception. As president of the American Peace Society, he opposed arming the Hungarians. Rev. Henry Ward Beecher and his paper, the *New York Independent*, however, welcomed Kossuth, presenting him with lead shot from the Battles of Bunker Hill and New Orleans. In Congress, Sumner and Seward defended Kossuth from the criticism of southerners. When Hale sought to amend a resolution welcoming Kossuth by Sen. Henry Foote of Mississippi to imply he was averse to slavery, Foote exploded in rage. Kossuth complained of his "cold reception" in the South, and the city of Richmond retracted its invitation to him. Congress's welcoming resolution for

Kossuth solicited six nays in the Senate and sixteen in the House, all cast by southerners.

The Garrisonian critique of Kossuth, though, had some effect. In an antislavery meeting in Cincinnati consisting of Garrisonians, Liberty Party men, and free soilers, black abolitionists passed a resolution rebuking Kossuth's conduct. When the abolitionist lawyer John Joliffe called for reconsideration of the resolution, John Mercer Langston chided Kossuth for preaching liberty in Europe and property in Kentucky, for riding two horses, and for linking the cause of liberty with men whose hands were "dripping with the blood" of over three million "oppressed men and women." William G. Allen and Henry Crozier disowned the AFASS address to Kossuth, which included the names of African Americans on its executive committee, Pennington and Cornish. Ward criticized a Liberty Party paper for lionizing Kossuth. McCune Smith had hoped that Kossuth would deliver "telling blows" against slavery but commented that African Americans had not been invited to meet him. Douglass argued that only fugitive slaves could have real sympathy for Kossuth, a fugitive himself, and initially commended him for abolishing serfdom. But if Kossuth took the "blood stained gold" of slaveholding America to liberate Hungary, he wrote, the slaves' curses would follow. The AASS's address to Kossuth stated that his "honors and laudations" had been purchased at too great a price. It predicted that he would not receive any help from what Douglass called "our slave-hunting, slave-extending" country.

Kossuth's very presence supported the cause of liberty wrote J.T. in *Frederick Douglass' Paper.* But his doctrine of nonintervention in the domestic affairs of another country did not serve his own cause well, as J. R. Johnson of Syracuse pointed out. When it came to soliciting aid from America, Kossuth evoked the principles of 1776 rather than noninterference. And when Kossuth pronounced himself in favor of Irish independence, Douglass angrily pointed out that he broke his rule of nonintervention only when it suited him. Other black leaders used the symbolism of the European revolutions to support their own struggle against the tyranny of slavery, imbuing their fight with revolutionary and transnational meaning. J.T., the one consistent black booster of the Hungarian, contended that Kossuth represented the forces of freedom, while regretting his silence on slavery. Kossuth's visit, he wrote, bolstered political antislavery and encouraged German Americans in particular to leave the Democratic Party and vote for the remnant of the Free Soil Party, the "Free Democracy."[36]

The emigration of German Forty-Eighters, refugees from the German republican revolution after the collapse of the Frankfurt Parliament, had an impact on the politics of abolition and free soil. Some of these freethinking, radical

German émigrés joined existing radical movements, the labor movement, land reform, and abolition while others became free soilers. Though some German, especially Catholic, immigrants voted Democratic, like their Irish counterparts, after the passage of the Kansas–Nebraska Act, many of them, especially urban workers and intellectuals, defected to the newly formed antislavery Republican Party. The Forty-Eighters formed alliances with abolitionists and brought a substantial section of the German immigrant population into the Republican Party. Antislavery Whigs like Seward and Lincoln repudiated nativism, and the Republican Party formally rejected the Know-Nothing platform in large part so as to not alienate their German supporters. The German radicals Adolf Douai, Friedrich Kapp, and Karl Heinzen published German-language free soil newspapers in Texas, Missouri, and Kentucky, until they were forced to leave. In the North, August Willich in Cincinnati, Fritz and Mathilde Anneke in Milwaukee, and Heinzen in Boston formed alliances with the abolitionists Moncure Conway, Peter Clark, Sherman and Mary Booth, and Phillips.

Radical freethinking Germans like the feminist Anneke and the socialists Willich and Heinzen, a close ally of Phillips in the war years, emerged as staunch abolitionists. In 1859 Willich presided over a German meeting organized by his Arbeiterverein (workers' association) to pay tribute to John Brown. Clark also addressed the meeting. After being hounded out of Lexington, Kentucky, Heinzen published the German *Die Pionier* in Boston. He asked Garrison to condemn an impending nativist amendment in Massachusetts that would make immigrants wait for two years before voting, scaled down considerably from the initial twenty-one- and fourteen-year bans but barring, he noted, men like Mazzini and Humboldt from the polls. Assuring Garrison of German support for abolition, he asked "the noble advocate of black rights" to say a word on behalf of the "rights of the immigrated." Garrison denounced the injustice of the nativist amendment, characterizing it as the last "expiring effort" of nativism that Republicans in the rest of the country had censured. Bailey had ridiculed the "proscriptive principles" of the Know-Nothing Party, going so far as to suggest that it was a proslavery plot to defeat the Republican Party and deflect attention from the slavery issue. The prominent Republicans Chase, Lincoln, Seward, and Sumner repudiated the amendment. The Liberty and Free Soil parties had opposed nativist restrictions on principle. Garrison welcomed the German turn toward free soilism and against the "slave oligarchy." He criticized European immigrants who denounced tyranny but had no sympathy for slaves. Germans, in his opinion, had passed the test.

While the Catholic Church exercised a conservative influence on the slavery issue among immigrants, radical institutions like the socialist Turnvereins were decidedly antislavery. A convention of German exiles in 1854 and the national Turnerbund the subsequent year came out strongly against slavery. The German Turners often came to the rescue of African Americans and abolitionists against mob attacks before and during the war. Douglass, who was close to the radical German journalist Ottilie Assing, claimed, "A German has only to be a German to be utterly opposed to slavery." He commended "those noble and high-minded men, most of whom, swept over by the tide of revolution in 1849, have become our active allies in the struggle against oppression and prejudice." McCune Smith noted, "The German immigrants are for the most part, a liberty-loving, caste despising people." The British and Foreign ASS even promoted German immigration to Texas to establish an antislavery population there.

German Texans would pay with their lives for their unionism during the Civil War. Many supported black suffrage and citizenship after it. Some of them, such as Carl Schurz and Francis Lieber, who had migrated before 1848 and lived in South Carolina, became well-known Republicans. Lieber, who became a professor at Columbia University, wrote Lincoln's war code that justified emancipation and racial equality. Schurz, who rallied German Americans to the Republican Party, wrote an exposé of southern atrocities during Reconstruction but eventually joined the Liberal Republican movement. Conservative rural German opposition to abolition and black rights, German dockworkers who joined the Irish in the Cincinnati race riot of 1862, and, ten years later, attacks on blacks and Douglass over the alleged rape of a German girl by a black man in Rochester qualify the simple notion that Germans were naturally antislavery and immune to the lures of racism in their adopted country. In the 1870s, when Germany was united by Otto von Bismarck's blood and iron policies, German immigrants reflected the conservative nationalism of policies back home. Like the North and the Republican Party, most of them moved ideologically away from antislavery.[37]

In the antebellum period, however, German immigrants had an antislavery reputation, thanks to the influence of the Forty-Eighters. The radical Forty-Eighters connected abolition to the labor movement. Willich promoted "the material and literary interests of the working classes against capitalism" and abolitionism in his *Cincinnati Republikaner*. According to him, without attacking the enslavement of black labor, white workers could not "have even set foot on the battlefield for the advancement of human rights." In turn, the Ohio black convention had expressed solidarity with Hungarian and German socialists. In New York, Joseph Wedemeyer's American Worker's League, founded in 1853, explicitly repudiated racial discrimination and supported the Republican Party. Both Willich and Wedemeyer were former associates of Marx and served in the Union army. Willich's ally, the black abolitionist and educator Peter Clark, briefly joined the Workingmen's, later the Socialist Labor Party, after the war. From a young age Clark was exposed to the principles of Fourierism and utopian socialism. Clark's socialism and admiration of Thomas Paine, for which he was fired from his job, were strengthened by his interaction with German socialists and freethinkers.

Marx, the premier socialist of the day, and his collaborator Engels were recruited by Charles Dana, a Fourierist, to become the London correspondents for Greeley's *Tribune* from 1852 to 1862. Their articles ranged from the opium wars in China, British imperialism in India, and the aftermath of the European revolutions to the labor and slavery questions in the Anglo-American world. Marx argued that land reform promoted communism and clearly viewed abolition as a species of labor reform. He became an ardent supporter of the Union cause during the war. Marx saw abolition as a necessary precondition for the emancipation of the working class in the United States, writing in *Das Kapital*, "Labor cannot emancipate itself in white skin where in the black it is branded." He composed a laudatory letter to Lincoln on behalf of the IWA and had a keen appreciation of the abolitionists Garrison, Smith, and Phillips, one of whose speeches he conveyed virtually verbatim, for having suffered for thirty years in the cause of the emancipation of slave labor.

After the war, an abolitionist–labor alliance found organizational expression briefly under Marxist auspices. Former abolitionists, Chartists, Owenites, utopian socialists, followers of Proudhon, labor, and "free love" advocates like Andrews and Victoria Woodhull joined the First International, begun with Marx's formation of the IWA in 1864 in London. Despite Marx's criticism of utopian socialism in contrast to his own brand of allegedly scientific socialism, many of these reformers were the first converts to Marxism. Abolitionists such as Richard Hinton, a follower of John Brown who led a black regiment during the Civil War, and William West, who had brought up the plight of wage slaves in the pages of the *Liberator* before the war, were prominent in the First International, which earned the support of Sumner and Phillips. Andrews translated and Woodhull published Marx's *Communist Manifesto* (1848) in the United States for the first time in her newspaper, *Woodhull and Claflin's Weekly*. While most denounced the Paris Commune of 1871, the NASS and the abolitionist Theodore Tilton's the *Independent* praised it. After the suppression of the commune, the IWA, now headquartered in New York, held a huge demonstration in sympathy that included an all-black Skidmore guard named after Thomas Skidmore. A black militia elected Tennessee Claflin, Woodhull's sister, as an officer. A radical gadfly, Woodhull supported labor rights and women's rights, experimented with spiritualism, and ran the first female brokerage firm on Wall Street with the help of Cornelius Vanderbilt, her sister's lover. She was eventually expelled from the First International by German Americans, who wanted to prioritize workers' participation, and arrested for violating obscenity laws in exposing the affair between Rev. Henry Ward Beecher and Tilton's wife. Marx not only dismissed her unconventional ideas on marriage and sexuality as a distraction but also voiced his skepticism about her dabbling in spiritualism and banking.

The attempt to form a progressive political platform under the IWA's auspices failed, but it is reductionist to accuse either German Marxists, many of whom were exiles from the revolution in 1848, of doctrinaire thinking, or American reformers, who advocated for the working class, of bourgeois reformism. Both sides had initially found enough common ground in the First International, and in the end both would face defeat. Counterrevolution soon followed the fall of Reconstruction, unleashing a massive reaction against the rights of African Americans and the working class during the age of capital in the United States, the Gilded Age. Some, like Hinton, moved on to Debsian socialism, or the American socialist party led by Eugene V. Debs.[38] For at least a few years the revolutionary ferment in Europe that exiled Marx to London and the international to New York drew socialists into the orbit of American radicalism, of which abolition had been the centerpiece.

THE ABOLITIONIST CRITIQUE OF IMPERIALISM

Despite being enamored of the tactics and success of British abolition, American abolitionists, especially Garrisonians, were staunch critics of British imperialism. The contrary view that hypocritical abolitionists were early supporters of European imperialism owes its origins to the defenders of slavery. Slaveholders were hardly shedding tears at the plight of British India or the use of indentured, or coolie, labor. The South Carolinian secessionist John Townsend reminded the British that the civilizing and subjection of an inferior race were goals they shared. In the 1850s expansionist-minded southern planters, dreaming of their own slaveholding empire that would encompass the Caribbean and Central and South America, led filibustering expeditions to Nicaragua and Cuba and debated plans to reopen the long-abolished African slave trade. Slaveholders, not their abolitionist critics, were the real champions of imperialism. The British and Foreign ASS passed resolutions against the new slave trade in indentured servants and coupled it with the revival of the African slave trade. It also condemned indentured servitude and the use of unfree labor in the British

Empire. Nor were abolitionists uncritical exponents of wage over slave labor. One British Garrisonian warned, "The English manufacturer cares less for the tears of the negro than for the rise of prices in the cotton market; — he sees insurrection in an abolition pamphlet & waits with philosophic composure till supplies from free labor will enable him to be humane without any sacrifice."[39]

Abolitionists had long distinguished their ideas from the imperialist logic of the ACS. Colonizationists greeted Buxton's founding of the African Civilization Society in London in 1840 to replace the slave trade with "legitimate commerce" and work for the civilization of Africa as essentially their program. But British abolitionists, despite Gurley's strenuous efforts, held themselves aloof from colonization. Buxton insisted he was not interested in encouraging black colonization or "extend[ing] the British Empire." Joseph Tracy, the secretary of the Massachusetts Colonization Society, linked the conversion of Africa with ending the slave trade, slavery, polygamy, and, more imaginatively, cannibalism and human sacrifices and called on "civilized men of African descent" to colonize the continent. Edward Everett, in an address before the ACS, said that the "proud white man . . . all daring Anglo-Saxon" cannot civilize central Africa, as they had India. British Garrisonians and Sturge, who was wary of Buxton because of his compromise on compensation and apprenticeship, opposed the African Civilization Society's disastrous Niger expedition as an imperialist one.[40]

Crummell and Garnet, who were in favor of the African Civilization Society's efforts to encourage the growth of "free cotton" in Africa, joined it to their efforts to revive the free produce movement. Crummell delivered a eulogy on Clarkson on the eve of his departure to England in 1846 that lauded the ethical progress of civilization epitomized by abolitionists. In one of his first speeches at the annual meeting of the British and Foreign ASS, Crummell recommended that the British stop their "immense consumption of slave-grown produce," particularly cotton and sugar. Garnet, who lectured with his old friend when he arrived in England in 1850, held up slave shackles, announcing that they were manufactured in the British iron heartland of Birmingham. Sarah Parker Remond declared that the profitability of the global cotton trade must be replaced by emancipation and a desirable and lasting prosperity for all. Crummell developed an incipient nationalist critique of European imperialism. Although in favor of commerce and Christianization, he noted that England was far more adept at exploiting the natural "resources of foreign lands to her own good" and that he was "not satisfied" that "Africa should make *other* men wealthy and not ourselves." Crummell was convinced black emigrants would undo the "history of rapine and murder, and wide-spread devastation" of western Africa by the slave trade.[41]

Garnet, who repeated Crummell's message of an economic embargo against slavery, lectured in Britain on behalf of the free produce movement. Understanding full well that capitalists had only commercial motives in promoting the production of free labor cotton, he maintained that it would still benefit the abolition cause. The skeptical Douglass critiqued Garnet's reasoning. Garnet complained to Ward, "I am annoyed to see anyone who, like you and I, has tasted the bitter cup of slavery, withholding his influence and talents from this good cause." Garnet did not return home but in 1852 became the United Presbyterian Church of Scotland's first black missionary to Jamaica. His wife, Julia Garnet, and children, whose travel to England was financed by Smith and British abolitionists, accompanied him. Garnet was eager to prove the superiority of free labor over slave in the West Indies, but he was also interested in establishing black economic independence. He was impressed by instances of black landownership in Jamaica and highly critical of the exploitation of black labor by planters. In a letter to Chamerovzow, Garnet wrote that black Jamaicans were "superiors in morality" to whites. He noted the preference of black workers for tilling their own provision grounds and planters' opposition to black landownership and determination to keep them as wageworkers. He concluded, "The emancipated people use their liberty with more moderation and propriety than their former masters exercise government over them." Ward also proposed establishing plantations to experiment in growing free labor sugar and cotton. In 1855 he left for Jamaica, where he was deeded fifty acres of land by a Quaker abolitionist. Ward deplored the exploitation of Jamaicans but opposed what he called the mulatto leadership of the Morant Bay rebellion, writing a pamphlet condemning it. He died in poverty in 1866.[42]

Before Ward and Garnet, Pennington traveled to Jamaica in 1846 and stayed there for two years. He formed the Jamaican Hamic Association to promote contact between African Americans and Jamaicans in a global fight against slavery and racism. To Tappan and Phelps, Pennington described Jamaica as a wonderful, ripe field for an abolitionist mission. The AMA established a Jamaican Mission, which owed its origins to Phelps's West India Mission. It sent abolitionists like Loren Thompson, who was converted to abolition at a young age by Rev. Lemuel Haynes and had studied at Oberlin, to work with freedpeople in Jamaica. To Phelps and Thompson, landownership was the essential precondition for black freedom and equality. The AMA missionaries opened schools for and employed black Jamaicans but complained that their work was severely handicapped by the opposition of local landowners who, determined to keep them as cheap laborers, refused to sell land to black people. While the missionaries' puritanical attitudes toward alcohol, sexuality, gender, and native religious practices like Obeah and Myalism did not help, they were leery of colonial authorities, especially after the violent suppression of the Morant Bay rebellion, when the government evicted black Jamaicans from abandoned lands. AMA missionaries believed in Christianization but also took issue with the entrenched political and economic inequalities of postemancipation Jamaica. After the Civil War they devoted themselves to the uplift and education of freedpeople nearer home.[43]

To a much greater extent and in an ideologically more consistent fashion than proslavery writers, abolitionists opposed British imperialism. In 1839 Joseph Pease, the father of Elizabeth Pease, founded the British India Society. Its original purpose was to combat slavery in India, but it soon became a critic of the "accumulated wrongs inflicted" on the Indian people by British rule. British Garrisonians such as William Adam and Thompson, both of whom had stayed in India, were prescient critics of imperialism. They joined the British India Society, which included Indians like Dwarkanath Tagore, the father of the Nobel Prize–winning nationalist author Rabindranath Tagore. Adam was also a close associate of the crusading Indian social reformer and nationalist Raja Rammohun Roy and introduced him to Unitarianism. Estlin provided medical care to Roy before his death. He sent locks of Roy's hair to the Boston antislavery bazaar to sell, just as British abolitionists had earlier sent to the Americans locks of hair from Wilberforce and Clarkson. The personal relationships between abolitionists and early Indian nationalists bore testimony to the anti-imperialism of the movement.

Garrison published Adam's and Thompson's speeches criticizing British rule in India, proceedings of the British India Society that condemned colonial misgovernment and slavery in India, and their correspondence with such Indian reformers as Ram Gopal Ghose. Garrison surmised that Indians had been "ground to the dust" by "British exactions." Writing from Dublin, Henry C. Wright agreed: "The history of England in India is one of systematic plunder and murder"; he prayed for the annihilation of the British Empire. He wrote that the "landed and titled and monied aristocracy" of Britain was little better than the "lords of the cowskin" in Mississippi plantations. Tappan admired Thompson's speeches on British India and wished that his cause would prosper. In England, Garrison and Remond gave speeches to the British India Society and linked the cause of the American slave with the oppressed millions of India. At a society meeting in 1841 presided over by Adam, Webb alluded to the dreadful famines caused by British government policy, which forced Indian farmers to grow cash crops such as cotton instead of food. Later that year the society deplored the ousting of the Rajah of Sattara by the British. British abolitionists elected Dwarkanath as an honorary member of the GES.

Thompson in particular was associated with the Indian cause. He recommended that abolitionists should turn their attention to the Indian subjects of British rule after the abolition of American slavery. Thompson had left the East India Company (EIC) forces in disgust, was an agent for the deposed Rajah and the last Mughal emperor, Bahadur Shah, who was executed after the Great Revolt of 1857. In his speech on Dwarkanath's induction, Thompson insisted that Indian reformers like him and Roy, rather than the colonial government, were responsible for the abolition of *sati*, or widow burning, and slavery in India. Nearly seventy years before Mahatma Gandhi led the famous Dandi march against it, he gave a brilliant lecture lambasting the salt monopoly instituted by the British government. Thompson complained that he was virtually the only Englishman to publicly impeach the EIC for its crimes against the Indian people. On Thompson's second abolition tour of the United States, Garrison introduced him as one who had exposed British injustice and tyranny in India as well as the horrors of slavery.

Abolitionists adopted an anticolonial discourse that took up the cause of subject peoples all over the world. O'Connell, who linked the oppression of India with that of Ireland, accused the British government of spreading misery and affliction among Indian masses, thereby deconstructing the imperialist logic that the British were the saviors of the Indian masses against their tyrannical native rulers. Elizabeth Pease criticized Dwarkanath even for accepting a medal from the EIC, the de facto ruling authority in British India before it became a royal colony. In 1842 Adam moved to America and taught at Harvard as a professor of Oriental languages and society. Illustrating the transnational radicalism of abolition, he gave a remarkable speech in which he criticized the British government for compensating West Indian slaveholders, for disfranchising the British working class represented by the Chartists, and for oppressing the masses of Ireland and India. In a letter to Elizabeth Pease, Angelina Grimké Weld wrote, "What a curse have civilized nations invariably been to the barbarians among whom they have settled, what a hissing and a by word must we be among the heathen! Look not only at India but the World." She went on to list the extermination of native populations in the Americas, the enslavement of Africans, and imperialism in Asia as examples. Sarah Grimké also predicted, "Signal judgment would ere long be poured out on Eu. and Am." for the crimes of slavery and imperialism.[44]

When the Indian revolt broke out in 1857, starting as a mutiny by sepoys (soldiers) and ending as a mass uprising of Indian rulers and their subjects against British rule, Garrison was horrified at the "calls for vengeance" in Britain. Abolitionists and slaveholders viewed the revolt through the lens of slave rebellion, and British stories of native cruelty and repressive measures smacked of slaveholders' fears. In a letter Garrison published prominently in the *Liberator,* Haughton wrote that he was sickened by the cry for "Blood Blood Blood" in the British press and held that it was sheer hypocrisy for the British to condemn alleged Indian atrocities: "And is Britain guiltless of such atrocities she now thirsts to avenge?" He concluded, "Our rule in India is one continued war against her people" and the sooner "we leave her people to govern themselves," the better. To Garrison, it was a mockery "for a people to subjugate nations, rob them, apply physical tortures, and goad them to insurrection, and then go over the solemn farce of Fast days and prayers." Notwithstanding his theory of Asiatic despotism and British imperialism as a progressive force of destruction, Marx, in his *Tribune* article, criticized the British for annexing the independent principality of Awadh "violently . . . in open infraction of the acknowledged treaties." It would be left to Lenin to develop a systematic critique of European imperialism as the highest stage of capitalism.[45]

Like the early Quaker abolitionists, second-wave abolitionists opposed the wars and militarism that accompanied Western imperialism. While Garrisonians espoused nonresistance, other abolitionists and antislavery people were active in the mainstream peace movement. The American Peace Society (APS) was founded in 1828 when William Ladd brought together a number of state peace societies. William Ellery Channing and May were admirers of Rev. Noah Worcester, whose opposition to the War of 1812 led to the formation of the Massachusetts Peace Society in 1815. Anglo-American abolitionists, however, internationalized the movement. In 1843, at Sturge's suggestion, they convened the first general peace convention in London, in which Scoble, Leavitt, and Tappan participated. Tappan offered a resolution condemning Britain's involvement in opium trafficking in China, and Ladd proposed a Congress of Nations to settle national disputes, anticipating by nearly a century the League of Nations and the United Nations.

Abolitionists viewed slavery as a state of undeclared war against African Americans and joined the international peace movement. The American peace reformer Elihu Burritt organized a peace congress in Brussels in 1848, and a year later he convened the Second Peace Congress in Paris, attended by Pennington and Wells Brown. To the discomfort of conservative pacifists, Pennington seconded Brown's notion that slavery was an "element of war." In 1850 Pennington attended the Frankfurt peace congress with Garnet, their color creating a sensation. Their visit led to the formation of a German ASS. Garnet traveled to Bavaria, Prussia, and France with Sturge, lecturing for peace and free labor. Sturge convened the last peace congress in London in 1851. In the decade following, the Crimean War, the Taiping rebellion in China, and the Great Revolt in India dealt a deathblow to the first international movement for peace.

While the peace movement collapsed, earlier opposition to the Mexican War (1846–48) as a land grab for slavery had married the cause of peace with that of antislavery. Abolitionists and their radical antislavery allies concentrated on combating slaveholding militarism and imperialism in the United States. Sumner's brilliant speech before the APS in 1849 was considered far too radical by most of its members, many of whom, for example, Frelinghuysen, were colonizationists. Garrisonian nonresistants considered the APS too mainstream. By the early 1850s antislavery politicians such as Sumner and Robert Rantoul as well as the abolitionists Ellis Gray Loring, Samuel Fessenden, and Gerrit Smith were officers of the APS. Its president was William Jay, who was succeeded by Smith. The Civil War permanently divided abolitionists such as Garrison, Sumner, and Tappan and pacifists like Burritt, Ballou, and Joseph Blanchard. Abolitionists viewed the war not as overthrowing their peace principles but as an opportunity to put an end to the violence of slavery as well as to slaveholders' expansionist adventurism in Central America and the Caribbean. Pacifists like Ballou, who opposed the war, would nevertheless assist contraband slaves during it.[46]

However much the British government used the moral capital of abolition to justify its imperial goals, radical abolitionists would deprecate both the theory and practice of imperialism. Abolitionists linked their denunciation of racism and persecution of people defined as nonwhite. In England, Thompson was involved in the Aborigines Protection Society, organized to protest the exploitation of indigenous people in Australia and the British colonies and before whom O'Connell gave an address. Thompson's son-in-law Frederick William Chesson became the society's secretary. The society also protested the use of Indian and Chinese coolie labor in various parts of the British Empire. Alfred Webb, the son of the Irish abolitionist, was elected honorary president of the Indian National Congress in 1894. Webb credited Garrisonian universalism for his anti-imperialist views. In 1898 William Lloyd Garrison Jr. helped found the Anti-Imperialist League, which adopted his father's abolitionist slogan. American abolitionism also became the prototype for international abolition, inspiring a comparable movement in Brazil. The abolition of slavery in Cuba and Puerto Rico came about with the demise of the Spanish Empire, just as it had in earlier Spanish colonies a generation ago. If European nations moved from empires of slavery to the "Scramble for Africa," abolitionists and their descendants remained critics of imperialism.[47]

In the United States, abolitionists had criticized settler colonialism from the start and drew attention to the plight of Native Americans. Benjamin Lundy, like most early Quaker abolitionists, had denounced the "slaveholding, land-jobbing, and Indian exterminating" character of the American Republic. Many evangelical abolitionists honed their skills in protest against Andrew Jackson's Indian removal policies. Since the very first issue of the *Liberator*, Garrison had written of the Cherokees forcibly removed from Georgia. He censured paternalistic missionaries and colonizationists like Lyman Beecher, who were against Indian removal but advocated the colonization of African Americans, and argued that African colonization was based on the same principle of removal. In their opposition to colonization, abolitionists also drew attention to the genocidal nature of the European conquest of the New World. Critiquing the missionary purpose of the ACS, Elizur Wright pointed to attempts to Christianize Indians that had resulted in the extermination of native cultures. The principle of colonization, Garrison observed, evoking the history of American colonists and the British in India, does not lead to "a very warm friendship" between colonists and natives.

Abolitionists and their allies were strong opponents of Indian dispossession. In 1838 David Lee Child denounced "the atrocious plot" of southern slaveholders and the U.S. government to deprive Indians of their lands and expand slavery. Antislavery politicians such as John Quincy Adams and Joshua Giddings opposed the Second Seminole War in 1835 as proslavery and anti-Indian. Tappan observed caustically in the midst of the *Amistad* trials, when Spanish authorities demanded extradition of the African rebels on the basis of treaties signed between Spain and the United States, that the American government was known to honor all treaties except when they were made with Native American nations. Before the war, Tappan's AMA, which was critical of slaveholding and the abusive missionaries of the American Board of Commissioners for Foreign Missions in Indian territories, had a small missionary presence among the Ojibwe Indians. During the Sand Creek massacre of Cheyennes and Arapahoes in 1864, Capt. Silas Soule, an abolitionist whose younger brother was named after Garrison, exposed the crime of his commanding officer John Chivington, a devout Methodist minister who was not "a committed abolitionist."

After the Civil War, abolitionists criticized the attempt to use the newly empowered nation-state to despoil rather than guarantee Indian rights. Before the war, the plight of "the disappearing Indian" had populated abolitionist literature from Lydia Maria Child's *Hobomok* (1824) to Henry Wadsworth Longfellow's *Song of Hiawatha* (1855). Indian resistance to European encroachment also acted as a model for many radical abolitionists' defiance of slavery. Lydia Maria Child and Phillips became staunch advocates of Native Americans even though both visualized the eventual incorporation of Indian nations into American society. On the other hand, southern slaveholding politicians from Jackson to Calhoun supported the idea of racial separation and the creation of a separate Indian territory, or reservations. Complicating matters further was the adoption of the southern institution of racial slavery by civilized southern Indian nations like the Creeks, Cherokees, and Choctaws, who would end up fighting for the Confederacy and opposing emancipation. Many leading abolitionists during Reconstruction, however, connected the cause of the former slaves with that of the Plains Indians. In 1867 Lydia Maria Child published *An Appeal for the Indians*, modeled after her pamphlet of 1833 on behalf of African Americans. Cora Daniels Tappan suggested at the twenty-sixth meeting of the AASS after the Civil War that abolitionists form a society protesting exterminating wars against Indians. In his speech of 1880 before Congress, Blanche K. Bruce, one of the first black senators from Mississippi during Reconstruction, called for a reversal of federal policy toward Native Americans, so as "not to exterminate them but to perpetuate them on this continent." He criticized the government, Indian agents, and the army as well as missionaries for trampling on Indian rights. Bruce's notion of Indians as equal citizens had abolitionist roots. He envisioned a relationship of equality rather than conquest between the newly empowered state and Indian nations.[48]

More than any of their contemporaries, abolitionists waged a principled battle against racially restrictive notions of democracy. Garrison reprimanded Sen. James Blaine's attempt to pass a Chinese exclusion bill just before his death in 1879 and warned Republicans of introducing another species of racial proscription into the country under the guise of antislavery. When Blaine defended the prohibition of coolie labor and maligned Chinese culture, Garrison wrote an extended reply. "The Chinese are our fellow-men," he said, and they have the right to follow their customs, culture, and religion. Confucius, he schooled Blaine, who had trumpeted the superiority of Christian "Anglo Saxon freemen" peopling the west, had preceded Christ in advocating the Golden Rule. Abolitionists like Phillips, Sumner, Douglass, and Garrison parted company again with the labor movement over the issue of race, rejecting racist calls for the exclusion of the Chinese. Phillips argued that the Chinese must be allowed to immigrate freely and that no racial exceptions should be made for coercing labor. Nor did abolitionists justify the use of coolie labor, seeing it as a new species of slavery. Men and women of antislavery convictions spearheaded the fight against various kinds of unfree labor and servitude in the west.[49]

Abolition expanded rather than contracted radical horizons. Abolitionists for the most part challenged rather than shored up the status quo. From women's rights, the abolition of capital punishment, the peace movement, and immigrants' and workingmen's rights to the rights of native populations trampled by European settlers and imperialism, abolitionists contributed to a variety of causes. Garrisonians like Phillips, William H. Channing, Theodore Parker, and Lydia Maria Child bolstered Charles Spear's movement to abolish capital punishment, and abolitionists in Massachusetts led petition campaigns against it. In 1843–44, at the height of the campaign, abolitionists sent over forty petitions to the General Court requesting the abolition of capital punishment in the Commonwealth. Garrison excoriated "hangman clergymen" who supported the death penalty and the inhumane notion of retributive justice. He even developed an incipient critique of the criminalization of blackness.[50]

Abolitionist ideas on racial inequality are a starting point in an interracial discourse of democratic radicalism in the modern world, their concerns relentlessly internationalist and eclectic. The struggle against slavery did not normalize or rationalize other forms of injustice but gave birth to diverse radical passions. It was the eclipse rather than the triumph of the abolitionist mentalité after the fall of Reconstruction that led to the most egregious crimes against humanity at home and abroad.

SLAVE RESISTANCE

"Rather die freemen than live to be slaves," the revolutionary slogan deployed by Henry Highland Garnet in his "An Address to the Slaves of the United States of America" of 1843, reveals that abolitionists conceived of the enslaved as central to their movement. The political significance of slave resistance in the making of abolition and the sectional conflict over slavery is understudied.[1] Slave resistance gave abolition its most enduring issue, the fugitive slave controversy, and provided the movement with its most dynamic exponents.

Slaves voted against slavery with their feet, giving rise not just to national but also international debates over the boundaries and legitimacy of slavery, a dress rehearsal for their momentous actions during the Civil War. From the early days of the Republic abolitionists assisted slaves who were seeking freedom. Slave resistance moved abolition into northern state- and courthouses and inspired grassroots militancy. Slave rebels and runaways put slavery on trial. The argument that most Americans saw slaves as complicit in their enslavement for not resisting it flies in the face of the history of slave resistance and its impact on national politics, international law, diplomacy, and popular sentiment.[2] Slave resistance revolutionized abolitionist discourse and practice.

FUGITIVE SLAVES AND THEIR ALLIES

Fugitive slaves offer a counternarrative of American history. For colonial slaves the land of freedom was not their home, but rather Spanish Florida or Indian territory, much as Canada, Mexico, Haiti, the British West Indies, and the northern states symbolized free spaces for their nineteenth-century descendants.[3] Enslaved "freedom seekers" contributed to the breakdown of comity between southern and northern states and had a wide-ranging impact on the rise of sectional tensions.

Individual acts of slave resistance became the stuff of politics. The Fugitive Slave Act of 1793 had not only granted extraterritoriality to southern laws of slavery in the free North but also facilitated the kidnapping of free blacks into slavery. In the 1820s states like Pennsylvania and New York passed personal liberty laws to protect free blacks from kidnapping and gave some legal protections to suspected runaways. By the antebellum period the lines between illegal kidnapping and legal rendition of fugitive slaves became increasingly blurry as southern laws of slavery came into conflict with northern laws of freedom. Northern black communities contained fugitive slaves who intermarried with free African Americans and came to resemble Maroon communities of runaways determined to defend their freedom at all costs.[4]

Slaves ran away frequently and in so doing displayed considerable political sophistication in discerning the social geography of slavery and freedom. A majority were young men from the border slave states. Conservative estimates of 1,000 runaways per year based on the U.S. Census records of 1850 and 1860—an official account of an essentially illegal activity and the first completed under the proslavery propagandist J. D. B. DeBow—are an obvious undercount. Today, historians count the number of fugitive slaves in 1830–60 at 150,000, higher than Albert Bushnell Hart's original estimate of 60,000. According to a recent estimate that includes runaway slaves who remained in the South and absconded temporarily, around 50,000 slaves ran away each year. Marronage, or the formation of communities of runaway slaves, within the slave South, as in the Dismal Swamp, was also more common than previously thought. There are no figures for those who made good their escape to Mexico or by sea to the Caribbean and even England. The exact number of fugitive slaves, some of whom were recaptured, may never be known. So ubiquitous were runaways that Samuel Cartwright diagnosed slaves' tendency to run away as a disease, "draepetomania."[5]

Contrary to the self-serving claims of their masters, fugitive slaves voting with their feet inspired abolitionism rather than vice versa. Early abolitionist societies and black leaders laid the legal foundations for the defense of blacks kidnapped into slavery and to bring southern slaves under the purview of northern emancipation laws. Abolitionists launched a concerted effort to restrict the reach of slaveholders in the North, an endeavor that inspired antislavery attempts to restrict slavery's political and geographic reach.

Outstanding abolitionists such as the Quakers Isaac T. Hopper, Levi Coffin, and the Presbyterian minister John Rankin, whose careers bridge the two waves of abolition, made assistance to fugitive slaves a quintessential form of abolitionist activism. Born in New Jersey, Hopper was a member of the PAS and particularly adept at confronting slaveholders, slave hunters, and kidnappers on the streets of Philadelphia, assisting hundreds of fugitive slaves and free blacks kidnapped into slavery. Working with the PAS and black leaders, he became widely known as "the friend and legal adviser of colored people upon all emergencies." In the life of Hopper compiled by Lydia Maria Child on his death in 1853, hundreds of these "tales of oppression" that had first appeared in the NASS acted as both inspiration and cautionary tales for latter-day activists. They not only revealed Hopper's street smarts but also portrayed black men like John Miller, who indented himself to buy the freedom of another, and Cyrus Field, whose struggle for freedom cost him his life, an enslaved woman who married a free man but was remanded as a fugitive, and the rescue of a young African boy, Wagelma. Nearly all of Hopper's stories can be verified from contemporary newspaper accounts and court records. Hopper moved to New York, where he worked with David Ruggles and his pioneering New York Committee of Vigilance.[6]

Like Hopper, two "migrants against slavery," Coffin, who moved from North Carolina to Indiana and eventually to Cincinnati, and Rankin, who left Tennessee by way of Kentucky to Ripley, Ohio, where his hilltop home became a beacon to slaves fleeing across the Ohio River, were founders of fugitive slave abolitionism. Both men had ties to short-lived abolition societies in the upper south. The Coffin family began helping free blacks kidnapped into slavery and fugitive slaves in North Carolina. Levi Coffin, who also ran a free produce store, was called the President of the Underground Railroad by his baffled opponents, and his reminiscences are dotted with the stories of many fugitives. He eventually "resigned" from the "presidency" of the UGRR and became active in freedmen's aid until his death in 1877. Coffin suffered a loss of business because of his activities, and Rankin's open assistance to fugitives resulted in the near burning of his house and barn. Rankin, whose letters inspired Garrison, became an agent of the AASS and a founding member of the Ohio and Ripley ASS.

Both men relied mainly on free blacks to operate the abolitionist underground for over thirty years. Coffin's expatriate North Carolina Quaker community adjoined that of free blacks emancipated by them in Indiana. When he moved to Cincinnati, its activist black community assisted him. Intrepid men like John Hudson, who ferried runaway slaves across the Ohio River, and the former slave John Parker, who always traveled armed, were part of Ripley's clandestine network, which included Parker's large family, free blacks, antislavery politicians, and members of abolitionist societies and churches. Like Harriet Tubman, the relatively unknown Parker helped "run off" hundreds of slaves. The history of the UGRR, however, must rise above the story of heroic individuals or be dismissed as the stuff of myth and memory.[7] It must be placed in its proper historical context, the growth of the abolition movement.

Black abolitionists established the permanent, organizational apparatus of the abolitionist underground, the vigilance committees of the 1830s. A decade earlier African Americans in Philadelphia, Baltimore, and Boston had formed protection societies against kidnapping. In 1834 Elizur Wright published a series of essays, "Chronicles of Kidnapping in New York," detailing many instances of "legalized kidnapping" of free blacks and runaways into slavery. Ruggles, who helped found and became the secretary of the New York Committee of Vigilance in 1835, was the person most responsible for this tactical innovation. The committee had a predominantly black membership but included a few white abolitionists like William Johnson, its treasurer, and, later, Lewis Tappan. It embodied abolitionist defiance of slaveholding laws and prerogatives. Ruggles built on the strategies developed by Hopper, Barney Corse of the NYMS, and the antislavery lawyer Theodore Sedgwick, but the committee was his brainchild, and he ran it virtually single-handedly. He "outed" kidnappers and slave catchers, publishing the committee's first annual report in 1837. Calling themselves the friends of human rights, the Committee of Vigilance assisted fugitive slaves and rescued kidnapped southern and local free blacks, the enslaved in ships involved in the illegal international slave trade, and slaves in transit with their masters. Often denied trial by jury and legal rights by their enslavers and law enforcement officers in cahoots with them, the committee hired lawyers to represent African Americans caught between slavery and freedom. Its executive committee included Cornish, Wright, Johnson, Van Rensselaer, and the grocer J. W. Higgins. It galvanized grassroots black activism, its large, so-called Effective Committee ready to intimidate would-be enslavers. Black women not only raised funds for the vigilance committee but also took part in street action, to the dismay of Cornish.

In his years with the committee Ruggles assisted hundreds of black men and women, including Douglass. At personal risk he confronted slaveholders, slave catchers, and sea captains involved in slaving numerous times, matching wits with the "kidnapping club" consisting of city officials and policemen. Calling "self defense the first law of nature" and urging direct action against enslavement, Ruggles uncovered a plot to kidnap and sell him into slavery. In 1838 he started an antislavery reading library and published the *Mirror of Liberty*, a magazine devoted to "the restoration of Equal Liberty and the full enfranchisement of my down-trodden countrymen." The committee's second annual report concluded that a "want of funds" hampered its activities. Ruggles was bankrupted trying to retrieve William Dixon, a free black man kidnapped into slavery. The next year Ruggles resigned from the committee after a libel case and became involved in a fractious dispute with Wright, Johnson, Cornish, Bell, and Ray. He sued the committee for back pay and aired his grievances in a pamphlet. The editors of the *CA* denounced him and demanded that he be held liable for damages from the libel suit, which nearly destroyed their paper. Garrisonians rallied to Ruggles's defense against the black clergymen associated with the Tappans. Virtually blind after his incarceration in the Darg case (Arthur Tappan and Higgins bailed him out), Ruggles ceased publication of his paper in 1841 and joined the Northampton Association. Ruggles, like many other black abolitionists, supported the Free Soil Party on the eve of his death in 1849. Wright and Ray, aided by the AFASS, led the Committee of Vigilance. By 1847 Hopper headed a reorganized New York State Vigilance Committee, which linked the city with vigilance committees in upstate New York in an underground railroad. Smith became its president a year later.[8]

Ruggles's brand of practical abolitionism was replicated in Boston, where blacks took the lead in fugitive slave rescues. In 1836 a group of black women stormed the courtroom of Chief Justice Shaw to whisk two enslaved women, Eliza Small and Polly Ann Bates, to safety. The two had been freed on a writ of habeas corpus brought by the abolitionist lawyer Samuel Sewall and the BFASS after their master's agent had them apprehended aboard a ship. When the agent tried again to have them remanded under the provisions of the federal fugitive slave law, the women, on Sewall's signal, acted. The "abolition riot" involving the women and the alleged dereliction of duty of Sheriff C. P. Sumner, a man of antislavery convictions and Sumner's father, led northern conservatives to warn of a new phase in the abolitionist war against slavery.

The same year, in *Commonwealth v. Aves*, Shaw denied slaveholders the right of transit with their slaves, citing the *Somerset* decision. While Benjamin and Charles Curtis argued that the state should recognize Louisiana's law of slavery, the abolitionist Ellis Gray Loring, with his cocounsel Rufus Choate, called for applying the *Somerset* principle to Massachusetts, especially since the case involved not just the right to transit but also residence in a free state. Southern states evoked instead the legal precedent of *The Slave Grace*. The *Aves* case, also brought by the BFASS, involved a six-year-old slave girl named Med and, unlike the case of the fugitives Eliza and Polly, made for much criticism of abolitionist interference in separating the child from the absent slave mother. But Med's owners had first separated her from her mother by bringing her to

Massachusetts, and abolitionists did not treat her as an adult. Garrison, who published the arguments in the case, consistently referred to Med as a slave child. In 1832 the NEASS had brought a writ of habeas corpus to free a Cuban slave boy, Francisco, through Sewall, but Shaw remanded him to his mistress on ascertaining his wishes and on his mistress's assurance that she would no longer hold the boy as a slave. In another case involving a slave child in 1837, a free black couple, the Robinsons, were judged guilty of kidnapping and were forced to pay court costs.

Some, like John Darg's slave Thomas Hughes, who was assisted by Hopper, Corse, and Ruggles, and Catherine Linda in Massachusetts, rejected freedom for family. Ruggles was involved in the Linda case too. He probably inspired the abolitionist E. D. Hudson, who was imprisoned for allegedly luring Linda at her master's behest. As abolitionists maintained, talk of free will made little sense in cases involving even adult slaves like Hughes, whose master tricked him into returning to slavery and eventually sold off his wife. Abolitionists managed to secure his release a second time. Massachusetts and other northern states after *Aves* moved to deny slaveholders the "right" to transit with slaves. In 1837 a legislative report by the abolitionist James Alvord questioned the constitutionality of the Fugitive Slave Act of 1793, and Massachusetts restored the right of trial by jury to suspected fugitives.[9]

Abolitionist activism bore similar fruit in New York. Alvan Stewart, arguing for two black boys hauled in as fugitive slaves in Utica, used the writ of habeas corpus to hinder rendition. Legal and political controversy over fugitive slaves soon involved antislavery politicians and lawyers. In 1839 Governor Seward refused to extradite three free black seamen involved in a fugitive slave rescue to the state of Virginia. In his public letter to Gov. Thomas Gilmer of Virginia, in response to Gilmer's proclamation posting a reward for the three men, Stewart, the Liberty Party candidate for the governorship, wrote that New York would not let its citizens be dragged to Virginia and asked whether Virginia was willing to extradite kidnappers to New York. Stewart called for the overthrow of the fugitive slave law of 1793, arguing that it allowed black people to be "*judicially kidnapped*" into slavery. In overturning the act, the North would "place Canada on the Mason's Dixon line," and every slave could theoretically walk to freedom.

Abolitionists fought to establish the freedom principle in the North. Ruggles's Committee of Vigilance petitioned for a trial by jury for suspected fugitives and an end to slaveholders' right to transit with their slaves in New York. In 1840 New York granted fugitives the right of trial by jury as a result of abolitionist and the state black conventions' petition campaigns, and the next year it repealed the nine-month transit provision for slaveholders enacted in 1817. Three years earlier Maine had turned down an extradition request from Georgia for two men accused of assisting runaway slaves. Georgia was threatening war, and the Maine ASS asked if Georgians planned to invade the state and "carry off the men by force." In 1845 Stewart represented two slaves in New Jersey who were born before 1804, when that state passed its gradual emancipation law freeing slaves born after that year, illustrating the porous lines between slavery and freedom in the North. The suit was brought at the instigation of the small New Jersey ASS, allied with the Liberty Party. Stewart stressed the unconstitutionality of slavery: it contradicted natural law, the state's constitution of 1844, which declared all men free and equal, the Constitution, and a republican form of government. Though he was unsuccessful, his eloquence held the court spellbound. Only the antislavery chief justice, Joseph Hornblower, who later joined the Republican Party, dissented.[10]

Confrontations over fugitive slaves instigated by abolitionists challenged federal and constitutional guarantees on rendition in the North. In 1837 the case of Basil Dorsey, who had escaped slavery with his brothers a year earlier, led black abolitionists to resurrect PAS efforts to help runaway slaves from the neighboring slave states of Maryland, Delaware, and Virginia. The abolitionist David Paul Brown argued the case. Dorsey, hustled out of the courtroom by Purvis when he was freed on a technicality, made his way north with the assistance of Leavitt and Ruggles in New York. He ended up in Northampton, where he became active in the UGRR himself. That year Purvis founded the Philadelphia Vigilant Committee, which included the PAS member Edward Needles, the Quaker abolitionist Edwin Coates as vice president, James Needham as treasurer, and the tailor Robert Ayres as secretary. Its standing committee included the black abolitionists Stephen H. Gloucester and Samuel Hastings, but its most active member was its agent, Jacob C. White, a barber. White kept a meticulous "Minute Book of the Vigilant Committee of Philadelphia" from 1839 to 1844, which still survives, though Purvis destroyed all his documents relating to fugitive slave rescues after the passage of the fugitive slave law of 1850.

White's record attests to the prominence of the black abolitionist network in Pennsylvania that facilitated slave escapes, with Whipper and Stephen Smith in Columbia, "a port of entry for flying fugitives," Purvis in Byberry, John and Lucy Ann Freeman in Woodbury, and Gloucester, McCrummell, the Vigilance Committee's first president, Charles Gardner, Daniel Payne, and Robert Forten in Philadelphia. The committee's purview extended beyond the state, as it prosecuted cases in New Jersey and regularly sent individual as well as groups of escaping slaves to New York and New England, White personally accompanying one group to Canada. In 1840 an acting committee led by Purvis replaced

White as agent. The PFASS funded the Vigilance Committee's activities as well as a black Female Vigilant Association of fifteen led by Elizabeth White, Sarah McCrummell, Mary Bustill, and Hetty Reckless. In 1847 McKim reorganized the Vigilance Committee. Five years later its name was changed to Philadelphia Vigilance Committee (PVC), and over the years it became famous. Its most active member, William Still, documented its history.[11]

Black vigilance committees inspired by Ruggles's committee arose all over the North. Detroit's Colored Vigilant Committee, founded in 1840 by William Lambert, a Quaker-educated black abolitionist from New Jersey, and George DeBaptiste, a free black man from Virginia, also acted as an abolition society and fought for the desegregation of the public school system. It operated as both a secret fraternal order and an emigration society. Black vigilance committees spread to Canada among fugitive slave communities in Toronto, Chatham, and Amherstburg. Black abolitionists such as Rev. Jermaine Loguen in Syracuse, Still in Philadelphia, Stephen and Harriet Myers in Albany, Thomas and Frances Brown in Pittsburgh, and Lewis Hayden in Boston founded local vigilance committees and led the shock troops involved in fugitive slave rescues. Many of them were fugitive slaves themselves. Loguen and DeBaptiste claimed to have helped thousands of runaway slaves. The homes of Pennington in Brooklyn, Douglass in Rochester, Garnet in Troy, Wells Brown in Buffalo, and John Jones in Chicago were well known as safe houses for fugitives. AME churches founded by the itinerant minister and later bishop William Paul Quinn in Pennsylvania, Illinois, and Indiana were havens for escaped slaves.[12] By the 1840s and 1850s organized abolitionist assistance to "freedom seekers," that is, the abolitionist underground, became popularly known as the UGRR.

In the borderlands between slavery and freedom, runaway slaves not only sparked abolitionist activism but also became a growing irritant in interstate relations between free and slave states. Ohio, bordering Kentucky and a center of abolitionism, was the site of important legal battles over fugitive slave rendition. In 1837 the case of Matilda Lawrence, who fled to freedom in Cincinnati with the help of a black barber and was employed by the Birney family, ended badly. She was captured by a slave hunter and sold into slavery in New Orleans. The state supreme court dropped the indictment against Birney for knowingly violating the state's law of 1804 against harboring a fugitive. Lawrence and Birney's lawyer was the young Salmon P. Chase, who joined the Liberty Party and founded the Free Soil and Republican parties. Chase adopted Birney's argument that the fugitive slave law was unconstitutional and repugnant to the Fourth and Fifth Amendments on unreasonable seizures and due process of law and to northern state laws as well. The constitutional clause on recaption, he contended ingeniously, applied to servants and did not "recognize right of property in man." The presumption of freedom should guide all cases where a human being may be consigned to perpetual bondage.

Like other antislavery lawyers, Chase rested his defense of Lawrence on a vindication of habeas corpus, "the surest safeguard of personal liberty." He also evoked the *Aves* decision, the Northwest Ordinance, the birthright of all citizens of Ohio, and the state's antikidnapping law of 1831. Birney published Chase's arguments in a widely circulated pamphlet and wrote to Lewis Tappan that it had done "much for the cause," though Lawrence lost her dearly won freedom. Launching his career as the "attorney general for fugitive slaves," Chase fought many cases whose decisions effectively nullified slaveholders' right to transit in Ohio. In a case in 1845 of a Virginian runaway, Samuel Watson, Judge Read, who had argued on the side of the prosecution in *Matilda*, conceded Chase's argument on transit. To commemorate the decision, Cincinnati's black community presented Chase with a silver pitcher for his "eloquent advocacy of the rights of man." In his speech A. J. Gordon also commended Chase for his opposition to Ohio's black laws. Chase responded, "I arraign the whole policy of our legislation in relation to our colored population" and promised to fight "until the sun . . . shall not behold, in all our broad and glorious land, the foot print of a single slave."

In 1838 it took a resolution of the Ohio legislature, after being deluged with abolitionist petitions, to free a black woman, Eliza Jane Johnson, a member of the Ripley ASS, kidnapped into slavery in Kentucky. Commenting on her case, Thomas Morris argued that the federal fugitive slave law had produced a state of war between the states. The same year John B. Mahan of Sardinia, who was also part of Rankin's underground network in southern Ohio, was arrested, extradited, tried, and imprisoned for over two months in Kentucky. His case was widely reported in the abolitionist press. Even though Mahan was eventually freed, he died bankrupt and sick from tuberculosis contracted in prison. His epitaph read, "Victim of the Slave Power." Bucking the trend in most northern states, Ohio, at the request of state commissioners from Kentucky, passed a fugitive slave law in 1839 ordering sheriffs and state officials to assist in fugitive slave rendition and stipulating a fine of five hundred dollars and sixty days in prison for hindering recaption. A group of antislavery Whigs led by Benjamin F. Wade, who had presented petitions against the state's black laws and defended blacks' right to petition the legislature, vigorously opposed its passage. Wade made an abolitionist argument: "Every slave in the South has an unalienable right to his liberty, and a right to defend that liberty against all aggression, if need be, even unto the death of the assailant." His radicalism cost him his seat. The law was widely reviled and often observed in the breach by abolitionists.[13]

Northern challenges to the fugitive slave clause of the Constitution and federal law reached the U.S. Supreme Court in the famous *Prigg v. Pennsylvania* case in 1842. In 1837 the slave catcher Edward Prigg captured Margaret, who had married a free man, and her three children and carried them back to Maryland without legal proceedings, as required by Pennsylvania's personal liberty law of 1826. Margaret's former master had freed most of his slaves, but his wife initiated the action on his death. Prigg and his associates were convicted of kidnapping by a grand jury, a conviction upheld by state courts. Prigg appealed his case all the way to the U.S. Supreme Court. Chief Justice Joseph Story's majority decision upheld the constitutionality of the Fugitive Slave Act of 1793 and declared all northern state laws that contravened it unconstitutional. To Garrison, the decision meant that "the slaveholding power could roam without molestation in the Northern states" and pushed him to advocate disunion. Stephen Myers pointed to the hypocrisy of southern constitutional claims while they continued to jail free black sailors in clear violation of the Constitution. While Story's proslavery decision in one fell swoop got rid of all the legal protections painstakingly won by abolitionists and their antislavery allies, it also made recaption a federal responsibility, leaving a wide loophole for northern noncooperation. Whether Story, a distinguished nationalist jurist from Massachusetts and Sumner's mentor, did this on purpose is debatable. But his decision outlawed not only personal liberty laws but also Ohio's notorious fugitive slave law, which was promptly repealed in 1843.

The Supreme Court's decision in *Jones v. Van Zandt* further upheld the federal fugitive slave law. In this Ohio case a poor elderly farmer named John Van Zandt was convicted of aiding the Kentucky slaveholder Wharton Jones's nine runaway slaves, one of whom, Abraham, managed to make good his escape. Jones sued Van Zandt for recovery costs and the "value" of Abraham. The case was argued by Chase and Morris initially and made its way to the Supreme Court in 1846, where Van Zandt was represented by Chase and Seward. Chief Justice Roger Taney predictably did not overturn Van Zandt's conviction. Chase pointed out not only that Van Zandt was not harboring or concealing a fugitive since Abraham had long since disappeared, a strict construction of the law of 1793, but also that the law itself was unconstitutional. Van Zandt died that year, telling Chase he would not utter a single word that would reenslave Abraham; his small estate was liable for all costs. He had gone, Chase noted, to "another bar where aid to the weak and suffering will not be imputed as a crime." In the initial Van Zandt case in Ohio, the charge to the jury by Judge John McLean, notwithstanding his antislavery reputation and dissent in *Prigg*, upheld fugitive slave rendition but denied slaveholders the right to transit. Two years later, in the Indiana case *Vaughn v. Williams*, McLean freed in absentia a runaway family of three slaves belonging to the Missouri slaveholder Livingston Vaughn, as the slaves had resided in Illinois. McLean deplored the actions of the abolitionist Owen Williams, who had assisted them, but did not convict him.[14]

Abolitionists were not interested in parsing the legal differences between fugitive slave escapes and residence or transit in free states. *Kidnapping* was a term they applied to actual instances of kidnapping of free blacks as well as to the recapture of fugitive slaves. They did not end their crusade to make the fugitive law a dead letter in the North. The first fallout from *Prigg* occurred when George Latimer was apprehended in Boston in October 1842 by a Virginian slaveholder from Norfolk and lodged in jail to prevent a "hostile crowd" of blacks from rescuing him. Latimer and his wife, Rebecca, also a fugitive, had escaped earlier that year. She was kept hidden after his arrest, and once Latimer was freed her master gave up on the idea of recovering her. The timeworn abolitionist tactics of using habeas corpus and a writ of personal replevin served by Sewall to free Latimer did not work, but the presiding judge allowed for a delay in order to investigate Latimer's claim that his master had freed him. The delay allowed abolitionists to launch a massive protest campaign. A Latimer Committee formed by Henry I. Bowditch, William F. Channing, and Frederick Cabot started publishing the first fugitive slave abolitionist paper, the *Latimer Journal and North Star*, to give voice to "the moral feeling and strength of the community." Twenty thousand copies of the journal, the editors claimed, were circulated in Massachusetts. The paper featured an interview with the jailed Latimer, who told abolitionists stories of his mistreatment by his master and assured them he would be given the customary thirty-nine lashes and washed with "pickle" if he was remanded back to Virginia.

A group of black men, probably the New England Freedom Association (NEFA) formed by Nell and Remond in 1842, stood ready, Sewall informed Latimer, to spirit him away. Modeled after the mostly black vigilance committees, it was a successor to Boston's first vigilance committee, formed in 1841. Lasting for five years, well after the Latimer Committee had disbanded, and including women, the NEFA raised money, food, and clothing for fugitives. The *Liberator* reported on mass protest meetings led by black abolitionists in Boston and New Bedford. A runaway himself, Douglass wrote and spoke about Latimer's plight as a man, husband, and father. Nell singled out Bowditch for special praise, whose Latimer Committee threatened a petition drive to remove the sheriff of Suffolk County if he did not order the release of Latimer. Abolitionist mobilization and popular pressure achieved what legal writs failed to do. Latimer was released to the custody of his claimant, who agreed to sell him. Black Bostonians raised the money to buy his freedom.

Unprecedented cooperation between Garrisonians and Liberty Party men in the Latimer case revealed how the fugitive slave issue united the movement and gained it new adherents. Abolitionists across the ideological spectrum, the Garrisonians Quincy, Phillips, Foster together with political abolitionists like Leavitt, Sewall, and Bowditch, spoke at a Latimer meeting held in Faneuil Hall, though racist rowdies refused to let Remond speak and disrupted the meeting. Its resolutions stated that Latimer embodied the rights and immunities of all citizens of Massachusetts and that his enslavement literally meant the enslavement of the state. Similar meetings in Lynn, Weymouth, Salem, and Sherburne challenged fugitive slave rendition.

Outraged that Latimer could be hunted as a slave in the Bay State, abolitionists there disseminated a petition through local post offices to prevent recaption under the federal law. Latimer himself became involved in the petition campaign. The Latimer, or Great Massachusetts, Petition, with over sixty-four thousand signatures demanding a law forbidding the use of state officials and jails in fugitive slave rendition and separating the people of Massachusetts from slavery, was sent to the General Court. Another with around fifty-one thousand signatures was sent to John Quincy Adams in Congress asking for the repeal of the federal law. Sewall and Phillips gave testimony before a Joint Special Committee calling for a new personal liberty law. Headed by Charles Francis Adams, the son of John Quincy, the committee issued a lengthy report recommending a personal liberty law along the lines suggested by abolitionist petitions and in conformity with *Prigg*. The so-called Latimer law forbidding the use of state facilities in fugitive slave rendition passed across partisan lines virtually unanimously in both houses with only a handful of negative votes. Years later, Latimer, who befriended the abolitionist Hutchinson family singers, dictated his story to them. He thanked Garrison and all "those who . . . aroused the North in an agitation that made freedom possible for me and mine." His son Lewis Latimer, born in freedom, became a famous inventor employed by Thomas Edison.

Abolitionists in Massachusetts united in action, yet philosophical differences remained. In 1846, when a slave stowaway, Joe, escaped from a ship in Boston, the ship's owners managed to recapture and send him back to New Orleans before anyone could be alerted to his plight. The city's leading abolitionists and antislavery men, Samuel Gridley Howe, Elizur Wright, John Andrew, and

Richard Hildreth, met at the home of Bowditch and called a meeting at Faneuil Hall. Sumner and Howe convinced Quincy Adams to attend. In his speech Howe protested the fact that the runaway had not benefited from laws for his protection and had been apprehended without a legal warrant. Anticipating the fugitive slave crisis of the 1850s, Phillips protested that all recaption, even those constitutionally sanctioned, should be prevented. Political abolitionists were careful to appeal to constitutional authority, while Garrisonians argued for conscientious objection to proslavery laws and the Constitution. The meeting led to the formation of an interracial forty-man Vigilance Committee consisting of, among others, Nell, Phillips, May, Francis Jackson, Robert Morris, Joshua B. Smith, Theodore Parker, Bowditch, Hildreth, Stanton, Andrew, and Sumner, to prevent such occurrences in the future. Its executive committee petitioned the legislature, recommended the formation of a Northern League, posted a one-hundred-dollar reward for information on fugitive slaves, and appointed Smith as its agent. The next year Pennsylvania followed suit at the height of the Wilmot Proviso controversy, passing a personal liberty law along the lines of the Massachusetts one.[15] Fugitive slaves fostered abolitionist organization and antislavery sentiment and laws.

JOHN BROWN'S FORERUNNERS

Some abolitionists did not just oppose the extraterritoriality of the laws of slavery in the North but invaded the slave South itself to run off slaves. This form of daring activism came at considerable cost and entailed personal loss and danger that often put those involved in close companionship with the enslaved. These abolitionists were indeed "John Brown's forerunners."[16]

Unprotected by law or public opinion, abolitionists who went south became subject to laws of slavery even as fugitives who made their way north benefited from laws of freedom. As the abolitionist Alanson Work, who was whipped in prison, put it, "I am a *prisoner* in a land, where to tell a man, made in the image of his Maker, that he has a right to *freedom*, is a crime of the deepest dye." In 1841 George Thompson, educated at Oberlin and in the Mission Institute in Quincy, Illinois, was arrested in Palmyra, Missouri, with Work and James Burr for planning the flight of slaves. Though not as active as the Ohio–Kentucky border, the Missouri–Illinois border witnessed the frequent flight of slaves, at times aided by sympathetic abolitionists in the Mission Institute. Rev. David Nelson headed the institute until a posse of Missourians burned it down in 1843. Thompson and his coconspirators were sentenced to twelve years of hard labor. They were pardoned after a few years, as their imprisonment generated international sympathy and proved to be an embarrassment to the state of Missouri. Thompson, who affirmed that "helping the poor is *right*" and not a crime involving slaveholders' property, was the most defiant of the three and the last to leave prison. Work was banished and ordered to return to his home state of Connecticut but not before his daughter "grieved herself to death." Burr, who broke his right hand and was frequently sick, was released next. Radicalized by his imprisonment, during which he saw slaves sold and whipped, was threatened with plots to assassinate him, and was tortured, Thompson published his prison reflections, containing the letters, poems, prayers, and sermons of the three imprisoned abolitionists, in 1847. As he put it in a letter to his parents, "My spirit they cannot confine, my thoughts they cannot chain." It was reprinted in six editions in the next ten years and sold thousands of copies, Work and Thompson embarking on successful lecture tours.[17]

Eighteen forty-four was a banner year for abolitionists who ran off slaves. That year Jonathan Walker, a sea captain from Harwich, Massachusetts, was fined over six hundred dollars, pilloried, and imprisoned in Pensacola, Florida, for attempting to set sail with seven runaway slaves. His hand was branded SS for "slave stealer," but abolitionists rechristened him "slave savior." A working-class abolitionist, Walker and his wife, Jane, named their children after Garrison, Lydia Maria Child, and Wilberforce. He had befriended local blacks in Florida and planned the escape with a slave named Charles Johnson. Pensacola, with its diverse population, had long acted as a gateway to freedom for enslaved blacks. Though Walker tried to shield the slaves from responsibility, four of them were imprisoned and given fifty blows with a wooden paddle. Abolitionists held meetings and picnics in Massachusetts, from Lynn to Waltham, to raise money to pay Walker's fine, who was released after a year. Walker and his "branded hand," which inspired Whittier's abolitionist poem of that title, wrote about his experiences and became a sensation on the abolitionist lecture circuit as the hero of Pensacola. He eventually moved with his family to Wisconsin and Michigan and remained active in the UGRR. In 1854 Garrison reported his death owing to his "excessive labors."

In his narrative Walker described his treatment by "the tribunals of my own country." He had lived in Pensacola, a common destination and haven for enslaved runaways, for five to six years with his family and was called before the authorities twice for being on "good terms with colored people." After his arrest Walker was kept in irons in the filthy hold of a steamboat for six days before being delivered up to the magistrate. He described the even worse condition of his prison, being chained, ill, and given food fit for and shared by animals until he found a way to get decent food from a Danish grocer. But the most gruesome experience Walker described was seeing the prison floor stained with the blood of a slave who had "committed suicide by cutting open his belly and throat with a razor." Like all imprisoned abolitionists, Walker was radicalized even further by his encounter with the enslaved while in prison. He could "see and feel the same chain attached to my leg" that was used to hold another slave and recorded the whipping of a slave woman in his journal.

Abolitionists imprisoned for slave stealing became international causes cé-lèbres. Walker received letters of sympathy from Clarkson and Scoble. On behalf of the state of Massachusetts, John G. Palfrey protested to the Florida governor over the "illegal or unusual severity of his confinement." The Florida legislature justified Walker's treatment in the name of self-preservation. On his release Walker became an AASS agent and a regular contributor to the *Liberator*. In 1846 he wrote *A Brief View of American Chattelized Humanity*, arraigning northern ignorance and indifference on slavery. He stated that American citizens "partake" in the rights and wrongs of their government. Garrison also publicized less well known instances of imprisoned abolitionists, like John L. Brown of Maine, who was convicted the same year of helping a female slave escape in Charleston, South Carolina. His death sentence, commuted to a public whipping, drew the attention of British abolitionists as well.[18]

More famously, Rev. Charles T. Torrey was arrested for helping an enslaved woman and her children in Baltimore escape. Torrey had helped found the first Boston Vigilance Committee with Nell, which apprehended kidnappers and traced abducted free blacks in the South. In 1842 he worked with Rev. Abel Brown of the Eastern NYASS and the Albany Vigilance Committee in upstate New York. Brown, an evangelical abolitionist and supporter of women's rights and political action, was a regular contributor to the *Liberator*, writing exposés of the crimes of the Baptist church. Abolitionists like him defy easy categorization. When Brown formed the Eastern NYASS he invited not just Smith and Stanton but also Remond and Collins. He founded the *Tocsin of Liberty*, renamed the *Albany Patriot*, faced his share of violent anti-abolitionist mobs, had runaway slaves accompany him on his lecture tours, and preached in black churches. Brown died early at the age of thirty-four. In 1849 his wife published his memoir, which detailed how he had made the area a hotbed of underground activity. Thanks to abolitionists like him, Myers, Loguen, and Garnet, upstate New York became a frequent stop, or station, for fugitive slaves on their way to Canada. Brown's Vigilance Committee, his wife wrote, "often found themselves in personal contest with slaveholders and their abettors, on account of the infringement on the rights of colored citizens of Albany." The Albany committee mounted an effective offensive against kidnappers. According to its first annual report, it aided 350 fugitives and spent over a thousand dollars. On Brown's death, the "colored citizens of Canandaigua" mourned, "We are bereft of one of the most efficient advocates of the cause of our countrymen, and the eloquent narrator of the story of our wrongs."

Torrey moved to Washington, D.C., where he joined the capital's interracial community of abolitionists and antislavery politicians. In 1839 Leonard Grimes, a free black man who operated a successful carriage business was an important member of the capital's abolitionist underground. He served two years of hard labor in a Richmond prison and paid a one-hundred-dollar fine for assisting a slave mother and children about to be sold away from her free husband. Grimes moved to New Bedford on his release and became pastor of the Twelfth Baptist Church in Boston, known as the Fugitive's Church, as his congregation consisted of many runaways. Torrey's life story reveals who composed the abolitionist underground in Washington, among them the former slave Thomas Smallwood and a boardinghouse keeper, Mrs. Padgett. Born a slave in Maryland, Smallwood criticized the "mask of philanthropy" of the ACS that freed slaves on condition of deportation. Once free, he rejected offers to migrate to Liberia and secreted "lots of fugitives who had been sold to the traders and fled to me so that I might effect their escape." They came to him, Smallwood wrote, by "the scores," and he was able to aid all except seven. He dated the start of the formal UGRR to the arrival of his "beloved friend" Torrey. Smallwood's narrative is dotted with their escapades with runaway slaves. He noted that to build a case against Torrey, slaveholders and their agents needed proof that would pass muster in a court of law, "but with regard to myself it was different, I was a colored man." Smallwood eventually escaped with his family to Toronto with "slaveholders . . . in hot pursuit of me." Torrey's UGRR operators were mostly African American: Jacob R. Gibbs in Baltimore, John Bush in Washington, who was also arrested, and James J. G. Bias of the PVC. John H. Fountain of Winchester, Virginia, was imprisoned for ten weeks for aiding Torrey. He also cooperated with the Quaker abolitionist Thomas Garrett of Wilmington and Brown in Albany, helping fugitive slaves from the border south travel to upstate New York and on to Canada.

Torrey was first arrested in 1842 while covering a slaveholders' convention at Annapolis as a correspondent for Brown's paper. Forgetting past quarrels, Garrison denounced his arrest. Torrey, too, was radicalized by his imprisonment, especially by his encounters with slaves, and decided on a "solemn re-consecration of myself to the work of freeing the slaves, until no slave shall be found in our land." Arrested again in 1844, he wrote that the states of Maryland and Virginia would be put on "TRIAL BEFORE THE TRIBUNAL OF MANKIND." Garrison raised money for Torrey and later his widow, as did Torrey's confidante Amos Phelps, who visited him in prison. In a letter to Garrison, Torrey thanked him for his magnanimous actions and recalled Garrison's imprisonment in Baltimore, writing that "the death of the system was decreed" from that day. To McKim he wrote that differences between old and new organization did not matter and that all abolitionists should "act for the slave." The next year Garrison reported that Torrey was severely ill. Chase wrote to William H. Collins, a Baltimore lawyer, requesting his release on humanitarian grounds, saying, "Sympathy with him is deep and widespread" in America and Europe. Torrey appreciated a note written by Clarkson in a shaky hand and another from Scoble. After a failed escape attempt, Torrey died of tuberculosis contracted while in prison in 1846. Boston's black abolitionists had held fund-raising meetings for Walker, Fountain, and Torrey, with Ruggles holding one in Northampton, and they planned to erect a monument in his memory. A leading fund-raiser for Torrey was Lewis Washington, one of the first fugitives he had assisted. Joseph Lovejoy compiled Torrey's memoir and presided over his funeral services at Tremont Temple, which was addressed by abolitionists of all stripes. Condemnations of his death came from across the country and from the British and Foreign ASS. At an Oberlin meeting William Howard Day noted "the sufferings of a Work, a Burr and a Thompson . . . the branded hand of a Walker . . . the glorious martyr-death of a Torrey by Maryland law and in a Maryland prison."[19]

Rankin was wary of "slave running," which risked the lives of those involved and endangered long-standing underground operations. His misgivings were borne out when the abolitionist minister Calvin Fairbank and Delia Webster, a schoolteacher who had briefly studied at Oberlin, were arrested in Kentucky for helping the enslaved Hayden family escape to freedom in September 1844. Fairbank, whose encounter with fugitive slaves had radicalized him as a young boy growing up in New York, had been active along the Ohio–Kentucky border. Webster was from Vergennes, Vermont, where the Quaker Hoag, Robinson, and Stevens families sheltered fugitives. The Garrisonians Rowland and Rachel Robinson employed them on their farm, Rokeby. At the prompting of Rev. John Mifflin Brown in Cincinnati, Fairbank was sent to retrieve the family of an es- caped slave, Gilson Berry, whom Webster had assisted. Unable to locate Berry, Fairbank, on Webster's suggestion, helped Lewis Hayden and his wife and child to escape. The two abolitionists were caught, but Hayden made his way to free- dom in Boston, becoming known for his activism on behalf of fugitive slaves. An old slave, Israel, who drove the carriage in which the Haydens escaped, was also arrested and severely whipped.

When informed that Israel had implicated her and Fairbank, Webster re- torted that he had been tortured. Tried separately, Fairbank was sentenced to fifteen years and Webster to two years in prison, but she was pardoned within two months. In prison, Fairbank, in heavy irons, encountered slaves jailed "on suspicion for longing for freedom," one who broke the neck of his mistress, who had "abused him in ways too vile to be spoken of," and was handcuffed with a slave condemned to die. Gov. John J. Crittenden pardoned Fairbank in 1849 after Hayden raised money to buy himself on the condition that his rescuer be released. Fairbank's father, who gathered petitions for his release, died just before he was freed. But Fairbank returned to help a slave woman named Tamar escape, for which he was again arrested and sentenced to fifteen years in prison. He was pardoned only in 1864 in the midst of the war after suffering solitary confinement, a harsh labor regimen, and regular whippings. He was visited by his fiancée, the abolitionist Laura Haviland, famous herself for assisting fugitives.

Women involved in the abolitionist underground, including Catherine Coffin, Jane Rankin, Harriet Myers, Rachel Robinson, Harriet Purvis, and Rachel Mendinhall Garrett, were often the wives of abolitionists active in aiding runaways or, like Lucretia Mott, worked in female abolitionist societies that harbored, sewed clothes for, and provided food for fugitive slaves. The Quaker abolitionists Graceanna Lewis, the daughter of the AASS founder Evan Lewis, Elizabeth Buffum Chace, the daughter of Arnold Buffum, and Abigail Hopper Gibbons, the daughter of Hopper, were known to assist fugitive slaves. Webster's and Haviland's involvement in slave running took female activism in the UGRR a notch further. Haviland and her husband ran Raisin Institute, an interracial manual labor school in Michigan known for sheltering fugitive slaves, and she taught in Bibb's fugitive slave Canadian settlement. The state of Tennessee put a price of three thousand dollars on her head for foiling the recapture of a runaway female slave. After her husband's death, Haviland moved to Cincinnati and got involved in fugitive slave rescues through the city's interracial Vigilance Committee and the Coffins; she noted that abolitionist women met three times a month to sew clothes for fugitives. Like Webster, she traveled to Kentucky and Arkansas, apparently even staring down bloodhounds once, to spirit away slaves and escort runaways to Canada.

Women abolitionists involved in slave running, like their male counterparts, displayed considerable courage and bravado. Webster, on gaining her freedom, caused some confusion in abolitionist circles by avowing herself to be a Kentucky colonizationist and denouncing "*Negro Stealing*." Rejecting charges of seducing as opposed to aiding slaves, she had purposefully formed a relationship with her infatuated jailor, who put his children in her care. With the Vermont abolitionist Rev. Norris Day, she purchased a farm in Kentucky, which she touted as an experiment in free labor with German tenants and said was to be used for creating an Oberlin-like institution. Day and Webster were widely suspected by their neighbors and state authorities of helping slaves escape across the Ohio River, where the farm was strategically located. While Day left with his family, Webster was arrested again in 1854 on old charges of helping Berry and Lewis's wife, Harriet Hayden, escape. Though freed owing to a lack of evidence, she was pursued by her scorned jailor to Madison, Indiana. An antislavery lawyer successfully defended her, and the humiliated jailor narrowly escaped an irate crowd, returning home with a bullet in his body.[20]

Running off slaves was a risky business rather than the stuff of romance. The MASS started carrying a regular feature in its annual reports, "Northern prisoners in the South." In 1848 the young Quaker abolitionist Richard Dillingham from Ohio was arrested in Nashville after he journeyed there to assist enslaved relatives of blacks in Cincinnati who had solicited his services. Sentenced to three years' hard labor after delivering a moving courtroom address, Dillingham died of cholera in prison two years later. John Fairchild of Virginia, a "southern abolitionist" and "inveterate hater of slavery," was known to run off slaves pretending to be a slaveholder or slave trader. He was imprisoned a few times, settled in a free black community in Indiana briefly, and was probably killed in a slave insurrection scare in Tennessee on the eve of the Civil War.[21]

Fugitive slave escapes became more common in the late antebellum period, involving groups of runaway slaves, anticipating the flight of hundreds of slaves during the war. In 1847 a group of no fewer than forty-five fugitive slaves openly paraded and were housed and fed in Battle Creek, Michigan. Whipper wrote that between 1847 and 1850 he personally "passed hundreds to the land of freedom." At times these escapes resembled mini slave rebellions, with pitched battles between "freedom seekers" and their sympathizers, including free blacks, abolitionists, bystanders, and employers, and law enforcement authorities, slaveholders, and their agents. In 1848 around seventy slaves escaped to the Ohio River with E. J. "Patrick" Doyle, a student from Center College, Danville. They were apprehended by some hundred white men and became involved in a gun battle in which one black man and one white man died. Surrounded by a reinforcement of nearly four hundred white men, the slaves surrendered; fifty were tried, three executed, and Doyle was sentenced to twenty years in prison, where he died. Such incidents happened often enough to constitute a "border war" over slavery in the slave and free states that adjoined each other. A Maryland slaveholder and a black man lost their lives in a violent confrontation when two slaveholders tried to recapture three runaway slaves in a courtroom in Harrisburg, Pennsylvania, in 1847. Episodic clashes over fugitives periodically disrupted the proslavery consensus based on commercial and political ties in slavery's borderlands.[22]

The UGRR consisted not so much of the elaborate routes mapped by its first historian, Wilbur Seibert, but of distinct sites of activist interracial abolitionism and antislavery politics, like parts of Ohio, the port towns of New Bedford and Boston, south-central Pennsylvania and Philadelphia, Detroit, western Illinois, upstate New York and New York City, black settlements in Canada, and the area around the District of Columbia. Free black communities, especially in the racially hostile northwestern states and border slave states, were essential to the political geography of fugitive slave resistance.[23] Acknowledging the interracial nature of the UGRR changes the terms of the tired dichotomy over whether one should concentrate on the heroism of self-emancipated slaves, as Garrison called them, or the abolitionists who assisted them. Fugitives set in motion a chain of events that had far-reaching political effects, and it is fair to conclude that they inspired abolitionist resistance to laws of the slaveholding republic.

In 1848 slaveholding authorities tried unsuccessfully to permanently disable one of these nodes of underground activism. They arrested and convicted the Quaker abolitionists John Hunn and Thomas Garrett in Wilmington, Delaware, for assisting fugitive slaves. Garrett had long worked with a network of free blacks, Joseph Walker, Harry Craig, Severn Johnson, and Joseph Holland, who undertook the risky business of hiding fugitives in their homes. Garrett assisted two famous fugitive slave abolitionists from Maryland, the family of Henry Highland Garnet and Harriet Tubman. Wilmington, a center of black abolitionism, was the home of Abraham Shadd and the former slave Peter Spencer of the African Union Methodist Church, both known to help runaway slaves. Born in Pennsylvania, Garrett dated his abolitionism to the kidnapping of a free black woman who worked in his home. He became a member of the PAS and later a confidante of Garrison. While Shadd moved to Pennsylvania and assisted fugitives there, Garrett moved to Delaware in 1822. After the death of his first wife, he married into the abolitionist Mendinhall family, who, along with other Quaker families and free blacks, some runaways themselves, helped make Chester County, Pennsylvania, a common destination of fugitive slaves. Garrett aided over two thousand freedom seekers, many of them from Maryland and Virginia.

Hunn and Garrett were arrested for facilitating the escape of the enslaved Hawkins family, whose owners sued both. Six separate cases were tried against them. Garrett was fined the crippling sum of over five thousand dollars, reduced to fifteen hundred. The trial judge who sentenced him was none other than the ubiquitous Taney, riding the Supreme Court circuit. Garrett defiantly told the court to send more fugitives his way since he had nothing left to lose. Samuel D. Burris, a free black operator "of marked courage and daring" from Delaware, first brought the Hawkins family to Hunn and Garrett's attention. Burris moved to Philadelphia and, like Tubman, made several rescue missions to the South. He was eventually arrested and threatened with reenslavement in a public auction. Isaac Flint, an abolitionist under cover, bought his freedom with "abolition gold." Burris moved to San Francisco, where he became active in contraband relief efforts during the war, his "interest in the cause of freedom" never faltering until his death at the age of sixty. In the 1850s Garrett recuperated his losses and was an accomplice of Tubman and Still of the PVC. In 1860 Maryland put a bounty of ten thousand dollars on his head, but he lived to celebrate the Emancipation Proclamation with Wilmington's black community. All the pallbearers at his funeral were African American, bearing testimony, as Still put it, to "his practical devotion to the Slave."[24]

The same year as Garrett's trial, three seamen, Capt. Daniel Drayton, Chester English, and Edward Sayres aboard the *Pearl*, carrying seventy-seven black men, women, and children, were apprehended in Washington by a magistrate in a steamer in hot pursuit. These three working-class men were paid for the mass escape, though Drayton was a man of antislavery sympathies, the source of his conversion being the desperate runaways he encountered. His memoir, written with the help of Hildreth, opens a window into the waterborne UGRR. Like another sea captain involved in the abolitionist underground, Albert Fountain, Drayton's seafaring career in the Chesapeake Bay, he explained, had "brought me a good deal into contact with the slave population." The slaves, he wrote, were "pretty adroit" in determining if a ship originated from the North and would board them at night "in hopes of obtaining passage in her to a land of freedom." Drayton's views on slavery "had undergone a gradual change" as "his intercourse with the negroes" revealed that "they had the same desires, wishes, and hopes as myself." Especially horrible, he noted, was the idea of having one's children sold away, a common enough occurrence in that area. The proslavery idea that slaves were content would do well, he said, only "for those who know nothing of the matter personally." A year before the *Pearl* episode he helped a slave mother married to a free black man and her children escape. A few of the fugitives aboard the *Pearl* were free and married to slaves, most members of the city's black churches, and some, like the Bells and Edmundsons, were fleeing to protect enslaved family members from sale to the South. When they were apprehended Drayton reported, "The black men came to the cabin, and asked if they should fight." He discouraged them, as resistance was futile.

The escape took place at the instigation of the slaves and the interracial abo-litionist network that stretched from the District of Columbia to Philadelphia. William Chaplin, who replaced Torrey, was involved in freedom suits and cases involving self-purchase as well as in assisting runaways. Daniel Bell, for instance, had scraped together money to buy his freedom; his wife, Mary, with Chaplin's assistance, was involved in a freedom suit against the widow of her deceased master, who had promised her freedom. Chaplin and his benefactor Gerrit Smith, who financed his activities, supported the idea of emancipation through purchase. He planned the *Pearl* escape with Charles Dexter Cleveland of the Philadelphia ASS. Chaplin and Cleveland hired Drayton, who in turn hired Sayres and his schooner *Pearl* along with English. After their arrest, the three were threatened with lynching by a proslavery mob led by local slave trad-ers. Of the three, only English, who was briefly imprisoned, did not know the nature of their undertaking. The simultaneous disappearance of so many slaves, many of whom were the property of Washington's political elite, caused great consternation. Slaves from the District were either whipped to extract informa-tion about the escape or, like Thomas Ducket, whose family was on the *Pearl*, and Anthony Blow, who worked in the Navy Yard, sold. Blow escaped to Phila-delphia six years later, but Ducket languished in Louisiana. Dolley Madison, the former first lady, sold her errant slave Ellen Steward to a Baltimore slave trader, but Steward, like a few others, was purchased and freed by abolitionists. Bell managed to purchase his wife and youngest child but lost his nine other children to slavery.

Tragically, most of the *Pearl* runaways were sold south. Their sale became a matter of controversy when Congressman John I. Slingerland from upstate New York witnessed their departure and the House chaplain, a Methodist min-ister, fraternizing with the slave trader, and wrote about it. The plight of the remarkable Edmundson family, half free and half slave, attracted the attention of abolitionists, who raised money for the purchase and education of Mary and Emily Edmundson. Paul, a free man who owned a farm, and his enslaved wife, Amelia, had twelve children, six of whom were free, five enslaved, and one sold for an attempted escape. Four brothers, one of whom was free, and Mary and Emily were on board the *Pearl*. Held in slave pens in Washington and Baltimore, they were sold in New Orleans, but the two sisters made it back to the North. They were freed after their father managed to raise enough money among ab-olitionists to buy them, a transaction in which Rev. Henry Ward Beecher of Plymouth Church played a crucial role. The girls' saga continued well into the 1850s. Financed by Henry's sister Harriet Beecher Stowe, both went on to study at Oberlin, staying with the abolitionist Cowles family. When Mary died of tuberculosis, Stowe was convinced that her imprisonment following the *Pearl* affair had brought on her illness. Emily became an abolitionist lecturer and teacher and helped raise money to buy one of her brothers. Another managed to escape from New Orleans and ended up in Britain and Australia, while yet another remained in Louisiana.[25]

The *Pearl* became a matter of sectional controversy in Congress just as debate over the western expansion of slavery in the aftermath of the Mexican War was heating up. It helped to push the abolition of the slave trade in the District and a new fugitive slave law onto the national agenda. Giddings may have known about it, as one of the Edmundson brothers had approached him to secure the freedom of his sisters before the escape. Giddings was quick to offer his services to the imprisoned seamen and visited them even though threatened with violence. A proslavery mob of thousands stoned the office of the newly established national antislavery newspaper in the city, the *National Era*, despite the public disavowal of any involvement by Gamaliel Bailey, its editor. At his home, Bailey and his old father confronted the mob and its committee, refusing to give up the right of free speech and press on the subject of slavery. The arrest of the fugitives and attack on Bailey's paper provoked antislavery members of Congress such as Sen. John P. Hale, Giddings, and the newly elected Palfrey to move resolutions demanding information on the *Pearl* slaves and protection of the life and property of antislavery members of Congress from proslavery violence. Hale decried the loss of liberties, including the right to discussion.

Alexander Stephens accused Giddings of slave theft, Calhoun called it "piratical acts," and Jefferson Davis, slave stealing. Sen. Henry Foote outdid them all in calling for Hale to visit Mississippi, where a noose would be waiting for him, earning him the sobriquet Hangman Foote from the antislavery press. Slaveholders demanded a new fugitive slave law. In reply, Giddings drew attention to the wholesale bartering of men, women, and children in the capital. Palfrey, Mann, Giddings, and others involved in the debate over the *Pearl* escape were at the forefront of the fight to abolish the slave trade and slavery in the District of Columbia. As a freshman congressman from Illinois, Abraham Lincoln shared Mrs. Spring's antislavery boardinghouse with Giddings, Palfrey, and Daniel Gott, whose resolution abolishing the slave trade in the District passed the House in 1848. A year later Lincoln proposed a plan for gradual, compensated emancipation there.

Abolitionists and antislavery politicians rallied to the defense of the imprisoned seamen. The prosecutor in the case against Drayton and Sayres was Philip Barton Key, the son of Francis Scott Key, continuing the family tradition of prosecuting abolitionists. Mann, who occupied Quincy Adams's seat in Congress, represented them, overcoming what Phillips called his "timid silence" on Boston's school desegregation struggle. A large abolitionist meeting across factional lines, attended by the Libertyites Sewall, Wright, Bowditch, the Garrisonians May and Jackson, and black abolitionists like Robert Morris, among others, collected funds for Drayton and Sayres's defense, a good chunk of the money coming from Gerrit Smith. Hildreth was deputized to go to Washington, and another lawyer, James Carlisle, was hired at considerable expense. Arguing for the defense, Mann noted threats of lynching against the prisoners, mob action against antislavery politicians, and the *Era*, which made a mockery of the law. He protested the exorbitant bail of seventy-six thousand dollars and the over three hundred counts of indictment brought against the three men. If convicted, they would be condemned to eight hundred years in prison, and Key would profit handsomely from each trial. Mann defended the slaves' right to flee, arguing that they were well aware of the ideals of the Declaration of Independence and the speeches praising the recent European revolutions for freedom by congressmen, who would then also be complicit. The defense tried to prove that the slaves had run away on their own and that Drayton and Sayres were guilty only of unknowingly transporting them.

While disavowing illegal interference in the institution of slavery, Bailey expressed his abhorrence at the severe charges and punishment of Drayton and Sayres. After a series of trials before an unsympathetic judge, Drayton was convicted and sentenced to twenty years in prison for larceny, or stealing slaves, and fined over ten thousand dollars for transporting them. Sayres was found guilty of transporting fugitive slaves and fined over seven thousand dollars. Unable to pay these enormous amounts, the two languished in jail. Bailey continued to "appeal for mercy" on their behalf. In prison Drayton saw a "good deal what slaves were exposed to." Both men were pardoned in 1852 because of the intervention of the newly elected Free Soil senator Charles Sumner. Sumner strategically spent his first year in the Senate working behind the scenes for their release and suffering criticism for his silence on the subject of slavery. Drayton concluded that while men like Hale, Sumner, Giddings, and Mann could deliver strong antislavery speeches, he would never be able to "make myself heard in Congress, or by the nation at large, except in the way of action." On his release he joined the abolitionist lecture circuit but was severely debilitated by his long imprisonment. He committed suicide in 1857 in New Bedford. The town paid for his funeral, and an admirer erected a monument to him inscribed with Sumner's words.[26]

Fugitive slaves and their abolitionist allies exposed the republican pretensions of slaveholding politicians. In the early Republic, Hopper had braved the wrath of the South Carolinian planter-politician Pierce Butler in order to aid his runaway slave Ben. In the antebellum period they embarrassed slavehold-ers widely known for their statesmanship. The NASS published an article on President John Tyler's two runaway slaves, one who claimed to be his son. At least two of Henry Clay's slaves caused considerable embarrassment to him. One, Lewis Richardson, accused him of abuse, and the other, Lewis Hayden, of selling off his first wife, thereby instigating a war of words between Clay and abolitionists. In furious letters to Sydney Howard Gay, the editor of the NASS, Clay dismissed his former slaves as lying, worthless men. But to abolitionists like Abel Brown, Clay was nothing but a man stealer. In a public letter to Clay, Douglass systematically dismantled all his objections to immediate abolition and questioned the sincerity of his antislavery beliefs, as he was the "robber of nearly fifty human beings." He urged Clay to follow Washington's example and "emancipate your slaves" in the "winter" of his life. Clay freed ten of his slaves, including a personal manservant, and, according to his biographers, was a be-nevolent master. Douglass, referring to his disappointed presidential ambitions, quipped that Clay was the president of the ACS but of nothing else. In his last political act as the Great Pacificator, Clay recommended the abolition of the slave trade in the District and a stringent new fugitive slave law as part of the Compromise of 1850.[27]

That year Chaplin was arrested for aiding two runaway slaves who happened to belong to the Georgia Whig duo Sen. Robert Toombs and Representative Stephens. Besides his involvement with the *Pearl*, Chaplin had spent over six thousand dollars rescuing and purchasing slaves in the Washington area. He was arrested by John Goddard, the head of the city Night Watch, eager to earn the reward posted by the two slaveholding politicians. Bruised and bloodied in his attempt to elude capture, Chaplin served four months in Washington and Maryland prisons, where he encountered starving slave children and a man jailed for speaking out against slavery. Abolitionists, again across factional lines, set up a Chaplin Fund Committee in Boston. The committee included po-litical abolitionists such as Smith, Whittier, and Samuel Fessenden of Maine, Garrisonians like May and Jackson, Douglass, William Harned of the New York State Vigilance Commmittee, and the radical antislavery politicians Chase, Giddings, and George Julian of Indiana. The committee successfully raised twenty-five thousand dollars to bail Chaplin out, who quickly left, forfeiting his bond. Chaplin, his defenders argued, had triumphed against "all legal and illegal tyranny." Chaplin asked abolitionists to set aside their differences and act upon their "professions."[28]

Washington's black community, enslaved and free, made the nation's capi-tal a contested ground between slavery and freedom. As early as 1843 William

Jones, a free black man jailed and about to be sold into slavery, petitioned Congress with the help of David Hall, an antislavery lawyer known to assist fugitive slaves, for his freedom. His petition, introduced by Giddings, led to a fractious debate along sectional lines in the House. By 1850 the fugitive slave issue had made its way to the nation's highest court and to Congress many times, having an impact on national politics that paralleled the debate over slavery in the territories. It assumed international significance when British authorities repeatedly turned down American demands for an extradition treaty covering fugitive slaves.[29] Self-emancipated slaves and their allies compiled a formidable record of noncompliance, legal wrangling, and open defiance of slave laws as well as eliciting international law and sanction against the Slave Power of the United States.

SHIPBOARD REBELLIONS

Shipboard slave revolts in the age of abolition played out on a global political stage. Two famous rebellions, one by enslaved Africans and the other by American slaves, the *Amistad* (1839) and the *Creole* (1841), respectively, helped revolutionize the abolition movement. Enslaved rebels accrued the advantages of "liminal spaces" inhabited by slavers in the high seas, subject to differing national sovereignties and law. Already radicalized by their encounter with runaway slaves, all abolitionists and even antislavery politicians found themselves defending the slaves' right to rebel. The "trope of revolutionary struggle" employed by abolitionists did not rest simply on a mainstream American revolutionary model. It belonged to an abolitionist tradition of lauding the Haitian Revolution as well as domestic slave revolts, "an Atlantic geography" of slave resistance that extended to Africa.[30]

In June 1839 Cinque (Sengbe Pieh) and his comrades, part of a cargo of fifty-three Africans, forty-nine men and four children, being transported by Don José Ruíz and Don Pedro Montes on the schooner *La Amistad* from Havana to plantations in Puerto Principe, rose in revolt. The long journey of the mostly Mende slaves had begun on the west coast of Africa, where they had been bought by the Spanish slave trader Pedro Blanco and then housed in Havana's barracoons, or slave pens, before being sold to Ruíz and Montes. The cook aboard the ship taunted Cinque that their owners would cannibalize them, instigating the revolt. Seizing the sharp sugar cane knives and cutlasses on board, Cinque and his men, two of whom died during the revolt, made short work of the Spanish captain and the cook, and had Ruíz and Montes at their mercy. Two sailors disappeared, but the captain's Cuban slave, the sixteen-year-old

Antonio, was spared. The rebels demanded that Ruíz and Montes take them back to Africa, but the two steered west. As the ship ran short on supplies, eight Africans died before they landed in Long Island, New York. Apprehended by Lt. Thomas Gedney aboard a U.S. Navy ship, the Africans and the *Amistad* were claimed as salvage by Gedney and a group of men led by a Henry Green. The ship was towed to New London, Connecticut, and Cinque and the thirty-eight adult men were indicted for murder and piracy. Their arrival caused a sensation: hundreds paid to visit them in jail, artists sketched their portraits, and a play based on the rebellion soon opened in New York City.

The local abolitionist Dwight Janes, who argued that the Africans "had a perfect right to get their liberty by killing the crew and taking possession of the vessel," immediately alerted Lewis Tappan and Leavitt. Tappan, Leavitt, and Jocelyn organized the Amistad Committee to "receive donations, employ counsel and for the protection and relief of the African Captives." With the help of the Mende-speaking black sailors Charles Pratt and James Covey, who had spent time in a Portuguese slaver, Josiah Gibbs of Yale, a linguist, James Ferry, who could speak a West African language, Vai, and the pioneer in deaf education Rev. Thomas Hopkins Gallaudet, the abolitionists managed to communicate with the enslaved Africans and learn their story. The Africans' individual stories, names, and silhouettes, complete with a phrenologist's glowing analysis of Cinque's head, soon appeared in pamphlets. Abolitionists printed descriptions of African societies and culture given by the captives. Cinque and his chief lieutenant, Grabeau, gave details of their cruel treatment by the Spanish captors. The committee enlisted the help of an old colonizationist rival, Rev. Leonard Bacon, among others, for the "intellectual and religious instruction" of the Africans. Reminiscent of abolitionist actions against kidnappers, a countersuit against Ruíz and Montes in New York on behalf of the Africans charged them with assault, battery, and false imprisonment. The two men were arrested: Montes was released and went back to Cuba, while Ruíz refused bail and was imprisoned for four months.

The *Amistad* case also united abolitionists across factional lines, the appeals of the committee appearing regularly in Garrisonian newspapers. Garrison was unstinting in his praise of Tappan for his efforts on behalf of the Africans. The Amistad Committee became a model for abolitionist committees formed to free imprisoned abolitionists such as Torrey, Walker, Drayton, and Chaplin. The revolt, like the prominent fugitive slave cases, not only galvanized the abolition movement but also, because of the protracted legal proceedings, became a forum for abolitionists to make their case against the national recognition of slavery and to draw attention to the prolific illegal African slave trade. The

Amistad, after all, had been built in the shipyards of Baltimore, which, along with New York, outfitted hundreds of slavers used in the African slave trade to Cuba and Brazil, an industry specifically prohibited by American laws. The Amistad Committee hired lawyers of known abolitionist convictions: Theodore Sedgwick of New York, Seth Staples, and Roger Sherman Baldwin, the scion of a prominent Connecticut family who had defended fugitive slaves and stood up to the New Haven mob in 1831. The Africans' lawyers first tried the tactic used in fugitive slave cases to free them, presenting a writ of habeas corpus. They wanted to establish that the Africans were legally free and unlawfully detained and could not therefore be claimed either as salvage or as slaves by their Spanish captors.

Baldwin argued that the American government had no authority to hold the Africans even on a criminal charge for an incident that had occurred on the high seas. Next, Staples, evoking another legal precedent from the fugitive slave trials, pointed out that since the Africans had been brought "voluntarily" by their Spanish masters to free territory, they were free and not subject to the fugitive slave law. The defense lawyers did not just invoke the law, the prohibition of the African slave trade by the Spanish, and abolition in the northern states but also the slaves' right to revolution when deprived of their "natural liberty." The affidavit of one of the Africans, Bahoo (Bau), made it clear that the recaptives were from Africa and should be sent back to Africa as required by the law of 1819 against the African slave trade. In September Judge Smith Thompson denied the writ of habeas corpus, noting that even though the Constitution did not mention the word *slavery*, American laws recognized the institution.

The Van Buren administration, in a long opinion written by Attorney General Felix Grundy of Tennessee, supported the claims of the Spanish government to extradite the Africans and even sent a man-of-war to spirit them back to Cuba after they had been tried. Abolitionists too made plans to rescue the Africans if the decision went against them, Birney suggesting that they bail them out and then forfeit the bond. In April 1840 Judge Andrew Judson (of Prudence Crandall fame [see chapter 8]) in the district court granted the *Amistad* as salvage to Gedney but ruled in favor of the Africans, setting them free and not liable under American laws for crimes committed under Spanish jurisdiction. The testimony of the Irish abolitionist Richard Madden, who led a one-man battle against the illegal African slave trade in Havana, and that of Cinque, Grabeau, Fuliwa, and Kimbo on their journey from Africa proved to be decisive. A colonizationist, Judson was happy to recommend the transportation of the Africans back to Africa. The Van Buren administration appealed the decision of the district court to the circuit court presided over by Thompson and Judson, who reiterated it pro forma. In an effort to appease the powerful southern wing of the Democratic Party, the administration adopted the Spanish position, and Spanish representatives quoted Calhoun's defense of slave property to make their case for extradition.[31]

When the *Amistad* case was tried in the Supreme Court in 1841 on appeal, Tappan retained the services of Quincy Adams as senior counsel. Adams had followed the case from the start, communicating his views to Loring. He visited the imprisoned Africans in New Haven and was moved by their plight. Some began corresponding with him, assuring him that they were from Africa. As Kale, one of the Mende captives, wrote, "All we want is make us free." In his brief Adams argued that the life and liberty of the Africans were at stake. He arraigned the administration for "sympathy with the white, antipathy to the black" and for tampering with official documents on the case. Adams was particularly critical of the secretary of state, the Georgian John Forsyth, for his deference to the Spanish government. The AFASS sought the intervention of the British government through the British and Foreign ASS as a counterweight. The British also demanded the prosecution of Ruíz and Montes in Cuba for participating in the African slave trade, outlawed by the Anglo–Spanish treaty of 1817. Adams went further, holding that slavery, or property in humans, had originated in a state of war and was not recognized by the founding document of the country, the Declaration that had established a natural right to life and liberty. Baldwin also defended the natural right of the Africans to self-emancipation. In the published version of his speech, parts of which he was unable to deliver in court, Adams dismantled the legal precedent of the 1825 case of the *Antelope*, part of whose cargo of enslaved Africans had been returned to the Spanish. The *Antelope* decision, Adams wrote, had "baffled, defeated, prostrated, nullified" the laws of the United States for the "suppression of the execrable slave trade." He noted the apologetic nature of the decision and Chief Justice John Marshall's opinion that the case established no legal precedent. The court had acknowledged that the African slave trade violated the "laws of nature" and in 1827 returned most of the recaptives to Africa. Since then Spain had abolished the slave trade, making the *Antelope* case irrelevant.

Chief Justice Story, who conveyed the court's decision, argued that the Africans were born free and therefore could not be returned to Spain under the provisions of the treaties of 1795 and 1821 signed between the two countries. But the Spanish continued to press for monetary compensation until the eve of the Civil War, when the *Amistad* claims became entangled with the politics of slavery and efforts by the United States to acquire Cuba. While southerners and their northern Democratic allies pressed the *Amistad* claims and issued two reports, one in the House and, later, another one in the Senate, favoring them, antislavery politicians such as Adams and Giddings strongly resisted. As the presidential candidate of the Free Soil Party in 1848, Van Buren was forced to explain away his stance on the *Amistad* case. Story, accepting abolitionist reasoning, maintained that the Africans had been kidnapped and had a natural right to self-defense to claim their liberty. As Tappan argued, the *Amistad* case was about human rights that transcended national boundaries. Story, however, remanded Antonio back to slavery, making a distinction between the illegal African slave trade and legal slavery. Antonio, with the help of Tappan and the local Committee of Vigilance, fled to Montreal through the abolitionist underground. The NASS concluded that the *Amistad* Africans "*have but just escaped us.*"[32]

The Africans, Sturge reported during his visit to the United States, had proven to be "of immense service to the antislavery cause." The Amistad Committee printed thousands of copies of Baldwin's and Adam's speeches before the Supreme Court and emphasized their stature as descendants of revolutionary figures. Abolitionists, through a writ of habeas corpus, recovered the three young African girls living with the jailor, whom the Africans heartily disliked and accused of mistreatment, amidst a jeering crowd of Yale students. They soon joined the other captives in Farmington, a station in the UGRR, that is, safely abolitionist country. Cinque and some of his comrades addressed packed meetings, raising money for their return to Africa. Sturge recalled his fluency and his "animated and graceful" manner on hearing him. To Leavitt, who closely followed the Supreme Court proceedings, the *Amistad* decision had marked "the revival of the Common Law doctrines of the Revolution." In abolitionist print culture, Cinque was apotheosized as a black revolutionary hero, and flattering descriptions of him called him "a tall and stalwart African of commanding presence and stalwart spirit" who, in his own words, had fought against "the bondage of the white man." Commissioned by Purvis, his portrait (reprinted in this book) was memorably rendered by Nathaniel Jocelyn, the brother of Simeon Jocelyn. Abolitionists sought to counter racist depictions of the Africans, one accusing them of cannibalism—ironically, a fate the rebels had sought to avoid—and efforts to discredit Cinque as a slave trader begun by the prosecution, a fact that escaped historians who revived that untenable accusation. After Foone, one of the recaptives, drowned in a likely suicide, abolitionists redoubled their efforts to have the Africans sent home. The government refused to help, and British promises to supply a ship took too long. Tappan tirelessly raised private donations and funds from public meetings featuring the Mende Africans. The thirty-five survivors and three girls sailed back to Africa in

November, arriving there in January 1842. Five abolitionist missionaries, a black couple and three whites, accompanied the Africans, laying the foundations of the Mendi mission in Africa.

The *Amistad* case spurred abolitionist missionary work. In 1841 Pennington, who was also active in raising funds for the return of the Africans, and the British-educated Augustus Hanson had formed the mostly black Union Missionary Society (UMS) with forty-three delegates from six states and five Mende Africans, including Cinque, to begin the Christianization of Africa. Its officers included Pennington as president, Amos Beman from New Haven, George Hogarth and Amos Freeman from Brooklyn, Wright from Manhattan, and Garnet and Ward from upstate New York. The "Missionary Convention" supported *"the enterprize of African missions"* but disavowed colonization. Pennington warned against developing European and American colonies in Africa on the pretext of missionary work. Tappan and the UMS executive committee urged Pennington to go to Africa as a missionary, but he chose to stay in the United States. The UMS published the short-lived *Union Missionary Herald* until the Amistad Committee merged with it, with Pennington as president and Tappan as treasurer. The UMS and other organizations connected with the abolitionists' free missions movement against slaveholding in the American Board of Commissioners of Foreign Missions—namely, the Western Evangelical Missionary Society at Oberlin and Phelps's Committee for West Indian Missions, created to support missionary work among former slaves—formed the AMA, led by Tappan, in 1846.

The *Amistad* missionaries established a foothold in Africa, but the Mendeans preferred to rejoin the societies and cultures they had been forced to leave behind. Cinque, whose wife and children had been killed or sold as slaves, was caught between the world of the mission and that of the natives. The AMA recruited Thompson, whose imprisonment fostered a desire to live the life of an abolitionist missionary, to head the Mendi mission. Sarah Margru, one of the children aboard the *Amistad*, returned to study at Oberlin and became a teacher at the mission. Some African graduates of its school moved to the United States and joined the fight for black rights during Reconstruction, completing the circle of transnational abolitionism in which the Africans were active participants.[33]

At the very time the *Amistad* Africans were heading home, another shipboard rebellion, this one on the American brig *Creole* with 135 slaves, also had ramifications in national politics and international diplomacy, and it too inspired abolitionists to defend the slave's right to rebel. In November 1841 the fortuitously named Virginian slave Madison Washington, with Ben Blacksmith (also known as Ben Johnstone), Elijah Morris, Doctor Ruffin, and George Portlock, took over command of the *Creole*, engaged in the waterborne interstate slave trade from Virginia to Louisiana. Washington, who had successfully escaped to Canada, returned to Virginia to free his enslaved wife and was captured and sold. During the uprising, he and Morris prevented others from wreaking vengeance on the whites. Only one man, John Hewell, was killed, while the captain was severely injured, and two others who were injured were treated by the rebels. One rebel was killed and another injured.

After being told that sailing to Liberia was impossible, the rebels made the crew steer the *Creole* to Nassau in the Bahamas. Commanded by a British officer, black soldiers, African recaptives from the illegal foreign slave trade, guarded the vessel. Circumventing an attempt to recapture the ship at the behest of the American consul, the British authorities freed the slaves and refused to extradite the nineteen rebels. Only four enslaved women and a child, hiding in the hold, returned to the United States, and the rest left for the shore in small boats ferried by the local black population. Around sixty soon boarded a ship to an anonymous freedom in Jamaica. The surviving seventeen rebels held for piracy—George Grundy succumbed to his wounds, and Adam Carnay died in prison—were freed in April 1842, much to the chagrin of the American government. Most of the slave owners and traders, represented by the future Confederate secretary of state Judah P. Benjamin, lost their case for compensation for their human property from insurance companies in the New Orleans courts since the loss had occurred because of a rebellion. Of the eight policies on the *Creole* slaves, only two had to pay up, as they covered losses owing to insurrection.

The *Creole* rebellion was indeed "a story of the revolutionary Black Atlantic." The revolt smacked of cosmopolitan political sophistication rather than of the elemental and natural, terms in which writers and historians have described it. A year before the rebellion, the British had freed slaves from the shipwrecked *Formosa* (also known as the *Hermosa*). Coincidentally, the Richmond slave trader Robert Lumpkin owned slaves on both brigs. However obtained, the *Creole* rebels had knowledge of the international geopolitics of slavery and freedom and the acumen to use it to their advantage. Canadian and British authorities had long refused the demands of Americans for an extradition treaty for fugitive slaves, except in the case of a crime. In the case of the *Creole*, the British had set the rebels free, disclaiming jurisdiction on the high seas. Washington had lived for a year in Canada and attended Hiram Wilson's manual labor school. On his way back to Virginia he met abolitionists, the Quaker Moore family of Rochester, Purvis, in whose home he saw Cinque's portrait, Garnet, and the British Quaker abolitionist John Gurney. His "geo-political literacy" thus straddled the worlds not just of the slave trade and slavery but also of the interracial and transnational world of abolition. The nonresistant Garrison praised the "hero mutineers" of the *Creole*, especially Washington, arguing that slaves had a right to attain their freedom by any means possible, and published a call for a petition to hang a portrait of Washington in the Library of Congress.[34]

The *Creole* case was a source of ongoing friction between the United States and Britain. As a rule, the British freed slaves from American ships when they landed on British soil. In the 1830s three American slavers involved in the interstate trade, the *Comet*, the *Encomium*, and the *Enterprise*, were wrecked in the Bahamas and Bermuda. According to Calhoun, all three were involved in a legal slave trade and fell under American jurisdiction. The British government agreed to pay American claims for the slaves on the *Comet* and *Encomium* but not for those on the *Enterprise* because it had landed after the British had abolished slavery on August 1, 1834. Southerners led by the unyielding Calhoun and President Tyler demanded reparations for the *Creole* slaves, and northern conservatives like Secretary of State Daniel Webster insisted that, unlike the *Amistad* case, the *Creole* case involved slaves legally held by slaveholders and wanted for "murder and mutiny" by the United States. The British were eager to secure American cooperation against the African slave trade, as the Americans staunchly opposed Britain's right to search American ships suspected of participating in the illegal trade, and the British minister was loath to let the *Creole* case get in the way of a treaty. The Anglo-American claims commission, set up by the Webster–Ashburton treaty of 1842, awarded the American slaveholders just over $110,000 for the *Creole* slaves in 1853.

Abolitionists in Britain and the United States protested the recognition of slaveholders' claims in human property. According to the NASS, Webster had no authority to demand the return of the rebels or compensation for slave property. Slaveholders saved their ire for the eighth article, which stipulated the joint patrolling of the African coast against the Atlantic slave trade. In a public letter, Ruggles protested the tenth article of the treaty, which endangered fugitive slaves in Canada. It allowed for the extradition of criminals, but the clause was not applied to fugitive slaves or slave rebels. In one of the few cases that year, Nelson Hackett of Arkansas, who had been helped by Detroit's Colored Vigilant Committee, was extradited for theft of articles ranging from a horse to a coat and gold watch. Later, even fugitives accused of murder, like John Anderson, were not extradited because of abolitionists' protests. The normally sedentary Smith traveled to Canada West twice on his behalf. Anderson, who killed his pursuer in self-defense, had escaped after being sold away from his family and eventually migrated to England and then Liberia.[35] By their actions, slave rebels precipitated a confrontation with the Slave Power in the court of international opinion, law, and diplomacy.

THE SLAVES' RIGHT TO REBELLION

The *Creole* and *Amistad* rebellions led abolitionists and antislavery politicians not only to question the proslavery position of the government but to defend the slaves' right to rebel. The Whig congressman from Ohio, Joshua R. Giddings, Adams's chief lieutenant in the fight against the Gag Rule, leaned toward abolition. He was of poor, obscure Puritan stock and largely self-taught. Giddings read law with the colonizationist Elisha Whittlesey and was elected to his seat in Congress in 1838. Appalled by his encounter with the slave trade in Washington, Giddings became part of the group of antislavery northern Whigs that included Slade and Gates, and he led the fight to abolish the slave trade in the capital. These men worked closely with abolitionists such as Leavitt and Weld, who shared their living quarters, and Bailey. Given their antislavery position, Chase tried to woo Adams, Seward, and Giddings to the Liberty Party, but he failed to convince them to join the abolitionist third party.

Giddings became notorious for endorsing slave rebellion. His first major antislavery speech on the Second Seminole War in 1841 accused the federal government and army of playing the role of slave catchers since the Seminole nation included hundreds of fugitive slaves and free blacks who had intermarried with the Creeks. It was the most threatening and influential of slave Maroon communities. Giddings condemned the "war upon human rights" which stole land from the Indians and reenslaved African Americans. It was essentially a war "against the *fugitive slaves* . . . who had fled from the oppression of professed Christians, and sought protection of savage barbarians. Against them the warlike energies of this mighty nation were brought to bear, for no other reason than their love of liberty." The Seminoles were relocated to Indian territory west of the Mississippi in Oklahoma at the end of the war. Giddings criticized the federal government and army for paying bounties for runaway slaves and hunting them down with bloodhounds brought from Cuba, thereby making the United States literally a nation of slave catchers. Asking for more copies of his speech, William Jay praised Giddings's "fearless exposure" of the proslavery nature of the Seminole war. Giddings later wrote an abolitionist history of the Seminole wars as a story of resistance by Native Americans and fugitive slaves. In it, he argued that the national government and army had been prostituted to slavery.

Giddings presented his famous resolutions on the *Creole* case in Congress on March 21, 1842. Formulated by Weld, the *Creole* resolutions asserted that slavery, being an "abridgement of the natural rights of man," could exist only in "municipal law." They further stated that the *Creole* rebels were not liable to the "slave laws" of Virginia and "in resuming their natural right to liberty" had not violated any U.S. law. Without giving him a chance to defend himself, horrified southerners quickly moved to censure Giddings for his support of "mutiny and murder." Giddings resigned his seat and was overwhelmingly reelected from his abolitionist Western Reserve district. His reelection, coming on the heels of the failed attempt to censure Adams, was a triumph of antislavery and portended the defeat of the Gag Rule. In a speech on the difficulties between Britain and the United States stemming from the *Creole* and the right to search, Giddings argued that he was not willing for a single American soldier to give up his life in defense of the slave trade. He criticized Webster, remarking that the domestic slave trade, like the foreign, was piracy and that the *Creole* rebels were not guilty of murder since they had acted in self-defense.

The next year Giddings gave a stronger philippic against the domestic slave trade, protesting a bill facilitating the payment of claims for the *Comet* and *Encomium* slaves. Calling slaves the "moral superiors" of slave traders, he protested that while the country called the slave trade piracy in Africa, it aided those committing the same crime in America. Threatened by a representative from Louisiana, Giddings remained undeterred. In 1844 his speech against a report and bill for compensating the Spanish in the *Amistad* case, or, as he put it, compensating "foreigners for their losses while dealing with human flesh," led to the tabling of both. The "heroic Africans," he stated, were the property of no man in fact or law. By the end of the decade Giddings was in close correspondence with abolitionists, expressing his admiration for Garrison and Phillips, and received invitations from the AASS and AFASS to address their meetings.[36]

Abolitionists and their antislavery allies also invoked international law against southern slavery. In one of his last pamphlets on slavery before his death, *The Duty of the Free States; Or, Remarks Suggested by the Case of the "Creole,"* William E. Channing wrote that he was not pleading the cause of the rebels, who had already won their freedom, but was concerned that the northern states were being forced into defending slavery as a "national interest." Using Webster's defense of slave property as a departure point, he bemoaned the influence of the "slave power" on the U.S. government and condemned the idea of human bondage in universal terms. Claims of slaveholders' kindness, he wrote, were not an effective defense of slavery because that could not mitigate robbing slaves of their essential human rights. From this condemnation of slavery, Channing argued that slavery was a creature of local law, and because it violated natural rights and natural law it did not have a "[hair's] breadth of jurisdiction" beyond that. The American government, founded on principles of universal liberty, should not defend slaveholders' rights that were morally suspect. As for the charge that the British authorities had liberated the slaves, he retorted, "The slaves had liberated themselves." The British had, in fact, liberated the captive white crew and arrested the mutineers before releasing them.

In the lengthier second part of his pamphlet Channing went on to delineate the duty of the free states on slavery and differentiate his position from that of abolitionists. On the fugitive slave issue he argued that it was better to have a thousand fugitives escape slavery than to condemn one free colored citizen of the North to a fate similar to death. He defended the legal protections in place in the northern states to prevent kidnapping. And he came close to defending a higher law, which he believed should guide the actions of the northern states rather than southern laws of slavery, which violated human rights. Channing called for an amendment to the Constitution that would explicitly divorce slavery from "national concerns" and for the abolition of slavery and the slave trade in the District of Columbia. The federal government should not be obligated to defend slavery *"in its intercourse with foreign nations."* He opposed the annexation of Texas, which he predicted would lead to a war with Mexico, or any war fought on behalf of slavery. It was the duty of the North to actively cooperate with Britain in suppressing the "hideous traffic" in African slaves, which the laws of the United States had branded as piracy. At the same time, Channing distanced himself from abolitionists who actively ran off slaves, who justified the slaves' right to rebellion, or who, like the Garrisonians, recommended disunion.[37]

In his response to Webster's vindication of the American laws of slavery and slaveholders' property rights in the *Creole* case, Jay went further. He contended that municipal laws that violated natural human rights, like slavery, were not recognized in international law or entitled to the comity of nations. Slave law ceased to exist on the high seas, and slaves were entitled to their "natural freedom." Slaves had the right to resist their enslavement "even unto death," and they did not violate any law by resisting slavery. Slavery itself was against "Law and Right" since it violated "universal justice."[38] In defending the slave's right to rebel, abolitionist legal theory made human rights an essential attribute of domestic and international law.

On the eve of the Civil War, abolitionists' main constituency was neither slaveholders nor northern whites but the slaves themselves. This was exemplified in their "addresses to the slaves." In 1842 Smith composed an address to the slaves of the United States of America on behalf of the NYASS insisting that abolitionists must communicate with slaves rather than with slaveholders. The inspiration for his address lay in the shipboard rebellions as well as in "the rapid multiplication of escapes from the house of bondage." Full of homilies and advice for slaves, Smith encouraged them to run away and steal whatever provisions they might require to sustain themselves. He asked all abolitionists to promote the escape of slaves from their "prison-house." To Smith, fugitive slaves rather than slave rebellion represented the best chance of success both in terms of slave resistance and abolitionist activism. The Presbyterian abolitionist Nathaniel Johnson, collaborating with Tappan, responded to Smith's address. The law of slavery, he contended, commanded "no moral obligation from the slave," who follows it only as a "matter of prudence," for it violated both natural and divine law. Slavery was a state of war, and the slave was in "an enemy's land" and therefore allowed to use violence if necessary. Defending Smith, Johnson noted it was not a sin to steal for the slave to effect a more desired "*peaceful escape.*" Even evangelical abolitionists challenged rigid doctrines of religious sin and justified slave resistance.

Garrison, often caricatured as a nonviolent moralist, issued his abolitionist address to the slaves the next year. Despite his personal commitment to radical pacifism Garrison had never hesitated to defend the Haitian Revolution and slave rebels, starting with Nat Turner. As early as 1832 Garrison had argued that in the absence of the Union, "scenes of St. Domingo" would be witnessed throughout the South. Slaveholders were hypocritical oppressors who celebrated the Declaration while calling slave rebels murderers and monsters. Garrison borrowed freely from black abolitionists' call to action: "Hereditary Bondmen! know ye not, Who would be free, themselves must strike the blow." He presented the range of opinion among abolitionists on the use of violence, from those who believed that even the oppressed should avoid shedding blood to those who thought "it is right for the oppressed to rise and take their liberty by violence." Both parties, though, agreed that no slave rebellion could contend with the "military power of the nation." Garrison advised against rebellion not because he was a nonresistant but because he thought it doomed to failure. The course of action he recommended was not the "appeals, warnings, rebukes, arguments and facts" that abolitionists had deployed so far but one inspired by the "twenty thousand of your number [who] have successfully runaway, many of whom are now residing in the North, but a very large proportion of whom are living in Canada." Flight would destabilize slavery even though, he cautioned, "many dangers yet lurk in the path of every fugitive, and should any of you be caught, you know that your fate would be a terrible one." Like Smith, Garrison called for a fugitive slave rebellion. As "fellow-countrymen," he demanded "for you all that we claim for ourselves—liberty, equal rights, equal privileges." He concluded, "Your blood is the cement that binds the American Union together; your bodies are crushed between the massy weight of this Union; and its repeal or dissolution would ensure the downfall of slavery." The NEAS convention adopted his address without much debate.[39]

Black abolitionists were more radical. In 1843 Garnet delineated a revolutionary plan for the overthrow of slavery in an address to the slaves delivered at the national black convention in Buffalo. It attracted far more attention than Smith's and Garrison's speeches. At the convention, Garnet encountered the combined opposition of Douglass and Remond and, outside of it, of the formidable Maria Weston Chapman, who criticized his dual endorsement of ballots (that is, the Liberty Party) and bullets. Chapman responded to a report of the speech in the *Liberator* by E. A. Marsh, who called it eloquent despite its "inflammatory appeals" and suffused with Patrick Henry's revolutionary spirit. Garnet replied to her that he was born a slave and Chapman would make him into a slave by forcing him to think exactly like her. He pointed out that he was "the first colored man" to support the Liberty Party. He accused Chapman of not reading his address, which was influenced both by another black man and by his wife, "and if she did counsel me, it is no matter for 'we twain are one flesh.'" If Julia Garnet, an abolitionist in her own right, did participate in the writing of the address, as Garnet indicated, then the notion of appeals to slave resistance as a masculinist discourse must be rethought. Black women, it seems, were no less militant. According to McCune Smith, no other document brought before the black conventions elicited as much debate as Garnet's address, which lost by one vote. The national convention of 1847 in Troy, a roster of prominent black abolitionists, pointedly rejected bloodshed in its report on abolition.

When Garnet published his address along with David Walker's famous appeal in 1848 (apparently John Brown contributed to the cost of publication), he self-consciously situated it in a distinct black abolitionist tradition of protest. Garnet resurrected the memory of Walker by appending a life sketch of him in which he wrote that the appeal was "the boldest and most direct appeal in behalf of freedom, which was made in the early part of the Anti-Slavery Reformation." On the title page of his own address he added, "(REJECTED BY THE NATIONAL CONVENTION, 1843)." In his address Garnet evoked the special connection between slaves and black abolitionists: "While you have been oppressed, we have also been partakers with you; nor can we be free while you are enslaved," and, as a fugitive slave himself whose parents had stolen him from slavery when he was but a child, he noted the ties of family that bound slave and free. They had no reason, Garnet made clear, to hope for emancipation from their enslavers, who he said were "not ignorant of the principles of Liberty" but who added "new links to our chains."

Unlike Smith and Garrison, he urged that slaves not run away from slavery to the North or to British dominions and Mexico, where slaveholders were trying to plant the "black flag" of slavery after expending much of the nation's "blood and treasure." Garnet also thought a slave revolt "INEXPEDIENT," as it was doomed to failure, and recommended instead a general strike: "Cease to labor for tyrants who will not remunerate you." But his address was understood as a call for slave rebellion with good reason. The speculation that he had initially advised rebellion and then substituted that with a call to refuse to labor when he published his address is untenable. His speech explicitly referred not just to Anglo-American revolutionaries like Hampden, Tell, Washington, and Lafayette but also to Louverture, Vesey, Turner, Cinque, and Madison Washington. He surely knew that some of the most spectacular slave rebellions, like those in Demerara and Jamaica, had begun as strikes, as Douglass in his rebuttal contended. Garnet's advice to the slaves implied rebellion: "To such DEGRADATION IT IS SINFUL IN THE EXTREME FOR YOU TO MAKE VOLUNTARY SUBMISSION" and "IT IS YOUR SOLEMN AND IMPERATIVE DUTY TO USE EVERY MEANS, BOTH MORAL, INTELLECTUAL, AND PHYSICAL THAT PROMISE SUCCESS." Most tellingly, he repeated twice in his short address, "RATHER DIE FREEMEN, THAN LIVE TO BE SLAVES" and "LIBERTY OR DEATH." He ended by saying, "Let your motto be RESISTANCE! RESISTANCE! RESISTANCE! No oppressed people have ever secured their liberty without resistance. What kind of resistance you had better make, you must decide. . . . Remember that you are three millions." Garrison, who was never shy about expressing his opinions, did not render one criticism of Garnet's address. In the 1960s, with the rise of a new black struggle for equality, the 1848 pamphlet was republished from an extant copy found in the personal papers of Garrison signed by his son, Francis Jackson Garrison.[40]

The abolitionist move toward active resistance to slavery was exemplified in the ideas of the relatively unknown Jabez Delano Hammond, an Ostego County judge in upstate New York. Hammond was known more for his Jeffersonian politics and political histories of the state—one of which included a biography of the Barnburner Democrat (northern Democrats who opposed the expansion of slavery) Silas Wright—than for his abolitionism. Hammond, who was born in Massachusetts, studied medicine and law, and died in 1855, was a correspondent of Smith, and his wife was an abolitionist. As early as 1839 he had written to Smith that slavery could be abolished only by force, and he proposed forming two military academies in Canada and Mexico to train fugitive slaves to foment slave rebellion in the South. Hammond's remarkable plan anticipated John Brown and the military exploits of black Union troops, most of whom were former slaves. He also published a fictional slave narrative, *Life and Opinions of Julius Melbourne* (1847). Part narrative, part political tract, the book is an eclectic mixture of abolitionism, slave resistance, and political antislavery. It ends with Melbourne proclaiming his love for America despite its faults but predicting bloodshed in the "rich rice and cotton fields of the south" if emancipation does not come about peacefully.[41]

Long before the crisis decade of the 1850s, abolitionists justified the actions of slaves who stole themselves, fought back in self-defense, and rebelled. Slave resistance not only revolutionized the abolition movement but also impacted the national and international politics of slavery. The political significance of slave resistance complemented the simultaneous emergence of antislavery politics in the North, and fugitive slaves became abolition's most effective emissaries.

13

FUGITIVE SLAVE ABOLITIONISM

On February 24, 1844, the *Liberator* printed an admiring report on Frederick Douglass's "masterly and impressive" speech in Concord, New Hampshire. The fugitive slave was the master of his audience. Douglass, the writer fantasized, was like "Toussaint among the plantations of Haiti. . . . He was an insurgent slave, taking hold of the right of speech, and charging on his tyrants the bondage of his race."[1] In the two decades before the Civil War, a new generation of black abolitionists, most of them fugitive slaves, came to dominate the movement.

The narratives of fugitive slaves, their firsthand indictment of slavery, was an effective rebuttal to the growing sophistication of the proslavery argument in the antebellum period. Small wonder that slavery ideologues challenged their veracity and dismissed them as abolitionist propaganda. Scholars have also been too quick to ascribe to white editors and amanuenses the abolitionist content of slave narratives.[2] Fugitive slaves created an authentic, original, and independent critique of slaveholding, one which made their narratives potent antislavery material. No longer could slaveholders claim that their northern critics had no idea about the actual conditions of southern slaves. Their stories of family separations, torture, abuse of children and women, and the hypocrisy of slaveholders constituted the most compelling answer yet to proslavery ideology. Fugitive slaves were abolitionists in their own right. Their narratives and public careers as spokesmen and women against slavery shaped the abolition movement.

SLAVE NARRATIVES

Slave narratives were the movement literature of abolition. Abolitionists did not simply use or co-opt insurgent slaves, a popular and racialist interpretation

that portrays these extraordinary men and women as perpetual victims incapable of political and intellectual warfare against slavery. Fugitive slaves wrote
themselves not just into being but also into history. They were engaged in a political struggle against slavery and racism, writing direct rebuttals of slaveholder
paternalism, at times as letters to their erstwhile masters.[3] Art and politics fused
to making a compelling case for black freedom.

People of African descent wrote autobiographies from the early days of racial
slavery. Fugitive slave narratives published under abolitionists' auspices, however, constitute a distinct genre. In the 1820s former slaves such as Solomon
Bayley and William Grimes published their narratives. Bayley's narrative was
published in London by Robert Hunard, who hoped it would lead to abolition
in the West Indies and the United States. While Bayley's narrative reads like a
spiritual story reinforced by the tragic deaths of his children, he indicts slavery
by retelling the story of his "Guinea" grandmother and mother, who were held
by a cruel family and whose children were illegally sold. Even more than Bayley, Grimes showed slavery to be an unending catalogue of horrors. Published
first in New York in 1825, the work, for which he obtained a copyright, was
republished in 1855 with a new conclusion. Grimes describes his checkered
life of freedom in Connecticut and his constant fear of being recaptured. In
the conclusion he delivers a damning critique of slaveholding republicanism:
"If it were not for the stripes on my back which were made while a slave, I
would in my will leave my skin as a legacy to the government, desiring that it
might be taken off and made into parchment, and then bind the constitution
of glorious, happy, and *free* America. Let the skin of an American slave bind
the charter of American liberty!" Eager to represent the slave's perspective, the
abolitionist writer Richard Hildreth published a two-volume memoir of a fictitious slave, Archy Moore, in 1836. Republished in a longer version as *The White
Slave* in 1852, the book, which painted a portrait of a heroic, rebellious slave,
was not as popular as Harriet Beecher Stowe's *Uncle Tom's Cabin*. Hildreth
subverted the myth of the "tragic mulatto" in his story rather than reinforce
racial stereotypes.[4]

Fugitive slaves themselves monopolized the genre, its tropes, and its politics.
The amanuensis and editor of Charles Ball's narrative of 1837, Isaac Fisher,
inserted long, informative sections on the slave South and claimed to have deleted the author's opinions on slavery. But Ball begins his narrative with a searing condemnation of southern slavery, in which the "entire white population is
leagued together by a common bond of the most sordid interest, in the torture
and oppression of the poor descendants of Africa." In 1859 Ball republished his
narrative anonymously and clearly made his own editorial decisions this time.

He chose an epigraph from Whittier and deleted all of Fisher's comments. His story "was merely a recital of my life as a slave in the Southern States of the Union—a description of negro slavery in the 'model Republic.'" Contradicting assertions of slaveholding paternalism, Ball develops a systemic critique of the domestic slave trade that had resulted in his separation from his wife and children and the punitive, slave-driving regime of the new Cotton Kingdom. His story has no formulaic happy ending, for, having escaped slavery in Georgia and then been recaptured, he escapes again only to find that his wife and children have been sold.[5]

Whittier wrote the introduction to the fugitive slave narrative of James Williams, the first to be published, in 1838 by the AASS. As Williams's amanuensis, Whittier wrote that he refrained from adding his own comments and adhered to Williams's "precise language. THE SLAVE HAS SPOKEN FOR HIMSELF." Williams exposed the empty paternalism of his master, to whom he complained about an abusive overseer whose atrocities dotted his narrative. His master "told him [the overseer] to give the hands food enough, and not over-work them, and, having, thus satisfied his conscience, left us to our fate." Williams escaped to Philadelphia with the assistance of free blacks, who warned him to speak only to Quakers and abolitionists. Too scared to reunite with his wife and children, he set sail for England to escape his pursuers. While Garrison stood by the narrative when southerners challenged its authenticity, the AASS withdrew it from circulation.[6] From the start, slaveholders worried about and challenged slave testimony.

Unlike Williams, Moses Roper wrote his own narrative, published first in London in 1837 and a year later in Philadelphia. Encouraged by the "recommendation of anti-slavery meetings" and "the suggestion of many warm friends of the cause of the oppressed," Roper wanted to expose "the cruel system of slavery." He gives many instances of slave torture, accompanied by a graphic illustration of his whipping while strung up from a machine used to pack cotton. He regretted that his enslaved mother and siblings lived in the "land of the free": "This is a weight which hangs heavy on me." His narrative was reprinted in many editions and in 1848 was republished with an appendix on his lecture tour in England. He married an Englishwoman before migrating to Canada West. The narratives of Ball, Williams, and Roper, Garrison wrote, did not contain extraordinary instances of suffering but showed "ordinary usage" in the slave South.[7]

Some narratives, like those of Moses Grandy and Lunsford Lane, both from North Carolina, were written to raise money to buy relatives from slavery with the active assistance of abolitionists. Lane, who bought his freedom and was warned out of the state, became popular on the lecture circuit in Massachusetts.

He published his narrative in 1842. Lane was tarred and feathered when he returned to buy his family, but he continued to lecture before antislavery audiences in the North. George Thompson was the amanuensis of Grandy's narrative, published in London in 1843. He was forced to buy himself three times over and had six children sold into slavery. In England, Scoble organized his successful lecture tour to raise money to buy the rest of his family. He succeeded even in buying a grandchild. Grandy's identification with the abolition movement, "our untiring friends" who upheld the rights of fugitive slaves and "redeemed" runaway slaves, was complete. Both Roper and Grandy went to England armed with letters of introduction from Garrison, Phillips, Sewall, and Loring.[8]

In the 1840s, interviews and narratives of former slaves like Aaron graced abolitionist publications with increasing frequency. In his narrative, Andrew Jackson dwelt on his longing for freedom, to which he was legally entitled, as his mother was free. He appended abolitionist sermons, homilies, poems, a letter to his master, and a journal detailing his travels as an abolitionist lecturer. He argued that slaves had as much right to fight for their freedom as the "revolutionary patriots" and castigated the American Republic with its three million slaves as a "miserable farce."[9] Fugitive slave narratives reinforced a black abolitionist tradition, exposing the crimes of the slaveholding democracy.

The title of Lewis Clarke's narrative of 1845, dictated to Joseph C. Lovejoy, said it all: *Narrative of the Sufferings of Lewis Clarke, During a Captivity of More Than Twenty-Five Years, Among the Algerines of Kentucky, One of the So Called Christian States of America*. Clarke, the son of a Scottish revolutionary soldier and a slave woman who was the daughter of her master, looked virtually white, like his siblings. In a series of questions and answers Clarke explicitly disproved the propositions of slaveholding paternalism. He calculated that after providing their minimal needs, masters still owed slaves eighty-eight dollars of every hundred they earned. Applying a labor theory of value, he justifies the actions of a slave woman who regularly stole livestock, as "she had a right to eat of the work of her own hands." Loving their masters was the "hardest work" slaves were compelled to perform.

On learning that he might be sold in Louisiana, Clarke escaped to the North and continued on to Canada. He returned to meet his brother Milton, also a runaway, in Oberlin and went back to Kentucky to help his youngest brother, Cyrus, escape. Lewis and Milton became successful abolitionist lecturers, and a year later they published their joint narrative. Milton was briefly recaptured and rescued by an antislavery crowd. The "spirit of slaveholding," he noted, was not confined to territory south of the Ohio River. Cyrus settled in Hamilton, New York, where a racist judge refused to let him vote without meeting the state's property-holding qualification for black men. He used his nearly white appearance to get the better of the judge.[10]

An extraordinary group of fugitive slaves like the Clarkes, whose narratives comprised the best-selling literature of the day, became the most effective abolitionist lecturers, writers, and thinkers. Their narratives must be read not just as autobiographies but also as antislavery texts composed by fugitive slave abolitionists. The foremost among them was Douglass, and the trajectory of his triumphant abolitionist career illustrates how self-emancipated slaves came to lead the movement. Born in Maryland in 1818, Douglass was the son of a slave mother and an unknown white father, most probably his master, Aaron Anthony. Like many border state slaves, he experienced slavery in all its variety, urban and rural, as a house slave, an abused field hand, and as a slave for hire. Douglass's escape in 1838 was facilitated by free blacks, by his fiancée, Anna Murray, and by black abolitionists such as Ruggles and Pennington in New York, who married them. He settled in New Bedford's interracial abolitionist community. Garrison discovered him as an effective lecturer at an abolitionist meeting in Nantucket in 1841.

Along with Kelley and Phillips, Douglass emerged as one of the leading orators of Garrisonian abolition. Speaking from personal experience—"I am a slave"—Douglass gave speeches that were an abolitionist sensation. "My back is scarred by the lash—that I could show you. I would I could make visible the wounds of this system upon my soul," he said in one of his early speeches. One of the most effective agents of the MASS, Douglass participated in the "one hundred conventions" held in Massachusetts and in the west in 1843–44. After his break with Garrison in the 1850s, Douglass remembered that he had been asked to simply tell his story, but he developed a wide-ranging repertoire that indicted southern slavery, northern racism, and the government, and he lampooned proslavery Christianity by mimicking the "Slaveholder's Sermon." Douglass resented abolitionist condescension but recalled that William White probably saved his life when he was assaulted by an anti-abolitionist mob in Indiana and that some had suffered with him in contesting segregated public transportation. Indeed, all was not accolades, as Douglass broke his right hand in the Indiana fracas, endured the abolitionist baptism of being pelted with stones and rotten eggs, and was subjected to racist aspersions that he could not possibly have been a slave. It was to answer these suspicions and to capitalize on the popularity of his lectures that Douglass published his best-selling narrative in 1845 in multiple editions and to rave reviews.

To Douglass's iconic narrative belongs the credit for making the slave's indictment of slavery the most effective weapon in the abolitionist arsenal and for popularizing the genre. The opening testimonials by Garrison and Phillips were common in abolitionist literature and not restricted to black authors. Chapman, in her introduction to Jonathan Walker's narrative, had given a far more overt endorsement of his character and veracity and compared it to Douglass's narrative. Walker, like other white abolitionists, quoted Douglass at length, ending his book with Douglass's critique of slaveholding Christianity. The *Narrative of the Life and Times of Frederick Douglass,* with its riveting scenes of family separation and slave torture on the one hand and the brotherhood and resistance of slaves on the other, Douglass's struggle for literacy, "the pathway from slavery to freedom," and his violent showdown with the slave breaker Covey that "revived within me my own sense of manhood," made it a classic first-person account of slavery. Yet, as he did in his speeches, Douglass was able to interweave a broader political, moral, and religious indictment of slavery that tied the cause of the slave to that of humanity and freedom. Its extraordinary success made Douglass an instant celebrity, and he capped his fame as a fugitive slave abolitionist with a triumphant lecture tour of the British Isles, where he said he was "an outlaw in the land of my birth." Since he had revealed his identity and that of his erstwhile masters in his narrative, he was in danger of reenslavement.

Relying on financing from his British admirers, Douglass bought his freedom and started publishing the *North Star* in Rochester in 1847, dedicated to his "oppressed countrymen." Its title was resonant of the short-lived Latimer paper and of fugitive slave abolitionism, the most dynamic wing of the movement. As he put it, "It has long been our anxious wish to see, in this slave-holding, slave-trading, and negro-hating land, a printing-press and paper, permanently established, under the complete control and direction of the immediate victims of slavery and oppression." His list of agents included Nathan Johnson, Ruggles, McCune Smith, Delany, Rowland T. Robinson, McKim, James Buffum, and Sydney Howard Gay. Nell moved to Rochester to help him print the paper. Douglass appreciated Pennington and J. N. Gloucester, who "threw open" their churches, and Van Rensselaer, Downing, and Remond for their support. According to Whipper, it was as good an abolitionist newspaper as the *Liberator* or any "other Anti-Slavery periodical" and not just a "colored newspaper." The paper became the voice of black abolitionism, and his autobiography, which he expanded in 1855 and 1892, the "great enabling text" of fugitive slave narratives.[11]

Douglass's star turn in Britain made fugitive slave abolitionism an international sensation. His letters in the *Liberator* and the popularity of the British editions of his narrative documented his success. As Henry C. Wright, who was also abroad at this time, observed, British abolitionists had never failed to cheer these "crushed and wounded spirits of American republicanism and

American Christianity." While slaveholders sought to keep the reality of slavery hidden from the world's view, Douglass noted, quoting Calhoun's stricture to leave the South alone, black abolitionists sought to lift that veil. In one of his first speeches, in Dublin, he stated, "I am the representative of three million bleeding slaves." He asked his audiences to tell slaveholders to "give up their vile practices, or continue to be held in contempt by the whole civilized world." The title of one of his speeches, "International Moral Force can Destroy Slavery," encapsulated his appeal. At the World Temperance Convention he called out the racial exclusion practiced by the American temperance movement. He lectured against accepting slaveholders' contributions to the Free Church of Scotland—"send back the money"—and American slaveholding churches in the newly formed Evangelical Alliance in London. At events featuring other speakers, Garrison reported that Douglass was the lion of all occasions.

Douglass gave more speeches during his eighteen-month tour than any other American abolitionist. His topics ranged from the bloodthirsty nature of slaveholding Christianity to the connection between intemperance and slavery— *"All great reforms go together"*—Texas annexation, the heroism of abolitionists, "America's Bastard Republicanism" against notions of racial inferiority, his own life story, to numerous calls to arms directed at the British public. In England he emerged as a bona fide leader of the movement. Douglass chafed when Webb sought to give him friendly advice, and he resented Chapman's control of his finances. John Estlin wondered how he would resume a quiet family life after being feted by Englishwomen. Douglass encountered subtle and open racism alike, some imputing that he was an imposter, while the send-back-the-money campaign was met with large posters declaring, "Send back the Nigger." Even admirers condescendingly called him the only "intelligent slave" they had met.[12]

Douglass's fame put his freedom in jeopardy. In Britain the abolitionist Quaker Richardson sisters raised more than sufficient money to purchase his freedom. Loring retained lawyers in New York and Baltimore to mediate the transaction. Douglass followed in the footsteps of numerous American fugitive slaves who had purchased their freedom with British assistance. He, however, was no ordinary fugitive but a leading light of the movement, and his self-purchase aroused considerable controversy. When abolitionist newspapers expressed discomfort at a deal that seemed to recognize property in man, Garrison leapt to Douglass's defense, calling it "The Ransom of Douglass." Abolitionists, he wrote, were against compensating slaveholders as a "class" for emancipation, but they had always helped ransom individual slaves, conveying the illegitimacy of slaveholding as kidnapping. Garrison concluded that to be a victim of extortion was one thing but to sanction it was another. Few of Douglass's critics, he continued, endangered their own freedom in the manner that they demanded of fugitive slave abolitionists. Douglass himself had been ambivalent about the issue since he had criticized Lane's attempts to buy his family. When Wright worried that Douglass's power as a "self-emancipated slave" was diminished, Douglass replied that his "sphere of usefulness" was in the United States, where he was at his master's mercy.[13]

Douglass's meteoric rise inspired a talented group of fugitive slave abolitionists to publish their narratives. William Wells Brown had escaped slavery in 1834 but published his narrative in 1847. It was reprinted in four editions and in five editions in England. The narrative begins with a moving dedication to the Quaker Wells Brown, who had helped him escape and whose name he adopted. A letter from Quincy addressed the racist aspersion that slave narratives were ghostwritten by white abolitionists. As he put it, "I should be a bold man, as well as a vain one, if I should attempt to improve your descriptions of what you have seen and suffered." The son of a slave mother and a white man, Brown called his master "the man who stole me as soon as I was born." Brown moved with him from Kentucky to Missouri, where he was hired out to a succession of cruel masters, including a "soul driver," and separated from his mother and sister. Challenging the idea that the nasty business of the slave trade was somehow separate from the paternalistic dictates of slaveholding, he writes, "But though these men may cant about negro-drivers, and tell what despicable creatures they are, who is it, I ask, that supplies them with the human beings that they are tearing asunder?" Remarkably, Brown worked for a short time for Elijah Lovejoy, from whom he got "what little learning I obtained while in slavery." He condemned American hypocrisy on his escape to freedom: "But when I thought of slavery with its Democratic whips—its Republican chains— its evangelical blood-hounds, and its religious slave-holders—when I thought of all this paraphernalia of American Democracy and Religion behind me, and the prospect of liberty before me, I was encouraged to press forward."

Brown found work on Lake Erie steamboats running slaves to Canada. It was a literal and symbolic reversal of his life as a slave, during which he was forced to participate in the interstate slave trade on the Mississippi River. In 1842 alone he claimed to have aided sixty-nine fugitives. He subscribed to abolitionist newspapers, became a lecturer for the Western NYASS, organized a temperance society, and traveled to Haiti and Cuba to explore prospects for black emigration. By 1844 Brown had given his first national speech, at the annual meeting of the AASS. "I would have the Constitution torn to shreds," he said, "and scattered to the four winds of heaven." He was soon lecturing in Ohio, where he insisted on calculating his fare by his weight since he was consigned to the cargo car, and in New York with E. D. Hudson. Brown argued that the domestic slave trade was slavery's dominant feature and that the law and public sentiment are "all a dead letter to the Slave." In 1847 he was elected to the business committee of the AASS and moved to Boston. The next year Brown wrote an essay, "The American Slave Trade," for the *Liberty Bell* and edited a book of abolitionist songs, *The Anti-Slavery Harp*. The songs selected displayed his talents as an editor, as some warn of slave rebellion while another has a fugitive slave asking, "Will you send me back?" Brown included his "Jefferson's Daughter," a topic he would explore in his novel *Clotel*. His daughter, Josephine Brown, with whom he had a mysterious falling out later, apparently for something scandalous she did, wrote his biography in 1855.[14]

Brown's five-year stay abroad was a result of the passage of the Fugitive Slave Act of 1850. In a speech he gave before leaving, he wittily noted that if America was the cradle of liberty, it had rocked the baby to death. Black Bostonians led by Hilton held a meeting honoring him as a delegate to the Paris Peace Congress. Brown reported that his narrative was in demand among some passengers aboard the steamship *Canada* but angered the slaveholding and proslavery among them. In Paris a slaveholder who had abused him during the voyage sought his favor so that he could meet Victor Hugo and Richard Cobden. Brown felt no compunction at snubbing him. Much to the chagrin of the American consul he was introduced to Madame de Tocqueville at the reception for the delegates. While pacifists like Burritt and Rev. William Allen wished to avoid a collision over slavery, Brown insisted that the violence of slavery must be removed for true peace to reign. In a public letter Brown effectively refuted Allen's claim that slavery was a matter of states' rights by pointing to the fugitive slave law and a host of actions by the federal government on behalf of slavery, from the Seminole to the Mexican war. Like Douglass, he published a letter to his former master. Brown gave over a thousand speeches in England.[15]

Brown wrote a catalogue of the panorama of slavery he had painted to accompany his speeches. His panorama highlighted the domestic slave trade, the *Creole* and *Pearl* cases, his own story and escape, and his experience with fugitives. He became a regular contributor to British and abolitionist newspapers and published a travelogue, *Three Years in Europe* (1852). Brown appended to his travel memoir a statement drafted by a group of fugitive slaves protesting the law of 1850, "An Appeal to the People of Great Britain and the World." In one emphatic statement, it encapsulated the abolitionist critique that so angered representatives of the American government: "The history of the Negroes in America is but a history of repeated injuries and acts of oppression committed upon them by the whites." The nation, now a "hunting ground" for slaveholders, was complicit. Brown recommended that there be a "good abolitionist" in England at all times to counter American slaveholders and officials.

On his return Brown was welcomed by abolitionist meetings in Philadelphia led by Purvis and in Boston presided over by Jackson, Garrison, and Phillips. Despite his estranged wife's repeated attempts to discredit him, he had retained the confidence of his abolitionist colleagues. The only glitch in his English sojourn was Scoble's rumor mongering about his personal problems, which lasted until Brown threatened to sue him for libel. Just as British Garrisonians remained suspicious of black clergymen like Pennington and Garnet, who were affiliated with the AFASS, mainstream British abolitionists clashed with black Garrisonians like Brown. Yet these factional divisions were often expressed only in private letters, and black abolitionists usually steered clear of them. When Brown returned home he got into a dispute with Douglass, whom he accused of demeaning him to Elizabeth Pease. Brown's two daughters, who also traveled to England and were subject to racial ostracism aboard the *America*, were schooled as teachers in Paris and London. Scorning the idea of begging for money, Brown supported his daughters from his publications and writing. As they had done for Douglass, Ellen Richardson and her family raised money to buy his freedom. William I. Bowditch oversaw the transaction in Boston, and Brown came home a free man. In 1855 he published an expanded version of his travel memoir.[16]

In 1849, the year Brown published the first English edition of his narrative, three fugitive slave abolitionists, Henry Bibb, Josiah Henson, and Pennington, published their narratives. Bibb's is prefaced by the proceedings of an investigation by some Liberty men into the facts of his life after a "scandalous and libelous account" to discredit him and the free soil cause was published in the *Washington Union*, a Democratic paper. In a letter to Birney, Bibb vindicated his authenticity and the "right to plead my own cause & the cause of the enslaved." Bibb was born of a slave mother, Mildred Jackson, and white father, James Bibb, a Kentucky state senator. His narrative begins with a personal condemnation of slavery: "I received stripes without number, the object of which was to degrade and keep me in subordination. I can truly say, that I drank deeply of the bitter cup of suffering and woe. I have been dragged down to the lowest depths of human degradation and wretchedness, by Slaveholders." Separated from his mother and hired out to various masters, Bibb learned "the art of running away to perfection." He repeatedly returns to rescue his family and is recaptured and then sold in New Orleans with his wife, Malinda, and daughter to a particularly sadistic deacon. Bibb attempts to escape again, is recaptured, and sold successively to some "sporting gentlemen" and into Indian "heathen" slavery, which he opines is better than "Christian" slavery.

In 1841 Bibb escaped to Ohio and participated in the state black convention in Detroit, defiantly sending copies of its proceedings to his former master and to prominent slaveholders in Kentucky. When his master responded, Bibb replied that he ran away because of the ill-treatment of his wife and child and that he now "subscribes myself a friend to the oppressed, and of Liberty forever." Bibb developed a critique of slavery that cited a labor theory of value. He was compelled to work under the lash without wages and, he argued, "who had a better right to eat of the fruits of my own hard earnings than myself?" It is a crime for a slave to starve, he wrote, rather than to help himself to the fruits of his labor. Attempting to purchase his wife and daughter from slavery, he learns that they had been sold to a man who had made his wife his mistress. He writes that Malinda is dead to him. But Bibb blames slavery, writing, "Poor unfortunate woman, I bring no charge of it against her, for I know not all the circumstances connected with the case." He married a teacher from Boston, Mary Miles, and settled with her in Canada, publishing his *Voice of the Fugitive* and aiding runaway slaves there.[17]

Another fugitive slave abolitionist, Josiah Henson, had long headed the free black Dawn settlement in Canada. His amanuensis, Samuel Eliot, assured the reader that Henson's narrative had been dictated by him and read back to him to correct errors and that "very often the words, are his." Eliot, a colonizationist, earned the ire of abolitionists for his vote in Congress for the Fugitive Slave Act of 1850, and his connection to Henson became a matter of considerable controversy. Henson, who was born in Maryland, opens his narrative with his father being brutally beaten and having his right ear cut off for attacking an overseer who had whipped his mother. His father became "morose, disobedient and intractable" and was sold to Alabama. His mother and siblings were sold after the death of her master. Despite run-ins with an overseer that left him maimed, Henson got married and rose to a position of trust under his dissolute master, who, he noted in a Hegelian reversal of the proslavery argument, became dependent on him. When asked by his master to lead all his slaves to Kentucky to save them from being sold for debt, Henson does so despite being urged by free blacks in Cincinnati to flee for freedom. He admits that he had "painful doubts" about leading others to slavery, even though their escape would have been just retribution to his master. When they are sold off, Henson regrets his agency in their calamity and professes greater hatred of the system of slavery.

A Methodist preacher helps Henson raise money to purchase his freedom, and he becomes a preacher. But Henson's master tricks him and attempts to sell him in New Orleans. Knowing that being sold to the Deep South meant hard labor, Henson hatches a plot to kill his master's son. It would have been self-defense, justifiable and even praiseworthy, he writes, but in the end his conscience prevents him from committing murder. Henson compares the hollow paternalism of his master's son, who promises to sell him to a good master who would use him as a house servant, to his watchful care when he falls severely ill, emphasizing his moral superiority to his enslavers. He returns to Kentucky but realizes that whatever merit he had in the eyes of his master lay in his "money value." Absolved of all his obligations to his master, Henson escapes, assisted by a fellow slave who rows him and his family across the Ohio River, by free blacks in Cincinnati, and by Indians during their long trek in the wilderness. Henson the model slave became the model abolitionist. He devoted himself to black improvement in Canada, which he described as being helped by "immigration" from the United States. Henson also assisted fugitive slaves from Maryland and Kentucky, to which he ventured back, to escape "Egypt."[18]

Like Henson, Pennington wrote his narrative well after his escape in 1827. First published in London, it was reprinted rapidly in three editions in 1849 and 1850. Pennington wrote his own preface (as he did for other black writers), a telling critique of slaveholders' paternalism. The essence of slavery, he argued, was "the chattel principle," the reducing of human beings to property, marketable commodity. As he put it, "My feelings are always outraged when I hear them speak of 'kind masters,' — 'Christian masters,' — 'the mildest form of slavery,' — 'well fed and clothed slaves,' as extenuations of slavery; I am satisfied they either mean to pervert the truth, or they do not know what they say." The slave trade and the use of slaves "to toil without requite" to supply the world market "with *cotton, sugar, rice, tobacco, &c*" revealed the sordid material reality behind all talk of "kind Christian masters." In his speeches, too, Pennington criticized the paternalistic pretensions of slaveholders.

Pennington described his dreary childhood subjected to the abuse of his master's children and overseers, until he learned blacksmithing skills. He writes that his master was not particularly cruel but whipped him, his father, and a "deeply pious and exemplary slave" whose daughter he sold. His master "was a perpetualist. He was opposed to emancipation; thought free negroes a great nuisance, and was, as respects discipline, a thorough slaveholder." Pennington's escape to Pennsylvania stressed the trials of a fugitive slave forced to choose freedom over family, suffering from desperate hunger and privation, and dodging slave catchers. He is taken in by a Quaker abolitionist, William Wright, who teaches him how to read and write. On hearing that his master had posted a reward for him, Pennington moves to New York City with the help of Quakers and free

blacks, reminding his readers that he escaped before there were antislavery societies and vigilance committees. Pennington decided to work for the uplift of
free blacks, whose condition "the whites tortured into a defense of slavery." He
purchased himself, and his father and sisters escaped to Canada, but his mother
died in slavery, and three siblings remained enslaved after the botched escape
of his brother and nephews. In an appendix, Pennington published a letter he
had written to his master in 1844 indicting him for the abuse of his family.[19]

American fugitive slaves successfully exported their brand of abolitionism to
Britain. In 1848 Henry Watson published an account of his enslavement, his
escape by sea, and the assistance rendered to him by free people of color and
Garrison. Watson hoped his descriptions of slavery in Mississippi would fill a
gap since most fugitives hailed from the upper south. He referred to the United
States as a "land of Bibles and whips" on his departure to England. Watson sarcastically noted that he could provide more information on "what I have seen
and felt of the kindly influences of that patriarchal institution" and its "heavenly
character," quoting George McDuffie's claim that slavery lay "at the cornerstone of our republican edifice." William Powell, disgusted by the new fugitive
slave law, left for England and predicted a dissolution of the Union. Henson
lectured with Pennington, Garnet, and Crummell in Britain. Garnet agreed
to raise funds for the Weems family of Washington, whose free black father
was desperately trying to buy back his enslaved children. One of them, Stella
Weems, escaped and resided with the Garnets before dying in Jamaica. There
were instances of fugitive slaves stowing away on British ships in southern ports;
one of them was found nearly starved to death. Powell reported that he had assisted five stowaways in Liverpool. In 1853 the Ladies Society to Aid Fugitives
was formed in England to help such runaways.[20]

Black women also contributed to the slave narrative genre. The most significant was the narrative of Sojourner Truth (born Isabella Van Wagenen), written
by Olive Gilbert, who had befriended Truth in Northampton. The preface,
written by Garrison, drew attention to the abuse of enslaved women. Truth capitalized on the success of fugitive slave narratives. Her story, published in 1850,
is more biography than autobiography, though Gilbert relied on information
provided by Truth. One of the few extant female slave narratives, it contains
one of the rare descriptions of northern slavery. After she began her lecturing
career, Truth sold copies of her book and, later, her carte de visite, becoming
a potent symbol of radical reform. Despite her reliance on Gilbert and then
Frances Titus, Truth fashioned her own persona.

Born a slave in New York, Isabella, like many of her siblings, was sold away
from her parents. Her new master and mistress cruelly abused the nine-year-old

girl, who spoke Dutch, the language of her first master. As she pointedly told Gilbert, "Now the war begun." Gilbert quotes her as saying, "When I hear 'em tell of whipping women on the bare flesh, it makes my flesh crawl, and my very hair rise on my head!" Sold to John Dumont in 1810 on her father's intervention, Isabella forms an attachment to her master, whom she characterized as being kind, but was probably abused by his wife. Dumont reneged on a promise to free her, and, like many northern slaves, she walked away from him and slavery a year before New York's abolition law of 1827. She worked with the Van Wagenens, whose surname she adopted. The long shadow of slavery, however, haunted Truth, as her children served out long indentures, and one of them, Peter, was sold illegally to slavery in Alabama. With the help of Quaker abolitionists she lodged a complaint before a grand jury and obtained a writ against her son's kidnappers. Gilbert writes of Truth's perseverance to free her son, whose custody she is finally awarded by a judge. In what Truth understood as divine retribution, the Alabama slaveholder who had abused her son murdered his wife, the sister of the man who had sold her son. The narrative ends not with her conversion but with her former master being converted to antislavery.

Truth's unconventional religiosity led her to join the Kingdom of Matthias, a cult founded by a self-proclaimed prophet, and, like Angelina Grimké, to flirt with Millerism (after William Miller, who predicted the Second Coming of Christ in 1843) before emerging as the abolitionist feminist preacher Sojourner Truth. In 1851 she launched her abolitionist career, accompanying Garrison, Phillips, and Thompson on their lecturing tour. Truth's narrative was republished by Titus in 1875 and again in 1883 after her death. Titus added a second part, "a book of life," containing material on her later storied life as a spokeswoman for abolition, women's rights, and freedmen's relief. The book of life was the title Truth gave to her book of autographs of Lincoln, Garrison, Phillips and abolitionists involved in slave running, Walker, Fairbank, and Haviland. To Phillips, who, like others, noticed her wit, Truth occupied a special place in the movement as the only former northern slave active in it. Truth's life highlighted northern complicity in slavery and northern blacks' demands for citizenship. As she once reminded proslavery hecklers, "I am a citizen of the State of New York; I was born in it, and I was a slave in the State of New York; and now I am a good citizen of this State."[21]

Abolitionists promoted other writings by slaves besides narratives. The poems of the enslaved George Moses Horton first appeared in *Freedom's Journal*, which supported his campaign to buy his freedom. He published three volumes of poetry, *The Hope of Liberty* (1829), *Poetical Works of George M. Horton, the*

Colored Bard of North Carolina (1845), and *Naked Genius* (1865). An unpublished collection, *The Museum*, is lost to history. Joseph Gales, a colonizationist who became the official publisher of congressional records, and a Massachusetts woman named Caroline Hentz who had literary aspirations of her own and was Horton's editor, helped him publish his first collection. In 1834 Garrison printed Horton's poem on slavery: "Is it because my skin is black, / That thou should'st be so dull and slack, / And scorn to set me free?" In 1837 the Philadelphia abolitionists Joshua Coffin and Lewis Gunn republished his first collection as *Poems By a Slave*. The next year Garrison's printer, Knapp, published the collection appended to a *Memoir and Poems of Phillis Wheatley* to "present an unvarnished record of African genius."

Horton was a slave at the University of North Carolina and had been promised freedom on condition that he leave for Liberia. In 1844 he wrote to Garrison, but the president of the university, David Swain, to whom he had entrusted the letter, never mailed it. A year later Horton's collection of poems was published on a subscription taken out by Swain and students at the university. Horton had ingratiated himself with the students, for whom he ran errands and wrote love poems, and they shared their books with him. Horton also banked on the popularity of fugitive slave narratives, appending an account of his life "written by himself." Abolitionist newspapers continued to publish his poetry: the *NASS* republished "The Slave's Complaint" and the *Emancipator* republished "On Liberty and Slavery." In 1848 the *National Era* reported that the Black Bard of Chapel Hill was still in slavery. The next year William G. Allen published a book of the works of Wheatley, Banneker, and Horton in which he also introduced American audiences to the transnational world of black letters: the Russian writer Alexander Pushkin and the black revolutionary poet from Cuba named Plácido. Horton did not give up the attempt to purchase himself, addressing a poetic petition to Greeley, which Swain also did not mail.

Like many southern slaves, Horton became a fugitive during the war. He obtained his freedom by walking to Union army lines. The abolitionist content of Horton's last collection, published after the war by a sympathetic Union army officer, Capt. William H. S. Banks, was unmistakable. His poem "Slavery" remonstrates, "Slavery, thou peace-disturbing thief, / We can't but look with frowns on thee, / Without the balm which gives relief, / The balm of birthright—Liberty." The poem "Negro Speculation," with its plaintive chorus "Weep, Humanity weep!," condemns the slave trade. Horton's poems on Gen. Ulysses S. Grant and "Sherman the Great," two poems mocking the defeat and flight of Jefferson Davis, and three dedicated to Lincoln reveal the author's ardent unionism, now linked to black freedom. His "Song of Liberty" celebrates "liberation" that no "treason can destroy." Child included a section on Horton, "The Slave Poet," in her freedmen's book of 1865.[22]

The countless enslaved writers and artists who perished along with slavery are unknown. Dave the Potter in Edgefield, South Carolina, etched his poetry in clay pots, writing about Nat Turner and slave sales, including his own, one with the sorrowful title "Where is My Family?" He faithfully, yet mockingly, reproduced the views of nullifiers, secessionists, and slaveholders' prohibition of slave literacy. The fugitive slave narratives, however, give one an inkling of the worldview of the enslaved. As Phillips put it, "It is the slave, the fugitive slave from the plantation, whose tongue inspired by oppression, speaks most forcibly to the American people."[23]

ABOLITIONIST ROMANTICISM

In the decade before the war, slave narratives and abolitionist fiction inspired by them took a romanticist turn. Presenting improbable and daring stories of escape, they captured the public imagination and showcased both the ingenuity of self-emancipated slaves, who matched their wits and daring with slaveholders' immense political and legal powers, and the abolitionist underground. Abolitionist fiction, inspired by the stories of fugitives and instances of slave revolt, blossomed. The abolitionists created a literature of protest that popularized antislavery and replaced newspapers, pamphlets, and petitions as the most potent tools in abolitionist print culture.

In 1849 two remarkable escape stories, the flight of a young slave couple named William and Ellen Craft in disguise and of Henry "Box" Brown, who shipped himself to freedom, became popular in abolitionist circles and beyond. William Craft published the Crafts' story long after the fact in 1860, but Brown's narrative was published a few months after his escape. Dictated to the abolitionist Charles Stearns, Brown's narrative, like others, recounted the physical cruelties of slavery and the sale of his wife and children, but the story of his remarkable escape is its centerpiece. Maiming his finger to get reprieve from work, Brown enlisted a northerner, Samuel Smith, and a free black man, James C. A. Smith Jr., whom he identified as a UGRR conductor in Richmond, to help him. He had himself boxed and mailed to the PASS office in Philadelphia. Confined for over twenty-four hours in the box, which had holes and a "bladder" of water, and being placed upside down many times, Brown emerged singing a thanksgiving hymn before McKim and Still. He stayed with the Motts before moving to Boston. Brown's mode of escape made him an instant draw at the annual convention of the NEASS, where he spoke on being introduced by Wells Brown. Benjamin Roberts painted a panorama of his escape for his lecture tour in Massachusetts. The next year the *Liberator* reported an attempt to kidnap him, and Brown sailed to England shortly thereafter.

In England he lectured, as Wells Brown had, with an elaborate panorama of slavery and even reenacted his escape, having himself shipped in a box again. Brown's narrative was republished in England in 1851. Though he eliminated Stearns's preface and letter, he included ample new abolitionist material, including a new preface written by himself, an introduction by British abolitionists, and letters from May and McKim. Garrison had criticized Stearns's "declamatory style" and his lose compilation of Brown's narrative. In his new preface Brown fashioned his own abolitionist indictment of slavery, the "bodily and mental" cruelties of the slave trade and his agony on losing his family: "Language is inadequate to express them." Samuel Smith was arrested for helping two young slaves emulate Brown by shipping themselves. He served a seven-year term and was welcomed by black Philadelphians as a martyr to the cause of freedom and the "poor, downtrodden slave." James Smith moved north and got into a controversy with Brown for not sharing the proceeds of their joint performances. Brown married again in England and became a successful lecturer and performer on disparate topics such as mesmerism. He returned to the United States as a performer doing magic tricks. Performance on an abolitionist stage prepared Brown for his later career.[24]

While Brown's showmanship excited some criticism from abolitionists, including Wells Brown, the Crafts remained active on the abolitionist circuit in England. The ingenuity of their escape excited wonder, just as Brown's had. *Running a Thousand Miles for Freedom*, William Craft pointed out, was not the story of their lives, but he could not refrain from writing about the breakup of their families. Like Pennington, he argued that southern custom offered no protection to slaves: "The practical working of slavery is worse than the odious laws by which it is governed." He wrote that "after puzzling our brains for years," the Crafts decided that "it was almost impossible to escape from slavery in Georgia, and travel a 1,000 miles across the slave states," until he got the idea to dress his nearly white wife as an invalid gentleman and pretend to be her slave. Ellen came up with the idea of covering her right hand and face with "poultice" to avoid signing her name in hotel registers. Traveling through many southern cities, the Crafts arrived in Philadelphia, where they were assisted by Purvis and the Quaker abolitionist Barkley Ivens, who sent them on to Boston. Wells Brown took them under his wing, and they lectured with him throughout the state and later in England.

The Crafts thought they would be safe in the abolitionist heartland, but the passage of the new fugitive slave law dispelled their sense of security, as their masters sent agents to recapture them. The Crafts outfoxed their captors with the help of the Boston Vigilance Committee. The committee confronted two "slave hunters" from Georgia, Hughes, a Macon jailer, and Knight, harassing them with frivolous lawsuits and warning Marshal Charles Devens against arresting the Crafts. The warrant for their arrest was issued with the help of the lawyer Seth Thomas, a close ally of Daniel Webster and of the federal commissioners Benjamin F. Hallet and George T. Curtis; it was executed by Judge Levi Woodbury. Theodore Parker, who led a vigilance committee delegation to warn the Georgia "slave catchers" out of town, hid Ellen Craft. The heavily armed William first barricaded himself in his carpentry shop and then, accompanied by Henry I. Bowditch, hid in Lewis Hayden's equally well-armed home. Parker officially married the Crafts before they left for Canada and England. It is known all over the world, William Craft wrote, that "Americans, as a people, are notoriously mean and cruel towards all coloured persons, whether they are bond or free." In 1852 Ellen, in response to reports that she wanted to return to Georgia, published a letter stating her preference for living in England. William lectured for free produce and traveled to Dahomey to fight against the slave trade. The Crafts helped found the London Emancipation Committee in 1859 with British abolitionists and returned to Georgia during Reconstruction, where they ran a plantation and school for freedpeople.[25]

If 1849 was the year of remarkable slave escapes, then surely the most important one was that of Harriet Tubman, who came to personify fugitive slave abolitionism. Though her biography was published after the Civil War, her story became legend. Mythologized in countless stories of the UGRR, Tubman's life was hardly romantic. Born in Maryland, she bore scars of whippings endured at the hands of successive masters and mistresses she was hired out to as well as a head injury from an overseer's blow intended for another slave. Her first biographer, Sarah Bradford, appended a piece called "Essay on Woman-Whipping" to her book to highlight the abuse of female slaves. Married to the free black man John Tubman, who abandoned her, she planned her escape with her brothers, who decided not to accompany her. Tubman was assisted in her flight by an anonymous white woman, Thomas Garrett in Wilmington, and the PVC. In the 1850s Tubman acquired a formidable reputation as the Moses of her people, making repeated forays into slave country to lead her family members and others out of bondage. In 1854 she spirited her three brothers to freedom, assisted by her father, Benjamin Ross, a free black man who bought his wife's freedom a year later. Tubman's parents remained in Maryland, assisting her in what might be called a family operation. By the end of 1855 Garrett wrote that Tubman had made four trips to her home state, rescuing seventeen family members and other slaves. She settled in St. Catherine's, Canada, with her brothers, leading slaves from "Egypt to de land of Canaan." She was also a member of a fugitive slave aid society. In an interview she gave to the abolitionist Benjamin Drew, she noted, "Slavery is the next thing to hell."

By the eve of the Civil War she had made thirteen clandestine trips and liberated around seventy slaves, her actions funded by leading abolitionists. In 1856 Maryland authorities announced a reward of twelve thousand dollars for her. The next year she brought her elderly parents from Maryland when state authorities threatened to arrest her father, saving "dem de expense ob de trial." In 1859 she moved with her family to Auburn, New York, where she purchased a farm from William Seward, a benefactor and her neighbor, and continued working in the UGRR. Jermaine Loguen, a fugitive slave himself, observed that Tubman was better known to the slaves than the Bible because she circulated among them so freely. John Brown anointed her General Harriet Tubman, referring to her in the masculine in recognition of her physical prowess. During the war Tubman was a Union army scout, nurse, and laundress. Long denied a pension despite repeated petitions, she married a Union army veteran named Nelson Davis in 1869 and finally received a widow's pension on his death. She died in 1913 but lived on as an icon of enslaved women's resistance, a "black Joan of Arc." Douglass's testimonial of 1868 best captured her activism: "The midnight sky and the silent stars have been witnesses of your devotion to freedom and your heroism."[26]

The incredible story of the kidnapping of Solomon Northup, a free black man from Saratoga, New York, who published his narrative in 1853, is now a major motion picture, *Twelve Years a Slave*. His work reinforced the romanticist trend in abolitionist literature. In 1841 two men kidnapped Northup on a promise of employment and sold him to a slave trader, James Burch. He left behind his wife and three children. Burch shipped Northup to New Orleans. While at sea Northup plotted a shipboard rebellion with two other black men, but their plans were foiled when one of them succumbed to smallpox. Northup managed to send a letter via a sympathetic sailor to Henry Northup, whose family had owned his. Henry Northup took the letter to the governor of New York, but, lacking knowledge of Solomon's whereabouts, they failed to rescue him. Though he was sold to a "good master," William Ford, Northup's narrative, like other slave stories, systematically dismantles the proslavery argument on slaveholder paternalism. Ford is unable to help a slave woman, Eliza, who is sold apart from her children, and she languished until her death. Northup himself is sold to successively abusive masters because of Ford's financial difficulties. He ends up the slave of Edwin Epps, the owner of a cotton plantation. He relates the plight of Patsey, an expert cotton picker but "an enslaved victim" of her master's lust and her mistress's hate. Cold calculus, under which slaves who did not meet the daily quota were whipped, governed the Cotton Kingdom. An institution that tolerates so much cruelty, he concluded, was unjust and barbarous, taking direct aim at men who "discourse flippantly from arm chairs of the pleasures of slave life."

Slaves passionately desired freedom, Northup wrote. The slaves of the bayou would hail an invading army, he told his readers. During the war a Union army soldier, John Burrud, who was familiar with the narrative, marched through Epps's farm, where he met slaves who knew Northup. His narrative, Burrud wrote, does "not portray the system as bad as it is it is not in the power of man to do it." Northup eventually found an antislavery Canadian carpenter, Samuel Bass, who sent word of his plight to New York. His wife, Anne, petitioned Gov. Washington Hunt, who appointed Henry Northup agent of the state of New York to recover him. Numerous black and white citizens from his hometown, Sandy Hill, gave affidavits on his behalf. By January 1853 Northup was back in Washington, where he brought charges of kidnapping against Burch. Arguing for the prosecution was Salmon Chase. Since Northup's testimony was inadmissible in Washington even though he was a citizen of New York, Burch got off scot-free. Burch had the temerity to sue Gamaliel Bailey for libel for publishing the details of Northup's story. The publication of the book led to the identification of Northup's two abductors, Alexander Merrill and Joseph Russell, who were charged with kidnapping. After much legal wrangling about whether they should be tried in New York, where Northup's testimony was admissible, or in Washington, the case was dropped, and the kidnappers were never brought to justice.

An antislavery lawyer and politician, David Wilson, helped Northup edit his narrative, but Northup, who was literate, was undoubtedly its author. He dedicated his narrative to Harriet Beecher Stowe, but he differentiated his factual account from her fictional one; as he put it, "This is no fiction, no exaggeration." Certain characters and events in his narrative seemed to echo Stowe's famous novel. Northup noted that his story appeared in Stowe's *A Key to Uncle Tom's Cabin*, evidence that Stowe compiled, in reply to her critics, to illustrate that her portrait of slavery was based on reality. When Northup's book sold thirty thousand copies, he managed to buy some property from the proceeds and joined the abolitionist lecture circuit. Douglass reported that Solomon and Henry Northup attended an antislavery meeting in Troy, where Douglass took up a collection for him, and another one in Albany. He also became active in the abolitionist underground, working with a Methodist minister, John L. Smith, in Vermont to aid runaways. Northup probably died in 1863, when he drops out of the historical record.[27]

The success of Northup's narrative owed a lot to the romantic antislavery novel *Uncle Tom's Cabin*, which borrowed freely from his and other slave narratives. Written in response to the enactment of the Fugitive Slave Act of 1850, Stowe's novel was published serially in Bailey's newspaper in 1851 and as a book a year later. A runaway best seller (pun intended), it made Stowe an international celebrity. The book was a literary phenomenon, selling over three hundred thousand copies in the United States in a year and a million in Britain and being translated into various European languages. Its diverse admirers included Douglass, Lenin, George Sand, José Martí, Mary Church Terrell, and Lincoln, who in the apocryphal story of their meeting called Stowe the "little lady" who had caused the "great war." A sentimental antislavery novel inspired by the death of Stowe's young son, it became the dominant representation of southern slavery in popular culture. Reproduced in countless plays and minstrel shows, at times shorn of its antislavery content, *Uncle Tom's Cabin* took on a life of its own. In the South it inspired a mini-industry, the highly forgettable "anti-Tom novels," which, Douglass opined, were "miserably bad."

Ironically, slave resistance inspired a novel commonly criticized for its portrayal of a submissive slave. The central characters of Stowe's book, Tom and George Harris, resembled real life fugitives such as Henson, Lewis Clarke, and Bibb; the story of Eliza escaping on the frozen Ohio River came from an actual slave mother who made that journey to Rankin's farmhouse; the Quaker Halliday couple were based on Levi and Catherine Coffin and on Thomas and Rachel Garrett; and Van Tromp on the Ohio farmer Van Zandt. The prolific interstate slave trade and the continuous stream of fugitive slaves to Canada gave *Uncle Tom's Cabin* its peculiar resonance, making it difficult for detractors to dismiss it as a mere work of sentimental fiction. One could argue that Stowe became an abolitionist after the stunning success of her book, which led Garrison to think it could be "eminently serviceable" to the slave's cause. Stowe started subscribing to the *Liberator*, assuring Garrison that she respected his paper. Her appeal in the novel, which adopted the language of appeasement long deployed by antislavery gradualists and colonizationists, to "the generous, noble-minded men and women of the South . . . whose virtue, and magnanimity, and purity of character, are the greater for the severer trial it has encountered," met with the same relentlessly hostile reception abolitionists had received. Her *Key*, published in 1853, made it evident that she had used slave narratives and stories from the abolitionist underground to compose her novel. Its extensive documentation included selections from Weld's *American Slavery As It Is*, which she imitated in reproducing runaway advertisements and articles from southern newspapers, famous fugitive slave cases, and testimonials from self-emancipated slaves. To Douglass, this more overtly abolitionist work proved "more and worse things against the murderous system than are alleged in the great book."

Stowe's family, her father, Lyman, and sister Catharine Beecher, was colonizationist, critical of the radicalism of abolition and women's rights. Her husband, Calvin Stowe, a professor at the Lane Seminary, was involved in the expelling of the abolitionist rebels led by Weld. In Cincinnati, Stowe was not a member of any female abolitionist society. Before the 1850s only Stowe's brother Edward Beecher identified as an abolitionist. Her sister Isabella Beecher Hooker became a spokeswoman for women's rights, and in 1851 another brother, Charles Beecher, published one of the most influential "higher law" tracts against the Fugitive Slave Act, *The Duty of Disobedience to Wicked Laws*, almost simultaneously with her serialized novel. According to him, no human law that violated God-given natural law and natural rights had any validity. The fugitive slave clause of the Constitution was wrong, as it "legalizes kidnapping." Stowe's younger brother Henry Ward Beecher, invited to be minister of the Plymouth Congregational Church in Brooklyn by Henry C. Bowen, Tappan's son-in-law, in 1847, also argued that the Constitution should not be obeyed if it "include requisitions which violate humanity." Henry made the church the most famous one in the country, his fiery antislavery sermons attracting huge crowds. The Fulton ferry to Brooklyn came to be known as "Beecher boats." Henry's position on the fugitive slave issue was equivocal, as he would aid fugitives but not "interrupt" official renditions. He was critical of Garrison's radicalism and, later, of John Brown. The Beechers were not abolitionists but, like some antislavery northerners, including the colonizationist clergyman Leonard Bacon and Lincoln, moved closer to abolition in the crisis decade.

Colonization rather than abolition brackets Stowe's novel. In the preface she calls for "an enlightened and Christianized community . . . on the shores of Africa, laws, language and literature drawn from us." In her concluding remarks she recommends the education of black people so that they "may put in practice the lessons they have learned in America." The novel ends with George Harris's endorsement of colonization, his rejection of Haiti as "a worn-out, effeminate" republic in comparison to the African nation of Liberia. Stowe had earlier advocated an "*intermediate* society" between abolition and colonization.

Stowe's novel reproduced sectional, racial, and gendered stereotypes: the mean Yankee slaveholder Simon Legree, the weak yet benevolent aristocratic southern slaveholder Augustine St. Clare, racialist descriptions of Topsy and Eva, and the mixed-race rebels Cassy and George. St. Clare predicts that "Anglo-Saxon blood will lead the way" in case of a Haiti-like rebellion. The novel is suffused with romantic racialism. Stowe refers to Africans as an exotic race, and she feminizes Uncle Tom as morally superior, a Christlike figure who is ennobled by his suffering. He became an enduring motif of black victimization that would linger on in antilynching literature. Tom is a resistant figure in his own fashion, refusing to rat on fellow slaves to the point of suffering death, but Stowe's portrayal of him as a pious martyr was out of sync with abolitionist activism, making Uncle Tom an epithet down to the present. The heroic slave women of Stowe's novel, like Eliza, were first and foremost devoted mothers. In a largely forgotten essay on Stowe, Terrell empathized with her trials as a wife and mother, paying back in full measure the gendered solidarity Stowe expressed with slave mothers. Her brother Henry's theatrical auctioning of "nearly white" slave women and their children in his church to help purchase their freedom replicated the worst features of the domestic slave trade and reinforced racist notions of female beauty. In 1856 he "auctioned" a slave woman, Sarah, who had been raising money for her own and her son's freedom, and four years later a nine-year-old slave girl, Sally Maria Diggs, or "Pinky." One writer to the *Liberator* compared his antics to those of the circus maven P. T. Barnum. Beecher's conservative politics during Reconstruction also made him anathema to abolitionists. During this time, Stowe wrote thirty books that had little to do with race or slavery. Like her brother and many fair-weather friends of abolition, she became a conservative on race and labor issues.[28]

Abolitionists, though, hailed Stowe's novel as a godsend, a mass conversion tool, but were alert to its problematic racialism. Garrison, who objected to the colonizationist ending of the novel, noted that Tom personified Christian nonresistance, but he went on to say, "Is there one law of submission and non resistance for the black man, and another law of rebellion and conflict for the white man?" How is it, he asked Stowe, that Christ approved of the American and European revolutions but not of slave rebellion? The Unitarian abolitionist minister Thomas Wentworth Higginson argued that the novel suffered from a great defect in that it had no heroism in it. He would have preferred it if Uncle Tom had resisted. Black abolitionists also critiqued Stowe's racialist and colonizationist sentiments. Uncle Tom displayed "too much piety," in the opinion of Allen, who recommended "resistance to tyrants, if need be, to the death" instead.

Purvis called Stowe's endorsement of colonization "a terrible blow." William J. Wilson, writing as Ethiop, worried at how quickly Uncle Tom had replaced the racially derogatory images of Zip Coon and Jim Crow. At the annual meeting of the AFASS, McCune Smith introduced resolutions commending Stowe, for she had struck the literary equivalent of "California gold," and called her advocacy of colonization spots in the sun. Tappan agreed, mentioning that he had asked Stowe to get rid of the colonization bits of her novel. H. O. Wagoner also thought her book would do good.

The most interesting debate over the political and racial meanings of *Uncle Tom's Cabin* took place between Douglass and Martin Delany. Douglass, who felt that it could be appropriated for the benefit of the movement, was a booster of Stowe from the start. An early review of the book in his paper, probably written by Julia Griffiths, predicted that it would enlist sympathies on behalf "of the oppressed African race" and create a "host of enemies" of slavery. Douglass got the national black convention to pass a resolution commending the novel and hoped to get Stowe to fund a national black college after her triumphant tour of England and Europe. Stowe backed out of the project and gave him the five hundred dollars or so she had raised for his personal use. Delany, who was increasingly on the outs with Douglass over emigration at this time, felt that Stowe had stolen the credit that properly belonged to the fugitive slaves, suggesting even that Henson should receive a portion of the royalties from her publisher. It was a nineteenth-century version of the Elvis Presley debate over highly successful white artists appropriating black art. Delany deplored Stowe's denigration of Haiti and condemned her as a colonizationist. In his short reply Douglass argued that Delany himself was a colonizationist of sorts and asked, "Who doubts that Mrs. Stowe is more of an abolitionist now than when she wrote that chapter?" Douglass viewed the novel as the most "efficient agent of change," going through the country like fire through a "dry stubble." The Douglass–Delany exchange established the contours of the debate over the novel still carried on today.[29]

The popularity of *Uncle Tom's Cabin*, based in part on its use of fugitive slave narratives, led to a revival of the genre. Besides Northup, Douglass published a larger and "novelized" version of his narrative in 1855, *My Bondage and My Freedom*. It sold fifteen thousand copies in the first two months of publication. It was, McCune Smith wrote in his new introduction to the narrative, Douglass's declaration of independence from Garrison, his reinvention as a political abolitionist, and his emergence as a race leader. "He is a Representative American man—a type of his countryman," he wrote. Douglass's new narrative was not a simple rejection of abolitionist interracialism, as his effusive dedication to Gerrit Smith revealed. Douglass sought to define himself against not just Garrison but also the one black abolitionist McCune Smith deliberately left out of his cast of contemporary black leaders, Delany. The politics of black protest, not only the politics of the abolition movement, form an essential backdrop to *My Bondage*. According to McCune Smith, the "real object" of abolition "is not only to disenthrall" but also "to bestow upon the negro the exercise of all those rights, from the possession of which he has been long debarred." After making it clear that Douglass's genius was a result of his black, not his Caucasian (a term McCune Smith adeptly deconstructs, making fun of ethnologists) heritage, he argues that Douglass, like Dumas, Aldridge, and the singer Elizabeth Greenfield, "the Black Swan," was an exemplar of a biological "grafting" of the Anglo-Saxon on "good, original negro stock." Like Egypt, the United States was a *"mixed race"* nation.

In the narrative Douglass put forward his compelling vision of race, democracy, and nation. An expanded meditation of the original *Narrative* of 1845, it is a more thoughtful dismantling of the notion that "the relation of master and slave is one of reciprocal benefits." The smaller part of the narrative describes Douglass's abolitionist career, and an appendix contains his best speeches. It is also a more philosophical account of his break with Garrison and a considered repudiation of Garrisonian views on the Union and Constitution as proslavery. By arguing for the "unconstitutionality and complete illegality of slavery in our land," Douglass claimed a spot for blacks in the nation and for himself the mantle of a "temperate revolutionary." But he coupled it with his rage at the racism he had experienced and a recognition that the problem of slavery was also the problem of racism. Douglass transcended the dialectic of resistance and accommodation to arrive at a compelling synthesis of the black presence in the United States. He would live out the rest of his life as the "Representative Colored Man of the United States," one who was identified with the struggles of the race. He claimed his identity as a black man to redefine what it meant to be an American.[30]

Others also banked on Stowe's success and published new editions of their narratives. Perhaps the fugitive slave who capitalized most on Stowe's novel was Henson. In 1858 Eliot published a new edition of Henson's narrative as *Truth Stranger Than Fiction*, for which Stowe wrote the preface. That year Henson got into an argument with Remond at a West India emancipation celebration in New Bedford on the advisability of slave rebellions. He recommended running away instead. Henson used the Uncle Tom comparison in fund-raising lectures for the Dawn settlement and its manual labor school. His narrative was reprinted several times in England and Canada from 1877 to 1890, with Henson repeatedly identified as Uncle Tom in the title. Thomas Jones, who published his narrative in the 1850s, also referenced Stowe's novel in the title, *Experience and Personal Narrative of Uncle Tom Jones*. His book contained a frontispiece with his picture and a cabin with the descriptor "Uncle Tom's Cabin."

While Jones's work followed fugitive slave narratives in graphically illustrating the cruelties of slavery, family separations, the slave trade, and whippings, it publicized a less known aspect of slave resistance, the manner in which many slaves scrimped and saved to buy themselves and their families out of slavery. After losing his first wife and three children when their mistress moved to Alabama, Jones bought the freedom of his second wife. She escaped with three of their children after being threatened with reenslavement, and he followed her. The story of Jones's escape, which he revealed in subsequent editions of his narrative after the war, was dramatic. Unable to withstand turpentine fumes in the hold of a ship in which he was hiding, he was discovered and then managed to escape in a raft before being picked up by a rescue boat. Assisted by abolitionists in Brooklyn, the Jones family moved to Massachusetts and then, fearful of being remanded back to slavery after the passage of the new fugitive law, to Canada. Jones's activism makes the Uncle Tom persona he adopted to sell his narrative incongruous. In Boston he pointed out that his children were not "in a free land," as they were excluded from the schools "because their skin is black." A successful preacher, he joined the MASS lecture circuit to purchase the freedom of his oldest son, left behind in slavery, and became an agent for the *Liberator* in Canada.

The second half of Jones's narrative—*Wild Tom*, a play on *Uncle Tom*—is a work of fiction set in South Carolina. Wild Tom is of "unmixed African blood" and still remembers his mother's stories of being kidnapped from Africa. In a nod to Hildreth's novel, his story is related by Archy Moore, the nearly white slave son of his master. When Tom's wife is whipped to death, he is transformed from a devout Methodist to a desperado, stealing rice from his master's fields with a gang of slaves, burning his master's home and rice mills, and killing the overseer. Wild Tom is caught and when asked who he belongs to, he defiantly answers, to God. He is burned alive in the end, smiling at his persecutors in "contemptuous defiance." Jones's novella acts as a definite counterfoil to Stowe's novel. In 1885 he published another version of his narrative, adding that he had managed to buy the freedom of his father and mother.[31]

Other stories by fugitive slaves blurred the line between fact and fiction. William Still's famous postwar book on the UGRR began with the poignant story of his brother Peter Still, who, with another brother, Levin, was sold into slavery by their Maryland master after their mother escaped to New Jersey. By sheer coincidence Peter purchased his freedom and met William, who figured out that he was his long-lost brother. But Peter pined for his wife and children in Alabama, and when Seth Concklin, an abolitionist "wholly insensible of fear," read about his story he offered to bring his family out of slavery. The plan, Still confided, was known only to him and McKim, and they never sought the approval of the PVC, whose activities did not include slave running. Concklin managed to spirit Peter's family all the way to Indiana, where his luck ran out when he was apprehended at Vincennes and the marshal of Evansville jailed the group. Peter's family was taken back to slavery, and Concklin "was found drowned, with his hands and feet in chains and his skull fractured."

Kate E. R. Pickard, a teacher at a female seminary at Tuscumbia, Alabama, who knew Peter, recounted a fictionalized version of his story in her book *The Kidnapped and the Ransomed* (1856). It was dedicated to the memory of Levin Still, the brother who died in slavery and after whom Peter named one of his sons. Pickard's book contained a foreword by Samuel J. May and an appendix by Rev. William Furness on the life of Concklin. A working-class abolitionist who dedicated all his "frugal means" and energies to abolition, Concklin, Furness wrote, had a life that was a "heroic poem." His only known words, besides his letters to Still, are a letter to his sister warning her of the "dreadful demon spirit" of racism in the colonization society. Peter did not give up the idea of redeeming his captive family after Concklin's death. Still entered into negotiations with Peter's master, who demanded five thousand dollars for his wife and their three children. Peter undertook a fund-raising tour on the abolitionist lecture circuit starting with May in Syracuse, speaking to the Garrisonians in Boston and in small towns all over New England and New York. He garnered funds and letters of support from antislavery celebrities such as Stowe, Greeley, Smith, and even Seward's Whig political manager, Thurlow Weed, and Bacon. By 1854 Peter had collected enough money to negotiate the ransom of his family, but one of his sons was forced to leave a child behind. On obtaining their freedom, Peter and his wife, Lavinia, legalized their marriage. Pickard's romanticized fictional version of the story has a happy ending.[32]

Abolitionist writers contributed to the popularity of fugitive slave literature. Mattie Griffith, a nineteen-year-old Kentucky orphan who freed her six slaves and became an abolitionist on hearing of the caning of Charles Sumner and reading his speech, published her *Autobiography of a Female Slave* in 1857. The book begins with the attempted sale of its young heroine Ann, and abolition is a constant theme, various characters declaiming at length against slavery. Its unconventional plot has Ann defending herself against abuse, for which she is imprisoned and whipped. Tragedy befalls her enslaved lover, Henry, whose master cheats him of his purchase money, leading him to commit suicide. Ann's mistress frees her, and she moves north to a quiet "puritanical little town" in Massachusetts. The women who befriend her are a free black woman and an Irish servant and her mistress.

The underlying feminist–abolitionist theme in the novel is hard to miss even though there are female characters who betray Ann and abuse her. Douglass is set up as the beau ideal of an abolitionist, disrupting the black slave / white abolitionist binary, as does Ann's romanticized view of Boston's free black community. "There I met full-blooded Africans," Griffith writes, "finely educated, in the possession of princely talents, occupying good positions, wielding a powerful political influence, and illustrating, in their lives, the oft-disputed fact, that the African intellect is equal to the Caucasian." The novel ends with an abolitionist call to the "mechanics" and workers of the North to check the spread of slavery. Griffith's mentor, Child, called her novel "sentimental and inflated." Like Child, Griffith wrote for the *Standard*, including the serialized self-referential novel *Madge Vertner*, about a woman who emancipates her slaves. In 1866 Griffith married Albert Gallatin Browne, a Union officer who had been indicted in the attempted rescue of the fugitive slave Anthony Burns.[33]

Black writers as well capitalized on Stowe's success. In 1853 Wells Brown published *Clotel*, reprinting his narrative as a preface to the novel, which was loosely based on Jefferson's relationship with Sally Hemings. Brown's main character, Clotel, Jefferson's fictional daughter, is sold into slavery, highlighting the hypocrisy and cruelty of slaveholders. Unlike direct rebuttals of Jefferson's racism, this fictional account of his black family is replete with real-life incidents and Brown's own experiences with slavery, the domestic slave trade, and the UGRR. It borrowed heavily from Child's *The Quadroons* and other abolitionists' words, but it is a multifaceted indictment of slavery and racism. The trope of the "tragic mulatto" in abolitionist literature disrupted racist binaries even when playing off them. Re-creating the act of a real female slave whose actions were commemorated in an abolitionist poem reprinted by Brown, Clotel commits suicide by jumping off a bridge as she is hemmed in by slave traders from Washington at one end and Virginian slaveholders on the other. Published later in different versions, Brown's pastiche of a novel alluded also to Turner's rebellion, the Crafts' escape, and the Haitian Revolution, blending protest and prose. The reception of Brown's novel in England was overshadowed by the thunderous success of *Uncle Tom's Cabin*, but today literary critics regard it as the first African American novel. Four years later he published a fugitive slave play, *The Escape, or, A Leap to Freedom* in five acts. Brown wrote in his preface that its main characters, Glen and Melinda, harassed by Melinda's owner Dr. Gaines and tormented by his jealous wife, were "actual characters" who "still reside in Canada." Melinda and Glen outwit their abusive owners. Brown gave successful dramatic readings of the play. During and after the war Brown wrote transnational black history and collective biographies of black abolitionists, writers, soldiers, and revolutionaries in the Americas. He was the most prolific black author of his time.[34]

Besides Brown, with whom she lectured in 1857, Frances Ellen Watkins emerged as a preeminent abolitionist writer. The niece of William Watkins, the orphaned Frances was educated by him and had worked as a teacher, seamstress, and domestic servant. Called the "bronze muse" of the abolition movement, Watkins spoke "eloquently of the wrongs of the slave" throughout the North and was hired as a lecturing agent by the Maine ASS. An abolitionist reporter described her as "a young lady of color, of fine attainments, of superior education, and an impressive speaker, leaving an impression, wherever she goes, which will not soon be forgotten." Watkins became known for her evocative recitation of her poetry as well as her finished abolitionist lectures. She published her first poetry collection, *Forest Leaves*, in 1845. In 1854 Watkins made her debut on the abolitionist lecture circuit and published her second collection, *Poems on Miscellaneous Subjects*, with a preface by Garrison. It was reprinted twenty times. Her poems on free produce and the reaction of Lovejoy's mother to the news of his death combined sentimental romanticism with activism. Two of her poems were based on characters from Stowe's novel: "Eliza Harris," depicting the flight across the Ohio, and "Eva's Farewell," on the death of Eva. One memorable stanza cast the female fugitive as the exemplary mother: "Oh! Poverty, danger and death she can brave,/For the child of her love is no longer a slave."

Fugitive slaves were the subject of Watkins's most famous poems, "The Slave Mother" and "The Fugitive's Wife." A Unitarian, Watkins, like the most famous Unitarian abolitionists of the day, Parker, William H. Channing, and Furness, was active in fugitive slave abolitionism. She was known to assist runaways, and Still listed her as "one of the most liberal contributors" to the UGRR. In Philadelphia she met many of the fugitives who inspired her poetry. In the expanded edition of her collection, published in 1857, she reworked "The Slave Mother" giving it the subtitle "A Tale of the Ohio," referencing Margaret Garner, who killed her children rather than see them enslaved. In its miscellaneous prose section she included her letter from Canada, "I have gazed for the first time upon Free Land!" Two years later she published the sentimental "The Dying Fugitive" in the *Anglo African Magazine*, where her feminist short story "The Two Offers" also appeared.

By the start of the war Watkins had become an astute political commentator whose works often graced the abolitionist press. She was a fierce advocate of emancipation and critic of Lincoln's colonization plans in her articles for the *Christian Recorder*. After the death of her husband and during Reconstruction, Frances Ellen Watkins Harper worked among freedmen and -women in the South. She became known for her advocacy of temperance and women's rights and was active in Frances Willard's Women's Christian Temperance Union. In her speech before the National Women's Rights Convention in 1866, Harper pointed out, "You white women here speak of rights. I speak of wrongs." She held up Tubman, "a woman who has gone down into the Egypt of slavery and brought out hundreds of our people into liberty" but was subject to Jim Crow railroad cars, as her feminist hero. A prolific author, she published the novel *Iola Leroy* (1892), which concentrated on the travails of enslaved women and reworked the tragic mulatto trope, and several books of poetry after the war. Harper's long literary and activist career make her an exceptional, if somewhat forgotten, abolitionist writer.[35]

Stowe fashioned herself as a patron of black writers. She wrote the preface for Frank J. Webb's novel *The Garies and their Friends* (1857), a portrait of free black life, which, like Wilson's autobiographical *Our Nig*, is an indictment of the pervasive nature of northern racism. The high point of the novel is the murder of Garies by a Philadelphia mob instigated by a lawyer who covets their property for being "amalgamationists." Garies is a former planter whose wife is black. Stowe befriended Webb's actress wife, Mary, for whom she wrote a dramatized account of her novel. Mary performed *The Christian Slave* (1855) in the North and in England. The Webbs, armed with Stowe's letters of introduction, visited England, where Webb published his novel.[36] Rather than view it in isolation, one must see the triumph of *Uncle Tom's Cabin* in the context of the slave narratives that preceded it and the renaissance of abolitionist literature that followed it.

LITERATURE OF RESISTANCE

Abolitionist writers developed a literature of resistance that upended the image of saintly suffering personified by Uncle Tom. The heroes and heroines of these books were rebels and fugitives, characters who challenged the military might and political power of the slaveholding republic. Starting with his confrontation with Covey, Douglass justified the notion of self-defense, even though he had opposed Garnet's address to the slaves. At the NEAS convention in 1848 Douglass vindicated the "slaves' right to revolt." There are many "Madison Washingtons and Nathaniel Turners" in the South, he claimed, who would rise if northerners "take your feet from their necks, and your sympathy and aid from their oppressors." He hoped that "the whole South will present again a scene something similar to the deck of the *Creole.*" Douglass enthralled an abolitionist meeting by saying he would welcome the news that "sable arms that had been engaged in beautifying and adorning the South were engaged in spreading death and devastation there." In January 1853 Douglass published his novella *The Heroic Slave* on Washington and the *Creole* shipboard rebellion in *Autographs of Freedom,* which Griffiths put together to raise funds for his paper. It was reprinted serially in four parts in March.

Douglass implies that Washington was more of a revolutionary than the slaveholding founders whose names he bore. In the very first scene, his manly appearance and words convert the white Ohioan Listwell, who resolves to be an abolitionist. The fugitive slave influences the white man rather than vice versa, as Listwell listens well. In the next scene Listwell aids Washington on his way to Canada and then encounters the black man again in a slave coffle, apprehended in an attempt to free his wife. Douglass's story adheres loosely to the actual story of the rebellion right down to the deliverance of the *Creole* rebels by black soldiers. Douglass's heroic Washington stands in contrast to Herman Melville's complex portrayal of the deceptively masterful slave rebel Babo in *Benito Cereno* (1855), also based on an actual shipboard rebellion described by Capt. Amasa Delano in his *A Narrative of Voyages and Travels in the Northern and Southern Hemispheres* (1817). It was not a coincidence that both Melville and Douglass wrote on the aesthetics of black resistance during this time. Stowe pronounced Douglass's novella excellent.[37]

Stowe herself contributed to the literature of resistance. In 1856 she published her lesser known novel *Dred,* which sold over two hundred thousand copies thanks to her celebrity. If *Uncle Tom's Cabin* appropriated material from fugitive slave narratives, *Dred* relied on the history of slave resistance. While it reads like a conventional plantation novel, Stowe introduces two notable instances of rebellion. An entire chapter is devoted to Vesey's conspiracy, and an appendix, which acts as a historical source à la *A Key,* to Nat Turner's confessions. *Dred* is a fugitive who lives in the Dismal Swamps, well known as the site of slave Maroon communities. He also happens to be the son of Vesey and a participant in Turner's rebellion. His armed presence is a constant menace to plantation society. Stowe also alludes to the Garner case and the caning of Sumner by the South Carolinian Preston Brooks. The brutal slaveholder Tom Gordon whips the antislavery Edward Clayton, making him eminently suitable for Congress, she wryly notes. *Dred's* runaway band rescues Clayton, reversing the order of fugitive slave "rescues" in the North, and breaks Tom's arm.

Stowe's romantic racialism, however, tinges her tale of black resistance. She describes the "unfathomable blackness and darkness" of Dred's "African eye," his overpowering physical presence. She draws attention to the "black velvet" skin of Aunt Milly, whom she calls an "African woman," a character perhaps inspired by Truth. Stowe's essay on Truth, the "Libyan Sibyl," portrayed the black New Yorker as a "native African." Major themes in *Uncle Tom's Cabin* are revisited in *Dred*, like the attempted abuse of the light-skinned slave Lisette by the abusive Gordon. Tom is the half brother of Nina Gordon, an adult version of Eva who dies of cholera in ministering to her slaves. She is the good slaveholder complicit in the system, and, like St. Clare, her abusive brother Tom inherits her slaves. The father of the antislavery Claytons, who free, educate, and settle their slaves in Canada, Judge Clayton delivers North Carolinian Thomas Ruffin's infamous *Mann* decision of 1829, which declared a master's power over his slaves absolute. Aunt Milly and Old Tiff are the seemingly Uncle Tom characters who escape from slavery, and Dred, the anti-Tom, dies a Tom-like martyr's death. Aunt Milly educates "destitute children" in freedom, and her son, Tomtit, grows up to be an abolitionist. Stowe's literary foray into the politics of black resistance was not a complete repudiation of her earlier views but more in keeping with abolitionist positions. Instead of Harris's colonizationist letter, we get Harry's letter, "the slave's argument," which evokes the Declaration on behalf of Vesey.[38]

Besides rebellion, works recovering the martial history of black men lent themselves to notions of violent resistance. William Cooper Nell's *The Colored Patriots of the American Revolution* (1855), for which Stowe wrote a preface, was the foremost. Often viewed as a simple black appropriation of the American revolutionary tradition, Nell's book teems with slave rebels as well as black patriots, fugitive slave rebellions, and outstanding leaders of the black community, valorization of revolutionary ideals as well as a critique of racism. It defies easy categorization. An expansion of his earlier pamphlet *Services of Colored Americans in the Wars of 1776 and 1812* (1851), which was popular enough to be printed in two editions, and inspired by the writings of Whittier and Child, the book recounts Nell's attempts to raise funds for a statue of Crispus Attucks, noting that the fugitive slaves Thomas Sims and Anthony Burns were remanded back to slavery on the very ground Attucks "trod." Attucks, Nell noted, was a fugitive slave. Black service in the Revolutionary War is coupled with early critiques of revolutionary republicanism in the New England slave petitions. The revolutionary hero Prince Whipple, Nell argued, did not hesitate to whip and shoot some white ruffians who attacked him. He presents a state-by-state account of black leaders and activism in which Turner, Vesey, and the "Virginia maroons" get the lion's share of attention in the chapters on southern slave states.

An eclectic appendix that includes the "claims of the red man," the words of Lafayette and Kościuszko, the *Amistad* revolt, and the Christiana uprising of 1851 illustrated Nell's refashioning of the American revolutionary heritage. In a letter to Garrison, Nell singled out European revolutionaries, known to sympathize with black Americans, as not being tainted with "American colorophobia." Abolitionists like Phillips, who wrote the introduction, Smith, and Garrison, he wrote, were "colored all over." Nell ended his book with the eloquent address of 1853 at the national black convention written by Douglass. It was a "sad, but true, confession," he concluded, that the "Revolution of 1776" necessitated another revolution. He called on black Americans to "nourish the tree of liberty" and "hasten . . . their claim to the title, 'Patriots of the Second Revolution.'" He asked them to join a "moral battle" against "American proslavery" and crown "Freedom's Army" with victory.

Nell, along with other black abolitionists in Massachusetts, namely, Morris, Hayden, Remond, and William J. Watkins, led a movement to form a black state militia. Their demand was no mere desire to dress up in fancy uniforms and parade around. At a time when Boston's courthouses had become battlegrounds over fugitive slaves, and federal troops and deputized marshals roamed the city streets to enforce the hated fugitive law, armed black men acting on behalf of the state could very well tip the scales in a confrontation. In 1852 sixty-five "colored citizens" petitioned the legislature and the following year petitioned the state constitutional convention for an "independent black military company." In his speech before the General Court, Watkins, apologizing for the "disabilities" of his education, viewed the exclusion of black men from the militia as an example of the "juggernaut of American Prejudice" crushing "the manhood out of us." It was an "inseparable concomitant" of American slavery, and Watkins made it clear that black men did not intend to "submit to your indignities with Christian meekness and becoming submission," like Uncle Tom. "Give us our rights," he demanded, as able-bodied male citizens of the Commonwealth. The Irish, often used in fugitive slave rendition, the Germans, and the Hungarians were allowed to form militias denied to "native born" black Americans, who, he said, quoting Nell's work, had fought for the country. Watkins's argument was no bow to nativism, as he concluded with the Garrisonian motto, "Our country is the world—Our countrymen all mankind."

Despite the support of radical Free Soilers such as Sumner and Henry Wilson, the opposition of conservatives like Benjamin F. Hallet, the bête noire of fugitive slaves and their abolitionist allies, killed the measure. The federal militia law of 1792 explicitly excluded black men, Hallet asserted. Not waiting for official permission, black abolitionists formed the Massasoit Guards, named after the Wampanoag chief, not after any of the revolutionary sires of the Commonwealth.

Nell regretted they could not take the name of Attucks, which black military companies in New York and Cincinnati had already adopted. In 1857 a black coachman named Lewis Gaul formed the Liberty Guard, the name of John Brown's militia in Kansas. White rowdies attacked them as they marched on city streets. Two years later Gov. Nathaniel Banks vetoed a bill allowing African Americans to join the militia. By one count there were twenty-seven black militias in the North and Canada West, most of them formed in the 1850s. Not until the Civil War was their dream of an armed black militia realized when one of the first black Union regiments, the Fifty-Fourth Massachusetts, was formed under the auspices of the state's radical governor John Andrews.[39]

Black abolitionists looked beyond America's shores to construct a cosmopolitan discourse of revolutionary resistance. In 1841 "R," probably Charles B. Ray, pointed to the Haitian Revolution rather than the American as an exemplar of black revolutionary resistance: "The immolations and martyrdoms on the plains of St. Domingo, in opposition to cruel and aristocratic oppression, though written as they are on the pages of history, in characters of blood, should be as 'balm to our souls, and incense to our worship.' They are sureties to us, that as a race, *we cannot be crushed.*" In defending the record of the Haitian Revolution from its racist detractors, McCune Smith, in his "Lecture on the Haytien Revolutions; With a Sketch of the Character of Toussaint L'Ouverture," anticipated the efforts of twentieth-century black radical intellectuals like C. L. R. James. In the talk, delivered as a fund raiser for the Colored Orphan Asylum, Smith set out to present a full, objective history of the revolution. Noting that five thousand African slaves died each year prior to the revolution, Smith asked his audience to compare this holocaust in black lives to the casualties of the *"wars, insurrections and massacres"* of the revolution. Jean-Jacques Dessalines, whom he called the Robespierre of Haiti, killed only those who were attempting to reinstall slavery. Smith divided his history into three revolutions, the formation of the French Republic, the abolition of slavery, and the independence of Haiti, over which Toussaint was the "presiding genius." His signal achievement, Smith wrote, was not just the abolition of slavery but also of the racial caste that had divided the island into whites, mixed race, and blacks.

Abolitionists had long laid claim to the heritage of the Haitian Revolution. In his lecture, which was published in 1855, Wells Brown found the American Revolution wanting: "Toussaint's government made liberty its watchword, incorporated it in its constitution, abolished the slave-trade, and freedom universal amongst the people. Washington's government incorporated slavery and the slave trade, and enacted laws by which chains were fastened upon the limbs of millions of people. Toussaint liberated his countrymen; Washington enslaved a portion of his, and aided in giving strength and vitality to an institution that will one day rent asunder the UNION that he helped form." Brown also used his history of Haiti to call for rebellion. Southern slaves, he argued, burned for revenge: "The indignation of the slaves of the south would kindle a fire so hot that would melt their chains, drop by drop, until not a single link would remain." Similarly, in his poem on the free black leader of Haiti, Vincent Ogé, George B. Vashon wrote, "Upon the slave's o'erclouded sky,/Your gallant actions traced the bow,/Which whispered of deliverance nigh—/The meed of one decisive blow." By 1861 Phillips had incorporated many of these ideas into his popular lecture "Toussaint L'Ouverture," which was more a history of the Haitian Revolution than a biography of Toussaint. He drove home the point: "There never was a race that, weakened and degraded by such chattel slavery, unaided, tore off its own fetters, forged them into swords, and won its liberty in the battle-field, but one, and that was the black race of St. Domingo."[40]

More than any other abolitionist, Delany imagined transnational black revolutionary resistance in his novel *Blake, or, The Huts of America*. Describing a Pan-African, hemispheric revolt against slavery, the novel was published serially in Thomas Hamilton's *Anglo-American Magazine* starting in February 1859. It was republished with an additional second part in the *Weekly Anglo-African* in 1861–62. Not published as a book until 1970, its last six chapters are lost to history. The central character is a fugitive slave in Mississippi called Henry Holland Blake, "a pure Negro—handsome, manly and intelligent." The novel starts with the sale of his wife, Maggie, to Cuba, which in turn leads to Henry's escape to Canada and his revolutionary plan to coordinate a rebellion in the slave south and Cuba, and along the way recover his wife's freedom. It is not clear if Delany wrote *Blake* as a response to *Uncle Tom's Cabin* or was influenced by *Dred*, as some scholars have claimed. He did not include the epigraphs by Stowe until the 1861–62 publication.

Blake visualized an international, Pan-African revolution as a response to proslavery imperialism and to the revival of plans to annex Cuba and reopen the African slave trade in the late 1850s. As early as 1849 Delany had written against slaveholding designs on Cuba, "the greatest western slave mart of the world," and held that the "redemption of Cuba" was central to black revolutionary politics. He advised the "oppressed in Cuba" to imitate the Haitians and "*take their cause in their own hands.*" In 1854 Mohammah Gardo Baquaqua published his narrative of enslavement in Africa, slavery in Brazil, and the gaining of his freedom through the intervention of the New York State Vigilance Committee in 1847. Baquaqua lived in Haiti and Canada and then traveled to England. Abolitionists like Rev. Cyrus Grosvenor, the president of New York

Central College, where Baquaqua enrolled, and Gerrit Smith helped him publish his book. He hoped to raise money to go back to Africa as a Baptist missionary. At the time Delany published *Blake*, black abolitionists in New York such as Pennington drew attention to the conduct of the illegal foreign slave trade to Cuba and Brazil, which involved American slavers and crew, and sought to ensure the freedom and safety of African recaptives, demanding that the children be housed in the Colored Orphan Asylum rather than in jail. An article in the *Anglo-African Magazine* asked free black people to take the lead against "the consummation of this astounding crime." In *Blake*, Henry turns out to be a Cuban kidnapped into southern slavery, and when he reaches Cuba, Delany has him meet Plácido, the revolutionary poet who was executed during the La Escalera slave conspiracy in 1844. Henry is Carolus Henrico Blacus, a long-lost cousin of Plácido, and the two plot revolution. Henry, unlike the characters Mammy Judy and Daddy Joe, who are Uncle Tom–like, is presented as an exemplary revolutionary leader, arguing that if he were to listen to "the advice of the old people here, and become reconciled to drag out a miserable life of degradation and bondage," his master would "crush out my lingering manhood, and reduce my free spirit to the submission of a slave." He is "General-in-chief" of an "Army of Emancipation."

The Western hemisphere, wrote Delany, was an inheritance of the colored races, of the original Indian people that inhabited the Americas, and of the black race. During his visit to Indian territory Henry posits a camaraderie between Indian masters and black slaves, quite unlike contemporary historical portrayals of Indian slavery. Delany, like the Haitian revolutionaries, saw the black revolution as reclaiming the Americas in the name of its indigenous inhabitants. Contrary to the dictates of the pseudoscience of race and social Darwinism, he wrote that while the colored races "increased and progressed," whites "decreased and continually retrograded." Henry sets sail for Africa, ironically in a slaver outfitted in Baltimore: "Goin' to Afraka," he says, "where de white man dare not stay." The last line of the extant novel reads, "Woe be unto those devils of whites, I say!"[41]

The most important narrative of female slave resistance, written by Harriet Jacobs, a fugitive from North Carolina, was published in 1861. An indictment of the sexual exploitation of enslaved women, it is a culmination of a theme running through slave narratives. The emphasis on female slave abuse, physical and sexual, stories of overseers who enjoyed whipping female slaves, jealous masters and mistresses who did not hesitate to scour them, the sale and mishandling of female slaves, and the rape of slave women populate slave narratives. Even those women who ostensibly formed long-term relationships with their owners were shown all too often to be at the mercy of the slave system and vengeful relatives after the demise of their protectors. If slave narratives are accepted as authentic black testimony about the workings of slavery, then the abuse of female slaves was an essential component of fugitive slave abolitionism rather than a figment of the supposed prurient and pornographic imagination of white abolitionists.

A failure to account for the essential place of fugitive slave abolitionists in the movement and their pivotal ideological contributions to it has led scholars to repeat uncritically an argument first put forward by slaveholders and their apologists. The long-held belief that Child, the editor of Jacobs's narrative, who confessed that she had not added more than forty words to the narrative itself, was its real author and that the narrative itself was abolitionist fiction underscores this point. Having adopted a pseudonym, Linda Brent, the author Jacobs was forgotten until her recovery by the literary scholar Jean Fagan Yellin. The fact that Jacobs rejected the editorial services of the famous Stowe and of her employer, whom she suspected of harboring proslavery sentiments, showed her determination not to lose control over her story. Of all abolitionist writers, Child had the largest role in the production of fugitive slave literature. In 1853 she wrote the life of Isaac Hopper, a pioneer of the abolitionist underground. Besides her numerous contributions to the abolitionist press, in 1858 she published a drama, pointedly titled *The Stars and Stripes*, based loosely on the escape of William and Ellen Craft. Like Brown's play, it ends with slave hunters failing to catch their prey at the Canadian ferry. By all accounts, Jacobs, who decided not to use the more famous yet condescending Stowe, and Child formed a mutually respectful and productive literary partnership.

Pitting the will of a young slave girl against her would-be abuser, Jacobs lays bare the underside of the patriarchal institution. She wrote memorably, "Slavery is terrible for men; but it is far more terrible for women. Superadded to the burden common to all, *they* have wrongs, and sufferings and mortifications peculiarly their own." Jacobs first foiled her master's designs by entering into a relationship with a prominent white lawyer by whom she has two children. She explained, "I feel that the slave woman ought not to be judged by the same standard as others," artfully challenging the sexual double standard that she knew most of her female readers experienced. Jacobs claimed the mantle of the virtuous slave mother rather than that of the fallen woman. She finally escaped the unwanted attentions of her lecherous old master by hiding in a crawl space in the attic of her grandmother's house for seven years, even sending him letters postmarked from New York. As she put it, "I resolved to match my cunning against his cunning." On escaping to the North in 1842, she is helped by the

abolitionist underground in Philadelphia and New York and becomes associated with the interracial abolitionist milieu in Boston and Rochester. Purvis
corroborated the main outlines of her story to Gay, though he was confused
about the details. Her brother John S. Jacobs was an abolitionist lecturer who
published his narrative serially in a British religious journal the same year as
Jacobs. Both narratives reveal that the Jacobses came from a family of rebels, a
proud father and a runaway uncle. John, who walked out on his relatively kind
master and father of his sister's children, left him a note signed simply, "no
longer yours." He ends his narrative with an abolitionist philippic. Even more
than Jacobs, her brother's lecturing career embodied the life of a fugitive slave
abolitionist. Jacobs's confidante in Rochester was the Quaker abolitionist Amy
Post, with whom she lived for a while. She worked in an antislavery reading
room above Douglass's newspaper office and wrote anonymous letters about
her experiences in abolitionist newspapers before publishing her narrative.

Like other slave narratives, Jacobs's destroyed the paternalistic image of slavery assiduously promoted by slaveholders and proslavery apologists, cataloguing
instances of abuse and the hypocrisy of slaveholding Christianity and directly
taking on slaveholders' claims that slaves were treated better than working-class
and poor whites in free societies. At one point she noted, "I would ten thousand
times rather that my children should be the half-starved paupers of Ireland
than to be the most pampered slaves in America." On her visit to England Jacobs insisted that the condition of the poorest and the meanest there was vastly
superior to that of American slaves. "I do not deny that the poor are oppressed
in Europe," but she did not subscribe to the "rose-colored" picture of slavery
painted by some who compared their condition to that of the slaves. Child,
whose editing of the narrative was minimal, mainly rearranging material, suggested deleting a concluding chapter on John Brown, and one is left to wonder
what abolitionist ending Jacobs had originally visualized. She advised Jacobs to
write a chapter on the terror inflicted on slaves and free blacks in the aftermath
of Turner's rebellion. During the war Jacobs, like other black women abolitionists, worked for the relief of contraband slaves and with her daughter established
schools for freed people in Alexandria and Savannah. She died in 1897.[42]

Unlike Jacobs's narrative, Hannah Craft's *The Bondwoman's Narrative*, a fictionalized account of the author's experiences and escape from slavery, never
saw the light of day. The literary scholar Henry Louis Gates Jr. published the rediscovered manuscript in 2002, and Greg Hecimovich has recently established
her identity as Hannah Bond. Her owner was John Wheeler, the master of
a famous fugitive, Jane Johnson. Like Jacobs, Bond, identifying herself as a
"fugitive slave recently escaped from North Carolina," emphasized the abuse
of slave women and unmistakably intended her story to be an argument for the

abolition of slavery. As she asks in the preface, "Have I succeeded in portraying any of the peculiar features of that institution whose curse rests over the fairest land the sun shines upon? Have I succeeded in showing how it blights the happiness of the white as well as the black race?" Like Ellen Craft, she escaped slavery disguised as a man. Her novel has a happy ending that many slave narratives lacked: she marries a black Methodist minister and teaches in a school for "colored children" in New Jersey. Bond's gothic novel, in which a mulatto mistress steadily descends into insanity before dying, her master commits suicide, and a slave trader and the man who sought to expose her mistress die, plays with notions of race and identity. The face of her mistress, Mrs. Wheeler, is temporarily blackened by powder, and she herself is fair enough to pass for white.[43]

Fugitive slaves presented the best riposte to proslavery thought. In 1856 Benjamin Drew, an abolitionist journalist and school principal from Massachusetts, published *A North-Side View of Slavery*, containing Canadian fugitive slave narratives. The title is a counterpoint to the proslavery tract by Garrison's clerical adversary Rev. Nehemiah Adams, who wrote *A South-Side View of Slavery*. The fugitives' experience, Drew wrote, "shed a peculiar lustre on the Institution of the South." Anticipating the WPA slave narratives, he recorded hundreds of interviews, admitting he could not publish all of them. His book remains one of the best sources on Canadian black communities composed primarily of fugitive slaves. He gave a census count of fourteen black settlements, a careful account of the churches and schools founded by them, and individual stories of escape and migration. Most of the narratives are of young men from the border states, a fair sampling of the fugitive slave population. One of the longer narratives, that of John Holmes, an escaped slave from Virginia, with its description of slaveholder brutality, was republished in the *Liberator*. Drew distilled the meaning of the narratives in his astute introduction. To him, slavery was "the oppression of the laboring portion of the community . . . to an entire deprivation of their civil and personal rights" and punishes "with bodily tortures the least infraction of its mandates." Only the authentic accounts of the slaves themselves told the real truth about slavery, that it was not a workers' paradise, the motif so belabored by southern defenders of slavery. They alone could recite "the history of their sufferings and wrongs, of their bondage and their escape." They were "the most irritating subject of discussion between the North and the South" and thwarted southern designs "to preserve, extend, and perpetuate slavery." In action and words, fugitive slave abolitionists were the true adversaries of southern slaveholders.

These self-emancipated Canadian "refugees" from American slavery, many of whom served in the Union army, contributed to the formation of emancipation policy. During the Civil War, the American Freedmen's Inquiry Commission, which included Samuel Gridley Howe and Robert Dale Owen, was formed to report on the transition from slavery to freedom by gathering information from former slaves, Union army officials, missionaries, and teachers. Their report led to the formation of the Freedmen's Bureau. Howe published a separate book on black communities in Canada in 1864, borrowing liberally from Drew's narratives, as his own sampling of interviews of former slaves, which he reproduced verbatim, was much smaller. Unlike Drew, Howe interviewed not just former slaves but many white teachers, who vouched for their ability. Howe wanted to prove the capacity of black people for self-government, even in the midst of an "unsympathizing population," and his work was geared to convince skeptical whites about the wisdom of emancipation and the ability of African Americans to thrive in freedom.[44]

Fugitive slave abolitionists represented a substantial countermovement to the slavery expansionism and proslavery imperialism of southern slaveholders in the 1850s. For them, the war against slavery had started long before the booming of guns involved the rest of the nation. It is no surprise that the ordinances of secession of southern states included the fugitive slave controversy as one of the major causes of disunion. And fugitive slaves en masse, acting like many of their predecessors, initiated the emancipation process during the war. Self-emancipated slaves were at the cutting-edge of the abolition movement.

14

THE POLITICS OF ABOLITION

In *Despotism in America* (1840) Richard Hildreth pointed out that the American Republic, commonly thought of as an experiment in democracy, was also an experiment in racial despotism. His *Theory of Politics* (1853) warned that "chattel slavery" and the "accumulation of wealth" and power were the bane of American democracy. Hildreth argued that all wealth was an "element of aristocracy," and "social slavery" left the masses "to labor, suffer and submit." He asked, "Is there never to be an *Age of the People*—of the working classes?" The socialist question about the "distribution of wealth" could not be "blinked out of sight." Hildreth linked the cause of the American slave to that of American democracy and the working classes. Suffering from ill health, he was appointed by Lincoln as consul in Trieste, Italy, at the request of Sumner and Seward. He died there in 1865.[1]

Antislavery politics, or free soilism, grew out of abolition. Nearly all Radical Republicans began their careers as abolitionists or allies of abolition. They occupied the vanguard of their party. Political abolitionists established the precedent of third-party politics, the vehicle for antislavery success in the North. They developed arguments on the unconstitutionality of slavery, the unrepublican character of the Slave Power, and a free labor critique of slavery that enlisted the mass of northern citizens in the fight for the future of the country. Free labor ideology appealed across class lines: both to labor, for whom it signified economic independence, and to the middle classes, for whom mobility offset the rise of a permanent class of wageworkers. It included the abolitionist critique of the perceived aristocratic classes, the slaveholders and the doughface merchants of the North, who presided over the political economy of slavery in antebellum America. Free soilism visualized eventual abolition, slowly choking slavery to death by curtailing its expansion into western territories, but it was not abolition.[2] The politics of abolition continued to exist beyond the structures of state and party. Its diverse political traditions encompassed women's rights, black citizenship, and, for Garrisonians, a critique of the state. It never became an uncritical valorization of free society.

BALLOTS FOR FREEDOM

Abolitionists first espoused constitutional ideas and legislative strategies to not just contain but abolish slavery. They predicted various scenarios in which the power of the state could be harnessed against rather than for slavery. The abolitionist petition campaigns of the 1820s and 1830s demanded that the federal government abolish both slavery in the District of Columbia and in the federal territories and the domestic slave trade. Some had called even for a constitutional amendment to abolish slavery. In 1838 Weld published *The Power of Congress over the District of Columbia* during the petition campaign. Responding to southern claims that Congress had no authority to legislate over slavery, Weld argued that the constitutional power of the federal government to legislate for the District was so clear it "defies misconstruction." But beyond that narrow question, Weld maintained that slavery could be abolished by legislative authority, as it had been in the northern states, or by Congress, as in the case of the Northwest Ordinance and the abolition of the African slave trade. Weld contended that slavery was brought into existence by "*statute law*" and since slavery was a "creature of legislation," it could be abolished by it. In rejecting the idea that legislative abolition was barred by the constitutional sanction against the confiscation of property without due process, Weld was upholding not a bourgeois sanctity of property but the abolitionist notion that there could be no property in human beings. The political abolitionist Samuel B. Treadwell, the editor of the short-lived *Michigan Freeman*, asserted that it was the duty of Congress to abolish the slave trade, which treated human beings as "articles of commerce." Like Hildreth, he warned of how "slaveholding politicians . . . devised ways and means for the monied, political, and ecclesiastical aristocracies in the north to blind, entrap, ensnare and finally *enslave*, the entire laboring population of the free states." In his extended defense of abolitionists' right to discuss slavery, Treadwell illustrated how its "despotic power" acted against American constitutional liberties and, as Wright and Cornish commended, the human rights of black people.

Abolitionists hitched their politics to black citizenship. Three years later Weld vindicated the "rights of colored citizens under the U.S. Constitution."

Despite holding "our fathers" guilty of the constitutional compromises over slavery, William Jay (the son of John Jay was speaking literally here) held that the Constitution recognized no differences based on color. But the federal government "OPPRESS[ES] AND DEGRADE[S] THE FREE PEOPLE OF COLOR," he noted, with its racist citizenship and militia laws. It aided slaveholders "in trampling upon those great principles of human rights." Jay listed the names and stories of free blacks held in prisons in the District of Columbia and at times sold, as they had no slaveholding claimants. Domestically and internationally the American government acted as the handmaiden of slavery: upholding the domestic slave trade and slavery, refusing to recognize the "heroic republic" of Haiti, warring against the Seminoles, demanding rendition of fugitives and compensation for slave rebels, tolerating an illegal African slave trade and infringements of civil liberties, and plotting to annex Texas. Jay predicted that if slaveholders seceded, their slaves would rise up in rebellion and, in the absence of the protection of the federal government, slavery was doomed. The "rapid sale" of his pamphlet led to a second edition in 1844.[3]

Abolitionists also put their words into action. Weld was part of Leavitt's "Abolitionist lobby" in Washington. They worked assiduously with the few congressmen representing abolitionist strongholds in the North to overturn the Gag Rule and nurture antislavery politics in the capital. Jay developed some of the most influential arguments defending the right to petition. Weld and Leavitt shared abolitionist ideas and living quarters, Ann Sprigg's boardinghouse, with antislavery Whigs. It came to be known as the "Abolition house." Hired slaves worked there to buy their freedom. Leavitt even received his mail care of Giddings to avoid paying postage. Leavitt saw the "true issue" as "SHALL SLAVERY GOVERN THE COUNTRY?" Weld did research for Adams's speeches, "ransacking the Library of Congress." He reasoned that one antislavery peroration in Congress reached many more northerners than abolitionist agents did.

Abolitionists' northern Whig allies were at the forefront of political antislavery in the nation's capital. Their antislavery "select committee" first opposed plans to annex Texas. Lundy and, later, David Lee Child, who also moved to Washington, sounded the alarm against slaveholders' designs on Texas to Adams, who spoke out against annexation. Giddings called for the admission of Florida as a free state and, as mentioned in chapter 12, condemned the government's war against the Seminoles. In 1843 Gates wrote an appeal against the annexation of Texas signed by Adams, Andrews, Slade, and Giddings. These men helped make anti-expansionism Whig policy on the eve of the Mexican War. With the founding of the Liberty Party in 1840, Leavitt criticized antislavery politicians for refusing to abandon the Whigs, but he, Weld, and even the allegedly apolitical Garrison came to appreciate their antislavery commitments. For most antislavery Whigs, the free trade economic policies of the Liberty Party and Leavitt leaned too Democratic. While Gates, who felt that Leavitt did him "an injustice" in questioning his antislavery, joined the Liberty Party, Giddings and Adams remained Whigs.[4]

The political influence of the abolitionist Liberty Party on northern politics cannot be gauged by electoral bean counting. While it significantly improved its national vote count in the presidential elections, growing steadily between 1840 and 1844 from 6,225 to nearly 62,000, it never came close to winning. Some Libertyites were better abolitionists than politicians, urging "moral action at the ballot box," and their perennial presidential nominee, James Birney, a reluctant candidate in 1840 who avoided campaigning, was not a huge electoral draw. Renominated in 1841, Birney started campaigning more, his letter of acceptance drawing attention to how slaveholders had used the federal government and Constitution to perpetuate their power as well as the persecution of African Americans, Native Americans, and Mormons. But as early as 1842 he avowed that not only the government and church but also the people themselves were corrupt. Birney's questioning of universal suffrage and his notion of giving immigrants the right to vote with "parsimony" made most abolitionists uncomfortable. Birney was specifically repudiating the "white man's democracy," swelled by the first great wave of European immigration, which did not hesitate to trample on the rights of racial minorities. The attempt to expand the Liberty platform from the "one idea" of abolition by adding a variety of other economic and political issues resulted in further confusion. As Garrison argued, partisan politics proved to be uncongenial to abolitionism pure and simple. But as a political pressure group, abolitionists of all factions did influence northern politics.

Notwithstanding Libertyites' accusation that Garrisonians voted for "proslavery parties," many Liberty Party voters were rank-and-file Garrisonians who paid little heed to abolitionist organizational divisions. In 1841 the Liberty Party in Massachusetts even nominated the Garrisonians Francis Jackson as mayor, Nathaniel Rodgers and Wendell Phillips as aldermen of Boston, while Samuel Sewall, the Liberty Party gubernatorial candidate in Massachusetts, remained with the old organization. Many old organization men, Edmund Quincy complained, voted for the Liberty Party. The strongholds of abolition, Massachusetts, upstate New York, and Ohio, gave the Liberty Party its largest vote counts. Despite Garrison's personal aversion to electoral politics and public debates between Garrisonians and Libertyites, AASS lecturing agents helped to increase the new party's vote count. Abby Kelley and Douglass debated political abolitionists in upstate New York and Ohio, Kelley trying even, in copious letters, to convince the stalwart Libertyite Gerrit Smith to see the error of his ways. The lines between Garrisonians and the Liberty Party were still not well drawn in upstate New York or Ohio, Kelley reported. Giles Stebbins wrote to Gay that many Liberty men subscribed to the Garrisonian NASS.

Garrison thought Adams and Giddings took antislavery stances far ahead of those of most northern politicians and was thus more complimentary of them than of his abolitionist rivals in the Liberty Party, who, he argued, lowered the abolitionist standard by entering partisan politics. So carried away were Garrisonians in their praise of Adams, wrote Birney, that they had forgotten he was not an abolitionist. Garrison conceded the "purity of purpose" of Libertyites in private but strongly resisted converting the abolition movement into a political party. That did not prevent him from supporting antislavery politicians. In 1845 he sent MASS agents to work for the reelection of the antislavery Democratic representative John P. Hale in New Hampshire, who was read out of his party for his opposition to the annexation of Texas. To Garrison, the political place of abolitionists lay in agitation, to move the political center to the left, rather than in party politics. Smarting under Garrison's criticism for confining abolitionism to the ballot box, Libertyites accused the nonvoting Garrisonians of harboring a "covert design" to vote for the Whigs.

The abolitionist ideology of the Liberty Party converted Democratic rhetoric against the "money power" into a critique of the Slave Power and harnessed Whigs' statist beliefs to demand action by the federal government against slavery. Appearing as vice presidential nominees on its presidential ticket were antislavery Democrats such as Thomas Earle in 1840 and Thomas Morris in 1844. But Morris's reluctance to endorse black citizenship discomfited abolitionists. While antislavery Whigs stole the party's abolitionist thunder, the presidency of the proslavery "His Accidency" John Tyler after the death of the Whig president William Henry Harrison in 1841 vindicated the case for independent abolitionist politics. As Leavitt noted, South Carolinian and Virginian slaveholders such as Calhoun, Abel T. Upshur, and Waddy Thompson dominated Tyler's administration and plotted the annexation of Texas.[5]

The Liberty Party made antislavery an essential component of the partisan loyalties of many northerners. It was a notable presence in states where abolitionists composed a substantial voting bloc. The party received support in Massachusetts, upstate New York, Ohio, and certain districts of upper northwestern states like Wisconsin and Michigan, where Birney eventually made his home and ran for the governorship. In Maine, the abolitionists Samuel Fessenden, Austin Willey, and Joseph Lovejoy urged voters to abandon old partisan loyalties for the Liberty Party, which elected town representatives in a number of cities. In Massachusetts, Whittier, among others, headed the Liberty Party congressional ticket. In Ohio, Liberty Party supporters were concentrated around Oberlin College, whose president, Asa Mahan, was an ardent Libertyite, as was Salmon Chase, though antislavery Whigs such as Giddings and Benjamin Wade in the Western Reserve also received abolitionist votes. A minority of Liberty voters was concentrated in the northern counties of Illinois and in Quaker-dominated counties in Indiana. Libertyites influenced state elections and were blamed by Whigs for putting New York in the Democratic column in the presidential election of 1844, which James Polk won over Henry Clay. Whigs used a local Democratic nomination of Birney in Michigan to perpetrate the so-called Garland forgery, claiming that Birney had endorsed the Democratic Party and Polk. The forgery and the efforts of Giddings, Wade, and Cassius Marcellus Clay, Clay's antislavery nephew, kept many in the Whig column.

Libertyites ran viable party newspapers like the *Emancipator*, which moved to Boston and continued to be a flashpoint in the quarrel between Garrisonians and political abolitionists, the *Liberty Press* and *Albany Patriot* in upstate New York, Gamaliel Bailey's the *Philanthropist* in Ohio, Zebina Eastman's *Western Citizen* in Chicago, the Quaker-run *Free Labor Advocate* in Indiana, Austin Willey's *Liberty Standard* in Maine, Sherman Booth's *American Freeman* in Wisconsin, the *New Jersey Freeman*, and Theodore Foster's the *Signal of Liberty* in Michigan, which pleaded with antislavery voters, "Don't throw away your votes." "One Idea" in the *Liberty Press* also urged voters to put aside economic issues that had separated Whigs and Democrats and vote abolitionist. The sixty-odd Liberty newspapers played a large role in determining party ideology and in electioneering.

In the burned-over districts of upstate New York, political abolitionists reaped the benefits of a potent combination of evangelical abolitionism with third-party politics. Their popular slogan "Vote as you pray" was designed to wean antislavery evangelical voters out of the Whig Party. The party press often carried news from abolitionist churches as much as political matters. Here, Birney wrote, the amalgamation of politics and religion was complete. Garrison rejected the church as inherently proslavery, and so did some of his detractors. Evangelical "come outers" established interdenominational abolitionist Union churches in New England and New York. These abolitionist congregations formed the voting base of the Liberty Party. Prominent leaders of the AFASS, including Tappan and Jay, followed Leavitt into Liberty Party ranks. The perfectionist "Bible politics" of Smith, who, like Garrison, rejected the sabbatarianism of the evangelicals, William Goodell, and Beriah Green also made upstate New York a hotbed of the Liberty Party. Voting for the Liberty Party, that is, to come out of old parties, was the political counterpart to religious "comeouterism."[6]

Ecclesiastical abolitionists were no lackeys of the emerging capitalist order in the countryside, as a simplistic social control model has long posited. Most were radical critics of their churches as well as of the commercialization of their society, which "elevate[d] property over humanity," as exemplified by the unholy alliance between northern manufacturers and southern slaveholders. According to Alvan Stewart, slavery degraded northern labor. He linked slaveholders' demands for shoes and tools to the unpaid labor of northern workers. In 1843 Jay issued an appeal to southern nonslaveholders to vote their class interests, anticipating Republican Party strategy. Goodell, Elizur Wright, and Smith fashioned themselves as champions of "universal reform" and labor. These Libertyites championed land reform and homestead legislation, progressive taxation, the abolition of war, the movement for a ten-hour workday, trade unions, and direct elections of federal officials, the aims of generations of labor and progressive reformers. One of the biggest criticisms Libertyites made of Clay, the Whig standard-bearer in 1844, besides being a slaveholder, was the fact that he had no sympathy for labor. Smith's wing of the Liberty Party fashioned itself as the "Poor Man's Party" that was faithful to the rights of black as well laboring white men. In Massachusetts, Libertyites formed coalitions with labor activists, successfully wooing working-class support. Wright called on Massachusetts voters to reject the "proslavery Whig aristocracy," the Cotton Whig manufacturers in cahoots with slaveholders, and to vote for "Birney and human rights." James C. Jackson's *Liberty Press* of Utica, appealing to working-class voters, drew attention to the impoverishing nature of the slave labor system. A careful study of the party's rank and file reveals that in upstate New York more laborers and mechanics voted for the Liberty Party than "nonabolitionist" parties. In the northwest the party garnered votes of farmers from the rural, agricultural hinterland.[7]

The Liberty Party attracted substantial African American support, especially in New York. In a public letter to Clay, Smith argued that the Constitution was antislavery and challenged not only Clay's criticisms of abolitionists but also his view that the Republic was constructed only for the defense of white men's liberties and rights. Black abolitionists attended national and state Liberty conventions as delegates, and the platform of 1844 welcomed "our colored fellow citizens to fraternity with us in the Liberty party." Black abolitionist clergymen such as Garnet and Ward, the editor of the party paper the *Impartial Citizen*, were ardent Libertyites, as were, to a lesser extent, Ray, Wright, Pennington, Gloucester, and the Bemans of Connecticut. William Lambert and George DeBaptiste in Michigan, the Langstons in Ohio, and John Jones of Illinois were Libertyites, and fugitive slave abolitionists like Bibb, the Clarke brothers, and Lunsford Lane became lecturers for the party. Martin Delany's newspaper *Mystery* favored the Liberty Party, which had strong support among Pittsburgh's black population.

Like Goodell and other Libertyites, Ward acquired a reputation as a champion of labor, arguing, "The poor mechanic and the laboring classes in almost every part of the country are becoming more and more depressed. Monopoly usurps the land, lowers wages, raises prices, contracts the circulation of money, holds all the offices, frames all the laws, and despising the poor, crushing him continually, and sets him at defiance." In 1848 Smith's National Liberty Party Convention elected Garnet as one of its vice presidents. An address to the colored population of the North sought their votes for the Liberty Party after most Libertyites had joined the new Free Soil coalition. Ward was the vice presidential candidate, with Smith heading the Liberty slate. The national black convention in Cleveland, however, backed the newly formed Free Soil Party, while claiming "the higher standard and more liberal views which have heretofore characterized us as abolitionists."[8]

Despite its racial inclusiveness, the Liberty Party remained bound by an ideology of "domestic feminism" that eschewed formal support of women's rights and suffrage. According to Stewart, "a wide door of usefulness" was still open for the "Liberty ladies." Women participated in Liberty meetings and formed Female Liberty Associations, though some Liberty Associations in New York and Connecticut included them. Like the colonizationist Whig women in Virginia, Liberty women entered national partisan politics even when they did not have the right to vote. A writer calling herself Maria published a Liberty Party appeal to the women of the free states during the presidential election of 1844. The Female Anti-Slavery Society of Dundee, Illinois, presented a banner proclaiming "Lovejoy and Liberty" to Millcreek's abolitionist voters for casting over 60 percent of its votes for the Libertyite Owen Lovejoy, the brother of Elijah Lovejoy, in the congressional elections of 1846. Apparently it was a tradition for Liberty women to make and present such banners to counties that gave the party its highest votes, as they did the same thing in Massachusetts. Like other abolitionist women, Liberty women also held fund-raising bazaars and fairs. In New York, women managed to secure Liberty Party support for married women's property rights and for the vote.

Women played prominent roles in the substantial Liberty Party press. Jane Van Vleet published the *Star of Freedom* in Michigan, and Mary Brown Davis contributed several articles to the *Western Citizen* after having published in Lundy's *Genius of Universal Emancipation*. The most famous Liberty newspaperwoman was Jane Grey Swisshelm, who began her journalism career as a writer for the *Spirit of Liberty* in Pittsburgh and became editor of the *Saturday Visitor*, which eventually supported the Free Soil Party and women's rights. Kelley addressed the Liberty Party nominating convention in 1843 after it voted her permission to do so, and Mott received five votes for the presidency at Smith's Liberty Party convention five years later. Women's widespread participation in the politics of abolition, however, did not translate into a formal endorsement of women's suffrage by the party platform. Some Libertyites like Smith, whose daughter Elizabeth Smith Miller designed and first wore bloomers, worked for women's equality.[9]

The Garrisonians emerged as more consistent advocates of women's rights, including the right to vote, than evangelical and political abolitionists. Garrisonian women like Kelley and Mott were organizers and participants in the antebellum women's movement. In Ohio abolitionist admirers of Kelley like Betsey Mix Cowles of the Ashtabula FASS, Jane Elizabeth Hitchcock Jones, and Josephine Griffing orchestrated women's rights state conventions in Salem and Akron. The one-thousand-strong gathering in Worcester, Massachusetts, in 1850 inaugurated the national women's rights conventions that met throughout the decade. It earned greetings from antislavery and feminist writers like Harriet Martineau in Britain, Frederika Bremer in Sweden, and Jeanne Deroin and Pauline Roland, who sent the best wishes of "socialist sisters of France" from their jail cell in Paris. The British feminist Harriet Taylor, the future wife of John Stuart Mill, wrote an influential review of the convention's proceedings, advocating the "Enfranchisement of Women." Stone, who had launched a petition campaign for woman suffrage in 1848–49 in Massachusetts, was the chief organizer of the national conventions. Wendell Phillips, Parker Pillsbury, Stephen Foster, and the Unitarian ministers James Freeman Clarke, Thomas Wentworth Higginson, Theodore Parker, and William H. Channing regularly attended the national and state women's rights conventions of the 1850s, voicing their support. In Massachusetts, Ohio, and New York abolitionist feminists launched petition campaigns to state legislatures and constitutional conventions for woman suffrage, finding allies among Liberty Party members.

Women activists infused fresh blood into the Garrisonian wing of the movement. Some of the most talented agents for the AASS were feminist-abolitionists such as Stone, Susan B. Anthony, and, ironically, Sallie Holley, the daughter of the founder of the Liberty Party, Myron Holley. Garrison opened the pages of the *Liberator* to women's rights advocates like Caroline Dall, Sarah E. Wall, and Elizabeth Oakes Smith. Garrison's critique of the church and clergy, staunch opponents of women's rights, resonated with early feminists. In 1860

Cady Stanton addressed the annual anniversary of the AASS on the invitation of Garrison. She insisted that women's rights were part of the abolitionist cause, which was a "great humanitarian one." In "settling the question of the negro's rights," she continued, in words that would come back to haunt her, "we find the exact limits of our own, for rights never clash or interfere."[10] "Woman rights" was an important, if divisive, component of the politics of abolition.

UNION AND CONSTITUTION

The emergence of political abolitionism forced Garrison and his allies to develop their own stance on politics, often mischaracterized either as an outmoded adherence to moral suasion or as apolitical. Garrisonians developed a politics of agitation that questioned the very foundations of the slaveholding Republic. In 1842, disgusted by the *Prigg* decision, Garrison announced his doctrine of disunion: "A repeal of the Union between northern liberty and southern slavery is essential to the abolition of one, and preservation of the other." For Garrisonians, disunionism was a concerted attack on slaveholders' political power, not a retreat into inaction. He was delighted when Adams's presentation of a disunion petition from Haverhill, Massachusetts, outraged southern members of Congress, some of whom regularly spewed threats of secession. According to Lydia Maria Child, the Union was a sham based on coercion rather than cooperation: it was the "disunited" states of America. The next year Garrison affirmed that he was in earnest about disunion, however much condemnation it evoked, even from abolitionists. In January 1843 the MASS approved the disunion program. By 1844 the official policy of the AASS became "no union with slaveholders" by a vote of fifty-nine to twenty-one, Earle, Loring, and David Lee Child among the dissenters.

Disunionism thinned the ranks of Garrisonians and drew a sharper line between them and political abolitionists. Child resigned as editor of the *NASS*, and Loring resigned from the MASS board of managers. Bradburn switched allegiances to the Liberty Party. Even for the black Garrisonian William Powell, disunion was too "cumbersome" an armor to bear. William I. Bowditch debated Gay on disunion. In 1845 Kelley and Foster established the Western Anti Slavery Society (WASS), and Benjamin and Jane Elizabeth Hitchcock Jones started publishing the *Anti-Slavery Bugle* on the new disunion platform, as many Garrisonians subscribed to Liberty Party newspapers. The OASS supported the Liberty Party, and the Garrisonian Ohio and American AS became the WASS. That year the NEAS convention, to thunderous applause, endorsed disunion overwhelmingly by a vote 250 to 24. Amasa Walker and Hildreth demurred.

Garrisonian disunion was a strategy to end northern complicity in the upholding of slavery. When Burritt expressed reservations at a warlike strategy, Garrison signed his reply, "Yours for the dissolution of every proslavery alliance." The Union, he noted in his "Address to the Friends of Freedom and Emancipation in the United States," was bought "*at the expense of the colored population of the country.*" Garrison expected opposition to so bold and revolutionary a step but argued that in advocating disunion the AASS had taken "the highest possible ground" against slavery. He called for a "peaceful revolution," one which deprived slavery of northern political support, saying, "In ceasing oppression we establish liberty." He said the Union was a "guilty compromise" over slavery and the Constitution, with its three-fifths and fugitive slave clauses and call to put down insurrections, a bulwark of the slaveholding oligarchy that made all American citizens prey on slaves. The next year he pronounced the founding document a "proslavery compact," a "covenant with death, and agreement with hell."[11]

Not known is the fact that Garrison lifted his famous condemnation of the Constitution from Pennington. In 1842, at the height of the Latimer affair (see chapter 12), Pennington delivered a sermon to his Hartford congregation titled "Covenants Involving Moral Wrong are not Obligatory Upon Man," which began with a quotation from the book of Isaiah: "And your Covenant with Death shall be Disannulled, and Your Agreement with Hell Shall not Stand." He argued that "laws and compacts designed to legalize the system of human bondage," like the constitutional obligation to deliver up fugitive slaves, ought to be swept away, as they involved disobedience to God. Pennington invoked the Declaration, the spirit of the Constitution, and divine law against the fugitive slave clause, a higher law, before it became popular with abolitionists and antislavery politicians. Garrison expanded Pennington's biblical condemnation of the fugitive slave clause into an indictment of the Constitution as a whole.[12]

While Garrisonians led the charge on political disunion, ecclesiastical abolitionists led the movement for religious disunion. Their failure to convert their churches to abolition had led to the formation of come outer abolitionist churches, the religious base of the Liberty Party. All abolitionists acted on the principle of "no Christian fellowship with slaveholders." Birney and Weld witnessed the Presbyterian schism of 1837–38 between Old and New Light, whose liberal theology was suspect on slavery. While the old school remained a bastion of proslavery sentiment, southern Presbyterians seceded from the new school twenty years later when it renewed a condemnation of slavery from 1818 under pressure from abolitionist Free Presbyterians. The first philippic against the church came from Birney's *The American Churches: The Bulwarks of American*

Slavery, published in England in 1841. It was an exposé of the actions and words of the major Christian denominations in the United States—the Presbyterian, Methodist, Baptist, and Episcopal Churches—on slavery and the unapologetically proslavery views of southern clergymen. He noted Presbyterian elders' involvement in the whipping of Amos Dresser and Bishop Onderdonk's persecution of black Episcopalians. That year Thomas Clarkson issued his reprimand of proslavery American clergymen and slaveholders. Goodell advocated secession from corrupt, proslavery churches in his pamphlet on "come-outerism," and Phillips endorsed it on behalf of the AASS despite political differences.

Anticlerical Garrisonians like Foster and Pillsbury liked Birney's formulation so much that they constantly quoted his phrase "bulwark of slavery." Foster, who had been imprisoned for debt, and Pillsbury, who had his license to preach revoked by the Congregational Church, were men of humble origins. In 1844 Foster published *The Brotherhood of Thieves*, which indicted the church, slavery, and anti-abolition mobs as the "queer trinity." Foster saw American clergymen as being guilty of crimes that would "disgrace an Algerine pirate." They upheld the violence, murder, and robbery that defined slavery, and were "watch-dogs" of southern plantations. Foster and Pillsbury were known to disrupt worship, many times being physically removed from churches.

The agitation of abolitionist clergymen and the Garrisonians' unrelenting criticism of the church made slavery a bone of contention among Methodists and Baptists. In a postscript to his pamphlet, Birney noted that abolitionists were "earnestly laboring to purify them [the churches] from the defilements of slavery." Abolitionist Methodists such as Orange Scott, LeRoy Sunderland, Luther Lee, and George Storrs founded the American Wesleyan Anti-Slavery Society in 1840 and established the Wesleyan Methodist Connection in 1843, their titles invoking the antislavery opinions of John Wesley. Abolitionist Baptists such as Elon Galusha, Nathaniel Colver, Charles Denison, and Cyrus P. Grosvenor organized an American Baptist Anti-Slavery Society in 1840 and the American Baptist Free Mission Society in 1843. The following year the Methodist general conference voted to suspend a slaveholding Georgian bishop, leading to the secession of the southern delegates and the formation of Methodist Episcopal Church, South, in 1845. The same year southern Baptists seceded over the issue of excluding slaveholding missionaries forming the Southern Baptist Convention.

Not just abolitionists but also conservative antislavery men like the Baptist minister and president of Brown University Rev. Francis Wayland debated the proslavery Baptist minister Richard Fuller of South Carolina, questioning the morality of slavery in his book on moral science. Many of the ideas antislavery and proslavery clergymen used in their religious fight over slavery borrowed from the political and constitutional discourses of federalism, states' rights, and disunion. Southern ministers evoked the Calhounian doctrine of state sovereignty to legitimize their secession. During the secession crisis, most southern clergymen were vocal proponents of disunion.[13] The sectional division of the two major evangelical denominations in 1844–45 over slaveholding foreshadowed political disunion.

Even after the breakup, abolitionists pushed their churches to take a more overt antislavery position. In 1846 Jay wrote the introduction to a book by Wilberforce's son, Bishop Samuel Wilberforce of the Anglican Church, that criticized the failure of American Episcopalianism to address the issue of slavery. Jay called the Episcopal Church a "mighty buttress" of slavery and excoriated its discriminatory attitude in the North, retelling the story of Onderdonk's persecution of "colored clergymen and colored Christians." In a public letter to Bishop L. Silliman Ives of North Carolina he defended Wilberforce's "reproof" of the American church, challenging southern claims on the religious instruction of slaves and using the testimony of its greatest proponent, Rev. Charles Colcock Jones, on slaves' dissatisfaction with proslavery doctrine.

The next year Pillsbury renewed the Garrisonian critique of the church, calling it the "forlorn hope of slavery," building on Birney's and Foster's arguments. Pillsbury's book read like a declension narrative, with the initial antislavery leanings of the various denominations corrupted by their consistently proslavery actions. He drew attention to the persecution of abolitionist clergymen like the anti-Garrisonian Galusha. Humanity, Pillsbury wrote, had grown tired of slavery's horrors, but the "religious sanction" of the church prevented its abolition. Garrison viewed come outerism as the second reformation of the church, and he linked his no union with slaveholders' stance to "no fellowship with pro-slavery ministers or churches."[14]

Political and religious abolitionist disunionism grew hand in hand. The AMA employed the abolitionist Kentucky clergyman and founder of the interracial Berea College, Rev. John G. Fee, after he was read out by his state's New School Presbyterian synod. Fee's conversion to abolition began with a long, disheartening struggle with his father over the freedom of a slave woman, Julett Miles, who died in prison for attempting to "steal" her children and grandchildren from slavery. Fee was educated at Lane Seminary until his father summoned him home and threatened to send him to Princeton, a bastion of proslavery theology. In 1849 Fee summarized the religious abolitionist argument in his *Non-Fellowship with Slaveholders the Duty of Christians*, which was first published as a series of articles in the newspaper of Cassius Clay, an antislavery politician

and Henry Clay's nephew, and then in the national organ of political abolitionism, Bailey's *National Era*. Foster linked his denunciation of the clergy with
that of politicians, calling Tyler a thief, his cabinet, congressmen, and Supreme
Court justices, negro thieves, and the American state, like the church, a "brotherhood of thieves." Pillsbury drew attention to the approval of most American
ministers to annex Texas and aggrandize territory from Mexico, and abolitionist
clergymen met in opposition to the Mexican War. Rankin, Goodell, Tappan,
Fee, and the slaveholding South Carolinian convert to abolition Rev. William
H. Brisbane attended the Christian Anti Slavery Convention in 1850.

Increasingly, ecclesiastical abolitionists trained their fire on proslavery ministers, with Fee producing the most influential scriptural arguments against slavery since Weld and Goodell, rather than on the Garrisonians, with whom they
seemed to have found some common ground. Jay issued an appeal on behalf of
the AFASS to the "Anti-slavery Christians of the United States" to unite against
slavery. It was signed by a number of northern clergymen. In 1854 he published
An Examination of the Mosaic Laws of Servitude to refute the argument that the
Old Testament sanctioned slavery. Rev. William Patton argued that while proslavery ministers accused the Garrisonians of religious infidelity, it was they who
brought disrepute to Christianity. Brisbane assured Garrison he would not rank
him as an infidel even though he differed from him in regard to their religious
opinions. By the 1850s the AASS had endorsed the Church ASS, and a reconciliation of sorts took place between Christian and Garrisonian abolitionists.
Garrison, who had been critical of abolitionist clergymen like George Cheever
because of their support of capital punishment, published their writings. In
his magnum opus *Slavery and Anti-Slavery*, Goodell compared Garrison to the
Hebrew prophets of old for his denunciations of a "priesthood that strikes hand
with oppressors" and northern "servility" to the Union, even though he thought
that the Union and Constitution "rightly construed" would lead to abolition.[15]

Political abolitionists shifted the sectional argument over slavery from the
Bible to the Constitution, also a sacred text for most Americans and part of their
civil religion. Alvan Stewart, in "A Constitutional Argument on the Subject of
Slavery," pronounced slavery unconstitutional on the basis of the Fifth Amendment, which stipulated that no person could be deprived of life, liberty, and
property without due process of law. Stewart's legal argument grew out of his
abolitionist conviction that African Americans were citizens under the Constitution and entitled to all its protections. Jay, Birney, Leavitt, Wright, and Bailey
rejected Stewart's claim that the federal government could abolish slavery in
order to fulfill the constitutional guarantee of republican government in the
southern states and in accordance with the general welfare. Until his death

in 1849 Stewart rejected antislavery moderation, and his constitutional views inspired radical political abolitionists such as Smith and Goodell. Even Garrison recommended G. W. F. Mellen's work of 1841 on the unconstitutionality of slavery as required reading for all abolitionists. Mellen was aware that Stewart had preceded him in arguing that under the Constitution neither the states nor Congress could establish slavery. Mellen's four-hundred-page book concluded that if the country's "courts decide that the descendants of Africa are to be thrown out of all government protection," then it would be better for "these United States to be broken up at once. . . . We saw no object in their Union." At the MASS meeting that year, Mellen reiterated that slavery was impossible under the Constitution.[16]

Garrisonians' and political abolitionists' stances on the nature of the Constitution hardened in response to each other. In 1844 Phillips, a lawyer by training, presented the full-blown Garrisonian argument in *The Constitution a Pro-Slavery Compact*. He went beyond the specific constitutional clauses dealing with slavery. He mined Madison's notes on the Constitutional Convention debates of 1787, which were published in 1840, to prove the intent of the founding fathers to protect slavery. Phillips concluded that the Constitution was an infamous bargain that proved "the melancholy fact" that "our fathers bartered honesty for gain, and became partners with tyrants, that they might profit from their tyranny," a radical critique of the sacrosanct reputation of the founders. He conceded that the Constitution had been put to proslavery use, but the Constitution in its original form, "as is," was also proslavery.

In a public letter to Whittier, Smith had called the Constitution "a noble and beautiful temple of liberty" based on the defense of human rights that had been perverted to proslavery ends. Even the three-fifths clause, he pointed out, could not prevent a northern white majority from voting in an antislavery government. In a response, Phillips asked how Smith could explain away the three-fifths clause as proliberty. A year later in *Can Abolitionists Vote or Take Office under the United States Constitution?* Phillips argued that the AASS's opposition to a proslavery government and laws should not be mistaken as endorsing a "no government" or nonresistant position. It had simply judged all institutions, no matter how venerable, by the "touchstone of anti-slavery principle" and found them wanting. The AASS published an expanded version of Phillips's pamphlet with an endorsement from its executive committee. It went through three editions, meriting a response from political abolitionists.

Goodell's *Views of American Constitutional Law in its Bearing upon American Slavery* (1844) and *The Unconstitutionality of Slavery* (1845) by the Massachusetts lawyer Lysander Spooner were the most detailed expositions of the political abolitionist position. Goodell's long treatise began with the deceptively simple premise that the American government and Constitution cannot be viewed as neutral or even partial on the subject of slavery; it must be either completely for or against liberty, as even a slight toleration of slavery endangered all liberty. If it was proslavery, as the Garrisonians argued, then abolitionists would have the option of the "right to revolution" or submission. But he argued that slaveholders' proslavery reading of the Constitution was based on their rejection of democracy, their defense of slavery, and their contempt for the laboring masses, black and white. The Constitution gave the federal government the power to act against slavery in the territories and the District. Going further, he noted that if republicanism is the basis of the Constitution, then even the domestic violence alluded to in the clause on republican governments was against the violence perpetrated in slavery, not slave rebellion. The democratic spirit of the Constitution, with its positive exhortations on liberty and rights, like that of English Common Law, the Declaration, and the New Testament, which also did not include a specific abolitionist injunction, was antislavery. Goodell's was the radical democratic interpretation that privileged ideas over the facts unearthed by Phillips.

Similarly, according to Spooner, all law, especially constitutional law, must be based on principles of natural rights and justice. Making a historical argument, Spooner wrote that slavery was not recognized in either the state constitutions or the Articles of Confederation, and if slavery did not have a "constitutional existence" earlier, it certainly did not under the Constitution, which recognized all people as citizens. The preamble referred to all the people of the United States, not just to whites or free people, as citizens of the country. The only guarantee in the Constitution concerned not slavery, despite the arrogant and bombastic claims of slaveholders, but a republican form of government, which slavery contravened. Spooner concluded that the antislavery nature of the Constitution guaranteed that all the children of slaves were born free and ought to be freed immediately by federal judges. In his review of Spooner's book in 1847, Phillips proceeded to dismantle each one of his historical and constitutional arguments but ended with genuine admiration for their ingenuity. While political abolitionists sought to harness the power of the state for abolition, Garrisonians, far from simply endorsing the proslavery constitutional argument of Calhounites, called for its revolutionary overthrow. Goodell recognized that despite their differences abolitionists shared enough common ground to recommend unity of purpose.[17]

Political abolitionists were more interested in dismantling slaveholders' constitutional claims than in sparring with Garrisonians. As in biblical interpretation, while slaveholders championed a literal and strict construction of the Constitution, they appealed to its liberal spirit. In 1846 the "Constitutional Abolitionist" Benjamin Shaw, in his "Illegality of Slavery," argued that since slavery sanctioned robbery, murder, and "all sorts of villainy" it could not be legal. Like Stewart, Goodell, and Spooner, whose works he recommended, Shaw based his argument on the Declaration and an antislavery reading of the Constitution. Three years later the abolitionist lawyer Joel Tiffany of Ohio declared slaveholders' claim that the Constitution guaranteed slavery absurd and ridiculous, as it went against the principles of the American Revolution. Tiffany contended that the Declaration disallowed slavery in the American Republic. He evoked state power, using the *Prigg* decision, to maintain that if the national government had the power to recapture fugitives, it also had the power to set them free. All people born in the United States, not just whites, the rich, or any such subset of the body politic, were entitled to citizenship. Tiffany insisted that "colored persons" were citizens entitled to the protections of habeas corpus and due process.[18]

Antislavery constitutional theory built on the idea that slavery was the creature of positive law and in contravention to the Constitution but dropped the abolitionist insistence on black citizenship and immediate abolition in the southern states. The person who best developed what he called constitutional antislavery was Chase. Just as he had used Birney's ideas to establish himself as the "attorney general of fugitive slaves," Chase elaborated abolitionist constitutionalism to convince northerners of the constitutional nature of the antislavery enterprise. Conceding ground to the Garrisonians, he argued that the Constitution protected slavery in the southern states but that the founding principles of the country were antislavery. The Constitution gave full powers to and made it the duty of the federal government to act against slavery in areas under its control, namely, the District of Columbia, the territories, the slave trade, and the fugitive slave clause. Chase's notion of the divorce of the federal government from slavery was incorporated into the Liberty Party platform of 1844. His slogan, the "DENATIONALIZATION OF SLAVERY," became the rallying cry of antislavery politicians. Chase argued that "the general government has the power to prohibit slavery everywhere outside of the slave States," and other radical antislavery politicians, like Sumner, popularized it under the slogan "Freedom National, Slavery Local." It was appropriate that this intrepid promoter of antislavery constitutional theory ended his career as the chief justice of the Supreme Court, appointed by Lincoln during Reconstruction and replacing Chief Justice Taney, who personified proslavery constitutionalism.

Chase, who joined the Liberty Party in 1841, became an advocate of broadening its appeal in the North. Maria Weston Chapman noted the emergence of Liberty men who seemed to be shunning the name of abolitionists. From the start, the party had been divided between politically savvy westerners led by Chase and Bailey, whose position was endorsed by a massive Liberty convention in Cincinnati in 1845, and abolitionist easterners like Stewart, Goodell, and Smith, who stressed abolition in the southern states and black rights. Smith suggested that Liberty men bury their differences by advocating a live-and-let-live policy. The western Ohio contingent could continue to stress "the rights and safety of the north," while the eastern wing of the party could advocate the abolition of slavery and black rights. Even in Ohio some abolitionists from the Western Reserve resisted the Cincinnati clique's control of the Liberty Party. Chase's attempt to replace Birney with more nationally known candidates such as Adams or Seward as the party's presidential nominee failed. Birney insisted that only an abolitionist should replace him. Tappan approached Jay as a possible candidate, but he declined.[19] With the rise of the controversy over the expansion of slavery, the Chase acolytes won the day.

FREE SOIL

The resurgence of the slavery expansion issue gave birth to a successful brand of antislavery politics. It all began with the annexation of Texas in 1845, which Calhoun, as Tyler's secretary of state, justified on specifically proslavery and racist grounds in his infamous letters to the British minister in Washington, Richard Pakenham. The plan, first conceived by Calhoun's predecessor Albert P. Upshur, a states' rights Whig from Virginia, infuriated abolitionists, who had led the anti-Texas movement since 1837. That year abolitionists sent 180,000 petitions to Congress against the admission of slaveholding Texas into the Union. The anti-Texas agitation contributed to the repeal of the Gag Rule in 1844. Moderate antislavery men such as Channing opposed annexation in his letter to Clay, the perennial Whig presidential nominee. Garrison noted that American slaveholders had reintroduced slavery into Texas; it had been abolished by the Mexican government, although Mexico implemented the ban indifferently. In Congress, Giddings argued that the annexation of Texas was for the express purpose of perpetuating slavery by opening new markets for the domestic slave trade. A Whig revolt defeated Tyler and Calhoun's attempt to ram through a treaty acquiring Texas in 1844.

Opposition to Texas annexation cost Clay the election. David Lee Child announced that he would vote for Clay, who came out against annexation, rather than Polk, causing much debate among both nonvoting Garrisonians and voting Libertyites. Under pressure from southern Whigs, Clay equivocated, and in the end twelve southern Whigs, including the future Confederate vice president

Alexander Stephens, voted for annexation. The Liberty press was particularly critical of Clay and his antislavery Whig supporters like Seward and Giddings. In New York a group of Barnburner Democrats, increasingly resentful of the southern dominance of their party that had denied Van Buren the Democratic presidential nomination because of his opposition to Texas, was led by his son John Van Buren, Preston King, and Silas Wright. Twenty-seven northern Democrats voted against annexation. The antislavery Democratic editor Theodore Sedgwick III opposed annexation for ensuring *"the perpetuity of slavery."*

But most Democrats fell in line with Sen. Robert J. Walker of Mississippi, writing an influential letter pleading for annexation and citing the old canard that expansion would lead to the diffusion and demise of slavery. The idea of stealth British influence in Texas, assiduously promoted by Calhoun's political manager Duff Green, also appealed to the spread eagle nationalism of "Young America," the country's "manifest destiny to overspread the continent," as the Democratic editor John L. O'Sullivan put it. Their heady brew of territorial and commercial expansion, with its proslavery baggage, won the day. In 1845 Congress annexed Texas by the constitutionally questionable measure of a joint resolution before Polk was inaugurated. To abolitionists and antislavery politicians, this was yet another instance of the federal government acting on behalf of slaveholders, who evoked strict construction only when it suited them.[20]

Abolitionist criticism of proslavery imperialism gave antislavery politicians their wedge issue. As early as 1843 the MASS characterized American policies toward Mexico as "eminently disgraceful." Rep. John P. Hale of New Hampshire first tried to append the "Hale proviso" to Texas annexation to ensure the exclusion of slavery and then opposed annexation as a proslavery plot. Opposed by the state's doughfaces, he was elected to the Senate the following year as an Independent Democrat by a coalition of political abolitionists, Whigs, and antislavery Democrats in a political "Hale storm." The New Hampshire alliance managed even to elect a Libertyite to serve out the senatorial term of Levi Woodbury. Like many pioneering free soilers, Hale ended his political career as a Lincoln appointee, the American minister to Spain. In Massachusetts a group of young so-called Conscience Whigs, among them Sumner, Palfrey, Henry Wilson, and the son of John Quincy Adams, Charles Francis Adams, whose party was already committed to nonexpansion, assumed leadership of the movement against Texas. Wilson, the "Natick cobbler," had been an indentured servant and became vice president in the Grant administration. Palfrey, a Unitarian minister and the former editor of the *North American Review*, had freed his Louisiana slaves. Educated with Phillips at Boston Latin and Harvard Law School, Sumner recalled that the *Liberator* was the first paper he had ever subscribed to and was an admirer of Lydia Maria Child's *Appeal*. Sumner imbibed the legal nationalism of his mentor, Chief Justice Story, and the antislavery ideas of Channing, Giddings, and Adams. His antiwar speech on the Fourth of July in 1845 alarmed conservatives but solicited high praise from abolitionists.

The anti-Texas movement created common antislavery ground among Garrisonians, Libertyites, and antislavery Whigs and Democrats. Abolitionists presided over a monster meeting with antislavery politicians in Faneuil Hall that generated an anti-Texas petition with over sixty-five thousand signatures. Wilson and Whittier carried the petition to Adams, who presented it in Congress. Whittier lobbied northern congressmen, especially the Van Buren Democrats, to vote against Texas. Lewis Tappan supported Stephen Pearl Andrews's scheme of compensated emancipation in Texas by the British government, and Garrison, politicized by the Texas issue, drummed up anti-Texas resolutions and reports in the MASS, the NEASS convention, and AASS. The ninth annual report of the AASS protested Texas annexation as a "scheme of slaveholding aggrandizement" designed to despoil Mexico of her territory. According to abolitionists, Garrison was "our Clarkson" and Adams "our Wilberforce" in the fight against Texas. Abolitionists published the antislavery speeches of Cassius Clay, calling him a "southern prodigy." Clay decried the "Texas treason." Garrison also published Henry Bowditch and Jay's arguments that Texas was part of a slaveholders' plot to perpetually expand slavery as well as Whittier's and Lowell's poems against annexation. Smith noted that antislavery politicians were holding a "looking glass" that abolitionists had been holding for years. Garrison attended all of the political meetings called by the Conscience Whigs, who also invited Clay to Massachusetts.

Whereas Garrison called for disunion on the admission of Texas, Stewart asked northerners to overthrow slavery and Texas through the ballot box. It was during this time, when antislavery became the stuff of politics, that Garrison stopped publishing the *Non Resistant* and parted ways with Nathaniel Rogers, who got into a dispute with his protégé Foster over the NHASS's control of the *Herald of Freedom*. Texas annexation protest meetings coordinated by the Massachusetts Anti-Texas Committee, consisting of Sumner, Wilson, Adams, and Palfrey and abolitionists like Phillips, Samuel May, Theodore Parker, Wright, and Stanton, were held throughout the state. The former Democratic governor Marcus Morton led antislavery Democrats into a political alliance with these men. The legislature condemned the summary expulsion of Judge Samuel Hoar, the state's emissary to South Carolina, to protest the treatment of Massachusetts's free colored seamen. Here was another unconstitutional act perpetrated by the Slave Power, a violation of the equal privileges clause on citizenship, a platform that abolitionists and antislavery politicians could unite on. Wright and Phillips predicted that slaveholders' overreaching would absorb the entire "political power of the north."[21]

This entente cordiale between abolitionists and antislavery politicians, or "A CORDIAL UNION OF EFFORTS," as Garrison called it, was strengthened during the Mexican War, when opposition to slavery expansionism united the antislavery wings of both parties with the Liberty Party. Antiwar sentiment gave a boost to the peace movement, which counted many abolitionists in its ranks. Garrison openly sympathized with "injured" Mexicans. Birney recommended the abolition of the army and navy, and Smith referred to all wars as "brutal, barbarous, and unnecessary." Richard Webb saw no difference between the imperialist wars of England in Asia and the robbery of Mexico by the United States. Abolitionists and antislavery politicians alike viewed the war started in 1846 under Polk, a Democratic slaveholding expansionist from Tennessee, as a land grab for slavery and a direct result of the disputed boundaries of Texas.

Barnburner Democrats, smarting under snubs from the Polk administration on patronage and its failure to pursue northern claims in Oregon against the British with the same vigor as American claims in the southwest, led a northern revolt within the party of Jackson. The result was the introduction of the Wilmot Proviso in Congress, named after Rep. David Wilmot of Pennsylvania, who first introduced it, and framed deliberately in the language of the Northwest Ordinance by Jacob Brinkerhoff of Ohio. Barring slavery in territories to be acquired from Mexico, it was attached to Polk's war appropriations bill. Reintroduced the next year by Preston King of New York, who widened its purview to include all future territories to be acquired by the United States, the proviso divided Congress along sectional lines, most northerners voting for it and virtually all southerners against it regardless of party affiliations. Giddings wrote to Smith that it made "slaveholders rave" and northern "doughfaces turn pale." Tappan noted the spread of antislavery sentiment in the North as a result of the war. Adams, who led the Whig opposition to it, gave his blessings to the proviso. He and Giddings had manned the congressional battle against slavery for years, as Adams wrote in his ode to Giddings: "Be ours the blessings to restore, / Our country's and the *rights of men*." Adams died at his post in the House two years later. Despite his reservations about Garrisonian disunion and the "peculiar views" of abolitionists, Giddings admired the "friends of humanity," of "the oppressed," and of "the slave," as he variously called them. He wrote to Gay that he was eager to meet Garrison and Phillips, and in 1847 he would get a chance to debate Garrison on disunion during Garrison's western tour. His daughter Maria was a Garrisonian abolitionist.

Whig stalwarts such as Clay, Thomas Corwin of Ohio, and a first-term congressman from Illinois, Abraham Lincoln, also opposed the war in Congress. The Democratic Party could agree on expansion but not on slavery. Northern Democrats such as Hannibal Hamlin of Maine, Lincoln's first vice president, and Gideon Welles of Connecticut, his secretary of the navy, opposed the extension of slavery in the southwest, and southern Democrats opposed the restriction of slavery in territories as far north as Oregon. Two exceptions to sectional alignment proved that slavery rather than territorial expansion was the real bone of sectional contention. Whereas Calhoun opposed the Mexican War because it might lead to the incorporation of a mixed race—revealing, according to Garrison, the "true spirit of slaveholding domination" in its "vulgar" regard for "the Caucasian" rather than for the "brotherhood of mankind"—Bailey supported it precisely on those grounds, in that the "dark skinned" Mexicans would undermine the racialist logic of American slavery.[22]

Although it failed to pass the Senate, the proviso became a rallying point for northern antislavery sentiment. Bailey moved to Washington, D.C., and started publishing the *National Era*, bankrolled by Tappan. He now called the war a "plundering [of] a weak neighbor of its territory, for the sake of extending human slavery" and advocated the passage of the proviso, writing that it was the sine qua non of political antislavery. The *National Era* became the largest-selling antislavery newspaper after Greeley's *Tribune* and an organ of the newly formed Free Soil Party, which adopted the proviso, or the nonextension of slavery, as its party platform. A coalition of the Liberty Party, whose presidential candidate, Hale, quickly withdrew from the race, Conscience Whigs, and Barnburner Democrats met at the Free Soil convention in Buffalo in 1848, nominating Martin Van Buren as its presidential and Charles Francis Adams, as its vice presidential candidate. Chase masterminded the party platform, which avowed itself to be in favor of "the rights of Free Labor against the aggressions of the Slave Power, and to secure Free Soil for a Free People." The new party stood for the national platform of freedom against the "sectional platform of slavery" under the twin slogans "No more Slave States and no more Slave Territory" and "Free Soil, Free Labor, Free Speech, and Free Men."

Though leading free soilers had fought for black rights, against the black laws of Ohio, and for voting rights in Wisconsin, Michigan, New York, and Connecticut, the party's antislavery appeal was directed at northern whites. Unlike the Liberty Party, the Free Soil Party did not formally endorse black rights. Douglass and Bibb addressed the Free Soil convention, which many abolitionists, including May, attended, causing some consternation among the Barnburners. The convention jettisoned the constitutionally suspect immediatism and racial egalitarianism of abolition for an antislavery platform that its largest contingent, the Barnburner Democrats led by Benjamin F. Butler of Massachusetts and Van Buren's supporters from New York, could back. Stanton suggested "Liberté, Fraternité, Egalité" as the slogan for the new party, evoking France's revolution of 1848 and its abolition of slavery. The Free Soil convention, he wrote, was a "motley assembly" with "abolitionists of all shades of opinion present"; the Barnburners were the "Girondists" of the coalition and presumably abolitionists, the Jacobins. Free soil was the lowest common denominator of antislavery, designed to appeal to the widest constituency.

The construction of an antislavery ideology that could appeal to states' rights Democrats by leaving southern slavery alone and to statist Whigs by demanding federal action against slavery in the territories and thereby unite all antislavery northerners was a free soil achievement. Giddings undertook a triumphant lecturing tour of Massachusetts feted by abolitionists. The state's Conscience Whigs followed him into the new party. Stanton, Chase, Bailey, and Leavitt led a majority of the Liberty men into the free soil coalition. According to Quincy, the Liberty Party had committed suicide, but Leavitt answered that it was not dead but "translated" into the Free Soil Party. Most Libertyites like Owen Lovejoy made the journey from abolitionism to free soilism. The alliance with the chastened Barnburners fell apart when most of them rejoined the Democratic Party after tipping New York into the Whig column and electing Zachary Taylor, a Louisiana slaveholder and war hero, to the presidency and the native son Millard Fillmore to the vice presidency. Antislavery Whigs like Seward, Lincoln's future secretary of state, Thaddeus Stevens, and Lincoln and antislavery Democrats like Hamlin, who, along with the free soilers Wilmot, King, and Brinkerhoff, was part of the group that had engineered the proviso, stayed with their parties. The Free Soil Party lost the presidential election of 1848, but its vote count was more than double that of the Liberty total in 1844. Unlike Giddings, Benjamin Wade also remained a Whig, though his brother Edward was a Liberty man and a free soiler. Bailey and Smith, who disagreed on free soilism, agreed that men like Greeley were one of the "wicked Whigs" who professed antislavery principles but ended up supporting their regular party ticket. Tappan's die-hard Democratic brother, Benjamin Tappan of Ohio, who had voted for the annexation of Texas, like most Van Burenites joined the Free Soil Party.

Despite its electoral defeat, the Free Soil coalition played a role in making antislavery a favored political principle in the North, as party regulars hurried to co-opt its platform. Sectional divisions delayed the organization of the House and election of a Speaker. Led by Giddings and Palfrey, antislavery Whigs refused to vote for the cotton Whig Robert Winthrop, who did not support the proviso. In 1848 the Treaty of Guadalupe Hidalgo, which ended the Mexican War, nearly doubled the size of the country by ceding a vast amount of Mexican territory and intensified the sectional battle over the territories. Both free soilers and slaveholders had long realized that their future status as slave or free states would determine the future of slavery, whether it would exist in perpetuity or be put on the road to extinction. Fifteen northern states and Delaware had endorsed the proviso, and ten southern states had repudiated it. The Free Soil Party elected a handful of staunch antislavery men like Giddings and the newcomer George Julian of Indiana, Giddings's future son-in-law, to Congress and, in coalition with Democrats, sent Chase to the Senate, where he joined Hale.

Bailey's home became the new antislavery headquarters in the capital, his Saturday night soirees a meeting point for abolitionists and their political allies. His newspaper kept the flag of the Free Soil remnant, the Free Democracy, flying long after the passage of the Compromise of 1850, which dealt a deathblow to both the Free Soil and Whig Parties. In 1852 Free Democrats nominated Hale for the presidency and Julian for the vice presidency on an abolitionist platform that repudiated the congressional compromise and the new Fugitive Slave Act, passed in 1850, calling slavery "a sin against God and a crime against man, which no human enactment nor usage can make right. . . . Christianity, humanity, and patriotism, alike demand its abolition." It called for the recognition of Haiti and justified the right of revolution. The convention elected Frederick Douglass as a secretary. Garrison viewed the Free Democracy as "an encouraging sign of the times" but argued that no union with slaveholders was the higher and truer position. The Free Democrats won just 5 percent of the vote in contrast to the 10 percent gained by free soilers in 1848, revealing that free soilism, not abolition, mobilized northern voters. The sectional compromise eclipsed political antislavery until the Kansas–Nebraska Act in 1854 reopened the question of slavery expansion.[23]

The simultaneous broadening and dilution of abolition into a northern antislavery party divided abolitionists. When the Liberty Party nominated Hale as its presidential candidate in 1847, Goodell and Smith formed the Liberty League, the "politico-religious" wing of the party, at Macedon Lock, New York. It stood on abolitionist ground, the abolition of southern slavery by the federal government, and for their brand of universal reform: abolition of all monopolies and debt, direct taxation instead of tariffs, land for the landless, and religious freedom. Ward joined them. Goodell complained that while the "one idea" Liberty men had objected to mixing abolition with other reforms, they had abandoned abolition for free soil. Green called the Free Soil Party a "poor concern." Garrison argued that Libertyites who advocated the constitutional abolition of slavery were actually close to his disunion position because if they implemented their program it would blow the Union "sky high." The Liberty League ran Smith for the presidency in 1848. In 1852 he was elected to Congress in coalition with free soilers. Garrison hailed Smith's election. With abolitionists in Congress, Gates wrote, Birney need not despair of the Republic.

Birney had suffered from a debilitating stroke in 1845 and had retired from active politics. In a series of articles for the *Albany Patriot* in 1847 he insisted that Congress had the power to abolish slavery not just in areas under federal jurisdiction but also in the southern states. Refuting Chase and Bailey's states' rights concession that the federal government did not possess the power to abolish southern slavery, Birney argued that Congress "should emancipate" under its war powers or to secure "domestic tranquility" and the "general welfare." If Calhoun and his followers argued that the Constitution carried slavery with it everywhere, in Birney's reading the Constitution, established to secure natural rights and justice, carried abolition. All who opposed this idea, Birney concluded, valued the "wrongs of the oppressor more than the rights of the oppressed." When Tappan's AFASS endorsed Hale as the Liberty Party's presidential candidate, Birney resigned, asserting that he could not abide by Hale's "low and false grounds" in supporting the restriction rather than abolition of slavery. Tappan had joined Chase and Bailey in developing a broad antislavery platform but balked at supporting Van Buren. He and Birney voted for Smith in 1848. Four years later Goodell headed the Liberty ticket, but for all intents and purposes the party was dead. Its political descendant was Smith's Radical Political Abolition Party, whose organ, the *Radical Abolitionist*, was edited by Goodell.

Disillusioned, Birney, in a letter to African Americans appended to his pamphlet on the Supreme Court decision of 1850 *Strader, Gorman and Armstrong v. Graham*, recommended emigration. The decision, which challenged the freedom principle in the North by holding that any slave who voluntarily returned to a slave state could not sue for his freedom based on residence in a free state, along with the new fugitive slave law weighed heavily on Birney, and he saw no prospects for black rights. At the same time, Birney remained critical of the ACS and argued that emancipation should not be made dependent on colonization. Sidelined from the abolition movement, he moved to Raritan Bay, where the Welds resided, and died there in 1857.[24]

Ironically, the political abolitionists who did not make the transition to free soilism were far more critical of it than Garrison, whose constitutional position aligned with free soilers' belief that the Constitution protected southern slavery. Unlike the Fosters and Pillsbury, who were suspicious of all politicians,

Garrison commended free soilism as a political advance but insisted that abolitionists must continue to agitate against slavery and for black rights. Garrison was especially fulsome in his praise of the Massachusetts abolitionist-minded free soilers, Sumner, Wilson, and Palfrey, for standing up to slaveholders' abuse. These men and Giddings, who had introduced a bill to abolish slavery in the District of Columbia that allowed free black men to vote on it, Garrison argued, set the "liberty ball . . . rolling." If the Van Burens and the Adamses could combine, the North was finally aroused, as was the South, Garrison noted. He reprinted Calhoun's address to southern members of Congress asking them to unite on slavery.

Quincy praised the rise of antislavery, a result, he observed, of abolitionists' labors, as earlier the nation had only a "slavery party." But he complained that many of "our old coadjutors" were joining the free soilers. Pillsbury noted with alarm that most abolitionists voted for the Free Soil Party and were abandoning the movement that inspired it. The Free Soil Party was not revolutionary, Garrison argued, until it forthrightly attacked slavery rather than its extension and supported black rights. It fell far short of the AASS standard, and abolitionists must still arouse the "conscience of the north." The AFASS also clarified that nonextension was not the same as abolition. Some political abolitionists, like Bradburn, who thought the Liberty League conventions were "within gunshot" of his own antislavery politics, agreed: "What is to be the end of Free Soilism? Shall we not have to content ourselves with or be, at least, resigned to getting one thing done at a time?" But Giddings pointed out that antislavery politicians like himself "regarded the high position and the labors of the American Anti Slavery Society as indispensable to the growth and efficacy of Free Soil, and all similar operations." Free soilism was not abolition, as its policy of forming a cordon sanitaire of freedom to strangle slavery to death was too gradual, and its failure to formally endorse black citizenship marked a red line between it and abolition. Garrison maintained that free soilism was derivative of abolition, a small step in the right direction. McKim, Phillips, and Pillsbury were critical of its watered-down antislavery.[25]

Free soil sentiment among Democrats and in the border slave states could be anti-abolitionist and antiblack. Thomas Hart Benton, the old Jacksonian Democrat from Missouri, was a convert. In West Virginia, Rev. Henry Ruffner, the president of Washington College, advocated both majority rule for the state's nonslaveholding white population, chafing under unequal representation, and gradual emancipation in a pamphlet of 1847. Employing anti-abolitionist rhetoric, Ruffner blamed the "meddlesome sect of abolitionists" for the failure of emancipation in the border states. He also denounced northern free soilers for threatening the bonds of union between slave and free states. Ruffner's critique of slavery was mainly economic, decrying its retarding effects on agriculture, manufacturing, public education, and white labor. He recommended laws to prohibit the importation of slaves to Virginia and encourage their "export" and post nati emancipation and to make slaveholders responsible for educating and colonizing their former slaves. His racialist antislavery ideas preceded those of the famous Hinton Rowan Helper in the 1850s.

The abolitionist Fee joined the free soiler Cassius Clay and antislavery colonizationists like Breckinridge and Henry Clay in a coalition to put gradual emancipation on the agenda in Kentucky's constitutional convention of 1849. To Fee, this was a continuation of the abolitionist legacy of David Rice. Cassius Clay started publishing the antislavery *True American* in 1845, until a proslavery mob shipped his press off to Cincinnati. A critic of Texas annexation, Clay had established a national reputation by giving antislavery speeches in Boston and New York. He expounded an economic, free labor critique of slavery, arguing that Kentucky would become *"the garden of the world"* without slavery. Despite participating in the Mexican War, for which abolitionists roundly criticized him, he was an advocate of free soil whose antislavery surpassed that of his slaveholding, colonizationist uncle. With financial help from Chase, Tappan, and Smith, Clay started publishing the *Louisville Examiner* and led an emancipationist movement in Kentucky. Despite a cholera epidemic that dampened voter turnout in antislavery urban areas, the emancipationists garnered around 35 percent of the vote to the state convention, higher than the national free soil vote count. But Kentucky ended up with a far more proslavery constitution after this defeat. Clay supported Taylor in the elections in 1848 but joined the Free Soil Party soon after. By 1852 both Fee, who established an antislavery colony and school in Berea, and Clay actively campaigned for the Free Democratic ticket, hosting its vice presidential candidate Julian on a lecture tour. The abolitionists Lucretia and James Mott also undertook a lecturing tour of the state. The pitiful strength of abolition in Kentucky was demonstrated by the 266 votes the Free Democrats won in the elections of 1852. Clay eventually joined the Republican Party and was appointed the American minister to Russia by Lincoln, and Fee allied with Smith's radical political abolitionists, for which he was forced to leave the state. He returned during the war to teach black Union soldiers and their families at Camp Nelson and at Berea College, a noteworthy experiment in interracial higher education. In the postwar years, he continued his abolitionist crusade against racial caste.[26]

The growing cultural appeal of antislavery matched slavery's national political spread. Henry Wadsworth Longfellow, one of the era's most beloved poets and a close friend of Sumner, published his *Poems on Slavery* in 1842. Though not critically acclaimed, the slim anthology of verses depicting slaves longing for liberty was welcomed by abolitionists. His "The Slave in the Dismal Swamp" evoked the image of the runaway slave, "the hunted negro." During the Mexican War, Walt Whitman lost his position as the editor of the Democratic *Brooklyn Eagle* when he became a free soiler. He attended the Free Soil convention in 1848 and briefly edited the *Daily Freeman*, writing political poems excoriating northern doughfaces and lauding the European revolutions. The abolitionist Whig poet James Russell Lowell in Boston published the satirical *The Biglow Papers* (1848), which, appearing first as a series in the *Boston Courier* in 1846, were against war and northern servility to the slave South. When Lowell joined the NASS staff, Douglass called his addition a most "fortunate one for the paper and the cause which it advocates." There were a few exceptions, the most prominent being Nathaniel Hawthorne, who shared the doughface politics of his friend Franklin Pierce, writing his campaign biography for the presidential election of 1852. Hawthorne had a decidedly jaundiced view of abolition and utopianism after his experience at Brook Farm, which he lampooned in *The Blithedale Romance.*[27]

The American romanticist movement, Transcendentalism, gave abolition its most acclaimed cultural figures. Transcendentalists' emphasis on spiritual universalism borrowed from German idealism and Hindu philosophy, and quintessential American notions of individual self-reliance and nature lent themselves to antislavery critique and inspired a literary renaissance. Transcendentalism led not to an anti-institutional individualism but to political engagement. Leading Transcendentalist thinkers such as Ralph Waldo Emerson, Margaret Fuller, and Henry David Thoreau became fellow travelers of abolition during the slavery expansion controversy in the 1840s, while others, like the radical Unitarian ministers Theodore Parker, Thomas Wentworth Higginson, William Henry Channing, William F. Channing, William Furness, James Freeman Clarke, and the Virginian Moncure Conway, were converts to abolition. Some, like William H. Channing, also espoused socialism, and most were critical of the soul-destroying materialism and inequality bred by early capitalism. The Transcendentalist Caroline Healey Dall was a regular contributor to the *Liberator* on women's rights.

Emerson, the country's most famous essayist and the founder of the Transcendental Club, shared his mentor William Ellery Channing's initial distaste for organized abolition despite the fact that his wife and brother were abolitionists. During the late 1830s, however, Emerson signed abolitionist petitions against the annexation of Texas, and Garrison praised his public letter to President Van Buren against Cherokee removal. At the height of the Texas controversy, Emerson became allied with the abolition movement, delivering the First of August oration at the annual MASS celebrations three times and calling emancipation a "moral revolution." In his speech in 1845 Emerson rejected the proslavery argument on the racial inferiority of Africans and instead drew attention to the barbarous nature of American slaveholders. With the start of the Mexican War, Emerson lent the prestige of his name to abolition, supporting the rescue of fugitive slaves and, together with Sumner, refusing to lecture before the racially segregated New Bedford Lyceum. Scholars have challenged the long-circulating myth that Emerson blackballed Douglass from his Town and Country Club, whose librarian was William Cooper Nell. Nell, a forgotten black Transcendentalist, was the founder of the Adelphic Union of the "most enterprising young men of color," which hosted lectures by leading Transcendentalists, including Emerson, abolitionists like Garrison, and antislavery politicians like Hale and Sumner. Thoreau, whose female family members also preceded him to abolition, famously protested against the Mexican War, the rendition of fugitive slaves, and the treatment of Native Americans by the government and refused to pay his poll taxes, for which he was briefly imprisoned. His famous lecture of 1848, "Resistance to Civil Government," published the following year, founded a tradition of civil disobedience that influenced Mahatma Gandhi, who in turn inspired Martin Luther King Jr. and Nelson Mandela.

More than Emerson and Thoreau, Parker, who had been taught by Palfrey at Harvard Divinity School and was known for his religious iconoclasm, became the face of transcendental abolitionism. Parker, like Emerson, defied the religious and political conservatism of Harvard Unitarianism. He shared Garrison's anticlericalism and biblical skepticism, attending his anti-Sabbath conventions. He also made his abolition debut at the MASS West India Day celebration in 1845. A couple of years later Parker issued his abolitionist letter on slavery to the American people. He became a regular speaker at AASS meetings and at his church, the Melodeon, a site for abolitionist meetings. One hundred and seventy Unitarian ministers had signed an antislavery protest composed by Clarke opposing Texas annexation. As early as 1842 Clarke delivered a sermon on the evils of slavery and two years later one against the annexation of Texas. In 1848 Parker and Clarke started publishing the *Massachusetts Quarterly Review*, hailed by abolitionists. Parker became known for his blistering sermons against the war, which he called "national infidelity," and supported the Conscience Whigs, delivering a moving eulogy of Adams. Parker, like Higginson, who also entered the abolitionist ranks in the 1840s, harnessed the romantic revolutionary spirit of the times in the slave's cause.[28] Antislavery popularized abolition among the North's leading political and cultural figures.

COMPROMISE

For abolitionists and antislavery men the free soil revolution against slaveholding despots of the New World was akin to the European revolutions of 1848 against Old World tyranny, its overthrow with the Compromise of 1850 similar to their defeat. The stalemate between the free soil movement and southern threats of secession over the future of the Mexican territories was broken by Henry Clay's perennial politics of sectional compromise. Stephen A. Douglas, the Democratic senator from Illinois, expedited the passage of the compromise by dividing Clay's "monster bill" into smaller, palatable parts for each section. The hopes of free soilers died with President Taylor, a slaveholding nationalist open to the idea of restricting the spread of slavery, and the succession of the conservative Fillmore. Clay's compromise, which allowed residents of the territories of New Mexico and Utah to vote slavery up or down, based on the losing Democratic presidential candidate Lewis Cass's "popular sovereignty" formula, was a decisive rejection of the free soil platform. Jay, who in an open letter to the inhabitants of New Mexico and California warned that slaveholders would not allow them the right of self-government without establishing "the dominion of the WHIP," opposed Clay's compromise because it denied the federal government the power to abolish slavery in the territories. Most galling to abolitionists was the passage of a draconian new federal fugitive slave law. In return, the North got the admission of California as a free state, expedited by the gold rush, and the abolition of the slave trade in Washington, D.C., facilitated by the retrocession of Alexandria, where most slave traders operated, to Virginia.

The opposition of the free soil contingent in Congress—Chase, Hale, and Benton in the Senate and nine representatives led by Giddings—failed to overcome Douglas's maneuvering, which involved putting each bill up for a separate vote, with each section, joined by a few defectors, voting for its interests, resulting in an "armistice" rather than a true compromise. Many northerners simply absented themselves or abstained from the vote on the fugitive law, illustrating their political cowardice to abolitionists. To drive home the point, Thaddeus Stevens had a congressional page inform the absent northern congressmen that they could safely enter the chambers as the slavery matter was disposed of. In a public letter to Samuel Eliot of Massachusetts excoriating his vote for the law, Jay argued that the compromise strengthened every provision of the

Constitution designed to protect and perpetuate slavery and decreed that every power for its curtailing remained dormant. Two men came in for special abolitionist criticism, Clay and Daniel Webster, who supported the compromise. Webster claimed that the deserts of the southwest and Mexican abolition would naturally deter the spread of slavery and made the proviso unnecessary. Of the "Great Triumvirate" in the Senate, abolitionists had always detested Clay, the slaveholding colonizationist who had rained abuse on abolitionists, and Calhoun, an unyielding spokesman for slaveholding interests, whose speeches regularly graced the *Liberator*'s "Refuge of Oppression" column. Calhoun now called the admission of California as a free state just cause for southern secession. Bailey distinguished "philanthropic Disunionists," or Garrisonians, from "the demagogues and politicians of the South who are aiming . . . to bring about a dissolution of the Union!"

But it was Webster's betrayal that shocked abolitionists and free soilers, who had underestimated his conservatism and presidential ambitions despite his course during the *Creole* affair. Abolitionists condemned his Seventh of March speech justifying the new fugitive law and calling for five new slave states to be carved out of Texas. While Whittier composed "Ichabod" for the fallen senator from Massachusetts, Parker and Phillips called him an "apostate to humanity." Garrison recommended a petition drive to censure Webster. By 1852 all three men were dead. Seward, who was behind Taylor's plan to admit California and New Mexico as free states, represented the antislavery position. In 1845 he had written to Smith that abolition was "the first, the leading, the paramount question of the day." Seward commanded the respect of abolitionists for his support of black voting rights and opposition to fugitive slave rendition when he was the governor of New York. He was also a political opponent of the conservative Fillmore, a Silver Grey Whig, who championed the compromise. In his famous "higher law" speech opposing the compromise, Seward equated the sectional quarrel over slavery with the fight between reaction and democracy and argued that emancipation represented a democratic revolution against capital. Seward reiterated an abolitionist idea, northerners' right to resist the fugitive slave law based on a higher calling to defend freedom. He called human rights the only "permanent foundations of society." At an abolitionist meeting in Faneuil Hall, Ward noted, Seward, "a Senator of my own State," unlike Webster, deserved "honorable mention." Tappan's AFASS printed ten thousand copies of his speech, and Greeley published it in a special edition of the *Tribune*.[29]

Garrison now distrusted the political world of compromise even more, but the rise of political antislavery facilitated Douglass's conversion to political abolitionism. On his return from England, Douglass had raised enough funds to start an independent newspaper, a venture that Garrison advised against as being risky, given the financial woes of the *Liberator,* and as jeopardizing Douglass's role as the star lecturer of the AASS. Instead, Garrisonians offered Douglass a paid column in the *NASS* and advised him to help Van Rensselaer's new paper, the *Ram's Horn.* On their joint western lecture tour in 1847, Douglass outshone his mentor, and when Garrison fell ill he was forced to carry on alone. Garrison complained about not receiving a letter from Douglass and about the fact that Douglass did not seek his advice on starting his newspaper. But it is a mistake to trace the break between the two to these incidents. Garrison's continued fulsome praise of Douglass in private and in the pages of his newspaper reveals that he was not resentful of Douglass's success or of his attempt to fashion himself as an independent spokesman of abolition. When Douglass moved to Rochester and started publishing the *North Star* in December, Garrison not only wished him well but also frequently reprinted material from his newspaper and solicited subscriptions for it. In his articles on the free soil movement Garrison often quoted Douglass, and both joined forces in dismissing the Bibles-for-slaves campaign launched by evangelical abolitionists. What was the point, they asked, when slaves were forbidden from acquiring literacy, the greater wrong in their eyes. When the *North Star* ran into trouble in 1849, Garrison wrote that his "enterprising and eloquent coadjutor['s]" paper "must continue to twinkle in the Antislavery firmament."

The break came in 1851, when Douglass publicly announced at the annual AASS meeting in Syracuse that he had changed his mind about the Constitution and now agreed with Smith, Goodell, Spooner, et al. that it was an antislavery document. Though not unexpected, given the drift of Douglass's paper, it surprised Garrison, who cried out, "There is roguery somewhere." A couple of months later the *North Star* received a much-needed infusion of funds from Smith and acquired the subscription lists of the *Liberty Party Paper,* with which it merged, and Ward's *Impartial Citizen.* Douglass renamed his paper *Frederick Douglass' Paper* and made it a Liberty Party organ. Garrison undiplomatically made it clear that he did not like either its new name or its politics. Douglass's conversion was not opportunistic but a result of his growing closeness to Smith, whose donations sustained his paper, and to New York's black political abolitionists. He was vice president of the national black convention in 1843 and its president in 1848. His actions were also a well-considered response to the growing potential of political antislavery. Nor did Douglass simply give way to expediency over principle, as he was constantly torn between supporting free soilism, with its promise of antislavery success, and his primary allegiance to Smith and political abolitionism. Garrison could not resist mocking his shifting support for the free soilers and the Liberty Party, claiming his paper represented both sides.

To reduce the Douglass–Garrison breach to a simple matter of race trivializes the serious political differences that developed between the two men. When Ward, also a Liberty man, accused Garrison of racism, Garrison responded that he had no qualms about criticizing a black man, as he did white men. At the next annual AASS meeting in Rochester, Douglass continued as one of the managers of the society, and Smith sent a letter noting that he had more in common with the Garrisonians on abolition, except for voting, than with Tappan's AFASS and the free soilers. Later, a vituperative debate between Douglass and Purvis and Remond also revealed that race was not the fault line in the break. While some black abolitionists split across the New York/Boston–Philadelphia axis, reflecting Garrisonian/anti-Garrisonian strength, others in Detroit and Chicago, except for a Libertyite meeting led by John Jones and one led by George T. Downing in Rhode Island, insisted on praising both men and refused to take sides. Garrisonians like Nell and Wells Brown also supported the Free Soil Party, although Wells Brown and Remond debated Douglass on the Constitution. Garrison was still printing Douglass's speeches and extracts from his paper after 1851 and praised the black convention's address in 1853 written by him as "an admirable document . . . impregnable in its positions."

But the truce did not last. The quarrel developed personal overtones starting with Douglass's criticism of the British abolitionist George Thompson and Richard Webb in defense of Smith and the Liberty Party. It became worse when Douglass accused Foster, Pillsbury, and Henry C. Wright of religious infidelity, a charge Garrison's clerical opponents had long hurled at him. Ironically, just as Garrison started being more generous in his appraisal of abolitionist clergymen after the schisms in the major denominations over slavery, even publishing a complimentary piece on Colver, Douglass revived the old accusation. Douglass also criticized Phillips's supercilious questioning of his presence at the MASS West India Day celebration, implying that Phillips had chosen to criticize him because he had lost his long public debate with Horace Mann over the Constitution and political action. While Garrison came to Phillips's defense, Douglass was clearly taken by Mann's arguments. Douglass also called Nell a "contemptible tool" after Nell, who had helped him start his paper, criticized him, and he alluded to Purvis's "blood-stained riches." Purvis responded in a letter that his white father was a merchant, not a slaveholder. Black Bostonians were suspicious of the free soiler Mann, who, unlike Henry I. Bowditch, had not lifted a finger to help them in their battle against school segregation when he was on the city's school committee. In the fall of 1853 Garrison began

publishing Douglass's attacks against "our white and colored friends" in his
"Refuge of Oppression." The wrath of the entire Garrisonian press, the NASS,
the *Pennsylvania Freeman,* and the *Anti-Slavery Bugle,* descended on Douglass,
who was forced to write a lengthy rebuttal. Garrison disowned Douglass, writing
that his "hostility to the American Anti-Slavery Society and its leading advocates
is unmitigated and unceasing." The two men stopped speaking to each other.

Garrison also did not take the high road, blaming the British abolitionist
Julia Griffiths, Douglass's editorial assistant, who worked hard to keep his paper
afloat, for causing unhappiness in Douglass's home. Abby Kelley Foster was
convinced that Griffiths exercised a pernicious influence on Douglass, as she
was allied with the evangelical wing of British abolitionists. A letter from Anna
Douglass, probably written by Douglass and Griffiths, put to rest any suggestion
of impropriety. In fact, Anna ordered Griffiths out of her home. Douglass, who
had until then been respectful of Garrison, was outraged that he had "seen fit
to invade my household" and given credence to scandalous rumors. Things
only got worse, each hitting the other below the belt: Garrison claimed that
fugitive slaves had no special insight into abolition, and Douglass accused him
of racism. Like Griffiths, the radical German journalist Ottilie Assing stayed in
Douglass's home. She referred derogatorily to Anna as an old woman who was
uneducated and ignorant. Assing, suffering from cancer and upon hearing of
Douglass's marriage to his second wife, Helen Pitts, later committed suicide in
Europe, leaving her estate to Douglass. When Douglass married Anna, he was
a slave and she a free woman; now he was an international celebrity and she the
mother of his children, who treated her husband as an "honored guest" in her
home. Their daughter, Rosetta, wrote in a tribute to Anna, who, she recalled,
was active in abolitionist circles in Massachusetts, that her "unswerving loyalty"
had made Douglass's success possible. Only those who knew her "intimately,"
she wrote, could appreciate her "enduring patience" as wife and mother.

By 1855 Douglass was lecturing on the antislavery movement, pointing out
that abolition predated Garrison. But Douglass continued to praise him alongside Smith, noting he would not deprive Garrison of any "honor justly his." As
a political abolitionist, Douglass criticized Garrisonian disunionism as well as
the free soilers. To Douglass belongs the last word on the abolitionist debate
over the Constitution. Like most political abolitionists, Douglass combined a
literal reading of the nation's founding legal document; he stressed that neither
slavery nor slaves were specifically mentioned in it, with the insistence that
constitutional guarantees of citizenship rights included African Americans. But
he went further. Douglass held that the original intent of the founders, many
of whom, he well knew, were slaveholders, was irrelevant. Instead, he treated

the Constitution as a living, breathing document whose democratic promise must be redeemed and extended by subsequent generations. As Douglass put it in 1860 in his speech, which was published as a pamphlet, *The Constitution of the United States: Is it Pro-slavery or Anti-Slavery*, slaveholders had given the Constitution a "proslavery interpretation," but the Constitution "will afford slavery no protection when it shall cease to be administered by slaveholders." By refusing to be held hostage to the intent of the founders, Douglass went well beyond slaveholding apologists like Calhoun, antislavery Republicans, and political abolitionists, all of whom claimed to have the founders on their side. He laid out the path to fundamentally remake the founders' Constitution along abolitionist lines. Slavery was abolished through political action but in the midst of the enormous bloodletting of the Civil War, indeed Garrison's covenant with death.[30]

Douglass's move to political abolitionism was facilitated by the election to Congress of the two men he most admired, Smith and Sumner. Sumner, a "one-idead abolitionist," was elected to the Senate on a fusion Free Soil–Democratic ticket after a drawn-out legislative battle in 1851. The presence of these men in Congress, along with Chase and Giddings, proved to be fortuitous when the next storm over slavery expansion erupted. In 1853 Stephen Douglas proposed a bill organizing Nebraska territory, a part of the Louisiana Purchase, to facilitate the building of a transcontinental railroad. As a price for southern support, the proslavery clique of senators in the F Street mess that included the Virginian James Mason, the author of the new fugitive slave law, and his partner in crime, Sen. Andrew Pickens Butler of South Carolina, proposed the rescinding of the Missouri Compromise line, allowing for the spread of slavery well to its north. Douglas viewed the Compromise of 1850 as taking precedence over the settlement of 1820: "popular sovereignty" in the territories would decide the fate of slavery. Like some other northwestern doughface politicians in the 1850s, he owned a Mississippi plantation and was indifferent to the spread of slavery. The antislavery minority in Congress was up to the challenge. Slavery and the Cotton Kingdom had expanded at such a rate in the antebellum American Republic that the Missouri Compromise line that had once been excoriated by abolitionists now stood as the last line of antislavery defense in the west.

Even before the passage of the Kansas–Nebraska Act of 1854, Chase, with the editorial help of Sumner and Smith, who were no doubt responsible for its abolitionist tone, composed an "Appeal of the Independent Democrats in Congress to the People of the United States." Published first in the *NE* and in a new, moderately antislavery newspaper, the *New York Times*, the appeal succeeded in doing what generations of abolitionists and antislavery politicians had sought,

to portray slavery as an existential threat to American democracy. It drew attention to the scheme to exclude Old World immigrants and northern free labor
from the territories, turning them into a "dreary region of despotism, inhabited
by masters and slaves." It delineated the vast area in the northwest, from the
newly acquired Mexican territories to Canada and from Missouri to the Pacific,
that the bill would affect. Starting with the Northwest Ordinance of 1787, the
Republic had pledged to keep this territory free. It targeted specific northern
antislavery constituencies, namely, the German language press, the working
classes, and Christian ministers. The appeal signed by Chase, Sumner, Giddings, Smith, and Alexander DeWitt of Massachusetts was a classic example of
tried-and-true abolitionist tactics, the ability of a radical minority to change the
course of public debate. Suffused with enough abolitionist logic and rhetoric,
it gained both Garrison's and Douglass's praise. The "atrocious plot" to spread
slavery was one against "EQUAL RIGHTS AND EXACT JUSTICE for all men." It asked
the American people not to become complicit in spreading "Legalized Oppression and Systematized Injustice."

The appeal did not displace concern for black freedom with white liberty;
instead, it warned of the designs of the Slave Power against both black and
white freedom in the Republic. It was an effective distillation of abolitionist
political thought, one that Chase said he was most proud of, and it planted the
seeds of a northern electoral rebellion against slavery. Douglas traveled home
to Chicago by the light of his burning effigies. Northern Democrats, who had
voted for the bill, were consigned to political oblivion. Abolitionist ministers
like Higginson and Parker took up the gauntlet, delivering fiery sermons against
it, and anti-Nebraska meetings spread like a prairie fire across the North. Over
three thousand clergymen in New England, including the longtime opponents of abolition Leonard Bacon and Lyman Beecher, signed a remonstrance
against rescinding the Missouri Compromise. Garrison called the passage of
the Kansas–Nebraska Act a triumph of the proslavery Union. In his speech reported as "Douglas vs. Douglass," Douglass characterized the accusation of his
"namesake" that opponents of the Nebraska bill were more solicitous of black
than of white rights as "mean, wicked and bitter." The appeal proved to be prescient, as the wars in "bleeding Kansas" between free-state and proslavery settlers illustrated. Missouri "border ruffians" who periodically raided the territory
to steal elections made a mockery of white democracy, leading even Douglas to
repudiate his handiwork.[31]

The aggressive nature of proslavery imperialism, or what Garrison called
"Slavery's Foreign Policy," facilitated by the Pierce administration also alarmed
abolitionists. Pierce used the weight of his presidency to give his blessing not
only to Kansas–Nebraska but also to designs to acquire Cuba. As early as 1848,

the Polk administration had tried to purchase Cuba. The Cuban adventurer Narciso López led illegal filibustering expeditions to the island from the United States until he was executed by Spanish authorities in 1851. Cuban annexation would "augment indefinitely the political power of slavery," according to Bailey. Southern Democratic slaveholding planter-politicians such as Pierre Soule of Louisiana and the former governor of Mississippi, the fire-eating secessionist John A. Quitman, were ardent backers of Cuban filibustering. In 1854 Soule, appointed the American minister to Spain, along with the ubiquitous Mason, the American minister in France, and James Buchanan, the northern dough-face minister in Britain, issued the Ostend Manifesto declaring the intent of the U.S. government to acquire Cuba. In Congress, Giddings and Hale led the charge against Cuban annexation, while southern expansionists warned against the "Africanization of Cuba." Coming on the heels of Kansas, Pierce repudiated the Ostend Manifesto, and Soule resigned, which Douglass sarcastically called "Mr. Soule's Flight."

Undeterred, Soule became a champion of the American filibusterer William Walker, whose private army, financed by the northern magnate Cornelius Vanderbilt, conquered Nicaragua the following year and reinstituted slavery there. The real war, Walker, "the gray eyed man of destiny," argued, was not to secure Kansas for slavery but to "re-establish slavery in Central America" and strengthen it through a tropical empire beyond the limits of the Union. Walker's proslavery government was overthrown, and he was executed in 1860, but the Buchanan administration revived the attempt to acquire Cuba. Parker listed Kansas, Cuba, fugitive slave renditions, filibustering, and the movement to reopen the African slave trade as revealing the alarming nature of proslavery imperialism in the 1850s. Douglass pointed to the revival of the African slave trade and filibustering as an illustration of the "Aggressions of the Slave Power." Writing as Ethiop, William J. Wilson warned that slavery gave rise to "every *monstrosity* of the age," fugitive slave laws, "Cuba invasions," and "Haytien subjugation schemes."[32]

The formation of the Republican Party was a direct result of the slavery expansion controversies. Despite competing cultural and political forces—temperance and the Maine prohibition law of 1851, and the nativism embodied in the rise of the Know-Nothing Party in 1854—antislavery came to dominate the northern political landscape, especially after the battle for Kansas escalated into an all-out war on the ground. A fusion of anti-Nebraska Democrats, antislavery Whigs, and free soilers in Michigan and one in Ripon, Wisconsin, adopting the Jeffersonian name Republican, and thirty congressmen in Washington who subsequently took the same name, signaled the rise of the new party. Bailey, a consistent booster of political antislavery, calculated by the end of 1855 fourteen to fifteen Republican or Republican-leaning senators, predicting that by the next year they would have twenty, a substantial advance from the two to three free soil senators before Kansas. On Christmas Day, Sumner, Chase, King, and Bailey met in Francis Blair's Missouri home to put the Republican coalition together, border state free soilism being the farthest removed from abolition.

The Republicans soon challenged the temporary ascendance of Know-Nothings, who swept into power in Massachusetts only to break apart like the traditional parties over slavery. Garrison predicted that nativism was a temporary excitement and indicative of the degraded "moral and mental condition" of northern whites. He saw nativism as linked to racism. Douglass argued that the slave should expect nothing from the nativist party and concluded, "Neither can we, oppressed as we are, consistently and conscientiously proscribe a man because of the accident of foreign birth." Bailey called the Know-Nothings a contemptible anti-Catholic movement that adopted abolitionist causes in Massachusetts and proslavery stances in the South. He was critical of attempts to form fusion tickets with the nativist party, arguing that its only tendency was to defeat Republicans, who sought "to rescue the Federal Government from Slaveholding tyranny." Writing on behalf of the Radical Political Abolition convention at Syracuse, the successor to Smith's Liberty League, Goodell maintained that whereas abolitionists' devotion to human rights made them reject nativism, free soilers made expedient alliances with it. Wilson found a temporary home in the Know-Nothing Party, using its legislative majority to get elected to the Senate and helping to divide the party by insisting on a stronger antislavery position. But Sumner, Seward, and Lincoln repudiated it. Giddings said nativism was "unjust, illiberal and un-American," contrasting it with antislavery, which "rejects all distinctions in political or civil rights, founded on birth, color, or religious creed or connection." Republicans viewed nativism as a competing political force. Mindful of German immigrants, the Republicans absorbed antislavery Know-Nothings but did not adopt the party's nativist platform.[33]

The Republican Party was neither rewarmed Whiggery, nor a resurgence of old Jacksonian Democrats, nor a nativist party; it was a free soil party whose radical vanguard was affiliated with the abolition movement. Douglass could barely contain his excitement at the success of Republicans in the anti-Nebraska elections of 1854. By 1856 Republicans had emerged as the dominant political opponent to the southern-based Democratic Party with a majority in the House of Representatives and a Speaker from its ranks. Its first presidential party platform condemned slavery and polygamy, an allusion to the Mormons, as the "twin relics of barbarism." Its candidate, John Frémont, an explorer and the son-in-law of Benton, gained the support of antislavery men because of his solid free soil credentials in California and Kansas. The so-called pathfinder was a dashing, romantic symbol of western freedom, and his ambitious wife, Jesse Benton Frémont, captured the imagination of free soil women. The Republicans presented a stark contrast to the relentlessly proslavery Democratic Party, which accused the "Black Republicans" of demolishing racial as well as gender hierarchies. Unlike abolitionists, Republicans had little to say about black rights or the dispossession of Native Americans on which their free soil program was predicated.

Abolitionists remained critical yet supportive of the party's first presidential campaign. Garrison, who was committed to nonvoting under a proslavery Constitution, said that he would like to bestow a million votes on Frémont. The "Rabolition" press was for Frémont. May wished for Frémont's election over the two "proslavery" candidates from the Democratic and nativist American Party, Buchanan and Fillmore, respectively. Douglass switched to Frémont after supporting Smith, the Radical Political Abolition candidate. Smith himself donated five hundred dollars to Frémont's campaign. Stanton organized a speaker's bureau for the new party. Greeley's paper and his election pamphlet on the history of slavery extension disseminated free soil ideology throughout the North. Frémont swept the upper north, Michigan, Wisconsin, and New England as well as New York and Ohio, areas that had given both the Liberty and Free Soil Parties their largest vote counts, and he made an impressive showing even in Pennsylvania and New Jersey, where the Democratic Party barely got over 50 percent of the vote. While the one-year-old party performed worse in states where it was disorganized or joined fusion People's Party tickets, it won a plurality of northern votes in an exciting election with an 83 percent voter turnout, high even by antebellum standards. Frémont lost to Buchanan in a "glorious defeat." The electoral math was clear: if the party could win the conservative lower north states, they could win without the slave south.[34]

Despite his criticisms of the Republican Party for its noncommitment to black rights, Garrison conceded that nonextension was antislavery, though not abolition. Radical political abolitionists such as Smith and Douglass, who inhabited the left wing of antislavery politics, and abolitionist free soilers like Sumner, Giddings, Julian, and Stevens made sure that the center of gravity of the new party remained antislavery. When Republicans moved to the right in order to woo moderate northern voters after the elections of 1856, abolitionists perfected their role as critical allies of the party. But abolitionist politics was not confined to an electoral strategy: its revolutionary edge lay revealed in the explosive fugitive slave controversies of the 1850s.

REVOLUTIONARY ABOLITIONISM

Indicted for rescuing the fugitive slave John Price in Ohio in 1859, Charles Langston declared that African Americans had the "right of self preservation," as the laws of the slaveholding republic offered them no protection. In his speech, which elicited the grudging admiration of even his opponents, Langston connected his own condition of rightslessness with the plight of the runaway slave.[1] The passage of the Fugitive Slave Act of 1850 crystallized abolitionists' commitment to direct action. The fugitive slave rebellions during this decade of crisis coalesced slave resistance, a tradition of self-defense among black communities, and revolutionary abolition.

The fugitive slave issue was no sideshow in the sectional conflict over slavery. Radical Republicans and antislavery lawyers, determined to keep the North free soil, lent their political and legal expertise to "freedom seekers" and their defenders. Abolitionist ideas about law, democracy, civil disobedience, and human rights received a national and international hearing.[2] As popular revulsion against fugitive rendition in the North grew with each minibattle, abolition took a revolutionary turn. Long influenced by slave resistance, the fugitive slave controversy dominated the movement on the eve of the war. Confronting slaveholders and their agents in their own backyard prepared abolitionists for a revolutionary, remorseless war against slavery.

KIDNAPPING LAW

The fugitive slave law was the most reviled part of the sectional Compromise of 1850 among abolitionists. *Prigg v. Pennsylvania* had swept aside personal liberty laws but encouraged state-level noncompliance. The new federal law bypassed the laws and practices of the free states and threatened the freedom principle in the North. Passed in response to growing opposition to fugitive slave rendition in the 1840s, it instigated a series of abolitionist rebellions. It bypassed the rule of law by requiring all fugitives to be brought before federal commissioners and flouted due process by disallowing the testimony of suspected fugitives, trial by jury, and habeas corpus. It criminalized any help rendered to suspected fugitives with up to six years' imprisonment and a thousand-dollar fine, encouraged the kidnapping of free blacks, and forced northern citizens to act as slave patrollers by allowing federal marshals to form a posse comitatus of adult armed citizens to apprehend runaways. It added, abolitionists noted, meanness to injustice by awarding federal commissioners a double stipend, ten dollars for a guilty verdict and five for innocence. The excuse given was the extra paperwork involved in rendition. The intrepid antislavery jurist George Stroud calculated that the certificates of rendition cost only sixty cents, at one cent for every ten words, making the ten dollars a bribe for officials.

The law wreaked havoc in northern black communities, and hundreds fled to Canada. Nearly half and sometimes the entire congregations of black churches in Boston and upstate New York fled for safety. More fugitives, nearly three hundred, were rendered back to the South under the new law—some in the border states being summarily kidnapped back into slavery—than were saved by vigilante action, according to Stanley Campbell. A recent study challenges Campbell's conclusion, noting how often he failed to account for attempted and successful rescues. Campbell also mischaracterized a number of kidnappings as renditions. Resistance to the law was greater in the upper north, where free soilism was ascendant. In the 1850s nearly eighty fugitive slave rescues were attempted in the North. Whatever the numbers, the impact of the law and renditions on northern antislavery sentiment is hard to underestimate. William H. Furness, who argued that "through the Fugitive Slave, Christ speaks to us," posed the sectional question. The South, he pointed out, threatened secession unless runaways were rendered back, and, to comply, the North "must forget our fathers . . . disown our Christianity . . . deny our God." "[Let us instead] resolve to be free and make free."[3]

Even before the bill became law, abolitionists issued a call to arms to resist it. In early August, Smith, as president of the New York State Vigilance Committee, and Ray, its secretary, convened a "fugitive slave convention" at Cazenovia. Nearly two thousand men and women met at an apple orchard. The convention, attended by Douglass, Loguen, the Edmonson sisters, and the fiancée of the incarcerated Chaplin, was a good representation of fugitive slave abolitionism, and the document it approved, Smith's "A Letter to the American Slave from those who have fled American Slavery," its most comprehensive statement. Douglass seconded its arguments. Calling slaveholders pirates and abolitionists in the AASS and the Liberty Party "friends and brothers to us," the address, written on behalf of the thousands of fugitive slaves, was suffused with revolutionary rhetoric, assuring slaves that when an insurrection takes place "the great mass of the colored men of the North . . . will be found by your side, with deep-stored and long-accumulated revenge in their hearts, and with death-dealing weapons in their hands." They would not hesitate to "shoot an American slaveholder," for "if the American revolutionists had excuse for shedding one drop of blood, then have the American slaves excuse for making blood flow 'even to the horse bridles.'" The Cazenovia address was a blueprint for radical abolitionist action during the fugitive slave crisis of the 1850s. It was not a cry in the dark, either, as David Yulee of Florida read excerpts from it in the Senate.[4]

The Fugitive Slave Act bolstered the emerging consensus among abolitionists that the use of violence in self-defense by slaves and their allies was justified. The WASS adopted the new slogan of the nonresistant Henry C. Wright: "Death to kidnappers." In a letter to Haughton, he warned that "our homes" would be "baptized" by either "our blood" or that of slave hunters and kidnappers. Wright's overnight conversion to physical resistance to slavery was a telling statement of the law's impact. His evangelical opponent, Nathaniel Colver, active in fugitive slave rescues, agreed. He argued that no constitution or law could allow a fugitive slave rendition from Massachusetts. The most radical statements of opposition came from black abolitionists. A meeting of Boston's colored citizens led by Hayden and Nell and addressed by Garrison, Hilton, John J. Smith as well as Henson, the Crafts, and Milton Clarke, issued a platform of "vigilant action," stating that the law left African Americans with no alternative but to "be prepared in the emergency for self-defense." At a massive meeting held to repudiate the law in Faneuil Hall, Douglass spoke on behalf of, in his words, a suffering, terrified, horror-stricken people. Joshua B. Smith remarked that if liberty was not worth fighting for, it was not worth possessing. William J. Watkins asserted that a slave hunter who assumed "the duties of a bloodhound" should be treated as such. Augustus Washington thought that if the Union could not exist without enslaving free black people, then its dissolution was certain. Remond advocated resisting the law "unto death," and Ward avowed, "Such crises as these leave us to the right Revolution, and if need be, that right we will, at whatever cost, most sacredly maintain." Meetings of colored citizens from Williamsport, Pennsylvania, to a "monster" meeting in New Bedford condemned the law and declared their intent of noncompliance.

Criticism of the unjust law was not confined to the North but emerged also from the abolitionist international in Canada and the West Indies, where fugitive slaves from southern ports, using their wits and at times the assistance of black sailors, had made their way to freedom. The Barbados ASS delivered the "indignant and unqualified reprobation" of the world against the "iniquitous" law, even though its purview was confined to the United States. In Toronto it led to the formation of the Canadian ASS to aid the extinction of slavery everywhere in the world. In Britain, abolitionists condemned the "New Slave Law," arguing that the American Republic "stands degraded" before the world. On their antislavery lecture tours in England, Pennington declared the law a nullity, and Garnet, two-thirds of whose congregation were fugitives, warned that if agents of slaveholders tried to abduct his family, he would not tamely submit.

Resistance and appeals to the law went hand in hand for abolitionists. The MASS reasoned that while the new law implemented the fugitive slave clause of the Constitution, it had disregarded the fundamental constitutional safeguards of trial by jury and habeas corpus and left self-emancipated slaves as well as free blacks vulnerable. The BFASS, with Helen Garrison as vice president, and the PASS also protested the illegalities of the law. The AFASS passed resolutions calling the bill inhumane and an "outrage on civil liberties." William Jay, in a public letter to George T. Downing and William Powell, opined that it illustrated slaveholders' contempt for all law. Sumner pronounced it unconstitutional and referred to it as a bill, refusing to call it a law. Josiah Quincy recalled that the original fugitive law of 1793 was hardly deficient and inspired "universal disgust." He urged northern states to not allow a single rendition without a trial by jury. Garrison complimented Spooner on his "very able" new book on the right of trial by jury.

The law united old adversaries and popularized states' rights theory in the North. By the end of the year Vermont had passed a new personal liberty law guaranteeing the writ of habeas corpus to suspected fugitives. To Bailey, the federal law was an invasion of free states' rights. Whittier proclaimed that he was now a nullifier. When Webster's hometown of Marshfield repudiated the law, Garrison rejoiced that they had disowned him. The *National Era* carried reports of protest meetings from all over the northern states. Jonathan Walker recommended the formation of vigilance committees in every town and village against the "kidnapping bill." Douglass reviled northern submission, especially by conservatives who upheld the "Bloodhound law" over human rights. He contended that it should be made a dead letter by making "two or three dead slaveholders." Abolitionists should make it unsafe for slave catchers and government officials to apprehend runaways.[5]

One of the first cases prosecuted under the new law, the very month it was passed in September 1850, occurred in New York City. Mary Brown of Baltimore obtained the rendition of James Hamlet, a "highly esteemed young man" and member of the AME Zion church. Her agents, including her son and son-in-law, brought the charge, and the federal commissioner Alexander Gardiner ordered Hamlet's arrest. Hamlet was quickly transported to Baltimore to prevent a rescue and jailed, his wife and children unaware of his fate. Douglass reported that the business of "slave catching" had commenced with "this female kidnapper." A mass black meeting in the Zion Chapel presided over by Powell, Downing, Patrick Reason, and Robert Hamilton, among others, protested the law and formed a Committee of Thirteen. In his speech Powell, alluding to Hamlet, fired off a series of questions asking if the black community would submit to the operations of the law and received a thunderous no, no in response. The law was read aloud amid cries of shame. Resolutions submitted by Downing asked fugitives to "arm themselves with the surest and most deadly weapons" and demanded the repeal of the law. After spirited speeches by Rev. Charles Gardner, Junius Morel, and John S. Jacobs, Ray appeared with eight hundred dollars to redeem Hamlet, one black man, Isaac Hollenbeck, contributing a hundred dollars.

On his return four to five thousand citizens greeted Hamlet, who, with tears running down his cheeks, listened as Ray, Hamilton, and Powell spoke. Albro Lyons and Louis Napoleon, active in the abolitionist underground in the city, were elected vice presidents. Albro and his wife, Mary Lyons, took over the Colored Sailors Home, which became known for housing runaways after Powell left for England. Black abolitionists also formed a Committee of Nine in Brooklyn and a Committee of Five in Williamsburg to assist fugitives. In a letter to the meeting, Thaddeus Stevens recommended that fugitives put themselves out of reach of the law. The AFASS published a pamphlet on the Hamlet case that made a wider argument on the unconstitutionality of the fugitive law, delineating the history of its passage, the names and post office addresses of the members of Congress who voted on the bill, and Chase's speech on its unconstitutionality. But Lewis Tappan, its likely author, concluded that "the law leaves the freeman of the North no alternative. HE MUST DISOBEY THE LAW." He recommended against fleeing to Canada, asking fugitives to avoid large cities and public places but to stand unmoved and unawed. Northerners must provide asylum for runaways and act on conscience against the unconstitutional and iniquitous law. Two editions of the pamphlet, thirteen thousand copies, were "disposed of in about three weeks." The AFASS circulated a pledge to disobey the law, which garnered over a thousand signatures.

If the Hamlet case had a happy ending, that of Henry Long, apprehended as a fugitive a year later, did not. Abolitionists like Tappan mobilized quickly to assist him. John Jay II, the son of William Jay, and others represented him. His master's agents received substantial assistance from the city's conservative unionist merchants, who were determined to uphold the law. Long was "dragged out of the city" by Rynders, who swore "vengeance against abolitionists." He was sent back to Richmond, Virginia, and sold to Georgia, where he was arrested for making "abolition speeches" to slaves. Long's lawyers were unable to get a writ of habeas corpus for him. That no attempt was made to rescue him "chilled" Douglass to the bone. "I felt myself degraded," he said. Nothing short of physical resistance by black people, he predicted, could stay the enormities of the law. John Bolding, an escaped slave from South Carolina, was arrested by Marshal Henry Tallmadge and remanded back to slavery, notwithstanding a grieving wife, eloquent appeals from his lawyer, Erastus D. Culver, and testimony by McCune Smith, who in his capacity as a doctor studied his "physiology" and determined that he was of Indian descent. In 1852 the fugitive Horace Preston of Williamsburg was dragged off after a summary hearing in which John Jay II and Culver represented him. Abolitionists raised sufficient money to redeem Bolding and Preston. Another runaway, however, James Trasker, the father of three children, was rendered back to slavery. The New York State Vigilance Committee was successful in two other cases, that of James Snowden and the daughter of a free black man and his enslaved wife. But two years later Pennington's brother Stephen Pembroke and his two sons were captured after being sent to New York by Still. Pennington's church and the "friends of humanity" raised sufficient money to redeem Pembroke, but his sons were sold down south. In all, twelve fugitive slaves were remanded back to slavery from New York, but abolitionists assisted well over a thousand.[6]

While there was talk of initiating a new petition campaign demanding the repeal of the fugitive law, much of the abolitionist opposition to it was on-the-ground resistance. The fiercest contestation occurred in Boston. The law reactivated the BVC, and a new Committee of Vigilance and Safety with over two hundred members was formed in 1850. The abolitionists Hilton, the Bowditches, May, Alcott, the Channings, Elizur Wright, Colver, Hildreth, Garrison, Spooner, Quincy, and antislavery politicians such as Anson Burlingame and John A. Andrew, the Civil War governor of the state, were members. The executive committee, composed of Parker, Phillips, Hayden, Howe, and Joshua B. Smith, the financial committee, consisting of Francis Jackson, its long-standing treasurer, Sewall, Loring, Henry I. Bowditch, Morris, and general agent Nell managed operations. The BVC was a grand coalition of black abolitionists,

Garrisonians, political abolitionists, transcendentalists, and working-class men such as Austin Bearse, the Barnstable seaman known to rescue fugitives at sea in his boat *Moby-Dick*. (Melville's novel was published in 1851.)

The BVC's black members and Bearse, its "doorkeeper," did most of the nitty-gritty work. Bearse's successful fund-raising and Jackson's account book reveal that abolitionists and antislavery societies from all over the state financed its activities. In nearly ten years it assisted over 430 slaves and transported more than 100 to Canada. Besides the Crafts, the BVC spirited unknown fugitives like William Jones, who was also sent to Canada. According to Jackson's account book, it secured clothes, money, work, and a place to reside for runaways. It employed 30 lawyers, and it financed lectures by abolitionists like Douglass at protest meetings. The BVC made frequent disbursements to Hayden, Nell, Smith, Leonard Grimes, Samuel May, Colver, Parker, Bowditch, Bearse; John S. Rock was its doctor on call. Hayden, whose basement at any given time housed dozens of runaways, was always armed. He once kept kegs of gunpowder to blow away slave catchers who trespassed. The BVC paid him for boarding and transporting fugitives and posting handbill warnings about slave catchers. Garrison's printers, J. B. Yerrington and Robert F. Wallcut, received frequent disbursements for postage and printing, and the BVC met often in the *Liberator* office.

As in New York, the city's conservative political and economic elites rallied in opposition to abolitionist defiance. Law-and-order rowdies disrupted an abolition meeting held to honor Thompson as Marshal Francis Tukey, who was notorious for his strict enforcement of the hated law, stood by. At a Union meeting in Faneuil Hall, Benjamin R. Curtis, appointed to the U.S. Supreme Court by Fillmore at Webster's prompting in 1851 and the brother of Commissioner George T. Curtis, likened fugitives to strangers and foreign convicts not entitled to the protection of the law, a claim that William Bowditch hotly contested. The fugitive slave clause, in fact, resembled an extradition treaty. Curtis had published an influential constitutional defense of the law. The Curtis brothers became the nemeses of fugitives and their abolitionist allies in Boston.[7]

The most spectacular rescue was that of Shadrach Minkins, their "doomed brother," by a "crowd of sympathetic colored persons" in 1851. Shadrach, a Virginian runaway, was arrested and hauled to the courthouse after George Curtis issued a warrant on behalf of the slave catcher John Caphart. Caphart was known for his brutality and was acting on behalf of Shadrach's owner, John DeBree. Deputy Marshal Patrick Riley quickly executed the warrant. The BVC lawyers Sewall, Loring, and Charles Davis pleaded Shadrach's case. Morris and Richard Henry Dana prepared a writ of habeas corpus for Chief Justice Shaw, who summarily dismissed it. A conservative unionist and narrow legalist, Shaw distinguished between fugitives such as Latimer and Shadrach, whose pleas he denied, and slaves like Med, who was brought voluntarily by her owner to the free states. The most famous former fugitive in the state, Latimer was paid nine dollars by the BVC for watching Caphart. Seth Thomas, representing Caphart, argued for a certificate of removal, but Shadrach's lawyers managed to win a delay in the proceedings. Successful fund-raising met the expenses of Loring, Sewall, and John King of the legal committee, the last hundred dollars coming from the coffers of the BVC, which also brought countersuits against Curtis, District Attorney George Lunt, and Caphart. Hundreds of black Bostonians gathered outside the courtroom where Shadrach was held, and a group led by Hayden broke in and rescued him. He was rushed to the house of Hayden's neighbor, Elizabeth Riley, and then to Joseph Lovejoy's home in Cambridge. Garrison commended the "peaceful rescue," while Parker and Phillips hearkened back to Boston's revolutionary past. The path of Shadrach's escape illumined the abolitionist network in the New England heartland. Hayden or John J. Smith drove Shadrach to Concord, where he stayed at the home of a blacksmith named Frances Edwin and his wife, Anne Bigelow, of the Concord FASS, whose members were known to shelter fugitives. Shadrach went on to Leominster, where he stayed with a Garrisonian couple, a shoemaker Jonathan and his wife, Frances Drake, and then on to Burlington, Vermont, whose activist black community had pledged resistance to the law. By the end of the month he was in Montreal.

The conservative reaction to Shadrach's rescue was not slow in coming and included racist allusions to the overthrow of "white power" in Boston and its transfer as a dominion of the "sooty" Haitian emperor. While Clay railed in the Senate that a government of black men had replaced that of whites, President Fillmore issued a warning proclamation to the citizens of Boston and called on all civil and military authorities to enforce the fugitive law. A number of abolitionists, including Davis, Elizur Wright, the editor of the *Commonwealth*, who was present at the fracas and had printed an extra edition on the rescue, Hayden, Morris, and eight other black men, were arrested. Besides Davis, who was not charged, District Attorney Benjamin F. Hallet indicted all the men. Wright's court costs were paid by the BVC. Sewall, Hildreth, Dana, and Hale successfully defended the rescuers, not one of whom was convicted. The cases against Hayden and James Scott, who led the rescue, resulted in hung juries. Dana later met the Concord blacksmith whose "obstinacy" had contributed to the deadlock. He confessed that he had taken part in the rescue himself. Morris also evaded conviction even though Judge Benjamin Curtis's charge to the jury construed resistance to the law as treason. Rebellions were in fact characterized as petty treason in slave codes, justifying capital punishment for rebels.

In April the authorities had their revenge when Secretary of State Webster, who also called the actions of Bostonians treasonous, personally supervised the rendition of a Georgia runaway, Thomas Sims. His ally Seth Thomas, representing John B. Bacon, the agent of Sims's master, James Potter, secured a warrant for his arrest from George Curtis. Deputy Marshal Asa O. Butman executed the warrant but not before Sims stabbed him in the thigh. Charles G. Loring, Robert Rantoul Jr., Sumner, Dana, and Sewall tried to procure his release. Rantoul, a talented Democratic lawyer who had been elected to Congress, was known for his defense of organized labor, his free soil sympathies, and his involvement in reform causes. He became the lead lawyer in Sims's case. Chief Justice Shaw, who was persuaded to convene a hearing on a writ of habeas corpus, rejected Rantoul's arguments and upheld the constitutionality of the Fugitive Slave Act. Rantoul then made his case before Curtis. He argued that a federal commissioner did not have the right to exercise judicial powers normally reserved for judges, that in a matter involving personal liberty a trial by jury was essential, that the evidence procured in Georgia for Sims's enslavement was "incompetent" and inadmissible in Massachusetts, as no opportunity for cross-examination was granted, and finally that the fugitive law that entailed such legal irregularities was itself unconstitutional. In his closing Loring conceded that the fugitive slave clause of the Constitution gave slaveholders a right to recapture runaways but questioned its implementation by the federal government. Curtis predictably rendered a verdict for Potter. Despite the loss, Rantoul's and Loring's arguments formed the bedrock of antislavery jurisprudence in subsequent cases.

The BVC tried various stratagems to release Sims, serving a writ of personal replevin on Marshal Charles Devens, making Hildreth, as justice of the peace, issue a warrant for Sims's arrest for attacking Butman and having Bacon briefly arrested on a conspiracy to kidnap. Hallet superseded Hildreth's warrant by charging Sims with a federal crime. Sewall, Dana, and Sumner tried again to have writs of habeas corpus issued by Judge Peleg Sprague, an anti-abolitionist who, predictably, refused, and by Judge Woodbury, who convened a hearing, with Benjamin Curtis arguing against it. Woodbury remanded Sims back to federal custody. To avoid a rescue like Shadrach's, the courthouse was heavily guarded and wrapped with heavy iron chains on orders from Tukey, its symbolism apparent to all. Hayden reported that most of Shadrach's black rescuers had been scattered by their recent prosecutions. Higginson's plan to have Sims jump out of a window onto a mattress below, conveyed to the prisoner by Grimes, was foiled by newly installed iron bars. Despite protest meetings at Tremont Temple and at the Commons, at which Phillips, Parker, Remond, and Colver counseled resistance, Sims was remanded back to slavery. He was marched to the brig *Acorn* surrounded by two hundred policemen and a hundred volunteers. The wealthy and most respectable, the merchants and bankers, raising three cheers for Webster and the Constitution as they watched Sims walk, had volunteered their services. Bacon thanked Boston's merchants for their assistance in a public letter.

In a MASS resolution, Phillips said that a man was sold into bondage so that State Street and Milk Street could make money. There was no disturbance when Sims was marched except for an occasional hissing and cries of "Shame" by a crowd of one hundred. Plans to have Bearse intercept at sea also came to naught. In Georgia, Sims was whipped and sold, "lost in the great multitude of the enslaved population" until, like scores of slaves, he fled to the Union army in 1863. The BVC stepped up its warnings and efforts to transport runaways to Canada after Sims's rendition. In the General Court, Joseph T. Buckingham reported a new personal liberty law crafted by Sumner and Dana, and a legislative committee convened hearings into the conduct of officials in the Sims affair, issuing a report highly critical of them. The legislature failed to pass a new law, but it did pass a resolution condemning the Fugitive Slave Act as abhorrent to the people of Massachusetts.[8] Initial confrontations over the implementation of the law soon gave way to full-fledged rebellions.

FUGITIVE SLAVE REBELLIONS

The famous fugitive slave rebellions of the 1850s occurred in places that had a long-standing abolitionist underground. The first violent confrontation took place in Christiana, Pennsylvania, exactly a year after the passage of the law. The area was rife with UGRR activity, facilitated by free blacks and Quaker families, whose antislavery roots stretched back to the eighteenth century. African Americans frequently defended themselves from slave hunters and kidnappers, especially the notorious Gap gang, known to kidnap its victims into slavery. In 1840 five black men in Gettysburg formed the Slave's Refuge Society to aid runaways. Still reported that after the passage of the new law, Hannah Dellum and her child were rendered back to slavery from Philadelphia, and Thomas Hall and his wife beaten and dragged off to slavery in Chester County. At least four black men were seized in 1850 in Lancaster County without any legal process.

A state of war over fugitives existed in southern Pennsylvania before the Christiana uprising. In September 1851 Edward Gorsuch, a Maryland slaveholder whose father's will stipulated that his slaves be freed when they turned twenty-eight, ended up there in hot pursuit of his four young male slaves who refused to wait for freedom. The four had found shelter and work at the home of William Parker, a former Maryland slave himself, who had escaped in 1839 with his brother. Parker rented a farm from a Quaker, Levi Pownell. A high point for Parker was hearing Garrison and Douglass at an abolitionist meeting. Parker believed that "sleepless vigilance" was the price of "stolen liberty" and ran a self-defense organization of black men. He was involved in the rescue of William Dorsey and Elizabeth, who worked for a Quaker, Moses Whitson. In the latter case Parker, Benjamin Whipper, and a few other black men gave a sound thrashing to the slave catchers. A year before Christiana, Parker and his men beat up a black man suspected of betraying a fugitive. In January Parker was not able to rescue John Williams, who was badly beaten and kidnapped back into slavery. That same month an armed standoff over the rendition of Stephen Bennett in Columbia led to the shattering of the sheriff's arm. Commissioner Edward Ingraham, who had wrongfully condemned a free black man, Abraham Gibson of Philadelphia, to slavery in one of the first renditions under the new law, remanded Bennett to slavery. The PASS and "several colored men" monitored the case, and seven hundred dollars was quickly raised to purchase his freedom.

Gorsuch was determined to recover his slaves, whom he accused of stealing grain and, along with a free black man named Abraham Johnston, trying to sell it. He got the governor of Maryland to send extradition requests for his slaves and Johnston, which the governor of Pennsylvania, an antislavery Whig, ignored. Gorsuch received a letter from William Padgett, a member of the Gap gang, informing him of his slaves' whereabouts. Padgett disappeared when the NASS published his letter. Accompanied by members of his family, neighbors, and Deputy Marshal Henry Kline and armed with warrants from the obliging Ingraham, Gorsuch led the slave-catching party to Parker's home. Still sent Samuel Williams, the keeper of the appropriately named revolutionary tavern Bolivar House, to warn Parker. Gorsuch's party confronted the Parkers, two of Gorsuch's runaway slaves, Johnston, and Parker's sister-in-law and her husband, Alexander and Hannah Pinckney. Parker's wife, Eliza, blew a horn, summoning an additional twenty armed black men, including the other two runaways. Other black men and a Quaker, Joseph Scarlett, also sounded the alarm. Two neighbors, the Quaker Elijah Lewis and Castner Hanway, a white miller, arrived at Parker's farm. They refused to be deputized by Kline. The shoot-out began with a confrontation between Gorsuch and his slaves. Although both Gorsuch and his son were riddled with bullets, only Gorsuch died. The slave catchers, some of whom belonged to the Gap gang, beat a hasty retreat. Parker reported that the women finished Gorsuch off, with unsubstantiated rumors circulating that they mutilated his body. Women certainly participated: Eliza, an escaped slave herself whose experience of slavery, Parker said, was worse than his, was a key player. She had been shot at when she sounded the alarm and had armed herself with a corn cutlass. With the help of the Pownell family, Parker, along with Johnson and Pinckney, escaped to Rochester, where he gave Douglass a valued memento, Gorsuch's revolver. Douglass hurried them on to Canada. In June 1852 Hiram Wilson wrote to Bibb that the "hero of Christiana" was in Elgin. Parker went on to assist fugitives in Detroit, and John Brown's son tried to recruit him for the Harper's Ferry raid.

In Pennsylvania the authorities, marines ordered by Fillmore to assist local law enforcement, and vigilante groups, including Marylanders and deputized Irish railroad workers, unleashed a manhunt, reenslaving suspected fugitives, arresting free blacks indiscriminately, and roughing up Cyrus Burleigh at an abolition meeting. A man named Miller was killed in Maryland when he went to retrieve a free black woman working for him who was kidnapped in retaliation for Gorsuch's murder; a large "indignation meeting" was held at Baltimore. Thirty-six black men, including Williams, the missing Parker, and Gorsuch's self-emancipated slaves, were indicted on charges of treason following the instruction of Judge John Kane. Of the thirty-six charged, twenty-seven were arrested. Five whites, Hanway, Lewis, Scarlett, James Jackson, an abolitionist who was not involved in Christiana, and Joseph Townsend, who had given a black man his loaded gun, were also indicted. Eliza Parker and Hannah Pinckney were arrested but not charged. They eventually joined their husbands in Canada, but their badly frightened mother was remanded back to slavery.

The Christiana trial in Philadelphia before Judges Kane and Grier became a legal contest between proslavery and antislavery politicians. The attorney general of Maryland, a sitting U.S. senator from Pennsylvania, District Attorney John Ashmead, and a few others argued for the prosecution. The prosecution's preoccupation with a nonexistent abolitionist conspiracy—they also subpoenaed a local abolitionist, Augustus Cain, a physician who had treated the Christiana rebels—considerably weakened its case. The defense, represented by Congressman Thaddeus Stevens from Lancaster, the abolitionist David Paul Brown, and others effectively discredited the character and testimony of Kline, who perjured himself, as did the prosecution's leading witness. As a state legislator, Stevens had blocked all attempts to restrict black migration to Pennsylvania. He employed a spy to report to him on the activities of slave catchers and kidnappers. Stevens represented the defendants at the initial hearings as well as at the trial, concentrating on the specifics of the case rather than on the validity of slavery and the fugitive law. Lucretia Mott sat next to the black defendants, all dressed alike with red, white, and blue kerchiefs around their necks, making identification by Kline difficult. The defense also presented testimony on the kidnapping and enslavement of free blacks in the area. To add insult to injury, Marshal Roberts, a Stevens man, was accused of stacking the jury and treating the defendants to a sumptuous Thanksgiving dinner courtesy of Judge Kane's abolitionist son. In his closing for the defense John Read decried kidnappers and man stealers who invaded the homes of the citizens of Pennsylvania, putting the onus for the violence on Gorsuch and his slave-hunting party.

Grier made it clear in his charge to the jury that, despite his disapproval of resistance to the law, the indictment for treason had not been proven. The jury declared Hanway, who was tried first, not guilty within fifteen minutes, and Lewis and Williams were released on bail. The rest of the men were sent back to Lancaster County, where they were released in short order. In an interesting coda, Kline arrested one of the black men released as a fugitive before he too escaped. In the last of the trials, Williams was arrested again and defended ably by Kane's other son, Robert P. Kane, and Kline was indicted for perjury. In the end no one was convicted. Radicalized by his experience, Hanway joined an abolitionist Quaker society; money for his defense had been raised by the Salisbury Friends Society. The court battle helped turn public opinion in favor of the defendants.

Abolitionists defended the actions of Parker and his men, Whittier writing an ode to the Quakers who refused to collaborate. At an antislavery meeting Giddings commended the black men's resistance. Mott demurred at the violence, but her actions at the trial spoke louder. The *Pennsylvania Freeman* pointed out that while the federal government had indicted the Christiana rebels for treason, it had interceded on behalf of American filbusterers plotting to overthrow the Spanish government in Cuba. In Edmund Quincy's view, the new law of treason called for a new "bloody revolution." It was the first genuine battle for freedom since the American Revolution had failed to rid the country of slavery. Garrison was unequivocal in his support, averring that the "resistance made by the gallant blacks" of Christiana, who were entitled to all the "rights of belligerents," was fully justified. Black meetings hailed the "Christiana heroes" throughout the North, in Columbus, in Chicago led by John Jones, and in Rochester. In New York, McCune Smith, Pennington, Ray, and Thomas Downing raised money for their defense. Detroit's Committee of Vigilance, led by Monroe, Baptiste, and Lambert, and Philadelphia's all-black Special Vigilance Committee, led by John Burr, William Forten, and Nathaniel W. Depee, also took up collections for them. Douglass commended the Christiana rebels for acting as men instead of what the law decreed, prey to be hunted. To Charles Langston they "were worthy the imitation of every colored man in the country." As Still put it, "Slave-holders [were] taught the wholesome lesson, that the Fugitive Slave Law was no guarantee against 'red hot shot.'"

Abolitionists had no illusions about slavery being an ongoing war in which they had to match wits, daring, and resources with slaveholders, who had the machinery of the state and the law at their disposal. That very year a fugitive was remanded back to slavery from Wilkes-Barre. Chastened by recent events, including the kidnapping of free blacks from Philadelphia, McKim convened a meeting on December 2, 1852, to revamp the PVC, as the old committee had become "disorganized and scattered." Black abolitionists took the lead: Purvis was named chairman of the new General Vigilance Committee, and Still was named secretary of the acting committee, which consisted of Jacob C. White, the agent of the first Vigilant Committee, Depee, and the Quaker abolitionist Passmore Williamson. As secretary, Still was a one-man action committee and left the most comprehensive account of the UGRR in his magnum opus, *The Underground Rail Road*, published after the Civil War. He personally assisted in over four hundred slaves' escape to freedom.[9]

Barely had the uproar over Christiana settled when Marshal Henry Allen arrested William Henry, known as Jerry, in Syracuse in October on behalf of James Lear, the agent of his Missouri owner, John McReynolds. Just two months earlier Commissioner Henry Smith had remanded a fugitive, John Davis, alias Daniel, in Buffalo back to slavery. When Davis was arrested he was assaulted in a "brutal and wanton" manner, his head clubbed and left lacerated and bloodied. His master's agent, Benjamin Rust, was prosecuted for assault and battery and fined fifty dollars. Davis's lawyers got a writ of habeas corpus, and he was spirited to Canada. In 1839 Syracuse's black community, with the assistance of Smith, secreted Harriet Pownell, visiting with her Mississippi owners, to Canada. The Syracuse VC (SVC), formed by May, Smith, Ward, and Loguen, to ensure that "no person is deprived of his liberty without 'due process of law,'" vowed to resist the "license for kidnapping." In January Syracuse hosted the New York State Anti–Fugitive Slave Law Convention. A few months later Webster, visiting Syracuse, threw down the gauntlet, demanding the rendition of fugitives in the middle of an "Anti-Slavery convention."

The SVC member Charles Wheaton witnessed Jerry's capture, and the news spread via the tolling of church bells to the Onondaga Agricultural Society's annual fair and a Liberty Party convention. Jerry, pleading for his liberty, nearly escaped through the huge crowd that quickly gathered. Bloodied and bruised, he was recaptured, shackled, and kept heavily guarded. At a meeting of the

SVC at the office of the physician Hiram Hoyt, Smith recommended a "bold and forcible rescue." Just a year earlier Hoyt had treated a runaway, William Harris, for self-inflicted wounds, the result of his being tormented by abusive seamen. Though William's daughter died, his tormenters were jailed, and he escaped with his wife, Catherine, to Canada. May met with Jerry to calm him down and had a carriage ready to spirit him away, admonishing the rescuers not to harm any of the officials. Loguen had no such qualms. In 1844 he had written, "If our rights are withheld any longer, then come war—let blood flow without measure." An interracial group of armed men overwhelmed the guards and managed to enter the jail by using a battering ram. Jerry was taken triumphantly to the home of two black sisters, where an abolitionist blacksmith broke apart his shackles, which were sent to Fillmore in a show of defiance. After being hidden at the home of a butcher, a proslavery Democrat who converted on seeing his plight, Jerry escaped to Kingston in Canada West through the abolitionist underground. He died two years later from tuberculosis but was immortalized by the annual Jerry rescue anniversary. Abolitionists from all factions used the occasion to proclaim their unified opposition to the law.

Most of the crowd that took part in the Jerry rescue were working-class men, many of whom lived alongside the city's black community. Twenty-five were indicted, of whom twelve were black. Among the first to post bail for the men was Seward. Of the five brought to trial, four white men, whose cases dragged on, were acquitted, while the trial of a mason named Ira Cobb, who managed to reach Jerry first, ended in a hung jury. Enoch Reed, a black laborer, the first rescuer tried and convicted, died before his appeal was decided. A law-and-order petition that upheld the Constitution and was critical of the rescue was signed by seven hundred people, the occupations of over four hundred of whom were identified as lawyers, merchants, landlords, barkeepers, and a few others. They were "gentlemen of property and standing." Abolitionists held protest meetings and formed a Jerry Rescue Committee led by Wheaton to raise funds for the defendants. Wheaton brought suit against Lear for kidnapping, but he too died before his case could be decided. Allen was charged with violating the state's personal liberty law. Smith pronounced the law unconstitutional, contending that the government was not meant to be a "gigantic slave catcher." Ward and Loguen left for Canada, and neither May nor Smith were tried. Governor Hunt ignored Loguen's plea for safe passage, but he returned, recommencing his work on the UGRR with his wife, Caroline.

Loguen, a runaway from Tennessee, had long settled in upstate New York as a minister and teacher. He lectured for the Liberty Party and was nominated for the state senate. Loguen advertised his name and address in newspapers so runaways could seek him out and refused to purchase his own freedom. Loguen's attempt to buy his mother failed because his master refused to sell her unless he paid for himself also. When his mistress, after selling off his siblings, asked him for a thousand dollars to relinquish her claims on him and pay for a mare he had used to escape, Loguen responded, "Wretched woman! Be it known to you that I value my freedom, to say nothing, of my mother, brother, and sisters, more than your whole body." The fugitive community became his family: his sister-in-law married Lewis Clarke, and his daughter Amelia married Douglass's son, Lewis. About the fugitive law he declared, "I don't respect this law—I don't fear it—I won't obey it! It outlaws me, and I outlaw it." Loguen wrote to Garrison in 1854 that he had personally dissolved the Union and that "my brethren should do as I have done; they should strike a blow for themselves and not wait for the hair-splitting of politicians and speakers." In 1856 Loguen helped found the Fugitive Aid Society, with May at its head, and was appointed its general agent a year later. Loguen published his narrative with the help of his amanuensis, John Thomas, the erstwhile editor of the *Liberty Party Paper*, in 1859. The narrative detailed Loguen's sale by his own father to Manasseth Logue, his uncle, who treated him brutally. Loguen whipped his master, threw him down to the ground, nearly breaking his neck, and ran away. After escaping to Canada, he attended Oneida Institute and settled in Syracuse in 1841. The last half of his narrative is devoted to the Jerry rescue. Thomas wrote that Loguen had "set slave laws at defiance, and trample[d] them under his feet." Douglass admired Loguen's refusal to buy himself, calling him "the man who does not lie down at night, nor rise in the morning, without being under the liability of being kidnapped!" Loguen, he estimated, had assisted over a thousand fugitives.[10]

Widely publicized instances of abolitionist defiance of the law made northern conservatives and the federal government determined to enforce it. In May 1854 they got their Pyrrhic victory with the arrest of Anthony Burns in Boston on a warrant issued by Commissioner Edward G. Loring and executed by the notorious Butman, who "made the hunting of fugitive slaves his special avocation." Burns's Virginian owner, Charles F. Suttle's agent William Brent, initiated the arrest. Both Jerry and Burns were arrested on the pretext of stealing, a nineteenth-century version of stop-and-frisk. Grimes, whose "fugitive slave church" Burns attended, soon got wind of his arrest, and Dana delayed the proceedings. The BVC lawyer Seth Webb served a writ of personal replevin, which Marshal Watson Freeman ignored, and got Suttle and Brent charged for kidnapping. The men were released on bond posted by Hallet's son and Freeman, but Hayden kept a conspicuous watch on them. The BVC was divided on the forcible rescue recommended by Hayden, Grimes, and Higginson or the employment of legal means, a result of the differing orientations of its members. Lawyers such as Charles Mayo Ellis, who had advised against forcible rescue during the Sims case, and Dana were appalled at how easily abolitionists spoke of direct action. "Advocates for an assault on the Court House" were outvoted at the committee's emergency meeting. A thirty-man rescue committee consisting of Higginson, Parker, Phillips, Howe, and Bearse nevertheless planned Burns's rescue. Phillips and Parker made fiery speeches at a five-thousand-strong protest meeting at Faneuil Hall led by Sewall, Bowditch, Howe, and Morris. Phillips urged that the people of Massachusetts must fall back on their own sovereignty. Parker addressed them as "subjects of Virginia" whose ancient writs, liberties, and constitutional protections had to bow down before the law of slavery.

Informed that a "mob of negroes" was going to assault the courthouse, many in the protest meeting adjourned there, according to a plan hatched by Higginson and Martin Stowell, who had taken part in the Jerry rescue. Higginson, who had left his conservative Unitarian congregation in Newburyport for a friendlier, radical one in Worcester in 1852, on Stowell's suggestion purchased axes to break down the doors. In Worcester, Higginson regularly escorted fugitives to the Fosters' farmhouse, but that, according to him, was minor antislavery work compared to the Burns rescue. Soon, the crowd, "the white and the colored race, the freeborn sons of Massachusetts and fugitive slaves from the South, here cooperated together" and attacked the courthouse, throwing bricks and stones, shattering its windows. Led by Hayden and Higginson, one group managed to open the heavy doors with a battering ram. Stowell tried to hack it down with his ax and was arrested. The men who participated in the attempted rescue of Burns were working-class radicals and black Bostonians. Two other men besides Stowell were arrested, a mechanic named John Roberts, for snuffing out the streetlights, and a black man, Walter Phoenix, for hurling a brick. The courthouse crowd included John Cluer, a mill worker from Scotland, a Chartist, and a leader of the ten-hour-a-day movement. He was a member of the BVC and, like Bearse, a fund raiser for it. Cluer and Stowell had witnessed Sims's rendition. The crowd also included the future labor leader Ira Steward. In the melee a deputized Irish truckman, James Batchelder, who was blocking the entry was stabbed to death. The Boston Irish, some of whom, like Riley, were known for slave hunting, and the Catholic Church came down on the side of enforcing the law. There were exceptions, like the BVC member Henry Kemp, an Irishman. Joseph K. Hayes, a BVC infiltrator, resigned from the city police rather than participate in Burns's rendition.

After the failed assault the mayor called out the militia, and Freeman requested the presence of two companies of U.S. Marines, making the courthouse impregnable. In the Jerry rescue Wheaton had dissuaded both from participating. The law President Pierce wrote must be executed, no matter what the cost. Two hundred radicals from the Worcester Freedom Club marched outside the courthouse. The BVC had no choice but to fall back on legal means. Shaw shut down the Supreme Judicial Court as armed men took over the courthouse. Boston was under virtual martial law. Meanwhile, Grimes raised a subscription of twelve hundred dollars, Suttle's price for Burns, but Suttle changed his mind. His northern as well as southern backers were determined to foil the abolitionists. Despite an effective defense by Dana and testimony from black and white workers at the Mattapan Iron Works that Burns was working there before his owner claimed he had escaped, Loring, whose mother had married into the Curtis family after the death of his father and who was a staunch defender of the fugitive law, ruled in favor of Suttle. Ironically, his cousin Charles G. Loring was a BVC lawyer. Two southern Harvard men participated: Moncure Conway, a student at the Divinity School, attended BVC meetings and became an abolitionist; Charles C. Jones Jr., the son of the proslavery Georgia minister, who volunteered as a guard, was appalled at the use of "negro testimony."

Exactly a week after his arrest Burns was escorted by the armed might of the government back to Virginia. Unlike the Sims rendition witnessed mainly by BVC members, thousands lined the streets; buildings were draped in black, American flags were outlined in black, and a coffin with the word *Liberty* on it was displayed. The tide of public sentiment had clearly turned. James Freeman Clarke evoked the scene: "Hung be the Heavens in black." The law could be enforced only "at the point of a bayonet." Coming on the heels of the Kansas–Nebraska Act, Burns's rendition converted some of Boston's cotton Whigs, including Amos Lawrence. They signed a petition for the repeal of the Fugitive Slave Act, and some contributed funds to purchase Burns. John Pearson, who had helped with the Sims rendition, refused permission to a U.S. cutter to dock at his wharf. Whittier's "The Rendition" and Whitman's "A Boston Ballad" captured antislavery angst.

Riding a wave of popular revulsion and hostility against immigrants, including Irish involvement in the Burns rendition, the Know-Nothing Party swept into power in Massachusetts. The nativist legislature passed the Personal Liberty Law of 1855, which nullified the federal fugitive law. It required a suspected fugitive to be brought for trial before state courts on a writ of habeas corpus and prohibited not only state lawyers like Seth Thomas, who had represented the claimants of the Crafts, Sims, Shadrach, and Burns, from representing slaveholders, but also the use of state facilities to hold fugitives and state officials from participating in rendition. It made claimants subject to fines and imprisonment for kidnapping, and being a commissioner enforcing the fugitive law became an impeachable offense. Despite a legislative hearing in which Phillips, Parker, Grimes, and Ellis gave testimony, the abolitionist campaign to impeach Loring failed, mainly owing to the opposition of Dana and the nativist governor Henry Gardner. In 1858, with Garrison invited to witness the proceedings, Republicans in the legislature voted for the removal of Loring, and the new governor, Nathaniel Banks, signed off on it. Benjamin Curtis, Shaw, and a bunch of die-hards signed a petition for the repeal of the new personal liberty law. Shaw resigned from the Supreme Judicial Court in 1860, his judicial legacy intertwined with the defense of slavery and racial segregation. His son-in-law Melville captured his tortured commitment to judicial formalism in the character of Captain Vere in *Billy Budd*.

In May 1855 Curtis and Judge Sprague presided over the trial of eight men, including Higginson, Stowell, Cluer, a black man named Wesley (alias Walter) Bishop as well as Parker and Phillips, indicted for inciting riot and for the murder of Batchelder. Hale, Ellis, and Andrew defended them. Hayden was not arrested or tried. Hallet, at the prompting of Pierce and his doughface attorney general from Massachusetts Caleb Cushing, and Elias Merwin, Curtis's law partner, prosecuted the case. They changed their minds, Curtis releasing Stowell on a technicality and the government entering a nolle prosequi, or refusal to proceed, for the others, not wanting to give abolitionists another forum to make their case. Parker foiled these plans when he published *The Trial of Theodore Parker*, in which he vindicated the "great Human Right to Freedom of Speech." It was not the abolitionists but government itself that was lawless. Parker argued that slavery was at war with democratic institutions and the independence of the judiciary corrupted by denying fugitives common law protections of trial by jury and habeas corpus. His long disquisition on the history of "judicial tyranny" in England, the use of torture by corrupt judges, and cruel laws preceded his indictment of the fugitive law, which read, "Its sins outrun my powers of speech." The sorry history of its enforcement resulted in "one huge Despotism, a House of Bondage for African Americans, a House of Bondage also for Saxon Americans." For good measure, he reproduced his speeches against slavery and the fugitive law, advocating revolutionary resistance.

Higginson marveled that the fugitive law had turned "honest American men into conscientious law-breakers." To him, antislavery was no longer a reform but a revolution. The Worcester radicals had their revenge. In October, Butman, on a fact-finding trip, ran afoul of the Worcester VC and was arrested for carrying a concealed weapon. He barely made it out of the city alive, being surrounded by a crowd of thousands and protected, ironically, by Higginson and Stowell. He first hid in a toilet at the train station and then rode posthaste back to Boston, swearing never to come back. Stephen Foster, who had urged the crowd to rough up Butman but not kill him, was arrested along with three others, but a black man was indicted for assault. In Boston some drunk toughs assaulted Dana, and threats were made against Phillips and Parker. Burns bore the brutality of slave law, locked in an airless cell in the slave trader Robert Lumpkin's pen for four months in shackles, with no privies and barely enough rotten food to keep him alive. He was sold to David McDaniel of North Carolina. When news of him trickled back to Massachusetts, Grimes and Charles C. Barry, the secretary of the Pine Street ASS, collected enough money to purchase him. Burns was excommunicated from his Virginia church for disobeying the law by running away, to which he replied, "I was stolen and made a slave as soon as I was born. . . . The manstealer who stole me . . . committed an outrage on the law of God. . . . I disobeyed no law of God revealed in the Bible. . . . You charge me with disobeying the *laws of men*. . . . To be real laws, they must be founded in equity. You have thrust me out of your church fellowship. . . . You cannot exclude me from heaven." On his return, Burns attended Oberlin and became a minister in Indianapolis before Indiana's black laws compelled him to leave for Canada. In 1862 Rev. Anthony Burns died of tuberculosis in St. Catherines, Ontario. He was the last fugitive to be recaptured in New England.[11]

The Burns rendition inspired Garrison, who called it a "deed of infamy," to make one of his most celebrated protests against slavery. On the Fourth of July the MASS converted its annual celebration in Framingham into a day of mourning, with black bunting surrounding an upside-down American flag. Phillips, Lucy Stone, Abby Kelley Foster, and Sojourner Truth, who said that if whites repaid blacks all that they owed they would not have enough left to seed, made speeches. Thoreau's "Slavery in Massachusetts" was one of the best statements on the abolitionists' understanding of the law caricatured by conservatives as higher law doctrine. "The law," Thoreau wrote, "will never make men free; it is men who have got to make the law free. They are the lovers of law and order, who observe the law when the government breaks it." Emerson made a similar argument in his speech on the fugitive slave law in 1851 justifying Shadrach's rescue: "An immoral law makes it a man's duty to break it, at every hazard." In the twentieth century these ideas would find new resonance in the conviction of Nazis for following immoral and unjust orders. Furness's three discourses on the rendition of Burns and Pennington's family urged the "Christian duty" of northerners to withhold "all aid and countenance from the work of oppression." Garrison read the Declaration and then proceeded to burn the Fugitive Slave Act, Loring's decision, the grand jury's charge against the courthouse protesters, and the Constitution with its fugitive slave clause, "the source and parent of the other atrocities." He concluded, "So perish all compromises with tyranny." Even antislavery allies who disagreed respected the sheer boldness of his gesture. Garrison's disunionism seemed less unreasonable in the age of the fugitive law, when an antislavery conscience was deemed seditious. Remond, who had pushed for the deliverance of Burns in a dramatic speech at the NEAS convention, defended Garrison's protest in the name of the three million slaves with whom he was identified by complexion. He gave it his "hearty approbation," as the Constitution and the law had outlawed black people.[12]

The same year as Burns's rendition, a successful fugitive slave rebellion occurred in Racine, Wisconsin. The arrest and rescue of Joshua Glover, a runaway slave of Benammi Garland of Missouri, precipitated another long contest in the courts. Garland came armed with a certificate of removal from a St. Louis court and a federal warrant for Glover's arrest from Judge Andrew Miller of the Eastern District of Wisconsin. It took two marshals—Deputy Marshal John Kearney landed a blow on Glover's head—and their four assistants to subdue the resistant Glover, who had escaped from slavery two years earlier. A black man named William Alby, who was with Glover at the time of his seizure, soon spread the word of his arrest, and the sheriff arrested Kearney and his assistant on charges of kidnapping, assault, and battery. The next day Racine abolitionists tolled church bells and held a protest meeting condemning the kidnapping of Glover, "a faithful laborer and honest man," demanding that a trial by jury be held for him and that the "Slave catching law of 1850" be repealed. Deputy Marshal Charles Cotton whisked Glover off to Milwaukee, where the abolitionist editor of the *Daily Free Democrat*, Sherman Booth, received the resolutions of the Racine meeting. As a student at Yale, Booth had taught the *Amistad* rebels English. A Liberty Party man, he had moved to Wisconsin from Connecticut, following his mentor, Ichabod Codding, and, like Chase, had made the transition to the Free Soil Party. Booth published a handbill on Glover's arrest and rode around Milwaukee, including the German Second Ward, a nineteenth-century Paul Revere summoning people to the courthouse. Another Liberty man, James Paine, who had moved to Milwaukee from Ohio, served a writ of habeas corpus on Cotton.

Led by the physician Edward B. Wolcott, Booth, Paine, his son Byron, and Abram Henry Bielfeld, who was born in Bremen and made a speech in German, a courthouse meeting passed resolutions demanding a trial by jury for

Glover. The meeting also formed a twenty-five man Vigilance Committee. A nervous Cotton, backed by the federal judge Miller and District Attorney John Sharpstein, whose request for military reinforcements was ignored, did not obey the writs of habeas corpus served on him by the local sheriff. Meanwhile, a contingent of one hundred from Racine joined the meeting, and the abolitionist Charles Watkins recommended taking the law into their own hands. A blacksmith, James Angove, led the predominantly working-class crowd, using a battering ram to break open the jail, and they carried Glover away. Glover doffed his cap to the crowd, crying, "Glory, Hallelujah," and disappeared in the abolitionist underground to Canada.

Glover's escape led to a flurry of lawsuits: Watkins and Paine appeared on behalf of Racine County seeking the arrest of Garland for disturbing the peace, and Garland sued Booth for the value of Glover and costs incurred to recapture him. A grand jury handed down indictments against Wolcott, the Paines, Watkins, and Herbert Reed, the chairman of the Milwaukee Vigilance Committee. The Pierce administration was determined that some heads should roll for the Glover rescue, so Booth, who had advised against violence, and John Ryecraft, who had helped break down the jail door, were arrested by Marshal Stephen Abelman for violating the fugitive slave law. In his hearing before Commissioner Winfield Smith, Booth raised issues of trial by jury and habeas corpus, and his attorney Paine, of the freedom of assembly and speech. Sharpstein made his distaste for radicalism clear, saying, "The whole matter of abolitionism, women's rights, Fourierism, Etc., is intended only to enable men to violate and trample on the laws. I despise the whole of it. I despise any man who preaches it, and I despise any man who defends him." Edward Ryan, an Irish immigrant and self-described proslavery Democrat, joined him in prosecuting the case against Booth and Ryecraft in federal court. Despite a plea from Byron Paine, both were found guilty.

Abolitionists, not conservative judges in the federal judiciary, built legal precedents for modern law stemming from the fugitive slave cases, including the reading of Miranda rights. In addition, it was not clear which side perpetrated more violence. By the eve of the war, slave-catching posses and officials took to operating by stealth, at night and by surprise, and to violently implement the fugitive law in the North. Booth and his lawyers constantly alluded to the violence of Glover's arrest and the abusive nature of the law. They secured a writ of habeas corpus from the state supreme court justice Abram Smith, known for his abolitionist leanings, who declared the law unconstitutional. In his famous brief before Smith, Byron Paine had challenged the constitutionality of the Fugitive Slave Act by disputing the power of Congress to enact it and its subversion of trial by jury; further, he questioned the constitutionality of giving federal commissioners judicial powers. He referred to the authority of Spooner, used Rantoul's argument from the Sims case, and impressed Sumner, who asked for a copy of his brief. The state supreme court upheld Smith's decision by two to one. In Wisconsin, state judges set themselves up as defenders of citizens' liberties and distinguished their version of states' rights from nullification, South Carolina's attempt to overthrow federal law during the tariff controversy.

State and federal officials worked at cross-purposes. Booth and Ryecraft were found guilty of violating the fugitive law in federal court. The court sentenced Booth to one month in prison and a thousand-dollar fine, but the Wisconsin Supreme Court unanimously discharged Booth and Ryecraft in February 1855. Evoking Jefferson's and Madison's Virginia and Kentucky resolutions against the Alien and Sedition Acts, as had Paine, but, significantly, not South Carolina's nullification of federal tariff laws, the court interposed itself between the state's citizens and the federal law and courts. It was not simply a matter of states' rights vis-à-vis federal power, but the protection of the civil liberties and constitutional rights of Wisconsin's citizens. Two years later Republicans in the state legislature passed a personal liberty law establishing the writ of habeas corpus, right to trial by jury, and legal counsel in fugitive slave cases. It punished the kidnapping of free blacks and prevented a lien on the personal property or real estate of persons who refused to obey the law. This section of the state law helped Booth get a writ of replevin against unlawful seizure of property when the zealous Abelman started impounding his press and printing materials to execute the judgment against him in *Garland v. Booth.* On appeal, the U.S. Supreme Court in *US v. Booth* and *Abelman v. Booth* in 1859 unanimously upheld the supremacy of federal law, overturning the decisions of the Wisconsin Supreme Court. Coming after *Dred Scott,* the decision of the Taney court came as no surprise, and the state legislature passed a joint resolution promising "positive defiance" of it. For good measure, the people of Wisconsin elected the young Byron Paine to the state supreme court.

The persistent Abelman arrested Booth again in 1860, but his supporters managed to spirit him out of the U.S. Custom House where he was being held. Booth surrendered himself later that year after campaigning for Lincoln. He languished in jail until President James Buchanan pardoned him just before leaving office in March 1861. Booth had lost much of his credibility after his arrest and trial in 1859 for seducing his fourteen-year-old babysitter, which ended in a hung jury but led to the breakdown of his marriage. He remarried after his wife's death and died at the ripe age of ninety-one in 1904. Glover died in Canada in 1888.

Abolitionists and black Wisconsinites led by Lewis Johnson saw resistance to the fugitive law and the fight for African American rights as two sides of the same coin. According to the 1850 Census, the state had slightly over six hundred free black people in a total population of more than three hundred thousand. The state hosted speaking tours by Lewis Washington, a fugitive slave, in 1847 and by Douglass in the 1850s. Like J. B. Smith, whose restaurant refused to serve soldiers in Boston, the black barber William Noland of Madison, who managed to hold state office without attracting much attention, refused to shave kidnappers. Abolitionists such as Booth and Rufus King, named for his antislavery Federalist father, the editor of the antislavery *Milwaukee Sentinel*, and Rev. Byrd Parker, a "Bird of African plumage," as racist Democrats called him, launched a campaign for black suffrage in the 1850s, but in 1857 the referendum was defeated by a vote of 45,157 to 31,964. Although the Republican Party never officially endorsed the measure, 95 percent of the vote for black suffrage came from Republicans. In 1865 Ezekiel Gillespie, a leader of Milwaukee's black community, accompanied by Booth, attempted to vote but was turned back by election officials. Byron Paine brought suit on Gillespie's behalf, holding that Wisconsin had established black suffrage in 1849, when a small majority had voted in its favor. The results had been disallowed because of the low number of votes cast. In March 1866 the Wisconsin Supreme Court ruled in Gillespie's favor, making the state one of a handful in the North to grant black suffrage before the passage of the Fourteenth and Fifteenth Amendments.[13]

The last well-known fugitive slave rebellion, in 1858, occurred in the abolitionist stronghold of Oberlin. In August a Kentuckian named Anderson Jennings who was looking for a fugitive slave recognized John Price, a fugitive belonging to his neighbor John Bacon. Price had run away with his cousin, Dinah, and Frank, who belonged to a Richard Lloyd, in the winter of 1856 when the Ohio River had frozen over. Price lived among Oberlin's activist black community, which, together with the college, was an important stop in the abolitionist underground. Deputy Marshal Anson Dayton was always on the lookout for fugitives and was known to write about their whereabouts to their Kentucky owners. Dayton, Deputy Marshal Jacob K. Lowe of Columbus, and two Kentucky slave catchers had tried to seize a black family, the Wagoners, in a midnight raid before being scared away by Wagoner, who was armed. It was Dayton who had brought Price to Jennings's attention. Bacon and Lloyd sent a slave catcher, Richard Mitchell, to recover their slaves. Though watched closely by a black community always on the alert for slave hunters, Jennings and Mitchell managed to abduct Price with some help from locals. Malachi Warren, an Alabama planter who had moved to the area with his "slave wife," and the Boynton family, who tricked Price with an offer of employment, assisted them. Lowe also got a warrant to arrest Price.

As the slave hunters made their way to Wellington, Ohio, they ran into an abolitionist student from Oberlin, Anson Lyman, who had ridden with John Brown in Kansas. Price cried out for help. Lyman raised an alarm, and soon a large, armed interracial crowd surrounded the Wellington hotel, where Price was being held. John Watson, a black grocer and leading member of the state black conventions, got a warrant for the arrest of Price's kidnappers, and Langston tried to negotiate his release. News that troops might arrive by train to reinforce the men guarding Price compelled action. An abolitionist named Charles Griffin advised the crowd, "Pay no attention to the laws." Two rescue parties, a group of Oberlin students led by Lyman, John Cowles, and the British-born William Lincoln, who had worked for the AMA, and a group of black men led by the former North Carolina slave John Scott, Jeremiah Fox, a fugitive himself, and a free black man, John A. Copeland, converged on the attic of the hotel. Richard Winsor, who was Price's Sunday school teacher, managed to spirit him out into a waiting buggy procured by Scott. Another student, Simeon Bushnell, rode the buggy with Price and Winsor to the home of the Oberlin bookseller James Fitch. Fitch's home was a known stop on the UGRR, so they took Price instead to the home of James Fairchild, a professor at Oberlin, where he hid for several days before being sent to Canada. A triumphant antislavery meeting at Oberlin celebrated what came to be known as the Oberlin–Wellington rescue, with three cheers for liberty and three groans for the informer Dayton and the federal government. Dayton was run out of town, as was Warren, who, disowned by his children and accused of whipping his wife, returned to Alabama. President Buchanan, like his predecessors, was determined to enforce the law and harshly punish all who defied it. A stacked, all-Democratic federal grand jury, including a member of the Boynton family, indicted thirty-seven men for the rescue, of whom twenty-five were from Oberlin, eleven from Wellington, and one from Pittsfield. Most of the Wellington defendants, farmers and one bricklayer, were listed as "Known member of the Underground Railroad." Of the Oberlin men, four were students, one a professor, and three were born in England and Scotland. Twelve were African American, including fugitive slaves like Fox and John Hartwell.

The rescuers' protracted trials in Cleveland became a political spectacle. Governor Chase's political allies Rufus Spalding and Albert Riddle acted as counsel for the defense before an unsympathetic Democratic district judge, Hiram Willson, and all-Democratic juries. The prosecution, led by District Attorney George Belden, got rid of the Wellington rescuers, striking deals or releasing them on bond or, in the case of the seventy-four-year-old "Father" Matthew Gillet, forcing him out of jail. One of them, Loring Wadsworth, was elected mayor. The government wanted to concentrate its fire on the "Oberlitionists." The college was a breeding ground for sedition and treason in the opinion of the prosecuting attorney George Bliss. Bushnell and Langston were tried first. In the Bushnell case, Riddle and Spalding justified the defendant's actions and called for the overthrow of the fugitive law. Langston's lawyers, the Oberlin graduate Seneca Griswold and Franklin Backus, commended his actions and character.

On his conviction, Langston gave a moving speech (see above), which was reproduced as an abolitionist pamphlet. He justified resistance to the law. It was his revolutionary duty as a colored man, an *"outlaw of the United States,"* to rescue the fugitive. The courts and the law of the country, Langston noted, were made to "oppress and outrage colored men." He had not been tried, he observed pointedly, by a "jury of my peers"—state conventions had long protested the exclusion of blacks from juries. He had no rights that a white man was bound to respect, repeating Taney's obiter dicta from the Dred Scott decision, but he had the right of self-preservation. Willson, who was moved enough by the speech to recommend a light sentence, threatened the audience at the courtroom with removal because of their prolonged applause. In Boston, Wells Brown, Nell, Hayden, Grimes, and J. Sella Martin, the newly installed pastor of the Joy Street Baptist church, led a meeting of colored citizens, commending Langston's "thrilling eloquent speech." Self-taught, Martin had escaped from slavery in 1856. He moved to Massachusetts in 1859 as a pastor for a white church in Lawrence, filling in at the famous Tremont Temple too.

Charles and John Mercer Langston were the sons of a Virginia planter and his common-law enslaved wife, Lucy Langston. They moved to Ohio in 1834 after the death of their parents, and both attended Oberlin. Charles was a teacher in black schools in Chillicothe and Columbus and sent some of his pupils on to Oberlin. His more famous younger brother John became the state's first black lawyer, after training with the Republican lawyer Philemon Bliss, and officeholder. He replaced Dayton as town clerk. After the war he became a Republican congressman from Virginia and the American minister to Haiti. Both were active in the state black conventions and the Ohio Colored American League, founded in 1850. Referring to the rescue at the state black convention in 1858, Mercer Langston argued that black people would trample the fugitive slave law under their foot. As secretary of the Ohio State ASS, Charles Langston continued to assist fugitives. He helped found Wilberforce University and became a superintendent in the Freedman's Bureau.

The black rescuers continued their war against slavery well after the Price rebellion. Copeland, who was not indicted, joined John Brown and died at Harper's Ferry. James Monroe, an abolitionist professor who had been present at Fairchild's home when Price arrived, vainly tried to recover Copeland's body from southern medical students, who desecrated the graves of the raiders and used their bodies for dissection. The brothers Henry Evans and Wilson Bruce Evans were cabinetmakers, and both were married to the sisters of another Harper's Ferry raider, Lewis Sheridan Leary. Langston married Leary's widow, who was pregnant when he was killed at Harper's Ferry. Her daughter Louise attended Oberlin and was the mother of the poet Langston Hughes. She named her son after her stepfather. James L. Patton served as a chaplain in one of Ohio's first black regiments during the war, and Orindatus S. B. Wall, whose sister married John Mercer Langston, was the first black man commissioned as a captain in 1865. Wilson Evans and Fox also served in the Union army.

The Oberlin–Wellington trials attracted national attention. The reporter covering them for the *New York Tribune* was John Brown's coconspirator, John Kagi. A widely reproduced photograph of the rescuers appeared in *Frank Leslie's Illustrated Magazine*. James A. Thome, a professor at Oberlin and one of the original Lane rebels, visited them in prison. John Brown, who was under federal indictment for running slaves from Missouri at that time, attended a meeting held in their support. At the "felon's feast" when the rescuers met their lawyers, Mercer Langston predicted they would "go to prison, or if necessary, go out on the battlefield to meet the Slave Oligarchy." To Pillsbury, it was a "PROVIDENTIAL CALL" to "buckle on his armor for the conflict." Frances Ellen Watkins raised twenty dollars for the rescuers. The rescuer Jacob Shipherd, a nephew of one of the founders of Oberlin, compiled a history of the affair dedicated to the thirty-seven indicted. An introduction by the rescuers Henry Peck, a professor, and Ralph Plumb portrayed the government, "a gigantic tyranny" that knows no law but its "own despotic will," as the real lawless entity in the country. The prisoners started printing their own paper, the *Rescuer*, in jail and protested their incarceration in a written statement to the court. A massive antislavery meeting held outside the jail breathed defiance and was addressed by Giddings, who recommended forming a new Sons of Liberty to thwart the fugitive law, and by Governor Chase, the former congressman Joseph Root, and Edward Wade, among others. Chase vowed to use the state militia to free the prisoners if called to enforce a writ of habeas corpus. The old antislavery congressman Judge Sherlock Andrews joined the counsel for the defense.

Despite all the publicity, the Oberlin rescuers did not emerge unscathed. The trials of Bushnell and Langston resulted in guilty verdicts, fines, and imprisonment. The two men, neither of whom had much personal wealth, were dunned for the fines and court costs long after the trial. The Ohio Supreme Court, with Republican appointees, stunned everyone by refusing to issue a writ of habeas corpus for the prisoners despite an eloquent appeal by the state's attorney general, Christopher P. Wolcott. He called the fugitive law a "FLA- GRANT USURPATION OF DELEGATED POWERS," opining that the very "CAUSE OF CONSTITUTIONAL GOVERNMENT" was at stake. The Western ASS saw the refusal as proof that the state government was powerless to protect its citizens. One of the architects of the Wilmot Proviso, Justice Jacob Brinkerhoff, and Justice Sutliff dissented. Radicals in the Ohio Republican convention repudiated the majority opinion of Judge Joseph Swan, refused to renominate him, and passed a resolution calling for the repeal of the Fugitive Slave Act of 1850. In uphold- ing the letter of the law, Swan, like Shaw and Loring, retreated to "mechanis- tic formalism." Meanwhile, a Loraine County jury indicted Price's captors for kidnapping. In a final settlement, the remaining rescuers, with the exception of Bushnell, who served an additional five days, were released on July 6, 1859, in exchange for the release of the four indicted kidnappers, Jennings, Mitch- ell, Lowe and Davis. Their prosecutor was W. W. Boynton, who, unlike other members of his family, was antislavery. He also joined the battle to expunge the word *white* from the state constitution. Abolitionist meetings welcomed back the rescuers in Oberlin. Henry Evans was satisfied that he had done his duty. A choir sang the "Marseillaise."[14]

THE ABOLITIONIST UNDERGROUND

During the fugitive slave controversy, the abolitionist underground kicked into high gear. The vigilance committees of the 1850s, Still writes, were orga- nized not only to rescue self-emancipated slaves from being reenslaved but also to free slaves brought by their masters to the North. In July 1855 Col. John H. Wheeler, the U.S. minister plenipotentiary designate to Nicaragua, traveled to Philadelphia with his slave Jane Johnson and her two sons. Wheeler warned Johnson to steer clear of free blacks, especially the "colored waiters" in the ho- tel, and kept her in a hotel room while he went out for dinner, checking on her periodically. Johnson managed to get word out of her desire for freedom. Still received an anonymous note, probably from one of the black hotel staff, de- scribing her plight. Enlisting Passmore Williamson, the two men hurried to the ferry, where they found Johnson and Wheeler. Williamson, who arrived first, informed Johnson that she was entitled to her freedom and released her from Wheeler's grasp. Wheeler pleaded with her not to leave her son behind and even promised her freedom. Her son had been sold away from her, and Johnson had little hope of ever seeing him again. She left with Still and Williamson and boarded a hack ready to carry her and her two other sons to freedom. A heated exchange and scuffle occurred between Still, Williamson, and Wheeler, who was held down by two of five black dockworkers present, William Curtis, James P. Braddock, John Ballard, James Martin, and Isaiah Moore, of whom, Still wrote, "too much cannot be said in commendation."

After Johnson's disappearance, Williamson was served a writ of habeas corpus. First released on a bond of five thousand dollars, he was imprisoned on contempt of court by none other than Judge Kane. Abolitionists were appalled that habeas corpus was being used to enslave rather than free a person and suspected that Kane held Williamson in contempt rather than perjury because he wanted to avoid a trial by jury, a "troublesome element" of "American jurisprudence" for slaveholders. The Pennsylvania Supreme Court refused to grant a writ of habeas corpus to release Williamson, with the "honorable exception" of Judge Knox, who wrote the sole dissent. Williamson, who had worked for years anonymously in the PVC, became an overnight abolitionist celebrity, visited by Douglass and Tubman and feted in the antislavery press. The national black convention, which met at Philadelphia that year, sent a delegation to wait on him. He languished in jail for three months. In his massive compendium on "Atrocious Judges" in Anglo-American history, "Infamous as Tools of Tyrants and Instruments of Oppression," Hildreth, with probably Shaw and Kane in mind, reproduced Williamson's petition for a writ of habeas corpus as a "native citizen of Pennsylvania" and the decision of the court along with Knox's dissent. In England, Hildreth wrote, tyrannical judges were part of the "Norman yoke" that subverted democratic "Anglo Saxon" traditions of trial by jury, and despotism was personified in the divine right of monarchs to rule their subjects. In the American Republic, "some two hundred thousand petty tyrants . . . in the shape of slaveholders" exercised the divine right to rule through congressional prerogative and corrupt judges.

At an antislavery meeting in Norristown led by Abby Kimber and Sarah Pugh of the PFASS and Purvis, McKim, and James Mott of the PASS, called to express sympathy with Williamson, Johnson appeared on stage. McKim criticized Kane, and Purvis contended that he should be treated as an outlaw, a murderer, vagabond, and outcast. Douglass too lit into Kane's "tyrannical position." Pennsylvania abolitionists launched a petition drive to impeach Kane, and the newly formed Republican Party nominated Williamson for the office of canal commissioner while he was still in prison. In Boston, Garrison called for Kane's impeachment, seeing him as akin to Loring. The primary moving force in the

Johnson case, it became clear as the trial proceeded, was Johnson herself. It was she who had initiated her rescue; abolitionists had not foisted a choice on her. Jacob Bigelow, the successor to Torrey and Chaplin in the Washington underground, affirmed that Johnson had indicated her desire for freedom while there, and he had planned to send a man to Philadelphia to give notice of her case. Johnson sent in an affidavit from New York stating, "Nobody forced me away; nobody pulled me, and nobody led me; I went away of my own free will; I always wished to be free and meant to be free when I came North." In a dramatic courtroom appearance, where she appeared veiled and surrounded by women of the PFASS, Mott, Pugh, and Sarah McKim, she repeated her testimony in person. Williamson was released on a nolle prosequi. Johnson left with Mott and McKim, accompanied by state police officers, as District Attorney Van Dyke threatened to arrest her under the fugitive law. The PASS commended Judge Kelley and District Attorney Mann for their protection and determination to uphold Pennsylvania laws. Johnson made her home in Boston, where she lived happily, as Nell reported. One of her sons served in the Fifty-Fifth Massachusetts during the war.

Still and the five dockworkers were arrested for riot, assault, battery, and "highway robbery" for stealing slave property in transit. The men were summarily locked up, denied food, and given an "exorbitant bail" of seven thousand dollars each. The highway robbery charge was eventually dropped and the bail reduced by Judge Kelley. Still was defended by Charles Gibbons and the others by William Pierce, "one of the oldest, ablest and most faithful lawyers to the slave" and known to take even hopeless cases, and William Birney, the son of James Birney. Of the five, Ballard and Curtis were convicted, fined ten dollars each, and imprisoned for a week. The five men sued Alderman James Freeman for "corrupt and malicious conduct" and for the inhumane conditions they endured during their imprisonment. Williamson sued Kane for false imprisonment. Wheeler was recalled from Nicaragua in disgrace for extending recognition to the government of the filibusterer William Walker without sanction from Washington.[15]

Like Johnson, other enslaved women who struggled for freedom became causes célèbres in the abolition movement. In January 1856 a family of eight Kentucky slaves—Simon, Mary, and their twenty-one-year-old son, Robert Garner, who all belonged to one James Marshall, along with Robert's pregnant twenty-two-year-old wife Margaret Garner and her four children, Thomas, Sam, Mary, and Cilla, belonging to Archibald Gaines—crossed over the "Fugitive Slaves' bridge," the frozen Ohio River. They went straight to the cabin of the Kites, a free black family headed by Margaret's uncle, who had bought his children from slavery. Her cousin Elijah Kites alerted Levi Coffin in Cincinnati of their arrival, and Coffin advised that the Garners be moved immediately. Soon after Elijah returned, however, Deputy Marshal George Bennet, armed with a warrant from the federal commissioner John L. Pendery and accompanied by Marshal Calvin Butts and deputies from Kentucky, Gaines, and Thomas Marshall, the son of James, surrounded the cabin. The Garners refused to surrender and as the authorities forced their way into the cabin, Robert Garner fired and injured one of the deputies. At the prospect of being captured, Margaret decapitated her two-year-old-daughter, Mary, with a carving knife and attempted to kill her other children. They "fought with the ferocity of tigers."

The couple had borne their share of the cruelties of border state slavery and had no intention of returning. Robert, called Samuel by his owners and in court records, had been incessantly hired out, and Margaret, called Peggy by her owners, after having their first child, had given birth to three mixed-race children. A white neighbor of the Kites testified that he saw Gaines sobbing and carrying Mary's body. He had most likely abused Margaret over a long period. During her trial, when asked about a scar on her face, Garner responded, "White man struck me." She calmly reiterated her determination to kill her children rather than have them grow up in slavery. In proslavery telling, Garner was an unfeeling monster, but to abolitionists like Garrison, Henry C. Wright, and Parker she was a proud slave mother saving her daughters from a life of degradation. In a widely reproduced speech in the abolitionist press, Rev. Henry Bushnell anointed her a "heroic wife" and noble mother. The black women of Cincinnati waved their handkerchiefs in support when she appeared after her arrest.

As Margaret's example shows, enslaved women were just as capable of violent resistance to slavery as men. A year earlier a young, pregnant slave in Missouri, Celia, whose middle-aged widower master had bought her when she was just fourteen, had killed him after suffering years of abuse. Having borne two of his children and wanting to marry a fellow slave, Celia had dispatched him and burned his body when he tried to rape her while she was pregnant. Garrison reported the case in his "Catalogue of Southern Crimes and Horrors," but modern historians have only recently discovered it. Celia was tried for murder and convicted; her case was appealed to the Missouri Supreme Court, which stood by the decision of the lower court. Unable to make a self-defense plea stick and having attempted escape, Celia was hanged. The rape of a black woman was not recognized in slave law, and Missouri had been whipped into a proslavery frenzy over the battle for Kansas by its fire-eating senator David Atchinson and the Irish-born president of the University of Missouri, James Shannon. Like Celia, Margaret had been abused since she was a teenager.

The man who defended Margaret and became the lead counsel for the entire Garner family was the abolitionist attorney John Jolliffe. A lapsed Quaker from Virginia, Jolliffe was known to defend runaways and those accused of slave running, like John Mahan. Jolliffe's antislavery activism stretched back to the late 1830s, and he was a member and fund raiser for the AASS and a trustee of the Colored Orphan Asylum; his wife, Synthelia, was a member of the Ladies Antislavery Sewing Circle, which provided the Garners with fresh clothes during their imprisonment. Joliffe denounced the fugitive law and in 1852 ran unsuccessfully for Congress on the Free Democratic ticket. In the 1850s he worked pro bono in seventeen fugitive cases. He secured the freedom of an enslaved mistress of a slaveholder at personal expense. In one instance, a runaway named Louis being defended by Jolliffe and the future Republican president Rutherford B. Hayes surreptitiously made his way to freedom through a "crowd of colored people" in the court into a passage "crowded with Germans." Black Cincinnatians like Peter Clark and Frances Scroggins Brown, who had long been active in the abolitionist underground, brought such cases to white antislavery lawyers like Jolliffe.

Jolliffe had a personal connection to the Garner family: he had successfully defended Margaret's uncle Joe Kite against his master in a case arising from a dispute over the purchase of Elijah. In 1854 he defended a group of runaways belonging to three Kentucky slaveholders, one of whom was John Gaines, Margaret's original owner and Archibald's cousin. During the Garner trials, Margaret's mother was among a group of four Gaines slaves who escaped to Canada through the abolitionist underground. In 1853 an Irish proslavery Democratic judge, Jacob Flinn, before whom Joliffe had unsuccessfully argued a fugitive slave case, assaulted him and was fined seventy dollars plus court costs. Unrepentant, Flinn positioned himself as amicus curiae, or friend of the court, making unsolicited interjections during the Garner cases. After the Garners were transported back to Kentucky, he accompanied the victorious slave-catching party in celebration. Rowdies nearly beat a *Cincinnati Gazette* reporter to death on suspicion of his being an abolitionist.

Cincinnati's Irish population was largely incorporated into its Democratic machine. The city's elite had political and business ties across the river, and half the city's population was southern born. The state's Democratic governor had distributed Sharps rifles to two Irish militias during the so-called Irish Filibuster Case. They were hired as deputy marshals by Marshal Hiram Robinson, the owner of the *Cincinnati Enquirer,* in a moneymaking scheme as well as a plan to intimidate would-be black rescuers during the Garner affair. None of this appeased proslavery nativists like the Garners' owners. The Kentucky lawyer representing Marshall and Gaines, John W. Finnell, alluding to the Irish abolitionist James Elliot, who had immigrated twenty-five years earlier, argued, "That man fresh from the bog, had better stayed there and removed the shackles from his own enslaved brethren than come here to meddle with our institutions." Gaines joined the Know-Nothing Party and in 1857 was booked on charges of assaulting Jolliffe and let off with a minor fine.

The Garner cases, along with the Marshall and Gaines claims being tried separately before Commissioner Pendery, put slavery itself on trial. The affair was widely followed in the national press. Jolliffe pursued two main legal strategies, one the old antislavery tactic of getting Judge John Burgoyne, known for his antislavery views, to issue a writ of habeas corpus to remand the Garners into state custody, and the other was to prove that all the adult Garners had visited Ohio earlier with their masters, making them and Margaret's later offspring free. To prove the latter, he marshaled testimony from Cincinnati's black community as well as from the German butcher Jacob Rice (Riis) and his daughter, with whom Robert Garner and his family had stayed. In contrast to the witnesses for the defense, the lawyers for the claimants called on the slaveholding chivalry of Kentucky to vouch for their clients. Jolliffe protested the authorities' attempt to keep black people out of the hearing, and when Coffin attended, a belligerent deputy knocked his hat off. Jolliffe's main argument was the unconstitutionality of the fugitive law, which gave precedence to one clause of the Constitution over all other constitutional protections, as well as its inhumanity: "It had driven a frantic mother to murder her own child, rather than see it carried back to the seething Hell of American Slavery."

In response, Finnell recalled the "old negro woman" who had reared him, whom he loved "as dearly as any white person on earth." This sentimental picture of Finnell's mammy sought to shift the focus from the reality of Garner's actions. It became clear that Pendery would rule in favor of the claimants, using the decision of the Supreme Court in *Strader v. Graham* (1850), in which Taney argued that if a slave voluntarily returned to a slave state, then residence in a free state did not entitle him or her to freedom. Jolliffe then tried to have Garner remain in Ohio to stand trial on criminal charges of murdering her daughter, contending that the Garners would go singing to the gallows rather than be returned to slavery. But Robinson steadfastly refused to obey any writ issued by the state courts, for which he was held in contempt. He succeeded in getting a countermanding writ issued by the federal court judge Humphrey Leavitt to free himself. Short of an armed standoff, Ohio officials yielded to federal law and Pendery's rulings against the Garners. The following year Governor Chase, in another case, brokered a compromise between federal marshals, represented by the future copperhead Democrat Clement Vallandigham, and state officials. A local sheriff had been pistol whipped by federal marshals during the rendition of a runaway named Addison White of Mechanicsburg. Townspeople raised sufficient funds to purchase him, and White went on to serve in the Union army.

Abolitionists, who raised a subscription of eight hundred dollars when the Garners were remanded back to slavery, were bitterly disappointed at the outcome of the case. May wrote, "Alas for her" after "so terrible a struggle, so bloody a sacrifice, so near to deliverance . . . to be, by the villainy and lying of her 'respectable' white owner, again engulphed in the abyss of Slavery!" During the trial, Lucy Stone, who had tried to persuade Gaines to sell the Garners, made a courthouse speech in which she argued that Margaret had "a right to deliver herself" and her children from slavery. Rev. William H. Brisbane and an antislavery Baptist minister named P. S. Bassett visited Garner in prison, the latter reporting her determination to kill her children rather than subject them to "a life more bitter than death." Phillips called her "the noblest American woman that this generation has produced." With the Garner case, Giddings proclaimed, the war against slavery had been brought to "our shores." The WASS called it "an outrage." In her speech in Dublin, Sarah Parker Remond referred to Garner as "without protection from the licentiousness of a brutal master." Garner inspired contemporary abolitionist poems and novels, most notably, in our own times, Toni Morrison's *Beloved*.

Governor Chase, criticized by Kelley Foster, Parker, Phillips, and Pillsbury for not doing enough, in a long, carefully argued requisition request, asked for the rendition of Margaret Garner and her family as accessories in a crime committed on Ohio soil. In his annual message to the legislature, he argued that the Garner case had subverted the sovereignty of the state. By the time the Kentucky governor received and agreed to the request, Gaines had shipped Margaret and her family to his brother's plantation in Arkansas. En route, Garner's ferry collided with another, and she either jumped or was pitched into the Mississippi with the infant Cilla in her arms. She was rescued, but Cilla drowned. Playing cat and mouse with the authorities, Gaines rendered Margaret back to Louisville in formal compliance with the governor's orders, but before Ohio deputies could claim her he shipped her off again with her family to New Orleans, where another brother sold them to a cotton plantation in Mississippi. Margaret succumbed to typhoid in 1858 but not before she told Robert never to marry again in slavery. Robert joined the Union army. He settled in Cincinnati and married in freedom.[16]

The last fugitive slave rescue was led by the most famous female slave runaway, Harriet Tubman, in April 1860, in Troy. Troy was part of the abolitionist underground in upstate New York and had a local vigilance committee, the TVC. It was an important hub of black activism, the national black convention was held here in 1847, and it hosted the state conventions in 1841 and 1855 and a suffrage convention in 1858. Garnet pastored the Liberty Street Presbyterian church from 1839 to 1848 and was a member of the executive committee of the Eastern NYASS, known for its fugitive slave activism. Troy's most prominent abolitionist was Garnet's mentor, Rev. Nathan S. S. Beman, whose estranged wife's son was the rabid secessionist from Alabama William Lowndes Yancey. Black Trojans like William Rich, the barbers Peter Baltimore and James Harden, Tubman's cousin John H. Hooper, William J. Bowley, and John Bowley, who was married to Tubman's niece Kessiah, ran the TVC. In 1857 alone the TVC assisted fifty-five fugitives at a cost of $125. The runaway slave Charles Nalle came to Troy and boarded with the black grocer and TVC member William Henry. Nalle had escaped from his owner, Blucher Hansbrough, of Culpeper County, Virginia, with a fellow slave, Jim, in 1858. His manumitted wife, Kitty, and six children lived in Washington, and despite repeated requests Hansbrough had not allowed Nalle to hire himself out to earn enough money to buy his freedom, while demanding an exorbitant sum of over two thousand dollars.

Nalle escaped with help from the abolitionist underground. In the District he was assisted by the black schoolteacher Anthony Bowen and by Bigelow, whose activities were financed by Tappan and whose code name was William Penn. These men had taken over the Smallwood–Torrey–Chaplin network and regularly shipped runaways to Still's PVC, as they did Nalle. Kitty was jailed in Washington and would have been sold into slavery had not a white man bailed her out. She moved to Columbia, Pennsylvania, and was reunited with her husband. Hansbrough sold two of Nalle's brothers after his escape. From Philadelphia, Nalle journeyed to Troy, where he worked as a coachman for a prominent local Republican, Uri Gilbert. Two years later a local Democratic lawyer, Horatio Averill, intercepted one of Nalle's letters and informed his master, who sent the slave catcher Henry J. Wale to recover his property. Local Democrats besides Averill assisted Wale: William Beach acted as a lawyer for the claimant, his son Miles Beach was the federal commissioner who issued the warrant for Nalle's arrest, and Deputy Marshal John L. Holmes arrested him. The black-dominated TVC sprung into action. Harden spread the word about Nalle's arrest, and Henry contacted Martin I. Townsend, a Republican lawyer. A Barnburner Democrat, Townsend had joined the Free Soil and then the Republican Parties. He had successfully defended the fugitive slave Antonio Lewis as early as 1842. While Townsend rushed to get a writ of habeas corpus for

Nalle, a large interracial crowd gathered outside the commissioner's office in the Mutual Bank building where he was being held.

Tubman, who was passing through town from her home in Auburn to meetings in Boston, pushed herself into the bank, refusing to budge. Townsend appeared with Sheriff Nathaniel Upham and a writ of habeas corpus from the New York Supreme Court judge George Gould. As Nalle was being moved to Gould's office down the road, Tubman grabbed him and did not let go, even as club blows rained down on her head. She and other members of the crowd engaged in hand-to-hand combat with law enforcement officials and got the best of them. Tubman acted in form, "like a heroine," noted the *Weekly Anglo-African.* She instructed the crowd to drag Nalle to the docks, where he was put in a skiff and rowed across the Hudson to West Troy. Authorities in Troy telegraphed the mayor of West Troy, who promptly had Nalle rearrested and guarded by policemen in Justice Daniel Stewart's office. But the crowd in Troy did not give up. Led by Tubman, they commandeered the local ferry and many boats present and headed to West Troy, "a sizeable armada carrying several hundred warriors." After an exchange of stones, projectiles, and bullets—Harden had bullet holes in his hat and coat—the crowd managed to get ahold of the bleeding Nalle, who was taken to Schenectady and disappeared into the countryside.

A local newspaper reported that a number of the most respectable citizens of both towns were in the crowd, but "the rank and file . . . were black, and African fury is entitled to claim the greatest share in the rescue." After the people of Troy and West Troy raised $650 to purchase Nalle, he returned to the city a free man and resumed his employment with Gilbert. Democratic officials had indictments issued against a number of local "Black Republicans" such as Townsend, and Tubman was the only black rescuer indicted. None of them were tried owing to the onset of the war. By the end of the year, Still records Tubman in Maryland conducting her last group of slaves, an enslaved family joined by a young man and pregnant woman, to freedom. During the war Troy, like New York City, witnessed a massive draft riot led by Irish workers that quickly degenerated into an all-out attack on the black community. Perhaps the event had something to do with Nalle's decision to move to Washington.[17]

Highly publicized conflicts laid bare the abolitionist underground, which for the most part operated in stealth. In 1852 Jonathan and Juliet Lemmon of Virginia and their eight slaves traveled to New York on their way to Texas. The intrepid Louis Napoleon procured a writ of habeas corpus on behalf of the Lemmon slaves. Jay and Culver argued the case for the slaves, and Judge Elijah Paine decreed their freedom, as Lemmon had voluntarily brought his slaves to a free state. To be safe, Tappan, Ray, Pennington, and Napoleon decided to send them to Canada. The brother of one of the Lemmon slaves, Richard Johnson, who had escaped slavery earlier and contributed to their defense fund, joined them. Governor Howell Cobb of Georgia said the decision represented a breakdown of comity unheard of among civilized nations. New York's merchants took out a subscription for the Lemmon slaves and compensated their owners in the amount of $5,280. The case, *Lemmon v. Napoleon,* was appealed to the New York Supreme Court by the state of Virginia, with Culver, Joseph Blunt, and William M. Evarts representing Napoleon and the state of New York. In 1857 the court upheld Paine's decision, and the legislature passed resolutions stipulating that the state would not recognize slavery in any form within its borders. Culver was greeted like a celebrity at the annual AASS meeting. In 1860 the New York Court of Appeals by a 5–3 decision affirmed the Lemmon slaves' freedom, the proslavery Democrat Charles O'Conor representing the appellant, and the future president Chester A. Arthur, replacing Culver, Blunt, and Evarts, the people of New York. O'Conor's arguments were a mash of blatant appeals to racism, to New York's laws, which elevated the "African-negro" to "political equality" with whites if they owned a "speck of property," and to proslavery constitutionalism. He quoted the proslavery jurist and brother of Cobb, T. R. R. Cobb, that the constitutional recognition of slave property overrode the laws of New York. The Lemmon case gave substance to northern fears of a concerted southern plot to expand slavery or at least the purview of slave laws in the free states. After *Dred Scott,* an adverse Supreme Court ruling, as Virginia threatened to appeal, no longer seemed out of the realm of possibility.[18]

These famous cases reveal how the abolitionist underground precipitated the sectional conflict over fugitive slaves. The best description of it, as noted, is *The Underground Rail Road,* in which Still meticulously documented the many runaways that came through the PVC, most of them from 1857 to 1860. Still's massive book tells many stories, but perhaps the one of a fifteen-year-old enslaved girl, Anna Maria Weems, best illustrates the inventiveness of runaways, the desperate struggles of enslaved families, and the network of abolitionists stretching from Delaware, Maryland, and Washington to southern Pennsylvania and Philadelphia and on to New York City, upstate New York, and Canada. Weems escaped from her slave-trading owner "attired in male habiliments" as "Joe Wright," a coachman for the physician Ellwood Harvey. Her case was well known to abolitionists: her mother, Earro Weems, had purchased her own freedom and that of a daughter, but her three sons had been sold down south. The Weems Ransom Fund set up by Tappan and Ray not only created friction between the two men but also failed to redeem Anna Maria, as her owner refused to sell her. After much planning she escaped through the interracial abolitionist underground: Bigelow, in the District, accompanied Harvey, who drove her to Still in Philadelphia and then to New York, where Ray took her to Tappan's home. Rev. A. N. Freeman, the pastor of the Siloam Presbyterian church in Brooklyn, took her by train to an uncle and aunt in Buxton, Canada. Abolitionists managed to purchase her brothers. In another story, Still relates the escape of John Henry Hill to Canada. Hill fought off his enslavers after being told by his owner that he was being sold and disappeared into Richmond's black underground. He made his way to Still and the PVC. Hill arranged to have his free wife and children brought over. Eventually his uncle and brother also escaped to Canada, with Still's help. Hill's letters to Still reveal that he "never forgot those with whom he had been a fellow-sufferer in Slavery." Hill started assisting other freedom seekers. Like many fugitive slave abolitionists, he was done with prayers and believed that "the fire and sword would affect more good."

Unlike Still's published volume, many records of the abolitionist underground never saw the light of day at the time. One such is the two-volume "Record of Fugitives" found in the papers of the Garrisonian Sydney Howard Gay, the editor of the *Standard* in New York City. Gay recorded the fugitives sent to him by Still and Thomas Garrett, whom he mostly forwarded to Loguen in Syracuse, Myers in Albany, a handful to New Bedford and Boston and at times all the way to Canada. He even worked with Tubman. His most complete records were for the years 1855 and 1856. Gay collaborated with Ray and Tappan across factional lines and recorded the escape of over two hundred fugitive slaves. Antislavery fairs conducted by women abolitionists from as far away as Scotland financed their work. The central figure in the city's abolitionist underground was Napoleon. Napoleon was illiterate—his petition in the Lemmon case bore his mark "X"—and he left no record of his activities. He was known to be on the lookout constantly for fugitives in the city's streets and docks. Gay wrote to Still, "When it is possible I wish you would advise me two days before a shipment of your intention, as Napoleon is not always on hand to look out for them on short notice." He suggested using a telegraph and the code "One M. (or F.)," which would give notice of one male or female runaway arriving in New York. The success of the New York underground depended on Napoleon's savvy. In one case he was sent after a slave, Sarah Moore, who had escaped from New Bern, North Carolina, hidden for seven days by a steward aboard a ship. She was living in New Haven and believed to be betrayed by her husband. Napoleon was taking her by train to Albany when he spotted the New York marshal who had caught Pennington's family. Thinking on his feet, he and Moore got off at Springfield, and he sent her on to Syracuse instead. Napoleon also recovered her children and saw them reunited with her. Napoleon and the black printer William Leonard continued to operate the abolitionist underground from the NASS office after Gay left to edit the *Tribune*. Napoleon was reputed to have assisted three thousand fugitives.[19]

Besides Gay's record, the recently discovered narrative of John Parker, a former slave and an active participant in what he called the Borderland war over slavery in Ohio offers a glimpse into the mindset of the black foot soldiers of the abolitionist underground. Parker not only describes his own struggle for freedom but also gives one of the best eyewitness accounts of conflict along the Ohio River between "the friends and enemies of the fugitive." A frequent accomplice of Father Rankin, whom he called "a man of deeds as well as words," and of Coffin, Parker recounted "my own little personal war against slavery." Perhaps the most noteworthy characteristic of Parker's narrative is the words he chooses to describe this war, his hatred of slavery even though he had relatively kind owners who allowed him to purchase his freedom, his reference to the land south of the river as enemy territory, and his martial references to the "fortunes of war" and "council of war" when talking about his work, which resembled the tactics of guerilla warfare and insurgency. Claiming to have assisted 315 slaves before and 440 after the passage of the fugitive law, some coming from as far south as Tennessee, Parker described many dangerous escapades as he rowed back and forth across the Ohio River with a bounty of a thousand dollars on his head. He did not just assist fugitives but, like Tubman, went into slave territory repeatedly to run off slaves. Parker came close to being captured and killed at many points. After the passage of the Fugitive Slave Act, he burned his "memorandum book," in which, like Still, he had recorded the names and stories of slaves he had assisted. The abolitionists in Ripley, Ohio, came within an "ace" of anticipating John Brown, he claimed. A revolutionary abolitionist, Parker was not blind to the potential of antislavery politics: he named one of his sons Hale Giddings.[20]

Abolitionists did not manufacture the fugitive slave controversy but were enlisted and radicalized by self-emancipated slaves. After the Burns case, Boston abolitionists formed the Anti–Man Hunting League (AMHL), whose purpose was to fight slaveholders and slave hunters with their own methods, that is, to restrain and kidnap them. The leading organizers of the AMHL were veterans of the BVC, like its record keeper Bowditch, Loring, Sewall, Bearse, Howe, Parker, Higginson, Clarke, William F. Channing, Alcott, Garrisonians like the MASS agent Samuel May Jr., David Lee Child, Phillips, and the political abolitionists Elizur Wright, Charles Slack, Andrew, F. W. Bird of Walpole, and black abolitionists like Hayden and Joshua B. Smith, "the famous black caterer—as brave as a lion and 'upto anything for one of his race.'" Its membership was restricted to those over the age of eighteen, and, although women were not excluded, it did not have a single female member. Applicants for membership had to go through a "process of initiation," answering a series of questions on the fugitive slave law and the idea of direct action in self-defense. Its constitution called for bimonthly meetings and set up local leagues and even a sort of shadow government with a militia, committees, a senate, and a council. Procedures for secret meetings stipulated two doorkeepers, one inner and one outer.

The AMHL of Massachusetts had 469 members, Boston 80, Abington 29, Concord 24, Leominster 30, and Worcester 16, and there were local leagues in Marblehead and Newburyport. Bowditch noted, "*Unanimously the leagues first proclaimed organized action of a physical character against the Slaveholder himself.*" It conducted drills diagrammed by Bowditch on how to restrain a slave hunter: four members holding a limb each and surrounded in a circle by twelve other members armed with the "billies" stored in Bowditch's basement. The purpose was not to injure but to disable and transport the perpetrator out of the state through various "secure lodges." Its purpose, outlined in the "Constitution of the Defensive League of Freedom," was to "make it difficult for a slave hunter to come and remain among us." The league also took over most of the BVC's functions, issuing broadsides warning black Bostonians about slave catchers and collaborators, petitioning the state government, and assisting fugitives. But the main aim of the AMHL, or the Defensive League of Freedom, was to make Massachusetts unsafe for slave hunters or, as its printed circular put it, "Our purpose is to see that no man is beaten down by the slave power and the immense resources of the US government, that no man is ruined for simple acts of humanity."

The league also included fugitive slave abolitionists such as Abraham Galloway from New Bern, North Carolina. Galloway had managed to stow away in a ship, enduring its fumigation meant to get rid of runaways as well as disease, and, with the help of Still and the PVC, escaped to Canada. He was at home in Boston's radical abolitionist milieu, developing connections to Garrison and James Redpath's revolutionary plans to undermine slavery from Haiti. He may have also been a member of a black abolitionist society League of Freedom, known as the Liberators, operating out of Canada West to guide fugitive slaves. Galloway became a spy for the Union army and a leader in North Carolina during Reconstruction until his death in 1870.[21]

Some members of the abolitionist underground entered the historical record when they were prosecuted under the Fugitive Slave Act. In 1852 Rush Sloane, a lawyer in Sandusky, Ohio, whose strategic location on Lake Erie made it a common stopover for freedom seekers headed to Canada, was fined three thousand dollars and over a thousand dollars in court costs for assisting seven Kentucky runaways. The black community of Sandusky presented the bankrupt Sloane with a silver-headed cane in appreciation of his efforts. He went on to serve as a probate judge in Erie County and eventually as mayor of Sandusky after the war. In 1854 a sixty-year-old Irish peddler, Thomas Brown, who had moved from Cincinnati to Kentucky, was arrested for assisting fugitive slaves from Union, Henderson, Davies, and Hopkins Counties, the citizens of these counties paying five hundred dollars to ensure his conviction. In 1857 he published an account of his imprisonment in Kentucky in which he described the brutal treatment he was subjected to as well as his fellow prisoners, some of whom were part of the abolitionist underground in the border states. These included a mechanic who had given a runaway some food and a black man from Evansville, Indiana, who died after a jailer gave him a blow to the head. A number of "antislavery prisoners" in Kentucky had working-class origins. Some were foreign born, like the German laborer William Green, who was imprisoned in 1859 for helping a slave woman, Hagar, and her children escape slavery.

Nineteen "free persons of color" were arrested for antislavery activities, five of whom were common laborers, one a cooper, and another a blacksmith. Elijah Anderson, a skilled blacksmith born in Virginia who was known to make forays into slave territory to assist runaways, died in a Kentucky prison in 1861. Anderson's last trip to rescue a free man's enslaved wife and four daughters had resulted in his capture. He was part of a black underground that operated out of Evansville, where Thomas Brown hawked his goods, and Madison, Indiana. William Anderson was a fugitive slave abolitionist who left a narrative not just of his life in slavery but also of the Indiana underground. As he put it, "My two wagons, and carriage, and five horses were always at the command of the liberty-seeking fugitive. Many times have my teams conveyed loads of fugitive slaves away while the hunters were close upon their track." He was arrested in 1856. The trial, Anderson wrote, "cost me all the money I could raise, and jeopardized my only piece of property, and has left me penniless and destitute."[22] It is not clear whether both of the Andersons belonged to the shadowy Anti-Slavery League known to assist fugitives in southern Indiana. The emergence of abolitionist leagues committed to self-defense marked a militant phase in the abolitionist resistance to slave law.

The implementation of the fugitive law also claimed countless victims and caused the kidnapping of free blacks to surge. Rev. Samuel May Jr. compiled a list of such victims that was published in 1856 and reissued in a revised, en-

larged edition by the AASS in 1861. May painstakingly combed through northern newspapers to include each and every known instance of fugitive slave
rendition and kidnapping of free blacks in the 1850s. He remarked that he was
not able to include those cases in which fugitives had been overtaken before
they reached the free states, concluding that it was a mockery to refer to them
as free. Besides the notorious Gap gang in southern Pennsylvania, a criminal
kidnapping gang called the Black Birders operated out of the Five Points district
in New York. May included not just the famous instances of rebellion but also
hundreds of cases of rendition, like that of a Virginian family who claimed they
were not fugitives but visiting Pennsylvania with their master's consent. Unimpressed, a federal commissioner remanded them back to slavery. There were
other stories that illustrated abolitionist success. In Philadelphia the PASS had
long fought George Alberti, a known kidnapper, who was finally caught, fined
a thousand dollars, and imprisoned in 1851 for the illegal kidnapping of Gibson.
Interviewed by a NASS reporter in 1859, Alberti turned out to be a true believer,
claiming that the Bible sanctioned slavery and that he had enslaved a hundred
blacks. That year the PVC won a landmark victory in the case of the fortuitously
named Daniel Webster, who was arrested, tried, and released by a federal commissioner in Harrisburg. The commissioner, a scion of a Quaker family, was
scrupulously fair, giving equal weight to the testimony of black Pennsylvanians
and to the Virginians who testified on behalf of the prosecution. In 1860 the
black Baptist and member of Ohio's Vigilance Committee Rev. William M.
Mitchell published the first history of the UGRR, in which he highlighted the
heroism of slave runaways and their free black allies.[23]

Abolitionist legal theory justified resistance to unjust laws. In 1853 William
Goodell published his legal indictment of slavery, *The American Slave Code in
Theory and Practice*. Ranging widely over statute law, judicial cases, instances
of extralegal violence, and even the Choctaw and Cherokee laws of slavery,
Goodell examined the treatment, lack of formal legal rights, and punishment
of slaves. A pertinent chapter on the fugitive laws, state and national, detailed
the elaborate police and legal system set up to prevent slave escapes and facilitate renditions. Published by the AFASS, his book inspired the Georgian
Thomas R. R. Cobb's massive legal defense of slavery published five years later.
In *Despotism in America*, which was reprinted in the wake of the Burns rendition, Hildreth added a one-hundred-page chapter on the fugitive slave question.
The fugitive slave law, he argued, personified the legal and political despotism
of slavery. In her tract *The Duty of Disobedience* (1860), Lydia Maria Child
reasoned, "You have learned that the law offers colored men nothing but its

penalties; that the white man engrosses all its *protections*." The work was part of the abolitionist offensive as northern states deliberated repealing their personal liberty laws to appease southern secessionists.[24]

In its defiance of the Fugitive Slave Act, abolition took on a revolutionary character, personified by the fugitive slave rebellions and the abolitionist underground. The abolitionists' critique of the law of slavery and of the criminalization of blackness by the fugitive law first addressed the issue of racial inequality in law enforcement that continues to bedevil American society.

ABOLITION WAR

When John Brown announced his intention to "mingle my blood further with . . . the blood of millions in this Slave country, whose rights are disregarded by wicked, cruel and unjust enactments," he signaled the final phase in the abolition war against slavery.[1] Brown was not sui generis or an aberrant lone wolf: he was the product of the abolition movement.

The simultaneous radicalization of abolition and the emergence of antislavery politics set the stage for war and emancipation. These two streams, one revolutionary and the other electoral, often seen as distinct, were symbiotic. During the Kansas wars, slaveholders and their allies used the powers of the federal government to subvert not only black freedom but also the norms of representative government. An aggressively expansionist Slave Power convinced a majority of northerners, including Lincoln, that the fate of democracy was irrevocably tied to the destruction of slavery. With Lincoln's election to the presidency and the secession of most of the slave states, antislavery could finally harness the power of the state: the political legitimacy and military might of the United States government. Hubris overtook the slaveholding class, who for much of the country's history had dominated it.

As a radical social movement, abolition did not become irrelevant or transformed into an establishment party. During the war, abolitionists and their Radical Republican allies pushed the Lincoln administration from nonextension to abolition to black rights. And as they had done before, the enslaved initiated the emancipation process by voting with their feet. Wars by themselves do not inexorably lead to emancipation, as the history of modern racial slavery in the Americas makes amply clear. Slave resistance, abolitionist pressure—often forgotten in the history of emancipation—an antislavery president and Congress,

and the military victory of the Union army made the Civil War into an abolition war.[2]

KANSAS WARS

John Brown's abolition war was long in the making. His father, Owen Brown,
was a trustee of Oberlin College and a founding member of a pioneering antislavery society. Owen Brown traced his beliefs to early Connecticut abolitionists
and was known to shelter fugitives. John Brown was born in 1800 in Torrington.
His so-called conversion to abolition is usually attributed to a single moment in
which, seeing an enslaved boy being beaten with an iron shovel, he swears *"eternal war* with slavery." Upon hearing about the death of Lovejoy, he decides to
"consecrate" his "life to the destruction of slavery." One of his sons argued that
a "colored preacher" influenced his father. Brown gathered his family, making
a "solemn compact" for an "active war" on slavery. He proposed a black school
and said "young blacks" would act as "firing powder" on slavery. The radical
abolitionist spent the 1830s and 1840s struggling with business failures and the
deaths of his first wife and five children.[3]

Brown identified with abolitionism. He subscribed to the *Liberator*, which he
read aloud to his family, and defied segregated church seating. He published
"Sambo's mistakes" (1848) in *Ram's Horn*, intertwining uplift with resistance.
Assuming a black voice, Brown, like generations of black abolitionists, criticized intemperance, vice, disunity, and sectarianism. Most fatal, he wrote, was
submitting to injustice, which would gain blacks as much respect as northern doughfaces, who lick the "spittle" of slaveholders. Between 1846 and 1848
Brown lived in Springfield, Massachusetts. He met Douglass, who said of him,
"Though a white gentleman, [he] is in sympathy a black man, and as deeply
interested in our cause, as though his soul had been pierced with the iron of
slavery." To Douglass, Brown proposed his "Subterranean Pass Way," a plan
to spirit slaves to the Allegheny Mountains and create a conduit for their escape to Canada. In 1851 Brown organized the all-black United States League of
Gileadites against the fugitive law. Evoking Lovejoy, Torrey, and the "branded
hand" of Walker, Brown recommended that Gileadites "outnumber your adversaries" with "weapons exposed to view" to prevent renditions. If indicted,
Gileadites must go to *"your most prominent and most influential white friends"*
for help. No jury would convict them, but he suggested creating a tumult in
the court by burning gunpowder if indicted. Forty-four blacks, including four
women and the abolitionist Henry Johnson, signed on.[4]

Brown began his war against slavery in earnest in Kansas. Historians often view the Kansas wars as a prelude to the Civil War. A struggle between settlers from the free states and those from the slave states broke out almost immediately after the passage of the Kansas–Nebraska Act of 1854. The Massachusetts (later the New England) Emigrant Aid Company, founded by Eli Thayer, funneled money and provisions to free-state emigrants. Abolitionists such as Hildreth, Sewall, and Howe as well as the free soilers Bird, Wilson, and Burlingame joined the company, its "plan for freedom" promising a contest of the people versus slavery. Amos Lawrence held the purse strings. But a majority of free-state emigrants came from the old northwest. They carried with them the antislavery and antiblack attitudes of their states. Seward predicted that northern emigrants, their numbers swelled by European immigration, were sure to win the battle of popular sovereignty or, as southerners called it, squatter sovereignty. Men like Sen. David Atchison of Missouri, who led proslavery forces, refused to accept that.

The Kansas wars blew apart the theory of American republicanism holding that white liberty was based on black slavery. In March 1855, despite the state's free-state majority, thousands of Missouri border ruffians invaded the territory and stole the elections, as noted in chapter 14. A proslavery territorial legislature passed a law that made it criminal to speak or write against slavery, prescribed ten years' hard labor or death for assisting fugitive slaves, and the death penalty for instigating a slave rebellion. Further, it restricted jury service to proslavery settlers in any case arising under this draconian law. President Pierce removed from office his appointee, Gov. Andrew Reeder, who refused to endorse the fraudulent elections. In response, free staters organized their own territorial government in Topeka. Abolitionists like Augustus Wattles and Clarina Nichols were a minority, though some northern emigrants were radicalized by their experience. Brown's sons hoped to find land and fight against slavery. John Brown Jr., who liberated two slaves, complained that free staters wanted to make Kansas a whites-only state, proposing "outrageous restrictions upon the colored man." Douglass promoted the emigration of a "LARGE AND WELL DISCIPLINED BODY OF FREE COLORED PEOPLE FROM THE NORTHERN STATES," but blacks stayed away from Kansas, especially after the law required settlers to uphold slavery.

Brown followed his sons, who set up Brown's Station in Osawatomie. Before leaving he attended a convention in Syracuse, presided over by Smith, Goodell, McCune Smith, and Douglass, to form the Radical Political Abolition Party. It became the first national political convention to call a black man to the chair, McCune Smith, who was nominated for secretary of state on its state ticket headed by Smith. Members of the defunct AFASS, including Tappan, Jocelyn, George Whipple of the AMA, and William Whiting, joined in the call for the convention. The slogan of the new party was "Slavery an Outlaw—And Forbidden by the Constitution which provides for its Abolition." It called slaveholding a crime, and since it was the duty of civil governments to suppress crime, those that did not were bound to be overthrown. The party recommended abolition through the ballot box or the dissolution of the Union and revolution, encouraging free soilers to correct their course after their "disappointments" in pursuing nonextension. The convention endorsed armed resistance, with Tappan dissenting. It called for opposition to the fugitive law and assistance for the cause of freedom in Kansas. Smith read letters from Brown's sons recommending the formation of military companies. Douglass took up a collection for Brown, who received sixty dollars, an assortment of pistols, broadswords, and muskets to avenge the murder of free-state settlers.

In May 1856 border ruffians and "southern rights" men from South Carolina and Alabama led by Jefferson Buford and Atchison and carrying banners proclaiming "SUPREMACY OF THE WHITE RACE," sacked Lawrence, the free-state stronghold named after its benefactor. The free staters, outnumbered and outgunned, offered no fight, and their leaders, Charles Robinson and James H. Lane, were arrested. The proslavery army destroyed the press of the antislavery *Herald of Freedom* and *Kansas Free State*, burned Robinson's house and the free-state hotel, and looted and laid the town to waste. Robinson appointed Brown a captain of the Liberty Guards in the First Brigade of Kansas Volunteers. While Brown prepared for a nighttime attack on the Missourians, a truce was brokered between Robinson, soon elected governor of the Topeka government, Lane, the Indiana congressman who ironically had voted for the Kansas–Nebraska Act but presided over the Topeka convention, and the new governor, Wilson Shannon. The Emigrant Aid Company sent money and Sharpe's rifles, called Beecher's Bibles, after Henry Ward Beecher recommended sending rifles rather than Bibles to Kansas.[5]

Bleeding Sumner soon joined bleeding Kansas as potent symbols of slaveholder aggression. On May 22 the South Carolinian representative Preston Brooks beat Sumner senseless after he delivered a speech called "The Crime Against Kansas." Abolitionists took the assault on Sumner, known for his virtually one-man fight in the Senate to repeal the fugitive law, personally. The abolitionist tone of Sumner's speeches had gained him high praise. Parker called him a "Senator with a conscience." Douglass wrote to him, "All the friends of freedom, in every State, and of every color, may claim you, just now, as their representative." Brooks's caning of Sumner is often portrayed as a retaliation for his Kansas speech, in which Sumner allegedly insulted his relative Sen. A. P. Butler unjustifiably. But southerners and their allies had rained abuse on Sumner, accusing him of advocating the "cause of niggerism." Butler, whose coarseness in debate has eluded historians' attention, was a rabid supporter of the fugitive and Kansas laws. He had asked Sumner to write a play about a "negro princess in search of a husband" and a white man's repulsion to "her white teeth . . . black skin and kinky hair." Butler claimed that when Sumner "speaks with so much fervor of the black race as equal to the white, let him recollect that, according to the judgment of history, they were once regarded something like puppies when they were weaned, and their mothers and fathers could be disposed of with a profit." Sumner's allusion to the "blunders" and "loose expectoration" that poured forth from Butler's mouth (owing to a defect in his lip) was in response to this crude race baiting. He likened Butler's devotion to slavery to Don Quixote's devotion to his ugly mistress and Stephen Douglas to Sancho Panza. Sumner's speech epitomized gendered abolitionist rhetoric, the rape of the virgin territory of Kansas by the brutal violence of slavery: "Border sorrows and African wrongs are revived together on American soil, while, for the time being, all protection is annulled, and the whole territory is enslaved." Garrison, not given to praising antislavery politicians indiscriminately, gushed at the speech's "power and grandeur."

Brooks's assault on Sumner was not just a matter of personal honor but a deliberate attempt, as he explained, to chastise an abolitionist, or, as the *Richmond Enquirer* put it, "They must be lashed into submission." Brooks beat Sumner the way a slaveholder whipped a slave, or a slave's ally. He had argued that the African was incapable of self-government and that slavery "has been the greatest blessing to the country," as it acted as a conservative check against fanatical movements that would have convulsed the entire nation in a "social explosion." When the House expelled Brooks, he asked if they intended to follow him to his plantation, where such punishment was doled out regularly to his slaves. Despite previous confrontations on the congressional floor, the enactment of a slaveholding ritual in the halls of Congress on a white man, a senator no less, shocked the North and no doubt helped the Republicans in the presidential election of 1856. Not only was Brooks reelected but most southerners approved of his conduct. The Massachusetts legislature passed resolutions that equated the assault on Sumner with a blow against representative government and free speech. As a standing rebuke, Sumner's chair lay vacant for nearly four years while he recuperated. Black Bostonians led by Nell, Morris, and Rock met at Reverend Grimes's Twelfth Baptist church to protest the assault on "our" senator, "that in this dastardly attempt to crush out free speech, we painfully recognize the abiding prevalence of that Spirit of Injustice which for two centuries upon this continent, ground our progenitors and ourselves under the iron hoof of Slavery . . . that we hereby express to Mr. Sumner our entire confidence in him as a faithful friend of the slave." Abolitionists led indignation meetings throughout the North. Brooks, previously a unionist Democrat, became a secessionist, vowing to "tear the Constitution of the United States, trample it under foot, and form a Southern Confederacy, every State of which will be a slave-holding State." A year later he died of a throat infection.[6]

Brown, who later insisted on viewing Sumner's bloodied coat, decided "to fight fire with fire." On May 24 he and his sons killed proslavery settlers in Pottawatomie, some of whom had accused them of abolitionism in court: the Sherman brothers, known to harass free staters and force Indian women into prostitution, James Doyle, a nonslaveholder from Tennessee who had threatened Henry Thompson, Brown's son-in-law, for using "incendiary language" on racial equality, and Allen Wilkinson, also of Tennessee, the district attorney. Seventy-five percent of the fifty-plus people killed in Kansas were free-state settlers, and twenty-eight were murdered outright. Of the eight proslavery men killed at Pottawatomie, five were hacked to death with broadswords by Brown's party in a summary execution. Brown spared only Doyle's youngest son, when his mother begged for his life. They killed the men Indian style, in a sudden nighttime reprisal. Kansas settlers were anti-Indian, bent on aggrandizing their land. Rev. Tom Johnson of the Shawnee Mission, the first proslavery settlement, was keen on exterminating Native Americans and enslaving African Americans. The Browns were an exception, befriending local Indians who hired them to survey their land. After the Pottawatomie massacre, the "half-breed" John Tecumseh Ottawa Jones sheltered the Browns.

Higginson, a Brown admirer, thought Pottawatomie put an "immediate check to the armed aggressions of the Missourians." Not used to being victims, the proslavery press called to "let slip the dogs of war," which plagued Kansas through the Civil War when Confederate raiders sacked Lawrence again and killed two hundred people. The first African Americans to serve in the Union army did so in the First Kansas Colored Volunteer Infantry organized by Lane. They raided Missouri and liberated slaves. The legend of Old Osawatomie Brown grew when he led forty free soilers to victory against a larger force of Missourians under Henry Clay Pate. Pate captured and tortured Brown's two sons and destroyed Brown's Station. He served in the Confederate army. Despite being a wanted man, Brown continued to fight in Kansas. In the Battle of Osawatomie he lost his son Frederick, whom he buried in North Elba under the headstone (procured from Connecticut) of his great-grandfather, a Revolutionary War soldier.[7]

The Kansas outrages were a matter of debate among abolitionists. The NEAS convention condemned the failure of the government to protect the political and civil rights of free staters. Garrison's correspondent Charles Stearns, a nonresistant, advocated armed self-defense. Garrison, who had defended slave rebellions, conceded that the settlers had a right to defend themselves, but he could not stomach the Kansas wars. Violence and bowie knives, he argued, were the tools of slavery. He sharply criticized Beecher's exulting in the exploits of the Puritans, who used their Bibles and guns against Native Americans, when it was used as an example for free soil Kansans. Garrison wrote that Indian blood was still crying out to heaven for retribution. Even Parker agreed that Sharpe's rifles could not be reconciled with the Gospel. Stearns respectfully dissented, asserting that the doctrine of nonresistance was useless in Kansas. Garrison was also bothered that free-state Kansans left out the colored citizen and were conducting a selfish and partial struggle. Usually not one to evoke the Constitution, he argued that the racially exclusive Topeka government was in violation of it.

Although Garrison criticized the violence in Kansas, he refused to join the compensated emancipation movement led by Burritt. Garrison admired the multilingual, working-class intellectual. An advocate of universal peace and labor education, Burritt was known by a moniker he disliked, "the learned blacksmith." Following his attempt to lead an international peace movement, Burritt edited a number of influential peace journals, ending with *The North and the South*, to prevent the descent into war. He advocated the revival of the free produce movement; if British markets were shut against slave-grown produce, southerners would be forced to abandon slavery. He recommended free labor depots that would trade in cotton, rice, and sugar grown in the West Indies and India. At the individual level, he asked consumers to abstain from participating in the crime and guilt of receiving stolen goods. By the end of the decade, Burritt was touting his compensated emancipation scheme as another way to end slavery without conflict. He revived an old antislavery idea, namely, the sale of public lands to purchase southern slaves. Burritt's National Compensated Emancipation Convention, held in Cleveland in 1857, had few southern backers and virtually no abolitionists, who opposed any compensation for slaveholders as a class. Only Smith attended. Smith, connecting compensated abolition to land reform, posited that slaveholders receive $150 from the federal government and an additional $75 from their states for each slave they emancipated. The freed slave would receive $25 and a plot of land. William Watkins maintained that if anyone deserved compensation it was the slaves, for years of stolen labor. Douglass worried that compensation made emancipation more a matter for the counter than the conscience. Garrison predicted that the slave south "will listen to no proposition" for abolition when it declares slavery as "essential to her safety and prosperity" and as "the normal condition of mankind." Even though he is often characterized as being purely for moral suasion, Garrison recognized that an aggressively expansionist South could no longer be "reasoned with." The present value of slaves, he pointed out, was "unparalleled in history," far greater than Burritt offered (an individual adult male slave was worth thousands). The compensated emancipation movement petered out with Burritt holding his last, sparsely attended convention in Albany in 1859. He blamed "old John Brown" and the Harper's Ferry raid.[8]

Brown gained his staunchest supporters among abolitionists. During his northeastern lecture tour he met members of the National and Massachusetts Kansas Committees, formed to aid free-state emigrants, giving speeches in the legislature and in small towns across New England and gaining the admiration of Emerson, Thoreau, and the "secret six" who financed his plan to start a slave rebellion. Higginson called him a "genuine warrior of the Revolution." Besides Higginson, Parker, Howe, Smith, and the transcendentalist schoolteacher Franklin Sanborn signed on. The Medford industrialist George L. Stearns, who was put in charge of recruiting black Union soldiers, rounded up the secret six. Higginson, Howe, and Stearns were also members of the Kansas committee. Brown's efforts at fund-raising were not very successful, but Sanborn, acting as an agent for Lawrence and Stearns, paid Smith over a thousand dollars for Brown's farm in North Elba. Phillips alone contributed twenty-five dollars. Abolitionists respected Brown for his willingness to take on proslavery forces in Kansas. The Kansas committees provided him with arms presumably to be used there. Brown ordered pikes and bowie knives mounted on poles from a blacksmith, collecting them on the eve of his raid. Brown revealed his plans for a "Rail Road business on a somewhat extended scale" to the secret six, a plan to invade Virginia, run off slaves, spread rebellion, and create a Maroon community in the Appalachians, a base from which to attack slave society and attract runaways.[9]

No anachronistic attempt to label Brown a terrorist can deny the abolitionist vision that motivated him. He spent the years before his raid seeking recruits. He stockpiled weapons in Iowa, where Hugh Forbes, a British soldier and the author of a manual on revolutionary fighting, drilled his Kansas followers. Brown was forced to postpone his raid because of the betrayal of Forbes, who, upset at not being paid, wrote to Seward, Sumner, Wilson, and Greeley. Brown discussed creating a free State of Topeka which would give the right to vote to African Americans and women, its state seal a black man atop a cannon holding a drawn sword and the motto "Justice to all Mankind." While staying with Douglass in 1858, Brown composed a "Provisional Constitution and Ordinances for the People of the United States." It called slavery a "most barbarous unprovoked and unjustifiable War of one portion of its citizens upon another portion" and was written in the name of black citizens. Brown's revolutionary black state encompassed women's rights and decreed all property be held in common and used for common benefit. A victim of the boom and bust economy of slavery's capitalism, Brown was a critic of private property. He also wrote "A Declaration of Liberty by the Representatives of the Slave Population of the United States of America" modeled after the Declaration. It promised to "secure equal rights, privileges, and Justice to *all, Irrespective of Sex*; or Nation." Calling out slave traders, slaveholders, and "idle, haughty, tyrannical, *Arrogant Land Monopolists*," he declared the right of slaves to rise up and change a government of such "Base Piratical Rulers."

Prominent black abolitionists did not accompany Brown on his raid, but he apprised them of his plans and solicited funds from them. He wrote to John Jones and H. O. Wagoner in Chicago, Downing in Providence, and Garnet in New York. As Nelson Hawkins, he visited Gloucester in Brooklyn, who wished him "Gods speed in his glorious work," Loguen in Syracuse, and he met with Still, Douglass, and Garnet. Gloucester's wife, Elizabeth, sent him twenty-five dollars. Accompanied by Loguen, he journeyed to St. Catherine's, where he met "General Tubman." Brown referred to Tubman in the masculine and hoped to persuade her and Douglass to join him. After meeting with Delany, Brown attended the Chatham convention, where he revealed his plan to start a rebellion. When some voiced doubts, Brown pointed to Haiti. The convention unanimously accepted Brown's provisional constitution, but the emigrationists Delany, William Monroe, and J. G. Reynolds, who led the radical League of Liberty, opposed an article disavowing the overthrow of the U.S. government. William Howard Day printed copies of the constitution for Brown to carry to Harper's Ferry, and he gained a recruit, Osborne Perry Anderson, a printer who wrote an account of the convention and the raid.

Brown was back in Kansas in 1859 under another assumed name, Shubel Morgan. A year earlier the Georgian Charles Hamilton, a future colonel in the Confederate army, frustrated at their success in the polls, rounded up eleven free staters, of whom he killed five, wounded five, and left one unhurt. At this time Brown and his son John Brown Jr., who, as noted, had been tortured by

Pate, ran a secret organization known as Black Strings in Ohio, recognizable by their black ribbons, to liberate slaves. Fighting with James Montgomery's free-state army, Brown gained two more recruits. He carried out a dramatic raid into Missouri, rescuing the enslaved Daniels family and six other slaves, eleven in all, and killing a slaveholder who drew his gun. In a letter to the *Tribune*, Brown's "Parallels," he compared the slave raid, which "forcibly restored" the slaves' natural rights, with Hamilton's killings, still unpunished. With a price of $3,000 on his head by the state of Missouri, Brown eluded capture and even briefly imprisoned some federal troops. When the Buchanan administration added $250 to that amount, Brown retorted that he had put a price of $2.50 on Buchanan's head. He escorted the slaves to Canada with the help of Jones in Chicago and Lambert and DeBaptiste in Detroit. DeBaptiste proposed an even more incendiary plan to Brown, the coordinated burning of southern churches on Sunday. On the way, John Daniels's wife had a baby. They named him John Brown.[10]

JOHN BROWN'S WAR

John Brown personified the abolition war against slavery, the growing use of armed resistance by runaways, abolitionists, and free soilers in the 1850s. He gained adherents among veterans of fugitive slave rebellions. In Cleveland his Kansas followers recruited John Anthony Copeland, who had participated in the Oberlin–Wellington rescue and his uncle Lewis Sheridan Leary, a fugitive who had heard Brown speak. The most personally motivated was Dangerfield Newby, a former slave from Virginia who was freed by his father but whose wife and six children were in slavery. Newby carried his wife's letters telling him of her master's plans to sell her, the last pleading, "If . . . I should never see you this earth would have no charms for me." Brown tried to persuade Douglass, who foresaw the suicidal nature of his enterprise, at their last meeting in Chambersburg, Pennsylvania, to join him. Douglass's companion Shields Green, a South Carolinian fugitive, decided to go "with the old man." He recruited Osborne Anderson, as noted earlier, in Canada.

Brown's black recruits and his extended family comprised nearly half of the twenty-three Harper's Ferry raiders. His three sons, Owen, Oliver, and Watson, and the brothers of his son-in-law, Dauphin and William Thompson, constituted his family army. Besides them, the Kansas veterans John Henry Kagi, Charles Tidd, Jeremiah Anderson, Albert Hazlett, John E. Cook, Albert Dwight Stevens, Charles W. Moffet, and William H. Leeman formed the largest contingent. A Canadian, Stewart Taylor, who had settled in Iowa, and Edwin and Barclay Coppoc, the "fighting Quaker" brothers, also signed on. Hayden recruited the last raider, Francis Jackson Merriam, the nephew of the Garrisonian Francis Jackson, while raising funds for Brown in Boston. Despite Brown's stockpile of weapons and months of preparation, the plan to take over the federal armory at Harper's Ferry and start a slave uprising with this small band, as Douglass realized, was a death trap. The raid took place between October 16 and 19, 1859, and ended with Brown, most of his men, and nearly thirty hostages trapped in the Harper's Ferry engine house.

Brown's contemporary critics, including Lincoln, pointed out that slaves failed to rise up during his raid, but it is doubtful that most of them had any precise knowledge of it. The first accidental victim was a free black porter, Hayward Shepherd, recast by the United Daughters of the Confederacy as a representative of faithful slaves. A smaller raiding party freed and recruited the slaves of Col. Lewis Washington, a great-grandnephew of George Washington. In an act rife with symbolism, the raiders confiscated the sword Frederick the Great had given to Washington and gave it to Osborne Anderson. Lewis's coachman Jim fought with the raiders "like a tiger" and drowned while fleeing from Harper's Ferry. Another, Mason, helped load weapons for them. The raiders also took a hostage, John Allstadt, freeing his slaves, one of whom, Phil, died fighting, and another, his brother Ben, died in jail. Anderson and others distributed pikes to slaves, of whom seventeen joined Brown and another ten ended up at his Maryland hideout. Recent research shows that black people from Virginia and Maryland to Pennsylvania may have known about Brown's plans, but whether they had any idea of the exact timing and of Brown's specific target is unclear. Brown revealed the details to the raiders themselves just a couple of days before the raid. A handful of slaves escaped amidst the confusion. Despite a heavy troop presence after the raid, fires broke out in the region, the suspicion being they were started by slaves.

The violence unleashed on the raiders and the innocent was far greater than any they perpetrated. Nearly all of the raiders Brown sent to negotiate under a white flag were shot. The death of Newby was particularly egregious: a mob desecrated his corpse, cutting off his ears and genitals and leaving it in the gutter for rooting hogs. Two of the raiders, Will Thompson and Will Leeman, were used for target practice long after they were dead, and Leeman and Leary were killed after they tried to surrender. In all, ten raiders lost their lives, including two of Brown's sons, Watson and Oliver. Watson's body was given to a local medical college for dissection, a fate that often befell slave rebels, including Nat Turner. The raiders shot Mayor Fontaine Beckham besides three others, including one marine who stormed the engine house. Brown and his men captured more than they killed. The hostages testified to Brown's considerate treatment of them.

Harper's Ferry is commonly viewed as a militarily inept disaster. Brown allowed a train on the Baltimore–Ohio line to proceed, spreading news of his raid, a false confidence instilled perhaps by the manner in which he had eluded authorities since 1856. But his few men managed to keep at bay hundreds of militia men and townspeople for nearly three days and were taken only after most were dead and severely wounded by marines commanded by the future Confederates Robert E. Lee and J. E. B. Stuart, who recognized Brown from his Kansas days. Only Owen Brown, Merriam, Barclay Coppoc, Tidd, and Anderson escaped. The abolitionist underground facilitated their escape: blacks in Chambersburg, Pennsylvania, Still, and Charles Langston assisted Anderson, and Merriam received assistance from Redpath, Thoreau, and Higginson, who sheltered him and Tidd. Most of the survivors fought in the Union army, recruiting and serving in units with black soldiers. Higginson, Anderson, Merriam, and the Kansas veteran Richard J. Hinton even devised plans in early 1861 to raid the newly formed Confederacy and start a slave rebellion. For them, the Civil War was a continuation of Brown's war against slavery.

Seven raiders stood trial for treason. Five, including Brown, were executed by the end of the year, and Hazlett and Stevens were executed in March 1860. Sanborn, Stearns, Howe, and Douglass escaped to Canada when letters implicating them were found at the Kennedy farm in Maryland. In his confessions Cook named some abolitionists who supported Brown. Douglass traveled on to England, while Parker hailed the raid from Italy, where he lay terminally ill with tuberculosis. Smith committed himself to an insane asylum, denying his connection to Brown. Higginson stood his ground, daring the authorities to arrest him. A Senate committee headed by Mason, the author of the Fugitive Slave Act, tried to pin the raid on the Republican Party and let Brown's coconspirators Howe and Stearns, who testified before it, go scot free. John Brown Jr., Redpath, and Sanborn, who escaped federal marshals sent to arrest him, refused to appear before the committee. The committee summoned Hayden and "George DeBapt" (DeBaptiste), but Mason revoked the summons when he found out that they were black, maintaining the façade of black docility.[11]

Brown's courageous demeanor won him the admiration of many northerners and the grudging respect of his enemies who got to know him, his "kind" jailor, Capt. John Avis, and the less sympathetic Gov. Henry Wise of Virginia. Brown rejected all plans to rescue him as well as legal stratagems to declare him insane in order to save his life. His detractors portrayed him as insane or criminal or both. Americans, Douglass wrote, mistook heroism for insanity. Brown's trial, like those accorded to convicted slaves, had the trappings of procedural fairness. His answers to Mason, Vallandigham, and state officials, numerous letters to friends and family, and courtroom declarations conveyed his deeply held abolitionism and stole victory from failure. Brown wanted the world to understand that he respected "the rights of the poorest and weakest of colored people" as much as those of the "most wealthy and most powerful." In a farewell note to Stearns, Brown wrote that he did not want hypocritical religious prayers said on his behalf; like most abolitionists, he particularly detested slaveholding ministers and refused to have them at his execution. He wrote, "When I am publicly *murdered* . . . my only *religious attendants* be poor *little, dirty, ragged, bare headed & barefooted Slave boys & girls*; led by some old *grey-headed Slave Mother.*" His only design was to "free the slaves." His dying conviction, that the "crimes of this *guilty land: will* never be purged *away*, but with blood," written on the day of his execution, "Charlestown, Va. 2nd, December, 1859."[12]

Brown's raid crystallized the debate over the capacity of the enslaved to rebel. J. Sella Martin argued that the problem was not that Brown shed blood but that he did not shed enough of it, leaving the slaves confused about his plans. In his lyric war poem *The Hero and the Slave* (1862), "founded on fact," Martin reversed the racial order of rescue, as a slave saves a white soldier. In the *Anglo-African Magazine* Thomas Hamilton warned that either the North will adopt Brown's method to end slavery or the enslaved will adopt Turner's. (He published Turner's confessions.) Higginson would publish articles in the *Atlantic Monthly* on the Maroons of the New World, Vesey, and Turner. One of the secret six most actively involved with Brown's plans, Higginson had traveled to Kansas and was briefly arrested with Redpath. He commanded an all-black regiment in the Civil War and wrote in his memoir, "Till the blacks were armed, there was no guaranty of their freedom."

Parker's letters from Italy proclaimed that a slave has a natural right to kill his oppressor and a freeman the natural right to assist him. His letters, though, were tinged with the romantic racialism for which Rock had criticized him. In a speech from 1858 Parker argued that the African was the "most docile and pliant of races," as they had "strong affections" and lacked the ferocity of Anglo-Saxon, Teutonic, and Celtic peoples. Slavery could be settled with the "stroke of an axe" but for the submissive nature of slaves. Rock had established his intellectual prowess with his much-admired speeches on the "unity of the human race." According to him, it was impossible to classify humankind into different races. His ideas anticipated the black is beautiful movement by a century. He declared his preference for black skin, hair, and features. Rock was quick to respond to Parker. He professed to have a poor estimate of whites since it took thirteen million armed whites to keep five million black people (there were four million slaves in the United States) in slavery. Parker backed down: slavery, he predicted, would succumb to a "general rising of the African race." Phillips joined in contending that all nations had been enslaved at one point or another in their history, but only the "colored race" had overthrown slavery by the force of arms in Haiti. Remond declared that Parker's Anglo-Saxonism had no place in an "Anti Slavery platform." Despite his romantic racialism, Parker, like Rock, was a severe critic of the pseudoscience of race, challenging Harvard's Agassiz for his belief in polygenesis. A year later Parker joined the secret six and backed Brown's plan to start a slave rebellion.[13]

Not just the secret six but all abolitionists claimed Brown as one of their own. In an editorial published on October 28, Garrison wrote that no one could deny that "Captain Brown" was "honest, brave, truthful, conscientious and disinterested"; he voiced his own reaction: "How many hearts will be thrilled and inspired by his utterances!" Shall a more "undaunted spirit" be found? He predicted, "It will be a terrible losing day for all of Slavedom when John Brown and his associates are brought to the gallows. It will be sowing seed broadcast for a harvest of retribution." In his speech at an antislavery meeting in Tremont Temple, held to mark Brown's execution, the nonresistant Garrison reiterated, "Success to every slave insurrection at the South, and in every slave country." He published all criticisms of Brown, north and south, under the "Refuge of Oppression." Reacting to Beecher's denigration of the raid and going back to his disagreement with him on Kansas, Garrison pointed out that Beecher apparently believed that Sharpe's rifles were suitable for white men but not for black. Beecher said Brown's execution was a good thing, as it made his failure a heroic success and redeemed his blundering and miserable deeds.

Thoreau, who had met and admired Brown, made the most eloquent appeal on his behalf, "A Plea for Captain John Brown," on October 30. Scholars who claim that Thoreau preceded Garrison in his defense of Brown are off the mark by two days. Thoreau wished "to correct the tone and statements" about Brown appearing in newspapers throughout the country, as even the *Liberator*, he claimed, had initially called the raid a misguided effort. Thoreau likened the U.S. government to the tyrannies of the Old World, keeping a "coffle of four millions slaves" and crucifying "a million Christs every day." Brown was their "heroic liberator." The only free area in the country was the underground railroad managed by vigilant committees, Thoreau argued, while defending the abolitionists who ran them. He viewed Brown's war as part of the slaves' war.

Higginson and Hinton claimed that Brown's exploits marked a "new era in the history of Anti Slavery," but it was actually a culmination of abolitionists' attempt to look to the slaves rather than to slaveholders in their fight against slavery. In his speech delivered at Beecher's church on November 1, Phillips proclaimed that the "lesson of the hour is insurrection," while reasserting his belief in moral suasion: the "age of ideas" must replace the "age of bullets." Phillips defended the enslaved, saying if Brown had marched across Virginia he would have gained as many followers as Turner. Henry C. Wright led a large antislavery meeting in Natick that unanimously passed the following resolution: "Whereas, resistance to tyrants is obedience to God; therefore *Resolved*, that it is the right and duty of the slaves to resist their masters." Wright opined that the "God of the oppressed" was with Brown, and his execution would be the start of the "death struggle" with slaveholders. He sent copies of the Natick resolution to Brown, Wise, and Avis, whom he commended for his kindness to Brown, and to the *Richmond Enquirer*. Wise's slaves had as much right to enslave him, Wright reasoned, as he to enslave them. In a letter to Garrison, he wrote that Brown's actions were compatible with nonresistant doctrine, as it opposed the violence of slavery. Abolitionists, he urged, should form a league of offense and defense with southern slaves to attack slavery. Foster also recommended an alliance with slaves, saying, "Revolution [is] the only remedy." The nonresistant Ballou objected to a "Pro War Anti Slavery."

At the executive committee meeting of the AASS on November 4, Garrison asked all northern towns and cities to mark the "murder of John Brown" by tolling their church bells. Like many, he evoked the image of Christ's crucifixion. The most popular conceit was coined by Mattie Griffiths: Brown would "make the gallows glorious like the cross," a saying made famous by Emerson. Garrison published a supplemental issue of the *Liberator* devoted to Brown at the end of the year. On the day of Brown's death commemorative meetings were held in Tremont Temple, and in New York they were led by Tappan and Cheever. In Worcester church bells tolled for half the day. Brown's wife, Mary, Phillips, and McKim accompanied his body for burial to North Elba, Brown's home among Smith's black land grantees. In his eulogy Phillips noted that Harper's Ferry was "the flowering out of fifty years of single-hearted devotion" to the slave's cause. Brown's neighbors the Epps family sang his favorite spiritual, "Blow ye the trumpet, blow . . . the year of Jubilee has come."[14]

Radical Republicans joined abolitionists in praising Brown, subverting their party's strategy of appealing to the conservative lower north in the presidential election of 1860. Wright took Henry Wilson to task for backtracking when he was asked in Congress about attending the pro-Brown Natick meeting. But John Andrews proclaimed that "John Brown himself was right." Giddings was suspected of sympathizing with Brown. He had corresponded with and invited

Brown to lecture and raise funds for Kansas in Ohio. Brown had admired Giddings's book *The Exiles of Florida* (1858) on the Seminole Maroons. In a card he issued after the raid Giddings blamed the murder of Brown's son and other "barbarities" in Kansas for the raid while denying any role in it. Democrats in Ohio publicized a donation Governor Chase had made to Brown in 1856. When Wise warned against any attack from Ohio to rescue Brown, Chase responded with his own warning against any Virginian invasion to recapture fugitives. Calling Brown's raid rash and criminal, Chase wrote, "Yet how hard to condemn him, when we remember the provocation, the unselfish desire to set free the oppressed, the bravery, the humanity towards his prisoners, which defeated his purposes!" The real "guiltiness" lay "upon slavery itself." Sumner, who resumed his senatorial seat in December 1859, commented that Brown's raid "must be deplored," yet he could not "refuse my admiration to many things in the *man.*"

Seward and Greeley were more critical, foreshadowing their conservative turn during and after the war. Greeley noted that Brown and his men "dared and died for what they felt to be right, though in a manner which seems to us fatally wrong." To Seward, Brown had acted "on earnest though fatally erroneous convictions" and committed an "act of sedition and treason." While Seward, Wade, and the colonizationist Joseph Doolittle voted for the formation of Mason's committee, Sumner and Hale voted against it. Sumner also presented a memorial from Sanborn asking for redress and one from black citizens protesting the arrest of Thaddeus Hyatt, the head of the National Kansas Committee, who refused to testify before the committee. In response to what he viewed as the Republican exculpation of Brown, Sen. Andrew Johnson of Tennessee called him a "thief and a murderer" and his raid a "legitimate result of the teachings" of abolition.[15]

Southerners challenged abolitionists' consecration of Brown. They drew attention to the Pottawatomie massacre. Mahala Doyle, James's wife, rejoiced at Brown's sons' death so that he might know her sorrow. Lydia Maria Child instead evoked the grief of slave mothers and requested permission from Wise to nurse Brown in prison. Brown responded that he was well looked after but asked one that was "so gifted and so kind" to raise money for his destitute family. Child, who felt that abolitionists should die for but not kill for the slave's cause, had condoned the use of violence in self-defense by free-state settlers in her *The Kansas Emigrants* (1856), first published in the *Tribune.* Its gutsy heroine, Kate Bradford, who protects her husband from certain death, was inspired by the experience of free-state women. Introducing herself to Wise as an "uncompromising abolitionist" who believed in "peace principles," Child argued that if she thought men should fight for their freedom, the enslaved were "best entitled to that right." Wise accused her of inciting murder and mayhem and made their correspondence public. Brown, Child replied, was no criminal but a "martyr to righteous principles." In her abusive letter, Margaretta Mason, the wife of James Mason, accused Child of not knowing the Bible and questioned whether she deserved the name of a woman. She evoked benevolent slaveholding mistresses ministering to their slaves even when their "sorrows resulted from their own misconduct." She asked whether Child, who had written extensively about the plight of the working poor in the NASS, had ever done as much. Child responded that abolitionists did *"not sell . . . babies."* According to Garrison, Child "pulverized" the statesman and "used up" the southern lady. The AASS sold three hundred thousand copies of the exchange. Taking advantage of her success, Child republished *The Patriarchal Institution* and *The Right Way the Safe Way*, expanded versions of her pamphlet of 1836 calling for immediate emancipation in 1860.

Other abolitionist women entered the fray. Frances Harper thanked Child for defending Brown, who had "reached out his brave and generous hand to the crushed and blighted of my race." The PFASS passed a resolution calling the raid a "solemn warning." Mott, with whom Mary Brown stayed during her husband's imprisonment, defined herself as a "belligerent non-resistant" rather than an "advocate of passivity." Brown, she felt, was a moral hero and a martyr. Kelley Foster held that the use of force against tyranny was both justifiable and Christian. Susan B. Anthony organized a pro-Brown meeting in which Pillsbury contended that he was greater than Washington. The Brown women, some of whom had participated in the Kansas wars, called for armed resistance to slavery long after his death.[16]

Black abolitionists in particular revered the "race traitor" Brown and apotheosized him as a martyr to black freedom. Douglass and Langston wrote disclaimers about their involvement in the raid but praised Brown lavishly. Wise had put marshals and a private investigator on Douglass's trail. Douglass, who had no desire to be *"bagged"* by the government of Virginia, said, "It can never be wrong [for slaves and their] friends, to hunt, harass, and even strike down the traffickers in human flesh." Langston confessed to having the "very deepest sympathy with the Immortal John Brown" and his actions to "let the oppressed go free" and "to put to death . . . those who steal men and sell them." Lambert in Detroit and John Peck in Pittsburgh commemorated Brown's hanging, which Garnet anointed "Martyr's Day." Garnet's church celebrated it every year for twenty years. The Martyr's Day meetings passed resolutions promising to hold Brown's memory "in sacred remembrance" and raised money for his family. In

Boston people at a meeting in Reverend Grimes's church, led by Remond and Nell, sang antislavery songs. In Worcester and Hartford blacks displayed public signs of mourning. In Providence Wells Brown gave a speech titled "The Heroes of Insurrection." In Philadelphia a crowd of four thousand listened to Mott, Grew, and Tilton, but confusion broke out when Purvis hoped that "the coward fiends of Virginia" would reap the wrath of God. In Canada West Harvey C. Jackson called for meetings of colored persons in every locality to collect money for the raiders' families and sent it to Sewall in Boston, who was put in charge of the fund. Black women in New York sent their contributions to Mary Brown, "desir[ing] to express our deep, undying gratitude to him who has given his life so freely to obtain for us our defrauded rights." Harper, who promptly sent a contribution, published a story on the "old man and his brave companions."

African Americans also marked the hanging of the two black raiders, John Copeland and Shields Green, raising money for their families. Both were buried in an unmarked grave, but medical students from Winchester Medical College dug up Copeland's body. After many inquiries to Wise went unanswered, Copeland's parents sent James Monroe, a professor at Oberlin, to reclaim his body. The refusal of the students to give up the body forced Monroe to return empty-handed. Oberlin's interracial abolitionist community commemorated their deaths in a large meeting attended by over three thousand people. In his address Henry Peck, one of the Oberlin–Wellington rescuers, said that the black raiders at Harper's Ferry were "not less firm, heroic and Christlike" than Brown. The next year the Oberlin Monument Committee put together enough funds from all over the North to erect a memorial to Copeland, Lewis Leary, and Green, who had left behind no known survivors and became an adopted "colored citizen" of Oberlin. It bore a tribute to "the heroic associates of John Brown" who "gave their lives for the slave." In a letter to his brother, Copeland had asked rhetorically if he could die in a nobler cause. The Union army burned Winchester Medical College to the ground during the Civil War.

The lone black survivor of Brown's raid, Osborne Anderson, published the first account of it, *A Voice from Harper's Ferry* in January 1861. Anderson viewed Brown not only through the lens of a global history of liberation stretching from Moses to the European revolutions of the nineteenth century but also in the context of slave rebellion, comparing his tactics and the raid specifically to Turner's rebellion. Black Bostonians led by Martin, Grimes, Nell, Downing, and Morris held a meeting to promote his book and raised nearly a hundred dollars. Anderson lectured and sold his book until the start of the war. He died in Washington, D.C., in 1872. His pallbearers included Downing, Douglass's son Lewis, and Purvis and his son Charles. Purvis called him "the last survivor of the only army of freedom ever recruited in the United States."

The emancipationist meaning of Brown's war was evoked by African Americans long after the Civil War. It did her soul good, Charlotte Forten wrote from St. Helena's Island in South Carolina, to teach black children to sing "John Brown's Body" in the freedmen's school. She wished their former masters could hear them. Martin argued that the song was not just a marching song for the Union army but "a creed as well, to the great majority of slaves." In 1882 Watson's "prepared body" after dissection was recovered and brought back for burial at his father's side. Seventeen years later the decomposed remains of the ten raiders, including Leary and Green, were buried in a single coffin draped with an American flag at North Elba with the Twenty-Sixth United States Infantry firing a gun salute before fifteen hundred spectators. With the fall of Reconstruction, the *Colored Citizen* of Kansas, noting the "brutal murders and barbarous outrages in the South," published "Wanted, a Few Black John Browns." In his speech on Brown delivered at Storer College, Harper's Ferry, in 1881, Douglass recalled that "his zeal in the cause of my race, was far greater than mine—it was as the burning sun to my taper light—mine was bounded by time, his stretched away to the boundless shores of eternity. I could live for the slave, but he would die for them." In 1906 the "Niagara movement," a black civil rights organization that preceded the NAACP, met at Harper's Ferry. The NAACP would long commemorate Brown and the death anniversaries of Garrison and Sumner. Du Bois wrote, "Of all Americans, [Brown has] perhaps come nearest to touching the real souls of black folk."[17]

Radical abolitionists, too, embraced Brown's revolutionary war. Many of them, like Kagi, who reported for the *Era*, William Phillips, Redpath, who wrote for the *Tribune*, Hinton, and Richard Realf, were journalists and veterans of the Kansas wars. The latter three were British and were influenced by Chartism. Hinton, a socialist, became the corresponding secretary of Marx's International Workingmen's Association. Redpath was known for his John Ball Jr. letters, his pseudonym the name of a radical priest involved in a fourteenth-century English peasant revolt. They detailed his clandestine conversations with slaves and free blacks during his travels to the south from 1854 to 1856. The slaves Redpath interviewed combined deep pessimism with an intense longing to be free. One claimed, "*I know hundreds and hundreds and almost all of them are as dissatisfied a they kin be.*" He documented the "underground telegraph," or the grapevine, among the slaves and the Maroons at Dismal Swamp, which he called the Canada of the South. Redpath dedicated his book to the "old hero" Brown. He encapsulated his abolition creed in a few sentences: he was a Republican who opposed not just the extension of slavery but its "protection" where it exists; an emancipationist opposed to all gradualism, even if it meant wresting the supposed rights of slaves "with torch and rifle"; an abolitionist who was a "Reparationist," believing that the slaves deserved not just freedom but compensation for "unrequited services"; a "Peace Man" willing to kill for peace; a "Non Resistant" willing to slay all those who opposed the liberation of slaves; an American who believed that natives and immigrants should enjoy citizenship rights; and a Democrat who believed in human rights. As he put it, "Southern Rights are human wrongs."

Redpath was convinced that the South would never liberate its slaves and that abolitionists "must carry the war into the south" in a series of border raids, echoing Brown's conviction to "carry the war into Africa." His suggestion that abolitionists should infiltrate the South and hand slaves a compass, money, food, and guns to make good their escape was put into practice by the twenty-four-year-old Canadian abolitionist, the physician Alexander Milton Ross, who started running off slaves to Canada in 1857 under the guise of being an ornithologist. Redpath's model was the immensely successful southern travelogues by Frederick Law Olmsted, a free labor indictment of slavery. But Redpath made clear that overthrowing the Slave Power and replacing it with a "Mill Power" was not the solution. The southern cotton-raising aristocracy and the northern cotton-manufacturing oligarchy were two branches of the same root. Unlike Thayer's *The North and South* (1856), a statistical comparison of the two regions that revealed the superiority of free to slave labor (Thayer advocated a "free labor invasion" of Virginia), Redpath called for the emancipation of labor from capital.[18]

Redpath was commissioned to write Brown's biography, causing Child to give up her plans to do so. In January 1860 it was rushed into print. Written with the cooperation of Mary Brown and Brown's associates, including Higginson and Sanborn, this first in a genre unto itself, the Brown biography, cast the abolitionist in a heroic mold. Redpath admitted, "I loved and reverenced the noble old man." Harper's Ferry was no "crazy scheme," he wrote. "Brown did right by invading Virginia and attempting to liberate her slaves." It was dedicated to the abolitionists and transcendentalists who had best vindicated Brown: Phillips, Emerson, and Thoreau, who cried, "Saint" when others said, "Madman." That year Redpath also published an accompanying set of documents on Brown, *Echoes of Harper's Ferry*, pro-Brown sermons, speeches, and poetry. Among these was Whittier's poem on Brown as well as Garrison's critique of it for its allusions to Brown's "rash and bloody hand" and to the raid as "folly that seeks evil through good." No such qualifications marked Whittier's poems in praise of the American revolutionaries, Garrison wrote. Garrison published Louisa May Alcott's "With a Rose that Bloomed on the Day of John Brown's Martyrdom" and Child's "The Hero's Heart," which, like Whittier's poem, forever imagined Brown kissing an enslaved baby held up by a slave mother. A fictitious account, the story owed its origins to Brown's last wishes and became the motif of a popular painting on his execution (see the illustration). After the war, Melville and Whitman likened Brown to a foreboding, a "meteor of war" in their poetry. In the twentieth century Brown continued to inspire writers and artists like Jacob Lawrence.[19]

Redpath represented the coming together of emigrationism and revolutionary abolitionism. Brown was an admirer of Haiti and the Jamaican Maroons. Redpath dedicated *Echoes* to the Haitian president Fabre Geffrard. The black republic officially mourned Brown and through Redpath contributed two thousand dollars to Mary Brown. Geffrard employed Redpath, who published *A Guide to Hayti* in 1861, as his agent. Filled with information on the history and geography of the island, Redpath touted Haiti as the future of the "African race." Redpath saw the empowering of the black republic as a way to counter proslavery imperialism and as a launching pad for a second raid on the South. Redpath bought the *Anglo-African*, rechristened it the *Pine and Palm*, and made it the official organ of Haitian emigration. Along with Redpath, the black abolitionist George Lawrence and Hinton served as its editors. The first issue contained a large portrait of Toussaint Louverture, "the first of the blacks." Redpath called for the "immediate eradication of slavery" through a constitutional amendment, the "national equality and power" of blacks with whites, and the establishment of "tropical confederacies" in the Caribbean to encircle and attack the slave South. He formed the Haytian Emigration Bureau in Boston, with branches in New York, Chicago, and Canada, and employed James T. Holly, Garnet, H. Ford Douglas, Langston, and John Brown Jr. in Canada and and Rev. Samuel Berry, an Episcopalian black minister, in Brooklyn. Delany, who named his sons after Toussaint and Emperor Faustin I, nevertheless remained critical of Haitian emigration. When he questioned having a white man at the head of the Haitian movement, Holly pointed out that Redpath was merely a servant of the Haitian government.

Holly had led the Haitian emigration movement in the 1850s. An abolitionist and Episcopalian minister, he advocated the establishment of a black "Christian Nationality" in Haiti. In 1855 he visited Haiti to explore the possibilities of emigration and met Faustin. Two years later Holly published *A Vindication of the Capacity of the Negro Race for Self-Government*. A history of the Haitian

Revolution, it argued that black rights were better respected among the "monarchical negroes" of Haiti than in the "bastard democracy" of America. In 1859 Holly published his "Thoughts on Hayti" series in the *Anglo-African Magazine*. Holly viewed Haiti as representative of "Black nationality in the New World." He lauded its "self-emancipating" history in contrast to West Indian apprenticeship and Liberia, which was propped up by a "questionable system of American philanthropy." Black Protestant emigrants would regenerate Haiti and create *"a strong, powerful, enlightened and progressive negro nationality."* In 1861, as Holly prepared to leave for Haiti with 150 emigrants, mostly from Canada, came the bombshell. Douglass, the inveterate foe of emigration, announced that he would accompany Holly to Haiti after writing sympathetically about Haitian emigration in his monthly.

As early as 1853 Douglass, in a speech before the AFASS, had approved of emigration to a place near the United States where free blacks would be within "hearing distance" of the enslaved. Other anti-emigrationists, like Wells Brown, Watkins, and Vashon, now supported Haitian emigration, Wells Brown acting as a recruiting agent in Canada West. He explained that the Haitian movement, unlike the "hateful" colonization movement, was "originated by a colored nation" in the "interests of the colored race." Initially disillusioned by the compromise-oriented stand of the Lincoln administration, Douglass immediately gave up on emigration when the war started. He joined anti-emigrationists like Pennington, McCune Smith, who restarted the *Weekly Anglo-African* to oppose emigration, and Downing. Douglass now rejected the idea of an independent black nationality, arguing that, as Americans, black people shall rise or fall with the American nation. The solution to racial inequality, he asserted, lay in "Human Brotherhood," not in "exclusive nationalities." John C. Bowers, too, warranted that black hopes must remain in this "Republican land of liberty where the great battle for freedom is to be fought and won." Gloucester dismissed emigration as *"Bumkim."* On Downing's urging, Garrison warned that emigration could play into racist hands, hobbling the battle for equal rights at home. But Holly emigrated to Haiti and became an Episcopalian bishop. In 1899 he attended one of the first Pan-African meetings held in London to oppose European imperialism in Africa, illustrating the abolitionist roots of anti-imperialism. Douglass's Haitian connection continued as well. From 1889 to 1891 he was the American consul to Haiti and chargé d'affaires to Santo Domingo. His critics accused him of showing too much sympathy for the black nation and of not representing American interests, which included acquiring a military base. Protesting the exclusion of blacks at the World's Columbian Exposition in Chicago in 1893, Douglass continued the abolitionist tradition of vindicating the emancipationist history of Haiti.

Redpath sent 2,000 black emigrants, free blacks from the North, the South, and Canada, to Haiti. Worsening conditions for southern free blacks, threatened with reenslavement in many slave states after Brown's raid, led over 200 from Louisiana to emigrate to Haiti, 150 in 1859 alone. Haitian emigration failed owing to the experiences of emigrants, which replicated those who had migrated to Haiti in the 1820s. Confronting disease, death, and a different culture, religion, and language, they returned telling stories of disillusionment. Redpath and Sumner lobbied the Lincoln administration for the recognition of Haiti, which, unlike the Spanish and British in the Caribbean, supported the Union blockade of the Confederacy. Lincoln recognized Haiti as well as Liberia to further his colonization plans. After his ill-fated attempt to set up a colony of freed slaves in Ile a Vache, the government brought black emigrants home. In September 1862, with the announcement of Lincoln's preliminary Emancipation Proclamation, Redpath resigned his agency, and his paper folded. But his interest in Haiti remained. A year later he reprinted a book on Louverture. After the war he promoted the Irish Land League Movement, the abolition of capital punishment, and Henry George's antipoverty campaign.[20]

Brown elicited admiration from abolitionists and radicals abroad. In Britain, Douglass, Martin, and Sarah Parker Remond mobilized the abolitionist international behind Brown. A graduate of Philadelphia's Institute for Colored Youth and a black student at the University of Edinburgh, Jesse Ewing Glasgow published the first account of the raid there in 1860. It ran through four editions, although its young author died the next year. George Thompson contended that Brown was "one of whom the world was not worthy" and the *Anti-Slavery Reporter* argued that Brown "was one of that class who figure as heroes in the history of nations." To Martineau, "The only clear thing to us about the Harper's Ferry business is the moral greatness of John Brown."

European revolutionaries viewed Brown as a comrade in arms. Some of Brown's men were veterans of the revolutions of 1848. August Bondi, a Jewish immigrant from Austria, had fought with Brown in Kansas and Lajos Kossuth in Hungary, and Forbes with Giuseppe Garibaldi in Italy, whom he rejoined after Harper's Ferry. Brown's "hangman," wrote Victor Hugo, was "the whole American republic. . . . It is Washington killing Spartacus." The day of Brown's hanging was also the day of Louis Napoleon's coup against the Second French Republic.

Marx wrote to Engels, "The most significant thing happening in the world today is the slave movement . . . initiated by the death of Brown. . . . This promises great things." Four years later, Pierre Vesnier, a member of the International and later elected to the General Council of the Paris Commune, published his book on Brown. Vesnier regarded the extermination of southern slaveholders as necessary to the liberation of blacks. The book was dedicated to the nonwhite peoples of the world and to the European proletariat. Garibaldi called Lincoln an "heir of the aspirations of Christ and Brown."[21] Unlike Lincoln, Brown never became an American icon, but he assumed that status in the eyes of African Americans, abolitionists, and revolutionaries all over the world.

LINCOLN'S WAR

Antislavery politics grew out of abolition, and to most northerners it appeared as the constitutional way to contain an aggressively expansionist slave system. The Republican Party, however, was not abolition writ large. In order to create a free soil electoral majority, its platform remained the lowest common denominator of antislavery commitment, the nonexpansion of slavery. Radical Republicans such as Sumner, Stevens, Giddings, and Chase had abolitionist roots, while others, like Hale, Seward, and Greeley, were fellow travelers. Radicals and abolitionists knew that containment was not abolition but hoped it would lead to emancipation. During the war they played a crucial role in realizing that goal, pushing moderates in their party to take higher antislavery ground.

Perhaps no one represented Republicans better than Lincoln, who claimed to hate slavery as much as any abolitionist but whose competing loyalties to the Union and the Constitution moderated his antislavery. Lincoln's first public statement on slavery came in 1837, when, as an Illinois legislator, he wrote a protest against a resolution condemning abolitionists. It stated that slavery was "founded on both injustice and bad policy" but that abolitionism tended to "increase rather than abate its evils." Lincoln distanced himself from both the proslavery resolution and abolition. A year later he deplored proslavery mob violence, alluding to Elijah Lovejoy's murder, McIntosh's lynching, which Lovejoy had witnessed, and the Mississippi slave insurrection scare of 1835, as the greatest threat to the rule of law and American democracy. But whereas his law partner, William Herndon, subscribed to abolitionist newspapers, Lincoln represented the legal claims of slaves as well as of slaveholders.[22]

Lincoln developed an antislavery reputation only with the emergence of the slavery expansion issue in national politics. As a one-term Whig congressman, he opposed the Mexican War and supported the Wilmot Proviso. Like Seward, he did not join the Free Soil Party in 1848 but boarded with free soilers like Giddings and Palfrey. In 1849 he proposed a bill for gradual, compensated emancipation in the District of Columbia. It contained a fugitive slave clause but prohibited the sale of slaves. Unlike Giddings's original proposal, it allowed only white men to vote on it in a referendum. Lincoln never introduced the bill. Like Clay, his "beau ideal of a statesman," he was for the Compromise of 1850 and was a colonizationist, and his commitment to the Union and the Constitution always won out.

The rise of Lincoln paralleled that of the Republican Party when antislavery increasingly became the guiding principle of his politics. In his Peoria speech of 1854 after the passage of the Kansas–Nebraska Act Lincoln called slavery a "monstrous injustice" that deprived the American Republic of "its just influence in the world—enables the enemies of free institutions, with plausibility, to taunt us as hypocrites—causes the real friends of freedom to doubt our sincerity." He waffled on colonization, admitting that sending black people to "their own native land" was practically impossible but argued that his "own feelings" would not allow for racial equality, and even if they did, "the great mass of white people will not." This politically expedient concession to racism, "a universal feeling, whether ill or well founded," stood in contrast to his unequivocal condemnation of slavery. To Lincoln, the great travesty of allowing the expansion of slavery was that it made slavery into a moral right and not an unfortunate necessity that the Republic would eventually do away with. He delivered over one hundred speeches for Frémont in 1856. Lincoln's reaction to *Dred Scott* put him on the path to the presidency.[23]

The Supreme Court's decision in 1857 struck a simultaneous blow at both abolitionist claims of black citizenship and the Republican program of nonextension. Dred Scott and his wife, Harriet Scott, of Missouri sued for their freedom based on their residence in the free territory of Illinois. They continued the long tradition of freedom suits stretching back to the colonial era, which had resulted in the establishment of the Somerset, or freedom, principle in Anglo-American jurisprudence, limiting the legal sway of slavery. The political significance of slave resistance lies hidden in plain sight, in the case titles derived from the names of their enslaved plaintiffs. Over two hundred slaves like the Scotts contested their enslavement in antebellum St. Louis. The seventeen-year-old Harriet Robinson, who grew up amidst frontier slavery in the old northwest, married the forty-year-old Etheldred (Dred) Scott, the moving force behind the idea to sue for their freedom. His first wife had been sold down south. Dred's master, the physician John Emerson, and the officers who hired him were paid a subsidy by the army; in effect the army was subsidizing slavery on the frontier. The U.S. government employed slave labor throughout the antebellum period, making a mockery of the free soil slogan, "Freedom national, slavery local."

The story of the Scotts complicates conventional narratives of the history of free soilism, for the enslaved as much as antislavery politicians pushed the movement forward. At the time Harriet first sued for her freedom in St. Louis, other enslaved women, laundresses like Harriet, had sued and won their own and their children's freedom. The indomitable Polly Wash escaped to Chicago, was recaptured and beaten, yet sued for her own and her daughter Lucy's freedom based on their residence in the free state of Illinois and won. Lucy Delaney wrote an account of their freedom suits after the war. Enslaved plaintiffs displayed considerable legal acumen to challenge their enslavement, exploiting the boundaries between slavery and freedom in the Missouri–Illinois borderland. St. Louis also boasted a free black population. John Berry Meachum, a minister in the African Baptist church, claimed in his address of 1846 to the colored citizens of St. Louis that he had purchased twenty people. His pamphlet, a mixture of anticolonization, racial uplift, and messianic nationalism, epitomized black abolitionism, albeit in more circumspect terms for a slave state. Twelve years later Cyprian Clamorgan wrote of the wealthy "colored aristocracy" of the city. According to Clamorgan, "wealth is power," but there was not a single colored man who "would not cheerfully part with his last dollar to effect the elevation of his race."

Abolitionists played a role in the Scotts' quest for freedom. Their first lawyer was Francis B. Murdoch from Alton, who had unsuccessfully tried to prosecute Lovejoy's killers and represented Polly and Lucy. On Emerson's death, his widow acquired legal title to Dred and his family. Emerson had not bought Harriet, whose Pennsylvania master was certainly subject to that state's gradual emancipation law. Irene Sanford Emerson refused Dred's request to purchase himself. Her slaveholding planter father, Colonel Sanford, was a proslavery man, and the family made good money hiring out and garnishing the wages of the Scotts. On April 4, 1846, Harriet and Dred filed separate suits accusing Emerson of illegally imprisoning them and depriving them of their liberty. Making a freedom claim was risky business in a slave society, leaving them vulnerable to retaliation. Murdoch's creditors foreclosed on his property, forcing him to move and leaving the Scotts without a lawyer. As the editor of a free labor newspaper in California, Murdoch wrote of the difficulty of pursuing freedom suits in a slave society. Dred Scott lost his case, Harriet's was never brought up because Emerson could not be legally established as her owner. The Scotts appealed the decision, a young lawyer from Massachusetts, David Hall, representing them. Hall was known to take on freedom suits, and Edward Bates, Lincoln's future attorney general who would declare the *Dred Scott* decision void, assisted him in the case of another slave, Pierre, and represented Lucy Delaney.

The Scotts' freedom claims became intertwined with the fortunes of the Republican Party. In 1850 they won their suit, with Harriet's case subsumed under Dred Scott's. After Colonel Sanford's death, Irene Emerson moved to Massachusetts and married a free soiler. Her brother John F. A. Sanford, the executor of her husband's estate, inherited their father's estate. The man managing the case on behalf of Sanford was Benami S. Garland, the Missouri slaveholder whose runaway slave Joshua Glover had outwitted him. Garland appealed the decision on a technicality. In a reversal of legal precedent, the Missouri Supreme Court by a two-to-one decision—the dissenter, Hamilton Gamble, became the wartime governor of the state—revoked the freedom of the Scotts. On the advice of their new lawyer from Vermont, Roswell Field, the Scotts then sued Sanford in federal court and accused him of assault. In 1854 the Scotts lost that case. The lawyer for Sanford, Hugh Garland, died, and his executors allowed one of his slaves, Elizabeth Keckley, to purchase her freedom. Keckley became Mary Todd Lincoln's dressmaker and confidante. The Scotts appealed their case to the U.S. Supreme Court. Field recruited Montgomery Blair, the scion of the free soil Blair family and Lincoln's future postmaster general, to represent them. Bailey's *National Era* was enlisted to raise money for the case. Appearing on behalf of Sanford was Henry Geyer, who had defeated Thomas Hart Benton in the senatorial elections for being weak on slavery.[24]

The politics of slavery determined the outcome of the case. Taney planned to settle once and for all the slavery question, but his proslavery, antiblack decision only inflamed sectional passions. He had a long record of judicial activism on behalf of slavery in fugitive slave cases and in early controversies involving the rights of free blacks stemming from the southern Negro Seamen laws. Whatever antislavery sentiments Taney harbored—in 1818 he defended an abolitionist minister and freed his eight slaves—had died long ago. Nearly half of Taney's decision was devoted to the question of black citizenship, the rest to the status of slavery in the territories, upon which Scott based his suit. Taney believed that a "Negro" brought as a slave to the country and treated as an "article of property" by colonial statutes, could never aspire to citizenship. The framers of the Constitution had erected a "perpetual and impassable barrier" between the two races. In his egregiously racist formulation, people of African descent were "regarded as beings of an inferior order, and altogether unfit to associate with the white race, either in social or political relations; and so far inferior, that they had no rights which a white man was bound to respect; and that the negro might be justly and lawfully reduced to slavery for his benefit." There was a legal precedent for Taney's decision, the slave codes. Taney, noting that Indians could be naturalized, marked people of African descent for special degradation.

Evoking original intent and strict construction, Taney adopted Calhoun's proslavery theory that the Constitution recognized slave property in all areas under it. The territories were co-owned by the states, and the federal government had no right to legislate on slavery in the territories, a reading that was in direct contravention to the constitutional clause that put territories under federal jurisdiction. Labeling the Northwest Ordinance, the basis of Scott's freedom claim, an unwarranted assumption of power under the Articles of Confederation and superseded by the Constitution, and calling all restrictions on slavery in the territories, including the Missouri Compromise, unconstitutional, the decision of the majority in *Scott v. Sandford* (Sanford's name was misspelled) essentially declared the free soil platform of the Republican Party unconstitutional. Taney was joined by four southern judges in separate opinions, one of the longest by Peter Daniel of Virginia, a "brooding proslavery fanatic." Daniel's history of racial inferiority surpassed that of Taney. Going back to Emmerich de Vattel and the Roman law of slavery, he argued that "the African negro race never have been acknowledged as belonging to the family of nations." Two northern Democratic doughfaces, Samuel Nelson of New York and Robert Grier of Pennsylvania, known for his run-in with abolitionists over fugitive rendition, went with the majority.

Political abolitionists and free soilers had labored to find a constitutional way to attack slavery, one which the Supreme Court now designated unconstitutional. The two dissenters were John McLean of Ohio, suspected of hankering after the Republican presidential nomination, and Massachusetts's Benjamin R. Curtis, whose brother George T. Curtis was Blair's cocounsel. Even northern conservatives like "the Curtti" and Blairs dissented from Taney's extreme proslavery formulation. Benjamin Curtis would return to form during the war, challenging the constitutionality of the Emancipation Proclamation and the impeachment of Andrew Johnson. McLean concluded that the court was obliged to respect not just Missouri's law of slavery but Illinois's law of freedom. Descendants of African slaves in Massachusetts, Curtis added, were not only "native born citizens" but also given the right to vote. He evoked the immunities and privileges clause on citizenship. Both judges affirmed the constitutional power of the federal government to legislate for the territories, deeming them "constitutional and valid laws."[25]

The fallout from *Dred Scott* was immediate, with abolitionists leading the charge. Garrison, who printed the decision in his "Refuge of Oppression," proposed a resolution at the NEAS convention that condemned it as "unjust, inhumane and unconstitutional," founded on "falsifications of history and perversions of law," and an "outrage and insult to all decency, morality and Christianity." Cheever famously called it "the moral assassination of a race," a case that made slaveholders a "LEGALIZED BANDITTI OF MEN-STEALERS." According to Smith, the Supreme Court had rebelled against the Republic itself. At a meeting of the colored citizens of Philadelphia, Purvis remarked that the decision confirmed that black people were "an alien, disfranchised and degraded class." Remond noted that it was in perfect accord with American practice, Taney had simply made it law. McCune Smith argued that free blacks had always exercised the basic rights of citizenship, and Douglass appealed "this hell-black judgment of the Supreme Court, to the court of common sense and common humanity."[26]

Republicans condemned the decision as obiter dictum—Taney's opinion had no force of law behind it—and vindicated the constitutional power of the federal government to restrict slavery in the territories. Many, including Lincoln, averred that it nationalized slavery. If the Constitution carried slavery with it, it surely did so in the free states under its jurisdiction. It overturned the freedom principle, affirming slaveholders' alleged right to travel and reside in free territory with their slaves. In Congress, Hale, Seward, Fessenden, and Wade lit into this exercise in "judicial tyranny." The most elaborate response came from Benton, who had spent a lifetime combating Calhoun's proslavery heresies. A slaveholder himself, he argued that slave owners had the right to carry their slaves to the territories with them but not their state laws of slavery. The old Jacksonian Democrat died in 1858 trying to reconcile his devotion to the Union with slavery.

Calvin Chaffee, the Republican congressman who had married Irene Emerson, was embarrassed by charges of hypocrisy. The Chaffees (Sanford died in an insane asylum) quickly transferred Scott's ownership to the Blows, Scott's original owners who had helped him with his freedom suit, perhaps guilt-ridden at having sold him to Emerson in the first place. Missouri laws stipulated that only a resident could free Scott. Dred and Harriet's two teenaged daughters, who had been missing since their parents' freedom was revoked, miraculously reappeared. It was probably concern about their fate that had motivated the Scotts to engage in the long, drawn-out legal battle. Irene Emerson Chaffee made sure she received Dred Scott's wages for the entire time the trials took place. Forever stigmatized, Calvin Chaffee did not run for political office ever again. Scott's benefactor Taylor Blow helped him post the thousand-dollar bond that Missouri law required from free blacks. The entire family, Dred, Harriet, Eliza, and Jane, posed for *Frank Leslie's Illustrated Magazine*. They were the most famous enslaved family in the country, one whose freedom struggles had spurred the contest over slavery. Like other enslaved freedom seekers, they helped emancipate their people. Dred Scott died a year later.[27]

Lincoln's growth in antislavery politics can be traced from his support of the Fugitive Slave Act (though he had suggested protections for free blacks) to his repudiation of *Dred Scott*. He excoriated the decision, not only because it declared the Republican platform unconstitutional but also because it questioned the humanity of black people. Lincoln's description of the plight of the slave in the aftermath of the case is memorable:

> All the powers of earth seem rapidly combining against him. Mammon is after him; ambition follows, and philosophy follows, and the Theology of the day is fast joining the cry. They have him in the prison house; they have searched his person, and left no prying instrument with him. One after another they have closed the heavy iron doors upon him, and now they have him, as it were, bolted in with a lock of a hundred keys, which can never be unlocked without the concurrence of every key; the keys in the hand of a hundred different men, and they scattered to a hundred different and distant places; and they stand musing as to what invention, in all the dominions of mind and matter, can be produced to make the impossibility of his escape more complete than it is.

Lincoln's "A House Divided" speech, which critiqued *Dred Scott* for nationalizing slavery, inaugurated his senatorial campaign. Douglass applauded "Abram" Lincoln's "great speech." Seward's "The Irrepressible Conflict" also argued that the country would become either "entirely a slave-holding nation or entirely a free labor nation."

Lincoln distinguished the Republican position, the active restriction of slavery by the federal government, from that of his Democratic opponent Stephen Douglas, who had broken with his party over Kansas's Lecompton Constitution. In 1857 a proslavery minority representing less than 10 percent of the territory's population elected a constitutional convention. The resulting Lecompton Constitution gave Kansans no choice on slavery: voters could either allow slavery or not allow it but were required to recognize the slaves already in the territory. Lecompton led Douglas to repudiate his own handiwork, as it violated popular sovereignty and the white man's democracy. When Buchanan, buckling to southern pressure, tried to force the admission of Kansas as a slave state under Lecompton, Douglas rebelled. Forced by Lincoln to explain his position, Douglas, in their second debate, in Freeport, Illinois, contended that even if the Constitution carried slavery to the territories, as Taney argued, the territorial legislatures, by refusing to pass laws to police slavery, could get rid of it. Lecompton and the "Freeport Doctrine" permanently estranged the southern wing of the Democratic Party, its base, from Douglas, dividing the Democrats along sectional lines during the presidential election of 1860. Lauded by Greeley's *Tribune*, Douglas, whose followers cooperated with Republicans in opposing Lecompton, was heralded as a candidate Republicans could live with. Lincoln, who distinguished between the active restriction of slavery that would lead to its "ultimate extinction" and Douglas's moral indifference to its spread, disagreed. For Douglas, a majority of white voters could establish slavery, a principle violated by Lecompton. The English compromise of 1858, named after the Democratic representative and northern doughface William English of Indiana, sent Lecompton back to Kansas voters, who were given a so-called choice to enter the Union with slavery or remain a territory and who proceeded to defeat it by an overwhelming majority. Neither the bribe of a federal land grant nor the political benefits of statehood changed the opinions of the large free-state majority. Kansas entered the Union in 1861 as a free state.[28]

The famous Lincoln–Douglas debates in 1858 represented a contest between antislavery and the white man's democracy. Lincoln was always on the defensive when speaking about racial equality, openly displaying his displeasure: "Let us discard all this quibbling about this man and the other man—this race and that race and the other race being inferior, and therefore they must be placed in an inferior position." He accused Democrats of fostering racism. Republicans argued that "the negro is a man; that his bondage is cruelly wrong, and the field of his oppression should not be enlarged. The Democrats deny his manhood; deny, or dwarf to insignificance, the wrong of his bondage; so far as possible, crush all sympathy for him, and cultivate and excite hatred and disgust against him." He was mercilessly race-baited by Douglas, who charged that Lincoln changed his views with the political geography of Illinois, appearing more progressive in the north half and less so in the southern, settled by white southerners. In Douglas's eyes, citizenship ought to be confined to people of European descent, excluding "Ethiopians," Native Americans, and other nonwhite people. Like most Democrats, he charged "Black Republicans" with espousing "racial amalgamation." Lincoln lost to Douglas, but the debates set the stage for his nomination as the Republican presidential candidate.

Lincoln stuck to his position that black people were entitled to natural rights, but he clarified that those did not include political rights. Lincoln said he personally was not in favor of black citizenship but, unlike Taney, believed that individual states had the power to confer citizenship on free blacks. He deliberately chose the example of a black woman to argue for natural but not social or political equality. He was "against the counterfeit logic which concludes that, because I do not want a black woman for a *slave* I must necessarily want her for a *wife*. I need not have her for either, I can just leave her alone. In some respects she is certainly not my equal; but in her natural right to eat the bread that she earns with her own hands without asking leave of anyone else, she is my equal, and the equal of all others." Lincoln usually characterized sectional differences in terms of political economy, what he called the "mudsill" view of society, referring to Hammond's King Cotton speech, versus free labor. He was appalled by Fitzhugh's argument that in an ideal society labor should be enslaved. To him, blacks and whites, men and women, could aspire to the promise of free labor even though all were not citizens.

Though Lincoln refused to sign a petition for black suffrage brought to him by black abolitionists like H. Ford Douglas, his views on race were far ahead of those of most people in the country. Privately, he belittled racist ideas. In a brilliant reductio ad absurdum refutation of the racial logic of slavery, Lincoln wrote if A can enslave B because of color, then by this rule the first man with a lighter skin you meet has the right to enslave you. He went on, "You mean the whites are *intellectually* the superiors of blacks," by this rule the first man you meet with "an intellect superior to your own" has the right to enslave you. Unlike Jefferson, Lincoln's favoring of colonization was not predicated on crude racist ideas, though his refusal to endorse black citizenship put him behind abolitionists and radicals in his own party.[29]

Throughout the 1850s, while Lincoln remained committed to colonization, a parallel movement for emigration arose among abolitionists. The black abolitionist most responsible for this was Martin Delany. Born free in Virginia in 1812, Delany became a leading abolitionist in Pittsburgh. In the 1840s he edited the *Mystery*, which, remarkably, lives on today as the *Christian Recorder* of the AME church. As the coeditor of Douglass's *North Star*, he undertook a western tour to raise subscriptions and glean information on the condition of African Americans. On the recommendation of Francis J. Le Moyne, a founding member of the PASS and the mayor of Pittsburgh, he was admitted to Harvard Medical School in 1850. He and two other black students sponsored by the ACS were forced to withdraw because of the objections of southern students. In *The Condition, Elevation, Emigration, and Destiny of the Colored People* (1852) Delany announced emigration as a solution to the plight of blacks. He differentiated emigration from colonization, calling the ACS one of the most "arrant enemies of the colored man." Delany gave a classic formulation of the position of blacks in the United States: they were "a nation within a nation." He thought that South and Central America or the eastern coast of Africa could be the site of a modern, commercial black nation. He proposed a transcontinental railroad linking Africa's two coasts.[30]

Delany's book forced abolitionists to reconsider emigration. Garrison noted Delany's "spirit of despondency," yet Delany thanked him for his "favorable and generous notice." Smith sent Delany a "letter of approval of the work," and

Bibb gave it a favorable notice in the *Voice of the Fugitive*. But Oliver Johnson, the editor of the *Pennsylvania Freeman*, in a ham-handed critique, drew attention to the book's printing errors and the author's alleged egotism. Obviously stung, Delany wrote to Johnson, "I . . . despise your sneers and defy your influence." More than Johnson's dismissive review, Douglass's silence, which he called unjustifiable, irritated Delany. The national black convention of 1853 in Rochester, led by Douglass and attended by blacks from the eastern states, came out against emigration. Only the poet from Buffalo, James M. Whitfield, Rev. William C. Monroe, and Rev. Augustus R. Green represented emigrationists. Whitfield, who published poems on Cinque, John Quincy Adams, and the First of August in Douglass's newspaper, dedicated his collection of poems to Delany. His poem *America* pronounced, "AMERICA, it is to thee, / Thou boasted land of liberty, / —It is to thee I raise my song, / Thou land of blood, and crime and wrong." Whitfield debated Douglass's associate editor, William J. Watkins, on emigration. Bibb's paper and William Howard Day's *Aliened American* reprinted Whitfield's letters arguing that blacks in Haiti, Canada, and South and Central America acted as potent challenges to slaveholders. Educated at Oberlin, Day married the college's first black woman graduate, Lucy Stanton. He migrated to Ontario and became a corresponding editor of Shadd's *Provincial Freeman*.

Delany's critique of entrenched racism influenced his critics. In 1852 Douglass, in his famous "What to the Slave is the Fourth of July?" speech, said, "This Fourth is *yours*, not *mine*. You may rejoice, I must mourn," accusing the American Republic of crimes against black people that would shame "a nation of savages." The speech ended tamely, however, vindicating the antislavery nature of the Constitution. The Rochester convention's address, written mostly by Douglass and McCune Smith, claimed, "We are Americans, and as Americans, we would speak to Americans," but it condemned American racism: "Our white fellow country-men do not know us. . . . The great mass of American citizens estimate us as being a characterless and purposeless people; and hence we hold up our heads, if at all, against the withering influence of a nation's scorn and contempt." That year Douglass gave one of his most brilliant (and relatively unknown) speeches, "A Nation in the Midst of a Nation," adopting Delany's formulation. The history of black people, he said, using O'Connell's allusion to Irish history, may be traced like the blood of a wounded man in a crowd. African Americans were treated as aliens in their own land. White Americans had sympathy for "the Hungarian, the Italian, the Irishman, the Jew, and the Gentile . . . but for my poor people enslaved—blasted and ruined—it would appear, that America has neither justice, mercy nor religion."[31]

In 1854 Delany called a national emigration convention in Cleveland. It was dominated by blacks from the northwestern states with discriminatory black laws but excluded all colonizationists, calling them "enemies of the race." It demanded that African Americans form the *"ruling element"* of a nation. Munroe, who had visited Haiti as a missionary, presided. Twenty-nine black women attended, and Mary Bibb was elected vice president. The convention formed the emigrationist National Board of Commissioners, a competing national body to Douglass's National Council. Delany's keynote address, "Political Destiny of the Colored Race on the American Continent," was its most significant outcome. Black people, he maintained, were neither freemen nor citizens of the country; their degradation was marked by their color regardless of anything they might have attained, just as white was viewed as a "mark of distinction and superiority." Dismissing the demand for suffrage, Delany counseled black sovereignty. His speech was an original Pan-African critique of European colonialism. The colored races were the global majority that a white minority sought to rule. A black nation must "meet and combat" the European politicians, economists, and "civil engineers" who direct the "nations and powers of the earth." Recounting a short history of the colonization of North America, Delany identified Indians as "identical subjects of American wrongs" with black people.

Emigrationists debated their opponents. H. Ford Douglas, who was born in Virginia and lived in Ohio, supported Delany, and John Mercer Langston opposed him. George B. Vashon, who returned from Haiti and became a contributor to Douglass's paper, was against and Martin H. Freeman for emigration. A year later the National Board of Commissioners meeting in Pittsburgh claimed that "the principles of Emigration are fast becoming the leading policy among our people in this country." But the board soon ceased to exist, and Delany migrated to Canada in 1856, after holding another emigration convention in Cleveland. Douglass's National Council also died a quick death after the last antebellum meeting of the national black convention in Philadelphia in 1855. Black Garrisonians, not emigrationists, opposed Douglass there.[32]

On the eve of the Civil War, antislavery colonizationists and black emigrationists joined forces to promote emigration to Africa. When Garnet returned from Jamaica in 1856, he became a leading advocate of African emigration. Two years later the Chatham Convention, which bolstered Brown's plans to found a revolutionary black state, also promoted emigration. It divided over choice of place, Day favoring Canada, Holly, Haiti, and Delany receiving an "African Commission." That year Garnet, with Rev. Theodore Bourne, the son of the abolitionist George Bourne, formed the African Civilization Society, using the name of the abolitionist British society rather than that of the ACS. Garnet joined forces with Delany, who founded the African Civilization Society of Canada. The new society soon found itself in bed with the ACS. Delany and the Jamaican-born teacher Robert Campbell formed the Niger River Valley Exploring Party, which was backed by antislavery colonizationists such as Benjamin Coates and William Coppinger in Philadelphia, Rev. John B. Pinney in New York, and Joseph Tracy in Massachusetts. Coates, the Quaker benefactor of the Institute for Colored Youth, where Campbell taught, was a member of both the PAS and PCS. He corresponded with leading black abolitionists, and his pamphlet of 1858 on cotton cultivation in Africa influenced Garnet. Active in the free produce movement, he argued that African sugar, coffee, and cotton grown by black migrants would undercut the market for slave produce and lead to the peaceful abolition of slavery. H. O. Wagoner recognized the sincerity of Coates's efforts, telling him, "I do not look upon *your enterprise* in the same light" as the ACS. Coates's attempt to convert Douglass on colonization failed. Douglass contended that Coates, rather than Garnet, was the mastermind behind the African Civilization Society. When black Bostonians refused to let Garnet promote his society in Grimes's church, Martin let him speak at his Joy Street church. Garnet insisted that he was "*not* a colonizationist." His aim was "to establish the grand center of Negro nationality, from which shall flow streams of commercial, intellectual, and political power which shall make colored people respected everywhere."[33]

Emigrationist sentiment became increasingly popular among black abolitionists. In their opening editorial in the *Weekly Anglo-African* in 1859, Robert and Thomas Hamilton, the sons of William Hamilton, announced their support for emigration. Their paper became a major outlet for emigrationists. That year Delany left in the Liberian-owned *Mendi*, and Blyden wrote of his triumphant welcome in Monrovia, where he gave a well-attended lecture portraying emigration as a natural evolution of black abolitionism. Campbell, who raised funds in England, assisted by the British and Foreign ASS, joined him in Liberia. With the help of the African Anglican missionary Rev. Samuel Ajayi Crowther in Lagos, Delany and Campbell signed a treaty with the Alake and other ruling chiefs of the Egba at Abeokuta for the land between the two cities. In April 1860 both men left for England, and the Egba, advised by a British missionary, repudiated the treaty. The accounts they left of the expedition reveal that the cultural distance between them and native Africans was mediated by their political commitment to a composite black nationality. Campbell's description of the beautiful country of highly cultivated, industrious Africans was an exercise in boosterism. Emigrants, he wrote, should make efforts to raise native Africans to the "proper standard" rather than "supercede or crush them" and follow the "laws" of the Egbas. Thomas Hamilton published Campbell's *A Journey to My Motherland*. Dedicated to Coates, it praised native governments and the beauty of the "African form." Campbell settled in Africa with his family and published the *Anglo-African* there.[34]

Delany wrote an official account of the expedition in London. Ever the medical doctor and mindful that one of the greatest objections to African emigration was mortality, Delany devoted large sections to the diseases of Africa. Like Campbell, Delany was struck by the natural beauty of Yoruba land and its people. According to him, the continent needed civilization, that is, Western modernization, directed by black emigrants, "a *new element* introduced into their midst. . . . This element must be *homogenous* in all the *natural* characteristics, claims, sentiments, and sympathies—the *descendants of Africa* being the only element that can effect it." His motto, "*Africa for the African race, and black men to rule them,*" was not simply a black counterpart to white imperialism but a prescient call for Pan-African nationalism and modernization that could have resisted the Scramble for Africa among European powers at the turn of the century. Delany also embarked on a successful lecturing tour for emigration. His introduction by Lord Brougham and speech at the International Statistical Congress led to a walkout by the entire American delegation except for Edward Jarvis, who is often misidentified as a racist but who had praised McCune Smith's exposé of Calhoun's faulty use of census data to prove black inferiority. The incident made Delany a celebrity in Britain and contributed to the success of his lectures. He gained the support of the Africa Aid Society, a descendant of Buxton's African Civilization Society. On his return to the States in 1861, Delany introduced two new articles to the African Civilization Society's original constitution, restating its goal as "Self Reliance and Self-Government, on the principle of African Nationality, the African race being the ruling element of the nation, controlling and directing their own affairs." He added Pennington's name to the list of all present at the meeting of the society, but to Pennington the African Civilization Society was a "one horse team." He preferred the prospects of Jamaican emigration but later came out against all forms of emigration. The society's list of vice presidents included Delany, Whipper, Daniel A. Payne, Coates, Wayland, Giddings, Robert Hamilton, Tunis Campbell (the author of a guide to housekeeping, hotel management, and waiting on tables that included recipes), destined to become a prominent Reconstruction leader in Georgia, and Rev. R. H. Cain. Garnet followed Delany to Britain, lecturing on behalf of the Africa Aid Society and the Yoruba settlement.[35]

Conservative Republican exponents of colonization tried to woo the emigration movement. In 1860, Joseph Dennis Harris, an emigrationist from Cleve-

land, published *A Summer on the Borders of the Caribbean Sea*. A series of letters containing an extensive account of the Haitian Revolution, the work touted
the economic potential and natural scenic beauty of the area to black emigrants.
Harris, who emigrated to Haiti, predicted the rise of an Anglo-African empire
ruled by colored men. In his introduction to Harris's book, George W. Curtis
pointed out the affinity of a number of Republicans like Francis P. Blair Jr. of
Missouri, the brother of Montgomery Blair, and Sen. James R. Doolittle of
Wisconsin for colonization. Like some slaveholders who dreamed of an empire
for slavery in the Caribbean and Central America, the Blairs imagined a commercial southern American empire. Blair championed the acquiring of land in
Central or South America to establish a black colony as a dependency of the
United States, holding that it would be the best way to prevent the expansion
of slavery. Black emigrationists corresponded with Blair, setting up a land company for emigration. Blair recommended following British imperial policies and
creating "our India" in South America. A staunch believer in the separation of
the races, he also judged that free blacks, like Native Americans, should be removed from the country. Blair trumpeted his plans before mercantile societies,
citing the advantages of commerce and empire for American business while
getting rid of an unwanted race. Like Blair, Doolittle, in his speech against the
acquisition of Cuba, advised the "peaceful emigration" of free blacks to Central or South America. The "colored race," he opined, was ordained by nature
and God to occupy the tropical regions of the hemisphere. During the war, he
opposed any plans for emancipation without colonization, and during Reconstruction he wanted to save the white South from "Africanization and Military
despotism." The Blairs, also foes of black equality, and Doolittle defected back
to the Democratic Party after the war.[36]

The Civil War marked the waning of Republican colonization and black emigration. Lincoln experimented with plans to send black Americans to Chiriqui,
Panama, and to Haiti. James Mitchell of the ACS, Lincoln's "Commissioner
of Emigration," insisted that the survival of republican institutions depended
on the removal of African Americans. The report in 1862 of the House select
committee on emancipation and colonization, of which Blair was a member,
included Delany's Cleveland address from 1854. At Lincoln's behest, Congress
appropriated six hundred thousand dollars on emancipation in the District of
Columbia for colonization. Sen. Samuel Pomeroy of Kansas announced that
thousands of blacks had signed up to emigrate to Central America. Henry Winter Davis of Maryland, Sumner, Hale, Lovejoy, and Seward opposed colonization. When Lincoln invited a black delegation from Washington to recommend
colonization, Frances Harper wrote, "We neither see the wisdom or expediency

of our self-exportation from a land which has in great measure [been] enriched by our toil for generations, till we have a birth-right on the soil, and the strongest claims on the nation for the justice and equity which has been withheld from us for ages." Abolitionist criticism, black military service, and the failure of his colonization schemes led Lincoln to abandon colonization and favor suffrage for black soldiers and the educated. In 1863 Delany was commissioned a major in the Union army. Garnet, who had tried unsuccessfully to solicit funds for emigration from Mitchell, became the first black man after emancipation to address Congress on Lincoln's birthday. He was later appointed the American minister and consul general to Liberia and died shortly after arriving there in 1882.

The idea of black nationhood never completely died out among African Americans. In 1861 Crummell visited the United States. His speeches on Liberian emigration made a convert of Rev. Henry McNeal Turner, destined to become the major black spokesman for emigration in the post-Reconstruction South. Crummell, who made the reverse journey back to the States in 1872, became an intellectual idol of Du Bois, who wrote of the "world-wandering of a soul in search of itself." Despite receiving a land grant in Lagos, Delany never returned to Africa, although he returned to advocating emigration after Reconstruction. After falling from grace for endorsing the Democrat and former Confederate Wade Hampton's gubernatorial campaign in South Carolina, he was reduced to soliciting the "Office of Door Keeper of the US Senate." He died in 1885. That year Crummell debated Douglass at Harper's Ferry. Douglass wanted "black people to remember slavery and forget they were black," while Crummell wanted them "to remember that they were black and forget slavery."[37]

On the eve of the war the Republican Party appealed to the white majority even as the abolition movement made slave resistance its lodestar. Southerners connected the two, referring to Republicans as the "Brown-Helper" party, after John Brown and the North Carolinian critic of slavery Hinton Rowan Helper. Helper's *The Impending Crisis* was a scathing economic indictment of slavery for oppressing nonslaveholding whites. During the congressional speakership controversy of 1859, Democrats blocked the election of any Republican who, like John Sherman, had endorsed the book. Abolitionists and Republicans appeared to slaveholders as an existential threat, inciting the subaltern classes of southern society, slaves and nonslaveholding whites. Helper's antislavery morphed into a racist ethnic cleansing of the South after the war. He became a paranoid segregationist, advocating the deportation of the entire black population. Helper committed suicide in 1909.

Republican attempts to fashion itself as a "white man's party" confused abolitionists. At the MASS meeting in 1859, Garrison opposed Pillsbury and Kelley Foster's resolution characterizing the party as the biggest hindrance to emancipation. Garrison admitted that the party was a "heterogeneous coalition" but asked abolitionists to judge it not by abolition standards but by its commitment to free soil. Abolitionists who arraigned the party as proslavery, Garrison editorialized, lacked judgment and discernment. To Douglass, the Republican Party was the source of both hope for presenting the possibility of attacking slavery through mainstream politics and despair over its relatively backward position on racial equality. When New York went heavily Republican but defeated a black suffrage amendment, he complained that the "black baby of Negro suffrage was thought too ugly to exhibit on so grand an occasion." Similarly, the *Weekly Anglo-African* noted, "Where it is clearly in their power to do anything for the oppressed colored man, why they are too nice, too conservative, to do it." H. Ford Douglas criticized a party that "wants to make the Territories free" but was unwilling to give free blacks all their rights. But both he and Douglass, who loyally voted for Smith's tiny abolitionist party rather than for Lincoln, recognized the "antislavery tendencies" of the party. Garrison as well, after criticizing the Republican Party for its "timeserving" tactics, avowed that it had "materials for growth." Rock placed the party on a graded antislavery scale, with abolitionists at the forefront. According to Child, abolitionists constituted the "van" and the Republicans the rear of the antislavery movement.

The Republican Party, most abolitionists conceded, was antislavery, and radicals such as Owen Lovejoy and Sumner impressed them. Phillips pointed out that the radicals acknowledged the existence of slavery, not just its extension as a problem. Lovejoy, who was reelected to his congressional seat in 1858 by a huge majority, drew attention to the "Fanaticism of the Democratic Party," its attempt to annex Cuba, reopen the slave trade, and extend slavery. The abolitionist press had publicized the very public instances of violation of the African slave trade laws in the lower south in the two years before the war and the aggressive nature of proslavery imperialism. Two years later Lovejoy delivered a speech in Congress in which he refused to "curse John Brown." The speech nearly resulted in fisticuffs on the floor of the House, southerners calling Lovejoy a "nigger-stealing thief" for his well-known involvement in the UGRR.

Similarly, Sumner's philippic "The Barbarism of Slavery," delivered in the Senate, spoke the mind of most abolitionists. In response to proslavery assertions of the historical ubiquity of human bondage, Sumner deduced that slavery was a relic of "ancient barbarism" that must recede with the advance of human civilization. He rigorously critiqued the pretension of the "alleged inferiority of

the African race," reminding the Senate that Polish aristocrats used the same
myths to justify the serfdom of their peasants. New threats of violence reached
Sumner, and some men attempted to assault him again. Douglass wrote that
Sumner had "exceeded our hopes and filled up the measure of all that we have
long desired in Senatorial discussions of Slavery." Letters of praise from Purvis,
Still, Rock, Joshua B. Smith, and H. O. Wagoner came pouring in, and Frances
Harper wrote an ode to the radical senator:

> Thank God that thou hast spoken
> Words earnest, true and brave;
> The lightning of thy lips has smote
> The fetters of the slave.
> Thy words were not soft echoes,
> Thy tones no siren song;
> They fell as battle-axes
> Upon our giant wrong.

The speeches of Lovejoy and Sumner embarrassed conservative Republicans,
but they rallied abolitionists. Sumner attempted to rescind the racial restriction
in the federal militia law at the request of his black constituents, foreshadowing
his wartime and Reconstruction career as a champion of black equality. Giddings, who had challenged Phillips's description of Lincoln as the "slave hound
from Illinois" for his sanctioning of fugitive slave rendition, along with Lovejoy
and Sumner, led most abolitionists into backing Lincoln. Sumner and Lovejoy
became Lincoln's confidantes, pressuring him to move on emancipation.[38]

Before the war Lincoln presented himself as an antislavery man who would
do nothing to interfere with southern slavery. In his address of 1860 at Cooper
Union in New York, he distanced Republicans from John Brown. He emphasized the constitutional nature of the free soil platform of the party. He agreed
to speak at Beecher's Brooklyn church, but the venue was changed at the last
minute, possibly to avoid identification with the abolition movement. Lincoln
argued that his party, unlike abolitionists, did not endorse slave insurrections.
During the presidential elections of 1856 and 1860, slave conspiracy scares had
cropped up, especially in Texas. Addressing southern fears, he contended that
rebellions were usually not possible given slaves' scattered locations, lack of
communication, and the loyalty of the few who betrayed conspiracies. The Haitian Revolution had succeeded because of "exceptional" circumstances. And
if slaves rebelled, it was their masters' fault, whose loud mischaracterizations
taught them to hope for the assistance of "Black Republicans." Lincoln reiterated that the Republican program was eminently conservative and stood on the

same ground as that of the founding fathers, that is, to restrict the expansion of slavery and let it continue in the states until they themselves decided to abolish it. The northern states, however, could not agree with the notion that slavery was right, even though they would honor constitutional compromises on slavery, and they would not impair the foundations of democratic government, free speech, civil liberties, and fair elections in order to perpetuate or expand slavery.

Lincoln's candidacy was acceptable to all Republicans since Chase and Seward, with their support of fugitive slaves and black rights, were too closely identified with abolition to carry the lower north. He was everyone's second choice. Lincoln shared the radicals' moral abhorrence of slavery, the moderates' reverence for the Union and the Constitution, and the conservatives' pet project of colonization. The Republican platform of 1860 stuck to nonextension and, on Giddings's suggestion, contained an endorsement of the Declaration, which had come under increasing proslavery criticism. It contained not a word on the divisive issues of black citizenship or colonization. The result of the four-way presidential election revealed sectional polarization but also unionist sentiment in the upper south. The South divided between a majority for the southern Democratic proslavery candidacy of John Breckinridge of Kentucky and the unionist ticket of John C. Bell of Tennessee and Massachusetts's Edward Everett. A northern antislavery majority of over 50 percent elected Lincoln, who did not appear on the ballot in most southern states, garnering nonnegligible votes only in the nearly free state of Delaware and among Missouri free soilers. New Jersey split its electoral vote between the northern Democratic candidate, Douglas, and Lincoln. Ironically, Douglas only won Missouri, whose citizens had made a mockery of popular sovereignty in Kansas. Lincoln carried every county in the abolitionist heartland of New England and nearly all the northern states, and he received more votes than all three of his opponents combined.[39] Abolitionists had sowed the seeds Republicans reaped. The northern antislavery majority that elected Lincoln to the presidency was the product of at least three decades of arduous and persistent abolitionist work.

All agreed that Lincoln's election marked a historic turning point in the progress of antislavery. Chase declared, "The Slave Power is overthrown." Douglass wrote that it had "vitiated" the slaveholders' "authority, and broken their power" and "demonstrated the possibility of electing, if not an Abolitionist, at least an anti-slavery reputation to the Presidency." Phillips enthused that for "the first time in our history the *slave* has chosen a President of the United States. We have passed the Rubicon." Disunion soon followed Lincoln's election, as the secessionist state par excellence, South Carolina, led the lower south out of the Union on December 20, 1860. Throughout the North abolitionists became victims of mob attacks led by conservative unionists who blamed them for secession. Garrison printed a book-length pamphlet on the "new reign of terror" in the South against suspected rebels and abolitionists after Brown's raid, which had resulted in the expulsion of John G. Fee and his followers from Kentucky and continued until the presidential election and secession. Garrison distinguished between his revolutionary commitment to disunion, chiding Henry C. Wright and Greeley for advocating a peaceful separation, and southerners' claim that the right to secession was a constitutional one. Everything changed with the firing on Fort Sumter on April 12, 1861. Four more upper south states seceded, and abolitionists were now seen as farseeing prophets. Rock speculated that out of the "rebellion for slavery . . . emancipation must spring." Once again forced to choose between peace principles and abolition, Garrison and most abolitionists chose an antislavery war over a proslavery peace. Slaveholders, who refused to abide by the results of an election and fired the first shot, linked the cause of the slave with the survival of American democracy.[40] They solved Lincoln's dilemma: abolition, union, and the Constitution became compatible, not competing, values.

The Civil War, as Douglass insisted, was an "abolition war." It proved to be the midwife of emancipation. Military emancipation, however, was far from being a foregone conclusion. Starting with the colonial wars and the American Revolution to the war between Brazil and Paraguay, military confrontations had not, after all, resulted in complete emancipation. The Haitian Revolution and the American Civil War were the only two wars that became unqualified abolition wars. Historical events seldom occur with an inexorable logic of their own. For wartime emancipation to occur, abolition must first be an option, and that option must be exercised. The slaves who defected to Union army lines initiated the process of emancipation, and their abolitionist and radical Republican allies enacted familiar roles, calling for abolition, black recruitment in the Union army, and, as uncompromising critics of gradualism, compensation and colonization. They helped make the Civil War into an abolition war, a "remorseless revolutionary struggle" against slavery. Lincoln did not move from Union to abolition but from nonextension to abolition. He achieved greatness by adopting the slave's cause. Before his death, Lincoln inhabited abolition ground, the possibility of black citizenship. And just as the Gettysburg Address was his best articulation of the connection between the cause of the slave and American democracy, Lincoln's Second Inaugural Address best defined the meaning of the abolition war: it would not end "until all the wealth piled by the bondsman's two hundred and fifty years of unrequited toil shall be sunk, and until every drop of blood drawn by the lash, shall be paid by another drawn by the sword."

Wartime emancipation was not a singular event; it was a historical process that involved many actors, great and small, the enslaved, abolitionists, congressional Republicans, the Union army, and the president. Lincoln understood that process. Modestly, he claimed that events had ruled him and that he was merely the instrument of emancipation: "The logic and moral power of Garrison and the anti-slavery people of the country and the army, have done all." Mindful of the history of the conflict over slavery, he had written before the war that every schoolboy recognized the names of Sharp and Wilberforce (at least they did then) but few could recall the names of their opponents. With the issuing of the Emancipation Proclamation in 1863 Lincoln was well on his way to becoming the Great Emancipator, and abolitionists, who had agitated so long for emancipation, the forgotten emancipationists. The slaves themselves lay forgotten as the architects of their own liberation.[41]

EPILOGUE: THE ABOLITIONIST ORIGINS OF AMERICAN DEMOCRACY

In May 1865 Garrison realized that the movement he had founded would outlive him. His resolution to disband the AASS because of the imminent ratification of the Thirteenth Amendment abolishing slavery in the United States was defeated decisively by a vote of 118 to 48 at its annual meeting. Phillips and Douglass argued that unless the government enfranchised all its black citizens, emancipation was not complete, and the dual goals of the AASS, ending slavery and achieving black equality, were not realized. Garrison was hardly opposed to black suffrage; he had championed it from the start and would continue to do so until he died fourteen years later. The division between him, along with the few who supported him, and the movement was not over principles. Garrison was exhausted after manning the guns for so long, and his wife lay debilitated by a paralytic stroke. But personal travails had never interfered with his ability to fight the good fight. The AASS still offered him the presidency, which he declined. In his valedictory address he said he was president of the society when it was unpopular, but "to-day, it is popular to be President of the American Anti-Slavery Society. Hence, my connection with it terminates here and now, both as a member and as its presiding officer." He set the type for the December 29 issue of the *Liberator* for the last time after thirty-five years of "unremitting labor." And Garrison left the movement he had started. Phillips was elected president, and he and Douglass would spearhead the abolitionist fight for black citizenship during Reconstruction, America's first experiment with interracial democracy after the Civil War.

The division between Phillips and Garrison began over Lincoln. Initially, both men were united in criticizing the president as a "slow coach" for not acting expeditiously on emancipation and black recruitment into the Union army and for experimenting with colonization, gradualism, and compensation for border-state slaveholders. Garrison formed the Emancipation League in 1861 to goad the president to abolish slavery and upbraided him severely for advocating colonization. After emancipation Lincoln won Garrison over. He was impressed by the president's capacity for growth, but Phillips continued to view him as a laggard in the cause of black rights. Before the war Phillips and Garrison had united against Pillsbury's and Foster's resolution denouncing the Republican Party as the greatest hindrance to emancipation. At the annual meeting of the AASS in 1864 Phillips joined Pillsbury and Foster. His resolution, stating that the Republicans were "ready to sacrifice" northern interests and freedpeople, was amended by Garrison to read "are in danger of sacrificing," but there was no rapprochement. Phillips joined the movement to replace Lincoln with Frémont as the Republican presidential nominee, while Garrison journeyed to the Republican National Convention in Baltimore to lend his support to Lincoln's renomination. Garrison, who was more nervous about Confederates and copperheads overturning emancipation, was wary of the Frémont movement. In his eagerness to support the president's reelection he defended Lincoln's wartime reconstruction of Louisiana, which did not guarantee black suffrage. Designed to expedite the end of the war rather than to be a blueprint for reconstruction, Lincoln's plan left open the possibility of black voting, and he privately urged Louisiana's governor to consider it. McKim assured Garrison that Lincoln was ahead of a majority in his own party on black suffrage. Most abolitionists led by Phillips were critical of the president's pocket veto of the Wade–Davis bill, which contained civil protections for freedpeople but not the right to vote.

Garrison, like Lincoln, prioritized a constitutional amendment that would make emancipation irreversible and immune from political vicissitudes. When Stanton and Anthony formed the Women's National Loyal League in 1863 to coordinate a national petition campaign for a congressional act of emancipation, Garrison recommended they change their demand to a constitutional amendment to abolish slavery, an idea that *Freedom's Journal* had first proposed in 1827. The women's league conducted the most successful petition campaign in abolitionist history for the Thirteenth Amendment, resulting in one million signatures in rolls carried by two black pages to Sumner's desk in the Senate. Lincoln campaigned for it tirelessly as a necessary and fitting conclusion to the war and endorsed partial black voting, for Union army soldiers and the educated, before his death. All abolitionists, even those who had criticized him relentlessly, regarded his death as a calamity.[1]

Garrison thought the center of gravity of antislavery had shifted to the government. Abolitionists, he felt, should concentrate their energies on freedpeople's relief and education, as had Lewis Tappan's AMA, McKim, Coffin, and many other abolitionist men and women. Phillips and Douglass argued that the movement must continue as standard-bearers in the fight for equal rights and warned of backsliders who might undo an abolition victory. The work of abolition, Douglass declared, would not be complete until "black men" had been admitted to the "body politic of America." In 1866 the Emancipation League became the Impartial Suffrage League. While Garrison and Phillips united to excoriate Andrew Johnson's opposition to black citizenship, they differed once again over the Fourteenth Amendment, which established national birthright citizenship and guaranteed all citizens equality before the law. Phillips, Douglass, and Sumner feared that the amendment had sacrificed the principle of black suffrage, though Sumner ended up voting for it. Abolitionists and radicals like Stevens also demanded the redistribution of land among freedpeople. Except for a few wartime grants, most of which Johnson revoked, land reform never became a part of Radical Reconstruction. Labor radicals, too, looked beyond equality to demand a social reconstruction of class relations and industrial democracy. Abolitionists and their radical allies, assisted by the northern backlash against the obduracy of the former Confederate states, which, under Johnson, had hastened to reestablish the substance of slavery without its form, made black citizenship Reconstruction's cornerstone. When Phillips and Douglass got their amendment, the Fifteenth, which gave black men the right to vote, they disbanded the AASS in 1870, overriding Foster's objections that they should continue to agitate for land redistribution.

Women abolitionists especially, including Stanton, Anthony, and Stone, cried foul at the Fourteenth and Fifteenth Amendments, which introduced the word *male*, or a gender restriction, into the Constitution, though Stone ended up supporting the Fifteenth Amendment. The American Equal Rights Association, formed to campaign for blacks and women's suffrage, fell apart. Stanton and Anthony formed the National Woman Suffrage Association, and Stone led most abolitionist feminists into the American Woman Suffrage Association in 1869. Black women like Harper and Truth refused to separate the two causes; as Harper had put it in her speech to the national women's rights convention in 1866, "We are all bound up together in one great bundle of humanity." The Reconstruction amendments remade the Constitution and substantially realized the abolitionist vision of an interracial democracy, even though they did not entirely live up to the abolitionist principle of equal rights. If Sumner, Phillips, Douglass, and Garrison were willing to sacrifice women's rights to "the negro's hour," some women's rights activists, led by Stanton and Anthony, were willing to sacrifice the abolitionist commitment to racial equality for the rights of women.[2]

Perhaps that is why abolitionists never really became popular and have come down to us as perpetual naysayers: they continued to focus on the shortcomings of the present to prepare the way for the achievements of the future. They refused to be satisfied by the success of their movement and warned of the dangers lurking ahead. In his letters published in the *Tribune*, Garrison inveighed against the government's campaign against the Plains Indians, Chinese exclusion, and "bloody misrule" in the South that disfranchised "colored citizens," and he supported the eight-hour-a-day demand and woman suffrage before his death. Phillips viewed the labor movement as a natural progression of abolition. Now that the struggle against those who asserted that "the laborer must necessarily be owned by capitalists" was over, the fight was for the refusal of labor to be "vassals of wealth." To Douglass, Ida B. Wells's campaign against lynching continued the abolitionist crusade for black liberation. He anointed her "Brave Woman" for doing an immeasurable service to the race. His last speech was against the new "Southern Barbarism."

Garrison, Phillips, Weld, and Douglass lived long enough to see abolitionist gains undone, while the deaths of many others, like Tappan, Sumner, and Stevens, spared them. Stevens was interred in an integrated cemetery, his dying protest against racial inequality. In 1883 the Supreme Court overturned Sumner's dying legacy, the Civil Rights Act of 1875, which presciently outlawed segregation in public spaces. Phillips and Garrison would unite once again in backing the Republican Party against the Liberals, who helped overthrow Reconstruction in the name of reforming government, preparing the way for the reunion between southern reaction and northern capital. Most abolitionists insisted that active government intervention was needed to safeguard the rights of former slaves and that the reconstruction of American democracy should not end. The Republican Party would be transformed from the party of antislavery and free labor to the party of big business, small government, laissez-faire, and states' rights. The equal protection clause of the Fourteenth Amendment, designed to safeguard the rights of former slaves, was deployed on behalf of large corporations. Only in modern times has it been put to good use. In the late twentieth century the political base of the party of Lincoln shifted ironically to the former Confederate states, which had not given Lincoln a single electoral vote.

Garrison and Douglass had parted over state action decades earlier. In the end they both proved to be right. Emancipation and enfranchisement had been enacted by the actions of an antislavery government, but as long as a majority of white Americans remained immune to the abolitionist commitment to racial equality, they could be vitiated. As Douglass noted, "Until it shall be safe to leave the lamb in the hold of the lion, the laborer in the power of the capitalist, the poor in the hands of the rich, it will not be safe to leave a newly emancipated people completely in the power of their former masters, especially when such masters have ceased to be such not from enlightened moral convictions but by irresistible force." The two men differed one last time. Whereas Douglass opposed the movement of former slaves, the Exodusters, from Mississippi to Kansas after the fall of Reconstruction, Garrison lent his support from his deathbed. Pioneering women abolitionists, among them Prudence Crandall Philleo, who had made her home in Kansas, Haviland, and Truth rushed to their aid. Douglass's moving eulogy for Garrison, "the chief apostle of the immediate and unconditional emancipation of all the slaves in America" in 1879, while not shying away from the differences between them, was also a eulogy for the abolition movement.[3]

Individual abolitionists and their successors continued the struggle for black equality and criticized the narrowing of democracy after the overthrow of Reconstruction in the most dismal circumstances: the golden age of imperialism, social Darwinism, scientific racism, robber barons, and assaults on the rights of blacks, Native Americans, labor, and immigrants. Abolitionists wrote their memoirs even as disfranchisement, segregation, debt peonage, and lynching made a mockery of black freedom, the nadir of black history, as Rayford Logan called it. It made for narratives of defeat, not triumph.[4] The tragedy of the Civil War was not that the abolitionist vision briefly triumphed over inertia and conservatism but that the opponents of the abolitionists, of their moral urgency and devotion to black rights, plunged the nation into yet another long racial nightmare. It would take a new movement in another century to realize abolitionist goals and unleash again a wave of radical social movements that pushed at the boundaries of American democracy.

For American radicals ever since, abolition has remained a model of activism, the template of a social movement. The interracial Knights of Labor viewed their project of a cooperative commonwealth as "the legitimate heir to mid-century abolitionism." The Populists adopted the abolitionists' lecturing agency system. Even the relatively conservative trade unionist Samuel Gompers of the American Federation of Labor recalled that "the great struggle against human slavery which was convulsing America was of vital interest to wage-earners" everywhere. The crusading black journalist William Monroe Trotter set type in the *Liberator*'s old office. Garrison was his beau ideal. In his *Crisis* editorials, the great intellectual and activist W. E. B. Du Bois repeatedly referred to the National Association for the Advancement of Colored People, cofounded by black radicals and a few white descendants of abolitionists, as the "New Abolition Movement." Eugene Debs invoked the abolitionists to prove that socialism was an American ideal, not a subversive, foreign import. Labor radicals in the Industrial Workers of the World, the wobblies, revived the abolitionist struggle for free speech. Communists in the Popular Front era called their movement the new Americanism, evoking both Lincoln and Douglass. The labor leader A. Philip Randolph, the first black vice president of the AFL-CIO, looked to the UGRR for inspiration. Civil rights activists saw themselves as the new abolitionists and named their movement "the second Reconstruction" of American democracy. Rev. Martin Luther King Jr. was fond of quoting Theodore Parker, the arc of the moral universe is long but it bends toward justice. This was no blind faith in inexorable progress but a call to radical action. A black nationalist magazine took the name the *Liberator*, and today a journal of "insurgent politics" is called *Abolition*. Even activists against mass incarceration, who find fault with the Thirteenth Amendment's exception for those legally convicted of a crime, call for the abolition of the prison industrial complex; their paper is the *Abolitionist*. Contemporary movements against human trafficking and labor exploitation continue to struggle against slavery in the name of abolition.[5]

The abolitionist legacy for American democracy lies hidden in plain sight. Deval Patrick, the first African American governor of Massachusetts, took his oath of office on the Bible presented by Cinque to John Quincy Adams. Loretta Lynch, the first black woman to occupy the office of U.S. attorney general, chose Douglass's Bible. Barack Obama, the forty-fourth president of the United States, used Lincoln's Bible. A racist critic once asked if Garrison could ever imagine voting for a black president, to which Garrison replied he surely would if a worthy candidate came along. In 2008 Obama compared his unlikely victory in the Iowa Democratic presidential caucuses to the way in which a band of ordinary men and women, black and white, the abolitionists, had achieved the destruction of slavery. His wife and children are descendants of American slaves. In 2015 he sang that old abolitionist hymn written by a repentant British slave trader, "Amazing Grace," in a church founded by black abolitionists. The age of Obama, like the age of Lincoln, has its critics and its admirers, but neither would have been possible without the abolition movement.

The enduring heritage of the abolition movement is even broader: its unyielding commitment to human rights and a call to action, however much abolitionists disagreed on tactics and ideas until the end. Demonstrating the potential of democratic radicalism is no mean achievement. Their wide-ranging activism was, as Du Bois put it, "the finest thing in American history."[6]

NOTES

ABBREVIATIONS

Abbreviations of the organizations mentioned in the notes may be found in the list of abbreviations in the front matter. The notes refer to the black abolitionist papers (BAP) both as a digitized source, in microfilm (with reel numbers) and print editions (with publication information and page numbers).

AHR	*American Historical Review*
ARCJ	*African Repository and Colonial Journal*
ASB	The *Anti-Slavery Bugle*
BAP	*Black Abolitionist Papers*
BPL	Boston Public Library
CA	*Colored American*
CU	Columbia University
CWH	*Civil War History*
DM	*Douglass' Monthly*
FDP	*Frederick Douglass' Paper*
FJ	*Freedom's Journal*
FOM	*Friend of Man*
GUE	*Genius of Universal Emancipation*
HSP	Historical Society of Pennsylvania
JAH	*Journal of American History*
JBS	*Journal of Black Studies*
JER	*Journal of the Early American Republic*
JNH	*Journal of Negro History*
JSH	*Journal of Southern History*
LC	Library of Congress
MHR	*Massachusetts Historical Review*
MHS	Massachusetts Historical Society

MVHR   *Mississippi Valley Historical Review*
NASS   *National Anti Slavery Standard*
NE   *National Era*
NEQ   *New England Quarterly*
NR   *National Reformer*
NS   *North Star*
NYHS   New-York Historical Society
PF   *Pennsylvania Freeman*
PH   *Pennsylvania History*
PMHB   *Pennsylvania Magazine of History and Biography*
S&A   *Slavery and Abolition*
TAE   *The Anti-Slavery Examiner*
TASR   *The Anti Slavery Record*
TE   *The Emancipator*
TEFA   *The Emancipator and Free American*
TL   *The Liberator*
TLP   *The Liberty Press*
TP   *The Philanthropist*
VMHB   *Virginia Magazine of History and Biography*
WMQ   *William and Mary Quarterly*

INTRODUCTION

1. Andrew Delbanco, *The Abolitionist Imagination* (Cambridge, Mass., 2012); also see Robin D. G. Kelley, *Freedom Dreams: The Black Radical Imagination* (Boston, 2002); Nick Bromell, *The Time Is Always Now: Black Thought and the Transformation of US Democracy* (New York, 2013).

2. C. L. R. James, *The Black Jacobins: Touissant L'Ouverture and the San Domingo Revolution* (New York, 1963); Laurent Dubois, "An Enslaved Enlightenment: Rethinking the Intellectual History of the French Atlantic," *Social History* 31 (February 2006): 1–14; Edward Rugemer, "Slave Rebels and Abolitionists: The Black Atlantic and the Coming of the Civil War," *Journal of the Civil War Era* 2 (June 2012): 179–202.

3. Frederick Cooper, "Elevating the Race: The Social Thought of Black Leaders, 1827–50," *American Quarterly* 24 (December 1972): 604–25; Stephen Kantrowitz, *More than Freedom: Fighting for Black Citizenship in a White Republic, 1829–1889* (New York, 2012), 4; Manisha Sinha, "An Alternative Tradition of Radicalism: African American Abolitionists and the Metaphor of Revolution," in Sinha and Penny Von Eschen, eds., *Contested Democracy: Freedom, Race, and Power in American History* (New York, 2007), 9–30.

4. John Stauffer, *The Black Hearts of Men: Radical Abolitionists and the Transformation of Race* (Cambridge, Mass., 2002); Ellen Carol DuBois, *Feminism and Suffrage: The Emergence of an Independent Women's Movement in America, 1848–1869* (Ithaca, 1978); Robert H. Abzug, *Cosmos Crumbling: American Reform and the Religious*

Imagination (New York, 1994); Aileen S. Kraditor, *Means and Ends in American Abolitionism: Garrison and His Critics on Strategy and Tactics, 1834–1850* (New York, 1967).

5. Eric Williams, *Capitalism and Slavery* (Chapel Hill, 1944); Seymour Drescher, "Capitalism and Slavery: After Fifty Years," in Heather Cateau and S. H. H. Carrington, eds., *Capitalism and Slavery: Fifty Years Later* (New York, 2000), 81–98; Seth Rockman, "The Unfree Origins of American Capitalism," in Cathy Matson, ed., *The Economy of Early America: Historical Perspectives and New Directions* (University Park, Pa., 2006), 335–61; Sven Beckert, *Empire of Cotton: A Global History* (New York, 2014); Calvin Schermerhorn, *The Business of Slavery and the Rise of American Capitalism, 1815–1860* (New Haven, 2015); Thomas Piketty, *Capital in the Twenty-First Century* (Cambridge, Mass., 2014); Edward E. Baptist, *The Half Has Never Been Told: Slavery and the Making of American Capitalism* (New York, 2014).

6. Bruce Laurie, *Beyond Garrison: Antislavery and Social Reform* (Cambridge, Eng., 2005); W. Caleb McDaniel, *The Problem of Democracy in the Age of Slavery: Garrisonian Abolitionists and Transatlantic Reform* (Baton Rouge, 2013); McDaniel, "The Bonds and Boundaries of Antislavery," *Journal of the Civil War Era* 4 (March 2014): 84–104; Thomas Bender, ed., *The Antislavery Debate: Capitalism and Abolitionism as a Problem in Historical Interpretation* (Berkeley, 1992).

7. Karen Haltunnen, "Humanitarianism and the Pornography of Pain in Anglo-American Culture," *AHR* 100 (April 1995): 303–34; Elizabeth B. Clark, "'The Sacred Rights of the Weak': Pain, Sympathy, and the Culture of Individual Rights in Antebellum America," *JAH* 82 (September 1995): 463–93; Carol Lasser, "Voyeuristic Abolitionism: Sex, Gender, and the Transformation of Antislavery Rhetoric," *JER* 28 (Spring 2008): 83–114; Marcus Wood, *Slavery, Empathy, and Pornography* (New York, 2002); Stauffer, *The Black Hearts of Men*, 39; Joseph Yannielli, "George Thompson Among the Africans: Empathy, Authority, and Insanity in the Age of Abolition," *JAH* 96 (March 2010): 979–1000; Saidiya V. Hartman, *Scenes of Subjection: Terror, Slavery, and Self-Making in Nineteenth-Century America* (New York, 1997); Margaret Abruzzo, *Polemical Pain: Slavery, Cruelty, and the Rise of Humanitarianism* (Baltimore, 2011).

8. Walter Johnson, *River of Dark Dreams: Slavery and Empire in the Cotton Kingdom* (Cambridge, Mass., 2013); Robert E. May, *Slavery, Race, and Conquest in the Tropics: Lincoln, Douglas, and the Future of Latin America* (Cambridge, Eng., 2013); Manisha Sinha, *The Counterrevolution of Slavery: Politics and Ideology in Antebellum South Carolina* (Chapel Hill, 2000); James Oakes, *The Scorpion's Sting: Antislavery and the Coming of the Civil War* (New York, 2014); James Brewer Stewart, *Abolitionist Politics and the Coming of the Civil War* (Amherst, Mass., 2005); David Ericson, *Slavery in the American Republic: Developing the Federal Government, 1791–1861* (Lawrence, Kan., 2011).

9. W. E. B. Du Bois, *Black Reconstruction: An Essay Toward a History of the Part Black Folk Played in the Reconstruction of Democracy in America, 1860–1880* (New York, 1935); James Oakes, *Freedom National: The Destruction of Slavery, 1861–1865* (New York, 2013); Eric Foner, *Reconstruction: America's Unfinished Revolution, 1863–1877*

(New York, 1988); Amy Dru Stanley, *From Bondage to Contract: Wage Labor, Marriage, and the Market in the Age of Slave Emancipation* (Cambridge, Eng., 1998); Steven Hahn, *A Nation Under Our Feet: Black Political Struggles in the Rural South from Slavery to the Great Migration* (Cambridge, Mass., 2003).

10. Robin Blackburn, *The American Crucible: Slavery, Emancipation and Human Rights* (London, 2011); Seymour Drescher, *Abolition: A History of Slavery and Antislavery* (Cambridge, Eng., 2009); David Brion Davis, *The Problem of Slavery in the Age of Emancipation* (New York, 2014).

CHAPTER ONE. PROPHETS WITHOUT HONOR

1. Eric Robert Taylor, *If We Must Die: Shipboard Insurrections in the Era of the Atlantic Slave Trade* (Baton Rouge, 2006), 21, 90, 113, 167–68; Sylviane A. Diouf, ed., *Fighting the Slave Trade: West African Strategies* (Athens, Ohio, 2003); Michael A. Gomez, *Exchanging Our Country Marks: The Transformation of African Identities in the Colonial and Antebellum South* (Chapel Hill, 1998), 160, 199–214; Randy J. Sparks, *Where the Negroes Are Masters: An African Port in the Era of the Slave Trade* (Cambridge, Mass., 2014).

2. David Brion Davis, *The Problem of Slavery in Western Culture* (Ithaca, 1966), 111–14; Robin Blackburn, *The Overthrow of Colonial Slavery, 1776–1848* (London, 1988), chap. 1; Blackburn, *The Making of New World Slavery: From the Baroque to the Modern 1492–1800* (London, 1997), 135–37, 150–56; Special Issue on Free Soil, *S&A* 32 (2011).

3. Bartolomé de las Casas, *An Account, Much Abbreviated, of the Destruction of the Indies With Related Texts*, Franklin W. Knight, ed. (Indianapolis, 2003); Daniel Castro, *Another Face of Empire: Bartolomé de las Casas, Indigenous Rights, and Ecclesiastical Imperialism* (Durham, 2007); Alonso de Sandoval, S.J., *Treatise on Slavery: Selections from De instuaranda Aethiopum salute*, ed. and trans. Nicole von Germeten (Indianapolis, 2008), introduction, 50–59, 66–84; Davis, *The Problem of Slavery in Western Culture*, 169–96; Christopher Schmidt-Nowara, *Slavery, Freedom and Abolition in Latin America and the Atlantic World* (Albuquerque, 2011), 22–23; Richard Gray, *Black Christians and White Missionaries* (New Haven, 1990), chap. 1.

4. Roger Bruns, ed., *Am I Not a Man and a Brother: The Antislavery Crusade of Revolutionary America, 1688–1788* (New York, 1977), 3, 6, 8; Henry J. Cadbury, "An Early Quaker Anti-Slavery Statement," *JNH* 22 (October 1937): 488–93; Katherine Gerbner, "'We Are Against the Traffick of Men-Body': The Germantown Quaker Protest of 1688 and the Origins of American Abolitionism," *PH* 74 (Spring 2007): 149–72; Kenneth L. Carroll, "William Sotheby, Early Quaker Antislavery Writer," *PMHB* 89 (October 1965): 416–27; Mary Stoughton Locke, *Antislavery in America from the Introduction of African Slaves to the Prohibition of the Slave Trade (1619–1808)* (Boston, 1901), 21–40; Brycchan Carey, *From Peace to Freedom: Quaker Rhetoric and the Birth of American Antislavery, 1657–1761* (New Haven, 2012).

5. George Fox, *To The Ministers, Teachers, and Priests (so called and so Stileing your Selves) in Barbados* (London, 1672), 5; G. F. [George Fox], *Gospel Family=Order,*

Being a Short Discourse Concerning the Ordering of Families, Both of Whites, Blacks and Indians (repr., Philadelphia, 1701), 14–17; J. William Frost, ed., *The Quaker Origins of Antislavery* (Norwood, Pa., 1980), introduction; Edmundson quoted on p. 68; Thomas E. Drake, *Quakers and Slavery in America* (New Haven, 1950), chaps. 1, 2; Jean R. Soderlund, *Quakers and Slavery: A Divided Spirit* (Princeton, 1985).

6. Henry J. Cadbury, *John Hepburn and His Book Against Slavery, 1715* (Worcester, Mass., 1949), 90–91, 104–5, 117; Elihu Coleman, *A Testimony Against the Anti-Christian Practice of Making Slaves of Men* (1733; repr., New Bedford, 1825), 22; Benjamin Lay, *All Slave-Keepers that Keep the Innocent in Bondage, Apostates . . .* (Philadelphia, 1737), 271; James Oliver and Lois E. Horton, *In Hope of Liberty: Culture, Community and Protest Among Northern Free Blacks, 1700–1860* (New York, 1997), chap. 2; Peter Linebaugh and Marcus Rediker, *The Many-Headed Hydra: Sailors, Slaves, Commoners, and the Hidden History of the Revolutionary Atlantic* (Boston, 2000).

7. Cadbury, *John Hepburn and His Book Against Slavery*, 122, 149, 153; Ralph Sandiford, *The Mystery of Iniquity . . .* , 2d ed. (Philadelphia, 1730), 7–8, 81–86, 100–107; Lay, *All Slave-Keepers*, 21–22, 229; Roberts Vaux, *Memoirs of the Lives of Benjamin Lay and Ralph Sandiford: Two of the Earliest Public Advocates for the Emancipation of the Enslaved Africans* (Philadelphia, 1815); David Brion Davis, *The Problem of Slavery in the Age of Revolution, 1770–1823* (Ithaca, 1975), chap. 5; Philip Gould, *Barbaric Traffic: Commerce and Antislavery in the 18th Century Atlantic World* (Cambridge, Eng., 2003), esp. chap. 1.

8. Christopher Hill, *The World Turned Upside Down: Radical Ideas During the English Revolution* (New York, 1972); John Donoghue, " 'Out of the Land of Bondage': The English Revolution and the Atlantic Origins of Abolition," *AHR* 115 (October 2010): 943–74; Richard Baxter, *A Christian directory, or, A summ of practical theologie . . .* (London, 1673), 557–60; Thomas Tryon, *Friendly Advice to the Gentleman Planters of the East and West Indies in Three Parts* (London, 1684), 75–224; James G. Basker, ed., *Amazing Grace: An Anthology of Poems About Slavery, 1660–1810* (New Haven, 2002), 25; Philippe Rosenberg, "Thomas Tryon and the Seventeenth-Century Dimensions of Antislavery," *WMQ* 61 (2004): 609–42; Kim F. Hall, " 'Extravagant Viciousness': Slavery and Gluttony in the Works of Thomas Tryon," in Philip D. Beidler and Gary Taylor, eds., *Writing Race Across the Atlantic World* (New York, 2005), 93–112; David Waldstreicher, "Benjamin Franklin, Religion, and Early Antislavery," in Steven Mintz and John Stauffer, eds., *The Problem of Evil: Slavery, Freedom, and the Ambiguities of American Reform* (Amherst, Mass., 2007), 162–73.

9. Morgan Godwyn, *The Negros and Indians Advocate, Suing for their Admission into the Church: or A Persuasive to the Instructing and Baptizing of the Negros and Indians in our Plantations* (London, 1680), 3–5, 7, 9–86, 164–65; Alden T. Vaughn, *Roots of American Racism: Essays on the Colonial Experience* (New York, 1995), chap. 3; Sylvia R. Frey and Betty Wood, *Come Shouting to Zion: African American Protestantism in the American South and British Caribbean to 1830* (Chapel Hill, 1988), chap. 2.

10. Thomas Bacon, *Two Sermons Preached to a Congregation of Black Slaves* (London, 1749); John Bell, "An Epistle to Friends (1741)," in Frost, ed., *Quaker Origins of Antislavery*, 134–37; Samuel Davies, *The Duty of Christians to Propagate their Religion*

among Heathens, Earnestly Recommended to the Masters of Negroe Slaves in Virginia (London, 1758); Travis Glasson, "'Baptism Does Not Bestow Freedom': Missionary Anglicanism, Slavery, and the Yorke–Talbot Opinion," *WMQ* 67 (April 2010): 279–318; John C. Van Horne, ed., *Religious Philanthropy and Colonial Slavery: The American Correspondence of the Associates of Dr. Bray, 1717–1777* (Urbana, 1985); Jeffrey H. Richards, "Samuel Davies and the Transatlantic Campaign for Slave Literacy in Virginia," *VMHB* 111 (2003): 333–78; Harry S. Stout, *The Divine Dramatist: George Whitefield and the Rise of Modern Evangelicalism* (Grand Rapids, 1991), 197–99; Terry L. Myers, "Benjamin Franklin, the College of William and Mary, and the Williamsburg Bray School," *Anglican and Episcopal History* 368 (2010); Maurice Jackson, *Let This Voice Be Heard: Anthony Benezet, Father of Atlantic Abolitionism* (Philadelphia, 2009), 2–9.

11. Cotton Mather, *A Good Master Well Served* (Boston, 1696); Mather, *The Negro Christianized: An Essay to Excite and Assist the Good Work, the Instruction of Negro-Servants in Christianity* (Boston, 1706), 19; Mather, *Rules for the Society of Negroes. 1693* (Boston, 1714); Christopher Cameron, "The Puritan Origins of Black Abolitionism in Massachusetts," *Historical Journal of Massachusetts* (Summer 2011): 78–107; Lorenzo J. Greene, *The Negro in Colonial New England, 1620–1776* (New York, 1942), 263–87; William D. Piersen, *Black Yankees: The Development of an Afro-American Subculture in Eighteenth-Century New England* (Amherst, Mass., 1998), 40, 50–59; Craig Steven Wilder, *Ebony and Ivy: Race, Slavery, and the Troubled History of America's Universities* (New York, 2013), 123, 190–91.

12. [Samuel Sewall], *The Selling of Joseph: A Memorial* (Boston, 1700), 1–3; Locke, *Antislavery in America*, 15–18; Mel Yazawa, ed., *The Diary and Life of Samuel Sewall* (Boston, 1988), 3; Mark A. Peterson, "The Selling of Joseph: Bostonians, Antislavery, and the Protestant International, 1689–1733," *MHR* 4 (2002): 1–22.

13. John Saffin, *A Brief and Candid Answer to a Late printed Sheet, Entitled, The Selling of Joseph* (Boston, 1701); George H. Moore, *Notes on the History of Slavery in Massachusetts* (New York, 1866), 89–97, 112, 251–56; Abner C. Goodell Jr., "John Saffin and His Slave Adam," *Transactions 1892–94*, vol. 1 of *Publications of the Colonial Society of Massachusetts* (Boston, 1895), 87–112; Lawrence W. Towner, "The Sewall–Saffin Dialogue on Slavery," *WMQ* 21 (January 1964): 40–52; "Early Negro Petitions for Freedom," in Herbert Aptheker, ed., *A Documentary History of the Negro People in the United States* (New York, 1950), 1:1–4; Bruns, ed., *Am I Not a Man*, 30; Sandiford, *Mystery of Iniquity*, 28.

14. Bruns, ed., *Am I Not a Man*, 64–68; Graham Russell Hodges and Alan Edward Brown, eds., *"Pretends to be Free": Runaway Slave Advertisements from Colonial and Revolutionary New York and New Jersey* (New York, 1994); Harvey Jackson, "The Darien Antislavery Petition of 1739 and the Georgia Plan," *WMQ* 34 (1977): 618–31; Jackson, "Hugh Bryan and the Evangelical Movement in Colonial South Carolina," *WMQ* 43 (October 1986): 594–614; Jill LePore, *New York Burning: Liberty, Slavery and Conspiracy in Eighteenth-Century Manhattan* (New York, 2005); Aptheker, ed., *A Documentary History*, 1:4–5; Peter Wood, *Black Majority: Negroes in Colonial South*

Carolina from 1670 through the Stono Rebellion (New York, 1974), chap. 12; Jane G. Landers, "The Atlantic Transformations of Francisco Menéndez," in Lisa A. Lindsay and John Wood Sweet, eds, *Biography and the Black Atlantic* (Philadelphia, 2014), 209–23; Allan Gallay, "The Origins of Slaveholders' Paternalism: George Whitefield, the Bryan Family, and the Great Awakening in the South," *JSH* 53 (August 1987): 369–94.

15. Lay, *All Slave-Keepers*, 32–40, 44–45, 87, 93, 178; Carey, *From Peace to Freedom*, 164–76.

16. [John Woolman], *A Journal of the Life, Gospel Labours, and Christian Experiences of that Faithful Minister of Jesus Christ John Woolman*, in *The Works of John Woolman in Two Parts*, 2d ed. (Philadelphia, 1775), 15–16, 64–65, 91–95, 120; Vincent Brown, *Slave Revolt in Jamaica, 1760–1761: A Cartographic Narrative* (2012) http://revolt.axismaps .com/project.html; Mike Heller, ed., *The Tendering Presence: Essays on John Woolman* (Wallingford, Pa., 2003); Carey, *From Peace to Freedom*, 207–19.

17. [John Woolman], *Some Considerations on the Keeping of Negroes Recommended to the Professors of Christianity of every Denomination First printed in the Year 1754*, in *The Works of John Woolman*, 253, 262; Woolman, *Considerations on the Keeping of Negroes. Recommended to the Professors of Christianity, of every Denomination Part Second* (Philadelphia, 1762), 8, 12, 29–30, 52; "A Plea for the Poor or A Word of Remembrance and Caution to the Rich," in Phillips P. Moulton, ed., *The Journal and Major Essays of John Woolman* (New York, 1971), 238–72; James Proud, ed., *John Woolman and the Affairs of Truth: The Journalist's Essays, Epistles, and Ephemera* (San Francisco, 2010), 62–86; Thomas P. Slaughter, *The Beautiful Soul of John Woolman, Apostle of Abolition* (New York, 2008), 269–71; Geoffrey Plank, *John Woolman's Path to the Peaceable Kingdom: A Quaker in the British Empire* (Philadelphia, 2012), chap. 5; Ellen M. Ross, "'Liberation Is Coming Soon': The Radical Reformation of Joshua Evans (1731–1798)," in Brycchan Carey and Geoffrey Plank, eds., *Quakers and Abolition* (Urbana, 2014), 15–28.

18. George S. Brookes, *Friend Anthony Benezet* (Philadelphia, 1937), chap. 6, 475–77; Frost, ed., *Quaker Origins of Antislavery*, 167–69; James G. Basker, ed., *Early American Abolitionists: A Collection of Anti-Slavery Writings, 1760–1820* (New York, 2005), 9–15; David L. Crosby, "Anthony Benezet's Transformation of Anti-Slavery Rhetoric," *S&A* 23 (2002): 39–58; Maurice Jackson, "Anthony Benezet: Working the Antislavery Cause inside and outside of 'The Society,'" in Carey and Plank, eds., *Quakers and Abolition*, 106–19.

19. Bruns, ed., *Am I Not a Man*, 80–81, 90–91, 95–96; Jonathan D. Sassi, "Africans in the Quaker Image: Anthony Benezet, African Travel Narratives and Revolutionary-Era Antislavery," *Journal of Early Modern History* 10 (2006): 95–130; Roger A. Bruns, "Anthony Benezet's Assertion of Negro Equality," *JNH* 56 (1971): 230–38; Maurice Jackson, "The Social and Intellectual Origins of Anthony Benezet's Antislavery Radicalism," *PH* 66 (Special Issue, 1999): 86–112; Nancy Slacom Hornick, "Anthony Benezet and the African's School: Toward a Theory of Full Equality," *PMHB* 99 (1975): 399–421.

20. Granville Sharp, *A Representation of the Injustice and Dangerous Tendency of Tolerating Slavery; Or, Of Admitting the Least Claim of Private Property in the Persons of Men, in England* . . . (London, 1769); Prince Hoare, *Memoirs of Granville Sharp, Esq.* . . . (London, 1820), chap. 4; Adam Hochschild, *Bury the Chains: Prophets and Rebels in the Fight to Free an Empire's Slaves* (New York, 2005), 43–51; Steven M. Wise, *Though the Heavens May Fall: The Landmark Trial that Led to the End of Human Slavery* (Cambridge, Mass., 2005); Mark S. Weiner, "New Biographical Evidence on Somerset's Case," *S&A* 23 (April 2002): 121–36; Sue Peabody, *"There Are No Slaves in France": The Political Culture of Race and Slavery in the Ancient Regime* (New York, 1996), 57–71, 88–94, 97–105.

21. Bruns, ed., *Am I Not a Man*, 193–99, 262–67, 269–70, 302–6; Hoare, *Memoirs of Granville Sharp*, 39–43, 95–104; Granville Sharp, *The Law of Retribution; or, a Serious Warning to Great Britain and her Colonies* . . . (London, 1776), 1–3, 11–57, 176, 206–7, 262–63, 300–316, appendix 1, *An Essay on Slavery* . . . (first published in Burlington, N.J., 1773); Sharp, *The Just Limitation of Slavery in the Laws of God, compared with the Unbounded Claims of the AFRICAN TRADERS and BRITISH AMERICAN SLAVEHOLDERS* (London, 1776), 2–3, 10–12, 33–50, 54–55; Sharp, *The Law of Passive Obedience, or Christian Submission to Personal Injuries* . . . (London, 1776), 7–20; Sharp, *The Law of Liberty, or Royal Law, by which all Mankind Shall be Judged! Earnestly Recommended to the Serious Consideration of all Slaveholders and Slavedealers* (London, 1776), esp. 5–10, 30–34, 48–49; E. C. P. Lascelles, *Granville Sharp and the Freedom of Slaves in England* (London, 1928); Christopher Leslie Brown, *Moral Capital: Foundations of British Abolitionism* (Chapel Hill, 2006), chap. 3.

22. Anthony Benezet, *Some Historical Account of Guinea* . . . (Philadelphia, 1771), 78, 117; Anthony Benezet and John Wesley, *Views of American Slavery* (repr., New York, 1969), 71–104; Jackson, *Let This Voice Be Heard*.

23. Brookes, *Friend Anthony Benezet*, 207–472; Bruns, ed., *Am I Not a Man*, 139–41, 267–69, 308–16, 379–84; Anthony Benezet, *Short Observations on Slavery, Introductory to some Extracts from the writing of the Abbé Raynal, on that important Subject* (Philadelphia, 1781), 12; dated to 1783 by David L. Crosby, ed., *The Complete Antislavery Writings of Anthony Benezet, 1754–1783* (Baton Rouge, 2013), 243; L. H. Butterfield, ed., *Letters of Benjamin Rush*, vol. 1, 1761–1792 (Princeton, 1951), 80.

24. Henry Louis Gates Jr., ed., *"Race," Writing, and Difference* (Chicago, 1986), introduction; Paul Gilroy, *The Black Atlantic: Modernity and Double Consciousness* (Cambridge, Mass., 1993); David Scott, *Conscripts of Modernity: The Tragedy of Colonial Enlightenment* (Durham, 2004); Laura Doyle, *Freedom's Empire: Race and the Rise of the Novel in Atlantic Modernity, 1640–1940* (Durham, 2008), 3–15.

25. J. Mira Seo and John Quinn, eds., *The Complete Works of Juan Latino, the First Black Poet* (Forthcoming), with permission to cite from Mira Seo; V. B. Spratlin, *Juan Latino, Slave and Humanist* (New York, 1938); Baltasar Fra Molinero, "Juan Latino and His Racial Difference," *Black Africans in Renaissance Europe* (2005), 326–44; Lisa Voigt, *Writing Captivity in the Early Modern Atlantic: Circulations of Knowledge and Authority in the Iberian and English Worlds* (Chapel Hill, 2009), 33–34.

26. Burchard Brentjes, *Anton Wilhelm Amo: der schwarze Philosoph in Halle* (Leipzig, 1976); Reginald Bess, "A. W. Amo: First Great Black Man of Letters," *JBS* 19 (June 1989): 387–93; Marilyn Sephocle, "Anton Willhelm Amo," *JBS* 23 (December 1992): 182–87; Andrej Krause, "Anton Wilhelm Amo's Ontology," *Philosophia Africana* 12 (Fall 2009): 141; Grant Parker, trans. and ed., *The Agony of Asar: A Thesis on Slavery by a Former Slave, Jacobus, Elisa Johannes Capitein, 1717–1747* (Princeton, 2001); Henri Grégoire, *An Enquiry Concerning the Intellectual and Moral Faculties, and Literature of Negroes*, ed. Graham Russell Hodges (Armonk, N.Y., 1997), 76–77, 85–90.

27. Thomas Bluett, *Some Memoirs of the Life of Job, the Son of Solomon the High Priest of Boonda in Africa* . . . (London, 1734); Philip D. Curtin, ed., *Africa Remembered: Narratives by West Africans from the Era of the Slave Trade* (Madison, 1967), chap. 1; Paul Edwards and James Walvin, *Black Personalities in the Era of the Slave Trade* (Baton Rouge, 1983), 211–17; [William Dodd], *The African Prince, Now in England to Zara at His Father's Court* (London, 1749); [Dodd], *Zara at the Court of Annamaboe to the African Prince, Now in England* (London, 1749); Randy J. Sparks, *The Two Princes of Calabar: An Eighteenth-Century Atlantic Odyssey* (Cambridge, Mass., 2004).

28. Lucy Terry Prince, "Bars Fight," in Vincent Carretta, ed., *Phillis Wheatley: Complete Writings* (New York, 2001), 199–200; Frances Smith Foster, *Written by Herself: Literary Production by African American Women, 1746–1892* (Bloomington, 1993), 23–30; David R. Proper, "Lucy Terry Prince: 'Singer of History,'" *Contributions in Black History* 9 (1990–92): 187–214; Sharon M. Harris, *Executing Race: Early American Women's Narratives of Race, Society and the Law* (Columbus, 2005), 150–84; Gretchen Holbrook Gerzina, Researched with Anthony Gerzina, *Mr. and Mrs. Prince: How an Extraordinary Eighteenth-Century Family Moved Out of Slavery and into Legend* (New York, 2008).

29. Dorothy Porter, ed., *Early Negro Writing, 1760–1837* (Boston, 1971), 522–28; Karen A. Weylar, "Race, Redemption and Captivity in A Narrative of the Lord's Wonderful Dealings with John Marrant, a Black, and Narrative of the Uncommon Sufferings and Surprizing Deliverance of Briton Hammon, a Negro Man," and Robert Desrochers Jr., "'Surprizing Deliverance'?: Slavery and Freedom, Language, and Identity in the Narrative of Briton Hammon, 'A Negro Man,'" in Vincent Carretta and Philip Gould, eds., *Genius in Bondage: Literature of the Early Black Atlantic* (Lexington, Ky., 2001), 43–45, 153–74.

30. *A NARRATIVE OF THE Most Remarkable Particulars in the LIFE of James Albert Ukawsaw Gronniosaw* . . . (Bath, Eng., 1772), 37–39; Henry Louis Gates Jr., *The Signifying Monkey: A Theory of Afro-American Literary Criticism* (New York, 1988), 132–42.

31. Henry J. Cadbury, "Negro Membership in the Society of Friends," *JNH* 21 (April 1936): 151–213; James D. Essig, *The Bonds of Wickedness: American Evangelicals Against Slavery, 1770–1808* (Philadelphia, 1982), chaps. 1, 2; Dee E. Andrews, *The Methodists and Revolutionary America, 1760–1800: The Shaping of an Evangelical Culture* (Princeton, 2005), esp. chap. 5; Albert J. Raboteau, "The Slave Church in the Era of the American Revolution," in Ira Berlin and Ronald Hoffman, eds., *Slavery and Freedom in the Age of the American Revolution* (Charlottesville, Va., 1983), 193–213;

Mechal Sobel, *Trabelin' On: The Slave Journey to an Afro-Baptist Faith* (Princeton, 1979); Jon Sensbach, *Rebecca's Revival: Creating Black Christianity in the Atlantic World* (Cambridge, Mass., 2005), esp. 85–158.

32. Nathan O. Hatch, *The Democratization of American Christianity* (New Haven, 1989); Eddie Glaude Jr., *Exodus! Religion, Race, and Nation in Early Nineteenth-Century Black America* (Chicago, 2000); Joanna Brooks, *American Lazarus: Religion and the Rise of African-American and Native American Literatures* (New York, 2003), introduction, 93; Catherine Adams and Elizabeth H. Pleck, *Love of Freedom: Black Women in Colonial and Revolutionary New England* (New York, 2010), 6–8; Erik R. Seeman, "'Justise Must Take Plase': Three African Americans Speak of Religion in Eighteenth-Century New England," *WMQ* 56 (April 1999): 393–414; Peter H. Wood, *Strange New Land: Africans in Colonial America* (New York, 1996), 90; J. William Harris, *The Hanging of Thomas Jeremiah: A Free Black Man's Encounter with Liberty* (New Haven, 2009), 72–78, 84–86.

33. [Margaretta Matilda Odell], *Memoir and Poems of Phillis Wheatley, A Native African and a Slave Also, Poems By a Slave*, 3d ed.(Boston, 1838); Henry Louis Gates Jr., *The Trials of Phillis Wheatley: America's First Black Poet and Her Encounters with the Founding Fathers* (New York, 2003); John C. Shields, "Phillis Wheatley's Struggle for Freedom in Her Poetry and Prose," in *The Collected Works of Phillis Wheatley* (New York, 1988), 229–70; William H. Robinson, "On Phillis Wheatley and Her Boston," in *Phillis Wheatley and Her Writings* (New York, 1984), 3–69; David Grimsted, "Anglo-American Racism and Phillis Wheatley's 'Sable Veil,' 'Length'ned Chain,' and 'Knitted Heart,'" in Ronald Hoffman and Peter J. Albert, eds., *Women in the Age of the American Revolution* (Charlottesville, Va., 1989), 338–444; Julian D. Mason, ed., *The Poems of Phillis Wheatley*, enl. ed. (Chapel Hill, 1989), 1–34; Thomas Jefferson, *Notes on the State of Virginia; written in the year 1781, Somewhat Corrected and Enlarged in the Winter of 1782* (London, 1787), 257; Vincent Carretta, *Phillis Wheatley: Biography of a Genius in Bondage* (Athens, Ga., 2011).

34. Orlando Patterson, *Slavery and Social Death: A Comparative Study* (Cambridge, Mass., 1982); Vincent Brown, *The Reaper's Garden: Death and Power in the World of Atlantic Slavery* (Cambridge, Mass., 2008); [Odell], *Memoir and Poems of Phillis Wheatley*, 12–20; Carretta, *Phillis Wheatley*, 34–35, 40, 70, 75, 87; William H. Robinson, "On Phillis Wheatley's Poetry," in *Phillis Wheatley and Her Writings* (New York: Garland, 1984), 87–126; John C. Shields, "Phillis Wheatley's Subversive Pastoral," *Eighteenth-Century Studies* 27 (Summer 1994): 631–47.

35. [Odell], *Memoir and Poems of Phillis Wheatley*, 21–22; James G. Basker, ed., *American Antislavery Writings: Colonial Beginnings to Emancipation* (New York, 2012), 49; Carretta, *Phillis Wheatley*, 13, 223–24; Winthrop Jordan, *White Over Black: American Attitudes Toward the Negro, 1550–1812* (Chapel Hill, 1968), chap. 6.

36. Oscar Wegelin, *Jupiter Hammon, American Negro Poet: Selections from His Writings and a Bibliography* (Miami, 1969), 7–28, 33, 42; Sondra A. O'Neale, *Jupiter Hammon and the Biblical Beginnings of African-American Literature* (Metuchen, N.J., 1993), introduction.

37. Carretta, ed., *Phillis Wheatley*, 59–60, 141–43, 148–49, 150, 153–54, 156–57, 161, 162; R. Lynn Matson, "Phillis Wheatley—Soul Sister?" *Phylon* 33 (Fall 1972): 222–30; Carretta, *Phillis Wheatley*, 44, 107.
38. Carretta, *Phillis Wheatley*, 40, 93, 153; Dwight A. McBride, *Impossible Witnesses: Truth, Abolitionism, and Slave Testimony* (New York, 2001), chap. 4; Charles W. Akers, "'Our Modern Egyptians': Phillis Wheatley and the Whig Campaign Against Slavery in Revolutionary Boston," *JNH* 60 (July 1975): 397–410; Phillip M. Richards, "Phillis Wheatley and Literary Americanization," *American Quarterly* 44 (June 1992): 163–91.
39. [Odell], *Memoir and Poems of Phillis Wheatley*, 9–10, 24–29, 37; Carretta, *Phillis Wheatley*, 10, 89, 150, 152, 172–202; Frank Shuffleton, "On Her Own Footing: Phillis Wheatley on Freedom," in Carretta and Gould, eds., *Genius in Bondage.*, 175–89; Henry Weincek, *An Imperfect God: George Washington, His Slaves and the Creation of America* (New York, 2003), 205–14; Vincent Carretta and Ty M. Reese, eds., *The Life and Letters of Philip Quaque: The First African Anglican Missionary* (Athens, Ga., 2010), introduction, 111–16; Margot Minardi, *Making Slavery History: Abolitionism and the Politics of Memory in Massachusetts* (New York, 2010): 100–101.

CHAPTER TWO. REVOLUTIONARY ANTISLAVERY IN BLACK AND WHITE

1. William C. Nell, *The Colored Patriots of the American Revolution . . .* (Boston, 1855), 14–18; Charles R. Foy, "Seeking Freedom in the Atlantic World, 1713–1783," *Early American Studies* (Spring 2006): 46–77; James Oliver and Lois E. Horton, *In Hope of Liberty: Culture, Community and Protest Among Northern Free Blacks, 1700–1860* (New York, 1997): 51–54; Stephen Kantrowitz, *More than Freedom: Fighting for Black Citizenship in a White Republic, 1829–1889* (New York, 2012), chap. 5.
2. David Brion Davis, *The Problem of Slavery in the Age of Revolution, 1770–1823* (Ithaca, 1975); Eric J. Hobsbawm, *The Age of Revolution, 1789–1848* (London, 1962); for a corrective, see Jeremy Adelman, "An Age of Imperial Revolutions," *AHR* 113 (April 2008): 319–40.
3. Manisha Sinha, "To 'Cast Just Obliquy' on Oppressors: Black Radicalism in the Age of Revolution," *WMQ* 64 (January 2007): 149–60; Douglas R. Egerton, *Death or Liberty: African Americans and Revolutionary America* (New York, 2009).
4. Laurent Dubois, *Avengers of the New World: The Story of the Haitian Revolution* (Cambridge, Mass., 2004); Robin Blackburn, "Haiti, Slavery, and the Age of the Democratic Revolution," *WMQ* 63 (October 2006): 643–74; Sibylle Fischer, *Modernity Disavowed: Haiti and the Cultures of Slavery in the Age of Revolution* (Durham, 2004).
5. Roger Bruns, ed., *Am I Not a Man and a Brother: The Antislavery Crusade of Revolutionary America, 1688–1788* (New York, 1977), 226, 239; David Freeman Hawke, *Benjamin Rush: Revolutionary Gadfly* (Indianapolis, 1971), 104–9; Srividhya Swaminathan, "Developing the West Indian Proslavery Position after the *Somerset* Decision," *S&A* 24 (2003): 40–60; John Locke, *Of Civil Government: Two Treatises* (repr., London, 1924);

Charles W. Mills, *The Racial Contract* (Ithaca, 1997); C. B. Macpherson, *The Political Theory of Possessive Individualism: From Hobbes to Locke* (London, 1962); Edmund S. Morgan, *American Slavery, American Freedom: The Ordeal of Colonial Virginia* (New York, 1975); Duncan J. MacLeod, *Slavery, Race and the American Revolution* (Cambridge, Eng., 1974); Woody Holton, *Forced Founders: Indians, Debtors, Slaves, and the Making of the American Revolution in Virginia* (Chapel Hill, 1999).

6. Bernard Bailyn, *The Ideological Origins of the American Revolution* (Cambridge, Mass., 1967), 232–46; Bruns, ed., *Am I Not a Man*, 104, 112, 128–29, 188, 239, 273, 335; James G. Basker, ed., *American Antislavery Writings: Colonial Beginnings to Emancipation* (New York, 2012), 46–48; Jacob Green, *Observations on the Reconciliation of Great Britain and the Colonies*, ed. Larry L. Gerlach (Trenton, 1976), 29.

7. Bruns, ed., *Am I Not a Man*, 338–39, 376–79, 385–86; James Lynch, "The Limits of Revolutionary Radicalism: Tom Paine and Slavery," *PMHB* 123 (July 1999): 177–99.

8. Bruns, ed., *Am I Not a Man*, 273, 335, 293–302.

9. Ibid., 316–37, 340–48, 358–65; Kenneth P. Minkema, "Jonathan Edwards on Slavery and the Slave Trade," *WMQ* 54 (October 1997): 823–34; Robert L. Ferm, *Jonathan Edwards the Younger, 1745–1801: A Colonial Pastor* (Grand Rapids, 1976), 93–95; Kenneth P. Minkema and Harry S. Stout, "The Edwardsean Tradition and the Antislavery Debate, 1740–1865," *JAH* 92 (June 2005): 47–74.

10. *The Works of Samuel Hopkins, D.D. . . .* (Boston, 1854), 1:114–38; Catherine A. Brekus, *Sarah Osborn's World: The Rise of Evangelical Christianity in Early America* (New Haven, 2013); Bruns, ed., *Am I Not a Man*, 290–93; J. William Frost, ed., *The Quaker Origins of Antislavery* (Norwood, Pa., 1980), 257–58; Edmund S. Morgan, *The Gentle Puritan: A Life of Ezra Stiles, 1727–1795* (New Haven, 1962); Oliver Wendell Elsbree, "Samuel Hopkins and His Doctrine of Benevolence," *NEQ* 8 (December 1935): 534–50; David S. Lovejoy, "Samuel Hopkins: Religion, Slavery, and the Revolution," *NEQ* 40 (June 1967): 227–43.

11. *The Works of Samuel Hopkins, D.D. . . .* (Boston, 1854), 2:549, 569, 571, 576, 589; Joseph A. Conforti, *Samuel Hopkins and the New Divinity Movement: Calvinism, the Congregational Ministry, and Reform in New England Between the Great Awakenings* (Grand Rapids, 1981), 128–31.

12. Bruns, ed., *Am I Not a Man*, 475–86; Basker, ed., *American Antislavery Writings*, 50–51; François Furstenberg, "Atlantic Slavery, Atlantic Freedom: George Washington, Slavery, and Transatlantic Abolitionist Networks," *WMQ* 68 (April 2011): 247–86; Richard Price, *Observations on the Importance of the American Revolution . . .* (Dublin, 1785), 83–84.

13. F. Nwabueze Okoye, "Chattel Slavery as the Nightmare of the American Revolutionaries," *WMQ* 37 (January 1980): 3–28; An American, *An Essay in Vindication of the Continental Colonies of America, from a Censure of Mr. Adam Smith . . .* (London, 1764), 9–16, 29–46; Bruns, ed., *Am I Not a Man*, 107–11; Basker, ed., *American Antislavery Writings*, 39–45; Louis W. Potts, *Arthur Lee: A Virtuous Revolutionary* (Baton Rouge, 1981), 27–30; David Waldstreicher, *Runaway America: Benjamin Franklin, Slavery and the American Revolution* (New York, 2004).

14. [Thomas Jefferson], *A Summary View of the Rights of British America* . . . (Williamsburg, Va., 1774), 17; Sidney Kaplan and Emma Nogrady Kaplan, eds., *The Black Presence in the Era of the American Revolution, 1770–1800* (Washington, 1973), 26; Pauline Maier, *American Scripture: Making the Declaration of Independence* (New York, 1997); David Armitage, *The Declaration of Independence: A Global History* (Cambridge, Mass., 2007).

15. Bruns, ed., *Am I Not a Man*, 222; Henry Mayer, *A Son of Thunder: Patrick Henry and the American Republic* (New York, 1986), 166–70; Gregory D. Massey, "The Limits of Antislavery Thought in the Revolutionary Lower South: John Laurens and Henry Laurens," *JSH* 63 (August 1997): 495–530; Basker, ed., *American Antislavery Writings*, 96–97; Milton E. Flower, *John Dickinson Conservative Revolutionary* (Charlottesville, Va., 1983); Andrew Levy, *The First Emancipator: The Forgotten Story of Robert Carter, the Founding Father Who Freed His Slaves* (New York, 2004); William W. Freehling, "The Founding Fathers and Slavery," *AHR* 77 (1972): 81–93; Paul Finkelman, *Slavery and the Founders: Race and Liberty in the Age of Jefferson* (New York, 1996), chap. 5; Paul Stephen Clarkson, *Luther Martin of Maryland* (Baltimore, 1970); Patricia Bradley, *Slavery, Propaganda and the American Revolution* (Jackson, Miss., 1998).

16. John R. Howe Jr, "John Adams' View of Slavery," *JNH* 49 (July 1964): 201–6; David Waldstreicher, "'The Origins of Antislavery in Pennsylvania: Early Abolitionists and Benjamin Franklin's Road Not Taken," in Richard Newman and James Mueller, eds., *Antislavery and Abolition in Philadelphia: Emancipation and the Long Struggle for Racial Justice in the City of Brotherly Love* (Baton Rouge, 2011), 45–65; Ron Chernow, *Alexander Hamilton* (New York, 2004), 210–16; Walter Stahr, *John Jay* (New York, 2005), 236–39; Daniel C. Littlefield, "John Jay, the Revolutionary Generation and Slavery," *New York History* 81 (2000): 91–96; R. B. Bernstein, *The Founding Fathers Reconsidered* (New York, 2009).

17. Herbert Aptheker, ed., *A Documentary History of the Negro People in the United States* (New York, 1951), 1:6–7.

18. Bruns, ed., *Am I Not a Man*, 200, 260–62; *The Appendix: or, Some Observations on the Expediency of the Petition of the Africans living in Boston &c* . . . (Boston, 1773), 1–14; *Massachusetts Spy*, June 21, 1775; Christopher Cameron, *To Plead Our Own Cause: African Americans in Massachusetts and the Making of the Antislavery Movement* (Kent, Ohio, 2014).

19. Aptheker, ed., *A Documentary History*, 1:7, 9, 12–13; Kaplan and Kaplan, eds., *The Black Presence*, 12, 29; George Livermore, *An Historical Research Respecting the Opinions of the Founders of the Republic on Negroes as Slaves, as Citizens, and as Soldiers* (Boston, 1863), 116–17; Thomas J. Davis, "Emancipation Rhetoric, Natural Rights and Revolutionary New England: A Note on Four Black Petitions in Massachusetts, 1773–1777," *NEQ* 57 (1989): 248–64.

20. Kaplan and Kaplan, eds., *The Black Presence*, 26–27; Aptheker, ed., *A Documentary History*, 1:9–12; Sinha, "To 'Cast Just Obliquy' on Oppressors," 151–53.

21. Aptheker, ed., *A Documentary History*, 1:7–8, 9–10; Kaplan and Kaplan, eds., *The Black Presence*, 15.

22. Bruns, ed., *Am I Not a Man*, 338–39; *Massachusetts Spy*, February 10, 1774.

23. Timothy Mather Cooley, *Sketches of the Life and Character of the Rev. Lemuel Haynes* . . . (New York, 1837), viii, 28, 69; John Saillant, *Black Puritan, Black Republican: The Life and Thought of Lemuel Haynes, 1753–1833* (New York, 2003).

24. Richard D. Brown, "'Not Only Extreme Poverty, but the Worst Kind of Orphanage': Lemuel Haynes and the Boundaries of Racial Tolerance on the Yankee Frontier, 1770–1820," *NEQ* 75 (March 2002): 509; Richard Newman, ed., *Black Preacher to White America: The Collected Writings of Lemuel Haynes, 1774–1833* (Brooklyn, N.Y., 1990), 12; Ruth Bogin, "'The Battle of Lexington': A Patriotic Ballad by Lemuel Haynes," *WMQ* 42 (October 1985): 499–506.

25. "Liberty Further Extended," in Newman, ed., *Black Preacher to White America*, 17–20, 22–24; Ruth Bogin, "'Liberty Further Extended': A 1776 Antislavery Manuscript by Lemuel Haynes," *WMQ* 40 (January 1983): 85–105; Rita Roberts, "Patriotism and Political Criticism: The Evolution of Political Consciousness in the Mind of a Black Revolutionary Soldier," *Eighteenth-Century Studies* 27 (Summer 1994): 569–88.

26. Cooley, *Life and Character of the Rev. Lemuel Haynes*, 89, 93, 124, 317; "Liberty Further Extended," 29–30; John Saillant, "Slavery and Divine Providence in New England Calvinism: The New Divinity and a Black Protest, 1775–1805," *NEQ* 68 (December 1995): 584–608.

27. *A Sermon on the Present Situation of the Affairs of America and Great-Britain Written By a Black* . . . (Philadelphia, 1782), 1–5, 9, 10–11.

28. Newman, ed., *Black Preacher to White America*, 32, 43–62, 175–200; Sondra A. O'Neale, *Jupiter Hammon and the Biblical Beginnings of African-American Literature* (Metuchen, N.J., 1993), 84, 99–100, 102–3, 171–73.

29. Peter Linebaugh and Marcus Rediker, *The Many-Headed Hydra: Sailors, Slaves, Commoners, and the Hidden History of the Revolutionary Atlantic* (Boston, 2000), chap. 7; Gary B. Nash, *The Unknown American Revolution: The Unruly Birth of Democracy and the Struggle to Create America* (New York, 2005), 45–62; Sylvia Frey, *Water from the Rock: Black Resistance in a Revolutionary Age* (Princeton, 1991); Michael Mullin, *Africa in America: Slave Acculturation and Resistance in the American South and the British Caribbean, 1736–1831* (Urbana, 1992), chap. 9; Richard B. Sheridan, "The Jamaican Slave Insurrection Scare of 1776 and the American Revolution," *JNH* 61 (July 1976): 290–308; Peter H. Wood, "'Liberty Is Sweet': African American Freedom Struggles in the Years Before White Independence," in Alfred F. Young, ed., *Beyond the American Revolution: Explorations in the History of American Radicalism* (DeKalb, Ill., 1993), 149–84; J. William Harris, *The Hanging of Thomas Jeremiah: A Free Black Man's Encounter with Liberty* (New Haven, 2009).

30. Christopher Leslie Brown and Philip D. Morgan, eds., *Arming Slaves: From Classical Times to the Modern Age* (New Haven, 2006); Jane G. Landers, *Atlantic Creoles in the Age of Revolutions* (Cambridge, Mass., 2010); Benjamin Quarles, "Lord Dunmore as Liberator," *WMQ* 15 (October 1958): 494–507; Michael A. McDonnell, *The Politics of War: Race, Class and Conflict in Revolutionary Virginia* (Chapel Hill, 2007), 139–44; Alan Gilbert, *Black Patriots and Loyalists: Fighting for Emancipation in the*

War for Independence (Chicago, 2012), 15–37; Cassandra Pybus, *Epic Journeys of Freedom: Runaway Slaves of the American Revolution and Their Global Quest for Liberty* (Boston, 2006), chap. 1.

31. George H. Moore, *Notes on the History of Slavery in Massachusetts* (New York, 1862), 4–7; Moore, *Historical Notes on the Employment of Negroes in the American Army of the Revolution* (New York, 1866), 243–50; Nell, *Colored Patriots*, 20–21; William Lloyd Garrison, "The Loyalty and Devotion of Colored Americans in the Revolution and War of 1812," in *The Negro Soldier: A Select Compilation* (Boston, 1861); Livermore, *Historical Research*, 92–97, 110, 111–13, 153; Gary Nash, *The Forgotten Fifth: African Americans in the Age of Revolution* (Cambridge, Mass., 2006), 7–15; Margot Minardi, *Making Slavery History: Abolitionism and the Politics of Memory in Massachusetts* (New York, 2010), 51–52, 56–58; Peter M. Bergman and Jean McCarroll, eds., *The Negro in the Continental Congress* (New York, 1969), 1:4–5.

32. Nell, *Colored Patriots*, 24–25, 50–51, 126–28, 167–71, 198–99; Moore, *Historical Notes*, 15–22; Livermore, *Historical Research*, 114–16, 117–28; Lorenzo Greene, "Some Observations on the Black Regiment of Rhode Island in the American Revolution," *JNH* 37 (January 1952): 142–72; Kaplan and Kaplan, *The Black Presence*, 64–69; Philip S. Foner, *History of Black Americans: From Africa to the Emergence of the Cotton Kingdom* (Westport, Conn., 1975), 1:328; Benjamin Quarles, "The Revolutionary War as a Black Declaration of Independence," in Ira Berlin and Ronald Hoffman, eds., *Slavery and Freedom in the Age of the American Revolution* (Charlottesville, Va., 1983), 283–301; John Wood Sweet, *Bodies Politic: Negotiating Race in the American North, 1730–1830* (Baltimore, 2003), 197–209, 215–21; Gilbert, *Black Patriots and Loyalists*, 98–111; Henry Weincek, *An Imperfect God: George Washington, His Slaves and the Creation of America* (New York, 2003), 242–48; Dubois, *Avengers of the New World*, 67.

33. McDonnell, *The Politics of War*, 261, 282, 338, 417, 475–77, 486–87; Gregory D. Massey, *John Laurens and the American Revolution* (Columbia, S.C., 2000); Gilbert, *Black Patriots and Loyalists*, 73–94, 120–21, 168–73.

34. Nell, *Colored Patriots*, 23, 166–71, 175, 198–99; Moore, *Historical Notes*, 7–15, 23–24; Foner, *History of Black Americans*, 1:329–40; Gilbert, *Black Patriots and Loyalists*, 108, 284; Michael Lee Lanning, *African Americans in the Revolutionary War* (New York, 2005); Benjamin Quarles, *The Negro in the American Revolution* (Chapel Hill, 1961), 60–67, 158–81; Eric Grundset, Briana L Diaz, Hollis L Gentry, Jean D Strahan, *Forgotten Patriots: African American and American Indian Patriots of the Revolutionary War; A Guide to Service, Sources and Studies*, 2d ed. (Washington, 2008); Julie Winch, *A Gentleman of Color: The Life of James Forten* (New York, 2002), chap. 2; Charles Foy, "Freedom in Revolutionary Philadelphia: James Forten and Stephen Decatur's Prize Negroes," manuscript in author's possession; Minardi, *Making Slavery History*, 63–69; Mark J. Sammons and Valerie Cunningham, *Black Portsmouth: Three Centuries of African-American Heritage* (Durham, N.H., 2004): 68–70.

35. Gerald Horne, *The Counter-Revolution of 1776: Slave Resistance and the Origins of the United States of America* (New York, 2014); Gilbert, *Black Patriots and Loyalists*,

128–51; Graham Russell Hodges, *Root and Branch: African Americans in New York and East Jersey, 1613–1863* (Chapel Hill, 1999), chap. 5; Philip Ranlet, "The British, Slaves, and Smallpox in Revolutionary Virginia," *JNH* 84 (Summer 1999): 217–26; George Liele, "An ACCOUNT of Several Baptist Churches, consisting chiefly of NEGRO SLAVES: particularly of one at *Kingston*, in JAMAICA; and another at *Savannah* in GEORGIA," in Vincent Carretta, ed., *Unchained Voices: An Anthology of Black Authors in the English-Speaking World of the Eighteenth Century* (Lexington, Ky., 1996), 325–29; John W. Davis, "George Liele and Andrew Bryan, Pioneer Negro Baptist Preachers," *JNH* 3 (April 1918): 119–27.

36. David George, "An Account of the Life of Mr. DAVID GEORGE, from Sierra Leone in Africa . . . ," and Boston King, "Memoirs of the Life of BOSTON KING, a Black Preacher," in Carretta, ed., *Unchained Voices*, 333, 352–53; Herbert Aptheker, *The Negro in the American Revolution* (New York, 1940), 20; Lathan Algerna Windley, *A Profile of Runaway Slaves in Virginia and South Carolina from 1730 through 1787* (New York, 1995); Landers, *Atlantic Creoles*, chap. 1; Cassandra Pybus, "Jefferson's Faulty Math: The Question of Slave Defections in the American Revolution," *WMQ* 62 (April 2005): 243–64; Bergman and McCarroll, eds., *The Negro in the Continental Congress*, 1:86–88, 96, 99, 106, 117, 120, 124–35, 138–39; Nash, *The Unknown American Revolution*, 339, 435.

37. Pybus, *Epic Journeys of Freedom*, chap. 4; Simon Schama, *Rough Crossings: Britain, the Slaves and the American Revolution* (New York, 2006): 93–156; Graham Russell Hodges, ed., *The Black Loyalist Directory: African Americans in Exile After the American Revolution* (New York, 1996), introduction; Boston King, "Memoirs," 356; Gilbert, *Black Patriots and Loyalists*, 178–206; Maya Jasanoff, *Liberty's Exiles: American Loyalists and the Revolutionary World* (New York, 2011).

38. Prince Hoare, *Memoirs of Granville Sharp, Esq. . . .* (London, 1820), part 3; Mary Beth Norton, "The Fate of Some Black Loyalists of the American Revolution," *JNH* 58 (October 1973): 402–26; Schama, *Rough Crossings*, part 2; James W. St. G. Walker, *The Black Loyalists: The Search for a Promised Land in Nova Scotia and Sierra Leone, 1783–1870* (1976; repr., Toronto, 1992); Ellen Gibson Wilson, *The Loyal Blacks* (New York, 1976); George, "An Account," 340; King, "Memoirs," 363; Cassandra Pybus, "Henry 'Harry' Washington (1750s–1790s): A Founding Father's Slave," in Karen Racine and Beatriz G. Mamigonian, eds., *The Human Tradition in the Atlantic World, 1500–1850* (Lanham, Md., 2010), 101–16; Catherine Hall, *Macaulay and Son: Architects of Imperial Britain* (New Haven, 2012); Alexander X. Byrd, *Captives and Voyagers: Black Migrations Across the Eighteenth-Century British Atlantic World* (Baton Rouge, 2008), 124.

39. C. L. R. James, *The Black Jacobins: Touissant L'Ouverture and the San Domingo Revolution* (New York, 1963); Laurent Dubois, "The Revolutionary Abolitionists of Haiti," in Richard Bessel, Nicholas Guyatt, and Jane Rendall, eds., *War, Empire and Slavery, 1770–1830* (New York, 2010), 44–60; Nick Nesbitt, *Universal Emancipation: The Haitian Revolution and the Radical Enlightenment* (Charlottesville, Va., 2008); Blackburn, "Haiti, Slavery, and the Age of the Democratic Revolution," 672.

40. Laurent Dubois and John D. Garrigus, eds., *Slave Revolution in the Caribbean, 1789–1804: A Brief History with Documents* (Boston, 2006), 69, 84, 116, 120–25, 129–32, 189–90, 192–93, 196; Dubois, *Avengers of the New World*, 298–300; John D. Garrigus, *Before Haiti: Race and Citizenship in French Saint-Domingue* (New York, 2006); Carolyn E. Fick, *The Making of Haiti: The Saint Domingue Revolution from Below* (Knoxville, 1990); Jeremy D. Popkin, *You Are All Free: The Haitian Revolution and the Abolition of Slavery* (Cambridge, Eng., 2010); Florence Gauthier, "The Role of the Saint-Domingue Deputation in the Abolition of Slavery," in Marcel Dorigny, ed., *The Abolitions of Slavery: From Léger Félicité Sonthonax to Victor Schoelcher, 1793, 1794, 1848* (New York, 2003), 169–79; Touissant Louverture, *The Haitian Revolution*, Nick Nesbitt, ed., with introduction by Jean-Bertrand Aristide (London, 2008), 28; Madison Smartt Bell, *Touissant Louverture: A Biography* (New York, 2007); Philippe R. Girard, *The Slaves Who Defeated Napoleon: Touissant Louverture and the Haitian War of Independence, 1801–1804* (Tuscaloosa, 2011).

41. Laurent Dubois, "An Enslaved Enlightenment: Rethinking the Intellectual History of the French Atlantic," *Social History* 31 (February 2006): 4–7; J. R. Oldfield, *Trans-atlantic Abolitionism in the Age of Revolution: An International History of Anti-Slavery, c. 1787–1820* (Cambridge, Eng., 2013), 17–18; Marie Jean de Caritat, "Reflections on Negro Slavery," in Lynn Hunt, ed., *The French Revolution and Human Rights: A Brief Documentary History* (Boston, 1996), 55–57; Mercer Cook, "Julien Raimond," *JNH* 26 (April 1941): 139–70; John D. Garrigus, "Opportunist or Patriot? Julien Raimond (1744–1801) and the Haitian Revolution," *S&A* 48 (April 2007): 1–27; Marcel Dorigny, "Mirabeau and the Société des Amis des Noirs: Which Way to Abolish Slavery?," in Dorigny, ed., *The Abolitions of Slavery*, 121–32; Eloise Ellery, *Brissot de Warville: A Study in the History of the French Revolution* (Boston, 1915), chap. 8.

42. Marcel Dorigny, "The Abbé Grégoire and the *Société des Amis des Noirs*," and Alyssa Goldstein Sepinwall, "Exporting the Revolution: Grégoire, Haiti and the Colonial Laboratory, 1815–1827," in J. D. Popkin and R. H. Popkin, eds., *The Abbé Grégoire and His World* (Dordrecht, Netherlands, 2000), 27–69; Ruth F. Necheles, *The Abbé Grégoire, 1787–1831: The Odyssey of an Egalitarian* (Westport, Conn., 1971).

43. Thomas Clarkson, *The True State of the Case, Respecting the Insurrection at St. Domingo* (Ipswich, 1792), 2–8; Earl Leslie Griggs and Clifford H. Prato, eds., *Henri Christophe and Thomas Clarkson: A Correspondence* (New York, 1968); Robert Isaac Wilberforce and Samuel Wilberforce, eds., *The Correspondence of William Wilberforce* (London, 1840), 1:357–63, 366–95; Henry Brougham, *A Concise Statement of the Question Regarding the Abolition of the Slave Trade* (London, 1804); Brougham, *An Inquiry into the Colonial Policies of the European Powers*, 2 vols. (Edinburgh, 1803); David Geggus, "Haiti and the Abolitionists: Opinion, Propaganda and International Politics in Britain and France, 1804–1838," in David Richardson, ed., *Abolition and Its Aftermath: The Historical Context, 1790–1816* (London, 1986), 113–40.

44. Marcus Rainsford, *An Historical Account of the Black Empire of Hayti* . . . (London, 1805), x, 103, 210–11, 364, 371, 376; Marlene Daut, "Un-Silencing the Past: Boisrond-Tonnerre, Vastey, and the Re-Writing of the Haitian Revolution," *South Atlantic*

Review 74 (Winter 2009): 35–64; Michel-Rolph Trouillot, *Silencing the Past: Power and the Production of History* (Boston, 1995).

45. Julius S. Scott, "The Common Wind: Currents of Afro-American Communication in the Era of the Haitian Revolution" (Ph.D. diss., Duke University, 1986); David Geggus, "The Influence of the Haitian Revolution on Blacks in Latin America and the Caribbean," in Nancy Priscilla Naro, ed., *Blacks, Coloureds and National Identity in Nineteenth-Century Latin America* (London, 2003), 38–59; Alfred N. Hunt, *Haiti's Influence on Antebellum America: Slumbering Volcano in the Caribbean* (Baton Rouge, 1988), 26–30; Landers, *Atlantic Creoles*, 148–59; Matt D. Childs, *The 1812 Aponte Rebellion and the Struggles Against Atlantic Slavery* (Chapel Hill, 2006); see chapters by Matt D. Childs, Aline Helig, and Marixa Lasso in David Geggus, ed., *The Impact of the Haitian Revolution in the Atlantic World* (Columbia, S.C., 2001); Anne Eller, "'All would be equal in the effort': Santo Domingo's 'Italian Revolution,' Independence and Haiti, 1809–1822," *Journal of Early American History* 1 (2011): 105–41; Christopher Schmidt-Nowara, *Slavery, Freedom, and Abolition in Latin America and the Atlantic World* (Albuquerque, 2011), chap. 3; Ada Ferrer, "Haiti, Free Soil, and Antislavery in the Revolutionary Atlantic," *AHR* 117 (February 2012): 40–66.

46. Ashli White, *Encountering Revolution: Haiti and the Making of the Early Republic* (Baltimore, 2010), chap. 4; Robert Alderson, "Charleston's Rumored Slave Revolt of 1793," in Geggus, ed., *The Impact of the Haitian Revolution*, 93–111; James Sidbury, "Saint Domingue in Virginia: Ideology, Local Meanings, and Resistance to Slavery, 1790–1800," *JSH* 63 (August 1997): 540–43; Douglas R. Egerton, *Gabriel's Rebellion: The Virginia Slave Conspiracies of 1800 and 1802* (Chapel Hill, 1993); Manisha Sinha, *The Counterrevolution of Slavery: Politics and Ideology in Antebellum South Carolina* (Chapel Hill, 2000), 15.

47. Daniel Rasmussen, *American Uprising: The Untold Story of America's Largest Slave Rebellion* (New York, 2011), 102; Junius Rodriguez, "Rebellion on the River Road: The Ideology and Influence of Louisiana's German Coast Slave Insurrection of 1811," in John R. McKivigan and Stanley Harrold, eds., *Antislavery Violence: Sectional, Racial, and Cultural Conflict in Antebellum America* (Knoxville, 1999), 65–88; Adam Rothman, *Slave Country: American Expansion and the Origins of the Deep South* (Cambridge, Mass., 2005), 106–17; Douglas R. Egerton, *He Shall Go Out Free: The Lives of Denmark Vesey* (Madison, 1999); Ira Berlin, "Documents: After Nat Turner: A Letter from the North," *JNH* 55 (1970): 144–51; Aptheker, *A Documentary History*, 1:53–57.

48. Tim Matthewson, "Abraham Bishop, 'The Rights of Black Men,' and the American Reaction to the Haitian Revolution," *JNH* 67 (1982): 148–54; McLeod is quoted in Hunt, *Haiti's Influence on Antebellum America*, 92; White, *Encountering Revolution*, 207–10; David Brion Davis, *Revolutions: Reflections on American Equality and Foreign Liberations* (Cambridge, Mass., 1990), 49–54.

49. Donald R. Hickey, "America's Response to the Slave Revolt in Haiti, 1791–1806," *JER* 2 (Winter 1982): 361–79; Ronald Angelo Johnson, *Diplomacy in Black and White: John Adams, Toussaint Louverture and Their Atlantic World Alliance* (Athens, Ga.,

2014); Gordon S. Brown, *Touissant's Clause: The Founding Fathers and the Haitian Revolution* (Jackson, Miss., 2005); Tim Matthewson, *A Proslavery Foreign Policy: Haitian American Relations during the Early Republic* (Westport, Conn., 2003); Garry Wills, *"Negro President": Jefferson and the Slave Power* (New York, 2003), chap. 2; Michael Zuckerman, *Almost Chosen People: Oblique Biographies in the American Grain* (Berkeley, 1993), chap. 6; Dubois and Garrigus, eds., *Slave Revolution in the Caribbean*, 161; Rayford W. Logan, *The Diplomatic Relations of the United States with Haiti, 1776–1891* (Chapel Hill, 1941); Arthur Scherr, "Jefferson's 'Cannibals' Revisited: A Closer Look at His Notorious Phrase," *JSH* 67 (May 2011): 251–82.

50. Hunt, *Haiti's Influence on Antebellum America*, chap. 2; Kenneth Roberts and Anna M. Roberts, eds., *Moreau de St. Méry's American Journey (1793–1798)* (New York, 1947); François Furstenberg, *When the United States Spoke French: Five Refugees who Shaped a Nation* (New York, 2014); White, *Encountering Revolution*, 126–33, 174, 180–202; NYMS, NYHS, vol. 7, May 18 1791–February 13, 1807, pp. 13, 141; vol. 10, March 11, 1807–July 8, 1817, p. 6; *Reflections on Slavery, with Recent Evidence on its Inhumanity Occasioned by the Melancholy Death of Romain, A French Negro, by Humanitas* (Philadelphia, 1803); Kimberly S. Hangar, *Bounded Lives, Bounded Spaces: Free Black Society in Colonial New Orleans, 1763–1803* (Durham, 1997), 167; Caryn Cosse Bell, *Revolution, Romanticism and the Afro-Creole Protest Tradition in Louisiana, 1718–1868* (Baton Rouge, 1997); Sara E. Johnson, *The Fear of French Negroes: Transcolonial Collaboration in the Revolutionary Americas* (Berkeley, 2012); Rebecca J. Scott and Jean M. Hebrad, "Rosalie of the Poulard Nation: Freedom, Law, and Dignity in the Era of the Haitian Revolution," in Lisa A. Lindsay and John Wood Sweet, eds, *Biography and the Black Atlantic* (Philadelphia, 2014), 248–67; Diane Batts Morrow, *Persons of Color and Religious at the Same Time: The Oblate Sisters of Providence, 1829–1860* (Chapel Hill, 2002).

51. Hannah Sawyer Lee, *Memoir of Pierre Touissant, Born a Slave in St. Domingo*, 2d rev. ed. (Sunbury, Pa., 1992); Arthur Jones, *Pierre Touissant* (New York, 2003); Susan Branson and Leslie Patrick, "Étrangers dans un Pays Étrange: Saint-Domingan Refugees of Color in Philadelphia," in Geggus, ed., *The Impact of the Haitian Revolution*, 199, 202.

52. White, *Encountering Revolution*, 145; John H. Bracey Jr. and Manisha Sinha, eds., *African American Mosaic: A Documentary History from the Slave Trade to the Twenty-First Century, Volume One — To 1877* (Upper Saddle River, N.J., 2004), 68–73; Sara C. Fanning, "The Roots of Early Black Nationalism: Northern African Americans' Invocations of Haiti in the Early Nineteenth Century," *S&A* 28 (April 2007): 61–85; Mitch Kachun, "Antebellum African Americans, Public Commemoration, and the Haitian Revolution: A Problem of Historical Mythmaking," *JER* 26 (Summer 2006): 249–69; Prince Saunders, *Haytian Papers: A Collection of the Interesting Proclamations and Other Official Documents, Together with some Account of the Rise, Progress, and Present State of the Kingdom of Hayti* (Boston, 1818), 81.

53. Jeremiah Gloucester, *An Oration Delivered on January 1, 1823 in Bethel Church on the Abolition of the Slave Trade* (Philadelphia, 1823), 10; *GUE*, August 1825; September 12, 1825; Winch, *A Gentleman of Color*, 161, 210; Chris Dixon, *African America*

and Haiti: Emigration and Black Nationalism in the Nineteenth Century (Westport, Conn., 2000), 31.

54. Winston James, *The Struggles of John Brown Russwurm: The Life and Writings of a Pan-Africanist Pioneer, 1799–1851* (New York, 2010), 5–25, 131–34; Monroe Fordham, "Nineteenth-Century Black Thought in the United States: Some Influences of the Santo Domingo Revolution," *JBS* 6 (December 1975): 115–26; Maurice Jackson and Jacqueline Bacon, eds., *African Americans and the Haitian Revolution: Selected Essays and Historical Documents* (New York, 2010).

CHAPTER THREE. THE LONG NORTHERN EMANCIPATION

1. Sidney Kaplan and Emma Nogrady Kaplan, eds., *The Black Presence in the Era of the American Revolution, 1770–1800* (Washington, 1973), 246.

2. Arthur Zilversmit, *The First Emancipation: The Abolition of Slavery in the North* (Chicago, 1967); Robert Fogel and Stanley Engerman, "Philanthropy at Bargain Prices: Notes on the Economics of Gradual Emancipation," *Journal of Legal Studies* 3 (June 1974): 377–401.

3. Mary Stoughton Locke, *Antislavery in America from the Introduction of African Slaves to the Prohibition of the Slave Trade (1619–1808)* (Boston, 1901), 67–69; Zilversmit, *The First Emancipation*, 46–52, 78–83; J. William Frost, ed., *The Quaker Origins of Antislavery* (Norwood, Pa., 1980), 238–46; Thomas E. Drake, *Quakers and Slavery in America* (New Haven, 1950), chap. 4; Roger Bruns, ed., *Am I Not a Man and a Brother: The Antislavery Crusade of Revolutionary America, 1688–1788* (New York, 1977), 493–502; Peter M. Bergman and Jean McCarroll ed., *The Negro in the Continental Congress* (New York, 1969), 1:96.

4. Leslie Harris, *In the Shadow of Slavery: African Americans in New York City, 1626–1863* (Chicago, 2003); Edgar J. McManus, *Black Bondage in the North* (Syracuse, 1973); John Wood Sweet, *Bodies Politic: Negotiating Race in the American North, 1730–1830* (Baltimore, 2003), 61; James A. Rawley, *The Transatlantic Slave Trade: A History* (New York, 1981), 264–330; Robert E. Desrochers Jr., "Slave-For-Sale Advertisements and Slavery in Massachusetts, 1704–1781," *WMQ* 59 (July 2002): 623–64.

5. George H. Moore, *Notes on the History of Slavery in Massachusetts* (New York, 1866), 111–15; Bruns, ed., *Am I Not a Man*, 105–7, 429–32; Christopher Cameron, "The Puritan Origins of Black Abolitionism in Massachusetts," *Historical Journal of Massachusetts* (Summer 2011): 92–98; James J. Allegro, "'Increasing and Strengthening the Country': Law, Politics, and the Antislavery Movement in Early-Eighteenth-Century Massachusetts Bay," *NEQ* 75 (March 2002): 5–23; Emily Blanck, "The Legal Emancipations of Leander and Caesar: Manumission and the Law in Revolutionary South Carolina and Massachusetts," *S&A* 28 (August 2007): 235–54; Blanck, "Seventeen Eighty-Three: The Turning Point in the Law of Slavery and Freedom in Massachusetts," *NEQ* 75 (March 2002): 27–28; Robert H. Romer, *Slavery in the Connecticut Valley of Massachusetts* (Florence, Mass., 2009), 168, 211, 233.

6. Bruns, ed., *Am I Not a Man*, 429–32; Harvey Amani Whitfield, *The Problem of Slavery in Early Vermont, 1777–1810: Essay and Primary Sources* (Barre, Vt., 2014), 13–39;

Locke, *Antislavery in America*, 80; Gary Nash, *The Unknown American Revolution: The Unruly Birth of Democracy and the Struggle to Create America* (New York, 2005), 282; Romer, *Slavery in the Connecticut Valley*, 221.

7. Moore, *Notes on the History of Slavery*, 148–54, 182–95; Zilversmit, *The First Emancipation*, 112–13; Elaine MacEacheren, "Emancipation of Slavery in Massachusetts: A Reexamination 1770–1790," *JNH* (October 1970): 302–3; Romer, *Slavery in the Connecticut Valley*, 217.

8. Moore, *Notes on the History of Slavery*, 211–21; Robert M. Spector, "The Quock Walker Cases (1781–83)—Slavery, Its Abolition, and Negro Citizenship in Early Massachusetts," *JNH* 53 (January 1968): 12–32; William O'Brien, "Did the Jennison Case Outlaw Slavery in Massachusetts?" *WMQ* 17 (April 1960): 219–41; Bruns, ed., *Am I Not a Man*, 474–75; John D. Cushing, "The Cushing Court and the Abolition of Slavery in Massachusetts: More Notes on the 'Quock Walker Case,'" *American Journal of Legal History* 5 (April 1961): 139–40; cf. Margot Minardi, *Making Slavery History: Abolitionism and the Politics of Memory in Massachusetts* (New York, 2010), 16–20; Romer, *Slavery in the Connecticut Valley*, 216; Emily Blanck, *Tyrannicide: Forging an American Law of Slavery in Revolutionary South Carolina and Massachusetts* (Athens, Ga., 2014).

9. Warren Billings, "The Cases of Fernando and Elizabeth Key: A Note on the Status of Blacks in Seventeenth-Century Virginia," *WMQ* 30 (July 1973): 464–74; Moore, *Notes on the History of Slavery*, 210–11; Chester W. Gregory, "Black Women in Pre-Federal America," in Mabel E. Deutrich and Virginia C. Purdy, eds., *Clio Was a Woman: Studies in the History of American Women* (Washington, 1980), 53–70; Blanck, *Tyrannicide*, 101–2; Catherine Adams and Elizabeth H. Pleck, *Love of Freedom: Black Women in Colonial and Revolutionary New England* (New York, 2010), 127–29.

10. Arthur Zilversmit, "Quok Walker, Mumbet, and the Abolition of Slavery in Massachusetts," *WMQ* 25 (October 1968): 614–24; Bruns, ed., *Am I Not a Man*, 468–69; Harold W. Felton, *Mumbet: The Story of Elizabeth Freeman* (New York, 1970); Blanck, "Seventeen Eighty-Three," 38–42; Adams and Pleck, *Love of Freedom*, 139–48; Richard E. Welch, *Theodore Sedgwick, Federalist: A Political Portrait* (Middletown, Conn., 1965), 51–52, 102, 249; Nash, *The Unknown American Revolution*, 409; *The Practicability of the Abolition of Slavery: A Lecture Delivered to the Lyceum in Stockbridge, February 1831* (New York, 1831), 14–18; Minardi, *Making Slavery History*, 125–30.

11. John H. Bracey Jr. and Manisha Sinha, eds., *African American Mosaic: A Documentary History from the Slave Trade to the Twenty-First Century, Volume One—To 1877* (Upper Saddle River, NJ, 2004), 56–57; Roy E. Finkenbine, "Belinda's Petition: Reparations for Slavery in Revolutionary Massachusetts," *WMQ* 64 (January 2007): 95–104; Adams and Pleck, *Love of Freedom*, 167–76; C. S. Manegold, *Ten Hills Farm: The Forgotten History of Slavery in the North* (Princeton, 2010), 154–55, 236; Sharon M. Harris, *Executing Race: Early American Women's Narratives of Race, Society and the Law* (Columbus, 2005), chap. 2.

12. Paul Cuffe and John Cuffe, Petition to the Massachusetts General Court, February 10, 1780, Cuffe Papers, New Bedford Library, and Letter from Paul Cuffe and John Cuffe to the Selectmen in the Town of Dartmouth, April 24, 1781, *BAP*; Moore, *Notes on*

the History of Slavery, 196–98; Sheldon H. Harris, *Paul Cuffe: Black America and the African Return* (New York, 1972), 33–37.

13. Bruns, ed., *Am I Not a Man*, 384–85; Edward Needles, *An Historical Memoir of the Pennsylvania Society, for Promoting the Abolition of Slavery* . . . (Philadelphia, 1848), 14–17; James G. Basker, ed., *Early American Abolitionists: A Collection of Antislavery Wrtings, 1760–1820* (New York, 2005), 79–80; Gary B. Nash and Jean Soderlund, *Freedom by Degrees: Emancipation in Pennsylvania and Its Aftermath* (New York, 1991), 80, 113–30; Kirsten Sword, "Remembering Dinah Nevil: Strategic Deceptions in Eighteenth-Century Antislavery," *JAH* 97 (September 2010): 315–43.

14. Bruns, ed., *Am I Not a Man*, 445–50; Needles, *An Historical Memoir*, chap. 3; Nash and Soderlund, *Freedom by Degrees*, 41–46; Zilversmit, *The First Emancipation*, 124–37.

15. Nash and Soderlund, *Freedom by Degrees*, 139–41, 203–4; Gary B. Nash, *Forging Freedom: The Formation of Philadelphia's Free Black Community, 1720–1840* (Cambridge, Mass., 1988), 63–65; Kaplan and Kaplan, eds., *The Black Presence*, 30–31; "To 'Mr. Printer' by 'Cato,'" Postscript to the *Freeman's Journal*, September 21, 1781.

16. Needles, *An Historical Memoir*, chap. 4; Bruns, ed., *Am I Not a Man*, 510–15; Basker, ed., *Early American Abolitionists*, 99; Nash and Soderlund, *Freedom by Degrees*, 115–27; Nash, *The Unknown American Revolution*, 411–13; Richard S. Newman, *The Transformation of American Abolitionism: Fighting Slavery in the Early Republic* (Chapel Hill, 2002), 4–5, 23–31.

17. Zilversmit, *The First Emancipation*, 118–24; David Menschel, "'Abolition Without Deliverance': The Law of Connecticut Slavery, 1784–1848," *Yale Law Journal* 111 (October 2001): 183–222; Sweet, *Bodies Politic*, 247–48, 252, 257–59.

18. *Life of James Mars, A Slave Born and Sold in Connecticut. Written by Himself* (Hartford, 1864), 4, 21–25; Bruns, ed., *Am I Not a Man*, 365–69; Joanne Pope Melish, *Disowning Slavery: Gradual Emancipation and "Race" in New England, 1780–1860* (Ithaca, 1998), 57–64, 68–73.

19. James B. Hedges, *The Browns of Providence Plantation: Colonial Years* (Cambridge, Mass., 1951), 72, 79–83; *The Works of Samuel Hopkins, D.D.* . . . (Boston, 1854), 2:43–48; Joseph A. Conforti, *Samuel Hopkins and the New Divinity Movement* (Washington, 1981), 133–41; *Constitution of a Society for Abolishing the Slave-Trade With Several Acts of the Legislatures of Massachusetts, Connecticut, and Rhode-Island for that Purpose* (Providence, 1789); Charles Rappleye, *Sons of Providence: The Brown Brothers, the Slave Trade, and the American Revolution* (New York, 2006); Mack Thompson, *Moses Brown: Reluctant Reformer* (Chapel Hill, 1962), 105; Sweet, *Bodies Politic*, 246, 260–62.

20. Zilversmit, *The First Emancipation*, 117; Dinah Mayo-Bobee, "Servile Discontents: Slavery and Resistance in Colonial New Hampshire, 1645–1785," *S&A* 30 (September 2009): 339–60; Romer, *Slavery in the Connecticut Valley*, 218.

21. Robin L. Einhorn, *American Taxation, American Slavery* (Chicago, 2006); David Waldstreicher, *Slavery's Constitution: From Revolution to Ratification* (New York, 2009); George William Van Cleve, *A Slaveholders' Union: Slavery, Politics, and the*

Constitution in the Early American Republic (Chicago, 2010); Staughton Lynd, *Class Conflict, Slavery and the United States Constitution* (Indianapolis, 1967); Paul Finkelman, *Slavery and the Founders: Race and Liberty in the Age of Jefferson* (New York, 1996), chaps. 1–3; William W. Freehling, *The Reintegration of American History: Slavery and the Civil War* (New York, 1994), chap. 2; Howard A. Ohline, "Republicanism and Slavery: Origins of the Three-Fifths Clause in the United States Constitution," *WMQ* 28 (October 1971): 563–84; Don E. Fehrenbacher, *The Slaveholding Republic: An Account of the United States Government's Relations to Slavery* (New York, 2001), chap. 2.

22. Gordon S. Wood, *The Creation of the American Republic, 1776–1787* (New York, 1972), 510–13; John P. Kaminski, ed., *A Necessary Evil? Slavery and the Debate over the Constitution* (Madison, 1995), 70–77, 116–17, 128–29, 147–8, 150, 152–53, 166–67, 172–75; Bruns, ed., *Am I Not a Man*, 520–21, 529–31; Gary B. Nash, *Race and Revolution* (Madison, 1990), 142–43; David Waldstreicher, *Runaway America: Benjamin Franklin, Slavery and the American Revolution* (New York, 2004), 232–35; David Freeman Hawke, *Benjamin Rush: Revolutionary Gadfly* (Indianapolis, 1971), 345, 360–63; Locke, *Antislavery in America*, 86–87; Frost, ed., *The Quaker Origins of Antislavery*, 259; Henry Mayer, *A Son of Thunder: Patrick Henry and the American Republic* (New York, 1986), 433–34; Robin L. Einhorn, "Patrick Henry's Case Against the Constitution: The Structural Problem with Slavery," *JER* 22 (2002): 549–73; Jeff Broadwater, *George Mason: Forgotten Founder* (Chapel Hill, 2006).

23. David N. Gellman, *Emancipating New York: The Politics of Slavery and Freedom, 1777–1827* (Baton Rouge, 2006), chap. 3; David N. Gellman and David Quigley, eds., *Jim Crow New York: A Documentary History of Race and Citizenship, 1777–1877* (New York, 2003), 25–32; Patrick Rael, "The Long Death of Slavery," in Ira Berlin and Leslie Harris, eds., *Slavery in New York* (New York, 2005), 111–46.

24. Bruns, ed., *Am I Not a Man*, 504–6; Minutes of the First Meeting of Individuals to Form the Society for the Manumission of Slaves and Protecting Such of them as have been or May be Liberated, January 25, 1785, 4 February [1785], 10 [February 1785], Report of Committee on Resolutions Affecting Members of the Society Holding Slaves ND, Records of the New York Manumission Society, NYHS, vol. 7, May 18 1791–February 13 1807, pp. 144–45, 148–49, 157; Harris, *In the Shadow of Slavery*, 56; Gellman, *Emancipating New York*, chap. 4; Gellman and Quigley, eds., *Jim Crow New York*, 33–38; Graham Russell Hodges, *Root and Branch: African Americans in New York and East Jersey, 1613–1863* (Chapel Hill, 1999), 166–68; Rob Weston, "Alexander Hamilton and the Abolition of Slavery in New York," *Afro-Americans in New York Life and History* 18 (January 1994): 31–45; Daniel C. Littlefield, "John Jay, the Revolutionary Generation, and Slavery," *New York History* 87 (January 2000): 91–132; Nancy Isenberg, *Fallen Founder: The Life of Aaron Burr* (New York, 2007).

25. Gellman, *Emancipating New York*, chap. 6; Shane White, "Impious Prayers: Elite and Popular Attitudes Towards Blacks and Slavery in the Middle Atlantic States, 1783–1810," *New York History* 67 (July 1986): 261–83; Sondra A. O'Neale, *Jupiter Hammon and the Biblical Beginnings of African-American Literature* (Metuchen, N.J., 1993),

230–41; Craig Wilder, *In the Company of Black Men: The African Influence on African American Culture in New York City* (New York, 2001), 64–71.

26. Philip S. Foner and Robert James Branham, *Lift Every Voice: African American Oratory, 1787–1900* (Tuscaloosa, 1998), 20–26; Anna Bustill Smith, "The Bustill Family," *JNH* 10 (October 1925): 638–44; Henry J. Cadbury, "Negro Membership in the Society of Friends," *JNH* 21 (April 1936): 189–94.

27. Shane White, *Somewhat More Independent: The End of Slavery in New York City, 1770–1810* (Athens, Ga., 1991), chap. 5; Graham Russell Hodges and Alan Edward Brown, *"Pretends to be Free": Runaway Slave Advertisements from Colonial and Revolutionary New York and New Jersey* (New York, 1994); Harris, *In the Shadow of Slavery,* 68–70; Carter G. Woodson, *Negro Orators and Their Orations* (New York, 1925), 14–25.

28. Woodson, *Negro Orators,* 25–30; Winthrop D. Jordan, *White Over Black: American Attitudes Towards the Negro, 1550–1812* (Chapel Hill, 1968), 8–9, 37–40.

29. *The Constitution of the New-York Society for Promoting the Manumission of Slaves, and Protecting Such of Them as Have Been, or May Be, Liberated. Revised, October, 1796* (New York, 1796); *A Discourse Delivered April 12, 1797 . . . By Samuel Miller A.M. . . .* (New York, 1797), 9–14, 15, 23–26, 27, 30–32.

30. *A Discourse, Delivered April 11, 1798 . . . By E. H. Smith . . .* (New York, 1798), 5–8, 11–12, 15–16, 23–25; White, *Somewhat More Independent,* 167, 185; James E. Cronin, ed., *The Diary of Elihu Hubbard Smith, 1771–1798* (Philadelphia, 1973).

31. Letter from Wm. Hamilton a black man to his excellency John Jay Esqr Governor of the State of New York, 8 March 1796, John Jay Papers, CU; Gellman and Quigley, eds., *Jim Crow New York,* 52–55, 67–72; Zilversmit, *The First Emancipation,* 200–214; Melish, *Disowning Slavery,* 76; Romer, *Slavery in the Connecticut Valley,* 218–19; Menschel, "Abolition Without Deliverance," 183–222; Edward Raymond Turner, "The Abolition of Slavery in Pennsylvania," *PMHB* 36 (1912): 139.

32. Bruns, ed., *Am I Not a Man and Brother,* 440–43, 456–59; Larry R. Gerlach, ed., *New Jersey in the American Revolution, 1763–1783: A Documentary History* (Trenton, 1975), 437–40; Simeon Moss, "The Persistence of Slavery in a Free State," *JNH* 35 (1950): 289–314; Hodges, *Root and Branch,* chap. 3; Hodges and Brown, eds.,"*Pretends to be Free*"; Graham Russell Hodges, *Slavery and Freedom in the Rural North: African Americans in Monmouth County, New Jersey, 1665–1865* (Madison, 1997), 114–16, 124–36.

33. *The Constitution of the New Jersey Society for Promoting the Abolition of Slavery . . .* (Burlington, N.J., 1793); Marion Thompson Wright, "New Jersey Laws and the Negro," *JNH* 28 (April 1943): 156–99; Locke, *Antislavery in America,* 82; Zilversmit, *The First Emancipation,* 140–46, 152–53, 173–76, 184–89, 192–99; Romer, *Slavery in the Connecticut Valley,* 220; James J. Gigantino II, *The Ragged Road to Abolition: Slavery and Freedom in New Jersey, 1775–1865* (Philadelphia, 2015).

34. Bruns, ed., *Am I Not a Man and Brother,* 470–71; Hilda Justice, comp., *Life and Ancestry of Warner Mifflin . . .* (Philadelphia, 1905), 38–40; *The Defence of Warner Mifflin . . .* (Philadelphia, 1796), 4, 18; Stephen B. Weeks, *Southern Quakers and*

Slavery: A Study in Institutional History (Baltimore, 1896), chap. 9; A. Glenn Crothers, *Quakers Living in the Lion's Mouth: The Society of Friends in Northern Virginia, 1730–1865* (Gainesville, Fla., 2012), 58–60; Michael L. Nicholls, "'The Squint of Freedom': African-American Freedom Suits in Post-Revolutionary Virginia," *S&A* 20 (August 1999): 47–62; "Documents: Manumission Papers of Free People of Color of Petersburg, Virginia, Deeds of Emancipation of Negroes Freeing Negroes," *JNH* 4 (October 1928): 534–38; Eva Sheppard Wolf, *Race and Liberty in the New Nation: Emancipation in Virginia from the Revolution to Nat Turner's Rebellion* (Baton Rouge, 2006), chaps. 1–3.

35. Bruns, ed., *Am I Not a Man and Brother*, 389, 465–67, 506–9; *The Constitution of the Virginia Society, for Promoting the Abolition of Slavery . . .* (Richmond, 1795); Kaminski, ed., *A Necessary Evil*, 24–26, 269; James D. Essig, *The Bonds of Wickedness: American Evangelicals Against Slavery, 1770–1808* (Philadelphia, 1982), chap. 3; Frederika Teute Schmidt and Barbara Ripel Wilhelm, "Early Proslavery Petitions in Virginia," *WMQ* 30 (1973): 133–46; Lacy K. Ford, *Deliver Us from Evil: The Slavery Question in the Old South* (New York, 2009), 23–26; Henry Wiencek, *An Imperfect God: George Washington, His Slaves, and the Creation of America* (New York, 2003): 321–24.

36. *Notes on the State of Virginia; written in the year 1781, Somewhat Corrected and Enlarged in the Winter of 1782* (London, 1787), 250–58, 262–65, 298–301; Peter S. Onuf, *The Mind of Thomas Jefferson* (Charlottesville, Va., 2007), part 4; Onuf, "'To Declare Them a Free and Independent People': Race, Slavery, and National Identity in Jefferson's Thought," *JER* 18 (Spring 1998): 1–46; Jordan, *White Over Black*, chap. 12; Bruce Dain, *A Hideous Monster of the Mind: American Race Theory in the Early Republic* (Cambridge, Mass., 2002), 26–39; Alexander Boulton, "The American Paradox: Jeffersonian Equality and Racial Science," *American Quarterly* 47 (September 1995): 467–92; "Forum: Thomas Jefferson and Sally Hemmings Redux," *WMQ* 57 (January 2000): 121–210; Annette Gordon-Reed, *Thomas Jefferson and Sally Hemings: An American Controversy* (Charlottesville, Va., 1997); Gordon-Reed, *The Hemingses of Monticello: An American Family* (New York, 2008).

37. Gilbert Imlay, *A Topographical Description of the Western Territory of North America . . .* (London, 1797), 222–31; Wil Verhoeven, *Gilbert Imlay: Citizen of the World* (London, 2008); *An Essay on the Causes of the Variety of Complexion and Figure in the Human Species . . . By the Rev. Samuel Stanhope Smith* (Philadelphia, 1787); Jordan, *White Over Black*, 517–21; Louis Ruchames, ed., *Racial Thought in America*, vol. 1, *From the Puritans to Abraham Lincoln, A Documentary History* (Amherst, Mass., 1969), 197–99, 218–25; Dain, *A Hideous Monster of the Mind*, chap. 2.

38. Finkelman, *Slavery and the Founders*, chap. 6; William W. Freehling, *The Road to Disunion: Secessionists at Bay, 1776–1854* (New York, 1990), 1:121–31, 138–43; Gary Wills, *"Negro President": Jefferson and the Slave Power* (New York, 2003), chap. 1; Gary B. Nash and Graham Russell Gao Hodges, *Friends of Liberty: Thomas Jefferson, Tadeusz Kościuszko and Agrippa Hall, A Tale of Three Patriots, Two Revolutions, and a Tragic Betrayal of Freedom in the New Nation* (New York, 2008), 162–70, 213–45; Adam Rothman, *Slave Country: American Expansion and the Origins of the Deep*

South (Cambridge, Mass., 2005); Lucia Stanton, "'Those who Labor for my Happiness': Thomas Jefferson and His Slaves," in Peter Onuf, ed., *Jeffersonian Legacies* (Charlottesville, Va., 1993), 147–80; Henry Wiencek, *Master of the Mountain: Thomas Jefferson and His Slaves* (New York, 2012), chaps. 1–4; Peter Onuf, "Thomas Jefferson, Missouri, and the 'Empire of Liberty,'" in James P. Ronda, ed., *Thomas Jefferson and the Changing West* (Albuquerque, 1997), 111–53.

39. Gary B. Nash, *The Forgotten Fifth: African Americans in the Age of Revolution* (Cambridge, Mass., 2006), chap. 2; Nash, *Race and Revolution*, 43–48, 146–50; [Jeremy Belknap], *Queries respecting the introduction, progress and abolition of Slavery in Massachusetts* (Boston, 1795); St. George Tucker, *A Dissertation on Slavery with a Proposal for the Gradual Abolition of it, in the State of Virginia* (Philadelphia, 1796); Jordan, *White Over Black*, 457; Philip Hamilton, "Revolutionary Principles and Family Loyalties: Slavery's Transformation in the St. George Tucker Household of Early National Virginia," WMQ 55 (1998): 531–56; Paul Finkelman, "The Dragon St. George Could Not Slay: Tucker's Plan to End Slavery," 1213–43, and Michael Kent Curtis, "St. George Tucker and the Legacy of Slavery," 1157–1212, *William and Mary Law Review* 47 (2006), http://scholarship.law.wm.edu/wmlr/vol47/iss4/5; Alan Taylor, *The Internal Enemy: Slavery and War in Virginia, 1772–1832* (New York, 2013), 85–102, 106–10; Douglas R. Egerton, *Gabriel's Rebellion: The Virginia Slave Conspiracies of 1800 and 1802* (Chapel Hill, 1993), 152–62.

40. *Constitution of the Maryland Society for Promoting the Abolition of Slavery, and the Relief of Free Negroes, and Others, Unlawfully held in Bondage* (Baltimore, 1789); *Constitution of the Chester-Town Society, for Promoting the Abolition of Slavery, and the Relief of Free Negroes, and Others, Unlawfully held in Bondage* (Baltimore, 1791); William Pinckney, *Speech of William Pinckney, Esq., in the House of Delegates of Maryland, at their Session in November 1789* (Philadelphia, 1790); George Buchanan, *An Oration Upon the Moral and Political Evil of Slavery . . .* (Baltimore, 1793), 6–11; T. Stephen Whitman, *The Price of Freedom: Slavery and Manumission in Baltimore and Early National Maryland* (Lexington, Ky., 1997), chaps. 4, 5; Barbara Jeanne Fields, *Slavery and Freedom on the Middle Ground: Maryland During the Nineteenth Century* (New Haven, 1985), 141–65, 241; *Constitution of the Delaware Society for Promoting the Abolition of Slavery and for the Relief and Protection of Free Blacks and People of Colour, Unlawfully Held in Bondage, or Otherwise Oppressed* (Wilmington, 1801); Patience Essah, *A House Divided: Slavery and Emancipation in Delaware, 1638–1865* (Charlottesville, Va., 1996), chap. 2; Monte Calvert, "The Abolition Society of Delaware, 1801–1807," *Delaware History* 10 (1963): 295–321; William H. Williams, *Slavery and Freedom in Delaware, 1639–1865* (Wilmington, Del., 1996), 141–65, 241.

41. Essig, *The Bonds of Wickedness*, 74–78, 84–88, 117–19; Locke, *Antislavery in America*, 42–44, 119–23, 170, 183; David Rice, *Slavery Inconsistent with Justice and Good Policy . . .* (New York, 1812), 17–21, 28–29; Asa Martin, *The Antislavery Movement in Kentucky Prior to 1850* (Louisville, Ky., 1918); Martin, "The Anti-Slavery Societies of Tennessee," *Tennessee Historical Magazine* 1 (1915): 261–80; Lowell H. Harrison, *The Antislavery Movement in Kentucky* (Lexington, Ky., 1978), 18–25; Alice Dana Adams,

The Neglected Period of Anti-Slavery in America, 1808–1831 (Williamstown, Mass., 1973), 34–38; Ford, *Deliver Us from Evil*, 38–46.

42. Aptheker, ed., *A Documentary History*, 1:13–14; Douglas R. Egerton, *Death or Liberty: African Americans and Revolutionary America* (New York, 2009), 158–59; Kevin T. Barksdale, *The Lost State of Franklin: America's First Secession* (Lexington, Ky., 2009); John Hope Franklin, *The Free Negro in North Carolina, 1790–1860* (Chapel Hill, 1943), 41–45.

43. Davis, *The Problem of Slavery in the Age of Revolution*, 196–212; Jed Handelsman Shugerman, "The Louisiana Purchase and South Carolina's Reopening of the Slave Trade in 1803," *JER* 22 (Summer 2002): 263–90; James A. McMillin, *The Final Victims: Foreign Slave Trade to North America, 1783–1810* (Columbia, S.C., 2004); Lewis Dupré, *An Admonitory Picture and a Solemn Warning . . .* (Charleston, S.C., 1810), esp. 19–24, 34–41; Adams, *The Neglected Period of Anti-Slavery*, 30–31.

44. Leon Litwack, *North of Slavery: The Negro in the Free States, 1790–1820* (Chicago, 1961), 18–19, 31; Finkelman, *Slavery and the Founders*, chap. 4; Paul Finkelman, "The Kidnapping of John Davis and the Adoption of the Fugitive Slave Law of 1793," *JSH* 56 (August 1990): 397–422; Stanley Harrold, *Border War: Fighting Over Slavery before the Civil War* (Chapel Hill, 2010), 21–23; Matthew Mason, *Slavery and Politics in the Early American Republic* (Chapel Hill, 2006), 17–18; Fehrenbacher, *The Slaveholding Republic*, chap. 7.

45. *The Works of Samuel Hopkins, D.D. . . .* (Boston, 1854), 2:613–24; *The Defence of Warner Mifflin*, 21–24; James O'Kelly, *Essay on Negro Slavery* (Philadelphia, 1789); Essig, *The Bonds of Wickedness*, 81; Buchanan, *An Oration*, 12–16; Melish, *Disowning Slavery*, 150–62.

CHAPTER FOUR. THE ANGLO-AMERICAN ABOLITION MOVEMENT

1. *Centennial Anniversary of the Pennsylvania Society for Promoting the Abolition of Slavery . . .* (Philadelphia, 1876), 22.

2. Don E. Fehrenbacher, *The Slaveholding Republic: An Account of the United States Government's Relations to Slavery* (New York, 2001); Michael A. Morrison and James Brewer Stewart, eds., *Race and the Early Republic: Racial Consciousness and Nation-Building in the Early Republic* (Lanham, Md., 2002); Dale W. Tomich, *Through the Prism of Slavery: Labor, Capital, and World Economy* (Lanham, Md., 2004), chap. 3.

3. Paul Polgar, "To Raise Them to an Equal Participation: Early National Abolitionism, Gradual Emancipation, and the Promise of African American Citizenship," *JER* 31 (Summer 2011): 229–58; Richard Newman, "The Pennsylvania Abolition Society and the Struggle for Racial Justice," in Newman and James Mueller, eds., *Antislavery and Abolition in Philadelphia: Emancipation and the Long Struggle for Racial Justice in the City of Brotherly Love* (Baton Rouge, 2011), 118–46.

4. [J. Philmore], *Two Dialogues on the Man-Trade* (London, 1760), 4–10, 20–32, 40–57, 61–62; [Maurice Morgann], *A Plan for the Abolition of Slavery in the West Indies* (London, 1772), esp. 25–26; Sankar Muthu, *Enlightenment Against Empire* (Princeton,

2003), 210–51; Christopher Leslie Brown, *Moral Capital: Foundations of British Abolitionism* (Chapel Hill, 2006).

5. *The Case of Our FELLOW-CREATURES* . . . (repr., Philadelphia, 1784); *The Epistle from the Yearly-Meeting* . . . (London, 1785); David Brion Davis, *The Problem of Slavery in the Age of Revolution, 1770–1820* (Ithaca, 1975), chap. 5; Seymour Drescher, "The Shocking Birth of British Abolitionism," *S&A* 33 (2012): 571–93; James Walvin, "The Slave Trade, Quakers, and the Early Days of British Abolition," in Brycchan Carey and Geoffrey Plank, eds., *Quakers and Abolition* (Urbana, 2014), 165–79; Marcus Wood, *Blind Memory: Visual Representations of Slavery in England and America* (New York, 2000), 14–27; Maurie D. McInnis, *Slaves Waiting for Sale: Abolitionist Art and the American Slave Trade* (Chicago, 2011); Jacqueline Francis, "The *Brooks* Slave Ship Icon: A 'Universal Symbol'?" *S&A* 30 (2009): 327–38.

6. Thomas Clarkson, *An Essay on the Slavery and Commerce of the Human Species* . . . (London, 1786); Clarkson, *An Essay on the Impolicy of the African Slave Trade In Two Parts* (London, 1788); Clarkson, *The Substance of the Evidence of Sundry Persons on the Slave Trade* . . . (London, 1789); Clarkson, *An Essay on the Comparative Efficiency of Regulation or Abolition, as Applied to the Slave Trade* (London, 1789); Clarkson, *Letters on the Slave-Trade* . . . (London, 1790); Ellen Gibson Wilson, *Thomas Clarkson: A Biography*, 2d ed. (New York, 1996); Earl Leslie Griggs, *Thomas Clarkson: The Friend of Slaves* (Ann Arbor, 1938); J. R. Oldfield, *Popular Politics and British Anti-Slavery: The Mobilisation of Public Opinion against the Slave Trade, 1787–1807* (London, 1998), chap. 3; Dee E. Andrews and Emma Jones Lapansky-Werner, "Thomas Clarkson's Quaker Trilogy: Abolitionist Narrative as Transformative History," in Carey and Plank, eds., *Quakers and Abolition*, 194–208.

7. James Ramsay, *An Essay on the Treatment and Conversion of African Slaves in the British Sugar Colonies* (London, 1784), esp. 68–69, 85–86, 198–248, 286–93; Ramsay, *An Enquiry into the Effects of Putting a Stop to the African Slave Trade* . . . (London, 1784), 9–10; Ramsay, *Objections to the Abolition of the Slave Trade, with Answers* . . . (London, 1788); F. O. Shyllon, *James Ramsay: The Unknown Abolitionist* (Edinburgh, 1977); John Newton, *The Journal of a Slave Trader (John Newton) 1750–1754* . . . (London, 1962), 98–113; D. Bruce Hindmarsh, *John Newton and the English Evangelical Tradition: Between the Conversions of Wesley and Wilberforce* (New York, 1996), 58; William E. Phipps, *Amazing Grace in John Newton: Slave-Ship Captain, Hymnwriter, and Abolitionist* (Macon, Ga., 2001); Marcus Wood, *The Poetry of Slavery: An Anglo-American Anthology 1764–1865* (New York, 2003), 77–93.

8. Hannah More, *Slavery* (Philadelphia, 1788); James G. Basker, ed., *Amazing Grace: An Anthology of Poems About Slavery, 1660–1810* (New Haven, 2002), 218; Lilla Maria Crisafulli, "Women and Abolitionism: Hannah More's and Anne Yearsley's Poetry of Freedom," in Cora Kaplan and J. R. Oldfield, eds., *Imagining Transatlantic Slavery* (New York, 2010), 110–24; Clare Midgley, *Women Against Slavery: The British Campaigns, 1780–1870* (London, 1992), esp. 29–35; Marcus Rediker, *The Slave Ship: A Human History* (New York, 2007), chap. 5; Moira Ferguson, *Subject to Others: British Women Writers and Colonial Slavery, 1670–1834* (London, 1992); Brycchan Carey,

British Abolitionism and the Rhetoric of Sensibility: Writing, Sentiment, and Slavery, 1760–1807 (New York, 2005).

9. J. R. Oldfield, *Transatlantic Abolitionism in the Age of Revolution: An International History of Anti-Slavery, c. 1787–1820* (Cambridge, Eng., 2013), chap. 4; Seymour Drescher, *Capitalism and Antislavery: British Mobilization in Comparative Perspective* (London, 1986); Leo D'Anjou, *Social Movements and Cultural Change: The First Abolition Campaign Revisited* (New York, 1996), part 2; Jürgen Habermas, *The Theory of Communicative Action: Reason and the Rationalization of Society*, vol. 1, trans. Thomas McCarthy (Boston, 1985).

10. Seymour Drescher, *Econocide: British Slavery in the Era of Abolition* (Pittsburgh, 1977); Thomas Bender, ed., *The Antislavery Debate: Capitalism and Abolitionism as a Problem in Historical Interpretation* (Berkeley, 1992); Ian Baucom, *Specters of the Atlantic: Finance Capital, Slavery and the Philosophy of History* (Durham, 2005); Srividhya Swaminathan, *Debating the Slave Trade: Rhetoric of British National Identity, 1759–1815* (Surrey, Eng., 2009).

11. *An Abstract of the Evidence Delivered Before a Select Committee of the House of Commons in the Years 1790 and 1791 . . .* (London, 1791); Davis, *The Problem of Slavery in the Age of Revolution*, 184–95; Oldfield, *Transatlantic Abolitionism*, chap. 5; [William Preston], *A Letter to Bryan Edwards, Esquire . . .* (London, 1795); Seymour Drescher, *Abolition: A History of Slavery and Antislavery* (Cambridge, Eng., 2009), 205–28; Roger Anstey, *The Atlantic Slave Trade and British Abolition, 1760–1810* (London, 1975); Robin Blackburn, *The Overthrow of Colonial Slavery, 1776–1848* (London, 1988), chap. 8; Granville Sharp, *Serious Reflections on the Slave Trade and Slavery . . .* (London, 1805), esp. 7–13, 39–40.

12. William Wilberforce, *A Letter on the Abolition of the Slave Trade . . .* (London, 1807); Robert Isaac Wilberforce and Samuel Wilberforce, *The Life of William Wilberforce*, 5 vols. (London, 1838); Matthew Mason, "Slavery Overshadowed: Congress Debates Prohibiting the Atlantic Slave Trade to the United States, 1806–1807," *JER* 20 (Spring 2000): 59–81; Padraig Riley, "Slavery and the Problem of Democracy in Jeffersonian America," in John Craig Hammond and Matthew Mason, eds., *Contesting Slavery: The Politics of Bondage and Freedom in the New American Nation* (Charlottesville, Va., 2011), 236–37.

13. PAS to the London Committee, SEAST, and the Société Française des Amis des Noir, 1790, reel 15, PAS Papers, HSP; Edward Needles, *An Historical Memoir of the Pennsylvania Society, for Promoting the Abolition of Slavery . . .* (Philadelphia, 1848), 30–35; *Essays on the Subject of the Slave . . .* (Philadelphia, 1791); *Description of a Slave Ship* (London, 1789); Sir William Elford, *Plan of an African Ship's Lower Deck* (Philadelphia, 1789); *Extract from the American Museum for May, 1789* (Philadelphia, 1789); *Letter from Granville Sharp, Esq. of London to the Maryland Society for Promoting the Abolition of Slavery . . .* (Baltimore, 1793); J. P. Brissot de Warville, *An Oration Upon the Necessity of Establishing at Paris, A Society to Cooperate with those in America and London, Towards the Abolition of the Trade and Slavery of the Negroes . . .* (Philadelphia, 1788); Betty Fladeland, *Men and Brothers: Anglo-American Antislavery Cooperation* (Urbana, 1972), 40–41.

14. J. P. Brissot de Warville, *New Travels in the United States of America 1788* (Cambridge, Mass., 1964), trans. Mara Soceanu Vamos and ed. Durand Esceverria, xiv–xvii, xxii, xxiii, 162–67, 217–52; Oldfield, *Transatlantic Abolitionism*, 90–91; Marie-Jeanne Rossignol, "The Quaker Antislavery Commitment and How It Revolutionized French Antislavery through the Crèvecoeur–Brissot Friendship, 1782–1789," in Carey and Plank, eds., *Quakers and Abolition*, 180–93; Eloise Ellery, *Brissot de Warville: A Study in the History of the French Revolution* (Boston, 1915), chap. 4; François Furstenberg, "Atlantic Slavery, Atlantic Freedom: George Washington, Slavery, and Transatlantic Abolitionist Networks," *WMQ* 68 (April 2011): 247–86; Davis, *The Problem of Slavery in the Age of Revolution*, 195.

15. Loose Correspondence from Giroud, Society of the Friends of the Blacks and Commissioners in St. Domingue, 17 January 1797, 1798, Undated letters from Raimond and Sonthonox, Zachary Macaulay to PAS, June 4, 1806, Wilberforce to the American Convention, August 28, 1806, reel 12, PAS Papers, HSP; Oldfield, *Transatlantic Abolitionism*, chap. 7; Drescher, *Abolition*, 228–41.

16. Peter M. Bergman and Jean McCarroll, eds., *The Negro in the Congressional Record, 1789–1801* (New York, 1969), 2:14–19, 20–24, 25–27, 29–35, 36–40; Kaminski, ed., *A Necessary Evil?*, 212–30; William C. diGiacomantonion, "'For the Gratification of a Volunteering Society': Antislavery and Pressure Group Politics in the First Federal Congress," *JER* 15 (Summer 1995): 169–97; Richard S. Newman, "Prelude to the Gag Rule: Southern Reaction to Antislavery Petitions in the First Federal Congress," *JER* 16 (Winter 1996): 571–99; Robert Parkinson, "'Manifest Signs of Passion': The First Federal Congress, Antislavery, and Legacies of the Revolutionary War," in Hammond and Mason, eds., *Contesting Slavery*, 49–68; Louis Ruchames, ed., *Racial Thought in America*, vol. 1, *From the Puritans to Abraham Lincoln, A Documentary History* (Amherst, Mass., 1969), 206–11; James G. Basker, ed., *Early American Abolitionists: A Collection of Antislavery Writings, 1760–1820* (New York, 2005), 242–72.

17. *Memorials Presented to the Congress of the United States of America . . .* (Philadelphia, 1792), 8; Memorials to Congress on Slavery and the Slave Trade, reel 25, PAS Papers, HSP; Warner Mifflin, *A Serious Expostulation with the Members of the House of Representatives of the United States* (Philadelphia, 1793), 11, 14; Bergman and McCarroll, eds., *The Negro in the Congressional Record*, 2:50–52; diGiacomantonion, "For the Gratification of a Volunteering Society," 188–89.

18. Simeon Baldwin, *An Oration Pronounced Before the Citizens of New-Haven, July 4th 1788 . . .* (New Haven, 1788), 15–16; *The Constitution of the Connecticut Society for the Promotion of Freedom, and for the Relief of Persons Unlawfully Holden in Bondage* (New Haven, 1790); James Dana, *The African Slave Trade . . .* (New Haven, 1791), 5–33; William Patten, *On the Inhumanity of the Slave Trade . . .* (Providence, 1793), 5–14; James D. Essig, "Connecticut Ministers and Slavery, 1790–1795," *Journal of American Studies* 15 (April 1981): 27–44; Edmund S. Morgan, *The Gentle Puritan: A Life of Ezra Stiles, 1727–1795* (New Haven, 1962); John Fitzmier, *New England's Moral Legislator: Timothy Dwight, 1752–1817* (Bloomington, 1998); James King Morse, *Jedidiah Morse: A Champion of New England Orthodoxy* (New York, 1939); Jonathan D. Sassi,

A *Republic of Righteousness: The Public Christianity of the Post-Revolutionary New England Clergy* (New York, 2001); Christopher Grasso, *A Speaking Aristocracy: Transforming Public Discourse in Eighteenth-Century Connecticut* (Chapel Hill, 1999).

19. Zephaniah Swift, *An Oration on Domestic Slavery . . .* (Hartford, 1791), 3–23; Basker, ed., *Early American Abolitionists,* 141–71; James G. Basker, ed., *American Antislavery Writings: Colonial Beginnings to Emancipation* (New York, 2012), 75–77, 140–41.

20. Noah Webster, *Effects of Slavery on Morals and Industry* (Hartford, 1793), esp. 5–8, 11, 31–42; Joshua Kendall, *The Forgotten Founding Father: Noah Webster's Obsession and the Creation of an American Culture* (New York, 2010): 178–79; Eva Sheppard Wolf, "Early Free Labor Thought and the Contest over Slavery in the Early Republic," in Hammond and Mason, eds., *Contesting Slavery,* 32–48.

21. David Blight, ed., *The Columbian Orator* (New York, 1998), introduction.

22. Theodore Dwight, *An Oration Spoken Before the Connecticut Society for the promotion of Freedom, and the Relief of Persons Unlawfully Holden in Bondage . . .* (Hartford, 1794), 3–24; Basker, ed., *Amazing Grace,* 486–88; Peter Hinks, "Timothy Dwight, Congregationalism, and Early Antislavery," in Steven Mintz and John Stauffer, eds., *The Problem of Evil: Slavery, Freedom, and the Ambiguities of American Reform* (Amherst, Mass., 2007), 148–61; Matthew Mason, "Federalists, Abolitionists, and the Problem of Influence," *American Nineteenth-Century History* 10 (March 2009): 1–27; Marc M. Arkin, "The Federalist Trope: Power and Passion in Abolitionist Rhetoric," *JAH* 9 (June 2001): 75–98; Paul Finkelman, *Slavery and the Founders: Race and Liberty in the Age of Jefferson* (Armonk, N.Y., 2001), chap. 5; Rachel Hope Cleves, *The Reign of Terror in America: Visions of Violence from Anti-Jacobinism to Antislavery* (Cambridge, Eng., 2009).

23. *Constitution of a Society for Abolishing the Slave-Trade . . .* (Providence, 1789); George Benson to PAS, September 5, 1806, reel 12, PAS Papers, HSP; *Works of Samuel Hopkins,* 2:595–612; Joseph A. Conforti, *Samuel Hopkins and the New Divinity Movement* (Washington, 1981), 153–55.

24. *Minutes of the Proceedings of a Convention of Delegates from the Abolition Societies . . .* (Philadelphia, 1794); *Minutes of the proceedings of the Second Convention of Delegates from the Abolition Societies . . .* (Philadelphia, 1795), 29; Abolition Society of Delaware Minute Book, 1810–1819, reel 30, PAS Papers, HSP; David Scholfield and Edmund Haviland, "The Appeal of the American Convention of Abolition Societies to Anti-Slavery Groups," *JNH* 6 (April 1921): 200–240; Needles, *An Historical Memoir,* 50–52, 55; Mary Staughton Locke, *Antislavery in America: African Americans in New York City, 1626–1863* (Chicago, 2003), 101–11.

25. *Minutes of the Proceedings of the Ninth Convention . . .* (Philadelphia, 1804): 40–49; *Minutes of the Proceedings of the Tenth American . . .* (Philadelphia, 1805), appendix; *Minutes of the Proceedings of the Eleventh American . . .* (Philadelphia, 1806), 28, 30–31.

26. *Minutes of the Proceedings of the Twelfth American Convention . . .* (Philadelphia, 1809), 23–24, 26–31; *Minutes of the Proceedings of the Thirteenth American Convention . . .* (Philadelphia, 1812), 16–17, 21–22, 28–29; Constitution of the Kentucky Abolition Society, 1808, reel 30, Carter Tarrant to PAS, May 27, 1809, reel 12, PAS Papers, HSP.

27. Burns ed., *Am I Not a Man and Brother*, 386–89; Basker ed., *Amazing Grace*, 494–96, 674–75; Basker ed., *Early American Abolitionists*, 172–215; Heather S. Nathans, "Staging Slavery: Representing Race and Abolitionism On and Off the Philadelphia Stage," in Newman and Mueller eds., *Antislavery and Abolition in Philadelphia*, 200–207.

28. John Parrish, *Remarks on the Slavery of the Black People . . .* (Philadelphia, 1806), 3–8, 12, 24, 36–37, 41–44; John L. Brooke, "Consent, Civil Society, and the Public Sphere in the Age of Revolution and the Early American Republic," in Jeffrey L. Pasley, Andrew W. Robertson, and David Waldstreicher, eds., *Beyond the Founders: New Approaches to the Public History of the Early American Republic* (Chapel Hill, 2004), 207–50.

29. Thomas Branagan, *A Preliminary Essay on the Oppression of the Exiled Sons of Africa . . .* (Philadelphia, 1804); Branagan, *Avenia: or, A Tragical Poem . . .* (Philadelphia, 1805); Branagan, *The Penitential Tyrant . . .* (Philadelphia, 1805), vii–xxxvi, 55; Branagan, *Serious Remonstrances, Addressed to the Citizens of the Northern States . . .* (Philadelphia, 1805), 36–89; Branagan, *The Guardian Genius of the Federal Union . . .* (New York, 1839); Beverly Tomek, "'From Motives of Generosity, as well as Self-Preservation': Thomas Branagan, Colonization, and the Gradual Emancipation Movement," *American Nineteenth-Century History* 6 (June 2005): 121–47.

30. David Freeman Hawke, *Benjamin Rush: Revolutionary Gadfly* (Indianapolis, 1971), 360–63; L. H. Butterfield, ed., *Letters of Benjamin Rush*, vol. 2, 1793–1819 (Princeton, 1951), 756–58; *Works of Samuel Hopkins*, 2:608.

31. *An Address to the Public from the Pennsylvania Society for Promoting the Abolition of Slavery, and the Relief of Free Negroes, unlawfully held in Bondage* (Philadelphia, 1789); Needles, *An Historical Memoir*, 37, 40, 43; Reports of PAS Sub Committees, March 25, 1791, March 1792, March 1793, August 1797, reel 6, PAS Papers, HSP; Report of the Committee to Prevent Irregular Conduct in Free Negroes, Read February 21, 1788, New York Manumission Society Records, NYHS; *The Constitution of the New-York Society for Promoting the Manumission of Slaves*, 3–4; Leslie Harris, *In the Shadow of Slavery: African Americans in New York City, 1626–1863* (Chicago, 2003), 65; John L. Rury, "Philanthropy, Self Help, and Social Control: The New York Manumission Society and Free Blacks, 1785–1810," *Phylon* 46 (1985): 231–41.

32. *Minutes of the Proceedings of the Second Convention*, 10–11; *Minutes of the Proceedings of the Third Convention . . .* (Philadelphia, 1796), 12–15; *Minutes of the Proceedings of the Fourth Convention . . .* (Philadelphia, 1797), 16–18; *Minutes of the proceedings of the Fifth Convention . . .* (Philadelphia, 1798), 17–18; American Convention of Abolition Societies, "Advice Given to Negroes a Century Ago," *JNH* 6 (January 1921): 103–12.

33. *An Address from the Pennsylvania Abolition Society to the Free Black People . . .* (Philadelphia, 1800), 3–8; *Minutes of the Proceedings of the Fifth Convention . . .* (Philadelphia, 1800), 6–7, 21; *Minutes of the Proceedings of the Fifteenth American . . .* (Philadelphia, 1817), 16; *Minutes of the Proceedings of the Eighth Convention . . .* (Philadelphia, 1803), 6–7, 22–23; Harris, *In the Shadow of Slavery*, 100–101.

34. *Address of the American Convention . . .* (Philadelphia, 1804), 3–8; *Minutes of the proceedings of the Fourteenth American . . .* (Philadelphia, 1816), 20; *Minutes of the*

Proceedings of the Tenth American Convention, 28, 37–38; *Minutes of the Proceedings of the Eleventh American Convention*, 17–18; *Minutes of the Fifteenth Convention* . . . (Philadelphia, 1818), 43–47; Address of the PAS to the Free People of Color, April 13, 1820, and Address of the PAS on behalf of Colored People, October 1821, reel 25, PAS Papers, HSP.

35. *Minutes of the Proceedings of the Seventh Convention of Delegates* . . . (Philadelphia, 1801), 12, 16–17, 22, 32, 37–41; Locke, *Antislavery in America*, 104; *Minutes of the Proceedings of the Twelfth American Convention*, 26–31.

36. *The Constitution of the Society for the Free Instruction of the Black people, formed in the Year 1789* (Philadelphia, 1808); Committee for Improving the Condition of Free Blacks, December 25, 1792, reel 9, Absalom Jones to PAS, July 15, 1795, Quomony Clarkson to PAS, July 27, 1802, reel 12, PAS Committee of Education Lists in PAS schools and the Clarkson Institute and Education Society, 1790–1800, reels 25 and 26, PAS Papers, HSP; Margaret Hope Bacon, "The Pennsylvania Abolition Society's Mission for Black Education," *Pennsylvania Legacies* 5 (November 2005): 21–26; Leroy Graham, *Baltimore: The Nineteenth Century Black Capital* (New York, 1982), 21–23, 62–63.

37. *Minutes of the Proceedings of the Fifth Convention*, 13; *Minutes of the Proceedings of the Fourth Convention*, 32–33; John L. Rury, "The New York African School, 1827–1836: Conflict over Community Control of Black Education," *Phylon* 44 (Third Quarter 1983): 187–97; Robert J. Swan, "John Teasman: African-American Educator and the Emergence of Community in Early Black New York City, 1787–1815," *JER* 12 (Autumn 1992): 331–56; Carla Peterson, *Black Gotham: A Family History of African Americans in Nineteenth-Century New York City* (New Haven, 2011), 66–69, 74–92.

38. *Minutes of the Proceedings of the Ninth American*, 5; *Minutes of the Proceedings of the Tenth American Convention*, 27; Report of the Trustees of the African Free School, November 10, 1818, New York Manumission Society Records, NYHS; Charles C. Andrews, *The History of the New-York African Free-Schools* . . . (New York, 1830), 7–24; *Minutes of the Proceedings of the Thirteenth American Convention* . . . (Philadelphia, 1812), 7, 21; *Minutes of the Adjourned Session of the Twentieth Biennial American Convention* . . . (Philadelphia, 1828), 62–68; Harris, *In the Shadow of Slavery*, 64–66, 128–44; Leslie M. Alexander, *African or American? Black Identity and Political Activism in New York City, 1784–1861* (Urbana, 2008), 13–14, 44–45.

39. New York Manumission Society Records, NYHS, vol. 6, pp. 5–7, 15–17, 25–28; vol. 7, May 18, 1791–February 13, 1807, pp. 7, 14, 20–23, 31, 59, 80, 141, 163, 165–67, 176, 178, 180, 182, 185–87, 193, 196, 204–5, 213, 217–18, 238–39, 242, 256–57, 282, 284, 304–8, 313–15, 321–22, 339, 342; vol. 10, March 11, 1807–July 8, 1817, pp. 7, 32–33, 36, 53, 68, 74, 90, 113, 134, 171, 188, 207, 216, 239, 259, 271–76, 329; vol. 11, July 15, 1817–January 17, 1842, pp. 11, 15–16, 19, 24, 33, 44, 65; Martha S. Jones, "Time, Space and Jurisdiction in Atlantic World Slavery: The Volunbrun Household in Gradual Emancipation New York," *Law and History Review* 29 (November 2011): 1031–60; John Teasman, *An Address Delivered in the African Episcopalian Church* . . . (New York, 1811), 7; cf. Thomas Robert Moseley, "A History of the New York Manumission Society 1785–1849" (Ph.D. diss., New York University, 1963).

40. Robert Layton to James Forten, May 2, 1825, Thomas Garrett to Thomas Shipley, July 1, 1826, reel 13; PAS Memorial to Governor Thomas Mifflin, reel 15, PAS Papers, HSP; Richard Newman, *The Transformation of American Abolitionism: Fighting Slavery in the Early Republic* (Chapel Hill, 2002), 18–31, 60–85; Dee E. Andrews, "Reconsidering the First Emancipation: Evidence from the Pennsylvania Abolition Society Correspondence, 1785–1810," *PH* 64 (Summer 1997): 230–49.

41. *Minutes of the Proceedings of the Eleventh American Convention*, 35–38; John H. Hewitt, "Peter Williams, Jr.: New York's First African-American Episcopal Priest," *New York History* 79 (April 1998): 101–29.

42. Prince Hoare, *Memoirs of Granville Sharp* . . . (London, 1820), 254–55; Vincent Carretta, ed., *Olaudah Equiano: The Interesting Narrative and Other Writings* (New York, 1995), 224–25; *The Life Experience and Gospel Labors of the Rt. Rev. Richard Allen* . . . (repr., Nashville, 1960), 75–89; Dorothy Porter, ed., *Early Negro Writing, 1760–1837* (Boston, 1971), 39, 98–100, 340, 344, 350–51, 362, 365, 388, 398; Adam Carman, *An Oration Delivered at the Fourth Anniversary of the Abolition of the African Slave Trade* . . . (New York, 1811), 15–18; Jeremiah Gloucester, *An Oration Delivered on January 1, 1823 in Bethel Church on the Abolition of the Slave Trade* (Philadelphia, 1823), 8–9.

43. *Constitution of the Brooklyn Woolman African Benevolent Society Adopted March 16, 1810* (Brooklyn, N.Y., 1820); John J. Zuille, *Historical Sketch of the New York African Society for Mutual Relief Organized in the City of New York 1808* . . . (New York, 1892); Porter, ed., *Early Negro Writing*, 37–50; Craig Wilder, "Black Life in Freedom: Creating a Civic Culture," in Ira Berlin and Leslie Harris, eds., *Slavery in New York* (New York, 2005), 217–37; Gloucester, *An Oration*, 14.

44. [John S. Tyson], *Life of Elisha Tyson, the Philanthropist By a Citizen of Baltimore* (Baltimore, 1825); Graham, *Baltimore*, chap. 2; Elisha Tyson to William Master, July 18, August 20, September 4, November 11, December 10, 1812, reel 13, PAS Papers, HSP; Isaac Parrish, *Brief Memoirs of Thomas Shipley and Edwin P. Atlee* . . . (Philadelphia, 1838); Parrish, *Remarks on the Slavery*, 49–66; Robert Purvis, A *Tribute to the Memory of Thomas Shipley, the Philanthropist* (Philadelphia, 1836), iii, 6–7, 16–17; Newman, *The Transformation of American Abolitionism*, 30, 63–64; William Staughton, *An Eulogium in Memory of the Late Dr. Benjamin Rush* (Philadelphia, 1813), 30; Richard Allen, *Articles of Association of the African Methodist Episcopal Church* . . . (Philadelphia, 1799), 17–19; Richard S. Newman, *Freedom's Prophet: Bishop Richard Allen, the AME Church, and the Black Founding Fathers* (New York, 2008), 142–44; L. H. Butterfield ed., *Letters of Benjamin Rush*, vol 2, 1793–1819 (Princeton, 1951), 639, 713.

45. Paul Gilroy, *The Black Atlantic: Modernity and Double Consciousness* (Cambridge, Mass., 1993); Deborah Gray White, "'Yes,' There is a Black Atlantic," *Itinerario* 23 (1999): 127–40; Henry Louis Gates Jr., *The Signifying Monkey: A Theory of Afro-American Literary Criticism* (New York, 1988), chap. 4; Houston Baker, *Modernism and the Harlem Renaissance* (Chicago, 1987).

46. Joanna Brooks and John Saillant, eds., *"Face Zion Forward": First Writers of the Black Atlantic, 1785–1798* (Boston, 2002), 47–75, 93–160; Arthur A. Schomburg, "Two Negro Missionaries to the American Indians: John Marrant and James Stewart," *JNH* 21

(October 1936): 394–400; Joanna Brooks, *American Lazarus: Religion and the Rise of African-American and Native American Literatures* (New York, 2003), chap. 3; John Saillant, "'Wipe Away all Tears from their Eyes': John Marrant's Theology in the Black Atlantic, 1785–1808," *Journal of Millenial Studies* 1 (Winter 1999): 1–23, www .mille.org/Journal.html.

47. Vincent Carretta, ed., *Letters of the Late Ignatius Sancho, An African* (New York, 1998), xix–xx; Reyhan King, ed., *Ignatius Sancho: An African Man of Letters* (London, 1997); Keith A. Sandiford, *Measuring the Moment: Strategies of Protest in Eighteenth-Century Afro-English Writing* (London, 1988), chap. 3.

48. Carretta, ed., *Letters of the Late Ignatius Sancho*, 46, 73–74, 93, 111–12, 130–31, 189, 200, 208, 210, 215, 216, 219; Paul Edwards and James Walvin, *Black Personalities in the Era of the Slave Trade* (Baton Rouge, 1983), 223–37; Felicity A. Nussbaum, "Being a Man: Olaudah Equiano and Ignatius Sancho," and Markman Ellis, "Ignatius Sancho's Letters: Sentimental Libertinism and the Politics of Form," in Vincent Carretta and Philip Gould, eds., *Genius in Bondage: Literature of the Early Black Atlantic* (Lexington, Ky., 2001), 63–69, 199–217.

49. Quobna Ottobah Cugoano, *Thoughts and Sentiments on the Evil of Slavery and Other Writings*, Vincent Carretta, ed. (New York, 1999), introduction, 7; Sandiford, *Measuring the Moment*, chap. 4; James Sidbury, *Becoming African in America: Race and Nation in the Early Black Atlantic* (New York, 2007), 59–64.

50. Cugoano, *Thoughts and Sentiments on the Evil of Slavery*, 9–17, 19–20, 22, 24–46, 52–53, 60–84, 88–91, 96–111; Roxann Wheeler, "'Betrayed by Some of My Own Complexion': Cugoano, Abolition, and the Contemporary Language of Racialism," in Carretta and Gould, eds., *Genius in Bondage*, 17–38.

51. Vincent Carretta, "Olaudah Equiano or Gustavus Vassa? New Light on an Eighteenth-Century Question of Identity," *S&A* 20 (December 1999): 96–105; Paul E. Lovejoy, "Autobiography and Memory: Gustavus Vassa, alias Olaudah Equiano, the African," *S&A* 27 (2006): 317–47; Lovejoy, "Issues of Motivation: Vassa/Equiano and Carretta's Critique of the Evidence"; and Vincent Carretta, "Response to Paul Lovejoy's 'Autobiography and Memory: Gustavus Vassa, alias Olaudah Equiano, the African,'" *S&A* 28 (2007): 115–19, 121–25; James H. Sweet, "Mistaken Identities? Olaudah Equiano, Domingos Alvares, and the Methodological Challenges of Studying the African Diaspora," *AHR* 114 (April 2009): 279–306.

52. Geraldine Murphy, "Olaudah Equiano: Accidental Tourist," *Eighteenth-Century Studies* 27 (Summer 1994): 551–68; James Green, "The Publishing History of Olaudah Equiano's *Interesting Narrative*," *S&A* 16 (1995): 362–75; Akiyo Ito, "Olaudah Equiano and the New York Artisans: The First American Edition of The Interesting Narrative of the Life of Olaudah Equiano, or Gustavus Vassa, the African," *Early American Literature* 32 (1997): 82–92.

53. Vincent Carretta, ed., *Olaudah Equiano: The Interesting Narrative and Other Writings* (New York, 1995), 328–40; Carretta, *Equiano the African: Biography of a Self-Made Man* (Athens, Ga., 2005), chap. 11; James Walvin, *The Zong: A Massacre, the Law and the End of Slavery* (New Haven, 2011).

54. Carretta, ed., *Olaudah Equiano*, 55–59, 61, 63–92, 104–12, 122–50, 158–64, 171–72, 205–21; Adam Potkay, "Olaudah Equiano and the Art of Spiritual Autobiography," *Eighteenth-Century Studies* 27 (Summer 1994): 677–92; George E. Boulukos, "Olaudah Equiano and the Eighteenth-Century Debate on Africa," *Eighteenth-Century Studies* 40 (Winter 2007): 241–57.

55. Carretta, ed., *Olaudah Equiano*, chap. 12; Adam Hochschild, *Bury the Chains: Prophets and Rebels in the Fight to Free an Empire's Slaves* (New York, 2005), 244–50.

CHAPTER FIVE. BLACK ABOLITIONISTS IN THE SLAVEHOLDING REPUBLIC

1. Richard S. Newman, *Freedom's Prophet: Bishop Richard Allen, the AME Church, and the Black Founding Fathers* (New York, 2008), 63–68; James Wood Sweet, *Bodies Politic: Negotiating Race in the American North, 1730–1830* (Baltimore, 2003), 336–40.

2. Joanna Brooks, "The Early American Public Sphere and the Emergence of a Black Print Counterpublic," *WMQ* 62 (January 2005): 67–98; Manisha Sinha, "An Alternative Tradition of Radicalism: African Americans and the Metaphor of Revolution, 1775–1865," in Manisha Sinha and Penny Von Eschen, eds., *Contested Democracy: Freedom, Race, and Power in American History* (New York, 2007), 9–30; Black Public Sphere Collective, *The Black Public Sphere: A Public Culture Book* (Chicago, 1995).

3. Richard S. Newman and Roy E. Finkenbine, "Black Founders in the New Republic," *WMQ* 64 (January 2007): 83–94.

4. Ira Berlin, "The Revolution in Black Life," in Alfred P. Young, ed., *The American Revolution: Explorations in the History of American Radicalism* (DeKalb, Ill., 1976), 349–82; William D. Piersen, *Black Yankees: The Development of an Afro-American Subculture in Eighteenth-Century New England* (Amherst, Mass., 1988), part 4; Joseph P. Reidy, "'Negro Election Day' and Black Community Life in New England, 1750–1860," *Marxist Perspectives* 1 (1978): 102–17; Theda Skocpol, Ariane Liazos, and Marshall Ganz, *What a Mighty Power We Can Be: African American Fraternal Groups and the Struggle for Racial Equality* (Princeton, 2006); William J. Novak, "The American Law of Association: The Legal–Political Construction of Civil Society," *Studies in American Political Development* 15 (Fall 2001): 163–88.

5. William H. Robinson, ed., *The Proceedings of the Free African Union Society and the African Benevolent Society* (Providence, 1976), introduction, 16, 58–59; James Campbell, *Middle Passages: African American Journeys to Africa, 1787–2005* (New York, 2006), 20–21, 54–56; Sweet, *Bodies Politic*, 328–35.

6. Robinson, ed., *Proceedings*, 19, 25, 32, 86–87; Gaillard Hunt, "William Thornton and Negro Colonization," *Proceedings of the American Antiquarian Society* 30 (April 14, 1921): 40–61; Floyd J. Miller, *The Search for Black Nationality: Black Emigration and Colonization, 1787–1863* (Urbana, 1975), 4–11.

7. Robinson, ed., *Proceedings*, 17–21, 24–34, 36–37, 43–47; George E. Brooks, "The Providence African Society," *International Journal of African Historical Studies* 7 (1974):

183–202; Conforti, *Samuel Hopkins*, 150–53; Miller, *The Search for Black Nationality*, 12–20.

8. Robinson, ed., *Proceedings*, 49–50, 81–82, 145–47, 153, 158–65, 171–72; William Patten, *A Sermon delivered at the Request of the African Benevolent Society* . . . (Newport, R.I., 1808), 10–15; *A Short History of the African Union Meeting and School-House* . . . (Providence, 1821), 5–9, 14–28.

9. Sidney Kaplan and Emma Nogrady Kaplan ed., *The Black Presence in the Era of the American Revolution, 1770–1800* (Washington, 1973), 202–14; Charles H. Wesley, *Prince Hall: Life and Legacy* (Washington, 1977); Lorenzo Johnston Greene, "Prince Hall: Massachusetts Leader in Crisis," *Freedomways* 1 (Fall 1961): 238–58; Corey D. B. Walker, *A Noble Fight: African American Freemasonry and the Struggle for Democracy in America* (Urbana, 2008), 7–12, 48–73; Chernoh Momodu Sesay Jr., "Emancipation and the Social Origins of Black Freemasonry, 1775–1800," in Peter P. Hinks and Stephen Kantrowitz, eds., *All Men Free and Brethren: Essays on the History of African American Freemasonry* (Ithaca, 2013), 21–39.

10. Wesley, *Prince Hall*, 66–72; Kaplan and Kaplan, eds., *The Black Presence*, 204–5, 207–11; Corey D. B. Walker, "Nation and Oration: The Political Language of African American Freemasonry in the Early Republic," in Hinks and Kantrowitz, eds., *All Men Free and Brethren*, 84–94; Christopher Cameron, *To Plead Our Own Cause: African Americans in Massachusetts and the Making of the Antislavery Movement* (Kent, Ohio, 2014).

11. Wesley, *Prince Hall*, 77–81; *A Sermon Preached* . . . *By the Right Reverend Marrant, Chaplain* (Boston, 1789), 3, 17–21; Joanna Brooks, *American Lazarus: Religion and the Rise of African-American and Native American Literatures* (New York, 2003), 126–35; Peter P. Hinks, "John Marrant and the Meaning of Free Black Masonry," *WMQ* 64 (January 2007): 105–16.

12. Wesley, *Prince Hall*, 72, 77; Dorothy Porter, ed., *Early Negro Writing, 1760–1837* (Boston, 1971), 63–69; John H. Bracey Jr. and Manisha Sinha, eds., *African American Mosaic: A Documentary History from the Slave Trade to the Twenty-First Century, Volume One — To 1877* (Upper Saddle River, N.J., 2004): 68–73.

13. Porter, ed., *Early Negro Writing*, 9–27; Hilary J. Moss, *Schooling Citizens: The Struggle for African American Education in Antebellum America* (Chicago, 2009), 136–37; James Oliver Horton and Lois E. Horton, *Black Bostonians: Family Life and Community Struggle in the Antebellum North* (New York, 1979), 28–30, 40–52; George A. Levesque, "Inherent Reformers–Inherited Orthodoxy: Black Baptists in Boston, 1800–1873," *JNH* 4 (1975): 491–525; Arthur O. White, "The Black Leadership Class and Education in Antebellum Boston," *Journal of Negro Education* 42 (Fall 1973): 504–15.

14. *Annals of the First African Church in the United States of America* . . . *By the Rev. Wm. Douglass, Rector* (Philadelphia, 1862), 15–40; Gary B. Nash, *Forging Freedom: The Formation of Philadelphia's Black Community, 1720–1840* (Cambridge, Mass., 1988), 66–79, 94–99.

15. *Annals of the First African Church*, 23–24, 40–85, 93–110, 118–22; *Constitution and Rules Observed Kept by the Friendly Society of St. Thomas' African Church, of*

Philadelphia (Philadelphia, 1799); Bracey and Sinha, eds., *African American Mosaic*, 63–64; Dagobert D. Runes, ed., *The Selected Writings of Benjamin Rush* (New York, 1947), 24–25; Nash, *Forging Freedom*, 109–20.

16. Bracey and Sinha, eds., *African American Mosaic*, 60–68; Charles H. Wesley, *Richard Allen: Apostle of Freedom* (Washington, 1935); Carol V. R. George, *Segregated Sabbaths: Richard Allen and the Emergence of Independent Black Churches, 1760–1840* (New York, 1973), chaps. 1–3.

17. *Articles of Association of the African Methodist Episcopal Church* . . . (Philadelphia, 1799); "African Supplement," in *The Life Experience and Gospel Labors of the Rt. Rev. Richard Allen* . . . (repr., Nashville, 1960), 37–41; Newman, *Freedom's Prophet*, 70–73, 130–36, 159–81; Dee Andrews, *The Methodists and Revolutionary America, 1760–1800* (Princeton, 2000), 139–50.

18. *Annals of the First African Church*, 110–13; L. H. Butterfield, ed., *Letters of Benjamin Rush*, vol. 2, 1793–1819 (Princeton, 1951), 639, 1071; John Gloucester to Benjamin Rush, January 11, 1812, Benjamin Rush Collection, BAP; Julie Winch, *Philadelphia's Black Elite: Activism, Accommodation and the Struggle for Autonomy, 1787–1848* (Philadelphia, 1988), 4–15; Winch, "'A Late Thing I Guess': The Early Years of Philadelphia's African Masonic Lodge," in Hinks and Kantrowitz, eds., *All Men Free and Brethren*, 63–83; Nash, *Forging Freedom*, 12, 199–210; Newman, *Freedom's Prophet*, 73–76.

19. Richard S. Newman, Roy E. Finkenbine, and Douglass Mooney, "Philadelphia Emigrationist Petitions, Circa 1792: An Introduction," *WMQ* 64 (January 2007): 161–66; Ruth Bogin, "Petitioning and the New Moral Economy of Post-Revolutionary America," *WMQ* 45 (July 1988): 391–425.

20. Herbert Aptheker, ed., *A Documentary History of the Negro People in the United States* (New York, 1951), 1:39–44.

21. Peter M. Bergman and Jean McCarroll, eds., *The Negro in the Congressional Record, 1789–1801* (New York, 1969), 2:154, 165–76; John Craig Hammond, *Slavery, Freedom, and Expansion in the Early American West* (Charlottesville, Va., 2007), 23–27.

22. Bracey and Sinha, eds., *African American Mosaic*, 58–59; Bergman and McCarroll, eds., *The Negro in the Congressional Record*, 2:55, 230–45.

23. "Letter from James Forten to George Thatcher, January 1800," BAP; Julie Winch, *A Gentleman of Color: The Life of James Forten* (New York, 2002); Ray Allen Billington, "James Forten, Forgotten Abolitionist," in John H. Bracey Jr., August Meier, and Elliot Rudwick, eds., *Blacks in the Abolitionist Movement* (Belmont, Calif., 1971), 4–16.

24. *A Short Account of the Rise and Progress of the African M.E. Church in America Written By Christopher Rush* . . . (New York, 1843), 57; Carla Peterson, *Black Gotham: A Family History of African Americans in Nineteenth-Century New York City* (New Haven, 2011), 50–55; Leslie M. Alexander, *African or American? Black Identity and Political Activism in New York City, 1784–1861* (Urbana, 2008), 8–13.

25. Craig Wilder, *In the Company of Black Men: The African Influence on African American Culture in New York City* (New York, 2001), chap. 2; Peterson, *Black Gotham*, 44–46; Leslie Harris, *In the Shadow of Slavery: African Americans in New York City, 1626–1863* (Chicago, 2003), 82–85; John H. Hewitt, "Peter Williams, Jr.: New

York's First African-American Episcopal Priest," *New York History* 79 (April 1998): 101–29.

26. John J. Zuille, *Historical Sketch of the New York African Society for Mutual Relief Organized in the City of New York . . .* (New York, 1892), 5–9, 15–18, 41–47, 52–53; Porter, ed., *Early Negro Writing*, 37–50; Wilder, *In the Company of Men*, chaps. 4–6; Craig Wilder, "Black Life in Freedom: Creating a Civic Culture," in Ira Berlin and Leslie Harris, eds., *Slavery in New York* (New York, 2005), 217–37; Daniel Perlman, "Organizations of the Free Negro in New York City, 1800–1860," *JNH* 56 (July 1871): 181–97.

27. Wilder, *In the Company of Men*, 45–47, 81–83, 138–40, 154–55, 161–64; Carla Peterson, "Black Life in Freedom: Creating an Elite Culture," in Berlin and Harris, eds., *Slavery in New York*, 183–214; Peterson, *Black Gotham*, 64–66.

28. Shane White, "'It was a Proud Day': African Americans, Festivals, and Parades in the North, 1741–1834," *JAH* (June 1994): 13–50; White, "Black Life in Freedom: Creating a Popular Culture," in Berlin and Harris, eds., *Slavery in New York*, 165–80; White, *Stories of Freedom in Black New York* (Cambridge, Mass., 2002); David Waldstreicher, *In the Midst of Perpetual Fetes: The Making of American Nationalism, 1776–1820* (Chapel Hill, 1997), esp. chap. 6.

29. Christopher Phillips, *Freedom's Port: The African American Community of Baltimore, 1790–1860* (Urbana, 1997), 127–38; Leroy Graham, *Baltimore: The Nineteenth Century Black Capital* (New York, 1982), 63, 72–75; Leonard P. Curry, *The Free Black in Urban America, 1800–1850: The Shadow of a Dream* (Chicago, 1981), chap. 11; John W. Davis, "George Liele and Andrew Bryan, Pioneer Negro Baptist Preachers," *JNH* 3 (April 1918): 119–27.

30. Herbert Aptheker, "Eighteenth-Century Petition of South Carolina Negroes," *JNH* 31 (January 1946): 98–99; Aptheker, ed., *A Documentary History*, 1:29–31; Robert L. Harris Jr., "Early Black Benevolent Associations, 1780–1830," *Massachusetts Review* 20 (Autumn 1979): 603–26; Jane G. Landers, ed., *Against the Odds: Free Blacks in the Slave Societies of the Americas* (London, 1996) (see esp. chapters by Olwell, Hangar, and Lachance); Ira Berlin, *Slaves Without Masters: The Free Negro in the Antebellum South* (New York, 1974).

31. *Memoir of Benjamin Banneker . . . By John H. B. Latrobe, Esq.* (Baltimore, 1845); *Banneker, The Afric-American Astronomer. From the Posthumous Papers of Martha E[llicott] Tyson. Edited by her Daughter* (Philadelphia, 1884); Porter, ed., *Early Negro Writing*, 324–29; Kaplan and Kaplan, eds., *The Black Presence*, 132–51; cf. Richard Newman, "'Good Communications Corrects Bad Manners': The Banneker–Jefferson Dialogue and the Project of White Uplift," in John Craig Hammond and Matthew Mason, eds., *Contesting Slavery: The Politics of Bondage and Freedom in the New American Nation* (Charlottesville, Va., 2011), 69–93.

32. Silvio A. Bedini, *The Life of Benjamin Banneker: The Definitive Biography of the First Black Man of Science* (New York, 1972), 164, 279–83; Louis Ruchames, ed., *Racial Thought in America*, vol. 1, *From the Puritans to Abraham Lincoln* (Amherst, Mass., 1969), 257.

33. Aptheker, ed., *A Documentary History*, 1:23; Bedini, *The Life of Benjamin Banneker*, 96–102, 143–201, 323; L. H. Butterfield, ed., *Letters of Benjamin Rush*, vol. 1, 1761–1792 (Princeton, 1951), 497.

34. Benjamin Banneker, *Banneker's Almanac and Ephemeris for the Year of our Lord 1793* . . . (Philadelphia, 1793), and *Banneker's Almanac, For the Year 1795* . . . (Philadelphia, 1795); Sandy Perot, "'But what are colours? Do complexions change human intellects?' Abolitionism and Benjamin Banneker's *Almanack*," unpublished manuscript; Bedini, *The Life of Benjamin Banneker*, 283–300.

35. Bracey and Sinha, eds., *African American Mosaic*, 1:32–45; Chandler B. Saint and George A. Krimsky, *Making Freedom: The Extraordinary Life of Venture Smith* (Middletown, Conn., 2009); Philip Gould, "'Remarkable Liberty,'" in Carretta and Gould, eds., *Genius in Bondage*, 123–28; Robert E. Desrochers Jr., "'Not Fade Away': The Narrative of Venture Smith, an African American in the Early Republic," *JAH* 84 (June 1997): 40–66; James Brewer Stewart, ed., *Venture Smith and the Business of Slavery and Freedom* (Amherst, Mass., 2010).

36. *The Life Experience and Gospel Labors of the Rt. Rev. Richard Allen*, 48–65; Butterfield, ed., *Letters of Benjamin Rush*, 2:731–32; Brooks, *American Lazarus*, chap. 5; Newman, *Freedom's Prophet*, chaps. 3, 4.

37. *The Life Experience and Gospel Labors of the Rt. Rev. Richard Allen*, 69–71.

38. Philip S. Foner and James Branham, eds., *Lift Every Voice: African American Oratory, 1787–1900* (Tuscaloosa, 1998), 58; Henry Weincek, *An Imperfect God: George Washington, His Slaves and the Creation of America* (New York, 2003); Richard S. Newman, "'We Participate in Common': Richard Allen's Eulogy of Washington and the Challenge of Interracial Appeals," *WMQ* 64 (January 2007): 117–28; François Furstenberg, *In the Name of the Father: Washington's Legacy, Slavery and the Making of a Nation* (New York, 2006), chap. 2.

39. *A Collection of Hymns and Spiritual Songs. From Various Authors. By the Rev. Richard Allen* . . . (Philadelphia, 1801), 11–12, 16, 33, 69–70; *The Life Experience and Gospel Labors of the Rt. Rev. Richard Allen*, 42–47, 72–74; Newman, *Freedom's Prophet*, chap. 6.

40. William L. Andrews, *To Tell a Free Story: The First Century of Afro-American Autobiography, 1760–1865* (Urbana, 1986), 49–51; *The Narrative and Confession of Thomas Powers* . . . (Norwich, Conn., 1796); [Richard Allen], *Confessions of John Joyce* . . . (Philadelphia, 1808), 5; [Allen], *Confession of Peter Mathias* . . . (Philadelphia, 1808), 30–35; Richard Newman, ed., *Black Preacher to White America: The Collected Writings of Lemuel Haynes, 1774–1833* (Brooklyn, N.Y., 1990), 223, 225.

41. Manisha Sinha, "To 'Cast Just Obliquy' on Oppressors: Black Radicalism in the Age of Revolution," *WMQ* 44 (January 2007): 149–60; William B. Gravely, "The Dialectic of Double Consciousness in Black American Freedom Celebrations, 1808–1863," *JNH* 67 (Winter 1982): 302–17; Genevieve Fabre, "African-American Commemorative Celebrations in the Nineteenth Century," in Genevieve Fabre and Robert O'Meally, eds., *History and Memory in African-American Culture* (New York, 1994), 77–80; Mitch Kachun, *Festivals of Freedom: Memory and Meaning in African American Emancipation Celebrations* (Amherst, Mass., 2003), chap. 1.

42. Porter, ed., *Early Negro Writing*, 336–37, 346–48, 384, 396.

43. Ibid., 348–49, 369, 396; Henry Johnson, *An Oration on the Abolition of the African Slave Trade With an Introductory Address by Adam Carman* . . . (New York, 1810), 8, 10; Jeremiah Gloucester, *An Oration Delivered on January 1, 1823 in Bethel Church on the Abolition of the Slave Trade* (Philadelphia, 1823), 7.

44. Adam Carman, *An Oration Delivered at the Fourth Anniversary of the Abolition of the African Slave Trade* . . . (New York, 1811), 3, 11–13; Ian Baucom, *Specters of the Atlantic: Finance Capital, Slavery and the Philosophy of History* (Durham, 2005); Philip Gould, *Barbaric Traffic: Commerce and Antislavery in the Eighteenth-Century Atlantic World* (Cambridge, Mass., 2003).

45. Porter, ed., *Early Negro Writing*, 347, 380, 395–98; Carman, *An Oration*, 19; Gloucester, *An Oration*, 11; John Teasman, *An Address Delivered in the African Episcopal Church* . . . (New York, 1811), 5–11; Michael A. Morrison and James Brewer Stewart, eds., *Race and the Early Republic: Racial Consciousness and Nation Building in the Early Republic* (New York, 2002).

46. *A Discourse, Delivered at the African-Meeting House* . . . *By Jedidiah Morse* . . . (Boston, 1808), 17; *A Sermon Delivered in Boston, Before the African Society* . . . *By Thomas Gray* . . . (Boston, 1818), 3–5; *A Discourse Delivered before the African Society* . . . *By Paul Dean* . . . (Boston, 1819), 6, 10–15; *A Discourse Delivered Before the African Society* . . . *By Rev. Thaddeus Mason Harris, DD* (Boston, 1822).

47. Porter, ed. *Early Negro Writing*, 36–37, 360–62; Baker, ed., "A Slave to Thomas Jefferson, November 30, 1808," and Thomas N. Baker, "Sources and Interpretations: 'A Slave' Writes Thomas Jefferson," *WMQ* 68 (January 2011): 127–39, 140–54.

48. Porter, *Early Negro Writing*, 353, 357–58, 373, 379, 382.

49. *A Dialogue between a Virginian and an African Minister, written by the Rev Daniel Coker* . . . (Baltimore, 1810), 4–6, 7–8, 10–13, 15–18, 20–25, 28–29, 30–31, 35, 38–40.

50. George W. Williams, *History of the Negro Race in America from 1619 to 1860: Negroes as Slaves, as Soldiers, and as Citizens*, vol. 2, 1800 to 1880 (New York, 1883), chaps. 2, 3; William C. Nell, *The Colored Patriots of the American Revolution* . . . (Boston, 1855), 181–88, 286–306; Gerald Horne, *Negro Comrades of the Crown: African Americans and the British Empire Fight the U.S. Before Emancipation* (New York, 2012), chaps. 1–6; W. Jeffrey Bolster, *Black Jacks: African American Seamen in the Age of Sail* (Cambridge, Mass., 1997), chap. 4; Gerard T. Altoff, *Amongst My Best Men: African Americans and the War of 1812* (Put-in-Bay, Ohio, 1996); Frank A. Cassell, "Slaves of the Chesapeake Bay Area and the War of 1812," *JNH* 57 (April 1972): 144–55; Alan Taylor, *The Internal Enemy: Slavery and War in Virginia, 1772–1832* (New York, 2013), 208–13; Nathaniel Millett, *The Maroons of Prospect Bluff and Their Quest for Freedom in the Atlantic World* (Gainesville, Fla., 2013); Harvey Amani Whitfield, *Blacks on the Border: The Black Refugees in British North America, 1815–1860* (Hanover, N.H., 2006).

51. James Forten, *Letters from a Man of Colour, on a late bill before the Senate of Pennsylvania* (Philadelphia, 1813), 1–11; Winch, *A Gentleman of Color*, 169–74.

52. *A Search for Truth* . . . *By Jacob Oson A Descendant of Africa* (New York, 1817), 3–11; Stephen G. Hall, *A Faithful Account of the Race: African American Historical Writing in Nineteenth-Century America* (Chapel Hill, 2009), 28–32.

53. Graham Russell Hodges, ed., *Black Itinerants of the Gospel: The Narratives of John Jea and George White* (Madison, 1993), 52–53, 60–61; Andrews, *To Tell a Free Story*, 52–56.

54. Hodges, ed., *Black Itinerants of the Gospel*, 89–94, 97–105, 111–19, 147–58, 168; Henry Louis Gates Jr., *The Signifying Monkey: A Theory of Afro-American Literary Criticism* (New York, 1988); Dickson D. Bruce, *The Origins of African American Literature 1680–1865* (Charlottesville, Va., 2001), 103–4; Andrews dates Jea's narrative to 1811, *To Tell a Free Story*, 48; David Kazanjian, *The Colonizing Trick: National Culture and Imperial Citizenship in Early America* (Minneapolis, 2003), 69–73.

55. Newman, ed., *Black Preacher to White America*, 74–75, 82, 119, 152–54, 157, 158, 167.

56. Henri Grégoire, *An Enquiry Concerning the Intellectual and Moral Faculties, and Literature of Negroes*, Graham Russell Hodges, ed. (Armonk, N.Y., 1997), 115; Ruchames ed., *Racial Thought in America*, 256–r7.

CHAPTER SIX. THE NEGLECTED PERIOD OF ANTISLAVERY

1. Jesse Torrey, A *Portraiture of Domestic Slavery in the United States* . . . (Philadelphia, 1817), 42–44.

2. Alice Dana Adams, *The Neglected Period of Anti-Slavery in America, 1808–1831* (Williamstown, Mass., 1973); Ousmane Power-Greene, *Against Wind and Tide: The African American Struggle Against the Colonization Movement* (New York, 2014); cf. David Brion Davis, *The Problem of Slavery in the Age of Emancipation* (New York, 2014), 84–86, 107.

3. Robert Pierce Forbes, *The Missouri Compromise and Its Aftermath: Slavery and the Meaning of America* (Chapel Hill, 2007); John Craig Hammond, *Slavery, Freedom, and Expansion in the Early West* (Charlottesville, Va., 2007); Matthew Mason, *Slavery and Politics in the Early American Republic* (Chapel Hill, 2006), chaps. 5, 6; David Brion Davis, "The Emergence of Immediatism in British and American Antislavery Thought," *MVHR* 49 (1962): 797–878.

4. Rosalind Cobb Wiggins, ed., *Captain Paul Cuffe's Logs and Letters, 1807–1817: A Black Quaker's "Voice from within the Veil"* (Washington, 1996), 103, 119, 148; James Pemberton to Paul Cuffe, June [8], September 27, 1808, Paul Cuffe to William Allen, April 22, 24, 1811, August 10, 1813, Elisha Tyson to Paul Cuffe, May 12, July 20, 1813, John Murray Jr. to Paul Cuffe, November 18, 1816, Cuffe Papers, New Bedford Public Library, *BAP*; Moses Brown to Paul Cuffe, June 10, 1812, Moses Brown Papers, Rhode Island Historical Society, *BAP*; James Sidbury, *Becoming African in America: Race and Nation in the Early Black Atlantic* (New York, 2007), 145–55; Kevin G. Lowther, *The African American Odyssey of John Kizell: A South Carolina Slave Returns to Fight the African Slave Trade in His African Homeland* (Columbia, S.C., 2011), chap. 7; Wayne Ackerson, *The African Institution (1807–1823) and the Antislavery Movement in Great Britain* (Lewiston, N.Y., 2005), 72–76; Lamont D. Thomas, *Paul Cuffe: Black Entrepreneur and Pan-Africanist* (Urbana, 1988), 35.

5. Paul Cuffe to James Madison, June 20, 1812, Prince Saunders to Paul Cuffe, June 25, August 3, 1812, Perry Locks to Paul Cuffe, July 15, 1813, Thomas Clarkson and William

Allen to Paul Cuffe, July 1, William Allen to Paul Cuffe, August 4, 13, October 29, 1812, Samuel J. Mills to Paul Cuffe, July 10, 1814, July 10, December 26, 1816, July 14, 1817, March 12, 1817, James Forten to Paul Cuffe, January 5, February 15, 1815, January 25, 28, April 14, July 25, 1817, Robert Finley to Paul Cuffe, December 5, 1816, Peter Williams Jr. to Paul Cuffe, March 22, 1817, John Gloucester to Paul Cuffe, July 22, 1817, Cuffe Papers, New Bedford Public Library, *BAP*.

6. Wiggins, ed., *Captain Paul Cuffe's Logs and Letters,*145, 252–53, 271, 276, 434–35, 436, 446, 455, 509; *A Brief Account of the Settlement and Present Situation of the Colony of Sierra Leone . . .* (New York, 1812), 3–12; Sheldon H. Harris, *Paul Cuffe: Black America and the African Return* (New York, 1972), 182–85; Floyd J. Miller, *The Search for a Black Nationality: Black Emigration and Colonization, 1787–1863* (Urbana, 1973), chap. 2.; Peter Williams, Jun., *A Discourse Delivered on the Death of Capt. Paul Cuffe . . .* (New York, 1817), 4–6, 8–9, 11–12, 15–16.

7. Robert Finley, *Thoughts on the Colonization of Free Blacks* [Washington, 1816], 1–2, 4–7; *ARCJ*, March 1825; P. J. Staudenraus, *The African Colonization Movement, 1816–1865* (New York, 1961), chap. 2; Hugh Davis, *Leonard Bacon: New England Reformer and Antislavery Moderate* (Baton Rouge, 1998), chap. 3; Mathew Spooner, "'I Know this Scheme is from God': Toward a Reconsideration of the Origins of the American Colonization Society," *S&A* (2013): 1–15.

8. *A Letter from General Harper, of Maryland, to Elias Caldwell . . .* (Baltimore, 1818), 7–11, 15–19, 29–32; *Memorial of the President and Board of Managers of The American Colonization . . .* (Washington, 1820), 3–6; *First Report of the New York Colonization Society . . .* (New York, 1823), 30–33; *ARCJ*, April 1826; *The Twelfth Annual Report of the American Society for the Colonizing of Free People of Colour . . .* (Washington, 1829), v–ix, 1, 22–24, 50–56; Staudenraus, *The African Colonization Movement*, chaps. 3, 5; Andrew Shankman, "Neither Infinite Wretchedness nor Positive Good: Mathew Carey and Henry Clay on Political Economy and Slavery during the Long 1820s," in John Craig Hammond and Matthew Mason, eds., *Contesting Slavery: The Politics of Bondage and Freedom in the New American Nation* (Charlottesville, Va., 2011), 247–66; Douglas R. Egerton, *Charles Fenton Mercer and the Trial of National Conservatism* (Jackson, Miss., 1989), 106–12, 161–73; Egerton "'Its Origin is Not a Little Curious': A New Look at the American Colonization Society," *JER* 5 (Winter 1985): 463–80; Eric Robert Papenfuse, *The Evils of Necessity: Robert Goodloe Harper and the Moral Dilemma of Slavery* (Philadelphia, 1997), chap. 3; Nicholas Guyatt, "'The Outskirts of Our Happiness': Race and the Lure of Colonization in the Early Republic," *JAH* 95 (March 2009): 986–1011.

9. Wm. Lloyd Garrison, *Thoughts on African Colonization . . .* (Boston, 1832), 9–13; Wiggins, ed., *Captain Paul Cuffe's Logs and Letters*, 502; Julie Winch, *A Gentleman of Color: The Life of James Forten* (New York, 2002), chap. 8.

10. Staudenraus, *The African Colonization Movement*, 34; Marie Tyler-McGraw, *An African Republic: Black and White Virginians in the Making of Liberia* (Chapel Hill, 2007); Eric Burin, *Slavery and the Peculiar Solution: A History of the American Colonization Society* (Gainesville, Fla., 2005); Douglas R. Egerton, "Averting a Crisis: The Proslavery Critique of the American Colonization Society," *CWH* 43 (June 1997):

142–56; Claude A. Clegg III, *The Price of Liberty: African Americans and the Making of Liberia* (Chapel Hill, 2004).

11. *ARCJ*, March 1825; November 1827; Archibald Alexander, *A History of Colonization on the Western Coast of Africa*, 2d ed. (Philadelphia, 1849), 98–218; Staudenraus, *The African Colonization Movement*, chaps. 4, 6; Leonard Bacon, *A Plea for Africa . . .* (New Haven, 1825), 9–12, 16–19; Bacon, *A Discourse Preached in the Center Church . . .* (New Haven, 1828), 9–14, 23; Davis, *Leonard Bacon*, 55–64; Ralph Randolph Gurley, *Life of Jehudi Ashmun . . .* (Washington, 1835), 73–89, 113–17, 134–37, 148–49, 154, 182–92, 390–94; *The Twelfth Annual Report*, vii, 2–4, 47; *First Report of the New York Colonization Society*, 12–14.

12. *ARCJ*, April 1825; May 1825; March 1826; July 1826; August 1826; October 1826; May 1827; September 1827; November 1827; May 1828; December 1828; October 1837; *A Concise History of the Commencement, Progress and Present Condition of the American Colonies in Liberia By Samuel Wilkeson* (Washington, 1839), 73; *A Sketch of the Origin and Progress of the American Colonization Society . . .* (Hartford, 1833); R. R. Gurley, *A Discourse . . .* (Washington, 1825), 14–19; Elizabeth Varon, "Evangelical Womanhood and the Politics of the African Colonization Movement in Virginia," in John R. McKivigan and Mitchell Snay, eds., *Religion and the Antebellum Debate over Slavery* (Athens, Ga., 1998), 169–93.

13. *Journal of Daniel Coker . . .* (Baltimore, 1820), 12, 17–19, 31–34, 42–48; Amos J. Beyan, *The American Colonization Society and the Creation of the Liberian State: A Historical Perspective, 1822–1900* (Lanham, Md., 1991), chaps. 2, 4; Leroy Graham, *Baltimore: The Nineteenth Century Black Capital* (New York, 1982), 75–77; Lowther, *The African American Odyssey*, 209–25.

14. Gurley, *Life of Ashmun*, 29–34, 134–36; *ARCJ*, October 1825; October 1827; December 1827; March 1828; October 1828; March 1829; June 1829; March 1830; June 1830; February 1832; May 1834; September 1837; *The Twelfth Annual Report*, 19–21; Bell I. Wiley, ed., *Slaves No More: Letters from Liberia 1833–1869* (Lexington, Ky., 1980); Beyan, *The American Colonization Society*, chap. 2; Howard Temperley, "African American Aspirations and the Settlement of Liberia," *S&A* 21 (2000): 67–92; Frankie Hutton, "Economic Considerations in the American Colonization Society's Early Effort to Emigrate Free Blacks to Liberia, 1816–1836," *JNH* 68 (Autumn 1983): 376–89; Tyler-McGraw, *An African Republic*, 64–70; James Wesley Smith, *Sojourners in Search of Freedom: The Settlement of Liberia by Black Americans* (Lanham, Md., 1987), 14–78; Tom W. Schick, *Behold the Promised Land: A History of Afro-American Settler Society in Nineteenth-Century Liberia* (Baltimore, 1977), chap. 2; Jeremiah Gloucester, *An Oration Delivered on January 1, 1823 . . .* (Philadelphia, 1823), 13.

15. Prince Saunders, *Haytian Papers . . .* (Boston, 1818), *An Address Delivered at Bethel Church, Philadelphia . . .* (Philadelphia, 1818), *A Memoir Presented to the American Convention for Promoting the Abolition of Slavery and Improving the Condition of the African Race . . .* (Philadelphia, 1818), 13–17; Thomas Clarkson to Prince Saunders, February 3, 1819, Miscellaneous Manuscripts, Henry E. Huntington Library, *BAP*; Arthur O. White, "Prince Saunders: An Instance of Social Mobility Among Antebellum

New England Blacks," *JNH* 60 (October 1975): 526–35; *Niles Weekly Register* 18 (July 1820): 326; *GUE*, Third Month 1821; Ninth Month 1822; September 17, 1825; Chris Dixon, "An Ambivalent Black Nationalism: Haiti, Africa, and Antebellum African American Emigrationism," *Australasian Journal of American Studies* 10 (December 1991): 10–25; Sara C. Fanning, "The Roots of Early Black Nationalism: Northern African Americans' Invocations of Haiti in the Early Nineteenth Century," *S&A* 28 (April 2007): 61–85.

16. *GUE*, January, March, April, August 1825; *Correspondence Relative to Emigration to Hayti . . .* (New York, 1824), 2–6, 7–10, 18–22, 29–31; *Information for the Free People of Colour, who are inclined to emigrate to Haiti* (New York, 1824), 3–6, 10; Newman, *Freedom's Prophet*, 20; Dorothy Porter, ed., *Early Negro Writing, 1760–1837* (Boston, 1971), 279–80; *Narrative of the Life and Adventures of Paul Cuffe . . .* (Vernon, Conn., 1839), 5; Alfred N. Hunt, *Haiti's Influence on Antebellum America: Slumbering Volcano in the Caribbean* (Baton Rouge, 1988), 165–70; Leon D. Pamphile, *Haitians and African Americans: A Heritage of Tragedy and Hope* (Gainesville, Fla., 2001), 34–46; Chris Dixon, *African America and Haiti: Emigration and Black Nationalism in the Nineteenth Century* (Westport, Conn., 2000), 34–49; Sara Fanning, *Caribbean Crossing: African Americans and the Haitian Emigration Movement* (New York, 2014).

17. *GUE*, Sixth Month, 1824; October, November 1824; January, February, March, June, October 8, 1825; June 3, 10, 1826; December 4, 1829; H. M. Wagstaff, ed., *Minutes of the N.C. Manumission Society, 1816–1834* (Chapel Hill, 1934), 82–84; Bruce Dain, *A Hideous Monster of the Mind: American Race Theory in the Early Republic* (Cambridge, Mass., 2002), 93–104; *The Life, Travels and Opinions of Benjamin Lundy . . .* (Philadelphia, 1847), 191–94; Merton L. Dillon, *Benjamin Lundy and the Struggle for Negro Freedom* (Urbana, 1966), chap. 6.

18. *Minutes of the Eighteenth Session of the American Convention . . .* (Philadelphia, 1823), 28–31; Edward Needles, *An Historical Memoir of the Pennsylvania Society for Promoting the Abolition of Slavery . . .* (Philadelphia, 1848), 81–82; vol. 11, July 15, 1817–January 17, 1842, pp. 26, 39, 61, 69–70, 73–74, 82–83, New York Manumission Society Records, NYHS.

19. Elias Hicks, *Observations on the Slavery of the Africans and Their Descendants . . .* (New York, 1811), 3–14, 23–24; Paul Buckley, ed., *The Journal of Elias Hicks* (San Francisco, 2009), introduction; Larry Ingle, *Quakers in Conflict: The Hicksite Reformation* (Knoxville, 1986); Kathleen G. Velsor, *The Underground Railroad on Long Island: Friends in Freedom* (Charleston, S.C., 2013); Thomas D. Hamm, "George F. White and Hicksite Opposition to the Abolitionist Movement," in Brycchan Carey and Geoffrey Plank, eds., *Quakers and Abolition* (Urbana, 2014), 43–55; Ryan P. Jordan, *Slavery and the Meetinghouse: Quakers and the Abolitionist Dilemma, 1820–1865* (Bloomington, 2007).

20. *An Exposition of the Treatment of Slaves in the Southern States . . .* (New Brunswick, N.J., 1815), iii, iv, 6–7, 16–18, 21–22, 24, 29–34.

21. John W. Christie and Dwight L. Dumond, *George Bourne and The Book and Slavery Irreconcilable* (Baltimore, 1969), 106–9, 113–17, 120–21, 126–27, 135–38, 140–46, 162–67,

186–92; Lester B. Scherer, *Slavery and the Churches in Early America, 1619–1819* (Grand Rapids, 1975), 134; *TL*, August 25, 1832.

22. John Kenrick, *Horrors of Slavery in Two Parts . . .* (Cambridge, 1817), 1–4; *TL*, February 2, June 8, 1833.

23. Torrey, *A Portraiture of Domestic Slavery*, 18–22, 28–30, 37–62; *TL*, February 2 1833.

24. *Minutes of the Proceedings of the Fourteenth American Convention for Promoting the Abolition of Slavery, and Improving the Condition of the African Race: Assembled at Philadelphia* (Philadelphia, 1816), 30–32; *Minutes of the Proceedings of the Fifteenth American Convention for Promoting the Abolition of Slavery, and Improving the Condition of the African Race: Assembled at Philadelphia* (Philadelphia, 1817), 31; Benjamin Quarles, *Black Abolitionists* (New York, 1969), 12; *Minutes of the Proceedings of a Special Meeting of the Fifteenth American Convention for Promoting the Abolition of Slavery, and Improving the Condition of the African Race: Assembled at Philadelphia* (Philadelphia, 1818), 47–54; *Minutes of the Seventeenth Session of the American Convention for Promoting the Abolition of Slavery, and Improving the Condition of the African Race. Convened at Philadelphia* (Philadelphia, 1821), 50–55; "Reports of the American Convention of Abolition Societies on Negroes and on Slavery, their Appeals to Congress, and their Addresses to the Citizens of the United States," *JNH* 6 (July 1921): 349–57; Adams, *The Neglected Period of Anti-Slavery*, 154–207.

25. David Barrow, *Involuntary, Unmerited, Absolute, Hereditary Slavery, Examined . . .* (Lexington, Ky., 1808), 11, 17–18, 28; *Address from the Manumission Society of Tennessee to the Free Men of the State, On Account of the Oppressed Africans Therein* (Rogersville, Tenn., 1816), 3–5; *The Emancipator (Complete) . . .* (Nashville, 1932), v–x, 2, 17, 60–61, 91, 111–12; *Minutes of the Eighteenth Session of the American Convention*, 16–19; James D. Essig, *The Bonds of Wickedness: American Evangelicals Against Slavery, 1770–1808* (Philadelphia, 1982), 140–51; Scherer, *Slavery and the Churches*, 135–37; Jeffrey Brook Allen, "Were Southern White Critics of Slavery Racists? Kentucky and the Upper South, 1791–1824," *JSH* 44 (May 1978): 169–90; James Brewer Stewart, "Evangelicalism and the Radical Strain in Southern Antislavery Thought During the 1820s," *JSH* 39 (August 1973): 379–96.

26. H. M. Wagstaff, ed., *Minutes of the N.C. Manumission Society, 1816–1834* (Chapel Hill, 1934), 37–39, 57–60, 62, 75–79, 81–93; *Minutes of an Adjourned Session of the American Convention for Promoting the Abolition of Slavery and Improving the Condition of the African Race . . .* (Baltimore, 1826), 32–39; Letitia Woods Brown, *Free Negroes in the District of Columbia, 1790–1846* (New York, 1972), 124–25; Gordon Finnie, "The Antislavery Movement in the Upper South before 1840," *JSH* 35 (August 1969): 319–34; Kenneth M. Stampp, "The Fate of the Southern Antislavery Movement," *JNH* 28 (January 1943): 10–22; Scherer, *Slavery and the Churches*, 131–34; A. Glenn Crothers, *Quakers Living in the Lion's Mouth: The Society of Friends in Northern Virginia, 1730–1865* (Gainesville, Fla., 2012), chaps. 4, 7; Patricia Hickin, "Gentle Agitator: Samuel M. Janney and the Antislavery Movement in Virginia, 1842–1851," *JSH* 37 (May 1971): 159–88.

27. *Minutes of the Proceedings of the Sixteenth American Convention . . .* (Philadelphia, 1819), 30–32; Hammond, *Slavery, Expansion, and Freedom in the Early American*

West, 139–45; [John S. Tyson], *Life of Elisha Tyson, the Philanthropist By a Citizen of Baltimore* (Baltimore, 1825), 99–102; Thomas D. Morris, *Free Men All: The Personal Liberty Laws of the North, 1780–1861* (Baltimore, 1974), 220–22; Mason, *Slavery and Politics*, 130–45; Adams, *The Neglected Period of Anti-Slavery*, chap. 20; Brown, *Free Negroes in the District of Columbia*, 125–28.

28. *An Oration Delivered before the Semi-Annual Meeting of the Union Humane Society . . . By Thos. H. Genin, Esq.* (Mount Pleasant, Ohio, 1818), 3–5, 7–9, 29, 31–32, 35–36.

29. *The Life, Travels and Opinions of Benjamin Lundy*, 9–23; Benjamin Lundy, *Circular To The Advocates of African Emancipation . . .* [St. Clairsville, Ohio, 1816]; *Minutes of the Eighteenth Session of the American Convention*, 42; GUE, Seventh Month, Twelfth Month 1821, First Month 1822; Needles, *An Historical Memoir*, 83–84; Dillon, *Benjamin Lundy*, chap. 1; Jane H. Pease and William H. Pease, *Bound with Them in Chains: A Biographical History of the Antislavery Movement* (Westport, Conn., 1972), chap. 5.

30. *Minutes of the Eighteenth Session of the American Convention*, 42–65; GUE, November 1824; W. Wilberforce, *An Appeal to the Religion, Justice and Humanity of the Inhabitants . . .* (London, 1823); T. Clarkson, *Thoughts on the Necessity of Improving the Condition of Slaves in the British Colonies . . .* (London, 1823); *Antislavery Recollections in A Series of Letters Addressed to Mrs. Beecher Stowe Written by Sir George Stephen*, 2d ed. (London, 1971), with a new introduction by Howard Temperley; F. J. Klingberg, *The Anti-Slavery Movement in England: A Study in English Humanitarianism* (New Haven, 1926); Betty Fladeland, *Men and Brothers: Anglo-American Antislavery Cooperation* (Urbana, 1972), 168–81; Seymour Drescher, *From Slavery to Freedom: Comparative Studies in the Rise and Fall of Atlantic Slavery* (New York, 1999), chap. 3; Robin Blackburn, *The Overthrow of Colonial Slavery, 1776–1848* (London, 1988), 421–23; David Turley, *The Culture of English Antislavery, 1780–1860* (New York, 1991).

31. *Minutes of the Adjourned Session of the Twentieth Biennial American Convention*, 44–52; *Minutes of the Twenty-First Biennial American Convention*, 37–47; GUE, Fifth Month 1823; Fifth Month 1824; December 1826; Charles Marriott, *An Address to the Members of the Religious Society of Friends . . .* (New York, 1835), 5, 15; *Minutes of Proceedings of the Requited Labor Convention . . .* (Philadelphia, 1838), 28; Ruth Ketring Nueremberger, *The Free Produce Movement: A Quaker Protest Against Slavery* (New York, 1942); Clare Midgley, "Slave Sugar Boycotts, Female Activism and the Domestic Base of British Anti-Slavery Culture," *S&A* 17 (December 1996); Carol Faulkner, "The Root of the Evil: Free Produce and Radical Antislavery, 1820–1860," *JER* 27 (Fall 2007): 377–405; Lawrence B. Glickman, "'Buy for the Sake of the Slave': Abolitionism and the Origins of Consumer Activism," *American Quarterly* 56 (December 2004): 889–912.

32. [Elizabeth Heyrick], *Immediate not Gradual Abolition . . .* (New York, 1825), 3–5, 9–16; Clare Midgley, *Women Against Slavery: The British Campaigns of 1780–1870* (London, 1992), 43–51, 58–71, 103–8; Seymour Drescher, *Abolition: A History of Slavery and Antislavery* (Cambridge, Eng., 2009), 248–52.

33. *Minutes of the Twenty-First Biennial American Convention for Promoting the Abolition of Slavery*, 48; GUE, January 7, 14, 21, 1825; September 2, 16, December 4, 1829;

Elizabeth Margaret Chandler, *Essays, Philanthropic and Moral Principally Relating to the Abolition of Slavery in America* (Philadelphia, 1845), 7–9, 37–39, 43–48, 51–52, 75–76, 115–17; Benjamin Lundy, *The Poetical Works of Elizabeth Margaret Chandler With a Memoir of Her Life and Character* (Philadelphia, 1845), 11–13, 16–25, 40–41, 59, 70–71; Marcia J. Heringa Mason, *Remember the Distance that Divides Us: The Family Letters of Philadelphia Quaker Abolitionist and Elizabeth Margaret Chandler, 1830–1842* (East Lansing, 2004), xxxvi–xxxix; Gay Gibson Cima, *Performing Anti-Slavery: Activist Women on Antebellum Stages* (Cambridge, Eng., 2014).

34. Benjamin Lundy, *A Plan for the Gradual Emancipation of Slavery in the United States Without Danger to the Citizens of the South* (Baltimore, 1825); *The Life, Travels and Opinions of Benjamin Lundy*, 29–30; *GUE*, February 24, 1827; May, June, October 1830; *Niles Weekly Register*, May 19, 1827; Dillon, *Benjamin Lundy*, 133–39.

35. *GUE*, November 26, December 10, 27, 1825; January 28, February 11, 1826; February 24, August 25, 1827; February 23, March 8, 15, 21, 1828; October 1830; Robert Dale Owen, *Twenty-Seven Years of Autobiography: Threading My Way* (London, 1874), 101–12, 264–72; Josephine M. Elliot, ed., *Robert Dale Owen's Travel Journal, 1827* (Indianapolis, 1977), 28; Dillon, *Benjamin Lundy*, chap. 7; Celia Morris Eckhart, *Fanny Wright: Rebel in America* (Cambridge, Mass., 1984), 86–102, 108–67; Sean Wilentz, *Chants Democratic: New York City and the Rise of the American Working Class, 1788–1850* (New York, 1984), 176–216; Philip Sheldon Foner, *History of the Labor Movement in the United States* (New York, 1947): 1:129–40; Arthur E. Bestor, *Backwoods Utopia: The Sectarian and Owenite Phases of Communitarian Socialism in America, 1663–1829* (Philadelphia, 1950); Robert Dale Owen, *The Policy of Emancipation . . .* (Philadelphia, 1863).

36. Nathan Perkins, *The National Sins, and National Punishment in the Recently Declared War . . .* (Hartford, 1812), 16–18; E. Parish, *A Protest Against the War . . .* (Newburyport, Mass., 1812), 13–17; Rachel Hope Cleves, *The Reign of Terror in America: Visions of Violence from Anti-Jacobinism to Antislavery* (Cambridge, Eng., 2009), 153–93, 230–48; Matthew Mason, "Federalists, Abolitionists, and the Problem of Influence," *American Nineteenth-Century History* 10 (March 2009): 1–27; Marc M. Arkin, "The Federalist Trope: Power and Passion in Abolitionist Rhetoric," *JAH* 9 (June 2001): 75–98; Leonard L. Richards, *The Slave Power: The Free North and Southern Domination, 1780–1860* (Baton Rouge, 2000), chap. 2; Albert F. Simpson, "The Political Significance of Slave Representation, 1787–1821," *JSH* 7 (August 1941): 333–42; Linda Kerber, *Federalists in Dissent: Imagery and Ideology in Jeffersonian America* (Ithaca, 1970), chap. 2; Sean Wilentz, *The Rise of American Democracy: Jefferson to Lincoln* (New York, 2005), 159–68; John L. Thomas, *The Liberator: William Lloyd Garrison, A Biography* (Boston, 1963), 28–35.

37. John Craig Hammond, *Slavery, Expansion, and Freedom in the Early American West* (Charlottesville, Va., 2007); Mason, *Slavery and Politics*, 145–56; Philip J. Schwartz, *Migrants Against Slavery: Virginians and the Nation* (Charlottesville, Va., 2001); Susan Cooper Guasco, *Confronting Slavery: Edward Coles and the Rise of Anti-Slavery Politics in Nineteenth-Century America* (DeKalb, Ill., 2013); Eugene Berwanger, *The Frontier Against Slavery: Western Anti-Negro Prejudice and the Slavery Extension Con-*

troversy (Urbana, 1967), chap. 1; Christopher P. Lehman, *Slavery in the Upper Mississippi Valley, 1787–1865: A History of Human Bondage in Illinois, Iowa, Minnesota and Wisconsin* (Jefferson, N.C., 2011).

38. Glover Moore, *The Missouri Controversy, 1819–1821* (Lexington, Ky., 1953), 1–64, 84–128, 281–87, 314–15; Hammond, *Slavery, Expansion, and Freedom,* chap. 8; Mason, *Slavery and Politics,* chap. 8; Major L. Wilson, *Space, Time, and Freedom: The Quest for Nationality and the Irrepressible Conflict, 1815–1861* (Westport, Conn., 1974), chap. 2; Forbes, *The Missouri Compromise and Its Aftermath,* chap. 2; Richards, *The Slave Power,* chap. 3; *Speech of the Honorable James Tallmadge, Jr . . .* (New York, 1819), 5, 13–15; *Remarks of Mr. Taylor* [Philadelphia, 1819], 1–6; *Select Speeches of John Sergeant of Pennsylvania* (Philadelphia, 1832), 185–233; *Substance of Two Speeches, Delivered in the Senate of the United States on the Subject of the Missouri Bill by the Hon. Rufus King of New York* (New York, 1819), 9–19, 23–25, 27–32; Robert Ernst, *Rufus King: American Federalist* (Chapel Hill, 1968), 369–78; Joshua Michael Zeitz, "The Missouri Compromise Reconsidered: Antislavery Rhetoric and the Emergence of the Free Labor Synthesis," *JER* 20 (Autumn 2000), 447–85; John R. Howe Jr., "John Adam's View of Slavery," *JNH* 49 (July 1964), 201–6.

39. Moore, *The Missouri Controversy,* 218–73; Russel Kirk, *John Randolph of Roanoke: A Study in American Politics, With Selected Speeches and Letters* (Indianapolis, 1978), 183–89; Norman K. Risjord, *The Old Republicans: Southern Conservatives in the Age of Jefferson* (New York, 1965), 213–22; John Chester Miller, *The Wolf by the Ears: Thomas Jefferson and Slavery* (New York, 1977); William W. Freehling, *The Road to Disunion: Secessionists at Bay, 1776–1854* (New York, 1990), 1: chaps. 7, 8; Lacy K. Ford, *Deliver Us from Evil: The Slavery Question in the Old South* (New York, 2009), 74–76; Manisha Sinha, *The Counterrevolution of Slavery: Politics and Ideology in Antebellum South Carolina* (Chapel Hill, 2000), 16.

40. Moore, *The Missouri Controversy,* chaps. 4, 5; Forbes, *The Missouri Compromise and Its Aftermath,* chap. 3; Mason, *Slavery and Politics,* chap. 9; Richards, *The Slave Power,* chap. 4; Sinha, *The Counterrevolution of Slavery,* 14–15.

41. *Minutes of the Proceedings of the Fifteenth American Convention,* 42–43; *The Life, Travels and Opinions of Benjamin Lundy,* 18–19; *Life of Elisha Tyson,* 102–6; *At a Numerous Meeting of the Citizens of Boston and its Vicinity . . .* [Boston, 1819]; *Minutes of the Proceedings of the Sixteenth American,* 10–11, 16, 18–27, 33, 60–62; *Minutes of the Seventeenth Session of the American Convention,* 22–25, 46–48; James G. Basker, ed., *Early American Abolitionists: A Collection of Anti-Slavery Writings, 1760–1820* (New York, 2005), 319–51; *Speech of the Honorable James Tallmadge, Jr.,* 17–20; Needles, *An Historical Memoir,* 68–69; *The Emancipator,* 87–89, 105–11; *GUE,* I Seventh Month 1821; "Reports of the American Convention of Abolition Societies on Negroes and on Slavery," 328–33.

42. Daniel Raymond, Esq. *The Missouri Question* (Baltimore, 1819), 3–7, 9–23, 25–26, 29–39; Raymond, *Thoughts on Political Economy* (Baltimore, 1820), 456; *Select Speeches of John Sergeant,* 237–56; Allen Kaufman, *Capitalism, Slavery and Republican Values, 1819–1848* (Austin, 1982), 243–314.

43. Fladeland, *Men and Brothers*, 170–71; Robert Walsh Jr., *An Appeal From the Judgments of Great Britain Respecting the United States of America . . .* (Philadelphia, 1819), 306–424; [Robert Walsh], *Free Remarks on the Spirit of the Federal Constitution . . .* (Philadelphia, 1819), 32–33, 83–84, 98–100; [Joseph Blunt], *An Examination of the Expediency and Constitutionality of Prohibiting Slavery in the State of Missouri By Marcus* (New York, 1819), 3–7, 13, 17–22; *Niles' Weekly Register*, May 15, 22, June 19, 26, July 17, August 14, 21, 1819; Padraig Riley, "Slavery and the Problem of Democracy in Jeffersonian America," in Hammond and Mason, eds., *Contesting Slavery*, 228–46.

44. [James (misidentified as William) Hillhouse], *The Crisis. No. 1 or Thoughts on Slavery Occasioned by the Missouri Question* (New Haven, 1820), 3–4, 6–7; *The Crisis. No. 2 or Thoughts on Slavery Occasioned by the Missouri Question . . .* (New Haven, 1820), 3–5, 7–10, 14–19; *Pocohontas; A Proclamation: With Plates* [New Haven, 1820], 3, 9–13; Gary Nash, "Race and Citizenship in the Early Republic," in Richard Newman and James Mueller, eds., *Antislavery and Abolition in Philadelphia: Emancipation and the Long Struggle for Racial Justice in the City of Brotherly Love* (Baton Rouge, 2011), 90–117; Martin Ohman, "Perfecting Independence: Tench Coxe and the Political Economy of Western Development," *JER* 31 (Fall 2011): 397–433; Sven Beckert, *Empire of Cotton: A Global History* (New York, 2014), chap. 2.

45. *Minutes of the Nineteenth Session of the American Convention . . .* (Philadelphia, 1825), 10–16, 33–35; *Minutes of the Adjourned Session*, 7, 28–29, 44–47; *Minutes of the Twentieth Session of the American Convention . . .* (Baltimore, 1827), 22–25, 29–31; *Minutes of the Adjourned Session of the Twentieth Biennial American Convention . . .* (Philadelphia, 1828), 17–24, 33–35; *GUE*, September 12, 1825; *Minutes of the Twenty-First Biennial American . . .* (Philadelphia, 1829), 19–35, 37–48; "Reports of the American Convention of Abolition Societies on Negroes and on Slavery," 310–16, 326–28, 342–49, 364–74; *The Life, Travels and Opinions of Benjamin Lundy*, 30; David G. Smith, *On the Edge of Freedom: The Fugitive Slave Issue in South Central Pennsylvania, 1820–1870* (New York, 2013), 74–78; Dwight Lowell Dumond, *Antislavery: The Crusade for Freedom in America* (Ann Arbor, 1961), 236–37.

CHAPTER SEVEN. INTERRACIAL IMMEDIATISM

1. *An Address Delivered on the Celebration of the Abolition of Slavery in the State of New York . . . By Nathaniel Paul . . .* (Albany, 1827), 23; *FJ*, December 19, 1828.

2. Ann C. Loveland, "Evangelicalism and 'Immediate Abolition' in American Antislavery Thought," *Journal of Social History* (1966): 172–88; David W. Blight, "Perceptions of Southern Intransigence and the Rise of Radical Antislavery Thought, 1816–1830," *JER* 3 (Summer 1983): 139–63.

3. Nathan O. Hatch, *The Democratization of American Christianity* (New Haven, 1989); Robert H. Abzug, *Cosmos Crumbling: American Reform and the Religious Imagination* (New York, 1994); John R. McKivigan, *The War Against Proslavery Religion: Abolitionism and the Northern Churches, 1830–1865* (Ithaca, 1984), 19–24.

4. Benjamin Quarles, *Black Abolitionists* (New York, 1969); Paul Goodman, *Of One Blood: Abolitionism and the Origins of Racial Equality* (Berkeley, 1998), chap. 3; Rich-

ard S. Newman, *The Transformation of American Abolitionism: Fighting Slavery in the Early Republic* (Chapel Hill, 2002); Manisha Sinha, "Coming of Age: The Historiography of Black Abolitionism," in Timothy Patrick McCarthy and John Stauffer, eds. *Prophets of Protest: Reconsidering the History of American Abolitionism* (New York, 2006), 23–38.

5. Vincent Harding, *There Is a River: The Black Struggle for Freedom in America* (New York, 1981); Sterling Stuckey, *Slave Culture: Nationalist Theory and the Foundations of Black America* (New York, 1987); Merton L. Dillon, *Slavery Attacked: Southern Slaves and Their Allies, 1619–1865* (Baton Rouge, 1990); Gelien Matthews, *Caribbean Slave Revolts and the British Abolitionist Movement* (Baton Rouge, 2006).

6. Lionel H. Kennedy and Thomas Parker, eds., *An Official Report of the Trials of Sundry Negroes . . .* (Charleston, S.C., 1822); James Hamilton Jr., *An Account of the Late Intended Insurrection Among a Portion of the Blacks of this City* (Charleston, S.C., 1822); GUE, Twelfth Month, 1822; "The Making of a Slave Conspiracy, Part I," *WMQ* 58 (October 2001): 913–76; "The Making of a Slave Conspiracy, Part II," *WMQ* 59 (January 2002): 153–268; Douglas R. Egerton, *He Shall Go Out Free: The Lives of Denmark Vesey* (Madison, 1999); Egerton "Of Facts and Fables: New Light on the Denmark Vesey Affair," *South Carolina Historical Magazine* 105 (January 2004): 8–48; Robert L. Paquette, "From Rebellion to Revisionism: The Continuing Debate about the Denmark Vesey Affair," *Journal of the Historical Society* 4 (Fall 2004): 8–48; James O"Neil Spady, "Power and Confession: On the Credibility of the Earliest Reports of the Denmark Vesey Slave Conspiracy," *WMQ* 68 (April 2011): 287–304.

7. *Niles Weekly Register*, September 14, 1822; Manisha Sinha, *The Counterrevolution of Slavery: Politics and Ideology in Antebellum South Carolina* (Chapel Hill, 2000), 14–16; John Lofton, *Denmark Vesey's Revolt: The Slave Plot that Lit a Fuse to Fort Sumter* (Kent, Ohio, 1964); Peter P. Hinks, *To Awaken My Afflicted Brethren: David Walker and the Problem of Antebellum Slave Resistance* (University Park, Pa., 1997); *Slave Insurrection in Southampton County, Va. . . . Compiled and Published by Henry Bibb* (New York, 1850), 1–7; Egerton, *He Shall Go Out Free*, xxiii, xxiv, 203–28; *Christian Recorder*, March 6, 1869.

8. L. Glen Inabinet, "'The July Fourth Incident' of 1816: An Insurrection Plotted by Slaves in Camden, South Carolina," in Herbert A. Johnson, ed., *South Carolina Legal History* (Spartanburg, S.C., 1980), 209–21; Emilia Viotti da Costa, *Crowns of Glory, Tears of Blood: The Demerara Slave Rebellion of 1823* (New York, 1994); Michael Craton, *Testing the Chains: Resistance to Slavery in the British West Indies* (Ithaca, 1982), chaps. 20, 21; GUE, First Month, 1824; [Elizabeth Heyrick], *Immediate not Gradual Abolition . . .* (New York, 1825), 7–8, 13, 21–22.

9. *Truth, Self-Supported . . . By Robert Wedderburn . . .* (London, [1795]); Iain McCalman ed., *The Horrors of Slavery and Other Writings by Robert Wedderburn* (Princeton, 1991), introduction, 47, 59, 81–83, 85–87, 89–103, 105–10, 133, 139; McCalman, "Anti-Slavery and Ultra-Radicalism in Early Nineteenth-Century England: The Case of Robert Wedderburn," *S&A* 7 (September 1986): 99–117.

10. [John S. Tyson], *Life of Elisha Tyson . . .* (Baltimore, 1825), 107–10; *The Farewell Address of Elisha Tyson . . .* (Baltimore, 1824), 8; GUE, April 1830; Leroy Graham,

Baltimore, the Nineteenth Century Black Capital (Lanham, Md., 1982), 70, 82–85, 95–107.

11. *ARCJ*, December 1826, July 1829; Andrew Diemer, "The Quaker and the Colonist: Moses Sheppard, Samuel Ford McGill, and Transatlantic Antislavery across the Color Line," in Brycchan Carey and Geoffrey Plank, eds., *Quakers and Abolition* (Urbana, 2014), 135–48; Christopher Phillips, *Freedom's Port: The African American Community of Baltimore, 1790–1860* (Urbana, 1997), 186–87; 214–15; 230–31.

12. Graham Russell Hodges, *Roots and Branch: African Americans in New York and East Jersey, 1619–1863* (Chapel Hill, 1999), 192; David N. Gellman and David Quigley, eds., *Jim Crow New York: A Documentary History of Race and Citizenship, 1777–1877* (New York, 2003), 64–66, 73–83, 87–200; Joanne Pope Melish, *Disowning Slavery: Gradual Emancipation and "Race" in New England, 1780–1860* (Ithaca, 1998), 172–83; John Wood Sweet, *Bodies Politic: Negotiating Race in the American North, 1730–1830* (Baltimore, 2003), 378–90; Shane White, *Stories of Freedom in Black New York* (Cambridge, Mass., 2002).

13. Porter, ed., *Early Negro Writing*, 100–104; *FJ*, June 1, 27, 29, July 6, 13, 20, 27, October 12, 1827; Philip S. Foner and Robert James Branham, eds., *Lift Every Voice: African American Oratory, 1787–1900* (Tuscaloosa, 1998), 107–8; Mitch Kachun, *Festivals of Freedom: Memory and Meaning in African American Emancipation Celebrations, 1808–1915* (Amherst, Mass., 2003), 42–53.

14. *FJ*, April 20, 1827; July 11, 18, 1828; *An Address Delivered on the Celebration of the Abolition of Slavery in the State of New York*, 5–6, 11–12; Nathaniel Paul, *An Address Delivered at Troy on the Celebration of the Abolition of Slavery . . .* (Albany, 1829), 8–12; Robert S. Levine, "Fifth of July: Nathaniel Paul and the Construction of Black Nationalism," in Vincent Carretta and Philip Gould, eds., *Genius in Bondage: Literature of the Early Black Atlantic* (Lexington, Ky., 2001), 242–60; Leonard I. Sweet, "The Fourth of July and Black Americans in the Nineteenth Century: Northern Leadership Opinion within the Context of the Black Experience," *JNH* 61 (July 1976): 256–75.

15. *A Selection from The Freedom's Journal . . .* (New York, 1987); *FJ*, March 16, September 14, 1827; David E. Swift, *Black Prophets of Justice: Activist Clergy Before the Civil War* (Baton Rouge, 1989), chap. 3; Jane H. Pease and William H. Pease, *Bound with Them in Chains: A Biographical History of the Antislavery Movement* (Westport, Conn., 1972), chap. 7.

16. *FJ*, March 16, 23, 30, April 6, 4, 13, July 6, September 28, 1827; *GUE*, September 15, 1827, November 8, 1828; Jacqueline Bacon, *Freedom's Journal: The First African-American Newspaper* (Lanham, Md., 2007); Timothy Patrick McCarthy, "'To Plead Our Own Cause': Black Print Culture and the Origins of American Abolitionism," in McCarthy and Stauffer, eds., *Prophets of Protest*, 114–33; David Kazanjian, *The Colonizing Trick: National Culture and Imperial Citizenship in Early America* (Minneapolis, 2003), 126–32.

17. *FJ*, June 15, August 17, 24, 1827; July 25, October 17, 31, 1828; Dain, *A Hideous Monster of the Mind*, 123–36.

18. *FJ*, March 16, April 6, 20, 27, May 4, 11, 18, June 14, 29, October 12, 1827; January 18, 25, February 8, 15, 1828; Jacqueline Bacon, "'A Revolution Unexampled in the History of

Man': The Haitian Revolution in Freedom's Journal, 1827–1829," in Maurice Jackson and Bacon, eds., *African Americans and the Haitian Revolution: Selected Essays and Historical Documents* (New York, 2010), 81–92.

19. *FJ*, May 18, June 8, July 6, August 24, 31, September 7, 14, 21, 28, October 5, 12, 19, 26, November 2, 9, 16, 23, 30, December 7, 1827; January 2, March 7, 1829; *African Colonization: Proceedings of the Formation of the New York State Colonization Society . . .* (Albany, 1829).

20. *FJ*, February 14, 21, 1829; Sandra Sandiford Young, "A Different Journey: John Brown Russwurm, 1799–1851" (Ph.D. diss., Boston College, 2004), 75–217, 241–50; Young, "John Brown Russwurm's Dilemma: Citizenship or Emigration?," in McCarthy and Stauffer, eds., *Prophets of Protest*, 90–113; *ARCJ*, April, May, June 1830; March 1831; Winston James, *The Struggles of John Brown Russwurm: The Life and Writings of a Pan-Africanist Pioneer, 1799–1851* (New York, 2010), chaps. 2, 3; Amos J. Beyan, *African American Settlements in West Africa: John Brown Russwurm and the American Civilizing Efforts* (New York, 2005).

21. *FJ*, March 16, 1827; April 25, October 24, December 19, 1828; Terry Alford, *Prince Among Slaves: The True Story of an African Prince Sold into Slavery in the American South* (New York, 1977); Hinks, *To Awaken My Afflicted Brethren*, chaps. 1–3; Stuckey, *Slave Culture*, 98–121; Quarles, *Black Abolitionists*, 16–17; Donald M. Jacobs, "David Walker: Boston Race Leader, 1825–1830," *Essex Institute Historical Collections* 107 (January 1971): 94–107; George R. Price and James Brewer Stewart, eds., *To Heal the Scourge of Prejudice: The Life and Writings of Hosea Easton* (Amherst, Mass., 1999), 6, 51–62.

22. *Walker's Appeal with a Brief Sketch of His Life By Henry Highland Garnet . . .* (New York, 1848), 11–13, 17–22, 25–27, 29–33, 38–46, 48–56, 66–81, 84–87; Herbert Aptheker, *One Continual Cry: David Walker's Appeal to the Coloured Citizens of the World, 1829–1830: Its Setting and Its Meaning, Together with the full text of the third, and last, edition of the Appeal* (New York, 1965); Rufus Burrow Jr., *God and Human Responsibility: David Walker and Ethical Prophecy* (Macon, Ga., 2003), chaps. 3–5; Mia Bay, *The White Image in the Black Mind: African-American Ideas About White People, 1830–1925* (New York, 2000), 32–36; Hinks, *To Awaken My Afflicted Brethren*, chaps. 4, 6–8.

23. Richard Newman, Patrick Rael, and Phillip Lapansky, eds., *Pamphlets of Protest: An Anthology of Early African American Protest Literature, 1790–1860* (New York, 2001), 84–89; Dain, *A Hideous Monster of the Mind*, 136–48.

24. John Malvin, *North into Freedom: The Autobiography of John Malvin, Free Negro, 1795–1880*, Allan Peskin, ed. (Cleveland, 1966), 38–44, 66–67; *FJ*, December 5, 1828; *ARCJ*, August, October 1829; Nikki Marie Taylor, *Frontiers of Freedom: Cincinnati's Black Community, 1802–1868* (Athens, Ohio, 2005), introduction, chaps. 1–3; Marilyn Baily, "From Cincinnati, Ohio to Wilberforce, Canada: A Note on Antebellum Colonization," *JNH* 58 (October 1973): 427–40; Harry E. Davis, "John Malvin, a Western Reserve Pioneer," *JNH* 23 (October 1938): 426–38.

25. *Rights of All*, May 29, June 12, August 14, September 12, 1829; Bella Gross, "*Freedom's Journal* and the *Rights of All*," *JNH* 17 (1932): 281–86.

26. Porter, ed., *Early Negro Writing*, 281–85, 295–99, 301; ARCJ, March 1831.

27. Howard Holman Bell, ed., *Minutes of the Proceedings of the National Negro Conventions, 1830–1864* (New York, 1969), iii, iv, 5, 9–12, Bell, *A Survey of the Negro Convention Movement, 1830–1861* (New York, 1969), chap. 2; Harry Reed, *Platform for Change: The Foundations of the Northern Free Black Community, 1775–1865* (East Lansing, 1994), 135–41.

28. *Minutes and Proceedings of the First Annual Convention of the People of Colour . . .* (Philadelphia, 1831), 3–7, 10–15, in Bell, ed., *Minutes*; Herbert Aptheker, ed., *A Documentary History of the Negro People in the United States: From the Colonial Times to the Civil War* (New York, 1951), 1:109–11; Julie Winch, ed., *The Elite of Our People: Joseph Willson's Sketches of Black Upper-Class Life in Antebellum Philadelphia* (University Park, Pa., 2002), 103–5.

29. Aptheker, *A Documentary History*, 1:111–14; FJ, May 11, 1827; Gary B. Nash, *Forging Freedom: The Formation of Philadelphia's Black Community, 1720–1840* (Cambridge, Mass., 1988), 253–59; Julie Winch, *Philadelphia's Black Elite: Activism, Accommodation, and the Struggle for Autonomy, 1787–1848* (Philadelphia, 1988), chap. 5; Theodore Hershberg, "Free Blacks in Antebellum Philadelphia: A Study of Ex-Slaves, Freeborn, and Socio Economic Decline," *Journal of Social History*, 183–209; Porter, ed., *Early Negro Writing*, 113–14, 119; David Zimmerman, "William Whipper in the Black Abolitionist Tradition," http://www.millersville.edu/~ugrr/resources/columbia/whipper.html; Richard P. McCormick, "William Whipper, Moral Reformer," PH 43 (January 1976): 22–46; Winch, *A Gentleman of Color*, 233–35.

30. *The Confessions of Nat Turner . . .* (Baltimore, 1831), 3; Louis Masur, *1831: Year of Eclipse* (New York, 2001), 9–34; Hinks, *To Awaken My Afflicted Brethren*, chap. 5; Glenn M. McNair, "The Elijah Burritt Affair: David Walker's *Appeal* and Partisan Journalism in Antebellum Milledgeville," *Georgia Historical Quarterly* 83 (Fall 1999): 448–78; Clement Eaton, "A Dangerous Pamphlet in the Old South, JSH 2 (August 1936): 323–34; Marshall Rachleff, "Document: David Walker's Southern Agent," JNH 62 (January 1977): 100–103; William H. Pease and Jane H. Pease, "Walker's *Appeal* Comes to Charleston: A Note and Documents," JNH 59 (July 1974): 287–92; Harding, *There Is a River*, 77–85, 94.

31. *The Confessions of Nat Turner*, 3–5, 7–11, 18–19; [Bibb], *Slave Insurrection in Southampton County*, 8–12; Peter H. Wood, "Nat Turner: The Unknown Slave as Visionary Leader," in Leon Litwack and August Meier, eds., *Black Leaders of the Nineteenth Century* (Urbana, 1988), 21–40; Herbert Aptheker, *Nat Turner's Slave Rebellion Together with the Full Text of the So-Called "Confessions" of Nat Turner Made in Prison in 1831* (New York, 1966); Kenneth S. Greenberg, ed., *Nat Turner: A Slave Rebellion in History and Memory* (New York, 2003), parts 1, 3; Stephen B. Oates, *The Fires of Jubilee: Nat Turner's Fierce Rebellion* (New York, 1975); Scot French, *The Rebellious Slave: Nat Turner in American Memory* (Boston, 2004), chaps. 1–3; Jean Fagan Yellin, *The Intricate Knot: Black Figures in American Literature, 1776–1863* (New York, 1972), chap. 9.

32. Thomas R. Dew, *Review of the Debate in the Virginia Legislature . . .* (Richmond, 1832); Eva Sheppard Wolf, *Race and Liberty in the New Nation: Emancipation in*

Virginia from the Revolution to Nat Turner's Rebellion (Baton Rouge, 2006), 185–238; Alison Goodyear Freehling, *Drift Toward Dissolution: The Virginia Slavery Debate of 1831–1832* (Baton Rouge, 1982); Penelope Campbell, *Maryland in Africa: The Maryland Colonization Society, 1831–1857* (Urbana, 1971), chaps. 1–3; William W. Freehling, *The Road to Disunion: Secessionists at Bay, 1776–1854* (New York, 1990): 1: chaps. 10, 11.

33. [Samuel Warner], *Authentic and Impartial Narrative of the Tragical Scene . . .* (New York, 1831), 6, 19–31, 35–38; Ira Berlin, "Documents: After Nat Turner: A Letter from the North," *JNH* 55 (1970): 144–51; *The Letter of Appomattox to the People of Virginia . . .* (Richmond, 1832), 21–27.

34. Henry Bleby, *Death Struggles of Slavery . . .* (London, 1853), 1–2, 116–18; Craton, *Testing the Chains*, 291–323; Gad Heuman, *Between Black and White: Race, Politics, and the Free Coloreds in Jamaica, 1792–1865* (Westport, Conn., 1995); Vincent Brown, *The Reaper's Garden: Death and Power in the World of Atlantic Slavery* (Cambridge, Mass., 2008), 232–35; Blackburn, *The Overthrow of Colonial Slavery*, 423–36, 451–52; Drescher, *Abolition*, 260–63.

35. Sara Salih, ed., *The History of Mary Prince: A West Indian Slave* (London, 2000), 3, 8–12, 16–21, 24–25, 31–38, 55, 64; Barbara Baumgartner, "The Body as Evidence: Resistance, Collaboration, and Appropriation in 'The History of Mary Prince,'" *Callaloo* 24 (Winter 2001): 253–75; Edlie L. Wong, *Neither Fugitive nor Free: Atlantic Slavery, Freedom Suits, and the Legal Culture of Travel* (New York, 2009), 36–63; Clare Midgley, *Women Against Slavery: The British Campaigns of 1780–1870* (London, 1992), 86–92.

36. [Francis Jackson Garrison and Wendell Phillips Garrison], *William Lloyd Garrison, 1805–1879: The Story of His Life told By His Children*, vol. 1, 1805–1835 (New York, 1885), chaps. 1–4; *GUE*, November 8, 1828; Henry Mayer, *All on Fire: William Lloyd Garrison and the Abolition of Slavery* (New York, 1998), 3–60.

37. *William Lloyd Garrison*, 1:126–38; Mayer, *All on Fire*, 68–69; Thomas, *The Liberator*, 101–3.

38. *GUE*, November 27, December 18, 1829; January 15, 29, May, June, October, November 1830; Bettye J. Gardner, "William Watkins: Antebellum Black Teacher and Anti-Slavery Writer," *Negro History Bulletin* 39 (September/October 1976): 623–25; Graham, *Baltimore*, chap. 2; *William Lloyd Garrison*, 1:148–49; Mayer, *All on Fire*, 79–82.

39. *William Lloyd Garrison*, 1:174–99, 202–4; Walter M. Merrill, *Against Wind and Tide: A Biography of William Lloyd Garrison* (Cambridge, Mass., 1963), 9; *TL*, January 1, 15, 1831; Mayer, *All on Fire*, 94.

40. *GUE*, December 1830; *The Life, Travels, and Opinions of Benjamin Lundy*, 30–186; Oliver Johnson, *William Lloyd Garrison and His Times . . .* (Boston, 1880), 28–31, 39; Dillon, *Benjamin Lundy and the Struggle for Negro Freedom*, chaps. 10–14.

41. *TL*, March 5, 12, April 9, 23, 30, May 14, 28, September 3, November 26, 1831, April 21, 1832; *William Lloyd Garrison*, 1:199–202, 212–24; James Forten to Garrison, December 31, 1830; February 2, 23, August 9, 1831; July 28, 1832; George Cary to Garrison, June 6, 1831; Joseph Cassey to Garrison, October 16, 1832; February 15, 1834;

February 12, 1835; William Watkins to Garrison, July 2, September 13, 1835, *BAP*, reel 1; Deborah Bingham Van Broekhoven, *The Devotion of These Women: Rhode Island in the Antislavery Network* (Amherst, Mass., 2002), 10–11, 15; Quarles, *Black Abolitionists*, 18–22; Charles H. Wesley, "The Negro in the Organization of Abolition," *Phylon* 2 (Third Quarter 1941): 223–25; Donald M. Jacobs, "William Lloyd Garrison's *Liberator* and Boston's Blacks, 1830–1865," *NEQ* 44 (June 1971): 259–61.

42. TL, January 1, January 8, January 15, March 12, June 4, November 26, 1831; *William Lloyd Garrison*, 1:351.

43. TL, January 1, 8, 15, 22, 29, February 26, April 30, May 14, 28, September 3, 10, 17, 24, October 1, 8, 1831; January 14, March 10, 1832; *The Abolitionist*, January 1833; Walter M. Merrill ed., *The Letters of William Lloyd Garrison*, vol. 1, *I Will be Heard! 1822–1835* (Cambridge, Mass., 1971), 149, 151–53, 195–96; Donald M. Jacobs, "David Walker and William Lloyd Garrison: Racial Cooperation and the Shaping of Boston Abolition," in Jacobs, ed., *Courage and Conscience: Black and White Abolitionists in Boston* (Bloomington, 1993), 7–17; Johnson, *William Lloyd Garrison*, 51–52, 60–66; Mayer, *All on Fire*, 116.

44. TL, March 12, April 2, July 2, 30, August 20, September 3, 17, November 5, December 10, 17, 1831; January 21, 1832; Louis R. Mehlinger, "The Attitude of the Free Negro Towards African Colonization," *JNH* 1 (July 1916): 283–88.

45. *American Colonization Society, and the Colony at Liberia Published by the Massachusetts Colonization Society* (Boston, 1831), 15; Wm. Lloyd Garrison, *Thoughts on African Colonization* . . . (Boston, 1832), preface, part 1: 5–9, 54, 57, 71–72, 78–80, 90, 103–10, 122–24, 129–34, 141–50; part 2: 4–6, 8; TL, September 17, 1831; January 28, October 27, 1832; Bruce Rosen, "Abolition and Colonization, The Years of Conflict, 1829–1834," *Phylon* 33 (Second Quarter 1972): 181–88.

46. TL, September 17, October 1, 1831; January 14, August 20, October 20, 1832; March 23, 30, April 13, May 4, June 22, 1833; Merrill ed., *The Letters of William Lloyd Garrison*, 1:217, 220–22, 261–62, 267–69; R. J. M. Blackett, *Building an Antislavery Wall: Black Americans in the Atlantic Abolitionist Movement, 1830–1860* (Baton Rouge, 1983), 52–69; *Reply to Mr. Joseph Phillips' Enquiry . . . By the Rev. Nathaniel Paul . . .* (N.p. [1832]); *A Letter to Thomas Clarkson by James Cropper: And Prejudice Vincible . . . By C. Stuart* (New York, 1833); Betty Fladeland, *Men and Brothers: Anglo-American Antislavery Cooperation* (Urbana, 1972), 204–20; David B. Davis, "James Cropper and the British Anti-Slavery Movement, 1823–1833," *JNH* 46 (April 1961): 154–73; Anthony J. Barker, *Captain Charles Stuart: Anglo-American Abolitionist* (Baton Rouge, 1986), chap. 3; *The Abolitionist*, June, October, December 1833.

47. *Speeches Delivered at the Anti-Colonization Meeting in Exeter Hall . . .* (Boston, 1833), 3–4, 7, 11, 13–15, 29–30, 39–40; TL, October 1, 1831; July 6, 13, August 10, 31, September 7, October 12, 19, November 2, 1833; *The Abolitionist*, January, March 1833; *Second Annual Report of the Board of Managers of the New England Anti Slavery Society . . .* (Boston, 1834), 31–48; *William Lloyd Garrison*, 1:372–73; Foner and Branham, eds., *Lift Every Voice*, 130–35; *First Annual Report of the Board of Managers of the New England Anti Slavery Society . . .* (Boston, 1833), 51–53; TE, January 7, 1841.

48. Merrill, ed., *The Letters of William Lloyd Garrison*, 1:215; *TL*, July 6, August 31, September 7, October 19, 1833; *William Lloyd Garrison*, 1:379; Porter, ed., *Early Negro Writing*, 6, 29, 32; Van Gosse, "'As a Nation, the English Are Our Friends': The Emergence of African American Politics in the British Atlantic World, 1776–1861," *AHR* 113 (October 2008): 1003–28; *The Abolitionist*, July 1833.

49. *TL*, May 28, July 2, 1831; February 18, April 14, June 23, September 22, October 13, December 1, 22, 1832; March 23, April 6, June 8, 1833; *The Abolitionist*, January, February, May, June 1833; Johnson, *William Lloyd Garrison*, 84–88; Samuel J. May, *Some Recollections of Our Antislavery Conflict* (Boston, 1869), 17–20, 31; Donald Yacovone, *Samuel Joseph May and the Dilemmas of the Liberal Persuasion, 1797–1871* (Philadelphia, 1991), chap. 3; Nina Moore Tiffany, *Samuel E. Sewall: A Memoir* (Boston, 1898), 33–42; Gilbert H. Barnes and Dwight L. Dumond, eds., *Letters of Theodore Dwight Weld, Angelina Grimké Weld and Sarah Grimké, 1822–1844* (Gloucester, Mass., 1965), 1:94–99; Charles A. Jarvis, "Admission to Abolition: The Case of John Greenleaf Whittier," *JER* 4 (Summer 1984): 161–76; Roman J. Zorn, "The New England Anti-Slavery Society: Pioneer Abolitionist Organization," *JNH* 52 (July 1957): 157–76; Lawrence B. Goodheart, *Abolitionist, Actuary, Atheist: Elizur Wright and the Reform Impulse* (Kent, Ohio, 1990), chaps. 4, 5; Milton C. Sernett, *Abolition's Axe: Beriah Green, Oneida Institute, and the Black Freedom Struggle* (Syracuse, 1986), 18–30; Lewis Tappan, *The Life of Arthur Tappan* (New York, 1871), 73–76, 88–142; Bertram Wyatt-Brown, *Lewis Tappan and the Evangelical War Against Slavery* (Cleveland, 1969), 45–52; Mayer, *All on Fire*, 131; Newman, *The Transformation of American Abolitionism*, 188–90.

50. *TL*, August 25, September 1, 15, 22, 29, October 6, 13, 20, 1832; May, *Some Recollections of Our Antislavery Conflict*, 10; Samuel J. May, *On Prejudice* (Boston, 1830), 6; John Rankin, *Letters on American Slavery . . .* (Boston, 1833), 7, 12–15, 20, 29, 35, 46, 52, 58, 116–18; James Duncan, *A Treatise on Slavery . . .* (1824; repr., New York, 1840), 25–38, 44–45, 50–55, 61, 73–74, 107–11, 123–24; *TE*, February 6, 1840; Dwight Lowell Dumond, *Antislavery: The Crusade for Freedom in America* (Ann Arbor, 1961), 140–41.

51. *The Abolitionist*, April, May, July, September, October, December 1833; *TL*, August 31, October 12, 19, December 14, 1833; *Third Annual Report of the Board of Managers of the New England Anti Slavery Society . . .* (Boston, 1835), 6–7; Gilbert Hobbs Barnes, *The Antislavery Impulse, 1830–1844* (New York, 1933), chaps. 1, 2; Hugh Davis, *Joshua Leavitt: Evangelical Abolitionist* (Baton Rouge, 1990), 94–109; Whitney R. Cross, *The Burned-Over District: The Social and Intellectual History of Enthusiastic Religion in Western New York, 1800–1850* (Ithaca, 1950); Wyatt-Brown, *Lewis Tappan*, 98–104; Robert H. Abzug, *Passionate Liberator: Theodore Dwight Weld and the Dilemma of Reform* (New York, 1980), chap. 3; Barnes and Dumond, eds., *Letters of Theodore Dwight Weld, Angelina Grimké Weld and Sarah Grimké*, 1:99–105, 114–17; Goodman, *Of One Blood*, 65–68, 77–78, 81–90, 99–102.

52. *Proceedings of the Anti-Slavery Convention Assembled in Philadelphia . . .* (New York, 1833), 3–4, 23–24; *First Annual Report of the Board of Managers of the New England Anti Slavery Society*, 8; John G. Whittier, *The Antislavery Convention of 1833 (Written in 1874)* [Boston, 1897], 1–6; Edward Needles, *An Historical Memoir of the*

Pennsylvania Society, for Promoting the Abolition of Slavery . . . (Philadelphia, 1848), 90–91, 97; *TL*, February 2, October 12, December 14, 1833; *The Abolitionist*, December 1833; *William Lloyd Garrison*, 1:392–401; May, *Some Recollections of Our Antislavery Conflict*, 81–91; Mary Grew, *James Mott: A Biographical Sketch* (New York, ca. 1868), 8–9; Barnes and Dumond, eds., *Letters of Theodore Dwight Weld, Angelina Grimké Weld and Sarah Grimké*, 1:117–20; Quarles, *Black Abolitionists*, 23–25; Wesley, "The Negro in the Organization of Abolition," 228.

53. *Proceedings of the Anti-Slavery Convention*, 7–16; Whittier, *The Antislavery Convention*, 7–12; *The Abolitionist*, December 1833; John G. Whittier, *Anti-Slavery Reporter* . . . (New York, 1833), 51–63; *William Lloyd Garrison*, 1:402–14; Johnson, *William Lloyd Garrison*, 147–53; Samuel T. Pickard, *Life and Letters of John Greenleaf Whittier* (Cambridge, Mass., 1894), 1:130–36; Barnes and Dumond, eds., *Letters of Theodore Dwight Weld, Angelina Grimké Weld and Sarah Grimké*, 1:121–31; Sernett, *Abolition's Axe*, 37–38.

54. Sinha, *The Counterrevolution of Slavery*, chaps. 1, 2; cf. Brian Schoen, *The Fragile Fabric of Union: Cotton, Federal Politics and the Global Origins of the Civil War* (Baltimore, 2009); Edward Rugemer, *The Problem of Emancipation: The Caribbean Roots of the American Civil War* (Baton Rouge, 2008).

CHAPTER EIGHT. ABOLITION EMERGENT

1. Robert H. Abzug, *Passionate Liberator: Theodore Dwight Weld and the Dilemma of Reform* (New York, 1980), 147–49.

2. Daniel Walker Howe, *What God Hath Wrought: The Transformation of America, 1815–1848* (New York, 2007); Lawrence Goodwyn, *Democratic Promise: The Populist Movement in America* (New York, 1976).

3. Alexis de Tocqueville, *Democracy in America*, trans. Henry Reeve, 2 vols. (London, 1836); Russel Nye, *Fettered Freedom: Civil Liberties and the Slavery Controversy* (East Lansing, 1949).

4. *College for Colored Youth* . . . (New York, 1831), 2–3, 5–7, 10–11, 13–15, 17–18, 20–24; *TL*, July 9, September 17, October 8, November 5, 1831; Walter M. Merrill, ed., *The Letters of William Lloyd Garrison, vol. 1, I Will be Heard! 1822–1835* (Cambridge, Mass., 1971), 119–21; "Abolition Letters Collected by Col. Arthur B. Spingarn," *JNH* 18 (January 1933): 79–80; Lewis Tappan, *The Life of Arthur Tappan* (New York, 1871), 146–52; Paul Goodman, "The Manual Labor Movement and the Origins of Abolitionism," *JER* 13 (Autumn 1993): 355–88; Hilary J. Moss, *Schooling Citizens: The Struggle for African American Education in Antebellum America* (Chicago, 2009), chap. 2; Robert H. Abzug, *Cosmos Crumbling: American Reform and the Religious Imagination* (New York, 1994), 116–24.

5. *TL*, May 25, June 15, August 3, 31, 1833; September 27, 1834; *The Abolitionist*, April, July, September, November 1833; [Francis Jackson Garrison and Wendell Phillips Garrison], *William Lloyd Garrison, 1805–1879: The Story of His Life told By His Children*, vol. 1, *1805–1835* (New York, 1885), 315–23, 340–42; Samuel J. May, *Some Recollections*

of Our Antislavery Conflict (Boston, 1869), 39–72, May, *The Right of Colored People to Education Vindicated* . . . (Brooklyn, Conn., 1833), 6, 9–11, 15–18, 21–24; "Abolition Letters," 80–84; *Second Annual Report of the Board of Managers of the New England Anti Slavery Society* . . . (Boston, 1834), 14–16; *Proceedings of the New England Anti Slavery Convention* . . . (Boston, 1834), 23; John Bowers to Garrison, May 14, 1834, *BAP*, reel 1; *First Annual Report of the American Anti-Slavery Society* . . . (New York, 1834), 47–48; Susan Strane, *A Whole-Souled Woman: Prudence Crandall and the Education of Black Women* (New York, 1990); Philip S. Foner and Josephine F. Pacheco, *Three Who Dared: Prudence Crandall, Margaret Douglass, Myrtilla Miner—Champions of Antebellum Black Education* (Westport, Conn., 1984), 5–54; Carl R. Woodward, "A Profile in Dedication: Sarah Harris and the Fayerweather Family," *New England Galaxy* 15 (Summer 1973): 3–14; Donald Yacovone, *Samuel Joseph May and the Dilemmas of the Liberal Persuasion, 1797–1871* (Philadelphia, 1991), chap. 4.

6. *Herald of Freedom*, March 7, July 25, September 5, 19, 1835; *TL*, October 25, 1834; February 28, May 16, July 25, 1835; *Second Annual Report of the New Hampshire Anti-Slavery Society* . . . (Concord, N.H., 1836), 11–17; *Third Annual Report of the American Anti-Slavery Society* . . . (New York, 1836), 52–54; Russell W. Irvine and Donna Zani Dunkerton, "The Noyes Academy, 1834–35: The Road to the Oberlin Collegiate Institute and the Higher Education of African-Americans in the Nineteenth Century," *Western Journal of Black Studies* 22 (1998): 260; Wilson Jeremiah Moses, *Alexander Crummell: A Study of Civilization and Discontent* (New York, 1989), 20–21; Martin B. Pasternak, *Rise Now and Fly to Arms: The Life of Henry Highland Garnet* (New York, 1995), 3–15; Joel Schor, *Henry Highland Garnet: A Voice of Black Radicalism in the Nineteenth Century* (Westport, Conn., 1977), 3–15; Milton C. Sernett, *Abolition's Axe: Beriah Green, Oneida Institute, and the Black Freedom Struggle* (Syracuse, 1986), chap. 4; Parker Pillsbury, *Acts of the Anti-Slavery Apostles* (Concord, N.H., 1883), chap. 2.

7. Merrill, ed., *The Letters of William Lloyd Garrison*, 1:137–38; *TL*, October 12, December 14, 1833; Leonard L. Richards, *"Gentlemen of Property and Standing": Anti-Abolition Mobs in Jacksonian America* (New York, 1970); David Grimsted, *American Mobbing, 1828–1861: Toward Civil War* (New York, 1998), 33–66; Hazel Catherine Wolf, *On Freedom's Altar: The Martyr Complex in the Abolition Movement* (Madison, 1952).

8. *TL*, January 4, July 12, 19, 26, August 2, 1834; Harriet Martineau, *The Martyr Age of the United States* (Boston, 1839), 20–21; Tappan, *The Life of Arthur Tappan*, chap. 12; Bertram Wyatt-Brown, *Lewis Tappan and the Evangelical War Against Slavery* (Cleveland, 1969), 115–22; Richards, "Gentlemen of Property and Standing," 113–22; Linda K. Kerber, "Abolitionists and Amalgamators: The New York City Race Riots of 1834," *New York History* 48 (January 1967): 28–39; John H. Hewitt, "Peter Williams, Jr.: New York's First African-American Episcopal Priest," *New York History* 79 (April 1998): 119–23; John Runcie, "'Hunting the Nigs' in Philadelphia: The Race Riot of August 1834," *Pennsylvania History* 39 (April 1972): 187–218; Grimsted, *American Mobbing*, 36; Carl E. Prince, "The Great 'Riot Year': Jacksonian Democracy and Patterns of Violence in 1834," *JER* 5 (1985): 1–19.

9. [William Thomas], *The Enemies of the Constitution Discovered . . . By Defensor* (New York, 1835), 48–103, 167–75; *TL*, January 13, 1834; October 3, 1835; *TE*, November 1835; *Third Annual Report of the American Anti-Slavery Society*, 63–65; Richards, "Gentlemen of Property and Standing," 85–92; Oliver Johnson, *William Lloyd Garrison and His Times . . .* (Boston, 1880), 208–10; Frederick J. Blue, *No Taint of Compromise: Crusaders in Antislavery Politics* (Baton Rouge, 2005), 17–19.

10. *TL*, August 23, October 11, 18, November 1, 22, December 6, 13, 1834; January 3, April 13, June 6, September 12, 26, 1835; *The Abolitionist*, May 1835; George Thompson to Robert Purvis, November 10, 1834, *BAP*, reel 1; *Second Annual Report of the American Anti-Slavery Society . . .* (New York, 1835), 16–23; *Third Annual Report of the American Anti-Slavery Society*, 37–38; *William Lloyd Garrison*, 1:434–53.

11. *TL*, October 4, November 22, 1834; September 5, 12, 19, October 10, 17, 31, November 7, 14, 28, 1835; *Right and Wrong in Boston: Report of the Boston Female Anti Slavery Society . . .* (Boston, 1836), 10–37, 55–73, 96–99; *Third Annual Report of the American Anti-Slavery Society*, 61–63; Merrill, ed., *The Letters of William Lloyd Garrison*, 1:496–526, 530–36, 541–42; *William Lloyd Garrison*, 1:486–514; [Francis Jackson Garrison and Wendell Phillips Garrison], *William Lloyd Garrison, 1805–1879: The Story of His Life told By His Children*, vol. 2, *1835–1840* (New York, 1885), 2–36; Johnson, *William Lloyd Garrison*, 195–201; Martineau, *The Martyr Age*, 30–33; C. Duncan Rice, "The Anti-Slavery Mission of George Thompson to the United States, 1834–1835," *Journal of American Studies* 2 (April 1968): 13–31; Henry Mayer, *All on Fire: William Lloyd Garrison and the Abolition of Slavery* (New York, 1998), 199–210.

12. *TL*, December 20, 27, 1834; January 3, 17, 24, 31, February 7, 28, November 14, December 12, 1835; January 9, 30, April 2, November 5, 1836; Merrill, ed., *The Letters of William Lloyd Garrison*, 1:436–42, 444–63, 578–84; Louis Ruchames, ed., *The Letters of William Lloyd Garrison*, vol. 2, *House Dividing Against Itself, 1836–1840* (Cambridge, Mass., 1971), 43–46; William E. Channing, *Slavery* (Boston, 1835); *Fourth Annual Report of the Board of Managers of the Massachusetts Anti-Slavery Society . . .* (Boston, 1836), 24; *TASR*, July 1836; Johnson, *William Lloyd Garrison*, 202–3; May, *Some Recollections*, 157–85; [Thomas], *The Enemies of the Constitution*, 157–66; John L. Thomas, *The Liberator, William Lloyd Garrison: A Biography* (Boston, 1963), 206–8; James Brewer Stewart, *Wendell Phillips: Liberty's Hero* (Baton Rouge, 1986), 42–46; Stephen P. Budney, *William Jay: Abolitionist and Anticolonialist* (Westport, Conn., 2005), 2–3, 30–35; John Stauffer, *The Black Hearts of Men: Radical Abolitionists and the Transformation of Race* (Cambridge, Mass., 2001), 99–102; Andrew Delbanco, *William Ellery Channing: An Essay on the Liberal Spirit in America* (Cambridge, Mass., 1981).

13. *Third Annual Report of the American Anti-Slavery Society*, 50; *TE*, October 13, 1836; Edwin A. Miles, "The Mississippi Insurrection Scare of 1835," *JNH* 42 (January 1957): 48–60; Christopher Morris, "An Event in Community Organization: The Mississippi Slave Insurrection Scare of 1835," *Journal of Social History* 22 (1988): 93–111; Laurence Shore, "Making Mississippi Safe for Slavery: The Insurrection Panic of 1835," in Orville Vernon Burton and Robert C. McMath Jr., eds., *Class, Consensus, and Conflict:*

Antebellum Southern Community Studies (Westport, Conn., 1982), 96–127; Joshua D. Rothman, *Flush Times and Fever Dreams: A Story of Capitalism and Slavery in the Age of Jackson* (Athens, Ga., 2012), 280–90.

14. *The Narrative of Amos Dresser* . . . (New York, 1836), 6–14; Martineau, *The Martyr Age*, 23–26; *TL*, September 26, 1835; January 21, February 11, 1837; *TASR*, November 1835; *TE*, October 1835; December 8, 1836; January 19, 1837; *TP*, November 25, 1836; *Third Annual Report of the American Anti-Slavery Society*, 48–50.

15. *The Trial of Reuben Crandall* . . . *By a Member of the Bar* (Washington, 1836), 3–5, 8–19, 24–32, 37–48; *TE*, March 8, 1838; *Third Annual Report of the American Anti-Slavery Society*, 54–55; Neil S. Kramer, "The Trial of Reuben Crandall," *Records of the Columbia Historical Society, Washington DC* 50 (1980): 123–39; Jefferson Morley, *Snow-storm in August: Washington City, Francis Scott Key, and the Forgotten Race Riot of 1835* (New York, 2012).

16. *Second Annual Report of the American Anti-Slavery Society*, 37, 76–82; *Narrative of the Late Riotous Proceedings Against the Liberty of the Press, in Cincinnati* . . . (Cincinnati, 1836), 8–20, 23–45; *A Collection of Valuable Documents* . . . (Boston, 1836), 5–6, 9–15, 26–30, 67–75; *TP*, September 27, October 14, 21, December 23, 1836; March 31, 1837; *TL*, April 4, May 23, 1835; February 13, August 27, October 1, 1836; *TE*, September 1835; August 11, 18, 1836; February 25, 1841; *TASR*, June 1836; Dwight L. Dumond, ed., *Letters of James Gillespie Birney, 1831–1857* (Gloucester, Mass., 1966), 1:112–25, 127–40, 147–52, 161–63, 170–82, 185–91, 201–22, 227–35, 239–44, 251–77, 280–302, 310–22, 342–60, 371–75; Ruchames, ed., *The Letters of William Lloyd Garrison*, 2:66–68; *Letter of William E. Channing to James G. Birney* (Boston, 1836), 7–13, 18–28; William Birney, *James G. Birney and His Times* . . . (New York, 1890), chaps. 21, 23; Betty Fladeland, *James Gillespie Birney: Slaveholder to Abolitionist* (New York, 1955), chaps. 1–7; Nikki M. Taylor, *Frontiers of Freedom: Cincinnati's Black Community, 1802–1868* (Athens, Ohio, 2005), 109–13, 118–26.

17. Joseph C. Lovejoy and Owen Lovejoy, *Memoir of the Rev. Elijah P. Lovejoy* . . . (New York, 1838); Edward Beecher, *Narrative of the Riots at Alton* (Alton, Ill., 1838); *Alton Observer Extra* . . . (Alton, Ill., 1838), 3–5, 9–10, 21–25; *TP*, May 6, May 27, 1836; November 21, 28, 1837; January 2, 1838; *TL*, August 13, 1836; September 15, November 17, 24, December 1, 8, 15, 22, 29, 1837; January 5, 12, February 23, April 27, 1838; Beriah Green, *The Martyr* . . . (New York, 1838), 8–16; *William Lloyd Garrison*, 2:182–96; May, *Some Recollections*, 221–30; *TE*, March 30, October 26, November 23, 30, December 7, 14, 21, 28, 1837; January 11, February 15, 1838; Wendell Phillips, *Speeches, Lectures, and Letters* (Boston, 1872), 1–10; Merton L. Dillon, *Elijah P. Lovejoy: Abolitionist Editor* (Urbana, 1961); Stewart, *Wendell Phillips*, 58–63; Mayer, *All on Fire*, 216, 237–39; Paul Simon, *Freedom's Champion Elijah Lovejoy* (Carbondale, 2000).

18. Martineau, *The Martyr Age*, 58–74; Isaac Stearns, *Right and Wrong in Mansfield, Massachusetts* . . . (Pawtucket, Mass., 1837), 1–10; *TL*, February 14, July 4, 1835; January 9, April 16, June 25, July 2, 1836; *TE*, June 7, 1838; January 31, 1839; *TP*, March 3, 1837; Ruchames, ed., *The Letters of William Lloyd Garrison*, 2:115; Gilbert H. Barnes and Dwight L. Dumond, eds., *Letters of Theodore Dwight Weld, Angelina Grimké*

Weld and Sarah Grimké, 1822–1844 (Gloucester, Mass., 1965), 1:205–8; *William Lloyd Garrison*, 2:210–18; May, *Some Recollections*, 150–57; Dwight Lowell Dumond, *Antislavery: The Crusade for Freedom in America* (Ann Arbor, 1961), 220; Russel B. Nye, "Marius Robinson, A Forgotten Abolitionist Leader," *Ohio State Archeological and Historical Quarterly* 55 (April–June 1946): 138–54; *History of Pennsylvania Hall . . .* (Philadelphia, 1838); Samuel T. Pickard, *Life and Letters of John Greenleaf Whittier* (Cambridge, Mass., 1894), 1:231–36; Henry B. Stanton, *Random Recollections* (New York, 1887), 51–55; *Fourth Annual Report of the Board of Managers of the Massachusetts Anti-Slavery Society*, 1–10; Beverly C. Tomek, *Pennsylvania Hall: A Legal Lynching in the Shadow of the Liberty Bell* (New York, 2014); Deborah A. Logan, "The Redemption of a Heretic: Harriet Martineau and Anglo-American Abolitionism," in Kathryn Kish Sklar and James Brewer Stewart, eds., *Women's Rights and Transatlantic Antislavery in the Era of Emancipation* (New Haven, 2007), 242–65.

19. Mathew Carey, *To the Public* (Philadelphia, 1832); Carey, *Reflections on the Causes that Led to the Formation of the Colonization Society . . .* (Philadelphia, 1832); Carey, *Letters on the Colonization Society . . .* (Philadelphia, 1832), 25–28; Carey, *Letters on the Colonization Society . . .* , 4th ed. (Philadelphia, 1832), 3; Carey, *Letters on the Colonization Society . . .* (Philadelphia, 1834), 1–3; Carey, *Address of the Managers of the American Colonization Society . . .* (Washington, 1832), 4–5; TL, January 28, 1832; George M. Fredrickson, *The Black Image in the White Mind: The Debate on Afro-American Character and Destiny, 1817–1914* (New York, 1971), 12–21.

20. TL, March 23, 1833; Wilbur D. Fisk, *Substance of an Address delivered before the Middletown Colonization Society . . .* (Middletown, Conn., 1835), 12–15; ARCJ, December, November 1832; *Remarks on African Colonization . . .* (Windsor, Vt., 1833), 3, 25, 31–34, 39–47; J. K. Converse, *A Discourse on the Moral, Legal, and Domestic Condition of Our Colored . . .* (Burlington, Vt., 1832), 9–15, 18–20; Converse, *The History of Slavery and Means of Elevating the African Race . . .* (Burlington, Vt., 1840), 22; A. [Mariah] Chandler, *A Discourse . . .* (Greenfield, Conn., 1833), 25; Honorable Elisha Whittlesey and Charles Whittlesey, *Two Addresses Delivered Before the Tallmadge Colonization Society . . .* (Ravena, Ohio, 1833), 8–10, 22–27; *A Sketch of the Colonization Enterprise . . .* (Newark, 1838), 8; *Professor Fowler's Discourse . . .* (Middlebury, 1834), 11–21; Hon. Caleb Cushing, *An Oration Pronounced at Boston Before the Colonization Society of Massachusetts . . .* (Boston, 1833), 6, 12–21; Joseph Tracy, *Natural Equality: A Sermon before the Vermont Colonization Society . . .* (Windsor, Vt., 1833), 10–14; *Abolition A Sedition By a Northern Man* (Philadelphia, 1839), 1–3, 12, 36–56, 72–85, 133–40, 159–69; *A Cursory Examination of the Respective Pretensions of the Colonizationists and Abolitionists* (New York, 1837), 8–11; *An Inquiry into the Condition and Prospects of the African Race in the United States . . .* (Philadelphia, 1839), 27–42, 111, 126–53, 183–91; TE, September 22, 1835.

21. Robert J. Breckinridge, *An Address Delivered Before the Colonization Society of Kentucky . . .* (Frankfort, Ky., 1831), 3, 19–24; *Review of Pamphlets on Slavery and Colonization* (New Haven, 1833), 3–12, 20–22; Hugh Davis, *Leonard Bacon: New England Reformer and Antislavery Moderate* (Baton Rouge, 1998), chaps. 4, 5; ARCJ, February,

March, November 1834; *TL,* January 17, February 7, 1835; Ebenezer Baldwin, *Observations on the Physical, Intellectual, and Moral Qualities of our Colored Population* . . . (New Haven, 1834), 10–38, 40–51; F. Freeman, *Yaradee* . . . (Philadelphia, 1836); R. R. Gurley, *Address at the Annual Meeting of the Pennsylvania Colonization Society* . . . (Philadelphia, 1839), 13–20, 26–40; [Calvin Colton], *Colonization and Abolition Contrasted* [Philadelphia, 1839], 2–5, 9–13.

22. Elizur Wright Jr., *The Sin of Slavery and its Remedy* . . . (New York, 1833), 3–5, 8–11, 13–18, 25–29, 32–37, 40–47; *TL,* March 24, July 21, September 1, 1832; January 5, February 2, 16, May 25, 1833; January 25, August 15, 16, 1834; January 3, August 8, 22, 1835; June 2, August 13, 20, 1836; *The Abolitionist,* February, July 1833; *TE,* August 11, 18, October 13, November 10, December 22, 1836; April 6, June 8, August 5, 10, 17, November 9, 1837; January 11, May 3, 1838; *TP,* September 27, October 14, December 2, 1836; September 29, 1837; *First Annual Report of the American Anti-Slavery Society,* 42; Dumond, ed., *Letters of James Gillespie Birney,* 1:440–44; Betty Fladeland, *Men and Brothers: Anglo-American Antislavery Cooperation* (Urbana, 1972), 236–37.

23. *Debate at the Lane Seminary, Cincinnati* . . . (Boston, 1834), 3–7, 10–11; Barnes and Dumond, eds., *Letters of Theodore Dwight Weld, Angelina Grimké Weld and Sarah Grimké,* 1:132–46, 170–73, 178–99, 247–49, 256–65, 270–89, 315–29; Dumond, ed., *Letters of James Gillespie Birney,* 1:136–40, 145–47; *TL,* April 5, 12, June 13, November 1, 1834; January 10, May 2, 1835; April 16, 1836:; *Third Annual Report of the Board of Managers of the New England Anti Slavery Society* . . . (Boston, 1835), 10–11; Stanton, *Random Recollections,* 46–49; *William Lloyd Garrison,* 2:116–17; *First Annual Report of the American Anti-Slavery Society,* 6–12, 23–28, 62–64; *Second Annual Report of the American Anti-Slavery,* 40–43; Lawrence Thomas Lesick, *The Lane Rebels: Evangelicalism and Antislavery in Antebellum America* (Metuchen, N.J., 1980), 70–173; J. Brent Morris, *Oberlin, Hotbed of Abolitionism: College, Community, and the Fight for Freedom and Equality in Antebellum America* (Chapel Hill, 2014), 22; Abzug, *Passionate Liberator,* chaps. 5–7; Deborah Bingham Broekhoven, *The Devotion of These Women: Rhode Island in the Antislavery Network* (Amherst, Mass., 2002), 21–24; John L. Myers, "Organization of 'The Seventy': To Arouse the North Against Slavery," *Mid-American: An Historical Review* 42 (1966): 29–46.

24. *Debate at Lane Seminary,* 11–16; *TE,* December 15, 1836; *First Annual Report of the American Anti-Slavery Society,* 4–6, 15–16, 28–31; Amos A. Phelps, *Lectures on Slavery* . . . (Boston, 1834), v–xi, 13–24, 27–30, 36–43, 58, 65–80, 145–60, 179–88, 213, 219–30, 239–50, 269–84; *TL,* January 25, 1834; August 11, 1836.

25. John Hersey, *An Appeal to Christians* . . . (Baltimore, 1833), 87–88; *Maryland Colonization Society* (Baltimore, 1833); *TL,* January 25, February 1, August 2, 1834; July 4, 1835; January 14, 1837; Bettye J. Gardner, "Opposition to Emigration: A Selected Letter of William Watkins (A Colored Baltimorean)," *JNH* 67 (Summer 1982): 155–58; *The Maryland Scheme* . . . (Boston, 1834), 4–14, 18–20; "Extract from Governor Russwurm's letter to the President of the Maryland State Colo. Society, Extracts from Dispatches of Governor Russwurm June 1839" and "Letters from John B. Russwurm to John H. B. Latrobe August 1839," *Maryland Colonization Journal, BAP*; Winston James, *The*

Struggles of John Brown Russwurm: The Life and Writings of a Pan-Africanist Pioneer, 1799–1851 (New York, 2010), chap. 5; Penelope Campbell, *Maryland in Africa: The Maryland State Colonization Society, 1831–1857* (Urbana, 1971).

26. *News from Africa* . . . (Baltimore, 1832); Amos J. Beyan, *African American Settlements in West Africa: John Brown Russwurm and the American Civilizing Efforts* (New York, 2005), chaps. 4, 5; Sandra Sandiford Young, "A Different Journey: John Brown Russwurm, 1799–1851" (Ph.D. diss., Boston College, 2004), 250–90; *ARCJ*, May, September, October 1832; April, July 1835; May, June, July, October 1836; April 1837; February, August 1839; March 1, 1840; *A Brief Account of the Colony of Liberia by Solomon Bayley* [Wilmington, Del., 1833]; *A Collection of Facts in Regard to Liberia* . . . (Woodstock, Vt., 1839); *Examination of Mr. Thomas C. Brown* . . . (New York, 1834).

27. Hon. James G. Birney, *Letter on Colonization* . . . (Boston, 1834), 7–10, 18–22, 43–44; *Third Annual Report of the Board of Managers of the New England Anti Slavery Society*, 13–14; William Jay, *Miscellaneous Writings on Slavery* (New York, 1853), 28–58, 64–74, 153–60, 170–96; *TL*, April 13, 1835; *TASR*, February 1837; *Third Annual Report of the American Anti-Slavery Society*, 3–4.

28. David Meredith Reese, *A Brief Review of the "First Annual Report of the American Anti-Slavery Society* . . ." (New York, 1834), 4–8, 14–17, 28–33; *The "Extinguisher" Extinguished! Or David M. Reese, M.D., "Used Up." By David Ruggles* . . . (New York, 1834), 3–5, 11–15; *A Brief Review of the First Annual Report of the American Anti-Slavery Society by David M. Reese, M.D. of New York Dissected by Martin Mar Quack* . . . (Boston, 1834); David Meredith Reese, *Letters to the Honorable William Jay* . . . (New York, 1835), x, xi; Reese, *Humbugs of New York* . . . (New York, 1838), 195–204; *An Antidote for a Poisonous Combination* . . . (New York, 1838), 1–2, 22–23, 31–32; *CA*, March 15, 22, April 12, June 16, 26, 1838; Graham Russell Gao Hodges, *David Ruggles: A Radical Black Abolitionist and the Underground Railroad in New York City* (Chapel Hill, 2010).

29. *CA*, May 13, 1837; January 27, March 29, June 16, August 11, 1838; January 12, 19, March 2, 1839; May 30, 1840; March 20, June 12, 19, 26, July 3, 10, 31, October 2, November 13, 20, 1841; *TE*, December 20, 1838; January 17, 1839; *TP*, January 17, March 5, 1839; P. J. Staudenraus, *The African Colonization Movement, 1816–1865* (New York, 1961), 201–23.

30. *First Annual Report of the American Anti-Slavery Society*, 16; *First Annual Report of the Board of Managers of the New England Anti Slavery Society* . . . (Boston, 1833), 9–43; *Second Annual Report of the Board of Managers of the New England Anti Slavery Society*, 22–29; *Third Annual Report of the Board of Managers of the New England Anti Slavery Society*, 17; *TASR*, February 1835; Cyrus Pitt Grosvenor, *Address Before the Anti-Slavery Society of Salem* . . . (Salem, Mass., 1834), 5–7, 9–10, 21–24, 28–29, 42–43; Amos Savage, *National Sins, The Cause of National Judgments* . . . (Utica, N.Y., 1835), 15–18; *Address of the Starksborough and Lincoln Anti Slavery Society* . . . (Middlebury, 1835), 3–5; James H. Eells, *The American Revolution Compared with the Present Struggle for the Abolition of Slavery in the United States* . . . (Elyria, Ohio, 1836), 9–12; Enoch Mack, *The Revolution Unfinished* . . . (Dover, 1838): 3–5; Edward A. Barber, *An Oration Delivered Before the Addison County Anti-Slavery Society*

... (Middlebury, 1836), 4–5, 11–14; John Rankin, *An Address to the Churches* ... (Medina, Ohio, 1836), 2–3, 6–8.

31. Grosvenor, *Address Before the Anti-Slavery Society of Salem*, 26; James T. Dickinson, *A Sermon Delivered in the Second Congregational Church* . . . (Norwich, Conn., 1834), 16, 31; W. D. Wilson, *A Discourse on Slavery* . . . (Concord, N.H., 1839), 14; David L. Child, *The Despotism of Freedom* . . . (Boston, 1833), 65–67; *Proceedings of the New England Anti-Slavery Convention* . . . 1834, 47, 63; *Proceedings of the New England Anti-Slavery Convention* . . . (Boston, 1836), 74; *Proceedings of the Fourth New England Anti- Slavery Convention*, 110–16; Oliver Johnson, *An Address Delivered in the Congregational Church* . . . (Montpelier, Vt., 1835), 12–13; Dumond, ed., *Letters of James Gillespie Birney, 1831–1857*, 1:286, 292–93; *TL*, August 6, 1831; May 17, 1834; June 16, 30, 1837; August 17, 1838; *TE*, January 26, 1837; July 12, 1838; *TASR*, April, November, December 1835; March, December 1836; December 1837; *TP*, January 1, 22, 1839; *Address of the New York City Anti-Slavery Society* . . . (New York, 1833), 7–11.

32. *First Annual Report of the American Anti-Slavery Society*, 26, 50–52; Birney, *Letter on Colonization*, 14–15; *Second Annual Report of the American Anti-Slavery Society*, 3–16, 43; Henry Peterson, *An Address Delivered Before the Junior Anti-Slavery Society* . . . (Philadelphia, 1837), 9; Jas. A Thome and J. Horace Kimball, *Emancipation in the West Indies* . . . (New York, 1838), 264, 330–41, 401–5; Alex Tyrell, *Joseph Sturge and the Moral Radical Party in Early Victorian Britain* (London, 1987); *TP*, May 5, 1837; *TE*, March 8, 1838; *TL*, April 20, July 6, August 17, 1838; *An Address to the Citizens of the United States, on the Subject of Slavery* (Philadelphia, 1838), 7–13; Fladeland, *Men and Brothers*, 246–52.

33. David Paul Brown, *An Oration Delivered* . . . (Philadelphia, 1834), 13–20, 28–30; *Proceedings of the New England Anti-Slavery Convention* . . . 1834, 15; *Second Annual Report of the New Hampshire Anti-Slavery Society*, 3–6; Johnson, *An Address Delivered*, 5–7; James G. Birney, *Letter to the Ministers and Elders* . . . [New York, 1834]; Samuel J. May, *Letter Addressed to the Editor of the Christian Examiner* (Boston, 1835), 5–7; *Proceedings of the Indiana Convention* . . . (Cincinnati, 1838), 7; *TP*, January 22, February 12, 1839; Beriah Green, *The Chattel Principle* . . . (New York, 1839), 18–20; Green, *Four Sermons* . . . (Cleveland, 1833), 7–19.

34. Green, *Four Sermons*, 30–52; Green, *The Chattel Principle*, 42; Rankin, *An Address to the Churches*, 5–8; *First Annual Report of the American Anti-Slavery Society*, 12–16; *Third Annual Report of the American Anti-Slavery Society*, 4–11, 67–74; *Constitution of the Anti-Slavery Society of Worcester County, North Division* (n.p., 1835), 4–5; Theodore Dwight Weld, *The Bible Against Slavery* . . . (New York, 1837), vii, 16–28, 86–98, 145–53; *TASR*, March, June, November 1835; December 1836; September 1837; *TP*, July 2, 23, 1839; *TAE* 3 (New York, 1837), 3–8, 18–24, 36–49; cf. Molly Oshatz, *Slavery and Sin: The Fight Against Slavery and the Rise of Liberal Protestantism* (New York: Oxford University Press, 2012).

35. *Human Rights*, July 1835; *Proceedings of the Rhode Island Anti-Slavery Convention* . . . (Providence, 1836), 18–21; David Root, *The Abolition Case Eventually Triumphant* . . . (Andover, 1836), 6–7; *TE*, August, October, November 1835; Channing, *Slavery*.

36. [Theodore D. Weld], *American Slavery As It Is: Testimony of a Thousand Witnesses* (New York, 1839), 8; Dumond, *Antislavery,* chap. 30; Abzug, *Passionate Liberator,* 210–18; Fladeland, *Men and Brothers,* 240; Eugene D. Genovese, *Roll, Jordan, Roll: The World the Slaves Made* (New York, 1972).

37. *TL,* February 26, 1831; August 23, 1835; February 20, 27, April 2, 9, May 7, 28, August 5, 1836; *TE,* October, November 1835; April 1836; *Third Annual Report of the American Anti-Slavery Society,* 11–19, 42–48, 55–60; Tappan, *The Life of Arthur Tappan,* 243–52; *William Lloyd Garrison,* 2:73–77, 95–97, 102–6; May, *Some Recollections,* 185–202; Martineau, *The Martyr Age,* 43–48; Theodore Sedgwick Jr., ed., *A Collection of the Political Writings of William Leggett* (New York, 1840), 2:7–64; Clement Eaton, *Freedom-of-Thought Struggle in the Old South* (Durham, 1940); Richard R. John, *Spreading the News: The American Postal System from Franklin to Morse* (Cambridge, Mass., 1995), chap. 7; Susan Wyly-Jones, "The 1835 Anti-Abolition Meetings in the South: A New Look at the Controversy over the Abolition Postal Campaign," *CWH* 47 (2001): 289–309.

38. *TL,* December 26, 1835; January 2, 9, 8, 16, 30, February 6, 13, 20, 27, March 12, June 18, July 9, October 8, 1836; February 11, March 4, April 7, 14, 21, June 2, 1837; February 16, 23, July 20, December 14, 1838; *TE,* June 22, August 31, 1837; January 16, February 1, 8, April 26, October 4, 25, 1838; January 31, February 7, 28, March 7, 1839; *TASR,* February, July, December 1836; March, April, November 1837; *TP,* June 17, 1836; June 2, 30, July 31, September 23, 29, 1837; Ruchames, ed., *The Letters of William Lloyd Garrison,* 2:84–85; *Third Annual Report of the American Anti-Slavery Society,* 83–86; May, *Some Recollections,* 211–21; *Fifth Annual Report of the Board of Managers of the Massachusetts Anti-Slavery Society . . .* (Boston, 1837), 17–70; B. F. Morris, ed., *The Life of Thomas Morris: Pioneer and Long a Legislator of Ohio, and U.S. Senator from 1833 to 1839* (Cincinnati, 1856), chaps. 11–15, quote from 85; *A Collection of Valuable Documents,* 41–66; Martineau, *The Martyr Age,* 75–81; *TAE* 9 (New York, 1839), 3–18; Leonard L. Richards, *The Life and Times of Congressman John Quincy Adams* (New York, 1986), 89–131; Richards, *The Slave Power: The Free North and Southern Domination, 1790–1860* (Baton Rouge, 2000); William Lee Miller, *Arguing About Slavery: The Great Battle in the United States Congress* (New York, 1996); William W. Freehling, *The Road to Disunion: Secessionists at Bay, 1776–1854* (New York, 1990) 1: chaps. 17–19; George C. Rable, "Slavery, Politics, and the South: The Gag Rule as a Case Study," *Capitol Studies* 3 (1975): 69–88; Daniel Wirls, "'The Only Mode of Avoiding Everlasting Debate': The Overlooked Senate Gag Rule of Antislavery Petitions," *JER* 27 (Spring 2007): 115–38; Edward B. Rugemer, "Caribbean Slave Revolts and the Origins of the Gag Rule: A Contest Between Abolitionism and Democracy, 1707–1835," in John Craig Hammond and Matthew Mason, eds., *Contesting Slavery: The Politics of Bondage and Freedom in the New American Nation* (Charlottesville, Va., 2011), 94–113.

39. *TL,* January 2, 1836; April 28, 1837; *TE,* April 20, 1837; *Second Annual Report of the American Anti-Slavery Society,* 83–87; *Third Annual Report of the American Anti-Slavery Society,* 89–99; *TAE* 8 (New York, 1838), 6–17; Teresa A. Goddu, "The Massa-

chusetts Anti-Slavery Society's Weekly Contribution Box," *Common-Place* (Fall 2014): http://www.common-place.org/vol-15/no-01/notes/; Louis Filler, *The Crusade Against Slavery, 1830–1860* (New York, 1960), 67, 70; Benjamin Quarles, "Sources of Abolitionist Income," in John R. McKivigan, ed., *Abolitionism and American Reform* (New York, 1999), 207–20; Gerald Sorin, *The New York Abolitionists: A Case Study of Radicalism* (Westport, Conn., 1971), chap. 4; John Jentz, "The Antislavery Constituency in Jacksonian New York City," *CWH* 27 (June 1981): 101–22; Jentz, "Artisans, Evangelicals and the City: A Social History of Abolition and Labor Reform in Jacksonian New York" (Ph.D. diss., City University of New York, 1977), chap. 5; Edward Magdol, *The Antislavery Rank and File: A Social Profile of the Abolitionists Constituency* (Westport, Conn., 1986); Magdol, "A Window on the Abolitionist Constituency: Antislavery Petitions, 1836–1839," in Alan M. Kraut, ed., *Crusaders and Compromisers: Essays on the Relationship of the Antislavery Struggle to the Antebellum Party System* (Westport, Conn., 1983), 45–70; John W. Quist, "'The Great Majority of Our Subscribers Are Farmers': The Michigan Abolitionist Constituency of the 1840s," *JER* 14 (Autumn 1994): 325–58; Ford Risley, *Abolition and the Press: The Moral Struggle Against Slavery* (Evanston, Ill., 2008); Robert Fanuzzi, *Abolition's Public Sphere* (Minneapolis, 2003).

40. *TL*, August 21, 1831; January 5, 12, October 10, 1833; March 14, 1835; June 4, July 23, 1836; October 13, 1837; October 12, 1838; *The Abolitionist*, August 1833; *TP*, June 17, 1836; Ruchames, ed., *The Letters of William Lloyd Garrison*, 2:85–88; *First Annual Report of the American Anti-Slavery Society*, 42–44; *Second Annual Report of the American Anti-Slavery Society*, 49–50; *Apology for Anti-Slavery Theological Seminary, Andover, August 22, 1833* (n.p., n.d.), 1–3; Child, *The Despotism of Freedom*, 5–11; *Address of the New York Young Men's Anti-Slavery Society*, 19–28; *First Annual Report of the New York Young Men's Anti-Slavery Society* . . . (New York, 1835), 3–4, 13–14; *Constitution of the New Bedford Young Men's Anti-Slavery Society* . . . (New Bedford, Mass., 1836), 6–7; Peterson, *An Address*, 3–4; Hermann R. Muelder, *Fighters for Freedom: A History of Anti-Slavery Activities of Men and Women Associated with Knox College* (New York, 1959); Robert Samuel Fletcher, *A History of Oberlin College: From Its Foundations Through the Civil War*, 2 vols. (New York, 1971).

41. *TL*, May 28, 1831; May 17, December 20, 1834; January 14, 1837; Ruchames, ed., *The Letters of William Lloyd Garrison*, 2:60; *Second Annual Report of the American Anti-Slavery Society*, 52–53; Harriet Hyman Alonso, *Growing Up Abolitionist: The Story of the Garrison Children* (Amherst, Mass., 2002); *Proceedings of the New England Anti Slavery Convention* . . . *1834*, 19; Lois A. Brown, ed., *Memoir of James Jackson: The Attentive and Obedient Scholar Who Died in Boston, October 31, 1833, Aged Six Years and Eleven Months by His Teacher Miss Susan Paul* (Cambridge, Mass., 2000), introduction, 71–72, 79–81, 88–90, 106–10, 117–27; Lois A. Brown, "Out of the Mouths of Babes: The Abolitionist Campaign of Susan Paul and the Juvenile Choir of Boston," *NEQ* 75 (March 2002): 52–79.

42. *Proceedings of the Fourth New England Anti Slavery Convention*, 45; Henry C. Wright, *A Kiss for a Blow* . . . (Boston, 1842); *The Slave's Friend*, I, II 1836; II, V, VI, VII, XI,

XII 1837; I, II, III, V, VII, VIII, IX, XII, IV 1838; I, II 1839; *TL*, April 19, 1839; January 8, 1841; September 9, 1842; Lewis Perry, *Childhood, Marriage, and Reform: Henry Clarke Wright, 1797–1870* (Chicago, 1980), chap. 1; Holly Keller, "Juvenile Antislavery Narrative and Notions of Childhood," *Children's Literature* 24 (1996): 86–100.

43. Aileen S. Kraditor, *Means and Ends in American Abolitionism: Garrison and His Critics on Strategy and Tactics, 1834–1850* (New York, 1967); Gilbert Hobbs Barnes, *The Anti-Slavery Impulse, 1830–1844* (New York, 1933).

44. *First Annual Report of the American Anti-Slavery Society*, 17; *Second Annual Report of the American Anti-Slavery Society*, 29; *Fourth Annual Report of the Board of Managers of the Massachusetts Anti-Slavery Society*, 16–17; *Sixth Annual Report of the Board of Managers of the Massachusetts Anti-Slavery Society* . . . (Boston, 1838), x–xii, xx–xxvii; Johnson, *Garrison and His Times*, chap. 14; Filler, *The Crusade Against Slavery*, 115–16, 123–26; John R. McKivigan, *The War Against Proslavery Religion: Abolitionism and the Northern Churches, 1830–1865* (Ithaca, 1984); Hugh Davis, *Joshua Leavitt: Evangelical Abolitionist* (Baton Rouge, 1990): 121–30.

45. *TL*, October 26, 1838; *TP*, May 20, 27, June 3, 1836; Ruchames, ed., *The Letters of William Lloyd Garrison*, 2:147–49, 172, 188, 208; *The "Negro Pew."* . . . (Boston, 1837), 3–14, 84–96, 102–8; *Second Annual Report of the American Anti-Slavery Society*, 32.

46. *TL*, August 11, 18, 19 Extra, September 1, 8, 15, 20, October 13, 27, November 3, 1837; January 12, 19, 26, March 2, April 27, June 29, July 6, 13, 27, 1838; September 14, 21, 28, October 26, November 2, 9, December 14, 21, 28, 1838; January 4, 11, 18, 25, February 22, March 8, 1839; *Right and Wrong in Boston . . . in 1837*, 83; May, *Some Recollections*, 236–48; Ruchames, ed., *The Letters of William Lloyd Garrison*, 2:234–51, 292–307, 311–22, 365, 383–85, 401–8, 413–19, 432–38, 440–44, 447–49, 459, 461–63, 493, 538–48; [Mara Weston Chapman], *Right and Wrong in Massachusetts* (Boston, 1839), 3–54; *William Lloyd Garrison*, 2:136–82, 199–207, 222–42; *Fifth Annual Report of the Board of Managers of the Massachusetts Anti-Slavery Society*, xxxvi; Johnson, *Garrison and His Times*, 271–81; *Principles of the Non-resistance Society* (Boston, 1839), 5; Mayer, *All on Fire*, 222–28, 249–51; Lewis Perry, *Radical Abolitionism: Anarchy and the Government of God in Antislavery Thought* (Ithaca, 1973), chaps. 3, 5; Kraditor, *Means and Ends*, chap. 4; Wyatt-Brown, *Lewis Tappan*, 185–91; Goodheart, *Abolitionist*, 101–5.

47. *Third Annual Report of the American Anti-Slavery Society*, 27, 30; *TP*, May 20, 27, December 30, 1836; July 31, August 4, 1837; April 30, 1839; *TL*, October 29, 1836; June 30, July 7, August 25, October 6, 1837; January 26, February 2, March 16, 23, 1838; *TE*, November 23, 1837; *William Lloyd Garrison*, 2:245–47; Kraditor, *Means and Ends*, chap. 5.

48. *Remarks of Henry B. Stanton* . . . (Boston, 1837); Stanton, *Random Recollections*, 49–50, 60–61; *TAE* 8 . . . 28–42; *TE*, February 14, 28, March 7, 1839; *TP*, July 23, 1839; Dumond, ed., *Letters of James Gillespie Birney*, 1:274, 381–91, 404–12, 417–28, 464–68, 478–79; Birney, *James G. Birney*, chap. 25; Kraditor, *Means and Ends*, chap. 6.

49. *TL*, February 1, 8, 22, April 12, May 3, 1839; *TE*, January 24, April 4, 11, June 6, 20, 1839; James G. Birney, *A Letter on the Political Obligations of Abolitionists* . . . (Boston, 1839), 3–4, 8–13, 14–15, 20–34; *Seventh Annual Report of the Board of Managers of the*

Massachusetts Anti-Slavery Society . . . (Boston, 1839), 6–16, 26–38; *Right and Wrong in Massachusetts*, 55–151; William Lloyd Garrison, 2:260–95; Mayer, *All on Fire*, 257–58; Tappan, *The Life of Arthur Tappan*, 279–82; Dumond, ed., *Letters of James Gillespie Birney*, 1:481–84, 489–95, 502–8; Alvan Stewart, *The Causes of Hard Times* (Boston, 1840); Joshua Leavitt, *The Financial Power of Slavery* . . . (New York, 1841); Johnson, *Garrison and His Times*, 282–85; Stauffer, *The Black Hearts of Men*, chap. 4; Julian P. Bretz, "The Economic Background of the Liberty Party," in John R. McKivigan, ed., *Abolition and American Politics and Government* (New York, 1999), 88–102; Rothman, *Flush Times*, epilogue; Edward Baptist, "Toxic Debt, Liar Loans, and Securitized Human Beings: The Panic of 1837 and the Fate of Slavery," *Common-Place* (April 2010): http://www.common-place.org/vol-10/no-03/baptist/; Jessica Lepler, *The Many Panics of 1837: People, Politics, and the Creation of a Transatlantic Financial Crisis* (New York, 2013).

50. *TL*, March 8, April 19, May 17, June 28, July 12, September 13, August 9, 30, November 15, 22, 29, December 13, 1839; January 2, 31, February 16, March 6, 13, 20, 27, April 24, May 8, 15, 19, July 3, 17, August 21, September 11, October 30, 1840; *TE*, May 16, 30, August 8, 15, October 2, 24, December 12, 1839; January 9, February 27, March 12, 1840; Ruchames, ed., *The Letters of William Lloyd Garrison*, 2:497–516, 523–27, 563–69, 577–87; *Eighth Annual Report of the Board of Managers of the Massachusetts Anti-Slavery Society* . . . (Boston, 1840), 4–32; [Elizur Wright], *Myron Holley* . . . (Boston, 1882), chaps. 20, 28; Dumond, ed., *Letters of James Gillespie Birney*, 1:511–19; William Lloyd Garrison, 2:296–320; Johnson, *Garrison and His Times*, 286–87; *TP*, September 3, November 1, October 8, December 31, 1839; Barnes and Dumond, eds., *Letters of Theodore Weld*, 2:849; Reinhard O. Johnson, *The Liberty Party, 1840–1848: Antislavery Third Party Politics in the United States* (Baton Rouge, 2009), 13–16; Frederick J. Blue, *No Taint of Compromise: Crusaders in Antislavery Politics* (Baton Rouge, 2005), 23–25; Fladeland, *James Gillespie Birney*, 166–70; Richard H. Sewell, *Ballots for Freedom: Antislavery Politics in the United States, 1837–1860* (New York, 1976), chap. 3.

51. *TL*, June 7, 28, September 6, October 18, December 6, 20, 1839; April 3, May 15, 22, 1840; *Eighth Annual Report of the Board of Managers of the Massachusetts Anti-Slavery Society*, 36–37; *TE*, May 8, 15, 22, July 2, 1840; Ruchames, ed., *The Letters of William Lloyd Garrison*, 2:607–18; *Ninth Annual Report of the Board of Managers of the Massachusetts Anti-Slavery Society* . . . (Boston, 1841), 5–53; William Lloyd Garrison, 2:342–51; Schor, *Henry Highland Garnet*, 30–35; [Wright], *Myron Holley*, 259–75; Stanley Harrold, *Gamaliel Bailey and Antislavery Union* (Kent, Ohio, 1986), 19–40; John B. Pickard, "John Greenleaf Whittier and the Abolitionist Schism of 1840," *NEQ* 37 (June 1964): 250–54; Mayer, *All on Fire*, chap. 13; Birney, *James G. Birney*, 299–313; Davis, *Joshua Leavitt*, 148–63.

52. *TL*, June 19, 1840; *TE*, June 5, 1840; McKivigan, *The War Against Proslavery Religion*, chaps. 4, 6; Wyatt-Brown, *Lewis Tappan*, 198–200; Gale L. Kenny, *Contentious Liberties: American Abolitionists in Post-Emancipation Jamaica, 1834–1866* (Athens, Ga., 2010); Clifton Herman Johnson, "The American Missionary Association, 1846–1861:

A Study of Christian Abolitionism" (Ph.D. diss., University of North Carolina, 1958); J. Brent Morris, "'All The Truly Wise or Truly Pious have one and the Same End in View': Oberlin, the West, and Abolitionist Schism," *CWH* 57 (2011): 234–67.

53. C. Peter Ripley, ed., *The Black Abolitionist Papers*, vol. 3, *The United States, 1830–1846* (Chapel Hill, 1991) 298–310, 329–39, 352–55; *Mirror of Liberty*, August 1838; *CA*, February 10, 17, 1838; March 21, April 4, May 2, 23, 30, August 22, October 3, 10, 24, 31, 1840; January 23, 30, April 24, May 8, 1841; *TL*, August 30, 1839, May 29, 1840.

54. Barnes and Dumond, eds., *Letters of Theodore Weld*, 2:966–67.

CHAPTER NINE. THE WOMAN QUESTION

1. *TL*, September 19, 1835; *Governor Hammond's Letters on Southern Slavery . . .* (Charleston, S.C., 1845), 32.

2. Barbara Welter, "The Cult of True Womanhood, 1820–1860," *American Quarterly* 18 (Summer 1966), 151–74; Nancy F. Cott, *The Bonds of Womanhood: "Woman's Sphere" in New England, 1780–1835* (New Haven, 1977); Nancy A. Hewitt, *Women's Activism and Social Change: Rochester, New York, 1822–1872* (Ithaca, 1984); Christine Stansell, *City of Women: Sex and Class in New York, 1789–1860* (New York, 1986); Lori D. Ginzberg, *Women and the Work of Benevolence: Morality, Politics and Class in the Nineteenth-Century United States* (New Haven, 1990); Carolyn J. Lawes, *Women and Reform in a New England Community, 1815–1860* (Lexington, Ky., 2000); Judith Wellman, "Women and Radical Reform in Antebellum Upstate New York: A Profile of Grassroots Female Abolitionists," in Mabel E. Deutrich and Virginia C. Purdy, eds., *Clio Was a Woman: Studies in the History of American Women* (Washington, 1980), 113–27; Julie Roy Jeffrey, "Permeable Boundaries: Abolitionist Women and Separate Spheres," *JER* 21 (Spring 2001): 79–93.

3. *FJ*, August 10, November 2, 1827; February 1, September 26, 1828; Dorothy Sterling, ed., *We Are Your Sisters: Black Women in the Nineteenth Century* (New York, 1984), 105–7; James Horton, "Freedom's Yoke: Gender Conventions among Antebellum Free Blacks," *Feminist Studies* 12 (Spring 1986), 51–76; Ann Firor Scott, "Most Invisible of All: Black Women's Voluntary Associations," *JSH* 56 (February 1990), 3–7; Elizabeth McHenry, *Forgotten Readers: Recovering the Lost History of African American Literary Societies* (Durham, 2002), 50–57, 84–102; Anne M. Boylan, "Benevolence and Antislavery Activity among African American Women in New York and Boston, 1820–1840," in Jean Fagan Yellin and John C. Van Horne, eds., *The Abolitionist Sisterhood: Women's Political Culture in Antebellum America* (Ithaca, 1994), 119–38; Linda Perkins, "The Impact of the 'Cult of True Womanhood' on the Education of Black Women," in Darlene Clark Hine, ed., *Black Women in United States History* (Brooklyn, N.Y., 1990), 3:1065–69; Gayle T. Tate, *Unknown Tongues: Black Women's Political Activism in the Antebellum Era, 1830–1860* (East Lansing, 2003).

4. Marilyn Richardson, ed., *Maria W. Stewart: America's First Black Woman Political Writer* (Bloomington, 1987), introduction, 28–30, 37–38, 40–41, 45–49, 56–74, 89, 92; James Oliver and Lois E. Horton, "The Affirmation of Manhood: Black Garrisonians

in Antebellum Boston," in Donald M. Jacobs, ed., *Courage and Conscience: Black and White Abolitionists in Boston* (Bloomington, 1993), 134–35; Kristin Waters, "Crying Out for Liberty: Maria W. Stewart and David Walker's Revolutionary Liberalism," *Philosophia Africana* 15 (Winter 2013): 35–60; Lena Ampadu, "Maria W. Stewart and the Rhetoric of Black Preaching: Perspectives on Womanism and Black Nationalism," in Kristin Waters and Carol B. Conaway, eds., *Black Women's Intellectual Traditions: Speaking Their Minds* (Burlington, Vt., 2007), 38–54 .

5. Richardson, ed., *Maria W. Stewart,* 79–109; Maria W. Stewart, "Two Texts on Children and Christian Education," introd. Eric Gardner, *Publications of the Modern Language Association* 123 (January 2008): 156–65; Marilyn Richardson, "'What if I am a Woman?' Maria W. Stewart's Defense of Black Women's Political Activism," in Jacobs, ed., *Courage,* 191–206.

6. Richardson, ed., *Maria W. Stewart,* 43–44, 53, 55, 127–28; *TL,* June 18, 1831; January 28, September 1, 1832; February 16, 1833; March 8, December 20, 1834; Sterling, ed., *We Are Your Sisters,* 108–9, 113; *Second Annual Report of the Board of Managers of the New England Anti-Slavery Society,* 49; Erica Armstrong Dunbar, *A Fragile Freedom: African American Women and Emancipation in the Antebellum City* (New Haven, 2008), 60–62, 101–2; Ann M. Boylan, *The Origins of Women's Activism: New York and Boston, 1797–1840* (Chapel Hill, 2002), 34–37, 44; Lois A. Brown, "William Lloyd Garrison and Emancipatory Feminism in Nineteenth-Century America," in James Brewer Stewart, ed., *William Lloyd Garrison at Two Hundred: History, Legacy, and Memory* (New Haven, 2008), 41–76; Shirley J. Yee, *Black Women Abolitionists: A Study in Activism, 1828–1860* (Knoxville, 1992), 18–19; Puritan, *The Abrogation of the Seventh Commandment by the American Churches* (New York, 1835), 4.

7. *TL,* June 18, 1831; August 18, 1832; February 9, 1838; *TE,* July 20, 1833; Sterling, ed., *We Are Your Sisters,* 103–4, 111–14, 127–33; Dorothy Porter, ed., *Early Negro Writing, 1760–1837* (Boston, 1971), 127–28; Sarah M. Douglass to Garrison, February 29, December 6, 1832; Garrison to Douglass, March 5, 1832, *BAP,* reel 1; Anna Bustill Smith, "The Bustill Family," *JNH* 9 (1925): 638–44; Julie Winch, "'You Have Talents–Only Cultivate Them': Philadelphia's Black Female Literary Societies and the Abolitionist Crusade," in Yellin and Van Horne, eds., *The Abolitionist Sisterhood,* 101–18; Erica Armstrong Dunbar, "Writing for True Womanhood: African-American Women's Writing and the Antislavery Struggle," in Kathryn Kish Sklar and James Brewer Stewart, eds., *Women's Rights and Transatlantic Antislavery in the Era of Emancipation* (New Haven, 2007), 299–308; April Haynes, "'Abuse Not': Flesh and Bones in Sarah Mapps Douglass' Classroom," paper presented at the AAS, 2010.

8. *TL,* April 23, 1831; January 28, 1832; Sterling, ed., *We Are Your Sisters,* 114–17, 119–26; Gilbert H. Barnes and Dwight L. Dumond, eds., *Letters of Theodore Dwight Weld, Angelina Grimké Weld and Sarah Grimké, 1822–1844* (Gloucester, Mass., 1965), 1:379–82; Janice Sumler-Lewis, "The Forten–Purvis Women of Philadelphia and the American Anti-Slavery Society," *JNH* 66 (Winter 1981): 281–88; Julie Winch, "Sarah Forten's Anti-Slavery Networks," in Sklar and Stewart, eds., *Women's Rights and Transatlantic Antislavery,* 143–57; Carolyn Williams, "The Female Antislavery Movement:

Fighting Against Racial Prejudice and Promoting Women's Rights in Antebellum America," in Yellin and Horne, eds., *The Abolitionist Sisterhood*, 159–77.

9. Porter, ed., *Early Negro Writing*, 494–514; William L. Andrews, ed., *Sisters of the Spirit: Three Black Women's Autobiographies of the Nineteenth Century* (Bloomington, 1986), introduction; Julyanne Dodson, "Nineteenth-Century A.M.E. Preaching Women," in Hine, ed., *Black Women in United States History*, 1:333–49; Nell Painter, *Sojourner Truth: A Life, A Symbol* (New York, 1996), 187.

10. Porter identifies L.H. as a black woman in *Early Negro Writing*, 123–26; TL, April 19, 1834; Tiya Miles, "Laura Smith Haviland in Abolitionist Women's History," *Michigan History* 39 (Fall 2013): 1–20; Anna Davis Hallowell, *James and Lucretia Mott: Life and Letters* (Boston, 1884), 110–27; Mary Grew, *James Mott: A Biographical Sketch* (New York, ca. 1868), 8–9, 29; Beverly Wilson Palmer, ed., *Selected Letters of Lucretia Coffin Mott* (Urbana, 2002), 20–35; Carol Faulkner, *Lucretia Mott's Heresy: Abolition and Women's Rights in Nineteenth-Century America* (Philadelphia, 2011); Ira V. Brown, "Cradle of Feminism: The Philadelphia Female Anti-Slavery Society, 1833–1840," *PMHB* 102 (April 1978): 143–66; Brown, *Mary Grew: Abolitionist and Feminist (1813–1896)* (Cranbury, N.J., 1992); Jean R. Soderlund, "Priorities and Power: The Philadelphia Female Anti-Slavery Society," in Yellin and Horne, eds., *The Abolitionist Sisterhood*, 67–88.

11. *Right and Wrong in Boston . . . Annual Meeting of 1835*, 4, 39, 81–86, 102–3; *Right and Wrong in Boston in 1836 . . .* (Boston, 1836), 22–25, 41; *Fourth Annual Report of the Board of Managers of the Massachusetts Anti-Slavery Society . . .* (Boston, 1836), 6; *The Liberty Bell . . .* (Boston, 1841); *The Liberty Bell . . .* (Boston, 1842), 164–204; *The Liberty Bell . . .* (Boston, 1843), 71–110, 170–74; Debra Gold Hansen, *Strained Sisterhood: Gender and Class in the Boston Female Anti-Slavery Society* (Amherst, Mass., 1993), chaps. 1, 4; Clare Taylor, *Women of the Anti-Slavery Movement: The Weston Sisters* (New York, 1995), chaps. 2, 3.

12. Mrs. Child, *An Appeal in Favor of that Class of Americans called Africans* (New York, 1836): 10–11, 23–24, 29–30, 32–34, 41–42, 73, 78–81, 84–88, 109–12, 117–21, 130–31, 134, 148, 166–68, 170–71, 191–94, 214–16; *TL*, September 7, 1833, 141; Jean Fagan Yellin, *Women and Sisters: The Antislavery Feminists in American Culture* (New Haven, 1989), chap. 3; Carolyn L. Karcher, *The First Woman of the Republic: A Cultural Biography of Lydia Maria Child* (Durham, 1994); Deborah Pickman Clifford, *Crusader for Freedom: A Life of Lydia Maria Child* (Boston, 1992).

13. Mrs. Child, ed., *The Oasis* (Boston, 1834), vi, viii; *Authentic Anecdotes of American Slavery* [Newburyport, 1835]; Mrs. Child, *Anti-Slavery Catechism* (Newburyport, 1836); Mrs. Child, *The Evils of Slavery and the Cure of Slavery* (Newburyport, 1836), 19; Mrs. D. L. Child, *The History of the Condition of Women in Various Ages and Nations*, vol. 1, *Comprising the Women of Asia and Africa*; vol. 2, *Comprising Women of Europe, America and South Sea Islands* (Boston, 1835); Karcher, *The First Woman of the Republic*, chap. 10; *Right and Wrong in Boston . . . Annual Meeting of 1835*, 90–96; Karen Sanchez-Eppler, *Touching Liberty: Abolition, Feminism, and the Politics of the Body* (Berkeley, 1993), chap. 1.

14. *First Annual Report of the Ladies New York City Anti-Slavery Society* (New York, 1836), 4–6, 15–19; *Right and Wrong in Boston . . . Annual Meeting of 1835*, 86–90; Amy Swerdlow, "Abolition's Conservative Sisters: The Ladies' New York City Anti-Slavery Societies, 1834–1840," in Yellin and Horne, *The Abolitionist Sisterhood*, 31–44; Betty Fladeland, *Men and Brothers: Anglo-American Antislavery Cooperation* (Urbana, 1972), 227.

15. *Second Annual Report of the American Anti-Slavery Society*, 50–53, 83–87; *First Annual Report of the Ladies Anti-Slavery Society of Concord . . .* (Concord, N.H., 1836), 5–10; *Right and Wrong in Boston in 1836*, 28–32, 72–75, 78: *TL*, November 2, 1833; March 19, May 21, August 13, 27, September 7, October 15, December 10, 27, 1836; January 2, 1837; *TP*, December 9, 1836; Deborah Bingham Van Broekhoven, *The Devotion of These Women: Rhode Island in the Antislavery Network* (Amherst, Mass., 2002), 11–17, 25–26, 85–87, 92; Beth A. Salerno, *Sister Societies: Women's Antislavery Organizations in Antebellum America* (DeKalb, Ill., 2005), chap. 2; Julie Roy Jeffrey, *The Great Silent Army of Abolitionism: Ordinary Women in the Antislavery Movement* (Chapel Hill, 1998), 36–95; Stacey M. Robertson, *Hearts Beating for Liberty: Women Abolitionists in the Old Northwest* (Chapel Hill, 2010), 15–20; Thomas Dublin, *Women at Work: The Transformation of Work and Community in Lowell, Massachusetts, 1826–1860* (New York, 1979).

16. John M. Putnam, *An Address Delivered at Concord . . .* (Concord, N.H., 1836), 12–13; James A. Thome, *Address to the Females of Ohio . . .* (Cincinnati, 1836), 1–5, 8–9, 11–15.

17. *TL*, October 15, December 10, 1836; January 1, 1841; July 22, 1842; Louis Ruchames, ed., *The Letters of William Lloyd Garrison*, vol. 2, *House Dividing Against Itself, 1836–1840* (Cambridge, Mass., 1971), 194; Jeffrey, *The Great Silent Army of Abolitionism*, 108–26; Van Broekhoven, *The Devotion of These Women*, chap. 7; Robertson, *Hearts Beating for Liberty*, chap. 4; Lee Chambers-Schiller, "'A Good Work Among the People': The Political Culture of the Boston Antislavery Fair," in Yellin and Horne, eds., *The Abolitionist Sisterhood*, 249–74.

18. *TE*, July 21, 1836; *TL*, March 11, April 28, June 16, 1837; July 20, 1838; Ruchames, ed., *The Letters of William Lloyd Garrison*, 2:326; Gerda Lerner, "The Political Activities of Antislavery Women," in *The Majority Finds Its Past: Placing Women in History* (New York, 1979), 112–28; Mary Hershberger, "Mobilizing Women, Anticipating Abolition: The Struggle against Indian Removal in the 1830s," *JAH* 86 (June 1999): 15–40; Deborah Bingham Van Broekhoven, "'Let Your Names be Enrolled': Method and Ideology in Women's Antislavery Petitioning," in Yellin and Horne, eds., *The Abolitionist Sisterhood*, 179–99; Susan Zaeske, *Signatures of Citizenship: Petitioning, Antislavery, and Women's Political Identity* (Chapel Hill, 2003); Daniel Carpenter and Colin D. Moore, "When Canvassers Become Activists: Antislavery Petitioning and the Political Mobilization of American Women," *American Political Science Review* 108 (August 2014): 479–98.

19. Charles Wilbanks, ed., *Walking by Faith: The Diary of Angelina Grimké 1828–1835* (Columbia, S.C., 2003), 107, 211–13; A. E. Grimké, *Appeal to the Christian Women of the*

South (New York, 1836), 1–2, 10–12, 14–20, 26–31, 35–36; *TL*, October 8, 1836; May 5, 1837; Sarah M. Grimké, *An Epistle to the Clergy of the Southern States* [New York, 1836], 1–4, 10–12; Barnes and Dumond, eds., *Letters of Theodore Dwight Weld, Angelina Grimké Weld and Sarah Grimké*, 1:366–72; Larry Ceplair, ed., *The Public Years of Sarah and Angelina Grimké: Selected Writings, 1835–1839* (New York, 1989), 33–36.

20. Catherine Birney, *The Grimké Sisters . . .* (Boston, 1885), 159–67, 177–95; *TL*, December 3, 1836; February 25, July 28, August 11, October 27, 1837; [Francis Jackson Garrison and Wendell Phillips Garrison], *William Lloyd Garrison, 1805–1879: The Story of His Life told By His Children* (New York, 1885), 2:133–35, 160–61; Palmer, ed., *Selected Letters of Lucretia Coffin Mott*, 36–37; *Right and Wrong in Boston in 1836*, 88–90; *Right and Wrong in Boston . . .* (Boston, 1837), 42–69, 94–101; Nathaniel P. Rogers, *An Address Delivered Before the Concord Female Anti-Slavery Society . . .* (Concord, N.H., 1838), 3–4, 10–12, 17–19; Barnes and Dumond, eds., *Letters of Theodore Dwight Weld, Angelina Grimké Weld and Sarah Grimké*, 1:374–75, 389–92, 395–97, 411–19, 423–36, 441–45; Ceplair, ed., *The Public Years*, 280–85, 289–94; Gerda Lerner, *The Grimké Sisters from South Carolina: Rebels Against Slavery* (Boston, 1967), 163–204; Katharine Du Pre Lumpkin, *The Emancipation of Angelina Grimké* (Chapel Hill, 1974), 94–101, 108–30; Yellin, *Women and Sisters*, 36, 45.

21. Catharine E. Beecher, *An Essay on Slavery and Abolitionism . . .* (Philadelphia, 1837), 6–9, 13–17, 21–28, 39–47, 96–107, 120–22; Kathryn Kish Sklar, *Catharine Beecher: A Study in American Domesticity* (New Haven, 1973), 98–101, 132–37, 235–43, 266–70; Du Pre Lumpkin, *The Emancipation of Angelina Grimké*, 115–17; Jeanne Boydston, Mary Kelley, and Anne Margolis, *The Limits of Sisterhood: The Beecher Sisters on Women's Rights and Women's Sphere* (Chapel Hill, 1988); Alisse Theodore Portnoy, "'Female Petitioners can be Lawfully Heard': Negotiating Female Decorum, United States Politics, and Political Agency, 1829–1831," *JER* 23 (Winter 2003): 573–610; Zaeske, *Signatures of Citizenship*, 164–66.

22. *Letters to Catharine E. Beecher . . .* (Boston, 1838), 4–7, 10–13, 15–17, 31–34, 36–41, 45–47, 89–93; *TL*, June 23, July 21, August 11, 25, September 15, 20, October 13, November 3, 1837; Kathryn Kish Sklar, "'The Throne of My Heart': Religion, Oratory, and Transatlantic Community in Angelina Grimké's Launching of Women's Rights, 1828–1838," in Sklar and Stewart, eds., *Women's Rights and Transatlantic Antislavery*, 211–41; Stephen Howard Browne, *Angelina Grimké: Rhetoric, Identity, and the Radical Imagination* (East Lansing, 1999), chap. 4.

23. *Letters to Catharine E. Beecher*, 106–29; *Letters on the Equality of the Sexes . . .* (Boston, 1838), 3, 11, 14–21, 45, 118–22; *TL*, January 5, 12, 19, 26, February 2, 9, 16, 1838; Elizabeth Ann Bartlett, *Liberty, Equality, Sorority: The Origin and Interpretation of American Feminist Thought: Frances Wright, Sarah Grimké, and Margaret Fuller* (Brooklyn, N.Y., 1994), chap. 4; Gerda Lerner, ed., *The Feminist Thought of Sarah Grimké* (New York, 1998), for her later writings.

24. *Right and Wrong in Boston . . . in 1837*, 32–41; *Proceedings of the Anti-Slavery Convention of American Women . . .* (New York, 1837), 3–9, 11–13, 15, 17; *An Appeal to the Women of the Nominally Free States . . .* (New York, 1837), 3–6, 14–28, 54–61, 66–67.

25. Barnes and Dumond, eds., *Letters of Theodore Dwight Weld, Angelina Grimké Weld and Sarah Grimké*, 2:540–43, 552–53, 564, 567–68; *TL*, March 2, 30, May 25, 1838; Ceplair, ed., *The Public Years*, 310–12, 318–23; *Proceedings of the Anti-Slavery Convention of American Women* . . . (Philadelphia, 1838), 3–5, 6–10, 12–14, 18; *Address to Antislavery Societies* (Philadelphia, 1838), 3–7, 9–10; *Address to the Free Colored People of the United States* (Philadelphia, 1838), 3–11; *Address to the Senators and Representatives of the Free States* . . . (Philadelphia, 1838), 3–10; Du Pre Lumpkin, *The Emancipation of Angelina Grimké*, 130–52.

26. *Proceedings of the Third Anti-Slavery Convention of American Women* . . . (Philadelphia, 1839), 3–10, 13, 15–28.

27. Barnes and Dumond, eds., *Letters of Theodore Dwight Weld, Angelina Grimké Weld and Sarah Grimké*, 2:532–683; Robert K. Nelson, "The Forgetfulness of Sex: Devotion and Desire in the Courtship Letters of Angelina Grimké and Theodore Dwight Weld," *Journal of Social History* 37 (Spring 2004): 663–79; Carol Berkin, *Civil War Wives: The Lives and Times of Angelina Grimké Weld, Varina Howell Davis, and Julia Dent Grant* (New York, 2009), chaps. 6–8.

28. Henry Mayer, *All on Fire: William Lloyd Garrison and the Abolition of Slavery* (New York, 1998), 177–87; Walter M. Merrill, ed., *The Letters of William Lloyd Garrison*, vol. 1, *I Will be Heard! 1822–1835* (Cambridge, Mass., 1971), 279–409; Hallowell, *James and Lucretia Mott*, 40–44; Palmer, ed., *Selected Letters of Lucretia Coffin Mott*, 188; Grew, *James Mott*, 16; John Stauffer, *The Black Hearts of Men: Radical Abolitionists and the Transformation of Race* (Cambridge, Mass., 2002), 215–18, 228–32; Karcher, *The First Woman of the Republic*, chap. 9; Lori D. Ginzberg, *Elizabeth Cady Stanton: An American Life* (New York, 2009), 86–89; Nancy H. Burkett, *Abby Kelley Foster and Stephen S. Foster* (Worcester, Mass., 1976); Leslie Wheeler, ed., *Loving Warriors: Selected Letters of Lucy Stone and Henry B. Blackwell, 1853 to 1893* (New York, 1981), introduction; Robertson, *Hearts Beating for Liberty*, 22–24, 145–53; Chris Dixon, *Perfecting the Family: Antislavery Marriages in Nineteenth-Century America* (Amherst, Mass., 1997); Blanche Glassman Hersh, *The Slavery of Sex: Feminists-Abolitionists in America* (Urbana, 1978), chap. 7; Yee, *Black Women Abolitionists*, chap. 1; Frances Smith Foster, ed., *Love and Marriage in Early African America* (Boston, 2008), 71.

29. *TL*, May 3, August 9, September 6, 1839; *TE*, August 8, 1839; *Seventh Annual Report of the Board of Managers of the Massachusetts Anti-Slavery Society* . . . (Boston, 1839), 31–33; *Eighth Annual Report of the Board of Managers of the Massachusetts Anti-Slavery Society* . . . (Boston, 1840), 27–29; Aileen S. Kraditor, *Means and Ends in American Abolitionism: Garrison and His Critics on Strategy and Tactics, 1834–1850* (New York, 1967), 49–52; Salerno, *Sister Societies*, 92–101; Ellen Carol DuBois, *Feminism and Suffrage: The Emergence of an Independent Women's Movement in America, 1848–1869* (Ithaca, 1978), 31–40; Betty Fladeland, *James Gillespie Birney: Slaveholder to Abolitionist* (Ithaca, 1955), 161–64.

30. *TL*, March 20, April 19, May 17, June 28, August 16, December 20, 1839; January 20, March 20, May 22, 29, 1840; *TE*, June 19, 1840; November 25, 1841; *Ninth Annual Report of the Board of Managers of the Massachusetts Anti-Slavery Society* . . . (Boston,

1841), 50–52; John B. Pickard, "John Greenleaf Whittier and the Abolitionist Schism of 1840," *NEQ* 37 (June 1964): 250–54; Dorothy Sterling, *Ahead of Her Time: Abby Kelley and the Politics of Antislavery* (New York, 1991); Keith Melder, "Abby Kelley and the Process of Liberation," in Yellin and Van Horne, eds., *The Abolitionist Sisterhood*, 231–40; Martha S. Jones, *All Bound Up Together: The Woman Question in African American Public Culture, 1830–1900* (Chapel Hill, 2007), 54–57; Salerno, *Sister Societies*, 101–17; Swerdlow, "Abolition's Conservative Sisters," 31–44.

31. *Seventh Annual Report of the Boston Female Anti-Slavery Society . . .* (Boston, 1840), 1–7, 28–30; Hansen, *Strained Sisterhood*, chap. 5; Margaret Hope Bacon, "By Moral Force Alone: The Antislavery Women and Nonresistance," in Yellin and Van Horne, eds., *The Abolitionist Sisterhood*, 275–97.

32. Palmer, ed., *Selected Letters of Lucretia Coffin Mott*, 47–50, 64–66, 71–73; Brown, "Cradle of Feminism," 143–66; "The Philadelphia Female Anti-Slavery Society," 84–88; Bruce Dorsey, *Reforming Men and Women: Gender in the Antebellum City* (Ithaca, 2002), 171–81; Faulkner, *Lucretia Mott's Heresy*, 81–83; Brown, *Mary Grew*, 52.

33. TL, July 23, 1841; March 18, April 15, 1842; Salerno, *Sister Societies*, chap. 5; Lawes, *Women and Reform*, 4–80; Jeffrey, *The Great Silent Army of Abolitionism*, 96–106; Robertson, *Hearts Beating for Liberty*; Michael D. Piersen, *Free Hearts and Free Homes: Gender and American Antislavery Politics* (Chapel Hill, 2003); Wendy Hamand Venet, *Neither Ballots nor Bullets: Women Abolitionists and the Civil War* (Charlottesville, Va., 1991).

34. Hersh, *The Slavery of Sex*; Alex Tyrell, *Joseph Sturge and the Moral Radical Party in Early Victorian Britain* (London, 1987); *William Lloyd Garrison*, 2:351–52; Douglas H. Maynard, "The World's Anti-Slavery Convention of 1840," *MVHR* 47 (December 1970): 452–71.

35. Elizabeth Cady Stanton, *Eighty Years and More: Reminiscences, 1815–1897* (1898; repr., New York, 1971), 54, 78–84; Ann D. Gordon, ed., *The Selected Papers of Elizabeth Cady Stanton and Susan B. Anthony: In the School of Anti-Slavery, 1840–1860* (New Brunswick, N.J., 1997), 1:8–15; Elizabeth Cady Stanton, Susan B. Anthony, and Matilda Jocelyn Gage, eds., *History of Woman Suffrage*, vol. 1, *1848–1861* (New York, 1881), 52, 61–62, 407–31; *William Lloyd Garrison*, 2:383; Ginzberg, *Elizabeth Cady Stanton*; Elisabeth Griffith, *In Her Own Right: The Life of Elizabeth Cady Stanton* (New York, 1984); Lois W. Banner, *Elizabeth Cady Stanton: A Radical for Women's Rights* (Boston, 1980).

36. TL, June 26, July 3, 24, 31, October 23, 1840; February 12, April 23, 1841; April 29, 1842; TE, June 18, July 9, 16, 23, 30, 1840; January 7, 1841; NASS, July 23, August 6, September 10, October 22, 1840; Stanton, Anthony, and Gage, eds., *History of Woman Suffrage*, 1:53–62; *Proceedings of the General Anti-Slavery Convention . . .* (London, 1841); Frederick B. Tolles ed., *Slavery and "The Woman Question": Lucretia Mott's Diary of Her Visit to Britain to Attend the World's Anti-Slavery Convention of 1840* (Haverford, Pa., 1952); James Mott, *Three Months in Great Britain* (Philadelphia, 1841); *Memorial of Sarah Pugh . . .* (Philadelphia, 1888), 22–30; Palmer, ed., *Selected Letters of Lucretia Coffin Mott*, 77–81; Hallowell, *James and Lucretia Mott*, chap. 7; Grew, *James Mott,*

14; *William Lloyd Garrison,* 2:366–407; Ruchames, ed., *The Letters of William Lloyd Garrison,* 2:659–71; *Ninth Annual Report of the Board of Managers of the Massachusetts Anti-Slavery Society,* 54–56; Anthony J. Barker, *Captain Charles Stuart: Anglo-American Abolitionist* (Baton Rouge, 1986), 189; Donald R. Kennon, "'An Apple of Discord': The Woman Question at the World's Antislavery Convention of 1840," *S&A* 5 (1984): 244–66; Kathryn Kish Sklar, "'Women Who Speak for an Entire Nation': American and British Women at the World Anti-Slavery Convention, London, 1840," in Yellin and Van Horne, eds., *The Abolitionist Sisterhood,* 301–33; Clare Midgley, "British Abolition and Feminism in Transatlantic Perspective," in Sklar and Stewart, eds., *Women's Rights and Transatlantic Antislavery,* 121–37; Fladeland, *Men and Brothers,* 227–28, 258–71.

37. *TL,* August 28, September 11, 25, October 23, 30, December 8, 1840; February 26, March 6, 12, 1841; *NASS,* May 23, 1844; *William Lloyd Garrison,* 2:361, 381; Brown, *Mary Grew,* 55–56.

38. Thomas Wentworth Higginson, *Margaret Fuller Ossoli* (Boston, 1884); *Love Letters of Margaret Fuller, 1845–1846* . . . (New York, 1903), 216, 222; Patricia Okker, *Our Sister Editors: Sarah J. Hale and the Tradition of Nineteenth-Century American Women Editors* (Athens, Ga., 1995); Charles Capper, *Margaret Fuller: An American Romantic Life,* vol. 2, *The Private Years* (New York, 1992), 332; Meg McGavran Murray, *Margaret Fuller: Wandering Pilgrim* (Athens, Ga., 2008), 1, 137; Joan Von Mehren, *Minerva and the Muse: A Life of Margaret Fuller* (Amherst, Mass., 1994); Megan Marshall, *Margaret Fuller: A New American Life* (New York, 2013).

39. Margaret Fuller Ossoli, *Woman in the Nineteenth Century* . . . (New York, 1869), 28–31, 37–43, 110–16, 140–48, 167–77; Robert N. Hudspeth, ed., *"My Heart Is a Large Kingdom": Selected Letters of Margaret Fuller* (Ithaca, 2001), 135–36; Capper, *Margaret Fuller . . . The Private Years,* 2:292, 306; Charles Capper, *Margaret Fuller: An American Romantic Life,* vol. 1, *The Public Years* (New York, 2007), 17, 106–22, 177–93; *Memoirs of Margaret Fuller Ossoli,* 2 vols. (Boston, 1857), 1:107, 319–50; Murray, *Margaret Fuller,* 218–27; Stanton, Anthony, and Gage, eds., *History of Woman Suffrage* 1:801–2.

40. Judith Mattson Bean and Joel Myerson eds., *Margaret Fuller, Critic: Writings from the New-York Tribune, 1844–1846* (New York, 2000), 28–29, 65–70, 119–20, 131–33, 233–39, 386–89; Capper, *Margaret Fuller . . . The Public Years,* 1:268–70.

41. *Memoirs of Margaret Fuller Ossoli,* 2 vols. (Boston, 1857), 2:169–352; Capper, *Margaret Fuller . . . The Public Years,* 1:487–89; Bonnie S. Anderson, "Frauen-emancipation and Beyond: The Use of the Concept of Emancipation by Early European Feminists," and Ellen Carol DuBois, "Ernestine Rose's Jewish Origins and the Varieties of Euro-American Emancipation in 1848," in Sklar and Stewart, eds., *Women's Rights and Transatlantic Antislavery,* 82–97, 279–96; Bonnie S. Anderson, *Joyous Greetings: The First International Women's Movement, 1830–1860* (New York, 2000); Margaret H. McFadden, *Golden Cables of Sympathy: The Transatlantic Sources of Nineteenth-Century Feminism* (Lexington, Ky., 1998); Mischa Honeck, *We Are the Revolutionists: German-Speaking Immigrants and American Abolitionists after 1848* (Athens, Ga., 2011), chap. 4.

42. Stanton, Anthony, and Gage, eds., *History of Woman Suffrage*, 1:63–67, 98–100; Paulina W. Davis, *A History of the National Woman's Rights Movement* . . . (New York, 1871), 12; Michael S. Kimmel and Thomas E. Mosmiller, eds., *Against the Tide: Pro-Feminist Men in the United States, 1776–1900* (Boston, 1992), 76–78, 82–93, 94–97; Lisa Tetrault, *The Myth of Seneca Falls: Memory and the Woman's Suffrage Movement, 1848–1898* (Chapel Hill, 2014); Norma Basch, *In the Eyes of the Law: Women, Marriage and Property in Nineteenth-Century New York* (Ithaca, 1982); Lori D. Ginzberg, *Untidy Origins: A Story of Woman's Rights in Antebellum New York* (Chapel Hill, 2005); Stansell, *City of Women*; Boyd Guest, "John Neal and 'Women's Rights and Women's Wrongs,'" *NEQ* 18 (December 1945): 508–15; Jane L. Silver-Isenstadt, *Shameless: The Visionary Life of Mary Gove Nichols* (Baltimore, 2002); Diane Eickhoff, *Revolutionary Heart: The Life of Clarina Nichols and the Pioneering Crusade for Women's Rights* (Kansas City, Kan., 2006); Marilyn S. Blackwell and Kristen T. Oertel, *Frontier Feminist: Clarina Howard Nichols and the Politics of Motherhood* (Lawrence, Kan., 2010); Lewis Perry, *Childhood, Marriage, and Reform: Henry Clarke Wright, 1797–1870* (Chicago, 1980), 218–55.

43. Samuel J. May, *Some Recollections of Our Antislavery Conflict* (New York, 1968), 236; *TL*, December 31, 1841; November 18, December 30, 1842; May 5, November 24, December 8, 1843; January 26, 1844; *NASS*, March 7, 1844; Judith Wellman, *The Road to Seneca Falls: Elizabeth Cady Stanton and the First Woman's Rights Convention* (Urbana, 2004), part 2; Donald Yacovone, *Samuel Joseph May and the Dilemmas of the Liberal Persuasion, 1797–1871* (Philadelphia, 1991), 119–25; Sterling, *Ahead of Her Time*, 150–186; Melder, "Abby Kelley and the Process of Liberation," 240–48; Nancy Hewitt, "'Seeking a Larger Liberty': Remapping First Wave Feminism," in Sklar and Stewart, eds., *Women's Rights and Transatlantic Antislavery*, 266–78; Rosalyn Terborg-Penn, *African American Women in the Struggle for the Vote, 1850–1920* (Bloomington, 1998), 14.

44. Gordon, ed., *The Selected Papers* 1:69, 75–88; Stanton, Anthony, and Gage, eds., *History of Woman Suffrage*, 1:67–75; Stanton, *Eighty Years and More*, 127–51; *Proceedings of the Woman's Rights Convention* . . . (New York, 1870); Hallowell, *James and Lucretia Mott*, 298–301; Grew, *James Mott*, 12; DuBois, *Feminism and Suffrage*, 40–41; Wellman, *The Road to Seneca Falls*, chaps. 7, 8; Philip S. Foner, ed., *Frederick Douglass on Women's Rights* (Greenwood, Conn., 1976); Sue Davis, *The Political Thought of Elizabeth Cady Stanton: Women's Rights and the American Political Traditions* (New York, 2008); Vivian Gornick, *The Solitude of Self: Thinking about Elizabeth Cady Stanton* (New York, 2005); Barbara Caine, "Elizabeth Cady Stanton, John Stuart Mill, and the Nature of Feminist Thought," in Ellen Carol DuBois and Richard Candida Smith, eds., *Elizabeth Cady Stanton: Feminist as Thinker, A Reader in Documents and Essays* (New York, 2007), 50–65; Paul A. Cimbala, "Elizabeth Cady Stanton and the Woman's Rights Movement," in Cimbala and Miller, eds., *Against the Tide*, 41–53; Sylvia D. Hoffert, *When Hens Crow: The Woman's Rights Movement in Antebellum America* (Bloomington, 1995), chap. 2.

45. *Proceedings of the Woman's Rights Convention*, 3–6, 8–12; Stanton, Anthony, and Gage, eds., *History of Woman Suffrage*, 1:808–10; Wellman, *The Road to Seneca Falls*,

211–16; Nancy A. Hewitt, "The Spriritual Journey of an Abolitionist: Amy Kirby Post, 1802–1889," in Brycchan Carey and Geoffrey Plank, eds., *Quakers and Abolition* (Urbana, 2014), 73–86; Keith E. Melder, *Beginnings of Sisterhood: The American Woman's Rights Movement, 1800–1850* (New York, 1977), chap. 10.

46. Gordon, ed., *The Selected Papers,* 1:88–123; Ginzberg, *Elizabeth Cady Stanton,* 66–84; Banner, *Elizabeth Cady Stanton,* chap. 4; Hallowell, *James and Lucretia Mott,* 487–506; Dana Greene, ed., *Lucretia Mott: Her Complete Speeches and Sermons* (New York, 1980): 143–62.

47. Du Bois, *Feminism and Suffrage;* Gayle V. Fischer, *Pantaloons and Power: A Nineteenth Century Dress Reform in the United States* (Kent, Ohio, 2001); Joelle Million, *Woman's Voice, Woman's Place: Lucy Stone and the Birth of the Woman's Rights Movement* (Westport, Conn., 2003); Aileen S. Kraditor, *The Ideas of the Woman Suffrage Movement, 1890–1920* (New York, 1981); Nancy F. Cott, *The Grounding of Modern Feminism* (New Haven, 1987), 6–9; Christine Stansell, *The Feminist Promise: 1792 to the Present* (New York, 2010).

CHAPTER TEN. THE BLACK MAN'S BURDEN

1. *Weekly Advocate,* January 7, 1837; Benjamin Quarles, *Black Abolitionists* (New York, 1969), introduction; Jane H. Pease and William H. Pease, *They Who Would Be Free: Blacks' Search for Freedom, 1830–1861* (New York, 1974), 297–99; Patrick Rael, ed., *African-American Activism Before the Civil War* (New York, 2008), 39–49, 58–77, 134–67; James Oliver and Lois E. Horton, *In Hope of Liberty: Culture, Community and Protest Among Northern Free Blacks, 1700–1860* (New York, 1997); Steven Kantrowitz, *More than Freedom: Fighting for Black Citizenship in a White Republic, 1829–1889* (New York, 2012).

2. *TL,* May 28, 1831; June 30, 1832; May 9, 1835; Howard Holman Bell, *A Survey of the Negro Convention Movement, 1830–1861* (1953, repr., New York, 1969); Harry Reed, *Platform for Change: The Foundation of the Northern Free Black Community, 1775–1865* (East Lansing, 1994), 141–52.

3. *Minutes and Proceedings of the Second Annual Convention . . .* (Philadelphia, 1832), 4–6, 8–11, 15–20, 32–36, and *Minutes and Proceedings of the Third Annual Convention . . .* (New York, 1833), 8–11, 14–19, 22–23, 26–36, in Howard Holman Bell, ed., *Minutes of the Proceedings of the National Negro Conventions, 1830–1864* (New York, 1969); *First Annual Report of the American Anti-Slavery Society . . .* (New York, 1834), 34–36; *Second Annual Report of the American Anti-Slavery Society . . .* (New York, 1835), 26–27; *Third Annual Report of the American Anti-Slavery Society,* 25; Donald Yacovone, "The Transformation of the Black Temperance Movement, 1827–1854: An Interpretation," *JER* 8 (Autumn 1988): 281–86; Leslie M. Alexander, *African or American?: Black Identity and Political Activism in New York City, 1784–1861* (Urbana, 2008), 81–82, 85.

4. *Minutes of the Fourth Annual Convention . . .* (New York, 1834), 3–7, 21–25, 27–36, in Bell, ed., *Minutes;* C. Peter Ripley, ed., *The Black Abolitionist Papers,* vol. 3, *The United States, 1830–1846* (Chapel Hill, 1991), 133; Jane H. Pease and William H. Pease,

"Negro Conventions and the Problem of Black Leadership," *Journal of Black Studies* 2 (September 1971): 30–31; Elizabeth Rauh Bethel, *The Roots of African American Identity: Memory and History in Antebellum Free Communities* (New York, 1997), 136–38.

5. *TL*, May 9, 1835; *Minutes of the Fifth Annual Convention . . .* (Philadelphia, 1835), 5, 10–14, 16–19, 25–32, in Bell, ed., *Minutes*.

6. Julie Winch, ed., *The Elite of Our People: Joseph Willson's Sketches of Black Upper-Class Life in Antebellum Philadelphia* (University Park, Pa., 2002), 84–85, 111–19; *Minutes and Proceedings of the Third Annual Convention*, 14; *TL*, June 4, 1831; *Weekly Advocate*, January 14, 28, February 4, 25, 1837; *NR*, January 1839; *CA*, October 5, 1839; Craig Steven Wilder, "Black Life in Freedom: Creating a Civic Culture," in Ira Berlin and Leslie Harris, eds., *Slavery in New York* (New York, 2005), 217–37; Dorothy Porter, "The Organized Educational Activities of Negro Literary Societies, 1828–1846," *Journal of Negro Education* 5 (Fall 1936): 555–75; Tony Martin, "The Banneker Literary Institute of Philadelphia: African American Intellectual Activism before the War of the Slaveholders' Rebellion," *JAH* 87 (Summer 2002): 303–22; Peter P. Hinks and Stephen Kantrowitz, *All Men Free and Brethren: Essays on the History of Free Black Masonry* (Ithaca, 2013), introduction; John Ernest, *A Nation within a Nation: Organizing African-American Communities before the Civil War* (Lanham, Md., 2011).

7. Ripley, ed., *The Black Abolitionist Papers*, 3:119–29, 189–94; *An Address Delivered Before the Moral Reform Society . . .* (Philadelphia, 1836), 5–7, 12–14.

8. *The Minutes and Proceedings of the First Annual Meeting of the American Moral Reform Society . . .* (Philadelphia, 1837): 20–25, 30–55; Ripley, ed., *The Black Abolitionist Papers*, 3:154–67; "John P. Burr, James Forten Jr.: A Circular *Pennsylvania Freeman*, July 5, 1838" and "Benjamin Wilson, The Council for the Philadelphia Association for the Moral and Mental Improvement of the People of Color, June 20, 1839," *BAP*; Howard H. Bell, "The American Moral Reform Society, 1836–1841," *Journal of Negro Education* 27 (Winter 1958): 34–40; Julie Winch, *Philadelphia's Black Elite: Activism, Accommodation, and the Struggle for Autonomy, 1787–1848* (Philadelphia, 1988), chap. 6; *Third Annual Report of the American Moral Reform Society . . .* (New York, 1838), 5–8, 13–33.

9. *Minutes of the Fifth Annual Convention*, 15; *NASS*, July 30, 1840; Richard P. McCormick, "William Whipper, Moral Reformer," *PH* 43 (January 1976), 22–46; Patrick Rael, *Black Identity and Black Protest in the Antebellum North* (Chapel Hill, 2002), 110–13; Karen E. Fields and Barbara J. Fields, *Racecraft: The Soul of Inequality in American Life* (New York, 2012); Jaqueline Jones, *A Dreadful Deceit: The Myth of Race from the Colonial Era to Obama's America* (New York, 2013).

10. *Weekly Advocate*, January 7, 14, 28, February 4, 18, 1837; *CA*, March 4, November 11, 18, 1837; January 13, February 3, 17, March 15, June 2, 9, 16, 23, August 4, September 1, 15, October 6, December 15, 22, 1838; July 13, September 14, 1839; *TL*, September 7, 1838; March 13, 1839; Ripley, ed., *The Black Abolitionist Papers*, 3:320–22; I. Garland Penn, *The Afro-American Press and Its Editors* (Springfield, Mass., 1891); David E. Swift, *Black Prophets of Justice: Activist Clergy Before the Civil War* (Baton Rouge, 1989), 82–85; Jane H. Pease and William H. Pease, *Bound with Them in Chains: A*

Biographical History of the Antislavery Movement (Westport, Conn., 1972), 148–49; M. N. Work, "The Life of Charles B. Ray," *JNH* 4 (October 1919): 361–71.

11. CA, August 26, September 2, 9, 16, 23, November 11, December 2, 9, 23, 30, 1837; February 3, 10, March 15, 22, 29, May 3, June 2, 23, 30, July 21, August 4, 25, September 22, 1838; January 12, June 8, 1839; Ripley, ed., *The Black Abolitionist Papers*, 3:288–93; Floyd Miller, "The Father of Black Nationalism: Another Contender," *CWH* 17 (December 1971): 310–19; Sterling Stuckey, *The Ideological Origins of Black Nationalism* (Boston, 1972), 13–15; Tunde Adeleke, "Afro-Americans and Moral Suasion: The Debate in the 1830s," *JNH* 83 (Spring 1998): 127–42.

12. CA, August 26, September 16, 23, 1837; March 3, June 9, August 25, September 22, 1838; September 28, 1839; NR, January 1839; TP, June 18, 1839; Ripley, ed., *The Black Abolitionist Papers*, 3:238–51.

13. I am grateful to Marieta Joyner for donating all her copies of the *National Reformer* to me. NR, September, October, November, December 1838; January, February, March, April, September, November, December 1839; TP, February 20, 1838; TE, December 27, 1838; "George Cary et al." and "A Colored Baltimorean to Editor," NE, February 1, 1838," BAP; CA, September 15, December 22, 1838; September 19, 1840; Yacovone, "The Transformation of the Black Temperance Movement," 281–97; Rita Roberts, *Evangelicalism and the Politics of Reform in Northern Black Thought, 1776–1863* (Baton Rouge, 2010), 104–14.

14. CA, September 23, October 7, 1837; February 10, March 22, 1838; February 13, 20, March 6, 13, 1841; TL, January 26, 1838, p. 15; Stuckey, *The Ideological Origin*, 17–19; Joel Schor, *Henry Highland Garnet: A Voice of Black Radicalism in the Nineteenth Century* (Westport, Conn., 1977), 36–40; Earl Ofari Hutchinson, *Let Your Motto Be Resistance: The Life and Thought of Henry Highland Garnet* (Boston, 1972), 18–22.

15. CA, March 11, 18, April 1, 15, June 3, September 9, October 7, 14, 28, November 18, 1837; February 3, 10, 17, June 2, 9, 23, 30, July 7, 14, 28, August 4, September 1, 8, 22, October 6, November 17, December 22, 1838; January 12, June 8, July 13, October 5, 1839; TL, May 25, 1838.

16. George R. Price and James Brewer Stewart, eds., *To Heal the Scourge of Prejudice: The Life and Writings of Hosea Easton* (Amherst, Mass., 1999), 16, 22–25, 74, 76, 81, 85, 91, 100–101, 104–6, 111–12, 115; *Second Annual Report of the American Anti-Slavery Society*, 31; TL, September 6, 1834, February 11, 1837; Patrick Rael, "A Common Nature, A United Destiny: African American Responses to Racial Science from the Revolution to the Civil War," in Timothy Patrick McCarthy and John Stauffer, eds., *Prophets of Protest: Reconsidering the History of American Abolitionism* (New York, 2006), 183–99; Mia Bay, *The White Image in the Black Mind: African American Ideas about White People, 1830–1925* (New York, 2000), 46–50, 77, 84–85; Bruce Dain, *A Hideous Monster of the Mind: American Race Theory in the Early Republic* (Cambridge, Mass., 2002), 170–96.

17. Robert Benjamin Lewis, *Light and Truth: From Ancient and Sacred History* (Portland, Me., 1836), 108–10, 132–39, 152–53, 155–56, 171–72, and *Light and Truth* . . . (Boston, 1844), v, 304–5, 386–98, 400; Laurie F. Maffly-Kipp, *Setting Down the Sacred Past:*

African American Race Histories (Cambridge, Mass., 2010); Stephen G. Hall, *A Faithful Account of the Race: African American Historical Writing in Nineteenth-Century America* (Chapel Hill, 2009), 62–64, 71–74, 79–84; John Ernest, *Liberation Historiography: African American Writers and the Challenge of History, 1794–1861* (Chapel Hill, 2004), 101–13.

18. Stephen Jay Gould, *The Mismeasure of Man* (New York, 1981); Ann Fabian, *The Skull Collectors: Race, Science, and America's Unburied Dead* (Chicago, 2010); James W. C. Pennington, A *Text Book of the Origin and History, &c. &c. of the Colored People* (Hartford, 1841), 3, 12, 43–44, 45, 48, 52–54, 56, 74–80, 85, 89; *CA,* January 9, 1841; R. J. M. Blackett, *Beating Against the Barriers: The Lives of Six Nineteenth-Century Afro-Americans* (Ithaca, 1989), chap. 1; David E. Swift, *Black Prophets of Justice: Activist Clergy before the Civil War* (Baton Rouge, 1989), chap. 9; Herman E. Thomas, *James W. C. Pennington: African American Churchman and Abolitionist* (New York, 1995); Christopher Webber, *American to the Backbone: The Life of James W. C. Pennington: The Fugitive Slave Who Became One of the First Abolitionists* (New York, 2011).

19. Ann Plato, *Essays Including Biographies and Miscellaneous Pieces, in Prose and Poetry* (Hartford, 1841), xviii, 41, 55, 60, 111–12, 114–15; Ripley, ed., *The Black Abolitionist Papers,* 3:326–28; Ann Allen Shockley, ed., *Afro-American Woman Writers, 1746–1933: An Anthology and Critical Guide* (New Haven, 1988), 26–28; Joan R. Sherman, *Invisible Poets: Afro-Americans of the Nineteenth Century* (Urbana, 1974), 33–34; Ron Welburn, *Hartford's Ann Plato and the Native Burden of Identity* (Albany, 2015).

20. Harriet E. Wilson, *Our Nig; or, Sketches from the Life of a Free Black* (New York, 1983), introduction, 3, 15, 126–29; JerriAnne Boggis, Eve Allegra Raimon, and Barbara A. White, eds., *Harriet Wilson's New England: Race Writing and Region* (Durham, N.H., 2007); Eric Gardner, "'This Attempt of Their Sister': Harriet Wilson's *Our Nig* from Printer to Readers," *NEQ* 66 (1993): 226–46; P. Gabrielle Foreman and Katherine Flynn, "Mrs. H. E. Wilson, Mogul? The Curious New History of an American Literary Original," *Boston Globe,* February 15, 2009.

21. *TL,* June 1, 1838; February 16, May 10, 1844; NASS, February 8, April 18, 1844; John Stauffer, ed., *The Works of James McCune Smith: Black Intellectual and Abolitionist* (New York, 2006), introduction, 51–52, 57–65, part 4, 265–66, 280; Stauffer, *The Black Hearts of Men: Radical Abolitionists and the Transformation of Race* (Cambridge, Mass., 2002), 65–68, 86–88; David W. Blight, "In Search of Learning, Liberty, and Self Definition: James McCune Smith and the Ordeal of the Antebellum Black Intellectual," *Afro-Americans in New York Life and History* 9 (July 1985), 7–26; Ivy G. Wilson, *Specters of Democracy: Blackness and the Aesthetics of Politics in the Antebellum United States* (New York, 2011), chap. 7.

22. Henry Highland Garnet, *The Past and Present Condition and the Destiny of the Colored Race* (Troy, N.Y., 1848), 6, 25–29; Hall, A *Faithful Account of the Race,* 56–57; Schor, *Henry Highland Garnet,* 89–91.

23. Frederick Douglass, *The Claims of the Negro Ethnologically Considered . . .* (Rochester, 1854), 5, 7–10, 13–16, 28–31, 34; Martin R. Delany, *Principia of Ethnology . . .* (Philadelphia, 1879); Robert S. Levine, *Martin Delany, Frederick Douglass, and the*

Politics of Representative Identity (Chapel Hill, 1997); Robert S. Levine, ed., *Martin R. Delany: A Documentary Reader (Chapel Hill, 2003)*: introduction.

24. *TL*, January 15, January 22, December 10, 1831; January 26, June 23, August 11, October 13, 1832; April 4, 1835; David L. Child, *The Despotism of Freedom; or The Tyranny and Cruelty of American Republican Slave-Masters Shown to be the Worst in the World* . . . (Boston, 1833), 5, 8, 11; *Proceedings of the New England Anti-Slavery Convention* . . . (Boston, 1834), 13.

25. *Proceedings of the New England Anti-Slavery Convention* . . . *1834*, 13–18; *First Annual Report of the American Anti-Slavery Society*, 45–47; *Proceedings of the New England Antislavery Convention* . . . (Boston, 1836), 57–58, 69–71; *Proceedings of the Fourth New England Anti-Slavery Convention* . . . (Boston, 1837), 46–49; Ripley, ed., *The Black Abolitionist Papers*, 3:269–71, 275–77, 294–97.

26. *Second Annual Report of the American Anti-Slavery Society*, 35–37; *Report on the Condition of the People of Color in the State of Ohio* . . . (Boston, 1836), 1–4, 10–15; *Third Annual Report of the American Anti-Slavery Society*, 27, 29.

27. Ripley, ed., *The Black Abolitionist Papers*, 3:181–88, 375–79; *Proceedings of the New England Antislavery Convention* . . . *1836*, 48–49, 55–56; *TL*, June 25, July 2, 1836; October 13, 1837; *TP*, November 25, 1836; Carter G. Woodson, ed., *Negro Orators and Their Orations* (Washington, 1925), 85–95; *CA*, October 14, 1837; *TE*, October 26, 1837; March 14, 1839; Swift, *Black Prophets of Justice*, 47–55, 60–71, 90–97, 100–101.

28. *An Apology for Abolitionists Addressed by the Anti-Slavery Society of Meriden* . . . (Middletown, Conn., 1837), 4, 7; *Proceedings of the Rhode Island Anti-Slavery Convention* . . . (Providence, 1836), 16; *Proceedings of the Indiana Convention* . . . (Cincinnati, 1838), 7–10, 13; *Proceedings of the Fourth New England Anti-Slavery Convention*, 122; *TL*, August 6, 1831; February 25, 1837; *TE*, May 17, 1838; *The "Negro Pew"* . . . (Boston, 1837), 9–14, 24–43, 52.

29. Christopher Malone, *Between Freedom and Bondage: Race, Party, and Voting Rights in the Antebellum North* (New York, 2008); *To the Honorable The Senate and House of Representatives of the Commonwealth of Pennsylvania The Memorial of the People of Colour of the City of Philadelphia and its vicinity* . . . [1832], 3–8; Winch, *Philadelphia's Black Elite*, 131–34; [John F. Denny], *An Enquiry into the Political Grade of the Free Colored Population* . . . [Chambersburg, 1834], 2–3, 21–23; *TE*, May 18, 1837; Ripley, ed., *The Black Abolitionist Papers*, 3:206–12; "Charles W. Gardner et al., Address to the Ministers of the Gospel in Pennsylvania," "Charles W. Gardner et al., Circular," and "Charles W. Gardner and Frederick A. Hinton, Memorial," *BAP*; *CA*, March 25, June 17, July 1, 29, 1837; March 15, 1838; *TL*, May 19, November 17 1837; David McBride, "Black Protest against Racial Politics: Gardner, Hinton, and Their Memorial of 1838," *Pennsylvania History* 46 (April 1979): 149–62; Winch, *Philadelphia's Black Elite*, 134–40.

30. Robert Purvis, *Appeal of Forty Thousand Threatened with Disfranchisement to the People of Pennsylvania* (Philadelphia, 1838), 3–6, 16–18; *CA*, January 27, February 3, March 3, 22, 29, April 19, May 3, June 2, 1838; Ripley, ed., *The Black Abolitionist*

Papers, 3:252, 389–92; *NASS*, August 25, 1842; Nicholas Wood, "'A Sacrifice on the Altar of Slavery': Doughface Politics and Black Disfranchisement in Pennsylvania, 1837–1838," *JER* 31 (Spring 2011): 75–106; Eric Ledell Smith, "The End of Black Voting Rights in Pennsylvania: African Americans and the Pennsylvania Constitutional Convention of 1837–1838," *Pennsylvania History* 65 (Summer 1998): 279–99; Nikki M. Taylor, *Frontiers of Freedom: Cincinnati's Black Community, 1802–1868* (Athens, Ohio, 2005), 118–26; Margaret Hope Bacon, *But One Race: The Life of Robert Purvis* (Albany, 2007), 59–65, 73, 98–99.

31. *Remarks of Henry B. Stanton in the Representatives Hall . . .* (Boston, 1837), 35; [Pennsylvania Anti-Slavery Society], *Address to the Colored People of the State of Pennsylvania* (Philadelphia, 1837), 3–7; *The Present State and Condition of the Free People of Color . . .* (Philadelphia, 1838); *TL*, August 27, 1831; William Jackson, *Views of Slavery . . .* (Philadelphia, 1838), 5.

32. William Yates, *Rights of Colored Men to Suffrage, Citizenship and Trial by Jury . . .* (Philadelphia, 1838), 3–4, 36–38, 52–63; *CA*, September 30, 1837; January 13, April 19, 29, March 3, 15, September 1, October 20, 1838; March 7, 14, 21, 1840.

33. William Jay, "Condition of the Free People of Color," in *Miscellaneous Writings on Slavery* (New York, 1853), 371–95; *CA*, January 26, 1837; April 1, 1839.

34. *CA*, March 4, 11, July 22, August 12, 19, September 23, December 30, 1837; March 15, April 12, May 3, June 16, September 8, October 20, 1838; Carla L. Peterson, *Black Gotham: A Family History of Nineteenth Century New York City* (New Haven, 2011), 121–24; Roberts, *Evangelicalism and the Politics of Reform*, 125; Celeste Michelle Condit and John Louis Lucaites, *Crafting Equality: America's Anglo-African Word* (Chicago, 1993), chap. 4.

35. *NASS*, June 25, July 2, 1840; September 23, 1841; Ripley, ed., *The Black Abolitionist Papers*, 3:340–51; *CA*, March 18, 1837; October 6, 24, 31, November 17, 24, 1838; June 6, 13, 20, 27, July 4, 11, 18, 25, August 1, 8, 15, 29, September 5, 12, 19, 1840; March 13, September 4, 18, 1841; Craig Steven Wilder, "Patrick and Charles Reason," in Berlin and Harris, eds., *Slavery in New York*, ed. 228; Willard Gatewood, ed., *Free Man of Color: The Autobiography of Willis Augustus Hodges* (Knoxville, 1992), introduction; Alexander, *African or American*, 97–107; Jane H. Pease and William H. Pease, "Black Power—The Debate in 1840," *Phylon*, 19–26.

36. Philip S. Foner and George E. Walker, eds., *Proceedings of the Black State Conventions*, vol. 1, *1840–1865* (Philadelphia, 1979), 2–42; *CA*, August 29, September 12, November 14, 21, December 5, 19, 26, 1840; January 2, 9, 16, 23, February 6, March 20, April 3, 24, May 8, June 12, 19, 26, July 10, 24, August 14, 21, 28, September 4, 11, October 30, November 13, December 4, 25, 1841; *NASS*, May 19, 1842; Schor, *Henry Highland Garnet*, 36–44; Jay Rubin, "Black Nativism: The European Immigrant in Negro Thought, 1830–1860," *Phylon* 39 (Fall 1978): 193–20.

37. Leon Litwack, *North of Slavery: The Negro in the Free States, 1790–1860* (Chicago, 1961), 88–89; David M. Gellman and David Quigley, eds., *Jim Crow New York: A Documentary History of Race and Citizenship, 1777–1877* (New York, 2003), 249–59; *An Address to the Three Thousand Colored Citizens of New York . . .* (New York, 1846);

Benjamin Quarles, ed., "Letters from Negro Leaders to Gerrit Smith," *JNH* 27 (October 1942): 432–53; Ripley, ed., *The Black Abolitionist Papers*, 3:479–81; Stauffer, *The Black Hearts of Men*, 136–58, 169–74; Phyllis E. Field, *The Politics of Race in New York: The Struggle for Black Suffrage in the Civil War Era* (Ithaca, 1982).

38. *TL*, March 5, 19, 1831; *CA*, March 6, 13, 27, June 12, July 3, 17, 24, 31, September 11, 18, 1841; Foner and Walker, eds., *Proceedings of the Black State Conventions*, 1:104–38; Erik Chaput, *The People's Martyr: Thomas Wilson Dorr and His 1842 Rhode Island Rebellion* (Lawrence, Kan., 2013); Robert J. Cottrol, *The Afro-Yankees: Providence's Black Community in the Antebellum Era* (Westport, Conn., 1982), 67–90; Julian Rammelkamp, "The Providence Negro Community, 1820–1841," in John H. Bracey, Elliot Rudwick, and August Meier, eds., *Free Blacks in America 1800–1860* (Belmont, Calif., 1970), 85–94; Wilson Jeremiah Moses, *Alexander Crummell: A Study of Civilization and Discontent* (New York, 1989), 34–35; *Memorial of Thirty Thousand Disfranchised Citizens of Philadelphia, to the Honorable Senate and House of Representatives* (Philadelphia, 1855), 1–2.

39. *Minutes of the National Convention of Colored Citizens: Held at Buffalo* . . . (New York, 1843), 7; *Proceedings of the National Convention of Colored People, and their Friends held in Troy* . . . (Troy, 1847), 13–14, 32; *Report of the Proceedings of the Colored National Convention, Held at Cleveland* . . . (Rochester, 1848), 5–6, 11, 17–20, in Bell, ed., *Minutes of the Proceedings of the National Negro Conventions.*

40. Foner and Walker, eds., *Proceedings of the Black State Conventions*, 1:173–97; Emma Lou Thornbrough, *The Negro in Indiana Before 1900* (Bloomington, 1993), chap. 3; Michael J. McManus, *Political Abolitionism in Wisconsin, 1840–1860* (Kent, Ohio, 1998); Paul Finkelman, "Prelude to the Fourteenth Amendment: Black Legal Rights in the Antebellum North," *Rutgers Law Journal* 17 (1985–86): 415–82.

41. Philip S. Foner and George E. Walker, eds., *Proceedings of the Black State Conventions*, vol. 2, 1840–1865 (Philadelphia, 1980), 306–21; "Morris Brown At a Meeting *Pennsylvania Freeman* December 6, 1838," *BAP;* Paul Finkelman, "Race, Slavery and the Law in Antebellum Ohio," in Michael Les Benedict and John F. Winkler, eds., *The History of Ohio Law* (Athens, Ohio, 2004), 2:748–81; Stephen Middleton, *The Black Laws: Race and Legal Process in Early Ohio* (Athens, Ohio, 2005), chap. 3.

42. *TP*, February 5, September 24, 1839; Foner and Walker, eds., *Proceedings of the Black State Conventions*, 1:214–73; Litwack, *North of Slavery*, 69–74; Blackett, *Beating Against the Barriers*, 288–97; William F. Cheek and Aimee Lee Cheek, *John Mercer Langston and the Fight for Black Freedom* (Urbana, 1989), chaps. 4, 5; Middleton, *The Black Laws*, chap. 4.

43. Foner and Walker, eds., *Proceedings of the Black State Conventions*, 2:2–6, 18–38; Graham Russell Hodges, *Root and Branch: African Americans in New York and East Jersey, 1613–1863* (Chapel Hill, 1999), 255–56; Marion Thompson Wright, "Negro Suffrage in New Jersey, 1776–1875," *JNH* 33 (April 1948): 168–224.

44. *TE*, August 23, November 8, 1838; May 16, 1839; *CA*, September 7, December 7, 1839; October 24, 1840; February 20, March 20, 26, June 5, 26, July 10, 1841; Jay, *Miscellaneous Writings on Slavery*, 442–48; *TL*, July 21, 1843; "Letter from Alexander Crummell

to Caste in the Church, 1839," "Letter from George T. Downing and John J. Zuille to Alexander Crummell, 1839," "Letter from James McCune Smith to Gerrit Smith 31 July 1839," "Letter to John Jay from Alexander Crummell 24 October 1839," *BAP*; "Letters from Negro Leaders to Gerrit Smth," *JNH* 27 (October 1942): 445–46; *FDP*, 1854, 1855, 1856; Moses, *Alexander Crummell*, 26–30, 38–40; Kyle G. Volk, *Moral Minorities and the Making of American Democracy* (New York, 2014), chap. 5; Gellman and Quigley, eds., *Jim Crow New York*, 291.

45. "Letter to William Cooper Nell from Jeremiah B. Sanderson and David Ruggles, 26 June 1841," *BAP*; *TL*, March 19, July 2, 9, August 20, September 10, 17, October 15, November 19, 1841; February 4, 11, 25, 1842; *Tenth Annual Report of the Board of Managers of the Mass. Anti-Slavery Society . . .* , 72–81; *Eleventh Annual Report . . .* , 28–29; *Twelfth Annual Report, Presented to the Massachusetts Anti-Slavery Society . . .* , 5–8; Stephen Kendrick and Paul Kendrick, *Sarah's Long Walk: The Free Blacks of Boston and How Their Struggle for Equality Changed America* (Boston, 2004), chap, 4; Louis Ruchames, "Race, Marriage, and Abolition in Masschusetts," *JNH* 40 (July 1955): 250–73; Ruchames, "Jim Crow Railroads in Masschusetts," *American Quarterly* 8 (Spring 1956): 61–75; George S. Levesque, "Politicians in Petticoats: Interracial Sex and Legislative Politics in Antebellum Massachusetts," *New England Journal of Black Studies* 3 (1983): 40–59; Graham Russell Gao Hodges, *David Ruggles: A Radical Black Abolitionist and the Underground Railroad in New York City* (Chapel Hill, 2010), 164–67; Kathryn Grover, *The Fugitive's Gibraltar: Escaping Slaves and Abolitionism in New Bedford, Massachusetts* (Amherst, Mass., 2001), 172–75; Bruce Laurie, *Beyond Garrison: Antislavery and Social Reform* (Cambridge, Eng., 2005), 108–16.

46. NASS, March 10, April 21, May 19, 1842; *Tenth Annual Report of the Board of Managers of the Mass. Anti-Slavery Society*, 63–72; Ripley, ed., *The Black Abolitionist Papers*, 3:314–19, 368–74; James Oliver Horton and Lois E. Horton, *Black Bostonians: Family Life and Community Struggle in the Antebellum North* (New York, 1979), 67–70; Grover, *The Fugitive's Gibraltar*, 176–81; William E. Ward, "Charles Lenox Remond: Black Abolitionist, 1838–1873" (Ph. D. diss., Clark University, 1977); Sibyl Ventress Brownlee, "Out of the Abundance of the Heart: Sarah Ann Parker Remond's Quest for Freedom" (Ph.D. diss., University of Massachusetts, Amherst, 1997), 98–100.

47. Dorothy Porter Wesley and Constance Porter Uzelac, eds., *William Cooper Nell, Nineteenth-Century African-American Abolitionist, Historian, Integrationist: Selected Writings 1832–1874* (Baltimore, 2002), 5–21, 30–33, 132–44, 150–51, 159–60, 253–56, 259–60, 380–84, 435–46; Robert P. Smith, "William Cooper Nell: Crusading Black Abolitionist," *JNH* (July 1970): 182–99; *Argument of Charles Sumner Esq. against the Constitutionality of Separate Colored . . .* (Boston, 1849); Kendrick and Kendrick, *Sarah's Long Walk*, 71–182, 217–39; *TL*, December 28, 1849; January 18, 25, April 26, December 28, 1850; Laurie, *Beyond Garrison*, 119–21, 277–82; Hilary J. Moss, *Schooling Citizens: The Struggle for African American Education in Antebellum America* (Chicago, 2009), chap. 6; Louis Ruchames, "Race and Education in Massachusetts," *Negro History Bulletin* 13 (December 1949): 53–71; Carleton Mabee, "A Negro Boycott to Integrate Boston Schools," *NEQ* 41 (September 1968): 341–61; *Triumph of Equal School Rights in Boston . . .* (Boston, 1856); Kantrowitz, *More than Freedom*, 167–71;

Barbara Ann White, *A Line in the Sand: The Battle to Integrate Nantucket Public Schools, 1825–1847* (New Bedford, Mass., 2009).

48. *TL*, February 24, 1860; Lawrence Grossman, "George T. Downing and Desegregation of Rhode Island Public Schools, 1855–1866," *Rhode Island History* 36 (November 1977): 99–105; Cottrol, *The Afro-Yankees*, 90–101; C. Vann Woodward, *The Strange Career of Jim Crow* (New York, 1955).

49. Floyd J. Miller, *The Search for a Black Nationality: Black Emigration and Colonization, 1787–1863* (Urbana, 1975); Kwando M. Kinhasa, *Emigration v. Assimilation: The Debate in the African American Press, 1827–1861* (Jefferson, N.C., 1988); Ousmane K. Power-Greene, *Against Wind and Tide: The African American Struggle against Colonization* (New York, 2014); Ifeoma Kiddoe Nwanko, *Black Cosmopolitanism: Racial Consciousness and Transnational Identity in the Nineteenth-Century Americas* (Philadelphia, 2005), 9–15.

50. Austin Steward, *Twenty-Two Years a Slave . . .* (New York, 1856), 176–95, 232–44, 251–73, 341–60; Ripley, ed., *The Black Abolitionist Papers*, 2:3–62, 76–83, 104–18, 316–20; *CA*, February 16, 1839; "Letter from James C. Brown to William Goodell July 24, 1839," *BAP*; William H. Pease and Jane H. Pease, *Black Utopia: Negro Communal Experiments in America* (Madison, 1963), chaps. 3–6; Robin W. Winks, *The Blacks in Canada: A History* (New Haven, 1971), chap. 7; Harvey Amani Whitfield, *Blacks on the Border: The Black Refugees in British North America, 1815–1860* (Burlington, Vt., 2006); Daniel G. Hill, *The Freedom Seekers: Blacks in Early Canada* (Agincourt, Canada, 1981), chaps. 4, 5; Donald G. Simpson, *Under the North Star: Black Communities in Upper Canada before Confederation (1867)*, ed. Paul E. Lovejoy (Trenton, 2005); Clara Merritt DeBoer, *Be Jubilant My Feet: African American Abolitionists in the American Missionary Association, 1839–1861* (New York, 1994), 153–59, 160–83; W. B. Hartgrove, "The Story of Josiah Henson," *JNH* 13 (January 1918): 1–21; Fred Landon, "Henry Bibb, a Colonizer," *JNH* 5 (October 1920): 437–47; Victor Ullman, *Look to the North Star: A Life of William King* (Boston, 1969).

51. *NS*, February 19, March 23, June 8, 1849; Ripley, ed., *The Black Abolitionist Papers*, 2:143–76, 184–92, 200–203, 208–11, 245–55, 270–78; Mary A. Shadd, *A Plea for Emigration*, Richard Almonte, ed. (Toronto, 1998), introduction, 53, 70–71, 81–85, 89–95; Jane Rhodes, *Mary Ann Shadd Cary: The Black Press and Protest in the Nineteenth Century* (Bloomington, 1998); Jason H. Silverman, "Mary Ann Shadd and the Search for Equality," in Darlene Clark Hine, ed., *Black Women in United States History* (Brooklyn, N.Y., 1990), 4:1260–74; Carol B. Conaway, "Mary Ann Shadd Cary: A Visionary of the Black Press," in Kristin Waters and Carol B. Conaway eds., *Black Women's Intellectual Traditions: Speaking Their Minds* (Burlington, Vt., 2007): 216–247.

52. Ripley, ed., *The Black Abolitionist Papers*, 2:136–37, 177–81, 224–37; Samuel Ringgold Ward, *Autobiography of a Fugitive Slave: His Anti-Slavery Labours in the United States, Canada, and England* (London, 1855), 12–13, 33–34, 43, 51, 139–50, 218–24, 303, 382–84; *Weekly Anglo-African*, August 20, 1859; DeBoer, *Be Jubilant My Feet*, 90–93; Ronald K. Burke, *Samuel Ringgold Ward: Christian Abolitionist* (New York, 1995).

53. *CA*, November 18, 1837; April 19, May 3, October 13, November 10, 1838; July 27, August 17, 31, September 14, October 5, 12, November 16, 1839; March 7, 14, April 4, 11,

18, May 2, 9, 16, June 6, July 18, 25, September 12, October 17, 31, December 26, 1840; February 6, 13, 27, March 6, 20, April 3, June 5, 26, July 5, November 13, December 4, 1841; *TE*, September 26, 1839; "Letter from Frederick A. Hinton to John G. Whittier 7 November 1839" and "Letter to James G. Barbadoes from Lewis Tappan 2 December 1839," *BAP*; Nancy Prince, *The West Indies . . .* (Boston, 1841); Miller, *The Search for a Black Nationality*, 94–101; P. J. Staudenraus, *The African Colonization Movement, 1816–1865* (New York, 1961), 244.

54. *ARCJ*, July 1838; April 1, 15, June 1, 1840; January 1, March 1, 1841; John H. B. Latrobe, *Maryland in Liberia . . .* (Baltimore, 1885), 72–79; Latrobe, *Memoir of Benjamin Banneker . . .* (Baltimore, 1845), 14–16; Mark J. Fleszar, "Zephaniah Kingsley, Slavery, and the Politics of Race in the Atlantic World" (Ph.D. diss., Georgia State University, 2009), esp. chaps. 4, 5.

55. *Letter of John McDonogh, on African Colonization . . .* (New Orleans, 1842), 4–8, 14–16; *Emigration to Liberia . . .* (New York, 1848), 5–14; Bell I. Wiley, ed., *Slaves No More: Letters from Liberia, 1833–1869* (Lexington, Ky., 1980), 116–19, 153; Eric Burin, *Slavery and the Peculiar Solution: A History of the American Colonization Society* (Gainesville, Fla., 2005); Claude A. Clegg, *The Price of Liberty: African Americans and the Making of Liberia* (Chapel Hill, 2004); Staudenraus, *The African Colonization Movement*, 240–46.

56. Samuel S. Cornish and Theodore E. Wright, *The Colonization Scheme Considered . . .* (Newark, 1840), 4–7, 10–15, 17–24; Robert J. Eells, *Forgotten Saint: The Life of Theodore Frelinghuysen: A Case Study of Christian Leadership* (Lanham, Md., 1987).

57. *ARCJ*, February 15, July 1842; May, June, September 1846; January, February, June, July 1847; January, March, April, June 1848; January, February 1849; *The Twenty-Fourth Annual Report of the American Colonization Society . . .* (Washington, 1841), 45–48; David Christy, *Ethiopia: Her Gloom and Glory . . .* (Cincinnati, 1857); [Ephraim Peabody], *Slavery in the United States . . .* (Boston, 1851), 22–29; *The Annual Reports of the American Society Colonizing the Free People of Color in the United States*, vols. 34–43, 1851–60 (New York, 1969): 35–52; Archibald Alexander, *A History of Colonization on the Western Coast of Africa* (Philadelphia, 1849), 646–59; *Calumny Refuted by Facts from Liberia . . .* (London, 1848), 3–6; James Wesley Smith, *Sojourners in Search of Freedom: The Settlement of Liberia by Black Americans* (Lanham, Md., 1987), chap. 11; Tom W. Shick, *Behold the Promised Land: A History of Afro-American Settler Society in Nineteenth-Century Liberia* (Baltimore, 1977), 44–50.

58. Robert J. Breckinridge, *The Black Race . . .* (Frankfort, Ky., 1851), 7–9, 12–13; *Colonization of the Western Coast of Africa . . .* (New York, 1851); *Information about going to Liberia . . .* (Washington, 1852), 19–23; *Circular of the Massachusetts Colonization Society* (Boston, 1855); Jacob Dewees, *The Great Future of America and Africa . . .* (Philadelphia, 1854), 49, 99–107, 156–62, 186–89, 210–20; C. Van Rensselaer, *Slaveholding and Colonization . . .* (Philadelphia, 1858), 15–17, 19–24.

59. *ARCJ*, November 1843; August 1844; *Information about going to Liberia*, 11; Wilson Jeremiah Moses, *The Golden Age of Black Nationalism, 1850–1925* (Hamden, Conn., 1978), 10–11; Winston James, *The Struggles of John Brown Russwurm: The Life and*

Writings of a Pan-Africanist Pioneer, 1799–1851 (New York, 2010), 236, 251; Penelope Campbell, *Maryland in Africa: The Maryland Colonization State Society, 1831–1857* (Urbana, 1970), 211–43; *Land of Hope* . . . (Hartford, 1852), 10, 13–14, 30–32, 52, 103, 185–94, 210–11; *The Looking-Glass* . . . (New York, 1854), 13–14, 18–20, 26–29, 121–32; Wilson Jeremiah Moses, ed., *Liberian Dreams: Back-to-Africa Narratives from the 1850s* (University Park, Pa., 1998), xxviii, xxix; Wiley, ed., *Slaves No More*, 216, 233.

60. Alexander Crummell, *Destiny and Race: Selected Writings, 1840–1898*, Wilson Jeremiah Moses, ed. (Amherst, Mass., 1992), 158–64, 269–88; Alexander Crummell, B.A., *The Future of Africa* . . . (1862; repr., New York, 1969), 89–90, 148, 216, 327–54; Moses, *Alexander Crummell*, chap. 6; Hollis Lynch, ed., *Selected Letters of Edward Wilmot Blyden* (New York, 1978), 29–30; Lynch, *Edward Wilmot Blyden, Pan-Negro Patriot, 1832–1912* (New York, 1967); Moses, *The Golden Age of Black Nationalism*, 20–21; Tunde Adeleke, *Unafrican Americans: Nineteenth-Century Black Nationalism and the Civilizing Mission* (Lexington, Ky., 1998), esp. chap. 4.

61. FDP, July 31, September 4, November 13, 1851; April 15, 1852; November 25, 1853; December 2, 1854; Alexander, *African or American?*, 142–45; *Weekly Anglo-African*, April 14, 1860; Moses, ed., *Liberian Dreams*, 181–224.

CHAPTER ELEVEN. THE ABOLITIONIST INTERNATIONAL

1. Cf. W. Caleb McDaniel, *The Problem of Democracy in the Age of Slavery: Garrisonian Abolitionists and Transatlantic Reform* (Baton Rouge, 2013); John T. Cumbler, *From Abolition to Rights for All: The Making of a Reform Community in the Nineteenth Century* (Philadelphia, 2008).

2. Howard Temperley, "Capitalism, Slavery and Ideology," *Past and Present* 75 (May 1977): 94–118; Richard Huzzey, *Freedom Burning: Anti-Slavery and Empire in Victorian Britain* (Ithaca, 2012); Marcus Cunliffe, *Chattel Slavery and Wage Slavery: The Anglo-American Context, 1830–1860* (Athens, Ga., 1979).

3. R. J. M. Blakett, *Building an Antislavery Wall: Black Americans in the Atlantic Abolitionist Movement, 1830–1860* (Baton Rouge, 1983); Fionnghuala Sweeney and Alan Rice, "Liberating Sojourns? African Americans and Transatlantic Abolition, 1845–1865," *S&A* 33 (June 2012): 181–89.

4. David Lee Child, *Oration in Honor of Universal Emancipation in the British Empire* . . . (Boston, 1834); [Samuel Cornish], *Address in Commemoration of the Great Jubilee on the 1st of August, 1834* (n.p., n.d.), 2–4; *TL*, August 17, 24, 1838; J. W. C. Pennington, *An Address Delivered at Newark, NJ, at the First Anniversary of West India Emancipation* . . . (Newark, 1839), 1, 3, 8; *NE*, August 17, 1836; *Anti-Slavery Reporter*, August 9, 1843, *BAP*; *CA*, July 15, 29, 1837; July 21, 28, August 11, 18, 1838; July 27, August 17, 24, 31, 1839; July 25, August 1, 15, 17, September 5, 1840; July 17, 24, 1841; *NASS*, August 5, September 2, 1841; June 23, 1842; Van Gosse, "'As a Nation the English Are Our Friends': The Emergence of African American Politics in the Atlantic World, 1772–1861," *AHR* 113 (October 2008): 1003–28; Benjamin Quarles, *Black Abolitionists* (New York, 1969), 116–29; J. R. Kerr-Ritchie, *Rites of August First: Emancipation Day*

in the Black Atlantic World (Baton Rouge, 2007); Mitch Kachun, *Festivals of Freedom: Memory and Meaning in African American Emancipation Celebrations, 1808–1915* (Amherst, Mass., 2003), chap. 2.

5. *TL*, November 15, 1834; June 30, 1843; August 8, 15, 1845; July 31, August 7, 21, 1846, July 30, August 13, 1847; August 25, September 1, 1848; July 13, August 17, 1849; August 9, 1850; August 15, 22, 29, 1851; August 6, 1852; August 12, 1853; August 4, 1854; August 10, 1855; August 8, 1856; August 7, 1857; August 6, 1858; August 5, 1859; John A. Collins, *The Anti-Slavery Picknick . . .* (Boston, 1842); Martha Schoolman, *Abolitionist Geographies* (Minneapolis, 2014), 69–74; W. Caleb McDaniel, "The Fourth and the First: Abolitionist Holidays, Respectability, and Radical Interracial Reform," *American Quarterly* 57 (2005): 129–51.

6. *NS*, May 28, 1848; April 29, June 29, August 31, 1849; June 13, 1850; *FDP*, August 26, 1853; August 11, 18, 25, 1854; J. W. C. Pennington, D.D., *An Address Delivered at Hartford, Conn., on the First of August, 1856* (Hartford, 1856); *Voice of the Fugitive*, July 16, 1851; *Weekly Anglo-African*, July 30, August 6, 13, 20, 1859; *Pine and Palm*, August 17, 1861, *BAP*; *Weekly Anglo-African*, October 15, November 19, 1859; Kerr-Ritchie, *Rites of August First*, 129, 133–43, 154–63; John R. McKivigan and Jason H. Silverman, "Monarchical Liberty and Republican Slavery: West India Celebrations in Upstate New York and Canada West," *Afro-Americans in New York Life and History* 10 (January 1986): 7–18.

7. *TL*, July 31, August 28, November 13, 1840; February 26, March 6, May 21, June 4, 25, July 9, 30, September 10, 24, November 19, 1841; *NASS*, July 1, September 9, 1841; C. Peter Ripley ed., *The Black Abolitionist Papers*, vol. 1, *The British Isles, 1830–1865* (Chapel Hill, 1985), 65–103; [Francis Jackson Garrison and Wendell Phillips Garrison], *William Lloyd Garrison, 1805–1879: The Story of His Life Told By His Children*, vol. 2, *1835–1840* (1885; repr., New York, 1969), 416–17; Clare Taylor, ed., *British and American Abolitionists: An Episode in Transatlantic Understanding* (Edinburgh, Scotland, 1974), 31; Betty Fladeland, *Men and Brothers: Anglo-American Antislavery Cooperation* (Urbana, 1972), 276–77; Miriam L. Usrey, "Charles Lenox Remond, Garrison's Ebony Echo: World Anti-Slavery Convention, 1840," *Essex Institute Historical Collection* 106 (April 1970): 113–25; Quarles, *Black Abolitionists*, 129–42; Blackett, *Building an Antislavery Wall*, 75–80.

8. Ripley, ed., *The Black Abolitionist Papers*, 1:104–33, 155–60, 182–83; *NASS*, August 31, September 7, 1843; *TL*, October 11, 1844; Christopher L. Webber, *American to the Backbone: The Life of James W. C. Pennington, the Fugitive Slave Who Became One of the First Black Abolitionists* (New York, 2011), chaps. 12, 16; R. J. M. Blackett, *Beating Against the Barriers: The Lives of Six Nineteenth-Century Afro-Americans* (Ithaca, 1989), 27–30, 42–51; Fladeland, *Men and Brothers*, 292–93; Manisha Sinha, "James W. C. Pennington and Transatlantic Abolitionism," *Annual Report 2010–2011 of the Heidelberg Center for American Studies* (Heidelberg, Germany, 2011), 165–66, 173; Mischa Honeck, "Liberating Sojourns? African American Travelers in Mid-Nineteenth Century Germany," Paper in author's possession, 4–12.

9. Ripley, ed., *The Black Abolitionist Papers*, 1:142–51, 469–73; *CA*, September 9, 1837; February 17, 1838; Margaret Hope Bacon, *But One Race: The Life of Robert Purvis*

(Albany, 2007), 44–47; *TL*, January 2, 1846; Ripley, ed., *The Black Abolitionist Papers*, 2:181; John W. Blassingame, ed., *The Frederick Douglass Papers, Series One: Speeches, Debates, and Interviews*, vol. 1, *1841–46* (New Haven, 1979), 90–92, 139–43; *A Narrative of the Life and Travels of Nancy Prince* (Boston, 1850); David F. Dorr, *A Coloured Man Round the World by a Quadroon* (Cleveland, 1858).

10. Samuel Ringgold Ward, *Autobiography of a Fugitive Slave: His Anti-Slavery Labours in the United States, Canada, and England* (London, 1855), 12–13, 33–34, 43, 51, 139–50, 218–24, 303, 382–84; *Impartial Citizen*, February 28, 1849; *Weekly Anglo-African*, August 20, 1859; Blackett, *Building an Antislavery Wall*, 149–53, 173–74; Ronald K. Burke, *Samuel Ringgold Ward: Christian Abolitionist* (New York, 1995); Jeffrey R. Kerr-Ritchie, "Samuel Ward and the Making of an Imperial Subject," *S&A* 33 (June 2012): 205–19.

11. Ripley, ed., *The Black Abolitionist Papers*, 1:349–54; Alexander Crummell, *The Future of Africa . . .* (1862; repr., New York, 1969), 327–54; Alexander Crummell, *Destiny and Race: Selected Writings, 1840–1898*, Wilson Jeremiah Moses, ed. (Amherst, Mass., 1992), 158–64; Wilson Jeremiah Moses, *Alexander Crummell: A Study in Civilization and Discontent* (New York, 1989), 46–88.

12. Wilson Armistead, *A Tribute to the Negro . . .* (London, 1848); John Stauffer, *The Black Hearts of Men: Radical Abolitionists and the Transformation of Race* (Cambridge, Mass., 2002), 50–51; Blackett, *Building an Antislavery Wall*, 155–61.

13. Ripley, ed., *The Black Abolitionist Papers*, 1:474; William Farmer, ed., *Three Years in Europe . . .* (Boston, 1852), 216–19, 246–49; Schoolman, *Abolitionist Geographies*, 109–14; Thomas C. Holt, *The Problem of Freedom: Race, Labor, and Politics in Jamaica and Britain, 1832–1938* (Baltimore, 1992), 280–86; Edward Bartlett Rugemer, *The Problem of Emancipation: The Caribbean Roots of the American Civil War* (Baton Rouge, 2008), 263, 270–71; Ezra Greenspan, *William Wells Brown: An African American Life* (New York, 2014), 242.

14. Ripley, ed., *The Black Abolitionist Papers*, 1:259–67; L. A. Chamerovzow, ed., *Slave Life in Georgia: A Narrative of the Life, Sufferings, and Escape of John Brown . . .* (London, 1855), 35–38, 45–48, 54–61, 68, 88, 171; Audrey A. Fisch, *American Slaves in Victorian England: Abolitionist Politics in Popular Literature and Culture* (Cambridge, Eng., 2000), chap. 3.

15. William G. Allen, *The American Prejudice Against Colour . . .* (London, 1853); *TL*, May 21, 1846; December 20, 1850; October 29, 1852; July 22, 1853; May 5, 1854; *FDP*, April 29, June 10, August 13, October 22, November 5, 1852; Ripley, ed., *The Black Abolitionist Papers*, 1:367–78, 423–26; R. J. M. Blackett, "William G. Allen: The Forgotten Professor," *CWH* 26 (March 1980): 39–52; Sarah Elbert, "An Inter-Racial Love Story in Fact and Fiction: William and Mary King Allen's Marriage and Louisa May Alcott's Tale, 'M.L.'" *History Workshop Journal* 53 (Spring 2002): 17–42.

16. *TL*, February 11, April 22, 1859; Sarah P. Remond, "The Negroes of the United States of America," *JNH* 27 (April 1942): 216–18; Sibyl Ventress Brownlee, "Out of the Abundance of the Heart: Sarah Ann Parker Remond's Quest for Freedom" (Ph.D. diss., University of Massachusetts, Amherst, 1997), chap. 4; Dorothy Sterling, ed., *We Are Your Sisters: Black Women in the Nineteenth Century* (New York, 1984), 175–80; Ruth

Bogin, "Sarah Parker Remond: Black Abolitionist from Salem," *Essex Institute Historical Collection* (April 1974): 120–50; Dorothy Porter, "Sarah Parker Remond, Abolitionist and Physician," *JNH* 20 (July 1935): 287–93; Clare Midgley, *Women Against Slavery: The British Campaigns, 1780–1870* (London, 1992), 143–45; Amanda Foreman, *A World on Fire: Britain's Crucial Role in the American Civil War* (New York, 2010).

17. *TE*, May 12, 1835; August 1, 1839; Theodore Sedgwick Jr., ed., *A Collection of the Political Writings of William Leggett* (New York, 1840), 1:28–40; *Proceedings of the New England Anti Slavery Convention . . . 1834*, 10; *Proceedings of the Fourth New England Anti Slavery Convention*, 45–46, 100; Sean Wilentz, *The Rise of American Democracy: From Jefferson to Lincoln* (New York, 2005), 422–25; Philip S. Foner and Herbert Shapiro, eds., *Northern Labor and Antislavery: A Documentary History* (Westport, Conn., 1994), 120–25; Herbert Shapiro, "Labor and Antislavery: Reflections on the Literature," *Nature, Society, and Thought* 2 (1989): 471–90; Paul Goodman, *Of One Blood: Abolitionism and the Origins of Racial Equality* (Berkeley, 1998), chaps. 11, 12; W. D. Wilson, *A Discourse on Slavery . . .* (Concord, N.H., 1839), 29–30; Bernard Mandel, *Labor: Free and Slave Workingmen and the Antislavery Movement in the United States* (New York, 1955), 61–95; Eric Foner, *Politics and Ideology in the Age of the Civil War* (New York, 1980), chap. 4.

18. *TE*, April 1836; *Proceedings of the Rhode Island Anti Slavery Convention*, 24–25, 31–33, 36–38, 57; David Root, *The Abolition Case Eventually Triumphant . . .* (Andover, 1836), 18–20; Isaac Stearns, *Right and Wrong in Mansfield, Massachusetts . . .* (Pawtucket, Mass., 1837), 11–12, 24–25; *Second Annual Report of the New Hampshire Anti Slavery Society*, 6; Beriah Green, *The Chattel Principle . . .* (New York, 1839), 53; Jonathan Glickstein, "The Chattelization of Northern Whites: An Evolving Abolitionist Warning," *American Nineteenth-Century History* 4 (2003): 25–58.

19. *TL*, January 1, 1831; November 22, December 13, 20, 1834; January 3, 31, February 7, 1835; January 2, 9, 1836; June 16, 1837; May 11, 1838; May 15, June 9, 12, October 23, December 18, 1840; August 22, 1845; January 9, February 13, 1846; April 23, 1847; *TE*, July 2, October 1, 1840; October 7, November 18, 1841; John A. Collins to Garrison, December 7, 1840, William Lloyd Garrison Papers, Antislavery Collection, BPL; Foner and Shapiro, eds., *Northern Labor and Antislavery*, 2–6, 184–85, 236–41; *William Lloyd Garrison*, 1:435, 469–75; *William Lloyd Garrison*, 2:358; Walter M. Merrill, ed., *The Letters of William Lloyd Garrison*, vol. 1, *I Will be Heard! 1822–1835* (Cambridge, Mass., 1971), 168; *TASR*, September 1835; September 1836; O. A. Brownson, *The Laboring Classes . . .* (Boston, 1840), 10; Taylor, ed., *British and American Abolitionists*, 133–35; Annie Heloise Abel and Frank J. Klingberg, eds., *A Side-Light on Anglo-American Relations, 1839–1858: Furnished by the Correspondence of Lewis Tappan and Others with the British and Foreign Anti-Slavery Society* (Washington, 1927), 66–69; Alex Gourevitch, *From Slavery to Cooperative Commonwealth: Labor and Republican Liberty in the Nineteenth Century* (Cambridge, Eng., 2015), 37, 41–46; Jonathan A. Glickstein, "'Poverty Is Not Slavery': American Abolitionists and the Competitive Labor Market," in Lewis Perry and Michael Fellman, eds., *Antislavery Reconsidered: New Perspectives on the Abolitionists* (Baton Rouge, 1979), 195–218.

20. William Lloyd Garrison, *American Slavery . . .* (London, 1846); *TL,* March 25, May 6, 1842; January 13, February 9, March 3, May 5, June 22, July 28, October 13, 1843; February 9, 1844; January 24, April 4, August 22, 1845; September 4, 25, October 2, 16, November 13, 1846; *TP,* July 2, October 29, 1839; *NASS,* July 31, 1845; *William Lloyd Garrison,* 2:159–73; Louis Ruchames, ed., *The Letters of William Lloyd Garrison: A House Dividing Against Itself,* vol. 2, *1836–1840* (Cambridge, Mass., 1971), 707–31; Walter M. Merrill, ed., *The Letters of William Lloyd Garrison,* vol. 3, *No Union with Slaveholders, 1841–1849* (Cambridge, Mass., 1973), 344–45, 368, 372–73, 377–79, 393–95, 455–59; Taylor, ed., *British and American Abolitionists,* 151, 160, 183, 185–86, 188, 225–26, 275–76, 278, 284–87, 289–92, 296, 308; Betty Fladeland, "'Our Cause Being One and the Same': Abolitionists and Chartism," in James Walvin, ed., *Slavery and British Society, 1776–1846* (Baton Rouge, 1982), 69–99; Fladeland, *Abolitionists and Working-Class Problems in the Age of Industrialization* (Baton Rouge, 1984); Gareth Stedman Jones, *Languages of Class: Studies in English Working Class History, 1832–1982* (Cambridge, Eng.,1983), 90–178; R. K. Webb, *Harriet Martineau: A Radical Victorian* (New York, 1960); Alex Tyrell, *Joseph Sturge and the Moral Radical Party in Early Victorian Britain* (London, 1987); Douglas B. A. Ansdell, "William Lloyd Garrison's Ambivalent Approach to Labour Reform," *Journal of American Studies* 24 (December 1990): 402–7; McDaniel, *The Problem of Democracy,* 143–58.

21. Ripley, ed., *The Black Abolitionist Papers,* 1:252–54, 379–82; William S. McFeely, *Frederick Douglass* (New York, 1991), 104–8, 138–41; Sarah P. Remond, "The Negroes of the United States of America," *JNH* 27 (April 1942): 217–18; Samuel Gompers, *Seventy Years of Life and Labor: An Autobiography* (New York, 1925), 1:20–21; Blackett, *Building an Antislavery Wall,* 14–25; Seymour Drescher, *Capitalism and Antislavery: British Mobilization in Comparative Perspective* (New York, 1986).

22. Jonathan H. Earle, *Jacksonian Antislavery and the Politics of Free Soil, 1824–1854* (Chapel Hill, 2004), chap. 1; Foner and Shapiro, eds., *Northern Labor and Antislavery,* 7–10, 91–98; James L. Huston, "Abolitionists, Political Economists, and Capitalism," *JER* 20 (2000): 487–521; *The Democracy of Christianity . . . ,* vol. 1 (New York, 1849); Goodman, *Of One Blood,* chap. 7; Jonathan Glickstein, "The Specter of White Chattelization: William Goodell's Abolitionist Thought," in Steven Mintz and John Stauffer, eds., *The Problem of Evil: Slavery, Freedom, and the Ambiguities of American Reform* (Amherst, Mass., 2007), 174–82; Sean Wilentz, *Chants Democratic: New York City and the Rise of the American Working Class, 1788–1850* (New York, 1984), 335–43; Jeffrey J. Pilz, *The Life, Work and Times of George Henry Evans, Newspaperman, Activist and Reformer 1829–1849* (New York, 2001); *TL,* October 1, 1847; February 16, 1849; Foner, *Politics and Ideology in the Age of the Civil War,* 69–73, 150–52; Stauffer, *The Black Hearts of Men,* 136–39; Henry George to Sarah Mifflin Gay, November 4, November 11, 1880, Sydney Howard Gay Papers, CU.

23. Foner and Shapiro, eds., *Northern Labor and Antislavery,* 19–22, 127–30; Abel and Klingberg, eds., *A Side-Light on Anglo-American Relations,* 219–20; Lawrence B. Goodheart, *Abolitionist, Actuary, Atheist: Elizur Wright and the Reform Impulse* (Kent, Ohio, 1990), chap. 9; Bruce Laurie, *Beyond Garrison: Antislavery and Social Reform* (Cambridge, Eng., 2005), 67–71; Adam Tuchinsky, *Horace Greeley's New-York Tribune:*

Civil War–Era Socialism and the Crisis of Free Labor (Ithaca, 2009); Mitchell Snay, *Horace Greeley and the Politics of Reform in Nineteenth-Century America* (Lanham, Md., 2011), chap. 4; Wilentz, *Chants Democratic*, 382–84, 387; Paul Goodman, "The Emergence of the Homestead Exemption in the United States: Accommodation and Resistance to the Market Revolution, 1840–1880," *JAH* 80 (September 1993): 482–87; Mark A. Lause, *Young America: Land, Labor and the Republican Community* (Urbana, 2005), chap. 7; Lawrence Goldmand, "Republicanism, Radicalism and Sectionalism: Land Reform and the Languages of American Working Men, 1820–1860," in Rebecca Starr, ed., *Articulating America: Fashioning a National Political Culture in Early America* (Lanham, Md., 2000), 177–236; Jamie Bronstein, *Land Reform and Working-Class Experience in Britain and the United States, 1800–1862* (Stanford, Calif., 1999).

24. Merrill, ed., *The Letters of William Lloyd Garrison*, 3:145, 184–85, 240–41, 267; TL, September 1, 1843; January 5, 1844; August 28, 1846, p. 139; Taylor, ed., *British and American Abolitionists*, 137; Abby Kelley Foster to Gay, December 14, 1846, Sydney Howard Gay Papers, CU; Albert Brisbane, *Social Destiny of Man: or Association and Reorganization of Industry* (Philadelphia, 1840); Lewis Perry, *Radical Abolitionism: Anarchy and Government of God in Antislavery Thought* (Ithaca, 1973), chap. 5; Carl J. Guarneri, *The Utopian Alternative: Fourierism in Nineteenth-Century America* (Ithaca, 1991); John L. Thomas, "Antislavery and Utopia," in Martin Duberman, ed., *The Antislavery Vanguard: New Essays on the Abolitionists* (Princeton, 1965), 249–69.

25. TL, July 28, 1843; February 15, 1856; Giles B. Stebbins, *Upward Steps of Seventy Years . . .* (New York, 1890), 51–62; Adin Ballou, *Practical Christian Socialism . . .* (Hopedale, Mass., 1854); John Humphrey Noyes, *History of American Socialisms* (1870; repr., New York, 1961); Walter M. Merrill, *Against Wind and Tide: A Biography of William Lloyd Garrison* (Cambridge, Mass., 1963), 216–17; Spencer Klaw, *Without Sin: The Life and Death of the Oneida Community* (New York, 1993); Anne C. Rose, *Transcendentalism as a Social Movement, 1830–1850* (New Haven, 1981); Christopher Clark, *The Communitarian Moment: The Radical Challenge of the Northampton Association* (Ithaca, 1995), 57–74, 88–134; Arthur E. Bestor, "Fourierism at Northampton: A Critical Note," *NEQ* 13 (March 1940): 110–22; Wendy E. Chmielewski, "Sojourner Truth: Utopian Visions and Search for Community, 1797–1883," in Chmielewski, Louis J. Kern, and Marlyn Klee-Hartzwell, eds., *Women in Spiritual and Communitarian Societies in the United States* (Syracuse, 1993); Guarneri, *The Utopian Alternative*, 322–26, 354–67.

26. CA, January 27, March 2, August 18, December 15, 1838; On Seneca village, see http://projects.ilt.columbia.edu/seneca/start.html and http://www.centralparknyc.org/visit/things-to-see/great-lawn/seneca-village-site.html; Roy Rosenzweig and Elizabeth Blackmar, *The Park and the People: A History of Central Park* (Ithaca, 1992), 65–73; Judith Wellman, *Brooklyn's Promised Land: The Free Black Community of Weeksville, New York* (New York, 2014); Sundiata Keita Cha-Jua, *America's First Black Town: Brooklyn, Illinois, 1830–1915* (Urbana, 2000); Juliet E. K. Walker, *Free Frank: A Black Pioneer on the Antebellum Frontier* (Lexington, Ky., 1983); Stephen A. Vincent, *Southern Seed, Northern Soil: African-American Farm Communities in the Midwest, 1765–1900* (Bloomington, 1999); William H. Pease and Jane H. Pease, *Black Utopia: Negro*

Communal Experiments in America (Madison, 1963), 26–27, 39–45; On Carthagena, see http://www.ohiohistorycentral.org/entry.php?rec=676.

27. *Governor Hammond's Letters on Southern Slavery* . . . (Charleston, S.C., 1845), 10–11, 16–19; *TL*, June 14, 1850; April 9, 1858; Foner and Shapiro, eds., *Northern Labor and Antislavery*, 152–60; Aileen S. Kraditor, *Means and Ends in American Abolitionism: Garrison and His Critics on Strategy and Tactics, 1834–1850* (New York, 1967), 243–47; Stacey M. Robertson, *Parker Pillsbury: Radical Abolitionist, Male Feminist* (Ithaca, 2000), 11–24; *The War a Rebellion of Capital Against Labor* . . . (n.p., 1864), 1–2; Henry Mayer, *All on Fire: William Lloyd Garrison and the Abolition of Slavery* (New York, 1998), 379; David Montgomery, *Beyond Equality: Labor and the Radical Republicans, 1862–72* (New York, 1967), 114–26; David Roediger, "Ira Steward and the Anti-Slavery Origins of American Eight-Hour Theory," *Labor History* 27 (June 1986): 410–26.

28. *TL*, December 4, 1846; March 26, June 4, 11, 1847; April 7, 28, 1848; May 17, 1850; *William Lloyd Garrison*, 2:280–300; Wilentz, *Chants Democratic*, 327–35; Tyler Anbinder, "Isaiah Rynders and the Ironies of Popular Democracy in Antebellum New York," in Manisha Sinha and Penny Von Eschen, eds., *Contested Democracy: Freedom, Race and Power in American History* (New York, 2007), chap. 2.

29. *TL*, December 13, 20, 1834; January 3, February 7, 1835; *TE*, July 11, December 26, 1839; June 18, 1840; *TASR*, September 1835; Jonathan Walker, *A Brief View of American Chattelized Humanity* . . . (Boston, 1846), 29–30; Noel Ignatiev, *How the Irish Became White* (New York, 1995), 75–79; David Roediger, *The Wages of Whiteness: Race and the Making of the American Working Class* (New York, 1991).

30. *TL*, September 10, October 8, 1840; February 18, March 3, 1841; March 11, 25, April 22, May 13, September 2, 1842; April 14, 28, May 13, June 30, July 7, 14, 21, 28, August 25, September 8, October 6, November 17, December 8, 1843; January 26, July 12, 1844; February 28, May 8, September 12, 26, 1845; February 5, 12, July 2, 1846; July 2, 1847; August 10, 24, September 7, 14, 28, October 5, 1849; May 24, 1850; May 9, 1856; *NASS*, April 21, June 2, August 11, 25, November 3, 1842; July 5, November 16, 1843; January 4, 1844; May 8, 1845; Merrill, ed., *The Letters of William Lloyd Garrison*, 3:229–33; Taylor, ed., *British and American Abolitionists*, 168–72, 174; *Daniel O'Connell upon American Slavery* . . . (New York, 1860); Gilbert Osofsky, "Abolitionists, Irish Immigrants, and the Dilemma of Romantic Nationalism," *AHR* 80 (October 1975): 889–912; Ignatiev, *How the Irish Became White*, 1–31; Angela F. Murphy, *American Slavery, Irish Freedom: Abolition, Immigrant Citizenship, and the Transatlantic Movement for Irish Repeal* (Baton Rouge, 2010); W. Caleb McDaniel, "Repealing Unions: American Abolitionists, Irish Repeal, and the Origins of Garrisonian Disunionism," *JER* 28 (Summer 2008): 243–69; John F. Quinn, "The Rise and Fall of Repeal: Slavery and Irish Nationalism in Philadelphia," *PMHB* 130 (January 2006): 45–78; Quinn, "Expecting the Impossible? Abolitionist Appeals to the Irish in Antebellum America," *NEQ* 82 (December 2009): 667–710; Quinn, *Father Mathew's Crusade: Temperance in Nineteenth-Century Ireland and Irish America* (Amherst, Mass., 2002), 160–64.

31. *TL*, February 3, March 17, May 19, 1854; September 18, 1857; December 10, 1858; Ignatiev, *How the Irish Became White*, 68–70; Bryan P. McGovern, *John Mitchel: Irish Nationalist, Southern Secessionist* (Knoxville, 2009); Iver Bernstein, *The New*

York City Draft Riots: Their Significance for American Society and Politics in the Age of the Civil War (New York, 1990); Leslie Harris, *In the Shadow of Slavery: African Americans in New York City, 1629–1863* (Chicago, 2001), 279–86; Kevin McGruder, 'A Fair and Open Field': The Responses of Black New Yorkers to the Draft Riots," *Afro-Americans in New York Life and History* 37 (July 2013): 7–40; Kevin Kenny, "Diaspora and Comparison: The Global Irish as a Case Study," *JAH* 90 (June 2003): 155–59; Montgomery, *Beyond Equality*, 126–34; Foner, *Politics and Ideology in the Age of the Civil War*, chap. 8; Edward T. O'Donnell, *Henry George and the Crisis of Inequality: Progress and Poverty in the Gilded Age* (New York, 2015), chap. 4.

32. *Proceedings of the New England Anti Slavery Convention . . . 1834*, 11–12; *First Annual Report of the New Hampshire Anti Slavery Society . . .* (Concord, N.H., 1835), 34–35; *Weekly Advocate*, January 21, 1837; *CA*, August 17, October 12, 1839; April 25, 1840; *TL*, August 9, 1839; January 30, 1846; July 2, 1858; Taylor, ed., *British and American Abolitionists*, 294, 316; James W. Trent Jr., *The Manliest Man: Samuel G. Howe and the Contours of Nineteenth-Century American Reform* (Amherst, Mass., 2012).

33. *TL*, April 14, 21, 1848; Clare Taylor, *Women of the Anti-Slavery Movement: The Weston Sisters* (New York, 1995), chap. 5; Lawrence C. Jennings, *French Anti-Slavery: The Movement for the Abolition of Slavery in France, 1802–1848* (Cambridge, Eng., 2000); Marcel Dorigny, ed., *The Abolitions of Slavery from Léger Félicité Sonthonax to Victor Schoelcher, 1793, 1794, 1848* (Paris, 2003), 305–17; Timothy Mason Roberts, *Distant Revolutions: 1848 and the Challenge to American Exceptionalism* (Charlottesville, Va., 2009); Martin Duberman, *James Russell Lowell* (Boston, 1966); Adam-Max Tuchinsky, "'The Bourgeoisie Will Fall and Fall Forever': The *New York Tribune*, the 1848 French Revolution, and American Social Democratic Discourse," *JAH* 92 (September 2005): 498–526; Eric J. Hobsbawm, *The Age of Revolution, 1789–1848* (New York, 1962).

34. David Brion Davis, *Revolutions: Reflections on American Equality and Foreign Liberations* (Cambridge, Mass., 1990); Charles M. Wiltse, "A Critical Southerner: John C. Calhoun on the Revolutions of 1848," *JSH* 15 (August 1949): 299–310; Richard C. Rohrs, "American Critics of the French Revolution of 1848," *JER* 14 (Autumn 1994): 359–77; Timothy M. Roberts, "'Revolutions Have become the Bloody Toy of the Multitude': European Revolutions, the South, and the Crisis of 1850," *JER* 25 (2005): 259–83; Thomas, "Antislavery and Utopia," 240–49; Manisha Sinha, *The Counterrevolution of Slavery: Politics and Ideology in Antebellum South Carolina* (Chapel Hill, 2000), 91, 224–27.

35. *TL*, October 31, November 7, December 20, 1851; January 2, 9, 16, 23, February 20, 27, March 5, 12, 19, May 7, 14, 1852; Taylor, ed., *British and American Abolitionists*, 416–18, 441; [William Lloyd Garrison], *Letter to Louis Kossuth . . .* (Boston, 1852), 4–8, 52, 76; *Letters on American Slavery . . .* (Boston, 1860); Enrico Dal Lago, *William Lloyd Garrison and Giuseppe Mazzini: Abolition, Democracy, and Radical Reform* (Baton Rouge, 2013); Mischa Honeck, *We Are the Revolutionists: German-Speaking Immigrants and American Abolitionists After 1848* (Athens, Ga., 2011), 26; Michael A. Morrison, "American Reaction to European Revolutions, 1848–1852: Sectionalism, Memory, and the Revolutionary Heritage," *CWH* 49 (June 2003): 111–32.

36. *NE*, August 5, October 23, November 6, 13, 20, December 4, 11, 18, 25, 1851; January 29, February 26, July 1, September 9, 1852; *FDP*, November 6, 13, 20, 27, December 11, 18, 25, 1851; January 1, 8, 15, 22, 29, February 12, 25, 26, March 11, 22, 25, April 1, 8, June 3, 10, October 22, 1852; Mitch Kachun, "'Our Platform Is as Broad as Humanity': Transatlantic Freedom Movements and the Idea of Progress in Nineteenth-Century African American Thought and Activism," *S&A* 24 (December 2003): 1–23; Erica L. Ball, *To Live an Antislavery Life: Personal Politics and the Antebellum Black Middle Class* (Athens, Ga, 2012), 117–24.

37. *TL*, April 8, 22, 1859; *NE*, November 9, 23, 1854; April 5, June 7, September 20, October 11, 25, November 8, 29, December 13, 20, 27, 1855; Honeck, *We Are the Revolutionists*, 34, esp. 141–47; Mischa Honeck, "An Unexpected Alliance: August Willich, Peter H. Clark and the Abolitionist Movement in Cincinnati," in Larry A. Greene and Anke Ortlepp, eds., *Germans and African Americans: Two Centuries of Exchange* (Jackson, Miss., 2011), 17–36; Bruce Levine, *The Spirit of 1848: German Immigrants, Labor Conflict, and the Coming of the Civil War* (Urbana, 1992); Alison Clark Efford, *German Immigrants, Race, and Citizenship in the Civil War Era* (Cambridge, Eng., 2013).

38. *TL*, May 18, 1849; Honeck, "An Unexpected Alliance," 27, 30; Timothy Messer-Kruse, *The Yankee International, 1846–1876: Marxism and the American Reform Tradition* (Chapel Hill, 1998), esp. chap. 1; Nikki M. Taylor, *America's First Black Socialist: The Radical Life of Peter H. Clark* (Lexington, Ky., 2013); Karl Marx, *Dispatches for the New York Tribune: Selected Journalism of Karl Marx*, James Ledbetter, ed. (New York, 2007); Tuchinsky, *Horace Greeley's New-York Tribune*, 104–7; Robin Blackburn, *Marx and Lincoln: An Unfinished Revolution* (London, 2011), introduction, 177–78; Nick Salvatore, *Eugene V. Debs: Citizen and Socialist* (Urbana, 1982); Eric J. Hobsbawm, *The Age of Capital, 1848–1875* (New York, 1975).

39. John Townsend, *The Doom of Slavery in the Union . . .* (Charleston, S.C., 1860), 24; Taylor, ed., *British and American Abolitionists*, 144, 176, 219–20; Robert E. May, *The Southern Dream of a Caribbean Empire, 1845–1861* (Baton Rouge, 1973); Walter Johnson, *River of Dark Dreams: Slavery and Empire in the Cotton Kingdom* (Cambridge, Mass., 2013); Fladeland, *Men and Brothers*, chap. 16.

40. R. R. Gurley, *Mission in England . . .* (Washington, 1841), 17, 62–65, 84–85, 140, 190; *ARCJ*, October 1837; March 15, 1840; April 15, 1841; November 1845; *CA*, February 27, 1841; Thomas Fowell Buxton, *The African Slave Trade and its Remedy* (London, 1840); *Report of the Committee of the African Civilization Society . . .* (London, 1842); *Colonization . . .* (Baltimore, 1851); Joseph Tracy, *Colonization and Missions . . .* (Boston, 1846), 12–21, 38–40; *Address of the Honorable Edward Everett . . .* (n.p., n.d.), 4–7; Howard Temperley, *White Dreams, Black Africa: The Antislavery Expedition to the River Niger, 1841–1842* (New Haven, 1991), 1–15, 33–36, 55–58.

41. Ripley, ed., *The Black Abolitionist Papers*, 1:349–54; Alexander Crummell, B.A., *The Future of Africa . . .* (1862; repr., New York, 1969), 89–90, 148, 216, 327–54; Crummell, *Destiny and Race*, 158–64, 269–88; Remond, "The Negroes of the United States of America," 218; Moses, *Alexander Crummell*, 46–88; Joel Schor, *Henry Highland Garnet: A Voice of Black Radicalism in the Nineteenth Century* (Westport, Conn., 1977), 114.

42. Ripley, ed., *The Black Abolitionist Papers*, 1:225–27, 232–33; *NS*, March 2, June 22, July 6, 27, August 31, September 7, 1849; October 31, 1850; *TL*, August 10, 1849; *NASS*, March 10, 1855; Schor, *Henry Highland Garnet*, chap. 6; Ofari, *Let Your Motto Be Resistance*, 66–69, 72–75, 155–60; Martin B. Pasternak, *Rise Now and Fly to Arms: The Life of Henry Highland Garnet* (New York, 1995), 73–76; Burke, *Samuel Ringgold Ward*; Sven Beckert, "Emancipation and Empire: Reconstructing the Worldwide Web of Cotton Production in the Age of the American Civil War," *AHR* 109 (December 2004): 1405–38.

43. J. W. C. Pennington to Phelps, February 2, 1846, Amos Phelps Papers, Antislavery Collection, BPL; Webber, *American to the Backbone*, 232–37; Clara Merritt DeBoer, *Be Jubilant My Feet: African American Abolitionists in the American Missionary Association, 1839–1861* (New York, 1994), 191–93; Gale L. Kenny, *Contentious Liberties: American Abolitionists in Post-Emancipation Jamaica, 1834–1866* (Athens, Ga., 2010); Rugemer, *The Problem of Emancipation*, 282, 291–301

44. *TL*, August 9, 1839; February 16, March 6, 20, April 3, August 7, 28, 1840; January 28, 1841; January 20, March 3, December 29, 1843; May 23, 1845; June 13, 1851; *NASS*, July 1, October 21, December 1, 1841; December 1, 1842; Taylor, ed., *British and American Abolitionists*, 68–70, 72, 77–79, 81–82, 86–87, 102, 108, 112, 126, 165, 184, 225, 230–31, 233, 239, 254; Abel and Klingberg, eds., *A Side-Light on Anglo-American Relations*, 62, 66; Stebbins, *Upward Steps of Seventy Years*, 58, 100–101; Elizabeth Kelly Gray, "'Whisper to Him the Word India': Trans-Atlantic Critics and American Slavery, 1830–1860," *JER* 27 (Fall 2008): 379–91; Howard Temperley, "The Delegalization of Slavery in British India," in *After Slavery: Emancipation and Its Discontents* (London, 2000), 169–87.

45. *TL*, September 25, October 2, November 6, 1857; Gray, "Whisper to Him the Word India," 379–91; Rajmohun Gandhi, *A Tale of Two Revolts: India's 1857 and the American Civil War* (New Delhi, 2009); Shlomo Avineri, *Karl Marx on Colonialism and Modernization* (Garden City, N.J., 1968); V. I. Lenin, *Imperialism, the Highest Stage of Capitalism: A Popular Outline* (1917: rev. ed. Moscow, 1934).

46. *Proceedings of the First General Peace Convention . . .* (London, 1843), 23–24, 33–34; *Report of the Proceedings of the Second General Peace Congress . . .* (London, 1849); Ofari, *Let Your Motto Be Resistance*, 58–61; Rufus W. Clark, *An Address Delivered Before the American Peace Society . . .* (Boston, 1851), 38; Chas. Nothend, ed., *Elihu Burritt . . .* (New York, 1879); Valerie Ziegler, *The Advocates of Peace in Antebellum America* (Bloomington, 1992); Merle E. Curti, *The American Peace Crusade, 1815–1860* (Durham, 1929); Peter Brock, *Radical Pacifists in Antebellum America* (Princeton, 1968); George Fredrickson, *The Inner Civil War: Northern Intellectuals and the Crisis of the Union* (New York, 1968).

47. Taylor, ed., *British and American Abolitionists*, 67; Christopher Schmidt-Nowara, "The End of Slavery and the End of Empire: Slave Emancipation in Cuba and Puerto Rico" and Charles Swaisland, "The Aborigines Protection Society, 1837–1909," in Temperley, ed., *After Slavery*, 188–205, 265–80; McDaniel, *The Problem of Democracy*, 269; Cecilia Azevedo, *Abolitionism in the United States and Brazil: A Comparative Perspective* (New York, 1995); Seymour Drescher, "From Empires of Slavery to

Empires of Antislavery," in Josep M. Fradera and Christopher Schmidt-Nowara, eds., *Slavery and Antislavery in Spain's Atlantic Empire* (New York, 2013): 291–316.

48. *TL*, January 1, October 8, 1831; February 28, 1835; August 31, 1838; *TE*, September 19, 1839; Wright, *The Sin of Slavery*, 4, 36–35; [Garrison], *The Maryland Scheme of Expatriation*, 18; Linda K. Kerber, "The Abolitionist Perception of the Indian," *JAH* 62 (September 1975): 271–95; Bruce Cutler, *The Massacre at Sand Creek: Narrative Voices* (Norman, Okla., 1995); Ari Kelman, *A Misplaced Massacre: Struggling over the Memory of Sand Creek* (Cambridge, Mass., 2013), chap. 1; Barbara Krauthamer, *Black Slaves, Indian Masters: Slavery, Emancipation and Citizenship in the Native American South* (Chapel Hill, 2015); Stauffer, *The Black Hearts of Men*, chap. 6; John H. Bracey Jr. and Manisha Sinha, eds., *African American Mosaic: A Documentary History from the Slave Trade to the Twenty-First Century, Volume One—To 1877* (Upper Saddle River, N.J., 2004), 387–92.

49. [Francis Jackson Garrison and Wendell Phillips Garrison], *William Lloyd Garrison, 1805–1879: The Story of His Life Told By His Children*, vol. 4, *1861–1879* (London, 1889): 296–300; Timothy Messer-Kruse, "Eight Hours, Greenbacks, and 'Chinamen': Wendell Phillips, Ira Steward and the Fate of Labor Reform in Massachusetts," *Labor History* 42 (May 2001): 133–58; Gwendolyn Mink, *Old Labor and New Immigrants in American Political Development: Union, Party and State, 1875–1920* (Ithaca, 1986); cf. Moon Ho-Jung, *Coolies and Cane: Race, Labor, and Sugar in the Age of Emancipation* (Baltimore, 2006); Stacey L. Smith, *Freedom's Frontier: California and the Struggle over Unfree Labor, Emancipation, and Reconstruction* (Chapel Hill, 2013), esp. chap. 7.

50. *TL*, November 17, 1843; February 23, 1844; January 2, 1846; see "Abolition of Capital Punishment" petitions, D. Carpenter, N. Topich, and G. Griffin, Digital Archive of Massachusetts Anti-Slavery and Anti-Segregation Petitions, Massachusetts Archives, Boston, Harvard Dataverse; Louis Masur, *Rites of Execution: Capital Punishment and the Transformation of American Culture, 1776–1865* (New York, 1989), 117–21, 160–61; Jeannine Marie DeLombard, *In the Shadow of the Gallows: Race, Crime, and American Civic Identity* (Philadelphia, 2012), 249–51.

CHAPTER TWELVE. SLAVE RESISTANCE

1. *Walker's Appeal, With a Brief Sketch of His Life By Henry Highland Garnet and also Garnet's Address to the Slaves of the United States of America* (1848; repr., New York, 1969); James Oakes, "The Political Significance of Slave Resistance," in Patrick Rael, ed., *African-American Activism Before the Civil War* (New York, 2008), 188–205.

2. Merton L. Dillon, *Slavery Attacked: Southern Slaves and Their Allies, 1619–1865* (Baton Rouge, 1990); Henrietta Buckmaster, *Let My People Go: The Story of the Underground Railroad and the Growth of the Abolition Movement* (New York, 1941); Jeanine DeLombard, *Slavery on Trial: Law, Abolitionism and Print Culture* (Chapel Hill, 2007); François Furstenberg, "Beyond Freedom and Slavery: Autonomy, Virtue, and Resistance in Early American Political Discourse," *JAH* 89 (March 2003): 1295–1330.

3. Marion Gleason McDougall, *Fugitive Slaves* (New York, 1891); Jane G. Landers, *Atlantic Creoles in the Age of Revolutions* (Cambridge, Mass., 2010); Sarah E. Cornell, "Citizens of Nowhere: Fugitive Slaves and Free African Americans in Mexico, 1833–1857," JAH 100 (September 2013): 351–74; Fergus M. Bordewich, *Bound for Canaan: The Epic Story of the Underground Railroad, America's First Civil Rights Movement* (New York, 2005); Charles L. Blockson, *The Underground Railroad* (Baltimore, 1994).

4. Carol Wilson, *Freedom at Risk: The Kidnapping of Free Blacks in America, 1780–1865* (Lexington, Ky., 1994); Thomas D. Morris, *Free Men All: The Personal Liberty Laws of the North, 1780–1861* (Baltimore, 1974), chap. 3; Paul Finkelman, *An Imperfect Union: Slavery, Federalism and Comity* (Chapel Hill, 1981); Steven Hahn, *The Political Worlds of Slavery and Freedom* (Cambridge, Mass., 2009), 29–44.

5. Stanley Harrold, *Border War: Fighting Over Slavery Before the Civil War* (Chapel Hill, 2010), 40; John Hope Franklin and Loren Schweninger, *Runaway Slaves: Rebels on the Plantation* (New York, 1999), 283–86; Sylviane A. Diouf, *Slavery's Exiles: The Story of the American Maroons* (New York, 2014); Sean Kelley, "'Mexico in His Head': Slavery and the Texas–Mexico Border, 1810–1860," *Journal of Social History* 37 (Spring 2004): 718; R. J. M. Blackett, *Making Freedom: The Underground Railroad and the Politics of Slavery* (Chapel Hill, 2013).

6. NASS, July 2, November 2, 26, December 31, 1840; January 11, March 4, April 29, May 13, 27, July 22, August 5, October 14, 28, November 25, December 16, 1841; January 20, March 24, October 20, 1843; July 13, November 9, 1844; L. Maria Child, *Isaac T. Hopper* . . . (Boston, 1853): 47, 70–73, 77–80, 208–9; Isaac T. Hopper, *Narrative of the Life of Thomas Cooper* (New York, 1832); Daniel Meaders, "Kidnapping Blacks in Philadelphia: Isaac Hopper's Tales of Oppression," JNH 80 (Spring 1995): 47–65; Meaders, *Kidnappers in Philadelphia: Isaac Hopper's Tales of Oppression 1780–1843* (New York, 1994).

7. *Reminiscences of Levi Coffin* . . . , 3d ed. (Cincinnati, 1898); Ann Hagedorn, *Beyond the River: The Untold Story of the Heroes of the Underground Railroad* (New York, 2002); Larry Gara, *The Liberty Line: The Legend of the Underground Railroad* (Lexington, Ky., 1961), 94–96; David W. Blight, ed., *Passages to Freedom: The Underground Railroad in History and Memory* (Washington, 2004).

8. Peter P. Hinks, "'Frequently Plunged into Slavery': Free Blacks and Kidnapping in Antebellum Boston," *Historical Journal of Massachusetts* (Winter 1992): 16–31; Lawrence B. Goodheart, "'The Chronicles of Kidnapping in New York': Resistance to the Fugitive Slave Law, 1834–1835," *Afro-Americans in New York Life and History* 8 (January 1984): 7–15; "Proceeding of a Meeting of the New York Committee of Vigilance . . . November, 1836," and "Second Annual Report of the New York Committee of Vigilance, 1838," BAP; *First Annual Report of the Committee of Vigilance* . . . (New York, 1837), 3–4, 8–14, 31–32, 73, 81–83; *The Mirror of Liberty*, August 1838; January 1839; David Ruggles, *A Plea for "A Man and a Brother"* (New York, 1839), 11–16; CA, October 20, November 3, 1838; January 26, February 23, March 9, July 27, August 31, September 7, 14, 1839; September 5, 1840; NASS, June 25, August 13, 20, October 15,

1840; March 25, May 6, September 9, 1841; May 26, 1842; May 11, 1843; February 10, 1848; *TL*, June 19, 1840; August 6, 20, November 3, September 9, 1841; August 31, September 13, 1844; December 21, 1849; Graham Russell Gao Hodges, *David Ruggles: A Radical Black Abolitionist and the Underground Railroad in New York City* (Chapel Hill, 2010), chaps. 3–5; Dorothy B. Porter, "David Ruggles, an Apostle of Human Rights," *JNH* 28 (January 1943): 23–50.

9. *TL*, August 6, October 15, 22, 1836; September 12, 19, October 3, 1845; November 20, 1846; Thomas Aves, *Case of the Slave-Child, Med . . .* (Boston, 1836), 4, 13–16, 21–31; Nina Moore Tiffany, *Samuel E. Sewall: A Memoir* (New York, 1898), 58–69; Walter M. Merrill, ed., *The Letters of William Lloyd Garrison*, vol. 3, *No Union with Slaveholders, 1841–1849* (Cambridge, Mass., 1973), 320–21; Leonard W. Levy, "The 'Abolition Riot': Boston's First Slave Rescue," *NEQ* 25 (1952): 85–92; Edlie L. Wong, *Neither Fugitive nor Free: Atlantic Slavery, Freedom Suits, and the Legal Culture of Travel* (New York, 2009), 81–104.

10. *CA*, May 30, 1840; April 17, May 15, 1841; Luther Rawson Marsh, ed., *Writings and Speeches of Alvan Stewart on Slavery* (New York, 1860), 94, 219–33, 377–88; Glyndon G. Van Deusen, *William Henry Seward* (New York, 1967), 64–67; Daniel R. Ernst, "Legal Positivism, Abolitionist Litigation and the New Jersey Slave Case of 1845," *Law and History Review* 4 (Autumn 1986): 337–65; Frederick Blue, *No Taint of Compromise: Crusaders in Antislavery Politics* (Baton Rouge, 2005), chap. 2.

11. Jacob C. White Sr., "Minute Book of the Vigilant Committee of Philadelphia," Elizabeth White and Sarah McCrummill, "Preamble, 5 July, 1838," "At a Meeting of the Vigilant Committee . . . 20 June 1839," "Robert Purvis to J. Miller McKim, October 31, 1844," *BAP*; *CA*, August 18, 1838; William Still, *The Underground Railroad . . .* (Philadelphia, 1872), 508, 525–28; Robert C. Smedley, *History of the Underground Railroad in Chester and the Neighboring Counties of Pennsylvania* (Lancaster, Pa., 1883), 355–61; Margaret Hope Bacon, *But One Race: The Life of Robert Purvis* (Albany, 2007), 75–82, 117–21; Joseph Borome, "The Vigilant Committee of Philadelphia," *PMHB* 92 (1968): 320–51; Richard S. Newman, " 'Lucky to be Born in Pennsylvania': Free Soil, Fugitive Slaves, and the Making of Pennsylvania's Anti-Slavery Borderland," *S&A* 32 (September 2011): 413–30.

12. C. Peter Ripley, ed., *The Black Abolitionist Papers*, 3:397–402; C. Peter Ripley, ed., *The Black Abolitionist Papers*, vol. 2, *Canada, 1830–1865* (Chapel Hill, 1986), 2:26–30; Katharine Du Pre Lumpkin, " 'The General Plan Was Freedom': A Negro Secret Order on the Underground Railroad," *Phylon* 28 (Spring 1967): 63–77; Keith P. Griffler, *Frontline of Freedom: African Americans and the Forging of the Underground Railroad in the Ohio River* (Lexington, Ky., 2004), 90–93; Carol M. Hunter, *To Set the Captive Free: Reverend Jermain Wesley Loguen and the Struggle for Freedom in Central New York, 1835–1872* (New York, 1993).

13. William Birney, *James G. Birney and His Times . . .* (New York, 1890), 260–66; *Speech of Salmon P. Chase in the Case of the Colored Woman, Matilda . . .* (Cincinnati, 1837), 7, 10–12, 19–27, 30–35; Dwight L. Dumond, ed., *Letters of James Gillespie Birney, 1831–1857* (Gloucester, Mass., 1966), 1:379; *The Address and Reply on the Presentation*

of a Testimonial to S. P. Chase by the Colored People of Cincinnati (Cincinnati, 1845), 11, 27, 35; Betty Fladeland, *James Gillespie Birney: Slaveholder to Abolitionist* (Ithaca, 1955), 149–54; Stephen Middleton, *Ohio and the Antislavery Activities of the Attorney Salmon Portland Chase, 1830–1849* (New York, 1990), 50–73, 92–113; Hagedorn, *Beyond the River*, 124–28, 140–93, 226–30; Hans Louis Trefousse, *Benjamin Franklin Wade: Radical Republican from Ohio* (New York, 1963), 32–38; Harrold, *Border War*, 79–93; Matthew Salafia, "Searching for Slavery: Fugitive Slaves in the Ohio River Valley Borderland, 1830–1860," *Ohio Valley History* 8 (Winter 2008): 38–63.

14. *TL*, March 11, April 22, May 13, 1842; *NASS*, April 21, 1842; Ripley, ed., *The Black Abolitionist Papers*, 3:380–84; S. P. Chase, *An Argument for the Defendant . . .* (Cincinnati, 1847), 6–9; Salmon P. Chase to Gay, April 28, 1847, Sydney Howard Gay Papers, CU; *Diary and Correspondence of Salmon P. Chase* (New York, 1971), 113–15; Paul Finkelman, "*Prigg v. Pennsylvania* and Northern State Courts: Anti-Slavery Use of a Pro-Slavery Decision," *CWH* 25 (March 1979): 5–35; Robert M. Cover, *Justice Accused: Antislavery and the Judicial Process* (New Haven, 1975), 166–74, 232–49; R. Kent Newmyer, *Supreme Court Justice Joseph Story: Statesman of the Old Republic* (Chapel Hill, 1985), 370–78; H. Robert Baker, *Prigg v. Pennsylvania: Slavery, the Supreme Court and the Ambivalent Constitution* (Lawrence, Kan., 2012).

15. *TL*, October 28, November 4, 11, 18, 25, December 9, 16, 23, 1842; January 13, February 3, March 24, April 7, May 12, 1843; November 26, 1847; *The Latimer Journal and North Star*, November 11, 1842; May 10, 1843; *NASS*, November 17, 24, December 8, 15, 1842; Austin G. Elbridge, *Statement of the Facts Connected with the Arrest and Emancipation of George Latimer* (Boston, 1842); Asa Davis, "The Two Autobiographical Fragments of George W. Latimer," *Journal of Afro-American Historical and Genealogical Magazine* 1 (Summer 1980); Vincent Y. Bowditch, *Life and Correspondence of Henry Ingersoll Bowditch*, 2 vols. (Boston, 1902), 1: chaps. 7–9; Tiffany, *Samuel E. Sewall*, 69–70; Book 8, Boston Vigilance Committee Records, 1846–47, Boston Anti-Man Hunting League Papers, MHS; *Address of the Committee Appointed by a Public Meeting . . .* (Boston, 1846); James W. Trent Jr., *The Manliest Man: Samuel G. Howe and the Contours of Nineteenth-Century Reform* (Amherst, Mass., 2012), 157–59; Bruce Laurie, *Beyond Garrison: Antislavery and Social Reform* (Cambridge, Eng., 2005), 78–79, 116–19.

16. Stanley Harrold, *The Abolitionists and the South* (Lexington, Ky., 1995), chap. 4.

17. *NASS*, November 25, December 2, 1841; William Beardsley et al., *Narrative of Facts Respecting Alanson Work, Jas E. Burr and Geo. Thompson . . .* (Quincy, Ill., 1842); George Thompson, *Prison Life and Reflections . . .* (Oberlin, 1847), 21, 62, 114, 170, 417; Harrold, *Border War*, 50–51; Joseph Yanielli, "George Thompson among the Africans: Empathy, Authority and Insanity in the Age of Abolition," *JAH* 96 (March 2010): 982–88; Benjamin G. Merkel, "The Underground Railroad and the Missouri Borders, 1840–1860," *Missouri Historical Review* 37 (April 1943): 271–85; Terrell Dempsey, *Searching for Jim: Slavery in Sam Clemens's World* (Columbia, Mo., 2003), chaps. 15, 16; Carol Pirtle, *Escape Betwixt Two Suns: A True Tale of the Underground Railroad in Illinois* (Carbondale, 2000).

18. *TL*, April 19, May 17, June 21, August 16, 31, September 6, December 6, 13, 1844; January 3, August 8, 15, 1845; January 23, February 20, March 20, July 24, 1846; February 12, March 5, April 9, August 20, October 15, 1847; February 11, March 31, May 26, 1848; November 30, 1849; March 29, 1850; May 19, 1854; *NASS*, October 3, 1844; February 27, July 17, 24, August 7, 1845; Henry Ingersoll Bowditch to Sydney Howard Gay, November 11, 1845, Sydney Howard Gay Papers, CU; Jonathan Walker, *Trial and Imprisonment of Jonathan Walker . . .* (Boston, 1845), 9, 11, 24–33, 44–51, 74–93, 105–6; Jonathan Walker, *A Brief View of American Chattelized Humanity, and Its Supports* (Boston, 1846), 3–4; *Thirteenth Annual Report, Presented to the Massachusetts Anti-Slavery Society, By its Board of Managers, January 22, 1845 . . .* , 23–25, 39–40, and *Fourteenth Annual Report, Presented to the Massachusetts Anti-Slavery Society, By its Board of Managers, January 28, 1846 . . .* (repr., Westport, Conn., 1970), 51–52; Frank Edward Kittredge, *The Man with the Branded Hand: An Authentic Sketch of the Life and Services of Capt. Jonathan Walker* (Rochester, 1899); Matthew J. Clavin, *Aiming for Pensacola: Fugitive Slaves on the Atlantic and Southern Frontiers* (Cambridge, Mass., 2015).

19. *TL*, January 21, 1842; August 9, 22, 31, September 6, 13, December 13, 20, 27, 1844; January 2, December 5, 1845; January 9, February 27, March 6, April 3, May 8, 15, July 3, 1846; *NASS*, October 3, November 28, 1844; *Memoir of Rev. Abel Brown by his Companion C. S. Brown* (Worcester, 1849), 100–128, 138–41, 150–52, 190–205, 212, 226–27; Torrey to Phelps, July 24, November 4, 1844, Phelps to Torrey, December 10, 1844, Amos A. Phelps Papers, Antislavery Collection, BPL; J. C. Lovejoy, ed., *Memoir of Reverend Charles T. Torrey . . .* (Boston, 1847), 89–99, 126–214, 282–308, 322–24; *A Narrative of Thomas Smallwood . . .* (Boston, 1851), 13–43; *Diary and Correspondence of Salmon P. Chase*, 107–8; Merrill, ed., *The Letters of William Lloyd Garrison*, 3:338; Stanley Harrold, *Subversives: Antislavery Community in Washington DC, 1828–1865* (Baton Rouge, 2003), 52–53, 64–93; Harrold, "On the Borders of Slavery and Race: Charles T. Torrey and the Underground Railroad," *JER* 20 (Summer 2000): 273–92; James L. Huston, "The Experiential Basis of the Northern Antislavery Impulse," *JSH* 56 (November 1990): 609–40; E. Fuller Torrey, *The Martyrdom of Abolitionist Charles Torrey* (Baton Rouge, 2013).

20. *TL*, November 29, 1844; August 1, September 12, 1845; February 27, 1846; April 23, 1852; December 29, 1854; January 26, 1855; February 8, March 7, 28, May 9, 1856; *NASS*, March 6, 1845; *Reminiscences of Levi Coffin*, 719–26; Delia Ann Webster, *Kentucky Jurisprudence . . .* (Vergennes, Vt., 1845), 21–23, 83–84; *Fourteenth Annual Report, Presented to the Massachusetts Anti-Slavery Society*, 52–53; Laura S. Haviland, *A Woman's Life-Work . . .* (Chicago, 1887), 139–61; Tiya Miles, "The Radical Mrs. Haviland," *Michigan History Magazine* (November–December 2012), 15–20; *Reverend Calvin Fairbank During Slavery Times . . .* (Chicago, 1890), 12–25, 50–52, 85–105; Randolph Paul Runyon, *Delia Webster and the Underground Railroad* (Lexington, Ky., 1996); Jane Williamson, "Rowland T. Robinson, Rokeby, and the Underground Railroad in Vermont," *Vermont History* 69 (2011): 19–31; Stanley J. Robboy and Anita W. Robboy, "Lewis Hayden: From Fugitive Slave to Statesman," *NEQ* 46 (December 1973):

591–613; Hallie Quinn Brown, *Homespun Heroines and Other Women of Distinction* (New York, 1988).

21. *Fifteenth Annual Report, Presented to the Massachusetts Anti-Slavery Society, By Its Board of Managers, January 27, 1847 . . .* (repr., Westport, Conn., 1970), 62–63; *Reminiscences of Levi Coffin*, 305–12, 428–46, 713–18.

22. Still, *The Underground Railroad*, 525, 527; Bordewich, *Bound for Canaan*, 312, 346; Runyon, *Delia Webster*, 123; Harrold, *Border War*, chaps. 5, 6; Mathew Salafia, *Slavery's Borderland: Freedom and Bondage Along the Ohio River* (Philadelphia, 2013).

23. Wilbur H. Seibert, *The Underground Railroad from Slavery to Freedom* (New York, 1898); J. Blaine Hudson, *Fugitive Slaves and the Underground Railroad in the Kentucky Borderland* (Jefferson, N.C., 2002); Keith P. Griffler, *Front Line of Freedom: African Americans and the Forging of the Underground Railroad in the Ohio Valley* (Lexington, Ky., 2004); Kathryn Grover, *The Fugitive's Gibraltar: Escaping Slaves and Abolitionism in New Bedford, Massachusetts* (Amherst, Mass., 2001), chap. 3; William C. Kashatus, *Just Over the Line: Chester County and the Underground Railroad* (Chester, Pa., 2002); David G. Smith, *On the Edge of Freedom: The Fugitive Slave Issue in South Central Pennsylvania, 1820–1870* (New York, 2012); Owen W. Muelder, *The Underground Railroad in Western Illinois* (Jefferson, N.C., 2008); Cheryl Janifer LaRoche, *Free Black Communities and the Underground Railroad: The Geography of Resistance* (Urbana, 2013); Tom Calarco, *The Underground Railroad in the Adirondack Region* (Jefferson, N.C., 2004); Calarco, *Places of the Underground Railroad* (Santa Barbara, Calif., 2011); William J. Switala, *Underground Railroad in Delaware, Maryland, and West Virginia* (Mechanicsburg, Pa., 2004); Switala, *Underground Railroad in Pennsylvania* (Mechanicsburg, Pa., 2001); Eric Foner, *Gateway to Freedom: New York City, the Underground Railroad, and the Irrepressible Conflict* (New York, 2015).

24. *PF*, June 1, 8, 1848; *TL*, November 12, 1852; March 2, 1860; Still, *The Underground Railroad*, 448–62, 511–14, 531–33; James A. McGowan, *Station Master of the Underground Railroad: The Life and Letters of Thomas Garrett* (Jefferson, N.C., 2005); Smedley, *History of the Underground Railroad in Chester*, 237–45, 249–59, 337, 355.

25. *Personal Memoir of Daniel Drayton . . .* (Boston, 1854), 20–26, 32–34, 38–62, 72–102, 111, 115, 122; *Slavery at Washington, Narrative of the Heroic Adventures of Drayton, an American Trader* (London, 1848); *TL*, April 28, May 26, 1848; *NE*, May 11, November 2, 1848; Josephine F. Pacheo, *The Pearl: A Failed Slave Escape on the Potomac* (Chapel Hill, 2005), chaps. 2–5; Mary K. Ricks, *Escape on the Pearl: The Heroic Bid for Freedom on the Underground Railroad* (New York, 2007); Harrold, *Subversives*, chaps. 4, 5.

26. Horace Mann, *Slavery: Letters and Speeches* (1851), 84–118; *TL*, August 18, December 15, 1848; April 27, May 4, 11, 1849; May 21, 1851; May 21, June 11, August 13, 27, September 3, 10, 1852; December 30, 1853; *NE*, July 13, August 3, 10, 24, December 21, 1848; May 31, 1849; October 31, 1850; November 6, 1851; April 29, January 29, September 16, 1852; January 12, 1854; Pacheo, *The Pearl*, chaps. 6–9; James B. Stewart, "Christian Statesmanship, Codes of Honor, and Congressional Violence: The Antislavery Travails and Triumphs of Joshua Giddings," Stanley Harrold, "Gamaliel Bailey, Anti-

slavery Journalist and Lobbyist," and Jonathan Earle, "Saturday Nights at the Baileys': Building an Antislavery Movement in Congress, 1838–1854," in Paul Finkelman and David R. Kennon, eds., *In the Shadow of Slavery: The Politics of Slavery in the Nation's Capital* (Athens, Ohio, 2011), 53, 62–65, 92–93; Eric Foner, *The Fiery Trial: Abraham Lincoln and American Slavery* (New York, 2010), 55–59.

27. Lydia Maria Child, *Isaac Hopper: A True Life (Boston, 1853)*, 98–103; Lewis Richardson, BAP; Henry Clay to Sydney Howard Gay, June 25, December 1, 22, 1847, Sydney Howard Gay Papers, CU; Runyon, *Delia Webster and the Underground Railroad*, 113–16; *Memoir of Rev. Abel Brown*, 130–37, 143–44; TL, April 3, 17, 1846; June 8, October 25, 1849; NS, December 13, 1847; NASS, December 30, 1841; August 25, 1842; Robert V. Remini, *Henry Clay: Statesman for the Union* (New York, 1991), 670.

28. *The Case of William Chaplin* (Boston, 1851), 14–21, 22–39, 49–51; *Circular From the Chaplin Fund Committee* [1850]; TL, August 16, 1850; April 25, 1851; NE, August 15, September 26, November 21, December 26, 1850; May 5, August 11, 1853; NS, September 5, October 3, 24, 1850; January 23, 1851; Pacheo, *The Pearl*, 219–22.

29. Ripley, ed., *The Black Abolitionist Papers*, 2:4–6, 3:428–29; Jason H. Silverman, *Unwelcome Guests: Canada West's Response to American Fugitive Slaves, 1800–1865* (Millwood, N.Y., 1983), 36–42; Irwin D. S. Winsboro and Joe Knetsch, "Florida Slaves, the 'Saltwater Railroad' to the Bahamas and Anglo-American Diplomacy," JSH 79 (February 2013): 51–78.

30. Howard Jones, *Mutiny on the* Amistad: *The Saga of a Slave Revolt and Its Impact on American Abolition, Law, and Diplomacy* (New York, 1987); Iyunolu Folayan Osagie, *The* Amistad *Revolt: Memory, Slavery, and the Politics of Identity in the United States and Sierra Leone* (Athens, Ga., 2000); Maggie Montesinos Sale, *The Slumbering Volcano: American Slave Ship Revolts and the Production of Rebellious Masculinity* (Durham, 1997), 6–7, 21–28; Marcus Rediker, *The* Amistad *Rebellion: An Atlantic Odyssey of Slavery and Freedom* (New York, 2012), 21.

31. *The African Captives . . .* (New York, 1839), iii–vi, 9–20, 22–27, 44–47; John W. Barber, *A History of the* Amistad *Captives . . .* (New Haven, 1840), 6–15, 17–18, 20–31; Augustus Field Beard, *The Story of the* "Amistad" (New York, n.d.); TE, September 5, 12, 19, 26, November 21, 1839; May 1, September 3, 1840; TL, September 13, October 18, 1839; January 17, 24, 1840; NASS, November 19, December 3, 1840; December 30, 1841; Rediker, *The* Amistad *Rebellion*, 168–71; Sydney Kaplan, "Black Mutiny on the *Amistad*," *Massachusetts Review* 10 (Summer 1969): 493–532; Leon O. Broin, *The Irish Abolitionist: Richard Madden and the Subversion of Empire*, trans. Michael O. hAodha (Dublin, 1971), chap. 5; Bertram Wyatt Brown, *Lewis Tappan and the Evangelical War Against Slavery* (Cleveland, 1969), 205–12.

32. *Argument of John Quincy Adams . . .* (New York, 1841), 4–6, 88–89, 113–15, 121–32; *Argument of Roger S. Baldwin . . .* (New York, 1841); Charles Francis Adams, ed., *Memoirs of John Quincy Adams, Comprising Portions of His Diary from 1795 to 1848* (Philadelphia, 1876), 5:128, 131–35, 427–37, 450–55; TE, February 11, March 18, 25, April 1, November 18, 1841; TL, March 5, 19, 26, April 16, November 3, 1841; March 19, 1847; NASS, January 21, March 4, 11, 25, April 1, 1841; April Anne Heloise Abel and Frank J. Klingberg, eds., *A Side-Light on Anglo-American Relations, 1839–1858, Furnished by*

the Correspondence of Lewis Tappan and Others with the British and Foreign Anti-Slavery Society (Lancaster, Pa., 1927), 60–66, 69–70, 83–84; Leonard L. Richards, *The Life and Times of Congressman John Quincy Adams* (New York, 1986), 135–39; John T. Noonan Jr., *The Antelope: The Ordeal of the Recaptured Africans in the Administration of James Monroe and John Quincy Adams* (Berkeley, 1977); Newmyer, *Supreme Court Justice Joseph Story*, 345–58, 368–69; Cover, *Justice Accused*, 109–12.

33. Joseph Sturge, *A Visit to the United States in 1841* (London, 1842), 68, 74, appendix liv; Jones, *Mutiny on the* Amistad, 196; Simeon E. Baldwin, "The Captives of the Amistad," *Papers of the New Haven Historical Society* 4 (New Haven, 1888), 331–70; Horatio T. Strother, *The Underground Railroad in Connecticut* (Middletown, Conn., 1962), chap. 4; Hugh Davis, *Joshua Leavitt, Evangelical Abolitionist* (Baton Rouge, 1990), 177–79; Howard Jones, "Cinque of the *Amistad* a Slave Trader? Perpetuating a Myth," and responses by Paul Finkelman, Bertram Wyatt Brown, and William S. Mc-Feely, *JAH* 87 (December 2000): 923–50; CA, July 31, September 4, December 4, 25, 1841; *TL*, April 22, 1842; Ripley, ed., *The Black Abolitionist Papers*, 3:365–67; Celeste Marie Bernier, *Characters of Blood: Black Heroism in the Transatlantic Imagination* (Charlottesville, Va., 2012), chap. 3; Rediker, *The* Amistad *Rebellion*, 196–217; Lewis Tappan, *History of the American Missionary Association . . .* (New York, 1855); Clara Merritt DeBoer, *Be Jubilant My Feet: African American Abolitionists in the American Missionary Association, 1839–1861* (New York, 1994), chaps. 2–5; Christopher L. Webber, *American to the Backbone: The Life of James W. C. Pennington, the Fugitive Slave Who Became One of the First Black Abolitionists* (New York, 2011), 158–72, 180–81; Clifton Herman Johnson, "The American Missionary Association, 1846–1861: A Study of Christian Abolitionism" (Ph.D. diss., University of North Carolina, 1958), chaps. 2, 3, 10, 11; Osagie, *The* Amistad *Revolt*, chap. 3; Yanneilli, "George Thompson among the Africans," 988–1000.

34. NASS, January 6, 1842; *TL*, January 7, June 10, 1842; January 20, 1843; George Hendrick and Willene Hendrick, *The* Creole *Mutiny: A Tale of Revolt Aboard a Slave Ship* (Chicago, 2008); Edward D. Jervey and C. Harold Huber, "The *Creole* Affair," *JNH* 65 (Summer 1980): 196–211; Phillip Troutman, "Grapevine in the Slave Market: African American Geo-Political Literacy and the 1841 *Creole* Slave Revolt," in Walter Johnson, ed., *The Chattel Principle: Internal Slave Trades in the Americas* (New Haven, 2004), 203–33; Walter Johnson, "White Lies: Human Property and Domestic Slavery Aboard the Slave Ship *Creole*," *Atlantic Studies* 5 (August 2008): 237–56.

35. Abel and Klingberg, eds., *A Side-Light on Anglo-American Relations*, 121–29; NASS, March 10, 17, September 1, 15, 22, 1842; January 12, April 6, 1843; Ripley, ed., *The Black Abolitionist Papers*, 2:4–6; Silverman, *Unwelcome Guests*, 42–43; Howard Jones, "The Peculiar Institution and National Honor: The Case of the *Creole* Slave Revolt," *CWH* 21 (March 1975): 28–50; Robin W. Winks, *The Blacks in Canada: A History* (New Haven, 1971), 169–76; Harper Twelvetrees, ed., *The Story and Life of John Anderson, the Fugitive Slave*" (London, 1863).

36. Joshua R. Giddings, *Speeches in Congress* (1853; repr., New York, 1968), 6–12, 15–19, 22–31, 33–38, 46–51, 76–81, 89–95; Giddings, *History of the Rebellion: Its Authors and Causes* (New York, 1864), 173–94, 205–11; NASS, February 9, 1843; Joshua R. Giddings

to Sydney Howard Gay, January 12, March 15, May 6, 25, 1846; April 17, May 27, 1848, Sydney Howard Gay Papers, CU; Matthew Clavin, " 'It is a Negro, not an Indian War': Southampton, St. Domingo, and the Second Seminole War," in William S. Belko, ed., *America's Hundred Years' War: U.S. Expansion to the Gulf Coast and the Fate of the Seminole, 1763–1858* (Gainesville, Fla., 2011), 181–208; George W. Julian, *The Life of Joshua R. Giddings* (Chicago, 1892), chaps. 3–5; James Brewer Stewart, *Joshua R. Giddings and the Tactics of Radical Politics* (Cleveland, 1970), 32–78.

37. "The Duty of the Free States," in *The Works of William E. Channing, D.D.* (Boston, 1903), 853–907; *TL*, June 17, 24, July 8, 1842.

38. *The Creole Case, and Mr. Webster's Dispatch* . . . (New York, 1842), 11–24, 29–31, 36; Cover, *Justice Accused*, 113–16.

39. *TL*, February 11, March 4, 1842; June 2, 1843; *NASS*, February 24, 1842; June 15, 1843; Stanley Harrold, *The Rise of Aggressive Abolitionism: Addresses to the Slaves* (Lexington, Ky., 2004), 77–80, 163–67; Dillon, *Slavery Attacked*, 217.

40. *TL*, September 8, 22, December 8, 1843; *Walker's Appeal* . . . *and also Garnet's Address to the Slaves of the United States of America*, 89–96; *Proceedings of the National Convention of Colored People and Their Friends, Held in Troy, N.Y. on the 6th, 7th, 8th and 9th October, 1847* (Troy, 1847), 31–32, in Howard Holman Bell, ed., *Minutes of the Proceedings of the National Negro Convention, 1830–1864* (New York, 1969); Earl Ofari, *Let Your Motto Be Resistance: The Life and Thought of Henry Highland Garnet* (Boston, 1972), 34–45; Joel Schor, *Henry Highland Garnet: A Voice of Black Radicalism in the Nineteenth Century* (Westport, Conn., 1977), 50–64; Martin B. Pasternak, *Rise Now and Fly to Arms: The Life of Henry Highland Garnet* (New York, 1995), 45–48.

41. Jabez Delano Hammond to Smith, May 18, 1839, Gerrit Smith Papers, SU; [Jabez Delano Hammond], *Life and Opinions of Julius Melbourne* . . . (Syracuse, 1847), 17, 37, 45, 58, 64–78, 119–20, 125–40, 236–38; Dillon, *Slavery Attacked*, 205–6.

CHAPTER THIRTEEN. FUGITIVE SLAVE ABOLITIONISM

1. *TL*, February 24, 1844.

2. John Sekora, "Black Message/White Envelop: Genre, Authenticity and Authority in the Antebellum Slave Narrative," *Callaloo* 10 (Summer 1987): 482–515; Dwight A. McBride, *Impossible Witnesses: Truth, Abolitionism and Slave Testimony* (New York, 2001), introduction.

3. Lara Langer Cohen and Jordan Alexander Stein, eds., *Early African American Print Culture* (Philadelphia, 2012), introduction; Kenneth W. Warren, *What Was African American Literature?* (Cambridge, Mass., 2011), 2–9; Eric Gardner, *Unexpected Places: Relocating Nineteenth-Century African American Literature* (Jackson, Miss., 2009): introduction; William L. Andrews, *To Tell a Free Story: The First Century of Afro-American Autobiography, 1760–1865* (Urbana, 1986); Charles T. Davis and Henry Louis Gates Jr., eds., *The Slave's Narrative* (New York, 1985), introduction, chapters by C. Vann Woodward, John Blassingame, James Olney, and Houston A. Baker Jr.

4. *A Narrative of Some Remarkable Incidents in the Life of Solomon Bayley* . . . (London, 1825), ix, 17–18, 37–41; Arna Bontemps, ed., *Five Black Lives* . . . (Middletown, Conn.,

1971), 104, 111, 119–20; William L. Andrews and Regina E. Mason, eds., *Life of William Grimes, the Runaway Slave* (New York, 2008), introduction; Charles Nichols, "The Case of William Grimes, the Runaway Slave," *WMQ* 8 (October 1951): 552–60; *The Slave: Or Memoirs of Archy Moore*, 2 vols. (Boston, 1836), 2:162; Moore, *The White Slave; or, Memoirs of a Fugitive* (Boston, 1852); Nancy Bentley, "White Slaves: The Mulatto Hero in Antebellum Fiction," *American Literature* 65 (September 1993): 501–22.

5. *Slavery in the United States . . .* (New York, 1837), 209–10; *Fifty Years in Chains; or, The Life of an American Slave* (New York, 1859), 9.

6. *Narrative of James Williams . . .* (Boston, 1838), xviii, xix, 70; *TL*, March 9, September 28, 1838; Davis and Gates, eds., *The Slave's Narrative*, 8–15; Henry Louis Gates Jr., "From Wheatley to Douglass: The Politics of Displacement," in Eric J. Sundquist, ed., *Frederick Douglass: New Literary and Historical Essays* (Cambridge, Eng., 1990), 57–60.

7. *A Narrative of the Adventures and Escape of Moses Roper . . .* (Philadelphia, 1838), 7–8, 87; *Narrative of the Adventures and Escape of Moses Roper . . .* (Berwick-Upon-Tweed, Eng., 1848); C. Peter Ripley, ed., *The Black Abolitionist Papers*, vol. 1, *The British Isles, 1830–1865* (Chapel Hill, 1985), 60–64; *TL*, March 30, 1838.

8. *The Narrative of Lunsford Lane . . .* (Boston, 1842); Lunsford Lane Speeches, *Western Citizen*, August 5, 1842, *Anti-Slavery Bugle*, May 19, 1855, Black Abolitionist Archive, University of Detroit, Mercy; *Narrative of the Life of Moses Grandy . . .* (London, 1843), 67–72; Ripley, ed., *The Black Abolitionist Papers*, 1:8; Bland Simpson, *Two Captains from Carolina: Moses Grandy, John Newland Maffitt, and the Coming of the Civil War* (Chapel Hill, 2012), 7–28, 40–65, 80–86, 122–30.

9. Lovejoy, ed., *Memoir of Reverend Charles T. Torrey*, 106–25; *TL*, February 23, 1844; *The Light and Truth of Slavery . . .* (Worcester, Mass., [1845]); *Narrative and Writings of Andrew Jackson . . .* (Syracuse, 1847), iii, iv, 7, 14, 22.

10. *Narrative of the Sufferings of Lewis Clarke . . .* (Boston, 1845), 9–12, 26, 37, 56–57; *NASS*, October 20, 27, 1842; April 6, 1843; *Narratives of the Sufferings of Lewis and Milton Clarke . . .* (Boston, 1846), 110, 112–13.

11. *TL*, August 27, December 31, 1841; January 14, 1842; May 12, 1843; January 12, 1844; May 9, 16, 23, 30, 1845; John W. Blassingame, ed., *The Frederick Douglass Papers, Series One: Speeches, Debates, and Interviews*, Vol. 1, *1841–46* (New Haven, 1979), 16; Jonathan Walker, *Trial and Imprisonment of Jonathan Walker* (Boston, 1845), iii–vi, 34–36; David W. Blight, ed., *Narrative of the Life of Frederick Douglass, An American Slave: Written by Himself, With Related Documents* (Boston, 2003), 31–32, 64, 89; *NS*, December 3, 1847; April 27, 1849; L. Diane Barnes, *Frederick Douglass: Reformer and Statesman* (New York, 2013), 66; Gregory P. Lampe, *Frederick Douglass: Freedom's Voice, 1818–1845* (East Lansing, 1998), 261; Sundquist, ed., *Frederick Douglass: New Literary and Historical Essays*; Deborah E. McDowell, "In the First Place: Making Frederick Douglass and the Afro-American Narrative Tradition," in William Andrews, ed., *African American Autobiography: A Collection of Critical Essays* (New York, 1992), 36–58.

12. Blassingame, ed., *The Frederick Douglass Papers*, 1:36, 58, 183, 228–29, 242–43, 249, 340; *TL*, January 16, 30, February 27, May 29, June 26, November 27, 1846; *NASS*,

November 27, 1846; Clare Taylor, ed., *British and American Abolitionists: An Episode in Transatlantic Understanding* (Edinburgh, Scotland, 1974), 241–44, 247–54, 258–60, 272–73, 277, 294; R. J. M. Blackett, *Building an Antislavery Wall: Black Americans in the Atlantic Abolitionist Movement, 1830–1860* (Baton Rouge, 1983), chap. 3; Betty Fladeland, *Men and Brothers: Anglo-American Antislavery Cooperation* (Urbana, 1972), 296–99.

13. *TL*, January 15, 29, March 5, April 16, 1847; William S. McFeely, *Frederick Douglass* (New York, 1991), 144; Aileen S. Kraditor, *Means and Ends in American Abolitionism: Garrison and His Critics on Strategy and Tactics, 1834–1850* (New York, 1967), 220–24.

14. *Narrative of William W. Brown* . . . (Boston, 1847), iii, iv, 13, 27, 70, 82–83, 109–10; *NASS*, August 29, 1844; January 30, 1845; *NS*, January 7, 1848; William W. Brown, *A Lecture Delivered Before the Female Anti-Slavery Society of Salem* . . . (Boston, 1847), 3, 5–7; Brown, *The Anti-Slavery Harp* . . . (Boston, 1849), 3, 6, 17, 23, 27–28, 45; William L. Andrews, ed., *From Fugitive Slave to Free Man: The Autobiographies of William Wells Brown* (New York, 1993), introduction, 81–83; *Biography of an American Bondman By His Daughter* (Boston, 1856): 96–99, 102–4; William Edward Farrison, *William Wells Brown: Author and Reformer* (Chicago, 1969), chaps. 1–9; Ezra Greenspan, *William Wells Brown: An African American Life* (New York, 2014).

15. William Farmer, ed., *Three Years in Europe* . . . (London, 1852), 2, 48–50, 176, 233–35, 252; *TL*, September 28, November 2, December 14, 1849; June 28, July 12, 1850; May 30, 1851; November 19, 1852; September 22, 1854; *NS*, April 17, 1851; Ripley, ed., *The Black Abolitionist Papers*, 1:155, 161–181; Fladeland, *Men and Brothers*, 344–47.

16. Farmer, ed., *Three Years in Europe*, 246–49; Ripley, ed., *The Black Abolitionist Papers*, 1:190–224, 283–92; *TL*, July 4, 25, September 26, 1851; Farrison, *William Wells Brown*, chaps. 10–12, 15; Paul Jefferson, ed., *The Travels of William Wells Brown* (New York, 1991), introduction.

17. *Narrative of the Life and Adventures of Henry Bibb* . . . (New York, 1849), 13–15, 24–25, 40, 50–51, 175–78, 187–90, 194–95; Bibb to Smith, December, 1848, Gerrit Smith Papers, SU; Ripley, ed., *The Black Abolitionist Papers*, 3:460–62; *NS*, February 25, June 16, September 1, December 29, 1848; January 6, 19, August 3, September 28, 1849; Fred Landon, "Henry Bibb, a Colonizer," *JNH* 5 (October 1920), 437–47.

18. *The Life of Josiah Henson* . . . (Boston, 1849), iii, 1–2, 5, 21–28, 39–43, 47–48, 56–59, 70–76; *TL*, January 24, 1851; W. B. Hartgrove, "The Story of Josiah Henson," *JNH* 13 (January 1918): 1–21.

19. *The Fugitive Blacksmith* . . . (London, 1849): iv–v, xi, 4, 9–10, 52–55, 59, 80–84. Herman E. Thomas, *James W. C. Pennington: African American Churchman and Abolitionist* (New York, 1995); Christopher Webber, *American to the Backbone: The Life of James W. C. Pennington: The Fugitive Slave Who Became One of the First Abolitionists* (New York, 2011), 347.

20. *Narrative of Henry Watson* . . . (Boston, 1848), 39–40; Ripley, ed., *The Black Abolitionist Papers*, 1:234–51, 259–67, 271–75, 290–92, 327–29; Earl Ofari Hutchinson, *Let Your Motto be Resistance: The Life and Thought of Henry Highland Garnet* (Boston, 1972), 61–66; Fladeland, *Men and Brothers*, 247; Blackett, *Building an Antislavery Wall*, 168–73.

21. *Narrative of Sojourner Truth* . . . (Boston, 1850), vii, 26–27, 30–33, 44–59, 82–84, 100, 124–25; *Narrative of Sojourner Truth* . . . (Boston, 1875); Nell Irvin Painter, *Sojourner Truth: A Life, A Symbol* (New York, 1996); Painter, ed., *Narrative of Sojourner Truth* (New York, 1998), introduction, 232; Margaret Washington, *Sojourner Truth's America* (Urbana, 2009).

22. *FJ*, July 18, August 8, 15, 29, September 12, October 3, 1828; *TL*, March 29, 1834; October 20, 1837, p. 172; *Memoir and Poems of Phillis Wheatley* . . . (Boston, 1838), 9, 119–23, 130; *NE*, April 28, 1848; *The Poetical Works of George Moses Horton* . . . (Hillsborough, N.C., 1845), v, vii, xii, xv, xvii, 45–50; William G. Allen, *Wheatley, Banneker, and Horton* (Boston, 1849), 5–7, 39; George Moses Horton, *Naked Genius* (Raleigh, 1865), 23, 66, 104, 114–15; Joan R. Sherman, ed., *The Black Bard of North Carolina: George Moses Horton and His Poetry* (Chapel Hill, 1997), introduction; Blyden Jackson, "George Moses Horton, North Carolinian," *North Carolina Historical Review* 53 (April 1976): 140–47.

23. Jill Beute Koverman, ed., *I Made This Jar: The Life and Works of the Enslaved African American Potter, Dave* (Columbia, S.C., 1998); Leonard Todd, *Carolina Clay: The Life and Legend of the Slave Potter Dave* (New York, 2008); Angela Cheng, *Etched in Clay: The Life of Dave, Enslaved Potter and Poet* (New York, 2013); Michael A. Chaney, *Fugitive Vision: Slave Image and Black Identity in Antebellum Narrative* (Bloomington, 2008), chap. 6; *TL*, February 9, June 8, November 30, 1849.

24. *Narrative of Henry Box Brown* . . . (Boston, 1849), 11–12, 56–62, 67, 86, 89–91; *NS*, August 24, September 28, November 16, 1849; *TL*, May 31, 1850; July 11, 1851; Cynthia Griffin Wolff, "Passing Beyond the Middle Passage: Henry 'Box' Brown's Translations of Slavery," *Massachusetts Review* 37 (Spring 1996): 42–22; John Ernest, ed., *Narrative of the Life of Henry Box Brown, Written By Himself* (Chapel Hill, 2008), 41–42, 122–67; Jeffrey Ruggles, *The Unboxing of Henry Brown* (Richmond, 2003); Daphne Brooks, *Bodies in Dissent: Spectacular Performances in Race and Freedom, 1850–1910* (Durham, 2006), chap. 2; Britt Rusert, "The Science of Freedom: Counterarchives of Racial Science on the Antebellum Stage," *African American Review* 45 (Fall 2012): 291–308.

25. *Running a Thousand Miles for Freedom* . . . (London, 1860), 15, 18, 29, 35–36, 41, 82, 87–92, 111; *TL*, February 9, March 2, April 27, 1849; January 24, May 30, July 11, 1851; January 2, December 17, 1852; *NS*, July 20, 1849; December 5, 1850; William Still, *The Underground Railroad* . . . (Philadelphia, 1872), 267–69; Ripley, ed., *The Black Abolitionist Papers*, 1:330–31; Vincent Y. Bowditch, *Life and Correspondence of Henry Ingersoll Bowditch*, 2 vols. (Boston, 1902), 1:203–9; Blackett, *Beating Against the Barriers: The Lives of Six Nineteenth-Century Afro-Americans* (Ithaca, 1989), chap. 2; Barbara McCaskill, "'Yours Very Truly': Ellen Craft—The Fugitive as Text and Artifact," *African American Review* 28 (1994): 509–29; McCaskill, *Love, Liberation and Escaping Slavery: William and Ellen Craft in Cultural Memory* (Athens, Ga., 2015).

26. Sarah H. Bradford, *Scenes in the Life of Harriet Tubman* (Auburn, N.Y., 1869), 1, 5, 7, 13, 29, 48, 79–84, 117–29; Milton C. Sernett, *Harriet Tubman: Myth, Memory, and History* (Durham, 2007); Jean M. Humez, *Harriet Tubman: The Life and the Life Sto-*

ries (Madison, 2003), 32, 38, 352; Kate Gifford Larson, *Bound for the Promised Land: Harriet Tubman, Portrait of an American Hero* (New York, 2004), 251, 302; Catherine Clinton, *Harriet Tubman: The Road to Freedom* (New York, 2004).

27. *Twelve Years a Slave* . . . (Auburn, N.Y., 1853), xvi, 20, 25, 56, 68–75, 189, 206–7, 247–49, 265–321; *NE*, February 3, 25, 1853; July 20, September 7, 1854; *TL*, September 9, 1853; *FDP*, January 28, February 11, 18, 1853; David Fiske, *Solomon Northup: His Life Before and After Slavery* (Ballston Spa, N.Y., 2012); Judith Bloom and Dennis Brindell Frandin, *Stolen into Slavery: The True Story of Solomon Northup, Free Black Man* (Washington, 2012); Adam Rothman, "The Horrors '12 Years a Slave' Could Not Tell," http://america.aljazeera.com/opinions/2014/1/the-horrors-a-12yearsaslaveacouldnattello.html.

28. *NE*, May 15, 1851; Harriet Beecher Stowe, *Uncle Tom's Cabin* . . . (1852; repr., New York, 1962), 51–52, 494–97, 506–11; Stowe, *A Key to Uncle Tom's Cabin* . . . (Boston, 1853), iii–iv; Charles Beecher, *The Duty of Disobedience to Wicked Laws: A Sermon on the Fugitive Slave Law* (Newark, 1851), 6–7, 10–11, 21–22; *FDP*, October 8, 15, 22, 1852; April 29, 1853; *TL*, January 7, 1853; July 6, 1855; Charles Edward Stowe, *Harriet Beecher Stowe: The Story of Her Life* (Boston, 1911); Mary Church Terrell, *Harriet Beecher Stowe: An Appreciation* (Washington, 1911); Eric J. Sundquist, ed., *New Essays on Uncle Tom's Cabin* (Cambridge, Eng., 1986); David S. Reynolds, *Mightier than the Sword: Uncle Tom's Cabin and the Battle for America* (New York, 2011), 107–61, 166–67, 173–80; Sarah Meer, *Uncle Tom Mania: Slavery, Minstrelsy, and Transatlantic Culture in the 1850s* (Athens, Ga., 2005); cf. Heather S. Nathans, *Slavery and Sentiment in the American Stage, 1787–1861: Lifting the Veil of Black* (Cambridge, Eng., 2009); Debby Applegate, *The Most Famous Man in America: The Biography of Henry Ward Beecher* (New York, 2006), 243, 257–59, 357–62; Richard Whitman Fox, "Performing Emancipation," in Steven Mintz and John Stauffer, eds., *The Problem of Evil: Slavery, Freedom, and the Ambiguities of American Reform* (Amherst, Mass., 2007), 298–311; Prithi Kanakamedala, *In Pursuit of Freedom: Antislavery Activism and the Culture of Abolitionism in Antebellum Brooklyn, NY* (Brooklyn Historical Society, 2012), 125–32; Ethan J. Kytle, *Romantic Reformers and the Antislavery Struggle in the Civil War Era* (Cambridge, Eng., 2014), chap. 3.

29. *TL*, March 26, 1852; February 4, 1859; *FDP*, April 8, May 27, June 10, 17, July 30, 1852; Andrews, *To Tell a Free Story*, 181; Robert S. Levine, *Martin Delany, Frederick Douglass and the Politics of Representative Identity* (Chapel Hill, 1997), 71–90, 143; Levine, ed., *Martin R. Delany: A Documentary Reader* (Chapel Hill, 2003), 230–37; Susan Gilman, "Networking *Uncle Tom's Cabin*; or, Hyper Stowe in Early African American Print Culture," in Cohen and Stein, eds., *Early African American Print Culture*, chap. 13.

30. Frederick Douglass, *My Bondage and My Freedom*, William L. Andrews, ed. (Urbana, 1987), xi–xxvi, 2, 9–10, 17, 21–23, 168, 215–17, 242–45, 248; Levine, *Martin Delany, Frederick Douglass*, 102, 144–45; John Stauffer, *The Black Hearts of Men: Radical Abolitionists and the Transformation of Race* (Cambridge, Mass., 2002), 200–201; Waldo E. Martin Jr., *The Mind of Frederick Douglass* (Chapel Hill, 1984); David W.

Blight, *Frederick Douglass' Civil War: Keeping Faith in Jubilee* (Baton Rouge, 1989), 88–91; Peter Walker, *Moral Choices: Memory, Desire, and Imagination in Nineteenth-Century American Abolition* (Baton Rouge, 1978), 209–28, 236–54, 261.

31. *Truth Stranger Than Fiction . . .* (Boston, 1858), iii–v; *TL*, August 13, 1858; Andrews, *To Tell a Free Story*, 123, 184; Robin W. Winks, "The Making of a Fugitive Slave Narrative: Josiah Henson and Uncle Tom—A Case Study," in Davis and Gates Jr., eds., *The Slave's Narrative*, 112–46; *Experience and Personal Narrative of Uncle Tom Jones . . .* (Boston, n.d.), 4, 23–29, 54; *The Experience of Rev. Thomas H. Jones . . .* (New Bedford, 1885), 70–82; Kanakamedala, *In Pursuit of Freedom*, 114–17.

32. Still, *The Underground Railroad*, 1–13; Kate E. R. Pickard, *The Kidnapped and the Ransomed . . .* (New York, 1856), xix–xx, 307–38, 375–76, 388; Nancy Grant, ed., *The Kidnapped and the Ransomed* (Jackson, Miss., 2013), introduction; Edlie L. Wong, *Neither Fugitive nor Free: Atlantic Slavery, Freedom Suits, and the Legal Culture of Travel* (New York, 2009), 114–25.

33. *Autobiography of a Female Slave* (New York, 1857), 13–18, 31–36, 79–82, 98–100, 105–6, 122–35, 145–50, 199–209, 226–31, 255–78, 296–302, 307–9, 343, 398–401; Joe Lockard, ed., *Autobiography of a Female Slave by Mattie Griffith* (Jackson, Miss., 1998), afterword; Carolyn L. Karcher, *The First Woman in the Republic: A Cultural Biography of Lydia Maria Child* (Durham, 1994), 413.

34. William Wells Brown, *Clotel, or, the President's Daughter*, Robert S. Levine, ed. (Boston, 2000); J. Noel Heermance, *William Wells Brown and Clotelle: A Portrait of an Artist in the First Negro Novel* (Hamden, Conn., 1969); Jonathan Senchyne, "Bottles of Ink and Reams of Paper: *Clotel*, Racialization, and the Material Culture of Print," and Lara Langer Cohen, "Notes from the State of Saint Domingue: The Practice of Citation in *Clotel*," in Cohen and Stein, eds., *Early African American Print Culture*, chaps. 8, 9; Greenspan, *William Wells Brown*, 288–300; Paula Garrett and Hollis Robbins, eds., *The Works of William Wells Brown: Using His "Strong, Manly Voice"* (New York, 2006), 264–308; John Ernest, "The Reconstruction of Whiteness: William Wells Brown's *The Escape, Or, a Leap for Freedom*," *PMLA* 113 (October 1998): 1108–21.

35. *TL*, January 11, 7, February 1, 19, 1856; May 21, 1858, p. 82; Frances Ellen Watkins, *Poems on Miscellaneous Subjects* (Boston, 1855), 3–4, 9–11, 32; Watkins, *Poems on Miscellaneous Subjects* (Philadelphia, 1857), 40–42, 53; *Anglo-African Magazine* 1 (August 1859), 253–54; Still, *The Underground Railroad*, 538–58; Melba Joyce Boyd, *Discarded Legacy: Politics and Poetics in the Life of Frances E. W. Harper, 1825–1911* (Detroit, 1994), 58–70, 114–16; Meredith L. McGill, "Frances Ellen Watkins Harper and the Circuits of Abolitionist Poetry," in Cohen and Stein, eds., *Early African American Print Culture*, chap. 3; Frances Smith Foster, ed., *A Brighter Coming Day: A Frances Ellen Watkins Harper Reader* (New York, 1990); Maryemma Graham, ed., *The Complete Poems of Frances E. W. Harper: An Annotated Critical History* (New York, 1988); Carla L. Peterson, *"Doers of the Word": African-American Women Speakers and Writers in the North (1830–1880)* (New York, 1995), 120–35; Dorothy Sterling, ed., *We Are Your Sisters: Black Women in the Nineteenth Century* (New York, 1984), 159–75; Manisha Sinha, "Allies for Emancipation?: Lincoln and Black Abolitionists," in

Eric Foner ed., *Our Lincoln: New Perspectives on Lincoln and His World* (New York, 2008), 184.

36. Frank J. Webb, *The Garies and Their Friends* (Project Gutenberg ebook, 2004), 2–3; *The Christian Slave . . .* (Boston, 1855); Werner Sollors, *Frank J. Webb: Fiction, Essays, Poetry* (New Milford, Conn., 2004), introduction; Eric Gardner, "'A Gentleman of Superior Cultivation and Refinement': Recovering the Biography of Frank J. Webb," *African American Review* 35 (2001): 297–308; Gardner, "A Nobler End: Mary Webb and the Victorian Platform," *Nineteenth-Century Prose* 19 (Spring 2002): 103–16; Samuel Otter, *Philadelphia Stories: America's Literature of Race and Freedom* (New York, 2013), chap. 4.

37. John W. Blassingame, ed., *The Frederick Douglass Papers, Series One: Speeches, Debates, and Interviews*, vol. 2, 1847–1854 (New Haven, 1982), 131, 154–55; *TL*, June 8, 1849; *FDP*, January 21, March 4, 11, 18, 25, 1853; Richard Yarborough, "Race, Violence and Manhood: The Masculine Ideal in Frederick Douglass' 'The Heroic Slave,'" in Eric J. Sundquist, ed., *Frederick Douglass: New Literary and Historical Essays* (Cambridge, Eng., 1990), 177–83; Maggie Montesinos Sale, *The Slumbering Volcano: American Slave Ship Revolts and the Production of Rebellious Masculinity* (Durham, 1997), chaps. 4, 5; Krista Walter, "Trappings of Nationalism in Frederick Douglass's 'The Heroic Slave,'" *African American Review* 34 (2000): 233–46; Celeste Marie-Bernier, "Ambiguities in Frederick Douglass's Two Versions of 'The Heroic Slave,'" *S&A* 22 (2001): 69–86; Cynthia S. Hamilton, "Models of Agency: Frederick Douglass and 'The Heroic Slave,'" *Proceedings of the American Antiquarian Society* 114 (Worcester, Mass., 2005): 87–136; Sterling Stuckey, *African Culture and Melville's Art: The Creative Process in* Benito Cereno *and* Moby-Dick (New York, 2009); Greg Grandin, *The Empire of Necessity: Slavery, Freedom, and Deception in the New World* (New York, 2014).

38. Harriet Beecher Stowe, *Dred: A Tale of the Great Dismal Swamp*, Robert S. Levine, ed. (Chapel Hill, 2000), ix, 49–51, 162, 198, 203–12, 353–55, 435–36, 438, 493–94, 509–13, 520, 539–47; Painter, *Sojourner Truth*, chap. 17; Jeanine DeLombard, *Slavery on Trial: Law, Abolitionism and Print Culture* (Chapel Hill, 2007), chap. 5; Cynthia S. Hamilton, "Dred: Intemperate Slavery," *Journal of American Studies* 34 (2000): 257–67; Levine, *Martin Delany, Frederick Douglass*, 156–76.

39. Dorothy Porter Wesley and Constance Porter Uzelac, eds., *William Cooper Nell: Selected Writings 1832–1847* (Baltimore, 2002), 282–86; William C. Nell, *The Colored Patriots of the American Revolution . . .* (Boston, 1855), 5–6, 11, 18, 101–11, 198–99, 223–29, 253–55, 369, 380–81; *TL*, July 1, August 2, 1853; November 14, 1856; August 5, 1859; William K. Watkins, *Our Rights as Men . . .* (Boston, 1853), 3–4, 7, 11, 17–18; Mitch Kachun, "From Forgotten Founder to Indispensable Icon: Crispus Attucks, Black Citizenship, and Collective Memory, 1770–1865," *JER* 29 (2009): 249–86; John Ernest, *Liberation Historiography: African American Writers and the Challenge of History, 1794–1861* (Chapel Hill, 2004), 95–97, 132–53; Stephen G. Hall, *A Faithful Account of the Race: African American Historical Writing in Nineteenth-Century America* (Chapel Hill, 2009), 94–104; J. R. Kerr-Ritchie, *Rites of August First: Emancipation*

Day in the Black Atlantic World (Baton Rouge, 2007), chap. 6; Stephen Kantrowitz, *More than Freedom: Fighting for Black Citizenship in a White Republic, 1829–1889* (New York, 2012), 198–222.

40. *CA*, June 4, August 7, 28, October 2, 9, 1841; John Stauffer, ed., *The Works of James McCune Smith: Black Intellectual and Abolitionist* (New York, 2006), 25–47; William Wells Brown, *St. Domingo: Its Revolutions and Its Patriots, A Lecture* (Boston, 1855), 37–38; "The Haitian Revolution in Resolutions Adopted by African American State and Regional Conventions (1858, 1859, 1865)," in Maurice Jackson and Jacqueline Bacon, eds., *African Americans and the Haitian Revolution: Selected Essays and Historical Documents* (New York, 2010), 194–95; George B. Vashon, "Vincent Ogé," in Julia Griffiths, ed., *Autographs for Freedom* (Auburn, N.Y., 1854), 59; Wendell Phillips, *Speeches, Lectures, and Letters* (Boston, 1872), 492; Manisha Sinha, "An Alternative Tradition of Radicalism: African American Abolitionists and the Metaphor of Revolution," in Manisha Sinha and Penny Von Eschen, eds., *Contested Democracy: Freedom, Race, and Power in American History* (New York, 2007), 9–30; cf. Jenna M. Gibbs, *Performing the Temple of Liberty: Slavery, Theatre and Popular Culture in London and Philadelphia, 1760–1850* (Baltimore, 2014), chap. 7.

41. *Anglo-African Magazine* 1 (February 1859): 37; ibid. (August 1859): 301; Floyd J. Miller, ed., *Blake, or the Huts of America, A Novel by Martin R. Delany* (Boston, 1970), 16–17, 29, 39, 192–93, 210–11, 241–42, 287, 313; Levine, ed., *Martin R. Delany*,160–69; Levine, *Martin Delany, Frederick Douglass*, 191–223; Sharla Fett, "'The Ship of Slavery': Atlantic Slave Trade Suppression, Liberated Africans, and Black Abolition Politics in Antebellum New York," in Ana Lucia Araujo, ed., *Paths of the Atlantic Slave Trade: Interactions, Identities, and Images* (Amherst, N.Y., 2011); Ifeoma Kiddoe Nwanko, *Black Cosmopolitanism: Racial Consciousness and Transnational Identity in the Nineteenth-Century Americas* (Philadelphia, 2005), 54–80.

42. Harriet A. Jacobs, *Incidents in the Life of a Slave Girl: Written by Herself*, Jean Fagan Yellin, ed. (Cambridge, Mass., 1987), 31, 56, 77, 128, 184–85; Harriet A. Jacobs, *Incidents in the Life of a Slave Girl: Written by Herself*, Enlarged Edition Now With "A True Tale of Slavery" by John S. Jacobs, Jean Fagan Yellin, ed. (Cambridge, Mass., 2000), xxv–xli, 207–28, 254, 258, 264, 266; Robert Purvis to Gay, September 13, 1858, Sydney Howard Gay Papers, CU; Jean Fagan Yellin, *Harriet Jacobs, A Life: The Remarkable Adventures of the Woman Who Wrote* Incidents in the Life of a Slave Girl (New York, 2004); Yellin, ed., *The Harriet Jacobs Family Papers* (Chapel Hill, 2008); Peterson, *"Doers of the Word,"* 156–65; Karen Sanchez-Eppler, *Touching Liberty: Abolition, Feminism, and the Politics of the Body* (Berkeley, 1993), chap. 3; Frances Smith Foster, *Written by Herself: Literary Production by African American Women, 1746–1892* (Bloomington, 1993), 108–16.

43. Henry Louis Gates Jr., ed., *The Bondwoman's Narrative* (New York, 2002), introduction, 1, 3; Henry Louis Gates Jr. and Hollis Robbins, eds., *In Search of Hannah Crafts: Critical Essays on* The Bondwoman's Narrative (New York, 2004); "Professor Says He Has Solved Mystery over a Slave's Novel," *New York Times*, September 18, 2013, http:// www.nytimes.com/2013/09/19/books/professor-says-he-has-solved-a-mystery-over-a -slaves-novel.html?pagewanted=all&_r=0.

44. Benjamin Drew, *The Refugee: or, the Narratives of Fugitive Slaves in Canada . . .* (Boston, 1856), vi, 1–3, 13–16, 161–73; *TL*, May 18, 1855; May 29, July 12, 1857; S. G. Howe, *The Refugees from Slavery in Canada West . . .* (Boston, 1864), 1, 103–4, 110; James W.Trent Jr., *The Manliest Man: Samuel G. Howe and the Contours of Nineteenth-Century Reform* (Amherst, Mass., 2012), 225–29.

CHAPTER FOURTEEN. THE POLITICS OF ABOLITION

1. *Despotism in America . . .* (Boston, 1840), 8–34, 40, 47, 50, 54–57, 61, 66–71, 90–97, 146, 156, 176–78, 186; Richard Hildreth, *Theory of Politics . . .* (New York, 1853): 15–16, 32, 25–26, 55–56, 61, 142–47, 151–55; 199–200, 208, 229, 267–74; Donald E. Emerson, *Richard Hildreth* (Baltimore, 1946); Arthur Schlesinger Jr., "The Problem of Richard Hildreth," *NEQ* 13 (June 1940): 223–45.

2. Daniel J. McInerney, *The Fortunate Heirs of Freedom: Abolition and Republican Thought* (Lincoln, Neb., 1994); Eric Foner, *Fee Soil, Free Labor, Free Men: The Ideology of the Republican Party Before the Civil War* (1970; repr. New York, 1994), ix–xxxix; John Ashworth, *Slavery, Capitalism and Politics in the Antebellum Republic,* 2 vols. (Cambridge, Eng., 1995); Thomas G. Mitchell, *Antislavery Politics in Antebellum and Civil War America* (Westport, Conn., 2007); James Oakes, *The Scorpion's Sting: Antislavery and the Coming of the Civil War* (New York, 2014).

3. *The Power of Congress Over the District of Columbia* (New York, 1838), 3, 15–16, 39–47; Gilbert H. Barnes and Dwight L. Dumond, eds., *Letters of Theodore Weld, and Angelina Grimké Weld and Sarah Grimké, 1822–1844* (Gloucester, Mass., 1965), 2:923, 954–55, 958; Samuel B. Treadwell, *American Liberties and American Slavery . . .* (New York, 1838), xii, xxxix, 58, 355; William Jay, *A View of the Action of the Federal Government, in Behalf of Slavery* (Utica, N.Y., 1844), 3, 9–26, 55–72, 79; William Jay, *Miscellaneous Writings on Slavery* (New York, 1853), 209, 371–95; Bayard Tuckerman, *William Jay and the Constitutional Movement for the Abolition of Slavery* (New York, 1893).

4. Leavitt to Roger H. Leavitt, May 17, 1841, Leavitt to Col. R. Hooker Leavitt, December 10, 1841, Leavitt to his mother, May 10, 1842, Joshua Leavitt Family Papers, LC; Barnes and Dumond, eds., *Letters of Theodore Weld,* 2:879–86, 899–913; *TEFA,* January 15, 20, February 10, 17, 24, March 3, 10, 17, 24, 31, April 7, 14, 21, August 25, November 24, December 29, 1842; February 23, March 9, May 11, 18, November 30, 1843; *TLP,* November 15, 1842; February 21, March 14, April 4, May 23, September 19, October 3, 1843; January 16, 30, March 5, 1844; *TL,* December 16, 1842; January 6, 13, February 3, March 10, 1843; March 8, 29, 1844; Seth M. Gates to Smith, August 28, 1839; February 4, June 7, 10, 18, November 23, 1841; January 25, 28, February 4, March 24, April 8, May 13, 1842; September 18, October 16, 1843, Gerrit Smith Papers, SU; James Brewer Stewart, "Abolitionists, Insurgents, and Third Parties: Sectionalism and Partisan Politics in Northern Whiggery, 1836–1844," in Alan M. Kraut, ed., *Crusaders and Compromisers: Essays on the Relationship of the Antislavery Struggle to the Antebellum Party System* (Westport, Conn., 1983), 25–43; Corey Brooks, " 'Stoking the Abolition Fire in the Capitol': Liberty Party Lobbying and Antislavery in Congress," *JER* 33 (Fall 2013): 523–47.

5. *TEFA*, December 8, 1841; February 24, August 4, 25, December 1, 1842; April 20, June 8, September 14, 28, October 5, November 16, 1843; *TLP*, December 27, 1842; January 10, March 7, 28, July 25, August 1, 8, September 12, October 31, 1843; *TL*, September 22, 1843; Giles Stebbins to Gay, September 25, 1846, Abby Kelley Foster to Gay, September 19, 1847, Sydney Howard Gay Papers, CU; Abby Kelley Foster to Smith, July 26, 1843, January 1, 1852, Gerrit Smith Papers, SU; Gerrit Smith to Wright, April 20, 1840, Elizur Wright Jr. Papers, LC; William Birney, *James G. Birney and His Times* (New York, 1890), 327–28; Dwight L. Dumond, ed., *Letters of James Gillespie Birney, 1831–1857* (Gloucester, Mass., 1966), 2:603–5, 613–14, 627–28, 642–56, 704, 743–48, 761–62, 766–73, 776; *Tenth Annual Report of the Board of Managers of the Massachusetts Anti-Slavery Society Presented January 26 1842 . . .*, 17–19; *Eleventh Annual Report, Presented to the Massachusetts Anti-Slavery Society, By its Board of Managers January 25, 1843*, 61–69; *Twelfth Annual Report, Presented to the Massachusetts Anti-Slavery Society, By its Board of Managers, January 24, 1844 . . .* 53–57 (reprs., Westport, Conn., 1970); Walter M. Merrill, ed., *The Letters of William Lloyd Garrison*, vol. 3, *No Union with Slaveholders, 1841–1849* (Cambridge, Mass., 1973), 163, 248; Reinhard O. Johnson, *The Liberty Party, 1840–1848: Antislavery Third-Party Politics in the United States* (Baton Rouge, 2009), chaps. 1–3; Aileen S. Kraditor, *Means and Ends in American Abolitionism: Garrison and His Critics on Strategy and Tactics, 1834–1850* (Chicago, 1967), chap. 6; Alan M. Kraut, "Partisanship and Principles: The Liberty Party in Antebellum Political Culture," in Kraut, ed., *Crusaders and Compromisers: Essays on the Relationship of the Antislavery Struggle to the Antebellum Party System* (Westport, Conn., 1983), 71–99; Richard H. Sewell, *Ballots for Freedom: Antislavery Politics in the United States, 1837–1860* (New York, 1976), chap. 4.

6. *TEFA*, July 7, August 11, 25, September 22, 29, October 27, 1842; March 16, April 20, July 20, November 2, December 7, 1843; *TLP*, August 22, 1843; Henry B. Stanton to Wright, July 4, 1843, Elizur Wright Jr. Papers, LC; Dumond, ed., *Letters of James Gillespie Birney*, 2:623, 633–40, 643–45, 778, 857–922; Birney, *James G. Birney*, 353–56; Gerrit Smith Printed Circular, December 14, 1843, Amos Phelps Papers, Antislavery Collection, BPL; William Goodell, *Slavery and Anti-Slavery . . .* (New York, 1855), 468–77; Austin Willey, *The History of the Antislavery Cause . . .* (Portland, Me., 1886), 227, 242–43, 260–61; Johnson, *The Liberty Party*, chaps. 5–7; Theodore Clark Smith, *The Liberty and Free Soil Parties in the Northwest* (New York, 1897), chap. 5; Richard J. Carwardine, *Evangelicals and Politics in Antebellum America* (Knoxville, 1997), 134–39; Betty Fladeland, *James Gillespie Birney: Slaveholder to Abolitionist* (Ithaca, 1955), 245–51; John R. McKivigan, "'Vote as you Pray and Pray as you Vote': Church-Oriented Abolitionism and Antislavery Politics," in Kraut, ed., *Crusaders and Compromisers*, 179–87.

7. *FOM*, February 22, 1838; *TLP*, November 15, 22, December 6, 1842; April 11, 1843; *TEFA*, March 30, November 23, 1843; February 8, 1844; Samuel Sewall to Wright, September 9, 1840, Elizur Wright Jr. Papers, LC; Douglas M. Strong, *Perfectionist Politics: Abolitionism and the Religious Tensions of American Democracy* (Syracuse, 1999), 24, 134; Johnson, *The Liberty Party*, 64–65, 145, 229–30; Bruce Laurie, *Beyond*

Garrison: *Antislavery and Social Reform* (Cambridge, Eng., 2005), chap. 4; Alan M. Kraut, "The Forgotten Reformers: A Profile of Third Party Abolitionists in Antebellum New York," in Lewis Perry and Michael Fellman, eds., *Antislavery Reconsidered: New Perspectives on Abolitionists* (Baton Rouge, 1979), 119–45; Vernon L. Volpe, *Forlorn Hope of Freedom: The Liberty Party in the Old Northwest, 1838–1848* (Kent, Ohio, 1990); John W. Quist, "'The Great Majority of Our Subscribers Are Farmers': The Michigan Abolitionist Constituency in the 1840s," *JER* 14 (Fall 1994): 325–58.

8. *"Letter of Gerrit Smith to Hon. Henry Clay," TAE,* 9, 18–54; *TL,* January 15, 9, 1841; April 12, July 5, November 1, 1844; April 18, 1845; Dumond, ed., *Letters of James Gillespie Birney,* 2:624–25; Johnson, *The Liberty Party,* chap. 9; Johnson, "National Liberty Party Platform, 1844," 320; *NASS,* October 17, November 14, p. 93, 1844; C. Peter Ripley, ed., *The Black Abolitionist Papers,* vol. 3, *The United States, 1830–1846* (Chapel Hill, 1991), 413–15, 468–73; Willey, *The History of the Antislavery Cause,* 300, 330–31; *The Impartial Citizen,* February 28, 1849; Ronald K. Burke, *Samuel Ringgold Ward: Christian Abolitionist* (New York, 1995), 34, 108; *Report of the Proceedings of the Colored National Convention, Held at Cleveland, Ohio . . .* (Rochester, 1848), 5–6, 8, 11–12, 14, in Howard Holman Bell, ed., *Minutes of the Proceedings of the National Negro Conventions 1830–1864* (New York, 1969).

9. *TLP,* January 10, September 12, October 31, 1843; February 20, September 24, 1844; Michael D. Pierson, *Free Hearts and Free Homes: Gender and American Antislavery Politics* (Chapel Hill, 2003), chaps. 1, 2; Elizabeth Varon, *We Mean to Be Counted: White Women and Politics in Antebellum Virginia* (Chapel Hill, 1998); Johnson, *The Liberty Party,* 276–85; Julie Roy Jeffrey, "The Liberty Women of Boston: Evangelicalism and Antislavery Politics," *NEQ* 85 (March 2012): 38–77; Alice Taylor, "From Petitions to Partyism: Antislavery and the Domestication of Maine Politics in the 1840s and 1850s," *NEQ* 77 (March 2004): 70–88; Sylvia D. Hoffert, *Jane Grey Swisshelm: An Unconventional Life, 1818–1884* (Chapel Hill, 2004); John Stauffer, *The Black Hearts of Men: Radical Abolitionists and the Transformation of Race* (Cambridge, Mass., 2002), 212–15.

10. Paulina W. Davis, *A History of the National Woman's Rights . . .* (New York, 1871); Elizabeth Cady Stanton, Susan B. Anthony, and Matilda Jocelyn Gage, eds., *History of Woman Suffrage,* vol. 1, *1848–1861* (New York, 1881); *The Proceedings of the Woman's Rights Convention, Held at Worcester, October 23d and 24th, 1850* (Boston, 1851), 6–19, 20–36, 820–25; *TL,* June 9, September 6, November 1, 1850; October 15, 29, 1852; January 14, 1853; March 16, 23, April 20, 1854; August 8, 1856; February 19, March 26, June 4, 25, October 15, 29, 1858; June 10, September 30, 1859; Carol Faulkner, *Lucretia Mott's Heresy: Abolition and Women's Rights in Nineteenth-Century America* (Philadelphia, 2011), chap. 9; Keith Melder, "Abby Kelley and the Process of Liberation," in Jean Fagan Yellin and John C. Van Horne, eds., *The Abolitionist Sisterhood: Women's Political Culture in Antebellum America* (Ithaca, 1994), 139–58; Alice Stone Blackwell, *Lucy Stone: Pioneer of Women's Rights* (Boston, 1930); Ida Husted Harper, *The Life and Work of Susan B. Anthony . . . ,* vol. 1 (Indianapolis, Ind., 1898); Stacey M. Robertson, *Hearts Bleeding for Liberty: Women Abolitionists in the Old Northwest* (Chapel

Hill, 2010), chaps. 5, 7; Sylvia D. Hoffert, *When Hens Crow: The Woman's Rights Movement in Antebellum America* (Bloomington, 1995); Ellen Carol DuBois, *Feminism and Suffrage: The Emergence of an Independent Women's Movement in America, 1848–1869* (Ithaca, 1981).

11. TL, February 25, April 22, 29, May 13, September, 2, 1842; January 20, 1843; May 17, 24, 31, 1844; February 7, April 4, July 18, 1845; NASS, March 31, May 5, June 2, 1842; September 19, 1844; March 13, April 10, 24, 1845; *Thirteenth Annual Report, Presented to the Massachusetts Anti-Slavery Society, By its Board of Managers, January 22, 1845 . . .* (repr.; Westport, Conn., 1970), 27–34, 77–78; Merrill, ed., *The Letters of William Lloyd Garrison*, 3:265–66, 273, 298–301; Caroline Weston to Gay, June 27, 1844, Abby Kelley Foster to Gay, July 6, August 11, 1845, March 1, June 10, August 2, 1846, Kelley Foster to Elizabeth Neall Gay, November 11, 1845, Kelley Foster to the Gays, November 16, 1845, Edmund Quincy to Gay, March 29, 1845, Sydney Howard Gay Papers, CU; [Francis Jackson Garrison and Wendell Phillips Garrison], *William Lloyd Garrison, 1805–1879 The Story of His Life Told By His Children*, vol. 3, 1841–1860 (New York, 1889), 88–90, 96–119; Leonard L. Richards, *The Life and Times of Congressman John Quincy Adams* (New York, 1986), 139–45; Henry Mayer, *All on Fire: William Lloyd Garrison and the Abolition of Slavery* (New York, 1998), 327–29, 365–71; Elizabeth Varon, *Disunion! The Coming of the American Civil War, 1789–1859* (Chapel Hill, 2008), chap. 4.

12. J. W. C. Pennington, *Covenants Involving Moral Wrong . . .* (Hartford, 1842), 4–7, 11; NASS, September 7, 1843.

13. TLP, September 3, 1841; November 29, 1842; December 19, 1843; March 26, 1844; TL, November 3, 10, December 22, 1843; January 3, 1845; NASS, April 4, 1844; *The American Churches . . .* , 2d ed. (Newburyport, Mass., 1842), 8, 40–44; Thomas Clarkson, *A Letter to the Clergy . . .* (London, 1841); Stephen S. Foster, *The Brotherhood of Thieves . . .* (1844; repr., Concord, N.H., 1886), 9–15, 73–74; William Goodell, *Come-Outerism . . .* (New York, 1845); *Eleventh Annual Report, Presented to the Massachusetts Anti-Slavery Society*, 58; *Domestic Slavery Considered as a Scriptural Institution . . .* (New York, 1845); *Fourteenth Annual Report Presented to the Massachusetts Anti-Slavery Society, By its Board of Managers, January 28, 1846 . . .* (repr., Westport, Conn., 1970), 66–77; John R. McKivigan, *The War Against Proslavery Religion: Abolitionism and the Northern Churches, 1830–1865* (Ithaca, 1984); Troy Duncan and Chris Dixon, "Denouncing the Brotherhood of Thieves: Stephen Symonds Foster and the Abolitionist Critique of the Anti-Abolitionist Clergy," CWH 47 (2001): 97–117; Deborah Bingham Van Broekhoven, "Suffering with Slaveholders: The Limits of Francis Wayland's Antislavery Witness," Edward R. Crowther, "'Religion has Something . . . to do with Politics': Southern Evangelicals and the North," and John R. McKivigan, "The Sectional Division of the Methodist and Baptist Denominations as Measures of Northern Antislavery Sentiment," in John R. McKivigan and Mitchell Snay, eds., *Religion and the Antebellum Debate over Slavery* (Athens, Ga., 1998), 196–220, 317–64; C. C. Goen, *Broken Churches, Broken Nation: Denominational Schisms and the Coming of the American Civil War* (Macon, Ga., 1985); Mitchell Snay, *Gospel of Disunion: Religion and Separatism in the Antebellum South* (Cambridge, Eng., 1993), chap. 4.

14. Samuel Wilberforce, *A History of the Protestant Episcopal Church in America* (London, 1844); Jay, *Miscellaneous Writings*, 430, 442–50, 471–81; Stephen P. Budney, *William Jay: Abolitionist and Anticolonialist* (Westport, Conn., 2005), 80–83; Parker Pillsbury, *The Church As It Is . . .* (1847; repr., Concord, N.H., 1885), 3–4, 7, 13, 40, 76.

15. Lewis Tappan to Phelps, September 30, October 28, 1844, Amos Phelps Papers, Antislavery Collection, BPL; *FOM*, June 27, 1838; *TLP*, December 6, 1842; Silas McKeen, *A Scriptural Argument in Favor of Withdrawing . . .* (New York, 1848); John G. Fee, *Non-Fellowship with Slaveholders . . .* (New York, 1849); Samuel Brooke, *The Slaveholder's Religion* (Cincinnati, 1845); William W. Patton, *Slavery, the Bible, Infidelity . . .* (Hartford, 1846), 14–15; Foster, *The Brotherhood of Thieves*, 26–29; Pillsbury, *The Church As It Is*, 57–67; John G. Fee, *An Anti-Slavery Manual . . .* (1848; rpr., New York, 1851); Fee, *The Sin-fulness of Slaveholding . . .* (New York, 1851); *Autobiography of John G. Fee, Berea, Kentucky* (Chicago, 1891), 20, 34–57; Jay, *Miscellaneous Writings*, 634–40, 658–64; *TL*, October 6, 1843; March 1, 8, 1844; *NASS*, January 25, 1844; Goodell, *Slavery and Anti-Slavery*, 153–219, 425–33, 487–516, 541–58; Mark A. Noll, *The Civil War as a Theological Crisis* (Chapel Hill, 2006), chap. 3.

16. Alvan Stewart, "A Constitutional Argument on the Subject of Slavery," in Jacobus tenBroek, ed., *Equal Under Law* (New York, 1965), 281–95; *FOM*, June 13, June 27, 1838; G. W. F. Mellen, *An Argument on the Unconstitutionality of Slavery . . .* (Boston, 1841), 4–6, 433; *TL*, July 20, August 27, 1841; June 21, 1844; *NASS*, September 12, 1844; Robert Cover, *Justice Accused: Antislavery and the Judicial Process* (New Haven, 1975), chap. 9; Frederick J. Blue, *No Taint of Compromise: Crusaders in Antislavery Politics* (Baton Rouge, 2005), 20–21, 30–36; William M. Weicek, *The Sources of Antislavery Constitutionalism in America, 1760–1848* (Ithaca, 1977), chap. 9.

17. Wendell Phillips, *The Constitution, a Pro-Slavery Compact . . .* (Boston, 1844), 8; *TAE*, No. 13, *Can Abolitionists Vote or Take Office Under the United States Constitution?* (New York, 1845), 4; William Goodell, *Views of American Constitutional Law . . .* (Utica, N.Y., 1844), 10–11, 35–37, 63–65, 97–102, 149–51; *Gerrit Smith's Constitutional Argument* (Peterboro, N.Y., 1844), 4–8; Lysander Spooner, *The Unconstitutionality of Slavery* (Boston, 1845; Project Gutenberg ebook, 2010); Wendell Phillips, *Review of Lysander Spooner's Essay . . .* (Boston, 1847), 9–15, 93; *NASS*, September 28, November 9, 1843; September 12, 19, 1844; September 18, November 14, 1845; *TL*, August 16, September 6, 13, 20, 27, October 4, 25, November 22, 1844; Wendell Phillips to Gay, July 3, 1844, October 7, n.d., William Goodell to Gay, April 20, 1847, Lysander Spooner to Gay, March 22, April 24, 1847, Sydney Howard Gay Papers, CU; Staughton Lynd, "The Abolitionist Critique of the United States Constitution," in Martin Duberman, ed., *The Antislavery Vanguard: New Essays on the Abolitionists* (Princeton, 1965), chap. 10; Weicek, *The Sources of Antislavery Constitutionalism*, chaps. 10, 11; Hoan Gia Phan, *Bonds of Citizenship: Law and the Labors of Emancipation* (New York, 2013), 127–38.

18. Benjamin Shaw, *Illegality of Slavery* (Boston, 1846), 1–2; Joel Tiffany, *A Treatise on the Unconstitutionality of Slavery . . .* (Cleveland, 1849), 7–10, 16–17, 21, 54–57, 60–83, 87–88, 93–96, 122–29, 135.

19. *Diary and Correspondence of Salmon P. Chase* (New York, 1971), 115; J. W. Schuckers, *The Life and Public Services of Salmon Portland Chase* (New York, 1874), 67–74; John

Niven, ed., *The Salmon P. Chase Papers*, vol. 2, *Correspondence, 1823–1857* (Kent, Ohio, 1994), 84–87, 99–100, 119–20; *TEFA*, September 14, 1843; *TLP*, August 29, 1843; Maria Weston Chapman to Gay, May 22, 1834, Sydney Howard Gay Papers, CU; Joshua Leavitt to Roger H. Leavitt, February 9, 1842, Joshua Leavitt Family Papers, LC; Dumond, ed., *Letters of James Gillespie Birney*, 2:661–62, 670–72; Foner, *Free Soil, Free Labor, Free Men*, 73–87; Oakes, *Freedom National*, 26–33; Stanley Harrold, *Gamaliel Bailey and Antislavery Union* (Kent, Ohio, 1986), 48–69.

20. *TL*, October 14, 1842; September 1, November 3, December 1, 8, 1843; February 23, March 15, 29, April 19, May 3, June 7, 1844; *TLP*, December 20, 1842; February 20, 27, March 5, 26, April 9, 16, May 7, 14, 28, June 7, July 9, 16, 30, August 6, 1844; *NASS*, April 4, May 2, 9, June 20, July 4, August 29, September 5, 1844; Edmund Quincy to Gay, March 4, 1845, Sydney Howard Gay Papers, CU; Joshua R. Giddings, *Speeches in Congress* (New York, 1853), 97–147; *Tenth Annual Report of . . . the Mass. Anti-Slavery Society*, 26–28; *Eleventh Annual Report, Presented to the Massachusetts Anti-Slavery Society*, 99; *Twelfth Annual Report, Presented to the Massachusetts Anti-Slavery Society*, 17–21; Merrill, ed., *The Letters of William Lloyd Garrison*, 3:284; Norman Graebner, ed., *Manifest Destiny* (Indianapolis, 1968), 15–28, 41–56, 63–69; Joshua R. Giddings, *History of the Rebellion . . .* (New York, 1864), 213–15, 222–36, 247; George W. Julian, *The Life of Joshua R. Giddings* (Chicago 1892), 155–68, 182–92; *Fourteenth Annual Report Presented to the Massachusetts Anti-Slavery Society*, 4–16; Frederick Merk, *Fruits of Propaganda in the Tyler Administration* (Cambridge, Mass., 1971), 95–128, 221–52; Merk, *Slavery and the Annexation of Texas* (New York, 1972); Joel H. Silbey, *Storm over Texas: The Annexation Controversy and the Road to Civil War* (New York, 2005); David Zarefsky, "Debating Slavery by Proxy: The Texas Annexation Controversy," in Paul Finkelman and Donald R. Kennon, eds., *In the Shadow of Freedom: The Politics of Slavery in the National Capital* (Athens, Ohio, 2011), 125–37.

21. *Eleventh Annual Report, Presented to the Massachusetts Anti-Slavery Society*, 24; *Twelfth Annual Report, Presented to the Massachusetts Anti-Slavery Society*, 21–22; *Thirteenth Annual Report, Presented to the Massachusetts Anti-Slavery Society*, 41–44; *Fourteenth Annual Report Presented to the Massachusetts Anti-Slavery Society*, 90–91; *Fifteenth Annual Report, Presented to the Massachusetts Anti-Slavery Society . . .* (repr., Westport, Conn., 1970), 4–26; *NASS*, June 1, 8, 15, December 14, 1843; January 4, February 15, 22, March 21, May 16, 1844; January 2, 16, February 6, 13, 20, 27, March 6, 20, October 2, November 13, December 25, 1845; *TL*, February 2, March 1, 8, April 5, May 3, June 28, December 13, 27, 1844; January 10, 24, 31, February 7, 14, 1845; March 7, 14, 28, April 4, 11, May 9, 16, October 31, November 7, 14, 28, December 5, 1845; March 6, April 17, December 18, 1846; *TLP*, February 6, April 9, 16, 30, October 19, 1844; *TEFA*, February 14, 24, May 11, 1844; Cassius M. Clay to Gay, March 22, 1845, Edmund Quincy to Gay, October 30, 1845, February 4, 1846, September 12, 1847, Caroline Weston to Gay, November 2, 1846, Sydney Howard Gay Papers, CU; Gerrit Smith Printed Letter to the Proslavery Voters of Madison County, May 22, 1844, Amos Phelps Papers, Antislavery Collection, BPL; Merrill, ed., *The Letters of William Lloyd Garrison*, 3:285–87, 311, 319; *William Lloyd Garrison*, 3:120–29; Samuel T.

Pickard, ed., *Whittier as a Politician* (Boston, 1900), 33–43; Henry Wilson, *History of the Rise and Fall of the Slave Power in America* (Boston, 1872): vol. 1, chaps. 41–45; Richard H. Sewell, *John P. Hale and the Politics of Abolition* (Cambridge, Mass., 1965), 28–35, 48–85; Jonathan H. Earle, *Jacksonian Antislavery and the Politics of Free Soil, 1824–1854* (Chapel Hill, 2004), chaps. 3, 4; Bertram Wyatt-Brown, *Lewis Tappan and the Evangelical War Against Slavery* (Cleveland, 1969), 250–56; Frank Otto Gatell, *John Gorham Palfrey and the New England Conscience* (Cambridge, Mass., 1963); Edward L. Pierce, *Memoir and Letters of Charles Sumner,* vol. 1, *1811–1838* (Boston, 1877), 156–57; ibid., vol. 2, *1838–1845,* 191–96, 335–67; Elias Nason, *The Life and Public Services of Henry Wilson* . . . (New York, 1876), 61–87; Kinley J. Brauer, *Cotton versus Conscience: Massachusetts Whig Politics and Southwestern Expansion, 1843–1848* (Lexington, Ky., 1967).

22. John G. Palfrey, *Papers on the Slave Power* . . . (Boston, 1846); William Jay, *A Review of the Mexican War* (Boston, 1849); *TL,* January 30, April 24, 1846; February 19, 26, 1847; January 21, February 4, July 21, 1848; Joshua Giddings to Smith, January 25, 1847, Gerrit Smith Papers, SU; Joshua R. Giddings to Gay, January 12, March 15, 26, May 6, 8, 25, 1846, January 24, 28, 1847, Giddings to Maria Weston Chapman, June 14, 1846, Giles Stebbins to Gay, September 25, November 13, 1846, Richard Webb to Gay, January 20, 1848, Sydney Howard Gay Papers, CU; Lewis Tappan to Phelps, February 22, 1847, Amos Phelps Papers, Antislavery Collection, BPL; *Sixteenth Annual Report, Presented to the Massachusetts Anti-Slavery Society* . . . (repr., Westport, Conn., 1970), 4–14; Julian, *The Life of Joshua R. Giddings,* 170, 192–204, 238–40; Giddings, *History of the Rebellion,* 250–73; Henry Wilson, *History of the Rise and Fall of the Slave Power in America* (Boston, 1874), 2: chaps. 2–4; Bernard De Voto, *The Year of Decision 1846* (Boston, 1942); Amy S. Greenberg, *A Wicked War: Polk, Clay, Lincoln and the 1846 US Invasion of Mexico* (New York, 2012).

23. *NE,* January 21, 28, February 11, 18, October 21, 28, 1847; July 27, August 3, 10, 24, 31, September 14, 21, 28, October 12, 19, 26, November 2, 9, 16, 23, 1848; February 8, March 22, 29, May 3, 10, 17, 24, June 7, 28, August 16, November 8, 15, 1849; January 3, August 29, 1850; April 22, 1852; *TL,* November 5, 19, December 17, 1847; September 23, 1853; George Bradburn to Smith, April 21, May 26, 1850, Gerrit Smith Papers, SU; John Gorham Palfrey to Gay, December 15, 1847, April 8, 1848, Sydney Howard Gay Papers, CU; Charles Knowlton to Roger H. Leavitt, October 12, 1848, Printed Circular Boston Free Soil Club, October 19, 1848, D. S. Jones to Roger Leavitt, November 8, 1848, Joshua Leavitt to Roger H. Leavitt, April 4, 1851, Joshua Leavitt Family Papers, LC; *TLP,* September 12, 1843; Henry B. Stanton, *Random Recollections* (New York, 1887), 157–65; Julian, *The Life of Joshua R. Giddings,* 206–57, 271–85; Wilson, *History of the Rise and Fall,* vol. 2, chaps. 10–15; Sewell, *Ballots for Freedom,* chaps. 6–9; Frederick J. Blue, *The Free Soilers: Third Party Politics, 1848–54* (Urbana, 1973), 293–301; Eric Foner, "Politics and Prejudice: The Free Soil Party and the Negro," *JNH* 50 (October 1965): 239–56; Mitchell, *Antislavery Politics,* chaps. 3–4; Michael F. Holt, *The Rise and Fall of the American Whig Party: Jacksonian Politics and the Onset of the Civil War* (New York, 1999); Richard H. Sewell, "Slavery, Race, and the Free

Soil Party, 1848–1854," in Kraut, ed., *Crusaders and Compromisers*, 101–24; Joseph G. Rayback, *Free Soil: The Election of 1848* (Lexington, Ky., 1970); Sewell, *John P. Hale*, chap. 6; Stanley Harrold, "Gamaliel Bailey, Antislavery Journalist and Lobbyist," and Jonathan Earle, "Saturday Nights at the Baileys': Building an Antislavery Movement in Congress, 1838–1854," in Finkelman and Kennon, eds., *In the Shadow of Freedom*, 58–96; Daniel Feller, "A Brother in Arms: Benjamin Tappan and the Antislavery Democracy," *JAH* 88 (June 2001): 48–74; Edward Magdol, *Owen Lovejoy: Abolitionist in Congress* (New Brunswick, N.J., 1967).

24. Goodell, *Slavery and Anti-Slavery*, 475–86; James Birney, "Can Congress, under the Constitution, Abolish Slavery in the States?," in tenBroek, ed., *Equal Under Law*, 296–319; Dumond, ed., *Letters of James Gillespie Birney*, 2:1027–29, 1047–57, 1087–88, 1094–95, 1108–9, 1124; F. Freeman, *Africa's Redemption the Salvation of Our Country* (New York, 1852), 314–24; William Birney, *James G. Birney and His Times . . .* (New York, 1890), chap. 31; Fladeland, *James Gillespie Birney*, chap. 14; George Bradburn to Smith, December 28, 1848, June 29, 1849, Seth M. Gates to Smith, November 8, 1852, David Lee Child to Smith, January 20, 1852, Gerrit Smith Papers, SU; Stauffer, *The Black Hearts of Men*, 174–76; Burke, *Samuel Ringgold Ward*, 35; Wyatt-Brown, *Lewis Tappan*, 274–76, 278–81.

25. TL, March 5, 12, June 25, July 2, October 22, December 17, 24, 1847; January 7, February 11, 18, 25, March 3, June 23, 30, July 7, 14, August 4, 18, 25, September 8, 15, 29, October 6, November 17, 1848; January 12, 26, February 3, May 18, June 1, July 27, November 30, 1849; Edmund Quincy to Gay, n.d., Sydney Howard Gay Papers, CU; *Seventeenth Annual Report, Presented to the Massachusetts Anti-Slavery Society . . .* and *Eighteenth Annual Report, Presented to the Massachusetts Anti-Slavery Society . . .* (repr., Westport, Conn., 1970), 34–42, 96–97; Mayer, *All on Fire*, 382–85.

26. Elbert B. Smith, *The Magnificent Missourian: The Life of Thomas Hart Benton* (Philadelphia, 1958); Henry Ruffner, *Address to the People of West Virginia . . .* (Lexington, Va., 1847), 9; NASS, December 14, 1843; February 22, 1844; March 6, August 28, September 4, 1845; TL, July 3, 1846; January 22, 1847; NS, February 9, April 27, September 7, 1849; FDP, November 5, 1852; December 22, 1854; NE, March 18, June 24, 1847; June 28, 1849; April 20, 1848; January 25, April 19, May 17, July 19, August 16, 30, November 1, 1849; April 2, 1851; September 23, October 28, December 9, 1852; August 2, 16, September 25, 1855; Horace Greeley ed., *The Writings of Cassius Marcellus Clay . . .* (New York, 1848), vi–vii, 68–71, 77–96, 129, 183, 521–22, 530–35; *The Life of Cassius Marcellus Clay . . .* (Cincinnati, Ohio, 1886), vol. 1, chaps. 5, 6, 10; Harold D. Tallant, *Evil Necessity: Slavery and Political Culture in Antebellum Kentucky* (Lexington, Ky., 2003).

27. Henry Wadsworth Longfellow, *Poems on Slavery* (Cambridge, Mass., 1842), 18; TL, December 30, 1842; November 28, 1845; February 13, July 3, 1846; December 1, 1848; NE, November 25, 1847; August 31, October 20, November 30, 1848; January 17, 1850; November 13, 1851; NS, April 28, October 6, 1848; January 26, 1849; August 13, 1852; PF, June 17, 1854; George Lowell Austin, *Henry Wadsworth Longfellow: His Life, His Work, and His Friendships* (Boston, 1883); David S. Reynolds, *Walt Whitman*

(New York, 2005), 8–11; [James Rusell Lowell], *The Biglow Papers* (Boston, 1848); Martin B. Duberman, *James Russell Lowell* (Boston, 1966), 102–15; John Stauffer, "Fighting the Devil With His Own Fire," in Andrew Delbanco, *The Abolitionist Imagination* (Cambridge, Mass., 2012), 61–67.

28. *TL*, January 12, 1844; December 5, 1845; November 27, 1846; June 16, 1848; November 1, 1850; July 2, August 20, October 1, 1852; August 10, 1855; *NASS*, July 11, 1844; February 20, December 18, 1845; *NE*, February 10, 17, 24, March 2, 1848; *NS*, January 7, 27, February 3, 11, March 24, 31, April 7, 14, 21, May 5, June 30, 1848; January 6, 13, 20, March 23, June 15, August 10, 24, 31, 1849; Ralph Waldo Emerson, *Emerson's Antislavery Writings*, Len Gougeon and Joel Myerson, eds. (New Haven, 1995), introduction, 26, 35–38, 41–50; Henry David Thoreau, *A Vision of Thoreau: With His 1849 Essay, Civil Disobedience* (Norwalk, Conn., 1965); *American Slavery: A Protest Against American Slavery, By One Hundred and Seventy Three Unitarian Ministers* (Boston, 1845); James Freeman Clarke, *Slavery in the United States . . .* (Boston, 1843); Clarke, *The Annexation of Texas . . .* (Boston, 1844); Theodore Parker, *Sermons on War . . . from The Collected Works of Theodore Parker*, ed. Francis P. Cobbe (New York, 1973); Len Gougeon, *Virtue's Hero: Emerson, Anti-Slavery, and Reform* (Athens, Ga., 1990); Peter Field, "The Strange Career of Emerson and Race," *American Nineteenth-Century History* 2 (Spring 2001): 1–32; Peter Wirzbicki, "Black Intellectuals, White Abolitionists, and Revolutionary Transcendentalists: Creating the Radical Intellectual Tradition in Antebellum Boston," (Ph.D. diss., New York University, 2012); Sandra Petrulionis, *To Set This World Right: The Antislavery Movement in Thoreau's Concord* (Ithaca, 2006); Nick Aaron Ford, "Henry David Thoreau, Abolitionist," *NEQ* 19 (1946): 284–310; Lewis Perry, "Black Abolitionists and the Origins of Civil Disobedience," in Karen Haltunnen and Lewis Perry, eds., *Moral Problems in American Life: New Perspectives on Cultural History* (Ithaca, 1998), 103–22; Dean Grodzins, *American Heretic: Theodore Parker and Transcendentalism* (Chapel Hill, 2002), 469–75; Ethan J. Kytle, *Romantic Reformers and the Antislavery Struggle in the Civil War Era* (Cambridge, Eng, 2014), chaps. 1, 5.

29. *NE*, February 7, 14, 28, March 7, 14, 28, April 4, 11, 18, 25, May 2, 9, 16, 23, 30, June 13, 20, July 18, 25, August 1, 8, 22, 29, September 12, 26, October 3, 10, November 28, December 5, 1850; *TL*, February 8, March 8, 15, 22, 29, April 5, 12, May 3, July 19, 1850; Richard Webb to Gay, June 7, 1850, Sydney Howard Gay Papers, CU; Jay, *Miscellaneous Writings*, 496, 569, 617; *NS*, October 3, 1850; *Nineteenth Annual Report, Presented to the Massachusetts Anti-Slavery Society . . .* (repr., Westport, Conn., 1970), 4–24; Burke, *Samuel Ringgold Ward*, 137–40; Giddings, *History of the Rebellion*, 309–39; Wilson, *History of the Rise and Fall*, vol. 2, chaps. 17–24; Fergus M. Bordewich, *America's Great Debate: Henry Clay, Stephen A. Douglas and the Compromise that Preserved the Union* (New York, 2012); Holman Hamilton, *Prologue to Conflict: The Crisis and the Compromise of 1850* (Lexington, Ky., 1964); Mark J. Stegmaier, "Zachary Taylor versus the South," *CWH* 33 (1987): 217–41; A. Glenn Crothers, "The 1846 Retrocession of Alexandria: Protecting Slavery and the Slave Trade in the District of Columbia," in Finkelman and Kennon, eds., *In the Shadow of Freedom*, 141–68;

Merrill D. Peterson, *The Great Triumvirate: Webster, Clay, and Calhoun* (New York, 1987); Robert V. Remini, *Daniel Webster: The Man and His Time* (New York, 1997), 669–81; Glyndon G. Van Deusen, *William Henry Seward* (New York, 1967), 106–42; Frederic Bancroft, *The Life of William H. Seward* (New York, 1900): 1:242–68.

30. TL, July 23, December 17, 1847; January 14, October 6, November 3, 17, December 1, 1848; January 5, April 13, May 18, June 8, 1849; June 28, July 5, November 29, 1850; May 16, 23, June 13, 20, July 4, October 31, November 14, 1851; January 30, May 14, 21, October 1, 22, 1852; July 22, August 5, 22, 26, September 2, 16, November 18, 25, December 19, 1853; January 13, 27, 1854; February 9, May 11, 1855; Philip S. Foner, ed., *The Life and Writings of Frederick Douglass*, vol. 1, *Early Years, 1817–1849* (New York, 1950), 253–55, 256–69, 306–7, 369–70; John W. Blassingame, ed., *The Frederick Douglass Papers, Series One, Speeches, Debates and Interviews*, vol. 2, *1847–1854* (New Haven, 1982), 93–95, 114, 193–97, 447–50; FDP, November 6, 1851; April 22, August 6, 1852; December 9, 1853; March 31, 1854; Merrill, ed., *The Letters of William Lloyd Garrison*, 3:532–33, 614, 625; Louis Ruchames, ed., *The Letters of William Lloyd Garrison*, vol. 4, *From Disunionism to the Brink of War, 1850–1860* (Cambridge, Mass., 1975), 256–57, 329–30, 391–92, 693–94; Mayer, *All on Fire*, 428–34; Stauffer, *The Black Hearts of Men*, 158–68; John R. McKivigan, "The Frederick Douglass–Gerrit Smith Friendship and Political Abolitionism in the 1850s," in Eric J. Sundquist, ed., *Frederick Douglass: New Literary and Historical Essays* (Cambridge, Eng., 1990), 205–32; Benjamin Quarles, "The Break between Douglass and Garrison," *JNH* 23 (April 1938): 144–54; William S. McFeely, *Frederick Douglass* (New York, 1991), chap. 14; Maria Diedrich, *Love Across Color Lines: Ottilie Assing and Frederick Douglass* (New York, 1999); Rosetta Douglass Sprague, "Anna Murray Douglass—My Mother as I Recall Her," *JNH* 8 (January 1923): 93–101; John W. Blassingame, ed., *The Frederick Douglass Papers, Series One: Speeches, Debates, and Interviews*, vol. 3, *1855–63* (New Haven, 1985), 14–51; Philip S. Foner, ed., *The Life and Writings of Frederick Douglass*, vol. 2, *Pre–Civil War Decade, 1850–1860* (New York, 1950), 467–80; Phan, *Bonds of Citizenship*, 138–41, 206–7.

31. NE, February 2, 9, 1854; TL, February 10, March 3, 17, May 5, 12, 26, 1854; FDP, October 30, 1851; August 6, September 24, December 10, 1852; February 10, 24, May 26, June 2, 23, August 25, September 15, October 27, November 24, 1854; Blassingame, ed., *The Frederick Douglass Papers, Series One*, 2:555; Wilson, *History of the Rise and Fall*, vol. 2, chap. 30; John R. Wunder and Joann M. Ross, eds., *The Nebraska–Kansas Act of 1854* (Lincoln, Neb., 2008); Roy F. Nichols, "The Kansas–Nebraska Act: A Century of Historiography," *MVHR* 34 (1956): 187–212; Michael Todd Landis, *Northern Men with Southern Loyalties: The Democratic Party and the Sectional Crisis* (Ithaca, 2014).

32. NE, August 28, September 4, 1851; December 8, 1853; May 4, 1854; January 25, 1855; TL, December 31, 1852; April 2, 1854; May 18, 1855; FDP, September 4, 1851; September 3, December 3, 31, 1852; January 7, 14, February 4, 18, 1853; May 12, June 23, September 29, 1854; Blassingame, ed., *The Frederick Douglass Papers, Series One*, 3:116–20; *The War in Nicaragua, Written by Gen'l William Walker* (Mobile, 1860),

276–80; Graebner, ed., *Manifest Destiny*, 245–53, 285–307; Giddings, *History of the Rebellion*, 413–18; Tom Chaffin, *Fatal Glory: Narciso López and the First Clandestine U.S. War against Cuba* (Charlottesville, Va., 1996); Robert May, *Manifest Destiny's Underworld: Filibustering in Antebellum America* (Chapel Hill, 2002); Walter Johnson, *River of Dark Dreams: Slavery and Empire in the Cotton Kingdom* (Cambridge, Mass., 2013).

33. *NE*, November 23, 1854; May 10, 31, July 19, September 20, October 4, 11, 18, November 1, 2, 8, 15, 29, December 13, 20, 27, 1855; *TL*, October 6, November 10, 17, December 1, 1854; *FDP*, November 17, December 15, 1854; Wilson, *History of the Rise and Fall*, vol. 2, chap. 32; Sewell, *Ballots for Freedom*, chap. 11; Foner, *Free Soil, Free Labor, Free Men*, chap. 7; William E. Gienapp, *The Origins of the Republican Party, 1852–1856* (New York, 1987); Tyler Anbinder, *Nativism and Slavery: The Northern Know Nothings and the Politics of the 1850s* (New York, 1992).

34. *FDP*, November 24, December 1, 1854; *TL*, May 25, October 24, 31, 1856; Blassingame ed., *The Frederick Douglass Papers, Series One*, 3:132, 141; Horace Greeley, *History of the Struggle for Slavery Extension . . .* (New York, 1856); Allan Nevins, *Frémont, the West's Greatest Adventurer . . .* (New York, 1928); David W. Blight, *Frederick Douglass' Civil War: Keeping Faith in Jubilee* (Baton Rouge, 1989), 47–51; Mitchell, *Antislavery Politics*, chap. 6; Pierson, *Free Hearts and Free Homes*, chaps. 5, 6.

CHAPTER FIFTEEN. REVOLUTIONARY ABOLITIONISM

1. Jacob R. Shipherd, *History of the Oberlin–Wellington Rescue* (Boston, 1859), 175–78.

2. Steven Lubet, *Fugitive Justice: Runaways, Rescuers, and Slavery on Trial* (Cambridge, Mass., 2010); Robert M. Cover, *Justice Accused: Antislavery and the Judicial Process* (New Haven, 1975); Gordon S. Barker, *Fugitive Slaves and the Unfinished American Revolution: Eight Cases, 1848–1856* (Jefferson, N.C., 2013).

3. *NE*, October 3, 1850; June 5, September 18, 1851; January 22, October 21, 1852; George Stroud, *A Sketch of the Laws Relating to Slavery* (Philadelphia, 1856); Stanley Campbell, *The Slave Catchers: Enforcement of the Fugitive Slave Law, 1850–1860* (Chapel Hill, 1968); Carol Wilson, *Freedom at Risk: The Kidnapping of Free Blacks in America, 1780–1865* (Lexington, Ky., 1994), 54; Robert Churchill, "Fugitive Slave Rescues in the North: Toward a Geography of Antislavery Violence," *Ohio Valley History* 14 (Summer 2014): 51–75; Lois E. Horton, "Kidnapping and Resistance: Antislavery Direct Action in the 1850s," in David W. Blight ed., *Passages to Freedom: The Underground Railroad in History and Memory* (Washington, 2004), 149–73; W. H. Furness, *A Discourse Occasioned by the Boston Fugitive Slave Case . . .* (Philadelphia, 1851), 6, 14–15.

4. *NS*, September 5, 1850; *TL*, August 9, September 13, 1850; *NE*, October 10, 1850; John Stauffer, *The Black Hearts of Men: Radical Abolitionists and the Transformation of Race* (Cambridge, Mass., 2002), 163–64.

5. *TL*, April 5, September 27, October 4, 11, 18, 25, November 1, December 13, 20, 1850; January 10, 17, October 24, 1851; December 27, 1852; *NE*, August 14, October 10, 24, 31, November 14, 21, 28, 1850; February 6, 25, March 20, April 24, May 22, November 13,

December 4, 1851; July 8, 1852; NS, October 24, October 31, 1850; January 16, 23, March 20, April 3, 10, 1851; R. J. M. Blackett, "'Freemen to the Rescue': Resistance to the Fugitive Slave Law of 1850," in Blight, ed., *Passages to Freedom*, 133–47; David W. Blight, *Frederick Douglass' Civil War: Keeping Faith in Jubilee* (Baton Rouge, 1989), chap. 4.

6. NS, October 3, 24, 1850; January 16, 1851; NE, October 10, November 21, 1850; *The Fugitive Slave Bill* . . . (New York, 1850), 2–5, 21, 31–36; TL, October 25, 1850, p. 170; Samuel May, *The Fugitive Slave Law and Its Victims* . . . (New York, 1861), 12–13, 37–38; NASS, January 2, 9, February 6, 1851; FDP, April 8, 15, May 13, June 3, 1852; William Still, *The Underground Railroad* . . . (1872; repr. Medford, N.J., 2005), 120–23; Carla L. Peterson, *Black Gotham: A Family History of African Americans in Nineteenth-Century New York City* (New Haven, 2011), 194–96, 237–40; Christopher L. Webber, *American to the Backbone: The Life of James W. C. Pennington, the Fugitive Slave Who Became One of the First Black Abolitionists* (New York, 2011), 341–51; Prithi Kanakamedala, "In Pursuit of Freedom: Anti-Slavery Activism and the Culture of Abolitionism in Brooklyn, NY," (Brooklyn Historical Society, 2012), 67–72; Eric Foner, *Gateway to Freedom: The Hidden History of the Underground Railroad* (New York, 2015), chap. 5.

7. TL, October 18, November 1, 29, December 13, 30, 1850; *Account Book of Francis Jackson, Treasurer 1850–1860* . . . (Boston, 1924), 18, 20, 24; Austin Bearse, *Reminiscences of Fugitive-Slave Law Days* . . . (Boston, 1880), 3–6, 13–20, 24–33; Gary Collison, "The Boston Vigilance Committee: A Reconsideration," *Historical Journal of Massachusetts* 12 (October 1984): 104–16; Sidney Kaplan, "The *Moby Dick* in the Service of the Underground Railroad," *Phylon* 12 (1951): 173–76; Stanley J. Robboy and Anita W. Robboy, "Lewis Hayden: From Fugitive Slave to Statesman," *NEQ* 46 (December 1973): 591–613; Dean Grodzins, "'Slave Law' versus 'Lynch Law' in Boston: Benjamin Robbins Curtis, Theodore Parker and the Fugitive Slave Crisis, 1850–1855," *MHR* 12 (2010): 1–33; Stephen Kantrowitz, *More than Freedom: Fighting for Black Citizenship in a White Republic, 1829–1889* (New York, 2012): 180–84.

8. TL, February 21, March 14, April 11, 18, May 9, 1851; NE, March 6, April 10, 17, May 22, 1851; NS, April 10, 1851; NASS, February 27, March 13, April 10, 17, 24, July 17, November 20, 1851; May, *The Fugitive Slave Law*, 15–17; Thomas Wentworth Higginson, *Cheerful Yesterdays* (Boston, 1898), 135–46; *Trial of Thomas Sims* . . . (Boston, 1851), 4, 15–16 26–27; *The Fugitive Slave Law: Speech of Hon. Robert Rantoul, Jr.* . . . (Boston, 1851); Gary Collison, *Shadrach Minkins: From Fugitive Slave to Citizen* (Cambridge, Mass., 1997); Leonard W. Levy, "Sims' Case: The Fugitive Slave Law in Boston," *JNH* 35 (January 1950): 39–69; Merle E. Curti, "Robert Rantoul Jr., A Reformer in Politics," *NEQ* 5 (April 1932): 264–80.

9. Still, *The Underground Railroad*, 251–64, 438–40; W. U. Hensel, *The Christiana Riot* . . . (Lancaster, Pa., 1911), 16, 20–39, 40–46, 57–91, 99–100, 103–25; James R. Robbins, *Report of the Trial of Caster Hanway* . . . (Philadelphia, 1852), 89–90, 111–17, 216–20; NASS, February 13, March 20, September 18, October 2, 16, 23, November 20, December 4, 11, 18, 25, 1851; FDP, September 25, October 2, 9, 16, 23, November 13, 20,

27, December 11, 1851; January 1, 8, 22, February 19, June 24, 1852; *NE*, September 18, 25, October 2, 9, 16, 23, 30, November 13, 20, 27, December 11, 18, 1851; January 1, 29, 1852; *TL*, September 26, October 3, 10, November 28, 1851; Beverly Wilson Palmer, ed., *The Selected Papers of Thaddeus Stevens* (Pittsburgh, 1987), 1:136–37; Marion Gleason McDougall, *Fugitive Slaves [1619–1865]* (Boston, 1891), 51; R. C. Smedley, *History of the Underground Railroad in Chester and the Neighboring Counties of Pennsylvania* (Lancaster, Pa., 1883); Julie Winch, "Philadelphia and the Other Underground Railroad," *PMHB* 111 (January 1987): 3–25; William J. Switala, *Underground Railroad in Pennsylvania* (Mechanicsburg, Pa., 2001); William C. Kashatus, *Just Over the Line: Chester County and the Underground Railroad* (West Chester, Pa., 2002); David G. Smith, *On the Edge of Freedom: The Fugitive Slave Issue in South Central Pennsylvania, 1820–1870* (New York, 2013), 27–30; Roderick W. Nash, "William Parker and the Christiana Riot," *JNH* 96 (1961): 24–31; Thomas P. Slaughter, *Bloody Dawn: The Christiana Riot and Racial Violence in the Antebellum North* (New York, 1991); Jonathan Katz, *Resistance at Christiana: The Fugitive Slave Rebellion, Christiana, Pennsylvania, September 11, 1851, A Documentary Account* (New York, 1974); Hans L. Trefousse, *Thaddeus Stevens: Nineteenth-Century Egalitarian* (Chapel Hill, 1997), 13–15, 84.

10. *NASS*, June 5, August 28, September 4, October 30, 1851; *FDP*, October 9, 30, 1851; January 8, 29, October 8, 15, December 24, 1852; February 11, March 4, 1853; *NE*, October 9, 1851; March 17, October 6, 1853; *TL*, October 3, 10, 17, 24, 1851; May 14, October 8, 15, 22, 1852; May 26, 1854; *The Reverend J. W. Loguen, As a Slave and a Freeman* . . . (Syracuse, 1859), ix, 389–444, 451–55; Carol M. Hunter, *To Set the Captives Free: Reverend Jermain Wesley Loguen and the Struggle for Freedom in Central New York, 1835–1872* (New York, 1993), 78–79, 120–22, 128–31, 156–57; Earl E. Sperry, *The Jerry Rescue, October 1, 1851* (Syracuse, 1924), 18–27, 32, 36, 38, 54–56; W. Freeman Galpin, "The Jerry Rescue," *New York History* 26 (January 1945): 19–34; Jayme Sokolow, "The Jerry McHenry Rescue and the Growth of Northern Anti-Slavery Sentiment During the 1850s," *Journal of American Studies* (December 1982): 427–45; Angela F. Murphy, *The Jerry Rescue: The Fugitive Slave Law, Northern Rights, and the American Sectional Crisis* (New York, 2016).

11. Charles Emery Stevens, *Anthony Burns* . . . (Boston, 1856), 16, 29–30, 33, 41–47, 50–52, 62–72, 93–95, 124–25, 139–49, 187–90, 237–44, 273–74, 281–83; *Boston Slave Riot, and Trial of Anthony* . . . (Boston, 1854), 5–18, 35–40, 57–60, 77–79, 84–89; Higginson, *Cheerful Yesterdays*, 146–66; James Freeman Clarke, *Discourse on Christian Politics* . . . (Boston, 1854), 9, 19, 21; *NASS*, June 3, 10, 24, July 1, 8, 1854; *FDP*, June 2, 9, 23, November 3, 1854; *TL*, February 9, 16, 23, March 2, 9, 23, April 6, 20, 27, May 4, 18, 25, 1855; March 27, 1857; March 5, 12, 1858; Theodore Parker, *The Trial of Theodore Parker* . . . (Boston, 1855), v, xviii–xx, 6–9, 42–68, 133, 217; Jane H. Pease and William H. Pease, *The Fugitive Slave Law and Anthony Burns: A Problem in Law Enforcement* (Philadelphia, 1975); Albert J. Von Frank, *The Trials of Anthony Burns: Freedom and Slavery in Emerson's Boston* (Cambridge, Mass., 1998); Earl M. Maltz, *Fugitive Slave on Trial: The Anthony Burns Case and Abolitionist Outrage* (Lawrence,

Kan., 2010); Gordon S. Barker, *The Imperfect Revolution: Anthony Burns and the Landscape of Race in Antebellum America* (Kent, Ohio, 2010); Cover, *Justice Accused*, 1–7, 249–52.

12. TL, June 2, 9, 16, 23, 30, July 7, 14, 21, 1854; Len Gougeon and Joel Myerson, eds., *Emerson's Antislavery Writings* (New Haven, 1995), 57; *Christian Duty: Three Discourses . . .* (Philadelphia, 1854), 10, 28; Henry Mayer, *All on Fire: William Lloyd Garrison and the Abolition of Slavery* (New York, 1998), 443–45; Lewis Perry, *Civil Disobedience: An American Tradition* (New Haven, 2013), chap. 4.

13. TL, April 7, 1854; May 4, 1855; May 1, 1857; *Provincial Freeman*, March 25, 1854; FDP, December 1, 1854; NE, February 1, 22, 1855; NASS, March 26, 1859; Byron Paine, *Unconstitutionality of the Fugitive Slave Act . . .* [Milwaukee, 1854], 4; H. Robert Baker, *The Rescue of Joshua Glover: A Fugitive Slave, the Constitution, and the Coming of the Civil War* (Athens, Ohio, 2006), 1–25, 63–64, 77, 91, 96, 152–53, 173–74; Ruby West Jackson and Walter T. McDonald, *Finding Freedom: The Untold Story of Joshua Glover, Runaway Slave* (Madison, 2007); Frederick J. Blue, *No Taint of Compromise: Crusaders in Antislavery Politics* (Baton Rouge, 2005), chap. 6; Joseph A. Ranney, "Concepts of Freedom: The Life of Justice Byron Paine," *Wisconsin Lawyer* 75 (November 2002) http://www.wisbar.org/newspublications/wisconsinlawyer/pages/wisconsin-lawyer.aspx?Volume=75&Issue=11; Michael J. McManus, *Political Abolitionism in Wisconsin, 1840–1861* (Kent, Ohio: Kent State University Press, 1998).

14. Shipherd, *History of the Oberlin–Wellington Rescue*, vii, 2–3, 8, 11–12, 92–95, 131, 176–78, 180–84, 223–25, 247–59, 263–80; TL, January 28, February 18, May 27, June 3, 10, 1859; ASB, April 9, 23, May 28, June 18, July 9, 16, 30, September 10, October 29, 1859; NASS, April 23, June 25, July 2, 16, 23, 30, 1859; Philip S. Foner and George E. Walker, eds., *Proceedings of the Black State Conventions, vol. 1, 1840–1865* (Philadelphia, 1979), 248–49, 334, 338–39; Nat Brandt, *The Town that Started the Civil War* (Syracuse, 1990), 44–111, 204–59; R. J. M. Blackett, *Beating Against the Barriers: The Lives of Six Nineteenth-Century Afro-Americans* (Ithaca, 1989), 185–92; William F. Cheek and Aimee Lee Cheek, *John Mercer Langston and the Fight for Black Freedom, 1829–1865* (Urbana, 1989); Warren Guthrie, "The Oberlin–Wellington Rescue Case, 1859," in J. Jeffrey Auer, ed., *Antislavery and Disunion, 1858–1861* (New York, 1963), 85–97; Cover, *Justice Accused*, 232, 252–56; J. Brent Morris, *Oberlin Hotbed of Abolitionism: College, Community, and the Fight for Freedom and Equality in Antebellum America* (Chapel Hill, 2014), 368–90.

15. Still, *The Underground Railroad*, 53–60, 125; *Narrative of Facts in the Case of Passmore Williamson* (Philadelphia, 1855), 4–5, 8, 10, 12–16, 18–22; NASS, July 28, August 15, 25, September 8, 22, 29, October 20, 27, November 10, 1855; NE, July 26, August 2, September 8, 13, 20, 27, October 18, 25, November 1, 8, 1855; TL, August 3, September 7, 14, 21, October 19, November 9, December 7, 1855; FDP, August 10, September 28, October 19, 1855; *Case of Passmore Williamson . . .* (Philadelphia, 1856); Richard Hildreth, ed., *Atrocious Judges . . .* (New York, 1856), 9–36, 389–432; *Passmore Williamson v. John K. Kane . . .* (Philadelphia, 1856); Edlie L. Wong, *Neither Fugitive nor Free: Atlantic Slavery, Freedom Suits, and the Legal Culture of Travel* (New York, 2009),

104–14; Phil Lapansky, "The Liberation of Jane Johnson," http://www.librarycompany .org/JaneJohnson/; May, *The Fugitive Slave Law*, 47; Nat Brandt and Yanna Brandt, *In the Shadow of the Civil War: Passmore Williamson and the Rescue of Jane Johnson* (Columbia, S.C., 2007).

16. May, *The Fugitive Slave Law*, 50–62, 67–68; NASS, February 9, 16, 23, March 15, April 12, May 16, 1856; TL, February 29, March 7, 14, May 16, 23, 1856; May 22, 1857; July 16, 1858; ASB, February 16, December 27, 1856; October 3, November 14, December 12, 1857; January 23, February 25, March 27, June 5, July 31, 1858; June 11, 1859; Steven Weisenburger, *Modern Medea: A Family Story of Slavery and Child-Murder from the Old South* (New York, 1998), 44–75, 90–106, 123–25, 170–75, 302; Melton A. McLaurin, *Celia, A Slave* (Athens, Ga., 1991); Stephen Middleton, "The Fugitive Slave Crisis in Cincinnati, 1850–1860: Resistance, Reinforcement, and Black Refugees," *JNH* 72 (1987): 20–32; Julius Yanuck, "The Garner Fugitive Slave Case," *MVHR* 40 (1953): 47–66; Cynthia Griffin Wolff, "'Margaret Garner': A Cincinnati Story," *Massachusetts Review* 32 (1991): 417–40.

17. NASS, May 5, 1860; Still, *The Underground Railroad*, 123–27, 353–54, 384–85; May, *The Fugitive Slave Law*, 134–35; *Weekly Anglo-African*, May 12, 1860; Scott Christianson, *Freeing Charles: The Struggle to Free a Slave on the Eve of the Civil War* (Urbana, 2010), 52–75, 88–122.

18. *New York Court of Appeals: Report of the Lemmon Slave Case . . .* (New York, 1861), 4–14, 25, 31, 33–35, 42–44, 117; NASS, December 12, 1857; May, *The Fugitive Slave Law*, 24, 134; TL, May 20, 1859; Paul Finkelman, *An Imperfect Union: Slavery, Federalism, and Comity* (Chapel Hill, 1981), 296–343; Thomas J. Davis, "Napoleon vs. Lemmon: Antebellum New Yorkers, Antislavery and Law," *Afro-Americans in New York Life and History* 33 (January 2009): 27–46; Wong, *Neither Fugitive nor Free*, chap. 4; Marie Tyler-McGraw and Dwight T. Picaithley, "The Lemmon Case: Courtroom Drama, Constitutional Crisis, and the Southern Quest to Nationalize Slavery," *Common-Place* 14 (Fall 2013): http://www.common-place.org/vol-14/no-01/mcgraw/# .U9KBvShy_zI.

19. Still, *The Underground Railroad*, 15, 128–31, 133–46; Stanley Harrold, "Freeing the Weems Family: A New Look at the Underground Railroad," *CWH* 52 (1996): 289–306; Bryan Prince, *A Shadow on the Household: One Enslaved Family's Incredible Struggle for Freedom* (New York, 2009); Elizabeth Varon, "'Beautiful Providences': William Still, the Vigilance Committee, and Abolitionists in the Age of Sectionalism," in Richard Newman and James Mueller, eds., *Antislavery and Abolition in Philadelphia: Emancipation and the Long Struggle for Racial Justice in the City of Brotherly Love* (Baton Rouge, 2011), 229–45; "Record of Fugitives," July 25, August 10, 1855, Sydney Howard Gay Papers, CU; Foner, *Gateway to Freedom*, chap. 7.

20. Stuart Seely Sprague, ed., *His Promised Land: The Autobiography of John P. Parker, Former Slave and Conductor on the Underground Railroad* (New York, 1996), 25–27, 30–35, 63–68, 71–105, 118–51; Ann Hagedorn, *Beyond the River: The Untold Story of the Heroes of the Underground Railroad* (New York, 2002), 232–37.

21. Boston Anti-Man Hunting League Records, MHS; Vincent Y. Bowditch, *Life and Correspondence of Henry Ingersoll Bowditch*, 2 vols. (Boston, 1902), 1:272–80; Still, *The*

Underground Railroad, 102–4; David S. Cecelski, *The Fire of Freedom: Abraham Gal-loway and the Slaves' Civil War* (Chapel Hill, 2012), 13–28.

22. *Brown's Three Years in the Kentucky Prisons, From May 30, 1854 to May 18, 1857* (Indianapolis, 1858), 6–9, 13; James M. Prichard, "Into the Fiery Furnace: Anti-Slavery Prisoners in the Kentucky State Penitentiary, 1844–1870," http://www.ket .org/underground/research/prichard2.htm; Keith P. Griffler, *Front Line of Freedom: African Americans and the Forging of the Underground Railroad in the Ohio Valley* (Lexington, Ky., 2004), 115–18; *Life and Narrative of William J. Anderson* . . . (Chicago, 1857), 38–40, 53–57; William M. Cockrum, *History of the Underground Railroad as it was Conducted by the Anti-Slavery League* (1915; repr., New York, 1969).

23. May, *The Fugitive Slave Law*, 12, 31; *NE*, January 2, 1851; Wilson, *Freedom at Risk*, 51–54, 113–14; Daniel Webster, *The Arrest, Trial, and Release of Daniel Webster* . . . (Philadelphia, 1859); William M. Mitchell, *The Underground Railroad: From Slavery to Freedom* (London, 1860).

24. William Goodell, *The American Slave Code in Theory and Practice* . . . (New York, 1853), 11–12, 15–20, 150–54, 201–38, 305–8, 378–79; Thomas R. R. Cobb, *An Inquiry into the Law of Negro Slavery* . . . (Philadelphia, 1858); Richard Hildreth, *Despotism in America* . . . (Boston, 1854), chap. 5, appendix; L. Maria Child, *The Duty of Disobedi-ence to the Fugitive Slave Act* . . . (Boston, 1860), 10–17, 21–23, 36; Caroline L. Karcher, *The First Woman in the Republic: A Cultural Biography of Lydia Maria Child* (Dur-ham, 1994), 413, 433–38; Thomas D. Morris, *Free Men All: The Personal Liberty Laws of the North, 1780–1861* (Baltimore, 1974), 199–218.

CHAPTER SIXTEEN. ABOLITION WAR

1. *Address of John Brown to the Virginia Court* . . . (Boston, 1859).

2. James Oakes, *Freedom National: The Destruction of Slavery in the United States, 1861–1865* (New York, 2013); John Fabian Witt, *Lincoln's Code: The Laws of War in American History* (New York, 2012).

3. F. B. Sanborn, ed., *The Life and Letters of John Brown* . . . (London, 1885), 10–11, 39–41, 66–67, 96–103, 111–14; Richard J. Hinton, *John Brown and His Men* . . . , rev. ed. (New York, 1894), 654.

4. Sanborn, ed., *The Life and Letters*, 124–33; *NS*, February 11, 1848; Brown to Willis A. Hodges, December 2, 23, 1848, John Brown Manuscripts, CU; James Redpath, *The Public Life of Capt. John Brown* . . . (Boston, 1860), 62–64; Hinton, *John Brown*, chap. 2; John Stauffer, *The Black Hearts of Men: Radical Abolitionists and the Transformation of Race* (Cambridge, Mass., 2001), 88–92, 118–23, 168–74; Benjamin Quarles, *Allies for Freedom: Blacks and John Brown* (New York, 1974), 18–28.

5. Sanborn, ed., *The Life and Letters*, 160–66, 171–83, 188–90, 201–20; Edward Everett Hale, *Kansas and Nebraska* (New York, 1854); *Nebraska and Kansas* . . . (Boston, 1854), 4–5, 11, 28–32; *FDP*, September 15, 1854; *TL*, February 16, 23, July 6, September 7, 1855; *Proceedings of the Convention of the Radical Political Abolitionists* . . . (New York, 1855), 3–9, 11–22, 49–52, 55–56; William Phillips, *The Conquest of Kansas* . . .

(Boston, 1856), chaps. 5, 7, 9; Thomas H. Gladstone, *The Englishman in Kansas . . .* (New York, 1857), chaps. 2, 3, 11, 21; Karl Gridley, "'Willing to Die for the Causes of Freedom': Free State Emigration, John Brown, and the Rise of Militant Abolitionism in the Kansas Territory," in Timothy Patrick McCarthy and John Stauffer, eds., *Prophets of Protest: Reconsidering the History of American Abolitionism* (New York, 2006), 147–64; Michael Fellman, "Rehearsal for the Civil War: Antislavery and Proslavery at the Fighting Point in Kansas," in Lewis Perry and Fellman, eds., *Antislavery Reconsidered: New Perspectives on the Abolitionists* (Baton Rouge, 1979), 287–309; Walter C. Rucker, "Unpopular Sovereignty: African American Resistance and Reactions to the Kansas–Nebraska Act," in John R. Wunder and Joann M. Ross, eds., *The Nebraska–Kansas Act of 1854* (Lincoln, Neb., 2008), 144–47; Jonathan Earle and Diane Mutti Burke, eds., *Bleeding Kansas, Bleeding Missouri: The Long Civil War on the Border* (Lawrence, Kan., 2013).

6. *TL*, May 30, June 6, 27, July 11, 18, 1856; Manisha Sinha, "The Caning of Charles Sumner: Slavery, Race, and Ideology in the Age of the Civil War," *JER* 23 (Summer 2003): 233–62; Williamjames Hull Hoffer, *The Caning of Charles Sumner: Honor, Idealism and the Origins of the Civil War* (Baltimore, 2010).

7. Sanborn, ed., *The Life and Letters*, 230–48, 258–74, 298–300; Redpath, *The Public Life*, 120, 177–84; Phillips, *The Conquest of Kansas*, chaps. 11, 12, 21, 24, 27; Gladstone, *The Englishman in Kansas*, chaps. 14, 16, 17, 23; Hinton, *John Brown*, chap. 4; David S. Reynolds, *John Brown, Abolitionist: The Man Who Killed Slavery, Sparked the Civil War, and Seeded Civil Rights* (New York, 2005), chaps. 7–8; Thomas Wentworth Higginson, *Cheerful Yesterdays* (Boston, 1898), 208; Stauffer, *The Black Hearts of Men*, 195–200.

8. *TL*, April 27, May 4, 11, June 1, 8, July 27, August 17, October 5, December 21, 1855; January 4, 18, February 15, 29, March 14, April 11, May 23, December 5, 1856; April 10, 1857; Elihu Burritt, *Twenty Reasons for Total Abstinence from Slave-Labor Produce* (Bucklersbury, Eng., ca. 1855), 1–4; Chas. Nothend, ed., *Elihu Burritt . . .* (New York, 1879), chap. 13; *Compensated Emancipation . . .* (n.p., 1857), 1–3; *New York Times*, January 27, 1859; Stauffer, *The Black Hearts of Men*, 143; Betty Fladeland, "Compensated Emancipation: A Rejected Alternative," *JSH* 42 (May 1976): 183–86; Merle Curti, ed., *The Learned Blacksmith: The Letters and Journals of Elihu Burritt* (New York, 1937).

9. *TL*, January 16, 1857; Higginson, *Cheerful Yesterdays*, 215–20; Sanborn, ed., *The Life and Letters*, 110–13, 349–56, 466–68, 500–511; Hinton, *John Brown*, chap. 6, 7; Gladstone, *The Englishman in Kansas*, chap. 25; Jeffrey Rossbach, *Ambivalent Conspirators: John Brown, the Secret Six, and a Theory of Slave Violence* (Philadelphia, 1983); Reynolds, *John Brown, Abolitionist*, chap. 9.

10. Sanborn, ed., *The Life and Letters*, 113–14, 418–36, 450–53, 469–70, 481–83; John Stauffer and Zoe Trodd, eds., *The Tribunal: Responses to John Brown and the Harper's Ferry Raid* (Cambridge, Mass., 2012), 26–37; Benjamin Quarles, ed., *Blacks on John Brown* (Urbana, 1972), 3–6; C. Peter Ripley, ed., *The Black Abolitionist Papers*, vol. 4, *The United States, 1847–1858* (Chapel Hill, 1991), 377–81; Quarles, *Allies for Freedom*, 38–72; Reynolds, *John Brown, Abolitionist*, 244–55, 268–79, 300; Daniel C. Littlefield,

"Blacks, John Brown, and a Theory of Manhood," in Paul Finkelman, ed., *His Soul Goes Marching On: Responses to John Brown and the Harper's Ferry Raid* (Charlottesville, Va., 1995), 67–97.

11. Sanborn, ed., *The Life and Letters*, 538–40, 546–60; Hinton, *John Brown*, chaps. 9–11, 14; Stauffer and Trodd, eds., *The Tribunal*, 38–43; Quarles, *Allies for Freedom*, 93–108, 157–58, 182–84; Carolyn E. Janney, "Written in Stone: Gender, Race, and the Hayward Shepherd Memorial," *CWH* 52 (June 2006): 117–41; Hannah Geffert, "Regional Black Involvement in John Brown's Raid on Harper's Ferry," in McCarthy and Stauffer, eds., *Prophets of Protest*, 165–79; Geffert, "They Heard His Call: The Local Black Community's Involvement in the Raid at Harper's Ferry," in Peggy A. Russo and Paul Finkelman, eds., *Terrible Swift Sword: The Legacy of John Brown* (Athens, Ohio, 2005), 23–45; Tony Horwitz, *Midnight Rising: John Brown and the Raid that Sparked the Civil War* (New York, 2011); Steven Lubet, *John Brown's Spy: The Adventurous Life and Tragic Confession of John E. Cook* (New Haven, 2012); John R. McKivigan, "His Soul Goes Marching On: The Story of John Brown's Followers after the Harper's Ferry Raid," in McKivigan and Stanley Harrold, eds., *Antislavery Violence: Sectional, Racial, and Cultural Conflict in Antebellum America* (Knoxville, 1999), 274–97.

12. Sanborn, ed., *The Life and Letters*, 500, 562–85, 610–11, 621–32; *The Life, Trials and Execution of Captain John Brown . . .* (New York, 1859), 39–95; Thomas Drew, *The John Brown Invasion . . .* (Boston, 1860); *Weekly Anglo-African*, November, December 1859; Higginson, *Cheerful Yesterdays*, 231–34; Stauffer and Trodd, eds., *The Tribunal*, 117–19; Robert E. McGlone, "John Brown, Henry Wise, and the Politics of Insanity," in Finkelman, ed., *His Soul Goes Marching On*, 213–52; Brian McGinty, *John Brown's Trial* (Cambridge, Mass., 2009).

13. *TL*, May 11, 1855, April 11, 1856; February 12, March 12, June 4, 1858; C. Peter Ripley ed., *The Black Abolitionist Papers: The United States, 1859–1865* (Chapel Hill, 1992), 5:59, 65–66; J. Sella Martin, *The Hero and the Slave* (Boston, 1862); *Anglo-African Magazine*, December 1859; Thomas Wentworth Higginson, *Army Life in a Black Regiment and Other Writings*, R. D. Madison, ed. (New York, 1997), 194; Higginson, *Black Rebellion: Five Slave Revolts*, James M. McPherson, ed. (New York, 1969); Tilden G. Edelstein, *Strange Enthusiasm: A Life of Thomas Wentworth Higginson* (New Haven, 1968), 245–46; George E. Levesque, "Boston's Black Brahmin: Dr. John S. Rock," *CWH* 26 (December 1980): 326–46; Dean Grodzins, "Why Theodore Parker Backed John Brown: The Political and Social Roots of Support for Abolitionist Violence," in Russo and Finkelman, eds., *Terrible Swift Sword*, 3–22; Grodzins, "Theodore Parker vs. John S. Rock on the Anglo-Saxon and the African," in *A House Divided: The Antebellum Slavery Debates in America, 1776–1865* (Princeton, 2003), 299–310; Paul Teed, "Romantic Nationalism and Its Challengers: Theodore Parker, John Rock, and the Antislavery Movement," *CWH* 41 (June 1995): 142–60; Michael Fellman, "Theodore Parker and the Abolitionist Role in the 1850s," *JAH* 61 (1974): 666–84; Peter Wirzbicki, "Black Intellectuals, White Abolitionists, and Revolutionary Transcendentalists: Creating the Radical Intellectual Tradition in Antebellum Boston" (Ph.D. diss., New York University, 2012), chap. 7; Franny Nudelman, *John Brown's Body: Slavery, Violence, and the Culture of War* (Chapel Hill, 2004).

14. TL, February 4, October 21, 28, November 4, 11, 18, 25, December 2, 9, 16, 1859; Louis Ruchames, ed., *The Letters of William Lloyd Garrison*, vol. 4, *From Disunionism to the Brink of War, 1850–1860* (Cambridge, Mass., 1975), 660–61; Stauffer and Trodd, eds., *The Tribunal*, 102–4; Henry David Thoreau, *A Plea for Captain John Brown* . . . (Boston, 1859); Wendell Phillips, *Speeches, Lectures, and Letters* (Boston, 1872), 263–64, 268–72, 280–81, 292; Henry C. Wright, *The Natick Resolution* . . . (Boston, 1859), 3–6, 11–18, 22–24, 26–32; William H. Pease and Jane H. Pease, eds., *The Antislavery Argument* (Indianapolis, 1965), 474–79; Parker Pillsbury, *Acts of the Anti-Slavery Apostles* (Concord, N.H., 1883), 145; Lewis Perry, *Radical Abolitionism: Anarchy and the Government of God in Antislavery Thought* (Ithaca, 1973), chap. 8; Reynolds, *John Brown, Abolitionist*, 344–47, 363–69, 398–406; Paul Finkelman, "Manufacturing Martyrdom: The Antislavery Response to John Brown's Raid," in Finkelman, ed., *His Soul Goes Marching On*, 41–66.

15. Brown to Giddings, September 7, 1848, John Brown Manuscripts, CU; Joshua R. Giddings, *The Exiles of Florida* . . . (Columbus, 1858), vi; Joshua R. Giddings, *History of the Rebellion* . . . (New York, 1864), 437–41; George W. Julian, *The Life of Joshua R. Giddings* (Chicago, 1892), 365–71; Stauffer and Trodd, eds., *The Tribunal*, 77–78, 99, 126–27, 188–89, 210–12, 303–7; Edward L. Pierce, ed., *Memoir and Letters of Charles Sumner*, vol. 3, *1845–1860* (Boston, 1894), 602–3; John Niven, *Salmon P. Chase: A Biography* (New York, 1995), 211; Frederick J. Blue, *Salmon P. Chase: A Life in Politics* (Kent, Ohio, 1987), 119.

16. *Correspondence Between Lydia Maria Child and Gov. Wise and Mrs. Mason, of Virginia* (Boston, 1860), 3–7, 14–19, 26; Stauffer and Trodd, eds., *The Tribunal*, 226–27, 261; L. Maria Child, *The Patriarchal Institution* . . . (New York, 1860), 49–53; *The Right Way the Safe Way* . . . (New York, 1862), 95–96; Wendy Hamand Venet, "'Cry Aloud and Spare Not': Northern Antislavery Women and John Brown's Raid," in Finkelman, ed., *His Soul Goes Marching On*, 98–115; Bonnie Laughlin-Schultz, *The Ties That Bound Us: The Women of John Brown's Family and the Legacy of Radical Abolitionism* (Ithaca, 2013).

17. Quarles, ed., *Blacks on John Brown*, 7–44, 54–66, 85–91; *A Tribute of Respect* . . . (Cleveland, 1859), 16–23; TL, December 9, 1859; Stauffer and Trodd, eds., *The Tribunal*, 149–65, 192–93, 228–30, 277–81, 440–41, 451–53, 488–89, 515–17; Quarles, *Allies for Freedom*, 110, 114–19, 125–63, 171–82; R. Blakeslee Gilpin, *John Brown Still Lives! America's Long Reckoning with Violence, Equality and Change* (Chapel Hill, 2011), 56–61, 82–87.

18. James Redpath, *The Roving Editor, or Talks with Slaves in the Southern States*, John R. McKivigan, ed. (University Park, Pa., 1996), 3–4, 7–8, 34, 40–44, 46, 50, 55, 72, 85–87, 108, 117, 119–20, 157–58, 185–86, 221–29, 239–52; Alexander Milton Ross, *Recollections and Experiences of an Abolitionist* . . . (Toronto, 1875), 6–24, 48–65; Otis K. Rice, "Eli Thayer and the Friendly Invasion of Virginia," *JSH* 37 (November 1971): 575–96; Albert J. Von Frank, "John Brown, James Redpath, and the Idea of Revolution," *CWH* 52 (June 2006): 142–60.

19. Redpath, *The Public Life*, 3, 7–10; Redpath, *Echoes of Harper's Ferry* (Boston, 1860), 3–4, 74–75, 80–86, 92–93, 174, 306–9, 457–59; Stauffer and Trodd, eds., *The Tribunal*,

90–91, 198–99, 215–18, 459–61, 476–77; Higginson, *Cheerful Yesterdays*, chap. 7; William Keeney, "Hero, Martyr, Madman: Representations of John Brown in the Poetry of the John Brown Year, 1859–1860," in Russo and Finkelman, eds., *Terrible Swift Sword*, 141–61; John McKivigan, *Forgotten Firebrand: James Redpath and the Making of Nineteenth-Century America* (Ithaca, 2008).

20. James Redpath, *A Guide to Hayti* (Boston, 1861), 171–75; Howard H. Bell, ed., *Black Separatism in the Caribbean 1860* (Ann Arbor, 1970), introduction, 21–27, 63–66, 103, 167–68; *Anglo-African Magazine*, June, July, August, September, October, November 1859; *Weekly Anglo-African*, February 18, April 14, May 26, 1860; *Pine and Palm* May 18, 25, June 2, 15, 22, 29, July 6, 13, 20, 27, August 31, September 7, 14, 28, December 7, 1861; January 23, May 1, September 4, 1862; J. R. Beard, *Touissant L'Ouverture* . . . (Boston, 1863); Robert S. Levine, ed., *Martin R. Delany, A Documentary Reader* (Chapel Hill, 2003), 363–72; *DM*, November 1860; March, July 1861; Floyd J. Miller, *The Search for a Black Nationality: Black Emigration and Colonization, 1787–1863* (Urbana, 1975), 108–15, 232–49, 267; David M. Dean, *Defender of the Race: James Theodore Holly, Black Nationalist Bishop* (Boston, 1979); McKivigan, *Forgotten Firebrand*, chap. 4; Chris Dixon, *African America and Haiti: Emigration and Black Nationalism in the Nineteenth Century* (Westport, Conn., 2000), chaps. 3–5; David W. Blight, *Frederick Douglass' Civil War: Keeping Faith in Jubilee* (Baton Rouge, 1989), 130–47.

21. *TL*, December 31, 1858; February 11, March 11, April 22, 1859; John W. Blassingame, ed., *The Frederick Douglass Papers, Series One*, vol. 3, *Speeches, Debates, and Interviews 1855–63* (New Haven, 1985), 303–4, 315–18; Quarles, *Allies for Freedom*, 164–66; Sibyl Ventress Brownlee, "Out of the Abundance of the Heart: Sarah Ann Parker Remond's Quest for Freedom" (Ph.D. diss., University of Massachusetts, Amherst, 1997), chap. 4; R. J. M. Blackett, *Building an Antislavery Wall: Black Americans in the Atlantic Abolitionist Movement, 1830–1860* (Baton Rouge, 1983), 160; J. Ewing Glasgow, *The Harpers Ferry Insurrection* . . . (Edinburgh, 1860); Stauffer and Trodd, eds., *The Tribunal*, 340–41, 367–72, 386–90, 395–96, 399, 409–10, 457–58; Higginson, *Cheerful Yesterdays*, 220; Seymour Drescher, "Servile Insurrection and John Brown's Body in Europe," in Finkelman, ed., *His Soul Goes Marching On*, 253–95; Higginson, *Army Life in a Black Regiment*, 206.

22. Roy P. Basler, ed., *The Collected Works of Abraham Lincoln*, vol. 1, *1824–1848* (New Brunswick, N.J., 1953), 74–75, 109–15; Manisha Sinha, "Abraham Lincoln's Competing Political Loyalties: Antislavery, Union, and the Constitution," in Nicholas Buccola, ed., *Abraham Lincoln and Liberal Democracy* (Lawrence, Kan., Forthcoming); Dorothy Ross, "Lincoln and the Ethics of Emancipation: Universalism, Nationalism, and Exceptionalism," *JAH* 96 (September 2009): 379–99; Eric Foner, *The Fiery Trial: Abraham Lincoln and American Slavery* (New York, 2010), chaps. 1, 2.

23. Roy P. Basler, ed., *The Collected Works of Abraham Lincoln*, vol. 2, *1848–1858* (New Brunswick, N.J., 1959): 20–22, 121–32, 247–83; Lewis E. Lehrman, *Lincoln at Peoria: The Turning Point* (Mechanicsburg, Pa., 2008).

24. The Revised Dred Scott Case Collection, http://digital.wustl.edu/dredscott/browse .html; Lea VanderVelde, *Mrs. Dred Scott: A Life on Slavery's Frontier* (New York,

2009), 75, 130, 197–99, 227–29, 233–36, 243, 261–68, 276–83; Lea VanderVelde, *Re-demption Songs: Suing for Freedom Before* Dred Scott (New York, 2014); Lucy A. Delaney, *From the Darkness Cometh the Light or Struggles for Freedom* (St. Louis, ca. 1883); Kelly Marie Kennington, "Law, Geography, and Mobility: Suing for Freedom in Antebellum St. Louis," *JSH* 80 (August 2014): 575–604; Eric Gardner, *Unexpected Places: Relocating Nineteenth-Century African American Literature* (Jackson, Miss., 2009), 27–55; Cyprian Clamorgan, *The Colored Aristocracy of St. Louis*, Julie Winch, ed. (Columbia, Mo., 1999), 47; Julie Winch, *The Clamorgans: One Family's History of Race in America* (New York, 2011); Don E. Fehrenbacher, *The Dred Scott Case: Its Significance in American Law and Politics* (New York, 1978), chaps. 9–11.

25. Benjamin Howard, *Report of the Decision of the Supreme Court . . .* (Washington, 1857), 9–11, 14–17, 45–60, 79–81, 139, 156–95, 239; Austin Allen, *Origins of the* Dred Scott *Case: Jacksonian Jurisprudence and the Supreme Court, 1837–1857* (Athens, Ga., 2006); Earl. M. Maltz, *Dred Scott and the Politics of Slavery* (Lawrence, Kan., 2007); Mark A. Graeber, Dred Scott *and the Problem of Constitutional Evil* (New York, 2006); Timothy S. Huebner, "Roger B. Taney and the Slavery Issue: Looking Beyond—and Before—*Dred Scott*," *JAH* 97 (June 2010): 17–38; Michael A. Schoep-pner, "Status Across Borders: Roger Taney, Black British Subjects, and a Diplomatic Antecedent to the *Dred Scott* Decision," *JAH* 100 (June 2013): 46–67; Stuart Streichler, *Justice Curtis in the Civil War Era: At the Crossroads of American Constitutionalism* (Charlottesville, Va., 2005).

26. TL, March 13, 20, April 3, 10, 24, May 1, 8, June 5, 12, 1857; George B. Cheever, D.D., *Guilt of Slavery and the Crime of Slaveholding . . .* (Boston, 1860), iv, 179–80; *Anglo-African Magazine*, May 1859; Blassingame, ed., *The Frederick Douglass Papers*, 3:143–83.

27. *Historical and Legal Examination . . .* (New York, 1858), 30, 121–30; Fehrenbacher, *The Dred Scott Case*, 472–74; VanderVelde, *Mrs. Dred Scott*, 320–33.

28. Basler, ed., *The Collected Works of Abraham Lincoln*, 2:398–410, 461–69; ibid., vol. 3, *1858–1860*, 146–47, 408; Blassingame, ed., *The Frederick Douglass Papers*, 3:233–37; Don E. Fehrenbacher, *Prelude to Greatness: Lincoln in the 1850s* (Stanford, Calif., 1962), chaps. 3, 4.

29. Basler, ed., *The Collected Works of Abraham Lincoln*, 2:222–23, 553; ibid., 3:9, 15–16, 38, 127–34, 179, 249, 296–97, 306–18, 366–69, 400–424, 463–70; John Burt, *Lincoln's Tragic Pragmatism: Lincoln, Douglas, and Moral Conflict* (Cambridge, Mass., 2013); David Zarefsky, *Lincoln, Douglas and Slavery: In the Crucible of Public Debate* (Chicago, 1990); Allen C. Guelzo, *Lincoln and Douglas: The Debates That Defined America* (New York, 2008); James Oliver Horton, "Naturally Anti-Slavery: Lincoln, Race, and the Complexity of American Liberty," in Sean Wilentz, ed., *The Best American History Essays on Lincoln* (New York, 2009), 63–84; George M. Fredrickson, *Big Enough to Be Inconsistent: Abraham Lincoln Confronts Slavery and Race* (Cambridge, Mass., 2008); Brian Dirck, ed., *Lincoln Emancipated: The President and the Politics of Race* (DeKalb, Ill., 2007); Henry Louis Gates Jr., ed., *Lincoln on Race and Slavery* (Prince-ton, 2009); Lerone Bennet Jr., *Forced into Glory: Abraham Lincoln's White Dream* (Chicago, 2000).

30. Levine, ed., *Martin R. Delany*, 30, 66, 144–48, 187–88; NS, January 21, November 18, 1848; June 29, 1849; June 27, 1850; Martin Robison Delany, *The Condition, Elevation, Emigration, and Destiny of the Colored People . . .* (Philadelphia, 1852), 10, 12, 23–30, 48–49, 67, 147–60, 169, 209–14; *FDP*, July 23, 1852; Victor Ullman, *Martin R. Delany: The Beginnings of Black Nationalism* (Boston, 1971); Dorothy Sterling, *The Making of an Afro-American: Martin Robison Delany, 1812–1885* (New York, 1971); Cyril E. Griffith, *The African Dream: Martin R. Delany and the Emergence of Pan-African Thought* (University Park, Pa., 1975).

31. *FDP*, May 6, June 17, August 19, September 30, November 18, December 2, 1853; Levine, ed., *Martin R. Delany*, 175–79, 217–23, 238–44; Robert S. Levine and Ivy G. Wilson, eds., *The Works of James M. Whitfield: America and Other Writings by a Nineteenth-Century African American Poet* (Chapel Hill, 2011), introduction, 41, 109–68; *Proceedings of the Colored National Convention . . .* (Rochester, 1853), 3–5, 8–11, 16–18, 39–41, 57; David W. Blight, ed., *Narrative of the Life of Frederick Douglass, An American Slave: Written By Himself, with Related Documents* (New York, 2003), 156–59; Miller, *The Search for a Black Nationality*, 137–43; R. J. M. Blackett, *Beating Against the Barriers: The Lives of Six Nineteenth-Century Afro-Americans* (Ithaca, 1989), chap. 5; Robert S. Levine, *Martin Delany, Frederick Douglass and the Politics of Representative Identity* (Chapel Hill, 1997); Manisha Sinha, "An Alternative Tradition of Radicalism: African American Abolitionists and the Metaphor of Revolution," in Sinha and Penny Von Eschen, eds., *Contested Democracy: Freedom, Race, and Power in American History* (New York, 2007), 24–25.

32. *FDP*, January 13, March 31, 1853; September 8, 15, December 22, 1854; Levine, ed., *Martin R. Delany*, 245–90; Ullman, *Martin R. Delany*, 163–71; Griffith, *The African Dream*, 24–29, 122–26; Tunde Adeleke, *Without Regard to Race: The Other Martin Robison Delany* (Jackson, Miss., 2003); Adeleke, *Unafrican Americans: Nineteenth-Century Black Nationalism and the Civilizing Mission* (Lexington, Ky., 1998), chap. 3; Miller, *The Search for a Black Nationality*, 148–56; *Proceedings of the Colored National Convention, Held in Franklin Hall, Sixth Street, Below Arch, Philadelphia, October 16th, 17th and 18th 1855* (Salem, N.J., 1856), 4, 17, 30–33.

33. NS, March 2, 1849; *FDP*, August 20, September 2, 1853; Miller, *The Search for a Black Nationality*, 170–98; *Fortieth Annual Report of the American Colonization Society . . .* , in *The Annual Reports*, 35–38; Ripley, ed., *The Black Abolitionist Papers*, 2:270–78; *Anglo-African Magazine*, March 1859; *Weekly Anglo-African*, September 10, 19, October 22, 1859; Levine, ed., *Martin R. Delany*, 326; Benjamin Coates, *Cotton Cultivation in Africa . . .* (Philadelphia, 1858); Emma J. Lapansky and Margaret Hope Bacon, eds., *Back to Africa: Benjamin Coates and the Colonization Movement in America, 1848–1880* (University Park, Pa., 2005), 1–53, 60–68, 72–75, 105–6, 110–19, 122–23, 125–26, 135–39, 141–42, 145–47; Earl Ofari, *Let Your Motto Be Resistance: The Life and Thought of Henry Highland Garnet* (Boston, 1972), 79–93, 183–5; Joel Schor, *Henry Highland Garnet: A Voice of Black Radicalism in the Nineteenth Century* (Westport, Conn., 1977), chap. 8; Beverly C. Tomek, *Colonization and Its Discontents: Emancipation, Emigration, and Antislavery in Antebellum Pennsylvania* (New York, 2011), 171–75, 181–86.

34. M. R. Delany, *Official Report of the Niger Valley Exploring Party* (London, 1861), 10–27, 50–52; *Weekly Anglo-African*, July 23, August 13, September 24, October 1, 1859; Ripley, ed., *The Black Abolitionist Papers*, 1:447–52; Robert Campbell, *A Few Facts . . .* (Philadelphia, 1860), 4–8, 10–17; Campbell, *A Pilgrimage to My Motherland . . .* (New York, 1861), 11, 18, 29–30, 36–39, 60–65, 115; Miller, *The Search for a Black Nationality*, 198–216; Lamin Sanneh, *Abolitionists Abroad: American Blacks and the Making of Modern West Africa* (Cambridge, Mass., 1999), 145–47; James Campbell, *Middle Passages: African American Journeys to Africa, 1787–2005* (New York, 2006), 76–93; R. J. M. Blackett, "Return to the Motherland: Robert Campbell, a Jamaican in Early Colonial Lagos," *Phylon* 40 (December 1979): 375–86.

35. Delany, *Official Report*, 27–33, 35–50, 53–61, 71; *Weekly Anglo-African*, March 3, 31, 1860; Levine, ed., *Martin R. Delany*, 358–64; Frank A. Rollin, *Life and Public Services of Martin R. Delany* (Boston, 1883), chap. 12; Ullman, *Martin R. Delany*, 232–46; Ripley, ed., *The Black Abolitionist Papers*, 1:488–90, 497–509, 519–23; Griffith, *The African Dream*, 53–57; Miller, *The Search for a Black Nationality*, 217–32; Sanneh, *Abolitionists Abroad*, 170–77; Blackett, *Building an Antislavery Wall*, 175–94; African Civilization Society, *Constitution of the African Civilization Society . . .* (New Haven, 1861), 3–7, 32–38; Tunis Campbell, *Hotel Keepers, Head Waiters, and Housekeepers Guide* (Boston, 1848); Russell Duncan, *Freedom's Shore: Tunis Campbell and the Georgia Freedmen* (Athens, Ga., 1986); Ofari Hutchinson, *Let Your Motto Be Resistance*, 95–98; Schor, *Henry Highland Garnet*, 178–81.

36. Bell, ed., *Black Separatism in the Caribbean*, 73–75, 172–84; *Speech of Honorable Francis P. Blair, Jr. . . .* (Washington, 1858), 3, 10–13; Francis P. Blair Jr., *Colonization and Commerce . . .* (Cincinnati, 1859), 2–5; Blair, *The Destiny of Races of this Continent . . .* (Washington, 1859), 4–7, 21–26, 29–33; *The Acquisition of Cuba . . .* (Washington, 1859), 5–7; *Speech of J. R. Doolittle . . .* (Washington, 1862), 1–2; *An Appeal to the Senate . . .* (Washington, 1868), 7–12.

37. *Letter on the Relation of the White and African Races in the United States . . .* (Washington, 1862), 7–9, 17–22; *Report of the Select Committee on Emancipation and Colonization . . .* (Washington, 1862), 1, 19–24, 37–59; *Speech of Honorable H. Winter Davis of Maryland . . .* (Washington, 1864), 7; *Pine and Palm*, January 2, March 20, April 3, 10, May 15, 29, June 5, 12, 19, July 10, 24, 31, August 7, 21, 28, September 4, 1862; *Christian Recorder*, September 27, 1862; Eric Foner, "Lincoln and Colonization," in *Our Lincoln: New Perspectives on Lincoln and His World* (New York, 2008), 135–66; Levine, ed., *Martin R. Delany*, 485; W. E. B. Du Bois, *The Souls of Black Folk* (New York, 1903), 184; Miller, *The Search for a Black Nationality*, 250–66; Ofari, *Let Your Motto Be Resistance*, 122–23; Wilson Jeremiah Moses, *Alexander Crummell: A Study in Civilization and Discontent* (New York, 1989), 135–45, 196, 208–11, 225–28.

38. TL, February 4, March 4, June 17, July 1, 1859; April 20, 27, June 1, 8, 22, July 13, 20, August 24, September 28, October 26, 1860; July 12, 1861; *The Impending Crisis of the South . . .* (New York, 1857); David Brown, *Southern Outcast: Hinton Rowan Helper and the Impending Crisis of the South* (Baton Rouge, 2006); Caroline L. Karcher, *The First Woman in the Republic: A Cultural Biography of Lydia Maria Child* (Durham, 1994), 390; Blight, *Frederick Douglass' Civil War*, chap. 2; Edward Magdol, *Owen*

Lovejoy: Abolitionist in Congress (New Brunswick, N.J., 1967), 223–43; Sinha, "The Caning of Charles Sumner," 256–57; William F. Moore and Jane Ann Moore, *Collaborators for Emancipation: Abraham Lincoln and Owen Lovejoy* (Urbana, 2014).

39. Basler, ed., *The Collected Works of Abraham Lincoln*, 3:480, 522–50; *TL*, May 25, September 21, 1860; Harold Holzer, *Lincoln at Cooper Union: The Speech that Made Abraham Lincoln President* (New York, 2004); Donald E. Reynolds, *Texas Terror: The Slave Insurrection Panic of 1860 and the Secession of the Lower South* (Baton Rouge, 2007); Foner, *The Fiery Trial*, 144.

40. *TL*, December 21, 28, 1860; January 4, 25, 14, February 1, 8, 22, 29, April 5, 19, 24, 1861; [William Lloyd Garrison], *The New "Reign of Terror"* . . . (New York, 1860); Manisha Sinha, *The Counterrevolution of Slavery: Politics and Ideology in Antebellum South Carolina* (Chapel Hill, 2000).

41. *Proceedings of the American Anti-Slavery Society at Its Third Decade* . . . (New York, 1864), 112; James Oakes, *Freedom National: The Destruction of Slavery in the United States, 1861–1865* (New York, 2013); Witt, *Lincoln's Code*; Manisha Sinha, "Allies for Emancipation?: Lincoln and Black Abolitionists," in Eric Foner, ed., *Our Lincoln: New Perspectives on Lincoln and His World* (New York, 2008), 168–98; *William Lloyd Garrison, 1805–1879: The Story of His Life* . . . , vol. 4, *1861–1879* (New York, 1889), 132; Foner, *The Fiery Trial*, 90; Ira Berlin et al., *Slaves No More: Three Essays on Emancipation and the Civil War* (Cambridge, Eng., 1992); David Williams, *I Freed Myself: African American Self-Emancipation in the Civil War Era* (New York, 2014).

EPILOGUE

1. *William Lloyd Garrison, 1805–1879: The Story of His Life* . . . , vol. 4, *1861–1879* (New York, 1889), chaps. 4–6; *TL*, May 20, 27, November 18, 1864; May 19, December 29, 1865; James M. McPherson, *The Struggle for Equality: Abolitionists and the Negro in the Civil War and Reconstruction* (Princeton, 1964), chaps. 12, 13; W. Caleb McDaniel, *The Problem of Democracy in the Age of Slavery: Garrisonian Abolitionists and Transatlantic Reform* (Baton Rouge, 2013), chap. 10; La Wanda Cox, *Lincoln and Black Freedom: A Study in Presidential Leadership* (Columbia, S.C., 1981); Wendy Hamand Venet, *Neither Ballots nor Bullets: Women Abolitionists and the Civil War* (Charlottesville, Va., 1991), chap. 5; Manisha Sinha, "Did He Die an Abolitionist? Abraham Lincoln's Evolving Antislavery," *American Political Thought* 4 (Summer 2015): 439–52; Martha Hodes, *Mourning Lincoln* (New Haven, 2015).

2. *Proceedings of the American Anti-Slavery Society at Its Third Decade* . . . (New York, 1864), 111; McPherson, *The Struggle for Equality*, chap. 17; James Brewer Stewart, *Wendell Phillips: Liberty's Hero* (Baton Rouge, 1986), 294–95; Carol Faulkner, *Women's Radical Reconstruction: The Freedmen's Aid Movement* (Philadelphia, 2004); Eric Foner, *Reconstruction: America's Unfinished Revolution, 1863–1877* (New York, 1988); Amy Dru Stanley, "Instead of Waiting for the Thirteenth Amendment: The War Power, Slave Marriage, and Inviolate Human Rights," *AHR* (June 2010): 732–65; David Montgomery, *Beyond Equality: Labor and the Radical Republicans, 1862–72* (New York, 1967); A. J. Aiseirithe, "Piloting the Car of Human Freedom: Abolition-

ists, Woman Suffrage, and the Problem of Radical Reform" (Ph.D. diss., University of Chicago, 2007); Faye E. Dudden, *Fighting Chance: The Struggle over Woman Suffrage and Black Suffrage in Reconstruction America* (New York, 2011); *Proceedings of the Eleventh National Woman's Rights Convention* (New York, 1866), 45–48.

3. David Roediger, *Seizing Freedom: Slave Emancipation and Liberty for All* (New York, 2014); Henry Mayer, *All on Fire: William Lloyd Garrison and the Abolition of Slavery* (New York, 1998), 616; Louis Filler, ed., *Wendell Phillips on Civil Rights and Freedom* (New York, 1965), 192, 207; William S. McFeely, *Frederick Douglass* (New York, 1991), 360–62, 376–81; Heather Cox Richardson, *To Make Men Free: A History of the Republican Party* (New York, 2014); Nell Irvin Painter, *Sojourner Truth: A Life, A Symbol* (New York, 1996), 244–46; John W. Blassingame and John R. McKivigan, eds., *The Frederick Douglass Papers: Series One: Speeches, Debates and Interviews*, vol. 4, *1864–80* (New Haven, 1991), 503–8.

4. Manisha Sinha, "Memory as History, Memory as Activism: The Forgotten Abolitionist Struggle After the Civil War," *Common-place* 14 (Winter 2014): http://www.common-place.org/vol-14/no-02/sinha/#.VOJBCihy_zI; Julie Roy Jeffrey, *Abolitionists Remember: Antislavery Autobiographies and the Unfinished Work of Emancipation* (Chapel Hill, 2008).

5. Alex Gourevitch, *From Slavery to Cooperative Commonwealth: Labor and Republican Liberty in the Nineteenth Century* (Cambridge, Eng., 2015), 69; Lawrence Goodwyn, *Democratic Promise: The Populist Moment in America* (New York, 1976); Samuel Gompers, *Seventy Years of Life and Labor: An Autobiography* (New York, 1925), 1:18–19; Stephen Fox, *The Guardian of Boston: William Monroe Trotter* (New York, 1970); James M. McPherson, *The Abolitionist Legacy: From Reconstruction to the NAACP* (1975; repr. Princeton, 1995), 390; Nick Salvatore, *Eugene V. Debs: Citizen and Socialist* (Urbana, 1982); Melvyn Dubofsky, *We Shall Be All: A History of the Industrial Workers of the World* (Chicago, 1969); Lewis Perry, *Civil Disobedience: An American Tradition* (New Haven, 2013), 2; Howard Zinn, "Abolitionists, Freedom Riders, and the Tactics of Agitation," in Martin Duberman, ed., *The Antislavery Vanguard: New Essays on the Abolitionists* (Princeton, 1965), 446–51; Michelle Alexander, *The New Jim Crow: Mass Incarceration in the Age of Colorblindness* (New York, 2010); Joel Quirk, *The Anti-Slavery Project: From the Slave Trade to Human Trafficking* (Philadelphia, 2011).

6. *William Lloyd Garrison, 1805–1879: The Story of His Life . . .* (New York, 1885), 1:177; McPherson, *The Abolitionist Legacy*, x.

ILLUSTRATION CREDITS

Benjamin Lay, Courtesy of the Library Company of Philadelphia
John Woolman, Courtesy of the Historical Society of Pennsylvania
Anthony Benezet, Courtesy of the American Antiquarian Society
Phillis Wheatley, Courtesy of the American Antiquarian Society
Olaudah Equiano, Courtesy of the Library Company of Philadelphia
Absalom Jones, Courtesy of the Historical Society of Pennsylvania
Lemuel Haynes, Courtesy of the American Antiquarian Society
Granville Sharp, Courtesy of the Prints and Photographic Division, Library of Congress
Thomas Clarkson, Courtesy of the Library Company of Philadelphia
William Wilberforce, Courtesy of the Library Company of Philadelphia
Plan and Sections of a Slave Ship (*Brooks*), Courtesy of the Library Company of
    Philadelphia
James Forten, Courtesy of the Historical Society of Pennsylvania
Samuel Cornish, Courtesy of Photographs and Prints Division, Schomburg Center for
    Research in Black Culture, The New York Public Library, Astor, Lenox and Tilden
    Foundations
William Lloyd Garrison, Courtesy of the Historical Society of Pennsylvania
Theodore Dwight Weld, Courtesy of the Massachusetts Historical Society
House Unpassed Legislation, 1843 Session, Docket 1289, Petition of Benjamin Lewis,
    SC1/series 230, Massachusetts Archives, Boston
William Whipper, Courtesy of the American Antiquarian Society
James W. C. Pennington, Courtesy of the American Antiquarian Society
Charles Lenox Remond, Courtesy of General Research & Reference Division, Schom-
    burg Center for Research in Black Culture, The New York Public Library, Astor,
    Lenox and Tilden Foundations
Robert Purvis, Courtesy of the Library Company of Philadelphia
James McCune Smith, Courtesy of Manuscripts, Archives and Rare Books Division,
    Schomburg Center for Research in Black Culture, The New York Public Library,
    Astor, Lenox and Tilden Foundations

733

Martin R. Delany, Courtesy of the Library Company of Philadelphia

William Cooper Nell, Courtesy of the Massachusetts Historical Society

Alexander Crummell, Courtesy of the American Antiquarian Society

Lucretia Mott, Courtesy of the Library Company of Philadelphia

Angelina Grimké, Courtesy of the Massachusetts Historical Society

Abby Kelley Foster, Courtesy of the American Antiquarian Society

Sojourner Truth, Courtesy of the American Antiquarian Society

Lucy Stone, Courtesy of the Prints and Photographic Division, Library of Congress

Frances Ellen Watkins Harper, Courtesy of the American Antiquarian Society

Wendell Phillips, Courtesy of the Library Company of Philadelphia

Samuel J. May, Courtesy of Print Collection, Miriam and Ira D. Wallach Division of
   Art, Prints and Photographs, The New York Public Library, Astor, Lenox and Tilden
   Foundations

Henry C. Wright, Courtesy of the Massachusetts Historical Society

Lydia Maria Child, Courtesy of the Massachusetts Historical Society

Maria Weston Chapman, Courtesy of the Massachusetts Historical Society

Lewis Tappan, Courtesy of Manuscripts, Archives and Rare Books Division, Schomburg
   Center for Research in Black Culture, The New York Public Library, Astor, Lenox
   and Tilden Foundations

William Jay, Courtesy of Manuscripts, Archives and Rare Books Division, Schomburg
   Center for Research in Black Culture, The New York Public Library, Astor, Lenox
   and Tilden Foundations

Gerrit Smith, Courtesy of the Library Company of Philadelphia

William Goodell, Courtesy of Print Collection, Miriam and Ira D. Wallach Division of
   Art, Prints and Photographs, The New York Public Library, Astor, Lenox and Tilden
   Foundations

Joshua Leavitt, Courtesy of the Massachusetts Historical Society

Alvan Stewart, Courtesy of the Prints and Photographic Division, Library of Congress

James G. Birney, Courtesy of the Massachusetts Historical Society

Toussaint Louverture, Courtesy of General Research & Reference Division, Schomburg
   Center for Research in Black Culture, The New York Public Library, Astor, Lenox
   and Tilden Foundations

Cinque (Sengbe Pieh), Courtesy of the Library Company of Philadelphia

The Branded Hand, Courtesy of the American Antiquarian Society

The Disappointed Abolitionists, Courtesy of the Library Company of Philadelphia

The Christiana Tragedy, Courtesy of the American Antiquarian Society

Levi Coffin, Courtesy of the American Antiquarian Society

Thomas Garrett, Courtesy of the American Antiquarian Society

John Rankin, Courtesy of the Massachusetts Historical Society

Henry Bibb, Courtesy of the Library Company of Philadelphia

Jermaine W. Loguen, Courtesy of the Library Company of Philadelphia

Harriet Tubman, Courtesy of the Massachusetts Historical Society

Laura Haviland, Courtesy of the Massachusetts Historical Society

Theodore Parker, Courtesy of the Library Company of Philadelphia
William Still, Courtesy of the American Antiquarian Society
John Brown, Courtesy of the Library Company of Philadelphia
John Quincy Adams, Courtesy of the American Antiquarian Society
Joshua R. Giddings, Courtesy of the Library Company of Philadelphia
Salmon P. Chase, Courtesy of the Library Company of Philadelphia
Charles Sumner, Courtesy of the Library Company of Philadelphia
William H. Seward, Courtesy of the Library Company of Philadelphia
Thaddeus Stevens, Courtesy of the Library Company of Philadelphia
Owen Lovejoy, Courtesy of the Library Company of Philadelphia
Eminent Opponents of the Slave Power, Courtesy of Picture Collection, The New York
    Public Library, Astor, Lenox and Tilden Foundations
Distinguished Colored Men, Courtesy of the Library Company of Philadelphia

INDEX